Coll
German
School
Dictionary

HarperCollins Publishers
Westerhill Road
Bishopbriggs
Glasgow G64 2QT

Fifth Edition 2018

10 9 8 7 6 5 4 3 2 1

ISBN 978-0-00-825798-9

www.collinsdictionary.com
www.collins.co.uk

Typeset by Davidson Publishing Solutions, Glasgow

Printed in Italy by Grafica Veneta S.p.A.

A catalogue record for this book is available from the British Library.

Acknowledgements
We would like to thank those authors and publishers who kindly gave permission for copyright material to be used in the Collins Corpus. We would also like to thank Times Newspapers Ltd for providing valuable data.

EDITOR
Susie Beattie

CONTRIBUTORS
Joyce Littlejohn
Horst Kopleck
Maggie Seaton
Anna Stevenson
Silke Zimmerman

FOR THE PUBLISHER
Janice McNeillie
Laura Waddell
Sarah Woods

TECHNICAL SUPPORT
Agnieszka Urbanowicz

CONTENTS

Acknowledgements

We are grateful to all those teachers and students who have contributed to the development of the *Collins German School Dictionary* by advising us on how to tailor it to their needs. We also gratefully acknowledge the help of the examining boards.

USING THIS DICTIONARY

The *Collins German School Dictionary* is designed specifically for anyone starting to learn German, and has been carefully researched with teachers and students. It is very straightforward, with an accessible layout that is easy on the eye, guiding students quickly to the right translation. It also offers essential help on German culture.

This section gives useful tips on how to use the *Collins German School Dictionary* effectively.

▷ Make sure you look in the right side of the dictionary

There are two sides in a bilingual dictionary. Here, the **German–English** side comes first, and the second part is **English–German**. At the top of each page there is a reminder of which side of the dictionary you have open. The middle pages of the book have a grey border so you can see where one side finishes and the other one starts.

▷ Finding the word you want

To help you find a word more quickly, use the **alphabet tabs** down the side of the page, then look at the words in **black bold** at the top of pages. They show the first and last words on the two pages where the dictionary is open.

▷ Make sure you use the right part of speech

Some entries are split into several parts of speech. For example '**glue**' can either be a noun ("Can I borrow your **glue**?") or a verb ("**Glue** this into your exercise book"). Parts of speech within an entry are separated by a black triangle ▶ and are given on a new line. They are given in their abbreviated form (*n* for noun, *adj* for adjective, etc). For the full list of abbreviations, look at page viii.

> **glue** *n* Klebstoff *m* (*pl* Klebstoffe)
> ▶ *vb* kleben ...

▷ Choosing the right translation

The main translation of a word is underlined and is shown after the part of speech. If there is more than one main translation for a word, each one is numbered. You may also sometimes find bracketed words in *italics* which give you some context. They help you choose the translation you want.

> **pool** *n* ❶ *(puddle)* Pfütze *f* ❷ *(pond)* Teich *m (pl* Teiche) ❸ *(for swimming)* Schwimmbecken *nt* ...

Often you will see phrases in *italics*, preceded by a white triangle ▷. These are examples of the word being used in context.

> **kaum** *adv* hardly ▷ *Ich habe kaum geschlafen.* I hardly slept.

Phrases in **bold type** are phrases which are particularly common and important. Sometimes these phrases have a totally different translation.

> **Besserung** *f* improvement; **Gute Besserung!** Get well soon!

Once you have found the right translation, remember that you may need to adapt the German word you have found. You may need to make a **noun** feminine or plural or genitive. Remember that the feminine form is given for nouns and that irregular plurals and genitive forms are also given.

> **dancer** *n* Tänzer *m (pl* Tänzer), Tänzerin *f*
>
> **zip** *n* Reißverschluss *m (gen* Reißverschlusses, *pl* Reißverschlüsse)

You may also need to adapt the **verb**. Verbs are given in the infinitive form, but you may wish to use them in the present, past or future tense. To do this, use the **verb tables** in the last section of the dictionary. Many German verbs on both sides are followed by a number in square brackets. This number corresponds to a verb table number in the Verb Tables at the back of the dictionary.

In the example below, **kauen** follows the same pattern as **holen**, which is verb number **38** in the verb tables.

kauen *vb* [**38**] to chew

Verbs which have no number are followed by the main forms in brackets, but some irregular verbs have both a number and show the main forms, for clarity.

▷ Find out more

In the *Collins German School Dictionary*, you will find lots of extra information about the German language. These **usage notes** help you understand how the language works, draw your attention to false friends (words which look similar to English words but have a different meaning), and give you some word-for-word translations.

entgegen *prep*

entgegen takes the dative.

Chips *pl* crisps *pl*

Be careful! The German word **Chips** does not mean **chips**.

Wörterbuch (*pl* **Wörterbücher**) *nt* dictionary

Word for word, **Wörterbuch** means 'word book'.

You can also find out more about life in Germany and German-speaking countries by reading the **cultural notes**.

A levels *npl* Abitur *nt sg*

Germans take their **Abitur** at the age of 19. The students sit examinations in a variety of subjects to attain an overall grade. If you pass, you have the right to a place at university.

▷ Remember!

Never take the first translation you see without looking at the others. Always look to see if there is more than one translation, or more than one part of speech.

ABBREVIATIONS USED IN THIS DICTIONARY

abbr	abbreviation
adj	adjective
adv	adverb
art	article
conj	conjunction
excl	exclamation
f	feminine
gen	genitive
imperf	imperfect tense
m	masculine
mf	masculine and feminine
n	noun
nt	neuter
num	number
perf	perfect tense
pl	plural
prep	preposition
pres	present tense
pron	pronoun
sing	singular
vb	verb

SYMBOLS

▷	example
▶	new part of speech
❷	new meaning
[**38**]	verb table number (see Verb Tables section at the back of the dictionary)
accident	Key words which you need for your GCSE or other exams of a similar level are highlighted in light grey throughout both sides of the dictionary to help you find them more easily.

TIME

Wie spät ist es? What time is it?

ein Uhr

zehn nach eins

Viertel nach eins

halb zwei

zwanzig vor zwei

Viertel vor zwei

Um wie viel uhr? At what time?

um Mitternacht

um Mittag

um ein Uhr (nachmittags)

um acht Uhr (abends)

um 11:15 Uhr *or* elf Uhr fünfzehn

um 20:45 Uhr *or* zwanzig Uhr fünfundvierzig

DATES

▷ Days of the Week

Montag	Monday
Dienstag	Tuesday
Mittwoch	Wednesday
Donnerstag	Thursday
Freitag	Friday
Samstag	Saturday
Sonntag	Sunday

▷ Months of the Year

Januar	January	**Juli**	July
Februar	February	**August**	August
März	March	**September**	September
April	April	**Oktober**	October
Mai	May	**November**	November
Juni	June	**Dezember**	December

▷ Wann?

im Februar
am 1. Dezember
am ersten Dezember
2018
zweitausendachtzehn

▷ When?

in February
on 1 December
on the first of December
in 2018
in two thousand and eighteen

▷ Der Wievielte ist heute?

Heute ist...
Sonntag, der 1. Oktober *or*
Sonntag, der erste Oktober
Monntag, der 10. Februar *or*
Monntag, der zehnte Februar

▷ What day is it?

It's...
Sunday 1 October *or*
Sunday, the first of October
Monday 10 February *or*
Monday, the tenth of February

NUMBERS

▷ Cardinal numbers

0	null
1	eins
2	zwei
3	drei
4	vier
5	fünf
6	sechs
7	sieben
8	acht
9	neun
10	zehn
11	elf
12	zwölf
13	dreizehn
14	vierzehn
15	fünfzehn
16	sechzehn
17	siebzehn
18	achtzehn
19	neunzehn
20	zwanzig
21	einundzwanzig
22	zweiundzwanzig
30	dreißig
40	vierzig
50	fünfzig
60	sechzig
70	siebzig
80	achtzig
90	neunzig
100	(ein)hundert
101	(ein)hundert(und) eins
200	zweihundert
300	dreihundert
301	dreihundert(und) eins
1000	(ein)tausend
2000	zweitausend
1,000,000	eine Million

▷ Fractions etc

1/2	ein halb
1/3	ein Drittel
2/3	zwei Drittel
1/4	ein Viertel
3/4	drei Viertel
1/5	ein Fünftel
0.5	null Komma fünf (1,5)
10%	zehn Prozent
100%	hundert Prozent

NUMBERS

▷ Ordinal numbers

1st	erste(r, s)
2nd	zweite(r, s)
3rd	dritte(r, s)
4th	vierte(r, s)
5th	fünfte(r, s)
6th	sechste(r, s)
7th	siebte(r, s)
8th	achte(r, s)
9th	neunte(r, s)
10th	zehnte(r, s)
11th	elfte(r, s)
12th	zwölfte(r, s)
13th	dreizehnte(r, s)
14th	vierzehnte(r, s)
15th	fünfzehnte(r, s)
16th	sechzehnte(r, s)
17th	siebzehnte(r, s)
18th	achtzehnte(r, s)
19th	neunzehnte(r, s)
20th	zwanzigste(r, s)
21st	einundzwanzigste(r, s)
22nd	zweiundzwanzigste(r, s)
30th	dreißigste(r, s)
100th	(ein)hundertste(r, s)
101st	(ein)hundert(und)erste(r, s)
1000th	(ein)tausendste(r, s)

DEUTSCH - ENGLISCH | GERMAN - ENGLISH

a

ab *prep, adv*

> The preposition **ab** takes the dative.

❶ from ▷ *Kinder ab zwölf Jahren* children from the age of twelve ▷ *ab morgen* from tomorrow ❷ off ▷ *Die Straße geht nach links ab.* The road goes off to the left. ▷ *Der Knopf ist ab.* The button has come off. ▷ *Ab nach Hause!* Off you go home!; **ab sofort** as of now; **ab und zu** now and then

abbiegen (*imperf* **bog ab**, *perf* **ist abgebogen**) *vb* ❶ to turn off ▷ *Sie bog an der Kreuzung nach links ab.* At the crossroads she turned off to the left. ❷ to bend ▷ *Die Hauptstraße biegt nach rechts ab.* The main road bends to the right.

Abbildung *f* illustration

abbrechen *vb* **[11]** ❶ to break off ▷ *Sie brach einen blühenden Zweig ab.* She broke off a flowering branch. ❷ to pull down ▷ *Das alte Gebäude muss abgebrochen werden.* The old building will have to be pulled down. ❸ to stop ▷ *Es ist schon spät, wir sollten abbrechen.* It's late now; we ought to stop. ❹ to abort ▷ *Das dauert zu lang, du solltest das Programm abbrechen.* It's taking too long; you should abort the program.

Abend (*pl* **Abende**) *m* evening ▷ *Sie macht jeden Abend einen Spaziergang.* She goes for a walk every evening. ▷ *guten Abend* good evening; **zu Abend essen** to have dinner; **heute Abend** this evening

Abendbrot *nt* supper

Abendessen (*pl* **Abendessen**) *nt* dinner ▷ *Zum Abendessen gibt es Spaghetti.* There's spaghetti for dinner.

abends *adv* in the evening

Abenteuer (*pl* **Abenteuer**) *nt* adventure

aber *conj, adv* ❶ but ▷ *Er wollte mit uns mitkommen, aber seine Eltern haben es nicht erlaubt.* He wanted to come with us, but his parents wouldn't let him. ❷ however ▷ *Ich möchte nach Ägypten reisen. Ich habe aber kein Geld.* I'd like to go to Egypt. However, I haven't got any money.; **Das ist aber schön!** That's really nice.; **Nun ist aber Schluss!** Now that's enough!

abfahren *vb* **[21]** to leave ▷ *Wir fahren morgen sehr früh ab.* We're leaving very early tomorrow. ▷ *Wann fährt dein Zug ab?* When does your train leave?

Abfahrt *f* departure

Abfall (*pl* **Abfälle**) *m* rubbish

Abfalleimer (*pl* **Abfalleimer**) *m* rubbish bin

abfliegen *vb* **[25]** to take off ▷ *Die Maschine ist mit Verspätung abgeflogen.* The plane was late taking off.; **Um wie viel Uhr fliegt ihr ab?** What time does your plane leave?

Abflug (*pl* **Abflüge**) *m* ❶ departure ▷ *Wir müssen eine Stunde vor Abflug am Flughafen sein.* We have to be at the airport one hour before departure. ❷ to takeoff ▷ *Die Maschine stürzte kurz nach dem Abflug ab.* The plane crashed shortly after takeoff.

Abgas (*gen* **Abgases**, *pl* **Abgase**) *nt* exhaust fumes *pl*

abgeben *vb* [**28**] ❶ to hand in ▷ *Die Klassenarbeiten müssen am Ende der Stunde abgegeben werden.* Tests must be handed in at the end of the lesson. ❷ to pass ▷ *Er gab den Ball an den Mittelstürmer ab.* He passed the ball to the centre-forward.; **sich mit jemandem abgeben** to associate with somebody; **sich mit etwas abgeben** to bother with something; **jemandem etwas abgeben** to let somebody have something

abgelegen *adj* remote

abgemacht *adj* agreed ▷ *Wir trafen uns zur abgemachten Zeit.* We met at the agreed time.; **Abgemacht!** OK!

abgesehen *adj* **es auf jemanden abgesehen haben** to be out to get somebody; **es auf etwas abgesehen haben** to be after something; **abgesehen von ...** apart from ...

abgewöhnen *vb* [**38**] **sich etwas abgewöhnen** to give something up

Abhang (*pl* **Abhänge**) *m* slope

abhängen (1) (*perf* **hat abgehängt**) *vb* [**4**] ❶ to take down ▷ *Weil ihr das Bild nicht mehr gefiel, hängte sie es ab.* She took the picture down because she didn't like it any more. ❷ to unhitch ▷ *Er hängte den Wohnwagen ab, bevor er in die Stadt fuhr.* He unhitched the caravan before he drove into town. ❸ to shake off ▷ *Den Räubern gelang es, die Polizei abzuhängen.* The robbers managed to shake off the police.

abhängen (2) (*imperf* **hing ab**, *perf* **hat abgehangen**) *vb* [**35**] **von jemandem abhängen** to depend on somebody; **von etwas abhängen** to depend on something

abhängig *adj* **abhängig von** dependent on

abheben (*imperf* **hob ab**, *perf* **hat abgehoben**) *vb* ❶ to answer ▷ *Es scheint niemand zu Hause zu sein, es hebt nämlich keiner ab.* There doesn't seem to be anyone at home as nobody's answering the phone. ❷ to withdraw ▷ *Ich muss Geld vom Sparbuch abheben.* I'll have to withdraw some money from my savings account. ❸ to take off ▷ *Wir sahen zu, wie das Flugzeug abhob.* We watched the plane take off. ❹ to lift off ▷ *Die Rakete hob senkrecht ab.* The rocket lifted off vertically.; **sich von etwas abheben** to stand out against something

abholen *vb* [**4**] ❶ to collect ▷ *Der Müll wird einmal in der Woche abgeholt.* Rubbish is collected once a week. ❷ to pick up ▷ *Ich hole dich um sieben ab.* I'll pick you up at seven.

Abitur *nt* A levels

Abiturient (*gen* **Abiturienten**, *pl* **Abiturienten**) *m* A level student

Abiturientin *f* A level student

abkürzen *vb* [**36**] to abbreviate ▷ *Man kann 'bitte wenden' mit b. w. abkürzen.* You can abbreviate 'please turn over' to PTO.; **den Weg abkürzen** to take a short cut

Abkürzung *f* ❶ abbreviation ▷ *Die Abkürzung für Europäische Union ist EU.* The abbreviation for European Union is EU. ❷ short cut ▷ *Wir haben eine Abkürzung genommen.* We took a short cut.

abladen (*pres* **lädt ab**, *imperf* **lud ab**, *perf* **hat abgeladen**) *vb* to unload

ablaufen *vb* [**43**] ❶ to expire ▷ *Ihr Pass ist leider abgelaufen.* Unfortunately, your passport has expired. ❷ to drain away ▷ *Der Abfluss ist verstopft, und deshalb läuft das Wasser nicht ab.* The waste pipe is blocked, and that's why the water won't drain away.

ablehnen *vb* [**4**] ❶ to turn down ▷ *Sie hat das Amt der Klassensprecherin abgelehnt.* She turned down being class representative. ▷ *Mein Antrag auf ein Stipendium wurde abgelehnt.* My application for a grant was turned down. ❷ to disapprove of ▷ *Ich lehne eine solche Arbeitseinstellung ab.* I disapprove of such an attitude to work.

ablenken *vb* [**4**] to distract ▷ *Lenk ihn nicht von seiner Arbeit ab.* Don't distract him from his work.; **vom Thema ablenken** to change the subject

abliefern *vb* [**88**] ❶ to drop off ▷ *Wir haben die Kinder wieder wohlbehalten zu Hause abgeliefert.* We dropped the children off at home safe and sound. ❷ to hand in ▷ *Bis wann musst du das Referat abliefern?* When do you have to hand your assignment in by?; **etwas bei jemandem abliefern** to take something to somebody

abmachen *vb* [**4**] ❶ to take off ▷ *Weißt du, wie man den Deckel abmacht?* Do you know how to take the lid off? ❷ to agree ▷ *Wir haben abgemacht, dass wir uns um sieben Uhr treffen.* We agreed to meet at seven. ❸ to sort out ▷ *Ihr solltet das untereinander abmachen, wer heute aufräumt.* Sort out amongst yourselves who's going to clear up today.

Abmachung *f* agreement

Abnahme *f* decrease ▷ *eine weitere Abnahme der Teilnehmerzahlen* a further decrease in attendance

abnehmen *vb* [**52**] ❶ to remove ▷ *Bei diesem Auto kann man das Verdeck abnehmen.* You can remove the hood on this car.; **Als das Telefon klingelte, nahm sie ab.** When the telephone rang, she answered it.; **jemandem etwas abnehmen** to take something away from somebody ❷ to decrease ▷ *Die Zahl der Teilnehmer hat stark abgenommen.* The number of participants has decreased dramatically. ❸ to lose weight ▷ *Ich muss dringend abnehmen.* I really must lose weight. ▷ *Ich habe schon zwei Kilo abgenommen.* I've already lost two kilos. ❹ to buy ▷ *Wenn Sie mehr als zehn Stück abnehmen, bekommen Sie einen Rabatt.* If you buy more than ten you get a discount. ▷ *Hat sie dir diese Geschichte wirklich abgenommen?* *(informal)* Did she really buy that story?

abonnieren *vb* [**76**] to subscribe to

abräumen *vb* [**4**] to clear away ▷ *Sie räumte die Teller ab.* She cleared away the plates.; **den Tisch abräumen** to clear the table

Abreise *f* departure

abreisen (*perf* **ist abgereist**) *vb* [**4**] to leave

Absage *f* refusal

absagen *vb* [**4**] ❶ to call off ▷ *Die Vorstellung wurde abgesagt, weil ein Schauspieler krank war.* The performance was called off because one of the actors was ill. ❷ to turn down ▷ *eine Einladung absagen* to turn down an invitation

Absatz (*gen* **Absatzes**, *pl* **Absätze**) *m* ❶ heel ▷ *Die Absätze von deinen Schuhen sind ganz schief.* The heels of your shoes are worn down. ❷ paragraph ▷ *Hier solltest du einen Absatz machen.* You need to start a new paragraph here. ❸ sales *pl* ▷ *Der Absatz an elektrischen Geräten ist gestiegen.* Sales of electrical appliances have risen.

abschaffen *vb* [**4**] ❶ to abolish ▷ *Wann wurde in Deutschland die Todesstrafe abgeschafft?* When was the death sentence abolished in Germany? ❷ to get rid of ▷ *Ich werde mein Auto abschaffen.* I'm going to get rid of my car.

abscheulich *adj* abominable

abschicken *vb* [**4**] to send off

Abschied (*pl* **Abschiede**) *m* parting; **von jemandem Abschied nehmen** to say goodbye to somebody

abschleppen *vb* **[4]** to tow ▷ *ein Auto abschleppen* to tow a car; **jemanden abschleppen** *(informal)* to pick somebody up

abschließen (*imperf* **schloss ab**, *perf* **hat abgeschlossen**) *vb* ❶ to lock ▷ *Ich schließe meinen Schreibtisch immer ab.* I always lock my desk. ❷ to conclude ▷ *einen Vertrag abschließen* to conclude a contract

abschließend *adj, adv* in conclusion ▷ *Abschließend möchte ich noch Folgendes sagen: ...* In conclusion I would like to say this: ...

Abschlussprüfung *f* final exam

abschneiden *vb* **[60]** ❶ to cut ▷ *Kannst du mir bitte eine Scheibe Brot abschneiden?* Can you cut me a slice of bread, please? ❷ to do ▷ *Sie hat in der Prüfung sehr gut abgeschnitten.* She did very well in the exam.

abschrecken *vb* **[4]** to deter ▷ *Diese Maßnahmen sollen Jugendliche davon abschrecken, Drogen zu nehmen.* These measures are intended to deter young people from taking drugs.

abschreiben *vb* **[61]** to copy ▷ *Er wurde dabei erwischt, wie er von seinem Nachbarn abgeschrieben hat.* He was caught copying from his neighbour. ▷ *Schreibt diesen Satz bitte in eure Hefte ab.* Please copy this sentence into your exercise books.

absehbar *adj* foreseeable ▷ *in absehbarer Zeit* in the foreseeable future; **Das Ende ist absehbar.** The end is in sight.

abseits *adv* apart ▷ *Sie stand etwas abseits von den anderen.* She was standing somewhat apart from the others.

Absender (*pl* **Absender**) *m* sender

absetzen *vb* **[36]** ❶ to drop off ▷ *Ich setze dich am Bahnhof ab.* I'll drop you off at the station. ❷ to take off ▷ *Willst du nicht deinen Motorradhelm absetzen?* Don't you want to take your helmet off? ❸ to drop ▷ *Dieser Sprachkurs musste vom Programm abgesetzt werden.* This language course has had to be dropped from the syllabus.; **die Pille absetzen** to stop taking the pill

Absicht *f* intention ▷ *Das war nicht meine Absicht.* That was not my intention.; **mit Absicht** on purpose

absichtlich *adj, adv* deliberate ▷ *eine absichtliche Beleidigung* a deliberate insult; **etwas absichtlich tun** to do something deliberately

abspülen *vb* **[4]** to rinse ▷ *Er spülte die Teller ab.* He rinsed the plates.; **Geschirr abspülen** to wash up

Abstand (*pl* **Abstände**) *m* distance ▷ *Abstand halten* to keep one's distance

abstellen *vb* **[4]** ❶ to put down ▷ *Der Koffer ist so schwer, ich muss ihn kurz abstellen.* The case is so heavy that I'll have to put it down for a moment. ❷ to park ▷ *Wir haben das Auto am Stadtrand abgestellt.* We parked the car on the outskirts of town. ❸ to switch off ▷ *Kannst du bitte das Radio abstellen?* Can you switch the radio off, please?

Abstimmung *f* vote

abstreiten (*imperf* **stritt ab**, *perf* **hat abgestritten**) *vb* to deny

abstürzen (*perf* **ist abgestürzt**) *vb* **[36]** ❶ to fall ▷ *Mathis ist beim Klettern abgestürzt.* Mathis fell while climbing. ❷ to crash ▷ *Die Maschine ist kurz nach dem Start abgestürzt.* The plane crashed shortly after takeoff.

Abteil (*pl* **Abteile**) *nt* compartment

Abteilung *f* ❶ department ▷ *Sie wurde in eine andere Abteilung versetzt.* She was transferred to another department. ❷ ward ▷ *In welcher Abteilung liegt Mathis?* Which ward is Mathis in?

Abtreibung *f* abortion

abtrocknen *vb* **[53]** to dry

abwärts *adv* down

Abwasch *m* washing-up ▷ *den Abwasch machen* to do the washing-up

abwaschen *vb* [**89**] ❶ to wash ▷ *Wer muss heute das Geschirr abwaschen?* Who's turn is it to wash the dishes today? ❷ to wash off ▷ *Wasch dir mal die Soße vom Gesicht ab!* Wash that gravy off your face.
Abwechslung *f* change ▷ *zur Abwechslung* for a change
abwerten *vb* [**2**] to devalue
abwertend *adj, adv* derogatory ▷ *sich abwertend über etwas äußern* to talk in a derogatory way about something
abwesend *adj* absent
Abwesenheit *f* absence
abzählen *vb* [**4**] to count
Abzeichen (*pl* **Abzeichen**) *nt* badge
abziehen *vb* [**96**]

> For the perfect tense use **haben** when the verb has an object and **sein** when there is no object.

❶ to take out ▷ *Er zog den Zündschlüssel ab.* He took out the ignition key. ❷ to withdraw ▷ *Sie haben ihre Truppen aus der Stadt abgezogen.* They have withdrawn their troops from the town. ❸ to deduct ▷ *Die Steuer wird vom Gehalt abgezogen.* Tax is deducted from earnings.; **Er ist beleidigt abgezogen.** *(informal)* He went away in a huff.
Achsel *f* shoulder
acht *num* eight; **acht Tage** a week
Acht *f* eight ▷ *Schreibe eine Acht.* Write the figure eight.; **sich in Acht nehmen** to beware; **etwas außer Acht lassen** to disregard something; **Acht geben** *see* **achtgeben**
achte *adj* eighth ▷ *Sie wiederholte den Satz ein achtes Mal.* She repeated the sentence for an eighth time. ▷ *Er kam als Achter.* He was the eighth to arrive.
achten *vb* [**2**] to respect ▷ *Ich achte deine Meinung.* I respect your opinion. ▷ *Sie ist sehr geachtet.* She's highly respected.; **auf etwas achten** to pay attention to something; **auf jemanden achten** to take notice of somebody
achtgeben *vb* [**28**] to pay attention ▷ *Du solltest etwas mehr auf die Rechtschreibung achtgeben!* You should pay a bit more attention to spelling.; **auf jemanden achtgeben** to keep an eye on somebody; **Gib acht!** Look out!
achtmal *adv* eight times
Achtung *f* respect ▷ *Ich habe große Achtung vor ihr.* I've great respect for her.; **Achtung!** Look out!; **Achtung Stufe!** Mind the step.; **Achtung, Achtung, hier eine Durchsage!** Your attention, please. Here is an announcement.; **Alle Achtung!** Well done!
achtzehn *num* eighteen
achtzig *num* eighty
Acker (*pl* **Äcker**) *m* field
addieren *vb* [**76**] to add
Adel *m* nobility
Ader *f* vein
ADHS *abbr* (= *Aufmerksamkeitsdefizit/Hyperaktivitätsstörung*) ADHD
Adjektiv (*pl* **Adjektive**) *nt* adjective
Adler (*pl* **Adler**) *m* eagle
adlig *adj* noble
adoptieren *vb* [**76**] to adopt
Adoptiveltern *pl* adoptive parents *pl*
Adoptivkind (*pl* **Adoptivkinder**) *nt* adopted child
Adresse *f* address
adressieren *vb* [**76**] to address ▷ *An wen soll ich den Brief adressieren?* To whom should I address the letter?
Adventskalender (*pl* **Adventskalender**) *m* Advent calendar
Adverb (*pl* **Adverbien**) *nt* adverb
Affe (*gen* **Affen**, *pl* **Affen**) *m* monkey
Afrika *nt* Africa
Afrikaner (*pl* **Afrikaner**) *m* African
Afrikanerin *f* African
afrikanisch *adj* African
Ägypten *nt* Egypt
Ägypter (*pl* **Ägypter**) *m* Egyptian
Ägypterin *f* Egyptian
ägyptisch *adj* Egyptian
ähneln *vb* [**34**] **jemandem ähneln** to resemble somebody; **Sie ähneln sich.** They are alike.

ahnen *vb* **[38]** ❶ to know ▷ *Ich habe geahnt, dass er nicht kommen würde.* I knew he wouldn't come. ▷ *Das konnte ich doch nicht ahnen!* How was I supposed to know that? ❷ to sense ▷ *Das Tier hat die Gefahr geahnt und ist schnell verschwunden.* The animal sensed the danger and quickly disappeared.

ähnlich *adj* similar ▷ *Unsere Kleider sind sehr ähnlich.* Our dresses are very similar.; **Sein Auto sieht ähnlich aus wie meines.** His car looks like mine.; **Er ist seinem Vater sehr ähnlich.** He's very like his father.; **Das sieht ihr ähnlich!** That's typical of her.

Ähnlichkeit *f* similarity

Ahnung *f* ❶ idea ▷ *Ich habe keine Ahnung, ob er kommt.* I've no idea whether he's coming.; **Er hat von Computern keine Ahnung.** He doesn't know the first thing about computers. ❷ hunch ▷ *Er hatte eine Ahnung, dass etwas Schlimmes geschehen würde.* He had a hunch that something terrible would happen.

ahnungslos *adj* unsuspecting

Aids (*gen* **Aids**) *nt* AIDS *sg* (= *Acquired Immune Deficiency Syndrome*) ▷ *Gerd ist an Aids gestorben.* Gerd died of AIDS.

Akademiker (*pl* **Akademiker**) *m* university graduate

Akademikerin *f* university graduate

Akkusativ (*pl* **Akkusative**) *m* accusative

Akne *f* acne ▷ *Sie hat Akne.* She's got acne.

Akte *f* file; **etwas zu den Akten legen** to file something away

Aktentasche *f* briefcase

Aktie *f* share ▷ *in Aktien investieren* to invest in shares

Aktion *f* ❶ campaign ▷ *eine Aktion für den Frieden* a campaign for peace ❷ operation ▷ *Wir alle nahmen an der Aktion teil.* We all took part in the operation.; **in Aktion treten** to go into action

> Word for word, **in Aktion treten** means 'to step into action'.

aktiv *adj* active

Aktivität *f* activity

aktuell *adj* ❶ topical ▷ *ein aktuelles Thema* a topical issue ❷ up-to-date ▷ *ein aktueller Fahrplan* an up-to-date timetable

Akzent (*pl* **Akzente**) *m* ❶ accent ▷ *Sie spricht mit einem amerikanischen Akzent.* She speaks with an American accent. ❷ emphasis ▷ *Der Akzent liegt auf Benutzerfreundlichkeit.* The emphasis is on user-friendliness.

albern *adj* silly; **sich albern benehmen** to act silly

Albtraum (*pl* **Albträume**) *m* nightmare

Album (*pl* **Alben**) *nt* album

Alkohol *m* alcohol

alkoholfrei *adj* nonalcoholic

Alkoholiker (*pl* **Alkoholiker**) *m* alcoholic

Alkoholikerin *f* alcoholic

alkoholisch *adj* alcoholic

All *nt* space ▷ *Sie haben eine Rakete ins All geschossen.* They've sent a rocket into space.

alle *adj, pron* ❶ all the ▷ *Alle Schüler sollten kommen.* All the pupils should come. ❷ all ▷ *Nicht alle Kinder mögen Schokolade.* Not all children like chocolate. ❸ all of them ▷ *Wir haben alle gesehen.* We saw all of them.; **Sie kamen alle.** They all came.; **wir alle** all of us; **Ich habe alle beide eingeladen.** I've invited both of them. ❹ every ▷ *alle vier Jahre* every four years ▷ *alle fünf Meter* every five metres; **Die Milch ist alle.** The milk's all gone.; **etwas alle machen** to finish something up

Allee (*pl* **Alleen**) *f* avenue

allein *adj, adv, conj* ❶ alone ▷ *Sie lebt allein.* She lives alone. ▷ *Du allein kannst das entscheiden.* You alone can decide. ❷ on one's own ▷ *Sie hat das ganz allein* *geschrieben*. She wrote that all on her own. ▷ *Seit ich allein bin, habe ich mehr Zeit*. Since I've been on my own, I've had more time.; **Er fühlt sich allein.** He feels lonely.; **nicht allein** not only

alleinstehend *adj* single

Word for word, **alleinstehend** means 'standing alone'.

allerdings *adv* ❶ though ▷ *Der Urlaub war schön, allerdings etwas kurz*. The holiday was nice, though it was rather short. ❷ certainly ▷ *Das ist allerdings schwierig*. That's certainly difficult.

Allergie *f* allergy

allergisch *adj* allergic ▷ *Sie ist allergisch gegen Katzen*. She's allergic to cats.

Allerheiligen *nt* All Saints' Day

Allerheiligen (November 1st) is a public holiday in those parts of Germany where most of the population are Roman Catholics.

allerlei *adj* all sorts of ▷ *allerlei Sachen* all sorts of things

alles *pron* everything ▷ *Sie haben alles aufgegessen*. They've eaten everything up.; **alles, was er sagt** everything he says; **alles in Allem** all in all; **Alles Gute!** All the best!

allgemein *adj* general; **im Allgemeinen** in general

allmählich *adj, adv* ❶ gradual ▷ *eine allmähliche Besserung* a gradual improvement ❷ gradually ▷ *Es wird allmählich wärmer*. It's gradually getting warmer.; **Allmählich solltest du das wissen.** You should know that by now.

Alltag *m* everyday life

allzu *adv* all too ▷ *allzu oft* all too often; **allzu viel** far too much

Alm *f* alpine pasture

Alpen *fpl* Alps *pl*

Alphabet (*pl* **Alphabete**) *nt* alphabet

alphabetisch *adj* alphabetical ▷ *alphabetisch geordnet* arranged in alphabetical order

Alptraum (*pl* **Alpträume**) *m* nightmare

als *conj* ❶ when ▷ *Als ich ein Kind war ...* When I was a child ... ❷ as ▷ *Sie kam, als ich gerade gehen wollte*. She arrived as I was about to leave. ▷ *Ich als Lehrerin weiß, ...* As a teacher, I know ...; **gerade, als ...** just as ...; **als ob** as if ❸ than ▷ *Sie ist älter als ich*. She's older than me. ▷ *Ich kam später als er*. I came later than he did.; **lieber als ...** rather than ...; **nichts als Ärger** nothing but trouble

also *adv, conj, excl* ❶ then ▷ *Was sollen wir also tun?* What shall we do, then? ▷ *Du willst also nicht mit*. You don't want to come along, then. ▷ *Du hast es also gewusst*. You did know then. ❷ so ▷ *Es war schon spät, also bin ich nach Hause gegangen*. It had got late, so I went home. ❸ well ▷ *Also ich gehe jetzt!* Well, I'm off now. ▷ *Also, Sie fahren immer geradeaus ...* Well, keep going straight on ...; **Also gut!** Okay then.; **Also, so was!** Well really!; **Na also!** There you are then!

Be careful! The German word **also** does not mean **also**.

alt *adj* old ▷ *Wie alt bist du?* How old are you? ▷ *Felix ist zehn Jahre alt*. Felix is ten years old. ▷ *Sein Auto ist älter als unseres*. His car is older than ours.; **meine ältere Schwester** my elder sister; **alles beim Alten lassen** to leave everything as it was

Altar (*pl* **Altäre**) *m* altar

Alter (*pl* **Alter**) *nt* ❶ age ▷ *In deinem Alter sollte man das wissen*. You ought to know that at your age. ❷ old age ▷ *Im Alter sind die Menschen oft einsam*. People are often lonely in old age.; **im Alter von** at the age of

Altglas (*gen* **Altglases**) *nt* used glass

Altglascontainer (*pl* **Altglascontainer**) *m* bottle bank

altmodisch *adj* old-fashioned

Altpapier *nt* waste paper

Altstadt (*pl* **Altstädte**) *f* old town

Alufolie *f* tinfoil

Aluminium *nt* aluminium

am = **an dem**; **am fünften März** on the fifth of March; **am höchsten** the highest; **am schönsten** the most beautiful

Ameise *f* ant

Amerika *nt* America

Amerikaner (*pl* **Amerikaner**) *m* American

Amerikanerin *f* American

amerikanisch *adj* American

Ampel *f* traffic lights *pl* ▷ *Die Ampel ist grün.* The traffic lights are at green.

Amsel *f* blackbird

Amt (*pl* **Ämter**) *nt* office ▷ *Welches Amt ist für Kindergeld zuständig?* Which office deals with child benefit?

amtlich *adj* official

amüsant *adj* amusing

amüsieren *vb* [**76**] to amuse ▷ *Diese Geschichte hat uns sehr amüsiert.* The story amused us very much.; **sich amüsieren** to enjoy oneself

an *prep, adv*

> Use the accusative to express movement or a change of place. Use the dative when there is no change of place.

❶ on ▷ *Das Wort stand an der Tafel.* The word was written on the blackboard. ▷ *Der Lehrer schrieb das Wort an die Tafel.* The teacher wrote the word on the blackboard. ▷ *Köln liegt am Rhein.* Cologne is on the Rhine. ▷ *Christoph hat am neunten November Geburtstag.* Christoph's birthday is on the ninth of November. ▷ *an diesem Tag* on this day ❷ to ▷ *Er ging ans Fenster.* He went to the window. ▷ *Wir waren gestern am Meer.* We went to the seaside yesterday. ▷ *Wir wollen morgen ans Meer fahren.* We want to go to the seaside tomorrow. ▷ *Ich habe einen Brief an meine Mutter geschrieben.* I've written a letter to my mother. ❸ by ▷ *Ihr Haus liegt an der Autobahn.* Their house is by the motorway.; **an Ostern** at Easter; **an etwas denken** to think of something; **reich an Nährstoffen** rich in nutrients; **an etwas sterben** to die of something; **an und für sich** actually; **an die hundert** about a hundred; **von heute an** from today onwards; **Das Licht ist an.** The light's on.; **ohne etwas an** with nothing on; **eine Frage an dich** a question for you; **an diesem Ort** in this place; **unten am Fluss** down by the river

Ananas (*pl* **Ananas**) *f* pineapple

anbauen *vb* [**4**] ❶ to build on ▷ *eine Garage ans Haus anbauen* to build a garage onto the house ❷ to cultivate ▷ *Reis anbauen* to cultivate rice

anbei *adv* enclosed

anbieten *vb* [**8**] to offer ▷ *Ich bot ihr eine Tasse Kaffee an.* I offered her a cup of coffee.; **anbieten, etwas zu tun** to volunteer to do something

Anblick (*pl* **Anblicke**) *m* sight

anbrechen *vb* [**11**]

> For the perfect tense use **haben** when the verb has an object and **sein** when there is no object.

❶ to break into ▷ *Für den Kauf müsste ich meine Ersparnisse anbrechen.* To buy it, I'd have to break into my savings. ❷ to break ▷ *wenn der Tag anbricht* when day breaks ❸ to dawn ▷ *Ein neues Zeitalter ist angebrochen.* A new age has dawned.

andauernd *adj, adv* ❶ continual ▷ *diese andauernden Unterbrechungen* these continual interruptions ❷ constantly ▷ *Er stört andauernd.* He's constantly interrupting.

Andenken (*pl* **Andenken**) *nt* ❶ memory ▷ *zum Andenken an eine schöne Zeit* in memory of a wonderful time ❷ souvenir ▷ *Ich habe mir aus dem Urlaub einige Andenken mitgebracht.* I brought a few souvenirs back from my holiday.

andere *adj, pron* ❶ other ▷ *Nein, nicht dieses Buch, gib mir bitte das andere.* No, not that book, please give me the other one. ❷ different ▷ *Er hat jetzt eine* *andere Freundin*. He's got a different girlfriend now. ❸ another ▷ *ein anderes Mal* another time ▷ *Wir werden das an einem anderen Tag machen*. We'll do that another day.; **kein anderer** nobody else; **die anderen** the others; **etwas anderes** something else

andererseits *adv* on the other hand ▷ *Einerseits ..., andererseits ...* On the one hand ..., on the other hand ...

ändern *vb* [88] to alter ▷ *Ich habe das Kleid ändern lassen*. I've had the dress altered.; **sich ändern** to change

anders *adv* differently ▷ *So geht das nicht, du musst das anders machen*. Not like that – you have to do it differently.; **anders als** different from; **Wer anders?** Who else?; **jemand anders** somebody else; **irgendwo anders** somewhere else; **anders aussehen** to look different

anderthalb *adj* one and a half

Änderung *f* alteration

andeuten *vb* [2] to hint ▷ *Sie hat angedeutet, dass sie weiß, wer es war*. She's hinted that she knows who it was.

Andeutung *f* hint ▷ *Sie hat eine Andeutung gemacht, dass sie es weiß*. She hinted that she knew.

anerkennend *adj, adv* appreciative

Anerkennung *f* ❶ appreciation ▷ *Ihre Leistung fand nicht die entsprechende Anerkennung*. Her work didn't get the appreciation it deserved. ❷ recognition ▷ *Dieser neue Staat hofft auf Anerkennung durch die Bundesrepublik*. This new country is hoping for recognition by the Federal Republic.

Anfall (*pl* **Anfälle**) *m* fit ▷ *Sie hatte einen epileptischen Anfall*. She had an epileptic fit. ▷ *Wenn er das erfährt, bekommt er einen Anfall*. *(informal)* If he finds out, he'll have a fit.

Anfang (*pl* **Anfänge**) *m* beginning ▷ *von Anfang an* right from the beginning ▷ *am Anfang* at the beginning ▷ *Anfang Mai* at the beginning of May; **zu Anfang** first

anfangen *vb* [23] ❶ to begin ▷ *Es fängt an zu regnen*. It's beginning to rain. ❷ to start ▷ *Der Film hat schon angefangen*. The film's already started. ▷ *Hast du den Aufsatz schon angefangen?* Have you already started your essay?; **Damit kann ich nichts anfangen.** It doesn't mean anything to me.; **Das fängt ja gut an!** That's a good start!

Anfänger (*pl* **Anfänger**) *m* beginner

anfassen *vb* [31] ❶ to touch ▷ *Fass den Hund besser nicht an!* You'd better not touch the dog. ❷ to treat ▷ *Du solltest die Kinder nicht immer so rau anfassen!* You shouldn't treat the children so roughly.; **mit anfassen** to lend a hand; **sich anfassen** to feel

sich **anfreunden** *vb* [4] ❶ to make friends ▷ *Ich habe mich in den Ferien mit einer Engländerin angefreundet*. I made friends with an English girl during the holidays. ❷ to become friends ▷ *Die beiden haben sich angefreundet*. The two of them have become friends.

Angabe *f* ❶ information ▷ *Die Angaben waren falsch*. The information was wrong. ❷ *(tennis)* serve ▷ *Wer hat Angabe?* Whose serve is it?; **Das ist doch alles nur Angabe!** That's nothing but show.

angeben *vb* [28] ❶ to give ▷ *Geben Sie bitte Ihre Personalien an*. Please give your personal details. ❷ to state ▷ *Sie hat angegeben, dass sie zu dem Zeitpunkt zu Hause war*. She stated that she was at home at the time. ❸ to indicate ▷ *Alle Raststätten sind auf der Karte angegeben*. All service areas are indicated on the map. ❹ to show off ▷ *Glaub ihm kein Wort, er gibt nur an*. Don't believe a word he says – he's just showing off.

Angeber (*pl* **Angeber**) *m (informal)* show-off

angeblich *adj, adv* ❶ alleged ▷ *Sie ist die angebliche Täterin.* She's the alleged culprit. ❷ allegedly ▷ *Angeblich hat sie es getan.* Allegedly, she did it.

Angebot (*pl* **Angebote**) *nt* offer ▷ *Ich nehme dein Angebot an.* I accept your offer.; **ein Angebot an etwas** a selection of something; **Angebot und Nachfrage** supply and demand

angehen *vb* [**29**]

> For the perfect tense use **haben** when the verb has an object and **sein** when there is no object.

❶ to concern ▷ *Diese Angelegenheit geht mich nichts an.* This matter doesn't concern me.; **Was geht dich das an?** What business is it of yours?; **was ... angeht** as regards ... ❷ to tackle ▷ *Ich weiß noch nicht so richtig, wie ich das Thema angehen soll.* I'm not really sure how to tackle the subject. ❸ to go on ▷ *Das Licht ging an.* The light went on.

Angehörige (*gen* **Angehörigen**, *pl* **Angehörigen**) *mf* relative ▷ *Er ist ein Angehöriger von mir.* He's a relative of mine.

Angel *f* ❶ fishing rod ❷ (*of door*) hinge

> Be careful! The German word **Angel** does not mean **angel**.

Angelegenheit *f* ❶ matter ▷ *Ich werde diese Angelegenheit prüfen.* I'll look into the matter. ❷ affair ▷ *Das ist meine Angelegenheit.* That's my affair.

angeln *vb* [**34**] ❶ to catch ▷ *Er hat eine große Forelle geangelt.* He caught a large trout. ❷ to fish ▷ *Sonntags geht Alex immer angeln.* Alex always goes fishing on Sundays.

angenehm *adj, adv* pleasant; **Angenehm!** Pleased to meet you.

angesehen *adj* respected

Angestellte (*gen* **Angestellten**, *pl* **Angestellten**) *mf* employee ▷ *Er ist nur ein kleiner Angestellter.* He's just a lowly employee.

angewiesen *adj* **auf jemanden angewiesen sein** to be dependent on somebody; **auf etwas angewiesen sein** to be dependent on something

angewöhnen *vb* [**38**] **jemandem etwas angewöhnen** to teach somebody something; **sich etwas angewöhnen** to get into the habit of doing something

Angewohnheit *f* habit ▷ *Das ist so eine Angewohnheit von ihr.* That's a habit of hers.

angreifen (*imperf* **griff an**, *perf* **hat angegriffen**) *vb* ❶ to attack ▷ *Ich wurde von einem Hund angegriffen.* I was attacked by a dog. ❷ to criticize ▷ *Sie wurde wegen dieser Aussage von ihren Freunden angegriffen.* She was criticized by her friends for what she said.

Angriff (*pl* **Angriffe**) *m* attack; **etwas in Angriff nehmen** to make a start on something

Angst (*pl* **Ängste**) *f* fear; **vor jemandem Angst haben** to be afraid of somebody; **vor etwas Angst haben** to be afraid of something; **Ich habe Angst vor der Prüfung.** I'm worried about the exam.; **Angst um jemanden haben** to be worried about somebody; **jemandem Angst machen** to scare somebody

ängstlich *adj, adv* ❶ scared ▷ *Nun sei doch nicht so ängstlich, der Hund tut dir nichts!* There's no need to be scared, the dog won't harm you. ❷ anxious ▷ *'Wird er wieder gesund?', fragte sie ängstlich.* 'Will he get well again?', she asked anxiously.

anhaben *vb* [**32**] to have on ▷ *Sie hatte heute das rote Kleid an.* She had her red dress on today.; **jemandem nichts anhaben können** to have nothing on somebody

anhalten *vb* [**33**] ❶ to stop ▷ *Können wir bitte anhalten, mir ist schlecht.* Can we stop please? I feel sick. ▷ *Kannst du bitte das Auto anhalten?* Can you stop the car

please? ❷ to last ▷ *Das wird nicht lange anhalten.* It won't last long.; **die Luft anhalten** to hold one's breath
Anhalter (*pl* **Anhalter**) *m* hitchhiker; **per Anhalter fahren** to hitchhike
anhand *prep*

The preposition **anhand** takes the genitive.

with the help of ▷ *Wir werden das anhand der Unterlagen prüfen.* We'll check that with the help of the documents.
Anhang (*pl* **Anhänge**) *m* appendix
Anhänger (*pl* **Anhänger**) *m* ❶ supporter ▷ *Er ist Anhänger von Schalke.* He's a Schalke supporter. ❷ *(on car)* trailer ❸ label ▷ *Mach einen Anhänger mit deinem Namen und deiner Adresse an deinen Koffer.* Put a label with your name and address on your case. ❹ pendant ▷ *Sie trug eine Kette mit Anhänger.* She was wearing a chain with a pendant.
Anhängerin *f* supporter ▷ *Sie ist Anhängerin von Schalke.* She's a Schalke supporter.
anhören *vb* [**4**] to listen to ▷ *Wir haben CDs angehört.* We listened to CDs.; **jemandem etwas anhören** to hear something in somebody's voice; **sich anhören** to sound
Anker (*pl* **Anker**) *m* anchor
anklicken *vb* [**4**] *(computer)* to click on ▷ *ein Icon anklicken* to click on an icon
ankommen *vb* [**40**] to arrive ▷ *Wir kommen morgen Nachmittag an.* We'll arrive tomorrow afternoon. ▷ *Ist der Brief schon angekommen?* Has the letter arrived yet?; **bei jemandem gut ankommen** to go down well with somebody; **bei jemandem schlecht ankommen** to go down badly with somebody; **es kommt darauf an** it depends; **wenn es darauf ankommt ...** when it really matters ...; **es darauf ankommen lassen** to wait and see
ankreuzen *vb* [**36**] to mark with a cross
ankündigen *vb* [**4**] to announce
Ankunft (*pl* **Ankünfte**) *f* arrival
Anlage *f* ❶ gardens *pl* ▷ *Wir sind in der Anlage spazieren gegangen.* We went for a walk in the gardens. ❷ plant ▷ *Das ist eine neuartige Anlage zum Recycling von Kunststoff.* That's a new plastics recycling plant. ❸ investment ▷ *Wir raten zu einer Anlage in Immobilien.* We would advise investment in real estate.
Anlass (*gen* **Anlasses**, *pl* **Anlässe**) *m* occasion ▷ *ein festlicher Anlass* a festive occasion; **ein Anlass zu etwas** cause for something; **aus Anlass** on the occasion of; **Anlass zu etwas geben** to give cause for something
Anleitung *f* instructions *pl*
Anlieger (*pl* **Anlieger**) *m* resident ▷ *'Anlieger frei'* 'residents only'
anmachen *vb* [**4**] ❶ to put on ▷ *Mach bitte das Licht an.* Please put the light on. ❷ to light ▷ *Wir haben ein Feuer angemacht.* We lit a fire. ❸ to dress ▷ *Sie macht den Salat immer mit Zitrone an.* She always dresses her salads with lemon. ❹ *(informal)* to chat up ▷ *Ich glaube, der Typ versucht, dich anzumachen.* I think that bloke is trying to chat you up.
anmelden *vb* [**54**] ❶ to announce ▷ *Sie hat für morgen ihren Besuch angemeldet.* She's announced that she'll visit us tomorrow.; **jemanden anmelden** **(1)** to make an appointment for somebody ▷ *Er hat seinen Sohn für morgen beim Zahnarzt angemeldet.* He's made a dental appointment for his son for tomorrow. **(2)** to put somebody's name down ▷ *Habt ihr Max schon im Gymnasium angemeldet?* Have you already put Max's name down for grammar school?; **sich anmelden** **(1)** to make an appointment ▷ *Ich muss mich beim Zahnarzt anmelden.* I must make an appointment with the

dentist. **(2)** to put one's name down ▷ *Sie hat sich für einen Judokurs angemeldet.* She's put her name down for a judo course. ❷ to report ▷ *Alle Besucher müssen sich beim Pförtner anmelden.* All visitors must report to the gatehouse. ❸ to register ▷ *Haben Sie sich schon beim Einwohnermeldeamt angemeldet?* Have you already registered with the residents' registration office?

Anyone moving to a new address in Germany is required by law to register (**sich anmelden**) at the residents' registration office (**Einwohnermeldeamt**).

Anmeldung *f* registration ▷ *Schluss für Anmeldungen ist der erste Mai.* The deadline for registrations is the first of May.

annehmen *vb* [1] ❶ to accept ▷ *Sie wollte das Geschenk nicht annehmen.* She didn't want to accept the present. ▷ *Danke für die Einladung, ich nehme gerne an.* Thank you for the invitation, which I'm happy to accept. ❷ to take ▷ *Er hat den Namen seiner Frau angenommen.* He took his wife's name.; **ein Kind annehmen** to adopt a child ❸ to believe ▷ *Die Polizei nimmt an, dass er der Täter war.* The police believe he did it. ❹ to suppose ▷ *Nehmen wir einmal an, es wäre so.* Let's suppose that was the case.; **angenommen ...** supposing ...

anordnen *vb* [53] ❶ to arrange ▷ *Er ordnete die Blumen zu einem hübschen Gesteck an.* He arranged the flowers into a pretty bouquet. ❷ to order ▷ *Wer hat das angeordnet?* Who ordered that?

anprobieren *vb* [76] to try on

Anrede *f* form of address ▷ *Für verheiratete und unverheiratete Frauen benutzt man die Anrede 'Frau'.* 'Frau' is the form of address used for married and unmarried women.

Anruf (*pl* **Anrufe**) *m* phone call

Anrufbeantworter (*pl* **Anrufbeantworter**) *m* answering machine

anrufen *vb* [56] to phone ▷ *Hat jemand angerufen?* Did anyone phone? ▷ *Ich muss mal eben meine Eltern anrufen.* I must just phone my parents.

ans = **an das**

anschalten *vb* [2] to switch on

anschauen *vb* [4] ❶ to look at ▷ *Schau mich an!* Look at me. ▷ *Willst du dir mal die Fotos anschauen?* Do you want to look at the photos? ❷ to see ▷ *Den Film will ich mir unbedingt anschauen.* I must go and see that film.

anscheinend *adv* apparently

Anschlag (*pl* **Anschläge**) *m* ❶ notice ▷ *Sie machte einen Anschlag am Schwarzen Brett.* She put a notice on the notice board. ❷ attack ▷ *Es gab einen Anschlag auf den Präsidenten.* There's been an attack on the President.

anschließen (*imperf* **schloss an**, *perf* **hat angeschlossen**) *vb* to connect ▷ *Das Telefon ist noch nicht angeschlossen.* The telephone hasn't been connected yet.; **sich jemandem anschließen** to join somebody; **Ich schließe mich dieser Meinung an.** I endorse this view.

anschließend *adj, adv* ❶ subsequent ▷ *die daran anschließende Diskussion* the subsequent discussion ❷ adjacent ▷ *das anschließende Grundstück* the adjacent plot of land ❸ afterwards ▷ *Wir waren essen, und anschließend sind wir ins Kino gegangen.* We had a meal and afterwards went to the cinema.

Anschluss (*gen* **Anschlusses**, *pl* **Anschlüsse**) *m* connection ▷ *Sie haben Anschluss an einen Zug nach Paris.* You have a connection with a train to Paris.; **im Anschluss an** following; **Anschluss finden** to make friends

Word for word, **Anschluss finden** means 'to find a connection'.

sich **anschnallen** *vb* [**4**] to fasten one's seat belt
Anschrift *f* address
ansehen *vb* [**64**] ❶ to look at ▷ *Sieh mich an!* Look at me. ▷ *Willst du dir mal die Fotos ansehen?* Do you want to look at the photos? ❷ to see ▷ *Den Film will ich mir unbedingt ansehen.* I must go and see that film. ▷ *Man hat ihr ihre Enttäuschung angesehen.* You could see the disappointment in her face. ❸ to regard ▷ *Sie wird als eine Expertin auf diesem Gebiet angesehen.* She's regarded as an expert in this field.; **Sieh mal einer an!** Well, fancy that!
Ansehen *nt* ❶ respect ▷ *Sie genießt großes Ansehen bei ihren Kollegen.* She enjoys great respect among her colleagues. ❷ reputation ▷ *Ein solches Benehmen könnte unserem Ansehen schaden.* Behaviour like that could damage our reputation.
Ansicht *f* view ▷ *eine Postkarte mit der Ansicht des Matterhorns* a postcard with a view of the Matterhorn ▷ *Wenn Sie meine Ansicht in dieser Sache hören wollen ...* If you want to hear my view on this business ... ▷ *meiner Ansicht nach* in my view; **zur Ansicht** on approval
Ansichtskarte *f* picture postcard
ansprechen *vb* [**70**] ❶ to approach ▷ *Mich hat ein wildfremder Mann angesprochen.* I was approached by a complete stranger. ❷ to appeal to ▷ *Diese Art von Malerei spricht mich nicht an.* This style of painting doesn't appeal to me. ❸ to ask ▷ *Ich werde Herrn Arnold ansprechen, ob er uns vielleicht hilft.* I'll ask Mr Arnold if he'll maybe help us. ❹ to mention ▷ *Sie hat dieses Problem bis jetzt noch nicht angesprochen.* She hasn't mentioned this problem yet.; **auf etwas ansprechen** to respond to something
Anspruch (*pl* **Ansprüche**) *m* demand ▷ *Sie war den Ansprüchen ihres Berufs nicht gewachsen.* She wasn't up to the demands of her job.; **hohe Ansprüche haben** to demand a lot; **hohe Ansprüche an jemanden stellen** to demand a lot of somebody; **Anspruch auf etwas haben** to be entitled to something; **etwas in Anspruch nehmen** to take advantage of something; **Ihr Beruf nimmt sie sehr in Anspruch.** Her job's very demanding.
anständig *adj* decent ▷ *ein anständiges Essen* a decent meal; **sich anständig benehmen** to behave oneself
anstatt *prep, conj*

> The preposition **anstatt** takes the genitive.

instead of ▷ *Sie kam anstatt ihres Bruders.* She came instead of her brother.
anstecken *vb* [**4**] **Er hat die halbe Klasse mit seiner Grippe angesteckt.** He gave half the class his flu.; **Lachen steckt an.** Laughter is infectious.; **sich anstecken** to catch something
ansteckend *adj* infectious ▷ *eine ansteckende Krankheit* an infectious disease
anstelle *prep*

> The preposition **anstelle** takes the genitive.

instead of ▷ *Anstelle der Mutter hat seine Tante unterschrieben.* His aunt has signed instead of his mother. ▷ *Pralinen anstelle von Blumen* chocolates instead of flowers
anstellen *vb* [**4**] ❶ to turn on ▷ *Kannst du mal bitte den Fernseher anstellen?* Can you turn the television on, please? ❷ to employ ▷ *Sie ist bei einem Versandhaus angestellt.* She's employed by a mail-order company. ❸ to do ▷ *Wie soll ich es bloß anstellen, dass er es erlaubt?* What can I do to get him to allow it? ▷ *Was stellen wir denn heute Nachmittag an?* What shall we do this afternoon? ❹ (*informal*) to be up to

▷ *Was hat der Lümmel denn schon wieder angestellt?* What has that rascal been up to this time?; **sich anstellen (1)** to queue ▷ *Musstet ihr euch für die Karten lange anstellen?* Did you have to queue for long for the tickets? **(2)** to act ▷ *Sie hat sich wirklich dumm angestellt.* She acted really stupidly.; **Stell dich nicht so an.** Don't make such a fuss.

anstrengen *vb* [4] **Die Reise hat mich sehr angestrengt.** The journey took a lot out of me.; **Streng deinen Kopf an!** Use your head!; **sich anstrengen** to make an effort

anstrengend *adj* tiring

Anstrengung *f* effort

Antarktis *f* the Antarctic ▷ *in der Antarktis* in the Antarctic

Anteil (*pl* **Anteile**) *m* share ▷ *Ich möchte meinen Anteil am Gewinn haben.* I would like to have my share of the profit.; **Anteil nehmen an** to sympathize with

Antenne *f* aerial

antiautoritär *adj* anti-authoritarian

antik *adj* antique

Antiquitäten *fpl* antiques *pl*

Antrag (*pl* **Anträge**) *m* ❶ application ▷ *Sie stellte einen Antrag auf Arbeitslosenunterstützung.* She put in an application for unemployment benefit. ❷ motion ▷ *der Antrag der Opposition* the motion put by the opposition

antun *vb* [81] **jemandem etwas antun** to do something to somebody; **jemandem ein Unrecht antun** to wrong somebody; **sich Zwang antun** to force oneself; **sich etwas antun** to kill oneself

Antwort *f* answer ▷ *jemandem eine Antwort geben* to give somebody an answer

antworten *vb* [2] to answer ▷ *Antworte bitte!* Please answer.; **auf etwas antworten** to answer something; **jemandem antworten** to answer somebody

Anwalt (*pl* **Anwälte**) *m* lawyer

Anwältin *f* lawyer

Anweisung *f* instruction ▷ *Folgen Sie bitte den Anweisungen Ihres Führers.* Please follow your guide's instructions. ▷ *Anweisung haben, etwas zu tun* to have instructions to do something

anwenden (*imperf* **wendete** *or* **wandte an**, *perf* **hat angewendet** *or* **angewandt**) *vb* ❶ to use ▷ *Welche Software wenden Sie an?* What software do you use? ▷ *Gewalt anwenden* to use violence ❷ (*law, rule*) to apply

Anwendung *f* application

anwesend *adj* present

Anwesenheit *f* presence

Anzahl *f* number ▷ *je nach Anzahl der Teilnehmer* according to the number of participants ▷ *eine große Anzahl an Fehlern* a large number of mistakes

anzahlen *vb* [4] **fünfzig Euro anzahlen** to pay fifty euros deposit; **ein Auto anzahlen** to put down a deposit on a car

Anzahlung *f* deposit ▷ *eine Anzahlung leisten* to pay a deposit

Anzeichen (*pl* **Anzeichen**) *nt* sign

Anzeige *f* advertisement ▷ *Ich habe ihn über eine Anzeige kennengelernt.* I met him through an advertisement.; **Anzeige gegen jemanden erstatten** to report somebody to the police; **Ich möchte Anzeige wegen Diebstahls erstatten.** I wish to report a theft.

anzeigen *vb* [4] ❶ to show ▷ *Der Tachometer zeigt die Geschwindigkeit an.* The speedometer shows the speed. ❷ to report ▷ *Ich werde Sie wegen Ruhestörung anzeigen!* I'll report you for breach of the peace. ▷ *Ich habe einen Diebstahl anzuzeigen.* I wish to report a theft.

anziehen *vb* [96] ❶ to put on ▷ *Ich muss mir nur noch die Schuhe anziehen.* I just have to put my shoes on. ❷ to dress ▷ *Kannst du bitte die Kinder anziehen?* Can you dress the children, please? ▷ *Er war sehr schick angezogen.* He was dressed very elegantly. ❸ to attract ▷ *Der Zoo zieht viele Besucher an.* The zoo attracts a lot of visitors.; **sich von jemandem angezogen fühlen** to feel attracted to somebody ❹ *(screw)* to tighten; **sich anziehen** to get dressed

Anzug (*pl* **Anzüge**) *m* suit

anzünden *vb* [**54**] to light ▷ *Ich habe mir eine Zigarette angezündet.* I lit a cigarette.

Apfel (*pl* **Äpfel**) *m* apple

Apfelmus (*gen* **Apfelmuses**) *nt* apple purée

Apfelsaft (*pl* **Apfelsäfte**) *m* apple juice

Apfelsine *f* orange

Apotheke *f* chemist's ▷ *in der Apotheke* at the chemist's

Apotheker (*pl* **Apotheker**) *m* pharmacist ▷ *Er ist Apotheker.* He's a pharmacist.

Apparat (*pl* **Apparate**) *m* ❶ gadget ▷ *Mit diesem Apparat kann man Dosen zerkleinern.* You can crush tins with this gadget. ❷ camera ❸ telephone ▷ *Wer war am Apparat?* Who was on the telephone?; **Am Apparat!** Speaking! ❹ *(TV)* set

Appetit *m* appetite; **Ich habe keinen Appetit.** I'm not hungry.

> Word for word, **Ich habe keinen Appetit** means 'I don't have an appetite'.

Guten Appetit! Enjoy your meal!

> Word for word, **Guten Appetit!** means 'Good appetite!'.

Aprikose *f* apricot

April (*gen* **April** *or* **Aprils**, *pl* **Aprile**) *m* April ▷ *im April* in April ▷ *am dritten April* on the third of April ▷ *Ulm, den 3. April 2007* Ulm, 3 April 2007 ▷ *Heute ist der dritte April.* Today is the third of April.; **April, April!** April Fool!

Araber (*pl* **Araber**) *m* Arab

Araberin *f* Arab

arabisch *adj* **arabische Länder** Arab countries; **die arabische Sprache** Arabic

Arbeit *f* ❶ job ▷ *Das ist eine sehr anstrengende Arbeit.* That's a very tiring job. ▷ *Er sucht eine Arbeit auf dem Bau.* He's looking for a job on a building site. ❷ work ▷ *Ich habe im Moment viel Arbeit.* I've got a lot of work at the moment. ▷ *Sie hat keine Arbeit.* She's out of work. ▷ *Das war eine Arbeit!* That was hard work. ❸ dissertation ▷ *Sie schreibt eine Arbeit über englische Ortsnamen.* She's writing a dissertation on English place names. ❹ test ▷ *Ich habe in der Arbeit eine Fünf geschrieben.* I got an 'E' in the test. ▷ *Morgen schreiben wir in Mathe eine Arbeit.* We've got a maths test tomorrow.; **in Arbeit sein** to be in hand

arbeiten *vb* [**2**] to work ▷ *Sie arbeitet hart.* She works hard. ▷ *Er arbeitet als Elektriker bei der Firma Müller.* He works as an electrician for Müller's. ▷ *Seine Nieren arbeiten nicht richtig.* His kidneys don't work properly.; **sich durch etwas arbeiten** to work one's way through something

Arbeiter (*pl* **Arbeiter**) *m* worker

Arbeiterin *f* worker

Arbeitgeber (*pl* **Arbeitgeber**) *m* employer

Arbeitnehmer (*pl* **Arbeitnehmer**) *m* employee ▷ *Als Arbeitnehmer hat man gewisse Rechte.* As an employee you have certain rights.

Arbeitsamt (*pl* **Arbeitsämter**) *nt* job centre

Arbeitserlaubnis (*pl* **Arbeitserlaubnisse**) *f* work permit

arbeitslos *adj* unemployed

Arbeitslose (*gen* **Arbeitslosen**, *pl* **Arbeitslosen**) *mf* unemployed person ▷ *Ein Arbeitsloser hat die Stelle bekommen.* An unemployed person got the job.; **die Arbeitslosen** the unemployed

Arbeitslosigkeit *f* unemployment
Arbeitsort (*pl* **Arbeitsorte**) *m* place of work
Arbeitsplatz (*gen* **Arbeitsplatzes**, *pl* **Arbeitsplätze**) *m* ❶ job ▷ *Suchen Sie einen neuen Arbeitsplatz?* Are you looking for a new job? ❷ desk ▷ *Frau Marr ist im Moment nicht an ihrem Arbeitsplatz.* Ms Marr isn't at her desk at the moment.
Arbeitszeit *f* working hours *pl*; **gleitende Arbeitszeit** flexitime

> Word for word, **gleitende Arbeitszeit** means 'gliding working hours'.

Arbeitszimmer (*pl* **Arbeitszimmer**) *nt* study
Architekt (*gen* **Architekten**, *pl* **Architekten**) *m* architect ▷ *Er ist Architekt.* He's an architect.
Architektur *f* architecture
Argentinien *nt* Argentina
Ärger *m* ❶ anger ▷ *Er hat seinen Ärger über die Verspätung an mir ausgelassen.* He took out his anger at the delay on me. ❷ trouble ▷ *Wenn du das machst, bekommst du Ärger.* If you do that, you'll get into trouble.; **Ärger mit etwas haben** to have trouble with something
ärgerlich *adj* ❶ annoying ▷ *Diese dauernden Störungen sind sehr ärgerlich.* These constant interruptions are very annoying. ❷ angry ▷ *Ich bin auf ihn ärgerlich.* I'm angry with him. ▷ *Er ist über die Verzögerung ärgerlich.* He's angry at the delay.; **jemanden ärgerlich machen** to annoy somebody
ärgern *vb* [**88**] to annoy ▷ *Du sollst deine Schwester nicht immer ärgern!* Don't keep annoying your sister.; **sich ärgern** to be annoyed
Arktis *f* the Arctic ▷ *in der Arktis* in the Arctic
arm *adj* poor ▷ *Er ist ärmer als ich.* He's poorer than me.
Arm (*pl* **Arme**) *m* arm; **jemanden auf den Arm nehmen** *(informal)* to pull somebody's leg
Armband (*pl* **Armbänder**) *nt* bracelet
Armbanduhr *f* wristwatch
Armee *f* army
Ärmel (*pl* **Ärmel**) *m* sleeve
Ärmelkanal *m* the English Channel
Armut *f* poverty
arrangieren *vb* [**76**] to arrange ▷ *Sie hat ein Treffen der beiden arrangiert.* She arranged for them both to meet.
Art (*pl* **Arten**) *f* ❶ way ▷ *Ich mache das auf meine Art.* I do that my way. ❷ kind ▷ *Ich mag diese Art Obst nicht.* I don't like this kind of fruit. ▷ *Häuser aller Art* all kinds of houses ❸ species ▷ *Diese Art ist vom Aussterben bedroht.* This species is in danger of extinction.; **Es ist nicht seine Art, das zu tun.** It's not like him to do that.
Artikel (*pl* **Artikel**) *m* article
Arzneimittel (*pl* **Arzneimittel**) *nt* *(medicine)* drug
Arzt (*pl* **Ärzte**) *m* doctor ▷ *Helmut ist Arzt.* Helmut's a doctor.
Ärztin *f* doctor ▷ *Jutta ist Ärztin.* Jutta's a doctor.
ärztlich *adj* medical; **Die Wunde muss ärztlich behandelt werden.** The wound will have to be treated by a doctor.
As *nt see* **Ass**
Asche (*pl* **Aschen**) *f* ash
Aschenbecher (*pl* **Aschenbecher**) *m* ashtray
Aschermittwoch *m* Ash Wednesday ▷ *am Aschermittwoch* on Ash Wednesday
Asiat (*gen* **Asiaten**, *pl* **Asiaten**) *m* Asian
Asiatin *f* Asian
asiatisch *adj* Asian
Asien *nt* Asia
aß *vb see* **essen**
Ass (*gen* **Asses**, *pl* **Asse**) *nt* ace ▷ *das Herzass* the ace of hearts
Assistent (*gen* **Assistenten**, *pl* **Assistenten**) *m* assistant

Assistentin *f* assistant
Ast (*pl* **Äste**) *m* branch
Asthma *nt* asthma ▷ *Sie hat Asthma.* She's got asthma.
Astrologie *f* astrology
Astronaut (*gen* **Astronauten**, *pl* **Astronauten**) *m* astronaut ▷ *Er ist Astronaut.* He's an astronaut.
Astronomie *f* astronomy
Asyl (*pl* **Asyle**) *nt* asylum ▷ *um Asyl bitten* to ask for asylum; **ein Obdachlosenasyl** a hostel for the homeless
Asylbewerber (*pl* **Asylbewerber**) *m* asylum-seeker
Asylbewerberin *f* asylum-seeker
Atem *m* breath ▷ *außer Atem* out of breath
atemlos *adj* breathless
Atlantik *m* the Atlantic ▷ *eine Insel im Atlantik* an island in the Atlantic
Atlas (*gen* **Atlasses**, *pl* **Atlasse** *or* **Atlanten**) *m* atlas
atmen *vb* [3] to breathe
Atmosphäre *f* atmosphere
Atom (*pl* **Atome**) *nt* atom
Atombombe *f* atom bomb
Atomwaffen *fpl* atomic weapons *pl*
attraktiv *adj* attractive ▷ *attraktiv aussehen* to look attractive
ätzend *adj* ❶ (*informal*) rubbish ▷ *Die Musik ist ätzend.* The music's rubbish. ❷ corrosive ❸ caustic
auch *adv* ❶ also ▷ *Gummienten verkaufen wir auch.* We also sell rubber ducks. ❷ too ▷ *Das ist auch schön.* That's nice, too. ▷ *Ich auch.* Me too.; **Ich auch nicht.** Me neither.; **auch nicht** not ... either; **Auch das noch!** That's all we needed! ❸ even ▷ *Auch wenn das Wetter schlecht ist.* Even if the weather's bad. ▷ *ohne auch nur zu fragen* without even asking; **wer auch** whoever; **was auch** whatever; **wie dem auch sei** be that as it may; **wie sehr er sich auch bemühte** however much he tried

auf *prep, adv* ❶ on

> Use the accusative to express movement or a change of place. Use the dative when there is no change of place.

▷ *Stell die Suppe bitte auf den Tisch.* Please put the soup on the table. ▷ *Die Suppe steht auf dem Tisch.* The soup's on the table.; **auf dem Land** in the country; **auf der ganzen Welt** in the whole world; **auf Deutsch** in German; **bis auf ihn** except for him; **auf einmal** at once; **auf seinen Vorschlag hin** at his suggestion ❷ open ▷ *Das Fenster ist auf.* The window's open. ▷ *Die Geschäfte sind am Sonntag nicht auf.* The shops aren't open on Sunday. ❸ up ▷ *Ist er schon auf?* Is he up yet? ▷ *Ich bin schon seit sieben Uhr auf.* I've been up since seven.; **auf und ab** up and down; **auf und davon** up and away
aufatmen *vb* [4] to heave a sigh of relief
aufbauen *vb* [4] to build up
aufbekommen *vb* [40] ❶ to get open ▷ *Ich bekomme das Fenster nicht auf.* I can't get the window open. ❷ to be given homework ▷ *Wir haben heute nichts aufbekommen.* We weren't given any homework today.
aufbewahren *vb* [38] to keep ▷ *Sie bewahrt ihre Ersparnisse in einer Blechdose auf.* She keeps her savings in a tin.
aufbleiben *vb* [10] ❶ to stay open ▷ *Heute bleiben die Geschäfte länger auf.* The shops stay open longer today. ❷ to stay up ▷ *Heute dürft ihr ausnahmsweise länger aufbleiben.* Today you can stay up late for once.
aufbrechen *vb* [11]

> For the perfect tense use **haben** when the verb has an object and **sein** when there is no object.

❶ to break open ▷ *Die Diebe haben den Safe aufgebrochen.* The thieves broke the safe open. ❷ to open up ▷ *Die Wunde ist wieder aufgebrochen.* The wound has

a b c d e f g h i j k l m n o p q r s t u v w x y z

opened up again. ❸ to set off ▷ *Wann seid ihr aufgebrochen?* When did you set off?

aufbringen *vb* [**13**] ❶ to open ▷ *Ich bringe das Konservenglas nicht auf.* I can't open the jar. ❷ to raise ▷ *Wie soll ich nur das Geld für die Reparatur aufbringen?* However am I going raise the money for the repairs?; **Verständnis für etwas aufbringen** to be able to understand something

aufeinander *adv* on top of each other ▷ *Leg die Handtücher aufeinander.* Put the towels on top of each other.; **aufeinander schießen** to shoot at one another; **aufeinander vertrauen** to trust each other

Aufenthalt (*pl* **Aufenthalte**) *m* ❶ stay ▷ *Während unseres Aufenthalts in London ...* During our stay in London ... ❷ stop ▷ *Der Zug hat fünf Minuten Aufenthalt in Ulm.* The train has a five-minute stop in Ulm.

aufessen *vb* [**20**] to eat up

auffallen *vb* [**22**] to be conspicuous; **jemandem auffallen** to strike somebody

auffällig *adj* conspicuous; **auffällig gekleidet sein** to be dressed strikingly

auffangen *vb* [**23**] to catch

aufführen *vb* [**4**] ❶ to perform ▷ *ein Stück aufführen* to perform a play ❷ to list ▷ *Alle Fachausdrücke sind im Anhang aufgeführt.* All technical terms are listed in the appendix.; **sich aufführen** to behave

Aufführung *f* performance

Aufgabe *f* ❶ task ▷ *Vier Kinder zu erziehen ist eine schwierige Aufgabe.* Bringing up four children is a difficult task. ❷ question ▷ *Ich konnte die zweite Aufgabe in der Mathearbeit nicht lösen.* I couldn't solve the second question in the maths test. ❸ homework ▷ *Hast du deine Aufgaben schon gemacht?* Have you done your homework yet?

aufgeben *vb* [**28**] ❶ to give up ▷ *Du solltest das Rauchen aufgeben.* You should give up smoking. ❷ to post ▷ *Ich habe das Paket an dich vor drei Tagen aufgegeben.* I posted the parcel to you three days ago. ❸ to check in ▷ *Du kannst den Koffer ja vor der Reise aufgeben.* You can check in your suitcase before you travel.; **eine Anzeige aufgeben** to place an advertisement; **Ich gebe auf!** I give up.

aufgehen *vb* [**29**] ❶ to rise ▷ *Der Mond ist aufgegangen.* The moon has risen. ❷ to open ▷ *Die Tür ging auf, und Christoph kam herein.* The door opened and Christoph came in.; **Zwanzig durch sechs geht nicht auf.** Six into twenty doesn't go.

aufgeregt *adj* excited

aufgrund *prep*

> The preposition **aufgrund** takes the genitive.

❶ because of ▷ *Das Spiel ist aufgrund des schlechten Wetters ausgefallen.* The game was cancelled because of the bad weather. ❷ on the basis of ▷ *Sie wurde aufgrund von Indizien überführt.* She was convicted on the basis of circumstantial evidence.

aufhaben *vb* [**32**] ❶ to have on ▷ *Sie hatte einen roten Hut auf.* She had a red hat on. ❷ to have homework to do ▷ *Wir haben heute in Englisch nichts auf.* We haven't got any English homework to do today.

aufhalten *vb* [**33**] ❶ to detain ▷ *Ich möchte dich nicht aufhalten.* I don't want to detain you. ❷ to check ▷ *Wie kann die Vergrößerung des Ozonlochs aufgehalten werden?* How can the growth of the ozone hole be checked? ❸ to hold open ▷ *Kannst du mir bitte die Tür aufhalten?* Can you hold the door open for me, please?; **Sie hielt die Hand auf.** She held out her hand.; **sich aufhalten (1)** to live ▷ *Sie hat sich lange im Ausland aufgehalten.* She lived abroad for a long time. **(2)** to stay ▷ *Ich möchte mich nicht lange aufhalten.* I don't want to stay long.; **sich mit etwas aufhalten** to waste time over something ▷ *Mit solchen Kinderspielen halte ich mich doch nicht auf.* I'm not wasting my time over such childish games.

aufhängen *vb* [**35**] *(washing)* to hang up; **sich aufhängen** to hang oneself

aufheben (*imperf* **hob auf**, *perf* **hat aufgehoben**) *vb* ❶ to pick up ▷ *Sie hob das Heft, das auf den Boden gefallen war, auf.* She picked up the exercise book which had fallen on the floor. ❷ to keep ▷ *Sie hat alle seine Briefe aufgehoben.* She's kept all his letters.; **gut aufgehoben sein** to be well looked after

aufhören *vb* [**4**] to stop ▷ *Der Regen hat aufgehört.* The rain's stopped.; **aufhören, etwas zu tun** to stop doing something

Aufkleber (*pl* **Aufkleber**) *m* sticker

auflassen *vb* [**42**] ❶ to leave open ▷ *Lass bitte das Fenster auf.* Please leave the window open. ❷ to keep on ▷ *Kann ich meine Mütze auflassen?* Can I keep my hat on?

auflegen *vb* [**4**] to hang up ▷ *Sie hat einfach aufgelegt.* She simply hung up.

auflösen *vb* [**4**] ❶ to dissolve ▷ *Du solltest die Tablette in Wasser auflösen.* You should dissolve the tablet in water. ❷ to break up ▷ *Die Polizei hat die Demonstration aufgelöst.* The police broke up the demonstration.; **sich auflösen** to dissolve; **wenn sich der Nebel aufgelöst hat** when the fog has lifted; **in Tränen aufgelöst sein** to be in tears

aufmachen *vb* [**4**] ❶ to open ▷ *Kannst du bitte die Tür aufmachen?* Can you open the door, please? ▷ *Wann machen die Geschäfte auf?* When do the shops open? ❷ to undo ▷ *Ich schaffe es nicht, den Reißverschluss aufzumachen.* I can't undo the zip.; **sich aufmachen** to set out

aufmerksam *adj* attentive; **jemanden auf etwas aufmerksam machen** to point something out to somebody

Aufmerksamkeit *f* attention ▷ *Darf ich um Ihre Aufmerksamkeit bitten!* May I have your attention?; **Wir sollten ihnen eine kleine Aufmerksamkeit mitbringen.** We ought to take them a little something.

Aufnahme *f* ❶ welcome ▷ *Wir fanden eine sehr freundliche Aufnahme in unserer Partnerstadt.* We were given a very friendly welcome in our twin town. ❷ recording ▷ *Wir haben uns die Aufnahme des Konzerts angehört.* We listened to a recording of the concert. ❸ photograph ▷ *Möchtest du die Aufnahmen sehen, die ich in den Ferien gemacht habe?* Would you like to see the photographs I took on holiday?

Aufnahmeprüfung *f* entrance test

aufnehmen *vb* [**52**] ❶ to take ▷ *Wie hat sie die Nachricht aufgenommen?* How did she take the news? ❷ to record ▷ *eine Sendung aufnehmen* to record a programme ❸ to photograph ▷ *Diesen tollen Sonnenuntergang muss ich aufnehmen.* I must photograph this wonderful sunset. ❹ to admit ▷ *Was muss man tun, um in den Tennisklub aufgenommen zu werden?* What do you have to do to be admitted to the tennis club?; **es mit jemandem aufnehmen können** to be able to compete with somebody

aufpassen *vb* [**31**] to pay attention ▷ *Ich habe heute im Unterricht nicht aufgepasst.* I didn't pay attention in class today.; **auf jemanden aufpassen** to look after somebody; **auf etwas aufpassen** to look after something; **Aufgepasst!** Look out!

aufräumen *vb* [**4**] to tidy up ▷ *Ich darf erst raus, wenn ich mein Zimmer* *aufgeräumt habe.* I can't go out until I've tidied up my room.

aufrecht *adj* upright

aufregen *vb* [**4**] to excite; **sich aufregen** to get excited

aufregend *adj* exciting

aufs = **auf das**

Aufsatz (*gen* **Aufsatzes**, *pl* **Aufsätze**) *m* essay ▷ *Wir haben heute in Deutsch einen Aufsatz geschrieben.* We wrote an essay in today's German lesson.

aufschieben (*imperf* **schob auf**, *perf* **hat aufgeschoben**) *vb* ❶ to push open ▷ *Man kann diese Tür aufschieben.* You can push this door open. ❷ to put off ▷ *Wir haben unsere Abreise noch einmal aufgeschoben.* We put off our departure once again.

aufschlagen *vb* [**59**] ❶ to open ▷ *ein Buch aufschlagen* to open a book ▷ *Schlagt Seite 111 auf.* Open your books at page 111. ❷ to pitch ▷ *Sie schlugen ihre Zelte auf.* They pitched their tents. ❸ *(prices)* to go up ▷ *Butter ist wieder aufgeschlagen.* The price of butter has gone up again. ❹ *(tennis)* to serve ▷ *Du schlägst auf.* It's your turn to serve.

aufschließen (*imperf* **schloss auf**, *perf* **hat aufgeschlossen**) *vb* to unlock ▷ *Schließ bitte die Tür auf!* Please unlock the door. ▷ *Sie schloss auf und ging hinein.* She unlocked the door and went in.

aufschlussreich *adj* informative

Aufschnitt (*pl* **Aufschnitte**) *m* cold meat

aufschreiben *vb* [**61**] to write down

Aufsehen *nt* stir ▷ *Ihre Kleidung hat Aufsehen erregt.* Her outfit caused a stir.

aufsehenerregend *adj* sensational

auf sein *vb* [**65**] *see* **auf**

aufsetzen *vb* [**36**] to put on ▷ *Setz dir eine Mütze auf!* Put a hat on.; **Ich setze das Teewasser auf.** I'll put the kettle on.; **sich aufsetzen** to sit up

Aufsicht *f* supervision; **die Aufsicht haben** to be in charge

aufstehen *vb* [**72**]

> Use **sein** for 'to get up' and **haben** for 'to be open'.

❶ to get up ▷ *Wann bist du heute Morgen aufgestanden?* When did you get up this morning? ▷ *Sie stand auf und ging.* She got up and left. ❷ to be open ▷ *Die Tür hat aufgestanden, also ging ich hinein.* The door was open, so I went in.

aufstellen *vb* [**4**] ❶ to pitch ▷ *Wir haben unser Zelt am Waldrand aufgestellt.* We pitched our tent at the edge of the woods. ❷ to stand up ▷ *Der Sonnenschirm ist umgefallen, ich muss ihn wieder aufstellen.* The sunshade has fallen over. I'll have to stand it up again. ❸ to set up ▷ *Sie stellte die Schachfiguren auf.* She set up the chess pieces.; **eine Liste aufstellen** to draw up a list; **einen Rekord aufstellen** to set a record; **jemanden für ein Spiel aufstellen** to pick somebody for a game; **sich aufstellen** to line up

auftauchen (*perf* **ist aufgetaucht**) *vb* [**4**] to appear

auftauen (*perf* **hat/ist aufgetaut**) *vb* [**4**]

> For the perfect tense use **haben** when the verb has an object and **sein** when there is no object.

❶ to thaw ▷ *Der Schnee taute auf.* The snow thawed. ❷ to defrost ▷ *Ich habe die Pizza im Mikrowellenherd aufgetaut.* I've defrosted the pizza in the microwave.

Auftrag (*pl* **Aufträge**) *m* orders *pl* ▷ *Ich habe den Auftrag, Sie davon zu unterrichten, dass ...* I have orders to inform you that ...; **im Auftrag von** on behalf of

auftreten *vb* [**79**] ❶ to appear ▷ *Dieser Schauspieler tritt erst im dritten Akt auf.* This actor doesn't appear until the third act. ❷ to occur ▷ *Sollten Probleme auftreten, wende dich an uns.* If any problems occur, get in touch with us. ❸ to behave ▷ *Er ist ziemlich unbeliebt,* *weil er immer so überheblich auftritt.* He's quite unpopular because he always behaves so arrogantly.

aufwachen (*perf* **ist aufgewacht**) *vb* [**4**] to wake up

aufwachsen *vb* [**87**] to grow up

aufwecken *vb* [**4**] to wake up

aufzählen *vb* [**4**] to list

Aufzug (*pl* **Aufzüge**) *m* lift ▷ *Wir sind mit dem Aufzug nach oben gefahren.* We went up in the lift.

Auge (*pl* **Augen**) *nt* eye ▷ *Sie hat dunkle Augen.* She's got dark eyes.; **unter vier Augen** in private

Augenblick (*pl* **Augenblicke**) *m* moment; **im Augenblick** at the moment

Augenbraue *f* eyebrow

August (*gen* **Augustes** *or* **August**, *pl* **Auguste**) *m* August ▷ *im August* in August ▷ *am fünften August* on 5 August ▷ *Ulm, den 5. August 2008* Ulm, 5 August 2008 ▷ *Heute ist der fünfte August.* Today is the fifth of August.

Aula (*pl* **Aulen**) *f* assembly hall

aus *prep, adv*

> The preposition **aus** takes the dative.

❶ out of ▷ *Sie nahm ein Bonbon aus der Tüte.* She took a sweet out of the bag. ▷ *aus dem Fenster* out of the window ❷ from ▷ *Wenn er aus der Schule kommt, ist er immer sehr müde.* When he comes home from school he's always very tired. ▷ *Ich komme aus Deutschland.* I come from Germany. ▷ *Er ist aus Berlin.* He's from Berlin. ❸ made of ▷ *Die Vase ist aus Porzellan.* The vase is made of china.; **aus Erfahrung** from experience; **aus Spaß** for fun; **aus Freundschaft** out of a sense of friendship ❹ finished ▷ *wenn das Kino aus ist* when the film's finished ▷ *Komm sofort nach Hause, wenn die Schule aus ist.* Come straight home when school has finished.; **Wann ist die Schule aus?** When does school finish? ❺ off ▷ *Der Fernseher ist aus.* The television's off.; **Licht aus!** Lights out!; **Sie können meinen Mann nicht sprechen, er ist aus.** You can't speak to my husband. He's out.; **von sich aus** of one's own accord; **von ihm aus** as far as he's concerned

ausatmen *vb* [**2**] to breathe out

ausbilden *vb* [**54**] to train ▷ *Er bildet Lehrlinge aus.* He trains apprentices. ▷ *Sie ist ausgebildete Krankenschwester.* She's a qualified nurse.

Ausbildung *f* training ▷ *eine solide Ausbildung* a decent training

Ausbildungsplatz (*gen* **Ausbildungsplatzes**, *pl* **Ausbildungsplätze**) *m* training job

Ausdauer *f* stamina

ausdenken *vb* [**14**] **sich etwas ausdenken** to think something up

Ausdruck (1) (*pl* **Ausdrücke**) *m* expression ▷ *Sie hat in der Schule ein paar schlimme Ausdrücke gelernt.* She's learned a few nasty expressions at school. ▷ *Als Ausdruck meiner Dankbarkeit habe ich ihr Blumen geschenkt.* I gave her flowers as an expression of my gratitude. ▷ *Ich kann am Ausdruck in deinem Gesicht sehen, dass dir das nicht passt.* I can see by your expression that it doesn't suit you.

Ausdruck (2) (*pl* **Ausdrucke**) *m* printout ▷ *Kannst du mir von der Datei einen Ausdruck machen?* Can you do me a printout of the file?

ausdrucken *vb* [**4**] to print out ▷ *Soll ich dir die Namen ausdrucken?* Shall I print out the names for you?

ausdrücken *vb* [**4**] to express ▷ *Ich weiß nicht, wie man das auf Englisch ausdrückt.* I don't know how to express it in English.

ausdrücklich *adj* explicit ▷ *Sie hat dir das ausdrücklich verboten.* She explicitly forbade you to do it.

auseinander *adv* apart ▷ *weit auseinander* far apart

a b c d e f g h i j k l m n o p q r s t u v w x y z

Ausfahrt *f* exit ▷ *Wir müssen an der nächsten Ausfahrt raus.* We have to take the next exit.

ausfallen (*perf* **ist ausgefallen**) *vb* [**22**] (1) to be cancelled ▷ *Der Sportunterricht fällt heute aus.* PE has been cancelled today. (2) to break down ▷ *Die Heizung ist mal wieder ausgefallen.* The heating has broken down again.; **Wenn der Strom ausfällt, ...** If there's a power cut ... (3) to fall out ▷ *Ihm sind die Haare ausgefallen, als er noch ziemlich jung war.* His hair fell out when he was still quite young.; **Die Arbeit ist sehr schlecht ausgefallen.** The results of the test were awful.

Ausflug (*pl* **Ausflüge**) *m* outing ▷ *einen Ausflug machen* to go on an outing

ausfragen *vb* [**4**] to question

Ausfuhr *f* export

ausführen *vb* [**4**] (1) to carry out ▷ *Sie hat ihren Plan ausgeführt.* She carried out her plan. (2) to export ▷ *Waren ausführen* to export goods; **jemanden ausführen** to take somebody out; **einen Hund ausführen** to take a dog for a walk

ausführlich *adj, adv* (1) detailed ▷ *ein ausführlicher Bericht* a detailed report (2) in detail ▷ *Sie hat mir ausführlich erzählt, wie es in den Ferien war.* She told me in detail what her holidays were like.

ausfüllen *vb* [**4**] to fill in ▷ *Füllt bitte die Lücken im Text aus.* Please fill in the gaps in the text. ▷ *Hast du den Antrag schon ausgefüllt?* Have you filled in the application form yet?

Ausgabe *f* (1) expenditure ▷ *Wir hatten in der letzten Zeit viele Ausgaben.* We've had a lot of expenditure recently. (2) edition ▷ *Sie hat eine sehr alte Ausgabe von Goethes Werken.* She's got a very old edition of Goethe's works. (3) issue ▷ *Ich habe das in der letzten Ausgabe meines Computermagazins gelesen.* I read it in the last issue of my computer magazine.

Ausgang (*pl* **Ausgänge**) *m* (1) exit ▷ *Ich warte dann am Ausgang auf euch.* I'll wait for you at the exit, then.; **'Kein Ausgang'** 'No exit' (2) ending ▷ *Der Film hat einen sehr traurigen Ausgang.* The film has a very sad ending. (3) result ▷ *Welchen Ausgang hatte das Spiel?* What was the result of the match?

ausgeben *vb* [**28**] (1) to spend ▷ *Wir haben auf dem Volksfest hundert Euro ausgegeben.* We spent a hundred euros at the fair. (2) to distribute ▷ *Du musst dich da vorn anstellen, da werden die Karten ausgegeben.* You have to queue at the front there. That's where the tickets are being distributed.; **einen ausgeben** (*informal*) to stand a round; **sich für jemanden ausgeben** to pass oneself off as somebody; **sich als etwas ausgeben** to pretend to be something

ausgehen *vb* [**29**] (1) to go out ▷ *Sollen wir heute Abend ausgehen?* Shall we go out this evening? ▷ *Fritz will mit dir ausgehen.* Fritz wants to go out with you. ▷ *Plötzlich ging das Licht aus.* Suddenly the light went out. (2) to run out ▷ *Wir sollten tanken, bevor das Benzin ausgeht.* We ought to fill up before we run out of petrol. ▷ *Mir ging das Benzin aus.* I ran out of petrol.; **Wie ist das Spiel ausgegangen?** How did the game end?; **schlecht ausgehen** to turn out badly; **Wir können davon ausgehen, dass ...** We can assume that ...

ausgelassen *adj* exuberant

ausgenommen *conj* except ▷ *Alle kamen, ausgenommen Günter.* Everyone came except Günter.; **Anwesende sind ausgenommen.** Present company excepted.

ausgerechnet *adv* **ausgerechnet heute** today of all days; **ausgerechnet du** you of all people

ausgeschlossen *adj* impossible ▷ *Ich halte das für ausgeschlossen.* I think that's impossible.

ausgezeichnet *adj, adv* ❶ excellent ▷ *Werner ist ein ausgezeichneter Koch.* Werner's an excellent cook. ❷ excellently ▷ *Sie hat es ausgezeichnet gemacht.* She did it excellently.

aushalten *vb* [**33**] **Ich halte diese Hitze nicht aus!** I can't stand this heat.; **Das ist nicht zum Aushalten.** It's unbearable.

sich **auskennen** *vb* [**39**] ❶ to know about ▷ *Sie kennt sich mit Kindern gut aus.* She knows a lot about children. ❷ to know one's way around ▷ *Er kennt sich in Stuttgart aus.* He knows his way around Stuttgart.

auskommen *vb* [**40**] **mit jemandem auskommen** to get on with somebody; **mit etwas auskommen** to manage on something

Auskunft (*pl* **Auskünfte**) *f* ❶ information ▷ *Nähere Auskunft erhalten Sie unter der folgenden Nummer.* For further information ring the following number. ❷ information office ▷ *Fragen Sie bei der Auskunft, wann der nächste Zug nach Bremen geht.* Ask at the information office when the next train leaves for Bremen.; **Telefonauskunft** directory inquiries *pl*

auslachen *vb* [**4**] to laugh at ▷ *Sie hat mich nur ausgelacht.* She just laughed at me.

Ausland *nt* **im Ausland** abroad; **ins Ausland** abroad

Ausländer (*pl* **Ausländer**) *m* foreigner ▷ *Ihr Mann ist Ausländer.* Her husband's a foreigner.

Ausländerin *f* foreigner ▷ *Seine Frau ist Ausländerin.* His wife's a foreigner.

ausländisch *adj* foreign

Auslandsgespräch (*pl* **Auslandsgespräche**) *nt* international call

auslassen *vb* [**42**] ❶ to leave out ▷ *Die nächste Übung können wir auslassen.* We can leave out the next exercise.; **Ich lasse heute das Mittagessen aus.** I'm skipping lunch today. ❷ to leave off ▷ *Heute lass ich den Fernseher aus.* I'm leaving the television off today. ▷ *Bei der Hitze kannst du die Jacke auslassen.* You can leave your jacket off in this heat.; **seine Wut an jemandem auslassen** to take one's anger out on somebody

ausleihen (*imperf* **lieh aus**, *perf* **hat ausgeliehen**) *vb* to lend ▷ *Kannst du mir dein Moped ausleihen?* Can you lend me your moped?; **sich etwas ausleihen** to borrow something

ausloggen *vb* [**4**] (*computer*) to log off

ausmachen *vb* [**48**] ❶ to turn off ▷ *Mach bitte das Radio aus, die Musik stört mich.* Please turn the radio off. The music's disturbing me.; **das Licht ausmachen** to switch off the light ❷ to put out ▷ *Du solltest deine Zigarette ausmachen, bevor du hineingehst.* You should put your cigarette out before you go in. ❸ to arrange ▷ *Habt ihr schon einen Termin für das Fest ausgemacht?* Have you arranged a date for the party yet? ▷ *Ich habe mit ihr ausgemacht, dass wir uns um fünf Uhr treffen.* I've arranged to meet her at five. ❹ to settle ▷ *Macht das unter euch aus.* Settle the matter between you. ❺ to mind ▷ *Es macht mir nichts aus, wenn ich allein gehen muss.* I don't mind having to go alone. ▷ *Macht es Ihnen etwas aus, wenn ...?* Would you mind if ...?

Ausnahme *f* exception

ausnahmsweise *adv* for once

ausnützen *vb* [**4**] to use

auspacken *vb* [**4**] to unpack

ausprobieren *vb* [**4**] to try out

Auspuff (*pl* **Auspuffe**) *m* exhaust

ausrechnen *vb* [**4**] to calculate

Ausrede *f* excuse

ausreichen *vb* [**4**] to be enough

a b c d e f g h i j k l m n o p q r s t u v w x y z

ausreichend *adj* ❶ sufficient ▷ *ausreichend Geld* sufficient money ❷ adequate

German marks range from one (**sehr gut**) to six (**ungenügend**).

Ausreise *f* departure; **bei der Ausreise** when leaving the country

ausrichten *vb* [**4**] ❶ to tell ▷ *Ich werde es ihm ausrichten.* I'll tell him.; **Richte bitte an deine Eltern schöne Grüße aus.** Please give my regards to your parents. ❷ to gear to ▷ *Wir müssen unser Veranstaltungsangebot mehr auf Jugendliche ausrichten.* We must gear our events more to young people.

ausrufen *vb* [**56**] to cry out; **jemanden ausrufen lassen** to page somebody

Ausrufezeichen (*pl* **Ausrufezeichen**) *nt* exclamation mark

sich **ausruhen** *vb* [**4**] to rest

ausrüsten *vb* [**4**] to equip

Ausrüstung *f* equipment

ausschalten *vb* [**2**] to switch off

ausschlafen *vb* [**58**] to have a good sleep; **Morgen kann ich ausschlafen.** I can have a lie-in tomorrow.; **Ich bin nicht ausgeschlafen.** I didn't get enough sleep.

ausschließlich *adv, prep* ❶ exclusively ▷ *Der Schulhof ist ausschließlich für Schüler dieser Schule.* The school yard is exclusively for pupils of this school. ❷ except ▷ *Wir haben jeden Tag geöffnet ausschließlich Sonntag.* We're open every day except Sunday.

ausschneiden *vb* [**60**] to cut out

aussehen *vb* [**64**] to look ▷ *Sie sieht sehr hübsch aus.* She looks very pretty. ▷ *Wie siehst du denn aus?* What do you look like! ▷ *Es sieht nach Regen aus.* It looks like rain. ▷ *Es sieht schlecht aus.* Things look bad.

Aussehen *nt* appearance

aus sein *vb* [**65**] *see* **aus**

außen *adv* on the outside ▷ *Außen ist es rot.* It's red on the outside.

Außenseiter (*pl* **Außenseiter**) *m* outsider

außer *prep, conj*

The preposition **außer** takes the dative.

❶ apart from ▷ *Außer dir haben das alle verstanden.* Everyone has understood apart from you. ▷ *Wer war noch da außer Horst?* Apart from Horst, who was there?; **außer Haus** out; **außer Landes** abroad; **außer Gefahr** out of danger; **außer Betrieb** out of order; **außer sich sein** to be beside oneself ❷ if ... not ▷ *Wir machen morgen ein Picknick, außer es regnet.* We're having a picnic tomorrow if it doesn't rain.

außerdem *conj* in addition

äußere *adj* ❶ outer ▷ *Sie bildeten einen äußeren und einen inneren Kreis.* They formed an outer and an inner circle. ❷ external ▷ *Nur zur äußeren Anwendung.* For external use only.

außergewöhnlich *adj* unusual

außerhalb *prep, adv*

The preposition **außerhalb** takes the genitive.

❶ outside ▷ *Es liegt außerhalb der Stadt.* It's outside the town. ❷ out of town ▷ *Sie wohnt nicht in Ulm, sondern ziemlich weit außerhalb.* She doesn't live in Ulm, but quite a way out of town.; **außerhalb der Saison** out of season

äußern *vb* [**88**] to express ▷ *Sie hat den Wunsch geäußert, allein in die Ferien fahren zu dürfen.* She's expressed the wish to be allowed to go on holiday alone.; **eine Meinung äußern** to give an opinion; **sich äußern** to comment

äußerst *adv* extremely

äußerste *adj* utmost ▷ *Diese Sache ist von äußerster Wichtigkeit.* This matter is of the utmost importance.

Äußerung *f* remark

Aussicht *f* ❶ view ▷ *Vom Hotel aus hat man eine schöne Aussicht aufs Meer.* You have a wonderful view of the sea from the hotel. ❷ prospect ▷ *Die Aussicht auf* *diese Stelle hat ihr neuen Mut gegeben.* The prospect of this job gave her new hope. ▷ *Das sind ja schöne Aussichten!* What a prospect!; **etwas in Aussicht haben** to have the prospect of something

ausspannen *vb* [**4**] to relax

Aussprache *f* ❶ pronunciation ▷ *Die Aussprache der Wörter ist mit phonetischen Zeichen angegeben.* The pronunciation of the words is shown by phonetic symbols. ❷ frank discussion ▷ *Ich hatte gestern eine lange Aussprache mit ihm.* I had a long, frank discussion with him yesterday.

aussprechen *vb* [**70**] to pronounce ▷ *Wie spricht man dieses Wort aus?* How do you pronounce this word?; **sich mit jemandem aussprechen** to talk things out with somebody; **sich gegen etwas aussprechen** to speak out against something; **sich für etwas aussprechen** to speak out in favour of something; **Lass ihn doch aussprechen!** Let him finish.

aussteigen *vb* [**74**] to get off ▷ *Ich sah, wie sie aus der Straßenbahn ausstieg.* I saw her get off the tram.

ausstellen *vb* [**4**] ❶ to exhibit ▷ *Im Museum werden zurzeit Bilder von Chagall ausgestellt.* Pictures by Chagall are currently being exhibited in the museum. ❷ to be on display ▷ *Im Schaufenster war exotisches Obst ausgestellt.* Exotic fruit was on display in the window. ❸ to switch off ▷ *Die Heizung wird im Mai ausgestellt.* The heating's switched off in May. ❹ to write ▷ *Die Lehrerin hat ihm ein gutes Zeugnis ausgestellt.* The teacher wrote him a good report. ❺ to issue ▷ *Auf welchem Amt werden Pässe ausgestellt?* Which office issues passports?

Ausstellung *f* exhibition

aussterben *vb* [**75**] to die out

Ausstieg *m* ❶ exit ▷ *Der Ausstieg ist hinten.* The exit is at the back. ❷ abandonment ▷ *der Ausstieg aus der Atomenergie* abandonment of nuclear energy

aussuchen *vb* [**4**] to choose ▷ *Such dir ein Eis aus.* Choose yourself an ice cream.

austauschen *vb* [**4**] ❶ to replace ▷ *Ich habe die Festplatte ausgetauscht.* I've replaced the hard disk. ❷ to substitute ▷ *Der Mittelstürmer wurde ausgetauscht.* The centre-forward was substituted.

austeilen *vb* [**4**] to give out

austragen *vb* [**77**] ❶ to deliver ▷ *Morgens trägt er immer die Post aus.* In the morning he always delivers the post. ❷ to hold ▷ *Der Wettkampf wird im Olympiastadion ausgetragen.* The competition will be held in the Olympic stadium.

Australien *nt* Australia

Australier (*pl* **Australier**) *m* Australian

Australierin *f* Australian

australisch *adj* Australian

austreten *vb* [**79**] **aus etwas austreten** to leave something; **Ich muss mal austreten.** (*informal*) I need to go to the loo.

austrinken *vb* [**80**] ❶ to drink up ▷ *Er trank aus und ging.* He drank up and left. ❷ to finish ▷ *Lass mich noch schnell meinen Saft austrinken.* Let me just quickly finish my juice.

Ausverkauf (*pl* **Ausverkäufe**) *m* clearance sale

ausverkauft *adj* ❶ sold out ▷ *Die Vorstellung ist leider ausverkauft.* The performance is sold out, I'm afraid. ❷ full ▷ *Das Kino war ausverkauft.* The cinema was full.

Auswahl *f* selection ▷ *Sie haben eine große Auswahl an Schuhen.* They have a large selection of shoes.

auswählen *vb* [**4**] to select

auswandern *vb* [**88**] to emigrate ▷ *Sie sind nach Australien ausgewandert.* They emigrated to Australia.

a b c d e f g h i j k l m n o p q r s t u v w x y z

auswärts *adv* ❶ in another town ▷ *Sie wohnt in Calw, arbeitet aber auswärts.* She lives in Calw but works in another town. ❷ away ▷ *Unsere Mannschaft spielt nächste Woche auswärts.* Our team's playing away next week.; **auswärts essen** to eat out

Ausweis (*pl* **Ausweise**) *m* ❶ identity card ▷ *Der Polizist wollte meinen Ausweis sehen.* The policeman wanted to see my identity card. ❷ card ▷ *Wenn du Schüler bist und deinen Ausweis zeigst, bekommst du Ermäßigung.* If you're a student and show them your card, you get a reduction.

auswendig *adv* by heart ▷ *etwas auswendig lernen* to learn something by heart

ausziehen *vb* [**96**]

> For the perfect tense use **haben** when the verb has an object and **sein** when there is no object.

❶ to take off ▷ *Sie hat ihren Mantel nicht ausgezogen.* She didn't take off her coat. ❷ to undress ▷ *Kannst du bitte die Kinder ausziehen und ins Bett bringen?* Can you undress the children and put them to bed, please?; **sich ausziehen** to undress ❸ to move out ▷ *Meine Nachbarn sind letzte Woche ausgezogen.* My neighbours moved out last week.

Auszubildende (*gen* **Auszubildenden**, *pl* **Auszubildenden**) *mf* trainee

Auto (*pl* **Autos**) *nt* car; **Auto fahren** to drive

Autobahn *f* motorway

Autobus (*gen* **Autobusses**, *pl* **Autobusse**) *m* bus

Autofahrer (*pl* **Autofahrer**) *m* motorist

Autogramm (*pl* **Autogramme**) *nt* autograph

Automat (*gen* **Automaten**, *pl* **Automaten**) *m* machine

automatisch *adj* automatic ▷ *Die Türen schließen automatisch.* The doors close automatically.

Autor (*pl* **Autoren**) *m* author

Autoradio (*pl* **Autoradios**) *nt* car radio

Autorin *f* author

autoritär *adj* authoritarian

Autorität *f* authority

Autounfall (*pl* **Autounfälle**) *m* car accident

Axt (*pl* **Äxte**) *f* axe

b

Baby (*pl* **Babys**) *nt* baby
babysitten (*perf* **hat gebabysittet**) *vb* [**2**] to babysit
Babysitter (*pl* **Babysitter**) *m* babysitter
Babysitterin *f* babysitter
Bach (*pl* **Bäche**) *m* stream
Backe *f* cheek
backen (*pres* **bäckt**, *imperf* **backte** *or* **buk**, *perf* **hat gebacken**) *vb* to bake
Bäcker (*pl* **Bäcker**) *m* baker ▷ *beim Bäcker* at the baker's ▷ *zum Bäcker* to the baker's
Bäckerei *f* baker's
Backofen (*pl* **Backöfen**) *m* oven
Bad (*pl* **Bäder**) *nt* bath; **ein Bad im Meer** a swim in the sea
Badeanzug (*pl* **Badeanzüge**) *m* bathing suit
Badehose *f* swimming trunks *pl*
baden *vb* [**54**] to have a bath; **jemanden baden** to bath somebody; **sich baden** to have a bath
Baden-Württemberg *nt* Baden-Württemberg

- **Baden-Württemberg** is one of the 16 **Länder**. Its capital is Stuttgart. Baden-Württemberg is home to the cuckoo clock and to Mercedes-Benz and Porsche.

Badewanne *f* bath *(tub)*
Badezimmer (*pl* **Badezimmer**) *nt* bathroom
Bahn (*pl* **Bahnen**) *f* ❶ railway ▷ *Er arbeitet bei der Bahn.* He works for the railway.; **mit der Bahn fahren** to go by train ❷ tram ❸ lane ▷ *Die Schwimmerin auf Bahn drei liegt in Führung.* The swimmer in lane three is in the lead.; **auf die schiefe Bahn geraten** to go off the rails
Bahnfahrt *f* railway journey
Bahnhof (*pl* **Bahnhöfe**) *m* station ▷ *auf dem Bahnhof* at the station
Bahnhofshalle *f* station concourse
Bahnsteig (*pl* **Bahnsteige**) *m* platform
bald *adv* ❶ soon ▷ *Es wird bald Frühling.* It'll soon be spring.; **Bis bald!** See you later. ❷ almost ▷ *Ich hätte bald was gesagt.* I almost said something.; **Wird's bald!** Get a move on!
Balken (*pl* **Balken**) *m* beam
Balkon (*pl* **Balkons** *or* **Balkone**) *m* balcony
Ball (*pl* **Bälle**) *m* ball ▷ *Die Kinder spielen mit dem Ball.* The children are playing with the ball. ▷ *Mit wem kommst du zum Ball?* Who are you going to the ball with?
Ballett (*pl* **Ballette**) *nt* ballet
Ballon (*pl* **Ballons** *or* **Ballone**) *m* balloon
Bambus (*gen* **Bambusses**, *pl* **Bambusse**) *m* bamboo
Banane *f* banana
band *vb see* **binden**
Band (1) (*pl* **Bände**) *m* volume ▷ *ein Lexikon in fünf Bänden* an encyclopedia in five volumes

Band (2) (*pl* **Bands**) *f* band ▷ *Er spielt Gitarre in einer Band.* He plays the guitar in a band.

Band (3) (*pl* **Bänder**) *nt* ❶ ribbon ▷ *Sie hatte ein rotes Band im Haar.* She had a red ribbon in her hair. ❷ production line ▷ *Mein Vater arbeitet am Band.* My father works on the production line. ❸ tape ▷ *Ich habe diesen Song auf Band.* I've got this song on tape.; **am laufenden Band** nonstop

Bank (1) (*pl* **Bänke**) *f* bench ▷ *Sie saß auf einer Bank im Park.* She was sitting on a park bench.

Bank (2) (*pl* **Banken**) *f* bank ▷ *Ich muss Geld von der Bank holen.* I'll have to get money from the bank.

Bankkonto (*pl* **Bankkonten**) *m* bank account

Bankleitzahl *f* bank sort code

bankrott *adj* bankrupt ▷ *Die Firma ist bankrott.* The firm is bankrupt.; **Bankrott machen** to go bankrupt

bar *adj* **bares Geld** cash; **etwas bar bezahlen** to pay cash for something

Bar (*pl* **Bars**) *f* bar

Bär (*gen* **Bären**, *pl* **Bären**) *m* bear

barfuß *adj* barefoot

Bargeld *nt* cash

Barren (*pl* **Barren**) *m* parallel bars *pl*

Bart (*pl* **Bärte**) *m* beard

bärtig *adj* bearded

Basis (*pl* **Basen**) *f* basis

Bass (*gen* **Basses**, *pl* **Bässe**) *m* bass

basteln *vb* [**34**] to make things ▷ *Ich bastle gern.* I like making things.; **etwas basteln** to make something

bat *vb see* **bitten**

Batterie *f* battery

Bau (*pl* **Bauten**) *m* ❶ construction ▷ *Das Haus ist noch im Bau befindlich.* The house is still under construction. ❷ building ▷ *In New York gibt es viele beeindruckende Bauten.* There are many impressive buildings in New York. ❸ building site ▷ *In den Ferien arbeitet er auf dem Bau.* He works on a building site in the holidays.

Bauarbeiter (*pl* **Bauarbeiter**) *m* building worker

Bauch (*pl* **Bäuche**) *m* stomach ▷ *Mir tut der Bauch weh.* My stomach's sore.

Bauchnabel (*pl* **Bauchnabel**) *m* belly button

Bauchschmerzen *pl* stomachache *sg*

bauen *vb* [**38**] to build ▷ *Meine Eltern haben das Haus gebaut, in dem wir wohnen.* My parents built the house we live in.

Bauer (*gen* **Bauern**, *pl* **Bauern**) *m* ❶ farmer ▷ *Friedas Vater ist Bauer.* Frieda's father is a farmer. ❷ pawn ▷ *Sie zog mit dem Bauer.* She moved the pawn.

Bäuerin *f* ❶ farmer ▷ *Sie möchte Bäuerin werden.* She would like to be a farmer. ❷ farmer's wife

Bauernhof (*pl* **Bauernhöfe**) *m* farm

baufällig *adj* dilapidated

Baum (*pl* **Bäume**) *m* tree

Baumwolle *f* cotton ▷ *eine Tischdecke aus Baumwolle* a cotton tablecloth

Baustelle *f* building site

Bayer (*gen* **Bayern**, *pl* **Bayern**) *m* Bavarian

Bayerin *f* Bavarian

Bayern *nt* Bavaria

Bayern is one of the 16 **Länder**. Its capital is München (Munich). Bavaria has the longest political tradition of any of the Länder, and since 1945 has developed into an important industrial region.

bayrisch *adj* Bavarian

beabsichtigen (*perf* **hat beabsichtigt**) *vb* [**7**] to intend ▷ *Ich beabsichtige, ins Ausland zu fahren.* I intend to go abroad.

beachten (*perf* **hat beachtet**) *vb* [**2**] ❶ to pay attention to ▷ *Beachte ihn nicht!* Don't pay any attention to him. ▷ *Du solltest den Hinweis auf der Packung beachten.* You should pay attention to the instructions on the packet.

❷ to obey ▷ *Man muss die Verkehrsregeln beachten.* You have to obey the traffic regulations. ❸ to observe ▷ *Sie hat die Vorfahrt nicht beachtet.* She didn't observe the right of way.

Beamte (*gen* **Beamten**, *pl* **Beamten**) *m* ❶ official ▷ *Der Beamte stempelte meinen Pass ab.* The official stamped my passport. ❷ civil servant

In Germany, traditionally all public employees are civil servants. They enjoy many privileges.

▷ *Deutsche Lehrer sind Beamte.* German teachers are civil servants.

Beamtin *f* civil servant ▷ *Meine Mutter ist Beamtin.* My mother's a civil servant.

beantragen (*perf* **hat beantragt**) *vb* [**7**] to apply for

beantworten (*perf* **hat beantwortet**) *vb* [**2**] to answer

bearbeiten (*perf* **hat bearbeitet**) *vb* [**2**] ❶ to deal with ▷ *Welches Thema hat sie in ihrer Diplomarbeit bearbeitet?* What subject did she deal with in her dissertation? ❷ to process ▷ *Wir haben Ihren Antrag noch nicht bearbeitet.* We haven't processed your application yet. ❸ to treat ▷ *Sie hat den Fleck mit Fleckenmittel bearbeitet.* She treated the stain with stain remover.; **jemanden bearbeiten** (*informal*) to work on somebody

Becher (*pl* **Becher**) *m* ❶ mug ▷ *Auf ihrem Schreibtisch stand ein Becher mit Kaffee.* There was a mug of coffee on her desk. ❷ carton ❸ tub

Becken (*pl* **Becken**) *nt* ❶ sink ▷ *Er ließ Wasser ins Becken laufen.* He ran water into the sink. ❷ pool; **ein breites Becken** broad hips

sich **bedanken** (*perf* **hat sich bedankt**) *vb* [**7**] to say thank you ▷ *Hast du dich auch bedankt?* Did you say thank you?; **sich bei jemandem bedanken** to say thank you to somebody

Bedarf *m* demand ▷ *je nach Bedarf* according to demand; **bei Bedarf** if necessary; **Bedarf an etwas haben** to be in need of something

bedauerlich *adj* regrettable

bedauern (*perf* **hat bedauert**) *vb* [**88**] ❶ to be sorry for ▷ *Wir bedauern es sehr, dass wir nicht kommen können.* We're very sorry that we can't come.; **Ich bedaure!** I'm sorry!; **Ich bedaure kein Wort.** I don't regret a single word! ❷ to pity ▷ *Ich bedaure dich wirklich!* I really pity you!

Bedenken *pl* doubts *pl* ▷ *Ich habe Bedenken, ob das klappt.* I have my doubts as to whether it'll work.; **Hast du keine Bedenken, wenn du deine Eltern so anlügst?** Don't you feel bad about lying to your parents like that?

bedenklich *adj* ❶ dubious ▷ *Das sind sehr bedenkliche Methoden.* These are very dubious methods. ❷ dangerous ▷ *Die Lage ist bedenklich.* The situation is dangerous.; **Ihr Gesundheitszustand ist bedenklich.** Her state of health is giving cause for concern.

bedeuten (*perf* **hat bedeutet**) *vb* [**2**] to mean ▷ *Was bedeutet dieser Ausdruck?* What does this expression mean? ▷ *Was hat das zu bedeuten?* What's that supposed to mean? ▷ *Er bedeutet mir sehr viel.* He means a lot to me.

bedeutend *adj* ❶ important ▷ *Er ist ein bedeutender Wissenschaftler.* He's an important scientist. ❷ considerable ▷ *Sie haben eine bedeutende Summe dafür bezahlt.* They paid a considerable sum for it.; **bedeutend besser** considerably better; **bedeutend schlechter** considerably worse

Bedeutung *f* ❶ meaning ▷ *die Bedeutung eines Worts* the meaning of a word ❷ importance ▷ *eine Erfindung von großer Bedeutung* an invention of great importance

bedienen (*perf* **hat bedient**) *vb* [**7**] ❶ to serve ▷ *Wir wurden sehr schnell bedient.* We were served very quickly. ❷ to operate ▷ *Er bedient die Druckmaschine.*

a b c d e f g h i j k l m n o p q r s t u v w x y z

He operates the printing press.; **sich bedienen** to help oneself

Bedienung *f* ❶ service ▷ *In diesem Geschäft ist die Bedienung schlecht.* The service is very poor in this shop. ❷ waiter, waitress ▷ *Wir haben bei der Bedienung ein Bier bestellt.* We ordered a beer from the waitress. ❸ shop assistant ▷ *Die Bedienung im Kaufhaus war äußerst unfreundlich.* The shop assistant in the department store was extremely unfriendly. ❹ service charge ▷ *Die Bedienung ist im Preis enthalten.* The service charge is included in the price.

Bedingung *f* condition ▷ *unter der Bedingung, dass ...* on condition that ...

bedrohen (*perf* **hat bedroht**) *vb* [**7**] to threaten

Bedürfnis (*gen* **Bedürfnisses**, *pl* **Bedürfnisse**) *nt* need

sich **beeilen** (*perf* **hat sich beeilt**) *vb* [**7**] to hurry

beeindrucken (*perf* **hat beeindruckt**) *vb* [**7**] to impress

beeindruckend *adj* impressive

beeinflussen (*pres* **beeinflusst**, *imperf* **beeinflusste**, *perf* **hat beeinflusst**) *vb* [**7**] to influence

beenden (*perf* **hat beendet**) *vb* [**54**] to end

Beerdigung *f* funeral

Beere *f* ❶ berry ❷ grape

Befehl (*pl* **Befehle**) *m* command

befehlen (*pres* **befiehlt**, *imperf* **befahl**, *perf* **hat befohlen**) *vb* ❶ to order ▷ *Der General hat den Rückzug befohlen.* The general ordered his men to retreat. ❷ to give orders ▷ *Du hast hier nicht zu befehlen!* You're not the one who gives the orders here!; **jemandem etwas befehlen** to order somebody to do something

befestigen (*perf* **hat befestigt**) *vb* [**7**] to fix ▷ *Die Regalbretter sind mit Schrauben an der Wand befestigt.* The shelves are fixed to the wall with screws.

sich **befinden** (*imperf* **befand sich**, *perf* **hat sich befunden**) *vb* [**24**] to be ▷ *Er befindet sich zurzeit im Ausland.* He's abroad at the moment.

befolgen (*perf* **hat befolgt**) *vb* [**7**] to obey

befördern (*perf* **hat befördert**) *vb* [**88**] ❶ to carry ▷ *Die städtischen Busse befördern täglich viele Menschen.* The municipal buses carry many people every day. ❷ to promote ▷ *Sie ist zur Abteilungsleiterin befördert worden.* She's been promoted to head of department.

Beförderung *f* ❶ transport ▷ *Das Rote Kreuz übernimmt die Beförderung der Hilfsgüter.* The Red Cross undertakes the transport of emergency supplies. ❷ promotion ▷ *Bei einer Beförderung bekommt man auch mehr Geld.* Promotion also means more money.

befragen (*perf* **hat befragt**) *vb* [**7**] to question

befreien (*perf* **hat befreit**) *vb* [**7**] ❶ to set free ▷ *Die Geiseln sind noch nicht befreit.* The hostages haven't been set free yet. ❷ to exempt ▷ *Sie ist vom Sportunterricht befreit.* She's exempt from PE lessons.

befreundet *adj* **mit jemandem befreundet sein** to be friends with somebody

befriedigen (*perf* **hat befriedigt**) *vb* [**7**] to satisfy

befriedigend *adj* satisfactory

German marks range from one (**sehr gut**) to six (**ungenügend**).

befürchten (*perf* **hat befürchtet**) *vb* [**2**] to fear

begabt *adj* talented

Begabung *f* talent

begann *vb see* **beginnen**

begegnen (*perf* **ist begegnet**) *vb* [**53**] **jemandem begegnen** to meet somebody

begehen (*imperf* **beging**, *perf* **hat begangen**) *vb* [**29**] to commit ▷ *Er hat einen Mord begangen.* He committed a murder.
begehren (*perf* **hat begehrt**) *vb* [**7**] to desire
begehrt *adj* ❶ in demand ❷ eligible
begeistern (*perf* **hat begeistert**) *vb* [**88**] to thrill ▷ *Der Film hat mich begeistert.* I was thrilled with the film.; **sich für etwas begeistern** to get enthusiastic about something
begeistert *adj* enthusiastic
Beginn *m* beginning ▷ *zu Beginn* at the beginning
beginnen (*imperf* **begann**, *perf* **hat begonnen**) *vb* [**5**] to start
begleiten (*perf* **hat begleitet**) *vb* [**2**] to accompany ▷ *Er hat mich zum Ball begleitet.* He accompanied me to the ball.
beglückwünschen (*perf* **hat beglückwünscht**) *vb* [**7**] to congratulate ▷ *Alle meine Freunde haben mich zur bestandenen Prüfung beglückwünscht.* All my friends congratulated me on passing the exam.
begonnen *vb see* **beginnen**
begraben (*pres* **begräbt**, *imperf* **begrub**, *perf* **hat begraben**) *vb* to bury
begreifen (*imperf* **begriff**, *perf* **hat begriffen**) *vb* to understand
Begriff (*pl* **Begriffe**) *m* term ▷ *Das ist ein Begriff aus der Architektur.* That is an architectural term.; **im Begriff sein, etwas zu tun** to be about to do something; **schwer von Begriff** slow on the uptake; **sich einen Begriff von etwas machen** to imagine something
begründen (*perf* **hat begründet**) *vb* [**54**] to justify
Begründung *f* justification
begrüßen (*perf* **hat begrüßt**) *vb* [**31**] to welcome ▷ *Ich begrüße diese Änderung sehr.* I very much welcome this change.; **herzlich begrüßt werden** to receive a warm welcome
Begrüßung *f* welcome
behaglich *adj* cosy
behalten (*pres* **behält**, *imperf* **behielt**, *perf* **hat behalten**) *vb* [**33**] ❶ to keep ▷ *Kann ich das Buch noch ein paar Tage behalten?* Can I keep the book for another couple of days? ❷ to remember ▷ *Ich kann ihren Namen nie behalten.* I can never remember her name.
Behälter (*pl* **Behälter**) *m* container
behandeln (*perf* **hat behandelt**) *vb* [**34**] ❶ to treat ▷ *Wir wurden sehr freundlich behandelt.* We were treated in a very friendly manner. ▷ *Die Wunde muss behandelt werden.* The wound will have to be treated. ▷ *Welcher Arzt behandelt Sie?* Which doctor is treating you? ❷ to deal with ▷ *Der Film behandelt das Thema Jugendkriminalität.* The film deals with the subject of juvenile delinquency.
Behandlung *f* treatment
behaupten (*perf* **hat behauptet**) *vb* [**2**] to claim
beherrschen (*perf* **hat beherrscht**) *vb* [**7**] ❶ to master ▷ *Ich beherrsche diese Technik noch nicht.* I haven't mastered this technique yet. ❷ to control ▷ *Er konnte seine Wut nicht mehr beherrschen.* He couldn't control his anger any longer.; **sich beherrschen** to control oneself
behilflich *adj* helpful; **jemandem bei etwas behilflich sein** to help somebody with something
behindern (*perf* **hat behindert**) *vb* [**88**] to hinder
behindert *adj* disabled
Behinderte (*gen* **Behinderten**, *pl* **Behinderten**) *mf* disabled person; **die Behinderten** people with disabilities
Behörde *f* authorities *pl*
bei *prep*

> The preposition **bei** takes the dative.

❶ near ▷ *Unser Haus ist beim Bahnhof.* Our house is near the station. ▷ *bei München* near Munich ❷ at ▷ *Felix ist zurzeit bei seiner Großmutter.* Felix is at his grandmother's at the moment. ▷ *Wenn man bei fremden Leuten zu Besuch ist ...* When you're at other people's houses ... ▷ *beim Friseur* at the hairdresser's ▷ *bei Nacht* at night ▷ *bei uns* at our place ❸ with ▷ *bei seinen Eltern wohnen* to live with one's parents ▷ *Wenn du bei mir bist, habe ich keine Angst.* When you're with me, I'm not afraid.; **Ich habe kein Geld bei mir.** I don't have any money on me.; **bei einer Firma arbeiten** to work for a firm; **beim Militär** in the army ❹ on ▷ *bei meiner Ankunft* on my arrival ▷ *bei der Abreise* on departure ❺ during ▷ *beim Abendessen* during dinner; **beim Fahren** while driving; **bei solcher Hitze** in such heat; **bei Nebel** in fog; **bei Regen** if it rains

beibringen (*imperf* **brachte bei**, *perf* **hat beigebracht**) *vb* [**13**] **jemandem etwas beibringen** to teach somebody something

beide *adj, pron* both ▷ *Ich habe beide Bücher gelesen.* I've read both books. ▷ *Ich will beide.* I want both of them. ▷ *jeder der beiden* both of them ▷ *Meine Eltern haben das beide verboten.* Both my parents have forbidden it.; **meine beiden Brüder** both my brothers; **die ersten beiden** the first two; **wir beide** we two; **einer von beiden** one of the two

beides *pron* both ▷ *Ich möchte beides.* I want both of them. ▷ *Beides ist schön.* Both of them are lovely.; **alles beides** both of them

beieinander *adv* together

Beifall *m* applause; **Beifall spenden** to applaud

beige *adj* beige

Beil (*pl* **Beile**) *nt* axe

Beilage *f* ❶ supplement ▷ *eine Beilage zur Samstagszeitung* a supplement in Saturday's paper ❷ side dish

beilegen (*perf* **hat beigelegt**) *vb* [**4**] ❶ to enclose ▷ *Ich lege einen Scheck bei.* I enclose a cheque. ❷ to settle ▷ *Der Streit war schnell beigelegt.* The argument was quickly settled.

Beileid *nt* sympathy ▷ *Wir haben ihr unser Beileid ausgesprochen.* We offered her our sympathy.; **herzliches Beileid** deepest sympathy

beim = **bei dem**

Bein (*pl* **Beine**) *nt* leg

beinahe *adv* almost

beisammen *adv* together

beiseite *adv* to one side ▷ *Sie schob ihren Teller beiseite.* She pushed her plate to one side.

beiseiteschaffen *vb* [**4**] to put by ▷ *Er hat sehr viel Geld beiseitegeschafft.* He's put a lot of money by.

Beispiel (*pl* **Beispiele**) *nt* example; **sich an jemandem ein Beispiel nehmen** to take a leaf out of somebody's book; **zum Beispiel** for example

beispielsweise *adv* for example

beißen (*imperf* **biss**, *perf* **hat gebissen**) *vb* [**6**] ❶ to bite ▷ *Mein Hund beißt nicht.* My dog doesn't bite. ▷ *Sie biss in den Apfel.* She bit into the apple. ❷ to burn ▷ *Der Rauch beißt mich in den Augen.* The smoke's burning my eyes.; **sich beißen** to clash

Beitrag (*pl* **Beiträge**) *m* ❶ contribution ▷ *einen Beitrag zu etwas leisten* to make a contribution to something; **Beiträge für die Zeitung** articles for the newspaper ❷ membership fee ▷ *Der Beitrag für den Klub wird am Monatsanfang fällig.* Membership fees for the club are due at the beginning of the month. ❸ premium ▷ *die Beiträge zur Krankenversicherung* the health insurance premiums

beitragen (*pres* **trägt bei**, *imperf* **trug bei**, *perf* **hat beigetragen**) *vb* [**77**] **zu**

etwas **beitragen** to contribute to something
bekämpfen (*perf* **hat bekämpft**) *vb* [7] to fight ▷ *ein Feuer bekämpfen* to fight a fire; **sich bekämpfen** to fight
bekannt *adj* ❶ well-known ▷ *Sie ist eine bekannte Schauspielerin.* She's a well-known actress. ❷ familiar ▷ *Bekannte Wörter brauche ich nicht nachzuschlagen.* I don't have to look up familiar words. ▷ *Sie kommt mir bekannt vor.* She seems familiar. ▷ *Das kommt mir bekannt vor.* That sounds familiar.; **mit jemandem bekannt sein** to know somebody; **für etwas bekannt sein** to be known for something; **Das ist mir bekannt.** I know that.; **etwas bekannt geben** to announce something publicly; **etwas bekannt machen** to announce something
Bekannte (*gen* **Bekannten**, *pl* **Bekannten**) *mf* ❶ friend ▷ *Ein Bekannter von mir hat mir das erzählt.* A friend of mine told me. ❷ acquaintance ▷ *Sie hat viele Bekannte, aber wenig Freunde.* She has a lot of acquaintances but few friends.
bekanntgeben *vb* [28] *see* **bekannt**
bekanntlich *adv* as you know ▷ *Rauchen macht bekanntlich süchtig.* As you know, smoking is addictive.
bekanntmachen *vb* [48] *see* **bekannt**
sich **beklagen** (*perf* **hat sich beklagt**) *vb* [7] to complain ▷ *Die Schüler haben sich darüber beklagt, dass sie Hausaufgaben aufbekommen haben.* The pupils complained about being given homework.
Bekleidung *f* clothing
bekommen *vb* [40] ❶ to get ▷ *Was hast du zum Geburtstag bekommen?* What did you get for your birthday? ▷ *Sie hat in Englisch eine schlechte Note bekommen.* She got bad marks in English. ▷ *Wir haben nichts zu essen bekommen.* We didn't get anything to eat.; **Hunger bekommen** to feel hungry; **Durst bekommen** to feel thirsty; **Angst bekommen** to become afraid; **ein Kind bekommen** to have a baby ❷ to catch ▷ *Ich habe den letzten Bus gerade noch bekommen.* I just caught the last bus.; **Das fette Essen ist ihm nicht bekommen.** The fatty food didn't agree with him.; **Was bekommen Sie?** What would you like?; **Bekommen Sie schon?** Are you being served?; **Was bekommen Sie dafür?** How much do I owe you?

> Be careful! **bekommen** does not mean **to become**.

belasten (*perf* **hat belastet**) *vb* [2] ❶ to burden ▷ *Ich möchte dich nicht mit meinen Problemen belasten.* I don't want to burden you with my problems. ❷ to load ▷ *Der Aufzug darf mit maximal zehn Personen belastet werden.* The lift's maximum load is ten people. ❸ to pollute ▷ *Unsere Umwelt ist mit zu vielen Schadstoffen belastet.* The environment is polluted by too many harmful substances. ❹ to debit ▷ *Wir werden Ihr Konto mit diesem Betrag belasten.* We will debit this amount from your account. ❺ to incriminate ▷ *Die Zeugin hat den Angeklagten belastet.* The witness incriminated the accused.
belästigen (*perf* **hat belästigt**) *vb* [7] to pester; **jemanden sexuell belästigen** to sexually harass somebody
belegt *adj* **ein belegtes Brot** an open sandwich; **belegt sein** to be engaged ▷ *Die Nummer ist belegt.* The number's engaged.
beleidigen (*perf* **hat beleidigt**) *vb* [7] to insult
Beleidigung *f* insult
Belgien *nt* Belgium
Belgier (*pl* **Belgier**) *m* Belgian
Belgierin *f* Belgian
belgisch *adj* Belgian
beliebig *adj, adv* ❶ any you like ▷ *in beliebiger Reihenfolge* in any order you

like ▷ *eine beliebige Anzahl* any number you like ❷ as you like ▷ *beliebig oft* as often as you like ▷ *beliebig viel* as much as you like ▷ *beliebig viele* as many as you like

beliebt *adj* popular ▷ *sich bei jemandem beliebt machen* to make oneself popular with somebody

Beliebtheit *f* popularity

bellen *vb* [**38**] to bark

belohnen (*perf* **hat belohnt**) *vb* [**7**] to reward

Belohnung *f* reward ▷ *zur Belohnung* as a reward

belügen (*imperf* **belog**, *perf* **hat belogen**) *vb* [**47**] to lie to

bemerken (*perf* **hat bemerkt**) *vb* [**7**] to notice ▷ *Ich habe keine Änderung bemerkt.* I haven't noticed any change.

Bemerkung *f* remark

bemitleiden (*perf* **hat bemitleidet**) *vb* [**7**] to pity

sich **bemühen** (*perf* **hat sich bemüht**) *vb* [**7**] to make an effort ▷ *Er hat sich bemüht, höflich zu bleiben.* He made an effort to remain polite.; **Bemühen Sie sich nicht.** Don't trouble yourself.; **sich um eine neue Arbeit bemühen** to try and find a new job; **Ich werde mich bemühen!** I'll do my best!

benachrichtigen (*perf* **hat benachrichtigt**) *vb* [**7**] to inform

benachteiligt *adj* disadvantaged

sich **benehmen** (*pres* **benimmt sich**, *imperf* **benahm sich**, *perf* **hat sich benommen**) *vb* [**52**] to behave ▷ *sich anständig benehmen* to behave properly ▷ *Sie haben sich furchtbar benommen.* They behaved terribly. ▷ *Benimm dich!* Behave yourself!

Benehmen *nt* behaviour

beneiden (*perf* **hat beneidet**) *vb* [**54**] to envy ▷ *Er ist nicht zu beneiden.* I don't envy him.; **jemanden um etwas beneiden** to envy somebody something

beneidenswert *adj, adv* enviable; **Sie ist beneidenswert reich.** She's enviably rich.

benoten (*perf* **hat benotet**) *vb* [**2**] to mark

benutzen (*perf* **hat benutzt**) *vb* [**36**] to use

Benutzer (*pl* **Benutzer**) *m* user

benutzerfreundlich *adj* user-friendly

Benutzung *f* use

Benzin *nt* petrol

beobachten (*perf* **hat beobachtet**) *vb* [**2**] to observe

bequem *adj* ❶ comfortable ▷ *ein bequemer Stuhl* a comfortable chair; **eine bequeme Ausrede** a convenient excuse ❷ lazy ▷ *Er ist zu bequem, sich selbst etwas zu kochen.* He's too lazy to cook himself something.

beraten (*pres* **berät**, *imperf* **beriet**, *perf* **hat beraten**) *vb* ❶ to give advice ▷ *Der Mann vom Arbeitsamt hat mich gut beraten.* The man at the job centre gave me good advice.; **Lassen Sie sich von Ihrem Arzt beraten.** Consult your doctor. ❷ to discuss ▷ *Wir müssen das weitere Vorgehen beraten.* We have to discuss further action.; **gut beraten sein** to be well advised; **schlecht beraten sein** to be ill advised

berauben (*perf* **hat beraubt**) *vb* [**7**] to rob

berechnen (*perf* **hat berechnet**) *vb* [**53**] to charge ▷ *Was berechnen Sie für eine Beratung?* What do you charge for a consultation?

bereit *adj* ready ▷ *Wir sind bereit abzufahren.* We're ready to leave. ▷ *Das Essen ist bereit.* Dinner's ready.; **bereit sein, etwas zu tun** to be prepared to do something; **etwas bereit haben** to have something ready

bereiten (*perf* **hat bereitet**) *vb* [**2**] to cause ▷ *Das hat mir einige Schwierigkeiten bereitet.* That caused me some problems.; **Die Kinder bereiten mir sehr viel Freude.** The children give me a great deal of pleasure.

bereits *adv* already
bereuen (*perf* **hat bereut**) *vb* [7] to regret
Berg (*pl* **Berge**) *m* ❶ mountain ▷ *Im Winter fahren wir in die Berge zum Skifahren.* In winter we go skiing in the mountains. ❷ hill ▷ *Hinter unserem Haus ist ein kleiner Berg.* There's a small hill behind our house.
Bergsteigen *nt* mountaineering ▷ *Bergsteigen ist ihr Hobby.* Her hobby's mountaineering. ▷ *Sie ist beim Bergsteigen verunglückt.* She had a mountaineering accident.
Bergsteiger (*pl* **Bergsteiger**) *m* mountaineer
Bergwerk (*pl* **Bergwerke**) *nt* mine
Bericht (*pl* **Berichte**) *m* report
berichten (*perf* **hat berichtet**) *vb* [2] to report ▷ *Die Zeitungen haben nichts über diesen Zwischenfall berichtet.* The newspapers didn't report anything about this incident.
Berlin *nt* Berlin

Berlin is one of the 16 **Länder**. It is a 'city-state' like Bremen and Hamburg. From 1963 to 1989 it was divided by the Berlin Wall. Now it is again the German capital.

berücksichtigen (*perf* **hat berücksichtigt**) *vb* [7] to bear in mind
Beruf (*pl* **Berufe**) *m* occupation ▷ *Welchen Beruf hat dein Vater?* What's your father's occupation?; **Sie ist Lehrerin von Beruf.** She's a teacher by profession.
beruflich *adj* professional; **beruflich unterwegs sein** to be away on business
Berufsberater (*pl* **Berufsberater**) *m* careers adviser
Berufsschule *f* technical college
berufstätig *adj* working ▷ *Seit wann ist deine Mutter wieder berufstätig?* When did your mother start working again?
beruhigen (*perf* **hat beruhigt**) *vb* [18] to calm down ▷ *Dem Lehrer gelang es nicht, die Klasse zu beruhigen.* The teacher didn't manage to calm the class down. ▷ *Beruhige dich doch!* Calm down!; **sich beruhigen** to calm down
Beruhigungsmittel (*pl* **Beruhigungsmittel**) *nt* tranquillizer
berühmt *adj* famous
berühren (*perf* **hat berührt**) *vb* [18] ❶ to touch ▷ *Er berührte meinen Arm.* He touched my arm. ❷ to affect ▷ *Die Armut der Menschen hat mich sehr berührt.* The poverty of the people affected me deeply. ❸ to touch on ▷ *Ich kann diese Frage heute nur berühren.* I can only touch on this question today.; **sich berühren** to touch
Berührung *f* contact ▷ *mit etwas in Berührung kommen* to come into contact with something
beschädigen (*perf* **hat beschädigt**) *vb* [7] to damage
beschaffen (*perf* **hat beschafft**) *vb* [7] to get ▷ *Ich muss mir ein Visum beschaffen.* I have to get a visa. ▷ *Können Sie mir nicht einen Job beschaffen?* Can't you get me a job?
beschäftigen (*perf* **hat beschäftigt**) *vb* [18] ❶ to occupy ▷ *Kannst du nicht irgendwie die Kinder beschäftigen?* Can't you occupy the children somehow? ▷ *Diese Frage beschäftigt mich seit Langem.* This question has been occupying me for a long time. ❷ to employ ▷ *Unsere Firma beschäftigt zweihundert Leute.* Our company employs two hundred people.; **sich beschäftigen** to occupy oneself; **sich beschäftigen mit** to deal with
beschäftigt *adj* busy
Beschäftigung *f* work ▷ *Er sucht eine Beschäftigung.* He's looking for work.; **Sie ist zurzeit ohne Beschäftigung.** She is unemployed at the moment.
Bescheid (*pl* **Bescheide**) *m* information ▷ *Ich warte auf den Bescheid des Konsulats.* I'm waiting for information from the consulate.;

Bescheid wissen to know; **über etwas Bescheid wissen** to know a lot about something; **jemandem Bescheid sagen** to let somebody know

bescheiden *adj* modest

Bescheinigung *f* certificate ▷ *Du brauchst eine Bescheinigung über die Teilnahme am Kurs.* You need a certificate showing that you attended the course. ▷ *eine Bescheinigung des Arztes* a doctor's certificate

Bescherung *f* giving out of Christmas presents; **Da haben wir die Bescherung!** What did I tell you!

beschimpfen (*perf* **hat beschimpft**) *vb* [**18**] to swear at

beschleunigen (*perf* **hat beschleunigt**) *vb* [**7**] ❶ to increase ▷ *Wir müssen das Arbeitstempo beschleunigen.* We have to increase our work rate. ❷ to accelerate ▷ *Das Auto vor mir beschleunigte.* The car in front of me accelerated.

beschließen (*imperf* **beschloss**, *perf* **hat beschlossen**) *vb* to decide ▷ *Wir haben beschlossen, nach Spanien zu fahren.* We decided to go to Spain.

Beschluss (*gen* **Beschlusses**, *pl* **Beschlüsse**) *m* decision

beschränken (*perf* **hat beschränkt**) *vb* [**18**] to limit ▷ *Wir müssen unsere Ausgaben beschränken.* We have to limit our spending.; **sich auf etwas beschränken** to restrict oneself to something

beschränkt *adj* ❶ limited ▷ *Diese Regel hat nur beschränkte Gültigkeit.* This regulation only has limited validity. ❷ stupid ▷ *Wie kann man nur so beschränkt sein?* How can anyone be so stupid?

beschreiben (*imperf* **beschrieb**, *perf* **hat beschrieben**) *vb* [**61**] to describe ▷ *Können Sie den Täter beschreiben?* Can you describe the culprit?

Beschreibung *f* description

beschützen (*perf* **hat beschützt**) *vb* [**7**] to protect ▷ *Ich möchte euch vor diesen Gefahren beschützen.* I want to protect you from these dangers.

Beschwerde *f* complaint ▷ *Wenn Sie eine Beschwerde haben, dann wenden Sie sich an den Geschäftsführer.* If you have a complaint, then please contact the manager.; **Beschwerden** trouble

sich **beschweren** (*perf* **hat sich beschwert**) *vb* [**18**] to complain ▷ *Deine Lehrerin hat sich über dich beschwert.* Your teacher has complained about you.

beseitigen (*perf* **hat beseitigt**) *vb* [**7**] to remove

Besen (*pl* **Besen**) *m* broom

besetzen (*perf* **hat besetzt**) *vb* [**7**] ❶ to occupy ▷ *Napoleons Truppen haben weite Teile Deutschlands besetzt.* Napoleon's troops occupied large areas of Germany. ❷ to fill ▷ *Der Posten soll mit einer Frau besetzt werden.* The position is to be filled by a woman. ▷ *Die Stelle ist noch nicht besetzt.* The position hasn't been filled yet.

besetzt *adj* ❶ full ▷ *Der Zug war voll besetzt.* The train was full. ❷ engaged ▷ *Es ist besetzt.* It's engaged. ❸ taken ▷ *Ist der Platz hier besetzt?* Is this seat taken?

besichtigen (*perf* **hat besichtigt**) *vb* [**18**] to visit

Besichtigung *f* visit

besitzen (*imperf* **besaß**, *perf* **hat besessen**) *vb* [**68**] ❶ to own ▷ *Sie besitzen ein Haus am Meer.* They own a house by the seaside. ❷ to have ▷ *Sie besitzt das Talent, sich mit allen zu zerstreiten.* She has the talent of quarrelling with everyone.

Besitzer (*pl* **Besitzer**) *m* owner

besondere *adj* special ▷ *Das sind besondere Umstände.* Those are special circumstances.; **keine besonderen Kennzeichen** no distinguishing features

besonders *adv* particularly ▷ *Es hat mir nicht besonders gefallen.* I didn't particularly like it.

besorgen (*perf* **hat besorgt**) *vb* [18] to get ▷ *Kannst du mir nicht einen Ferienjob besorgen?* Can't you get me a holiday job? ▷ *Soll ich dir ein Taxi besorgen?* Shall I get you a taxi? ▷ *Ich muss Milch und Eier besorgen.* I'll have to get milk and eggs.

besorgt *adj* worried ▷ *Sie ist sehr besorgt um dich.* She's very worried about you.

besprechen (*pres* **bespricht**, *imperf* **besprach**, *perf* **hat besprochen**) *vb* [70] to discuss ▷ *Das muss ich mit deiner Mutter besprechen.* I'll have to discuss it with your mother.

Besprechung *f* ❶ meeting ▷ *Frau Airlie ist in einer Besprechung.* Ms Airlie is in a meeting. ❷ review ▷ *Hast du die Besprechung dieses Films gelesen?* Have you read the review of this film?

besser *adj, adv* better ▷ *eine bessere Note* a better mark ▷ *Du gehst jetzt besser nach Hause.* You'd better go home now.; **Es geht ihm besser.** He's feeling better.; **je schneller, desto besser** the quicker the better

sich **bessern** *vb* [88] to improve ▷ *Das Wetter hat sich gebessert.* The weather's improved.

Besserung *f* improvement; **Gute Besserung!** Get well soon!

bestätigen (*perf* **hat bestätigt**) *vb* [18] ❶ to confirm ▷ *Ich kann bestätigen, dass sie die Wahrheit gesagt hat.* I can confirm that she told the truth. ❷ to acknowledge ▷ *Hiermit bestätigen wir den Erhalt Ihres Briefes.* We hereby acknowledge receipt of your letter.; **sich bestätigen** to prove to be true

beste *adj* best ▷ *Sie ist die beste Schülerin der Klasse.* She's the best pupil in the class. ▷ *So ist es am besten.* It's best that way.; **Am besten gehst du gleich.** You'd better go at once.; **jemanden zum Besten haben** to pull somebody's leg; **einen Witz zum Besten geben** to tell a joke; **Es ist nur zu deinem Besten.** It's for your own good.

bestechen (*pres* **besticht**, *imperf* **bestach**, *perf* **hat bestochen**) *vb* to bribe

Bestechung *f* bribery

Besteck (*pl* **Bestecke**) *nt* cutlery

bestehen (*imperf* **bestand**, *perf* **hat bestanden**) *vb* [72] ❶ to be ▷ *Es besteht die Möglichkeit, einen Sprachkurs zu belegen.* There's the chance of registering for a language course. ▷ *Es besteht keine Hoffnung mehr, sie jemals wiederzusehen.* There's no more hope of ever seeing her again. ❷ to exist ▷ *Die Firma besteht seit hundert Jahren.* The firm has existed for a hundred years.; **etwas bestehen** to pass something; **auf etwas bestehen** to insist on something; **bestehen aus** to consist of

bestehlen *vb* [73] **jemanden bestehlen** to rob somebody

bestellen (*perf* **hat bestellt**) *vb* [7] ❶ to order ▷ *Ich habe im Versandhaus ein Kleid bestellt.* I've ordered a dress from a mail-order company. ▷ *Haben Sie schon bestellt?* Have you ordered yet? ▷ *Wir sollten ein Taxi bestellen.* We should order a taxi. ❷ to reserve ▷ *Ich habe einen Tisch beim Chinesen bestellt.* I've reserved a table at the Chinese restaurant. ❸ to send for ▷ *Der Direktor hat mich zu sich bestellt.* The headmaster sent for me.; **Bestell deiner Mutter schöne Grüße.** Give my regards to your mother.; **Soll ich ihr etwas von dir bestellen?** Shall I give her a message from you?

Bestellung *f* order; **auf Bestellung** to order

bestimmen (*perf* **hat bestimmt**) *vb* [7] to decide ▷ *Du kannst bestimmen, wer mitkommen soll.* You can decide who's coming. ▷ *Wer bestimmt hier, was gemacht werden muss?* Who decides what has to be done?; **Du hast hier nichts zu bestimmen!** You're not the one who decides here!; **für jemanden bestimmt sein** to be meant for somebody; **für etwas bestimmt sein** to be intended for something

bestimmt *adj, adv* ❶ certain ▷ *Wir treffen uns immer zu einer bestimmten Zeit.* We always meet at a certain time. ▷ *Die Teilnehmer sollten eine bestimmte Anzahl nicht überschreiten.* The participants shouldn't exceed a certain number. ❷ particular ▷ *Ich suche ein ganz bestimmtes Buch.* I'm looking for a particular book.; **Suchen Sie etwas Bestimmtes?** Are you looking for something in particular?; **der bestimmte Artikel** the definite article; **Ich habe ihn bestimmt gesehen.** I'm sure I've seen him.; **Das hat er bestimmt nicht so gemeint.** I'm sure that's not how he meant it.; **Das hat sie bestimmt vergessen.** She's bound to have forgotten.

bestrafen (*perf* **hat bestraft**) *vb* [7] to punish

Besuch (*pl* **Besuche**) *m* ❶ visit ▷ *Deutschland bereitet sich auf den Besuch der Königin vor.* Germany's preparing for the Queen's visit. ▷ *bei unserem Besuch in London* during our visit to London; **Der Schulbesuch ist Pflicht.** School attendance is compulsory. ❷ visitor ▷ *Ist euer Besuch noch da?* Is your visitor still there? ▷ *Besuch haben* to have visitors; **bei jemandem einen Besuch machen** to pay somebody a visit; **bei jemandem zu Besuch sein** to be visiting somebody; **zu Besuch kommen** to be visiting

besuchen (*perf* **hat besucht**) *vb* [7] ❶ to visit ▷ *Hast du schon das Planetarium besucht?* Have you visited the planetarium yet?; **Besuch uns mal wieder!** Come again! ❷ to attend ▷ *Sie besucht das Gymnasium.* She attends grammar school. ▷ *Der Vortrag war sehr gut besucht.* The lecture was very well attended.; **Wir haben ein Konzert besucht.** We went to a concert.

Besucher (*pl* **Besucher**) *m* visitor

betätigen (*perf* **hat betätigt**) *vb* [7] **die Hupe betätigen** to sound the horn; **einen Schalter betätigen** to press a switch; **die Bremse betätigen** to apply the brakes; **Du solltest dich sportlich betätigen.** You should do some sport.

beteiligen (*perf* **hat beteiligt**) *vb* [7] **sich an etwas beteiligen** to take part in something; **Alle werden am Gewinn beteiligt.** Everyone will share in the winnings.

beten *vb* [2] to pray

Beton (*pl* **Betons**) *m* concrete

betonen (*perf* **hat betont**) *vb* [7] to stress

Betonung *f* stress ▷ *Wo liegt die Betonung bei diesem Wort?* Where's the stress in this word?

beträchtlich *adj, adv* ❶ considerable ▷ *eine beträchtliche Summe* a considerable amount ❷ considerably ▷ *Es hat beträchtlich länger gedauert.* It took considerably longer.

Betrag (*pl* **Beträge**) *m* amount

betragen (*pres* **beträgt**, *imperf* **betrug**, *perf* **hat betragen**) *vb* [77] to come to ▷ *Die Reparatur betrug dreihundert Euro.* The repair came to three hundred euros.; **sich betragen** to behave

Betragen *nt* behaviour ▷ *Ich werde mich über dein schlechtes Betragen beschweren.* I'm going to complain about your bad behaviour.

betreffen (*pres* **betrifft**, *imperf* **betraf**, *perf* **hat betroffen**) *vb* [78] to concern; **was mich betrifft** as far as I'm concerned

betreten (*pres* **betritt**, *imperf* **betrat**, *perf* **hat betreten**) *vb* [79] to enter ▷ *Sie klopfte, bevor sie das Zimmer betrat.* She knocked before entering the room.; **'Betreten verboten'** 'Keep out'

Betrieb (*pl* **Betriebe**) *m* ❶ firm ▷ *Unser Betrieb beschäftigt dreihundert Menschen.* Our firm employs three hundred people. ❷ operation ▷ *Die Maschine ist jetzt in Betrieb.* The machine is now in operation.; **In der Stadt war heute viel Betrieb.** It was really busy in town today.; **außer Betrieb sein** to be out of order

sich **betrinken** (*imperf* **betrank sich**, *perf* **hat sich betrunken**) *vb* [**80**] to get drunk

betroffen *adj* ❶ full of concern ▷ *Sie machte ein betroffenes Gesicht.* Her face was full of concern. ❷ affected ▷ *von etwas betroffen sein* to be affected by something ▷ *Wir sind über diese Nachricht zutiefst betroffen.* We are deeply affected by the news.

betrügen (*imperf* **betrog**, *perf* **hat betrogen**) *vb* ❶ to cheat ▷ *Der Händler hat dich betrogen.* The dealer's cheated you. ❷ to defraud ▷ *Er hat seinen Arbeitgeber um Millionen betrogen.* He defrauded his employer of millions. ❸ to be unfaithful to ▷ *Hast du deine Freundin schon mal betrogen?* Have you ever been unfaithful to your girlfriend?

betrunken *adj* drunk

Bett (*pl* **Betten**) *nt* bed ▷ *ins Bett gehen* to go to bed ▷ *das Bett machen* to make the bed

Bettdecke *f* blanket

betteln *vb* [**34**] to beg

Bettlaken (*pl* **Bettlaken**) *nt* sheet

Bettler (*pl* **Bettler**) *m* beggar

Betttuch (*pl* **Betttücher**) *nt* sheet

Bettwäsche *f* bed linen

beugen *vb* [**38**] to bend ▷ *Ich kann den Arm nicht beugen.* I can't bend my arm.; **sich beugen** to bow

Beule *f* ❶ bump ▷ *eine Beule am Kopf* a bump on the head ❷ dent ▷ *Das Auto hat eine Beule.* The car has a dent in it.

beunruhigen (*perf* **hat beunruhigt**) *vb* [**7**] to alarm

beurteilen (*perf* **hat beurteilt**) *vb* [**7**] to judge ▷ *Ich beurteile die Leute nicht nach ihrem Aussehen.* I don't judge people on their appearance.

Beutel (*pl* **Beutel**) *m* ❶ bag ▷ *Sie tat die Einkäufe in den Beutel.* She put the shopping in the bag. ❷ purse ▷ *Er nahm einen Euro aus dem Beutel.* He took a euro from the purse.

Bevölkerung *f* population

bevor *conj* before ▷ *Sie war gegangen, bevor ich es ihr sagen konnte.* She left before I could tell her.

bevorstehen (*imperf* **stand bevor**, *perf* **hat bevorgestanden**) *vb* [**72**] to be imminent ▷ *Die Prüfung steht bevor.* The exam's imminent.; **jemandem bevorstehen** to be in store for somebody

sich **bewähren** (*perf* **hat sich bewährt**) *vb* [**7**] to prove oneself ▷ *Er hat sich als mein Freund bewährt.* He proved himself to be my friend. ▷ *Diese Methode hat sich bewährt.* This method has proved itself.

bewährt *adj* tried and tested ▷ *Das ist eine bewährte Methode.* That's a tried and tested method.; **Sie ist eine bewährte Mitarbeiterin.** She's a reliable colleague.

bewegen (*perf* **hat bewegt**) *vb* [**7**] to move; **sich bewegen** to move; **jemanden zu etwas bewegen** to persuade somebody to do something

beweglich *adj* ❶ movable ▷ *Die Puppe hat bewegliche Beine.* The doll has movable legs. ❷ agile ▷ *Sie ist trotz ihres Alters noch sehr beweglich.* She's still very agile despite her age.

bewegt *adj* ❶ eventful ▷ *Sie hatte ein bewegtes Leben.* She had an eventful life. ❷ touched ▷ *Wir waren von seinen Worten sehr bewegt.* We were very touched by his words.

Bewegung *f* ❶ movement ▷ *Mir fällt jede Bewegung schwer.* Every movement is difficult for me. ❷ motion ▷ *Er setzte das Fahrzeug in Bewegung.* He set the vehicle in motion. ❸ exercise ▷ *Du brauchst mehr Bewegung.* You need more exercise.

Beweis (*pl* **Beweise**) *m* ❶ proof ▷ *Die Polizei hat keine Beweise.* The police don't have any proof. ❷ sign ▷ *als Beweis meiner Freundschaft* as a sign of my friendship

beweisen (*imperf* **bewies**, *perf* **hat bewiesen**) *vb* ❶ to prove ▷ *Ich kann nicht beweisen, dass sie das gesagt hat.* I can't prove that she said it. ▷ *Die Polizei kann nichts beweisen.* The police can't prove anything. ❷ to show ▷ *Er hat sehr viel Mut bewiesen.* He showed great courage.

sich **bewerben** (*pres* **bewirbt sich**, *imperf* **bewarb sich**, *perf* **hat sich beworben**) *vb* [**90**] to apply ▷ *Es haben sich dreißig Kandidaten beworben.* Thirty candidates have applied. ▷ *Sie hat sich bei Siemens um einen Ausbildungsplatz beworben.* She applied to Siemens for an apprenticeship.

Bewerber (*pl* **Bewerber**) *m* applicant

Bewerbung *f* application

bewerten (*perf* **hat bewertet**) *vb* [**2**] to assess ▷ *Der Lehrer hat unsere Aufsätze zu bewerten.* The teacher has to assess our essays.

bewirken (*perf* **hat bewirkt**) *vb* [**7**] ❶ to bring about ▷ *Dieses Medikament wird eine schnelle Besserung bewirken.* This medicine will bring about a rapid improvement. ❷ to achieve ▷ *Meine Bitte hat nichts bewirkt.* My request didn't achieve anything.; **Ich konnte bei ihm nichts bewirken.** I couldn't get anywhere with him.

bewohnen (*perf* **hat bewohnt**) *vb* [**7**] to live in ▷ *Das Haus wird von drei Familien bewohnt.* Three families live in the house.

Bewohner (*pl* **Bewohner**) *m* ❶ inhabitant ▷ *die Bewohner des Landes* the inhabitants of the country ❷ resident ▷ *die Bewohner des Hauses* the residents of the house

bewölkt *adj* cloudy

Bewölkung *f* clouds *pl*

bewundern (*perf* **hat bewundert**) *vb* [**88**] to admire

Bewunderung *f* admiration

bewusst *adj* ❶ conscious ▷ *umweltbewusst* environmentally conscious ❷ deliberate ▷ *Er hat ganz bewusst gelogen.* He lied quite deliberately.; **sich einer Sache bewusst sein** to be aware of something; **Ihr wurde plötzlich bewusst, dass ...** She suddenly realized that ...

bewusstlos *adj* unconscious; **bewusstlos werden** to lose consciousness

Bewusstlosigkeit *f* unconsciousness

bezahlen (*perf* **hat bezahlt**) *vb* [**7**] to pay ▷ *Er bezahlte die Rechnung.* He paid the bill.

Bezahlung *f* payment

bezeichnen (*perf* **hat bezeichnet**) *vb* [**53**] ❶ to mark ▷ *Bezeichnen Sie die Stelle mit einem Kreuz.* Mark the spot with a cross. ❷ to call ▷ *Sie hat mich als Lügnerin bezeichnet.* She called me a liar.

bezeichnend *adj* typical ▷ *Das ist bezeichnend für sie!* That's typical of her!

beziehen (*imperf* **bezog**, *perf* **hat bezogen**) *vb* [**96**] ❶ to cover ▷ *Sie beschloss, alle Kissen zu beziehen.* She decided to cover all the cushions.; **das Bett beziehen** to change the bed ❷ to move into ▷ *Wann könnt ihr euer neues Haus beziehen?* When can you move into your new house? ❸ to get ▷ *Wir beziehen unsere Kartoffeln direkt vom Bauern.* We get our potatoes straight from the farm. ▷ *Sie beziehen Arbeitslosenhilfe.* They get unemployment benefit. ❹ to subscribe to ▷ *Ich beziehe eine Tageszeitung.* I subscribe to a daily newspaper.; **sich beziehen** to cloud over; **sich auf etwas beziehen** to refer to something

Beziehung *f* ❶ relationship ▷ *Er hat eine Beziehung mit einer verheirateten Frau.* He has a relationship with a married woman. ❷ relations *pl* ▷ *unsere Beziehungen zu dieser Firma* our relations with this company ▷ *diplomatische Beziehungen* diplomatic relations ❸ connection ▷ *Es besteht eine Beziehung zwischen den beiden Straftaten.* There's a connection between the two crimes.; **in dieser Beziehung** in this respect; **Beziehungen haben** to have contacts; **eine Beziehung zu etwas haben** to be able to relate to something

Bezirk (*pl* **Bezirke**) *m* district

Bezug (*pl* **Bezüge**) *m* cover ▷ *Das Sofa hatte einen bunten Bezug.* The sofa had a brightly-coloured cover.; **in Bezug auf** regarding; **Bezug nehmen auf** to refer to

bezweifeln (*perf* **hat bezweifelt**) *vb* **[34]** to doubt ▷ *Ich bezweifle das.* I doubt it.

BH (*pl* **BHs**) *m* (= *Büstenhalter*) bra

Bibel *f* Bible

Bibliothek (*pl* **Bibliotheken**) *f* library

biegen (*imperf* **bog**, *perf* **hat gebogen**) *vb* ❶ to bend ▷ *Sie bog den Draht zur Seite.* She bent the wire to one side. ❷ to turn ▷ *Du musst an der Ampel rechts in die Seitenstraße biegen.* You have to turn right at the lights, into the side street.; **sich biegen** to bend

Biene *f* bee

Bier (*pl* **Biere** *or* **Bier**) *nt* beer ▷ *Zwei Bier, bitte!* Two beers, please!

bieten (*imperf* **bot**, *perf* **hat geboten**) *vb* **[8]** ❶ to offer ▷ *Dieser Job bietet mir die Möglichkeit, meine Englischkenntnisse anzuwenden.* This job offers me the chance to use my knowledge of English. ❷ to bid ▷ *Sie hat zweihundert Euro für den Stuhl geboten.* She bid two hundred euros for the chair. ▷ *Wer bietet mehr?* Any more bids?; **sobald sich die Gelegenheit bietet** as soon as the opportunity arises; **sich etwas bieten lassen** to put up with something

Bild (*pl* **Bilder**) *nt* ❶ picture ▷ *ein Bild von Picasso* a picture by Picasso; **ein Bild der Verwüstung** a scene of destruction ❷ photo ▷ *Hast du ein Bild von deinem Freund?* Have you got a photo of your boyfriend?

bilden *vb* **[54]** ❶ to form ▷ *Bildet einen Kreis.* Form a circle. ▷ *Wie wird der Plural dieses Worts gebildet?* How do you form the plural of this word? ❷ to set up ▷ *Sie haben einen Ausschuss gebildet.* They set up a committee.; **sich eine Meinung bilden** to form an opinion; **sich bilden (1)** to form ▷ *Am Himmel bildeten sich dunkle Wolken.* Dark clouds formed in the sky. **(2)** to educate oneself ▷ *Sie macht Kurse, um sich zu bilden.* She attends courses in order to educate herself.

Bildschirm (*pl* **Bildschirme**) *m* screen

Bildschirmschoner (*pl* **Bildschirmschoner**) *m* screen saver

Bildung *f* ❶ education ▷ *Sie hat eine gute Bildung.* She has a good education. ❷ formation ▷ *Die Bildung des Plurals im Englischen ist ziemlich regelmäßig.* The formation of the plural in English is quite regular. ▷ *die Bildung der Regierung* the formation of the government

billig *adj* cheap

Billigflieger (*pl* **Billigflieger**) *m* low-cost airline

Binde *f* ❶ bandage ▷ *eine elastische Binde* an elastic bandage ❷ sanitary towel ▷ *Sie benützt lieber Binden als Tampons.* She prefers sanitary towels to tampons.

binden (*imperf* **band**, *perf* **hat gebunden**) *vb* to tie ▷ *Die Tomaten werden an einen Stock gebunden.* The tomatoes are tied to a cane. ▷ *Sie band die Haare zu einem Pferdeschwanz.* She tied her hair back into a ponytail.; **ein Buch binden** to bind a book; **sich binden** to get involved

Bindestrich (*pl* **Bindestriche**) *m* hyphen
Bindfaden (*pl* **Bindfäden**) *m* string
Bio- *prefix* organic
Biologie *f* biology
biologisch *adj* biological
Birke *f* birch
Birne *f* ❶ pear ▷ *Zum Nachtisch gab es Birnen mit Schokoladensoße.* There were pears with chocolate sauce for dessert. ❷ bulb ▷ *Die Lampe funktioniert nicht, weil die Birne kaputt ist.* The lamp isn't working because the bulb's gone.
bis *prep, conj*

The preposition **bis** takes the accusative.

❶ until ▷ *Sie bleibt bis Ende August in England.* She's staying in England until the end of August. ▷ *Du hast bis Montag Zeit.* You have until Monday. ▷ *bis es dunkel wird* until it gets dark; **bis auf weiteres** until further notice ❷ by ▷ *Das Referat muss bis nächsten Montag fertig sein.* The assignment must be finished by next Monday.; **bis in die Nacht** into the night; **bis bald** see you later; **bis gleich** see you soon ❸ as far as ▷ *Ich fahre bis Köln.* I'm going as far as Cologne.; **bis hierher** this far; **von ... bis ...** from ... to ... ❹ up to ▷ *Kinder bis drei fahren umsonst.* Children up to three travel free. ▷ *bis zu dreißig Grad* up to thirty degrees; **zehn bis zwanzig** ten to twenty; **bis zu** up to; **bis auf** apart from
bisher *adv* up to now
bisherig *adj* previous
biss *vb see* **beißen**
Biss (*gen* **Bisses**, *pl* **Bisse**) *m* bite
bisschen *adj, adv* bit ▷ *ein bisschen* a bit
bissig *adj* ❶ vicious; **Vorsicht, bissiger Hund!** Beware of the dog! ❷ cutting ▷ *Er machte eine bissige Bemerkung.* He made a cutting remark.
bist *vb see* **sein**
bitte *excl* ❶ please ▷ *Kann ich bitte noch etwas Saft haben?* Can I have some more juice, please? ▷ *Darf ich? — Aber bitte!* May I? — Please do.; **Wie bitte?** Pardon?; **Hier bitte!** Here you are.; **Bitte warten.** Please hold the line. *(phone)* ❷ don't mention it ▷ *Vielen Dank für die Hilfe! — Bitte!* Many thanks for your help! — Don't mention it!; **Bitte schön!** It was a pleasure.; **Bitte sehr!** You're welcome.
Bitte *f* request ▷ *Ich habe eine Bitte.* I have a request. ▷ *auf seine Bitte hin* at his request
bitten (*imperf* **bat**, *perf* **hat gebeten**) *vb* [**9**] **jemanden um etwas bitten** to ask somebody for something
bitter *adj* bitter
blamieren (*perf* **hat blamiert**) *vb* [**76**] **sich blamieren** to make a fool of oneself; **jemanden blamieren** to let somebody down
Blase *f* ❶ bubble ▷ *Die Blase platzte.* The bubble burst. ❷ blister ▷ *Ich habe Blasen an den Füßen.* I've got blisters on my feet. ❸ bladder ▷ *Sie hat eine schwache Blase.* She has a weak bladder.
blasen (*pres* **bläst**, *imperf* **blies**, *perf* **hat geblasen**) *vb* to blow
Blasinstrument (*pl* **Blasinstrumente**) *nt* wind instrument
Blasmusik *f* brass band music
blass *adj* pale ▷ *Als sie das hörte, wurde sie blass.* When she heard that, she turned pale.
Blatt (*pl* **Blätter**) *nt* ❶ leaf ▷ *Im Herbst fallen die Blätter von den Bäumen.* In autumn, the leaves fall from the trees. ❷ sheet ▷ *ein Blatt Papier* a sheet of paper ❸ newspaper ▷ *In welchem Blatt hast du die Anzeige aufgegeben?* Which newspaper did you place the advertisement in?
blau *adj* ❶ blue ▷ *Er hat blaue Augen.* He has blue eyes. ❷ *(informal)* sloshed ▷ *Gestern Abend warst du ganz schön blau.* You were absolutely sloshed yesterday evening.; **ein blaues Auge** a black eye

Word for word, **ein blaues Auge** means 'a blue eye'.

ein blauer Fleck a bruise

Word for word, **ein blauer Fleck** means 'a blue spot'.

eine Fahrt ins Blaue a mystery tour

Blech (*pl* **Bleche**) *nt* ❶ sheet metal ❷ baking tray

Blei *nt* lead

bleiben (*imperf* **blieb**, *perf* **ist geblieben**) *vb* [10] ❶ to stay ▷ *Wie lange bleiben Sie hier?* How long are you staying here? ▷ *Hoffentlich bleibt das Wetter schön.* I hope the weather will stay fine.; **bei etwas bleiben** to stick to something ❷ to be left ▷ *Vom Kuchen war nur noch ein Stück für mich geblieben.* There was only one piece of cake left for me.; **Bleibt es bei morgen zehn Uhr?** Is ten o'clock tomorrow morning still on?; **Wo bleibt sie denn?** Where's she got to?

bleich *adj* pale ▷ *Als er das hörte, wurde er bleich.* When he heard that, he turned pale.

bleifrei *adj* unleaded

Bleistift (*pl* **Bleistifte**) *m* pencil

Blick (*pl* **Blicke**) *m* ❶ glance ▷ *Ich habe mit einem Blick gesehen, dass das nicht gut gehen kann.* I saw at a glance that it couldn't work.; **Er warf einen Blick auf die Uhr.** He glanced at the clock. ❷ look ▷ *Sie warf mir einen verzweifelten Blick zu.* She gave me a desperate look. ❸ view ▷ *Das Zimmer hat einen herrlichen Blick auf die Berge.* The room has a wonderful view of the mountains.; **auf den ersten Blick** at first glance

blicken *vb* [48] to look ▷ *Sie blickte zur Seite.* She looked to one side.; **sich blicken lassen** to show one's face; **Das lässt tief blicken!** That's very revealing!

blieb *vb see* **bleiben**

blind *adj* ❶ blind ▷ *Er ist auf einem Auge blind.* He's blind in one eye. ❷ tarnished ▷ *Der Spiegel war blind geworden.* The mirror had become tarnished.; **ein blinder Passagier** a stowaway

Word for word, **ein blinder Passagier** means 'a blind passenger'.

Blinddarm (*pl* **Blinddärme**) *m* appendix ▷ *Er wurde am Blinddarm operiert.* He had his appendix out.

blinzeln *vb* [88] to blink

Blitz (*pl* **Blitze**) *m* lightning ▷ *Der Blitz schlug in den Baum ein.* The tree was struck by lightning.

blitzen *vb* [36] **Es blitzt.** There's a flash of lightning.

Blitzlicht (*pl* **Blitzlichter**) *nt* flashlight

Block (*pl* **Blöcke**) *m* ❶ block ▷ *Unsere Nachbarn aus dem nächsten Block haben uns gestern besucht.* Our neighbours from the next block visited us yesterday. ❷ pad ▷ *Er riss ein Blatt vom Block und fing an zu schreiben.* He tore a sheet from the pad and began to write.

Blockflöte *f* recorder

blöd *adj* stupid ▷ *Du bist blöd!* You're stupid!; **blöd fragen** to ask stupid questions

Blödsinn *m* nonsense

Blog (*pl* **Blogs**) *nt* blog

blond *adj* ❶ blond ▷ *Er hat blonde Haare.* He has blond hair. ❷ blonde ▷ *Meine Schwester ist blond.* My sister's blonde. ▷ *Sie hat ihre Haare blond gefärbt.* She dyed her hair blonde.

bloß *adv, adj* only ▷ *Er hat bloß einen Fehler gemacht.* He only made one mistake. ▷ *Wenn das bloß schon fertig wäre!* If only it was finished.; **Lass das bloß!** Don't do that!; **Wie ist das bloß passiert?** How on earth did that happen?; **Wo ist er bloß?** Where's he got to?; **mit bloßem Auge** with the naked eye; **der bloße Gedanke** the very thought; **bloßer Neid** sheer envy

blühen *vb* [38] to be in bloom ▷ *Zurzeit blüht der Flieder.* The lilac's in bloom at the moment.

Blume *f* flower ▷ *Sie hat mir einen Strauß Blumen mitgebracht.* She brought me a bunch of flowers.
Blumenbeet (*pl* **Blumenbeete**) *nt* flowerbed
Blumenkohl (*pl* **Blumenkohle**) *m* cauliflower
Bluse *f* blouse
Blut *nt* blood
Blutdruck *m* blood pressure
Blüte *f* blossom
bluten *vb* [2] to bleed ▷ *Meine Nase blutet.* My nose is bleeding.
Blutprobe *f* blood test
Bock *m* **Bock haben, etwas zu tun** *(informal)* to fancy doing something
Bockwurst (*pl* **Bockwürste**) *f* frankfurter
Boden (*pl* **Böden**) *m* ❶ soil ▷ *Der Boden ist in dieser Gegend sehr fruchtbar.* The soil in this area is very fertile. ▷ *auf deutschem Boden* on German soil ❷ floor ▷ *Wir haben auf dem Boden gesessen.* We sat on the floor. ❸ bottom ▷ *Das Schiff sank auf den Boden des Meers.* The ship sank to the bottom of the sea. ▷ *Das Fass hat einen hölzernen Boden.* The barrel has a wooden bottom. ❹ attic ▷ *Wir haben die alten Möbel auf den Boden gebracht.* We put the old furniture into the attic.
Bodensee *m* Lake Constance ▷ *eine Stadt am Bodensee* a town on Lake Constance
Bohne *f* bean
bohren *vb* [38] ❶ to bore ▷ *Sie bohrte ein Loch in das Brett.* She bored a hole in the shelf. ❷ to drill ▷ *Der Zahnarzt musste nicht bohren.* The dentist didn't have to drill. ▷ *In der Nordsee wird nach Erdöl gebohrt.* They're drilling for oil in the North Sea.; **in der Nase bohren** to pick one's nose
Bohrer (*pl* **Bohrer**) *m* drill
Bohrmaschine *f* drill
Bombe *f* bomb
Bonbon (*pl* **Bonbons**) *m* sweet
Boot (*pl* **Boote**) *nt* boat
Bord *m* **an Bord** on board
Bord (*pl* **Borde**) *nt* shelf ▷ *Er brachte über dem Schreibtisch ein Bord für seine Bücher an.* He put up a shelf over his desk for his books.
borgen *vb* [38] to borrow ▷ *Das gehört nicht mir, das habe ich mir geborgt.* That doesn't belong to me, I borrowed it.; **jemandem etwas borgen** to lend somebody something
Börse *f* ❶ purse ▷ *Sie nahm zehn Euro aus ihrer Börse.* She took ten euros out of her purse. ❷ stock exchange ▷ *Diese Aktien werden an der Börse gehandelt.* These shares are traded on the stock exchange.
böse *adj* ❶ bad ▷ *Er ist ein böser Mensch.* He's a bad man. ▷ *Die Kinder waren böse.* The children were bad. ▷ *Sie hat eine böse Erkältung.* She has a bad cold. ❷ angry ▷ *Ich habe ihm einen bösen Brief geschrieben.* I wrote him an angry letter.; **böse werden** to get angry ▷ *Wenn du das noch einmal tust, werde ich böse.* If you do that again, I'll get angry. ▷ *Bist du mir noch böse?* Are you still angry with me?; **auf jemanden böse sein** to be angry with somebody ▷ *Ich bin böse auf Martin, weil er nicht gekommen ist.* I'm angry with Martin because he didn't come.; **eine böse Überraschung** a nasty shock; **Mit ihm sieht es böse aus.** It doesn't look too good for him.
Bosnien *nt* Bosnia
bot *vb see* **bieten**
Botschaft *f* ❶ message ▷ *Kannst du ihm eine Botschaft übermitteln?* Can you give him a message? ❷ embassy ▷ *Sie müssen das Visum auf der Botschaft beantragen.* You have to apply to the embassy for a visa.
boxen *vb* [48] to box
Boxer (*pl* **Boxer**) *m* boxer
brach *vb see* **brechen**
brachte *vb see* **bringen**

Brand (*pl* **Brände**) *m* fire

Brandenburg *nt* Brandenburg

Brandenburg is one of the 16 **Länder**. Its capital is Potsdam, which is famous as Frederick the Great's residence. Agriculture and forestry are still important parts of the economy.

Brasilien *nt* Brazil

braten (*pres* **brät**, *imperf* **briet**, *perf* **hat gebraten**) *vb* ❶ to roast ▷ *Wir haben das Hähnchen im Backofen gebraten.* We roasted the chicken in the oven. ❷ to fry ▷ *Sie briet die Kartoffeln in der Pfanne.* She fried the potatoes in the frying pan.

Braten (*pl* **Braten**) *m* roast

Brathähnchen (*pl* **Brathähnchen**) *nt* roast chicken

Bratkartoffeln *fpl* fried potatoes *pl*

Bratwurst (*pl* **Bratwürste**) *f* fried sausage

Brauch (*pl* **Bräuche**) *m* custom

brauchbar *adj* ❶ usable ▷ *Dieses alte Gerät ist nicht mehr brauchbar.* The old appliance is no longer usable. ❷ capable ▷ *Sie ist eine sehr brauchbare Mitarbeiterin.* She's a very capable colleague.

brauchen *vb* **[48]** ❶ to need ▷ *Wir brauchen noch Brot und Butter.* We still need bread and butter. ▷ *Dazu brauche ich mindestens zwei Tage.* I'll need at least two days. ❷ to have to ▷ *Du brauchst heute nicht zu kommen.* You don't have to come today. ▷ *Du brauchst nur Bescheid zu sagen, dann helfe ich dir.* You only have to let me know and I'll help you.; **Das kann ich gut brauchen.** I could really do with that.

Brauerei *f* brewery

braun *adj* ❶ brown ▷ *Sie hat braune Haare und braune Augen.* She has brown hair and brown eyes. ❷ tanned ▷ *Wir kamen ganz braun aus den Ferien zurück.* We came back all tanned from our holidays.

Braut (*pl* **Bräute**) *f* bride

Bräutigam (*pl* **Bräutigame**) *m* bridegroom

Brautpaar (*pl* **Brautpaare**) *nt* bride and groom *pl*

brav *adj* good ▷ *Die Kinder waren brav.* The children were good.; **Er ist ganz brav ins Bett gegangen.** He went to bed as good as gold.

> Be careful! **brav** does not mean **brave**.

bravo! *excl* well done!

BRD *f* (= *Bundesrepublik Deutschland*) Federal Republic of Germany

brechen (*pres* **bricht**, *imperf* **brach**, *perf* **hat/ist gebrochen**) *vb* **[11]**

> For the perfect tense use **haben** when the verb has an object and **sein** when there is no object. Use **haben** for 'to vomit'.

❶ to break ▷ *Der Zweig ist gebrochen.* The branch broke. ▷ *Ich habe den Stock in zwei Teile gebrochen.* I broke the stick in two. ▷ *Ich habe mir den rechten Arm gebrochen.* I've broken my right arm. ▷ *Sie hat ihr Versprechen gebrochen.* She broke her promise. ▷ *einen Rekord brechen* to break a record ❷ to vomit ▷ *Ihm wurde schlecht, und er musste brechen.* He felt ill and had to vomit.

breit *adj* wide ▷ *Das ist ein breiter Fluss.* That's a wide river. ▷ *Das Brett ist fünfzehn Zentimeter breit.* The plank is fifteen centimetres wide.

Breitband *nt* broadband

Breitbandanschluss (*pl* **Breitbandanschlüsse**) *m* broadband connection

Breite *f* width ▷ *die Breite des Tisches* the width of the table

Bremen *nt* Bremen

The 'Free Hanseatic City of Bremen' is one of the 16 **Länder**. It is a 'city-state' like Berlin and Hamburg, and is made up of the cities Bremen and Bremerhaven. It is the smallest **Land**, but the second-oldest city-republic in the world.

Bremse *f* ❶ brake ▷ *Sie trat auf die Bremse.* She stepped on the brakes. ❷ horsefly ▷ *Wir sind von Bremsen gestochen worden.* We were bitten by horseflies.

bremsen *vb* [36] to brake ▷ *Als er das Kind sah, bremste er.* When he saw the child, he braked.; **Sie versuchte, das Auto zu bremsen.** She tried to stop the car.; **Sie ist nicht zu bremsen.** There's no stopping her.

brennen (*imperf* **brannte**, *perf* **hat gebrannt**) *vb* [12] ❶ to burn ▷ *Das Holz ist zu nass, es brennt nicht.* The wood's too wet, it won't burn. ▷ *Im Wohnzimmer brennt Licht.* There's a light burning in the living room. ▷ *Der Schnaps brennt auf der Zunge.* The schnapps burns your tongue. ▷ *ein Loch in etwas brennen* to burn a hole in something ❷ to be on fire ▷ *Das Haus brannte.* The house was on fire.; **sich brennen** to burn oneself; **darauf brennen, etwas zu tun** to be dying to do something

Brennnessel *f* stinging nettle

Brett (*pl* **Bretter**) *nt* ❶ board ▷ *Die Hütte bestand aus ein paar zusammengenagelten Brettern.* The hut consisted of a few boards nailed together. ▷ *Sie stellte die Schachfiguren aufs Brett.* She set up the chessmen on the board. ❷ shelf ▷ *Die Gewürze stehen auf einem Brett über dem Herd.* The spices are on a shelf above the cooker.; **das Schwarze Brett** the notice board

> Word for word, **das Schwarze Brett** means 'the black board'.

Ich hatte ein Brett vor dem Kopf. My mind went blank.

Brezel *f* pretzel

bricht *vb see* **brechen**

Brief (*pl* **Briefe**) *m* letter

Brieffreund (*pl* **Brieffreunde**) *m* pen friend

Brieffreundin *f* pen friend

Briefkasten (*pl* **Briefkästen**) *m* ❶ letterbox ❷ postbox

Briefmarke *f* stamp

Brieftasche *f* wallet

Briefträger (*pl* **Briefträger**) *m* postman ▷ *Günter ist Briefträger.* Günter's a postman.

Briefträgerin *f* postwoman ▷ *Meine Tante ist Briefträgerin.* My aunt's a postwoman.

Briefumschlag (*pl* **Briefumschläge**) *m* envelope

briet *vb see* **braten**

Brille *f* ❶ glasses *pl* ▷ *Lesley trägt eine Brille.* Lesley wears glasses. ▷ *eine Brille* a pair of glasses ❷ goggles *pl* ▷ *Beim Schweißen sollte man eine Brille tragen.* You should wear goggles when welding. ❸ toilet seat ▷ *Ich hasse es, wenn Männer die Brille oben lassen.* I hate it when men leave the toilet seat up.

bringen (*imperf* **brachte**, *perf* **hat gebracht**) *vb* [13] ❶ to bring ▷ *Unsere Gäste haben uns einen schönen Blumenstrauß gebracht.* Our guests have brought us a lovely bunch of flowers. ▷ *Kann ich meine Schwester mit zur Party bringen?* Can I bring my sister to the party? ❷ to take ▷ *Meine Freunde haben mich zum Flughafen gebracht.* My friends took me to the airport. ▷ *jemanden nach Hause bringen* to take somebody home ❸ to bring in ▷ *Diese Anlage bringt fünf Prozent Zinsen.* This investment brings in five per cent interest. ❹ to publish ▷ *Alle Zeitungen brachten diese Geschichte auf der ersten Seite.* All the newspapers published this story on the first page. ❺ to be on ▷ *Sieh mal in der Zeitung nach, was das Theater bringt.* Look in the paper to see what's on at the theatre.; **jemanden zu etwas bringen** to make somebody do something; **jemanden dazu bringen, etwas zu tun** to get somebody to do something; **es über sich bringen, etwas zu tun** to bring oneself to do something; **jemanden um etwas bringen** to cheat somebody out of something; **jemanden in Gefahr bringen** to put somebody in danger; **Unser Computer bringt's nicht.** *(informal)* Our computer's rubbish.; **Das bringt nichts!** That's no use!

Brite (*gen* **Briten**, *pl* **Briten**) *m* Briton; **die Briten** the British

Britin *f* Briton

britisch *adj* British

Brombeere *f* blackberry

Broschüre *f* brochure

Brot (*pl* **Brote**) *nt* ❶ bread ▷ *Haben wir noch Brot im Haus?* Do we still have some bread in the house? ❷ loaf ▷ *Kannst du für die Party drei Brote holen?* Can you get three loaves for the party?

Brötchen (*pl* **Brötchen**) *nt* roll

browsen (*perf* **hat gebrowst**) *vb* [**38**] to browse

Bruch (*pl* **Brüche**) *m* ❶ fracture ▷ *Sie wurde mit einem Bruch ins Krankenhaus eingeliefert.* She was taken to hospital with a fracture.; **zu Bruch gehen** to get broken ❷ hernia ▷ *Trag das nicht allein, du hebst dir sonst einen Bruch!* Don't carry that on your own, you'll give yourself a hernia! ❸ fraction ▷ *Das Rechnen mit Brüchen haben wir noch nicht gelernt.* We haven't learned fractions yet.

Brücke *f* bridge

Bruder (*pl* **Brüder**) *m* brother

brüllen *vb* [**38**] to roar ▷ *Der Löwe brüllte.* The lion roared.; **Er brüllte vor Schmerz.** He screamed with pain.

brummen *vb* [**38**] ❶ to growl ▷ *Der Bär brummte.* The bear growled. ❷ to buzz ▷ *Eine dicke Fliege brummte durchs Zimmer.* A huge fly buzzed around the room.; **etwas brummen** to mumble something

Brunnen (*pl* **Brunnen**) *m* ❶ fountain ▷ *Am Marktplatz steht ein Brunnen.* There's a fountain in the market square. ❷ well ▷ *Wasser aus dem Brunnen* water from the well

Brust (*pl* **Brüste**) *f* breast ▷ *Sie hat kleine Brüste.* She has small breasts.

brutal *adj* brutal

Brutalität *f* brutality

brutto *adv* gross

Buch (*pl* **Bücher**) *nt* book

buchen *vb* [**48**] to book ▷ *Wir haben eine Reise nach Kreta gebucht.* We've booked a trip to Crete.

Bücherei *f* library

Bücherregal (*pl* **Bücherregale**) *nt* bookcase

Buchhalter (*pl* **Buchhalter**) *m* accountant

Buchhandlung *f* bookshop

Buchladen (*pl* **Buchläden**) *m* bookshop

Büchse *f* tin ▷ *Sie bewahrt den Tee in einer Büchse auf.* She keeps her tea in a tin.

Büchsenöffner (*pl* **Büchsenöffner**) *m* tin opener

Buchstabe (*gen* **Buchstabens**, *pl* **Buchstaben**) *m* letter of the alphabet

buchstabieren (*perf* **hat buchstabiert**) *vb* [**76**] to spell

sich **bücken** *vb* [**48**] to bend down

Bude *f* stall ▷ *die Buden auf dem Jahrmarkt* the stalls at the fair; **Kommt ihr noch mit auf meine Bude?** Do you want to come back to my place?

Bügel (*pl* **Bügel**) *m* hanger

Bügeleisen (*pl* **Bügeleisen**) *nt* iron ▷ *Ich habe mir die Hand am Bügeleisen verbrannt.* I burnt my hand on the iron.

bügeln *vb* [**34**] to iron

Bühne *f* stage ▷ *auf der Bühne stehen* to be on stage

buk *vb see* **backen**

Bulgarien *nt* Bulgaria

Bummel (*pl* **Bummel**) *m* stroll ▷ *Wir machten einen Bummel an der Donau entlang.* We went for a stroll along the Danube.

bummeln *vb* [**88**]

> Use **sein** to form the perfect tense for 'to stroll' and **haben** for 'to dawdle'.

❶ to stroll ▷ *Wir sind durch die Stadt gebummelt.* We strolled through the town. ❷ to dawdle ▷ *Heute hast du auf dem Heimweg aber gebummelt.* You've really been dawdling on your way home today.

Bund (*pl* **Bünde**) *m* ❶ association ▷ *Die Bauern schlossen sich zu einem Bund zusammen.* The farmers formed an association.; **Bund und Länder** the Federal Government and the Länder ❷ waistband ▷ *Die Hose ist am Bund zu eng.* The trousers are too tight at the waistband.

Bundes- *prefix* Federal

Bundeskanzler (*pl* **Bundeskanzler**) *m* Federal Chancellor

Bundesland (*pl* **Bundesländer**) *nt* state

Bundesliga *f* Premier League

Bundesrat *m* upper chamber of the German Parliament

The **Bundesrat** is not directly elected, but is made up of representatives of the 16 **Länder**. In many cases, **Bundesrat** approval is required before laws (particularly amendments to the constitution) can be passed.

Bundesregierung *f* Federal government

Bundesrepublik *f* Federal Republic ▷ *die Bundesrepublik Deutschland* the Federal Republic of Germany

Bundestag *m* German Parliament

The **Bundestag** is the German parliamentary assembly, elected every four years.

Bundeswehr *f* German Armed Forces *pl*

bunt *adj* ❶ brightly-coloured ▷ *Sie hatte ein buntes Kleid an.* She was wearing a brightly-coloured dress. ❷ mixed ▷ *Unsere Klasse ist ein buntes Häufchen.* Our class is a mixed bunch.; **Mir wird es zu bunt.** It's getting too much for me.

Word for word, **Mir wird es zu bunt** means 'It's getting too colourful for me'.

Burg (*pl* **Burgen**) *f* castle

Bürger (*pl* **Bürger**) *m* citizen

bürgerlich *adj* ❶ civil ▷ *bürgerliche Rechte* civil rights ❷ middle-class ▷ *eine gute bürgerliche Familie* a good middle-class family

Bürgermeister (*pl* **Bürgermeister**) *m* mayor

Bürgersteig (*pl* **Bürgersteige**) *m* pavement

Büro (*pl* **Büros**) *nt* office

Büroklammer *f* paper clip

Bürste *f* brush

bürsten (*perf* **hat gebürstet**) *vb* [**2**] to brush

Bus (*gen* **Busses**, *pl* **Busse**) *m* bus ▷ *mit dem Bus fahren* to go by bus

Busbahnhof (*pl* **Busbahnhöfe**) *m* bus station

Busch (*pl* **Büsche**) *m* bush

Busen (*pl* **Busen**) *m* bosom

Busfahrer (*pl* **Busfahrer**) *m* bus driver

Bushaltestelle *f* bus stop

Buslinie *f* bus route

Bußgeld (*pl* **Bußgelder**) *nt* fine

Büstenhalter (*pl* **Büstenhalter**) *m* bra

Butter *f* butter

Butterbrot (*pl* **Butterbrote**) *nt* bread and butter

C

Café (*pl* **Cafés**) *nt* café ▷ *Sonntags gehen wir immer ins Café.* On Sundays we always go to a café.
Cafeteria (*pl* **Cafeterias**) *f* cafeteria
Callcenter (*pl* **Callcenter**) *nt* call centre
campen *vb* [**38**] to camp
Campingplatz (*gen* **Campingplatzes**, *pl* **Campingplätze**) *m* campsite
CD (*pl* **CDs**) *f* CD
CD-Spieler (*pl* **CD-Spieler**) *m* CD player
Cent (*pl* **Cents**) *m* cent
Champignon (*pl* **Champignons**) *m* button mushroom
Chance *f* chance
Chaos (*gen* **Chaos**) *nt* chaos
chaotisch *adj* chaotic
Charakter (*pl* **Charakter**) *m* character
charmant *adj* charming
Charterflug (*pl* **Charterflüge**) *m* charter flight
Chat (*pl* **Chats**) *m (internet)* chat
Chatroom (*pl* **Chatrooms**) *m* chat room
chatten *vb* [**2**] to chat ▷ *Wir haben im Internet gechattet.* We chatted on the Net.
Chef (*pl* **Chefs**) *m* ❶ head ▷ *Er ist Chef einer großen Firma.* He's the head of a large company. ❷ boss ▷ *Da muss ich den Chef fragen.* I'll have to ask my boss.
Chefin *f* boss
Chemie *f* chemistry
Chemiker (*pl* **Chemiker**) *m* industrial chemist
chemisch *adj* chemical; **chemische Reinigung** dry cleaning
Chile *nt* Chile
China *nt* China
Chinese (*gen* **Chinesen**, *pl* **Chinesen**) *m* Chinese; **die Chinesen** the Chinese
Chinesin *f* Chinese
chinesisch *adj* Chinese
Chips *pl* crisps *pl*

> Be careful! The German word **Chips** does not mean **chips**.

Chirurg (*gen* **Chirurgen**, *pl* **Chirurgen**) *m* surgeon
Chirurgie *f* surgery
Chor (*pl* **Chöre**) *m* choir ▷ *Sie singt im Chor.* She sings in a choir.
Christ (*gen* **Christen**, *pl* **Christen**) *m* Christian ▷ *Er ist Christ.* He's a Christian.
Christin *f* Christian ▷ *Sie ist Christin.* She's a Christian.
christlich *adj* Christian
cm *abbr (= Zentimeter)* cm
Cola (*pl* **Colas**) *f* Coke®
Computer (*pl* **Computer**) *m* computer
Computerspiel (*pl* **Computerspiele**) *nt* computer game
cool *adj* cool
Cousin (*pl* **Cousins**) *m* cousin
Cousine *f* cousin
Creme (*pl* **Cremes**) *f* ❶ cream ▷ *eine Handcreme* a hand cream ❷ polish

▷ *Hast du schwarze Schuhcreme?* Do you have any black shoe polish? ❸ mousse ▷ *eine Zitronencreme* a lemon mousse

Curry *m* curry powder

Currywurst (*pl* **Currywürste**) *f* curried sausage

d

da *adv, conj* ❶ there ▷ *Da ist es schön.* It's beautiful there. ▷ *da draußen* out there ▷ *Da haben wir Glück gehabt.* We were lucky there.; **da sein** to be there ❷ here ▷ *Da liegt meine Brille ja.* Here are my glasses. ▷ *Da bin ich.* Here I am.; **Ist noch Milch da?** Is there any milk left? ❸ since ▷ *Da du gerade hier bist ...* Since you're here ...

dabei *adv* **nahe dabei** close by; **Sie hatten ihren Hund dabei.** They had their dog with them.; **Was ist schon dabei?** What of it?; **Es ist doch nichts dabei, wenn ...** It doesn't matter if ...; **Bleiben wir dabei.** Let's leave it at that.; **Es bleibt dabei.** That's settled.; **dabei sein** to be there; **Er war gerade dabei, zu gehen.** He was just about to leave.

Dach (*pl* **Dächer**) *nt* roof

Dachboden (*pl* **Dachböden**) *m* attic

dachte *vb see* **denken**

Dackel (*pl* **Dackel**) *m* dachshund

dafür *adv* ❶ for it ▷ *Was hast du dafür bezahlt?* How much did you pay for it?

▷ *Was bekomme ich dafür?* What will I get for it?; **Er ist bekannt dafür.** He's well-known for that. ❷ instead ▷ *Wenn du nicht mit ins Schwimmbad kannst, dann komm dafür doch mit ins Kino.* If you can't come with us to the swimming pool, then come along to the cinema instead.; **Er kann nichts dafür.** He can't help it.

dagegen *adv, conj* ❶ against it ▷ *Was hast du dagegen?* What have you got against it? ▷ *Ich war dagegen.* I was against it.; **Ich habe nichts dagegen.** I don't mind.; **Dagegen kann man nichts tun.** You can't do anything about it. ❷ into it ▷ *Er sah den Baum nicht und rannte dagegen.* He didn't see the tree and ran into it. ❸ for it ▷ *Das ist jetzt mein Ball, ich habe meine Murmeln dagegen getauscht.* This is my ball now — I swapped my marbles for it. ❹ by comparison ▷ *Dagegen ist unser Haus klein.* Our house is small by comparison. ❺ however ▷ *Sie wollte gehen, er dagegen wollte bleiben.* She wanted to leave; however he wanted to stay.

daheim *adv* at home

daher *adv, conj* ❶ from there ▷ *Daher komme ich gerade.* I've just come from there. ❷ that's where ▷ *Das war ein schwerer Unfall; daher hat er sein kaputtes Bein.* It was a serious accident; that's where he got his bad leg. ❸ that's why ▷ *Sie war krank und konnte daher nicht mitkommen.* She was ill, and that's why she couldn't come.

dahin *adv* there ▷ *Dahin gehe ich jetzt.* I'm going there now.

dahinten *adv* over there

dahinter *adv* behind it ▷ *Er versteckte sich dahinter.* He hid behind it.

damals *adv* in those days

Dame *f* ❶ lady ❷ *(chess, cards)* queen ❸ draughts *sg* ▷ *Dame ist mein Lieblingsspiel.* Draughts is my favourite game.

damit *adv, conj* ❶ with it ▷ *Wisch damit den Tisch ab.* Wipe the table with it. ❷ by that ▷ *Was meint er damit?* What does he mean by that?; **Was willst du damit sagen?** What are you getting at?; **Genug damit!** That's enough of that!; **Damit eilt es nicht.** There's no hurry. ❸ so that ▷ *Ich sage dir das, damit du das weißt.* I'm telling you so that you know.

Dampf *m* steam

dampfen *vb* **[48]** ❶ to vape ❷ to puff

Dampfer (*pl* **Dampfer**) *m* steamer ▷ *mit dem Dampfer fahren* to go by steamer; **Du bist auf dem falschen Dampfer.** *(informal)* You've got the wrong idea.

> Word for word, **Du bist auf dem falschen Dampfer** means 'You're on the wrong steamer'.

danach *adv* ❶ afterwards ▷ *Ich habe etwas getrunken, und danach fühlte ich mich besser.* I had something to drink and afterwards felt much better. ❷ accordingly ▷ *Verhalte dich bitte danach.* Please behave accordingly.

Däne (*gen* **Dänen**, *pl* **Dänen**) *m* Dane

daneben *adv* ❶ beside it ❷ by comparison

Dänemark *nt* Denmark

Dänin *f* Dane

dänisch *adj* Danish

dank *prep*

> **dank** takes the genitive or dative.

thanks to ▷ *Dank meiner Schwester habe ich noch rechtzeitig davon erfahren.* Thanks to my sister I found out about it in time.

Dank *m* thanks *pl* ▷ *Unser Dank gilt vor allem Herrn Morris.* Our thanks to Mr Morris in particular.; **Vielen Dank!** Many thanks.

dankbar *adj* grateful ▷ *Ich bin dir sehr dankbar.* I'm very grateful to you.; **eine dankbare Aufgabe** a rewarding task

danke *excl* thank you; **Danke sehr!** Thank you.; **Danke schön!** Thank you very much.; **Nein, danke!** No, thanks.

danken *vb* [**38**] to thank ▷ *Ich möchte dir dafür danken.* I'd like to thank you for that.; **Nichts zu danken!** Don't mention it!

dann *adv* then; **dann und wann** now and then

daran *adv* ❶ on it ▷ *ein Päckchen mit einem Zettel daran* a parcel with a label on it ❷ of it ▷ *Er ist daran gestorben.* He died of it. ▷ *Ich habe nicht daran gedacht.* I didn't think of it.; **Es liegt daran, dass ...** This is because ...; **das Beste daran** the best thing about it; **Ich war nahe daran, zu gehen.** I was on the point of going.

darauf *adv* ❶ on it ▷ *Nimm einen Untersetzer und stelle den Topf darauf.* Take a mat and put the pan on it. ❷ afterwards ▷ *kurz darauf* shortly afterwards; **die Tage darauf** the following days; **am Tag darauf** the next day; **Er ging darauf zu.** He walked towards it.; **Es kommt ganz darauf an, ob ...** It all depends whether ...

daraus *adv* ❶ out of it ▷ *Sie nahm einen Keks daraus.* She took a biscuit out of it. ❷ of it ▷ *Was ist daraus geworden?* What became of it?; **Daraus geht hervor, dass ...** This means that ...

darf *vb see* **dürfen**

darin *adv* in it ▷ *eine Dose mit Keksen darin* a tin with biscuits in it; **Darin sehe ich kein Problem.** I don't see any problem there.

Darm (*pl* **Därme**) *m* intestine

darstellen (*perf* **hat dargestellt**) *vb* [**4**] to portray ▷ *etwas in einem günstigen Licht darstellen* to portray something in a good light

darüber *adv* ❶ over it ▷ *ein Tisch mit einer Lampe darüber* a table with a light over it ▷ *Da war eine Brücke, wir sind aber nicht darüber gefahren.* There was a bridge, but we didn't drive over it. ❷ about it ▷ *Wir haben darüber gesprochen.* We talked about it. ▷ *Denk mal darüber nach.* Think about it. ❸ more ▷ *Sie verdient fünftausend oder vielleicht sogar darüber.* She earns five thousand or maybe even more.

darum *adv, conj* ❶ round it ▷ *Sie machte ein rotes Band darum.* She put a red ribbon round it.; **Es geht darum, dass ...** The important thing is to ...; **Er würde viel darum geben, wenn ...** He would give a lot to ... ❷ that's why ▷ *Darum bin ich nicht gekommen.* That's why I didn't come.; **Ich tue es darum, weil ...** I'm doing it because ...

darunter *adv* ❶ under it ▷ *Der Topf ist heiß, leg einen Untersetzer darunter.* The pot's hot, put a mat under it.; **ein Stockwerk darunter** one floor below ❷ less ▷ *Er verdient nur dreitausend Euro oder vielleicht sogar darunter.* He earns only three thousand euros or maybe even less.; **Was verstehst du darunter?** What do you understand by that?

das *art, pron*

das is the definite neuter article.

❶ the ▷ *das Auto* the car; **das Leben** life; **Er hat sich das Knie verletzt.** He's hurt his knee. ❷ who ▷ *das Kind, das dir das gesagt hat* the child who told you; **das Kind, das du gesehen hast** the child you saw ❸ which ▷ *das Fahrrad, das du da siehst* the bike which you can see over there; **das mit dem roten Sattel** the one with the red saddle ❹ that ▷ *Das habe ich nicht gehört.* I didn't hear that.; **das da** that one

dass *conj* that ▷ *Ich bin böse, dass er nicht gekommen ist.* I'm annoyed that he didn't come. ▷ *Ich weiß, dass du besser in Mathe bist als ich.* I know you're better at maths than me.

dasselbe *pron* the same ▷ *dasselbe Kind* the same child

dastehen (*imperf* **stand da**, *perf* **hat dagestanden**) *vb* [**72**] to stand there

Datei *f* file

Daten *ntpl* data *pl*

Datenbank (*pl* **Datenbanken**) *f* data base
Datenverarbeitung *f* data processing
Dativ (*pl* **Dative**) *m* dative
Datum (*pl* **Daten**) *nt* date
Dauer *f* ❶ duration ▷ *für die Dauer meines Aufenthalts* for the duration of my stay ❷ length ▷ *die Dauer einer Reise* the length of a journey ▷ *die Dauer eines Anrufs* the length of a call; **von Dauer sein** to be permanent; **Ihr Glück war nur von kurzer Dauer.** Their happiness was only short-lived.; **auf die Dauer** **(1)** in the long run ▷ *Auf die Dauer wird ihm das langweilig werden.* He'll get bored with it in the long run. **(2)** indefinitely ▷ *Auf die Dauer geht das aber nicht.* That can't go on indefinitely.
dauern *vb* [**88**] to last ▷ *Der Krieg hat zehn Jahre gedauert.* The war lasted ten years.; **lange dauern** to take a long time; **Wie lange dauert das denn noch?** How much longer is this going to take?
dauernd *adj, adv* constant ▷ *Ich konnte sein dauerndes Stöhnen nicht ertragen.* I couldn't stand his constant moaning.; **Musst du mich dauernd stören?** Do you have to constantly interrupt me?
Daumen (*pl* **Daumen**) *m* thumb; **Ich drücke dir die Daumen.** I'll keep my fingers crossed for you.
davon *adv* ❶ of them ▷ *Sie nahm zwei davon.* She took two of them.; **Sie nahm hundert Gramm davon.** She took a hundred grams. ❷ away ▷ *Er lief davon.* He ran away. ❸ from it ▷ *Sie hat den Knopf davon abgetrennt.* She removed the button from it.; **Sie bekommt Kopfschmerzen davon.** It gives her a headache.; **davon abgesehen** apart from that ❹ about it ▷ *davon sprechen* to talk about it ▷ *Sie weiß nichts davon.* She doesn't know anything about it.; **Was habe ich davon?** What's the point?; **Das kommt davon!** That's what you get.
davonkommen (*imperf* **kam davon**, *perf* **ist davongekommen**) *vb* [**40**] to escape ▷ *Wir sind noch einmal davongekommen.* We've had a lucky escape.
davor *adv* ❶ in front of it ▷ *Ich stellte mich davor.* I stood in front of it. ❷ first ▷ *Du solltest davor aber noch zum Friseur.* You ought to go to the hairdresser's first.; **Ich habe dich davor gewarnt.** I warned you about it.
dazu *adv* with it ▷ *Was sollen wir dazu trinken?* What shall we drink with it?; **ein Beispiel dazu** an example of this; **seine Gedanken dazu** his thoughts on this; **dazu fähig sein** to be capable of it; **und dazu noch** and in addition
dazwischen *adv* ❶ in between ▷ *Wir können dazwischen ja eine Pause machen.* We can have a break in between. ❷ between them ▷ *Siehst du die beiden Pfosten, stell dich dazwischen.* You see the two posts? Go and stand between them. ▷ *der Unterschied dazwischen* the difference between them
DDR (*gen* **DDR**) *f* (= *Deutsche Demokratische Republik*) GDR ▷ *die ehemalige DDR* the former GDR
Decke *f* ❶ ceiling ▷ *Wir haben die Decke des Kinderzimmers gestrichen.* We've painted the ceiling of the children's room. ❷ blanket ▷ *eine Wolldecke* a woollen blanket; **eine Tischdecke** a tablecloth
Deckel (*pl* **Deckel**) *m* lid
decken *vb* [**38**] to cover ▷ *Er deckte die Hand über seine Augen.* He covered his eyes with his hand.; **den Tisch decken** to lay the table
dehnen *vb* [**38**] to stretch ▷ *Er dehnte sich und gähnte.* He stretched and yawned.
dein *adj* ❶ your ▷ *Dein Englischlehrer ist nett.* Your English teacher's nice. ▷ *Hat deine Mutter das erlaubt?* Did your mother let you? ▷ *Ist das dein Buch?* Is that your book? ▷ *Wo sind deine Eltern?*

Where are your parents? ❷ yours ▷ *Der Bleistift hier, ist das deiner?* Is this pencil yours? ▷ *Meine Mutter heißt Ulla, wie heißt deine?* My mother's called Ulla; what's yours called? ▷ *Mein Fahrrad ist kaputt, kann ich deins benutzen?* My bike's broken; can I use yours?

deinetwegen *adv* ❶ for your sake ▷ *Ich habe deinetwegen darauf verzichtet.* I did without for your sake. ❷ on your account ▷ *Er hat sich deinetwegen aufgeregt.* He got upset on your account.

deklinieren (*perf* **hat dekliniert**) *vb* [**76**] to decline

Delphin (*pl* **Delphine**) *m* dolphin

dem *art, pron*

> **dem** is the dative of **der** and **das**.

the ▷ *auf dem Tisch* on the table; **Gib es dem Mann.** Give it to the man.; **der Mann, dem ich es gegeben habe** the man I gave it to

demnächst *adv* shortly

Demokratie *f* democracy

demokratisch *adj* democratic

Demonstration *f* demonstration

demonstrieren (*perf* **hat demonstriert**) *vb* [**76**] to demonstrate

den *art, pron*

> **den** is the accusative of **der**.

the ▷ *Ich sehe den Mann.* I can see the man. ▷ *durch den Wald* through the wood; **Er hat sich den Fuß verletzt.** He's hurt his foot.; **der Mann, den ich gesehen habe** the man I saw

denen *pron*

> **denen** is the dative of **die** (plural).

❶ whom; **die Leute, denen ich die Bücher gegeben habe** the people I gave the books to; **die Leute, denen ich helfen wollte** the people I wanted to help ❷ which ▷ *Probleme, denen wir nicht gewachsen sind* problems which we can't cope with

denkbar *adj* conceivable

denken (*imperf* **dachte**, *perf* **hat gedacht**) *vb* [**14**] to think

Denkmal (*pl* **Denkmäler**) *nt* monument

denn *conj, adv* ❶ because ▷ *Ich habe sie nicht gesehen, denn sie war schon weg.* I didn't see her because she had already left. ❷ than ▷ *besser denn je* better than ever; **es sei denn ...** unless ...; **Warum denn?** But why?

dennoch *conj* nevertheless

der *art, pron*

> **der** is the definite masculine article and genitive and dative of **die**.

❶ the ▷ *der Mann* the man; **der Tod** death; **das Auto der Frau** the woman's car; **Gib es der Frau.** Give it to the woman. ❷ who ▷ *der, der dir das gesagt hat* the person who told you that; **die Frau, der ich es gegeben habe** the woman I gave it to ❸ which ▷ *der Computer, der mir gehört* the computer which belongs to me; **der mit der Brille** the one with glasses; **der da** that one

derselbe *pron* the same ▷ *derselbe Mann* the same man

deshalb *adv* that's why

dessen *pron*

> **dessen** is the genitive of **der** and **das**.

whose ▷ *mein Freund, dessen Schwester krank ist* my friend whose sister is ill

deswegen *conj* that's why ▷ *Hat er deswegen so geschimpft?* Is that why he was so mad?; **Es ist spät, deswegen gehen wir jetzt.** It's late, so we're leaving.; **Ich sage das deswegen, weil ...** The reason I'm saying this is that ...

deutlich *adj, adv* ❶ clear ▷ *mit deutlicher Stimme* in a clear voice ❷ clearly ▷ *Drück dich bitte deutlicher aus.* Please speak more clearly. ▷ *Es war deutlich zu sehen.* It was clearly visible.; **ein deutlicher Unterschied** a distinct difference

deutsch *adj* German

Deutsch (*gen* **Deutschen**) *nt* German ▷ *Er lernt Deutsch in der Schule.* He's learning German at school.; **auf Deutsch** in German

Deutsche (*gen* **Deutschen**, *pl* **Deutschen**) *mf* German; **Ich bin Deutscher.** I'm German.

Deutschland *nt* Germany

Dezember (*gen* **Dezember** *or* **Dezembers**, *pl* **Dezember**) *m* December ▷ *im Dezember* in December ▷ *am vierten Dezember* on the fourth of December ▷ *Ulm, den 5. Dezember 2014* Ulm, 5 December 2014 ▷ *Heute ist der sechste Dezember.* Today is the sixth of December.

d. h. *abbr* (= *das heißt*) i.e.

Dia (*pl* **Dias**) *nt* slide

Dialekt (*pl* **Dialekte**) *m* dialect

Diamant (*gen* **Diamanten**, *pl* **Diamanten**) *m* diamond

Diät *f* diet ▷ *Sie muss Diät halten.* She has to stick to a strict diet.

dich *pron* ❶ you ▷ *Ich habe dich gesehen.* I saw you. ❷ yourself ▷ *Sieh dich mal im Spiegel an.* Look at yourself in the mirror.

dicht *adj, adv* ❶ dense ▷ *dichte Wälder* dense woods ❷ thick ▷ *dichter Nebel* thick fog ❸ watertight ▷ *Ist der Behälter dicht?* Is the container watertight?; **Die Gasleitung war nicht dicht.** There was a leak in the gas pipe.; **dichter Verkehr** heavy traffic; **dicht an** close to

Dichter (*pl* **Dichter**) *m* poet

dick *adj* ❶ thick ▷ *Das Brett ist drei Zentimeter dick.* The plank's three centimetres thick. ❷ fat ▷ *Ich bin zu dick.* I'm too fat.

die *art, pron*

> **die** is the definite feminine article and the definite article plural.

❶ the ▷ *die Frau* the woman ▷ *die Kinder* the children; **die Liebe** love; **Er hat sich die Hand verletzt.** He's hurt his hand. ❷ who ▷ *die, die dir das gesagt hat* the person who told you that; **die Frau, die du gesehen hast** the woman you saw ❸ which ▷ *die Uhr, die mir gehört* the watch which belongs to me; **die mit der Brille** the one with glasses; **die da** that one

Dieb (*pl* **Diebe**) *m* thief

Diebstahl (*pl* **Diebstähle**) *m* theft

Diele *f* hall ▷ *Sie stand vor dem Spiegel in der Diele.* She stood in front of the mirror in the hall.

dienen (*perf* **hat gedient**) *vb* [38] to serve ▷ *Es dient einem guten Zweck.* It serves a useful purpose.; **Womit kann ich Ihnen dienen?** What can I do for you?

Dienst (*pl* **Dienste**) *m* service; **Dienst haben** to be on duty

Dienstag (*pl* **Dienstage**) *m* Tuesday ▷ *am Dienstag* on Tuesday

dienstags *adv* on Tuesdays

dies *pron* ❶ this ▷ *Dies ist unser Haus.* This is our house. ❷ these ▷ *Dies sind meine Bücher.* These are my books.

diese *pron* ❶ this ▷ *Dieses Kleid gefällt mir besonders gut.* I particularly like this dress. ❷ these ▷ *diese Bücher* these books ❸ this one ▷ *Ich möchte diesen hier.* I'd like this one. ❹ these ones ▷ *Ich suche ein Paar Sandalen, kann ich diese anprobieren?* I'm looking for a pair of sandals; can I try these ones on?

Diesel *m* diesel

dieselbe *pron* the same ▷ *dieselbe Frau* the same woman

diesmal *adv* this time

digital *adj* digital ▷ *die digitale Revolution* the digital revolution

Diktat (*pl* **Diktate**) *nt* dictation

Ding (*pl* **Dinge**) *nt* thing

Diplom (*pl* **Diplome**) *nt* diploma

Diplomatie *f* diplomacy

diplomatisch *adj* diplomatic

dir *pron*

> **dir** is the dative of **du**.

❶ you ▷ *Ich habe es dir doch gesagt.* I told you so. ❷ to you ▷ *Ich habe es dir gestern gegeben.* I gave it to you yesterday.

a b c d e f g h i j k l m n o p q r s t u v w x y z

direkt *adj* direct ▷ *Der Flug geht direkt.* It's a direct flight.
Direktor (*pl* **Direktoren**) *m* ❶ director ▷ *der Direktor der Firma* the director of the company ❷ headmaster ▷ *Mein Bruder musste gestern zum Direktor.* My brother was sent to the headmaster yesterday.
Diskette *f* diskette
Diskothek *f* disco
Diskussion *f* discussion; **zur Diskussion stehen** to be under discussion
Diskuswerfen *nt* throwing the discus
diskutieren (*perf* **hat diskutiert**) *vb* [**76**] to discuss ▷ *Wir haben über Politik diskutiert.* We discussed politics.
doch *adv, conj* ❶ after all ▷ *Sie ist doch noch gekommen.* She came after all. ❷ anyway ▷ *Du machst ja doch, was du willst.* You do what you want anyway. ❸ but ▷ *Ich habe ihn eingeladen, doch er hatte keine Lust.* I invited him, but he didn't feel like it. ▷ *Sie ist doch noch so jung.* But she's still so young. ❹ yes

doch is used to contradict a negative statement.

▷ *Du magst doch keine Süßigkeiten. — Doch!* You don't like sweets. — Yes I do. ▷ *Das ist nicht wahr. — Doch!* That's not true. — Yes it is!; **Komm doch.** Do come.; **Lass ihn doch.** Just leave him.
Doktor (*pl* **Doktoren**) *m* doctor ▷ *Er ist Doktor der Philosophie.* He's a doctor of philosophy.
Dokument *nt* document
Dokumentarfilm (*pl* **Dokumentarfilme**) *m* documentary
dolmetschen *vb* [**48**] to interpret
Dolmetscher (*pl* **Dolmetscher**) *m* interpreter
Dom (*pl* **Dome**) *m* cathedral
Donau *f* Danube
Donner (*pl* **Donner**) *m* thunder
donnern *vb* [**88**] to thunder ▷ *Es donnerte.* It was thundering.
Donnerstag (*pl* **Donnerstage**) *m* Thursday ▷ *am Donnerstag* on Thursday
donnerstags *adv* on Thursdays
doof *adj (informal)* thick
Doppelbett (*pl* **Doppelbetten**) *nt* double bed
Doppelfenster *ntpl* double glazing *sg*
Doppelhaus (*gen* **Doppelhauses**, *pl* **Doppelhäuser**) *nt* semidetached house
Doppelpunkt (*pl* **Doppelpunkte**) *m* colon
Doppelstunde *f* double period
doppelt *adj* ❶ double ▷ *die doppelte Menge* double the amount ❷ twice the ▷ *der doppelte Preis* twice the price ▷ *die doppelte Geschwindigkeit* twice the speed; **doppelt so viel** twice as much; **in doppelter Ausführung** in duplicate
Doppelzimmer (*pl* **Doppelzimmer**) *nt* double room
Dorf (*pl* **Dörfer**) *nt* village
dort *adv* there; **dort drüben** over there
dorther *adv* from there
dorthin *adv* there ▷ *Wir gehen jetzt dorthin.* We're going there now.
Dose *f* tin
Dosenöffner (*pl* **Dosenöffner**) *m* tin opener
Draht (*pl* **Drähte**) *m* wire; **auf Draht sein** to be on the ball
drahtlos *adj* wireless
Drama (*pl* **Dramen**) *nt* drama
dran *adv* **Jetzt bin ich dran!** It's my turn now.; **Wer ist dran?** Whose turn is it?; **gut dran sein** to be well-off; **schlecht dran sein** to be in a bad way
drauf *adv see* **darauf**
draußen *adv* outside
Dreck *m* dirt
dreckig *adj* dirty ▷ *Mach deine Kleider nicht dreckig.* Don't get your clothes dirty.
drehen *vb* [**38**] to turn ▷ *Dreh mal deinen Kopf zur Seite.* Turn your head to one side. ▷ *Du musst an dem Rad drehen.* You have to turn the wheel.; **eine**

Zigarette drehen to roll a cigarette; **einen Film drehen** to shoot a film; **sich drehen** to turn; **Es dreht sich um ...** It's about ...
drei *num* three
Drei *f* ❶ three ❷ satisfactory
German marks range from one (**sehr gut**) to six (**ungenügend**).
Dreieck (*pl* **Dreiecke**) *nt* triangle
dreihundert *num* three hundred
dreimal *adv* three times
dreißig *num* thirty
Dreiviertelstunde *f* three-quarters of an hour ▷ *Eine Dreiviertelstunde war vergangen.* Three-quarters of an hour had passed.
dreizehn *num* thirteen
drin *adv see* **darin**
dringend *adj* urgent
drinnen *adv* inside
dritte *adj* third ▷ *Sie nahm beim dritten Klingeln ab.* She answered on the third ring. ▷ *Er kam als Dritter.* He was the third to arrive.; **die Dritte Welt** the Third World; **das Dritte Reich** the Third Reich
Drittel (*pl* **Drittel**) *nt* third
Droge *f* drug
drogenabhängig *adj* addicted to drugs
Drogerie *f* chemist's shop
Drogist (*gen* **Drogisten**, *pl* **Drogisten**) *m* pharmacist
Drogistin *f* pharmacist
drohen *vb* [**38**] to threaten ▷ *jemandem drohen* to threaten somebody
drüben *adv* over there
Druck (*pl* **Drucke**) *m* ❶ pressure ▷ *Der Behälter muss viel Druck aushalten.* The container has to withstand a lot of pressure.; **jemanden unter Druck setzen** to put pressure on somebody ❷ printing ▷ *der Druck eines Buches* the printing of a book ❸ print ▷ *An der Wand hingen Drucke.* There were prints on the wall.
drücken *vb* [**38**] ❶ to press ▷ *Er drückte auf den Knopf.* He pressed the button.; **Sie drückte ihm die Hand.** She squeezed his hand. ❷ to pinch ▷ *Meine Schuhe drücken.* My shoes pinch.; **sich vor etwas drücken** to get out of something
Drucker (*pl* **Drucker**) *m* printer
Drucksache *f* printed matter
Dschungel (*pl* **Dschungel**) *m* jungle
du *pron* you ▷ *Hast du das gesehen?* Did you see that?; **du sagen** to use the 'du' form of address
The familiar form of address **du** (plural **ihr**) is used when addressing family members, friends, children under 16 and pets.
Dudelsack (*pl* **Dudelsäcke**) *m* bagpipes *pl* ▷ *Er spielt Dudelsack.* He plays the bagpipes.
Duft (*pl* **Düfte**) *m* scent
duften *vb* [**2**] to smell ▷ *Hier duftet es nach Kaffee.* It smells of coffee here.
dumm *adj* ❶ stupid ▷ *Das ist die dümmste Ausrede, die ich je gehört habe.* That's the stupidest excuse I've ever heard. ❷ bad ▷ *Es ist wirklich zu dumm, dass du nicht gekommen bist.* It's really too bad that you didn't come.; **der Dumme sein** to draw the short straw
dummerweise *adv* stupidly
Dummheit *f* ❶ stupidity ▷ *Deine Dummheit ist wirklich grenzenlos.* Your stupidity really knows no bounds. ❷ stupid mistake ▷ *Es war eine Dummheit, ihr das zu erzählen.* It was a stupid mistake telling her that.; **Dummheiten machen** to do something stupid
Dummkopf (*pl* **Dummköpfe**) *m* idiot
dunkel *adj* dark ▷ *Im Zimmer war es dunkel.* It was dark in the room.; **eine dunkle Stimme** a deep voice; **eine dunkle Ahnung** a vague idea; **dunkle Gestalten** sinister figures; **dunkle Geschäfte** shady dealings; **im Dunkeln tappen** to grope about in the dark; **ein Dunkles** a dark beer

a b c d e f g h i j k l m n o p q r s t u v w x y z

Dunkelheit *f* dark ▷ *Er hat Angst vor der Dunkelheit.* He's afraid of the dark.
dünn *adj* thin
Dunst (*pl* **Dünste**) *m* haze
durch *prep, adv*
The preposition **durch** takes the accusative.
❶ through ▷ *durch den Wald* through the wood ▷ *Ich habe die Stelle durch meinen Onkel bekommen.* I got the job through my uncle. ▷ *durch seine Bemühungen* through his efforts ❷ throughout ▷ *die ganze Nacht durch* throughout the night ▷ *den Sommer durch* throughout the summer ❸ owing to ▷ *Durch die Verspätung haben wir den Anschluss verpasst.* Owing to the delay we missed our connection.; **Tod durch Herzschlag** death from a heart attack; **durch die Post** by post; **durch und durch** completely
durcharbeiten (*perf* **hat durchgearbeitet**) *vb* [**15**] to work without a break
durcheinander *adv* ❶ in a mess ▷ *Warum ist dein Zimmer so durcheinander?* Why is your room in such a mess? ❷ confused ▷ *Ich war völlig durcheinander.* I was completely confused.; **Du bringst mich ganz durcheinander.** You completely confuse me.
Durcheinander *nt* mess ▷ *In ihrem Zimmer war ein völliges Durcheinander.* Her room was in a complete mess.
durchfahren (*pres* **fährt durch**, *imperf* **fuhr durch**, *perf* **ist durchgefahren**) *vb* [**21**] ❶ to drive through ▷ *Wir sind durch einen Tunnel durchgefahren.* We drove through a tunnel. ❷ to drive without a break ▷ *Wir sind die ganze Nacht durchgefahren.* We drove all night without a break.; **Der Zug fährt bis Hamburg durch.** The train runs direct to Hamburg.
Durchfahrt (*pl* **Durchfahrten**) *f* way through ▷ *auf unserer Durchfahrt durch Frankreich* on our way through France; **'Durchfahrt verboten'** 'no through road'
Durchfall *m* diarrhoea
durchfallen (*pres* **fällt durch**, *imperf* **fiel durch**, *perf* **ist durchgefallen**) *vb* [**22**] ❶ to fall through ▷ *Die Münze ist durch dieses Gitter durchgefallen.* The coin fell through this grating. ❷ to fail ▷ *Sie ist in der Prüfung durchgefallen.* She failed the exam.
durchführen (*perf* **hat durchgeführt**) *vb* [**4**] to carry out
durchgehen (*imperf* **ging durch**, *perf* **ist durchgegangen**) *vb* [**29**] ❶ to go through ▷ *durch einen Tunnel durchgehen* to go through a tunnel ❷ to break loose ▷ *Das Pferd ist durchgegangen.* The horse has broken loose.; **jemandem etwas durchgehen lassen** to let somebody get away with something; **ein durchgehender Zug** a through train
durchkommen (*imperf* **kam durch**, *perf* **ist durchgekommen**) *vb* [**40**] ❶ to get through ▷ *Obwohl die Öffnung sehr schmal war, sind wir durchgekommen.* Although the opening was very narrow, we got through. ❷ to pass ▷ *Es war knapp, aber ich bin durchgekommen.* It was a close shave, but I passed. ❸ to pull through ▷ *Er war schwer verletzt, ist aber durchgekommen.* He was seriously injured, but he pulled through.
durchlassen (*pres* **lässt durch**, *imperf* **ließ durch**, *perf* **hat durchgelassen**) *vb* [**42**] to let through ▷ *Der Ordner wollte uns nicht durchlassen.* The steward didn't want to let us through.; **Der Behälter lässt Wasser durch.** The container isn't watertight.
durchlesen (*pres* **liest durch**, *imperf* **las durch**, *perf* **hat durchgelesen**) *vb* [**45**] to read through

Durchmesser (*pl* **Durchmesser**) *m* diameter

durchnehmen (*pres* **nimmt durch**, *imperf* **nahm durch**, *perf* **hat durchgenommen**) *vb* [**52**] to do ▷ *Wir nehmen gerade Shakespeare durch.* We're doing Shakespeare just now.

Durchreise *f* journey through ▷ *die Durchreise durch die Schweiz* the journey through Switzerland; **Ich bin nur auf der Durchreise.** I'm just passing through.

durchs = **durch das**

Durchschnitt *m* average ▷ *über dem Durchschnitt* above average ▷ *unter dem Durchschnitt* below average; **im Durchschnitt** on average

durchschnittlich *adj, adv* ❶ average ▷ *Ich habe durchschnittliche Noten.* My marks are average. ❷ on average ▷ *Durchschnittlich brauche ich eine Stunde für die Hausaufgaben.* On average, my homework takes me an hour.

durchsetzen (*perf* **hat durchgesetzt**) *vb* [**15**] **sich durchsetzen** to assert oneself; **Du solltest dich mehr durchsetzen.** You should be more assertive.; **seinen Kopf durchsetzen** to get one's way

durchsichtig *adj* transparent

durchsuchen (*perf* **hat durchsucht**) *vb* [**18**] to search

dürfen (*pres* **darf**, *imperf* **durfte**, *perf* **hat gedurft** *or* **dürfen**) *vb* [**16**] to be allowed to ▷ *Ich darf das.* I'm allowed to do that. ▷ *Er darf das nicht.* He's not allowed to do that. ▷ *Ich habe leider nicht gedurft.* Unfortunately, I wasn't allowed.; **Darf ich?** May I?; **Darf ich ins Kino?** Can I go to the cinema?

The past participle **dürfen** is used when **dürfen** is a modal auxiliary.

Ich habe das nicht tun dürfen. I wasn't allowed to do that.; **darf nicht** must not; **Da darf sie sich nicht wundern.** That shouldn't surprise her.; **Das darf nicht wahr sein!** I don't believe it!; **Darf ich Sie bitten, das zu tun?** Could I ask you to do that?; **Was darf es sein?** What can I do for you?; **Das dürfen Sie mir glauben.** You can take my word for it.; **Das dürfte genug sein.** That should be enough.; **Es dürfte Ihnen bekannt sein, dass ...** As you will probably know ...

Durst *m* thirst; **Durst haben** to be thirsty

durstig *adj* thirsty

Dusche *f* shower

duschen *vb* [**48**] to have a shower; **sich duschen** to have a shower

düster *adj* ❶ dark ▷ *Hier drin ist es so düster.* It's so dark in here. ❷ gloomy

Dutzend (*pl* **Dutzende** *or* **Dutzend**) *nt* dozen ▷ *zwei Dutzend Bücher* two dozen books

duzen *vb* [**36**] to address someone as 'du'

The familiar form of address **du** (plural **ihr**) is used when addressing family members, friends, children under 16 and pets.

DVD-Player (*pl* **DVD-Player**) *m* DVD player

D-Zug (*pl* **D-Züge**) *m* through train

a b c d e f g h i j k l m n o p q r s t u v w x y z

e

Ebbe *f* low tide ▷ *bei Ebbe* at low tide
eben *adj, adv* ❶ flat ▷ *eine ebene Fläche* a flat surface ❷ just ▷ *Er ist eben erst gegangen.* He's just gone. ❸ exactly ▷ *Eben, das sage ich ja.* That's exactly what I'm saying.; **eben deswegen** that's precisely why
Ebene *f* ❶ plain ▷ *Wir sahen auf die Ebene hinunter.* We looked down onto the plain. ❷ level ▷ *Das muss auf höherer Ebene entschieden werden.* That has to be decided at a higher level.
ebenfalls *adv* likewise
ebenso *adv* just as ▷ *Sie ist ebenso groß wie ihr Bruder.* She's just as tall as her brother.
Echo (*pl* **Echos**) *nt* echo
echt *adj, adv* ❶ real ▷ *echtes Gold* real gold; **Der Geldschein ist nicht echt.** That banknote's a fake. ❷ really ▷ *Die Party war echt gut.* The party was really good.; **Echt?** Really?
Ecke *f* corner ▷ *um die Ecke* round the corner
Edelstein (*pl* **Edelsteine**) *m* precious stone
EDV *f* (= *elektronische Datenverarbeitung*) electronic data processing
egal *adj* all the same ▷ *Das ist mir egal.* It's all the same to me.; **Das ist egal.** That makes no difference.; **Egal, ob ...** It doesn't matter whether ...
egoistisch *adj* selfish
ehe *conj* before ▷ *Ehe ich es vergesse, ...* Before I forget, ...
Ehe *f* marriage
Ehefrau *f* wife
ehemalig *adj* former
Ehemann (*pl* **Ehemänner**) *m* husband
Ehepaar (*pl* **Ehepaare**) *nt* married couple *pl*
eher *adv* sooner ▷ *Das hättest du eher sagen müssen.* You should have said that sooner.; **Das kommt schon eher der Wahrheit nahe.** That's more like the truth.
Ehre *f* honour
ehrgeizig *adj* ambitious
ehrlich *adj* honest
Ehrlichkeit *f* honesty
Ei (*pl* **Eier**) *nt* egg
Eiche *f* oak
Eichhörnchen (*pl* **Eichhörnchen**) *nt* squirrel
Eid (*pl* **Eide**) *m* oath ▷ *einen Eid schwören* to swear an oath
Eifersucht *f* jealousy
eifersüchtig *adj* jealous ▷ *Er ist eifersüchtig auf seine kleine Schwester.* He's jealous of his little sister.
eifrig *adj* eager
Eigelb (*pl* **Eigelb**) *nt* egg yolk
eigen *adj* own ▷ *meine eigene Meinung* my own opinion
Eigenart *f* peculiarity ▷ *Wir haben alle unsere Eigenarten.* We all have our own peculiarities.
eigenartig *adj* peculiar
Eigenschaft *f* quality
eigensinnig *adj* obstinate

eigentlich *adj, adv* ❶ actual ▷ *Er ist der eigentliche Besitzer.* He's the actual owner. ❷ actually ▷ *Eigentlich wollte ich heute nicht weggehen.* Actually I didn't want to go out today.; **Eigentlich nicht.** Not really.
Eigentum *nt* property
Eigentümer (*pl* **Eigentümer**) *m* owner
sich **eignen** *vb* [**53**] to be suited ▷ *Er eignet sich nicht für diese Stelle.* He's not suited to this position.
eilen *vb* [**38**] to be urgent ▷ *Das eilt nicht.* It's not urgent.
eilig *adj* urgent ▷ *Ich muss zuerst die eiligen Dinge erledigen.* I'll have to do the urgent things first.; **es eilig haben** to be in a hurry
Eilzug (*pl* **Eilzüge**) *m* fast stopping train
Eimer (*pl* **Eimer**) *m* bucket
ein *num, art* ❶ one ▷ *Es war nur ein Kind da.* There was only one child there. ▷ *Ich möchte nur einen.* I only want one. ❷ somebody ▷ *Wenn einer dir das sagt, glaube es nicht.* If somebody tells you that, don't believe it. ❸ you ▷ *Da kann einem die Lust vergehen.* It's enough to put you off. ❹ a ▷ *ein Mann* a man ▷ *eine Frau* a woman ▷ *ein Kind* a child an ▷ *ein Ei* an egg ▷ *eine Stunde* an hour
einander *pron* each other
einatmen (*perf* **hat eingeatmet**) *vb* [**3**] to breathe in
Einbahnstraße *f* one-way street
einbilden (*perf* **hat eingebildet**) *vb* [**54**] **sich etwas einbilden** to imagine something
einbrechen (*pres* **bricht ein**, *imperf* **brach ein**, *perf* **ist eingebrochen**) *vb* [**11**] to break in ▷ *Bei ihnen wurde eingebrochen.* Their house has been broken into. ▷ *Er ist in das Haus eingebrochen.* He broke into the house.
Einbrecher (*pl* **Einbrecher**) *m* burglar
Einbruch (*pl* **Einbrüche**) *m* break-in ▷ *In dieser Gegend gibt es häufiger Einbrüche.* There are a lot of break-ins in this area.; **bei Einbruch der Nacht** at nightfall; **vor Einbruch der Nacht** before nightfall
eindeutig *adj* clear ▷ *eine eindeutige Antwort geben* to give a clear answer
Eindruck (*pl* **Eindrücke**) *m* impression
eindrucksvoll *adj* impressive
eine *see* **ein**
einer *see* **ein**
einerseits *adv* on the one hand ▷ *Einerseits ..., andererseits ...* On the one hand ..., on the other hand ...
einfach *adj, adv* ❶ easy ▷ *Das war eine einfache Frage.* That was an easy question. ▷ *Das ist nicht einfach.* That isn't easy. ❷ simple ▷ *aus dem einfachen Grund ...* for the simple reason ... ▷ *Sie leben in sehr einfachen Verhältnissen.* They live very simple lives. ❸ single ▷ *eine einfache Fahrkarte* a single ticket ❹ simply ▷ *Ich will das einfach nicht.* I simply don't want it. ▷ *Er wollte einfach nicht begreifen.* He simply didn't want to understand.
Einfachheit *f* simplicity
Einfahrt *f* entrance
Einfall (*pl* **Einfälle**) *m* idea ▷ *Das war so ein Einfall von mir.* It was just an idea. ▷ *Du hast manchmal Einfälle!* You do come up with strange ideas sometimes!
einfallen (*pres* **fällt ein**, *imperf* **fiel ein**, *perf* **ist eingefallen**) *vb* [**22**] **jemandem einfallen** to occur to somebody; **Das fällt mir gar nicht ein.** I wouldn't dream of it.; **sich etwas einfallen lassen** to come up with a good idea
einfarbig *adj* plain
Einfluss (*gen* **Einflusses**, *pl* **Einflüsse**) *m* influence ▷ *Er hat einen schlechten Einfluss auf dich.* He has a bad influence on you.
Einfuhr *f* import
Eingang (*pl* **Eingänge**) *m* entrance

eingeben (*pres* **gibt ein**, *imperf* **gab ein**, *perf* **hat eingegeben**) *vb* [**28**] to enter ▷ *Beate hat den Text in den Computer eingegeben.* Beate entered the text into the computer.

eingebildet *adj* conceited ▷ *Sie ist furchtbar eingebildet.* She's terribly conceited.; **Ihre Krankheit ist nur eingebildet.** Her illness is all in the imagination.

eingehen (*imperf* **ging ein**, *perf* **ist eingegangen**) *vb* [**29**] ❶ to die ▷ *Mir ist schon wieder eine Pflanze eingegangen.* Another of my plants has died. ❷ to shrink ▷ *Der Pulli ist in der Wäsche eingegangen.* The pullover shrank in the wash.; **auf etwas eingehen** to comment on something

eingenommen *adj* **eingenommen von** taken with

eingestellt *adj* **auf etwas eingestellt sein** to be prepared for something

eingreifen (*imperf* **griff ein**, *perf* **hat eingegriffen**) *vb* to intervene

Einheimische (*gen* **Einheimischen**, *pl* **Einheimischen**) *mf* local ▷ *Wir sollten einen Einheimischen fragen.* We should ask a local.

einholen (*perf* **hat eingeholt**) *vb* [**4**] ❶ to catch up with ▷ *Wir werden euch sicher bald einholen.* We'll soon catch up with you. ❷ to make up ▷ *Wir haben die Verspätung nicht mehr eingeholt.* We didn't make up the delay.

einhundert *num* a hundred

einig *adj* **sich einig sein** to be in agreement; **einig werden** to reach an agreement

einige *adj, pron* ❶ some ▷ *einige Bücher* some books ▷ *einige von uns* some of us; **einiges** quite a lot of things ❷ several ▷ *Wir sind dort einige Tage geblieben.* We stayed there several days. ▷ *Bei dem Konzert sind einige früher gegangen.* Several people left the concert early.

sich **einigen** *vb* [**38**] to agree ▷ *Wir haben uns auf diesen Termin geeinigt.* We agreed on this date.

einigermaßen *adv* ❶ somewhat ▷ *Ich war einigermaßen erstaunt.* I was somewhat surprised. ❷ reasonably ▷ *Diesmal hast du dich wenigstens einigermaßen angestrengt.* At least this time you've tried reasonably hard. ▷ *Das Wetter war einigermaßen trocken.* The weather was reasonably dry.

Einigung *f* agreement

Einkauf (*pl* **Einkäufe**) *m* purchase; **Einkäufe machen** to go shopping

einkaufen (*perf* **hat eingekauft**) *vb* [**4**] ❶ to buy ▷ *Wir müssen Brot einkaufen.* We'll have to buy bread. ❷ to shop ▷ *Wir kaufen meist samstags ein.* We usually shop on Saturdays.; **einkaufen gehen** to go shopping

Einkaufsbummel (*pl* **Einkaufsbummel**) *m* shopping spree

Einkaufswagen (*pl* **Einkaufswagen**) *m* shopping trolley

Einkaufszentrum (*pl* **Einkaufszentren**) *nt* shopping centre

Einkaufszettel (*pl* **Einkaufszettel**) *m* shopping list

Einkommen (*pl* **Einkommen**) *nt* income

einladen (*pres* **lädt ein**, *imperf* **lud ein**, *perf* **hat eingeladen**) *vb* ❶ to invite ▷ *Sie hat mich zu ihrer Party eingeladen.* She's invited me to her party.; **jemanden ins Kino einladen** to take somebody to the cinema; **Ich lade dich ein.** I'll treat you. ❷ to load ▷ *Kannst du bitte die Koffer ins Auto einladen?* Can you load the cases into the car, please?

Einladung *f* invitation

einlaufen (*pres* **läuft ein**, *imperf* **lief ein**, *perf* **ist eingelaufen**) *vb* [**43**] ❶ to come in ▷ *Das Schiff läuft in den Hafen ein.* The ship is coming into the harbour. ❷ to shrink ▷ *Mein Pullover ist eingelaufen.* My jumper has shrunk.

Einleitung *f* introduction

einleuchten (*perf* **hat eingeleuchtet**) *vb* [**4**] **jemandem einleuchten** to make sense to somebody

einleuchtend *adj* clear

einloggen (*perf* **hat eingeloggt**) *vb* [**4**] (*computer*) to log on

einlösen *vb* [**4**] to cash ▷ *Kann ich diesen Scheck einlösen?* Can I cash this cheque?; **ein Versprechen einlösen** to keep a promise

einmal *adv* ❶ once ▷ *Wenn du das erst einmal begriffen hast ...* Once you've understood it ...; **Es war einmal ...** Once upon a time there was ...; **noch einmal** once more; **auf einmal** all at once ❷ one day ▷ *Das wirst du schon einmal begreifen.* You'll understand it one day.; **Nehmen wir einmal an: ...** Let's just suppose: ...; **nicht einmal** not even

einmalig *adj* ❶ unique ▷ *Das ist eine einmalige Gelegenheit.* This is a unique opportunity. ❷ single ▷ *Das erfordert nur eine einmalige Überprüfung.* That requires only a single check. ❸ fantastic ▷ *Das war eine einmalige Party.* That was a fantastic party.

einpacken (*perf* **hat eingepackt**) *vb* [**4**] to pack ▷ *Hast du deine Zahnbürste eingepackt?* Have you packed your toothbrush?

Einreise *f* entry; **bei der Einreise** when entering the country

einreisen (*perf* **ist eingereist**) *vb* [**4**] **in ein Land einreisen** to enter a country

einrichten (*perf* **hat eingerichtet**) *vb* [**2**] ❶ to furnish ▷ *Sie haben ihr Haus antik eingerichtet.* They've furnished their house with antiques. ❷ to set up ▷ *Die Stadt hat eine Beratungsstelle eingerichtet.* The town has set up an advice bureau.; **sich auf etwas einrichten** to prepare for something

Einrichtung *f* ❶ furnishings *pl* ▷ *Die moderne Einrichtung gefiel mir gut.* I liked the modern furnishings. ❷ facility ▷ *städtische Einrichtungen* municipal facilities

eins *num* one ▷ *Ich habe nur eins bekommen.* I only got one.; **Es ist mir alles eins.** It's all the same to me.

Eins (*pl* **Einsen**) *f* ❶ one ❷ very good

German marks range from one (**sehr gut**) to six (**ungenügend**).

einsam *adj* ❶ lonely ▷ *Ich fühle mich einsam.* I'm feeling lonely. ❷ remote ▷ *eine einsame Gegend* a remote area

einsammeln (*perf* **hat eingesammelt**) *vb* [**4**] to collect

einschalten (*perf* **hat eingeschaltet**) *vb* [**2**] to switch on ▷ *Schalt mal das Radio ein.* Switch the radio on.

einschlafen (*pres* **schläft ein**, *imperf* **schlief ein**, *perf* **ist eingeschlafen**) *vb* [**58**] to fall asleep

einschließen (*imperf* **schloss ein**, *perf* **hat eingeschlossen**) *vb* ❶ to lock in ▷ *Sie hat mich im Badezimmer eingeschlossen.* She locked me in the bathroom. ❷ to lock away ▷ *Du solltest die Wertsachen einschließen.* You should lock away the valuables. ❸ to include ▷ *Der Preis schließt die Verpflegung ein.* The price includes all meals.; **sich einschließen** to lock oneself in

einschließlich *adv, prep*

The preposition **einschließlich** takes the genitive.

❶ inclusive ▷ *Wir sind vom zehnten bis einschließlich fünfzehnten Juni weg.* We're away from the tenth to the fifteenth of June inclusive. ❷ including ▷ *Das macht zwanzig Euro einschließlich Bedienung.* That's twenty euros including service.

einschränken (*perf* **hat eingeschränkt**) *vb* [**4**] ❶ to restrict ▷ *Dadurch wurde unsere Freiheit eingeschränkt.* This restricted our freedom. ❷ to reduce ▷ *Wir müssen die Kosten einschränken.* We'll have to reduce costs.; **sich einschränken** to cut down

sich **einschreiben** (*imperf* **schrieb sich ein**, *perf* **hat sich eingeschrieben**) *vb* [**61**] ❶ to register ▷ *Hast du dich für den Kurs eingeschrieben?* Have you registered for the course? ❷ to enrol ▷ *sich an der Universität einschreiben* to enrol at university

Einschreiben (*pl* **Einschreiben**) *nt* recorded delivery

einsehen (*pres* **sieht ein**, *imperf* **sah ein**, *perf* **hat eingesehen**) *vb* [**64**] to see ▷ *Siehst du das nicht ein?* Don't you see that?

einseitig *adj* one-sided

einsenden (*imperf* **sendete ein** *or* **sandte ein**, *perf* **hat eingesendet** *or* **hat eingesandt**) *vb* to send in

einsetzen (*perf* **hat eingesetzt**) *vb* [**36**] ❶ to put in ▷ *Setzt das richtige Wort ein.* Put in the correct word. ❷ to bet ▷ *Wie viel Geld hast du eingesetzt?* How much money did you bet? ❸ to use ▷ *An den Schulen werden immer mehr Computer eingesetzt.* More and more computers are being used in schools. ❹ to set in ▷ *Wenn der Winter einsetzt ...* When winter sets in ...; **sich einsetzen** to work hard; **sich für jemanden einsetzen** to support somebody

einsperren (*perf* **hat eingesperrt**) *vb* [**4**] to lock up

einsprachig *adj* monolingual

Einspruch (*pl* **Einsprüche**) *m* objection

einsteigen (*imperf* **stieg ein**, *perf* **ist eingestiegen**) *vb* [**74**] ❶ to get on ▷ *Wir sind in den Bus eingestiegen.* We got on the bus.; **Bitte einsteigen!** All aboard! ❷ to climb in ▷ *Wir sind durchs Kellerfenster ins Haus eingestiegen.* We climbed into the house through the cellar window.

einstellen (*perf* **hat eingestellt**) *vb* [**4**] ❶ to adjust ▷ *den Spiegel einstellen* to adjust the mirror; **eine Kamera einstellen** to focus a camera ❷ to tune in to ▷ *Welchen Sender hast du da eingestellt?* Which station have you tuned in to? ❸ to stop ▷ *Sie haben die Produktion eingestellt.* They've stopped production. ❹ to employ ▷ *Sie wurde als Sekretärin eingestellt.* She was employed as a secretary.; **sich auf etwas einstellen** to prepare oneself for something

Einstellung *f* attitude ▷ *Ich mag deine Einstellung nicht.* I don't like your attitude.

Einstieg *m* entrance ▷ *Der Einstieg ist vorn.* The entrance is at the front.

einstimmen (*perf* **hat eingestimmt**) *vb* [**4**] to join in ▷ *Alle stimmten in das Lied ein.* Everyone joined in the singing.; **sich auf etwas einstimmen** to get oneself in the right mood for something

eintägig *adj* one-day

eintausend *num* a thousand

eintönig *adj* monotonous

Eintopf (*pl* **Eintöpfe**) *m* stew

Eintrag (*pl* **Einträge**) *m* entry ▷ *ein Eintrag im Wörterbuch* a dictionary entry

eintragen (*pres* **trägt ein**, *imperf* **trug ein**, *perf* **hat eingetragen**) *vb* [**77**] to write ▷ *Tragt die Vokabeln in euer Heft ein.* Write the vocabulary in your exercise book.; **sich eintragen** to put one's name down

eintreffen (*pres* **trifft ein**, *imperf* **traf ein**, *perf* **ist eingetroffen**) *vb* [**78**] ❶ to arrive ▷ *Sobald die Gäste eintreffen ...* As soon as the guests arrive ... ❷ to come true ▷ *Die Prophezeiung ist tatsächlich eingetroffen.* The prophecy actually came true.

eintreten (*pres* **tritt ein**, *imperf* **trat ein**, *perf* **ist eingetreten**) *vb* [**79**] **eintreten in (1)** to enter ▷ *Er ist ins Zimmer eingetreten.* He entered the room. **(2)** to join ▷ *Wann bist du in den Tennisklub eingetreten?* When did you join the tennis club?; **Es ist eine Verzögerung eingetreten.** There has been a delay.

Eintritt (*pl* **Eintritte**) *m* admission ▷ *Wie viel kostet der Eintritt?* How much does the admission cost?; **'Eintritt frei'** 'Admission free'
Eintrittsgeld (*pl* **Eintrittsgelder**) *nt* admission charge
Eintrittskarte *f* admission ticket
einverstanden *adj* **einverstanden sein** to agree; **Einverstanden!** Okay!
Einwanderer (*pl* **Einwanderer**) *m* immigrant
einwandern (*perf* **ist eingewandert**) *vb* [**88**] to immigrate
Einwegflasche *f* nonreturnable bottle
einweihen (*perf* **hat eingeweiht**) *vb* [**4**] to open ▷ *Morgen wird die neue Brücke eingeweiht.* The new bridge is being opened tomorrow.; **jemanden in etwas einweihen** to initiate somebody into something; **jemanden in ein Geheimnis einweihen** to let somebody in on a secret
einwerfen (*pres* **wirft ein**, *imperf* **warf ein**, *perf* **hat eingeworfen**) *vb* [**92**] to smash ▷ *Ich habe eine Scheibe eingeworfen.* I've smashed a pane.; **einen Brief einwerfen** to post a letter; **Geld einwerfen** to insert money
Einwohner (*pl* **Einwohner**) *m* inhabitant
Einwohnermeldeamt (*pl* **Einwohnermeldeämter**) *nt* registration office

Anyone moving to a new address in Germany is required by law to register (**sich anmelden**) at the residents' registration office (**Einwohnermeldeamt**).

Einwurf (*pl* **Einwürfe**) *m* ❶ slot ▷ *Sie steckte den Brief in den Einwurf.* She put the letter through the slot. ❷ (*sport*) throw-in ▷ *Der Schiedsrichter gab einen Einwurf.* The referee gave a throw-in.
Einzahl *f* singular
einzahlen (*perf* **hat eingezahlt**) *vb* [**4**] to pay
Einzelbett (*pl* **Einzelbetten**) *nt* single bed
Einzelfahrschein (*pl* **Einzelfahrscheine**) *m* single ticket
Einzelheit *f* detail
einzeln *adj, adv* ❶ single ▷ *Jeder einzelne Schüler wurde befragt.* Every single pupil was asked. ❷ odd ▷ *Ich habe ein paar einzelne Socken.* I've got a couple of odd socks. ❸ one at a time ▷ *Bitte einzeln eintreten.* Please come in one at a time.; **einzeln angeben** to specify; **der Einzelne** the individual; **ins Einzelne gehen** to go into details
Einzelteil (*pl* **Einzelteile**) *nt* component
Einzelzimmer (*pl* **Einzelzimmer**) *nt* single room
einziehen (*imperf* **zog ein**, *perf* **ist/hat eingezogen**) *vb* [**96**]

For the perfect tense use **haben** when the verb has an object and **sein** when there is no object.

❶ to retract; **den Kopf einziehen** to duck one's head ❷ to collect ❸ to move in ▷ *Wann sind die neuen Nachbarn eingezogen?* When did the new neighbours move in?
einzig *adj* only ▷ *Er ist unser einziges Kind.* He's our only child.; **das Einzige** the only thing; **der Einzige** the only one
einzigartig *adj* unique
Eis (*pl* **Eis**) *nt* ❶ ice ▷ *Es war Eis auf dem See.* There was ice on the lake. ❷ ice cream ▷ *Möchtest du ein Eis?* Would you like an ice cream?
Eisbär (*gen* **Eisbären**, *pl* **Eisbären**) *m* polar bear
Eisberg (*pl* **Eisberge**) *m* iceberg
Eisen (*pl* **Eisen**) *nt* iron ▷ *Die Brücke ist aus Eisen.* The bridge is made of iron.
Eisenbahn *f* railway
eisern *adj* iron ▷ *eine eiserne Stange* an iron rod; **die eiserne Reserve** emergency reserves
Eishockey *nt* ice hockey
eisig *adj* icy

eiskalt *adj* ❶ ice-cold ▷ *ein eiskaltes Getränk* an ice-cold drink ❷ icy cold ▷ *In diesem Zimmer ist es eiskalt.* This room's icy cold.
Eiswürfel (*pl* **Eiswürfel**) *m* ice cube
eitel *adj* vain
Eiter *m* pus
Eiweiß (*pl* **Eiweiße**) *nt* ❶ egg white ▷ *Das Eiweiß zu Schnee schlagen.* Whisk the egg whites until stiff. ❷ protein ▷ *eine eiweißreiche Diät* a diet rich in protein
Ekel *m* disgust
ekelhaft *adj* disgusting
sich **ekeln** *vb* [**34**] to disgust; **sich vor etwas ekeln** to find something disgusting
Elefant (*gen* **Elefanten**, *pl* **Elefanten**) *m* elephant
elegant *adj* elegant
Elektriker (*pl* **Elektriker**) *m* electrician
elektrisch *adj* electric
Elektrizität *f* electricity
Elektrogerät *nt* electrical appliance
Elektroherd (*pl* **Elektroherde**) *m* electric cooker
Elektronik *f* electronics *sg* ▷ *Er studiert Elektronik.* He's studying electronics. ▷ *Die Elektronik am Auto ist kaputt.* There's something wrong with the electronics in the car.
elektronisch *adj* electronic ▷ *elektronische Post* electronic mail ▷ *elektronischer Briefkasten* electronic mailbox
Element (*pl* **Elemente**) *nt* element
elend *adj* miserable ▷ *Ich fühle mich so elend.* I feel so miserable.
Elend *nt* misery
elf *num* eleven ▷ *Sie ist elf.* She's eleven.
Elfmeter (*pl* **Elfmeter**) *m* penalty

> Word for word, **Elfmeter** means 'eleven metres'.

▷ *einen Elfmeter schießen* to take a penalty
Ellbogen (*pl* **Ellbogen**) *m* elbow
Eltern *pl* parents *pl*
Elterngeld (*pl* **Elterngelder**) *nt* child benefit
Elternschaft *f* parenthood
Elternteil (*pl* **Elternteile**) *m* parent ▷ *beide Elternteile* both parents
E-Mail (*pl* **E-Mails**) *f* email ▷ *Meine E-Mail-Adresse ist ...* My email address is ...
Emoticon (*pl* **Emoticons**) *nt* smiley
Empfang (*pl* **Empfänge**) *m* ❶ reception ▷ *Wart ihr auch bei dem Empfang?* Were you at the reception too? ❷ receipt ▷ *Bitte bestätigen Sie den Empfang der Ware.* Please acknowledge receipt of the goods.; **in Empfang nehmen** to receive
empfangen (*pres* **empfängt**, *imperf* **empfing**, *perf* **hat empfangen**) *vb* [**23**] to receive
Empfänger (*pl* **Empfänger**) *m* receiver
Empfängnisverhütung *f* contraception
empfehlen (*pres* **empfiehlt**, *imperf* **empfahl**, *perf* **hat empfohlen**) *vb* [**17**] to recommend ▷ *Dieses Restaurant ist zu empfehlen.* This restaurant is to be recommended.
empfinden (*imperf* **empfand**, *perf* **hat empfunden**) *vb* [**24**] to feel ▷ *Ich empfinde nichts für sie.* I don't feel anything for her.
empfindlich *adj* ❶ sensitive ▷ *Er ist ein sehr empfindlicher Mensch.* He's very sensitive. ❷ touchy ▷ *Sie ist schrecklich empfindlich.* She's terribly touchy.
empfohlen *vb see* **empfehlen**
Ende (*pl* **Enden**) *nt* end; **am Ende (1)** at the end ▷ *am Ende des Zuges* at the end of the train **(2)** in the end ▷ *Am Ende ist er dann doch mitgekommen.* He came in the end.; **zu Ende gehen** to come to an end; **zu Ende sein** to be finished; **Ende Dezember** at the end of December
enden *vb* [**54**] to end
endgültig *adj* definite
endlich *adv* finally ▷ *Ich bin endlich fertig.* I've finally finished. ▷ *Hast du das endlich begriffen?* Have you finally understood

it?; **Endlich!** At last!; **Komm endlich!** Come on!

endlos *adj* endless

Endspiel (*pl* **Endspiele**) *nt* final

Endstation *f* terminus

Endung *f* ending

Energie *f* energy ▷ *seine ganze Energie für etwas einsetzen* to devote all one's energies to something

energisch *adj* energetic

eng *adj* ❶ narrow ▷ *ein enger Durchgang* a narrow passageway ❷ tight ▷ *Die Hose ist mir zu eng.* The trousers are too tight for me. ❸ close ▷ *Wir sind eng befreundet.* We are close friends.

Enge *f* narrowness; **jemanden in die Enge treiben** to drive somebody into a corner

Engel (*pl* **Engel**) *m* angel

England *nt* England

Engländer (*pl* **Engländer**) *m* Englishman; **Er ist Engländer.** He's English.; **die Engländer** the English

Engländerin *f* Englishwoman; **Sie ist Engländerin.** She's English.

englisch *adj* English

Englisch (*gen* **Englischen**) *nt* English ▷ *Er lernt Englisch in der Schule.* He's learning English at school.

Enkel (*pl* **Enkel**) *m* grandson; **alle ihre Enkel** all her grandchildren

Enkelin *f* granddaughter

enorm *adj* enormous ▷ *Er verdient enorm viel Geld.* He earns an enormous amount of money.

entdecken (*perf* **hat entdeckt**) *vb* [18] to discover

Ente *f* duck

entfernen (*perf* **hat entfernt**) *vb* [18] to remove

entfernt *adj* distant ▷ *ein entfernter Verwandter* a distant relative; **weit entfernt** far away; **weit davon entfernt sein, etwas zu tun** to be far from doing something; **nicht im Entferntesten** not in the slightest

Entfernung *f* distance

entführen (*perf* **hat entführt**) *vb* [18] to kidnap

entgegen *prep*

> **entgegen** takes the dative.

contrary to ▷ *entgegen meinen Anweisungen* contrary to my instructions

entgegenkommen (*imperf* **kam entgegen**, *perf* **ist entgegengekommen**) *vb* [40] ❶ to come towards ▷ *Uns kam ein Lastwagen entgegen.* A lorry came towards us. ❷ to meet half way ▷ *Ich werde Ihnen entgegenkommen, sagen wir zwanzig Euro.* I'll meet you half way, let's say twenty euros.

entgehen (*imperf* **entging**, *perf* **ist entgangen**) *vb* [29] **jemandem entgehen** to escape somebody's attention; **sich etwas entgehen lassen** to miss something

enthalten (*pres* **enthält**, *imperf* **enthielt**, *perf* **hat enthalten**) *vb* [33] to contain ▷ *Dieses Fass enthält radioaktiven Müll.* This drum contains radioactive waste.; **sich enthalten** to abstain

entkommen (*imperf* **entkam**, *perf* **ist entkommen**) *vb* [40] to escape

entlang *prep*

> **entlang** takes the accusative or the dative.

along ▷ *Entlang der Mauer wuchs Efeu.* Ivy was growing along the wall. ▷ *Wir gingen den Fluss entlang.* We walked along the river.

entlassen (*pres* **entlässt**, *imperf* **entließ**, *perf* **hat entlassen**) *vb* [42] ❶ to release ▷ *Er wurde aus dem Gefängnis entlassen.* He was released from prison. ❷ to make redundant ▷ *500 Arbeiter mussten entlassen werden.* 500 workers had to be made redundant.

entrüstet *adj* outraged

entschädigen (*perf* **hat entschädigt**) *vb* [18] to compensate ▷ *jemanden für* *etwas entschädigen* to compensate somebody for something

entscheiden (*imperf* **entschied**, *perf* **hat entschieden**) *vb* to decide; **sich entscheiden** to make up one's mind

entscheidend *adj* decisive

Entscheidung *f* decision

entschieden *adj* ❶ decided ▷ *Es ist entschieden, wir fahren nach Rom.* It's been decided that we're going to Rome. ❷ resolute ▷ *ein sehr entschiedener Mensch* a very resolute person

sich **entschließen** (*imperf* **entschloss sich**, *perf* **hat sich entschlossen**) *vb* to decide

entschlossen *adj* determined

Entschluss (*gen* **Entschlusses**, *pl* **Entschlüsse**) *m* decision

entschuldigen (*perf* **hat entschuldigt**) *vb* [**18**] ❶ to excuse ▷ *Entschuldige bitte die Verspätung.* Please excuse the delay. ❷ to apologize ▷ *Du solltest dich besser bei ihm entschuldigen.* You'd better apologize to him.

Entschuldigung *f* ❶ apology ▷ *Hat er deine Entschuldigung angenommen?* Did he accept your apology?; **jemanden um Entschuldigung bitten** to apologize to somebody ❷ excuse ▷ *Krankheit ist keine Entschuldigung.* Illness is no excuse.; **Entschuldigung!** Sorry.

entsetzlich *adj* dreadful

entsetzt *adj, adv* horrified

Entsorgung *f* waste disposal

sich **entspannen** (*perf* **hat sich entspannt**) *vb* [**18**] ❶ to relax ▷ *Entspann dich!* Relax! ❷ to ease ▷ *Die Lage hat sich entspannt.* The situation has eased.

entsprechen (*pres* **entspricht**, *imperf* **entsprach**, *perf* **hat entsprochen**) *vb* [**70**] ❶ to meet ▷ *Sie hat den Anforderungen nicht entsprochen.* She didn't meet the requirements. ❷ to comply with ▷ *Dieses Gerät entspricht nicht den Normen.* This appliance doesn't comply with the standards.

entsprechend *adj, adv* ❶ appropriate ▷ *Die entsprechende Antwort ankreuzen.* Tick the appropriate answer. ❷ accordingly ▷ *Benimm dich entsprechend.* Behave accordingly.

enttäuschen (*perf* **hat enttäuscht**) *vb* [**18**] to disappoint

enttäuschend *adj* disappointing

Enttäuschung *f* disappointment

entweder *conj* either; **entweder ... oder ...** either ... or ...

entwerten *vb* [**18**] to cancel ▷ *Du musst die Fahrkarte erst entwerten.* You have to cancel your ticket first.

Entwerter (*pl* **Entwerter**) *m* ticket stamping machine

When you travel by train or tram (and sometimes by bus) you have to stamp your ticket in an **Entwerter**. The machines are either on the platforms or inside the vehicles.

entwickeln (*perf* **hat entwickelt**) *vb* [**34**] ❶ to develop ▷ *Fähigkeiten entwickeln* to develop skills ▷ *einen Film entwickeln* to develop a film ❷ to show ▷ *Sie hat eine enorme Energie entwickelt.* She showed terrific energy.; **sich entwickeln** to develop

Entwicklung *f* development

Entwicklungsland (*pl* **Entwicklungsländer**) *nt* developing country

sich **entzünden** (*perf* **hat sich entzündet**) *vb* [**18**] to become inflamed ▷ *Die Wunde hat sich entzündet.* The wound has become inflamed.

Entzündung *f* inflammation

entzwei *adv* broken ▷ *Die Vase ist entzwei.* The vase is broken.

er *pron* ❶ he ▷ *Er ist größer als ich.* He's taller than me. ❷ it ▷ *Schöner Ring, ist er neu?* Lovely ring, is it new? ❸ him ▷ *Er ist es.* It's him. ▷ *Er war es nicht, ich war's.* It wasn't him, it was me.

erben *vb* [**38**] to inherit
erbrechen (*pres* **erbricht**, *imperf* **erbrach**, *perf* **hat erbrochen**) *vb* [**11**] to vomit
Erbse *f* pea
Erdbeben (*pl* **Erdbeben**) *nt* earthquake
Erdbeere *f* strawberry
Erde *f* earth; **zu ebener Erde** at ground level; **auf der ganzen Erde** all over the world
Erdgas (*gen* **Erdgases**) *nt* natural gas
Erdgeschoss (*gen* **Erdgeschosses**, *pl* **Erdgeschosse**) *nt* ground floor ▷ *im Erdgeschoss* on the ground floor
Erdkunde *f* geography
Erdnuss (*pl* **Erdnüsse**) *f* peanut
Erdöl *nt* mineral oil
sich **ereignen** (*perf* **hat sich ereignet**) *vb* [**53**] to happen
Ereignis (*gen* **Ereignisses**, *pl* **Ereignisse**) *nt* event
erfahren (*pres* **erfährt**, *imperf* **erfuhr**, *perf* **hat erfahren**) *vb* [**21**] ❶ to hear ▷ *Ich habe erfahren, dass du heiraten willst.* I've heard that you want to get married. ❷ to experience ▷ *Sie hat im Leben viel Gutes erfahren.* She's experienced a lot of good things in her life.
▶ *adj* experienced ▷ *Er ist ein erfahrener Lehrer.* He's an experienced teacher.
Erfahrung *f* experience
erfassen (*perf* **hat erfasst**) *vb* [**31**] ❶ to understand ▷ *Ich habe den Text noch nicht erfasst.* I haven't understood the text yet. ❷ to register ▷ *Alle Aidsfälle werden erfasst.* All AIDS cases are registered.
erfinden (*imperf* **erfand**, *perf* **hat erfunden**) *vb* [**24**] to invent
Erfinder (*pl* **Erfinder**) *m* inventor
Erfindung *f* invention
Erfolg (*pl* **Erfolge**) *m* success; **Erfolg versprechend** promising; **Viel Erfolg!** Good luck!
erfolglos *adj* unsuccessful
erfolgreich *adj* successful
erforderlich *adj* necessary
erfreut *adj* pleased ▷ *Über mein gutes Zeugnis war ich sehr erfreut.* I was very pleased with my good report.
erfrieren (*imperf* **erfror**, *perf* **ist erfroren**) *vb* to freeze to death ▷ *Er ist erfroren.* He froze to death.; **Die Pflanze ist erfroren.** The plant was killed by frost.
Erfrischung *f* refreshment
erfüllen (*perf* **hat erfüllt**) *vb* [**7**] to fulfil ▷ *Er hat ihr den Wunsch erfüllt.* He fulfilled her wish.; **sich erfüllen** to come true
ergänzen (*perf* **hat ergänzt**) *vb* [**36**] to complete ▷ *Ergänzt den Satz.* Complete the sentence.; **sich ergänzen** to complement one another
Ergebnis (*gen* **Ergebnisses**, *pl* **Ergebnisse**) *nt* result
ergreifen (*imperf* **ergriff**, *perf* **hat ergriffen**) *vb* ❶ to seize ▷ *Er ergriff meine Hand.* He seized my hand. ▷ *die Gelegenheit ergreifen* to seize the opportunity; **einen Beruf ergreifen** to take up a profession; **Maßnahmen gegen etwas ergreifen** to take measures against something ❷ to move ▷ *Ihr Schicksal hat uns sehr ergriffen.* Her fate moved us deeply.
ergreifend *adj* moving
ergriffen *adj* deeply moved
erhalten (*pres* **erhält**, *imperf* **erhielt**, *perf* **hat erhalten**) *vb* [**33**] ❶ to receive ▷ *Sie hat den ersten Preis erhalten.* She received first prize. ❷ to preserve ▷ *Das Gebäude sollte erhalten werden.* The building should be preserved.; **gut erhalten** in good condition

Word for word, **gut erhalten** means 'well preserved'.

erhältlich *adj* obtainable
erhitzen (*perf* **hat erhitzt**) *vb* [**7**] to heat
sich **erholen** (*perf* **hat sich erholt**) *vb* [**19**] ❶ to recover ▷ *Der Patient muss sich nach der Operation erholen.* The patient

needs to recover after the operation. ❷ to have a rest ▷ *Wir haben uns in den Ferien gut erholt.* We had a good rest when we were on holiday.

erholsam *adj* restful

Erholung *f* rest ▷ *Wir fahren zur Erholung ans Meer.* We're going to the sea for a rest.

erinnern (*perf* **hat erinnert**) *vb* [**88**] **erinnern an** to remind of; **sich erinnern** to remember

Erinnerung *f* ❶ memory ▷ *Wir haben Erinnerungen ausgetauscht.* We swapped memories. ❷ souvenir ▷ *eine Erinnerung an meinen Russlandaufenthalt* a souvenir of my stay in Russia

erkältet *adj* **erkältet sein** to have a cold

Erkältung *f* cold

erkennbar *adj* recognizable

erkennen (*imperf* **erkannte**, *perf* **hat erkannt**) *vb* [**39**] ❶ to recognize ▷ *Ich hätte dich fast nicht erkannt.* I would hardly have recognized you. ❷ to see ▷ *Jetzt erkenne ich, dass das ein Fehler war.* I see now that it was a mistake.

erklären (*perf* **hat erklärt**) *vb* [**19**] to explain

Erklärung *f* explanation; **eine Liebeserklärung** a declaration of love

sich **erkundigen** (*perf* **hat sich erkundigt**) *vb* [**19**] **sich erkundigen nach** to inquire about; **Er hat sich nach dir erkundigt.** He was asking about you.

erlauben (*perf* **hat erlaubt**) *vb* [**19**] **jemandem etwas erlauben** to allow somebody to do something; **sich etwas erlauben** to allow oneself something; **Was erlaubst du dir denn eigentlich?** How dare you!

Erlaubnis (*pl* **Erlaubnisse**) *f* permission

erleben (*perf* **hat erlebt**) *vb* [**19**] ❶ to experience ▷ *Eine solche Frechheit habe ich selten erlebt.* I've seldom experienced such cheek.; **Wir haben in den Ferien viel Schönes erlebt.** We had a lovely time on holiday.; **Sie hat viel Schlimmes erlebt.** She's had a lot of bad experiences. ❷ to live through ▷ *Mein Opa hat den Zweiten Weltkrieg erlebt.* My grandpa lived through the Second World War. ❸ to live to see ▷ *Ich möchte die Geburt deines Kindes noch erleben.* I would like to live to see the birth of your child.

Erlebnis (*gen* **Erlebnisses**, *pl* **Erlebnisse**) *nt* experience

erledigen (*perf* **hat erledigt**) *vb* [**19**] ❶ to see to ▷ *Ich habe heute noch viel zu erledigen.* I've a lot to see to today. ❷ to do ▷ *Hast du deine Hausaufgaben schon erledigt?* Have you done your homework already? ❸ to wear out (*informal*) ▷ *Die Wanderung hat mich ziemlich erledigt.* The hike's really worn me out.

Erleichterung *f* relief ▷ *Das war eine Erleichterung!* That was a relief!

erlösen (*perf* **hat erlöst**) *vb* [**7**] to save ▷ *Sie erlöste ihn aus einer gefährlichen Lage.* She saved him from a dangerous situation.

Ermahnung *f* admonition

Ermäßigung *f* reduction

ermöglichen (*perf* **hat ermöglicht**) *vb* [**7**] **jemandem etwas ermöglichen** to make something possible for somebody

ermorden (*perf* **hat ermordet**) *vb* [**53**] to murder

ermüdend *adj* tiring

ermutigen (*perf* **hat ermutigt**) *vb* [**7**] to encourage

ernähren (*perf* **hat ernährt**) *vb* [**19**] to support ▷ *Er hat eine Familie zu ernähren.* He has a family to support.; **sich von etwas ernähren** to live on something

ernennen (*imperf* **ernannte**, *perf* **hat ernannt**) *vb* to appoint

erneuern (*perf* **hat erneuert**) *vb* [**88**] to renew

ernst *adj* serious

Ernst *m* seriousness; **Das ist mein Ernst.** I'm quite serious.; **im Ernst** in earnest
ernsthaft *adj, adv* serious ▷ *ein ernsthaftes Gespräch* a serious talk seriously ▷ *Glaubst du das ernsthaft?* Do you seriously believe that?
ernstlich *adj, adv* serious; **ernstlich besorgt** seriously concerned
Ernte *f* harvest
ernten *vb* [**2**] to harvest ▷ *Es ist Zeit, die Kirschen zu ernten.* It's time to harvest the cherries.; **Lob ernten** to earn praise
erobern (*perf* **hat erobert**) *vb* [**88**] to conquer
erotisch *adj* erotic
erpressen (*perf* **hat erpresst**) *vb* [**7**] ❶ to blackmail ▷ *Du willst mich wohl erpressen?* Are you trying to blackmail me? ❷ to extort ▷ *Er hat von ihm Geld erpresst.* He extorted money from him.
erraten (*pres* **errät**, *imperf* **erriet**, *perf* **hat erraten**) *vb* to guess
Erregung *f* excitement
erreichen (*perf* **hat erreicht**) *vb* [**19**] ❶ to reach ▷ *Wir haben Hamburg am späten Nachmittag erreicht.* We reached Hamburg in the late afternoon. ❷ to catch ▷ *Wir haben den Zug nicht mehr erreicht.* We didn't manage to catch the train. ❸ to achieve ▷ *seinen Zweck erreichen* to achieve one's purpose ▷ *Was willst du damit erreichen?* What do you aim to achieve by this?; **So erreichst du bei mir gar nichts.** You won't get anywhere with me by doing that.
Ersatzteil (*pl* **Ersatzteile**) *nt* spare part
erschaffen (*imperf* **erschuf**, *perf* **hat erschaffen**) *vb* to create
erscheinen (*imperf* **erschien**, *perf* **ist erschienen**) *vb* [**57**] to appear
erschießen (*imperf* **erschoss**, *perf* **hat erschossen**) *vb* to shoot dead
erschöpft *adj* exhausted
erschrecken (1) (*perf* **hat erschreckt**) *vb* [**19**] to frighten ▷ *Hast du mich erschreckt!* You really frightened me!
erschrecken (2) (*pres* **erschrickt**, *imperf* **erschrak**, *perf* **ist erschrocken**) *vb* to be frightened ▷ *Ich bin furchtbar erschrocken, als plötzlich das Licht ausging.* I was terribly frightened when the light suddenly went out.
erschreckend *adj* alarming
erschrocken *adj* frightened
ersetzen (*perf* **hat ersetzt**) *vb* [**36**] to replace ▷ *Du musst die Vase ersetzen.* You'll have to replace that vase.; **jemandem die Unkosten ersetzen** to pay somebody's expenses
erst *adv* ❶ first ▷ *Erst will ich wissen, was das kostet.* First I want to know what it costs. ▷ *Mach erst mal die Arbeit fertig.* Finish your work first.; **Wenn du das erst mal hinter dir hast, ...** Once you've got that behind you, ... ❷ only ▷ *Das ist erst gestern passiert.* That happened only yesterday. ▷ *Er ist gerade erst angekommen.* He's only just arrived. ❸ not until ▷ *Er hat es erst gemacht, als ich es ihm befohlen habe.* He didn't do it until I told him. ▷ *erst morgen* not until tomorrow ▷ *erst um 5 Uhr* not until 5 o'clock
erstaunlich *adj* astonishing
erstaunt *adj* astonished
erste *adj* first ▷ *Ich habe gerade mein erstes Auto gekauft.* I've just bought my first car. ▷ *Er kam als Erster.* He was the first to arrive.; **Erste Hilfe** first aid
erstechen (*pres* **ersticht**, *imperf* **erstach**, *perf* **hat erstochen**) *vb* to stab to death
erstens *adv* firstly
erstklassig *adj* first-class
erstmals *adv* for the first time
ertragen (*pres* **erträgt**, *imperf* **ertrug**, *perf* **hat ertragen**) *vb* [**77**] to stand ▷ *Ich kann die Schmerzen kaum ertragen.* I can hardly stand the pain. ▷ *Sie erträgt*

es nicht, wenn man ihr widerspricht. She can't stand being contradicted.

erträglich *adj* bearable

ertrinken (*imperf* **ertrank**, *perf* **ist ertrunken**) *vb* [**80**] to drown

erwachsen *adj* grown-up

Erwachsene (*gen* **Erwachsenen**, *pl* **Erwachsenen**) *mf* adult ▷ *Erwachsene können das nicht verstehen.* Adults can't understand that.

erwähnen (*perf* **hat erwähnt**) *vb* [**19**] to mention

erwarten (*perf* **hat erwartet**) *vb* [**2**] to expect ▷ *Er erwartet zu viel von uns.* He's expecting too much of us.; **Wir können es kaum erwarten, dass die Ferien beginnen.** We can hardly wait for the holidays to begin.

erweisen (*imperf* **erwies**, *perf* **hat erwiesen**) *vb* **sich erweisen als** to prove to be

erwerben (*pres* **erwirbt**, *imperf* **erwarb**, *perf* **hat erworben**) *vb* [**90**] to acquire

erzählen (*perf* **hat erzählt**) *vb* [**19**] to tell

Erzählung *f* story

erzeugen (*perf* **hat erzeugt**) *vb* [**19**] ❶ to produce ▷ *In dieser Gegend wird Wein erzeugt.* Wine is produced in this region. ❷ to generate ▷ *Strom erzeugen* to generate electricity

Erzeugnis (*gen* **Erzeugnisses**, *pl* **Erzeugnisse**) *nt* produce ▷ *ausländische Erzeugnisse* foreign produce

erziehen (*imperf* **erzog**, *perf* **hat erzogen**) *vb* [**96**] to bring up ▷ *Sie hat fünf Kinder erzogen.* She brought up five children. ▷ *Sie sollte ihre Kinder zu etwas mehr Höflichkeit erziehen.* She should bring her children up to be more polite.

Erziehung *f* education

es *pron* it ▷ *Es ist rot.* It's red. ▷ *Ich habe es nicht gesehen.* I didn't see it. ▷ *Es schneit.* It's snowing.

Esel (*pl* **Esel**) *m* donkey

essbar *adj* edible

essen (*pres* **isst**, *imperf* **aß**, *perf* **hat gegessen**) *vb* [**20**] to eat

Essen (*pl* **Essen**) *nt* ❶ meal ▷ *Komm doch am Freitag zum Essen.* Why don't you come for a meal on Friday?. ❷ food ▷ *Das Essen war lecker.* The food was delicious.

Essig (*pl* **Essige**) *m* vinegar

Esszimmer (*pl* **Esszimmer**) *nt* dining room

Etage *f* floor ▷ *Wir wohnen in der dritten Etage.* We live on the third floor.

Etikett (*pl* **Etikette** *or* **Etiketten**) *nt* label ▷ *Lies mal, was auf dem Etikett steht.* Read what's on the label.

etliche *pron pl* quite a few ▷ *etliche Leute* quite a few people

Etui (*pl* **Etuis**) *nt* case ▷ *ein Brillenetui* a glasses case

etwa *adv* ❶ about ▷ *Es waren etwa zwanzig.* There were about twenty. ❷ for instance ▷ *Leute wie etwa Jochen wissen das eben nicht.* People like Jochen, for instance, just don't know that.; **Soll das etwa heißen, dass ...** Is that supposed to mean that ...; **Du willst doch nicht etwa schon gehen.** You're not going already, are you?

etwas *pron, adv* ❶ something ▷ *Wir sollten ihr etwas schenken.* We should give her something. ❷ anything ▷ *Hast du nicht etwas gehört?* Haven't you heard anything? ❸ a little ▷ *Wir sollten uns etwas ausruhen.* We should have a little rest. ▷ *Nur etwas Milch bitte.* Just a little milk, please.

EU *f* (= *Europäische Union*) EU (= *European Union*)

euch *pron*

> **euch** is the accusative and dative of **ihr**.

❶ you ▷ *Ich habe euch gesehen.* I saw you. ▷ *Ich komme mit euch.* I'll come with you. ❷ yourselves ▷ *Seht euch mal im Spiegel an.* Look at yourselves in the mirror. ❸ to you ▷ *Sie hat es euch gegeben.* She gave it to you.

euer *pron, adj* ❶ your ▷ *Euer Deutschlehrer ist nett.* Your German teacher is nice. ▷ *Wenn das eure Mutter erlaubt.* If your mother lets you. ▷ *Ist das euer Haus?* Is that your house? ❷ yours ▷ *Das ist nicht unser Computer, das ist eurer.* That's not our computer, that's yours. ▷ *Unsere Mutter heißt Ulla, wie heißt eure?* Our mother's called Ulla, what's yours called? ▷ *Wenn es in unserem Haus nicht geht, feiern wir in eurem.* If it's not OK in our house, then we'll celebrate in yours.

Eule *f* owl

eure *see* **euer**

eures *see* **euer**

euretwegen *adv* ❶ for your sakes ▷ *Wir sind euretwegen nicht in Urlaub gefahren.* We didn't go on holiday for your sakes. ❷ on your account ▷ *Er hat sich euretwegen aufgeregt.* He got upset on your account.

Euro (*pl* **Euros** *or* **Euro**) *m* euro ▷ *Das kostet fünf Euro.* It costs five euros.

Europa *nt* Europe

Europäer (*pl* **Europäer**) *m* European

Europäerin *f* European

europäisch *adj* European

evangelisch *adj* Protestant

eventuell *adv, adj* perhaps ▷ *Eventuell komme ich später nach.* Perhaps I'll come on later.; **Eventuelle Fragen wird mein Kollege gerne beantworten.** My colleague will be pleased to answer any questions you may have.

> Be careful! **eventuell** does not mean **eventual**.

ewig *adj* eternal

Ewigkeit *f* eternity

Examen (*pl* **Examen**) *nt* exam

explodieren (*perf* **ist explodiert**) *vb* [**76**] to explode

Explosion *f* explosion

exportieren (*perf* **hat exportiert**) *vb* [**76**] to export

extra *adv, adj* ❶ separately ▷ *Schicke den USB-Stick lieber extra.* It'd be better to send the USB stick separately. ❷ specially ▷ *Das wurde extra für sie angefertigt.* That was made specially for her. ▷ *Ich bin extra wegen dir gekommen.* I came specially because of you. ❸ on purpose ▷ *Das hat er extra gemacht.* He did that on purpose. ❹ extra ▷ *Ich habe das extra schnell gemacht.* I did it extra quickly. ▷ *Das sind extra starke Pfefferminzbonbons.* These are extra strong peppermints.

extrem *adj* extreme

a b c d **e** f g h i j k l m n o p q r s t u v w x y z

f

Fabrik *f* factory

> Be careful! **Fabrik** does not mean **fabric**.

Fach (*pl* **Fächer**) *nt* ❶ shelf ▷ *Das ist mein Fach im Schrank.* This is my shelf in the cupboard. ❷ pigeonhole ▷ *Jeder Lehrer hat im Lehrerzimmer ein Fach.* Every teacher has a pigeonhole in the staff room. ❸ subject ▷ *In welchem Fach bist du am besten?* What subject are you best at?

Facharzt (*gen* **Facharztes**, *pl* **Fachärzte**) *m* specialist *(doctor)*

Fachärztin *f* specialist *(doctor)*

Fachfrau *f* expert

Fachhochschule *f* college

Fachmann (*pl* **Fachleute**) *m* expert

Fachschule *f* technical college

Fackel *f* torch

Faden (*pl* **Fäden**) *m* thread

fähig *adj* capable ▷ *Sie ist eine sehr fähige Lehrerin.* She's a very capable teacher.; **fähig sein, etwas zu tun** to be capable of doing something

Fähigkeit *f* ability

Fahne *f* flag; **eine Fahne haben** *(informal)* to stink of booze

Fahrausweis (*gen* **Fahrausweises**, *pl* **Fahrausweise**) *m* ticket ▷ *Die Fahrausweise, bitte.* Tickets, please.

Fahrbahn *f* carriageway

Fähre *f* ferry

fahren (*pres* **fährt**, *imperf* **fuhr**, *perf* **ist/hat gefahren**) *vb* [**21**]

> For the perfect tense use **haben** when the verb has an object and **sein** when there is no object.

❶ to drive ▷ *Er hat mich nach Hause gefahren.* He drove me home. ▷ *Er ist sehr schnell gefahren.* He drove very fast.; **ein Rennen fahren** to drive in a race ❷ to go ▷ *Der Intercity fährt stündlich.* The Intercity train goes every hour. ❸ to leave ▷ *Wann seid ihr gefahren?* When did you leave? ❹ to sail ▷ *Das Schiff fährt nach Amerika.* The ship's sailing to America. ▷ *Wir sind mit dem Schiff nach Amerika gefahren.* We sailed to America.; **Rad fahren** to cycle; **mit dem Auto fahren** to go by car; **mit dem Zug fahren** to go by train

Fahrer (*pl* **Fahrer**) *m* driver

Fahrerin *f* driver

Fahrgast (*pl* **Fahrgäste**) *m* passenger

Fahrgeld (*pl* **Fahrgelder**) *nt* fare ▷ *Bitte das Fahrgeld abgezählt bereithalten.* Please have exact fare ready.

Fahrkarte *f* ticket ▷ *Die Fahrkarten, bitte.* Tickets, please.

Fahrkartenautomat (*gen* **Fahrkartenautomaten**, *pl* **Fahrkartenautomaten**) *m* ticket machine

Fahrkartenschalter (*pl* **Fahrkartenschalter**) *m* ticket office

fahrlässig *adj* negligent

Fahrplan (*pl* **Fahrpläne**) *m* timetable

Fahrpreis (*gen* **Fahrpreises**, *pl* **Fahrpreise**) *m* fare

Fahrprüfung *f* driving test

Fahrrad (*pl* **Fahrräder**) *nt* bicycle

Fahrradweg (*pl* **Fahrradwege**) *m* cycle lane
Fahrschein (*pl* **Fahrscheine**) *m* ticket ▷ *Die Fahrscheine, bitte.* Tickets, please.
Fahrschule *f* driving school
Fahrstuhl (*pl* **Fahrstühle**) *m* lift
Fahrt *f* ❶ journey ▷ *Die Fahrt nach Hamburg war lang.* It was a long journey to Hamburg. ❷ trip ▷ *Am Wochenende haben wir eine Fahrt in den Schwarzwald gemacht.* We went on a trip to the Black Forest at the weekend.; **Gute Fahrt!** Have a good journey.
Fahrtkosten *pl* travelling expenses *pl*
Fahrzeug (*pl* **Fahrzeuge**) *nt* vehicle
fair *adj* fair ▷ *Das ist nicht fair!* That's not fair!
Faktor (*pl* **Faktoren**) *m* factor
Fakultät *f* faculty
Falke (*gen* **Falken**, *pl* **Falken**) *m* falcon
Fall (*pl* **Fälle**) *m* case ▷ *Die Polizei untersucht den Fall.* The police are investigating the case. ▷ *In diesem Fall mache ich eine Ausnahme.* I'll make an exception in this case. ▷ *Welcher Fall steht nach 'außer'?* Which case does 'außer' take?; **auf jeden Fall** definitely; **für alle Fälle** just in case; **Auf keinen Fall!** No way!
Falle *f* trap
fallen (*pres* **fällt**, *imperf* **fiel**, *perf* **ist gefallen**) *vb* [**22**] to fall; **etwas fallen lassen (1)** to drop something ▷ *Lass es nicht fallen!* Don't drop it! **(2)** to abandon something ▷ *Wir haben die Idee, in Frankreich Ferien zu machen, wieder fallen lassen.* We've abandoned the idea of spending our holidays in France.; **eine Bemerkung fallen lassen** to make a remark
fällen *vb* [**38**] **einen Baum fällen** to fell a tree; **ein Urteil fällen** to pronounce judgement
fallenlassen *vb* [**42**] *see* **fallen**
fällig *adj* due
falls *adv* if
Fallschirm (*pl* **Fallschirme**) *m* parachute
falsch *adj* ❶ wrong ▷ *Die Antwort war falsch.* The answer was wrong.; **jemanden falsch verstehen** to get somebody wrong ❷ false ▷ *falsche Zähne* false teeth
fälschen *vb* [**38**] to forge
Fälschung *f* forgery
Falte *f* ❶ fold ▷ *eine Falte im Papier* a fold in the paper ❷ crease ▷ *Die Hose ist voller Falten.* The trousers are all creased. ❸ wrinkle ▷ *Ihr Gesicht ist voller Falten.* Her face is all wrinkled. ❹ pleat ▷ *eine Rockfalte* a pleat in a skirt
falten *vb* [**2**] to fold
faltig *adj* ❶ wrinkled ▷ *Er hat ein faltiges Gesicht.* He's got a wrinkled face. ❷ creased ▷ *Deine Hose ist ganz faltig.* Your trousers are all creased.
Familie *f* family
Familienname (*gen* **Familiennamens**, *pl* **Familiennamen**) *m* surname
Fan (*pl* **Fans**) *m* fan ▷ *Sie ist ein Fan von Sting.* She's a Sting fan.
fand *vb see* **finden**
fangen (*pres* **fängt**, *imperf* **fing**, *perf* **hat gefangen**) *vb* [**23**] to catch
Fantasie *f* imagination
fantasieren (*perf* **hat fantasiert**) *vb* [**76**] to fantasize
fantastisch *adj* fantastic
Farbe *f* ❶ colour ▷ *Rosa ist Beates Lieblingsfarbe.* Pink is Beate's favourite colour. ❷ paint ▷ *Hast du Farben, ich möchte was malen?* I'd like to do some painting, have you got any paints?
farbecht *adj* colourfast
färben *vb* [**38**] to dye ▷ *Sie hat ihre Haare gefärbt.* She's dyed her hair.
farbenblind *adj* colour-blind
Farbfilm (*pl* **Farbfilme**) *m* colour film
Farbfoto (*pl* **Farbfotos**) *nt* colour photograph
farbig *adj* coloured
farblos *adj* colourless

Farbstift (*pl* **Farbstifte**) *m* coloured pencil
Farbstoff (*pl* **Farbstoffe**) *m* dye
Farbton (*pl* **Farbtöne**) *m* shade
Fasan (*pl* **Fasane** *or* **Fasanen**) *m* pheasant
Fasching (*pl* **Faschinge**) *m* carnival

The German carnival season lasts from 11 November to Shrove Tuesday but most events, fancy-dress processions and parties take place in the week leading up to Ash Wednesday.

Faser *f* fibre
Fass (*gen* **Fasses**, *pl* **Fässer**) *nt* barrel ▷ *ein Weinfass* a wine barrel; **ein Ölfass** an oil drum; **Bier vom Fass** draught beer
fassen (*perf* **hat gefasst**) *vb* [**31**] ❶ to grasp ▷ *Er fasste mich am Arm.* He grasped my arm. ❷ to hold ▷ *Der Behälter fasst zwanzig Liter.* The container holds twenty litres. ❸ to understand ▷ *Ich kann es nicht fassen, dass du das noch immer nicht gemacht hast.* I can't understand why you still haven't done it.; **nicht zu fassen** unbelievable; **sich fassen** to calm down
Fassung *f* ❶ composure ▷ *Sie hat die Fassung verloren.* She lost her composure.; **jemanden aus der Fassung bringen** to upset somebody ❷ version ▷ *der Text in einer neuen Fassung* the text in a new version
fassungslos *adj* speechless
fast *adv* almost

Be careful! The German word **fast** does not mean **fast**.

fasten *vb* [**2**] to fast
Fastenzeit *f* Lent
Fastnacht *f* carnival

The German carnival season lasts from 11 November to Shrove Tuesday but most events, fancy-dress processions and parties take place in the week leading up to Ash Wednesday.

faul *adj* ❶ rotten ▷ *Der Apfel ist faul.* The apple's rotten. ❷ lazy ▷ *Er ist der faulste Schüler.* He's our laziest pupil.; **eine faule Ausrede** a lame excuse; **Daran ist etwas faul.** *(informal)* There's something fishy about it.
faulen *vb* [**38**] to rot
faulenzen *vb* [**36**] to laze about
Faust (*pl* **Fäuste**) *f* fist; **auf eigene Faust** off one's own bat
faxen *vb* [**36**] to fax ▷ *jemandem etwas faxen* to fax something to somebody
FCKW *m* (= *Fluorchlorkohlenwasserstoff*) CFC (= *chlorofluorocarbon*)
Februar (*gen* **Februar** *or* **Februars**, *pl* **Februare**) *m* February ▷ *im Februar* in February ▷ *am dritten Februar* on the third of February ▷ *Bonn, den 3. Februar 2009* Bonn, 3 February 2009 ▷ *Heute ist der zweite Februar.* Today is the second of February.
fechten (*pres* **ficht**, *imperf* **focht**, *perf* **hat gefochten**) *vb* to fence
Feder *f* ❶ feather ▷ *Er hatte eine Feder am Hut.* He had a feather in his hat. ❷ spring ▷ *Die Federn des Betts sind ausgeleiert.* The bed springs have worn out.
Federbett (*pl* **Federbetten**) *nt* continental quilt
fegen *vb* [**38**] to sweep
fehl *adj* **fehl am Platz** out of place
fehlen *vb* [**38**] ❶ to be absent ▷ *Er hat gestern in der Schule gefehlt.* He was absent from school yesterday. ❷ to be missing ▷ *Da fehlt ein Knopf.* There's a button missing. ▷ *Wer fehlt?* Is anyone missing?; **Mir fehlt das nötige Geld.** I haven't got the money.; **Du fehlst mir.** I miss you.; **Was fehlt ihm?** What's wrong with him?
Fehler (*pl* **Fehler**) *m* ❶ mistake ▷ *Wie viele Fehler hast du gemacht?* How many mistakes did you make? ❷ fault ▷ *Sein einziger Fehler ist, dass er den Mund nicht halten kann.* His only fault is that he can't keep his mouth shut.

Feier *f* celebration
Feierabend (*pl* **Feierabende**) *m* clocking-off time; **Feierabend machen** to clock off; **Wann hat dein Vater Feierabend?** When does your father finish work?
feierlich *adj* solemn
Feierlichkeit *f* festivity
feiern *vb* [**88**] to celebrate
Feiertag (*pl* **Feiertage**) *m* holiday ▷ *ein öffentlicher Feiertag* a public holiday
feige *adj* cowardly
Feige *f* fig
Feigling (*pl* **Feiglinge**) *m* coward
Feile *f* file ▷ *eine Nagelfeile* a nailfile
fein *adj* ❶ fine ▷ *feiner Sand* fine sand ❷ refined ▷ *feine Leute* refined people; **Fein!** Great!
Feind (*pl* **Feinde**) *m* enemy
feindlich *adj* hostile
Feindschaft *f* hostility
Feld (*pl* **Felder**) *nt* ❶ field ▷ *Auf diesem Feld wächst Hafer.* There are oats growing in this field. ❷ pitch ▷ *ein Fußballfeld* a football pitch ❸ square ▷ *Er rückte mit seinem Bauern ein Feld vor.* He moved his pawn forward one square.
Fels (*gen* **Felsen**, *pl* **Felsen**) *m* rock; **die weißen Felsen von Dover** the white cliffs of Dover
feminin *adj* feminine
Fenster (*pl* **Fenster**) *nt* window
Fensterscheibe *f* windowpane
Ferien *pl* holidays *pl*; **Ferien haben** to be on holiday
Ferienjob (*pl* **Ferienjobs**) *m* holiday job
Ferienkurs (*gen* **Ferienkurses**, *pl* **Ferienkurse**) *m* vacation course
Ferienlager (*pl* **Ferienlager**) *nt* holiday camp
fern *adj*, *adv* distant ▷ *in ferner Zukunft* in the distant future; **fern von hier** a long way from here; **der Ferne Osten** the Far East
Fernbedienung *f* remote control
Ferngespräch (*pl* **Ferngespräche**) *nt* long-distance call
Fernglas (*gen* **Fernglases**, *pl* **Ferngläser**) *nt* binoculars *pl* ▷ *ein Fernglas* a pair of binoculars
Fernsehapparat (*pl* **Fernsehapparate**) *m* television set
fernsehen (*pres* **sieht fern**, *imperf* **sah fern**, *perf* **hat ferngesehen**) *vb* [**64**] to watch television
Fernsehen *nt* television ▷ *im Fernsehen* on television
Fernseher (*pl* **Fernseher**) *m* television set
Fernsehsendung *f* TV programme
Fernsehserie *f* TV series
Fernsprecher (*pl* **Fernsprecher**) *m* telephone
Fernsteuerung *f* remote control
Ferse *f* heel ▷ *Ich habe eine Blase an der Ferse.* I've got a blister on my heel.
fertig *adj* ❶ ready ▷ *Das Essen ist fertig.* Dinner's ready. ❷ finished ▷ *Der Aufsatz ist fertig.* The essay's finished. ▷ *Bist du mit deinen Hausaufgaben fertig?* Have you finished your homework?; **etwas fertig machen** to finish something; **sich fertig machen** to get ready
fertigbringen (*imperf* **brachte fertig**, *perf* **hat fertiggebracht**) *vb* [**13**] **es fertigbringen, etwas zu tun** to bring oneself to do something
Fertiggericht (*pl* **Fertiggerichte**) *nt* ready meal
fertigmachen *vb* [**48**] **jemanden fertigmachen (1)** to wear somebody out ▷ *Die Radtour hat mich fertiggemacht.* The cycling trip wore me out. **(2)** *(informal)* to tear somebody off a strip ▷ *Meine Englischlehrerin hat mich heute fertiggemacht.* My English teacher tore me off a strip today.
fesselnd *adj* captivating
fest *adj*, *adv* firm ▷ *Er hielt sie mit festem Griff.* He had a firm grip of her. ▷ *Er hat einen festen Händedruck.* He has a firm handshake.; **ein festes Einkommen** a

regular income; **fest schlafen** to sleep soundly; **feste Nahrung** solids *pl*

Fest (*pl* **Feste**) *nt* ❶ party ▷ *Fritz macht am Samstag ein Fest.* Fritz is having a party on Saturday. ❷ festival ▷ *das Backnanger Straßenfest* the Backnang Street Festival; **Frohes Fest!** Happy Christmas!

festhalten (*pres* **hält fest**, *imperf* **hielt fest**, *perf* **hat festgehalten**) *vb* [**33**] to keep hold of ▷ *Du musst das Steuer festhalten.* You must keep hold of the wheel.; **sich festhalten an** to hold on to

festlegen (*perf* **hat festgelegt**) *vb* [**4**] to fix ▷ *einen Termin festlegen* to fix a date; **sich festlegen** to commit oneself

festlich *adj* festive

festmachen (*perf* **hat festgemacht**) *vb* [**48**] ❶ to fix ▷ *Habt ihr den Termin schon festgemacht?* Have you fixed the date yet? ❷ to moor ▷ *Wir haben das Boot im Hafen festgemacht.* We moored the boat in the harbour.

festnehmen (*pres* **nimmt fest**, *imperf* **nahm fest**, *perf* **hat festgenommen**) *vb* [**52**] to arrest

Festplatte *f* hard disk

feststehen (*imperf* **stand fest**, *perf* **hat festgestanden**) *vb* [**72**] to be certain ▷ *So viel steht fest: ...* This much is certain: ...

feststellen (*perf* **hat festgestellt**) *vb* [**4**] ❶ to establish ▷ *Wir konnten nicht feststellen, wer das geschrieben hatte.* We couldn't establish who'd written it. ❷ to see ▷ *Ich stelle fest, dass du schon wieder nicht aufgepasst hast.* I see that you haven't been paying attention again. ❸ to detect ▷ *Wir haben da einen Fehler festgestellt.* We've detected an error.

Festtag *m* special day

fett *adj* fat ▷ *Er ist zu fett.* He's too fat.; **fettes Essen** greasy food; **fette Schrift** bold type

Fett (*pl* **Fette**) *nt* fat

fettarm *adj* low-fat

fettig *adj* greasy

Fetzen (*pl* **Fetzen**) *m* scrap ▷ *ein Fetzen Papier* a scrap of paper

feucht *adj* ❶ damp ▷ *etwas mit einem feuchten Tuch abwischen* to wipe something with a damp cloth ❷ humid ▷ *Das Klima ist sehr feucht.* The climate's very humid.

Feuchtigkeit *f* ❶ moisture ▷ *Salz zieht Feuchtigkeit an.* Salt attracts moisture. ❷ humidity ▷ *hohe Luftfeuchtigkeit* high humidity

Feuer (*pl* **Feuer**) *nt* fire

Feuerlöscher (*pl* **Feuerlöscher**) *m* fire extinguisher

Feuerwehr (*pl* **Feuerwehren**) *f* fire brigade

Feuerwehrauto (*pl* **Feuerwehrautos**) *nt* fire engine

Feuerwehrmann (*pl* **Feuerwehrleute** *or* **Feuerwehrmänner**) *m* fireman

Feuerwerk (*pl* **Feuerwerke**) *nt* fireworks *pl* ▷ *Wir waren beim Feuerwerk.* We went to the fireworks.

Feuerzeug (*pl* **Feuerzeuge**) *nt* lighter

Fieber (*pl* **Fieber**) *nt* ❶ fever ▷ *Das Fieber wird sich in ein paar Tagen senken.* The fever will pass in a couple of days. ❷ temperature ▷ *Hast du Fieber?* Have you got a temperature?

fiel *vb see* **fallen**

fies *adj* nasty

Figur *f* figure ▷ *Sie hat eine gute Figur.* She's got a good figure.; **eine Schachfigur** a chessman

Filiale *f* branch

Film (*pl* **Filme**) *m* film

filmen *vb* [**38**] to film

Filter (*pl* **Filter**) *m* filter

Filzstift (*pl* **Filzstifte**) *m* felt-tip pen

Finanzamt (*pl* **Finanzämter**) *nt* Inland Revenue Office

finanziell *adj* financial

finanzieren (*perf* **hat finanziert**) *vb* [**76**] to finance

finden (*imperf* **fand**, *perf* **hat gefunden**) *vb* [**24**] ❶ to find ▷ *Hast du deinen Radiergummi gefunden?* Have you found your rubber? ❷ to think ▷ *Ich finde, er sieht gut aus.* I think he's good-looking. ▷ *Ich finde sie nicht attraktiv.* I don't think she's attractive.; **Ich finde nichts dabei, wenn ...** I don't see what's wrong with ...; **Das wird sich finden.** Things will work out.
fing *vb see* **fangen**
Finger (*pl* **Finger**) *m* finger
Fingerabdruck (*pl* **Fingerabdrücke**) *m* fingerprint; **genetische Fingerabdrücke** genetic fingerprinting
Fingernagel (*pl* **Fingernägel**) *m* fingernail
Finne (*gen* **Finnen**, *pl* **Finnen**) *m* Finn
Finnin *f* Finn
finnisch *adj* Finnish
Finnland *nt* Finland
finster *adj* ❶ dark ▷ *Hier ist es aber finster.* It's dark in here. ❷ sinister ▷ *finstere Gestalten* sinister figures; **ein finsteres Gesicht** a grim face
Finsternis *f* darkness
Firma (*pl* **Firmen**) *f* firm
Fisch (*pl* **Fische**) *m* fish ▷ *Ich habe fünf Fische.* I've got five fish.; **Fische** Pisces *sg*
fischen *vb* [**48**] to fish ▷ *Sonntags geht Alex immer fischen.* Alex always goes fishing on Sundays.
Fischer (*pl* **Fischer**) *m* fisherman
fit *adj* fit ▷ *Ich halte mich mit Schwimmen fit.* I keep fit by swimming.
fix *adj* **fix und fertig (1)** finished ▷ *Alles war fix und fertig.* Everything was finished. **(2)** *(informal)* all in ▷ *Ich bin fix und fertig.* I'm all in.
Fixer (*pl* **Fixer**) *m (informal)* junkie
flach *adj* ❶ flat ▷ *Norddeutschland ist flach.* North Germany's flat. ❷ shallow ▷ *Ich brauche eine flache Schale.* I need a shallow bowl.
Flachbildschirm (*pl* **Flachbildschirme**) *m* flat screen ▷ *ein Fernseher mit Flachbildschirm* a flatscreen TV
Fläche *f* area ▷ *eine Fläche von hundert Quadratkilometern* an area of a hundred square kilometres
flackern *vb* [**88**] to flicker
Flagge *f* flag
Flamme *f* flame
Flasche *f* bottle ▷ *eine Flasche Mineralwasser* a bottle of mineral water
Flaschenöffner (*pl* **Flaschenöffner**) *m* bottle-opener
Fleck (*pl* **Flecke**) *m* ❶ stain ▷ *Der Wein hat einen Fleck auf dem Teppich gemacht.* The wine left a stain on the carpet. ❷ spot ▷ *Das ist ein hübscher Fleck.* This is a beautiful spot.
fleckig *adj* ❶ spotted ▷ *Ein Dalmatiner hat ein fleckiges Fell.* A Dalmatian has a spotted coat. ❷ stained ▷ *Die Tischdecke ist ganz fleckig.* The tablecloth's all stained.
Fledermaus (*pl* **Fledermäuse**) *f* bat
Fleisch *nt* meat ▷ *Ich esse kein Fleisch.* I don't eat meat.
Fleischer (*pl* **Fleischer**) *m* butcher
Fleischerei *f* butcher's
Fleiß (*gen* **Fleißes**) *m* hard work ▷ *Mit etwas Fleiß könntest du deine Noten verbessern.* With a bit of hard work you could improve your marks.
fleißig *adj* hard-working ▷ *Silke ist eine fleißige Schülerin.* Silke's a hard-working pupil.; **Ich war heute schon fleißig.** I've already done quite a bit of work today.
flexibel *adj* flexible
flicken *vb* [**48**] to mend
Fliege *f* ❶ fly ▷ *Er tut keiner Fliege etwas zuleide.* He wouldn't hurt a fly. ❷ bow tie ▷ *Er trug eine Fliege.* He was wearing a bow tie.
fliegen (*imperf* **flog**, *perf* **ist geflogen**) *vb* [**25**] to fly
fliehen (*imperf* **floh**, *perf* **ist geflohen**) *vb* [**26**] to flee

Fliese *f* tile
Fließband (*pl* **Fließbänder**) *nt* assembly line
fließen (*imperf* **floss**, *perf* **ist geflossen**) *vb* [**27**] to flow
fließend *adj, adv* ❶ running ▷ *fließendes Wasser* running water ❷ fluent ▷ *Sie spricht fließend Englisch.* She is fluent in English.
flink *adj* nimble
Flitterwochen *fpl* honeymoon *sg*
flitzen (*perf* **ist geflitzt**) *vb* [**48**] to dash
Flocke *f* flake ▷ *eine Schneeflocke* a snowflake
flog *vb see* **fliegen**
Floh (*pl* **Flöhe**) *m* flea
Flohmarkt (*pl* **Flohmärkte**) *m* flea market
floss *vb see* **fließen**
Flosse *f* ❶ fin ▷ *die Flosse eines Hais* a shark's fin ❷ flipper ▷ *Er hat seine Flossen mit ins Schwimmbad genommen.* He took his flippers with him to the swimming baths.
Flöte *f* ❶ flute ▷ *Cordula spielt Flöte.* Cordula plays the flute. ❷ recorder ▷ *Phil spielt Flöte.* Phil plays the recorder.
fluchen *vb* [**38**] to curse
flüchtig *adj* at large ▷ *Der Einbrecher ist noch flüchtig.* The burglar's still at large.; **jemanden nur flüchtig kennen** to know somebody only superficially
Flüchtling (*pl* **Flüchtlinge**) *m* refugee
Flug (*pl* **Flüge**) *m* flight ▷ *Der Flug nach Atlanta ist verspätet.* The flight to Atlanta's been delayed.
Flugblatt (*pl* **Flugblätter**) *nt* leaflet
Flügel (*pl* **Flügel**) *m* ❶ wing ▷ *die Flügel des Adlers* the eagle's wings ❷ grand piano ▷ *Im Musikzimmer steht ein Flügel.* There's a grand piano in the music room.
Fluggast (*pl* **Fluggäste**) *m* airline passenger
Fluggesellschaft *f* airline
Flughafen (*pl* **Flughäfen**) *m* airport
Fluglotse (*gen* **Fluglotsen**, *pl* **Fluglotsen**) *m* air traffic controller
Flugplan (*pl* **Flugpläne**) *m* flight schedule
Flugplatz (*gen* **Flugplatzes**, *pl* **Flugplätze**) *m* ❶ airport ▷ *Wir bringen dich zum Flugplatz.* We'll take you to the airport. ❷ airfield ▷ *Dieser Flugplatz ist nur für Privatflugzeuge.* This airfield is only for private planes.
Flugticket (*pl* **Flugtickets**) *nt* plane ticket
Flugzeug (*pl* **Flugzeuge**) *nt* aeroplane
Flugzeugentführung *f* hijacking
Flur (*pl* **Flure**) *m* corridor

> Be careful! **Flur** does not mean **floor**.

Fluss (*gen* **Flusses**, *pl* **Flüsse**) *m* river
flüssig *adj* liquid
Flüssigkeit *f* liquid
flüstern *vb* [**88**] to whisper
Flut (*pl* **Fluten**) *f* ❶ flood ▷ *Wir haben eine Flut von Briefen bekommen.* We received a flood of letters. ❷ high tide ▷ *Das Schiff läuft bei Flut aus.* The ship sails at high tide.
Flutlicht (*pl* **Flutlichter**) *nt* floodlight
Föhn (*pl* **Föhne**) *m* ❶ (*warm dry alpine wind*) foehn ❷ hair dryer
föhnen *vb* [**38**] to blow-dry
Folge *f* ❶ result ▷ *Er starb an den Folgen des Unfalls.* He died as a result of the accident.; **etwas zur Folge haben** to result in something; **Folgen haben** to have consequences ❷ episode ▷ *Hast du die letzte Folge der 'Lindenstraße' gesehen?* Did you see the latest episode of 'Lindenstraße'?; **ein Roman in Folgen** a serialized novel
folgen (*perf* **ist gefolgt**) *vb* [**38**] to follow ▷ *Uns ist ein grünes Auto gefolgt.* We were followed by a green car. ▷ *Folgen Sie dem Wagen da.* Follow that car. ▷ *Ich konnte ihm nicht folgen.* I couldn't follow what he was saying.; **Meine**

Kinder folgen nicht immer. My children don't always do what they're told.
folgend *adj* following
Folgerung *f* conclusion
folglich *adv* consequently
folgsam *adj* obedient
Folie *f* foil
foltern *vb* [**88**] to torture
Fön® (*pl* **Föne**) *m* hair dryer
fordern *vb* [**88**] to demand
Forderung *f* demand
Forelle *f* trout ▷ *drei Forellen* three trout
Form *f* ❶ shape ▷ *Das Auto hat eine elegante Form.* The car has an elegant shape. ❷ mould ▷ *Das Metall wird in eine Form gegossen.* The metal is poured into a mould. ❸ baking tin
Format (*pl* **Formate**) *nt* format
formatieren (*perf* **hat formatiert**) *vb* [**76**] to format
Formel *f* formula
formen *vb* [**38**] to form
förmlich *adj* formal
Formular (*pl* **Formulare**) *nt* form ▷ *ein Formular ausfüllen* to fill in a form
formulieren (*perf* **hat formuliert**) *vb* [**76**] to formulate
Forscher (*pl* **Forscher**) *m* ❶ research scientist ▷ *Die Forscher haben noch keinen Impfstoff gegen Aids entwickelt.* Research scientists have still not developed an AIDS vaccine. ❷ explorer ▷ *Ein Gruppe von Forschern ist im Amazonasgebiet verschollen.* A group of explorers is missing in the Amazon region.
Forschung *f* research
fort *adv* gone ▷ *Mein Geldbeutel ist fort.* My purse is gone.; **und so fort** and so on; **in einem fort** on and on; **Fort mit dir!** Away with you!
sich **fortbewegen** (*perf* **hat sich fortbewegt**) *vb* [**4**] to move
fortbleiben (*imperf* **blieb fort**, *perf* **ist fortgeblieben**) *vb* [**10**] to stay away
fortfahren (*pres* **fährt fort**, *imperf* **fuhr fort**, *perf* **ist fortgefahren**) *vb* [**21**] ❶ to leave ▷ *Sie sind gestern fortgefahren.* They left yesterday. ❷ to continue ▷ *Er fuhr in seiner Rede fort.* He continued with his speech.
fortgeschritten *adj* advanced
Fortschritt (*pl* **Fortschritte**) *m* progress ▷ *Fortschritte machen* to make progress
fortschrittlich *adj* progressive
fortsetzen (*perf* **hat fortgesetzt**) *vb* [**15**] to continue
Fortsetzung *f* ❶ continuation ▷ *die Fortsetzung des Krieges* the continuation of the war ❷ sequel ▷ *Hast du die Fortsetzung gelesen?* Have you read the sequel?; **Fortsetzung folgt** to be continued
Foto (*pl* **Fotos**) *nt* photo
Fotoapparat (*pl* **Fotoapparate**) *m* camera
Fotograf (*gen* **Fotografen**, *pl* **Fotografen**) *m* photographer
> Be careful! **Fotograf** does not mean **photograph**.

Fotografie *f* ❶ photography ▷ *Die Fotografie ist sein Hobby.* His hobby is photography. ❷ photograph ▷ *Ich habe eine Fotografie davon gesehen.* I've seen a photograph of it.
fotografieren (*perf* **hat fotografiert**) *vb* [**76**] ❶ to take a photo of ▷ *Kannst du uns mal fotografieren?* Can you take a photo of us? ❷ to take photographs ▷ *Ich fotografiere in den Ferien nie.* I never take photographs on holiday.
Fotohandy (*pl* **Fotohandys**) *nt* camera phone
Fotokopie *f* photocopy
Fracht *f* freight ▷ *Frachtkosten* freight charges
Frage *f* question ▷ *Könntest du bitte meine Frage beantworten?* Could you please answer my question? ▷ *jemandem eine Frage stellen* to ask somebody a question; **in Frage kommen/stellen** *see* **infrage**

Fragebogen (*pl* **Fragebogen**) *m* questionnaire

fragen *vb* [**38**] to ask ▷ *Kann ich dich was fragen?* Can I ask you something?

Fragezeichen (*pl* **Fragezeichen**) *nt* question mark

fraglich *adj* doubtful ▷ *Es ist sehr fraglich, ob wir kommen können.* It's very doubtful whether we can come.

Franken (*pl* **Franken**) *m* franc ▷ *Er bezahlte 50 Franken.* He paid 50 francs.; **der Schweizer Franken** the Swiss franc

frankieren (*perf* **hat frankiert**) *vb* [**76**] **einen Brief frankieren** to put a stamp on a letter; **ein frankierter Briefumschlag** a stamped self-addressed envelope

Frankreich *nt* France

Franzose (*gen* **Franzosen**, *pl* **Franzosen**) *m* Frenchman; **Er ist Franzose.** He's French.; **die Franzosen** the French

Französin *f* Frenchwoman; **Sie ist Französin.** She's French.

französisch *adj* French

Französisch (*gen* **Französischen**) *nt* French ▷ *Er lernt Französisch in der Schule.* He's learning French at school.

fraß *vb see* **fressen**

Frau *f* ❶ woman ▷ *Sie ist eine nette Frau.* She's a nice woman. ❷ wife ▷ *Herr Arnold ist mit seiner Frau gekommen.* Mr Arnold came with his wife.; **Sehr geehrte Frau Braun (1)** Dear Mrs Braun **(2)** Dear Ms Braun

- Generally **Frau** is used to address all women whether married or not.

Frau Doktor Doctor

Frauenarzt (*gen* **Frauenarztes**, *pl* **Frauenärzte**) *m* gynaecologist

Fräulein (*pl* **Fräulein**) *nt* Miss ▷ *Liebes Fräulein Dümmler* Dear Miss Dümmler

- **Fräulein** is hardly ever used nowadays and **Frau** is used instead to address all women whether married or not.

frech *adj* cheeky

Frechheit *f* cheek

frei *adj* free; **Ist der Platz hier frei?** Is this seat taken?; **Soll ich einen Platz für dich frei halten?** Shall I keep a seat for you?; **'Einfahrt frei halten'** 'Keep clear'; **Wir haben im Moment keine freien Stellen.** We haven't got any vacancies at the moment.; **ein freier Mitarbeiter** a freelancer; **im Freien** in the open air

Freibad (*pl* **Freibäder**) *nt* open-air swimming pool ▷ *Im Sommer gehe ich gern ins Freibad.* I like going to the open-air swimming pool in the summer.

freigebig *adj* generous

freihalten *vb* [**33**] *see* **frei**

Freiheit *f* ❶ freedom ❷ liberty ▷ *sich Freiheiten herausnehmen* to take liberties

freilassen (*pres* **lässt frei**, *imperf* **ließ frei**, *perf* **hat freigelassen**) *vb* [**42**] to free

Freiminuten *pl* free minutes

Freitag (*pl* **Freitage**) *m* Friday ▷ *am Freitag* on Friday

freitags *adv* on Fridays

freiwillig *adj* voluntary

Freizeit *f* spare time ▷ *Was machst du in deiner Freizeit?* What do you do in your spare time?

Freizeitbeschäftigung *f* leisure activity

fremd *adj* ❶ strange ▷ *eine fremde Umgebung* strange surroundings ❷ foreign ▷ *fremde Länder und Sprachen* foreign countries and languages; **Ich bin in London fremd.** I'm a stranger to London.

Fremdenverkehr *m* tourism

Fremdenzimmer (*pl* **Fremdenzimmer**) *nt* guest room

Fremdsprache *f* foreign language

fressen (*pres* **frisst**, *imperf* **fraß**, *perf* **hat gefressen**) *vb* to eat ▷ *Er frisst wie ein Schwein.* He eats like a pig.

Freude *f* ❶ joy ▷ *Welche Freude!* What joy! ❷ delight ▷ *Zu meiner Freude hatten* *wir gestern keine Schule.* To my delight we didn't have any school yesterday.; **Er hat viel Freude an seinem Mountainbike.** He's delighted with his mountain bike.; **Das wird den Kindern Freude machen.** That'll please the children.; **Ich wollte dir eine Freude machen.** I wanted to make you happy.

freuen *vb* [**38**] **sich freuen** to be glad; **sich auf etwas freuen** to look forward to something; **sich über etwas freuen** to be pleased with something; **Dein Brief hat mich sehr gefreut.** Your letter made me very happy.; **Freut mich!** Pleased to meet you.

Freund (*pl* **Freunde**) *m* ❶ friend ▷ *Alle meine Freunde waren da.* All my friends were there. ❷ boyfriend ▷ *Hast du einen Freund?* Have you got a boyfriend?

Freundin *f* ❶ friend ▷ *Wiltrud kommt mit ihrer Freundin.* Wiltrud's coming with her friend. ❷ girlfriend ▷ *Tobias hat keine Freundin.* Tobias hasn't got a girlfriend.

freundlich *adj* ❶ friendly ▷ *Die Leute waren sehr freundlich.* The people were very friendly. ▷ *ein freundliches Lächeln* a friendly smile ❷ kind ▷ *Das ist sehr freundlich von Ihnen.* That's very kind of you.

Freundlichkeit *f* friendliness

Freundschaft *f* friendship

Frieden (*pl* **Frieden**) *m* peace; **im Frieden** in peacetime

Friedhof (*pl* **Friedhöfe**) *m* cemetery

friedlich *adj* peaceful

frieren (*imperf* **fror**, *perf* **hat gefroren**) *vb* to freeze ▷ *Ich friere.* I'm freezing.; **Es friert mich.** I'm freezing.; **Letzte Nacht hat es gefroren.** It was frosty last night.

Frikadelle *f* rissole

frisch *adj* fresh ▷ *frische Milch* fresh milk ▷ *ein frischer Wind* a fresh wind ▷ *Nimm ein frisches Blatt.* Take a fresh sheet of paper.; **Frisch gestrichen!** Wet paint!; **sich frisch machen** to freshen oneself up

Friseur (*pl* **Friseure**) *m* hairdresser

Friseuse *f* hairdresser

frisieren (*perf* **hat frisiert**) *vb* [**76**] **jemanden frisieren** to do somebody's hair; **sich frisieren** to do one's hair

frisst *vb see* **fressen**

Frist *f* deadline ▷ *eine Frist einhalten* to meet a deadline

Frisur *f* hairdo

froh *adj* happy ▷ *frohe Gesichter* happy faces; **Ich bin froh, dass ...** I'm glad that ...

fröhlich *adj* cheerful

fromm *adj* devout

fror *vb see* **frieren**

Frosch (*pl* **Frösche**) *m* frog

Frost (*pl* **Fröste**) *m* frost ▷ *ein strenger Frost* a hard frost

frösteln *vb* [**88**] to shiver

Frucht (*pl* **Früchte**) *f* fruit

fruchtbar *adj* ❶ fruitful ▷ *ein fruchtbares Gespräch* a fruitful conversation ❷ fertile ▷ *fruchtbarer Boden* fertile soil

Fruchtsaft (*pl* **Fruchtsäfte**) *m* fruit juice

früh *adj, adv* early ▷ *Komm lieber etwas früher.* It's better if you come a bit earlier.; **heute früh** this morning

früher *adj, adv* ❶ former ▷ *eine frühere Schülerin unserer Schule* a former pupil of our school ❷ once ▷ *Hier stand früher ein Haus.* A house once stood here.; **Früher war das anders.** That used to be different.

Frühjahr (*pl* **Frühjahre**) *nt* spring ▷ *im Frühjahr* in spring

Frühling (*pl* **Frühlinge**) *m* spring ▷ *im Frühling* in spring

Frühstück *nt* breakfast

frühstücken *vb* [**38**] to have breakfast

frustrieren (*perf* **hat frustriert**) *vb* [**76**] to frustrate

Fuchs (*gen* **Fuchses**, *pl* **Füchse**) *m* fox

a b c d e f g h i j k l m n o p q r s t u v w x y z

fühlen *vb* [**38**] to feel ▷ *Fühl mal, wie weich das ist.* Feel how soft it is. ▷ *Ich fühle mich wohl.* I feel fine.

fuhr *vb see* **fahren**

führen *vb* [**38**] ❶ to lead ▷ *Sie führte uns nach draußen.* She led us outside.; **ein Geschäft führen** to run a business ❷ to be winning ▷ *Welche Mannschaft führt?* Which team's winning?

Führer (*pl* **Führer**) *m* ❶ leader ▷ *der Parteiführer* the party leader ❷ guide ▷ *Unser Führer zeigte uns alle Sehenswürdigkeiten.* Our guide showed us all the sights. ❸ guidebook ▷ *Hast du einen Führer von Rom?* Have you got a guidebook of Rome?

Führerschein (*pl* **Führerscheine**) *m* driving licence; **den Führerschein machen** to take one's driving test

Führung *f* ❶ lead ▷ *Unsere Mannschaft liegt in Führung.* Our team is in the lead. ❷ leadership ▷ *Er übernahm die Führung der Partei.* He took over the leadership of the party. ❸ management ▷ *Das Geschäft hat unter neuer Führung wiedereröffnet.* The business has reopened under new management. ❹ guided tour ▷ *Führungen durchs Museum finden stündlich statt.* There are guided tours of the museum every hour.

füllen *vb* [**38**] ❶ to fill ▷ *Sie füllte das Glas bis zum Rand.* She filled the glass to the brim. ❷ to stuff ▷ *Heute gibt es gefüllte Paprika.* We're having stuffed peppers today.

Füller (*pl* **Füller**) *m* fountain pen

Füllung *f* filling

Fundament (*pl* **Fundamente**) *nt* foundations *pl*

Fundbüro (*pl* **Fundbüros**) *nt* lost property office

fundiert *adj* sound ▷ *fundierte Englischkenntnisse* a sound knowledge of English

fünf *num* five

Fünf *f* ❶ five ❷ poor

German marks range from one (**sehr gut**) to six (**ungenügend**).

fünfte *adj* fifth ▷ *Ich erkläre dir das jetzt zum fünften Mal.* This is the fifth time I've explained this to you. ▷ *Er kam als Fünfter.* He was the fifth to arrive.

fünfzehn *num* fifteen

fünfzig *num* fifty

Funke (*gen* **Funkens**, *pl* **Funken**) *m* spark

funkeln *vb* [**88**] to sparkle

Funkloch (*pl* **Funklöcher**) *nt* (*mobile phone*) dead spot

Funktion *f* function

funktionieren (*perf* **hat funktioniert**) *vb* [**76**] to work

Funktionstaste *f* function key

für *prep*

The preposition **für** takes the accusative.

for ▷ *Das ist für dich.* This is for you.; **was für** what kind of; **das Für und Wider** the pros and cons

Word for word, **das Für und Wider** means 'the for and against'.

Furcht *f* fear

furchtbar *adj* terrible

fürchten *vb* [**2**] to be afraid ▷ *Ich fürchte mich vor diesem Mann.* I'm afraid of that man.

fürchterlich *adj* awful

fürs = **für das**

Fuß (*gen* **Fußes**, *pl* **Füße**) *m* ❶ foot ▷ *Mir tun die Füße weh.* My feet hurt. ❷ leg ▷ *Der Tisch hat vier Füße.* The table's got four legs.; **zu Fuß** on foot

Fußball (*pl* **Fußbälle**) *m* football

Fußballplatz (*gen* **Fußballplatzes**, *pl* **Fußballplätze**) *m* football pitch

Fußballspiel (*pl* **Fußballspiele**) *nt* football match

Fußballspieler (*pl* **Fußballspieler**) *m* footballer

Fußboden (*pl* **Fußböden**) *m* floor

Fußgänger (*pl* **Fußgänger**) *m* pedestrian

Fußgängerzone *f* pedestrian precinct
Fußweg (*pl* **Fußwege**) *m* footpath
Futter (*pl* **Futter**) *nt* ❶ feed ▷ *BSE entstand durch verseuchtes Futter.* BSE was the result of contaminated feed. ❷ food ▷ *Hast du Futter für die Katze gekauft?* Have you bought cat food? ❸ lining ▷ *Der Mantel hat ein Futter aus Pelz.* The coat has a fur lining.
füttern *vb* [88] ❶ to feed ▷ *Kannst du bitte das Baby füttern?* Can you feed the baby, please? ❷ to line ▷ *Der Mantel ist gefüttert.* The coat's lined.
Futur (*pl* **Future**) *nt* future

g

g *abbr* (= *Gramm*) g
gab *vb see* **geben**
Gabel *f* fork
gähnen *vb* [38] to yawn
Galerie *f* gallery
Gang (*pl* **Gänge**) *m* ❶ corridor ▷ *Häng deinen Mantel im Gang auf.* Hang your coat up in the corridor. ❷ aisle ▷ *Ich hätte gern einen Platz am Gang.* I'd like an aisle seat. ❸ gear ▷ *Mein Fahrrad hat zehn Gänge.* My bike has ten gears. ❹ course ▷ *Das war erst der zweite Gang, und ich bin schon satt.* That was only the second course and I'm full already. ▷ *der Gang der Dinge* the course of events; **etwas in Gang bringen** to get something off the ground
Gans (*pl* **Gänse**) *f* goose
Gänseblümchen (*pl* **Gänseblümchen**) *nt* daisy
Gänsehaut *f* goose pimples *pl*
ganz *adj, adv* ❶ whole ▷ *die ganze Welt* the whole world ▷ *ganz Europa* the whole of Europe; **sein ganzes Geld** all

his money ❷ quite ▷ *ganz gut* quite good; **ganz und gar nicht** not at all; **Es sieht ganz so aus.** It really looks like it.

ganztags *adv* full time ▷ *ganztags arbeiten* to work full time

gar *adj, adv* done ▷ *Die Kartoffeln sind gar.* The potatoes are done.; **gar nicht** not at all; **gar nichts** nothing at all; **gar niemand** nobody at all

Garage *f* garage *(for parking)*

garantieren (*perf* **hat garantiert**) *vb* [**76**] to guarantee; **Er kommt garantiert.** He's sure to come.

Garderobe *f* cloakroom ▷ *Ich habe meinen Mantel an der Garderobe abgegeben.* I left my coat in the cloakroom.

Gardine *f* curtain ▷ *die Gardinen zuziehen* to shut the curtains

Garten (*pl* **Gärten**) *m* garden

Gas (*gen* **Gases**, *pl* **Gase**) *nt* gas ▷ *Wir kochen mit Gas.* We cook with gas.; **Gas geben** to accelerate

Gasherd (*pl* **Gasherde**) *m* gas cooker

Gaspedal (*pl* **Gaspedale**) *nt* accelerator

Gasse *f* lane ▷ *die schmalen Gassen der Altstadt* the narrow lanes of the old town

Gast (*pl* **Gäste**) *m* guest ▷ *Wir haben Gäste aus England.* We've got guests from England.; **bei jemandem zu Gast sein** to be somebody's guest

gastfreundlich *adj* hospitable

Gastfreundschaft *f* hospitality

Gastgeber (*pl* **Gastgeber**) *m* host

Gastgeberin *f* hostess

Gasthaus (*gen* **Gasthauses**, *pl* **Gasthäuser**) *nt* inn

Gasthof (*pl* **Gasthöfe**) *m* inn

Gaststätte *f* pub

> In Germany there's practically no difference between pubs and restaurants. You can eat or drink in a **Gaststätte**, families are welcome and the opening hours are flexible.

Gebäck (*pl* **Gebäcke**) *nt* pastry ▷ *Kuchen und Gebäck* cakes and pastries

gebären (*pres* **gebiert**, *imperf* **gebar**, *perf* **hat geboren**) *vb* to give birth to

Gebäude (*pl* **Gebäude**) *nt* building

geben (*pres* **gibt**, *imperf* **gab**, *perf* **hat gegeben**) *vb* [**28**] to give ▷ *Gib ihm bitte das Geld.* Please give him the money. ▷ *Kannst du dieses Buch bitte deiner Mutter geben.* Could you give this book to your mother, please.; **Karten geben** to deal

> Word for word, **Karten geben** means 'to give cards'.

es gibt there is; **Was gibt's?** What's up?; **Was gibt es im Kino?** What's on at the cinema?; **sich geschlagen geben** to admit defeat; **Das wird sich schon geben.** That'll sort itself out.

Gebet (*pl* **Gebete**) *nt* prayer

gebeten *vb see* **bitten**

Gebiet (*pl* **Gebiete**) *nt* ❶ area ▷ *ein bewaldetes Gebiet* a wooded area ❷ field ▷ *Er ist Experte auf diesem Gebiet.* He's an expert in this field.

gebildet *adj* cultured

Gebirge (*pl* **Gebirge**) *nt* mountain chain ▷ *Die Alpen sind ein großes Gebirge.* The Alps are a large mountain chain.; **ins Gebirge fahren** to go to the mountains

Gebiss (*gen* **Gebisses**, *pl* **Gebisse**) *nt* ❶ teeth *pl* ▷ *Sie hat ein gesundes Gebiss.* She's got healthy teeth. ❷ dentures *pl* ▷ *Opas Gebiss lag auf dem Tisch.* Grandpa's dentures were lying on the table.

gebissen *vb see* **beißen**

geblieben *vb see* **bleiben**

geboren *vb see* **gebären**

▸ *adj* ❶ born ▷ *Wann bist du geboren?* When were you born? ❷ née ▷ *Frau Dümmler, geborene Schnorr* Mrs Dümmler, née Schnorr

geboten *vb see* **bieten**

gebracht *vb see* **bringen**

gebraten *adj* fried

gebrauchen (*perf* **hat gebraucht**) *vb* [**48**] to use
Gebrauchsanweisung *f* directions for use *pl* ▷ *Wo ist die Gebrauchsanweisung?* Where are the directions for use?
gebraucht *adj* used
Gebrauchtwagen (*pl* **Gebrauchtwagen**) *m* second-hand car
gebrochen *vb see* **brechen**
Gebühr *f* fee
Gebühreneinheit *f* unit *(telephone)*
gebührenpflichtig *adj* subject to a charge; **eine gebührenpflichtige Verwarnung** a fine
gebunden *vb see* **binden**
Geburt *f* birth ▷ *bei der Geburt* at the birth
gebürtig *adj* native of ▷ *ein gebürtiger Schweizer* a native of Switzerland
Geburtsdatum (*pl* **Geburtsdaten**) *nt* date of birth
Geburtsort (*pl* **Geburtsorte**) *m* birthplace
Geburtstag (*pl* **Geburtstage**) *m* birthday ▷ *Herzlichen Glückwunsch zum Geburtstag!* Happy Birthday!
gedacht *vb see* **denken**
Gedächtnis (*gen* **Gedächtnisses**, *pl* **Gedächtnisse**) *nt* memory ▷ *Ich habe ein schlechtes Gedächtnis.* I've got a bad memory.
Gedanke (*gen* **Gedankens**, *pl* **Gedanken**) *m* thought; **sich über etwas Gedanken machen** to think about something
gedeihen (*imperf* **gedieh**, *perf* **ist gediehen**) *vb* to thrive
Gedicht (*pl* **Gedichte**) *nt* poem
Gedränge *nt* crush ▷ *Vor der Kinokasse herrschte großes Gedränge.* There was a huge crush at the cinema box office.
Geduld *f* patience
sich **gedulden** (*perf* **hat sich geduldet**) *vb* [**7**] to be patient
geduldig *adj* patient
gedurft *vb see* **dürfen**
geehrt *adj* **Sehr geehrter Herr Butterfeld** Dear Mr Butterfeld
geeignet *adj* suitable
Gefahr *f* ❶ danger ▷ *in Gefahr schweben* to be in danger ❷ risk ▷ *Gefahr laufen, etwas zu tun* to run the risk of doing something ▷ *auf eigene Gefahr* at one's own risk
gefährden (*perf* **hat gefährdet**) *vb* [**7**] to endanger
gefährlich *adj* dangerous
Gefälle (*pl* **Gefälle**) *nt* gradient
gefallen (1) *vb* [**22**] *see* **fallen**
gefallen (2) (*pres* **gefällt**, *imperf* **gefiel**, *perf* **hat gefallen**) *vb* [**22**] to like ▷ *Es gefällt mir.* I like it. ▷ *Das Geschenk hat ihr gefallen.* She liked the present. ▷ *Er gefällt mir.* I like him. ▷ *Das gefällt mir an ihm.* That's one thing I like about him.; **sich etwas gefallen lassen** to put up with something
Gefallen (*pl* **Gefallen**) *m* favour ▷ *Könntest du mir einen Gefallen tun?* Could you do me a favour?
gefangen *vb see* **fangen**; **jemanden gefangen nehmen** to take somebody prisoner
Gefangene (*gen* **Gefangenen**, *pl* **Gefangenen**) *mf* prisoner ▷ *Ein Gefangener ist geflohen.* A prisoner has escaped.
gefangennehmen *vb* [**52**] *see* **gefangen**
Gefangenschaft *f* captivity
Gefängnis (*gen* **Gefängnisses**, *pl* **Gefängnisse**) *nt* prison
Gefängnisstrafe *f* prison sentence
Gefäß (*gen* **Gefäßes**, *pl* **Gefäße**) *nt* container
gefasst *adj* composed ▷ *Sie war sehr gefasst.* She was very composed.; **auf etwas gefasst sein** to be prepared for something
geflogen *vb see* **fliegen**
geflossen *vb see* **fließen**
Geflügel *nt* poultry

gefragt *adj* in demand ▷ *Er ist ein sehr gefragter Künstler.* He's an artist very much in demand. ▷ *Handwerker sind sehr gefragt.* Tradesmen are in great demand.
gefräßig *adj* greedy
Gefrierfach (*pl* **Gefrierfächer**) *nt* icebox
Gefriertruhe *f* deep-freeze
gefroren *adj* frozen
Gefühl (*pl* **Gefühle**) *nt* feeling ▷ *Sie hat ein Gefühl für Kunst.* She's got a feeling for art.; **etwas im Gefühl haben** to have a feel for something
gefüllt *adj* stuffed ▷ *gefüllte Auberginen* stuffed aubergines
gefunden *vb see* **finden**
gegangen *vb see* **gehen**
gegeben *vb see* **geben**
gegen *prep*

The preposition **gegen** takes the accusative.

❶ against ▷ *Ich bin gegen diese Idee.* I'm against this idea. ▷ *nichts gegen jemanden haben* to have nothing against somebody; **ein Mittel gegen Schnupfen** something for colds; **Maske gegen Botha** Maske versus Botha ❷ towards ▷ *gegen Osten* towards the east ▷ *gegen Abend* towards evening; **gegen einen Baum fahren** to drive into a tree ❸ round about ▷ *gegen drei Uhr* round about three o'clock
Gegend *f* area ▷ *die Gegend um Ulm* the area around Ulm
Gegensatz (*gen* **Gegensatzes**, *pl* **Gegensätze**) *m* contrast; **Im Gegensatz zu mir ist er gut in Mathe.** Unlike me, he's good at maths.
gegenseitig *adj* mutual ▷ *gegenseitiges Vertrauen* mutual trust; **sich gegenseitig helfen** to help each other
Gegenstand (*pl* **Gegenstände**) *m* object
Gegenteil *nt* opposite ▷ *Das ist das Gegenteil von schön.* That's the opposite of lovely.; **im Gegenteil** on the contrary
gegenüber *prep, adv*

The preposition **gegenüber** takes the dative.

❶ opposite ▷ *Die Apotheke ist gegenüber.* The chemist's is opposite. ▷ *Er saß mir gegenüber.* He sat opposite me.
❷ towards ▷ *Sie waren mir gegenüber sehr freundlich.* They were very friendly towards me.
Gegenverkehr *m* oncoming traffic
Gegenwart *f* present ▷ *in der Gegenwart leben* to live in the present
gegessen *vb see* **essen**
Gegner (*pl* **Gegner**) *m* opponent
Gehackte (*gen* **Gehackten**) *nt* mince ▷ *Ein Kilo Gehacktes, bitte.* A kilo of mince, please.
Gehalt (*pl* **Gehälter**) *nt* salary ▷ *Er verdient ein gutes Gehalt.* He earns a good salary.
gehässig *adj* spiteful
geheim *adj* secret ▷ *geheim halten* to keep secret
Geheimnis (*gen* **Geheimnisses**, *pl* **Geheimnisse**) *nt* ❶ secret ▷ *Kannst du ein Geheimnis behalten?* Can you keep a secret? ❷ mystery ▷ *die Geheimnisse der Erde* the Earth's mysteries
geheimnisvoll *adj* mysterious
Geheimnummer *f* ex-directory number; **Wir haben eine Geheimnummer.** We're ex-directory.
gehen (*imperf* **ging**, *perf* **ist gegangen**) *vb* [**29**] ❶ to go ▷ *Wir gehen jetzt.* We're going now. ▷ *schwimmen gehen* to go swimming ❷ to walk ▷ *Sollen wir gehen oder den Bus nehmen?* Shall we walk or go by bus?; **Wie geht es dir?** How are you?; **Wie geht's?** How are things?; **Mir geht's gut.** I'm fine.; **Ihm geht's gut.** He's fine.; **Es geht.** Not bad.; **Geht das?** Is that possible?; **Geht's noch?** Can you manage?; **Das geht nicht.** That's not on.; **um etwas gehen** to be about something; **Hier**

geht es um sehr viel Geld. There's a lot of money at stake here.
Gehirn (*pl* **Gehirne**) *nt* brain
Gehirnerschütterung *f* concussion
gehoben *vb see* **heben**
geholfen *vb see* **helfen**
gehorchen (*perf* **hat gehorcht**) *vb* [**48**] to obey ▷ *Du solltest deinem Vater gehorchen.* You should obey your father. ▷ *Ein Hund sollte lernen zu gehorchen.* A dog should learn to obey.
gehören (*perf* **hat gehört**) *vb* [**38**] **jemandem gehören** to belong to somebody; **Das gehört sich einfach nicht.** That just isn't done.
gehorsam *adj* obedient
Gehorsam *m* obedience
Gehweg (*pl* **Gehwege**) *m* pavement
Geier (*pl* **Geier**) *m* vulture
Geige *f* violin ▷ *Wiltrud spielt Geige.* Wiltrud plays the violin.
geil *adj* ❶ *(informal)* horny ▷ *Wenn er das sieht, wird er geil.* When he sees that, he'll get horny. ❷ *(informal)* cool ▷ *Das war eine geile Party.* That was a cool party. ▷ *ein geiler Song* a cool song
Geisel *f* hostage
Geist (*pl* **Geister**) *m* ❶ ghost ❷ mind ▷ *Er hat einen regen Geist.* He has a lively mind.; **Seine Rede sprühte vor Geist.** His speech was very witty.
geisteskrank *adj* mentally ill
Geisteskrankheit *f* mental illness
Geiz (*gen* **Geizes**) *m* meanness
Geizhals (*gen* **Geizhalses**, *pl* **Geizhälse**) *m* miser
geizig *adj* mean
gekannt *vb see* **kennen**
gekonnt *vb see* **können**
▶ *adj* skilful
Gel (*pl* **Gele**) *nt* gel
Gelächter *nt* laughter
geladen *vb see* **laden**
▶ *adj* ❶ loaded ▷ *eine geladene Waffe* a loaded weapon ❷ invited ▷ *geladene Gäste* invited guests; **geladen sein** to be furious
gelähmt *adj* paralysed
Gelände (*pl* **Gelände**) *nt* ❶ grounds *pl* ▷ *auf dem Gelände der Schule* on the school grounds ❷ terrain ▷ *unwegsames Gelände* difficult terrain; **durchs Gelände fahren** to go cross-country; **ein Baugelände** a building site
gelangweilt *adj* bored
gelassen *vb see* **lassen**
▶ *adj* calm ▷ *Sie blieb gelassen.* She remained calm.
geläufig *adj* common ▷ *ein geläufiger Begriff* a common term; **Das ist mir nicht geläufig.** I'm not familiar with that.
gelaunt *adj* **gut gelaunt** in a good mood; **schlecht gelaunt** in a bad mood; **Wie ist er gelaunt?** What sort of mood's he in?
gelb *adj* ❶ yellow ❷ amber ▷ *Die Ampel war gelb.* The traffic lights were at amber.
Geld (*pl* **Gelder**) *nt* money; **etwas zu Geld machen** to sell something off
Geldautomat (*gen* **Geldautomaten**, *pl* **Geldautomaten**) *m* cash machine
Geldschein (*pl* **Geldscheine**) *m* banknote
Geldstrafe *f* fine
Geldstück (*pl* **Geldstücke**) *nt* coin
Geldwechsel *m* changing of money ▷ *Beim Geldwechsel muss man eine Gebühr bezahlen.* There is a charge for changing money.; **'Geldwechsel'** 'bureau de change'
gelegen *vb see* **liegen**
Gelegenheit *f* ❶ opportunity ▷ *Sobald ich eine Gelegenheit bekomme ...* As soon as I get an opportunity ... ▷ *bei jeder Gelegenheit* at every opportunity ❷ occasion ▷ *Bei dieser Gelegenheit trug sie das blaue Kostüm.* On this occasion she wore her blue suit.
gelegentlich *adv* ❶ occasionally ▷ *Gelegentlich gehe ich ganz gern ins Kino.* I occasionally like going to the cinema.

a b c d e f g h i j k l m n o p q r s t u v w x y z

❷ some time or other ▷ *Ich werde mich gelegentlich darum kümmern.* I'll do it some time or other.
Gelenk (*pl* **Gelenke**) *nt* joint *(in body)*
gelenkig *adj* supple
gelernt *adj* skilled
geliehen *vb see* **leihen**
gelingen (*imperf* **gelang**, *perf* **ist gelungen**) *vb* to succeed ▷ *Sein Plan ist ihm nicht gelungen.* His plan didn't succeed.; **Es ist mir gelungen, ihn zu überzeugen.** I succeeded in convincing him.; **Der Kuchen ist gelungen.** The cake turned out well.
gelten (*pres* **gilt**, *imperf* **galt**, *perf* **hat gegolten**) *vb* to be valid ▷ *Dein Ausweis gilt nicht mehr.* Your passport is no longer valid.; **es gilt, etwas zu tun** it's necessary to do something; **jemandem gelten** to be aimed at somebody; **etwas gelten lassen** to accept something; **Was gilt die Wette?** What do you bet?
gelungen *vb see* **gelingen**
▶ *adj* successful
Gemälde (*pl* **Gemälde**) *nt* painting ▷ *ein Gemälde von Rembrandt* a painting by Rembrandt
gemein *adj* mean ▷ *Das war gemein!* That was mean!; **etwas gemein haben mit** to have something in common with
gemeinsam *adj, adv* ❶ joint ▷ *gemeinsame Anstrengungen* joint efforts ❷ together ▷ *Wir sind gemeinsam zum Lehrer gegangen.* We went together to the teacher. ▷ *ein gemeinsames Abendessen* dinner together; **etwas gemeinsam haben** to have something in common
gemischt *adj* mixed
gemocht *vb see* **mögen**
Gemüse (*pl* **Gemüse**) *nt* vegetables *pl* ▷ *Gemüse ist gesund.* Vegetables are healthy.
gemusst *vb see* **müssen**
gemütlich *adj* ❶ cosy ▷ *eine gemütliche Wohnung* a cosy flat; **ein gemütlicher Abend** a pleasant evening ❷ good-natured ▷ *Sie ist ein gemütlicher Mensch.* She's good-natured.
Gen (*pl* **Gene**) *nt* gene
genannt *vb see* **nennen**
genau *adj, adv* ❶ exact ▷ *Ich brauche genaue Zahlen.* I need exact figures. ❷ accurate ▷ *Diese Übersetzung ist nicht sehr genau.* This translation isn't very accurate. ❸ exactly ▷ *Genau das habe ich auch gesagt.* That's exactly what I said. ▷ *Sie hatte genau dasselbe Kleid an.* She was wearing exactly the same dress. ▷ *Das ist genau anders herum.* That's exactly the opposite.; **etwas genau nehmen** to take something seriously; **genau genommen** strictly speaking
genauso *adv* **genauso gut** just as good
genehmigen (*perf* **hat genehmigt**) *vb* [7] to approve; **sich etwas genehmigen** to treat oneself to something
Genehmigung *f* ❶ permission ▷ *Für den Umbau brauchen wir eine Genehmigung.* We need permission for the conversion. ❷ permit ▷ *Hier ist meine Genehmigung.* Here's my permit.
Generation *f* generation
Genf *nt* Geneva; **der Genfer See** Lake Geneva
genial *adj* brilliant
Genick (*pl* **Genicke**) *nt* back of the neck; **sich das Genick brechen** to break one's neck
Genie (*pl* **Genies**) *nt* genius
genießen (*imperf* **genoss**, *perf* **hat genossen**) *vb* to enjoy ▷ *Wir haben die Ferien genossen.* We enjoyed our holidays.
genmanipuliert *adj* genetically modified ▷ *genmanipulierte Lebensmittel* genetically modified food
genommen *vb see* **nehmen**
genug *adj* enough ▷ *Wir haben genug Geld.* We've got enough money. ▷ *gut genug* good enough

genügen (*perf* **hat genügt**) *vb* [38] to be enough ▷ *Das genügt noch nicht.* That isn't enough.; **jemandem genügen** to be enough for somebody
genügend *adj* sufficient
Genuss (*gen* **Genusses**, *pl* **Genüsse**) *m* ❶ pleasure ▷ *Es war ein Genuss!* That was sheer pleasure! ❷ consumption ▷ *der Genuss von Alkohol* the consumption of alcohol; **in den Genuss von etwas kommen** to receive the benefit of something
geöffnet *adj* open
Geografie *f* geography
Geometrie *f* geometry
Gepäck *nt* luggage
Gepäckannahme *f* luggage office
Gepäckausgabe *f* baggage reclaim
gepflegt *adj* ❶ well-groomed ▷ *gepflegte Hände* well-groomed hands ❷ well-kept ▷ *ein gepflegter Park* a well-kept park
gerade *adj, adv* ❶ straight ▷ *eine gerade Strecke* a straight stretch ❷ upright ▷ *eine gerade Haltung* an upright posture; **eine gerade Zahl** an even number ❸ just ▷ *Du kommst gerade richtig.* You've come just at the right time. ▷ *Das ist es ja gerade!* That's just it! ▷ *Er wollte gerade aufstehen.* He was just about to get up.; **gerade erst** only just; **gerade noch** only just; **gerade deshalb** that's exactly why; **gerade du** you of all people; **nicht gerade** not exactly
geradeaus *adv* straight ahead
gerannt *vb see* **rennen**
Gerät (*pl* **Geräte**) *nt* ❶ gadget ▷ *ein Gerät zum Papierschneiden* a gadget for cutting paper ❷ appliance ▷ *ein Haushaltsgerät* a household appliance ❸ tool ▷ *ein Gartengerät* a garden tool ❹ apparatus ▷ *Wir haben heute an den Geräten geturnt.* We did gymnastics on the apparatus today. ❺ equipment ▷ *Geräte zum Angeln* fishing equipment
geraten (*pres* **gerät**, *imperf* **geriet**, *perf* **ist geraten**) *vb* ❶ to thrive ▷ *Hier geraten die Pflanzen.* Plants thrive here. ❷ to turn out ▷ *Ihre Kinder sind alle gut geraten.* All their children have turned out well. ▷ *Der Kuchen ist mir nicht geraten.* The cake hasn't turned out well.; **in etwas geraten** to get into something; **in Angst geraten** to get frightened; **nach jemandem geraten** to take after somebody
geräuchert *adj* smoked
Geräusch (*pl* **Geräusche**) *nt* sound
gerecht *adj* fair ▷ *Das ist nicht gerecht!* That's not fair!
Gerechtigkeit *f* justice
Gerede *nt* gossip ▷ *Das ist alles nur Gerede.* That's all just gossip.
gereizt *adj* irritable
Gericht (*pl* **Gerichte**) *nt* ❶ court ▷ *Wir sehen uns vor Gericht.* I'll see you in court. ❷ dish ▷ *ein leckeres Gericht* a tasty dish; **das Jüngste Gericht** the Last Judgement
gerieben *vb see* **reiben**
gering *adj* ❶ small ▷ *eine geringe Menge* a small amount ❷ low ▷ *geringe Beteiligung* low participation; **eine geringe Zeit** a short time
geringste *adj* least ▷ *Das ist meine geringste Sorge.* That's the least of my worries.
geritten *vb see* **reiten**
gern *adv* gladly ▷ *Das habe ich gern getan.* I did it gladly.; **gern mögen** to like; **etwas gern tun** to like doing something; **Ich hätte gern ...** I'd like ...; **Ja, gern!** Yes, please.; **Gern geschehen!** It's a pleasure.
gerochen *vb see* **riechen**
Geruch (*pl* **Gerüche**) *m* smell
Gerücht (*pl* **Gerüchte**) *nt* rumour
gesalzen *vb see* **salzen**
▸ *adj* **gesalzene Preise** (*informal*) hefty prices

> Word for word, **gesalzene Preise** means 'salted prices'.

gesamt *adj* whole ▷ *die gesamte Klasse* the whole class; **die gesamten Kosten** the total cost; **gesamte Werke** complete works; **im Gesamten** all in all

Gesamtschule *f* comprehensive school

- **Gesamtschulen** are the exception rather than the rule in Germany.

gesandt *vb see* **senden**

Geschäft (*pl* **Geschäfte**) *nt* ❶ shop ▷ *In welchem Geschäft hast du das gekauft?* Which shop did you buy that in? ❷ business ▷ *Die Geschäfte gehen gut.* Business is good. ❸ deal ▷ *Ich schlage dir ein Geschäft vor.* I'll make a deal with you. ▷ *Das war ein gutes Geschäft.* That was a good deal.

Geschäftsfrau *f* businesswoman

Geschäftsmann (*pl* **Geschäftsmänner**) *m* businessman

geschehen (*pres* **geschieht**, *imperf* **geschah**, *perf* **ist geschehen**) *vb* to happen ▷ *Was ist geschehen?* What's happened? ▷ *Was ist mit ihm geschehen?* What's happened to him?

gescheit *adj* clever

Geschenk (*pl* **Geschenke**) *nt* present

Geschichte *f* ❶ story ▷ *eine lustige Geschichte* a funny story ❷ history ▷ *die deutsche Geschichte* German history ❸ business ▷ *die Geschichte mit dem verschwundenen Pass* the business of the missing passport

geschickt *adj* skilful

geschieden *vb see* **scheiden**
▶ *adj* divorced

geschienen *vb see* **scheinen**

Geschirr *nt* crockery ▷ *In welchem Schrank steht das Geschirr?* What cupboard is the crockery kept in?; **das Geschirr spülen** to do the dishes

Geschirrspülmaschine *f* dishwasher

Geschirrtuch (*pl* **Geschirrtücher**) *nt* dish cloth

Geschlecht (*pl* **Geschlechter**) *nt* ❶ sex ▷ *ein Kind weiblichen Geschlechts* a child of the female sex ❷ gender ▷ *Welches Geschlecht hat dieses Substantiv?* What gender is this noun?

Geschlechtskrankheit *f* sexually transmitted disease

geschlossen *vb see* **schließen**
▶ *adj* shut; **'Geschlossen'** 'Closed'

Geschmack (*pl* **Geschmäcke**) *m* taste ▷ *Das ist nicht nach meinem Geschmack.* This is not to my taste.; **Geschmack an etwas finden** to come to like something

geschmacklos *adj* ❶ tasteless ▷ *Die Suppe war ziemlich geschmacklos.* The soup was pretty tasteless. ❷ in bad taste ▷ *Das war ein geschmackloser Witz.* That joke was in bad taste.

geschmackvoll *adj* tasteful

geschnitten *vb see* **schneiden**

geschossen *vb see* **schießen**

geschrieben *vb see* **schreiben**

geschrien *vb see* **schreien**

geschützt *adj* protected

Geschwätz *nt* chatter

geschwätzig *adj* talkative

Geschwindigkeit *f* speed

Geschwindigkeitsbeschränkung *f* speed limit

Geschwister *pl* brothers and sisters *pl*

geschwommen *vb see* **schwimmen**

gesellig *adj* sociable

Gesellschaft *f* ❶ society ▷ *die Gesellschaft verändern* to change society ❷ company ▷ *jemandem Gesellschaft leisten* to keep somebody company

gesessen *vb see* **sitzen**

Gesetz (*gen* **Gesetzes**, *pl* **Gesetze**) *nt* law

gesetzlich *adj* legal; **gesetzlicher Feiertag** public holiday

Gesicht (*pl* **Gesichter**) *nt* face

gespannt *adj* ❶ strained ▷ *Die Lage im Nahen Osten ist gespannt.* The situation in the Middle East is strained. ❷ eager ▷ *gespannte Zuhörer* eager listeners; **Ich bin gespannt, ob ...** I wonder whether ...; **auf etwas gespannt sein** to look forward to something

Gespenst (*pl* **Gespenster**) *nt* ghost
gesperrt *adj* closed off
Gespräch (*pl* **Gespräche**) *nt* ❶ conversation ▷ *ein langes Gespräch* a long conversation ❷ call ▷ *Frau Morris, ein Gespräch für Sie.* Mrs Morris, there's a call for you.
gesprächig *adj* talkative
gesprochen *vb see* **sprechen**
gesprungen *vb see* **springen**
Gestalt *f* ❶ shape ▷ *die Gestalt der Skulptur* the shape of the sculpture; **Gestalt annehmen** to take shape ❷ figure ▷ *Ich konnte eine dunkle Gestalt im Garten erkennen.* I could see a dark figure in the garden.; **in Gestalt von** in the form of
gestalten (*perf* **hat gestaltet**) *vb* [**2**] to lay out ▷ *Wer hat euren Garten gestaltet?* Who laid out your garden?; **Wie gestaltest du deine Freizeit?** How do you spend your spare time?
gestanden *vb see* **stehen**
Geständnis (*gen* **Geständnisses**, *pl* **Geständnisse**) *nt* confession
Gestank *m* stench
gestatten (*perf* **hat/ist gestattet**) *vb* [**2**] to allow; **Gestatten Sie?** May I?
gestattet *adj* permitted ▷ *Das ist nicht gestattet.* That is not permitted.
Geste *f* gesture
gestehen (*imperf* **gestand**, *perf* **hat gestanden**) *vb* [**72**] to confess
gestern *adv* yesterday; **gestern Abend** yesterday evening; **gestern Morgen** yesterday morning
gestohlen *vb see* **stehlen**
gestorben *vb see* **sterben**
gestört *adj* disturbed
gestreift *adj* striped
gesund *adj* healthy; **wieder gesund werden** to get better
Gesundheit *f* health; **Gesundheit!** Bless you!
gesungen *vb see* **singen**
getan *vb see* **tun**
Getränk (*pl* **Getränke**) *nt* drink
Getreide (*pl* **Getreide**) *nt* cereals *pl*
getrennt *adj* separate
Getriebe (*pl* **Getriebe**) *nt* gearbox
getrieben *vb see* **treiben**
getroffen *vb see* **treffen**
getrunken *vb see* **trinken**
geübt *adj* experienced
gewachsen *vb see* **wachsen** ▶ *adj* **jemandem gewachsen sein** to be a match for somebody; **Sie ist den Kindern nicht gewachsen.** She can't cope with the children.; **einer Sache gewachsen sein** to be up to something
gewagt *adj* risky
Gewalt *f* ❶ force ▷ *die Gewalt des Aufpralls* the force of the impact ❷ power ▷ *die staatliche Gewalt* the power of the state ❸ violence ▷ *Gewalt gegen Kinder* violence against children; **mit aller Gewalt** with all one's might
gewaltig *adj* tremendous ▷ *eine gewaltige Menge* a tremendous amount; **Sie hat sich gewaltig angestrengt.** She tried tremendously hard.; **ein gewaltiger Irrtum** a huge mistake
gewalttätig *adj* violent
gewann *vb see* **gewinnen**
Gewässer (*pl* **Gewässer**) *nt* waters *pl*
Gewebe (*pl* **Gewebe**) *nt* ❶ fabric ▷ *ein feines Gewebe* a fine fabric ❷ tissue ▷ *Die Gewebeprobe hat ergeben, dass alles in Ordnung ist.* The tissue samples showed that there's nothing wrong.
Gewehr (*pl* **Gewehre**) *nt* gun
Gewerkschaft *f* trade union
Unions in Germany are mainly organized within the **Deutscher Gewerkschaftsbund (DGB)**.
gewesen *vb see* **sein**
Gewicht (*pl* **Gewichte**) *nt* weight ▷ *das Gewicht meines Koffers* the weight of my case
Gewinn (*pl* **Gewinne**) *m* profit ▷ *Wir haben dieses Jahr einen Gewinn gemacht.* We've made a profit this year. ▷ *etwas*

mit Gewinn verkaufen to sell something at a profit

gewinnen (*imperf* **gewann**, *perf* **hat gewonnen**) *vb* **[30]** to win ▷ *Sie hat den ersten Preis gewonnen.* She won first prize.; **im Lotto gewinnen** to have a win on the lottery; **an etwas gewinnen** to gain in something

Gewinner (*pl* **Gewinner**) *m* winner

gewiss *adj, adv* certain ▷ *Zwischen den beiden besteht eine gewisse Ähnlichkeit.* There's a certain similarity between them.; **Das weiß ich ganz gewiss.** I'm certain about that.; **Das hat sie gewiss vergessen.** She must have forgotten.

Gewissen (*pl* **Gewissen**) *nt* conscience

gewissenhaft *adj* conscientious

Gewitter (*pl* **Gewitter**) *nt* thunderstorm

gewöhnen (*perf* **hat gewöhnt**) *vb* **[75]** **sich an etwas gewöhnen** to get used to something; **jemanden an etwas gewöhnen** to teach somebody something

Gewohnheit *f* habit ▷ *Es ist so eine Gewohnheit von mir, morgens Kaffee zu trinken.* It's a habit of mine to drink coffee in the morning. ▷ *zur Gewohnheit werden* to become a habit; **aus Gewohnheit** from habit

gewöhnlich *adj* ❶ usual ▷ *Ich bin heute früh zu der gewöhnlichen Zeit aufgestanden.* I got up at my usual time this morning.; **Ich stehe gewöhnlich um sieben Uhr auf.** I usually get up at seven o'clock. ❷ ordinary ▷ *Das sind ganz gewöhnliche Leute.* They're quite ordinary people.; **wie gewöhnlich** as usual

gewohnt *adj* usual ▷ *Mir fehlt die gewohnte Umgebung.* I miss my usual surroundings.; **etwas gewohnt sein** to be used to something

gewonnen *vb see* **gewinnen**

geworden *vb see* **werden**

geworfen *vb see* **werfen**

Gewürz (*gen* **Gewürzes**, *pl* **Gewürze**) *nt* spice

gewusst *vb see* **wissen**

Gezeiten *pl* tides *pl*

gezogen *vb see* **ziehen**

gezwungen *vb see* **zwingen**

gibt *vb see* **geben**

Gier *f* greed

gierig *adj* greedy ▷ *gierig nach Geld* greedy for money

gießen (*imperf* **goss**, *perf* **hat gegossen**) *vb* to pour ▷ *Sie goss mir Wein ins Glas.* She poured wine into my glass.; **die Blumen gießen** to water the flowers; **Es gießt in Strömen.** It's pouring.

Gießkanne *f* watering can

Gift (*pl* **Gifte**) *nt* poison

> Be careful! The German word **Gift** does not mean **gift**.

giftig *adj* poisonous ▷ *eine giftige Pflanze* a poisonous plant

ging *vb see* **gehen**

Gipfel (*pl* **Gipfel**) *m* ❶ peak ▷ *die schneebedeckten Gipfel* the snow-covered peaks ❷ height ▷ *Das ist der Gipfel der Unverschämtheit.* That's the height of impudence.

Giraffe *f* giraffe

Girokonto (*pl* **Girokonten**) *nt* current account

Gitarre *f* guitar ▷ *Ich spiele Gitarre.* I play the guitar.

glänzen *vb* **[36]** to shine ▷ *Ihr Gesicht glänzte vor Freude.* Her face shone with joy.

glänzend *adj* ❶ shining ▷ *ein glänzendes Metall* shining metal ❷ brilliant ▷ *Das war eine glänzende Leistung.* That was a brilliant achievement.

Glas (*gen* **Glases**, *pl* **Gläser**) *nt* glass

Glasscheibe *f* pane

glatt *adj* ❶ smooth ▷ *Der Tisch hat eine glatte Oberfläche.* The table has a smooth surface. ❷ slippery ▷ *Pass auf, die Straßen sind glatt.* Be careful, the streets are slippery.; **eine glatte Absage** a flat refusal; **eine glatte Lüge** a downright lie; **Das habe ich glatt vergessen.** It completely slipped my mind.

Glatteis (*gen* **Glatteises**) *nt* black ice ▷ *Bei Glatteis sollte man vorsichtig fahren.* When there's black ice, you have to drive carefully.

glauben *vb* [38] ❶ to believe ▷ *Ich habe kein Wort geglaubt.* I didn't believe a word. ❷ to think ▷ *Ich glaube, wir sind hier nicht willkommen.* I don't think we're welcome here.; **jemandem glauben** to believe somebody; **an etwas glauben** to believe in something

glaubwürdig *adj* ❶ credible ▷ *Das ist keine besonders glaubwürdige Geschichte.* That story's not particularly credible. ❷ trustworthy ▷ *Er ist ein glaubwürdiger Mensch.* He's a trustworthy person.

gleich *adj, adv* ❶ same ▷ *Wir haben das gleiche Problem.* We have the same problem. ❷ identical ▷ *Bei einem Würfel sind alle Seiten gleich.* All the sides of a cube are identical. ❸ the same ▷ *Ich behandle alle meine Kinder gleich.* I treat all my children the same. ▷ *Sie waren genau gleich angezogen.* They were dressed exactly the same.; **gleich groß** the same size ❹ equal ▷ *Wir wollen für die gleiche Arbeit auch die gleiche Bezahlung.* We want equal pay for equal work. ❺ straight away ▷ *Ich werde ihn gleich anrufen.* I'll call him straight away.; **Ich bin gleich fertig.** I'll be ready in a minute.; **Es ist mir gleich.** It's all the same to me.; **Zwei mal zwei gleich vier.** Two times two equals four.; **gleich nach** right after; **gleich neben** right next to

gleichaltrig *adj* of the same age ▷ *gleichaltrige Schüler* pupils of the same age ▷ *Sie sind gleichaltrig.* They're the same age.

gleichartig *adj* similar

Gleichberechtigung *f* equal rights *pl* ▷ *die Gleichberechtigung der Frau* equal rights for women

gleichen (*imperf* **glich**, *perf* **hat geglichen**) *vb* **jemandem gleichen** to be like somebody; **einer Sache gleichen** to be like something; **sich gleichen** to be alike

gleichfalls *adv* **Danke gleichfalls!** The same to you.

Gleichgewicht *nt* balance

gleichgültig *adj* ❶ indifferent ▷ *Er zeigte sich ihr gegenüber ziemlich gleichgültig.* He seemed to be quite indifferent to her. ❷ not important ▷ *Es ist doch gleichgültig, wie wir das machen.* It's not important how we do it.

gleichzeitig *adv* at the same time ▷ *Ich kann doch nicht drei Dinge gleichzeitig tun.* I can't do three things at the same time.

Gleis (*gen* **Gleises**, *pl* **Gleise**) *nt* ❶ line ▷ *die Straßenbahngleise* the tram lines ❷ platform ▷ *Achtung auf Gleis drei.* Attention on platform three.

Gletscher (*pl* **Gletscher**) *m* glacier

gliedern *vb* [88] to structure ▷ *Du musst deinen Aufsatz besser gliedern.* You must structure your essay better.

glitzern *vb* [88] ❶ to glitter ▷ *Das Wasser glitzerte in der Sonne.* The water glittered in the sun. ❷ to twinkle ▷ *Die Sterne glitzerten.* The stars twinkled.

Globalisierung *f* globalization

Glocke *f* bell; **etwas an die große Glocke hängen** to shout something from the rooftops

> Word for word, **etwas an die große Glocke hängen** means 'to hang something from the big bell'.

Glück *nt* ❶ luck ▷ *Ein vierblättriges Kleeblatt bringt Glück.* A four-leaf clover brings good luck.; **Glück haben** to be lucky; **Viel Glück!** Good luck!; **zum Glück** fortunately ❷ happiness ▷ *Sie strahlte vor Glück.* She was beaming with happiness.

glücklich *adj* ❶ happy ▷ *Ich bin sehr glücklich mit ihm.* I'm very happy with him. ▷ *Das waren glückliche Tage.* Those were happy days. ❷ lucky ▷ *Das war ein glücklicher Zufall.* That was a lucky coincidence.

Glückwunsch (*pl* **Glückwünsche**) *m* congratulations *pl* ▷ *Herzlichen Glückwunsch zur bestandenen Prüfung.* Congratulations on passing your exam.; **Herzlichen Glückwunsch zum Geburtstag.** Happy Birthday.

Glühbirne *f* light bulb

GmbH *abbr* (= *Gesellschaft mit beschränkter Haftung*) limited company

Gold *nt* gold

golden *adj* golden

Goldfisch (*pl* **Goldfische**) *m* goldfish ▷ *Ich habe zwei Goldfische.* I've got two goldfish.

Golf (*pl* **Golfe**) *m* gulf ▷ *der Persische Golf* the Persian Gulf
▶ *nt* golf ▷ *Mein Vater spielt Golf.* My father plays golf.

Golfplatz (*gen* **Golfplatzes**, *pl* **Golfplätze**) *m* golf course

Golfstrom *m* the Gulf Stream

gönnen *vb* [**38**] **sich etwas gönnen** to treat oneself to something; **Sie gönnt mir meinen Erfolg nicht.** She begrudges me my success.

Gott (*pl* **Götter**) *m* god; **Mein Gott!** For heaven's sake!; **Um Gottes willen!** For heaven's sake!; **Grüß Gott!** Hello!; **Gott sei Dank!** Thank God!

Göttin *f* goddess

Grab (*pl* **Gräber**) *nt* grave

graben (*pres* **gräbt**, *imperf* **grub**, *perf* **hat gegraben**) *vb* to dig

Graben (*pl* **Gräben**) *m* ditch

Grad (*pl* **Grad**) *m* degree ▷ *dreißig Grad im Schatten* thirty degrees in the shade

Grafikkarte *f* graphics card ▷ *Welche Grafikkarte hast du in deinem PC?* What graphics card do you have in your PC?

grafisch *adj* graphic

Gramm (*pl* **Gramme** *or* **Gramm**) *nt* gram ▷ *hundert Gramm Käse* a hundred grams of cheese

Grammatik *f* grammar

Gras (*gen* **Grases**, *pl* **Gräser**) *nt* grass

Gräte *f* bone ▷ *Dieser Fisch hat zu viele Gräten.* This fish has too many bones in it.

gratis *adv* free of charge

gratulieren (*perf* **hat gratuliert**) *vb* [**76**] **jemandem gratulieren** to congratulate somebody; **Gratuliere!** Congratulations!

grau *adj* grey

Graubrot (*pl* **Graubrote**) *nt* brown bread

Gräuel (*pl* **Gräuel**) *m* horror ▷ *die Gräuel des Bürgerkriegs* the horrors of civil war; **Das ist mir ein Gräuel.** I loathe it.

grauenhaft *adj* horrible

grausam *adj* cruel

Grausamkeit *f* cruelty

greifen (*imperf* **griff**, *perf* **hat gegriffen**) *vb* **nach etwas greifen** to reach for something; **um sich greifen** to spread

grell *adj* harsh ▷ *eine grelle Farbe* a harsh colour; **ein greller Schrei** a piercing scream

Grenze *f* ❶ border ▷ *Wir sind an der Grenze kontrolliert worden.* Our papers were checked at the border.
❷ boundary ▷ *Der Zaun ist die Grenze zum Grundstück des Nachbarn.* The fence marks the boundary with our neighbour's property. ❸ limit ▷ *die Grenzen des guten Geschmacks* the limits of good taste

grenzen *vb* [**36**] **an etwas grenzen** to border on something; **Das grenzt an Wahnsinn.** It verges on madness.

grenzenlos *adj* boundless

Greuel *m* *see* **Gräuel**

Grieche (*gen* **Griechen**, *pl* **Griechen**) *m* Greek

Griechenland *nt* Greece

Griechin *f* Greek

griechisch *adj* Greek

Griff (*pl* **Griffe**) *m* ❶ handle ▷ *Halte dich da an dem Griff fest.* Hold on to the handle. ❷ hold ▷ *Ich habe Judogriffe geübt.* I've been practising judo holds.
griffbereit *adj* handy ▷ *etwas griffbereit halten* to keep something handy
Grill (*pl* **Grills**) *m* grill
grillen *vb* [**48**] ❶ to grill ▷ *gegrillter Fisch* grilled fish ❷ to have a barbecue ▷ *Wir wollen am Sonntag grillen.* We'd like to have a barbecue on Sunday.
grinsen *vb* [**38**] to grin
Grippe *f* flu
grob *adj* ❶ coarse ▷ *grober Sand* coarse sand ❷ rough ▷ *Sei nicht so grob zu deiner Schwester.* Don't be so rough with your sister. ❸ serious ▷ *ein grober Fehler* a serious mistake
groß *adj, adv* ❶ big ▷ *Das war mein größter Fehler.* That was my biggest mistake. ▷ *Sie haben ein großes Haus.* They have a big house. ❷ tall ▷ *Mein Bruder ist viel größer als ich.* My brother is much taller than me. ▷ *Wie groß bist du?* How tall are you? ❸ great ▷ *Das war eine große Leistung.* That was a great achievement. ▷ *Er war ein großer Politiker.* He was a great politician.; **großen Hunger haben** to be very hungry; **die großen Ferien** the summer holidays; **Er hat sich nicht groß angestrengt.** He didn't try very hard.; **im Großen und Ganzen** on the whole
großartig *adj* splendid
Großbritannien *nt* Great Britain
Größe *f* ❶ size ▷ *Welche Schuhgröße hast du?* What size shoes do you take? ❷ height ▷ *Im Pass steht bei den Angaben zur Person auch die Größe.* Your height's also included in your passport under personal details.
Großeltern *pl* grandparents *pl*
Großmutter (*pl* **Großmütter**) *f* grandmother
großschreiben (*imperf* **schrieb groß**, *perf* **hat großgeschrieben**) *vb* [**61**] to write in capitals
Großstadt (*pl* **Großstädte**) *f* city
größtenteils *adv* for the most part
Großvater (*pl* **Großväter**) *m* grandfather
großzügig *adj, adv* generous ▷ *Meine Eltern sind sehr großzügig.* My parents are very generous. ▷ *Sie hat großzügig darauf verzichtet.* She generously did without.
grün *adj* green ▷ *Die Ampel ist grün.* The traffic lights are at green.
Grund (*pl* **Gründe**) *m* ❶ reason ▷ *Nenn mir einen Grund, warum wir das nicht so machen können.* Give me one reason why we can't do it like this.; **Aus welchem Grund ist er so böse?** Why is he so angry? ❷ ground ▷ *Das Haus ist auf felsigem Grund gebaut.* The house is built on rocky ground. ❸ bottom ▷ *Das Schiff sank auf den Grund des Meeres.* The ship sank to the bottom of the sea.; **im Grunde genommen** basically; **auf Grund** *see* **aufgrund**; **zu Grunde** *see* **zugrunde**
gründen *vb* [**54**] to found ▷ *Wir haben einen Fanklub gegründet.* We've founded a fan club.
gründlich *adj, adv* thorough ▷ *eine gründliche Vorbereitung zur Prüfung* thorough preparation for the exam ▷ *Wir haben das Haus gründlich geputzt.* We cleaned the house thoroughly.; **Ich habe mich gründlich geirrt.** I was completely wrong.
Grundsatz (*gen* **Grundsatzes**, *pl* **Grundsätze**) *m* principle
grundsätzlich *adj, adv* ❶ fundamental ▷ *Es bleibt die grundsätzliche Frage, ob das erlaubt werden soll.* The fundamental question remains: should it be allowed? ❷ basically ▷ *Grundsätzlich bin ich ja dafür, aber ...* Basically I'm in favour, but ... ❸ on principle ▷ *Ich bin grundsätzlich gegen die Prügelstrafe.* I'm against corporal punishment on principle.
Grundschule *f* primary school

a b c d e f g h i j k l m n o p q r s t u v w x y z

Grüne *pl* **die Grünen** the Greens *pl*
grunzen *vb* [**36**] to grunt
Gruppe *f* group
Gruß (*gen* **Grußes**, *pl* **Grüße**) *m* greeting; **viele Grüße** best wishes; **mit freundlichen Grüßen** yours sincerely; **Grüße an** regards to
grüßen *vb* [**31**] to say hello ▷ *Sie hat mich nicht gegrüßt.* She didn't say hello to me.; **Grüß Lorna von mir.** Give Lorna my regards.; **Lorna läßt dich grüßen.** Lorna sends her regards.
gucken *vb* [**38**] to look
Gulasch (*pl* **Gulaschs**) *m* goulash
gültig *adj* valid
Gummi (*pl* **Gummis**) *nt*
You can also say **der Gummi**.
rubber ▷ *Die Reifen sind aus Gummi.* The tyres are made of rubber.
Gummiband (*pl* **Gummibänder**) *nt* elastic band ▷ *Sie machte ein Gummiband um das Geschenk.* She put an elastic band round the present.
günstig *adj* convenient ▷ *Morgen wäre günstig.* Tomorrow would be convenient.; **eine günstige Gelegenheit** a favourable opportunity; **Das habe ich günstig bekommen.** It was a bargain.
Gurke *f* cucumber ▷ *Sie mag Gurkensalat nicht.* She doesn't like cucumber salad.; **saure Gurke** gherkin
Gurt (*pl* **Gurte**) *m* belt
Gürtel (*pl* **Gürtel**) *m* belt
gut *adj, adv* ❶ good ▷ *Ich habe gute Noten bekommen.* I got good marks. ▷ *Sie ist ein guter Mensch.* She's a good person. ▷ *Das ist ein guter Witz.* That's a good joke.; **In Englisch habe ich 'gut'.** I got a B in English.
German marks range from one (**sehr gut**) to six (**ungenügend**).
Alles Gute! All the best.; **also gut** all right then ❷ well ▷ *Sie hat das gut gemacht.* She did it well. ▷ *Ich kenne ihn gut.* I know him well.; **gut schmecken** to taste good; **gut drei Stunden** a good three hours; **Das kann gut sein.** That may well be.; **Gut, aber ...** OK, but ...; **Lass es gut sein.** That'll do.; **Es ist zum Glück gut gegangen.** Fortunately it came off.; **Mir geht's gut.** I'm fine.; **gut gemeint** well-meant; **gut tun** *see* **guttun**
Güter *ntpl* goods *pl*
gutgehen *vb* [**29**] *see* **gut**
gütig *adj* kind
gutmütig *adj* good-natured
Gutschein (*pl* **Gutscheine**) *m* voucher
guttun (*imperf* **tat gut**, *perf* **hat gutgetan**) *vb* [**81**] **jemandem guttun** to do somebody good
Gymnasium (*pl* **Gymnasien**) *nt* grammar school
Gymnastik *f* keep-fit ▷ *Ich mache einmal in der Woche Gymnastik.* I do keep-fit once a week.

h

Haar (*pl* **Haare**) *nt* hair ▷ *Sie hat dunkle Haare.* She's got dark hair.; **um ein Haar** nearly
haben (*pres* **hat**, *imperf* **hatte**, *perf* **hat gehabt**) *vb* [**32**] to have ▷ *Ich habe einen neuen Pulli.* I've got a new pullover. ▷ *Sie hat ihn nicht gesehen.* She hasn't seen him.; **Welches Datum haben wir heute?** What's the date today?; **Hunger haben** to be hungry; **Angst haben** to be afraid; **Woher hast du das?** Where did you get that from?; **Was hast du denn?** What's the matter with you?; **Ich hätte gern ...** I would like ...
Hackfleisch *nt* mince
Hafen (*pl* **Häfen**) *m* harbour
Hafenstadt (*pl* **Hafenstädte**) *f* port
Hafer *m* oats *pl*
Haferflocken *fpl* porridge oats *pl*
haftbar *adj* responsible ▷ *Eltern sind für ihre Kinder haftbar.* Parents are responsible for their children.
haften *vb* [**2**] to stick ▷ *Der Klebstreifen haftet nicht.* The adhesive tape isn't sticking.; **haften für** to be responsible for
Haftpflichtversicherung *f* third party insurance
Hagel *m* hail
hageln *vb* [**88**] **Es hagelt.** It's hailing.
Hahn (*pl* **Hähne**) *m* ❶ cock ▷ *Der Hahn krähte.* The cock crowed. ❷ tap ▷ *Der Hahn tropft.* The tap's dripping.
Hähnchen (*pl* **Hähnchen**) *nt* chicken ▷ *Heute gibt es Hähnchen.* We're having chicken today.
Hai (*pl* **Haie**) *m* shark
Haken (*pl* **Haken**) *m* ❶ hook ▷ *Häng deinen Anorak an den Haken.* Hang your anorak up on the hook. ❷ catch ▷ *Die Sache hat einen Haken.* There's a catch.
halb *adj* half ▷ *ein halber Kuchen* half a cake ▷ *eine halbe Stunde* half an hour; **halb eins** half past twelve
halbieren (*perf* **hat halbiert**) *vb* [**76**] to halve
Halbjahr (*pl* **Halbjahre**) *nt* six months *pl*
halbtags *adv* **halbtags arbeiten** to work part-time
Halbtagsarbeit *f* part-time job
half *vb see* **helfen**
Hälfte *f* half
Halle *f* hall ▷ *eine Messehalle* an exhibition hall
Hallenbad (*pl* **Hallenbäder**) *nt* indoor swimming pool
hallo *excl* hello!
Hals (*gen* **Halses**, *pl* **Hälse**) *m* ❶ neck ▷ *Ich habe einen steifen Hals.* I've got a stiff neck. ❷ throat ▷ *Mir tut der Hals weh.* My throat's sore.; **Hals über Kopf** in a rush
Halskette *f* necklace
Halsschmerzen *pl* sore throat *sg* ▷ *Ich habe Halsschmerzen.* I've got a sore throat.
Halstuch (*pl* **Halstücher**) *nt* scarf
halt *excl* stop!
haltbar *adj* durable ▷ *Das ist ein sehr haltbares Material.* That's a very durable

material.; **Butter ist nur begrenzt haltbar.** Butter only keeps for a limited time.; **'Mindestens haltbar bis ...'** 'Best before ...'

halten (*pres* **hält**, *imperf* **hielt**, *perf* **hat gehalten**) *vb* **[33]** ❶ to hold ▷ *Er hielt sie an der Hand.* He held her by the hand. ▷ *Kannst du das mal halten?* Can you hold that for a moment? ❷ to keep ▷ *Obst hält nicht lange.* Fruit doesn't keep long. ❸ to last ▷ *Ihre Freundschaft hat lange gehalten.* Their friendship has lasted a long time. ❹ to stop ▷ *Der Bus hielt vor dem Rathaus.* The bus stopped in front of the town hall.; **halten für** to regard as; **Ich habe sie für deine Mutter gehalten.** I took her for your mother.; **halten von** to think of; **sich rechts halten** to keep to the right

Haltestelle *f* stop ▷ *die Haltestelle der Straßenbahn* the tram stop

haltmachen *vb* **[48]** to stop

Haltung *f* ❶ posture ▷ *Er hat eine aufrechte Haltung.* He has an upright posture. ❷ attitude ▷ *Ich bewundere deine Haltung in dieser Frage.* I admire your attitude in this issue.

Hamburg *nt* Hamburg

The 'Free Hanseatic City of Hamburg' is one of the 16 **Länder**. It is a 'city-state' like Bremen and Berlin, and is Germany's principal seaport.

Hammer (*pl* **Hämmer**) *m* hammer

Hand (*pl* **Hände**) *f* hand

Handarbeit *f* ❶ manual work ▷ *Handarbeit macht ihm mehr Spaß als geistige Arbeit.* He enjoys manual work more than intellectual work. ❷ needlework ▷ *In Handarbeit hat sie eine Zwei.* She got a B in needlework.

Handball *m* handball

Handbremse *f* handbrake

Handbuch (*pl* **Handbücher**) *nt* manual

Handel *m* ❶ trade ▷ *der Handel mit Osteuropa* trade with Eastern Europe; **Dieses Gerät ist überall im Handel erhältlich.** This appliance is available in all shops and retail outlets. ❷ deal ▷ *Wir haben einen Handel abgeschlossen.* We have concluded a deal.

handeln *vb* **[34]** ❶ to act ▷ *Wir müssen schnell handeln.* We'll have to act quickly. ❷ to trade ▷ *Er handelt mit Gebrauchtwaren.* He trades in second-hand goods.; **mit jemandem handeln** to bargain with somebody; **Es handelt sich um ...** It's about ...; **handeln von** to be about

Handelsschule *f* business school

Handgepäck *nt* hand luggage

Händler (*pl* **Händler**) *m* dealer ▷ *Ich habe meinen Computerhändler danach gefragt.* I asked my computer dealer about it.

handlich *adj* handy

Handlung *f* ❶ act ▷ *Das war eine unüberlegte Handlung.* That was a rash act. ❷ plot ▷ *Ich habe die Handlung des Buches nicht genau verstanden.* I didn't really understand the plot of the book. ❸ shop ▷ *eine Eisenwarenhandlung* an ironmonger's shop

Handschrift *f* handwriting

Handschuh (*pl* **Handschuhe**) *m* glove

Handtasche *f* handbag

Handtuch (*pl* **Handtücher**) *nt* towel

Handy (*pl* **Handys**) *nt* mobile phone

Hang (*pl* **Hänge**) *m* slope

hängen (1) (*imperf* **hängte**, *perf* **hat gehängt**) *vb* **[48]** to hang ▷ *Sie hat die Wäsche auf die Leine gehängt.* She hung her washing on the line. ▷ *Sie hängten den Verbrecher.* They hanged the criminal.

hängen (2) (*imperf* **hing**, *perf* **hat gehangen**) *vb* **[35]** to hang ▷ *An der Wand hing ein Bild von Picasso.* A painting by Picasso was hanging on the wall.; **hängen an** to be attached to

harmlos *adj* harmless

harmonisch *adj* harmonious

hart *adj* hard ▷ *hart wie Stein* as hard as stone ▷ *Wir haben hart gearbeitet.* We worked hard.; **harte Worte** harsh words; **Das ist hart.** That's tough.; **ein hart gekochtes Ei** a hard-boiled egg

hartnäckig *adj* stubborn

Haschisch (*gen* **Haschisch**) *nt* hashish

Hase (*gen* **Hasen**, *pl* **Hasen**) *m* hare

Haselnuss (*pl* **Haselnüsse**) *f* hazelnut

Hass (*gen* **Hasses**) *m* hatred

hassen (*perf* **hat gehasst**) *vb* [31] to hate

hässlich *adj* ❶ ugly ▷ *Sie ist das hässlichste Mädchen der Klasse.* She's the ugliest girl in the class. ❷ nasty ▷ *Es ist hässlich, so etwas zu sagen.* It's nasty to say things like that.

hast *vb see* **haben**

hastig *adj* hasty

Haufen (*pl* **Haufen**) *m* heap ▷ *In ihrem Schlafzimmer lag ein Haufen schmutziger Wäsche.* There was a heap of dirty washing lying in her bedroom.; **ein Haufen ...** (*informal*) heaps of ...

häufig *adj, adv* ❶ frequent ▷ *sein häufiges Fehlen* his frequent absences ❷ frequently ▷ *Er fehlt häufig.* He is frequently absent.

Hauptbahnhof (*pl* **Hauptbahnhöfe**) *m* main station

Hauptfach (*pl* **Hauptfächer**) *nt* main subject

Hauptgericht (*pl* **Hauptgerichte**) *nt* main course

Hauptsache *f* main thing ▷ *Hauptsache, du bist gesund.* The main thing is that you're healthy.

Hauptschule *f* secondary school

Hauptstadt (*pl* **Hauptstädte**) *f* capital ▷ *Berlin ist die Hauptstadt von Deutschland.* Berlin's the capital of Germany.

Hauptstraße *f* main street

Hauptverkehrszeit *f* rush hour

Hauptwort (*pl* **Hauptwörter**) *nt* noun

Haus (*gen* **Hauses**, *pl* **Häuser**) *nt* house; **nach Hause** home; **zu Hause** at home

Hausarbeit *f* ❶ housework ▷ *Am Wochenende hilft mein Vater bei der Hausarbeit.* My father helps with the housework at the weekend. ❷ homework ▷ *Wir haben eine Hausarbeit zum Thema Umweltverschmutzung auf.* We've got homework on the subject of pollution.

Hausarzt (*gen* **Hausarztes**, *pl* **Hausärzte**) *m* family doctor

Hausaufgaben *fpl* homework ▷ *Heute waren die Hausaufgaben nicht schwierig.* Our homework wasn't difficult today.

Hausfrau *f* housewife

Haushalt (*pl* **Haushalte**) *m* ❶ household ▷ *den Haushalt führen* to run the household ❷ budget ▷ *der Haushalt für 2014* the 2014 budget

Hausmeister (*pl* **Hausmeister**) *m* caretaker

Hausnummer *f* house number

Hausschlüssel (*pl* **Hausschlüssel**) *m* front-door key

Hausschuh (*pl* **Hausschuhe**) *m* slipper

Haustier (*pl* **Haustiere**) *nt* pet

Haustür *f* front door

Haut (*pl* **Häute**) *f* skin

Hbf. *abbr* (= *Hauptbahnhof*) central station

Hebel (*pl* **Hebel**) *m* lever

heben (*imperf* **hob**, *perf* **hat gehoben**) *vb* to lift

Hecke *f* hedge

Hefe *f* yeast

Heft (*pl* **Hefte**) *nt* ❶ exercise book ▷ *Schreibt die Verbesserung in euer Heft.* Write the correction in your exercise books. ❷ issue ▷ *Hast du noch das letzte Heft von 'Geo'?* Have you got the latest issue of 'Geo'?

Heftklammer *f* paper clip

Heftpflaster (*pl* **Heftpflaster**) *nt* sticking plaster

Heide *f* moor ▷ *Wir haben einen Spaziergang durch die Heide gemacht.* We went for a walk over the moor.; **die Lüneburger Heide** Lüneburg Heath

Heidekraut *nt* heather

Heidelbeere *f* blueberry

a b c d e f g h i j k l m n o p q r s t u v w x y z

heilbar *adj* curable
heilen (*perf* **hat/ist geheilt**) *vb* [38]

> For the perfect tense use **haben** when the verb has an object and **sein** when there is no object.

❶ to cure ▷ *Viele Arten von Krebs kann man heilen.* Many kinds of cancer can be cured. ❷ to heal ▷ *Die Wunde ist schnell geheilt.* The wound healed quickly.
heilig *adj* holy
Heiligabend (*pl* **Heiligabende**) *m* Christmas Eve
Heilmittel (*pl* **Heilmittel**) *nt* remedy
heim *adv* home ▷ *Ich muss jetzt heim.* I'll have to go home now.
Heim (*pl* **Heime**) *nt* home ▷ *ein Heim für Kinder mit Lernschwierigkeiten* a home for children with learning difficulties
Heimat *f* homeland ▷ *Deutschland ist meine Heimat.* Germany's my homeland.
heimatlos *adj* homeless
Heimfahrt *f* journey home
heimgehen (*imperf* **ging heim**, *perf* **ist heimgegangen**) *vb* [29] to go home
heimlich *adj* secret ▷ *Er hat das heimlich gemacht.* He did it secretly.
Heimreise *f* journey home
Heimweg (*pl* **Heimwege**) *m* way home
Heimweh *nt* homesickness
Heirat *f* marriage
heiraten *vb* [2] to get married ▷ *Sie heiraten morgen.* They're getting married tomorrow.; **jemanden heiraten** to marry somebody
heiser *adj* hoarse
Heiserkeit *f* hoarseness
heiß *adj* hot ▷ *Mir ist heiß.* I'm hot. ▷ *heiße Schokolade* hot chocolate
heißen (*imperf* **hieß**, *perf* **hat geheißen**) *vb* ❶ to be called ▷ *Er heißt Marek.* He's called Marek. ❷ to mean ▷ *Das heißt, dass wir morgen früh aufstehen müssen.* That means that we'll have to get up early tomorrow.; **Es heißt ...** It is said ...; **das heißt** that is to say
heiter *adj* ❶ cheerful ▷ *Ich war in heiterer Laune.* I was in a cheerful mood. ❷ bright ▷ *Das Wetter wird heiter bis bewölkt.* The weather will be cloudy with bright spells.
heizen *vb* [36] to heat
Heizung *f* heating
hektisch *adj* hectic
Held (*gen* **Helden**, *pl* **Helden**) *m* hero
Heldin *f* heroine
helfen (*pres* **hilft**, *imperf* **half**, *perf* **hat geholfen**) *vb* [37] to help ▷ *Kann ich dir helfen?* Can I help you? ▷ *Die Tablette hat geholfen.* The pill helped. ▷ *jemandem bei etwas helfen* to help somebody with something; **sich zu helfen wissen** to be resourceful; **Es hilft nichts, du musst ...** It's no use, you'll have to ...
hell *adj* bright ▷ *Hier ist es schön hell.* It's nice and bright here.; **Sie hat einen hellen Teint.** She has a clear complexion.; **eine helle Farbe** a light colour; **ein Helles** a light beer
hellblond *adj* ash-blond
Helm (*pl* **Helme**) *m* helmet
Hemd (*pl* **Hemden**) *nt* shirt; **ein Unterhemd** a vest
Hemmung *f* inhibition ▷ *Er hat furchtbare Hemmungen.* He has terrible inhibitions.
Henne *f* hen
her *adv* ago ▷ *Das ist fünf Jahre her.* That was five years ago.; **von ... her** from ...; **Wo bist du her?** Where do you come from?; **Komm her zu mir.** Come here.; **Her damit!** Hand it over!
herab *adv* down
heran *adv* **Näher heran!** Come closer!
herauf *adv* up ▷ *Komm hier herauf.* Come up here.
heraus *adv* out
herausfordern (*perf* **hat herausgefordert**) *vb* [15] to challenge
herauskommen (*imperf* **kam heraus**, *perf* **ist herausgekommen**) *vb* [40] to come out ▷ *Die Maus ist aus ihrem Loch herausgekommen.* The mouse came out

of its hole.; **Dabei kommt nichts heraus.** Nothing will come of it.

herausnehmen (*pres* **nimmt heraus**, *imperf* **nahm heraus**, *perf* **hat herausgenommen**) *vb* [**52**] to take out ▷ *Sie hat das Lesezeichen aus dem Buch herausgenommen.* She took the bookmark out of the book.; **sich etwas herausnehmen** to take liberties

herausziehen (*imperf* **zog heraus**, *perf* **hat herausgezogen**) *vb* [**96**] to pull out

herb *adj* bitter ▷ *eine herbe Enttäuschung* a bitter disappointment ▷ *ein herber Geschmack* a bitter taste

herbei *adv* over ▷ *Alle eilten herbei.* Everyone hurried over.

Herbergseltern *pl* wardens *pl* (*in youth hostel*)

herbringen (*imperf* **brachte her**, *perf* **hat hergebracht**) *vb* [**13**] to bring here

Herbst (*pl* **Herbste**) *m* autumn ▷ *im Herbst* in autumn

Herbstferien *pl* autumn holidays *pl*

herbstlich *adj* autumnal

Herd (*pl* **Herde**) *m* cooker ▷ *ein Herd mit vier Platten* a cooker with four rings

Herde *f* herd ▷ *eine Herde Kühe* a herd of cows; **eine Schafherde** a flock of sheep

herein *adv* in ▷ *Noch mehr Menschen drängten herein.* Even more people pushed their way in. ▷ *Das Wasser strömte herein.* The water poured in.; **Herein!** Come in!

hereinfallen (*pres* **fällt herein**, *imperf* **fiel herein**, *perf* **ist hereingefallen**) *vb* [**22**] **auf etwas hereinfallen** to fall for something

hereinkommen (*imperf* **kam herein**, *perf* **ist hereingekommen**) *vb* [**40**] to come in

hereinlassen (*pres* **lässt herein**, *imperf* **ließ herein**, *perf* **hat hereingelassen**) *vb* [**42**] to let in

hereinlegen (*perf* **hat hereingelegt**) *vb* [**4**] **jemanden hereinlegen** (*informal*) to take somebody for a ride

hergeben (*pres* **gibt her**, *imperf* **gab her**, *perf* **hat hergegeben**) *vb* [**28**] to hand over ▷ *Gib das Buch her!* Hand over the book!; **sich zu etwas hergeben** to lend one's name to something

hergehen (*imperf* **ging her**, *perf* **ist hergegangen**) *vb* [**29**] **hinter jemandem hergehen** to follow somebody; **Es geht hoch her.** (*informal*) There are a lot of goings-on.

Hering (*pl* **Heringe**) *m* herring

herkommen (*imperf* **kam her**, *perf* **ist hergekommen**) *vb* [**40**] to come ▷ *Komm mal her!* Come here!

Herkunft (*pl* **Herkünfte**) *f* origin

Heroin *nt* heroin

Herr (*gen* **Herrn**, *pl* **Herren**) *m* ❶ gentleman ▷ *Er ist ein feiner Herr.* He's a fine gentleman. ▷ *Meine Herren!* Gentlemen! ❷ Lord ▷ *Herr, gib uns Frieden!* Lord, give us peace. ❸ Mr ▷ *Herr Mosbacher* Mr Mosbacher; **Mein Herr!** Sir!

herrlich *adj* marvellous

herrschen *vb* [**48**] ❶ to reign ▷ *Wann hat Karl der Große geherrscht?* When did Charlemagne reign? ❷ to be ▷ *Hier herrschen ja schöne Zustände.* This is a fine state of affairs. ▷ *Es herrscht noch Ungewissheit, wann das gemacht werden soll.* It's still uncertain when it's to be done.

herstellen (*perf* **hat hergestellt**) *vb* [**4**] to manufacture

Hersteller (*pl* **Hersteller**) *m* manufacturer

Herstellung *f* manufacture

herüber *adv* ❶ over here ▷ *Er kam langsam zu uns herüber.* He came slowly over to us. ❷ across ▷ *Sie versuchte, zu uns herüberzuschwimmen.* She tried to swim across to us.

herum *adv* round ▷ *Mach ein rotes Band herum.* Tie a red band round it.; **um etwas herum** round something
herumführen (*perf* **hat herumgeführt**) *vb* [**4**] to show around
herumgehen (*imperf* **ging herum**, *perf* **ist herumgegangen**) *vb* [**29**] to walk about ▷ *Wir sind ein paar Stunden in der Stadt herumgegangen.* We walked about the town for a couple of hours.; **um etwas herumgehen** to walk round something
sich **herumsprechen** (*pres* **spricht sich herum**, *imperf* **sprach sich herum**, *perf* **hat sich herumgesprochen**) *vb* [**70**] to get around
herunter *adv* down
herunterkommen (*imperf* **kam herunter**, *perf* **ist heruntergekommen**) *vb* [**40**] ❶ to come down ▷ *Sie ist zu uns heruntergekommen.* She came down to us. ❷ to become run-down ▷ *Das Haus ist in den letzten Jahren ziemlich heruntergekommen.* The house has become rather run-down in the past few years.
herunterladen (*pres* **lädt herunter**, *imperf* **lud herunter**, *perf* **hat heruntergeladen**) *vb (computer)* to download ▷ *eine Datei herunterladen* to download a file
hervorbringen (*imperf* **brachte hervor**, *perf* **hat hervorgebracht**) *vb* [**13**] to produce
hervorragend *adj* excellent
hervorrufen (*imperf* **rief hervor**, *perf* **hat hervorgerufen**) *vb* [**56**] to cause
Herz (*gen* **Herzens**, *pl* **Herzen**) *nt* ❶ heart ▷ *Es bricht mir fast das Herz.* It almost breaks my heart. ❷ hearts *sg* ▷ *Herz ist Trumpf.* Hearts is trumps.
Herzinfarkt (*pl* **Herzinfarkte**) *m* heart attack
herzlich *adj* warm ▷ *ein herzlicher Empfang* a warm welcome; **Wir wurden herzlich begrüßt.** We were warmly welcomed.; **Herzlich willkommen in Bamberg.** Welcome to Bamberg.; **Herzlichen Glückwunsch!** Congratulations.; **Herzliche Grüße.** Best wishes.
herzlos *adj* heartless
Herzschlag (*pl* **Herzschläge**) *m* ❶ heartbeat ▷ *bei jedem Herzschlag* with every heartbeat ❷ heart attack ▷ *Er hat einen Herzschlag bekommen.* He had a heart attack.
Hessen *nt* Hesse

Hessen is one of the 16 **Länder**. Its capital is Wiesbaden, yet its biggest city is Frankfurt am Main, which is Germany's principal financial centre and home to the Bundesbank.

Heu *nt* hay; **Geld wie Heu** stacks of money
heulen *vb* [**38**] ❶ to howl ▷ *Die Wölfe heulten.* The wolves were howling. ❷ to cry ▷ *Jetzt fang nicht gleich an zu heulen.* Now don't start crying.
Heuschnupfen *m* hay fever ▷ *Sie leidet an Heuschnupfen.* She suffers from hay fever.
heute *adv* today; **heute Abend** this evening; **heute Morgen** this morning; **heute früh** this morning
heutig *adj* today's ▷ *die heutige Jugend* today's youth
heutzutage *adv* nowadays
Hexe *f* witch
hielt *vb see* **halten**
hier *adv* here ▷ *hier drinnen* in here; **Hier spricht Lisa.** This is Lisa.; **hier bleiben** to stay here
hierher *adv* here
hiesig *adj* local ▷ *die hiesige Bevölkerung* the local population
hieß *vb see* **heißen**
Hilfe *f* help; **Erste Hilfe** first aid; **Hilfe!** Help!
hilflos *adj* helpless
hilfreich *adj* helpful
hilfsbereit *adj* ready to help
hilft *vb see* **helfen**

Himbeere *f* raspberry

Himmel (*pl* **Himmel**) *m* ❶ sky ▷ *ein wolkenloser Himmel* a cloudless sky ❷ heaven ▷ *in den Himmel kommen* to go to heaven

Himmelsrichtung *f* **die vier Himmelsrichtungen** the four points of the compass

hin *adv* **hin und zurück** there and back; **hin und her** to and fro; **Wo ist er hin?** Where has he gone?; **auf meine Bitte hin** at my request

hinab *adv* down

hinauf *adv* up

hinaufsteigen (*imperf* **stieg hinauf**, *perf* **ist hinaufgestiegen**) *vb* [**74**] to climb ▷ *Wir sind auf den Berg hinaufgestiegen.* We climbed up the mountain.

hinaus *adv* out

hinausgehen (*imperf* **ging hinaus**, *perf* **ist hinausgegangen**) *vb* [**29**] to go out ▷ *Sie ist kurz hinausgegangen.* She's gone out for a minute.; **über etwas hinausgehen** to exceed something

hinausschieben (*imperf* **schob hinaus**, *perf* **hat hinausgeschoben**) *vb* to put off ▷ *Sie haben die Entscheidung hinausgeschoben.* They put the decision off.

hindern *vb* [**88**] **jemanden an etwas hindern** to prevent somebody from doing something

Hindernis (*gen* **Hindernisses**, *pl* **Hindernisse**) *nt* obstacle

hinein *adv* in ▷ *Hinein mit dir!* In you go!

hineingehen (*imperf* **ging hinein**, *perf* **ist hineingegangen**) *vb* [**29**] to go in ▷ *Geh doch hinein.* Go in.; **hineingehen in** to go into

Hinfahrt *f* outward journey

hinfallen (*pres* **fällt hin**, *imperf* **fiel hin**, *perf* **ist hingefallen**) *vb* [**22**] to fall ▷ *Sie stolperte und fiel hin.* She stumbled and fell.

Hinflug (*pl* **Hinflüge**) *m* outward flight

hinhalten (*pres* **hält hin**, *imperf* **hielt hin**, *perf* **hat hingehalten**) *vb* [**33**] to hold out ▷ *Sie hielt ihren Teller hin.* She held out her plate.; **jemanden hinhalten** to put somebody off

hinken *vb* [**38**] to limp

hinlegen (*perf* **hat hingelegt**) *vb* [**4**] to put down ▷ *Leg das Buch dort drüben hin.* Put the book down over there.; **sich hinlegen** to lie down

hinnehmen (*pres* **nimmt hin**, *imperf* **nahm hin**, *perf* **hat hingenommen**) *vb* [**52**] to put up with ▷ *Das kann ich nicht länger hinnehmen.* I can't put up with this any longer.

Hinreise *f* outward journey

sich **hinsetzen** (*perf* **hat sich hingesetzt**) *vb* [**15**] to sit down

hinstellen (*perf* **hat hingestellt**) *vb* [**4**] to put ▷ *Wo soll ich die Vase hinstellen?* Where shall I put the vase?; **Er stellte sich vor den Lehrer hin.** He went and stood in front of the teacher.

hinten *adv* at the back ▷ *Er sitzt ganz hinten.* He sits at the very back.

hinter *prep*

> Use the accusative to express movement or a change of place. Use the dative when there is no change of place.

❶ behind ▷ *Stell dich hinter deine Schwester.* Stand behind your sister. ▷ *Ich saß hinter ihr.* I was sitting behind her. ❷ after ▷ *Wir hatten kurz hinter Köln eine Panne.* We broke down just after Cologne.

hintere *adj* back ▷ *die hinteren Reihen* the back rows; **der hintere Reifen** the rear tyre

hintereinander *adv* one after the other; **dreimal hintereinander** three times in a row

Hintergrund (*pl* **Hintergründe**) *m* background

hinterher *adv* afterwards

Hintern (*gen* **Hintern**, *pl* **Hintern**) *m* bottom

Hinterrad (*pl* **Hinterräder**) *nt* back wheel
hinüber *adv* over
hinübergehen (*imperf* **ging hinüber**, *perf* **ist hinübergegangen**) *vb* **[29]** to go over
hinunter *adv* down
Hinweis (*gen* **Hinweises**, *pl* **Hinweise**) *m* ❶ hint ▷ *Er hat mir nicht den kleinsten Hinweis gegeben, wie ich das machen soll.* He didn't give me the slightest hint as to how I was supposed to do it. ❷ instruction ▷ *Hinweise zur Bedienung* operating instructions
hinweisen (*imperf* **wies hin**, *perf* **hat hingewiesen**) *vb* **jemanden auf etwas hinweisen** to point something out to somebody
hinzufügen (*perf* **hat hinzugefügt**) *vb* **[15]** to add
Hirn (*pl* **Hirne**) *nt* brain
Hirsch (*pl* **Hirsche**) *m* stag
historisch *adj* historic
Hitparade *f* charts *pl*
Hitze *f* heat
hitzefrei *adj* **hitzefrei haben** to have time off school because of excessively hot weather

If the temperature reaches 28°C – 30°C at 10 a.m., then German children are sent home early and any afternoon lessons are cancelled.

Hitzschlag (*pl* **Hitzschläge**) *m* heatstroke
hoch *adj* high ▷ *zehn Meter hoch* ten metres high

Before a noun or after an article, use **hohe**.

▷ *ein hoher Zaun* a high fence; **Das ist mir zu hoch.** That's beyond me.

Word for word, **Das ist mir zu hoch** means 'It's too high for me'.

Hoch (*pl* **Hochs**) *nt* ❶ cheer ▷ *Ein Hoch auf die Gastgeber!* Three cheers for the hosts! ❷ area of high pressure ▷ *ein Hoch über dem Atlantik* an area of high pressure over the Atlantic
hochachtungsvoll *adv* yours faithfully
hochbegabt *adj* extremely talented
Hochhaus (*gen* **Hochhauses**, *pl* **Hochhäuser**) *nt* multistorey building
hochheben (*imperf* **hob hoch**, *perf* **hat hochgehoben**) *vb* to lift up
Hochsaison (*pl* **Hochsaisons**) *f* high season
Hochschule *f* ❶ college ❷ university
Hochsommer (*pl* **Hochsommer**) *m* high summer
Hochsprung (*pl* **Hochsprünge**) *m* high jump
höchst *adv* extremely
höchste *adj* highest ▷ *Die Zugspitze ist der höchste Berg Deutschlands.* The Zugspitze is the highest mountain in Germany.
höchstens *adv* at most
Höchstgeschwindigkeit *f* maximum speed
Hochzeit *f* wedding
Hochzeitstag (*pl* **Hochzeitstage**) *m* ❶ wedding day ▷ *An ihrem Hochzeitstag trug sie ein wunderschönes Kleid.* She wore a beautiful dress on her wedding day. ❷ wedding anniversary ▷ *Morgen ist ihr zehnter Hochzeitstag.* It's their tenth wedding anniversary tomorrow.
Hocker (*pl* **Hocker**) *m* stool
Hof (*pl* **Höfe**) *m* ❶ yard ▷ *Die Kinder spielen im Hof.* The children are playing in the yard. ❷ farm ▷ *Dieser Bauer hat den größten Hof im Dorf.* This farmer has the largest farm in the village.
hoffen *vb* **[38]** to hope ▷ *Ich hoffe, er kommt noch.* I hope he's coming.; **auf etwas hoffen** to hope for something
hoffentlich *adv* hopefully ▷ *Hoffentlich kommt er bald.* Hopefully he'll come soon. ▷ *Das passiert hoffentlich nie wieder.* Hopefully that won't happen again.; **Hoffentlich nicht.** I hope not.
Hoffnung *f* hope
hoffnungslos *adj* hopeless
hoffnungsvoll *adj* hopeful
höflich *adj* polite

Höflichkeit *f* politeness
hohe *adj*
> **hohe** is the form of **hoch** used before a noun.

high ▷ *ein hoher Zaun* a high fence
Höhe *f* height
Höhepunkt (*pl* **Höhepunkte**) *m* climax ▷ *der Höhepunkt des Abends* the climax of the evening
höher *adj, adv* higher
hohl *adj* hollow
Höhle *f* cave
holen *vb* [**38**] to get ▷ *Ich hole ihn.* I'll get him.; **jemanden holen lassen** to send for somebody
Holland *nt* Holland
Holländer (*pl* **Holländer**) *m* Dutchman; **Er ist Holländer.** He's Dutch.; **die Holländer** the Dutch
Holländerin *f* Dutchwoman; **Sie ist Holländerin.** She's Dutch.
holländisch *adj* Dutch
Hölle *f* hell
Holz (*gen* **Holzes**, *pl* **Hölzer**) *nt* wood
Holzkohle *f* charcoal
homosexuell *adj* homosexual
Honig (*pl* **Honige**) *m* honey
Hopfen (*pl* **Hopfen**) *m* hops *pl*
hörbar *adj* audible
Hörbuch (*pl* **Hörbücher**) *nt* audio book
horchen *vb* [**48**] ❶ to listen ▷ *Er horchte auf das kleinste Geräusch.* He listened for the slightest noise. ❷ to eavesdrop ▷ *Du hast an der Tür gehorcht!* You've been eavesdropping at the door!
hören *vb* [**38**] to hear ▷ *Ich höre dich nicht.* I can't hear you.; **Musik hören** to listen to music; **Radio hören** to listen to the radio
Hörer (*pl* **Hörer**) *m* receiver ▷ *Sie hat einfach den Hörer aufgelegt.* She simply put down the receiver.
Horizont (*pl* **Horizonte**) *m* horizon ▷ *am Horizont* on the horizon
horizontal *adj* horizontal
Horn (*pl* **Hörner**) *nt* horn
Horror *m* horror
Horrorfilm (*pl* **Horrorfilme**) *m* horror film
Hose *f* trousers *pl* ▷ *eine Hose* a pair of trousers
> Be careful! The German word **Hose** does not mean **hose**.

Hosentasche *f* trouser pocket
Hosenträger (*pl* **Hosenträger**) *m* braces *pl*
Hotel (*pl* **Hotels**) *nt* hotel
hübsch *adj* pretty
Hubschrauber (*pl* **Hubschrauber**) *m* helicopter
Hufeisen (*pl* **Hufeisen**) *nt* horseshoe
Hüfte *f* hip
Hügel (*pl* **Hügel**) *m* hill
Huhn (*pl* **Hühner**) *nt* chicken ▷ *Huhn mit Reis* chicken with rice
Hummel *f* bumblebee
Humor *m* humour; **Humor haben** to have a sense of humour
humorvoll *adj* humorous
Hund (*pl* **Hunde**) *m* dog
hundert *num* a hundred
Hunger *m* hunger; **Hunger haben** to be hungry
hungrig *adj* hungry
Hupe *f* horn ▷ *auf die Hupe drücken* to sound the horn
hupen *vb* [**38**] to sound the horn
hüpfen (*perf* **ist gehüpft**) *vb* [**38**] to hop
husten *vb* [**2**] to cough
Husten *m* cough ▷ *Sie hat Husten.* She has a cough.
Hut (*pl* **Hüte**) *m* hat
Hut *f* **auf der Hut sein** to be on one's guard
Hütte *f* hut
Hybridauto (*pl* **Hybridautos**) *nt* hybrid car
hygienisch *adj* hygienic
hysterisch *adj* hysterical ▷ *Sie wurde hysterisch.* She became hysterical.

I

ICE *abbr* (= *Intercityexpress*) Intercity Express train
ich *pron* I ▷ *Ich weiß nicht.* I don't know.; **Ich bin's!** It's me!
ideal *adj* ideal
Ideal (*pl* **Ideale**) *nt* ideal
Idee *f* idea
identifizieren (*perf* **hat identifiziert**) *vb* [**76**] to identify
identisch *adj* identical
Ideologie *f* ideology
Idiot (*gen* **Idioten**, *pl* **Idioten**) *m* idiot
idiotisch *adj* idiotic
Igel (*pl* **Igel**) *m* hedgehog
ihm *pron*

ihm is the dative of **er** and **es**.

❶ him ▷ *Kannst du ihm sagen, wie spät es ist?* Can you tell him what the time is? ❷ to him ▷ *Gib es ihm!* Give it to him. ❸ it ▷ *Das Meerschweinchen hat Hunger, gib ihm was zu essen.* The guinea pig's hungry, give it something to eat.
ihn *pron*

ihn is the accusative of **er**.

him ▷ *Ich habe ihn gesehen.* I saw him.
ihnen *pron*

ihnen is the dative of **sie** (plural).

❶ them ▷ *Ich sage es ihnen.* I'll tell them. ❷ to them ▷ *Gib es ihnen.* Give it to them.
Ihnen *pron*

Ihnen is the dative of **Sie**.

❶ you ▷ *Darf ich Ihnen etwas zu trinken anbieten?* May I offer you something to drink? ❷ to you ▷ *Darf ich Ihnen das geben?* May I give this to you?
ihr *pron* ❶ you ▷ *Habt ihr das gesehen?* Did you see that?

The familiar form of address **ihr** (singular **du**) is used when addressing family members, friends, children under 16 and pets.

▷ *Ihr seid es.* It's you.

ihr is also the dative of **sie** (singular).

❷ her ▷ *Kannst du ihr das bitte ausrichten?* Can you please tell her? ▷ *Er steht neben ihr.* He's standing beside her. ❸ to her ▷ *Gib es ihr.* Give it to her.
▶ *adj* ❶ her ▷ *Ihr Vater ist nett.* Her father's nice. ▷ *Ihre Mutter hat mir das gesagt.* Her mother told me. ▷ *Das ist ihr Fahrrad.* That's her bike. ❷ hers ▷ *Das ist nicht ihr Füller, ihrer ist schwarz.* That's not her pen, hers is black. ▷ *Meine Mutter heißt Ulla, ihre auch.* My mother's called Ulla, so is hers. ▷ *Mein Fahrrad war kaputt, also habe ich ihres genommen.* My bike was broken, so I took hers. ❸ their ▷ *Das ist ihr Lehrer.* That's their teacher. ▷ *Ihre Englischlehrerin ist netter als unsere.* Their English teacher's nicer than ours. ▷ *Ihr Haus liegt gleich neben unserem.* Their house is right next door to ours. ❹ theirs ▷ *Das ist nicht ihr Lehrer, ihrer heißt Herr Schulz.* That's not their teacher, theirs is called Mr Schulz. ▷ *Unsere Schule macht einen Wandertag, ihre nicht.* Our school is going rambling, theirs isn't.

Ihr *adj* ❶ your ▷ *Ihr Vater ist nett.* Your father's nice. ▷ *Ihre Mutter hat mir das gesagt.* Your mother told me. ▷ *Ist das Ihr Fahrrad?* Is that your bike? ▷ *Leben Ihre Eltern noch?* Are your parents still alive? ❷ yours ▷ *Das ist nicht Ihr Füller, Ihrer ist hier.* That's not your pen, yours is here. ▷ *Meine Mutter heißt Ulla, wie heißt Ihre?* My mother's called Ulla, what's yours called? ▷ *Mein Fahrrad ist kaputt, kann ich Ihres nehmen?* My bike's broken, can I take yours?

ihretwegen *adv*

> **ihretwegen** refers to **sie** (singular or plural).

❶ for her sake ▷ *Ich habe ihretwegen auf den Urlaub verzichtet.* I went without a holiday for her sake. ❷ on her account ▷ *Er hat sich ihretwegen furchtbar aufgeregt.* He got terribly upset on her account. ❸ as far as she's concerned ▷ *Sie sagt, dass du ihretwegen ruhig gehen kannst.* She says that as far as she's concerned you can go. ❹ for their sake ▷ *Wir haben ihretwegen auf den Urlaub verzichtet.* We went without a holiday for their sake. ❺ on their account ▷ *Er hat sich ihretwegen furchtbar aufgeregt.* He got terribly upset on their account. ❻ as far as they're concerned ▷ *Sie sagen, dass du ihretwegen ruhig gehen kannst.* They say that as far as they're concerned you can go.

Ihretwegen *adv*

> **Ihretwegen** refers to **Sie**.

❶ for your sake ▷ *Ich habe Ihretwegen auf den Urlaub verzichtet.* I went without a holiday for your sake. ❷ on your account ▷ *Er hat sich Ihretwegen furchtbar aufgeregt.* He got terribly upset on your account.

Illustrierte (*gen* **Illustrierten**) *f* magazine

im = **in dem**

Imbiss (*gen* **Imbisses**, *pl* **Imbisse**) *m* snack

Imbissstube *f* snack bar

immatrikulieren (*perf* **hat immatrikuliert**) *vb* [**76**] to register (*at university*)

immer *adv* always ▷ *Du kommst immer zu spät.* You're always late.; **immer wieder** again and again; **immer noch** still; **immer noch nicht** still not; **für immer** forever; **immer wenn ich ...** every time I ...; **immer schöner** more and more beautiful; **immer trauriger** sadder and sadder; **wer auch immer** whoever; **was auch immer** whatever

immerhin *adv* at least

Imperfekt (*pl* **Imperfekte**) *nt* imperfect

impfen *vb* [**38**] to vaccinate ▷ *jemanden gegen etwas impfen* to vaccinate somebody against something

Impfstoff (*pl* **Impfstoffe**) *m* vaccine

Impfung *f* vaccination

Import (*pl* **Importe**) *m* import

importieren (*perf* **hat importiert**) *vb* [**76**] to import

imstande *adj* **imstande sein, etwas zu tun** to be able to do something

in *prep*

> Use the accusative to express movement or a change of place. Use the dative when there is no change of place.

❶ in ▷ *Es ist im Schrank.* It's in the cupboard. ▷ *Sie ist in der Stadt.* She's in town. ▷ *Sie wurde rot im Gesicht.* She went red in the face. ❷ into ▷ *Lege es in diese Schublade.* Put it into this drawer. ▷ *Sie geht in die Stadt.* She's going into town.; **in der Schule sein** to be at school; **in die Schule gehen** to go to school; **in diesem Jahr** this year; **heute in zwei Wochen** two weeks today; **in sein** to be in

inbegriffen *adv* included

Inder (*pl* **Inder**) *m* Indian

Inderin *f* Indian

Indianer (*pl* **Indianer**) *m* Native American

Indianerin *f* Native American

indianisch *adj* Native American
Indien *nt* India
indisch *adj* Indian
Industrie *f* industry
Industriegebiet (*pl* **Industriegebiete**) *nt* industrial area
Infektion *f* infection
Infinitiv (*pl* **Infinitive**) *m* infinitive
infizieren (*perf* **hat infiziert**) *vb* [**76**] to infect ▷ *Sie hat ihren Bruder infiziert.* She infected her brother.; **sich bei jemandem infizieren** to catch something from somebody
Inflation *f* inflation
infolge *prep*
The preposition **infolge** takes the genitive.
as a result of
infolgedessen *adv* consequently
Informatik *f* computer science
Informatiker (*pl* **Informatiker**) *m* computer scientist
Information *f* information ▷ *Weitere Informationen lassen wir Ihnen zukommen.* We will send you further information.
informieren (*perf* **hat informiert**) *vb* [**76**] to inform; **sich über etwas informieren** to find out about something; **sich über jemanden informieren** to make enquiries about somebody
infrage *adv* **etwas infrage stellen** to question something; **nicht infrage kommen** to be out of the question
Ingenieur (*pl* **Ingenieure**) *m* engineer
Ingwer *m* ginger
Inhaber (*pl* **Inhaber**) *m* owner ▷ *Wir müssen den Inhaber des Hauses fragen, ob das geht.* We'll have to ask the owner of the house if it's all right.; **der Inhaber einer Lizenz** the licence holder
Inhalt (*pl* **Inhalte**) *m* ❶ contents *pl* ▷ *Der Inhalt der Flasche war grün.* The contents of the bottle were green. ❷ content ▷ *Fasse den Inhalt dieser Geschichte zusammen.* Summarize the content of this story. ❸ volume ▷ *Berechne den Inhalt des Würfels.* Calculate the volume of the cube.
Inhaltsangabe *f* summary
Inhaltsverzeichnis (*gen* **Inhaltsverzeichnisses**, *pl* **Inhaltsverzeichnisse**) *nt* table of contents
inklusive *prep, adv*
The preposition **inklusive** takes the genitive.
❶ inclusive of ▷ *ein Computer inklusive Bildschirm* a computer inclusive of monitor ❷ included ▷ *Die Bedienung ist inklusive.* Service is included.
Inland *nt* **im In- und Ausland** at home and abroad
innen *adv* inside
Innenstadt (*pl* **Innenstädte**) *f* town centre
innere *adj* internal ▷ *innere Blutungen* internal bleeding ▷ *die inneren Angelegenheiten des Landes* the internal matters of the country
innerhalb *adv, prep*
The preposition **innerhalb** takes the genitive.
❶ within ▷ *Das muss innerhalb von zwei Tagen gemacht werden.* That must be done within two days. ❷ during ▷ *Der Bus fährt nur innerhalb der Woche, nicht an Wochenenden.* The bus only runs during the week, not at the weekend.
inoffiziell *adj* unofficial
ins = **in das**
insbesondere *adv* particularly
Insekt (*pl* **Insekten**) *nt* insect
Insel *f* island
insgesamt *adv* in all ▷ *Er hat insgesamt drei Fahrräder.* He has three bikes in all. ▷ *Insgesamt waren dreihundert Leute gekommen.* In all, three hundred people came.
Instinkt (*pl* **Instinkte**) *m* instinct
Instrument (*pl* **Instrumente**) *nt* instrument

intelligent *adj* intelligent
Intelligenz *f* intelligence
intensiv *adj* intensive
Intercityexpress (*gen* **Intercityexpresses**, *pl* **Intercityexpresse**) *m* Intercity Express train
interessant *adj* interesting
Interesse (*pl* **Interessen**) *nt* interest; **Interesse haben an** to be interested in
interessieren (*perf* **hat interessiert**) *vb* **[76]** to interest ▷ *Es interessiert mich, was du in den Ferien erlebt hast.* I'm interested to know what you did in your holidays.; **sich interessieren für** to be interested in
Internat (*pl* **Internate**) *nt* boarding school
international *adj* international
Internet *nt* internet
Internet-Anbieter (*pl* **Internet-Anbieter**) *m* Internet Service Provider
Internet-Café (*pl* **Internet-Cafés**) *nt* internet café
Internetseite (*pl* **Internetseiten**) *f* web page
interpretieren (*perf* **hat interpretiert**) *vb* **[76]** to interpret
intransitiv *adj* intransitive
inzwischen *adv* meanwhile
Irak *m* Iraq
irakisch *adj* Iraqi
Iran *m* Iran
iranisch *adj* Iranian
Ire (*gen* **Iren**, *pl* **Iren**) *m* Irishman; **die Iren** the Irish
irgend *adv* at all ▷ *Komm, wenn es irgend geht.* Come if it's at all possible.
irgendein *adj* ❶ some ▷ *Irgendein Mann hat mir das gesagt.* Some man told me. ▷ *Irgendeine Ausrede wird dir schon einfallen.* You'll think of some excuse. ❷ any ▷ *Ich will nicht irgendeinen Computer.* I don't just want any computer. ▷ *Gibt es nicht irgendeine Möglichkeit?* Isn't there any chance? ▷ *Welchen Kuli willst du? — Irgendeinen.* Which pen do you want? — Any one.
irgendetwas *pron* ❶ something ▷ *irgendetwas Schönes* something nice ❷ anything ▷ *Hast du irgendetwas gehört?* Did you hear anything?
irgendjemand *pron* ❶ somebody ▷ *Das hat mir irgendjemand gesagt.* Somebody told me. ❷ anybody ▷ *Hast du irgendjemanden gesehen?* Did you see anybody?
irgendwann *adv* sometime
irgendwas *pron* ❶ something ▷ *Er murmelte irgendwas.* He murmured something. ❷ anything ▷ *Was soll ich anziehen? — Irgendwas.* What shall I wear? — Anything.
irgendwie *adv* somehow
irgendwo *adv* somewhere
Irin *f* Irishwoman
irisch *adj* Irish
Irland *nt* Ireland
Ironie *f* irony
ironisch *adj* ironic ▷ *Das war ironisch gemeint.* That was meant to be ironic.
irre *adj, adv* ❶ mad ▷ *Wer ist denn auf diese irre Idee gekommen?* Who thought up this mad idea? ❷ fantastic ▷ *Das war ein irres Konzert.* That was a fantastic concert. ❸ incredibly ▷ *Er ist irre schnell gefahren.* He drove incredibly fast. ▷ *Die Party war irre gut.* The party was incredibly good.
irreführen (*perf* **hat irregeführt**) *vb* **[4]** to mislead
irren *vb* **[38]**

> Use **haben** to form the perfect tense for 'to be mistaken' but **sein** for 'to wander about'.

to wander about ▷ *Sie ist durch die Straßen geirrt.* She wandered about the streets.; **sich irren** to be mistaken ▷ *Du hast dich geirrt.* You were mistaken.
Irrtum (*pl* **Irrtümer**) *m* mistake
Islam *m* Islam
Island *nt* Iceland
Israel *nt* Israel

a b c d e f g h i j k l m n o p q r s t u v w x y z

Israeli (*pl* **Israelis**) *mf* Israeli ▷ *Sie ist mit einem Israeli verheiratet.* She is married to an Israeli.
israelisch *adj* Israeli
isst *vb see* **essen**
ist *vb see* **sein**
Italien *nt* Italy
Italiener (*pl* **Italiener**) *m* Italian
Italienerin *f* Italian
italienisch *adj* Italian

◆ J

ja *adv* ❶ yes ▷ *Hast du das gesehen? — Ja.* Did you see that? — Yes, I did.; **Ich glaube ja.** I think so. ❷ really? ▷ *Ich habe mir ein neues Auto gekauft. — Ach ja?* I've bought a new car. — Really?; **Du kommst, ja?** You're coming, aren't you?; **Sei ja vorsichtig!** Do be careful.; **Sie wissen ja, dass ...** As you know, ...; **Tu das ja nicht!** Don't you dare do that!; **Ich habe es ja gewusst.** I just knew it.; **ja, also ...** well ... ▷ *Ja, also wenn ihr alle geht, dann gehe ich mit.* Well, if you're all going, then I'm going too.
Jacht *f* yacht
Jacke *f* ❶ jacket ▷ *Sie trug einen blauen Rock und eine schwarze Jacke.* She was wearing a blue skirt and a black jacket. ❷ cardigan ▷ *Wenn es dir kalt ist, solltest du eine Jacke anziehen.* If you're cold, you should put on a cardigan.
Jackett (*pl* **Jacketts**) *nt* jacket
Jagd (*pl* **Jagden**) *f* ❶ hunt ▷ *Er fiel während der Jagd vom Pferd.* He fell off his horse during the hunt. ❷ hunting

▷ *Alan geht oft zur Jagd.* Alan often goes hunting.
jagen *vb* [**38**]

> Use **haben** to form the perfect tense for 'to hunt' or 'to chase' but **sein** for 'to race'.

❶ to hunt ▷ *Sonntags geht er jagen.* He goes hunting on Sundays. ▷ *Er hat in Afrika Löwen gejagt.* He hunted lions in Africa. ▷ *Meine Katze jagt Mäuse.* My cat hunts mice. ❷ to chase ▷ *Die Polizei hat die Bankräuber gejagt, aber nicht eingeholt.* The police chased the bank robbers but didn't catch them. ❸ to race ▷ *Wir sind mit ihr ins Krankenhaus gejagt.* We raced with her to the hospital.; **Damit kann man mich jagen.** I can't stand that.
Jahr (*pl* **Jahre**) *nt* year ▷ *Ich bin vierzehn Jahre alt.* I'm fourteen years old.; **die Neunzigerjahre** the nineties
Jahreszeit *f* season; **zu jeder Jahreszeit** throughout the year
Jahrhundert (*pl* **Jahrhunderte**) *nt* century
jährlich *adj, adv* yearly
Jahrmarkt (*pl* **Jahrmärkte**) *m* funfair
Jahrtausend (*pl* **Jahrtausende**) *nt* millennium
Jalousie *f* Venetian blind
jammern *vb* [**88**] to whine ▷ *Hör auf zu jammern!* Stop whining.
Januar (*gen* **Januar** *or* **Januars**, *pl* **Januare**) *m* January ▷ *im Januar* in January ▷ *am dritten Januar* on the third of January ▷ *Ulm, den 3. Januar 2008* Ulm, 3 January 2008 ▷ *Heute ist der dritte Januar.* Today is the third of January.
Japan *nt* Japan
Japaner (*pl* **Japaner**) *m* Japanese
Japanerin *f* Japanese
japanisch *adj* Japanese
je *adv, conj* ❶ ever ▷ *Warst du je in Italien?* Have you ever been to Italy? ▷ *Hast du so was je gesehen?* Did you ever see anything like it? ▷ *besser denn je* better than ever ❷ each ▷ *Wir haben je zwei Stück bekommen.* We got two pieces each. ▷ *Sie zahlten je zehn Euro.* They paid ten euros each.; **je nach** depending on; **je nachdem** it depends; **je nachdem, ob ...** depending on whether ...; **je ... umso ...** the ... the ...; **je eher, desto besser** the sooner the better
Jeans (*pl* **Jeans**) *f* jeans *pl*; **eine Jeans** a pair of jeans
jede *adj, pron* ❶ every ▷ *Jeder Schüler bekommt ein Zeugnis.* Every pupil receives a report. ▷ *Ich besuche sie jede Woche.* I visit her every week. ▷ *Er gab jedem Mädchen ein Bonbon.* He gave every girl a sweet.; **jeder** everybody ❷ each ▷ *Jeder von euch bekommt ein Stück.* Each of you will get a piece. ▷ *Jede seiner Freundinnen war anders.* Each of his girlfriends was different. ▷ *Jedes der Kinder hat mir etwas geschenkt.* Each child gave me something.; **jedes Mal** every time
jedenfalls *adv* in any case
jederzeit *adv* at any time
jedoch *adv* however
jemals *adv* ever
jemand *pron* ❶ somebody ▷ *Jemand hat mir gesagt, dass du krank bist.* Somebody told me that you were ill. ❷ anybody ▷ *War jemand zu Hause?* Was anybody at home?
jene *pron* ❶ that ▷ *in jener Zeit* at that time ❷ those ▷ *in jenen Tagen* in those days
jetzt *adv* now ▷ *Sie ist jetzt in der Schweiz.* She's in Switzerland now.
jeweils *adv* **jeweils zwei zusammen** two at a time; **zu jeweils fünf Euro** at five euros each
Job (*pl* **Jobs**) *m* (*informal*) job
Jod *nt* iodine
joggen *vb* [**48**]

> Use **haben** for the perfect tense when you describe the activity and **sein** when you describe the motion.

to jog ▷ *Früher habe ich oft gejoggt.* I used to jog a lot. ▷ *Wir sind durch den Wald gejoggt.* We jogged through the woods.
Jogging *nt* jogging
Jogginganzug (*pl* **Jogginganzüge**) *m* tracksuit
Joghurt (*pl* **Joghurts**) *m* yogurt
Jogurt (*pl* **Jogurts**) *m* yogurt
Johannisbeere *f* redcurrant ▷ *Johannisbeeren sind mir zu sauer.* Redcurrants are too sour for me.; **Schwarze Johannisbeere** blackcurrant
Journalist (*gen* **Journalisten**, *pl* **Journalisten**) *m* journalist
jubeln *vb* [**34**] to rejoice
Jubiläum (*pl* **Jubiläen**) *nt* anniversary ▷ *Nächstes Jahr feiert unsere Schule ihr zwanzigjähriges Jubiläum.* Our school's celebrating its twentieth anniversary next year.
jucken *vb* [**38**] to be itchy ▷ *Meine Nase juckt.* My nose is itchy. ▷ *Es juckt mich am Arm.* My arm's itchy.
Jude (*gen* **Juden**, *pl* **Juden**) *m* Jew
Jüdin *f* Jew
jüdisch *adj* Jewish
Jugend *f* youth ▷ *In meiner Jugend habe ich Fußball gespielt.* I used to play football in my youth. ▷ *die Jugend von heute* the youth of today
Jugendherberge *f* youth hostel
Jugendklub (*pl* **Jugendklubs**) *m* youth club
jugendlich *adj* youthful ▷ *Er hat ein jugendliches Gesicht.* He has a youthful face. ▷ *Sie sieht sehr jugendlich aus.* She looks very youthful.
Jugendliche (*gen* **Jugendlichen**, *pl* **Jugendlichen**) *mf* teenager ▷ *Ich habe einen Jugendlichen dabei beobachtet, wie er die Wand besprüht hat.* I watched a teenager spray the wall.
Jugendzentrum (*pl* **Jugendzentren**) *nt* youth centre
Juli (*gen* **Juli** *or* **Julis**, *pl* **Julis**) *m* July ▷ *im Juli* in July ▷ *am dritten Juli* on the third of July ▷ *Ulm, den 3. Juli 2008* Ulm, 3 July 2008 ▷ *Heute ist der dritte Juli.* Today is the third of July.
jung *adj* young ▷ *Er ist drei Jahre jünger als ich.* He's three years younger than me.
Junge (*gen* **Jungen**, *pl* **Jungen**) *m* boy ▷ *In unserer Klasse gibt es zehn Jungen und fünfzehn Mädchen.* There are ten boys and fifteen girls in our class.
▶ *nt* young animal; **eine Löwin mit ihren Jungen** a lioness with her young
Jungfrau *f* ❶ virgin ❷ Virgo ▷ *Veronika ist Jungfrau.* Veronika's Virgo.
jüngste *adj* ❶ youngest ▷ *Er ist der jüngste Schüler der Klasse.* He's the youngest pupil in the class. ❷ latest ▷ *die jüngsten Entwicklungen* the latest developments
Juni (*gen* **Juni** *or* **Junis**, *pl* **Junis**) *m* June ▷ *im Juni* in June ▷ *am fünfzehnten Juni* on the fifteenth of June ▷ *Ulm, den 3. Juni 2009* Ulm, 3 June 2009 ▷ *Heute ist der dritte Juni.* Today is the third of June.

k

Kabel (*pl* **Kabel**) *nt* ❶ wire ▷ *Das Kabel des Telefons ist zu kurz.* The telephone wire is too short. ❷ cable ▷ *Das Kabel der Seilbahn muss regelmäßig überprüft werden.* The cable on the cable car has to be checked regularly.

Kabelfernsehen *nt* cable television

Kabine *f* ❶ cabin ▷ *Wir hatten zu zweit eine Kabine auf dem Schiff.* The two of us shared a cabin on the ship. ❷ cubicle ▷ *Sie können das Kleid dort hinten in der Kabine anprobieren.* You can try the dress on in the cubicle over there.

Käfer (*pl* **Käfer**) *m* beetle

Kaffee (*pl* **Kaffees** *or* **Kaffee**) *m* coffee ▷ *Herr Ober, zwei Kaffee bitte.* Two coffees please, waiter.

Kaffeekanne *f* coffeepot

Kaffeepause *f* coffee break ▷ *Wir machten Kaffeepause.* We had a coffee break.

Käfig (*pl* **Käfige**) *m* cage

kahl *adj* bald ▷ *sein kahler Kopf* his bald head; **die kahlen Bäume im Winter** the bare trees in winter; **kahl geschoren** shaven

Kakao (*pl* **Kakaos** *or* **Kakao**) *m* cocoa ▷ *Herr Ober, zwei Kakao bitte.* Two cups of cocoa please, waiter.

Kalb (*pl* **Kälber**) *nt* calf *(animal)*

Kalbfleisch *nt* veal

Kalender (*pl* **Kalender**) *m* ❶ calendar ▷ *An der Wand hing ein Kalender mit Bildern von Picasso.* A calendar with pictures by Picasso was hanging on the wall. ❷ diary ▷ *Sie holte ihren Kalender aus der Tasche.* She got her diary out of her bag.

Kalorie *f* calorie

kalorienarm *adj* low in calories

kalt *adj* cold ▷ *Heute ist es kälter als gestern.* It's colder today than yesterday. ▷ *Mir ist kalt.* I'm cold.; **etwas kalt stellen** to chill something

Kälte *f* ❶ cold ▷ *Bei dieser Kälte gehe ich nicht raus.* I'm not going out in this cold. ❷ coldness ▷ *Die Kälte des Wassers hat uns vom Baden abgehalten.* The coldness of the water stopped us from bathing.

kam *vb see* **kommen**

Kamera (*pl* **Kameras**) *f* camera

Kamerad (*gen* **Kameraden**, *pl* **Kameraden**) *m* friend

Kamin (*pl* **Kamine**) *m* open fire; **Wir saßen am Kamin.** We sat by the fire.

Kamm (*pl* **Kämme**) *m* comb

kämmen *vb* [38] to comb ▷ *Sie kann es nicht leiden, wenn man sie kämmt.* She can't stand having her hair combed. ▷ *Ich muss meiner kleinen Schwester die Haare kämmen.* I have to comb my little sister's hair.; **sich kämmen** to comb one's hair

Kampf (*pl* **Kämpfe**) *m* ❶ fight ▷ *der Kampf zwischen Tyson und Bruno* the fight between Tyson and Bruno ❷ contest ▷ *Dieses Jahr findet der Kampf um den Pokal in Großbritannien statt.* The contest for the cup is taking place in Great Britain this year. ❸ struggle ▷ *Ich habe die Prüfung geschafft, aber es*

war ein Kampf. I passed the exam but it was a struggle.
kämpfen *vb* [**38**] to fight
Kanada *nt* Canada
Kanadier (*pl* **Kanadier**) *m* Canadian
Kanadierin *f* Canadian
kanadisch *adj* Canadian
Kanal (*pl* **Kanäle**) *m* ❶ canal ▷ *Diese beiden Flüsse sind durch einen Kanal verbunden.* These two rivers are connected by a canal. ❷ drain
Kanarienvogel (*pl* **Kanarienvögel**) *m* canary
Kandidat (*gen* **Kandidaten**, *pl* **Kandidaten**) *m* candidate
Känguru (*pl* **Kängurus**) *nt* kangaroo
Kaninchen (*pl* **Kaninchen**) *nt* rabbit
Kanister (*pl* **Kanister**) *m* can ▷ *ein Benzinkanister* a petrol can
kann *vb see* **können**
Kanne *f* ❶ *(for coffee)* pot ❷ *(for milk)* churn ❸ watering can
Kante *f* edge
Kantine *f* canteen ▷ *Mittags isst sie in der Kantine.* She eats in the canteen at lunchtime.
Kanu (*pl* **Kanus**) *nt* canoe; **Kanu fahren** to go canoeing
Kanzler (*pl* **Kanzler**) *m* chancellor
Kapital *nt* capital *(money)*
Kapitän (*pl* **Kapitäne**) *m* captain
Kapitel (*pl* **Kapitel**) *nt* chapter
Kappe *f* cap
kaputt *adj* ❶ broken ▷ *Mein Computer ist kaputt.* My computer's broken.; **Am Auto ist etwas kaputt.** There's something wrong with the car.; **kaputt machen** to break ❷ *(informal)* knackered ▷ *Ich bin von der Wanderung total kaputt.* I'm completely knackered after the walk.
kaputtgehen (*imperf* **ging kaputt**, *perf* **ist kaputtgegangen**) *vb* [**29**] ❶ to break ▷ *Mein Computer ist gestern kaputtgegangen.* My computer broke yesterday. ❷ *(material)* to wear out ❸ *(plant)* to die ❹ *(relationship)* to break up
kaputtmachen (*perf* **hat kaputtgemacht**) *vb* [**48**] to wear out ▷ *Die viele Arbeit macht mich noch kaputt.* All this work is wearing me out.; **sich kaputtmachen** to wear oneself out
Kapuze *f* hood ▷ *ein Anorak mit Kapuze* an anorak with a hood
Karfreitag *m* Good Friday
kariert *adj* ❶ checked ▷ *Sie hatte ein kariertes Kleid an.* She was wearing a checked dress. ❷ squared ▷ *Für Mathe brauchst du ein Heft mit kariertem Papier.* You need an exercise book with squared paper for maths.
Karies *f* tooth decay ▷ *Sie hat Karies.* She has tooth decay.
Karneval (*pl* **Karnevale** *or* **Karnevals**) *m* carnival

The German carnival season lasts from 11 November to Shrove Tuesday but most events, fancy-dress processions and parties take place in the week leading up to Ash Wednesday.

Karo (*pl* **Karos**) *nt* ❶ square ▷ *Das Muster bestand aus kleinen Karos.* The pattern was made up of little squares. ❷ diamonds *sg* ▷ *Karo ist Trumpf.* Diamonds is trumps.
Karotte *f* carrot
Karriere *f* career; **Karriere machen** to get on
Karte *f* ❶ card ▷ *Sie hat uns aus dem Urlaub eine Karte geschickt.* She sent us a card from her holiday. ▷ *Ich weiß nicht, welche Karte ich ausspielen soll.* I don't know which card I should play.; **die Gelbe Karte** the yellow card; **die Rote Karte** the red card ❷ map ▷ *Sieh mal auf der Karte nach, wie weit wir noch fahren müssen.* Look on the map to see how far we still have to go. ❸ menu ▷ *Der Ober brachte uns die Karte.* The waiter brought us the menu. ❹ ticket ▷ *Kannst du Karten fürs Konzert besorgen?* Can you get us tickets for the concert? ▷ *Ich fahre morgen nach Bonn, die Karte*

habe ich schon gekauft. I'm going to Bonn tomorrow, I've already bought my ticket.; **alles auf eine Karte setzen** to put all one's eggs in one basket

> Word for word, **alles auf eine Karte setzen** means 'to bet everything on one card'.

Kartenspiel (*pl* **Kartenspiele**) *nt* ❶ card game ▷ *Ich habe ein neues Kartenspiel gelernt.* I've learned a new card game. ❷ pack of cards ▷ *Hast du ein Kartenspiel da?* Have you got a pack of cards?

Kartoffel *f* potato

Kartoffelbrei *m* mashed potatoes *pl*

Kartoffelsalat (*pl* **Kartoffelsalate**) *m* potato salad

Karton (*pl* **Kartons**) *m* ❶ cardboard ▷ *Wir haben das Bild auf Karton aufgezogen.* We mounted the picture on cardboard. ❷ cardboard box ▷ *Sie packte die Bücher in einen Karton.* She packed the books in a cardboard box.

Karussell (*pl* **Karussells**) *nt* roundabout ▷ *Ich möchte Karussell fahren.* I'd like to go on the roundabout.

Käse (*pl* **Käse**) *m* cheese

Käsekuchen (*pl* **Käsekuchen**) *m* cheesecake

Kaserne *f* barracks *pl* ▷ *In unserer Nähe gibt es eine Kaserne.* There's a barracks near us.

Kasse *f* ❶ till ▷ *Die meisten Geschäfte haben elektronische Kassen.* Most shops have electronic tills. ❷ checkout ▷ *an der Kasse* at the checkout ▷ *Es war nur eine von fünf Kassen besetzt.* Only one of the five checkouts was open. ❸ box office ▷ *Sie können Ihre Karten telefonisch vorbestellen und an der Kasse abholen.* You may order your tickets in advance and collect them from the box office. ❹ ticket office ▷ *Karten fürs Fußballspiel bekommen Sie auch an der Kasse des Stadions.* You can also get tickets for the football match at the ticket office in the stadium. ❺ cash box ▷ *Alle Barbeträge bewahren wir in dieser Kasse auf.* We keep all the cash in this cash box. ❻ health insurance ▷ *Bei welcher Kasse sind Sie versichert?* What health insurance have you got?

> In Germany one can choose between different health insurance schemes. There is no 'National Health Service'.

gut bei Kasse sein (*informal*) to be in the money

Kassenzettel (*pl* **Kassenzettel**) *m* receipt

Kassette *f* ❶ tape ▷ *Diesen Song habe ich auf Kassette.* I've got this song on tape. ▷ *eine Videokassette* a video tape ❷ small box ▷ *Sie bewahrt ihren Schmuck in einer Kassette auf.* She keeps her jewellery in a small box.

kassieren (*perf* **hat kassiert**) *vb* [76] to take ▷ *Die Polizei hat seinen Führerschein kassiert.* The police took his driving licence.; **Der Parkwächter hat zehn Euro Parkgebühren kassiert.** The parking attendant charged us ten euros to park the car.; **Darf ich kassieren?** Would you like to pay now?

Kastanie *f* ❶ chestnut ❷ chestnut tree

Kasten (*pl* **Kästen**) *m* ❶ box ▷ *Er warf den Brief in den Kasten.* He put the letter in the box. ❷ case ▷ *Sie legte die Geige zurück in den Kasten.* She put the violin back in its case.; **ein Kasten Bier** a crate of beer

Katalog (*pl* **Kataloge**) *m* catalogue

Katalysator (*pl* **Katalysatoren**) *m* catalytic converter ▷ *ein Auto mit Katalysator* a car with catalytic converter

katastrophal *adj, adv* catastrophic; **katastrophal schlecht** appallingly bad

Katastrophe *f* disaster

Kategorie *f* category

Kater (*pl* **Kater**) *m* ❶ tomcat ▷ *Wir haben einen Kater und eine Katze.* We have a tomcat and a female cat.

❷ hangover ▷ *Nach der Party hatte ich einen furchtbaren Kater.* I had a terrible hangover after the party.

katholisch *adj* Catholic

Katze *f* cat; **für die Katz** for nothing

kauen *vb* [**38**] to chew

Kauf (*pl* **Käufe**) *m* purchase ▷ *der Kauf eines Autos* the purchase of a car; **ein guter Kauf** a bargain

kaufen *vb* [**38**] to buy

Käufer (*pl* **Käufer**) *m* buyer

Kauffrau *f* businesswoman

Kaufhaus (*gen* **Kaufhauses**, *pl* **Kaufhäuser**) *nt* department store

Kaufmann (*pl* **Kaufleute**) *m* ❶ businessman ▷ *ein erfolgreicher Kaufmann* a successful businessman ❷ grocer ▷ *zum Kaufmann gehen* to go to the grocer's

Kaugummi (*pl* **Kaugummis**) *m* chewing gum

kaum *adv* hardly ▷ *Ich habe kaum geschlafen.* I hardly slept.

Kehle *f* throat

Keil (*pl* **Keile**) *m* wedge

Keim (*pl* **Keime**) *m* ❶ shoot ▷ *Eine Woche nach der Aussaat zeigen sich die ersten Keime.* The first shoots appear a week after sowing. ❷ germ ▷ *Das Mittel tötete die Keime ab.* The medicine killed the germs.; **etwas im Keim ersticken** to nip something in the bud

kein *adj, pron*

> When combined with a noun, **kein** is used for masculine and neuter nouns, **keine** for feminine and plural nouns. On its own **keiner** is used for masculine, **keine** for feminine and plural, and **keines** or **keins** for neuter.

❶ not ... any ▷ *Ich habe keine Geschwister.* I don't have any brothers or sisters. ▷ *Ich will keinen Streit.* I don't want any quarrelling. ▷ *Er zeigt kein Interesse an Computern.* He doesn't show any interest in computers. ▷ *Von den Autos hat mir keines gefallen.* I didn't like any of the cars. ❷ no ▷ *Kein Tier könnte in diesem Klima überleben.* No animal could survive in this climate.; **'Kein Zutritt'** 'No entry'; **Ich habe keine Lust.** I don't feel like it.; **Ich habe keinen Hunger.** I'm not hungry. ❸ nobody ▷ *Alle waren eingeladen, es ist aber keiner gekommen.* Everybody was invited but nobody came.; **Ich kenne hier keinen.** I don't know anybody here.

Keks (*pl* **Kekse**) *m* biscuit

Keller (*pl* **Keller**) *m* cellar

Kellner (*pl* **Kellner**) *m* waiter

Kellnerin *f* waitress

kennen (*imperf* **kannte**, *perf* **hat gekannt**) *vb* [**39**] to know ▷ *Ich kenne ihn nicht.* I don't know him. ▷ *Ich kenne London gut.* I know London well.

kennenlernen *vb* [**4**] ❶ to meet ▷ *Sie hat ihren Freund bei einem Fußballspiel kennengelernt.* She met her boyfriend at a football match. ❷ to get to know ▷ *Ich würde ihn gern besser kennenlernen.* I'd like to get to know him better.; **sich kennenlernen (1)** to meet ▷ *Wir haben uns auf einer Party kennengelernt.* We met at a party. **(2)** to get to know each other ▷ *Wir haben uns im Laufe der Zeit immer besser kennengelernt.* We got to know each other better and better as time went on.

Kenntnis (*pl* **Kenntnisse**) *f* knowledge ▷ *Deutschkenntnisse wären von Vorteil.* Knowledge of German would be an advantage.; **etwas zur Kenntnis nehmen** to note something; **jemanden in Kenntnis setzen** to inform somebody

Kennzeichen (*pl* **Kennzeichen**) *nt* ❶ mark ▷ *unveränderliche Kennzeichen* distinguishing marks ❷ registration ▷ *das Auto mit dem Kennzeichen S-MJ 2714* the car with the registration S-MJ 2714

Kerl (*pl* **Kerle**) *m* bloke; **Sie ist ein netter Kerl.** She's a good sort.

Kern (*pl* **Kerne**) *m* ❶ pip ▷ *Klementinen haben keine Kerne.* Clementines don't have any pips. ❷ stone ▷ *der Kern der Kirsche* the cherry stone ❸ *(of nut)* kernel ❹ nucleus ❺ core ▷ *der Reaktorkern* the reactor core; **Wir sollten zum Kern des Problems kommen.** We should get to the heart of the problem.
Kernenergie *f* nuclear energy
Kernkraftwerk (*pl* **Kernkraftwerke**) *nt* nuclear power station
Kerze *f* ❶ candle ▷ *Sie zündete eine Kerze an.* She lit a candle. ❷ plug ▷ *Bei der Inspektion werden die Kerzen erneuert.* The plugs are changed while the car is being serviced.
Kette *f* chain
Keuchhusten *m* whooping cough ▷ *Meine Schwester hat Keuchhusten.* My sister has whooping cough.
Keule *f* ❶ club ▷ *Er schlug ihm mit einer Keule über den Kopf.* He hit him over the head with a club. ❷ leg ▷ *Beim Hähnchen mag ich am liebsten die Keule.* My favourite part of a chicken is the leg.
kg *abbr (= Kilogramm)* kg
kichern *vb* [**88**] to giggle
Kiefer (*pl* **Kiefer**) *m* jaw
▶ *f* pine tree
Kies *m* gravel
Kilo (*pl* **Kilos** *or* **Kilo**) *nt* kilo ▷ *Ich muss ein paar Kilos loswerden.* I need to lose a couple of kilos. ▷ *Ich hätte gern zwei Kilo Tomaten.* Can I have two kilos of tomatoes. ▷ *Ich wiege fünfzig Kilo.* I weigh eight stone.
Kilogramm (*pl* **Kilogramme** *or* **Kilogramm**) *nt* kilogram ▷ *zwei Kilogramm Äpfel* two kilograms of apples
Kilometer (*pl* **Kilometer**) *m* kilometre ▷ *mit achtzig Kilometern pro Stunde* at fifty miles per hour
Kind (*pl* **Kinder**) *nt* child; **von Kind auf** from childhood; **ein Kind bekommen** to have a baby
Kindergarten (*pl* **Kindergärten**) *m* kindergarten
Kindergärtnerin *f* kindergarten teacher
Kindergeld *nt* child benefit
Kinderkrippe *f* crèche
Kinderlähmung *f* polio ▷ *Sie hatte als Kind Kinderlähmung.* She had polio as a child.
Kindertagesstätte *f* day nursery
Kinderwagen (*pl* **Kinderwagen**) *m* pram
Kindheit *f* childhood
kindisch *adj* childish; **sich kindisch benehmen** to behave childishly
Kinn (*pl* **Kinne**) *nt* chin
Kino (*pl* **Kinos**) *nt* cinema ▷ *ins Kino gehen* to go to the cinema
Kiosk (*pl* **Kioske**) *m* kiosk
Kirche *f* church
Kirmes (*pl* **Kirmessen**) *f* funfair
Kirsche *f* cherry
Kissen (*pl* **Kissen**) *nt* ❶ cushion ▷ *Auf dem Sofa lagen bunte Kissen.* There were brightly-coloured cushions on the sofa. ❷ pillow ▷ *Er schläft ohne Kissen.* He sleeps without a pillow.
kitschig *adj* kitschy
kitzeln *vb* [**34**] to tickle
kitzlig *adj* ticklish ▷ *Ich bin kitzlig an den Füßen.* My feet are ticklish. ▷ *Das ist eine ganz kitzlige Angelegenheit.* That's a very ticklish matter.
klagen *vb* [**38**] ❶ to wail ▷ *'Hätte ich doch nur auf dich gehört', klagte er.* 'If only I had listened to you', he wailed. ❷ to complain ▷ *Sie klagt dauernd über ihre Kinder.* She's constantly complaining about her children. ▷ *Sie klagt in letzter Zeit oft über Kopfschmerzen.* She's been complaining of headaches a lot recently. ❸ to sue ▷ *Wir werden gegen ihn klagen.* We're going to sue him.; **Sie hat mir ihr Leid geklagt.** She poured out her sorrows to me.
Klammer (*pl* **Klammern**) *f* ❶ bracket ▷ *Sie schrieb in Klammern eine Erklärung*

dazu. She wrote an explanation in brackets. ❷ *(clothes peg)* peg ❸ *(for teeth)* brace ▷ *Viele Kinder müssen eine Klammer tragen*. Many children have to wear a brace.

Klang (*pl* **Klänge**) *m* sound

Klappe *f* ❶ flap ▷ *Über dem Briefkasten ist eine Klappe*. There's a flap over the letterbox. ❷ valve ▷ *Die Klappe an seinem Herzen hat ein Loch*. His heart valve has a hole in it. ❸ *(informal)* trap ▷ *Er soll die Klappe halten*. He should keep his trap shut.; **Sie hat eine große Klappe.** She's got a big mouth.

klappen *vb* [**48**] ❶ to work ▷ *Das kann ja nicht klappen*. That won't work. ▷ *Das Experiment hat geklappt*. The experiment worked. ❷ to tip ▷ *Sie klappte den Sitz nach oben*. She tipped up the seat. ▷ *Er klappte den Deckel der Kiste nach hinten*. He tipped the lid of the chest back.

klappern *vb* [**88**] to rattle

klar *adj* clear ▷ *Das Wasser ist sehr klar*. The water is very clear. ▷ *Ich brauche einen klaren Kopf*. I need a clear head. ▷ *eine klare Antwort* a clear answer ▷ *Mir ist nicht klar, was er eigentlich will*. I'm not clear about what he really wants.; **sich über etwas im Klaren sein** to be clear about something; **Na klar!** Of course!

klären *vb* [**38**] ❶ to clarify ▷ *Wir sollten diese Frage klären*. We should clarify this matter. ❷ to purify ▷ *In dieser Anlage wird das Abwasser geklärt*. The sewage is purified in this plant.; **sich klären** to clear itself up

Klarheit *f* ❶ clarity; **Wir brauchen in dieser Sache Klarheit.** This matter must be clarified. ❷ clearness ▷ *die Klarheit des Wassers* the clearness of the water

Klarinette *f* clarinet ▷ *Oliver spielt Klarinette*. Oliver plays the clarinet.

klarstellen (*perf* **hat klargestellt**) *vb* [**4**] to make clear ▷ *Ich möchte doch mal klarstellen, dass ich das nie gesagt habe*. I would like to make it quite clear that I never said that.

klasse *adj (informal)* smashing ▷ *Er ist ein klasse Lehrer*. He's a smashing teacher.

Klasse *f* class ▷ *Wir sind in der ersten Klasse gefahren*. We travelled first class. ▷ *Unsere Klasse fährt nach England*. Our class is going to England.; **große Klasse sein** to be great

Klassenarbeit *f* test

The **Klassenarbeit** is the main form of assessment in German schools. Over the school year, German pupils write between 6 and 8 **Klassenarbeiten**, usually 45 minutes long, in their core subjects (generally maths, German and English).

▷ *Wir schreiben morgen in Englisch eine Klassenarbeit*. We've got a written English test tomorrow.

Klassenbuch (*pl* **Klassenbücher**) *nt* class register

Klassenkamerad (*gen* **Klassenkameraden**, *pl* **Klassenkameraden**) *m* classmate

Klassenkameradin *f* classmate

Klassenlehrer (*pl* **Klassenlehrer**) *m* class teacher

Klassenlehrerin *f* class teacher

Klassensprecher (*pl* **Klassensprecher**) *m* class representative

Klassensprecherin *f* class representative

Klassenzimmer (*pl* **Klassenzimmer**) *nt* classroom

klassisch *adj* classical

Klatsch (*gen* **Klatsches**) *m* gossip ▷ *Hast du schon den neuesten Klatsch gehört?* Have you heard the latest gossip?

klauen (*perf* **hat geklaut**) *vb* [**38**] *(informal)* to pinch

Klavier *nt* piano ▷ *Bettina spielt Klavier*. Bettina plays the piano.

kleben *vb* [**38**] to stick ▷ *Ich habe die zerbrochene Vase wieder geklebt.* I've stuck the broken vase together again. ▷ *Das klebt nicht.* It doesn't stick.; **etwas an etwas kleben** to stick something on something; **an etwas kleben** to stick to something; **jemandem eine kleben** *(informal)* to thump somebody
klebrig *adj* sticky
Klebstoff (*pl* **Klebstoffe**) *m* glue
Klee *m* clover
Kleid (*pl* **Kleider**) *nt* dress ▷ *Sie trug ein rotes Kleid.* She was wearing a red dress.; **Kleider** clothes *pl*
Kleiderbügel (*pl* **Kleiderbügel**) *m* coat hanger
Kleiderschrank (*pl* **Kleiderschränke**) *m* wardrobe
Kleidung *f* clothing
klein *adj* small ▷ *ein kleines Kind* a small child ▷ *ein kleiner Betrag* a small amount; **als ich klein war** when I was little
Kleingeld *nt* small change
Klempner (*pl* **Klempner**) *m* plumber
klettern (*perf* **ist geklettert**) *vb* [**88**] to climb
klicken *vb* [**48**] *(computer)* to click ▷ *mit der Maus klicken* to click on the mouse
Klima (*pl* **Klimas**) *nt* climate
Klimaanlage *f* air conditioning
Klingel *f* bell
klingeln *vb* [**34**] to ring; **Es klingelte.** The doorbell rang.
Klingelton (*pl* **Klingeltöne**) *m (of mobile phone)* ringtone
klingen (*imperf* **klang**, *perf* **hat geklungen**) *vb* to sound ▷ *Das Klavier klingt verstimmt.* The piano sounds out of tune. ▷ *Der Vorschlag klingt gut.* The suggestion sounds good. ▷ *Du klingst deprimiert.* You sound depressed.
Klinik *f* clinic
Klinke *f* handle *(of door)*
Klippe *f* cliff
Klo (*pl* **Klos**) *nt (informal)* loo
klonen *vb* [**38**] to clone ▷ *ein geklontes Schaf* a cloned sheep
klopfen *vb* [**38**] ❶ to knock ▷ *Sie klopfte an die Tür.* She knocked on the door.; **Es klopft.** There's somebody knocking on the door. ❷ to pound ▷ *Mein Herz klopfte vor Aufregung.* My heart was pounding with excitement.; **jemandem auf die Schulter klopfen** to tap somebody on the shoulder
Kloster (*pl* **Klöster**) *nt* ❶ monastery ❷ convent
Klub (*pl* **Klubs**) *m (association)* club
klug *adj* intelligent
km *abbr (= Kilometer)* km
knabbern *vb* [**88**] to nibble ▷ *Sie knabberte an einem Keks.* She nibbled a biscuit.
Knäckebrot *nt* crispbread
Knall (*pl* **Knalle**) *m* bang ▷ *Die Tür schlug mit einem lauten Knall zu.* The door closed with a loud bang.
knapp *adj* ❶ tight ▷ *Sie hatte einen sehr knappen Pulli an.* She was wearing a very tight pullover. ❷ scarce ▷ *Benzin ist knapp.* Petrol is scarce.; **knapp bei Kasse** short of money ❸ just ▷ *Sie ist knapp fünfzehn Jahre alt.* She has just turned fifteen. ▷ *Wir haben knapp verloren.* We only just lost.; **eine knappe Stunde** just under an hour; **knapp unter** just under
kneifen (*imperf* **kniff**, *perf* **hat gekniffen**) *vb* ❶ to pinch ▷ *Er hat mich in den Arm gekniffen.* He pinched my arm. ❷ to back out ▷ *Als er springen sollte, hat er gekniffen.* When it was his turn to jump, he backed out.
Kneipe *f* pub
Knie (*pl* **Knie**) *nt* knee
Knoblauch *m* garlic
Knöchel (*pl* **Knöchel**) *m* ❶ knuckle ▷ *Ich habe mir die Knöchel an der rechten Hand geschürft.* I've scraped the knuckles of my right hand. ❷ ankle ▷ *Bei dem Sprung habe ich mir den Knöchel verstaucht.* I sprained my ankle when I jumped.

a b c d e f g h i j **k** l m n o p q r s t u v w x y z

Knochen (*pl* **Knochen**) *m* bone
Knödel (*pl* **Knödel**) *m* dumpling
Knopf (*pl* **Knöpfe**) *m* button
Knoten (*pl* **Knoten**) *m* ❶ knot ▷ *Sie machte einen Knoten in die Schnur.* She tied a knot in the string. ❷ bun ▷ *Sie trug das Haar in einem Knoten.* She wore her hair in a bun. ❸ lump ▷ *Sie hat einen Knoten in der Brust entdeckt.* She noticed a lump in her breast.
Knüppel (*pl* **Knüppel**) *m* ❶ cudgel ▷ *Die Robbenbabys werden mit Knüppeln erschlagen.* The baby seals are beaten with cudgels. ❷ truncheon ▷ *Die Polizisten gingen mit Knüppeln gegen die Demonstranten vor.* The police used truncheons against the demonstrators. ❸ joystick
Koch (*pl* **Köche**) *m* cook
kochen *vb* [**48**] ❶ to cook ▷ *Was kochst du heute?* What are you cooking today? ▷ *Ich koche gern.* I like cooking.; **Sie kann gut kochen.** She's a good cook. ❷ to boil ▷ *Das Wasser kocht.* The water's boiling.
Köchin *f* cook
Kochtopf (*pl* **Kochtöpfe**) *m* saucepan
Koffer (*pl* **Koffer**) *m* suitcase
Kofferraum (*pl* **Kofferräume**) *m* boot (*of car*)
Kohl *m* cabbage
Kohle *f* ❶ coal ▷ *Wir heizen mit Kohle.* We use coal for heating. ❷ charcoal ▷ *Wir brauchen noch Kohle zum Grillen.* We need charcoal for the barbecue. ❸ (*money*) dough; **Ich habe keine Kohle.** (*informal*) I'm broke.
Kohlensäure *f* carbon dioxide; **Mineralwasser mit Kohlensäure** sparkling mineral water
Kokosnuss (*pl* **Kokosnüsse**) *f* coconut
Kollege (*gen* **Kollegen**, *pl* **Kollegen**) *m* colleague
Kollegin *f* colleague
Köln *nt* Cologne
Komfort *m* luxury ▷ *ein Auto mit allem Komfort* a luxury car
Komfortzone *f* comfort zone
Komiker (*pl* **Komiker**) *m* comedian
komisch *adj* funny ▷ *ein komischer Film* a funny film ▷ *ein komisches Gefühl* a funny feeling
Komma (*pl* **Kommas**) *nt* comma; **zwei Komma drei (2,3)** two point three (2.3)
kommen (*imperf* **kam**, *perf* **ist gekommen**) *vb* [**40**] ❶ to come ▷ *Wann ist der Brief gekommen?* When did the letter come? ▷ *Kommst du auch zur Party?* Are you coming to the party too?; **Komm gut nach Hause!** Safe journey home. ❷ to get ▷ *Wie komme ich zum Bahnhof?* How do I get to the station?; **unter ein Auto kommen** to be run over by a car ❸ to appear ▷ *Es wird Frühling, die Schneeglöckchen kommen schon.* Spring is coming, the snowdrops are appearing. ❹ to go ▷ *Er ist gestern ins Krankenhaus gekommen.* He went into hospital yesterday. ▷ *Das kommt in den Schrank.* That goes in the cupboard.; **Mit sechs kommt man in die Schule.** You start school at six.; **Wer kommt zuerst?** Who's first?; **Jetzt kommst du an die Reihe.** It's your turn now.; **kommenden Sonntag** next Sunday; **kommen lassen** to send for; **auf etwas kommen** to think of something; **Wie kommst du auf die Idee?** What gave you that idea?; **Ich komme nicht auf seinen Namen.** His name escapes me.; **Er kommt aus Bayern.** He comes from Bavaria.; **Sie ist durchs Abitur gekommen.** She got through her Abitur.; **ums Leben kommen** to lose one's life; **Das kommt davon!** That's what you get!; **zu sich kommen** to come round; **zu etwas kommen (1)** to get something ▷ *Wie bist du zu dem Computer gekommen?* How did you get the computer? **(2)** to get round to something ▷ *Ich mache das, sobald ich dazu komme.* I'll do it as soon as I get round to it.

Kommunismus (*gen* **Kommunismus**) *m* communism
Komödie *f* comedy
kompatibel *adj* compatible
Kompliment (*pl* **Komplimente**) *nt* compliment ▷ *Er hat ihr zu ihrem Kuchen ein Kompliment gemacht.* He complimented her on her cake.
kompliziert *adj* complicated
Komponist (*gen* **Komponisten**, *pl* **Komponisten**) *m* composer
Kompott (*pl* **Kompotte**) *nt* compote
Konditor (*pl* **Konditoren**) *m* pastry cook
Konditorei *f* cake shop
Kondom (*pl* **Kondome**) *nt* condom
Konflikt (*pl* **Konflikte**) *m* conflict
König (*pl* **Könige**) *m* king
Königin *f* queen
Konjugation *f* conjugation
konjugieren (*perf* **hat konjugiert**) *vb* [**76**] to conjugate
Konjunktion *f* conjunction
Konjunktiv (*pl* **Konjunktive**) *m* subjunctive
Konkurrenz *f* ❶ competition ▷ *Auf diesem Sektor ist die Konkurrenz groß.* Competition is keen in this sector. ❷ competitors *pl* ▷ *Sie ist zur Konkurrenz gegangen.* She's gone over to our competitors.
können (*pres* **kann**, *imperf* **konnte**, *perf* **hat gekonnt** *or* **können**) *vb* [**41**]

The past participle **können** is used when **können** is a modal auxiliary.

❶ can ▷ *Kannst du schwimmen?* Can you swim? ▷ *Sie kann keine Mathematik.* She can't do mathematics. ▷ *Sie hat nicht früher kommen können.* She couldn't come earlier. ▷ *Kann ich mit?* Can I come with you? ▷ *Ich kann nicht ...* I can't ... ❷ to be able to ▷ *Morgen werde ich nicht kommen können.* I won't be able to come tomorrow.; **Ich kann nicht mehr.** **(1)** I can't go on. ▷ *Ich mache jetzt Schluss, ich kann nicht mehr.* I'll have to stop now, I can't go on. **(2)** I'm full up. ▷ *Willst du noch ein Stück Kuchen? — Nein danke, ich kann nicht mehr.* Would you like another piece of cake? — No thanks, I'm full up. ❸ may ▷ *Kann ich gehen?* May I go? ▷ *Sie könnten recht haben.* You may be right.; **Es kann sein, dass ...** It may be that ... ▷ *Es kann sein, dass ich etwas später komme.* It may be that I'll come a little later.; **Ich kann nichts dafür.** It's not my fault.; **Das kann sein.** That's possible. ❹ to know ▷ *Er kann viele Geschichtszahlen.* He knows a lot of historical dates.; **Können Sie Deutsch?** Can you speak German?
Können *nt* ability ▷ *Sie hat ihr Können bewiesen.* She has proved her ability.
konnte *vb see* **können**
konservativ *adj* conservative
Konserve *f* tinned food
Konsonant (*gen* **Konsonanten**, *pl* **Konsonanten**) *m* consonant
Kontakt (*pl* **Kontakte**) *m* contact
Kontaktlinsen *fpl* contact lenses *pl*
Kontinent (*pl* **Kontinente**) *m* continent
Konto (*pl* **Konten**) *nt* account ▷ *Geld auf ein Konto einzahlen* to pay money into an account
Kontrolle *f* control ▷ *die Passkontrolle* passport control ▷ *Sie hat die Kontrolle über das Fahrzeug verloren.* She lost control of the vehicle. ▷ *etwas unter Kontrolle haben* to have something under control
Kontrolleur (*pl* **Kontrolleure**) *m* inspector
kontrollieren (*perf* **hat kontrolliert**) *vb* [**76**] to check ▷ *Kann ich bitte Ihre Fahrkarten kontrollieren?* May I check your tickets please?
sich **konzentrieren** (*perf* **hat sich konzentriert**) *vb* [**76**] to concentrate ▷ *Ich kann mich nicht konzentrieren.* I can't concentrate.
Konzert (*pl* **Konzerte**) *nt* ❶ concert ▷ *Wir waren gestern Abend im Konzert.*

We were at a concert yesterday evening. ❷ concerto ▷ *ein Konzert für Klavier und Violine* a concerto for piano and violin

Kopf (*pl* **Köpfe**) *m* head

Kopfhörer (*pl* **Kopfhörer**) *m* headphones *pl*

Kopfkissen (*pl* **Kopfkissen**) *nt* pillow

Kopfsalat (*pl* **Kopfsalate**) *m* lettuce

Kopfschmerzen *pl* headache *sg* ▷ *Ich habe Kopfschmerzen.* I've got a headache.

Kopie *f* copy

kopieren (*perf* **hat kopiert**) *vb* [**76**] to copy ▷ *kopieren und einfügen* to copy and paste

Kopiergerät (*pl* **Kopiergeräte**) *nt* photocopier

Korb (*pl* **Körbe**) *m* basket; **jemandem einen Korb geben** to turn somebody down

> Word for word, **jemandem einen Korb geben** means 'to give somebody a basket'.

Korken (*pl* **Korken**) *m* cork

Korkenzieher (*pl* **Korkenzieher**) *m* corkscrew

Korn (*pl* **Körner**) *nt* corn

Körper (*pl* **Körper**) *m* body

korrigieren (*perf* **hat korrigiert**) *vb* [**76**] to correct

Kosmetik *f* cosmetics *pl*

Kost *f* ❶ food ▷ *Sie ernährt sich von gesunder Kost.* She eats healthy food. ❷ board ▷ *Für Kost und Unterkunft ist gesorgt.* Board and lodging will be provided.

kostbar *adj* precious ▷ *Du vergeudest meine kostbare Zeit.* You're wasting my precious time.

kosten *vb* [**2**] ❶ to cost ▷ *Mein Fahrrad hat zweitausend Euro gekostet.* My bike cost two thousand euros.; **Was kostet ...?** How much is ...? ❷ to taste ▷ *Willst du die Soße mal kosten?* Would you like to taste the sauce? ▷ *Koste mal, ob das schmeckt.* Taste it and see if it's good.

Kosten *pl* ❶ costs *pl* ▷ *die Kosten tragen* to bear the costs ❷ expense ▷ *Bei vielen Kindern hat man auch viele Kosten.* Lots of children mean a lot of expense.; **auf jemandes Kosten** at somebody's expense

kostenlos *adj* free of charge

köstlich *adj* ❶ hilarious ▷ *Das war ein köstlicher Film.* That was a hilarious film. ▷ *ein köstlicher Witz* a hilarious joke ❷ *(food)* delicious; **sich köstlich amüsieren** to have a marvellous time

Kostüm (*pl* **Kostüme**) *nt* costume; **ein Damenkostüm** a ladies' suit

Kotelett (*pl* **Koteletts**) *nt* chop

krabbeln (*perf* **ist gekrabbelt**) *vb* [**88**] to crawl

Krach *m* ❶ crash ▷ *Die Vase fiel mit einem lauten Krach zu Boden.* The vase fell on the ground with a loud crash. ❷ noise ▷ *Unsere Nachbarn machen viel Krach.* Our neighbours make a lot of noise. ❸ row ▷ *Sie hat Krach mit ihrem Freund.* She had a row with her boyfriend.

Kraft (*pl* **Kräfte**) *f* strength ▷ *Samson hat seine Kraft verloren.* Samson lost his strength.; **Er hat viel Kraft.** He's very strong.; **mit aller Kraft** with all one's might; **Kinder kosten viel Kraft.** Children require a lot of energy.; **Sie scheint magische Kräfte zu haben.** She seems to have magic powers.; **Das Gesetz tritt am ersten August in Kraft.** The law comes into effect on the first of August.

Kraftfahrzeug (*pl* **Kraftfahrzeuge**) *nt* motor vehicle

kräftig *adj, adv* ❶ strong ▷ *Er ist ein kräftiger Junge.* He is a strong boy. ❷ hard ▷ *ein kräftiger Schlag* a hard blow ▷ *kräftig schütteln* to shake hard; **kräftig üben** to practise a lot

Kraftwerk (*pl* **Kraftwerke**) *nt* power station

Kragen (*pl* **Kragen**) *m* collar

Kralle *f* ❶ claw ▷ *die Krallen der Katze* the cat's claws ❷ talon ▷ *die Krallen des Vogels* the bird's talons
krank *adj* ill ▷ *Ich bin krank.* I'm ill. ▷ *Ich habe eine kranke Mutter.* My mother's ill.
Krankenhaus (*gen* **Krankenhauses**, *pl* **Krankenhäuser**) *nt* hospital
Krankenkasse *f* health insurance
In Germany one can choose between different health insurance schemes. There is no 'National Health Service'.
Krankenpfleger (*pl* **Krankenpfleger**) *m* male nurse
Krankenschein (*pl* **Krankenscheine**) *m* health insurance card
Krankenschwester *f* nurse
Krankenwagen (*pl* **Krankenwagen**) *m* ambulance
Krankheit *f* illness
kratzen *vb* [**36**] to scratch; **sich kratzen** to scratch oneself
Kraut (*pl* **Kräuter**) *nt* ❶ herb ▷ *eine Salatsoße mit frischen Kräutern* a salad dressing with fresh herbs ❷ sauerkraut ▷ *Heute gibt es Würstchen mit Kraut.* We're having sausages and sauerkraut today.
Krawatte *f* tie
Krebs (*gen* **Krebses**, *pl* **Krebse**) *m* ❶ crab ▷ *Krebse bewegen sich seitlich voran.* Crabs move sideways. ❷ cancer ▷ *Sie ist an Krebs gestorben.* She died of cancer. ❸ Cancer ▷ *Beate ist Krebs.* Beate's Cancer.
Kredit (*pl* **Kredite**) *m* credit ▷ *auf Kredit* on credit
Kreditkarte *f* credit card
Kreide *f* chalk
Kreis (*gen* **Kreises**, *pl* **Kreise**) *m* ❶ circle ▷ *Stellt euch im Kreis auf.* Form a circle. ▷ *mein Freundeskreis* my circle of friends ▷ *im Kreis gehen* to go round in circles ❷ district ▷ *Blaubeuren liegt im Kreis Ulm.* Blaubeuren is in the district of Ulm.
kreischen *vb* [**38**] to shriek ▷ *Sie kreischte laut.* She shrieked loudly.
Kreislauf *m* circulation ▷ *Sie hat einen labilen Kreislauf.* She has bad circulation.
Kreisverkehr (*pl* **Kreisverkehre**) *m* roundabout
Kreuz (*gen* **Kreuzes**, *pl* **Kreuze**) *nt* ❶ cross ▷ *Sie markierte die Stelle mit einem Kreuz.* She marked the place with a cross. ❷ back ▷ *Mir tut das Kreuz weh.* My back's sore. ❸ clubs *sg* ▷ *Kreuz ist Trumpf.* Clubs is trumps.
Kreuzung *f* ❶ crossroads *sg* ▷ *An der Kreuzung fährst du links.* You go left at the crossroads. ❷ cross ▷ *Das ist eine Kreuzung zwischen Pferd und Esel.* It's a cross between a horse and a donkey.
Kreuzworträtsel (*pl* **Kreuzworträtsel**) *nt* crossword puzzle
kriechen (*imperf* **kroch**, *perf* **ist gekrochen**) *vb* ❶ to crawl ▷ *Das Baby kroch zur Tür.* The baby crawled towards the door. ▷ *Der Verkehr kriecht.* The traffic is crawling. ❷ to grovel ▷ *Er kriecht vor seinem Chef.* He's grovelling to his boss.
Krieg (*pl* **Kriege**) *m* war
kriegen *vb* [**38**] to get ▷ *Ich kriege einen Schnupfen.* I'm getting a cold.; **Sie kriegt ein Kind.** She's going to have a baby.
Krimi (*pl* **Krimis**) *m* thriller
Kriminalfilm (*pl* **Kriminalfilme**) *m* crime thriller
Kriminalroman (*pl* **Kriminalromane**) *m* detective story
kriminell *adj* criminal
Krise *f* crisis
kritisch *adj* critical
kritisieren (*perf* **hat kritisiert**) *vb* [**76**] to criticize
Krone *f* crown
Krug (*pl* **Krüge**) *m* ❶ jug ▷ *Sie stellte einen Krug Saft auf den Tisch.* She put a jug of juice on the table. ❷ beer mug ▷ *Er trinkt sein Bier immer aus einem Krug.* He always drinks his beer out of a beer mug.

krumm *adj* **ein krummer Rücken** a hunched back; **Mach nicht so einen krummen Rücken.** Don't slouch.; **Sitz nicht so krumm.** Sit up straight.

Küche *f* ❶ kitchen ❷ cooking ▷ *die französische Küche* French cooking

Kuchen (*pl* **Kuchen**) *m* ❶ cake ▷ *ein Marmorkuchen* a marble cake ❷ flan ▷ *ein Obstkuchen* a fruit flan

Kuckuck (*pl* **Kuckucke**) *m* cuckoo

Kuckucksuhr *f* cuckoo clock

Kugel *f* ❶ bullet ▷ *Er wurde von einer Kugel getroffen.* He was hit by a bullet. ❷ ball ▷ *Die Wahrsagerin hat eine Kugel aus Glas.* The fortune teller has a crystal ball.

Kugelschreiber (*pl* **Kugelschreiber**) *m* Biro®

Kuh (*pl* **Kühe**) *f* cow

kühl *adj* cool ▷ *Abends wurde es kühl.* In the evenings it got cool.

Kühler (*pl* **Kühler**) *m* radiator *(in car)*

Kühlschrank (*pl* **Kühlschränke**) *m* fridge

Kühltruhe *f* freezer

kühn *adj* bold

Kuli (*pl* **Kulis**) *m* Biro®

Kultur *f* ❶ culture; **Kultur haben** to be cultured ❷ civilization ▷ *die abendländische Kultur* Western civilization

kulturell *adj* cultural

Kummer *m* sorrow; **Hast du Kummer?** Have you got problems?

kümmern *vb* [**38**] to concern ▷ *Was kümmert mich seine Kritik?* Why should his criticism concern me?; **Das kümmert mich nicht.** That doesn't worry me.; **sich um jemanden kümmern** to look after somebody; **sich um etwas kümmern** to see to something

Kunde (*gen* **Kunden**, *pl* **Kunden**) *m* customer

kündigen *vb* [**38**] ❶ to hand in one's notice ▷ *Die Arbeit gefällt mir nicht, ich werde kündigen.* I don't like the job, I'm going to hand in my notice.; **Der Chef hat ihr gekündigt.** The boss gave her her notice.; **die Wohnung kündigen** to give notice on one's flat ❷ to cancel ▷ *Ich habe mein Abonnement gekündigt.* I've cancelled my subscription.

Kündigung *f* notice ▷ *Er reichte seine Kündigung ein.* He handed in his notice.

Kundin *f* customer

Kundschaft *f* customers *pl*

Kunst (*pl* **Künste**) *f* ❶ art ▷ *Sie interessiert sich für Kunst.* She's interested in art. ❷ knack ▷ *Er beherrscht die Kunst, andere zu überzeugen.* He's got the knack of persuading others.; **Das ist doch keine Kunst.** It's easy.

> Word for word, **Das ist doch keine Kunst** means 'It's not an art'.

Künstler (*pl* **Künstler**) *m* artist

Künstlerin *f* artist

künstlerisch *adj* artistic ▷ *künstlerisch begabt sein* to have artistic talents

künstlich *adj* artificial

Kunststoff (*pl* **Kunststoffe**) *m* synthetic material

Kunststück (*pl* **Kunststücke**) *nt* trick

Kunstwerk (*pl* **Kunstwerke**) *nt* work of art

Kupfer *nt* copper *(metal)*

Kupplung *f* clutch ▷ *Bei Automatikwagen gibt es keine Kupplung.* Automatic cars don't have a clutch.

Kur *f* health cure ▷ *eine Kur machen* to take a health cure

Kurs (*gen* **Kurses**, *pl* **Kurse**) *m* ❶ course ▷ *Ich mache einen Kurs, um Spanisch zu lernen.* I'm doing a course to learn Spanish. ❷ rate ▷ *Wie ist der Kurs des Pfunds?* What's the rate for the pound?

Kurve *f* ❶ bend ▷ *Ein Auto bog um die Kurve.* A car came round the bend. ❷ curve ▷ *die Kurve eines Schaubilds* the curve on a graph

kurz *adj* short ▷ *Sie hat kurze Haare.* She has short hair. ▷ *Sie hat eine kurze Rede gehalten.* She made a short speech.;

kurz gesagt in short; **zu kurz kommen** to come off badly; **den Kürzeren ziehen** to get the worst of it

> Word for word, **den Kürzeren ziehen** means 'to pull the shorter one'.

Kürze *f* shortness
kürzen *vb* [**36**] ❶ to shorten ▷ *Du solltest den Aufsatz etwas kürzen.* You should shorten your essay a little. ❷ to cut ▷ *Mein Vater hat mir das Taschengeld gekürzt.* My father has cut my pocket money.
Kurzgeschichte *f* short story
kürzlich *adv* recently
kurzsichtig *adj* short-sighted
Kusine *f* cousin
Kuss (*gen* **Kusses**, *pl* **Küsse**) *m* kiss
küssen *vb* [**48**] to kiss ▷ *Sie hat mich geküsst.* She kissed me.; **sich küssen** to kiss
Küste *f* coast

L

Labor (*pl* **Labore** *or* **Labors**) *nt* lab
lächeln *vb* [**34**] to smile
Lächeln *nt* smile
lachen *vb* [**48**] to laugh
lächerlich *adj* ridiculous
Lachs (*gen* **Lachses**, *pl* **Lachse**) *m* salmon ▷ *drei Lachse* three salmon
Lack (*pl* **Lacke**) *m* ❶ varnish ▷ *Er hat das Holz mit Lack behandelt.* He treated the wood with varnish. ❷ paint ▷ *Der Lack an meinem Auto ist stumpf geworden.* The paint on my car has become dull.
laden (*pres* **lädt**, *imperf* **lud**, *perf* **hat geladen**) *vb* ❶ to load ▷ *Wir haben das Gepäck ins Auto geladen.* We loaded the luggage into the car. ▷ *Das Programm wird geladen.* The program is being loaded. ▷ *eine Waffe laden* to load a weapon ❷ to charge ▷ *eine Batterie laden* to charge a battery ❸ to summon ▷ *Ich wurde als Zeugin geladen.* I was summoned as a witness.
Laden (*pl* **Läden**) *m* ❶ shop ▷ *In welchem Laden hast du das gekauft?* Which shop

did you buy it in? ❷ shutter ▷ *Im Sommer machen wir tagsüber die Läden zu.* In summer we close the shutters during the day.

Ladung *f* ❶ cargo ▷ *Das Flugzeug hatte zu viel Ladung an Bord.* The plane had too much cargo on board. ❷ loading ▷ *Ein Arbeiter ist bei der Ladung des Schiffes verunglückt.* A worker was injured while loading the ship. ❸ summons *sg* ▷ *Wenn Sie eine Ladung als Zeuge bekommen, müssen Sie erscheinen.* If you receive a summons to appear as a witness, you have to attend. ❹ charge ▷ *eine Ladung Dynamit* a charge of dynamite

Lage *f* ❶ situation ▷ *Die politische Lage auf dem Balkan ist brisant.* The political situation in the Balkans is explosive. ❷ layer ▷ *Die Torte bestand aus mehreren Lagen.* The gateau was made up of several layers.; **in der Lage sein, etwas zu tun** to be in a position to do something

Lager (*pl* **Lager**) *nt* ❶ camp ▷ *Er fährt im Sommer in ein Lager der Pfadfinder.* He's going to a scout camp in the summer. ❷ warehouse ▷ *Die Fabrik hat ein eigenes Lager.* The factory has its own warehouse. ❸ stockroom ▷ *Die Verkäuferin hat im Lager nachgesehen.* The sales assistant looked in the stockroom.

lagern *vb* **[88]** ❶ to store ▷ *kühl lagern* to store in a cool place ▷ *trocken lagern* to store in a dry place ❷ to lay down ▷ *Der Verletzte sollte auf der Seite gelagert werden.* The injured person should be laid down on his side. ❸ to camp ▷ *Die Indianer lagerten am Fluss.* The Indians camped by the river.

lahm *adj* ❶ lame ▷ *Das Pferd ist lahm.* The horse is lame. ❷ slow ▷ *Er ist furchtbar lahm.* He is terribly slow.

lähmen *vb* **[38]** to paralyse

Lähmung *f* paralysis

Laken (*pl* **Laken**) *nt* sheet *(on bed)*

Lamm (*pl* **Lämmer**) *nt* lamb

Lammfleisch *nt* lamb *(meat)*

Lampe *f* lamp

Land (*pl* **Länder**) *nt* ❶ country ▷ *Italien ist ein schönes Land.* Italy is a beautiful country. ▷ *Am Wochenende fahren wir aufs Land.* We're going to the country at the weekend.; **auf dem Land** in the country; **an Land** on land ❷ state ▷ *Die Bundesrepublik besteht aus sechzehn Ländern.* The Federal Republic consists of sixteen states.

Landebahn *f* runway

landen (*perf* **ist gelandet**) *vb* **[54]** to land

Landeskunde *f* regional and cultural studies *pl*

Landkarte *f* map

Landkreis (*gen* **Landkreises**, *pl* **Landkreise**) *m* administrative district

The German administrative hierarchy starts with the **Stadt/Gemeinde** (town/community), and continues via the **Landkreis** (administrative district) and **Land** (federal state) to the **Bund** (federation).

ländlich *adj* rural

Landschaft *f* ❶ countryside ▷ *Die toskanische Landschaft ist sehr schön.* The Tuscan countryside is very beautiful. ❷ landscape ▷ *Turner hat viele Landschaften gemalt.* Turner painted many landscapes.

Landstraße *f* country road

Landung *f* landing ▷ *Das Flugzeug verunglückte bei der Landung.* The plane crashed on landing.

Landwirtschaft *f* agriculture

lang *adj* ❶ long ▷ *Sie hat lange Haare.* She has long hair. ▷ *Das war eine lange Rede.* That was a long speech. ▷ *Sie war länger als erwartet weg.* She was away longer than expected. ▷ *Es wird nicht lang dauern.* It won't take long. ❷ tall ▷ *Mathis ist der Längste in unserer Klasse.* Mathis is the tallest in our class.

lange *adv* for a long time ▷ *Sie war lange krank.* She was ill for a long time.; **lange dauern** to last a long time; **lange brauchen** to take a long time
Länge *f* length ▷ *Sie hat die Länge und Breite des Zimmers ausgemessen.* She measured the length and breadth of the room. ▷ *die Länge eines Films* the length of a film
langen *vb* [**38**] to be enough ▷ *Das Fleisch hat nicht für alle gelangt.* There wasn't enough meat to go round. ▷ *Meinst du das Geld langt?* Do you think we have enough money?; **Es langt mir.** I've had enough.; **nach etwas langen** to reach for something
Langeweile *f* boredom
langfristig *adj, adv* long-term ▷ *eine langfristige Besserung* a long-term improvement ▷ *Wir müssen langfristig planen.* We have to plan long-term.
länglich *adj* longish
langsam *adj, adv* ❶ slow ❷ slowly ▷ *langsam fahren* to drive slowly; **Das wird langsam langweilig.** This is getting boring.
längst *adv* **Das ist längst fertig.** That was finished a long time ago.; **Das weiß ich längst.** I've known that for a long time.; **Er ist längst nicht so gescheit wie seine Schwester.** He's far from being as bright as his sister.
längste *adj* longest ▷ *der längste Tag des Jahres* the longest day of the year
langweilen *vb* [**38**] to bore ▷ *Langweile ich dich?* Am I boring you?; **sich langweilen** to be bored
langweilig *adj* boring
Lappen (*pl* **Lappen**) *m* rag ▷ *mit einem feuchten Lappen* with a damp rag
Lärm *m* noise
Laser (*pl* **Laser**) *m* laser
lassen (*pres* **lässt**, *imperf* **ließ**, *perf* **gelassen** *or* **lassen**) *vb* [**42**]

> The past participle **lassen** is used when **lassen** is a modal auxiliary.

❶ to stop ▷ *Du solltest das Rauchen lassen.* You should stop smoking. ▷ *Er kann das Trinken nicht lassen.* He can't stop drinking. ▷ *Sie kann's nicht lassen.* She won't stop doing it.; **Lass das!** Stop that! ❷ to leave ▷ *Kann ich die Kinder hier lassen?* Can I leave the children here? ▷ *jemanden allein lassen* to leave somebody alone ▷ *Wir haben das Auto zu Hause gelassen.* We left the car at home. ▷ *etwas lassen, wie es ist* to leave something as it is ▷ *Lass mal, ich mache das schon.* Leave it, I'll do it.; **Lassen wir das!** Let's leave it.; **Lass mich!** Leave me alone.; **jemanden irgendwohin lassen** to let somebody go somewhere; **etwas machen lassen** to have something done; **jemanden etwas tun lassen** to let somebody do something; **jemanden warten lassen** to keep somebody waiting; **Das lässt sich machen.** That can be done.; **Lass uns gehen.** Let's go.
lässig *adj* casual
Last *f* load ▷ *Er stöhnte unter der schweren Last.* He groaned under the heavy load.; **jemandem zur Last fallen** to be a burden to somebody
lästig *adj* tiresome
Lastwagen (*pl* **Lastwagen**) *m* lorry
Latein *nt* Latin
Lateinamerika *nt* Latin America
Laterne *f* ❶ lantern ❷ streetlamp
Lauch (*pl* **Lauche**) *m* leek
Lauf (*pl* **Läufe**) *m* ❶ run ▷ *Er machte einen Lauf durch den Wald.* He went for a run through the forest. ❷ race ▷ *Sie hat den Lauf über vierhundert Meter gewonnen.* She won the four-hundred-metre race. ❸ course ▷ *der Lauf des Flusses* the course of the river ▷ *im Laufe der Woche* in the course of the week ▷ *einer Sache ihren Lauf lassen* to let something take its course ❹ barrel ▷ *Er richtete den Lauf seiner Pistole auf mich.* He aimed the barrel of his pistol at me.

laufen (*pres* **läuft**, *imperf* **lief**, *perf* **ist gelaufen**) *vb* [**43**] ❶ to run ▷ *Sie liefen so schnell sie konnten.* They ran as fast as they could. ▷ *Er läuft Marathon.* He runs marathons. ❷ to walk ▷ *Wir mussten nach Hause laufen.* We had to walk home.

laufend *adj, adv* ❶ running ▷ *bei laufendem Motor* with the engine running ❷ current ▷ *die laufenden Ausgaben* current expenses; **auf dem Laufenden sein** to be up to date; **auf dem Laufenden halten** to keep up to date ❸ always ▷ *Musst du mich laufend stören?* Do you always have to interrupt me?

Läufer (*pl* **Läufer**) *m* ❶ runner ▷ *Die Läufer standen am Start.* The runners were at the start. ▷ *Im Flur liegt ein roter Läufer.* There's a red runner in the hall. ❷ bishop ▷ *Sie zog mit dem Läufer.* She moved her bishop.

Läuferin *f* runner

Laufwerk (*pl* **Laufwerke**) *nt* disk drive ▷ *Die Diskette in Laufwerk A einlegen.* Put the diskette in disk drive A.

Laune *f* mood ▷ *Was hat sie für eine Laune?* What kind of mood is she in? ▷ *Ich habe gute Laune.* I'm in a good mood. ▷ *Ich bin deine Launen leid.* I'm fed up with your bad moods.

launisch *adj* ❶ temperamental ▷ *Sie ist ein sehr launischer Mensch.* She's very temperamental. ❷ bad-tempered ▷ *Er war heute schrecklich launisch.* He was terribly bad-tempered today.

Laus (*pl* **Läuse**) *f* louse

laut *adj, adv, prep* ❶ loud ▷ *Ich mag laute Musik nicht.* I don't like loud music. ❷ noisy ▷ *Hier ist es schrecklich laut.* It's terribly noisy here. ❸ loudly ▷ *Sie schrie so laut sie konnte.* She screamed as loudly as she could.; **laut lesen** to read aloud ❹ according to ▷ *Laut unserem Vertrag ...* According to our contract ...

Laut (*pl* **Laute**) *m* sound

lauten *vb* [**2**] ❶ to go ▷ *Wie lautet die zweite Strophe des Lieds?* How does the second verse of the song go? ❷ to be ▷ *Das Urteil lautete auf zehn Jahre Gefängnis.* The sentence was ten years' imprisonment.

läuten *vb* [**2**] to ring ▷ *Die Glocken läuten.* The bells are ringing. ▷ *Ich habe geläutet, es hat aber niemand aufgemacht.* I rang but nobody answered.

lauter *adv* nothing but ▷ *Sie hat lauter Lügen erzählt.* She told nothing but lies.

Lautschrift *f* phonetics *pl*

Lautsprecher (*pl* **Lautsprecher**) *m* loudspeaker

Lautstärke *f* volume

lauwarm *adj* lukewarm

Lawine *f* avalanche

leben *vb* [**38**] to live

Leben (*pl* **Leben**) *nt* life; **ums Leben kommen** to lose one's life

lebend *adj* living

lebendig *adj* ❶ alive ▷ *Er konnte lebendig aus den Trümmern geborgen werden.* He was rescued from the ruins alive. ❷ lively ▷ *Sie ist ein sehr lebendiges Kind.* She's a very lively child.

Lebensgefahr *f* mortal danger ▷ *Die Geiseln waren in Lebensgefahr.* The hostages were in mortal danger.; **'Lebensgefahr!'** 'danger!'

lebensgefährlich *adj* ❶ dangerous ▷ *eine lebensgefährliche Kurve* a dangerous corner ❷ critical ▷ *eine lebensgefährliche Krankheit* a critical illness ▷ *lebensgefährlich verletzt* critically injured

lebenslänglich *adj* for life; **Er hat eine lebenslängliche Gefängnisstrafe bekommen.** He received a life sentence.

Lebenslauf (*pl* **Lebensläufe**) *m* CV (= *curriculum vitae*)

Lebensmittel *ntpl* food *sg*

Lebensmittelgeschäft (*pl* **Lebensmittelgeschäfte**) *nt* grocer's shop

Lebensversicherung *f* life insurance
Leber *f* liver
Leberwurst (*pl* **Leberwürste**) *f* liver sausage
Lebewesen (*pl* **Lebewesen**) *nt* creature
lebhaft *adj* lively
Lebkuchen (*pl* **Lebkuchen**) *m* gingerbread
lecken *vb* [**48**] ❶ to leak ▷ *Der Behälter leckt.* The container's leaking. ❷ to lick ▷ *Die Katze leckte sich das Fell.* The cat licked its fur. ▷ *Sie leckte am Eis.* She licked her ice cream.
lecker *adj* delicious ▷ *lecker schmecken* to taste delicious
Leder (*pl* **Leder**) *nt* leather
Lederhose *f* leather trousers *pl*
Lederhosen are the traditional dress in South Germany and Austria.
ledig *adj* single ▷ *'Familienstand: ledig'* 'Marital status: single'
leer *adj* empty ▷ *eine leere Flasche* an empty bottle ▷ *leere Drohungen* empty threats; **ein leeres Blatt Papier** a blank sheet of paper; **ein leerer Blick** a vacant expression; **leer machen** to empty
Leere *f* emptiness
leeren *vb* [**38**] to empty
legal *adj* legal
legen *vb* [**38**] ❶ to put ▷ *Sie legte das Kind ins Bett.* She put the child to bed. ▷ *Leg das Besteck in die Schublade.* Put the cutlery in the drawer. ▷ *Er legte das Buch aus der Hand.* He put the book down. ❷ to lay ▷ *Sie legten den Verletzten auf eine Decke.* They laid the injured man on a blanket. ▷ *Sie legte ihren Mantel über den Stuhl.* She laid her coat over the chair. ▷ *ein Ei legen* to lay an egg; **sich legen (1)** to lie down ▷ *Sie legte sich auf das Sofa.* She lay down on the sofa. ▷ *Ich lege mich ins Bett.* I'm going to lie down. **(2)** to drop ▷ *Der Wind hat sich gelegt.* The wind has dropped.; **Das wird sich legen.** That will sort itself out.
Lehne *f* ❶ arm ▷ *Sie saß auf der Lehne des Sofas.* She sat on the arm of the sofa. ❷ back ▷ *Der Sessel hat eine hohe Lehne.* The chair has a high back.
lehnen *vb* [**38**] to lean
Lehnstuhl (*pl* **Lehnstühle**) *m* armchair
Lehre *f* ❶ apprenticeship ▷ *bei jemandem in die Lehre gehen* to serve one's apprenticeship with somebody ❷ lesson ▷ *Lass dir das eine Lehre sein!* Let that be a lesson to you!
Lehrer (*pl* **Lehrer**) *m* teacher
Lehrerin *f* teacher
Lehrerzimmer (*pl* **Lehrerzimmer**) *nt* staff room
Lehrling (*pl* **Lehrlinge**) *m* apprentice
Lehrplan (*pl* **Lehrpläne**) *m* syllabus
Lehrstelle *f* apprenticeship
Leiche *f* corpse
leicht *adj* ❶ light ▷ *leichtes Gepäck* light luggage ❷ easy ▷ *Die Klassenarbeit war leicht.* The class test was easy.; **es sich leicht machen** to make things easy for oneself
Leichtathletik *f* athletics *sg*
leichtfallen *vb* [**22**] **jemandem leichtfallen** to be easy for somebody
leichtmachen *vb* [**48**] *see* **leicht**
leichtsinnig *adj* careless
leid *adj* **etwas leid sein** to be tired of something
Leid *nt* sorrow
leiden (*imperf* **litt**, *perf* **hat gelitten**) *vb* [**44**] to suffer ▷ *Sie leidet an Asthma.* She suffers from asthma. ▷ *Wir leiden unter der Hitze.* We're suffering from the heat.; **jemanden gut leiden können** to like somebody; **Ich kann ihn nicht leiden.** I can't stand him.
leider *adv* unfortunately ▷ *Ich kann leider nicht kommen.* Unfortunately I can't come.; **Ja, leider.** Yes, I'm afraid so.; **Leider nicht.** I'm afraid not.
leidtun (*imperf* **tat leid**, *perf* **hat leidgetan**) *vb* [**81**] **Es tut mir leid.** I'm sorry.; **Er tut mir leid.** I'm sorry for him.

leihen (*imperf* **lieh**, *perf* **hat geliehen**) *vb* to lend ▷ *Kannst du mir fünfzig Euro leihen?* Can you lend me fifty euros?; **sich etwas leihen** to borrow something

Leim (*pl* **Leime**) *m* glue

Leine *f* ❶ line ▷ *Sie hängte die Wäsche auf die Leine.* She hung the washing on the line. ❷ lead ▷ *Hunde müssen an der Leine geführt werden.* Dogs must be kept on a lead.

Leinen (*pl* **Leinen**) *nt* linen

leise *adj, adv* ❶ quiet ▷ *Seid bitte leise.* Please be quiet. ❷ quietly ▷ *Sie sprach mit leiser Stimme.* She spoke quietly. ▷ *Sie kam ganz leise ins Zimmer.* She came into the room very quietly.

leisten *vb* [**2**] ❶ to do ▷ *Du hast gute Arbeit geleistet.* You've done a good job. ❷ to achieve ▷ *Sie hat viel geleistet im Leben.* She's achieved a lot in her life.; **jemandem Gesellschaft leisten** to keep somebody company; **sich etwas leisten** to treat oneself to something; **sich etwas leisten können** to be able to afford something

Leistung *f* ❶ performance ▷ *Sie haben die Leistung des Motors verbessert.* They've improved the performance of the engine.; **schulische Leistungen** school results ❷ achievement ▷ *eine sportliche Leistung* a sporting achievement ▷ *Das war wirklich eine Leistung!* That really was an achievement.

leiten *vb* [**2**] ❶ to direct ▷ *Das Wasser wird durch Rohre geleitet.* The water is directed through pipes. ❷ to lead ▷ *eine Partei leiten* to lead a party ❸ to run ▷ *Wer leitet diese Firma?* Who runs this company? ❹ to chair ▷ *Wer hat die Versammlung geleitet?* Who chaired the meeting?; **Metall leitet Strom besonders gut.** Metal is a good conductor of electricity.

Leiter (*pl* **Leiter**) *m* head ▷ *der Leiter des Museums* the head of the museum ▶ *f* ladder ▷ *eine Leiter hinaufklettern* to climb a ladder

Leitung *f* ❶ management ▷ *Ihr wurde die Leitung der Abteilung übertragen.* She was entrusted with the management of the department. ❷ direction ▷ *der Jugendchor unter Leitung von ...* the youth choir under the direction of ... ❸ pipe ▷ *In unserer Straße werden neue Leitungen für Wasser und Gas verlegt.* They're laying new water and gas pipes in our road. ❹ cable ▷ *Die Leitung steht unter Strom.* The cable is live. ❺ line ▷ *Alle Leitungen waren besetzt.* All the lines were busy.; **eine lange Leitung haben** to be slow on the uptake

Lektion *f* lesson

Lektüre *f* ❶ reading ▷ *Stör sie nicht bei der Lektüre.* Don't disturb her while she's reading. ❷ reading matter ▷ *Das ist die richtige Lektüre für die Ferien.* That's the right reading matter for the holidays. ❸ set text ▷ *Welche Lektüre habt ihr dieses Jahr in Englisch?* What are your set texts in English this year?

> Be careful! **Lektüre** does not mean **lecture**.

lenken *vb* [**38**] to steer ▷ *ein Fahrzeug lenken* to steer a car

Lenkrad (*pl* **Lenkräder**) *nt* steering wheel

lernen *vb* [**38**] to learn

Lernplattform *f* VLE, virtual learning environment

Lesebuch (*pl* **Lesebücher**) *nt* reading book

lesen (*pres* **liest**, *imperf* **las**, *perf* **hat gelesen**) *vb* [**45**] to read

leserlich *adj* legible ▷ *eine leserliche Handschrift* legible handwriting ▷ *leserlich schreiben* to write legibly

letzte *adj* ❶ last ▷ *In der letzten Arbeit habe ich eine Zwei geschrieben.* I got a 'B' in the last test. ▷ *Ich habe noch einen letzten Wunsch.* I have one last wish. ▷ *letzte Woche* last week ▷ *zum letzten Mal* for the last time; **als Letzter** last ❷ latest ▷ *Laut letzten Informationen* *kam es zu schweren Unruhen.* According to latest reports there were serious riots.

letztens *adv* lately

leuchten *vb* [**2**] to shine ▷ *jemandem ins Gesicht leuchten* to shine a light in somebody's face

Leuchter (*pl* **Leuchter**) *m* candlestick

Leuchtstift (*pl* **Leuchtstifte**) *m* highlighter

Leute *pl* people *pl*

Lexikon (*pl* **Lexika**) *nt* encyclopedia

Licht (*pl* **Lichter**) *nt* light

Lid (*pl* **Lider**) *nt* eyelid

Lidschatten (*pl* **Lidschatten**) *m* eyeshadow

lieb *adj* dear ▷ *Liebe Bettina* Dear Bettina ▷ *Lieber Herr Schlüter* Dear Mr Schlüter; **Das ist lieb von dir.** That's nice of you.; **jemanden lieb haben** to be fond of somebody

Liebe *f* love

lieben *vb* [**38**] to love

liebenswürdig *adj* kind

lieber *adv* rather ▷ *Ich hätte jetzt lieber einen Kaffee.* I'd rather have a coffee just now. ▷ *Ich gehe lieber nicht.* I'd rather not go.; **Lass das lieber!** I'd leave that if I were you.; **etwas lieber haben** to prefer something

Liebesbrief (*pl* **Liebesbriefe**) *m* love letter

Liebeskummer *m* **Liebeskummer haben** to be lovesick

Liebesroman (*pl* **Liebesromane**) *m* romantic novel

liebevoll *adj* loving

liebhaben *vb* [**32**] *see* **lieb**

Liebling (*pl* **Lieblinge**) *m* darling

Lieblings- *prefix* favourite ▷ *Was ist dein Lieblingsfach?* What's your favourite subject?

liebste *adj* favourite ▷ *Der Winter ist meine liebste Jahreszeit.* Winter is my favourite season.; **am liebsten** best

Lied (*pl* **Lieder**) *nt* song

lief *vb see* **laufen**

liefern *vb* [**88**] ❶ to deliver ▷ *Wir liefern die Möbel ins Haus.* We deliver the furniture to your door. ❷ to supply ▷ *Das Kraftwerk liefert den Strom für die ganze Gegend.* The power station supplies electricity to the whole area.; **den Beweis liefern** to produce proof

Lieferwagen (*pl* **Lieferwagen**) *m* van

liegen (*imperf* **lag**, *perf* **hat gelegen**) *vb* [**46**] ❶ to lie ▷ *Sie lag auf dem Bett.* She lay on the bed. ▷ *Wir haben den ganzen Tag am Strand gelegen.* We lay on the beach all day. ▷ *Auf meinem Schreibtisch liegt eine Menge Papier.* There's a lot of paper lying on my desk.; **Es lag viel Schnee.** There was a lot of snow. ❷ to be ▷ *Unser Haus liegt sehr zentral.* Our house is very central. ▷ *Ulm liegt an der Donau.* Ulm is on the Danube.; **nach Süden liegen** to face south; **Mir liegt viel daran.** It matters a lot to me.; **Mir liegt nichts daran.** It doesn't matter to me.; **Es liegt bei dir, ob ...** It's up to you whether ...; **Sprachen liegen mir nicht.** Languages are not my thing.; **Woran liegt es?** How come?; **Das liegt am Wetter.** It's because of the weather.; **liegen bleiben (1)** to lie in ▷ *Morgen ist Sonntag, da kann ich liegen bleiben.* It's Sunday tomorrow, so I can lie in. **(2)** not to get up ▷ *Der verletzte Spieler blieb liegen.* The injured player didn't get up. **(3)** to be left behind ▷ *Der Schirm ist liegen geblieben.* The umbrella's been left behind.; **etwas liegen lassen** to leave something ▷ *Ich muss diese Arbeit liegen lassen.* I'll have to leave this job. ▷ *Ich habe meinen Schirm liegen lassen.* I've left my umbrella.

Liegestuhl (*pl* **Liegestühle**) *m* deck chair

Lift (*pl* **Lifte** *or* **Lifts**) *m* lift *(elevator)*

Liga (*pl* **Ligen**) *f* league

lila *adj* purple ▷ *Sie hatte einen lila Hut auf.* She was wearing a purple hat.

Limo (*pl* **Limos**) *f* lemonade

Limonade *f* lemonade

Lineal (*pl* **Lineale**) *nt* ruler ▷ *einen Strich mit dem Lineal ziehen* to draw a line with a ruler
Linie *f* line
linke *adj* left ▷ *In Großbritannien fährt man auf der linken Seite.* In Great Britain they drive on the left. ▷ *Mein linkes Auge tut weh.* My left eye's hurting. ▷ *Er hat sich den linken Arm gebrochen.* He broke his left arm.
Linke (*gen* **Linken**) *f* ❶ left ▷ *Zu Ihrer Linken sehen Sie das Rathaus.* On your left you'll see the town hall. ❷ left hand ▷ *Er schlug mit der Linken zu.* He hit out with his left hand.
links *adv* left ▷ *links abbiegen* to turn left; **links überholen** to overtake on the left; **Er schreibt mit links.** He writes with his left hand.; **Links sehen Sie das Rathaus.** On the left you'll see the town hall.; **links von der Kirche** to the left of the church; **links von mir** on my left; **links wählen** to vote for a left-wing party; **etwas mit links machen** to do something easily
Linkshänder (*pl* **Linkshänder**) *m* **Er ist Linkshänder.** He's left-handed.
Linkshänderin *f* **Sie ist Linkshänderin.** She's left-handed.
Linse *f* ❶ lentil ▷ *Linsensuppe* lentil soup ❷ lens ▷ *die Linse der Kamera* the camera lens
Lippe *f* lip
Lippenstift (*pl* **Lippenstifte**) *m* lipstick
Liste *f* list
Liter (*pl* **Liter**) *m*

> You can also say **das Liter**.

litre
Literatur *f* literature
Lizenz *f* licence
Lkw (*gen* **Lkw** *or* **Lkws**, *pl* **Lkws**) *m* (= *Lastkraftwagen*) lorry
Lob *nt* praise
loben *vb* [**38**] to praise
Loch (*pl* **Löcher**) *nt* hole
locker *adj* ❶ loose ▷ *ein lockerer Zahn* a loose tooth ❷ relaxed ▷ *eine lockere Atmosphäre* a relaxed atmosphere
Löffel (*pl* **Löffel**) *m* spoon; **ein Löffel Zucker** a spoonful of sugar
logisch *adj* logical
Lohn (*pl* **Löhne**) *m* ❶ wages *pl* ▷ *Freitags wird der Lohn ausbezahlt.* The wages are paid on Fridays. ❷ reward ▷ *Das ist jetzt der Lohn für meine Mühe!* That's the reward for my efforts.
lohnen *vb* [**38**] **Das lohnt sich.** It's worth it.

> Word for word, **Das lohnt sich** means 'It rewards itself'.

lohnend *adj* worthwhile
Lohnsteuer *f* income tax
Lokal (*pl* **Lokale**) *nt* pub
Lokomotive *f* locomotive
los *adj* loose ▷ *Die Schraube ist los.* The screw's loose.; **Dort ist viel los.** There's a lot going on there.; **Dort ist nichts los.** There's nothing going on there.; **Was ist los?** What's the matter?; **Los!** Go on!
Los (*gen* **Loses**, *pl* **Lose**) *nt* lottery ticket ▷ *Mein Los hat gewonnen.* My lottery ticket has won.
losbinden (*imperf* **band los**, *perf* **hat losgebunden**) *vb* to untie
löschen *vb* [**48**] to put out ▷ *ein Feuer löschen* to put out a fire ▷ *das Licht löschen* to put out the light; **den Durst löschen** to quench one's thirst; **eine Datei löschen** to delete a file
Löschtaste *f* delete key
lose *adj* loose ▷ *lose Blätter* loose sheets ▷ *etwas lose verkaufen* to sell something loose; **ein loses Mundwerk** a big mouth
lösen *vb* [**38**] ❶ to solve ▷ *ein Rätsel lösen* to solve a puzzle ▷ *ein Problem lösen* to solve a problem ❷ to loosen ▷ *Kannst du diesen Knoten lösen?* Can you loosen the knot?; **etwas von etwas lösen** to remove something from something ▷ *Sie löste das Etikett vom Glas.* She

removed the label from the jar.; **sich lösen (1)** to come loose ▷ *Eine Schraube hatte sich gelöst.* A screw had come loose. **(2)** to dissolve ▷ *Die Tablette löst sich in Wasser.* The pill dissolves in water. **(3)** to resolve itself ▷ *Das Problem hat sich inzwischen gelöst.* The problem has resolved itself in the meantime.; **eine Fahrkarte lösen** to buy a ticket

losfahren (*pres* **fährt los**, *imperf* **fuhr los**, *perf* **ist losgefahren**) *vb* [**21**] to leave

loslassen (*pres* **lässt los**, *imperf* **ließ los**, *perf* **hat losgelassen**) *vb* [**42**] to let go of

löslich *adj* soluble

Lösung *f* solution ▷ *Weißt du die Lösung des Rätsels?* Do you know the solution to the puzzle?

Lotto (*pl* **Lottos**) *nt* National Lottery

Lottozahlen *fpl* winning lottery numbers *pl*

Löwe (*gen* **Löwen**, *pl* **Löwen**) *m* ❶ lion ❷ Leo ▷ *Manfred ist Löwe.* Manfred's Leo.

Lücke *f* gap

Luft (*pl* **Lüfte**) *f* air ▷ *Ich brauche frische Luft.* I need some fresh air.; **in der Luft liegen** to be in the air; **jemanden wie Luft behandeln** to ignore somebody

> Word for word, **jemanden wie Luft behandeln** means 'to treat somebody like air'.

Luftballon (*pl* **Luftballons** *or* **Luftballone**) *m* balloon

Luftdruck *m* atmospheric pressure

Luftmatratze *f* air bed

Luftpost *f* airmail ▷ *per Luftpost* by airmail

Luftverschmutzung *f* air pollution

Lüge *f* lie

lügen (*imperf* **log**, *perf* **hat gelogen**) *vb* [**47**] to lie ▷ *Ich müsste lügen, wenn ...* I would be lying if ...; **Er lügt ständig.** He's always telling lies.

Lügner (*pl* **Lügner**) *m* liar

Lunge *f* lung

Lungenentzündung *f* pneumonia

Lupe *f* magnifying glass; **unter die Lupe nehmen** to scrutinize

Lust *f* **Lust haben, etwas zu tun** to feel like doing something; **keine Lust haben, etwas zu tun** not to feel like doing something; **Lust auf etwas haben** to feel like something

lustig *adj* funny ▷ *eine lustige Geschichte* a funny story

lutschen *vb* [**48**] to suck ▷ *am Daumen lutschen* to suck one's thumb

Lutscher (*pl* **Lutscher**) *m* lollipop

Luxemburg *nt* Luxembourg

Luxus (*gen* **Luxus**) *m* luxury

m

machen *vb* [**48**] ❶ to do ▷ *Hausaufgaben machen* to do one's homework ▷ *etwas sorgfältig machen* to do something carefully ▷ *Was machst du heute Nachmittag?* What are you doing this afternoon?; **eine Prüfung machen** to sit an exam; **den Führerschein machen** to take driving lessons ❷ to make ▷ *aus Holz gemacht* made of wood ▷ *Kaffee machen* to make coffee ▷ *einen Fehler machen* to make a mistake ▷ *Krach machen* to make a noise ▷ *jemanden traurig machen* to make somebody sad ▷ *Das macht müde.* It makes you tired.; **Schluss machen** to finish; **ein Foto machen** to take a photo ❸ to cause ▷ *Das hat mir viel Mühe gemacht.* This caused me a lot of trouble. ▷ *viel Arbeit machen* to cause a lot of work; **Das macht die Kälte.** It's the cold that does that. ❹ to be ▷ *Drei und fünf macht acht.* Three and five is eight. ▷ *Was macht das?* How much is that? ▷ *Das macht acht Euro.* That's eight euros.; **Was macht die Arbeit?** How's the work going?; **Was macht dein Bruder?** How's your brother doing?; **Das macht nichts.** That doesn't matter.; **Die Kälte macht mir nichts.** I don't mind the cold.; **sich machen** to come on; **sich nichts aus etwas machen** not to be very keen on something; **Mach's gut!** Take care!; **Mach schon!** Come on!

Macht (*pl* **Mächte**) *f* power

Mädchen (*pl* **Mädchen**) *nt* girl

mag *vb see* **mögen**

Magazin *nt* magazine ▷ *Ich habe das in einem Magazin gelesen.* I read it in a magazine.

Magen (*pl* **Magen** *or* **Mägen**) *m* stomach

Magenschmerzen *pl* stomachache *sg* ▷ *Ich habe Magenschmerzen.* I've got a stomachache.

mager *adj* ❶ lean ▷ *mageres Fleisch* lean meat ❷ thin ▷ *Sie ist furchtbar mager.* She's terribly thin.

Magnet (*gen* **Magnets** *or* **Magneten**, *pl* **Magneten**) *m* magnet

magnetisch *adj* magnetic

Mahlzeit *f* meal ▷ *Wir essen drei Mahlzeiten am Tag.* We eat three meals a day.

Mai (*gen* **Mai** *or* **Mais**, *pl* **Maie**) *m* May ▷ *im Mai* in May ▷ *am sechsten Mai* on 6 May ▷ *Ulm, den 6. Mai 2006* Ulm, 6 May 2006 ▷ *Heute ist der sechste Mai.* Today is the sixth of May.; **der Erste Mai** May Day

mailen (*perf* **hat gemailt**) *vb* [**38**] to email ▷ *Hast du es gemailt?* Did you email it?

Mailingliste (*pl* **Mailinglisten**) *f* mailing list

Mais (*gen* **Maises**) *m* maize

Majonäse *f* mayonnaise

mal *adv* times ▷ *zwei mal fünf* two times five ▷ *Wir haben sechsmal geklingelt.* We rang six times.; **Warst du schon mal in Paris?** Have you ever been to Paris?

Mal (*pl* **Male**) *nt* ❶ time ▷ *das fünfte Mal* the fifth time ▷ *zum ersten Mal* for the first time ▷ *Wie viele Male hast du es versucht?* How many times have you tried? ❷ mark ▷ *Sie hat ein rotes Mal im Gesicht.* She has a red mark on her face.

malen *vb* [**38**] to paint

Maler (*pl* **Maler**) *m* painter

malerisch *adj* picturesque

Mallorca *nt* Majorca

malnehmen (*pres* **nimmt mal**, *imperf* **nahm mal**, *perf* **hat malgenommen**) *vb* [**52**] to multiply

Malz (*gen* **Malzes**) *nt* malt

Mama (*pl* **Mamas**) *f* (*informal*) mum

man *pron* you ▷ *Man kann nie wissen.* You never know. ▷ *Wie schreibt man das?* How do you spell that?; **man sagt, ...** they say ...; **Man hat mir gesagt ...** I was told that ...

Manager (*pl* **Manager**) *m* manager

manche *pron* some ▷ *Manche Bücher sind langweilig.* Some books are boring.

manchmal *adv* sometimes

Mandarine *f* mandarin orange

Mandel *f* ❶ almond ▷ *ein Kuchen mit Nüssen und Mandeln* a cake with nuts and almonds ❷ tonsil ▷ *Sie hat entzündete Mandeln.* Her tonsils are inflamed.

Mangel (*pl* **Mängel**) *m* ❶ lack ▷ *Schlafmangel* lack of sleep ❷ shortage ▷ *Der Mangel an Arbeitsplätzen führt zu immer größerer Arbeitslosigkeit.* The shortage of jobs is causing rising unemployment. ❸ fault ▷ *Das Gerät weist mehrere Mängel auf.* The appliance has several faults.

mangelhaft *adj* ❶ poor ▷ *Er hat mangelhaft bekommen.* He got a poor mark.

> German marks range from one (**sehr gut**) to six (**ungenügend**).

❷ faulty ▷ *Mangelhafte Waren kann man zurückgehen lassen.* You can return faulty goods.

mangels *prep*

> The preposition **mangels** takes the genitive.

for lack of ▷ *Er wurde mangels Beweisen freigesprochen.* He was acquitted for lack of evidence.

Manieren *pl* manners *pl* ▷ *Sie hat keine Manieren.* She doesn't have any manners.

Mann (*pl* **Männer**) *m* ❶ man ▷ *Es war ein Mann am Telefon.* There was a man on the phone. ❷ husband ▷ *Frau Maier kam mit ihrem Mann.* Mrs Maier came with her husband.; **seinen Mann stehen** to hold one's own; **Alle Mann an Deck!** All hands on deck!

männlich *adj* ❶ male ▷ *meine männlichen Kollegen* my male colleagues; **eine männliche Person** a man ❷ masculine ▷ *ein männliches Substantiv* a masculine noun

Mannschaft *f* ❶ team ▷ *die deutsche Mannschaft* the German team ❷ crew ▷ *der Kapitän und seine Mannschaft* the captain and his crew

Mantel (*pl* **Mäntel**) *m* coat ▷ *Er hatte einen Mantel an.* He was wearing a coat.

Mappe *f* ❶ briefcase ❷ folder

> Be careful! **Mappe** does not mean **map**.

Märchen (*pl* **Märchen**) *nt* fairy tale

Margarine *f* margarine

Marine *f* navy ▷ *Er ist bei der Marine.* He's in the navy.

Marke *f* ❶ brand ▷ *Für diese Marke sieht man in letzter Zeit viel Werbung.* There's been a lot of advertising for this brand recently. ❷ make ▷ *Welche Marke fährt dein Vater?* What make of car does your father drive? ❸ voucher; **eine Briefmarke** a postage stamp

markieren (*perf* **hat markiert**) *vb* [**76**] to mark ▷ *Sie hat die Stelle mit Leuchtstift markiert.* She marked the place with a highlighter.

Markt (*pl* **Märkte**) *m* market

Marktplatz (*gen* **Marktplatzes**, *pl* **Marktplätze**) *m* market place

Marmelade *f* jam ▷ *Erdbeermarmelade* strawberry jam; **Orangenmarmelade** marmalade

Marmor (*pl* **Marmore**) *m* marble

März (*gen* **März** *or* **Märzes**, *pl* **Märze**) *m* March ▷ *im März* in March ▷ *am dritten März* on the third of March ▷ *Ulm, den 3. März 2008* Ulm, 3 March 2008 ▷ *Heute ist der dritte März.* Today is the third of March.

Masche *f* ❶ mesh ▷ *Das Netz hatte feine Maschen.* The net had a very fine mesh. ❷ stitch; **Das ist die neueste Masche.** That's the latest thing.

Maschine *f* ❶ machine ▷ *Werkzeug wird heutzutage von Maschinen hergestellt.* Nowadays tools are manufactured by machines. ▷ *Kannst du die schmutzige Wäsche bitte in die Maschine tun?* Can you put the dirty washing in the machine? ❷ engine ▷ *Dieses Motorrad hat eine starke Maschine.* This motorbike has a powerful engine. ❸ typewriter ▷ *Sie hat ihr Referat mit der Maschine geschrieben.* She typed her assignment. ❹ plane

Maschinengewehr (*pl* **Maschinengewehre**) *nt* machine gun

Masern *pl* measles *sg* ▷ *Masern sind bei Erwachsenen ziemlich gefährlich.* Measles is quite dangerous for adults.

Maske *f* mask

Maß (1) (*gen* **Maßes**, *pl* **Maße**) *nt* ❶ measure ▷ *In Deutschland werden metrische Maße verwendet.* Metric measures are used in Germany.; **Wie sind die Maße des Zimmers?** What are the measurements of the room? ❷ extent ▷ *Sie war zu einem hohen Maß selbst schuld.* To a large extent she had only herself to blame.

Maß (2) (*gen* **Maß**, *pl* **Maß** *or* **Maßen**) *f* litre of beer

Massage *f* massage

Masse *f* mass

massenhaft *adj (informal)* masses of ▷ *Du hast massenhaft Fehler gemacht.* You've made masses of mistakes.

Massenmedien *ntpl* mass media *pl*

mäßig *adj* moderate

Maßnahme *f* step ▷ *Maßnahmen ergreifen* to take steps

Maßstab (*pl* **Maßstäbe**) *m* ❶ standard ▷ *Dieses Gerät setzt neue Maßstäbe.* This appliance sets new standards. ❷ scale ▷ *In welchem Maßstab ist diese Karte?* What's the scale of this map?

Mast (*pl* **Maste** *or* **Masten**) *m* ❶ mast ▷ *Am Mast hing die britische Fahne.* The Union Jack was hanging from the mast. ❷ pylon ▷ *Neben unserem Garten steht ein Hochspannungsmast.* There's a high-tension pylon beside our garden.

Material (*pl* **Materialien**) *nt* material ▷ *Aus welchem Material ist das gemacht?* What material is it made of? ▷ *Ich sammle Material für mein Referat.* I'm collecting material for my assignment.

Mathe *f (informal)* maths *sg*

Mathematik *f* mathematics *sg* ▷ *Mathematik ist mein Lieblingsfach.* Mathematics is my favourite subject.

Matratze *f* mattress

Matrose (*gen* **Matrosen**, *pl* **Matrosen**) *m* sailor

Matsch *m* ❶ mud ▷ *Deine Schuhe sind voller Matsch.* Your shoes are covered in mud. ❷ slush

matschig *adj* ❶ muddy ▷ *Nach dem Regen war der Weg sehr matschig.* The path was very muddy after the rain. ❷ slushy ▷ *Bei matschigem Schnee macht das Skifahren keinen Spaß.* Skiing isn't fun when the snow is slushy.

matt *adj* ❶ weak ▷ *Bei der Hitze fühle ich mich so matt.* I feel so weak in this heat. ❷ dull ▷ *Ihre Augen waren ganz matt.* Her eyes were really dull. ❸ matt ▷ *Möchten Sie die Abzüge Hochglanz oder matt?* Would you like the prints glossy or matt? ❹ mate ▷ *Schach und matt* checkmate

Matte *f* mat
Mauer *f* wall
Maul (*pl* **Mäuler**) *nt* mouth ▷ *Die Katze hatte einen Vogel im Maul.* The cat had a bird in its mouth.; **Halt's Maul!** *(informal)* Shut your face!
Maulkorb (*pl* **Maulkörbe**) *m* muzzle
Maulwurf (*pl* **Maulwürfe**) *m* mole
Maurer (*pl* **Maurer**) *m* bricklayer
Maus (*pl* **Mäuse**) *f* mouse ▷ *Sie hat Angst vor Mäusen.* She's afraid of mice. ▷ *Du musst zweimal mit der Maus klicken.* You have to click the mouse twice.
Mausefalle *f* mousetrap
Mausklick (*pl* **Mausklicks**) *m* mouse click; **per Mausklick** by clicking the mouse
maximal *adj, adv* ❶ maximum ▷ *der maximale Betrag* the maximum amount ❷ at most ▷ *Wir können maximal eine Woche wegfahren.* We can go away for a week at most.
Mayonnaise *f* mayonnaise
Mechaniker (*pl* **Mechaniker**) *m* mechanic
mechanisch *adj, adv* ❶ mechanical ▷ *Das Gerät hat einen mechanischen Schaden.* The appliance has a mechanical fault. ❷ mechanically ▷ *etwas mechanisch tun* to do something mechanically
meckern *vb* [**88**] to moan ▷ *Müsst ihr über alles meckern?* Do you have to moan about everything?
Mecklenburg-Vorpommern *nt* Mecklenburg-Western Pomerania

Mecklenburg-Vorpommern is one of the 16 **Länder**. Its capital is Schwerin. It is Germany's most rural and thinly populated **Land**, and is becoming increasingly popular with tourists.

Medaille *f* medal
Medien *ntpl* media *pl*
Medikament (*pl* **Medikamente**) *nt* drug ▷ *verschreibungspflichtige Medikamente* prescribed drugs
Medizin *f* medicine
medizinisch *adj* medical
Meer (*pl* **Meere**) *nt* sea ▷ *Wir wohnen am Meer.* We live by the sea.
Meerschweinchen (*pl* **Meerschweinchen**) *nt* guinea pig
Mehl (*pl* **Mehle**) *nt* flour
mehr *adj, adv* more
mehrere *adj* several
mehreres *pron* several things
mehrfach *adj, adv* ❶ many ▷ *Dieses Gerät hat mehrfache Verwendungsmöglichkeiten.* This gadget has many uses. ❷ repeated ▷ *Es ist mir erst nach mehrfachen Versuchen gelungen.* I only managed after repeated attempts. ▷ *Ich habe mehrfach versucht, dich zu erreichen.* I've tried repeatedly to get hold of you.
Mehrheit *f* majority
mehrmalig *adj* repeated
mehrmals *adv* repeatedly
Mehrwertsteuer *f* value added tax
Mehrzahl *f* ❶ majority ▷ *Die Mehrzahl der Schüler besitzt einen Computer.* The majority of pupils have a computer. ❷ plural ▷ *Wie heißt die Mehrzahl von 'woman'?* What's the plural of 'woman'?
meiden (*imperf* **mied**, *perf* **hat gemieden**) *vb* to avoid
mein *adj, pron* ❶ my ▷ *Mein Englischlehrer ist nett.* My English teacher's nice. ▷ *Meine Mutter erlaubt es nicht.* My mother won't allow it. ▷ *Ich finde mein Buch nicht.* I can't find my book. ❷ mine ▷ *Das ist nicht mein Füller, meiner ist blau.* That's not my pen, mine's blue. ▷ *Seine Mutter heißt Anne, meine auch.* His mother's called Anne, so's mine. ▷ *Wenn dein Fahrrad kaputt ist, kannst du meins nehmen.* If your bike's broken you can use mine.
meinen *vb* [**38**] ❶ to think ▷ *Ich meine, wir sollten jetzt gehen.* I think we should go now. ▷ *Was meint deine Mutter zu deinem Freund?* What does your mother think about your boyfriend? ▷ *Sollen wir*

sie zur Party einladen, was meinst du? Should we invite her to the party, what do you think? ❷ to say ▷ *Unser Lehrer meint, wir sollten am Wochenende keine Aufgaben machen.* Our teacher says that we shouldn't do any homework at the weekend. ❸ to mean ▷ *Was meint er mit diesem Wort?* What does he mean by this word? ▷ *Ich verstehe nicht, was du meinst.* I don't understand what you mean. ▷ *So habe ich das nicht gemeint.* I didn't mean it like that.; **Das will ich meinen!** I should think so.

meinetwegen *adv* ❶ for my sake ▷ *Ihr müsst meinetwegen nicht auf euren Urlaub verzichten.* You don't have to do without your holiday for my sake. ❷ on my account ▷ *Hat er sich meinetwegen so aufgeregt?* Did he get so upset on my account? ❸ as far as I'm concerned ▷ *Meinetwegen kannst du gehen.* As far as I'm concerned you can go. ❹ go ahead ▷ *Kann ich das machen? — Meinetwegen.* Can I do that? — Go ahead.

Meinung *f* opinion ▷ *Er hat mich nach meiner Meinung zu diesem Punkt gefragt.* He asked for my opinion on this subject.; **meiner Meinung nach** in my opinion; **Ganz meine Meinung!** I quite agree.; **jemandem die Meinung sagen** to give somebody a piece of one's mind

> Be careful! **Meinung** does not mean **meaning**.

meist *adv* usually ▷ *Samstags bin ich meist zu Hause.* I'm usually at home on Saturdays.

meiste *adj* most ▷ *Die meisten Bücher habe ich schon gelesen.* I've already read most of the books. ▷ *Hast du die Bücher alle gelesen? — Ja, die meisten.* Have you read all the books? — Yes, most of them. ▷ *Die meisten von euch kennen dieses Wort sicher.* Most of you must know this word.; **am meisten (1)** most ▷ *Darüber hat sie sich am meisten aufgeregt.* This upset her most. **(2)** the most ▷ *Er hat am meisten gewonnen.* He won the most.

meistens *adv* usually ▷ *Samstags bin ich meistens zu Hause.* I'm usually at home on Saturdays.

Meister (*pl* **Meister**) *m* ❶ champion ▷ *Er ist deutscher Meister im Ringen.* He's the German wrestling champion. ❷ master craftsman ▷ *Der Meister bildet Lehrlinge aus.* The master craftsman trains apprentices.

Meisterschaft *f* championship ▷ *Wer hat die Meisterschaft gewonnen?* Who won the championship?

melden *vb* **[54]** to report ▷ *Er meldete den Diebstahl bei der Polizei.* He reported the theft to the police.; **sich melden (1)** to answer *(phone)* ▷ *Es meldet sich niemand.* There's no answer. **(2)** to put one's hand up *(in school)*; **sich polizeilich melden** to register with the police

Melodie *f* tune

Melone *f* ❶ melon ❷ bowler hat ▷ *Er trug eine Melone.* He was wearing a bowler hat.

Menge *f* ❶ quantity ▷ *etwas in großen Mengen bestellen* to order a large quantity of something ❷ crowd ▷ *Ich habe ihn in der Menge verloren.* I lost him in the crowd.; **eine Menge** a lot of

Mensch (*gen* **Menschen**, *pl* **Menschen**) *m* human being ▷ *Es heißt, dass sich der Mensch durch die Sprache vom Tier unterscheidet.* It's said that what distinguishes human beings from animals is language.; **Wie viele Menschen?** How many people?; **kein Mensch** nobody

Menschheit *f* mankind

menschlich *adj* human

Menü (*pl* **Menüs**) *nt* set meal

merken *vb* **[38]** to notice ▷ *Hat sie gemerkt, dass ich gefehlt habe?* Did she notice that I wasn't there? ▷ *Ich habe den Fehler nicht gemerkt.* I didn't notice the mistake.; **sich etwas merken** to

remember something; **Das werd' ich mir merken!** I won't forget that in a hurry!
merkwürdig *adj* odd; **sich merkwürdig benehmen** to behave strangely
Messe *f* ❶ fair ▷ *Auf der Messe wurden die neuesten Modelle gezeigt.* The latest models were shown at the fair. ❷ mass ▷ *Sie geht jeden Sonntag zur Messe.* She goes to mass every Sunday.
messen (*pres* **misst**, *imperf* **maß**, *perf* **hat gemessen**) *vb* to measure ▷ *Hast du die Länge gemessen?* Have you measured the length?; **bei jemandem Fieber messen** to take somebody's temperature; **Mit ihm kannst du dich nicht messen.** You're no match for him.
Messer (*pl* **Messer**) *nt* knife
Messgerät (*pl* **Messgeräte**) *nt* gauge
Metall (*pl* **Metalle**) *nt* metal
Meter (*pl* **Meter**) *m* metre
Methode *f* method
Metzger (*pl* **Metzger**) *m* butcher ▷ *Er ist Metzger.* He's a butcher. ▷ *beim Metzger* at the butcher's
Metzgerei *f* butcher's
mich *pron*

mich is the accusative of **ich**.

❶ me ▷ *Er hat mich zu seiner Party eingeladen.* He's invited me to his party. ❷ myself ▷ *Ich sehe mich im Spiegel.* I can see myself in the mirror.
Miene *f* look; **eine finstere Miene machen** to look grim
mies *adj* (*informal*) lousy ▷ *Mir geht's mies.* I feel lousy.
Miete *f* rent; **zur Miete wohnen** to live in rented accommodation
mieten *vb* [**2**] ❶ to rent

It is far more usual to live in rented accommodation in Germany than it is in Britain. Flats are mainly rented unfurnished.

▷ *Wir haben eine Ferienwohnung gemietet.* We've rented a holiday flat. ❷ to hire ▷ *Man kann am Flughafen ein Auto mieten.* You can hire a car at the airport.
Mietshaus (*gen* **Mietshauses**, *pl* **Mietshäuser**) *nt* block of rented flats
Mietvertrag (*pl* **Mietverträge**) *m* lease
Mietwagen (*pl* **Mietwagen**) *m* rental car
Mikrofon (*pl* **Mikrofone**) *nt* microphone
Mikroskop (*pl* **Mikroskope**) *nt* microscope
Mikrowelle *f* microwave
Milch *f* milk
mild *adj* ❶ mild ▷ *eine milde Seife* a mild soap ▷ *mildes Wetter* mild weather ❷ lenient ▷ *ein mildes Urteil* a lenient sentence ▷ *ein milder Richter* a lenient judge
Militär *nt* army ▷ *zum Militär gehen* to join the army
militärisch *adj* military
Milliarde *f* billion
Millimeter (*pl* **Millimeter**) *m* millimetre
Million *f* million
Millionär (*pl* **Millionäre**) *m* millionaire ▷ *Er ist Millionär.* He's a millionaire.
Minderheit *f* minority ▷ *in der Minderheit sein* to be in the minority
Minderjährige (*gen* **Minderjährigen**, *pl* **Minderjährigen**) *mf* minor ▷ *Minderjährige dürfen keinen Alkohol kaufen.* Minors are not allowed to buy alcohol.
minderwertig *adj* inferior
mindeste *adj* **das Mindeste** the least; **nicht im Mindesten** not in the least; **zum Mindesten** at least
mindestens *adv* at least
Mineral (*pl* **Minerale** *or* **Mineralien**) *nt* mineral
Mineralwasser (*pl* **Mineralwasser**) *nt* mineral water
Minister (*pl* **Minister**) *m* minister (*in government*)

Ministerium (*pl* **Ministerien**) *nt* ministry

Minute *f* minute

mir *pron*

mir is the dative of **ich**.

❶ me ▷ *Kannst du mir sagen, wie spät es ist?* Can you tell me the time? ❷ to me ▷ *Gib es mir!* Give it to me.; **mir nichts, dir nichts** just like that

mischen *vb* [**48**] to mix

Mischung *f* mixture

miserabel *adj* dreadful ▷ *Mir geht's miserabel.* I feel dreadful.

Missbrauch *m* abuse

Misserfolg (*pl* **Misserfolge**) *m* failure

misshandeln (*perf* **hat misshandelt**) *vb* [**88**] to ill-treat

missmutig *adj* sullen

misstrauen (*perf* **hat misstraut**) *vb* [**49**] **jemandem misstrauen** to mistrust somebody

Misstrauen *nt* suspicion

misstrauisch *adj* suspicious

Missverständnis (*gen* **Missverständnisses**, *pl* **Missverständnisse**) *nt* misunderstanding

missverstehen (*imperf* **missverstand**, *perf* **hat missverstanden**) *vb* [**72**] to misunderstand

Mist *m* ❶ manure ▷ *Im Frühling werden die Felder mit Mist gedüngt.* The fields are fertilized with manure in the spring. ❷ (*informal*) rubbish ▷ *Warum isst du so einen Mist?* Why do you eat such rubbish? ▷ *Heute kommt wieder nur Mist im Fernsehen.* There's nothing but rubbish on TV again today. ▷ *Du redest Mist.* You're talking rubbish.; **Mist!** Blast!

Be careful! The German word **Mist** does not mean **mist**.

mit *prep, adv*

The preposition **mit** takes the dative.

❶ with ▷ *Er ist mit seiner Freundin gekommen.* He came with his girlfriend. ▷ *mit Filzstift geschrieben* written with a felt-tip pen ❷ by ▷ *mit dem Auto* by car ▷ *mit der Bahn* by train ▷ *mit dem Bus* by bus; **mit zehn Jahren** at the age of ten; **Sie ist mit die Beste in ihrer Klasse.** She is one of the best in her class.; **Wollen Sie mit?** Do you want to come along?

Mitarbeiter (*pl* **Mitarbeiter**) *m* ❶ colleague ▷ *meine Mitarbeiter und ich* my colleagues and I ❷ collaborator ▷ *die Mitarbeiter an diesem Projekt* the collaborators on this project ❸ employee ▷ *Die Firma hat 500 Mitarbeiter.* The company has 500 employees.

mitbringen (*imperf* **brachte mit**, *perf* **hat mitgebracht**) *vb* [**13**] to bring along ▷ *Kann ich meine Freundin mitbringen?* Can I bring my girlfriend along?

miteinander *adv* with each another

mitfahren (*pres* **fährt mit**, *imperf* **fuhr mit**, *perf* **ist mitgefahren**) *vb* [**21**] to come too ▷ *Wir fahren nach Berlin. Willst du mitfahren?* We're going to Berlin. Do you want to come too?; **Ich fahre nicht mit.** I'm not going.; **Willst du mit uns im Auto mitfahren?** Do you want a lift in our car?

mitgeben (*pres* **gibt mit**, *imperf* **gab mit**, *perf* **hat mitgegeben**) *vb* [**28**] to give

Mitglied (*pl* **Mitglieder**) *nt* member

mitkommen (*imperf* **kam mit**, *perf* **ist mitgekommen**) *vb* [**40**] ❶ to come along ▷ *Willst du nicht mitkommen?* Wouldn't you like to come along? ❷ to keep up ▷ *In Mathe komme ich nicht mit.* I can't keep up in maths.

Mitleid *nt* ❶ sympathy; **Ich habe wirklich Mitleid mit dir.** I really sympathize with you. ❷ pity ▷ *Er kennt kein Mitleid.* He knows no pity.

mitmachen (*perf* **hat mitgemacht**) *vb* [**48**] to join in

mitnehmen (*pres* **nimmt mit**, *imperf* **nahm mit**, *perf* **hat mitgenommen**) *vb* [**52**] ❶ to take ▷ *Kannst du den Brief zur Post mitnehmen?* Can you take the letter to the post office? ▷ *Ich habe meine Freundin zur Party mitgenommen.* I took my girlfriend to the party. ❷ to take away ▷ *Die Polizei ist gekommen und hat ihn mitgenommen.* The police came and took him away. ❸ to affect ▷ *Die Scheidung ihrer Eltern hat sie sehr mitgenommen.* Her parents' divorce really affected her.; **zum Mitnehmen** to take away

Mitschüler (*pl* **Mitschüler**) *m* schoolmate

Mitschülerin *f* schoolmate

mitspielen *vb* [**4**] to join in ▷ *Willst du nicht mitspielen?* Don't you want to join in?; **Wer hat bei dem Match mitgespielt?** Who played in the match?

Mittag (*pl* **Mittage**) *m* midday ▷ *gegen Mittag* around midday; **zu Mittag essen** to have lunch; **heute Mittag** at lunchtime; **morgen Mittag** tomorrow lunchtime; **gestern Mittag** yesterday lunchtime

Mittagessen (*pl* **Mittagessen**) *nt* lunch

mittags *adv* at lunchtime

Mittagspause *f* lunch break

Mitte *f* middle

mitteilen *vb* [**4**] **jemandem etwas mitteilen** to inform somebody of something

Mitteilung *f* communication

Mittel (*pl* **Mittel**) *nt* means *sg* ▷ *Wir werden jedes Mittel einsetzen, um die Genehmigung zu bekommen.* We will use every means to gain approval. ▷ *ein Mittel zum Zweck* a means to an end; **ein Mittel gegen Husten** something for a cough; **ein Mittel gegen Flecken** a stain remover; **öffentliche Mittel** public funds

Mitteleuropa *nt* Central Europe

mittelmäßig *adj* mediocre

Mittelmeer *nt* the Mediterranean

Mittelpunkt (*pl* **Mittelpunkte**) *m* centre

Mittelstürmer (*pl* **Mittelstürmer**) *m* centre-forward

Mitternacht *f* midnight ▷ *um Mitternacht* at midnight

mittlere *adj* ❶ middle ▷ *Das mittlere von den Fahrrädern ist meins.* The bike in the middle is mine. ▷ *Der mittlere Teil des Buches ist langweilig.* The middle section of the book is boring. ❷ average ▷ *Die mittleren Temperaturen liegen bei zwanzig Grad.* The average temperature is twenty degrees.; **mittleren Alters** middle-aged; **mittlere Reife** O-levels *pl*

Mittwoch (*pl* **Mittwoche**) *m* Wednesday ▷ *am Mittwoch* on Wednesday

mittwochs *adv* on Wednesdays

Mobbing *nt* workplace bullying

Möbel *ntpl* furniture *sg*

Möbelwagen (*pl* **Möbelwagen**) *m* removal van

Mobiltelefon (*pl* **Mobiltelefone**) *nt* mobile phone

möchte *vb see* **mögen**

Mode *f* fashion

Modell (*pl* **Modelle**) *nt* model

modern *adj* modern

modernisieren (*perf* **hat modernisiert**) *vb* [**76**] to modernize

modisch *adj* fashionable ▷ *Jane trägt sehr modische Kleidung.* Jane wears very fashionable clothes.

mogeln *vb* [**88**] to cheat

mögen (*pres* **mag**, *imperf* **mochte**, *perf* **hat gemocht** *or* **mögen**) *vb* [**50**]

> The past participle **mögen** is used when **mögen** is a modal auxiliary.

to like ▷ *Ich mag Süßes.* I like sweet things. ▷ *Ich habe sie noch nie gemocht.* I've never liked her.; **Ich möchte ...** I'd like ...; **Ich möchte nicht, dass du ...** I wouldn't like you to ...; **Ich mag nicht**

a b c d e f g h i j k l m n o p q r s t u v w x y z

mehr. I've had enough.; **etwas tun mögen** to like to do something; **etwas nicht tun mögen** not to want to do something
möglich *adj* possible ▷ *Das ist gar nicht möglich!* That's not possible. ▷ *so viel wie möglich* as much as possible
möglicherweise *adv* possibly
Möglichkeit *f* possibility; **nach Möglichkeit** if possible
möglichst *adv* as ... as possible ▷ *Komm möglichst bald.* Come as soon as possible.
Möhre *f* carrot
Moment (*pl* **Momente**) *m* moment ▷ *Wir müssen den richtigen Moment abwarten.* We have to wait for the right moment.; **im Moment** at the moment; **Moment mal!** Just a moment.
momentan *adj, adv* ❶ momentary ▷ *Das ist nur eine momentane Schwäche.* It's only a momentary weakness. ❷ at the moment ▷ *Ich bin momentan sehr beschäftigt.* I'm very busy at the moment.
Monarchie *f* monarchy
Monat (*pl* **Monate**) *m* month
monatlich *adj, adv* monthly
Monatskarte *f* monthly ticket
Mond (*pl* **Monde**) *m* moon
monetarisieren *vb* [**76**] to monetize
Montag (*pl* **Montage**) *m* Monday ▷ *am Montag* on Monday
montags *adv* on Mondays
Moor (*pl* **Moore**) *nt* moor
Moral *f* ❶ morals *pl* ▷ *Sie hat keine Moral.* She hasn't any morals. ❷ moral ▷ *Und die Moral der Geschichte ist: ...* And the moral of the story is: ...
moralisch *adj* moral
Mord (*pl* **Morde**) *m* murder
Mörder (*pl* **Mörder**) *m* murderer

> Be careful! **Mörder** does not mean **murder**.

Mörderin *f* murderer
morgen *adv* tomorrow; **morgen früh** tomorrow morning; **Bis morgen!** See you tomorrow!
Morgen (*pl* **Morgen**) *m* morning ▷ *Wir haben den ganzen Morgen Unterricht.* We've got lessons all morning.; **Guten Morgen!** Good morning.
morgens *adv* in the morning ▷ *Morgens bin ich immer müde.* I'm always tired in the morning.; **von morgens bis abends** from morning to night
Mosel *f* Moselle
Motiv (*pl* **Motive**) *nt* motive ▷ *Was war sein Motiv?* What was his motive?
Motor (*pl* **Motoren**) *m* ❶ engine ▷ *Das Auto hat einen starken Motor.* The car has a powerful engine. ❷ motor ▷ *ein Außenbordmotor* an outboard motor
Motorboot (*pl* **Motorboote**) *nt* motorboat
Motorrad (*pl* **Motorräder**) *nt* motorcycle
Möwe *f* seagull
MP3-Spieler (*pl* **MP3-Spieler**) *m* MP3 player
MRT *abbr* (= **Magnetresonanztomographie**) MRI
Mücke *f* midge
müde *adj* tired ▷ *Ich bin sehr müde.* I'm very tired.
Müdigkeit *f* tiredness
Mühe *f* trouble ▷ *Das macht gar keine Mühe.* That's no trouble.; **mit Müh und Not** with great difficulty; **sich Mühe geben** to go to a lot of trouble; **sich mehr Mühe geben** to try harder
Mühle *f* mill ▷ *In dieser Mühle wird Korn gemahlen.* Corn is ground in this mill. ▷ *Hast du eine Mühle, um den Kaffee zu mahlen?* Do you have a coffee mill?
mühsam *adj, adv* ❶ arduous ❷ with difficulty
Müll *m* refuse
Müllabfuhr *f* ❶ disposal of rubbish ▷ *Die Gebühren für die Müllabfuhr sollen erhöht werden.* The charges for the disposal of rubbish are to be increased. ❷ dustmen *pl* ▷ *Morgen kommt die Müllabfuhr.* The dustmen come tomorrow.
Mülleimer (*pl* **Mülleimer**) *m* rubbish bin

Mülltonne *f* dustbin
multiplizieren (*perf* **hat multipliziert**) *vb* [**76**] to multiply
München *nt* Munich
Mund (*pl* **Münder**) *m* mouth; **Halt den Mund!** *(informal)* Shut up!
Mundharmonika *f* mouth organ
mündlich *adj* oral ▷ *eine mündliche Prüfung* an oral exam
Munition *f* ammunition
Münster (*pl* **Münster**) *nt* cathedral
munter *adj* lively
Münze *f* coin
murmeln *vb* [**34**] to mumble ▷ *Er murmelte irgendwas vor sich hin.* He mumbled something.
mürrisch *adj* sullen
Muschel *f* ❶ mussel ▷ *Ich esse gern Muscheln.* I like mussels. ❷ shell ▷ *Wir haben am Strand Muscheln gesammelt.* We collected shells on the beach. ❸ receiver ▷ *Du musst in die Muschel sprechen.* You have to speak into the receiver.
Museum (*pl* **Museen**) *nt* museum
Musik *f* music
musikalisch *adj* musical ▷ *musikalisch begabt sein* to be musically gifted
Musiker (*pl* **Musiker**) *m* musician
Musikinstrument (*pl* **Musikinstrumente**) *nt* musical instrument
Muskel (*pl* **Muskeln**) *m* muscle
Müsli (*pl* **Müsli**) *nt* muesli
müssen (*pres* **muss**, *imperf* **musste**, *perf* **hat gemusst** *or* **müssen**) *vb* [**51**]

> The past participle **müssen** is used when **müssen** is a modal auxiliary.

❶ must ▷ *Ich muss es tun.* I must do it. ❷ to have to ▷ *Er hat gehen müssen.* He had to go. ▷ *Ich musste es tun.* I had to do it. ▷ *Er muss es nicht tun.* He doesn't have to do it. ▷ *Muss ich?* Do I have to?; **Muss das sein?** Is that really necessary?; **Es muss nicht wahr sein.** It needn't be true.; **Sie hätten ihn fragen müssen.** You should have asked him.; **Es muss geregnet haben.** It must have rained.; **Ich muss mal.** *(informal)* I need the loo.
Muster (*pl* **Muster**) *nt* ❶ pattern ▷ *ein Kleid mit einem geometrischen Muster* a dress with a geometric pattern ❷ sample ▷ *Lass dir von dem Stoff doch ein Muster geben.* Ask them to give you a sample of the material.
Mut *m* courage; **Nur Mut!** Cheer up!; **jemandem Mut machen** to encourage somebody; **zu Mute** *see* **zumute**
mutig *adj* courageous
Mutter (1) (*pl* **Mütter**) *f* mother ▷ *Meine Mutter erlaubt das nicht.* My mother doesn't allow that.
Mutter (2) (*pl* **Muttern**) *f* nut ▷ *Hast du die Mutter zu dieser Schraube gesehen?* Have you seen the nut for this bolt?
Muttersprache *f* mother tongue
Muttertag (*pl* **Muttertage**) *m* Mother's Day
Mutti (*pl* **Muttis**) *f (informal)* mummy
Mütze *f* cap

n

Nabel (*pl* **Nabel**) *m* navel

nach *prep, adv*

The preposition **nach** takes the dative.

❶ to ▷ *nach Berlin* to Berlin ▷ *nach Italien* to Italy; **nach Süden** south; **nach links** left; **nach rechts** right; **nach oben** up; **nach hinten** back ❷ after ▷ *Ich fange nach Weihnachten damit an.* I'll start on it after Christmas. ▷ *die nächste Straße nach der Kreuzung* the first street after the crossroads ▷ *einer nach dem anderen* one after the other ▷ *Nach Ihnen!* After you! ▷ *Ihm nach!* After him! ❸ past ▷ *zehn nach drei* ten past three ❹ according to ▷ *Nach unserer Englischlehrerin wird das so geschrieben.* According to our English teacher, that's how it's spelt.; **nach und nach** little by little; **nach wie vor** still

Nachbar (*gen* **Nachbarn**, *pl* **Nachbarn**) *m* neighbour

Nachbarin *f* neighbour

Nachbarschaft *f* neighbourhood

nachdem *conj* ❶ after ▷ *Nachdem er gegangen war, haben wir Witze erzählt.* After he left we told jokes. ❷ since ▷ *Nachdem du sowieso zur Post gehst, könntest du mein Päckchen aufgeben?* Since you're going to the post office anyway, could you post my parcel?; **je nachdem** it depends; **je nachdem, ob** depending on whether

nachdenken (*imperf* **dachte nach**, *perf* **hat nachgedacht**) *vb* **[14]** **nachdenken über** to think about

nacheinander *adv* one after the other

nachgeben (*pres* **gibt nach**, *imperf* **gab nach**, *perf* **hat nachgegeben**) *vb* **[28]** ❶ to give way ▷ *Das Brett hat nachgegeben.* The plank gave way. ❷ to give in ▷ *Ich werde nicht nachgeben.* I won't give in.

nachgehen (*imperf* **ging nach**, *perf* **ist nachgegangen**) *vb* **[29]** **jemandem nachgehen** to follow somebody; **einer Sache nachgehen** to look into something; **Die Uhr geht nach.** The clock is slow.

nachher *adv* afterwards

Nachhilfeunterricht *m* extra tuition

nachholen (*perf* **hat nachgeholt**) *vb* **[4]** ❶ to catch up on ▷ *Weil er gefehlt hat, muss er jetzt viel nachholen.* As he was absent, he's got a lot to catch up on. ❷ to make up for ▷ *Wir konnten meinen Geburtstag nicht feiern, werden das aber nachholen.* We weren't able to celebrate my birthday, but we'll make up for it.; **eine Prüfung nachholen** to do an exam at a later date

nachkommen (*imperf* **kam nach**, *perf* **ist nachgekommen**) *vb* **[40]** to come later ▷ *Wir gehen schon mal, du kannst ja später nachkommen.* We'll go on and you can come later.; **einer Verpflichtung nachkommen** to fulfil an obligation

nachlassen (*pres* **lässt nach**, *imperf* **ließ nach**, *perf* **hat nachgelassen**) *vb* **[42]** ❶ to deteriorate ▷ *Seine Leistungen haben merklich nachgelassen.* His marks have deteriorated considerably.; **Ihr Gedächtnis lässt nach.** Her memory is going.; **Er hat nachgelassen.** He's got worse. ❷ to ease off ▷ *Die Schmerzen haben nachgelassen.* The pain has eased off. ❸ to die down ▷ *sobald der Sturm nachlässt* as soon as the storm dies down

nachlässig *adj* careless; **etwas nachlässig machen** to do something carelessly

nachlaufen (*pres* **läuft nach**, *imperf* **lief nach**, *perf* **ist nachgelaufen**) *vb* [**43**] **jemandem nachlaufen** to run after somebody to chase ▷ *Er läuft allen Mädchen nach.* He chases all the girls.

nachmachen (*perf* **hat nachgemacht**) *vb* [**4**] ❶ to copy ▷ *Macht alle meine Bewegungen nach.* Copy all my movements. ❷ to imitate ▷ *Sie kann unsere Mathelehrerin gut nachmachen.* She's good at imitating our maths teacher. ❸ to forge ▷ *ein Gemälde nachmachen* to forge a painting; **Das ist nicht echt, sondern nachgemacht.** This isn't genuine, it's a fake.

Nachmittag (*pl* **Nachmittage**) *m* afternoon ▷ *am Nachmittag* in the afternoon; **heute Nachmittag** this afternoon

nachmittags *adv* in the afternoon

Nachname (*gen* **Nachnamens**, *pl* **Nachnamen**) *m* surname ▷ *Wie heißt du mit Nachnamen?* What's your surname?

nachprüfen (*perf* **hat nachgeprüft**) *vb* [**4**] to check ▷ *nachprüfen, ob* to check whether

Nachricht *f* ❶ news *sg* ▷ *Wir haben noch keine Nachricht von ihr.* We still haven't had any news of her.; **die Nachrichten** the news ❷ message ▷ *Kannst du ihm eine Nachricht von mir übermitteln?* Can you give him a message from me?

nachschlagen (*pres* **schlägt nach**, *imperf* **schlug nach**, *perf* **hat nachgeschlagen**) *vb* [**59**] to look up (*in dictionary*)

nachsehen (*pres* **sieht nach**, *imperf* **sah nach**, *perf* **hat nachgesehen**) *vb* [**64**] to check ▷ *Sieh mal nach, ob noch genügend Brot da ist.* Check whether we've still got enough bread. ▷ *Ich habe im Wörterbuch nachgesehen.* I've checked in the dictionary. ▷ *Mein Vater sieht immer meine Englischaufgaben nach.* My father always checks my English homework.; **jemandem etwas nachsehen** to forgive somebody something; **das Nachsehen haben** to come off worst

nachsichtig *adj* lenient

nachsitzen (*imperf* **saß nach**, *perf* **hat nachgesessen**) *vb* [**68**] **nachsitzen müssen** to be kept in

Nachspeise *f* pudding ▷ *Was gibt's als Nachspeise?* What's for pudding?

nächste *adj* ❶ next ▷ *Wir nehmen den nächsten Zug.* We'll take the next train. ▷ *Beim nächsten Mal passt du besser auf.* Be more careful next time. ▷ *nächstes Jahr* next year; **als Nächstes** next; **Der Nächste bitte!** Next, please! ❷ nearest ▷ *Wo ist hier die nächste Post?* Where's the nearest post office?

Nacht (*pl* **Nächte**) *f* night; **Gute Nacht!** Good night.

Nachteil (*pl* **Nachteile**) *m* disadvantage

Nachthemd (*pl* **Nachthemden**) *nt* nightshirt

Nachtisch *m* pudding ▷ *Was gibt's zum Nachtisch?* What's for pudding?

Nachtklub (*pl* **Nachtklubs**) *m* night club

Nachtruhe *f* sleep ▷ *Ich brauche meine Nachtruhe.* I need my sleep.

nachts *adv* at night

Nacken (*pl* **Nacken**) *m* nape of the neck

nackt *adj* naked ▷ *Er war nackt.* He was naked.; **nackte Arme** bare arms; **nackte Tatsachen** plain facts

Nadel *f* ❶ needle ▷ *Ich brauche Nadel und Faden.* I need a needle and thread. ❷ pin ▷ *Ich habe mich an der Nadel des Ansteckers gestochen.* I've pricked myself on the pin of my badge.
Nagel (*pl* **Nägel**) *m* nail
Nagellack (*pl* **Nagellacke**) *m* nail varnish
nagelneu *adj* brand-new
nagen *vb* [**38**] to gnaw ▷ *an etwas nagen* to gnaw on something
nahe *adj, adv, prep* ❶ near ▷ *in der nahen Zukunft* in the near future; **nahe bei** near ❷ close ▷ *Der Bahnhof ist ganz nah.* The station's quite close. ▷ *nahe Verwandte* close relatives ▷ *nahe Freunde* close friends ▷ *Unser Haus ist nahe der Universität.* Our house is close to the university. ▷ *den Tränen nahe* close to tears ▷ *mit jemandem nah verwandt sein* to be closely related to somebody; **der Nahe Osten** the Middle East; **Die Prüfungen rücken näher.** The exams are getting closer.; **nahe daran sein, etwas zu tun** to be close to doing something
Nähe *f* **in der Nähe** near; **aus der Nähe** close up
nähen *vb* [**38**] to sew
näher *adj, adv* nearer ▷ *Die Straßenbahnhaltestelle ist näher als die Bushaltestelle.* The tram stop is nearer than the bus stop.; **Näheres** details *pl*; **näher kommen** to get closer
sich **nähern** *vb* [**88**] to get closer ▷ *Wir näherten uns dem Bahnhof.* We were approaching the station.
nahm *vb see* **nehmen**
Nähmaschine *f* sewing machine
nahrhaft *adj* nourishing
Nahrung *f* food ▷ *feste Nahrung* solid food
Nahrungsmittel (*pl* **Nahrungsmittel**) *nt* foodstuffs *pl*
Naht (*pl* **Nähte**) *f* seam ▷ *Die Hose ist an der Naht geplatzt.* The trousers have split along the seam.
Nahverkehr *m* local traffic
Nahverkehrszug (*pl* **Nahverkehrszüge**) *m* local train
Name (*gen* **Namens**, *pl* **Namen**) *m* name ▷ *Mein Name ist ...* My name is ...; **im Namen von** on behalf of
nämlich *adv* ❶ you see ▷ *Sie ist nämlich meine beste Freundin.* You see, she's my best friend. ❷ that is to say ▷ *Nächstes Jahr, nämlich im März ...* Next year, that is to say in March ...
nannte *vb see* **nennen**
Narbe *f* scar
Narkose *f* anaesthetic
naschen *vb* [**48**] **Sie nascht gern.** She's got a sweet tooth.; **Wer hat von der Torte genascht?** Who's been at the cake?
Nase *f* nose ▷ *Meine Nase blutet.* My nose is bleeding.
Nasenbluten *nt* nosebleed ▷ *Ich hatte Nasenbluten.* I had a nosebleed.
nass *adj* wet ▷ *Nach dem Regen war die Wäsche noch nässer.* After the rain, the washing was even wetter.
Nässe *f* wetness
Nation *f* nation
Nationalhymne *f* national anthem
Nationalität *f* nationality
Natur *f* ❶ country ▷ *Wir gehen gern in der Natur spazieren.* We like to go for a walk in the country. ❷ constitution ▷ *Sie hat eine robuste Natur.* She's got a strong constitution.
natürlich *adj, adv* ❶ natural ▷ *Das ist ihre natürliche Haarfarbe.* That's her natural hair colour. ❷ of course ▷ *Wir kommen natürlich.* Of course we'll come. ▷ *Sie hat das natürlich wieder vergessen.* She's forgotten it again, of course. ▷ *Ja, natürlich!* Yes, of course.
Naturschutzgebiet (*pl* **Naturschutzgebiete**) *nt* nature reserve
Naturwissenschaft *f* natural science
Navi *m* GPS, sat nav
Nebel (*pl* **Nebel**) *m* ❶ mist ❷ fog
nebelig *adj* ❶ misty ❷ foggy

neben *prep*

Use the accusative to express movement or a change of place. Use the dative when there is no change of place.

❶ next to ▷ *Dein Rad steht neben meinem.* Your bike's next to mine. ▷ *Stell dein Rad neben meines.* Put your bike next to mine. ❷ apart from

neben takes the dative in this sense.

▷ *Neben den Sehenswürdigkeiten haben wir uns auch ein Theaterstück angesehen.* Apart from the sights, we also saw a play.

nebenan *adv* next door

nebenbei *adv* ❶ at the same time ▷ *Ich kann nicht Hausaufgaben machen und nebenbei fernsehen.* I can't do my homework and watch TV at the same time. ❷ on the side ▷ *Sie hat nebenbei noch einen anderen Job.* She has another job on the side.; **Sie sagte ganz nebenbei, dass sie nicht mitkommen wollte.** She mentioned quite casually that she didn't want to come along.; **Nebenbei bemerkt, ...** Incidentally, ...

nebeneinander *adv* side by side

Nebenfach (*pl* **Nebenfächer**) *nt* subsidiary subject

Nebenfluss (*gen* **Nebenflusses**, *pl* **Nebenflüsse**) *m* tributary

Nebenstraße *f* side street

neblig *adj* ❶ misty ❷ foggy

Neffe (*gen* **Neffen**, *pl* **Neffen**) *m* nephew

negativ *adj* negative ▷ *HIV-negativ* HIV-negative

Negativ (*pl* **Negative**) *nt* negative ▷ *Kann ich von den Bildern das Negativ haben?* Can I have the negatives of these pictures?

nehmen (*pres* **nimmt**, *imperf* **nahm**, *perf* **hat genommen**) *vb* [**52**] to take ▷ *Sie nahm fünf Euro aus dem Geldbeutel.* She took five euros out of her purse. ▷ *Wir nehmen besser den Bus in die Stadt.* We'd better take the bus into town. ▷ *Hast du deine Medizin genommen?* Have you taken your medicine? ▷ *Nimm ihn nicht ernst!* Don't take him seriously.; **Ich nehme ein Erdbeereis.** I'll have a strawberry ice cream.; **Nimm dir doch bitte!** Please help yourself.

Neid *m* envy

neidisch *adj* envious ▷ *Sie ist neidisch auf ihren Bruder.* She's envious of her brother.

nein *adv* no ▷ *Hast du das gesehen? — Nein.* Did you see that? — No, I didn't.; **Ich glaube nein.** I don't think so.

Nelke *f* ❶ carnation ▷ *Er brachte mir einen Strauß Nelken.* He brought me a bunch of carnations. ❷ clove ▷ *Zum Glühwein braucht man Nelken.* You need cloves to make mulled wine.

nennen (*imperf* **nannte**, *perf* **hat genannt**) *vb* ❶ to call ▷ *Sie haben ihren Sohn Manfred genannt.* They called their son Manfred. ▷ *Die Band nennt sich 'Die Zerstörer'.* The band call themselves 'The Destroyers'. ▷ *Wie nennt man ...?* What do you call ...? ❷ to name ▷ *Kannst du mir einen Fluss in England nennen?* Can you name a river in England?

Nerv (*pl* **Nerven**) *m* nerve; **jemandem auf die Nerven gehen** to get on somebody's nerves

Nervenzusammenbruch (*pl* **Nervenzusammenbrüche**) *m* nervous breakdown

nervös *adj* nervous

Nervosität *f* nervousness

Nest (*pl* **Nester**) *nt* ❶ nest ▷ *Der Vogel hat ein Nest gebaut.* The bird has built a nest. ❷ (*informal*) dump ▷ *Wiblingen ist ein Nest.* Wiblingen is a dump.

nett *adj* ❶ lovely ▷ *Vielen Dank für den netten Abend.* Thanks for a lovely evening. ❷ nice ▷ *Wir haben uns nett unterhalten.* We had a nice talk. ❸ kind ▷ *Wären Sie vielleicht so nett, mir zu helfen?* Would you be so kind as to help

a b c d e f g h i j k l m **n** o p q r s t u v w x y z

me? ▷ *Das war sehr nett von dir.* That was very kind of you.

netto *adv* net ▷ *Sie verdient dreitausend Euro netto.* She earns three thousand euros net.

Netz (*gen* **Netzes**, *pl* **Netze**) *nt* ❶ net ▷ *Die Fischer werfen ihre Netze aus.* The fishermen cast their nets. ▷ *Der Ball ging ins Netz.* The ball went into the net. ❷ string bag ▷ *Sie packte die Einkäufe ins Netz.* She packed her shopping into a string bag. ❸ network ▷ *ein weitverzweigtes Netz an Rohren* an extensive network of pipes ▷ *einen Computer ans Netz anschließen* to connect a computer to the network

Netzwerk (*pl* **Netzwerke**) *nt* network

neu *adj* new ▷ *Ist der Pulli neu?* Is that pullover new? ▷ *Sie hat einen neuen Freund.* She's got a new boyfriend. ▷ *Ich bin neu hier.* I'm new here.; **neue Sprachen** modern languages; **neueste** latest; **seit Neuestem** recently; **neu schreiben** to rewrite; **Das ist mir neu!** That's news to me.

neuartig *adj* new kind of ▷ *ein neuartiges Wörterbuch* a new kind of dictionary

Neugier *f* curiosity

neugierig *adj* curious

Neuheit *f* new product ▷ *Auf der Messe werden alle Neuheiten vorgestellt.* All new products are presented at the trade fair.

Neuigkeit *f* news *sg* ▷ *Gibt es irgendwelche Neuigkeiten?* Is there any news?

Neujahr *nt* New Year

neulich *adv* the other day

neun *num* nine

neunte *adj* ninth ▷ *Heute ist der neunte Juni.* Today is the ninth of June.

neunzehn *num* nineteen

neunzig *num* ninety

Neuseeland *nt* New Zealand

Neuseeländer (*pl* **Neuseeländer**) *m* New Zealander

Neuseeländerin *f* New Zealander

neutral *adj* neutral

Neutrum (*pl* **Neutra** *or* **Neutren**) *nt* neuter

nicht *adv* not ▷ *Ich bin nicht müde.* I'm not tired. ▷ *Er ist es nicht.* It's not him. ▷ *Es regnet nicht mehr.* It's not raining any more.; **Er raucht nicht. (1)** He isn't smoking. **(2)** He doesn't smoke.; **Ich kann das nicht. — Ich auch nicht.** I can't do it. — Neither can I.; **Nicht!** Don't!; **Nicht berühren!** Do not touch!; **Du bist müde, nicht wahr?** You're tired, aren't you?; **Das ist schön, nicht wahr?** It's nice, isn't it?; **Was du nicht sagst!** You don't say!

Nichte *f* niece

Nichtraucher (*pl* **Nichtraucher**) *m* nonsmoker

nichts *pron* nothing ▷ *nichts zu verzollen* nothing to declare ▷ *nichts Neues* nothing new; **Ich habe nichts gesagt.** I didn't say anything.; **Nichts ist so wie früher.** Things aren't what they used to be.; **Das macht nichts.** It doesn't matter.; **für nichts und wieder nichts** for nothing

nicken *vb* **[48]** to nod

nie *adv* never ▷ *Das habe ich nie gesagt.* I never said that. ▷ *Das werde ich nie vergessen.* I'll never forget that. ▷ *Das habe ich noch nie gehört.* I've never heard that. ▷ *Ich war noch nie in Indien.* I've never been to India.; **nie wieder** never again; **nie mehr** never again; **nie und nimmer** no way

Niederlage *f* defeat

Niederlande *ntpl* the Netherlands *pl*; **aus den Niederlanden** from the Netherlands; **in den Niederlanden** in the Netherlands; **in die Niederlande** to the Netherlands

Niederländer (*pl* **Niederländer**) *m* Dutchman; **Er ist Niederländer.** He's Dutch.

Niederländerin *f* Dutchwoman; **Sie ist Niederländerin.** She's Dutch.

niederländisch *adj* Dutch
Niedersachsen *nt* Lower Saxony
Niedersachsen is one of the 16 **Länder**. Its capital is Hannover. Its most important industries are mining and car manufacturing (Volkswagen). The Hannover Industrial Fair is the largest in the world.
Niederschlag (*pl* **Niederschläge**) *m* precipitation; **heftige Niederschläge** heavy rain; **radioaktiver Niederschlag** radioactive fallout
niedlich *adj* sweet ▷ *niedlich aussehen* to look sweet
niedrig *adj* ❶ low ▷ *Die Decke ist sehr niedrig.* The ceiling is very low. ▷ *niedrige Temperaturen* low temperatures ❷ shallow ▷ *Hier ist der Fluss niedriger.* The river is shallower here. ❸ base ▷ *niedrige Motive* base motives
niemals *adv* never
niemand *pron* ❶ nobody ▷ *Niemand hat mir Bescheid gesagt.* Nobody told me. ❷ not ... anybody ▷ *Ich habe niemanden gesehen.* I haven't seen anybody. ▷ *Sie hat mit niemandem darüber gesprochen.* She hasn't mentioned it to anybody.
Niere *f* kidney
nieseln *vb* [**88**] to drizzle
niesen *vb* [**38**] to sneeze
Niete *f* ❶ stud ▷ *Jeans mit Nieten* jeans with studs ❷ blank ▷ *Ich habe eine Niete gezogen.* I've drawn a blank.; **In Mathe ist er eine Niete.** He's useless at maths.
nimmt *vb see* **nehmen**
nirgends *adv* ❶ nowhere ❷ not ... anywhere
nirgendwo *adv see* **nirgends**
noch *adv, conj* still ▷ *Ich habe noch Hunger.* I'm still hungry. ▷ *Das kann noch passieren.* That might still happen. ▷ *Das ist noch besser.* That's better still.; **Bleib doch noch ein bisschen!** Stay a bit longer.; **Das wirst du noch lernen.** You'll learn.; **Er wird noch kommen.** He'll come.; **heute noch** today; **noch am selben Tag** the very same day; **noch vor einer Woche** only a week ago; **Wer noch?** Who else?; **Was noch?** What else?; **noch nicht** not yet; **noch nie** never; **immer noch** still; **noch einmal** again; **noch dreimal** three more times; **noch einer** another one; **noch größer** even bigger; **Geld noch und noch** *(informal)* loads of money; **weder ... noch ...** neither ... nor ...
nochmals *adv* again
Nominativ (*pl* **Nominative**) *m* nominative
Nordamerika *nt* North America
Norden *m* north
Nordirland *nt* Northern Ireland
nördlich *adj, prep, adv* northerly ▷ *Wir fuhren in nördlicher Richtung.* We drove in a northerly direction.; **nördlich einer Sache** to the north of something; **nördlich von** north of
Nordpol *m* North Pole ▷ *am Nordpol* at the North Pole
Nordrhein-Westfalen *nt* North Rhine-Westphalia
Nordrhein-Westfalen is one of the 16 **Länder**. Its capital is Düsseldorf. It is Germany's most densely populated state, and includes the Ruhr district.
Nordsee *f* North Sea ▷ *Wir fahren an die Nordsee.* We're going to the North Sea. ▷ *Wir waren an der Nordsee.* We've been to the North Sea.
Norm *f* standard ▷ *Für die meisten technischen Geräte gibt es Normen.* There are set standards for most technical equipment.
normal *adj* normal
Normalbenzin *nt* regular petrol
normalerweise *adv* normally
Norwegen *nt* Norway
Norweger (*pl* **Norweger**) *m* Norwegian
Norwegerin *f* Norwegian

a b c d e f g h i j k l m n o p q r s t u v w x y z

norwegisch *adj* Norwegian
Not *f* **zur Not** if necessary
Notausgang (*pl* **Notausgänge**) *m* emergency exit
Notbremse *f* emergency brake
Notdienst (*pl* **Notdienste**) *m* emergency service
Note *f* ❶ mark ▷ *Max hat gute Noten.* Max has got good marks. ❷ note ▷ *Welche Note hast du eben gespielt?* What note did you just play?
Notfall (*pl* **Notfälle**) *m* emergency
notfalls *adv* if need be
notieren (*perf* **hat notiert**) *vb* [**76**] to note down
nötig *adj* necessary ▷ *wenn nötig* if necessary; **etwas nötig haben** to need something
Notiz *f* ❶ note ▷ *Sein Kalender ist voller Notizen.* His diary is full of notes. ❷ item ▷ *Das stand heute in einer kleinen Notiz in der Zeitung.* There was a short item on it in the newspaper today.; **Notiz nehmen von** to take notice of
Notizbuch (*pl* **Notizbücher**) *nt* notebook
notlanden (*perf* **ist notgelandet**) *vb* [**54**] to make an emergency landing
Notruf (*pl* **Notrufe**) *m* emergency call
notwendig *adj* necessary
November (*gen* **November** *or* **Novembers**, *pl* **November**) *m* November ▷ *im November* in November ▷ *am neunten November* on the ninth of November ▷ *Freiburg, den 9. November 2008* Freiburg, 9 November 2008 ▷ *Heute ist der neunte November.* Today is the ninth of November.
nüchtern *adj* ❶ sober ▷ *Nach drei Gläsern Wein bist du nicht mehr nüchtern.* After three glasses of wine you aren't sober any more. ▷ *nüchterne Tatsachen* sober facts ❷ with an empty stomach ▷ *Kommen Sie nüchtern ins Krankenhaus.* Come to the hospital with an empty stomach.; **auf nüchternen Magen** on an empty stomach; **eine Lage nüchtern betrachten** to look at a situation rationally
Nudel *f* noodle ▷ *Es waren Nudeln in der Suppe.* There were noodles in the soup.; **Nudeln** pasta *sg*
null *num* ❶ nil ▷ *Sie haben eins zu null gespielt.* They won one nil. ❷ no ▷ *Ich hatte null Fehler.* I had no mistakes.; **null Uhr** midnight; **null und nichtig** null and void
Null *f* ❶ zero ▷ *Du musst zuerst eine Null wählen.* You have to dial zero first. ❷ nonentity ▷ *Er ist doch eine völlige Null.* He's a complete nonentity.
Nullerjahre *pl* 2000s, noughties
Nummer *f* ❶ number ▷ *Ich kann seine Nummer auswendig.* I know his number by heart. ❷ size ▷ *Die Schuhe sind eine Nummer zu groß.* These shoes are a size too big.
nummerieren (*perf* **hat nummeriert**) *vb* [**76**] to number
Nummernschild (*pl* **Nummernschilder**) *nt* number plate
nun *adv, excl* ❶ now ▷ *von nun an* from now on ❷ well ▷ *Nun, was gibt's Neues?* Well, what's new?; **Das ist nun mal so.** That's the way it is.
nur *adv* only ▷ *Das hat nur zwanzig Euro gekostet.* It only cost twenty euros. ▷ *Es sind nur fünf Leute da gewesen.* There were only five people there.; **Wo bleibt er nur?** Where on earth can he be?; **Was hat sie nur?** What on earth's wrong with her?
Nuss (*pl* **Nüsse**) *f* nut
nutzen *vb* [**36**] to help ▷ *Sprachkenntnisse können dir im Ausland viel nutzen.* Knowing a language can help you a lot abroad.; **etwas nutzen** to make use of something; **Das nutzt ja doch nichts.** That's pointless.; **Es nutzt alles nichts, wir müssen ...** There's no getting around it, we'll have to ...
Nutzen *m* **von Nutzen** useful; **Das ist zu deinem Nutzen.** It's for your own good.

nützen *vb* [**36**] *see* **nutzen**
nützlich *adj* useful ▷ *sich nützlich machen* to make oneself useful
nutzlos *adj* useless

O

Oase *f* oasis
ob *conj* ❶ whether ▷ *Ich weiß nicht, ob ich kommen kann.* I don't know whether I can come. ❷ if ▷ *Sie fragt, ob du auch kommst.* She wants to know if you're coming too.; **Ob das wohl wahr ist?** Can that be true?; **Und ob!** You bet!
obdachlos *adj* homeless
oben *adv* on top ▷ *oben auf dem Schrank* on top of the cupboard; **oben auf dem Berg** up on the mountain; **Die Schlafzimmer sind oben.** The bedrooms are upstairs.; **nach oben** up; **von oben** down; **oben ohne** topless; **Befehl von oben** orders from above
Ober (*pl* **Ober**) *m* waiter; **Herr Ober!** Waiter!
obere *adj* upper ▷ *die oberen Stockwerke* the upper floors; **die oberen Klassen** the senior classes
Oberfläche *f* surface
Obergeschoss (*gen* **Obergeschosses**, *pl* **Obergeschosse**) *nt* upper storey

Oberschenkel (*pl* **Oberschenkel**) *m* thigh

oberste *adj* topmost ▷ *Das Buch steht auf dem obersten Regalbrett.* The book is on the topmost shelf.; **Sie ist in der obersten Klasse.** She's in the top class.

obgleich *conj* although ▷ *Obgleich sie müde war, blieb sie lange auf.* Although she was tired, she stayed up late.

Objekt (*pl* **Objekte**) *nt* object

objektiv *adj* objective

Objektiv (*pl* **Objektive**) *nt* lens *(of camera)*

Obst *nt* fruit

Obstkuchen (*pl* **Obstkuchen**) *m* fruit tart

obwohl *conj* although ▷ *Obwohl sie müde war, blieb sie lange auf.* Although she was tired, she stayed up late.

Ochse (*gen* **Ochsen**, *pl* **Ochsen**) *m* ox

öde *adj* dull ▷ *eine öde Landschaft* a dull landscape; **Diese Arbeit ist echt öde.** *(informal)* This job's really the pits.

oder *conj* or ▷ *entweder ich oder du* either me or you; **Das stimmt, oder?** That's right, isn't it?

Ofen (*pl* **Öfen**) *m* ❶ oven ▷ *Der Kuchen ist im Ofen.* The cake's in the oven. ❷ heater; **Mach bitte den Ofen an, mir ist kalt.** Put the fire on, I'm cold.

offen *adj* open ▷ *Das Fenster ist offen.* The window's open. ▷ *Die Banken sind bis sechzehn Uhr offen.* The banks are open until four o'clock. ▷ *Sie ist ein sehr offener Mensch.* She's a very open person.; **offen gesagt** to be honest; **Ich gebe dir eine offene Antwort.** I'll be frank with you.; **eine offene Stelle** a vacancy

offensichtlich *adj, adv* ❶ obvious ▷ *ein offensichtlicher Fehler* an obvious mistake ❷ obviously ▷ *Er ist offensichtlich nicht zufrieden.* He's obviously dissatisfied.

öffentlich *adj* public ▷ *öffentliche Verkehrsmittel* public transport

Öffentlichkeit *f* public ▷ *Die Öffentlichkeit wurde nicht informiert.* The public were not informed. ▷ *in aller Öffentlichkeit* in public

offiziell *adj* official

öffnen *vb* [**53**] to open ▷ *jemandem die Tür öffnen* to open the door for somebody

Öffner (*pl* **Öffner**) *m* opener

Öffnung *f* opening

Öffnungszeiten *fpl* opening times *pl*

oft *adv* often ▷ *Wie oft warst du schon in London?* How often have you been to London?

öfter *adv* more often ▷ *Ich würde dich gern öfter besuchen.* I would like to visit you more often.; **Sie war in letzter Zeit öfter krank.** She's been ill a lot recently.

öfters *adv* often

ohne *prep, conj*

> The preposition **ohne** takes the accusative.

without ▷ *Ich fahre ohne meine Eltern in Ferien.* I'm going on holiday without my parents. ▷ *Ich habe das ohne Wörterbuch übersetzt.* I translated it without a dictionary. ▷ *Sie ist gegangen, ohne Bescheid zu sagen.* She left without telling anyone. ▷ *ohne zu fragen* without asking; **Das ist nicht ohne.** *(informal)* It's not half bad.; **ohne weiteres** easily; **Du kannst doch nicht so ohne weiteres gehen.** You can't just leave.

ohnmächtig *adj* **ohnmächtig werden** to faint; **Sie ist ohnmächtig.** She's fainted.

Ohr (*pl* **Ohren**) *nt* ear; **Er hat sehr gute Ohren.** His hearing is very good.

Ohrenschmerzen *pl* earache *sg* ▷ *Sie hat Ohrenschmerzen.* She's got earache.

Ohrfeige *f* slap across the face

ohrfeigen *vb* [**38**] **jemanden ohrfeigen** to slap somebody across the face

Ohrring (*pl* **Ohrringe**) *m* earring

ökologisch *adj* ecological

Oktober (*gen* **Oktober** *or* **Oktobers**, *pl* **Oktober**) *m* October ▷ *im Oktober* in October ▷ *am dritten Oktober* on the third of October ▷ *Ulm, den 3. Oktober 2010* Ulm, 3 October 2010. ▷ *Heute ist der dritte Oktober.* Today is the third of October.
Oktoberfest (*pl* **Oktoberfeste**) *nt* Munich beer festival
Öl (*pl* **Öle**) *nt* oil
ölig *adj* oily
oliv *adj* olive-green
Olive *f* olive
Ölsardine *f* sardine
Ölwechsel (*pl* **Ölwechsel**) *m* oil change
Olympiade *f* Olympic Games *pl*
Olympiasieger (*pl* **Olympiasieger**) *m* Olympic champion
Olympiasiegerin *f* Olympic champion
olympisch *adj* Olympic
Oma (*pl* **Omas**) *f (informal)* granny
Omelett (*pl* **Omeletts**) *nt* omelette
Onkel (*pl* **Onkel**) *m* uncle
Opa (*pl* **Opas**) *m (informal)* grandpa
Oper *f* ❶ opera ▷ *eine Oper von Verdi* an opera by Verdi ❷ opera house ▷ *Die Mailänder Oper ist berühmt.* The Milan opera house is famous.
Operation *f* operation
Operationssaal (*pl* **Operationssäle**) *m* operating theatre
Operette *f* operetta
operieren (*perf* **hat operiert**) *vb* [**76**] to operate on ▷ *jemanden operieren* to operate on somebody; **Sie muss operiert werden.** She has to have an operation.; **Sie wurde am Auge operiert.** She had an eye operation.
Opfer (*pl* **Opfer**) *nt* ❶ sacrifice ▷ *Das war ein großes Opfer für ihn.* It was a great sacrifice for him. ❷ victim ▷ *Der Unfall hat viele Opfer gefordert.* The accident claimed a lot of victims.
Opposition *f* opposition
Optiker (*pl* **Optiker**) *m* optician
optimal *adj, adv* optimum ▷ *Das ist die optimale Lösung.* That's the optimum solution.; **Sie hat das optimal gelöst.** She solved it in the best possible way.; **Wir haben den Platz optimal genutzt.** We made the best possible use of the space available.
Optimismus (*gen* **Optimismus**) *m* optimism
Optimist (*gen* **Optimisten**, *pl* **Optimisten**) *m* optimist
optimistisch *adj* optimistic
orange *adj* orange
Orange *f* orange
Orangensaft (*pl* **Orangensäfte**) *m* orange juice
Orchester (*pl* **Orchester**) *nt* orchestra
ordentlich *adj, adv* ❶ tidy ▷ *Seine Wohnung ist sehr ordentlich.* His flat's very tidy. ▷ *Ich bin ein ordentlicher Mensch.* I'm a tidy person. ❷ decent ▷ *Das sind ordentliche Leute.* They're decent people. ▷ *Das ist doch kein ordentliches Gehalt.* That's not a decent wage. ▷ *eine ordentliche Portion* a decent portion; **Ich brauche jetzt etwas Ordentliches zu essen.** Now I need a decent meal. ❸ respectable ▷ *Das ist eine ordentliche Leistung.* That's a respectable achievement. ▷ *Du solltest dir einen ordentlichen Beruf aussuchen.* You ought to look for a respectable job. ❹ neatly ▷ *Du solltest ordentlicher schreiben.* You should write more neatly. ❺ properly ▷ *Kannst du dich nicht ordentlich benehmen?* Can't you behave properly?; **Es hat ordentlich geschneit.** There's been a fair bit of snow.; **Sie haben ihn ordentlich verprügelt.** *(informal)* They beat him up good and proper.
ordnen *vb* [**53**] to put in order
Ordner (*pl* **Ordner**) *m* file
Ordnung *f* order ▷ *Ruhe und Ordnung* law and order; **Sie liebt Ordnung.** She likes everything to be in its place.; **Das hat schon alles seine Ordnung.** Everything is as it should be.;

Ordnung machen to tidy up; **Mit meinem Auto ist etwas nicht in Ordnung.** Something's wrong with my car.; **etwas wieder in Ordnung bringen** to repair something; **Ist alles in Ordnung?** Is everything okay?; **In Ordnung!** Okay!

Organ (*pl* **Organe**) *nt* organ ▷ *die inneren Organe* internal organs; **Er hat ein lautes Organ.** He's got a loud voice.

Organisation *f* organization

organisch *adj* organic

organisieren (*perf* **hat organisiert**) *vb* [**76**] to organize ▷ *Wer hat das Fest organisiert?* Who organized the party?

Orgel *f* organ ▷ *Sie spielt Orgel.* She plays the organ.

sich **orientieren** (*perf* **hat sich orientiert**) *vb* [**76**] ❶ to find one's way around ▷ *Ich brauche einen Stadtplan, um mich besser orientieren zu können.* I need a city map to be able to find my way around better. ❷ to find out ▷ *Ich muss mich orientieren, wie das gehandhabt wird.* I'll have to find out what the procedure is.

originell *adj* original ▷ *ein origineller Einfall* an original idea

Orkan (*pl* **Orkane**) *m* hurricane

Ort (*pl* **Orte**) *m* place; **an Ort und Stelle** on the spot

Orthografie *f* spelling

örtlich *adj* local

Ortsgespräch (*pl* **Ortsgespräche**) *nt* local phone call

Osten *m* east

Osterei (*pl* **Ostereier**) *nt* Easter egg

Osterferien *pl* Easter holidays *pl*

Ostern (*pl* **Ostern**) *nt* Easter ▷ *an Ostern* at Easter

Österreich *nt* Austria

Österreicher (*pl* **Österreicher**) *m* Austrian

Österreicherin *f* Austrian

österreichisch *adj* Austrian

People in Austria speak a dialect of German.

östlich *adj, prep, adv* easterly ▷ *Wir fuhren in östlicher Richtung.* We drove in an easterly direction.; **östlich einer Sache** to the east of something; **östlich von** east of

Ostsee *f* Baltic ▷ *Wir fahren an die Ostsee.* We're going to the Baltic. ▷ *Wir waren an der Ostsee.* We've been to the Baltic.

oval *adj* oval

Ozean (*pl* **Ozeane**) *m* ocean

Ozon *nt* ozone

Ozonloch (*pl* **Ozonlöcher**) *nt* ozone hole

Ozonschicht *f* ozone layer

p

Paar (*pl* **Paare**) *nt* ❶ pair ▷ *Ich habe ein Paar Schuhe gekauft.* I've bought a pair of shoes. ❷ couple ▷ *Sie sind ein sehr glückliches Paar.* They're a very happy couple.; **ein paar** a few

paarmal *adv* **ein paarmal** a few times

Päckchen (*pl* **Päckchen**) *nt* ❶ small parcel ▷ *Wie viel kostet ein Päckchen ins Ausland?* How much does it cost to post a small parcel abroad? ❷ packet ▷ *Sie raucht ein Päckchen pro Tag.* She smokes a packet a day.

packen *vb* **[38]** ❶ to pack ▷ *Hast du deinen Koffer schon gepackt?* Have you already packed your suitcase? ❷ to grasp ▷ *Sie packte mich am Arm.* She grasped my arm.; **Er hat die Prüfung nicht gepackt.** He didn't manage to get through the exam.

Packung *f* ❶ packet ▷ *eine Packung Tee* a packet of tea ▷ *eine Packung Zigaretten* a packet of cigarettes ❷ box ▷ *eine Packung Pralinen* a box of chocolates

Paket (*pl* **Pakete**) *nt* ❶ packet ▷ *Ich habe ein Paket Waschpulver gekauft.* I bought a packet of washing powder. ❷ parcel ▷ *Die Gebühren für Pakete stehen in dieser Liste.* Parcel rates are in this list.

Palast (*pl* **Paläste**) *m* palace

Palme *f* palm tree

Pampelmuse *f* grapefruit

Panik *f* panic

panisch *adj* **panische Angst vor etwas haben** to be terrified of something; **panisch reagieren** to panic

Panne *f* ❶ breakdown ▷ *Wir hatten eine Panne auf der Autobahn.* We had a breakdown on the motorway. ❷ slip ▷ *Mir ist da eine kleine Panne passiert.* I made a slight slip.

Panzer (*pl* **Panzer**) *m* ❶ tank ▷ *Die Armee setzte Panzer ein.* The army used tanks. ❷ shell ▷ *der Panzer einer Schildkröte* a tortoise's shell

Papa (*pl* **Papas**) *m* *(informal)* daddy

Papagei (*pl* **Papageien**) *m* parrot

Papier (*pl* **Papiere**) *nt* paper

Papierkorb (*pl* **Papierkörbe**) *m* wastepaper basket

Papiertüte *f* paper bag

Pappe *f* cardboard

Paprika (*pl* **Paprikas**) *m* ❶ paprika ▷ *Ich habe das Hähnchen mit Paprika gewürzt.* I've seasoned the chicken with paprika. ❷ pepper ▷ *Heute gibt es gefüllte Paprikas.* We're having stuffed peppers today.

Papst (*pl* **Päpste**) *m* pope

Paradies (*gen* **Paradieses**, *pl* **Paradiese**) *nt* paradise

parallel *adj* parallel

paralympisch *adj* Paralympic

Pärchen (*pl* **Pärchen**) *nt* couple ▷ *Auf der Parkbank saß ein Pärchen.* There was a couple sitting on the bench in the park.

Parfüm (*pl* **Parfüms** *or* **Parfüme**) *nt* perfume

Park (*pl* **Parks**) *m* park

parken *vb* **[38]** to park

Parkett (*pl* **Parkette** *or* **Parketts**) *nt* stalls *pl* *(theatre)*
Parkhaus (*gen* **Parkhauses**, *pl* **Parkhäuser**) *nt* multistorey car park
Parkplatz (*gen* **Parkplatzes**, *pl* **Parkplätze**) *m* car park
Parkscheibe *f* parking disc
Parkschein *m* car-park ticket
Parkuhr *f* parking meter
Parkverbot (*pl* **Parkverbote**) *nt* **Hier ist Parkverbot.** You're not allowed to park here.
Parlament (*pl* **Parlamente**) *nt* parliament
Partei *f* party *(political)*; **Partei für jemanden ergreifen** to take somebody's side
Parterre (*pl* **Parterres**) *nt* ❶ ground floor ▷ *Wir wohnen im Parterre.* We live on the ground floor. ❷ stalls *pl* *(theatre)*
Partner (*pl* **Partner**) *m* partner
Partnerin *f* partner
Partnerstadt (*pl* **Partnerstädte**) *f* twin town
Party (*pl* **Partys**) *f* party ▷ *eine Party veranstalten* to have a party
Pass (*gen* **Passes**, *pl* **Pässe**) *m* ❶ passport ▷ *Für Indien brauchst du einen Pass.* You need a passport for India. ❷ pass ▷ *Im Winter ist der Pass gesperrt.* The pass is closed in winter.
Passage *f* passage; **eine Einkaufspassage** a shopping arcade
Passagier (*pl* **Passagiere**) *m* passenger
passen *vb* **[31]** ❶ to fit ▷ *Die Hose passt nicht.* The trousers don't fit. ▷ *Es ist zu groß und passt nicht in meinen Koffer.* It's too big and doesn't fit in my suitcase. ❷ to suit ▷ *Passt dir Dienstag?* Does Tuesday suit you? ▷ *Dieser Termin passt mir nicht.* That date doesn't suit me.; **Es passt mir nicht, dass du so frech bist.** I don't like you being so cheeky.; **zu etwas passen** to go with something; **zu jemandem passen** to be right for somebody ❸ to pass ▷ *Auf die Frage muss ich passen.* I'll have to pass on that question.
passend *adj* ❶ matching ▷ *Ich muss jetzt dazu passende Schuhe kaufen.* I now must buy some matching shoes. ❷ appropriate ▷ *Sie hat ein paar passende Worte gesprochen.* She said a few appropriate words. ❸ convenient ▷ *Das ist nicht die passende Gelegenheit.* This isn't a convenient time.
passieren (*perf* **ist passiert**) *vb* **[76]** to happen ▷ *Was ist passiert?* What happened? ▷ *Mir ist etwas Lustiges passiert.* Something funny happened to me.
passiv *adj, adv* passive ▷ *passives Rauchen* passive smoking ▷ *passiv zusehen* to watch passively
Passiv (*pl* **Passive**) *nt* passive
Passivrauchen *nt* passive smoking
Passkontrolle *f* passport control
Passwort (*pl* **Passwörter**) *nt* password
Pastete *f* pie *(savoury)*
Pate (*gen* **Paten**, *pl* **Paten**) *m* godfather
Patenkind (*pl* **Patenkinder**) *nt* godchild
Patent (*pl* **Patente**) *nt* patent
Patient (*gen* **Patienten**, *pl* **Patienten**) *m* patient
Patientin *f* patient
Patin *f* godmother
Patrone *f* cartridge
pauken *vb* **[38]** ❶ *(informal)* to swot ▷ *Vor der Arbeit habe ich ziemlich gepaukt.* I swotted quite a lot before the test. ❷ *(informal)* to swot up ▷ *Ich muss Vokabeln pauken.* I have to swot up my vocabulary.
Pauschalreise *f* package tour
Pause *f* ❶ break ▷ *eine Pause machen* to have a break ▷ *die große Pause* the long break ❷ interval ▷ *In der Pause haben wir über das Stück gesprochen.* We talked about the play during the interval.
Pazifik *m* Pacific

Pech *nt* bad luck ▷ *Das war Pech!* That was bad luck.; **Pech haben** to be unlucky; **Pech!** Hard luck!
Pedal (*pl* **Pedale**) *nt* pedal
peinlich *adj* ❶ embarrassing ▷ *eine peinliche Frage* an embarrassing question ❷ awkward ▷ *eine peinliche Angelegenheit* an awkward situation; **Das ist mir aber peinlich.** I'm dreadfully sorry.; **peinlich genau** painstakingly
Peitsche *f* whip
Pelle *f* skin
Pelz (*gen* **Pelzes**, *pl* **Pelze**) *m* fur
Pendel (*pl* **Pendel**) *nt* pendulum
pendeln (*perf* **ist gependelt**) *vb* [**34**] to commute ▷ *Er pendelt zwischen Tübingen und Stuttgart.* He commutes between Tübingen and Stuttgart.
Pendelverkehr *m* ❶ shuttle service ▷ *Die Fluggesellschaft hat einen Pendelverkehr zwischen Köln und Berlin eingerichtet.* The airline set up a shuttle service between Cologne and Berlin. ❷ commuter traffic ▷ *Zwischen Tübingen und Stuttgart besteht ein reger Pendelverkehr.* There is heavy commuter traffic between Tübingen and Stuttgart.
Pendler (*pl* **Pendler**) *m* commuter
Penis (*gen* **Penis**, *pl* **Penisse**) *m* penis
pennen *vb* [**48**] *(informal)* to kip ▷ *Ich habe auf dem Fußboden gepennt.* I kipped on the floor.; **Er pennt.** He's having a kip.
Penner (*pl* **Penner**) *m (informal)* dosser
Pension *f* ❶ pension ▷ *Er bezieht eine ordentliche Pension.* He gets a decent pension.; **in Pension gehen** to retire ❷ guesthouse ▷ *Wir haben in einer Pension übernachtet.* We stayed overnight in a guesthouse.
perfekt *adj* perfect ▷ *ein perfektes Alibi* a perfect alibi ▷ *perfekt passen* to fit perfectly
Perfekt (*pl* **Perfekte**) *nt* perfect
Periode *f* period
Perle *f* pearl
Person *f* person; **ich für meine Person ...** personally I ...
Personal *nt* staff ▷ *das Personal der Firma* the staff of the company ▷ *das Hotelpersonal* the hotel staff
Personalausweis (*gen* **Personalausweises**, *pl* **Personalausweise**) *m* identity card
Personenzug (*pl* **Personenzüge**) *m* passenger train
persönlich *adj, adv* ❶ personal ▷ *das persönliche Fürwort* the personal pronoun ▷ *persönlich werden* to get personal ❷ in person ▷ *persönlich erscheinen* to appear in person ❸ personally ▷ *jemanden persönlich kennen* to know somebody personally ▷ *Das war nicht persönlich gemeint.* It wasn't meant personally.
Persönlichkeit *f* personality
Perücke *f* wig
Pessimist (*gen* **Pessimisten**, *pl* **Pessimisten**) *m* pessimist
pessimistisch *adj* pessimistic
Pest *f* plague; **jemanden wie die Pest hassen** to loathe somebody
Petersilie *f* parsley
Pfad (*pl* **Pfade**) *m* path
Pfadfinder (*pl* **Pfadfinder**) *m* boy scout
Pfadfinderin *f* girl guide
Pfand (*pl* **Pfänder**) *nt* ❶ deposit ▷ *Auf der Flasche ist ein Pfand von siebzig Cent.* There's a deposit of seventy cents on the bottle. ❷ forfeit ▷ *Wer die Frage nicht beantworten kann, muss ein Pfand geben.* Anyone who cannot answer the question must pay a forfeit.
Pfandflasche *f* returnable bottle
Pfanne *f* frying pan
Pfannkuchen (*pl* **Pfannkuchen**) *m* pancake
Pfarrer (*pl* **Pfarrer**) *m* parish priest
Pfeffer (*pl* **Pfeffer**) *m* pepper
Pfefferkorn (*pl* **Pfefferkörner**) *nt* peppercorn

Pfefferminzbonbon (*pl* **Pfefferminzbonbons**) *nt* peppermint

Pfeife *f* ❶ whistle ▷ *die Pfeife des Schiedsrichters* the referee's whistle ❷ pipe ▷ *Mein Bruder raucht Pfeife.* My brother smokes a pipe.

pfeifen (*imperf* **pfiff**, *perf* **hat gepfiffen**) *vb* to whistle

Pfeil (*pl* **Pfeile**) *m* arrow

Pferd (*pl* **Pferde**) *nt* horse

Pferderennen (*pl* **Pferderennen**) *nt* ❶ race meeting ▷ *Er geht regelmäßig zu Pferderennen.* He regularly goes to race meetings. ❷ horse-racing ▷ *Ich interessiere mich nicht für Pferderennen.* I'm not interested in horse-racing.

Pferdeschwanz (*gen* **Pferdeschwanzes**, *pl* **Pferdeschwänze**) *m* ponytail

> Word for word, **Pferdeschwanz** means 'horse's tail'.

Pferdestall (*pl* **Pferdeställe**) *m* stable

Pfingsten (*gen* **Pfingsten**, *pl* **Pfingsten**) *nt* Whitsun ▷ *an Pfingsten* at Whitsun

Pfirsich (*pl* **Pfirsiche**) *m* peach

Pflanze *f* plant

pflanzen *vb* [36] to plant

Pflaster (*pl* **Pflaster**) *nt* ❶ plaster ▷ *Sie klebte ein Pflaster auf die Wunde.* She put a plaster on the cut. ❷ paving stones *pl* ▷ *Jemand hatte das Pflaster in der Fußgängerzone bemalt.* Somebody had been painting on the paving stones in the pedestrian precinct.

Pflaume *f* plum

Pflege *f* ❶ care ▷ *Diese Pflanze braucht nicht viel Pflege.* This plant doesn't need much care. ▷ *ein Mittel zur Pflege von Leder* a leather-care product ❷ nursing ▷ *Ein krankes Baby braucht viel Pflege.* A sick baby needs a lot of nursing.; **ein Kind in Pflege geben** to have a child fostered

Pflegeeltern *pl* foster parents *pl*

pflegen *vb* [38] ❶ to nurse ▷ *Sie pflegt ihre kranke Mutter.* She's nursing her sick mother. ❷ to look after ▷ *Briten pflegen ihren Rasen.* The British look after their lawns.; **gepflegte Hände** well-cared-for hands; **gepflegt aussehen** to look well-groomed

Pfleger (*pl* **Pfleger**) *m* male nurse

Pflicht *f* duty ▷ *Es ist deine Pflicht, dich darum zu kümmern.* It's your duty to take care of it.

pflichtbewusst *adj* conscientious

Pflichtfach (*pl* **Pflichtfächer**) *nt* compulsory subject

pflücken *vb* [48] to pick ▷ *Wir haben Himbeeren gepflückt.* We picked raspberries. ▷ *einen Strauß pflücken* to pick a bunch of flowers

Pförtner (*pl* **Pförtner**) *m* doorman

Pfosten (*pl* **Pfosten**) *m* post ▷ *Der Ball traf den Pfosten.* The ball hit the post.

Pfote *f* paw ▷ *Der Hund hat schmutzige Pfoten.* The dog's paws are dirty.

pfui *excl* ugh!

Pfund (*pl* **Pfunde** *or* **Pfund**) *nt* pound ▷ *drei Pfund Äpfel* three pounds of apples ▷ *dreißig britische Pfund* thirty pounds sterling

pfuschen *vb* [38] *(informal)* to be sloppy; **Die Handwerker haben gepfuscht.** The craftsmen produced sloppy work.; **jemandem ins Handwerk pfuschen** to stick one's nose into somebody's business

Pfütze *f* puddle

Phantasie *f see* **Fantasie**

phantasieren *vb see* **fantasieren**

phantastisch *adj see* **fantastisch**

Philosophie *f* philosophy

Photo *nt see* **Foto**

Physik *f* physics *sg* ▷ *Physik ist mein Lieblingsfach.* Physics is my favourite subject.

Physiker (*pl* **Physiker**) *m* physicist

Pickel (*pl* **Pickel**) *m* ❶ pimple ▷ *Du hast einen Pickel auf der Nase.* You've got a pimple on your nose. ❷ pickaxe ▷ *Die*

Arbeiter haben den Straßenbelag mit Pickeln aufgeschlagen. The workers broke up the road surface with pickaxes. ❸ ice axe ▷ *Die Bergsteiger hatten Seile und Pickel dabei.* The mountaineers had ropes and ice axes with them.

Picknick (*pl* **Picknicks**) *nt* picnic ▷ *Picknick machen* to have a picnic

Piepser (*pl* **Piepser**) *m (informal)* bleeper

Pik (*pl* **Pik**) *nt* spades *sg* ▷ *Pik ist Trumpf.* Spades is trumps.

pikant *adj* spicy

Pille *f* pill ▷ *Sie nimmt die Pille.* She's on the pill.

Pilot (*gen* **Piloten**, *pl* **Piloten**) *m* pilot

Pils (*gen* **Pils**, *pl* **Pils**) *nt* Pilsner lager

Pilz (*gen* **Pilzes**, *pl* **Pilze**) *m* ❶ mushroom ▷ *eine Soße mit Pilzen* a mushroom sauce ❷ toadstool ▷ *Der Fliegenpilz ist giftig.* The fly agaric is a toadstool.

pinkeln *vb* [**88**] *(informal)* to pee

Pinsel (*pl* **Pinsel**) *m* paintbrush

Pinzette *f* tweezers *pl* ▷ *eine Pinzette* a pair of tweezers

Pirat (*gen* **Piraten**, *pl* **Piraten**) *m* pirate

Piste *f* ❶ run ▷ *Wir sind die blaue Piste runtergefahren.* We skied down the blue run. ❷ runway ▷ *Das Flugzeug stand auf der Piste und wartete auf die Starterlaubnis.* The plane stood on the runway waiting for clearance for takeoff.

Pistole *f* pistol

Plakat (*pl* **Plakate**) *nt* poster

Plan (*pl* **Pläne**) *m* ❶ plan ▷ *Unser Plan war, vor ihm da zu sein.* Our plan was to arrive before him. ❷ map ▷ *Hast du einen Plan von München?* Have you got a map of Munich?

planen *vb* [**38**] to plan ▷ *Wir planen unseren nächsten Urlaub.* We're planning our next holiday.; **einen Mord planen** to plot a murder

Planet (*gen* **Planeten**, *pl* **Planeten**) *m* planet

planmäßig *adj* ❶ according to plan ▷ *Alles verlief planmäßig.* Everything went according to plan. ❷ scheduled ▷ *planmäßige Ankunft* scheduled arrival ❸ on time ▷ *Die Maschine ist planmäßig gelandet.* The plane landed on time.

Plastik *nt* plastic ▷ *Die meisten Spielzeuge sind heute aus Plastik.* Most toys these days are made of plastic.
▶ *f* sculpture

Plastikbeutel (*pl* **Plastikbeutel**) *m* plastic bag

Plastiktüte *f* plastic bag

platt *adj* flat ▷ *ein platter Reifen* a flat tyre ▷ *plattes Land* flat country; **etwas platt drücken** to flatten something; **Ich bin platt!** *(informal)* I'm flabbergasted!

plattdeutsch *adj* low German

Platte *f* ❶ plate ▷ *Sie stellte den Topf auf die Platte.* She put the saucepan on the plate.; **eine Platte mit Käseaufschnitt** a platter of assorted cheeses ❷ record ▷ *Sie hat alle Platten der Beatles.* She's got all the Beatles' records.

Plattenspieler (*pl* **Plattenspieler**) *m* record player

Platz (*gen* **Platzes**, *pl* **Plätze**) *m* ❶ place ▷ *Das ist ein schöner Platz zum Zelten.* That's a good place to pitch a tent. ▷ *Das Buch steht nicht an seinem Platz.* The book isn't in its place. ▷ *der erste Platz* the first place ❷ seat ▷ *Wir hatten Plätze in der ersten Reihe.* We had seats in the front row. ▷ *Ist hier noch ein Platz frei?* Are all these seats taken?; **Platz nehmen** to take a seat ❸ room ▷ *Das Sofa braucht zu viel Platz.* The sofa takes up too much room. ▷ *jemandem Platz machen* to make room for somebody ❹ square ▷ *Auf dem Platz vor der Kirche ist zweimal die Woche Markt.* There's a market twice a week on the square in front of the church. ❺ playing field; **Der Schiedsrichter schickte ihn vom Platz.** The referee sent him off.

Plätzchen (*pl* **Plätzchen**) *nt* ❶ spot ▷ *ein hübsches Plätzchen* a beautiful spot ❷ biscuit ▷ *Zum Kaffee gab es Plätzchen.* There were biscuits with the coffee.
platzen (*perf* **ist geplatzt**) *vb* [**36**] ❶ to burst ▷ *Der Luftballon ist geplatzt.* The balloon has burst. ❷ to explode ▷ *In der Innenstadt ist gestern eine Bombe geplatzt.* A bomb exploded in the town centre yesterday.; **vor Wut platzen** *(informal)* to be livid
Platzkarte *f* seat reservation
plaudern *vb* [**88**] to chat
pleite *adj (informal)* broke ▷ *Ich bin total pleite.* I'm stony-broke.
Pleite *f* ❶ bankruptcy ▷ *die Pleite einer Firma* the bankruptcy of a company; **Pleite machen** *(informal)* to go bust ❷ *(informal)* flop ▷ *Die Veranstaltung war eine Pleite.* The event was a flop.
Plombe *f* filling ▷ *Ich habe noch keine einzige Plombe.* I still haven't got a single filling.
plötzlich *adj, adv* ❶ sudden ▷ *ihr plötzliches Erscheinen* her sudden appearance ❷ suddenly ▷ *Sie war plötzlich weg.* Suddenly she was gone.
plump *adj* clumsy ▷ *plumpe Bewegungen* clumsy movements; **ein plumper Körper** a shapeless body; **eine plumpe Lüge** a blatant lie
Plural (*pl* **Plurale**) *m* plural
Plutonium *nt* plutonium
Po (*pl* **Pos**) *m (informal)* bum
Pokal (*pl* **Pokale**) *m* ❶ cup ▷ *Welche Mannschaft hat den Pokal gewonnen?* Which team won the cup? ❷ goblet ▷ *Sie tranken Wein aus Pokalen.* They drank wine out of goblets.
Pokalspiel (*pl* **Pokalspiele**) *nt* cup tie
Pol (*pl* **Pole**) *m* pole ▷ *am Pol* at the Pole
Pole (*gen* **Polen**, *pl* **Polen**) *m* Pole; **Er ist Pole.** He's Polish.
Polen *nt* Poland
Police *f* insurance policy
polieren (*perf* **hat poliert**) *vb* [**76**] to polish
Polin *f* Pole; **Sie ist Polin.** She's Polish.
Politik *f* ❶ politics *sg* ▷ *Politik interessiert mich nicht.* Politics doesn't interest me. ❷ policy ▷ *die Politik Großbritanniens in Bezug auf Immigration* Great Britain's policy on immigration
Politiker (*pl* **Politiker**) *m* politician
politisch *adj* political
Polizei *f* police

> Note that **Polizei** is used with a singular verb and 'police' with a plural verb.

▷ *Die Polizei ist noch nicht da.* The police haven't arrived yet.
Polizeibeamte (*gen* **Polizeibeamten**, *pl* **Polizeibeamten**) *m* police officer ▷ *Wir wurden von einem Polizeibeamten angehalten.* We were stopped by a police officer.
Polizeibeamtin *f* police officer ▷ *Sie ist Polizeibeamtin.* She's a police officer.
polizeilich *adj* **Er wird polizeilich gesucht.** The police are looking for him.
Polizeirevier (*pl* **Polizeireviere**) *nt* police station
Polizeiwache *f* police station
Polizist (*gen* **Polizisten**, *pl* **Polizisten**) *m* policeman ▷ *Dietmar ist Polizist.* Dietmar's a policeman.
Polizistin *f* policewoman ▷ *Ursula ist Polizistin.* Ursula's a policewoman.
polnisch *adj* Polish
Pommes *fpl* chips *pl* ▷ *Pommes mit Mayonnaise* chips with mayonnaise
Pommes frites *fpl* chips *pl* ▷ *Würstchen mit Pommes frites* sausages and chips
Pony (*pl* **Ponys**) *nt* pony ▷ *Wir sind auf Ponys geritten.* We rode ponies.
▸ *m* fringe ▷ *Sie trägt einen Pony.* She's got a fringe.
Pop *m* pop
Popmusik *f* pop music
Pore *f* pore
Pornografie *f* pornography
porös *adj* porous
Porree (*pl* **Porrees**) *m* leek

Portemonnaie (*pl* **Portemonnaies**) *nt* purse
Portier (*pl* **Portiers**) *m* porter
Portion *f* portion ▷ *eine große Portion* a big portion ▷ *Zwei Portionen Pommes frites, bitte.* Two portions of chips, please.; **Dazu gehört eine ordentliche Portion Mut.** You need quite a bit of courage for that.
Portmonee (*pl* **Portmonees**) *nt* purse
Porto (*pl* **Portos**) *nt* postage
Portugal *nt* Portugal
Portugiese (*gen* **Portugiesen**, *pl* **Portugiesen**) *m* Portuguese
Portugiesin *f* Portuguese
portugiesisch *adj* Portuguese
Porzellan *nt* ❶ porcelain ▷ *eine Figur aus Porzellan* a porcelain figurine ❷ china ▷ *Das Porzellan habe ich von meiner Oma geerbt.* I inherited the china from my grandma.
positiv *adj* positive ▷ *HIV-positiv* HIV-positive
Post *f* ❶ post office ▷ *Bring bitte das Päckchen zur Post.* Please take the parcel to the post office. ❷ mail ▷ *Ist Post für mich gekommen?* Was there any mail for me?
Postamt (*pl* **Postämter**) *nt* post office
Postausgang (*pl* **Postausgänge**) *m* outbox
Postbote (*gen* **Postboten**, *pl* **Postboten**) *m* postman
Postbotin *f* postwoman
Posteingang (*pl* **Posteingänge**) *m* inbox
Posten (*pl* **Posten**) *m* ❶ post ▷ *Sie hat einen guten Posten als Chefsekretärin.* She's got a good post as a director's secretary. ❷ sentry ▷ *Die Armee hat vor dem Gebäude Posten aufgestellt.* The army posted sentries in front of the building. ❸ item ▷ *Dieser Posten ist nicht auf der Preisliste aufgeführt.* This item doesn't appear on the price list.
Postfach (*pl* **Postfächer**) *nt* post office box
Postkarte *f* postcard
Postleitzahl *f* postcode
Pracht *f* splendour
prächtig *adj, adv* ❶ magnificent ▷ *ein prächtiges Haus* a magnificent house ❷ marvellous ▷ *Wir haben uns prächtig amüsiert.* We had a marvellous time.
prachtvoll *adj* splendid
Prädikat (*pl* **Prädikate**) *nt* predicate ▷ *Subjekt und Prädikat eines Satzes* subject and predicate of a sentence
prahlen *vb* **[38]** to brag
Praktikant (*gen* **Praktikanten**, *pl* **Praktikanten**) *m* trainee
Praktikantin *f* trainee
Praktikum (*gen* **Praktikums**, *pl* **Praktika**) *nt* practical training ▷ *Sie absolviert ihr Praktikum.* She's doing her practical training.
praktisch *adj* ❶ practical ▷ *ein praktischer Mensch* a practical person ▷ *eine praktische Lösung* a practical solution ▷ *praktische Erfahrung* practical experience ❷ handy ▷ *ein praktisches Gerät* a handy gadget; **praktischer Arzt** general practitioner; **praktisch begabt sein** to be good with one's hands
Praline *f* chocolate
Präposition *f* preposition
Präsens (*gen* **Präsens**) *nt* present tense
Präservativ (*pl* **Präservative**) *nt* condom
Präsident (*gen* **Präsidenten**, *pl* **Präsidenten**) *m* president
Praxis (*pl* **Praxen**) *f* ❶ practical experience ▷ *Ihr fehlt die Praxis.* She lacks practical experience.; **etwas in die Praxis umsetzen** to put something into practice ❷ surgery ▷ *Kommen Sie zur Behandlung in die Praxis.* Come to the surgery for treatment. ❸ practice ▷ *Mein Anwalt hat seine eigene Praxis aufgemacht.* My solicitor has opened his own practice.
Preis (*gen* **Preises**, *pl* **Preise**) *m* ❶ price ▷ *Die Preise für Computer sind gefallen.* Computer prices have fallen. ❷ prize ▷ *Ihr Hund hat einen Preis gewonnen.* Her dog's won a prize.; **um keinen Preis** not at any price

preisgünstig *adj* inexpensive
Preislage *f* price range
Preisschild (*pl* **Preisschilder**) *nt* price tag
Preisträger (*pl* **Preisträger**) *m* prizewinner
preiswert *adj* inexpensive
Prellung *f* bruise
Premierminister (*pl* **Premierminister**) *m* prime minister
Presse *f* press
pressen *vb* **[31]** to press
Priester (*pl* **Priester**) *m* priest
prima *adj* super ▷ *Es ist ein prima Hotel.* It's a super hotel.
Prinz (*gen* **Prinzen**, *pl* **Prinzen**) *m* prince
Prinzessin *f* princess
Prinzip (*pl* **Prinzipien**) *nt* principle; **aus Prinzip** as a matter of principle
privat *adj* private
Privatschule *f* fee-paying school
pro *prep*

The preposition **pro** takes the accusative.

per ▷ *zehn Euro pro Person* ten euros per person; **einmal pro Woche** once a week
Probe *f* ❶ test ▷ *Wir haben in Englisch morgen eine Probe.* We've got an English test tomorrow. ❷ sample ▷ *Die Probe wird im Labor untersucht.* The sample's being examined in the laboratory. ❸ rehearsal ▷ *die letzte Probe vor der Aufführung* the final rehearsal before the performance; **jemanden auf die Probe stellen** to test somebody
probieren (*perf* **hat probiert**) *vb* **[76]** to try ▷ *Probier mal eine andere Methode.* Try a different method. ▷ *Willst du mal von dem Käse probieren?* Would you like to try some of the cheese?; **Ich werde probieren, ob ich das kann.** I'll give it a try.
Problem (*pl* **Probleme**) *nt* problem ▷ *Kein Problem!* No problem.
Produkt (*pl* **Produkte**) *nt* product
Produktion *f* ❶ production ▷ *die Produktion von Luxusautos* the production of luxury cars ❷ output ▷ *Wir müssen unsere Produktion erhöhen.* We must increase our output.
produzieren (*perf* **hat produziert**) *vb* **[76]** to produce
Professor (*pl* **Professoren**) *m* professor
Profi (*pl* **Profis**) *m* (*informal*) pro ▷ *Er spielt wie ein Profi.* He plays like a pro.
Profit (*pl* **Profite**) *m* profit
profitieren (*perf* **hat profitiert**) *vb* **[76]** to profit
Programm (*pl* **Programme**) *nt* ❶ programme ▷ *das Programm des heutigen Abends* this evening's programme ❷ program ▷ *Für die Kalkulation arbeite ich mit einem anderen Programm.* I've got a different program for spreadsheets.
programmieren (*perf* **hat programmiert**) *vb* **[76]** to program
Programmierer (*pl* **Programmierer**) *m* programmer
Projekt (*pl* **Projekte**) *nt* project
Promi *mf* celebrity
Promille (*pl* **Promille**) *nt* alcohol level ▷ *Er hatte drei Promille.* He had an alcohol level of three hundred milligrams in a hundred millilitres of blood.
Pronomen (*pl* **Pronomen**) *nt* pronoun
Prospekt (*pl* **Prospekte**) *m* brochure

Be careful! **Prospekt** does not mean **prospect**.

prost *excl* cheers!
Prostituierte (*gen* **Prostituierten**) *f* prostitute
Prostitution *f* prostitution
Protest (*pl* **Proteste**) *m* protest
protestantisch *adj* Protestant
protestieren (*perf* **hat protestiert**) *vb* **[76]** to protest ▷ *Wir protestieren gegen diese Maßnahmen.* We're protesting against these measures.
Protokoll (*pl* **Protokolle**) *nt* ❶ minutes *pl* ▷ *Wer schreibt das Protokoll der*

heutigen Besprechung? Who is taking the minutes of today's meeting? ❷ statement ▷ *Der Zeuge muss das polizeiliche Protokoll unterschreiben.* The witness must sign the statement he made to the police.

Proviant (*pl* **Proviante**) *m* provisions *pl*

provisorisch *adj* provisional

provozieren (*perf* **hat provoziert**) *vb* [**76**] to provoke

Prozent (*pl* **Prozente**) *nt* per cent ▷ *zehn Prozent* ten per cent

Prozess (*gen* **Prozesses**, *pl* **Prozesse**) *m* trial ▷ *der Prozess gegen die Terroristen* the trial of the terrorists; **einen Prozess gewinnen** to win a case

prüfen *vb* [**38**] ❶ to test ▷ *Wir werden morgen in Chemie geprüft.* We're having a chemistry test tomorrow. ❷ to check ▷ *Vor der Reise sollte man den Ölstand prüfen.* You should check the oil before your journey.

Prüfer (*pl* **Prüfer**) *m* examiner

Prüfung *f* ❶ examination ▷ *Sie hat die Prüfung bestanden.* She's passed the examination. ❷ check ▷ *Bei der Prüfung der Bremsen haben wir einen Defekt festgestellt.* During a check on the brakes we found a fault.

Prügel (*pl* **Prügel**) *m* stick ▷ *Er schlug ihn mit einem Prügel.* He hit him with a stick.; **Prügel bekommen** *(informal)* to get a hiding; **Er hat von seinen Freunden Prügel bekommen.** His friends beat him up.

prügeln *vb* [**34**] to beat ▷ *Eltern sollten ihre Kinder nicht prügeln.* Parents shouldn't beat their children.; **sich prügeln** to fight; **Die beiden haben sich in der Pause geprügelt.** The two of them had a fight in the break.

psychisch *adj* psychological

Psychologe (*gen* **Psychologen**, *pl* **Psychologen**) *m* psychologist ▷ *Ihr Vater ist Psychologe.* Her father is a psychologist.

Psychologie *f* psychology

psychologisch *adj* psychological

Pubertät *f* puberty ▷ *während der Pubertät* during puberty

Publikum *nt* audience ▷ *Am Ende des Stückes klatschte das Publikum.* The audience clapped at the end of the play.

Pudding (*pl* **Puddinge** *or* **Puddings**) *m* blancmange

Puder (*pl* **Puder**) *m* powder

Pullover (*pl* **Pullover**) *m* pullover

Puls (*gen* **Pulses**, *pl* **Pulse**) *m* pulse; **jemandem den Puls fühlen** to take somebody's pulse

Pult (*pl* **Pulte**) *nt* desk

Pulver (*pl* **Pulver**) *nt* powder

Pumpe *f* pump

pumpen *vb* [**38**] ❶ to pump ▷ *Das Öl wird durch die Pipeline gepumpt.* The oil's pumped along the pipeline. ❷ to lend ▷ *Kannst du mir mal dein iPad® pumpen?* Can you lend me your iPad®? ❸ to borrow ▷ *Ich habe mir das Rad meiner Schwester gepumpt.* I've borrowed my sister's bike.

Punkt (*pl* **Punkte**) *m* ❶ full stop ▷ *Am Satzende steht ein Punkt.* A full stop goes at the end of a sentence. ❷ point ▷ *In diesem Punkt gebe ich dir recht.* On this point I agree with you. ❸ dot ▷ *Sie trug ein rotes Kleid mit weißen Punkten.* She was wearing a red dress with white dots.

pünktlich *adj, adv* ❶ punctual ▷ *Sie ist nicht sehr pünktlich.* She's not very punctual. ❷ on time ▷ *Der Zug kam pünktlich an.* The train arrived on time.

Puppe *f* doll

pur *adj* pure ▷ *Das ist pures Gold.* That's pure gold. ▷ *Das ist doch der pure Wahnsinn.* But that's pure madness.; **etwas pur trinken** to drink something neat; **Whisky pur** neat whisky

Pute *f* turkey

Puter (*pl* **Puter**) *m* turkey

putzen *vb* [**36**] ❶ to clean ▷ *Sie putzt jeden Samstag das Haus.* She cleans the house every Saturday. ❷ to wipe ▷ *Putz dir die Schuhe, bevor du reinkommst.* Wipe your shoes before you come in.; **sich die Nase putzen** to blow one's nose; **sich die Zähne putzen** to brush one's teeth

Putzfrau *f* cleaner

Putzmann (*pl* **Putzmänner**) *m* cleaner

Pyramide *f* pyramid

q

Quadrat (*pl* **Quadrate**) *nt* square

Quadratmeter (*pl* **Quadratmeter**) *m* square metre ▷ *eine Wohnung von achtzig Quadratmetern* a flat of eighty square metres

Qual *f* ❶ agony ▷ *Treppensteigen ist für sie eine Qual.* Climbing the stairs is agony for her. ❷ anguish ▷ *Die Qualen, die ich bei dieser Prüfung ausgestanden habe ...* The anguish I went through in that exam ...

quälen *vb* [**38**] to treat cruelly ▷ *Tiere quälen* to treat animals cruelly; **sich quälen (1)** to struggle ▷ *Sie quälte sich die Treppe hinauf.* She struggled up the steps. **(2)** to torment oneself ▷ *Quäl dich nicht so!* Don't torment yourself like that.; **Er muss sich in der Schule ziemlich quälen.** School's quite a trial for him.

Qualität *f* quality

Qualle *f* jellyfish ▷ *zwei Quallen* two jellyfish

Qualm *m* thick smoke

qualmen *vb* [**38**] to smoke ▷ *Der Schornstein qualmt.* The chimney is smoking.
Quark *m* quark
Quarz (*gen* **Quarzes**) *m* quartz
Quatsch *m (informal)* rubbish ▷ *Erzähl keinen Quatsch.* Don't talk rubbish.; **Quatsch machen** to fool around; **Mach keinen Quatsch!** Don't be foolish!
quatschen *vb* [**48**] *(informal)* to natter
Quelle *f* ❶ spring ▷ *heiße Quellen* hot springs ❷ source ▷ *aus zuverlässiger Quelle* from a reliable source
quer *adv* ❶ diagonally ▷ *Die Streifen auf dem Stoff verlaufen quer.* The stripes run diagonally across the material.; **quer auf dem Bett** across the bed ❷ at right angles ▷ *Die Mannstraße verläuft quer zur Müllerstraße.* Mann Street runs at right angles to Müller Street.
Querflöte *f* flute ▷ *Cordula spielt Querflöte.* Cordula plays the flute.
querschnittsgelähmt *adj* paraplegic
Querstraße *f* **eine Straße mit vielen Querstraßen** a road with a lot of side streets off it; **Biegen Sie an der zweiten Querstraße links ab.** Take the second street on the left.
quetschen *vb* [**48**] ❶ to squash ▷ *Pass auf, dass die Tomaten nicht gequetscht werden.* Mind the tomatoes don't get squashed. ❷ to cram ▷ *Sie quetschte das Kleid noch in ihren Koffer.* She crammed the dress into her case.; **Ich habe mir den Finger in der Tür gequetscht.** I trapped my finger in the door.
Quetschung *f* bruise
quitt *adj* quits ▷ *Jetzt sind wir quitt.* We're quits now.
Quittung *f* receipt ▷ *Brauchen Sie eine Quittung?* Do you need a receipt?

r

Rabatt (*pl* **Rabatte**) *m* discount
Rache *f* revenge
Rad (*pl* **Räder**) *nt* ❶ wheel ❷ bike ▷ *Wir sind mit dem Rad gekommen.* We came by bike.; **Rad fahren** to cycle
Radarkontrolle *f* radar-controlled speed check
radfahren *vb* [**21**] *see* **Rad**
Radfahrer (*pl* **Radfahrer**) *m* cyclist
Radfahrweg (*pl* **Radfahrwege**) *m* cycle track
Radiergummi (*pl* **Radiergummis**) *m* rubber
Radieschen (*pl* **Radieschen**) *nt* radish
Radio (*pl* **Radios**) *nt* radio
radioaktiv *adj* radioactive
Radioaktivität *f* radioactivity
Radrennen (*pl* **Radrennen**) *nt* ❶ cycle race ▷ *Er hat an dem Radrennen teilgenommen.* He took part in the cycle race. ❷ cycle racing ▷ *Sie begeistert sich für Radrennen.* She's a cycle racing fan.
Rahm *m* cream

Rahmen (*pl* **Rahmen**) *m* frame ▷ *der Rahmen eines Bildes* the frame of a picture; **im Rahmen des Möglichen** within the bounds of possibility

Rakete *f* rocket

Rand (*pl* **Ränder**) *m* ❶ edge ▷ *Er stand am Rand des Schwimmbeckens.* He stood on the edge of the swimming pool. ❷ rim ▷ *der Rand der Tasse* the rim of the cup; **eine Brille mit Goldrand** a pair of gold-rimmed glasses ❸ margin ▷ *Lass an der Seite des Blattes einen Rand.* Leave a margin at the edge of the page. ❹ ring ▷ *In der Badewanne waren dunkle Ränder.* There were dark rings in the bath tub. ❺ verge ▷ *Die Firma steht am Rand des Bankrotts.* The company's on the verge of bankruptcy.; **außer Rand und Band** out of control

Rang (*pl* **Ränge**) *m* ❶ rank *(military)* ▷ *Er steht im Rang eines Hauptmanns.* He has the rank of captain.; **ein Mann ohne Rang und Namen** a man without any standing ❷ circle *(theatre)* ▷ *erster Rang* dress circle ▷ *zweiter Rang* upper circle

Rappen (*pl* **Rappen**) *m* rappen ▷ *Der Schweizer Franken hat hundert Rappen.* There're one hundred rappen in a Swiss franc.

In the French-speaking part of Switzerland you talk about **centime** rather than **Rappen**.

rasch *adj, adv* quick ▷ *Das war rasch gemacht.* That was quickly done.; **Ich gehe noch rasch beim Bäcker vorbei.** I'll just pop round to the baker's.

rasen (*perf* **ist gerast**) *vb* [**88**] to race ▷ *Wir sind durch die engen Straßen gerast.* We raced along the narrow streets.

Rasen (*pl* **Rasen**) *m* lawn

Rasenmäher (*pl* **Rasenmäher**) *m* lawnmower

Rasierapparat (*pl* **Rasierapparate**) *m* shaver

Rasiercreme (*pl* **Rasiercremes**) *f* shaving cream

rasieren (*perf* **hat rasiert**) *vb* [**76**] to shave; **sich rasieren** to shave

Rasiermesser (*pl* **Rasiermesser**) *nt* razor

Rasse *f* ❶ race ▷ *Rassenunruhen* race riots ❷ breed ▷ *Welche Rasse ist Ihr Hund?* What breed is your dog?

Rassismus (*gen* **Rassismus**) *m* racism

Rast *f* rest; **Rast machen** to stop for a break

rasten *vb* [**2**] to rest

Rasthof (*pl* **Rasthöfe**) *m* services *pl (motorway)*

Raststätte *f* service area

Rasur *f* shaving

Rat (*pl* **Ratschläge**) *m* advice ▷ *Ich habe viele Ratschläge bekommen.* I've been given a lot of advice.; **ein Rat** a piece of advice; **Ich weiß keinen Rat.** I don't know what to do.; **jemanden zu Rate ziehen** to consult somebody

Rate *f* instalment

raten (*pres* **rät**, *imperf* **riet**, *perf* **hat geraten**) *vb* to guess ▷ *Rat mal, wie alt ich bin.* Guess how old I am.; **jemandem raten** to advise somebody

Rathaus (*gen* **Rathauses**, *pl* **Rathäuser**) *nt* town hall

rationalisieren (*perf* **hat rationalisiert**) *vb* [**76**] to rationalize

ratlos *adj* at a loss ▷ *Ich bin ratlos, was ich tun soll.* I'm at a loss as to what to do.; **Sie sah mich ratlos an.** She gave me a helpless look.

Ratschlag (*pl* **Ratschläge**) *m* piece of advice ▷ *Ich habe viele Ratschläge bekommen.* I've been given a lot of advice.

Rätsel (*pl* **Rätsel**) *nt* ❶ puzzle ▷ *Sie löst gern Rätsel.* She likes solving puzzles. ❷ mystery ▷ *Das ist mir ein Rätsel.* It's a mystery to me.

rätselhaft *adj* mysterious; **Es ist mir rätselhaft ...** It's a mystery to me ...

Ratte *f* rat

rau *adj* ❶ rough ▷ *raue Haut* rough skin ❷ husky ▷ *eine raue Stimme* a husky voice ❸ sore ▷ *ein rauer Hals* a sore throat ❹ harsh ▷ *raues Wetter* harsh weather ▷ *ein rauer Wind* a harsh wind; **Hier herrschen raue Sitten.** People here have rough-and-ready ways.

Raub *m* robbery

Raubtier (*pl* **Raubtiere**) *nt* predator

Rauch *m* smoke

rauchen *vb* [**48**] to smoke ▷ *Er raucht Pfeife.* He smokes a pipe.; **'Rauchen verboten'** 'No smoking'

Raucher (*pl* **Raucher**) *m* smoker

räuchern *vb* [**88**] to smoke ▷ *Fisch räuchern* to smoke fish

rauh *adj see* **rau**

Raum (*pl* **Räume**) *m* ❶ space ▷ *Sie haben eine Rakete in den Raum geschossen.* They launched a rocket into space. ▷ *Raum und Zeit* space and time ❷ room ▷ *Eine Wohnung mit vier Räumen ist nicht groß genug für uns.* A four-roomed flat isn't big enough for us. ▷ *Dieses Gerät braucht wenig Raum.* This appliance doesn't take up much room. ❸ area ▷ *Im Raum Stuttgart kommt es morgen zu Gewittern.* There will be thunderstorms in the Stuttgart area tomorrow.

räumen *vb* [**38**] ❶ to clear ▷ *Die Polizei hat das besetzte Haus geräumt.* The police cleared the squat. ❷ to vacate ▷ *Bitte räumen Sie Ihr Zimmer bis spätestens zehn Uhr.* Please vacate your room by ten o'clock at the latest. ❸ to clear away ▷ *Könnt ihr bitte das Geschirr vom Tisch räumen?* Could you clear away the dishes, please? ❹ to put away ▷ *Räum bitte deine Spielsachen in den Schrank.* Please put your toys away in the cupboard.

Raumfähre *f* space shuttle

Raumfahrt *f* space travel

räumlich *adj* spatial

Raumschiff (*pl* **Raumschiffe**) *nt* spaceship

Rausch (*pl* **Räusche**) *m* **einen Rausch haben** to be drunk; **seinen Rausch ausschlafen** to sleep it off

Rauschgift (*pl* **Rauschgifte**) *nt* drug

Rauschgiftsüchtige (*gen* **Rauschgiftsüchtigen**, *pl* **Rauschgiftsüchtigen**) *mf* drug addict ▷ *Gestern wurde ein Rauschgiftsüchtiger tot aufgefunden.* A drug addict was found dead yesterday.

sich **räuspern** *vb* [**88**] to clear one's throat

reagieren (*perf* **hat reagiert**) *vb* [**76**] ❶ to react ▷ *Wie hat sie auf diesen Vorwurf reagiert?* How did she react to the allegation? ❷ to respond ▷ *Die Bremsen haben nicht reagiert.* The brakes didn't respond.

Reaktion *f* reaction

Reaktor (*pl* **Reaktoren**) *m* reactor

realisieren (*perf* **hat realisiert**) *vb* [**76**] ❶ to fulfil ▷ *Er hat seine Träume realisiert.* He's fulfilled his dreams. ❷ to carry out ▷ *Wir sollten diese Pläne realisieren.* We ought to carry out these plans. ❸ to realize ▷ *Sie hat gar nicht realisiert, dass er schon längst weg war.* She simply didn't realize that he had long since left.

realistisch *adj* realistic

Realityshow *f* reality show

Realschule *f* secondary school

Pupils enter **Realschule** at the age of about ten, and leave after six years. It is not as academically oriented as the **Gymnasium**.

rechnen *vb* [**53**] to work out ▷ *Lass mich rechnen, wie viel das wird.* Let me work out how much that's going to be.; **gut rechnen können** to be good at arithmetic; **Schneider wird zu den besten Fußballspielern gerechnet.** Schneider is regarded as one of the best footballers.; **rechnen zu** to class as; **rechnen mit (1)** to reckon with ▷ *Mit wie vielen Besuchern können wir rechnen?* How many visitors can we reckon with? **(2)** to reckon on ▷ *Mit dieser Reaktion hatte ich nicht gerechnet.* I hadn't reckoned on this reaction.; **rechnen auf** to count on

Rechnen *nt* arithmetic ▷ *Bettina ist gut im Rechnen.* Bettina's good at arithmetic.

Rechner (*pl* **Rechner**) *m* ❶ calculator ▷ *Ich habe das mit meinem Rechner nachgerechnet.* I've checked it with my calculator. ❷ computer ▷ *Er hat sich für seinen Rechner einen neuen Prozessor gekauft.* He's bought a new CPU for his computer.

Rechnung *f* ❶ calculations *pl* ▷ *Meine Rechnung ergibt, dass wir noch zweihundert Euro haben.* According to my calculations, we still have two hundred euros left. ❷ invoice ▷ *Die Rechnung liegt der Sendung bei.* The invoice is enclosed.

recht *adj, adv* ❶ right ▷ *Es war nicht recht, dass du sie belogen hast.* It wasn't right of you to lie to her. ▷ *Dies ist nicht der rechte Moment, um darüber zu sprechen.* This isn't the right moment to talk about it.; **Wenn ich dich recht verstehe ...** If I understand you correctly ...; **Das geschieht dir recht!** Serves you right! ❷ quite ▷ *Das scheint recht einfach.* It seems quite simple.; **jemandem recht sein** to be all right with somebody; **Das ist mir recht.** That suits me.; **es jemandem recht machen** to please somebody; **recht haben** to be right; **jemandem recht geben** to agree with somebody; **Jetzt erst recht!** Now more than ever.

Recht (*pl* **Rechte**) *nt* ❶ right ▷ *Es ist mein Recht, das zu erfahren.* It's my right to know that. ▷ *Ich habe ein Recht auf eine Erklärung.* I've got a right to an explanation.; **im Recht sein** to be in the right; **etwas mit Recht tun** to be right to do something ❷ law ▷ *Sie wurde nach deutschem Recht zu zehn Jahren Gefängnis verurteilt.* She was sentenced under German law to ten years' imprisonment.; **Recht sprechen** to administer justice

rechte *adj* right ▷ *In Deutschland fährt man auf der rechten Seite.* They drive on the right in Germany. ▷ *Mein rechtes Auge tut weh.* My right eye's hurting. ▷ *Er hat sich den rechten Arm gebrochen.* He broke his right arm.

Rechte (*gen* **Rechten**) *f* ❶ right ▷ *Zu Ihrer Rechten sehen Sie das Rathaus.* On your right you'll see the town hall. ❷ right hand ▷ *Er schlug mit der Rechten zu.* He hit out with his right hand. ❸ right-wing ▷ *eine Partei der Rechten* a right-wing party
▶ *nt* right thing ▷ *Pass auf, dass du das Rechte sagst.* Make sure you say the right thing.

rechteckig *adj* rectangular

rechtfertigen *vb* [**38**] to justify ▷ *Wie kannst du dein Verhalten rechtfertigen?* How can you justify your behaviour?; **sich rechtfertigen** to justify oneself

rechtmäßig *adj* lawful

rechts *adv* right ▷ *rechts abbiegen* to turn right; **rechts überholen** to overtake on the right; **Er schreibt mit rechts.** He writes with his right hand.; **Rechts sehen Sie das Rathaus.** On the right you'll see the town hall.; **rechts von der Kirche** to the right of the church; **rechts von mir** on my right; **rechts wählen** to vote for a right-wing party

Rechtsanwalt (*pl* **Rechtsanwälte**) *m* lawyer

Rechtsanwältin *f* lawyer

Rechtschreibung *f* spelling

Rechtshänder (*pl* **Rechtshänder**) *m* **Er ist Rechtshänder.** He's right-handed.

Rechtshänderin *f* **Sie ist Rechtshänderin.** She's right-handed.

rechtzeitig *adj, adv* in time ▷ *Ich bitte um rechtzeitige Benachrichtigung.* Please let me know in time. ▷ *Wir sind rechtzeitig angekommen.* We arrived in time.

recyceln (*perf* **hat recycelt**) *vb* [**7**] to recycle

Redakteur (*pl* **Redakteure**) *m* editor
Redaktion *f* ❶ editorial staff ▷ *Die Redaktion hat das Manuskript abgelehnt.* The editorial staff rejected the manuscript. ❷ editorial office ▷ *Er arbeitet in unserer Redaktion.* He works in our editorial office.
Rede *f* speech ▷ *Er hat eine witzige Rede gehalten.* He made an amusing speech.; **jemanden zur Rede stellen** to take somebody to task
reden *vb* **[54]** ❶ to talk ▷ *Wir haben über das Wetter geredet.* We talked about the weather. ▷ *Du redest Unsinn.* You're talking nonsense. ❷ to speak ▷ *Ich werde mit deiner Mutter reden.* I'll speak to your mother. ▷ *Ich rede nicht gern vor so vielen Menschen.* I don't like speaking in front of so many people. ❸ to say ▷ *Was reden die Leute über uns?* What are people saying about us?
Redewendung *f* expression
Redner (*pl* **Redner**) *m* speaker
reduzieren (*perf* **hat reduziert**) *vb* **[76]** to reduce
Referat (*pl* **Referate**) *nt* ❶ assignment ▷ *Ich muss in Geografie ein Referat schreiben.* I have to write an assignment in geography. ❷ paper ▷ *Sie hat ein Referat über Shakespeare gehalten.* She gave a paper on Shakespeare. ❸ section ▷ *Er ist Leiter des Referats Umweltschutz.* He's head of the environmental protection section.
reflexiv *adj* reflexive
Reform *f* reform
Regal (*pl* **Regale**) *nt* ❶ bookcase ▷ *In ihrem Regal stehen viele Krimis.* There are a lot of detective stories in her bookcase. ❷ rack ▷ *ein Regal für Weinflaschen* a wine rack ❸ shelf ▷ *Auf dem Regal standen Kräuter.* There were herbs on the shelf.
Regel *f* ❶ rule ▷ *Keine Regel ohne Ausnahme.* The exception proves the rule. ❷ period ▷ *Meine Regel ist ausgeblieben.* I've missed a period.
regelmäßig *adj, adv* regular ▷ *in regelmäßigen Abständen* at regular intervals ▷ *Die Busse verkehren regelmäßig.* The buses run regularly.
Regelmäßigkeit *f* regularity
regeln *vb* **[34]** ❶ to direct ▷ *Ein Polizist regelte den Verkehr.* A policeman was directing the traffic. ❷ to control ▷ *die Lautstärke regeln* to control the volume ❸ to settle ▷ *Ich habe da noch eine Sache mit ihm zu regeln.* I've still got something to settle with him. ❹ to arrange ▷ *Wir haben das so geregelt, dass er abwäscht und ich putze.* We've arranged things so that he washes the dishes and I do the cleaning.; **sich von selbst regeln** to take care of itself
Regen (*pl* **Regen**) *m* rain
Regenbogen (*pl* **Regenbogen**) *m* rainbow
Regenmantel (*pl* **Regenmäntel**) *m* raincoat
Regenschauer (*pl* **Regenschauer**) *m* shower
Regenschirm (*pl* **Regenschirme**) *m* umbrella
regieren (*perf* **hat regiert**) *vb* **[76]** ❶ to govern ▷ *Wer regiert zurzeit Russland?* Who governs Russia nowadays? ❷ to reign ▷ *Wann hat Elisabeth die Erste regiert?* When did Elizabeth the First reign?
Regierung *f* ❶ government ▷ *die deutsche Regierung* the German government ❷ reign ▷ *England unter der Regierung von Elisabeth der Zweiten* England during the reign of Elizabeth the Second
regnen *vb* **[53]** to rain ▷ *Es regnet.* It's raining.
regnerisch *adj* rainy
Reh (*pl* **Rehe**) *nt* deer
reiben (*imperf* **rieb**, *perf* **hat gerieben**) *vb* ❶ to rub ▷ *Warum reibst du dir die Augen?* Why are you rubbing your eyes? ❷ to grate ▷ *Er rieb Käse über die*

Kartoffeln. He grated cheese over the potatoes.

Reibung *f* friction

reich *adj* rich

reichen *vb* [**48**] ❶ to be enough ▷ *Der Kuchen wird nicht für alle reichen.* There won't be enough cake for everybody. ❷ to give ▷ *Sie reichte mir die Hand.* She gave me her hand.; **jemandem etwas reichen** to pass somebody something; **Nur ein Salat reicht ihm nicht.** A salad won't be enough for him.; **Mir reicht's!** I've had enough.

reif *adj* ❶ ripe ▷ *Die Äpfel sind noch nicht reif.* The apples aren't ripe yet. ❷ mature ▷ *Für sein Alter ist er schon sehr reif.* He's very mature for his age.

Reifen (*pl* **Reifen**) *m* ❶ tyre ▷ *Mir ist ein Reifen geplatzt.* I've got a burst tyre. ❷ hoop ▷ *ein Hula-Hoop-Reifen* a hula hoop

Reifenpanne *f* puncture

Reihe *f* row ▷ *Stellt euch in einer Reihe auf.* Stand in a row. ▷ *Wir saßen in der zweiten Reihe.* We sat in the second row.; **der Reihe nach** in turn; **Er ist an der Reihe.** It's his turn.; **an die Reihe kommen** to have one's turn

Reihenfolge *f* order ▷ *alphabetische Reihenfolge* alphabetical order

Reihenhaus (*gen* **Reihenhauses**, *pl* **Reihenhäuser**) *nt* terraced house

rein *adj, adv* ❶ pure ▷ *Das ist reines Gold.* That's pure gold. ▷ *reine Seide* pure silk ❷ clean ▷ *Damit wird die Wäsche rein.* This will get the washing clean. ▷ *reine Luft* clean air ▷ *reine Haut* clear skin ❸ sheer ▷ *Das ist der reine Wahnsinn.* That's sheer madness. ▷ *Das ist das reinste Vergnügen.* It's sheer pleasure. ❹ purely ▷ *Rein technisch ist das machbar.* From a purely technical point of view it's feasible.; **rein gar nichts** absolutely nothing; **etwas ins Reine schreiben** to make a fair copy of something; **etwas ins Reine bringen** to clear something up ❺ in ▷ *Deckel auf und rein mit dem Müll.* Off with the lid and in with the rubbish. ▷ *Los rein mit dir, Zeit fürs Bett!* Come on, in you come, it's time for bed.

Reinheit *f* purity ▷ *die Reinheit des Biers* the purity of beer; **Für die Reinheit Ihrer Wäsche ...** To get your washing really clean ...

reinigen *vb* [**38**] to clean

Reinigung *f* ❶ cleaning ▷ *ein Mittel zur Reinigung der Polster* an cleaning agent for upholstery ❷ cleaner's *sg* ▷ *Bring bitte meine Hose in die Reinigung.* Please take my trousers to the cleaner's.; **chemische Reinigung (1)** dry cleaning ▷ *Bei diesem Stoff empfehlen wir eine chemische Reinigung.* We recommend dry cleaning for this material. **(2)** dry cleaner's ▷ *Im Einkaufszentrum gibt es auch eine chemische Reinigung.* There's also a dry cleaner's in the shopping mall.

Reis (*gen* **Reises**) *m* rice

Reise *f* journey ▷ *Auf meiner letzten Reise durch Ägypten habe ich viel gesehen.* I saw a lot on my last journey through Egypt.; **Reisen** travels; **Gute Reise!** Have a good journey.

Reiseandenken (*pl* **Reiseandenken**) *nt* souvenir

Reisebüro (*pl* **Reisebüros**) *nt* travel agency

Reiseführer (*pl* **Reiseführer**) *m* ❶ guidebook ▷ *Ich habe einen Reiseführer für Griechenland gekauft.* I've bought a guidebook to Greece. ❷ travel guide ▷ *Unser Reiseführer hat uns alles erklärt.* Our travel guide explained everything to us.

Reiseleiter (*pl* **Reiseleiter**) *m* courier

reisen (*perf* **ist gereist**) *vb* [**36**] to travel ▷ *Ich reise gern.* I like travelling.; **reisen nach** to go to

Reisende (*gen* **Reisenden**, *pl* **Reisenden**) *mf* traveller ▷ *Ein Reisender hat sich verirrt.* A traveller has got lost.

Reisepass (*gen* **Reisepasses**, *pl* **Reisepässe**) *m* passport
Reiseziel (*pl* **Reiseziele**) *nt* destination
reißen (*imperf* **riss**, *perf* **hat/ist gerissen**) *vb*

> Use **haben** to form the perfect tense. Use **sein** to form the perfect tense for 'to break'.

❶ to tear ▷ *Er riss ihren Brief in tausend Stücke.* He tore her letter into a thousand pieces. ▷ *Sie riss sich die Kleider vom Leib.* She tore her clothes off. ❷ to break ▷ *Das Seil ist gerissen.* The rope has broken. ❸ to snatch ▷ *Er hat mir den Geldbeutel aus der Hand gerissen.* He snatched my purse from my hand. ❹ to drag ▷ *Sie hat ihn zu Boden gerissen.* She dragged him to the floor. ❺ to wrench ▷ *Er riss das Steuer nach links.* He wrenched the steering wheel to the left. ❻ to tug ▷ *Er riss an der Leine.* He tugged at the rope.; **Witze reißen** to crack jokes; **etwas an sich reißen** to seize something; **sich um etwas reißen** to scramble for something
Reißverschluss (*gen* **Reißverschlusses**, *pl* **Reißverschlüsse**) *m* zip
reiten (*imperf* **ritt**, *perf* **ist geritten**) *vb* to ride
Reiter (*pl* **Reiter**) *m* rider
Reiz (*gen* **Reizes**, *pl* **Reize**) *m* ❶ charm ▷ *der Reiz dieser Stadt* the charm of this town ❷ appeal ▷ *der Reiz der Großstadt* the appeal of the big city
reizen *vb* [**36**] ❶ to appeal to ▷ *Diese Arbeit reizt mich sehr.* The work greatly appeals to me. ▷ *Es würde mich reizen, mal nach Kreta zu fahren.* The idea of going to Crete appeals to me. ❷ to annoy ▷ *Du musst den Hund nicht reizen.* Don't annoy the dog. ❸ to irritate ▷ *Der Rauch reizt die Augen.* Smoke irritates the eyes.
reizend *adj* charming
reizvoll *adj* attractive
Reklame *f* ❶ advertising ▷ *Im Fernsehen gibt es viel zu viel Reklame.* There's far too much advertising on television. ❷ advertisement ▷ *zehn Seiten Reklame* ten pages of advertisements
Rekord (*pl* **Rekorde**) *m* record ▷ *Der Rekord liegt bei zehn Metern.* The record is ten metres. ▷ *einen neuen Rekord aufstellen* to set a new record
Rektor (*pl* **Rektoren**) *m* ❶ headteacher ▷ *Der Rektor ist bei uns für die Stundenpläne zuständig.* At our school, the headteacher's in charge of timetables. ❷ vice-chancellor ▷ *Zu Semesterbeginn hält der Rektor eine Rede.* At the beginning of term the vice-chancellor gives a speech.
relativ *adv* relatively ▷ *Das ist relativ einfach.* That's relatively easy.
relaxt *adj* relaxed
Religion *f* religion
religiös *adj* religious
Rendezvous (*gen* **Rendezvous**, *pl* **Rendezvous**) *nt* date ▷ *Sie hatte gestern Abend ein Rendezvous mit Michael.* She had a date with Michael last night.
rennen (*imperf* **rannte**, *perf* **ist gerannt**) *vb* [**55**] to run
Rennen (*pl* **Rennen**) *nt* race ▷ *ein Pferderennen* a horse race ▷ *ein Autorennen* a motor race
Rennfahrer (*pl* **Rennfahrer**) *m* racing driver
Rennwagen (*pl* **Rennwagen**) *m* racing car
renovieren (*perf* **hat renoviert**) *vb* [**76**] to renovate
rentabel *adj* ❶ lucrative ▷ *eine rentable Arbeit* a lucrative job ❷ profitable ▷ *Das wäre nicht rentabel.* That wouldn't be profitable.
Rente *f* pension; **in Rente gehen** to retire

> Be careful! **Rente** does not mean **rent**.

sich **rentieren** (*perf* **hat sich rentiert**) *vb* [**76**] to be profitable ▷ *Das Geschäft rentiert sich nicht mehr.* The business is no longer profitable.; **Das hat sich rentiert.** That was worthwhile.
Rentner (*pl* **Rentner**) *m* pensioner
Reparatur *f* repair
Reparaturwerkstatt (*pl* **Reparaturwerkstätten**) *f* garage *(repair shop)*
reparieren (*perf* **hat repariert**) *vb* [**76**] to repair
Reportage *f* ❶ report ▷ *Ich habe eine Reportage über die Zustände in Rumänien gelesen.* I read a report about conditions in Romania. ❷ live commentary ▷ *Hast du im Radio die Reportage des Europapokalspiels gehört?* Did you hear the live commentary on the European cup game on the radio?
Reporter (*pl* **Reporter**) *m* reporter
Republik *f* republic
Reserve *f* reserve
Reserverad (*pl* **Reserveräder**) *nt* spare wheel
reservieren (*perf* **hat reserviert**) *vb* [**76**] to reserve ▷ *Ich habe einen Tisch für heute Abend reservieren lassen.* I've reserved a table for this evening.
Reservierung *f* reservation
Respekt *m* respect
respektieren (*perf* **hat respektiert**) *vb* [**76**] to respect
respektlos *adj* disrespectful
respektvoll *adj* respectful
Rest (*pl* **Reste**) *m* ❶ rest ▷ *Den Rest bezahle ich später.* I'll pay the rest later. ▷ *Die meisten sind früher gegangen, der Rest hat noch lange gefeiert.* Most left early, but the rest carried on celebrating for a long time. ❷ left-over ▷ *Heute gab's die Reste von gestern.* Today we had yesterday's left-overs.; **die Reste** the remains
Restaurant (*pl* **Restaurants**) *nt* restaurant
restlich *adj* remaining
Restmüll *m* non-recyclable waste
Resultat (*pl* **Resultate**) *nt* result
retten *vb* [**2**] to rescue
Rettich (*pl* **Rettiche**) *m* radish
Rettung *f* ❶ rescue ▷ *Alle zeigten bei der Rettung großen Mut.* They all showed great courage during the rescue. ❷ salvation ▷ *Das war meine Rettung.* That was my salvation. ❸ hope ▷ *seine letzte Rettung* his last hope
Rettungsboot (*pl* **Rettungsboote**) *nt* lifeboat
Rettungsdienst (*pl* **Rettungsdienste**) *m* rescue service
Rettungsring (*pl* **Rettungsringe**) *m* lifebelt
Rettungswagen (*pl* **Rettungswagen**) *m* ambulance
Reue *f* remorse ▷ *Der Täter zeigt keine Reue.* The culprit doesn't show any remorse.
Revier (*pl* **Reviere**) *nt* ❶ police station ▷ *Der Polizist nahm ihn mit aufs Revier.* The policeman took him to the police station. ❷ territory ▷ *Das männliche Tier verteidigt sein Revier.* The male animal defends his territory.
Revolution *f* revolution ▷ *die Revolution von 1789* the revolution of 1789
Revolver (*pl* **Revolver**) *m* revolver
Rezept (*pl* **Rezepte**) *nt* ❶ recipe ▷ *Kannst du mir mal das Rezept von deinem Käsekuchen geben?* Can you give me your cheesecake recipe? ❷ prescription ▷ *Dieses Medikament bekommt man nur auf Rezept.* You can only get this medicine on prescription.
Rezeption *f* reception
rezeptpflichtig *adj* available only on prescription; **rezeptpflichtige Medikamente** prescribed drugs
Rhabarber *m* rhubarb
Rhein *m* Rhine
The Rhine is 1320 km long and the entire 865 km which flows through Germany is navigable, making it an important inland waterway. It flows

past such important cities as Karlsruhe, Mannheim, Ludwigshafen, Mainz, Cologne, Düsseldorf and Duisburg.

Rheinland-Pfalz *nt* Rhineland-Palatinate

Rheinland-Pfalz is one of the 16 **Länder**. Its capital is Mainz. It is home to the BASF chemicals giant and to Germany's biggest television network, ZDF (Channel 2).

Rheuma *nt* rheumatism ▷ *Meine Oma hat Rheuma.* My granny's got rheumatism.

Rhythmus (*gen* **Rhythmus**, *pl* **Rhythmen**) *m* rhythm

richten *vb* [**2**] to point ▷ *Er richtete das Fernrohr zum Himmel.* He pointed the telescope at the sky.; **eine Waffe auf jemanden richten** to aim a weapon at somebody; **etwas an jemanden richten** to address something to somebody ▷ *Der Brief war an meine Eltern gerichtet.* The letter was addressed to my parents.; **Ich richte mich ganz nach dir.** I'll do whatever you want.; **sich nach etwas richten** **(1)** to conform to something ▷ *Auch du solltest dich danach richten, wie wir das hier machen.* You should conform to our way of doing things. **(2)** to be determined by something ▷ *Das Angebot richtet sich nach der Nachfrage.* Supply is determined by demand.

Richter (*pl* **Richter**) *m* judge

richtig *adj, adv* ❶ right ▷ *Es war nicht richtig von dir, ihn zu belügen.* It wasn't right of you to lie to him. ▷ *Das war nicht die richtige Antwort.* That wasn't the right answer.; **Bin ich hier richtig?** Have I come to the right place?; **der Richtige** the right person; **das Richtige** the right thing ❷ correctly ▷ *Du hast das nicht richtig geschrieben.* You haven't written that correctly. ❸ proper ▷ *Ich will ein richtiges Motorrad und kein Moped.* I want a proper motorbike, not a moped. ❹ really ▷ *Wir waren richtig froh, als es vorbei war.* We were really glad when it was over.

Richtung *f* direction ▷ *Wir gehen in die falsche Richtung.* We are going in the wrong direction. ▷ *in östlicher Richtung* in an easterly direction

rieb *vb see* **reiben**

riechen (*imperf* **roch**, *perf* **hat gerochen**) *vb* to smell ▷ *Ich rieche Gas.* I can smell gas. ▷ *Das riecht gut.* That smells good. ▷ *Ich kann nichts riechen.* I can't smell anything.; **an etwas riechen** to smell something; **nach etwas riechen** to smell of something; **Ich kann ihn nicht riechen.** I can't stand him.

Word for word, **Ich kann ihn nicht riechen** means 'I can't smell him'.

rief *vb see* **rufen**

Riegel (*pl* **Riegel**) *m* ❶ bolt ▷ *Sie schob den Riegel vor die Tür.* She bolted the door. ❷ bar ▷ *Für unterwegs haben wir einen Schokoriegel mitgenommen.* We've brought a bar of chocolate to eat on the way.

Riese (*gen* **Riesen**, *pl* **Riesen**) *m* giant

riesengroß *adj* gigantic

riesig *adj* huge

riet *vb see* **raten**

Rind (*pl* **Rinder**) *nt* ❶ *(male)* ox ❷ *(female)* cow; **Rinder** cattle ❸ beef ▷ *Wir essen kaum noch Rind.* We hardly eat beef any more.

Rinde *f* ❶ rind ▷ *Er schnitt die Rinde vom Käse ab.* He cut the rind off the cheese. ❷ crust ▷ *frisches Brot mit knuspriger Rinde* fresh crusty bread ❸ bark ▷ *Er ritzte ihren Namen in die Rinde einer Eiche.* He carved her name into the bark of an oak tree.

Rindfleisch *nt* beef

Ring (*pl* **Ringe**) *m* ring

Ringbuch (*pl* **Ringbücher**) *nt* ring binder

Ringen *nt* wrestling ▷ *Ringen ist sein Hobby.* His hobby is wrestling.

a b c d e f g h i j k l m n o p q r s t u v w x y z

Ringkampf (*pl* **Ringkämpfe**) *m* wrestling bout
Rippe *f* rib
Risiko (*pl* **Risiken**) *nt* risk
riskant *adj* risky
riskieren (*perf* **hat riskiert**) *vb* **[76]** to risk
Riss (*gen* **Risses**, *pl* **Risse**) *m* ❶ crack ▷ *Die Maus verschwand durch einen Riss in der Mauer.* The mouse disappeared into a crack in the wall. ▷ *Der trockene Boden war voller Risse.* The dry soil was full of cracks. ❷ tear ▷ *Er hatte einen Riss in der Hose.* There was a tear in his trousers.
rissig *adj* ❶ cracked ▷ *Von der Trockenheit ist die Erde rissig geworden.* The soil is cracked as a result of the drought. ❷ chapped ▷ *Vom vielen Waschen hat sie ganz rissige Hände.* Her hands are all chapped from doing so much washing.
ritt *vb see* **reiten**
Robbe *f* seal ▷ *ein Robbenbaby* a seal pup
Roboter (*pl* **Roboter**) *m* robot
roch *vb see* **riechen**
Rock (*pl* **Röcke**) *m* skirt
Roggen *m* rye
roh *adj* ❶ raw ▷ *rohes Fleisch* raw meat ▷ *Karotten esse ich am liebsten roh.* I like carrots best raw. ❷ callous ▷ *Sei nicht so roh.* Don't be so callous. ❸ rough ▷ *Er hat sie ziemlich roh mit sich gezogen.* He dragged her off pretty roughly.
Rohr (*pl* **Rohre**) *nt* ❶ pipe ▷ *Das Abwasser wird durch Rohre in die Kanalisation geleitet.* Sewage is fed into the sewer via pipes. ❷ cane ▷ *ein Stuhl aus Rohr* a cane chair ❸ reeds *pl* ▷ *In dem Teich wuchs Rohr.* Reeds were growing in the pond.
Rohstoff (*pl* **Rohstoffe**) *m* raw material
Rollbrett (*pl* **Rollbretter**) *nt* skateboard
Rolle *f* ❶ role ▷ *Der Schauspieler hat die Rolle des Königs gut gespielt.* The actor was good in the role of the king. ▷ *Die Rolle der Frau hat sich geändert.* The role of women has changed. ❷ castor ▷ *ein Stuhl mit Rollen* a chair with castors ❸ roll ▷ *eine Rolle Toilettenpapier* a roll of toilet paper ❹ reel ▷ *Sie hat den Faden von der Rolle abgewickelt.* She unwound the thread from the reel.; **keine Rolle spielen** not to matter; **eine wichtige Rolle spielen bei** to play a major role in
rollen (*perf* **hat/ist gerollt**) *vb* **[38]**

> For the perfect tense use **haben** when the verb has an object and **sein** when there is no object.

to roll ▷ *Sie haben den Stein den Berg hinuntergerollt.* They rolled the stone down the hill. ▷ *Der Ball ist direkt vor ein Auto gerollt.* The ball rolled right in front of a car.
Roller (*pl* **Roller**) *m* scooter
Rollladen (*pl* **Rollläden**) *m* shutter
Rollschuh (*pl* **Rollschuhe**) *m* roller skate
Rollstuhl (*pl* **Rollstühle**) *m* wheelchair
Rolltreppe *f* escalator
Rom *nt* Rome
Roman (*pl* **Romane**) *m* novel
romantisch *adj* romantic
röntgen *vb* **[54]** to X-ray
rosa *adj* pink ▷ *Sie hatte ein rosa Kleid an.* She was wearing a pink dress.
Rose *f* rose
Rosenkohl *m* Brussels sprouts *pl* ▷ *Rosenkohl ist mein Lieblingsgemüse.* Brussels sprouts are my favourite vegetable.
Rosine *f* raisin
Rost (*pl* **Roste**) *m* rust ▷ *An diesem Auto ist viel Rost.* This car has a lot of rust on it.; **ein Bratrost** a grill
rosten (*perf* **ist gerostet**) *vb* **[2]** to rust
rösten *vb* **[2]** ❶ to roast ▷ *geröstete Erdnüsse* roasted peanuts ❷ to toast ▷ *Brot rösten* to toast bread ❸ to grill ▷ *Würstchen auf dem Grill rösten* to grill sausages
rostig *adj* rusty
rot *adj* red ▷ *Sein Gesicht wurde immer röter.* His face got redder and redder.;

in den roten Zahlen in the red; **das Rote Meer** the Red Sea
Röteln *pl* German measles *sg* ▷ *Röteln sind für schwangere Frauen gefährlich.* German measles is dangerous for pregnant women.
rothaarig *adj* red-haired
Rotkohl *m* red cabbage
Rotwein (*pl* **Rotweine**) *m* red wine
Roulade *f* beef olive
Route *f* route
Routenplaner (*pl* **Routenplaner**) *m* route planner
Router *m* router
Rowdy (*pl* **Rowdys**) *m* hooligan
RSI-Syndrom *nt* (= *Repetitive-Strain-Injury-Syndrom*) RSI
Rübe *f* beet ▷ *Der Bauer füttert die Kühe mit Rüben.* The farmer feeds his cows on beet.; **Gelbe Rübe** carrot; **Rote Rübe** beetroot
rüber *adv* over ▷ *Komm hier rüber, da siehst du besser.* Come over here, you'll get a better view. ▷ *Ich geh mal zu den Nachbarn rüber.* I'm just going over to our neighbours.
rücken (*perf* **ist/hat gerückt**) *vb* [38]

> For the perfect tense use **haben** when the verb has an object and **sein** when there is no object.

❶ to move over ▷ *Rück mal ein bisschen.* Move over a bit. ❷ to shift ▷ *Sie rückten den Schrank zur Seite.* They shifted the cupboard to one side.
Rücken (*pl* **Rücken**) *m* back ▷ *Er schläft auf dem Rücken.* He sleeps on his back.
Rückenschmerzen *pl* backache *sg*
Rückfahrkarte *f* return ticket
Rückfahrt *f* return journey
Rückflug (*pl* **Rückflüge**) *m* return flight
Rückgabe *f* return
Rückgrat (*pl* **Rückgrate**) *nt* spine
Rückkehr *f* return ▷ *bei unserer Rückkehr* on our return
Rücklicht (*pl* **Rücklichter**) *nt* rear light
Rückreise *f* return journey
Rücksicht *f* consideration; **auf jemanden Rücksicht nehmen** to show consideration for somebody
rücksichtslos *adj* inconsiderate; **ein rücksichtsloser Fahrer** a reckless driver
rücksichtsvoll *adj* considerate
Rücksitz (*pl* **Rücksitze**) *m* back seat ▷ *Dieser Sportwagen hat keine Rücksitze.* This sports car has no back seats.; **auf dem Rücksitz** in the back
Rückspiegel (*pl* **Rückspiegel**) *m* rear-view mirror
Rückspiel (*pl* **Rückspiele**) *nt* return match
Rücktritt (*pl* **Rücktritte**) *m* resignation
rückwärts *adv* backwards ▷ *rückwärts zählen* to count backwards
Rückwärtsgang (*pl* **Rückwärtsgänge**) *m* reverse gear
Rückweg (*pl* **Rückwege**) *m* way back
Ruder (*pl* **Ruder**) *nt* ❶ oar ▷ *ein Boot mit zwei Rudern* a boat with two oars ❷ rudder ▷ *Der Steuermann steht am Ruder.* The helmsman stands at the rudder.
Ruderboot (*pl* **Ruderboote**) *nt* rowing boat
rudern (*perf* **hat/ist gerudert**) *vb* [88]

> Use **haben** for the perfect tense when you describe the activity and **sein** when you describe the motion.

to row ▷ *Zuerst hat er gerudert, dann sie.* First he rowed, then she did. ▷ *Wir sind über den See gerudert.* We rowed across the lake.
Ruf (*pl* **Rufe**) *m* ❶ shout ▷ *Wir hörten seine Rufe.* We heard his shouts. ❷ reputation ▷ *Das schadet seinem Ruf.* This will damage his reputation.
rufen (*imperf* **rief**, *perf* **hat gerufen**) *vb* [56] ❶ to call out ▷ *Ich habe gerufen, es hat mich aber niemand gehört.* I called out, but nobody heard me.; **Der Patient rief nach der Schwester.** The patient called for the nurse. ❷ to call ▷ *Wir sollten den Arzt rufen.* We ought to call the doctor. ▷ *Sie hat mir ein Taxi gerufen.* She called me a taxi. ❸ to

shout ▷ *Sie rief um Hilfe.* She shouted for help.

Rufnummer *f* telephone number

Ruhe *f* ❶ rest ▷ *Nach den anstrengenden Tagen brauche ich etwas Ruhe.* After the strain of the last few days I need a rest. ❷ peace ▷ *Jetzt kann ich in Ruhe arbeiten.* Now I can work in peace. ❸ peace and quiet ▷ *Die Kinder sind weg, ich genieße die Ruhe.* The children are out and I'm enjoying the peace and quiet.; **in aller Ruhe** calmly; **jemanden aus der Ruhe bringen** to unsettle somebody ❹ silence ▷ *Ich bitte um etwas mehr Ruhe.* I would ask you for a bit more silence.; **Ruhe!** Silence!; **jemanden in Ruhe lassen** to leave somebody alone; **sich zur Ruhe setzen** to retire

ruhig *adj, adv* ❶ quiet ▷ *Im Haus war alles ruhig.* The house was completely quiet. ▷ *Die Kinder haben ruhig gespielt.* The children played quietly. ▷ *Seid endlich ruhig!* Will you be quiet! ❷ still ▷ *Bleib ruhig stehen, dann tut dir der Hund nichts.* If you keep still the dog won't hurt you.; **eine ruhige Hand** a steady hand ❸ calm ▷ *Wie kannst du so ruhig bleiben?* How can you stay so calm? ▷ *Ich bin ganz ruhig in die Prüfung gegangen.* I went quite calmly into the exam.; **ein ruhiges Gewissen** a clear conscience; **Kommen Sie ruhig herein!** Come on in.

Ruhm *m* fame

Rührei (*pl* **Rühreier**) *nt* scrambled eggs *pl*

rühren *vb* [**38**] ❶ to stir ▷ *Sie rührte mit dem Löffel in der Soße.* She stirred the sauce with the spoon. ❷ to move ▷ *Ich kann meine Beine nicht rühren.* I can't move my legs.; **sich rühren** to move; **jemanden rühren** to move somebody

rührend *adj* touching ▷ *eine rührende Geschichte* a touching story ▷ *Er ist rührend naiv.* He's touchingly naive.

Ruine *f* ruin

ruinieren (*perf* **hat ruiniert**) *vb* [**76**] to ruin

Rumäne (*gen* **Rumänen**, *pl* **Rumänen**) *m* Romanian

Rumänien *nt* Romania

Rumänin *f* Romanian

rumänisch *adj* Romanian

Rummelplatz (*gen* **Rummelplatzes**, *pl* **Rummelplätze**) *m* fairground

rund *adj, adv* ❶ round ▷ *Sie hat ein rundes Gesicht.* She's got a round face. ❷ about ▷ *Das kostet rund hundert Euro.* It costs about a hundred euros.; **rund um etwas** around something

Runde *f* ❶ lap ▷ *Das Auto fuhr ein paar Runden.* The car drove a few laps. ❷ round ▷ *Diese Runde zahle ich.* I'll get this round.

It isn't usual to buy rounds in Germany. Normally people just order what they want from the waiter, and pay when they leave. You can, however, buy a round (**eine Runde schmeißen**) if you're feeling generous.

❸ lap ▷ *Er liegt in der letzten Runde in Führung.* He's in the lead on the last lap. ❹ party ▷ *Wir waren eine fröhliche Runde.* We were a merry party.

Rundfahrt *f* round trip

Rundfunk *m* broadcasting; **im Rundfunk** on the radio

runter *adv* ❶ off ▷ *Runter vom Tisch!* Get off the table! ❷ down ▷ *Dann ging's den Berg runter.* Then off we went down the mountain.

runterladen (*pres* **lädt runter**, *imperf* **lud runter**, *perf* **hat runtergeladen**) *vb* (*computer*) to download ▷ *eine Datei runterladen* to download a file

Ruß (*gen* **Rußes**) *m* soot

Russe (*gen* **Russen**, *pl* **Russen**) *m* Russian

Rüssel (*pl* **Rüssel**) *m* ❶ snout ▷ *der Rüssel eines Schweins* a pig's snout ❷ trunk ▷ *der Rüssel eines Elefanten* an elephant's trunk

rußig *adj* sooty
Russin *f* Russian
russisch *adj* Russian
Russland *nt* Russia
Rüstung *f* ❶ suit of armour ▷ *In der Burg standen ein paar rostige Rüstungen.* There were a couple of rusty suits of armour in the castle. ❷ armaments *pl* ▷ *Es wird viel Geld für Rüstung ausgegeben.* A lot of money is spent on armaments.
Rutschbahn *f* slide
rutschen (*perf* **ist gerutscht**) *vb* [**48**] ❶ to slip ▷ *Sie ist auf dem Eis gerutscht und hingefallen.* She slipped and fell on the ice. ▷ *Der Teller ist mir aus der Hand gerutscht.* The plate slipped out of my hand. ❷ to move over ▷ *Rutsch mal ein bisschen!* Move over a bit.

S

Saal (*pl* **Säle**) *m* hall
Saarland *nt* Saarland
The **Saarland** is one of the 16 **Länder**. Its capital is Saarbrücken. While its coal and steel industries have been in crisis, it still has flourishing ceramics and glass industries.
Sache *f* ❶ thing ▷ *Räum bitte deine Sachen weg.* Please put your things away. ▷ *Pack warme Sachen ein.* Pack warm things. ▷ *Was machst du denn für Sachen?* The things you do! ❷ matter ▷ *Wir sollten diese Sache ausdiskutieren.* We should discuss this matter fully. ▷ *Die Polizei wird dieser Sache nachgehen.* The police will investigate this affair. ❸ job ▷ *Es ist deine Sache, dich darum zu kümmern.* It's your job to see to it.; **Mach keine Sachen!** Don't be silly!; **zur Sache** to the point
sachlich *adj* ❶ objective ▷ *ein sehr sachlicher Bericht* a very objective report ▷ *Du solltest sachlich bleiben.* You should

remain objective. ❷ factual ▷ *Was er sagt, ist sachlich falsch.* What he says is factually inaccurate.

sächlich *adj* neuter

Sachsen *nt* Saxony

Sachsen is one of the 16 **Länder**. Its capital is Dresden. Its largest city, Leipzig, is famous for its industrial fair and was one of the main centres of the peaceful revolt against the DDR regime.

Sachsen-Anhalt *nt* Saxony-Anhalt

Sachsen-Anhalt is one of the 16 **Länder**. Its capital is Magdeburg. It has a rich cultural past: Martin Luther and Georg Friedrich Händel were born here, and the Bauhaus school of architecture was situated in Dessau.

sächsisch *adj* Saxon

sachte *adv* softly

Sack (*pl* **Säcke**) *m* sack

Sackgasse *f* cul-de-sac

Saft (*pl* **Säfte**) *m* juice

saftig *adj* juicy

Säge *f* saw

sagen *vb* **[38]** ❶ to say ▷ *Ich kann noch nicht sagen, ob ich komme.* I can't say yet if I'll come. ▷ *Habe ich etwas Falsches gesagt?* Have I said something wrong? ▷ *Wie sagt man 'danke' auf Japanisch?* How do you say 'thank you' in Japanese? ▷ *Was sagst du zu meinem Vorschlag?* What do you say to my suggestion?; **Man sagt, dass ...** It's said that ... ❷ to tell ▷ *Kannst du ihm bitte sagen, er soll seine Eltern anrufen.* Can you tell him to call his parents. ▷ *Ich werde es ihr sagen.* I'll tell her. ▷ *Sag ihm, er solle das nicht tun.* Tell him he shouldn't do it.; **etwas zu jemandem sagen** to call somebody something; **zu sagen haben** to have a say; **Das hat nichts zu sagen.** It doesn't mean anything.

sägen *vb* **[38]** to saw

sah *vb see* **sehen**

Sahne *f* cream

Saison (*pl* **Saisons**) *f* season

Saite *f* string

Saiteninstrument (*pl* **Saiteninstrumente**) *nt* stringed instrument

Salat (*pl* **Salate**) *m* ❶ salad ▷ *Es gab verschiedene Salate.* There were various salads. ❷ lettuce ▷ *Am liebsten mag ich grünen Salat.* I like lettuce best.

Salbe *f* ointment

Salz (*gen* **Salzes**) *nt* salt

salzen (*perf* **hat gesalzen**) *vb* to salt

salzig *adj* salty

Salzkartoffeln *fpl* boiled potatoes *pl*

Salzstange *f* pretzel stick

Samen (*pl* **Samen**) *m* seed ▷ *Hast du die Blumensamen schon ausgesät?* Have you sown the flower seeds yet?

sammeln *vb* **[34]** ❶ to collect ▷ *Er sammelt Briefmarken.* He collects stamps. ▷ *Sie sammeln für ein Waisenhaus.* They're collecting for an orphanage. ▷ *Altpapier wird gesammelt und wiederverwertet.* Waste paper is collected and recycled. ❷ to gather ▷ *Wir haben Pilze gesammelt.* We gathered mushrooms.

Sammlung *f* collection

Samstag (*pl* **Samstage**) *m* Saturday ▷ *am Samstag* on Saturday

samstags *adv* on Saturdays

samt *prep*

The preposition **samt** takes the dative.

with ▷ *Sie kamen samt Kindern und Hund.* They came with their children and dog.

Samt (*pl* **Samte**) *m* velvet

Sand *m* sand

Sandale *f* sandal

Sandkasten (*pl* **Sandkästen**) *m* sandpit

Sandstrand (*pl* **Sandstrände**) *m* sandy beach

sandte *vb see* **senden**

sanft *adj* gentle ▷ *etwas sanft berühren* to touch something gently

sang *vb see* **singen**
Sänger (*pl* **Sänger**) *m* singer
Sängerin *f* singer
Sarg (*pl* **Särge**) *m* coffin
saß *vb see* **sitzen**
Satellit (*gen* **Satelliten**, *pl* **Satelliten**) *m* satellite
Satellitenfernsehen *nt* satellite television
satt *adj* ❶ full ▷ *Ich bin satt.* I'm full.; **Wir sind nicht satt geworden.** We didn't get enough to eat.; **sich satt essen** to eat one's fill; **satt machen** to be filling; **jemanden satt sein** to be fed up with somebody ❷ rich ▷ *satte Farben* rich colours ▷ *ein sattes Rot* a rich red
Sattel (*pl* **Sättel**) *m* saddle
Satz (*gen* **Satzes**, *pl* **Sätze**) *m* ❶ sentence ▷ *Bitte antworte mit einem ganzen Satz.* Please answer in a complete sentence.; **ein Nebensatz** a subordinate clause; **ein Adverbialsatz** an adverbial clause ❷ theorem ▷ *der Satz des Pythagoras* Pythagoras' theorem ❸ set ▷ *Becker hat den ersten Satz verloren.* Becker lost the first set. ▷ *ein Satz Schraubenschlüssel* a set of screwdrivers ❹ rate ▷ *Die Krankenversicherung hat ihre Sätze erhöht.* The health insurance has increased its rates.
Satzzeichen (*pl* **Satzzeichen**) *nt* punctuation mark
sauber *adj* ❶ clean ▷ *Die Wäsche ist nicht sauber geworden.* The washing hasn't come up clean. ❷ fine ▷ *Du bist mir ein sauberer Freund!* You're a fine friend!; **sauber machen** to clean
Sauberkeit *f* cleanness
saubermachen *vb* [**48**] *see* **sauber**
Sauce *f* sauce
sauer *adj* ❶ sour ▷ *Der Apfel ist sauer.* The apple is sour. ▷ *Die Milch ist sauer geworden.* The milk has turned sour. ❷ acid ▷ *saurer Regen* acid rain ❸ cross ▷ *Ich bin sauer auf meine Freundin.* I'm cross with my girlfriend.
Sauerkraut *nt* sauerkraut *(pickled cabbage)*
Sauerstoff *m* oxygen
saufen (*pres* **säuft**, *imperf* **soff**, *perf* **hat gesoffen**) *vb (informal)* to booze
saugen (*imperf* **saugte** *or* **sog**, *perf* **hat gesaugt** *or* **gesogen**) *vb* to suck
Säugetier (*pl* **Säugetiere**) *nt* mammal
Säugling (*pl* **Säuglinge**) *m* infant
Säule *f* column
Sauna (*pl* **Saunas**) *f* sauna
Säure *f* acid ▷ *Die Säure hat den Stein zerfressen.* The acid has eaten away at the stone.
Saxofon (*pl* **Saxofone**) *nt* saxophone ▷ *Er spielt Saxofon.* He plays the saxophone.
Schach *nt* chess ▷ *Ich kann nicht Schach spielen.* I can't play chess.
Schachbrett (*pl* **Schachbretter**) *nt* chessboard
Schachfigur *f* chessman
Schachtel *f* box
schade *adj, excl* a pity ▷ *Es ist schade um das gute Essen.* It's a pity to waste good food. ▷ *Das ist aber schade.* That's a pity.; **Wie schade!** What a pity!; **für etwas zu schade sein** to be too good for something; **sich für etwas zu schade sein** to consider oneself too good for something
Schädel (*pl* **Schädel**) *m* skull
schaden *vb* [**54**] **jemandem schaden** to harm somebody; **einer Sache schaden** to damage something; **es kann nicht schaden ...** it can't do any harm ...
Schaden (*pl* **Schäden**) *m* ❶ damage ▷ *Der Schaden an seinem Auto war nicht so groß.* The damage to his car wasn't too bad. ❷ injury ▷ *Sie hat den Unfall ohne Schaden überstanden.* She came out of the accident without injury. ❸ disadvantage ▷ *Es soll dein Schaden nicht sein.* It won't be to your disadvantage.

schädigen (*perf* **hat geschädigt**) *vb* [**38**] to damage

schädlich *adj* harmful ▷ *Rauchen ist schädlich.* Smoking is harmful. ▷ *Alkohol ist für die Leber schädlich.* Alcohol is harmful to your liver.

Schadstoff (*pl* **Schadstoffe**) *m* harmful substance

Schaf (*pl* **Schafe**) *nt* sheep ▷ *zehn Schafe* ten sheep

Schäferhund (*pl* **Schäferhunde**) *m* Alsatian

schaffen (1) (*imperf* **schuf**, *perf* **hat geschaffen**) *vb* to create ▷ *Die Regierung will neue Arbeitsplätze schaffen.* The government wants to create new jobs.

schaffen (2) (*imperf* **schaffte**, *perf* **hat geschafft**) *vb* [**48**] to manage ▷ *Die Übersetzung schaffe ich heute noch.* I'll manage that translation today. ▷ *Er schafft das nicht allein.* He won't manage to do that on his own. ▷ *Wir haben den Zug gerade noch geschafft.* We just managed to catch the train.; **eine Prüfung schaffen** to pass an exam; **Ich bin geschafft!** I'm shattered!

Schal (*pl* **Schale** *or* **Schals**) *m* scarf

Schale *f* ❶ skin ▷ *eine Bananenschale* a banana skin ❷ peel ▷ *die Kartoffelschalen* the potato peel ▷ *eine Zitronenschale* lemon peel ❸ shell ▷ *Die Nussschalen nicht in den Kompost werfen.* Don't throw the nutshells onto the compost heap. ▷ *Diese Eier haben sehr dünne Schalen.* These eggs have very thin shells. ❹ bowl ▷ *Auf dem Tisch stand eine Schale mit Obst.* There was a bowl of fruit on the table.

schälen *vb* [**38**] ❶ to peel ▷ *einen Apfel schälen* to peel an apple ❷ to shell ▷ *Nüsse schälen* to shell nuts; **sich schälen** to peel

Schall *m* sound

Schallplatte *f* record

schalten *vb* [**2**] ❶ to switch ▷ *den Herd auf 'aus' schalten* to switch the oven to 'off' ❷ to change gear ▷ *Du solltest schalten.* You should change gear.; **in den vierten Gang schalten** to change into fourth ❸ *(informal)* to catch on ▷ *Ich habe zu spät geschaltet.* I caught on too late.

Schalter (*pl* **Schalter**) *m* ❶ counter ▷ *Zahlen Sie bitte am Schalter dort drüben.* Please pay at the counter over there. ❷ switch ▷ *Wo ist der Lichtschalter?* Where is the light switch?

Schaltjahr (*pl* **Schaltjahre**) *nt* leap year

sich **schämen** *vb* [**38**] to be ashamed ▷ *sich einer Sache schämen* to be ashamed of something

Schande *f* disgrace

scharf *adj* ❶ sharp ▷ *ein scharfes Messer* a sharp knife ▷ *eine scharfe Kurve* a sharp corner; **ein scharfer Wind** a biting wind ❷ hot ▷ *Indisches Essen ist schärfer als deutsches.* Indian food is hotter than German food.; **scharfe Munition** live ammunition; **scharf schießen** to shoot with live ammunition; **scharf nachdenken** to think hard; **auf etwas scharf sein** *(informal)* to be mad about something; **auf jemanden scharf sein** to fancy somebody

Schatten (*pl* **Schatten**) *m* ❶ shadow ❷ shade ▷ *Wir saßen im Schatten.* We sat in the shade.

schattig *adj* shady

Schatz (*gen* **Schatzes**, *pl* **Schätze**) *m* ❶ treasure ▷ *der Schatz der Piraten* the pirates' treasure ❷ darling ▷ *Du bist ein Schatz!* You're a darling! ▷ *Mein Schatz.* My darling.

schätzen *vb* [**36**] ❶ to guess ▷ *Schätz mal, wie viel das gekostet hat.* Guess how much that cost.; **Man kann sein Alter schlecht schätzen.** It's difficult to tell how old he is. ❷ to value ▷ *Ich werde die alte Uhr schätzen lassen.* I'm going to have the old clock valued. ❸ to appreciate ▷ *Ich schätze deine Hilfe sehr.* I really appreciate your help.

Schaubild (*pl* **Schaubilder**) *nt* diagram
schauen *vb* [**38**] to look ▷ *Schau mal an die Tafel.* Look at the board.
Schauer (*pl* **Schauer**) *m* ❶ shower ▷ *Für morgen sind Schauer angesagt.* Showers are forecast for tomorrow. ❷ shudder ▷ *Ein Schauer überlief sie.* A shudder ran through her body.
Schaufel *f* shovel
Schaufenster (*pl* **Schaufenster**) *nt* shop window
Schaufensterbummel (*pl* **Schaufensterbummel**) *m* window shopping
Schaukel *f* swing
schaukeln *vb* [**34**] to swing
Schaumgummi *m* foam rubber
Schauspiel *nt* play *(theatre)*
Schauspieler (*pl* **Schauspieler**) *m* actor
Schauspielerin *f* actress
Scheck (*pl* **Schecks**) *m* cheque
Scheckkarte *f* cheque card
Scheibe *f* slice ▷ *Sie belegte das Brot mit mehreren Scheiben Wurst.* She put several slices of cold meat on the bread.
Scheibenwischer (*pl* **Scheibenwischer**) *m* windscreen wiper
scheiden (*imperf* **schied**, *perf* **hat geschieden**) *vb* **sich scheiden lassen** to get a divorce; **geschieden sein** to be divorced
Scheidung *f* divorce
Schein (*pl* **Scheine**) *m* ❶ light ▷ *beim Schein einer Kerze* by the light of a candle ❷ appearance ▷ *Der Schein trügt.* Appearances are deceptive. ❸ note ▷ *Er hat in großen Scheinen bezahlt.* He paid in large notes. ❹ certificate ▷ *Am Ende des Semesters bekommt man einen Schein.* You get a certificate at the end of the semester.; **etwas zum Schein tun** to pretend to do something
scheinbar *adv* apparently
scheinen (*imperf* **schien**, *perf* **hat geschienen**) *vb* [**57**] ❶ to shine ▷ *Die Sonne scheint.* The sun is shining. ❷ to seem ▷ *Sie scheint glücklich zu sein.* She seems to be happy.
Scheinwerfer (*pl* **Scheinwerfer**) *m* ❶ headlamp ▷ *Die Scheinwerfer des entgegenkommenden Autos haben mich geblendet.* The headlamps of the approaching car blinded me. ❷ floodlight ▷ *Die Scheinwerfer beleuchteten das Stadion.* The floodlights lit the stadium. ❸ spotlight ▷ *Das Gemälde wird von einem Scheinwerfer angestrahlt.* The painting is lit up by a spotlight.
scheitern (*perf* **ist gescheitert**) *vb* [**88**] to fail
Schenkel (*pl* **Schenkel**) *m* thigh
schenken *vb* [**38**] ❶ to give ▷ *Was haben dir deine Eltern zum Geburtstag geschenkt?* What did your parents give you for your birthday? ▷ *Das habe ich geschenkt bekommen.* I was given it as a present. ❷ to pour ▷ *Sie schenkte ihm noch etwas Rotwein ins Glas.* She poured some more red wine into his glass.; **sich etwas schenken** to skip something ▷ *Die Geigenstunde werde ich mir heute schenken.* I'm going to skip my violin lesson today.; **Das ist geschenkt! (1)** That's a giveaway! **(2)** That's worthless!
Schere *f* ❶ scissors *pl* ▷ *eine Schere* a pair of scissors ❷ shears *pl* ▷ *Wo ist die Schere, um die Hecke zu schneiden?* Where are the shears for cutting the hedge?
Scherz (*gen* **Scherzes**, *pl* **Scherze**) *m* joke ▷ *Das war doch nur ein Scherz!* It was only a joke.; **zum Scherz** for fun
scheußlich *adj* dreadful ▷ *Das Wetter war scheußlich.* The weather was dreadful.; **Das tut scheußlich weh.** It hurts dreadfully.
Schi (*pl* **Schi** *or* **Schier**) *m* *see* **Ski**
Schicht *f* ❶ layer ▷ *Auf dem Weg lag eine Schicht Sand.* There was a layer of sand on the path. ❷ class ▷ *soziale Schichten*

social classes ❸ shift ▷ *Mein Vater arbeitet Schicht.* My father works shifts.

schick *adj* stylish ▷ *ein schicker Hosenanzug* a stylish trouser suit; **schick angezogen** stylishly dressed

schicken *vb* [**48**] to send ▷ *Ich habe ihr ein Päckchen geschickt.* I've sent her a parcel. ▷ *Sie hat ihren Sohn zum Bäcker geschickt.* She sent her son to the baker's.

Schicksal *nt* fate

schieben (*imperf* **schob**, *perf* **hat geschoben**) *vb* to push ▷ *Wir mussten das Auto schieben.* We had to push the car. ▷ *Könnt ihr mal schieben?* Could you lot push?; **die Schuld auf jemanden schieben** to put the blame on somebody

Schiedsrichter (*pl* **Schiedsrichter**) *m* ❶ referee ▷ *Der Schiedsrichter pfiff das Spiel an.* The referee blew the whistle to start the game. ❷ umpire ▷ *Bei einem Tennisspiel sagt der Schiedsrichter den Spielstand an.* In a tennis match the umpire gives the score.

schief *adj, adv* crooked ▷ *Die Wände des Hauses sind schief.* The walls of the house are crooked.; **Das Bild hängt schief.** The picture isn't hanging straight.; **der Schiefe Turm von Pisa** the Leaning Tower of Pisa; **ein schiefer Blick** a funny look; **Er hatte seinen Hut schief aufgesetzt.** He was wearing his hat at an angle.

schiefgehen (*imperf* **ging schief**, *perf* **ist schiefgegangen**) *vb* [**29**] to go wrong

schielen *vb* [**38**] to squint

schien *vb see* **scheinen**

Schiene *f* ❶ rail ▷ *Die Schienen sind verrostet.* The rails have rusted. ❷ splint ▷ *Sie hatte den Arm in einer Schiene.* She had her arm in a splint.

schießen (*imperf* **schoss**, *perf* **hat geschossen**) *vb* ❶ to shoot ▷ *Nicht schießen!* Don't shoot! ▷ *Er hat ein Kaninchen geschossen.* He shot a rabbit. ▷ *Er hat auf einen Polizisten geschossen.* He shot at a policeman. ❷ to kick ▷ *Sie schoss den Ball ins Tor.* She kicked the ball into the goal.

Schiff (*pl* **Schiffe**) *nt* ship

Schifffahrt *f* shipping

Schild (*pl* **Schilder**) *nt* sign ▷ *Das ist eine Einbahnstraße, hast du das Schild nicht gesehen?* This is a one-way street, didn't you see the sign?; **ein Namensschild** a nameplate

Schildkröte *f* ❶ tortoise ❷ turtle

Schimmel (*pl* **Schimmel**) *m* ❶ mould ▷ *Auf dem Käse ist Schimmel.* There's mould on the cheese. ❷ white horse ▷ *Sie ritt auf einem Schimmel.* She rode a white horse.

schimmelig *adj* mouldy

Schimpanse (*gen* **Schimpansen**, *pl* **Schimpansen**) *m* chimpanzee

schimpfen *vb* [**38**] to scold ▷ *Hat deine Mutter geschimpft?* Did your mother scold you?; **auf jemanden schimpfen** to curse somebody; **über etwas schimpfen** to complain about something

Schimpfwort (*pl* **Schimpfwörter**) *nt* term of abuse

Schinken (*pl* **Schinken**) *m* ham

Schirm (*pl* **Schirme**) *m* umbrella ▷ *Nimm einen Schirm mit!* Take an umbrella!; **der Sonnenschirm** the sunshade; **eine Mütze mit Schirm** a peaked cap

Schlacht *f* battle

schlachten *vb* [**2**] to slaughter

Schlachthof (*pl* **Schlachthöfe**) *m* slaughterhouse

Schlaf *m* sleep

Schlafanzug (*pl* **Schlafanzüge**) *m* pyjamas *pl* ▷ *ein Schlafanzug* a pair of pyjamas

schlafen (*pres* **schläft**, *imperf* **schlief**, *perf* **hat geschlafen**) *vb* [**58**] to sleep ▷ *Hast du gut geschlafen?* Did you sleep well? ▷ *Schlaf gut!* Sleep well.; **schlafen gehen** to go to bed

schlaff *adj* ❶ exhausted ▷ *Nach der Gartenarbeit war ich total schlaff.* I was completely exhausted after working in the garden. ❷ slack ▷ *Das Seil ist zu schlaff.* The rope is too slack.

schlaflos *adj* sleepless

Schlafsaal (*pl* **Schlafsäle**) *m* dormitory

Schlafsack (*pl* **Schlafsäcke**) *m* sleeping bag

Schlaftablette *f* sleeping pill

Schlafzimmer (*pl* **Schlafzimmer**) *nt* bedroom

Schlag (*pl* **Schläge**) *m* ❶ blow ▷ *ein Schlag auf den Kopf* a blow to the head ▷ *Ich bin durchgefallen, das ist ein Schlag.* I've failed, that's a blow. ❷ stroke ▷ *Mein Opa hat einen Schlag gehabt und ist gelähmt.* My granddad's had a stroke and he's now paralysed. ❸ shock ▷ *Fass nicht an den Draht, sonst bekommst du einen Schlag.* Don't touch that wire, otherwise you'll get a shock.; **Er hat von seinem Vater Schläge bekommen.** (*informal*) His father gave him a hiding.; **mit einem Schlag** all at once

schlagen (*pres* **schlägt**, *imperf* **schlug**, *perf* **hat geschlagen**) *vb* [59] ❶ to beat ▷ *Meine Eltern haben mich noch nie geschlagen.* My parents have never beaten me. ▷ *England hat Holland vier zu eins geschlagen.* England beat Holland four one. ▷ *Ihr Herz schlug schneller.* Her heart beat faster.; **Sahne schlagen** to whip cream ❷ to hit ▷ *Er schlug mit dem Hammer auf den Nagel.* He hit the nail with the hammer. ▷ *Sie schlug mit der Faust auf den Tisch.* She hit the table with her fist.; **Er schlägt den Nagel in die Wand.** He hammers the nail into the wall. ❸ to strike ▷ *Die Uhr schlägt zehn.* The clock strikes ten. ▷ *Es hat eben zehn geschlagen.* It's just struck ten.; **nach jemandem schlagen** to take after somebody; **sich gut schlagen** to do well

Schlager (*pl* **Schlager**) *m* hit

Schläger (*pl* **Schläger**) *m* ❶ thug ▷ *Franz ist ein Schläger.* Franz is a thug. ❷ bat ▷ *Baseball und Tischtennis spielt man mit einem Schläger.* You play baseball and table tennis with a bat. ❸ racket ▷ *Für Tennis, Federball und Squash braucht man einen Schläger.* You need a racket for tennis, badminton and squash.; **ein Golfschläger** a golf club; **ein Hockeyschläger** a hockey stick

Schlägerei *f* fight

schlagfertig *adj* quick-witted

Schlagsahne *f* whipped cream

Schlagzeile *f* headline

Schlagzeug (*pl* **Schlagzeuge**) *nt* drums *pl* ▷ *Er spielt Schlagzeug.* He plays the drums. ▷ *Am Schlagzeug: Freddy Braun.* On drums: Freddy Braun.

Schlamm *m* mud

Schlange *f* ❶ snake ▷ *eine giftige Schlange* a poisonous snake ❷ queue ▷ *Vor dem Kino stand eine lange Schlange.* There was a long queue outside the cinema.; **Schlange stehen** to queue

schlank *adj* slim ▷ *Sie ist sehr schlank.* She's very slim.

Schlankheitskur *f* diet ▷ *eine Schlankheitskur machen* to be on a diet

schlapp *adj* worn out ▷ *Ich fühle mich schlapp.* I feel worn out.

schlau *adj* cunning

Schlauch (*pl* **Schläuche**) *m* ❶ hose ▷ *Er hat den Garten mit dem Schlauch gespritzt.* He watered the garden with the hose. ❷ inner tube ▷ *Ich brauche einen neuen Schlauch für mein Fahrrad.* I need a new inner tube for my bike.

Schlauchboot (*pl* **Schlauchboote**) *nt* rubber dinghy

schlecht *adj, adv* ❶ bad ▷ *Er ist in Mathe schlecht.* He is bad at maths. ▷ *Meine Augen werden immer schlechter.* My eyes are getting worse.; **ein schlechtes Gewissen** a guilty conscience ❷ badly ▷ *Ich habe schlecht geschlafen.* I slept badly.; **schlecht gelaunt** in a bad mood; **Mir ist schlecht.** I feel sick.; **ein schlecht bezahlter Job** a poorly paid job; **Ihm geht es schlecht.** He's in a bad way.

schlechtmachen *vb* [**48**] **jemanden schlechtmachen** to run somebody down

schleichen (*imperf* **schlich**, *perf* **ist geschlichen**) *vb* to creep

Schleife *f* ❶ loop ▷ *Der Fluss macht eine Schleife.* The river makes a loop. ❷ bow ▷ *Sie hatte eine Schleife im Haar.* She had a bow in her hair.

Schleswig-Holstein *nt* Schleswig-Holstein

Schleswig-Holstein is one of the 16 **Länder**. Its capital is Kiel. It is Germany's northernmost state, bordered by the North Sea and the Baltic, and by Denmark in the north.

schleudern (*perf* **hat/ist geschleudert**) *vb* [**88**]

For the perfect tense use **haben** when the verb has an object and **sein** when there is no object.

❶ to hurl ▷ *Sie hat das Buch in die Ecke geschleudert.* She hurled the book into the corner. ❷ to spin ▷ *Du solltest die nasse Wäsche schleudern.* You should spin the wet washing. ❸ to skid ▷ *Das Auto ist geschleudert.* The car skidded.

schlief *vb see* **schlafen**

schließen (*imperf* **schloss**, *perf* **hat geschlossen**) *vb* to shut ▷ *Schließ bitte das Fenster.* Please shut the window. ▷ *Wann schließen die Geschäfte?* When do the shops shut? ▷ *Sie hatte die Augen geschlossen.* She had her eyes shut. ▷ *Der Betrieb wurde geschlossen.* The company was shut down.; **mit jemandem Freundschaft schließen** to make friends with somebody; **etwas aus etwas schließen** to gather something from something

schließlich *adv* finally; **schließlich doch** after all

schlimm *adj* bad

schlimmer *adj* worse

schlimmste *adj* worst ▷ *mein schlimmster Feind* my worst enemy

Schlips *m* tie *(necktie)*

Schlitten (*pl* **Schlitten**) *m* sledge ▷ *Im Winter sind wir viel Schlitten gefahren.* We went sledging a lot in the winter.

Schlittschuh (*pl* **Schlittschuhe**) *m* skate; **Schlittschuh laufen** to skate

Schlitz (*gen* **Schlitzes**, *pl* **Schlitze**) *m* ❶ slit ▷ *Der Rock hat hinten einen Schlitz.* The skirt has a slit at the back. ❷ slot ▷ *Du musst das Zwei-Euro-Stück in den Schlitz werfen.* You have to put the two-euro coin in the slot. ❸ flies *pl* ▷ *Der Schlitz an deiner Hose ist auf.* Your flies are open.

schloss *vb see* **schließen**

Schloss (*gen* **Schlosses**, *pl* **Schlösser**) *nt* ❶ lock ▷ *Sie steckte den Schlüssel ins Schloss.* She put the key in the lock. ❷ clasp ▷ *Kannst du mir bitte das Schloss an meiner Kette aufmachen?* Can you please open the clasp of my necklace? ❸ chateau ▷ *das Schloss in Versailles* the chateau of Versailles

Schluckauf *m* hiccups *pl* ▷ *Er hatte einen Schluckauf.* He had hiccups.

schlucken *vb* [**48**] to swallow

schlug *vb see* **schlagen**

Schluss (*gen* **Schlusses**, *pl* **Schlüsse**) *m* ❶ end ▷ *am Schluss des Jahres* at the end of the year ❷ ending ▷ *Das Buch hat einen traurigen Schluss.* The book has a sad ending. ❸ conclusion ▷ *Ich habe meine Schlüsse gezogen.* I've drawn my conclusions.; **zum Schluss** finally; **Schluss machen** to finish; **mit jemandem Schluss machen** to finish with somebody

Schlüssel (*pl* **Schlüssel**) *m* key ▷ *Wo ist mein Fahrradschlüssel?* Where's the key for my bike? ▷ *der Schlüssel zum Erfolg* the key to success

Schlüsselbund (*pl* **Schlüsselbunde**) *m* bunch of keys

Schlüsselring (*pl* **Schlüsselringe**) *m* keyring
Schlussverkauf *m* sales *pl* ▷ *Dieses Kleid habe ich im Schlussverkauf bekommen.* I got this dress in the sales.
schmal *adj* ❶ narrow ▷ *ein schmaler Durchgang* a narrow passageway ❷ thin ▷ *Sie hat ein schmales Gesicht.* She has a thin face.

> Be careful! **schmal** does not mean **small**.

schmecken *vb* **[48]** to taste ▷ *Wie schmeckt eine Mango?* What does a mango taste like? ▷ *Das schmeckt gut.* That tastes good.; **Es schmeckt ihm.** He likes it.
schmeicheln *vb* **[38] jemandem schmeicheln** to flatter somebody
schmeißen (*imperf* **schmiss**, *perf* **hat geschmissen**) *vb* to throw
schmelzen (*pres* **schmilzt**, *imperf* **schmolz**, *perf* **ist geschmolzen**) *vb* to melt ▷ *Das Eis ist geschmolzen.* The ice has melted.
Schmerz (*gen* **Schmerzes**, *pl* **Schmerzen**) *m* ❶ pain ▷ *ein stechender Schmerz in der Seite* a stabbing pain in the side ❷ grief ▷ *Sie verbarg ihren Schmerz über diesen Verlust.* She hid her grief over her loss.
schmerzen (*perf* **hat geschmerzt**) *vb* **[36]** to hurt
Schmerzmittel (*pl* **Schmerzmittel**) *nt* painkiller
Schmerztablette *f* painkiller
Schmetterling (*pl* **Schmetterlinge**) *m* butterfly
Schminke *f* make-up
schminken *vb* **[38]** to make up ▷ *Hast du dir die Augen geschminkt?* Have you made up your eyes?; **Ich schminke mich selten.** I seldom use make-up.
Schmuck *m* ❶ jewellery ▷ *Sie trägt selten Schmuck.* She seldom wears jewellery. ❷ decoration ▷ *bunte Kugeln als Schmuck für den Weihnachtsbaum* bright baubles as Christmas tree decorations
schmücken *vb* **[48]** to decorate
schmuggeln *vb* **[34]** to smuggle
schmusen *vb* **[38]** to cuddle ▷ *Sie hat mit Felix geschmust.* She cuddled Felix.
Schmutz (*gen* **Schmutzes**) *m* dirt
schmutzig *adj* dirty
Schnabel (*pl* **Schnäbel**) *m* beak ▷ *Der Schnabel der Amsel ist gelb.* The blackbird's beak is yellow.
Schnalle *f* buckle
Schnaps (*gen* **Schnapses**, *pl* **Schnäpse**) *m* schnapps
schnarchen *vb* **[48]** to snore
schnaufen *vb* **[38]** to puff
Schnauze *f* ❶ nose ▷ *Der Hund hat eine kalte Schnauze.* The dog has a cold nose. ❷ (*informal*) gob ▷ *Halt die Schnauze!* Shut your gob!; **die Schnauze von etwas voll haben** to be fed up to the back teeth of something

> Word for word, **die Schnauze von etwas voll haben** means 'to have one's gob full of something'.

sich **schnäuzen** *vb* **[36]** to blow one's nose
Schnecke *f* snail; **eine Nacktschnecke** a slug

> Word for word, **eine Nacktschnecke** means 'a naked snail'.

Schnee *m* snow ▷ *Heute Nacht ist viel Schnee gefallen.* A lot of snow fell last night.
Schneeball (*pl* **Schneebälle**) *m* snowball
Schneemann (*pl* **Schneemänner**) *m* snowman
schneiden (*imperf* **schnitt**, *perf* **hat geschnitten**) *vb* **[60]** to cut ▷ *Kannst du bitte Brot schneiden?* Can you cut some bread, please? ▷ *jemandem die Haare schneiden* to cut somebody's hair ▷ *Du solltest dir die Haare schneiden lassen.* You should have your hair cut.; **sich schneiden (1)** to cut oneself ▷ *Ich habe mich geschnitten.* I've cut myself. ▷ *Ich habe mir in den Finger geschnitten.*

I've cut my finger. **(2)** to intersect ▷ *Die beiden Geraden schneiden sich.* The two straight lines intersect.

schneien *vb* [**38**] **Es schneit.** It's snowing.

schnell *adj, adv* ❶ fast ▷ *Sie hat ein schnelles Auto.* She has a fast car. ▷ *Sie ist schnell gefahren.* She drove fast. ❷ quickly ▷ *Ich rief schnell einen Krankenwagen.* I quickly phoned for an ambulance.

Schnelligkeit *f* speed

Schnellimbiss (*gen* **Schnellimbisses**, *pl* **Schnellimbisse**) *m* snack bar

schnellstens *adv* as quickly as possible

Schnellzug (*pl* **Schnellzüge**) *m* express train

sich **schneuzen** *vb* [**36**] *see* **schnäuzen**

schnitt *vb see* **schneiden**

Schnitt (*pl* **Schnitte**) *m* ❶ cut ▷ *Der Schnitt blutet.* The cut's bleeding. ▷ *Das Kleid hat einen eleganten Schnitt.* The dress has an elegant cut. ❷ average ▷ *Ich habe im Zeugnis einen Schnitt von drei.* I've got an average of C in my report. ❸ pattern ▷ *Hast du zu dem Rock einen Schnitt?* Have you got a pattern for this skirt?

Schnitzel (*pl* **Schnitzel**) *nt* escalope ▷ *Ich bestelle mir ein Schnitzel.* I'm going to order an escalope.

schnitzen *vb* [**48**] to carve

Schnuller (*pl* **Schnuller**) *m* dummy ▷ *Das Baby saugte am Schnuller.* The baby sucked the dummy.

Schnupfen (*pl* **Schnupfen**) *m* cold ▷ *Meine Schwester hat Schnupfen.* My sister has a cold.

Schnur (*pl* **Schnüre**) *f* ❶ string ▷ *Du solltest eine Schnur um das Päckchen machen.* You should put string round the parcel. ❷ flex ▷ *Die Schnur von der Lampe ist zu kurz.* The flex of the lamp is too short.

Schnurrbart (*pl* **Schnurrbärte**) *m* moustache

Schnürsenkel (*pl* **Schnürsenkel**) *m* shoelace

Schock (*pl* **Schocks**) *m* shock

Schokolade *f* chocolate ▷ *eine heiße Schokolade* a hot chocolate

schon *adv* ❶ already ▷ *Ich bin schon fertig.* I've already finished. ❷ yet ▷ *Ist er schon da?* Is he there yet?; **Warst du schon einmal da?** Have you ever been there?; **Ich war schon einmal da.** I've been there before.; **Das war schon immer so.** That's always been the case.; **Hast du schon gehört?** Have you heard?; **schon oft** often; **schon der Gedanke** the very thought; **Du wirst schon sehen.** You'll see.; **Das wird schon noch gut.** That'll be OK.; **ja schon, aber ...** yes, but ...; **schon möglich** possible; **Schon gut!** OK!; **Du weißt schon.** You know.; **Komm schon!** Come on!

schön *adj* ❶ beautiful ▷ *Sie haben ein schönes Haus.* They have a beautiful house. ❷ nice ▷ *Es waren schöne Ferien.* The holidays were nice. ▷ *Schönes Wochenende!* Have a nice weekend.; **sich schön machen** to make oneself look nice; **Schöne Grüße an deine Eltern!** Regards to your parents.; **ganz schön frech** *(informal)* pretty damn cheeky; **na schön** very well

schonend *adj, adv* gentle ▷ *jemandem etwas schonend beibringen* to break something gently to somebody

Schönheit *f* beauty

schöpfen *vb* [**38**] to ladle ▷ *Sie schöpfte Suppe in die Teller.* She ladled soup into the plates.; **Luft schöpfen** to get some air

Schornstein (*pl* **Schornsteine**) *m* chimney

schoss *vb see* **schießen**

Schotte (*gen* **Schotten**, *pl* **Schotten**) *m* Scot; **Er ist Schotte.** He's Scottish.

Schottin *f* Scot; **Sie ist Schottin.** She's Scottish.

schottisch *adj* Scottish

Schottland *nt* Scotland

schräg *adj* sloping ▷ *Das Haus hat ein schräges Dach.* The house has a sloping roof.; **schräg gegenüber** diagonally opposite

Schrägstrich (*pl* **Schrägstriche**) *m* slash

Schrank (*pl* **Schränke**) *m* ❶ cupboard ▷ *Der Besen ist im Schrank in der Küche.* The broom's in the cupboard in the kitchen. ❷ wardrobe ▷ *Ich räume meine Kleider in den Schrank.* I'll put my clothes away in the wardrobe.

Schranke *f* barrier

Schraube *f* ❶ screw ❷ bolt

Schraubenschlüssel (*pl* **Schraubenschlüssel**) *m* spanner

> Word for word, **Schraubenschlüssel** means 'screw key'.

Schraubenzieher (*pl* **Schraubenzieher**) *m* screwdriver

Schreck *m* fright ▷ *Ich habe einen furchtbaren Schreck bekommen.* I got a terrible fright.

schreckhaft *adj* jumpy

schrecklich *adj, adv* ❶ terrible ▷ *Das Wetter war schrecklich schlecht.* The weather was terrible. ❷ terribly ▷ *Das tut schrecklich weh.* It hurts terribly. ▷ *Es tut mir schrecklich leid.* I'm terribly sorry.

Schrei (*pl* **Schreie**) *m* ❶ scream ▷ *Als sie die Spinne sah, stieß sie einen Schrei aus.* When she saw the spider she let out a scream. ❷ shout ▷ *Wir hörten einen Schrei um Hilfe.* We heard a shout for help.

schreiben (*imperf* **schrieb**, *perf* **hat geschrieben**) *vb* [61] ❶ to write ▷ *Ich habe ihr einen Brief geschrieben.* I've written her a letter. ▷ *Wir sollten uns schreiben.* We should write to each other. ❷ to spell ▷ *Wie schreibt man seinen Namen?* How do you spell his name?

Schreibmaschine *f* typewriter

Schreibtisch (*pl* **Schreibtische**) *m* desk

Schreibwaren *fpl* stationery *sg*

schreien (*imperf* **schrie**, *perf* **hat geschrien**) *vb* [62] ❶ to scream ▷ *Sie schrie vor Schmerzen.* She screamed with pain. ❷ to shout ▷ *Wir haben geschrien, du hast uns aber nicht gehört.* We shouted but you didn't hear us.

Schreiner (*pl* **Schreiner**) *m* joiner

schrieb *vb see* **schreiben**

Schrift *f* ❶ writing ▷ *Sie hat eine schöne Schrift.* She has lovely writing. ❷ font ▷ *Welche Schrift soll ich für das Dokument nehmen?* Which font should I use for the document?

schriftlich *adj, adv* written ▷ *eine schriftliche Entschuldigung* a written apology; **etwas schriftlich festhalten** to put something in writing

Schriftsteller (*pl* **Schriftsteller**) *m* writer

schrill *adj* shrill

Schritt (*pl* **Schritte**) *m* ❶ step ▷ *Er machte einen vorsichtigen Schritt nach vorn.* He took a careful step forward. ❷ walk ▷ *Ich habe dich an deinem Schritt erkannt.* I recognized you by your walk. ❸ pace ▷ *Sie ging mit schnellen Schritten nach Hause.* She walked home at a brisk pace.; **Schritt fahren** to drive at walking pace

Schrott *m* scrap metal

Schublade *f* drawer

schüchtern *adj* shy

Schuh (*pl* **Schuhe**) *m* shoe

Schuhcreme (*pl* **Schuhcremes**) *f* shoe polish

Schuhgröße *f* shoe size ▷ *Welche Schuhgröße hast du?* What shoe size are you?

Schulaufgaben *fpl* homework *sg* ▷ *Heute haben wir keine Schulaufgaben bekommen.* We didn't get any homework today.

Schulbuch (*pl* **Schulbücher**) *nt* school book

schuld *adj* **an etwas schuld sein** to be to blame for something; **Er ist schuld.** It's his fault.

Schuld *f* ❶ guilt ▷ *Seine Schuld konnte nicht bewiesen werden.* His guilt couldn't be proved. ❷ fault ▷ *Es war deine Schuld, dass wir zu spät kamen.* It was your fault that we arrived late.; **jemandem Schuld geben** to blame somebody

schulden *vb* [**54**] to owe ▷ *Was schulde ich dir?* How much do I owe you?

Schulden *fpl* debt *sg* ▷ *Ich muss noch meine Schulden bei dir bezahlen.* I still have to pay off my debts to you. ▷ *Staatsschulden* national debt

schuldig *adj* guilty ▷ *Meinst du, dass die Angeklagte schuldig ist?* Do you think that the accused is guilty?; **jemandem etwas schuldig sein** to owe somebody something

Schuldirektor (*pl* **Schuldirektoren**) *m* headmaster

Schuldirektorin *f* headmistress

Schule *f* school ▷ *in der Schule* at school

Schüler (*pl* **Schüler**) *m* pupil

Schülerin *f* pupil

Schulferien *pl* school holidays *pl*

schulfrei *adj* **ein schulfreier Tag** a holiday; **Sonntag ist schulfrei.** Sunday isn't a school day.

Schulhof (*pl* **Schulhöfe**) *m* playground

Schuljahr (*pl* **Schuljahre**) *nt* school year

schulpflichtig *adj* of school age

Schulstunde *f* period

Schultag (*pl* **Schultage**) *m* **mein erster Schultag** my first day at school

Schultasche *f* school bag

Schulter *f* shoulder

Schulzeugnis (*gen* **Schulzeugnisses**, *pl* **Schulzeugnisse**) *nt* school report

Schürze *f* apron

Schuss (*gen* **Schusses**, *pl* **Schüsse**) *m* shot ▷ *Wir hörten einen Schuss.* We heard a shot.

Schüssel *f* bowl

Schusswaffe *f* firearm

Schuster (*pl* **Schuster**) *m* cobbler

Schutt *m* rubble ▷ *Der Schutt von der Baustelle wird morgen weggebracht.* The rubble from the building site will be removed tomorrow.; **Schutt abladen verboten!** No dumping!

schütteln *vb* [**34**] to shake; **sich schütteln** to shake oneself

schütten *vb* [**2**] ❶ to pour ▷ *Soll ich dir Saft ins Glas schütten?* Shall I pour you some juice? ❷ to spill ▷ *Pass auf, dass du den Kaffee nicht auf die Tischdecke schüttest.* Be careful that you don't spill coffee on the tablecloth.; **Es schüttet.** It's pouring down.

Schutz (*gen* **Schutzes**) *m* ❶ protection ▷ *Zum Schutz gegen die Sonne solltest du dich eincremen.* You should put some cream on to protect against the sun. ❷ shelter ▷ *Sie suchten Schutz in der Berghütte.* They took shelter in a mountain hut.; **jemanden in Schutz nehmen** to stand up for somebody

Schütze (*gen* **Schützen**, *pl* **Schützen**) *m* ❶ marksman ▷ *Er ist ein guter Schütze.* He's a good marksman. ❷ Sagittarius ▷ *Martin ist Schütze.* Martin's Sagittarius.

schützen *vb* [**36**] to protect ▷ *Die Pflanzen sollten vor zu großer Hitze geschützt werden.* The plants should be protected from too much heat. ▷ *Diese Creme schützt die Haut gegen Sonnenbrand.* This cream protects the skin from sunburn.; **sich gegen etwas schützen** to protect oneself from something

schwach *adj* weak ▷ *Ihre Stimme wurde immer schwächer.* Her voice became weaker and weaker.; **Das war eine schwache Leistung!** That wasn't very good.

Schwäche *f* weakness

Schwachsinn *m* balderdash

Schwager (*pl* **Schwäger**) *m* brother-in-law

Schwägerin *f* sister-in-law

schwamm *vb see* **schwimmen**

Schwamm (*pl* **Schwämme**) *m* sponge

schwanger *adj* pregnant ▷ *Sie ist im dritten Monat schwanger.* She's three months pregnant.
schwanken *vb* [**38**] ❶ to sway ▷ *Das Schiff schwankte.* The ship swayed. ❷ to stagger ▷ *Er schwankte und fiel dann um.* He staggered and fell down. ❸ to fluctuate ▷ *Die Temperaturen schwanken.* Temperatures are fluctuating. ▷ *Der Kurs des Pfunds schwankt.* The exchange rate of the pound is fluctuating.
Schwanz (*gen* **Schwanzes**, *pl* **Schwänze**) *m* tail
schwänzen *vb* [**36**] *(informal)* to skive off ▷ *Ich habe heute die Turnstunde geschwänzt.* I skived off PE today.
Schwarm (*pl* **Schwärme**) *m* swarm ▷ *ein Schwarm Fliegen* a swarm of flies; **Er ist mein Schwarm.** *(informal)* I have a crush on him.
schwärmen (*perf* **hat/ist geschwärmt**) *vb* [**38**]

> Use **sein** to form the perfect tense for 'to swarm'.

to swarm ▷ *Die Bienen sind aus dem Bienenstock geschwärmt.* The bees swarmed out of the hive.; **schwärmen für** *(informal)* to have a crush on; **schwärmen von** to rave about
schwarz *adj* black ▷ *Der Himmel wurde immer schwärzer.* The sky turned blacker and blacker.; **Schwarzes Brett** notice board

> Word for word, **Schwarzes Brett** means 'black board'.

ins Schwarze treffen to hit the bull's eye
Schwarzbrot (*pl* **Schwarzbrote**) *nt* brown rye bread
Schwarze (*gen* **Schwarzen**, *pl* **Schwarzen**) *mf* black
schwarzfahren (*pres* **fährt schwarz**, *imperf* **fuhr schwarz**, *perf* **ist schwarzgefahren**) *vb* [**21**] **Sie fährt in der Straßenbahn immer schwarz.** She never pays her tram fare.
schwarzsehen (*pres* **sieht schwarz**, *imperf* **sah schwarz**, *perf* **hat schwarzgesehen**) *vb* [**64**] to look on the black side of things ▷ *Sieh doch nicht immer so schwarz.* Don't always look on the black side of things.
Schwarzwald *m* Black Forest
schwarz-weiß *adj* black and white
schwätzen *vb* [**48**] to chatter
Schwätzer (*pl* **Schwätzer**) *m (informal)* windbag
Schwede (*gen* **Schweden**, *pl* **Schweden**) *m* Swede; **Er ist Schwede.** He's Swedish.
Schweden *nt* Sweden
Schwedin *f* Swede
schwedisch *adj* Swedish
schweigen (*imperf* **schwieg**, *perf* **hat geschwiegen**) *vb* ❶ to be silent ▷ *Die Kinder finden es schwierig, mehr als fünf Minuten lang zu schweigen.* The children find it difficult to be silent for more than five minutes. ❷ to stop talking ▷ *Sag ihm, er soll schweigen.* Tell him to stop talking.
Schwein (*pl* **Schweine**) *nt* pig; **Schwein haben** to be really lucky
Schweinebraten (*pl* **Schweinebraten**) *m* roast pork
Schweinefleisch *nt* pork
Schweiß (*gen* **Schweißes**) *m* sweat
Schweiz *f* Switzerland
Schweizer (*pl* **Schweizer**) *m* Swiss ▷ *die Schweizer* the Swiss
Schweizerin *f* Swiss
schweizerisch *adj* Swiss
schwer *adj, adv* ❶ heavy ▷ *Ich habe einen schweren Koffer.* I have a heavy suitcase. ▷ *Er hat eine schwere Erkältung.* He has a heavy cold.; **Ich habe einen schweren Kopf.** I've got a headache.

> Word for word, **Ich habe einen schweren Kopf** means 'I have a heavy head'.

❷ difficult ▷ *Die Mathearbeit war schwer.* The maths test was difficult.; **Er ist schwer verletzt.** He's badly injured.

a b c d e f g h i j k l m n o p q r s t u v w x y z

schwerfallen (*pres* **fällt schwer**, *imperf* **fiel schwer**, *perf* **ist schwergefallen**) *vb* [**22**] **jemandem schwerfallen** to be difficult for somebody
Schwert (*pl* **Schwerter**) *nt* sword
Schwester *f* ❶ sister ▷ *Meine Schwester ist jünger als ich.* My sister's younger than me. ❷ nurse ▷ *Die Schwester hat mir eine Schmerztablette gegeben.* The nurse gave me a painkiller.
Schwiegereltern *pl* parents-in-law *pl*
Schwiegermutter (*pl* **Schwiegermütter**) *f* mother-in-law
Schwiegersohn (*pl* **Schwiegersöhne**) *m* son-in-law
Schwiegertochter (*pl* **Schwiegertöchter**) *f* daughter-in-law
Schwiegervater (*pl* **Schwiegerväter**) *m* father-in-law
schwierig *adj* difficult
Schwierigkeit *f* difficulty
Schwimmbad (*pl* **Schwimmbäder**) *nt* swimming pool
Schwimmbecken (*pl* **Schwimmbecken**) *nt* swimming pool
schwimmen (*imperf* **schwamm**, *perf* **ist geschwommen**) *vb* [**63**] ❶ to swim ▷ *Er kann nicht schwimmen.* He can't swim. ❷ to float ▷ *Auf dem Fluss schwammen Äste.* Branches were floating on the river.
Schwindel *m* ❶ dizzy spell ▷ *Bei hohem Fieber muss man auch mit Schwindel rechnen.* If you have a high temperature, you can also expect to have dizzy spells. ❷ fraud ▷ *Der Schwindel wurde entdeckt.* The fraud was discovered.
schwindelfrei *adj* **schwindelfrei sein** to have a good head for heights
schwindeln *vb* [**34**] (*informal*) to fib
schwindlig *adj* dizzy; **Mir ist schwindlig.** I feel dizzy.
schwitzen *vb* [**36**] to sweat
schwören (*imperf* **schwor**, *perf* **hat geschworen**) *vb* to swear
schwul *adj* gay
schwül *adj* close
Schwule (*gen* **Schwulen**, *pl* **Schwulen**) *mf* gay ▷ *Ich habe nichts gegen Schwule.* I have nothing against gays.
Schwung (*pl* **Schwünge**) *m* swing ▷ *Sie setzte das Pendel in Schwung.* She started the pendulum swinging.; **jemanden in Schwung bringen** to get somebody going
sechs *num* six
Sechs *f* ❶ six ❷ unsatisfactory
- German marks range from one (**sehr gut**) to six (**ungenügend**).

sechste *adj* sixth ▷ *Er kam als Sechster.* He was the sixth to arrive.
Sechstel (*pl* **Sechstel**) *nt* sixth
sechzehn *num* sixteen
sechzig *num* sixty
See *f* sea ▷ *auf See* at sea; **an die See fahren** to go to the seaside
▶ *m* lake ▷ *der Genfer See* Lake Geneva
Seehund (*pl* **Seehunde**) *m* seal
seekrank *adj* seasick
Seele *f* soul
Segel (*pl* **Segel**) *nt* sail
Segelboot (*pl* **Segelboote**) *nt* yacht
Segelflugzeug (*pl* **Segelflugzeuge**) *nt* glider
segeln (*perf* **ist gesegelt**) *vb* [**34**] to sail
Segelschiff (*pl* **Segelschiffe**) *nt* sailing ship
Segen (*pl* **Segen**) *m* blessing
sehen (*pres* **sieht**, *imperf* **sah**, *perf* **hat gesehen**) *vb* [**64**] ❶ to see ▷ *Hast du den Film schon gesehen?* Have you seen the film yet?; **siehe Seite fünf** see page five ❷ to look ▷ *Sieh mal an die Tafel.* Look at the board.; **schlecht sehen** to have bad eyesight; **mal sehen, ob ...** let's see if ...; **Kommst du mit? — Mal sehen.** Are you coming? — I'll see.
sehenswert *adj* worth seeing
Sehenswürdigkeiten *fpl* sights *pl*
sich **sehnen** *vb* [**38**] **sich sehnen nach** to long for
Sehnsucht (*pl* **Sehnsüchte**) *f* longing
sehnsüchtig *adj* longing

sehr *adv* ❶ very ▷ *Das ist sehr schön.* That's very nice.; **sehr gut** very good
German marks range from one (**sehr gut**) to six (**ungenügend**).
❷ a lot ▷ *Sie hat sehr geweint.* She cried a lot.; **zu sehr** too much; **Sehr geehrter Herr Ahlers** Dear Mr Ahlers
Seide *f* silk
Seife *f* soap
Seifenoper *f* soap opera
Seil (*pl* **Seile**) *nt* ❶ rope ▷ *Sie hatten ihn mit einem Seil gefesselt.* They had tied him up with a rope. ❷ cable ▷ *das Seil des Skilifts* the cable of the ski lift
Seilbahn *f* cable car
sein (*pres* **ist**, *imperf* **war**, *perf* **ist gewesen**) *vb* [**65**] to be ▷ *Ich bin müde.* I'm tired. ▷ *Du bist doof.* You're stupid. ▷ *Er ist reich.* He's rich. ▷ *Sie ist Lehrerin.* She's a teacher. ▷ *Es ist kalt.* It's cold. ▷ *Wir sind Schüler am Gymnasium.* We're pupils at the grammar school. ▷ *Wir waren dort.* We were there. ▷ *Wir sind im Schwimmbad gewesen.* We've been to the swimming pool. ▷ *Seien Sie nicht böse.* Don't be angry. ▷ *Morgen bin ich in Rom.* Tomorrow I'll be in Rome.; **Das wäre gut.** That would be a good thing.; **Wenn ich Sie wäre ...** If I were you ...; **Das wär's.** That's it.; **Mir ist kalt.** I'm cold.; **Was ist?** What's the matter?; **Ist was?** Is something the matter?; **es sei denn, dass ...** unless ...; **wie dem auch sei** be that as it may; **Wie wäre es mit ...?** How about ...?; **Lass das sein!** Stop that!
▶ *adj* ❶ his ▷ *Sein Deutschlehrer ist nett.* His German teacher's nice. ▷ *Seine Mutter erlaubt das nicht.* His mother doesn't allow it. ▷ *Das ist sein Buch.* That's his book. ▷ *Seine Eltern sind klasse.* His parents are great. ▷ *Das ist nicht mein Füller, das ist seiner.* That's not my pen, it's his. ▷ *Meine Mutter heißt Anne, seine auch.* My mother's called Anne, so is his. ❷ its ▷ *Der Fuchs kam aus seiner Höhle.* The fox came out of its lair. ▷ *Jedes Buch hat seinen Platz.* Each book has its place.
seiner *pron*
seiner is the genitive of **er**.
of him ▷ *Wir gedenken seiner.* We're thinking of him.
seinetwegen *adv* ❶ for his sake ▷ *Ihr müsst seinetwegen nicht auf euren Urlaub verzichten.* You don't have to do without your holiday for his sake. ❷ on his account ▷ *Hat sie sich seinetwegen so aufgeregt?* Did she get so upset on his account? ❸ as far as he's concerned ▷ *Er sagt, dass du seinetwegen gehen kannst.* He says that as far as he's concerned you can go.
seit *prep, conj*
The preposition **seit** takes the dative.
❶ since ▷ *Seit er verheiratet ist, spielt er nicht mehr Fußball.* He's stopped playing football since he got married. ▷ *Seit letztem Jahr habe ich nichts mehr von ihm gehört.* I haven't heard anything from him since last year. ❷ for ▷ *Er ist seit einer Woche hier.* He's been here for a week. ▷ *seit Langem* for a long time
seitdem *adv, conj* since ▷ *Seitdem sie im Gymnasium ist, hat sie kaum mehr Zeit.* Since she's been going to grammar school, she's hardly had any time.; **Ich habe seitdem nichts mehr von ihr gehört.** I haven't heard from her since then.
Seite *f* ❶ side ▷ *Die rechte Seite des Autos war beschädigt.* The right side of the car was damaged. ❷ page ▷ *Das steht auf Seite fünfzig.* It's on page fifty.
Sekretär *m* secretary
Sekretariat (*pl* **Sekretariate**) *nt* secretary's office
Sekretärin *f* secretary
Sekt (*pl* **Sekte**) *m* sparkling wine
Sekunde *f* second ▷ *zehn Sekunden* ten seconds
selber *pron* = **selbst**

selbst *pron, adv* ❶ on one's own ▷ *Das Kind kann sich selbst anziehen.* The child can get dressed on her own. ▷ *Ich werde schon selbst eine Lösung finden.* I'll find a solution on my own.; **ich selbst** I myself; **er selbst** he himself; **wir selbst** we ourselves; **Sie ist die Liebenswürdigkeit selbst.** She's kindness itself.; **Er braut sein Bier selbst.** He brews his own beer.; **von selbst** by itself ❷ even ▷ *Selbst meine Mutter findet Oasis gut.* Even my mother likes Oasis.; **selbst wenn** even if

selbständig *adj see* **selbstständig**

Selbstbedienung *f* self-service

selbstbewusst *adj* self-confident

Selbstmord (*pl* **Selbstmorde**) *m* suicide ▷ *Selbstmord begehen* to commit suicide

Selbstmordanschlag (*pl* **Selbstmordanschläge**) *m* suicide attack

selbstsicher *adj* self-assured

selbstständig *adj* ❶ independent ▷ *Du solltest langsam selbstständiger werden.* It's about time you started to become more independent. ▷ *ein selbstständiger Staat* an independent country ❷ on one's own ▷ *Kannst du das nicht selbstständig entscheiden?* Can't you decide on your own?; **sich selbstständig machen** to become self-employed

selbstverständlich *adj, adv* ❶ obvious ▷ *Das ist für mich durchaus nicht selbstverständlich.* It's not at all obvious to me.; **Es ist doch selbstverständlich, dass man da hilft.** It goes without saying that you should help.; **Ich halte das für selbstverständlich.** I take that for granted. ❷ of course ▷ *Ich habe mich selbstverständlich sofort bedankt.* Of course I said thank you immediately. ▷ *Kommt er mit? — Selbstverständlich.* Is he coming? — Of course. ▷ *Ich habe selbstverständlich nicht unterschrieben.* Of course I didn't sign.

Selbstvertrauen *nt* self-confidence

Sellerie *m* celeriac

selten *adj, adv* ❶ rare ▷ *eine seltene Pflanze* a rare plant ❷ rarely ▷ *Wir gehen selten ins Kino.* We rarely go to the cinema.

seltsam *adj* curious

Semester (*pl* **Semester**) *nt* semester

senden (*imperf* **sendete** *or* **sandte**, *perf* **hat gesendet** *or* **gesandt**) *vb* ❶ to send ▷ *Bitte senden Sie mir Ihren neuesten Katalog.* Please send me your latest catalogue. ❷ to broadcast ▷ *Der Spielfilm wird im dritten Programm gesendet.* The film will be broadcast on Channel three. ▷ *Wir senden bis Mitternacht.* We broadcast until midnight.

Sendereihe *f* series

Sendung *f* ❶ transmission ▷ *Während der Sendung darf das Studio nicht betreten werden.* Nobody's allowed to enter the studio during transmission. ❷ programme ▷ *Kennst du die Sendung 'Tiere im Zoo'?* Do you know the programme 'Animals in the Zoo'? ❸ consignment ▷ *Für Sie ist eine Sendung mit Mustern angekommen.* A consignment of samples has arrived for you.

Senf (*pl* **Senfe**) *m* mustard

Sensation *f* sensation

sensibel *adj* sensitive ▷ *Sie ist ein sehr sensibler Mensch.* She's a very sensitive person.

> Be careful! **sensibel** does not mean **sensible**.

sentimental *adj* sentimental ▷ *Nun werd nicht sentimental!* Now don't get sentimental.

September *m* September ▷ *im September* in September ▷ *am elften September* on the eleventh of September ▷ *Ulm, den 10. September 2007* Ulm, 10 September 2007 ▷ *Heute ist der elfte September.* Today is the eleventh of September.

Serie *f* series *sg*
seriös *adj* respectable
Be careful! **seriös** does not mean **serious**.
Server (*pl* **Server**) *m* server
Service (*gen* **Service** *or* **Services**, *pl* **Service**) *nt* set ▷ *Sie hat ein hübsches Teeservice aus Porzellan.* She has a lovely china tea set.
▶ *m* service ▷ *In dem Hotel ist der Service ausgezeichnet.* The service in the hotel is excellent.
Serviette *f* serviette
servus *excl* ❶ hello! ❷ goodbye!
Sessel (*pl* **Sessel**) *m* armchair
setzen *vb* [**36**] to put ▷ *Sie setzte das Kind auf den Stuhl.* She put the child on the chair. ▷ *Er setzte das Glas an den Mund.* He put the glass to his lips. ▷ *Hast du meinen Namen auf die Liste gesetzt?* Have you put my name on the list? ▷ *ein Komma setzen* to put a comma; **jemandem eine Frist setzen** to set somebody a deadline; **sich setzen** **(1)** to settle ▷ *Der Kaffeesatz hat sich gesetzt.* The coffee grounds have settled. **(2)** to sit down ▷ *Setz dich doch!* Do sit down! ▷ *Er setzte sich aufs Sofa.* He sat down on the sofa.; **auf etwas setzen** to bet on something ▷ *Er hat hundert Euro auf die Nummer zwei gesetzt.* He bet a hundred euros on number two.
Seuche *f* epidemic
seufzen *vb* [**36**] to sigh
sexuell *adj* sexual
Shampoo (*pl* **Shampoos**) *nt* shampoo
Sibirien *nt* Siberia
sich *pron* ❶ himself ▷ *Er redet mit sich selbst.* He's talking to himself. herself ▷ *Sie spricht nicht gern über sich selbst.* She doesn't like to talk about herself. ▷ *Sie wäscht sich.* She's washing herself. ▷ *Sie hat sich einen Pullover gekauft.* She bought herself a jumper. itself ▷ *Das Boot hat sich wieder aufgerichtet.* The boat righted itself. ❷ themselves ▷ *Meine Eltern haben sich ein neues Auto gekauft.* My parents have bought themselves a new car. ▷ *Sie bleiben gern unter sich.* They keep themselves to themselves. ❸ each other ▷ *Sie lieben sich.* They love each other.; **Sie wäscht sich die Haare.** She's washing her hair.; **Er schneidet sich die Nägel.** He's cutting his nails.; **Man fragt sich, ob ...** One wonders whether ...; **Sie wiederholen sich.** You're repeating yourself.; **Haben Sie Ihren Ausweis bei sich?** Do you have your pass on you?; **Dieser Artikel verkauft sich gut.** This article sells well.
sicher *adj, adv* ❶ safe ▷ *Das ist ein sehr sicheres Auto.* It's a very safe car. ❷ certain ▷ *Der Termin ist noch nicht sicher.* The date isn't certain yet.; **Ich bin nicht sicher.** I'm not sure. ❸ reliable ▷ *eine sichere Methode* a reliable method; **vor jemandem sicher sein** to be safe from somebody; **vor etwas sicher sein** to be safe from something ❹ definitely ▷ *Sie kommt sicher nicht mehr.* She's definitely not coming anymore.; **Er weiß das sicher schon.** I'm sure he knows that already.; **sicher nicht** surely not; **Aber sicher!** Of course!
Sicherheit *f* safety ▷ *Tragen Sie einen Helm zu Ihrer eigenen Sicherheit.* Wear a helmet for your own safety. ▷ *Diese Maßnahmen dienen der Sicherheit der Fluggäste.* These measures are for passenger safety.; **Hier sind wir in Sicherheit.** We're safe here.; **Ich kann nicht mit Sicherheit sagen, ob ich komme.** I can't say for sure if I'll come.
Sicherheitsgurt (*pl* **Sicherheitsgurte**) *m* seat belt
sicherlich *adv* certainly
sichern *vb* [**88**] to secure ▷ *Maßnahmen, die Arbeitsplätze sichern* measures to secure jobs; **Daten sichern** to back up

data; **jemandem etwas sichern** to secure something for somebody

Sicherung *f* ❶ securing ▷ *Maßnahmen zur Sicherung der Arbeitsplätze* measures for securing jobs ❷ fuse ▷ *Die Sicherung ist durchgebrannt.* The fuse has blown.

Sicht *f* view ▷ *Wir hatten eine gute Sicht auf die Berge.* We had a good view of the mountains. ▷ *Du versperrst mir die Sicht.* You're blocking my view.; **auf lange Sicht** on a long-term basis; **aus jemandes Sicht** as somebody sees it

sichtbar *adj* visible

sie *pron* ❶ she ▷ *Sie ist sehr hübsch.* She's very pretty. ❷ it ▷ *Schöne Tasche, ist sie neu?* Lovely bag, is it new? ▷ *Kann ich deine Tasche haben, oder brauchst du sie noch?* Can I have your bag or do you need it? ❸ her ▷ *Ich kenne sie nicht.* I don't know her. ❹ they ▷ *Sie sind alle gekommen.* They all came. ❺ them ▷ *Ich habe sie alle eingeladen.* I've invited all of them.

Sie *pron* you ▷ *Möchten Sie mitkommen?* Would you like to come? ▷ *Ich kenne Sie.* I know you.

The formal form of address **Sie** (singular and plural) is used when addressing people you don't know or your superiors. Teachers say **Sie** to children over the age of 16.

Sieb (*pl* **Siebe**) *nt* ❶ sieve ▷ *Wir sollten da Mehl durch ein Sieb schütten.* We should rub the flour through a sieve. ❷ strainer ▷ *Hast du ein Teesieb?* Have you got a tea strainer?

sieben *num* seven

siebte *adj* seventh ▷ *Er kam als Siebter.* He was the seventh to arrive.

siebzehn *num* seventeen

siebzig *num* seventy

Siedlung *f* ❶ settlement ▷ *eine indianische Siedlung* an Indian settlement ❷ estate ▷ *Sie wohnt in unserer Siedlung.* She lives on our estate.

Sieg (*pl* **Siege**) *m* victory

siegen *vb* [**38**] to win ▷ *Welche Mannschaft hat gesiegt?* Which team won?

Sieger (*pl* **Sieger**) *m* winner ▷ *Brasilien war 1994 Sieger der Fußballweltmeisterschaft.* Brazil was the winner of the 1994 World Cup.

siehe *vb see* **sehen**

siezen *vb* [**36**] to address as 'Sie'

The formal form of address **Sie** (singular and plural) is used when addressing people you don't know or your superiors. Teachers say **Sie** to children over the age of 16.

Silbe *f* syllable

Silber *nt* silver

Silvester (*pl* **Silvester**) *nt* New Year's Eve

singen (*imperf* **sang**, *perf* **hat gesungen**) *vb* [**66**] to sing

Singular (*pl* **Singulare**) *m* singular

sinken (*imperf* **sank**, *perf* **ist gesunken**) *vb* [**67**] ❶ to sink ▷ *Das Schiff ist gesunken.* The ship has sunk. ❷ to fall ▷ *Die Preise für Computer sind gesunken.* The prices of computers have fallen.

Sinn (*pl* **Sinne**) *m* ❶ sense ▷ *die fünf Sinne* the five senses ❷ meaning ▷ *Ich verstehe den Sinn dieses Satzes nicht.* I don't understand the meaning of this sentence. ▷ *Was ist der Sinn des Lebens?* What's the meaning of life?; **Sinn für etwas haben** to have a sense of something; **jemandem in den Sinn kommen** to come to somebody; **Es hat keinen Sinn.** There's no point.

sinnlos *adj* ❶ pointless ▷ *Es ist sinnlos, das zu tun.* It's pointless doing that. ❷ meaningless ▷ *Er hat sinnloses Zeug geredet.* He talked meaningless rubbish.

sinnvoll *adj* sensible ▷ *Das wäre eine sinnvolle Änderung.* That would be a sensible change.

Situation *f* situation

Sitz (*gen* **Sitzes**, *pl* **Sitze**) *m* seat

sitzen *vb* [**68**] ❶ to sit ▷ *Er saß auf dem Stuhl.* He was sitting on the chair.; **sitzen bleiben (1)** to remain seated ▷ *Bitte bleiben Sie sitzen.* Please remain seated. **(2)** to have to repeat a year

In Germany, pupils do not automatically move up (**versetzt werden**) to the next class at the end of the school year. If their performance is not good enough, they have to repeat the school year. This is known as **sitzen bleiben**.

▷ *Ich habe Angst, dass ich dieses Jahr sitzen bleibe.* I'm worried that I'll have to repeat this year. ❷ to fit ▷ *Diese Hose sitzt.* These trousers fit well.

Sitzplatz (*gen* **Sitzplatzes**, *pl* **Sitzplätze**) *m* seat

Sitzung *f* meeting

Skandal (*pl* **Skandale**) *m* scandal

Skandinavien *nt* Scandinavia

skandinavisch *adj* Scandinavian

Skelett (*pl* **Skelette**) *nt* skeleton

Ski (*pl* **Ski** *or* **Skier**) *m* ski; **Ski fahren** to ski

Skifahrer (*pl* **Skifahrer**) *m* skier

Skilaufen *nt* skiing

Skilehrer (*pl* **Skilehrer**) *m* ski instructor

Skilift (*pl* **Skilifte** *or* **Skilifts**) *m* ski lift

Skorpion (*pl* **Skorpione**) *m* ❶ scorpion ❷ Scorpio ▷ *Sie ist Skorpion.* She's Scorpio.

Slip (*pl* **Slips**) *m* pants *pl* ▷ *ein Slip* a pair of pants

Slowakei *f* Slovakia

so *adv, conj, excl* ❶ so ▷ *Ich hatte mich so darauf gefreut.* I was so looking forward to it. ▷ *so schön* so nice ▷ *zwanzig oder so* twenty or so ▷ *und so weiter* and so on; **so groß wie ...** as big as ... ❷ so much ▷ *Das hat ihn so geärgert, dass ...* That annoyed him so much that ... ❸ like that ▷ *Mach es nicht so.* Don't do it like that.; **... oder so was** ... or something like that; **so einer wie ich** somebody like me; **Na so was!** Well, well!; **so dass** so that; **So?** Really?

sobald *conj* as soon as

Söckchen (*pl* **Söckchen**) *nt* ankle sock

Socke *f* sock

sodass *conj* so that

Sofa (*pl* **Sofas**) *nt* sofa

sofort *adv* immediately

sogar *adv* even

sogleich *adv* straight away

Sohle *f* sole

Sohn (*pl* **Söhne**) *m* son

solch *pron* such ▷ *Sie ist solch eine nette Frau.* She's such a nice lady. ▷ *eine solche Frechheit* such a cheek; **ein solcher** a ... like that

Soldat (*gen* **Soldaten**, *pl* **Soldaten**) *m* soldier

solide *adj* ❶ solid ▷ *Dieser Tisch ist aus solidem Holz.* This table is made of solid wood. ❷ sound ▷ *Sie hat solide Grammatikkenntnisse.* She has a sound grasp of grammar. ❸ respectable ▷ *Wir führen ein solides Leben.* We lead a respectable life. ▷ *Er ist solide geworden.* He's become respectable.

sollen (*imperf* **sollte**, *perf* **hat gesollt** *or* **sollen**) *vb* [**69**]

The past participle **sollen** is used when **sollen** is a modal auxiliary.

❶ to be supposed to ▷ *Ich soll um fünf Uhr dort sein.* I'm supposed to be there at five o'clock. ▷ *Was soll das heißen?* What's that supposed to mean? ▷ *Morgen soll es schön werden.* It's supposed to be nice tomorrow. ❷ to have to ▷ *Du sollst sofort nach Hause.* You have to go home immediately. ▷ *Sie sagt, du sollst nach Hause kommen.* She says that you have to come home.; **Sag ihm, er soll warten.** Tell him he's to wait. ❸ should ▷ *Ich sollte meine Hausaufgaben machen.* I should do my homework. ▷ *Du hättest nicht gehen sollen.* You shouldn't have gone. ▷ *Was soll ich machen?* What should I do? ▷ *Ich hätte eigentlich nicht gesollt.* I really shouldn't have. ▷ *Das sollst du nicht.* You shouldn't do that.; **Sie soll verheiratet**

sein. She's said to be married.; **Man sollte glauben, dass ...** You would think that ...; **Soll ich dir helfen?** Shall I help you?; **Soll ich?** Shall I?; **Was soll das?** What's all this?; **Was soll's?** *(informal)* What the hell!

Sommer (*pl* **Sommer**) *m* summer ▷ *im Sommer* in summer

Sommerferien *pl* summer holidays *pl*

sommerlich *adj* ❶ summery ▷ *ein sommerliches Kleid* a summery dress ❷ summer ▷ *sommerliche Kleidung* summer clothes ▷ *sommerliches Wetter* summer weather

Sommerschlussverkauf (*pl* **Sommerschlussverkäufe**) *m* summer sale

Sommersprossen *fpl* freckles *pl*

Sonderangebot (*pl* **Sonderangebote**) *nt* special offer

sonderbar *adj* strange

sondern *conj* but; **nicht nur ..., sondern auch** not only ..., but also

Sonderpreis *m* special price

Sonnabend (*pl* **Sonnabende**) *m* Saturday ▷ *am Sonnabend* on Saturday

sonnabends *adv* on Saturdays

Sonne *f* sun

sich **sonnen** *vb* [**38**] to sun oneself

Sonnenbrand (*pl* **Sonnenbrände**) *m* sunburn

Sonnenbrille *f* sunglasses *pl* ▷ *Sie trug eine Sonnenbrille.* She was wearing sunglasses.

Sonnenenergie *f* solar power

Sonnenmilch *f* suntan lotion

Sonnenschein *m* sunshine

Sonnenschirm (*pl* **Sonnenschirme**) *m* sunshade

Sonnenstich *m* sunstroke

sonnig *adj* sunny

Sonntag (*pl* **Sonntage**) *m* Sunday ▷ *am Sonntag* on Sunday

sonntags *adv* on Sundays

sonst *adv, conj* ❶ normally ▷ *Was ist mit dir? Du bist doch sonst nicht so still.* What's wrong with you? You're not normally so quiet. ▷ *Die Kinder sind sonst eigentlich artiger.* The children normally behave better. ❷ else ▷ *Wer sonst?* Who else? ▷ *Was sonst?* What else? ▷ *Sonst war niemand da.* Nobody else was there. ▷ *sonst nichts* nothing else; **sonst noch** else; **Haben Sie sonst noch einen Wunsch?** Would you like anything else?; **Sonst noch etwas?** Anything else?; **sonst wo** somewhere else ❸ otherwise ▷ *Ich habe etwas Kopfschmerzen, aber sonst geht's mir gut.* I've got a headache, otherwise I feel fine.

sonstig *adj* other

Sorge *f* worry; **Ich mache mir Sorgen.** I'm worried.

sorgen *vb* [**38**] **für jemanden sorgen** to look after somebody; **für etwas sorgen** to see to something; **sich um jemanden sorgen** to worry about somebody

sorgfältig *adj* careful

Sorte *f* ❶ sort ▷ *Welche Sorte Äpfel ist das?* What sort of apple is that? ❷ brand ▷ *Welche Sorte Waschmittel verwenden Sie?* What brand of detergent do you use?

sortieren (*perf* **hat sortiert**) *vb* [**76**] to sort out

Soße *f* ❶ sauce ▷ *Eis mit Himbeersoße* ice cream with raspberry sauce ❷ gravy ▷ *Schweinebraten mit Soße* roast pork with gravy ❸ dressing ▷ *Salat mit einer Joghurtsoße* salad with a yoghurt dressing

Souvenir (*pl* **Souvenirs**) *nt* souvenir

soviel *adv see* **viel**
▶ *conj* as far as ▷ *soviel ich weiß* as far as I know

soweit *adv see* **weit**
▶ *conj* as far as ▷ *Soweit ich weiß, kann er nicht kommen.* As far as I know, he can't come.

sowenig *adv see* **wenig**

sowie *conj* as soon as ▷ *Ich rufe an, sowie ich Bescheid weiß.* I'll phone as soon as I know.

sowieso *adv* anyway
sowohl *conj* **sowohl ... als auch** both ... and
sozial *adj* social
Sozialhilfe *f* social security ▷ *Sozialhilfe bekommen* to be on social security
Sozialkunde *f* social studies *sg*
Spalte *f* ❶ crack ▷ *Durch die Trockenheit hatten sich tiefe Spalten gebildet.* Deep cracks had formed as a result of the dry spell. ❷ column ▷ *Der Text ist in zwei Spalten gedruckt.* The text is printed in two columns.
spalten *vb* [**2**] to split
Spanien *nt* Spain
Spanier (*pl* **Spanier**) *m* Spaniard; **Er ist Spanier.** He's Spanish.; **die Spanier** the Spanish
Spanierin *f* Spaniard; **Sie ist Spanierin.** She's Spanish.
spanisch *adj* Spanish
Spanisch (*gen* **Spanischen**) *nt* Spanish ▷ *Er lernt Spanisch in der Schule.* He's learning Spanish at school.
spannend *adj* exciting
Spannung *f* ❶ suspense ▷ *ein Film voller Spannung* a film full of suspense ❷ tension ▷ *Das führte zu Spannungen zwischen den beiden Ländern.* That caused tension between the two countries.
Sparbuch (*pl* **Sparbücher**) *nt* savings book
sparen *vb* [**38**] to save ▷ *Wir müssen sparen.* We have to save. ▷ *Sie hat zweihundert Euro gespart.* She's saved two hundred euros. ▷ *Energie sparen* to save energy ▷ *Er spart für ein Mountainbike.* He's saving for a mountain bike.; **sich etwas sparen (1)** not to bother with something ▷ *Den Film kannst du dir sparen.* Don't bother with that film. **(2)** to keep something to oneself ▷ *Spar dir deine Bemerkungen.* You can keep your remarks to yourself.; **mit etwas sparen** to be sparing with something; **an etwas sparen** to economize on something ▷ *Sie spart in letzter Zeit am Essen.* She's been economizing on food recently.

> Be careful! **sparen** does not mean **to spare**.

Spargel *m* asparagus
Sparkasse *f* savings bank
sparsam *adj* ❶ economical ▷ *ein sparsames Auto* an economical car ▷ *Wir sollten mit den Rohstoffen sparsam umgehen.* We should be economical with raw materials. ❷ thrifty ▷ *Sie ist sehr sparsam.* She's very thrifty.
Sparschwein (*pl* **Sparschweine**) *nt* piggy bank
Spaß (*gen* **Spaßes**, *pl* **Späße**) *m* fun ▷ *Wir hatten in den Ferien viel Spaß.* We had great fun in the holidays.; **Sie versteht keinen Spaß.** She has no sense of humour.

> Word for word, **Sie versteht keinen Spaß** means 'She doesn't understand fun'.

Skifahren macht mir Spaß. I like skiing.; **zum Spaß** for fun; **Viel Spaß!** Have fun!
spät *adj, adv* late ▷ *Es wird spät.* It's getting late. ▷ *Wir kamen zu spät.* We were late.; **Wie spät ist es?** What's the time?
später *adj, adv* later ▷ *Bis später!* See you later!
spätestens *adv* at the latest
Spatz (*gen* **Spatzen**, *pl* **Spatzen**) *m* sparrow
spazieren *vb* [**76**] **spazieren fahren** to go for a drive; **spazieren gehen** to go for a walk
Spaziergang (*pl* **Spaziergänge**) *m* walk ▷ *einen Spaziergang machen* to go for a walk
Speck *m* bacon
Speerwerfen *nt* throwing the javelin
Speicher (*pl* **Speicher**) *m* ❶ loft ▷ *Die alten Möbel sind auf dem Speicher.* The old furniture's in the loft. ❷ storehouse ▷ *Die alten Speicher am Hafen wurden zu*

Wohnungen umgebaut. The old storehouses at the harbour were converted into flats. ❸ memory ▷ *Ich will den Speicher meines Computers erweitern.* I want to expand the memory of my computer.

speichern (*perf* **hat gespeichert**) *vb* [**88**] ❶ to store ▷ *Energie speichern* to store energy ❷ to save ▷ *eine Datei speichern* to save a file

Speiseeis *nt* ice cream

Speisekarte *f* menu ▷ *Könnte ich bitte die Speisekarte haben?* Could I have the menu please?

Speisesaal *m* dining room

Speisewagen (*pl* **Speisewagen**) *m* dining car

Spende *f* donation

spenden *vb* [**54**] to donate ▷ *Ich habe zwanzig Euro gespendet.* I've donated twenty euros.; **Blut spenden** to give blood

> Be careful! **spenden** does not mean **to spend**.

Spender (*pl* **Spender**) *m* donor

spendieren (*perf* **hat spendiert**) *vb* [**76**] **jemandem etwas spendieren** (*informal*) to stand somebody something

Sperre *f* ❶ barrier ▷ *Vor dem Eingang befand sich eine Sperre.* There was a barrier in front of the entrance. ❷ ban ▷ *Er erhielt eine Sperre von drei Monaten.* He got a three-month ban.

sperren (*perf* **hat gesperrt**) *vb* [**38**] ❶ to close ▷ *Die Polizei hat die Straße gesperrt.* The police closed the road. ❷ to obstruct ▷ *Es ist verboten, gegnerische Spieler zu sperren.* Obstructing the opposition is not allowed. ❸ to lock ▷ *Diese Dateien sind gesperrt.* These files are locked.

Spezialität *f* speciality

Spiegel (*pl* **Spiegel**) *m* mirror ▷ *Er sah in den Spiegel.* He looked in the mirror.

Spiegelbild (*pl* **Spiegelbilder**) *nt* reflection

Spiegelei (*pl* **Spiegeleier**) *nt* fried egg

Spiel (*pl* **Spiele**) *nt* ❶ game ▷ *Sollen wir ein Spiel spielen?* Shall we play a game? ▷ *Hast du das Spiel England gegen Deutschland gesehen?* Did you see the England-Germany game? ❷ pack ▷ *Hast du ein Spiel Karten?* Do you have a pack of cards?; **ein Theaterspiel** a play

spielen *vb* [**38**] to play ▷ *Die Kinder spielen im Garten.* The children are playing in the garden. ▷ *Wollen wir Tennis spielen?* Shall we play tennis? ▷ *Wer spielt den Hamlet?* Who's playing Hamlet? ▷ *Wir haben um Geld gespielt.* We played for money.

Spieler (*pl* **Spieler**) *m* ❶ player ▷ *Wir brauchen noch einen dritten Spieler.* We still need a third player. ❷ gambler ▷ *Er ist ein leidenschaftlicher Spieler.* He's a passionate gambler.

Spielfeld (*pl* **Spielfelder**) *nt* pitch

Spielfilm (*pl* **Spielfilme**) *m* feature film

Spielplatz (*gen* **Spielplatzes**, *pl* **Spielplätze**) *m* playground

Spielzeug (*pl* **Spielzeuge**) *nt* toy

Spinat *m* spinach

Spinne *f* spider

spinnen (*imperf* **spann**, *perf* **hat gesponnen**) *vb* ❶ to spin ▷ *Wolle spinnen* to spin wool ❷ to be crazy ▷ *Du spinnst wohl!* You're crazy!

Spionage *f* espionage

spionieren (*perf* **hat spioniert**) *vb* [**76**] to spy

spitz *adj* pointed; **ein spitzer Winkel** an acute angle; **eine spitze Zunge** a sharp tongue; **eine spitze Bemerkung** a caustic remark

spitze *adj* (*informal*) great; **Das war spitze!** That was great!

Spitze *f* ❶ point ▷ *Die Spitze des Bleistifts ist abgebrochen.* The point of the pencil has broken off. ❷ peak ▷ *Die Spitzen der Berge waren schneebedeckt.* The peaks of the mountains were covered with snow. ❸ top ▷ *Welche Mannschaft liegt an der Spitze?* Which team is top? ❹ lace

▷ *An ihrem Kleid war ein Kragen aus Spitze.* Her dress had a lace collar.
Spitzer (*pl* **Spitzer**) *m* pencil sharpener
Spitzname (*gen* **Spitznamens**, *pl* **Spitznamen**) *m* nickname
Splitter (*pl* **Splitter**) *m* splinter
sponsern *vb* [**88**] to sponsor
Sport *m* sport
Sportart *f* sport ▷ *verschiedene Sportarten* various sports
Sportler (*pl* **Sportler**) *m* sportsman
Sportlerin *f* sportswoman
sportlich *adj* sporty ▷ *Bettina ist sehr sportlich.* Bettina is very sporty.
Sportplatz (*gen* **Sportplatzes**, *pl* **Sportplätze**) *m* sports field
Sportverein (*pl* **Sportvereine**) *m* sports club
Sportzentrum (*pl* **Sportzentren**) *nt* sports centre
sprach *vb see* **sprechen**
Sprache *f* language
Sprachführer (*pl* **Sprachführer**) *m* phrase book

Word for word, **Sprachführer** means 'language guide'.

Sprachlabor (*pl* **Sprachlabors** *or* **Sprachlabore**) *nt* language laboratory
sprachlich *adj* linguistic
sprachlos *adj* speechless
Sprachsteuerung *f* voice control
sprang *vb see* **springen**
sprechen (*pres* **spricht**, *imperf* **sprach**, *perf* **hat gesprochen**) *vb* [**70**] ❶ to talk ▷ *Seid bitte ruhig, wenn ich spreche.* Please be quiet, I'm talking. ▷ *Du sprichst so leise.* You talk so quietly. ▷ *Wir haben von dir gesprochen.* We were talking about you. ❷ to say ▷ *Sie hat kein Wort gesprochen.* She didn't say a word. ❸ to speak ▷ *Ich spreche Italienisch ziemlich schlecht.* I speak Italian pretty badly.; **jemanden sprechen** to speak to somebody; **mit jemandem über etwas sprechen** to speak to somebody about something; **Das spricht für ihn.** That's a point in his favour.
Sprechstunde *f* surgery (*doctor's*)
spricht *vb see* **sprechen**
Sprichwort (*pl* **Sprichwörter**) *nt* proverb
springen (*imperf* **sprang**, *perf* **ist gesprungen**) *vb* [**71**] ❶ to jump ▷ *Er sprang über den Zaun.* He jumped over the fence. ❷ to crack ▷ *Das Glas ist gesprungen.* The glass has cracked.
Spritze *f* ❶ syringe ▷ *Die Spritze muss steril sein.* The syringe has to be sterile. ❷ injection ▷ *Der Arzt hat mir eine Spritze gegeben.* The doctor gave me an injection. ❸ nozzle ▷ *Die Spritze am Gartenschlauch ist nicht dicht.* The nozzle on the garden hose leaks.
spritzen (*perf* **hat/ist gespritzt**) *vb* [**36**]

Use **haben** to form the perfect tense. Use **sein** to form the perfect tense for 'to spurt out'.

❶ to spray ▷ *Er hat sein Fahrrad grün gespritzt.* He's sprayed his bike green.; **den Garten spritzen** to water the garden; **jemanden nass spritzen** to splash somebody ❷ to spurt out ▷ *Das Blut spritzte aus der Wunde.* The blood spurted out of the wound.
Sprudel (*pl* **Sprudel**) *m* mineral water; **süßer Sprudel** lemonade
sprühen (*perf* **hat/ist gesprüht**) *vb* [**38**]

For the perfect tense use **haben** when the verb has an object and **sein** when there is no object. Use **haben** to form the perfect tense for 'to sparkle'.

❶ to spray ▷ *Sie hat Haarspray auf ihre Haare gesprüht.* She sprayed her hair with hairspray. ❷ to fly ▷ *In alle Richtungen sind Funken gesprüht.* Sparks flew in all directions. ❸ to sparkle ▷ *Er hat gestern Abend vor Witz gesprüht.* He was sparkling with humour yesterday evening.
Sprung (*pl* **Sprünge**) *m* ❶ jump ▷ *Das war ein weiter Sprung.* That was a long

jump. ❷ crack ▷ *Die Tasse hat einen Sprung.* There is a crack in the cup.

Sprungbrett (*pl* **Sprungbretter**) *nt* springboard

spucken *vb* [**38**] to spit

Spüle *f* kitchen sink

spülen *vb* [**38**] ❶ to rinse ▷ *Wollsachen muss man gut spülen.* Woollens have to be rinsed well. ❷ to wash up ▷ *Wenn du spülst, dann trockne ich ab.* If you wash up I'll dry.

Spülmaschine *f* dishwasher

Spülmittel (*pl* **Spülmittel**) *nt* washing-up liquid

Spur *f* ❶ track ▷ *Wir sahen Spuren im Sand.* We saw tracks in the sand. ❷ lane ▷ *Der Fahrer vor mir hat plötzlich die Spur gewechselt.* The driver in front of me suddenly changed lane. ❸ trace ▷ *Auf ihrem Gesicht sah man die Spuren der Anstrengung.* You could see the traces of strain on her face.; **eine Bremsspur** skidmarks *pl* ❹ trail ▷ *Die Polizei verfolgte seine Spur.* The police followed his trail.; **Das Essen war eine Spur zu scharf.** The meal was a touch too spicy.

spüren *vb* [**38**] to feel

Staat (*pl* **Staaten**) *m* state; **die Vereinigten Staaten von Amerika** the United States of America

staatlich *adj* ❶ state ▷ *staatliche Fördermittel* state subsidies ▷ *eine staatliche Schule* a state school ❷ state-run ▷ *eine staatliche Einrichtung* a state-run organization

stabil *adj* ❶ stable ▷ *Die Lage ist stabil.* The situation is stable. ▷ *Sie ist psychisch stabil.* She's mentally stable. ❷ sturdy ▷ *stabile Möbel* sturdy furniture

Stachel (*pl* **Stacheln**) *m* ❶ spike ▷ *Ich habe mir die Hose an einem Stachel aufgerissen.* I've torn my trousers on a spike. ❷ spine ▷ *Ein Igel hat Stacheln.* A hedgehog has spines. ▷ *Dieser Kaktus hat lange Stacheln.* This cactus has long spines. ❸ sting ▷ *Ich habe versucht, den Stachel der Biene herauszuziehen.* I tried to take the bee sting out.

Stachelbeere *f* gooseberry

Stacheldraht (*pl* **Stacheldrähte**) *m* barbed wire

Stadion (*pl* **Stadien**) *nt* stadium

Stadt (*pl* **Städte**) *f* town

Stadtkreis (*pl* **Stadtkreise**) *m* town borough

Stadtmitte *f* town centre

Stadtplan (*pl* **Stadtpläne**) *m* street map

Stadtrand (*pl* **Stadtränder**) *m* outskirts *pl*

Stadtrundfahrt *f* tour of the city

Stadtteil (*pl* **Stadtteile**) *m* part of town

Stadtzentrum (*pl* **Stadtzentren**) *nt* city centre

stahl *vb see* **stehlen**

Stahl *m* steel

Stall (*pl* **Ställe**) *m* stable ▷ *Die Pferde sind im Stall.* The horses are in the stable.; **ein Hühnerstall** a henhouse

Stamm (*pl* **Stämme**) *m* ❶ trunk ▷ *Der Baum hat einen dicken Stamm.* The tree has a thick trunk. ❷ tribe ▷ *Er gehört zum Stamm der Bantus.* He belongs to the Bantu tribe. ❸ stem ▷ *Die Endung wird an den Stamm des Verbs angehängt.* The ending's added to the stem of the verb.

stammen *vb* [**38**] **stammen aus** to come from

Stammgast (*pl* **Stammgäste**) *m* regular customer

Stammtisch (*pl* **Stammtische**) *m* table for the regulars

In Germany it is usual for a group of friends to reserve a table in the same pub or restaurant for the same time each week.

stand *vb see* **stehen**

Stand (*pl* **Stände**) *m* ❶ state ▷ *Was ist der Stand der Dinge?* What's the state of affairs? ❷ score ▷ *Sie sind beim Stand von eins zu eins in die Pause.* The score was one all at half-time. ❸ stand ▷ *An* *welchen Stand hast du den Luftballon gekauft?* Which stand did you buy the balloon at? ❹ level ▷ *Prüf mal den Ölstand.* Check the oil level.; **zu Stande** *see* **zustande**

ständig *adj* constant ▷ *Musst du ständig stören?* Do you constantly have to interrupt?

Standort (*pl* **Standorte**) *m* location

Stapel (*pl* **Stapel**) *m* pile

starb *vb see* **sterben**

stark *adj* ❶ strong ▷ *Mein Bruder ist stärker als du.* My brother's stronger than you. ❷ heavy ▷ *starke Regenfälle* heavy rain; **starke Kopfschmerzen** a splitting headache ❸ *(informal)* great ▷ *Das war stark!* That was great!

Start (*pl* **Starts**) *m* ❶ start ▷ *Es waren über hundert Läufer am Start.* There were over a hundred runners at the start. ❷ takeoff ▷ *Die Maschine war bereit zum Start.* The machine was ready for takeoff.

starten *vb* [2] ❶ to start ▷ *Wann startet das Rennen?* When does the race start? ❷ to take off ▷ *Das Flugzeug startet gleich.* The plane is about to take off.

statt *conj, prep*

> The preposition **statt** takes the genitive or the dative.

instead of ▷ *Statt nach Hause zu gehen, sind wir noch in die Disco.* Instead of going home, we went to the disco. ▷ *Sie kam statt ihres Bruders.* She came instead of her brother.

stattfinden (*imperf* **fand statt**, *perf* **hat stattgefunden**) *vb* [24] to take place

Stau (*pl* **Staus**) *m* traffic jam ▷ *Wir sind im Stau stecken geblieben.* We were stuck in a traffic jam.

Staub *m* dust; **Staub wischen** to dust

staubig *adj* dusty

staubsaugen (*perf* **hat staubgesaugt**) *vb* [38] to hoover

Staubsauger (*pl* **Staubsauger**) *m* vacuum cleaner

staunen *vb* [38] to be astonished

stechen (*pres* **sticht**, *imperf* **stach**, *perf* **hat gestochen**) *vb* ❶ to prick ▷ *Ich habe mich mit der Nadel gestochen.* I've pricked myself with the needle. ❷ to sting ▷ *Mich hat eine Biene gestochen.* A bee stung me. ❸ to bite ▷ *Reibe dich ein, damit du nicht gestochen wirst.* Rub something on so that you won't be bitten. ❹ to trump ▷ *Sie hat meine Dame gestochen.* She trumped my queen.

Steckdose *f* socket

stecken *vb* [48] ❶ to put ▷ *Sie steckte ihren Geldbeutel in die Tasche.* She put her purse in her bag. ❷ to insert ▷ *Stecken Sie die Münze in den Schlitz.* Insert the coin into the slot. ❸ to stick ▷ *Steck deinen Finger nicht in das Loch!* Don't stick your finger in the hole. ❹ to pin ▷ *Ich steckte das Abzeichen an meine Jacke.* I pinned the badge onto my jacket. ❺ to be stuck ▷ *Wir stecken im Stau.* We are stuck in a traffic jam.; **Wo steckt sie nur?** Where on earth is she?

Stecker (*pl* **Stecker**) *m* plug

stehen (*imperf* **stand**, *perf* **hat gestanden**) *vb* [72] ❶ to stand ▷ *Es war so voll, dass wir stehen mussten.* It was so full that we had to stand. ❷ to be ▷ *Vor unserem Haus steht eine Kastanie.* There's a chestnut tree in front of our house. ❸ to say ▷ *In der Zeitung steht, dass das Wetter besser wird.* It says in the newspaper that the weather will improve.; **zum Stehen kommen** to come to a halt; **Es steht schlecht um ihn.** Things are bad for him.; **jemandem stehen** to suit somebody; **Wie steht's? (1)** How are things? **(2)** What's the score?; **stehen bleiben** to stop

Stehlampe *f* standard lamp

stehlen (*pres* **stiehlt**, *imperf* **stahl**, *perf* **hat gestohlen**) *vb* [73] to steal

steif *adj* stiff

steigen (*imperf* **stieg**, *perf* **ist gestiegen**) *vb* [74] ❶ to rise ▷ *Der Ballon stieg zum Himmel.* The balloon rose into the sky. ❷ to climb ▷ *Sie ist auf die Leiter gestiegen.* She climbed up the ladder.; **in etwas steigen** to get into something; **Sie stieg in den Zug.** She got on the train.; **auf etwas steigen** to get on something

steil *adj* steep

Stein (*pl* **Steine**) *m* stone

Steinbock (*pl* **Steinböcke**) *m* Capricorn ▷ *Er ist Steinbock.* He's Capricorn.

steinig *adj* stony

Stelle *f* ❶ place ▷ *Ich habe mir die Stelle im Buch angestrichen.* I've marked the place in the book.; **an dieser Stelle** here ❷ job ▷ *Ich suche eine neue Stelle.* I'm looking for a new job. ❸ office ▷ *Bei welcher Stelle kann man einen Pass bekommen?* In which office can you get a passport?; **An deiner Stelle würde ich das nicht tun.** I wouldn't do it if I were you.

stellen *vb* **[38]** ❶ to put ▷ *Ich habe die Vase auf den Tisch gestellt.* I put the vase on the table. ❷ to set ▷ *Stell deine Uhr nach meiner.* Set your watch by mine. ❸ to supply ▷ *Die Lehrbücher werden gestellt.* The course books will be supplied.; **sich irgendwohin stellen** to stand somewhere; **sich stellen** to give oneself up; **sich dumm stellen** to pretend to be stupid

Stellenanzeige *f* job advertisement

Stellung *f* position ▷ *In welcher Stellung schläfst du?* Which position do you sleep in? ▷ *Er hat eine gute Stellung.* He has a good position.; **zu etwas Stellung nehmen** to comment on something

Stellvertreter (*pl* **Stellvertreter**) *m* deputy

Stempel (*pl* **Stempel**) *m* stamp

stempeln *vb* **[34]** to stamp; **jemanden zum Sündenbock stempeln** to make somebody a scapegoat

sterben (*pres* **stirbt**, *imperf* **starb**, *perf* **ist gestorben**) *vb* **[75]** to die

Stereoanlage *f* stereo

Stern (*pl* **Sterne**) *m* star ▷ *die Sterne am Himmel* the stars in the sky

Sternzeichen (*pl* **Sternzeichen**) *nt* star sign ▷ *Was ist dein Sternzeichen?* What star sign are you?

Steuer (*pl* **Steuer**) *nt* wheel ▷ *Wer saß am Steuer?* Who was at the wheel? ▶ *f* tax ▷ *Wir müssen viel Steuern bezahlen.* We have to pay a lot of tax.

Steuerrad (*pl* **Steuerräder**) *nt* steering wheel

Stich (*pl* **Stiche**) *m* ❶ bite ▷ *Das Mittel schützt vor Stichen.* This gives protection from bites. ▷ *ein Mückenstich* a midge bite; **ein Bienenstich** a bee sting ❷ stab ▷ *Er tötete sie mit zwölf Stichen.* He killed her by stabbing her twelve times. ❸ stitch ▷ *Sie hat den Aufhänger mit ein paar Stichen angenäht.* She sewed on the loop with a couple of stitches. ▷ *Die Wunde wurde mit drei Stichen genäht.* Three stitches were put in the wound. ❹ trick ▷ *Ich habe beim letzten Spiel keinen Stich gemacht.* I didn't win any tricks in the last game. ❺ engraving ▷ *ein Kupferstich* a copper engraving; **jemanden im Stich lassen** to leave somebody in the lurch

sticken *vb* **[38]** to embroider

Stickstoff *m* nitrogen

Stiefel (*pl* **Stiefel**) *m* boot

Stiefkind (*pl* **Stiefkinder**) *nt* stepchild

Stiefmutter (*pl* **Stiefmütter**) *f* stepmother

Stiefvater (*pl* **Stiefväter**) *m* stepfather

stiehlt *vb see* **stehlen**

Stiel (*pl* **Stiele**) *m* ❶ handle ▷ *der Stiel des Besens* the broom handle ❷ stem ▷ *Er hat den Stiel der Tulpe abgeknickt.* He snapped the stem off the tulip.

Stier (*pl* **Stiere**) *m* ❶ bull ▷ *Der Stier wurde getötet.* The bull was killed. ❷ Taurus ▷ *Brigitte ist Stier.* Brigitte's Taurus.

Stift (*pl* **Stifte**) *m* ❶ peg ▷ *Das Brett wird mit Stiften an der Wand befestigt.* The board is fixed to the wall with pegs.

❷ crayon ▷ *Sebastian hat lauter bunte Stifte bekommen.* Sebastian got lots of coloured crayons. ❸ pencil ▷ *Schreib lieber mit Kuli als mit einem Stift.* I'd rather you wrote with a Biro than a pencil.

stiften *vb* [**2**] **Sie hat eine Runde Eis gestiftet.** She bought us all an ice cream.; **Unruhe stiften** to cause trouble

Stil (*pl* **Stile**) *m* style

still *adj* quiet ▷ *Seid mal still.* Be quiet.; **Sie stand ganz still.** She stood quite still.

Stille *f* quietness; **in aller Stille** quietly

stillhalten (*pres* **hält still**, *imperf* **hielt still**, *perf* **hat stillgehalten**) *vb* [**33**] to keep still

stillschweigend *adv* tacitly

Stimme *f* ❶ voice ▷ *Er hat eine laute Stimme.* He has a loud voice. ❷ vote ▷ *Er bekam nur zwanzig Stimmen.* He only got twenty votes.; **Wem hast du deine Stimme gegeben?** Who did you vote for?

stimmen *vb* [**38**] ❶ to be right ▷ *Die Übersetzung stimmt nicht.* The translation isn't right. ▷ *Das stimmt nicht!* That's not right! ❷ to tune ▷ *ein Instrument stimmen* to tune an instrument ❸ to vote ▷ *stimmen für* to vote for ▷ *stimmen gegen* to vote against; **Stimmt so!** Keep the change.

Stimmung *f* mood

stinken (*imperf* **stank**, *perf* **hat gestunken**) *vb* to stink

stirbt *vb see* **sterben**

Stirn *f* forehead

Stock (1) (*pl* **Stöcke**) *m* stick ▷ *Er hat ihn mit einem Stock geschlagen.* He hit him with a stick.

Stock (2) (*pl* **Stock** *or* **Stockwerke**) *m* floor ▷ *Wir wohnen im dritten Stock.* We live on the third floor.

Stoff (*pl* **Stoffe**) *m* ❶ fabric ▷ *Das ist ein hübscher Stoff.* That's a pretty fabric. ❷ material ▷ *Ich sammle Stoff für mein Referat.* I'm collecting material for my assignment.

stöhnen *vb* [**38**] to groan

stolpern (*perf* **ist gestolpert**) *vb* [**88**] ❶ to stumble ▷ *Er ist gestolpert und gefallen.* He stumbled and fell. ❷ to trip ▷ *Er ist über einen Stein gestolpert.* He tripped over a stone.

stolz *adj* proud ▷ *Ich bin stolz auf dich.* I'm proud of you.

stören *vb* [**38**] to disturb ▷ *Störe ich?* Am I disturbing you? ▷ *Ich will nicht länger stören.* I won't disturb you any longer.; **Stört es dich, wenn ich rauche?** Do you mind if I smoke?; **Die Leitung war gestört.** It was a bad line.; **sich an etwas stören** to worry about something

Störung *f* ❶ interruption ▷ *Diese dauernden Störungen regen mich auf.* These constant interruptions are getting on my nerves. ❷ interference ▷ *Es war eine Störung beim Bild.* There was interference to the picture.

stoßen (*pres* **stößt**, *imperf* **stieß**, *perf* **hat gestoßen**) *vb* **den Kopf an etwas stoßen** to bump one's head on something; **sich stoßen** to bump oneself; **sich an etwas stoßen** to take exception to something; **an etwas stoßen** to bump into something; **auf etwas stoßen** to come across

stottern *vb* [**88**] to stutter

Strafarbeit *f* lines *pl* ▷ *Ich habe eine Strafarbeit bekommen.* I got lines.

Strafe *f* ❶ punishment ▷ *Zur Strafe müsst ihr länger bleiben.* You'll be kept in after school as a punishment.; **eine Gefängnisstrafe** a prison sentence ❷ fine ▷ *Er musste eine Strafe von fünfzig Euro bezahlen.* He had to pay a fifty euro fine.

Strahl (*pl* **Strahlen**) *m* ❶ ray ▷ *radioaktive Strahlen* radioactive rays ▷ *ein Sonnenstrahl* a ray of sunlight; **ein Lichtstrahl** a beam of light ❷ jet ▷ *ein Wasserstrahl* a jet of water

strahlen *vb* [**38**] ❶ to shine ▷ *Die Sterne strahlten hell.* The stars shone brightly. ❷ to beam ▷ *Sie strahlte, als sie das hörte.* She beamed when she heard that.

Strahlung *f* radiation

Strand (*pl* **Strände**) *m* ❶ beach ▷ *Wir haben den ganzen Tag am Strand gelegen.* We lay on the beach all day. ❷ shore ▷ *Das wurde an den Strand gespült.* That was washed up on the shore.

strapazieren (*perf* **hat strapaziert**) *vb* [**76**] ❶ to be hard on ▷ *Du hast heute deinen Computer ganz schön strapaziert.* You've been really hard on your computer today. ❷ to wear out ▷ *Die Wanderung hat uns ziemlich strapaziert.* The walk has really worn us out.

Straße *f* ❶ street ▷ *In welcher Straße wohnt Thomas?* Which street does Thomas live in? ❷ road ▷ *Wir sind die Straße entlang der Küste gefahren.* We drove along the coast road.

Straßenbahn *f* tram

Strauß (*gen* **Straußes**, *pl* **Sträuße**) *m* bunch of flowers ▷ *Wir haben unserer Gastgeberin einen Strauß mitgebracht.* We brought our hostess a bunch of flowers.

Strecke *f* ❶ distance ▷ *Wir haben diese Strecke an einem Tag zurückgelegt.* We covered this distance in one day. ▷ *Bis zu ihm ist es noch eine ziemliche Strecke.* It's still quite a distance to his place. ❷ line ▷ *Auf der Strecke zwischen Stuttgart und Ulm gab es ein Zugunglück.* There's been a train accident on the Stuttgart to Ulm line.

streicheln *vb* [**88**] to stroke

streichen (*imperf* **strich**, *perf* **hat gestrichen**) *vb* ❶ to stroke ▷ *Sie strich über seine Haare.* She stroked his hair. ❷ to spread ▷ *Sie strich Honig aufs Brot.* She spread honey on the bread. ❸ to paint ▷ *Ich muss dringend mein Zimmer streichen.* I really must paint my room. ❹ to delete ▷ *Den zweiten Satz kannst du streichen.* You can delete the second sentence. ❺ to cancel ▷ *Der Direktor hat den Schulausflug gestrichen.* The headmaster has cancelled the school trip.

Streichholz (*gen* **Streichholzes**, *pl* **Streichhölzer**) *nt* match

Streifen (*pl* **Streifen**) *m* strip

Streik (*pl* **Streiks**) *m* strike

streiken *vb* [**38**] to go on strike; **Sie streiken.** They're on strike.

Streit (*pl* **Streite**) *m* argument

sich **streiten** (*imperf* **stritt**, *perf* **hat gestritten**) *vb* to argue ▷ *Sie streiten sich ständig.* They argue constantly.; **Darüber lässt sich streiten.** That's debatable.

streng *adj* ❶ strict ▷ *Meine Eltern sind furchtbar streng.* My parents are terribly strict. ❷ severe ▷ *Es war ein strenger Winter.* It was a severe winter. ▷ *Das wird streng bestraft.* That will be severely punished. ❸ sharp ▷ *Wo kommt der strenge Geruch her?* Where's that sharp smell coming from?

Stress (*gen* **Stresses**) *m* stress; **Ich bin im Stress!** *(informal)* I'm stressed out.

stressen (*pres* **stresst**, *imperf* **stresste**, *perf* **hat gestresst**) *vb* [**48**] to put under stress

stressig *adj* stressful

Strich (*pl* **Striche**) *m* ❶ line ▷ *Mach einen Strich unter die Spalte.* Draw a line under the column. ❷ stroke ▷ *Mit ein paar Strichen zeichnete er ein Haus.* He drew a house with a couple of strokes.; **auf den Strich gehen** *(informal)* to be on the game

Strichkode (*pl* **Strichkodes**) *m* bar code

Strick (*pl* **Stricke**) *m* rope

stricken *vb* [**48**] to knit

Stroh *nt* straw

Strohhalm (*pl* **Strohhalme**) *m* drinking straw

Strom (*pl* **Ströme**) *m* ❶ current ▷ *der Wechselstrom* alternating current;

Vorsicht, auf dem Draht ist Strom. Be careful, the wire is live. ❷ electricity ▷ *Sie haben den Strom abgeschaltet.* They've cut off the electricity. ❸ stream ▷ *Ein Strom von Zuschauern kam aus dem Stadion.* A stream of spectators was coming out of the stadium.

Strömung *f* current

Strumpf (*pl* **Strümpfe**) *m* stocking

Strumpfhose *f* tights *pl* ▷ *eine Strumpfhose* a pair of tights

> Word for word, **eine Strumpfhose** means 'a pair of stocking trousers'.

Stück (*pl* **Stücke**) *nt* ❶ piece ▷ *Sie schnitt ein Stück Käse ab.* She cut off a piece of cheese. ❷ play ▷ *Wir haben ein Stück von Brecht angesehen.* We saw a play by Brecht.

Student (*gen* **Studenten**, *pl* **Studenten**) *m* student

Studentin *f* student

studieren (*perf* **hat studiert**) *vb* **[76]** to study ▷ *Mein Bruder studiert Physik.* My brother's studying physics.

Studium (*pl* **Studien**) *nt* studies *pl*

Stufe *f* ❶ step ▷ *Vorsicht, Stufe!* Mind the step! ❷ stage ▷ *Er hat bereits eine fortgeschrittene Stufe erreicht.* He's already reached an advanced stage. ▷ *eine Entwicklungsstufe* a stage of development

Stuhl (*pl* **Stühle**) *m* chair

stumm *adj* silent ▷ *Sie blieb stumm.* She remained silent.

stumpf *adj* blunt ▷ *Er wurde mit einem stumpfen Gegenstand am Kopf getroffen.* He was hit on the head with a blunt object.; **ein stumpfer Winkel** an obtuse angle

Stunde *f* ❶ hour ▷ *Ich komme in einer Stunde.* I'll come in an hour. ❷ lesson ▷ *Was haben wir in der letzten Stunde behandelt?* What did we do in the last lesson?

Stundenplan (*pl* **Stundenpläne**) *m* timetable

stündlich *adj* hourly ▷ *stündlich verkehren* to run hourly

stur *adj* obstinate

Sturm (*pl* **Stürme**) *m* storm

stürmen (*perf* **ist/hat gestürmt**) *vb* **[38]**

> Use **sein** to form the perfect tense for 'to storm (out)'. Use **haben** to form the perfect tense for all other meanings.

to storm ▷ *Er ist aus dem Zimmer gestürmt.* He stormed out of the room. ▷ *Die Polizei hat das Gebäude gestürmt.* The police stormed the building.; **Es stürmt.** There's a gale blowing.

stürmisch *adj* stormy

Sturz (*gen* **Sturzes**, *pl* **Stürze**) *m* ❶ fall ▷ *Bei dem Sturz hat sie sich das Bein gebrochen.* She broke her leg in the fall. ❷ overthrow ▷ *Alle freuten sich über den Sturz des Diktators.* Everybody was pleased about the overthrow of the dictator.

stürzen (*perf* **hat/ist gestürzt**) *vb* **[36]**

> Use **sein** to form the perfect tense. Use **haben** to form the perfect tense for 'to overthrow' and for **sich stürzen**.

❶ to fall ▷ *Sie ist vom Pferd gestürzt.* She fell off a horse. ❷ to rush ▷ *Er kam ins Zimmer gestürzt.* He rushed into the room. ❸ to overthrow ▷ *Die Regierung wurde gestürzt.* The government has been overthrown.; **sich stürzen** to plunge

Sturzhelm (*pl* **Sturzhelme**) *m* crash helmet

Stütze *f* support

Subjekt (*pl* **Subjekte**) *nt* subject

Substantiv (*pl* **Substantive**) *nt* noun

Suche *f* search

suchen *vb* **[48]** to look for ▷ *Ich suche meinen Radiergummi.* I'm looking for my rubber. ▷ *Wir haben gesucht, es aber nicht gefunden.* We looked for it but couldn't find it. ▷ *Er wird von der Polizei gesucht.* The police are looking for him.; **nach etwas suchen** to look for something

Suchmaschine *f (internet)* search engine
süchtig *adj* addicted ▷ *heroinsüchtig* addicted to heroin
Südafrika *nt* South Africa
Südamerika *nt* South America
Süden *m* south
südlich *adj, prep, adv* southerly ▷ *in südlicher Richtung* in a southerly direction; **südlich einer Sache** to the south of something; **südlich von** south of
Südpol *m* South Pole ▷ *am Südpol* at the South Pole
Summe *f* total
summen *vb* [**38**] ❶ to buzz ▷ *Die Bienen summten.* The bees were buzzing. ❷ to hum ▷ *Sie summte vor sich hin.* She was humming. ▷ *Er hat ein Lied gesummt.* He hummed a song.
Sünde *f* sin
Super *nt* four star ▷ *Ich tanke Super.* My car takes four star.
Superbenzin *nt* four-star petrol
Superlativ (*pl* **Superlative**) *m* superlative
Supermarkt (*pl* **Supermärkte**) *m* supermarket
Suppe *f* soup
Surfbrett (*pl* **Surfbretter**) *nt* surfboard
surfen (*perf* **hat gesurft**) *vb* [**38**] to surf; **im Internet surfen** to surf the Net
süß *adj* sweet
Süßigkeit *f* sweet ▷ *Sie isst gern Süßigkeiten.* She likes eating sweets.
Süßstoff (*pl* **Süßstoffe**) *m* sweetener
Süßwaren *pl* confectionery *sg*
Symbol (*pl* **Symbole**) *nt* symbol
sympathisch *adj* likeable ▷ *Er ist ein sympathischer Mensch.* He's a likeable person.; **Er ist mir sympathisch.** I like him.

> Be careful! **sympathisch** does not mean **sympathetic**.

synchronisieren (*perf* **hat synchronisiert**) *vb* [**76**] to dub ▷ *ein synchronisierter Film* a dubbed film
synthetisch *adj* synthetic
System (*pl* **Systeme**) *nt* system
systematisch *adj* systematic
Szene *f* scene

t

Tabak (*pl* **Tabake**) *m* tobacco
Tabelle *f* table
Tablett (*pl* **Tablette**) *nt* tray
Tablette *f* tablet
Tachometer (*pl* **Tachometer**) *m* speedometer
tadellos *adj* faultless
Tafel *f* blackboard ▷ *Der Lehrer schrieb das Wort an die Tafel.* The teacher wrote the word on the blackboard.; **eine Tafel Schokolade** a bar of chocolate
Tag (*pl* **Tage**) *m* ❶ day ▷ *Ich war den ganzen Tag weg.* I was away all day. ❷ daylight ▷ *Wir möchten noch bei Tag ankommen.* We want to arrive in daylight.; **an den Tag kommen** to come to light; **Guten Tag!** Hello!
Tageblatt (*pl* **Tageblätter**) *nt* daily newspaper
Tagebuch (*pl* **Tagebücher**) *nt* diary ▷ *ein Tagebuch führen* to keep a diary
tagelang *adv* for days
Tagesanbruch *m* dawn ▷ *bei Tagesanbruch* at dawn
Tagesgericht (*pl* **Tagesgerichte**) *nt* dish of the day
Tageskarte *f* ❶ menu of the day ❷ day ticket
Tageslicht *nt* daylight
Tageszeitung *f* daily paper
täglich *adj, adv* daily
tagsüber *adv* during the day
Taille *f* waist
Takt (*pl* **Takte**) *m* tact ▷ *Sie behandelte die Sache mit viel Takt.* She showed great tact in dealing with the matter.; **keinen Takt haben** to be tactless; **den Takt angeben** to keep time; **im Stundentakt** at hourly intervals
Taktik *f* tactics *pl* ▷ *Das ist die falsche Taktik.* Those are the wrong tactics.
taktisch *adj* tactical ▷ *Das war taktisch unklug.* That was a tactical mistake.
taktlos *adj* tactless
taktvoll *adj* tactful
Tal (*pl* **Täler**) *nt* valley
Talent (*pl* **Talente**) *nt* talent
talentiert *adj* talented
Tank (*pl* **Tanks**) *m* tank
tanken *vb* [38] to get petrol ▷ *Wir müssen noch tanken.* We still have to get petrol.
Tankstelle *f* petrol station
Tanne *f* fir
Tante *f* aunt
Tanz (*gen* **Tanzes**, *pl* **Tänze**) *m* dance
tanzen *vb* [36] to dance
Tanzschule *f* dancing school

It is very common for German boys and girls to go to a **Tanzschule** when they are about 14.

Tapete *f* wallpaper
tapezieren (*perf* **hat tapeziert**) *vb* [76] to wallpaper
tapfer *adj* brave
Tapferkeit *f* bravery
Tasche *f* ❶ pocket ▷ *Er hatte die Hände in der Hosentasche.* He had his hands in his trouser pockets. ❷ bag ▷ *Sie kann ihre Tasche nicht finden.* She can't find her bag.

Taschenbuch (*pl* **Taschenbücher**) *nt* paperback
Taschendieb *m* pickpocket
Taschengeld (*pl* **Taschengelder**) *nt* pocket money
Taschenlampe *f* torch
Taschenmesser (*pl* **Taschenmesser**) *nt* penknife
Taschenrechner (*pl* **Taschenrechner**) *m* pocket calculator
Taschentuch (*pl* **Taschentücher**) *nt* handkerchief
Tasse *f* cup ▷ *eine Tasse Tee* a cup of tea
Tastatur *f* keyboard
Taste *f* ❶ button ▷ *Welche Taste muss ich drücken, um die Waschmaschine anzustellen?* What button do I have to press to start the washing machine? ❷ key ▷ *Bei der Schreibmaschine und der Computertastatur gibt es eine Hochstelltaste.* There's a shift key on the typewriter and the computer keyboard.
tat *vb see* **tun**
Tat (*pl* **Taten**) *f* ❶ deed ▷ *Das war eine tapfere Tat.* That was a brave deed. ▷ *eine gute Tat* a good deed ❷ crime ▷ *Der Beschuldigte hat die Tat gestanden.* The accused confessed to the crime.; **in der Tat** indeed
Täter (*pl* **Täter**) *m* culprit
tätowieren (*perf* **hat tätowiert**) *vb* [**76**] to tattoo
Tatsache *f* fact
tatsächlich *adj, adv* ❶ actual ▷ *Der tatsächliche Grund war ein anderer als der, den sie angegeben hatte.* The actual reason was different from the one she gave. ❷ really ▷ *Das hat sie tatsächlich gesagt.* She really did say that. ▷ *Er ist tatsächlich rechtzeitig gekommen.* He really has come in time.
taub *adj* deaf ▷ *Sie ist auf dem rechten Ohr taub.* She's deaf in her right ear.
Taube *f* ❶ pigeon ▷ *die Tauben auf dem Marktplatz* the pigeons in the market square ❷ dove ▷ *die Friedenstaube* the dove of peace
tauchen (*perf* **hat/ist getaucht**) *vb* [**48**]

> Use **haben** for the perfect tense when you describe the activity and **sein** when you describe the motion.

❶ to dip ▷ *Sie hat ihren Zeh ins Wasser getaucht.* She dipped her toe into the water. ❷ to dive ▷ *Als Kind habe ich viel getaucht.* I used to dive a lot as a child. ▷ *Er ist nach dem versunkenen Schatz getaucht.* He dived in search of the sunken treasure.
tauen *vb* [**38**] **Es taut.** It's thawing.
Taufe *f* christening
taufen *vb* [**38**] to christen
taugen *vb* [**38**] **nichts taugen** to be no good
tauschen *vb* [**48**] to exchange
täuschen *vb* [**48**] ❶ to deceive ▷ *Du hast mich bewusst getäuscht.* You deliberately deceived me. ❷ to be deceptive ▷ *Der äußere Anschein täuscht oft.* Appearances are often deceptive.; **sich täuschen** to be wrong
tausend *num* thousand
Taxi (*gen* **Taxis**, *pl* **Taxis**) *nt* taxi
Taxifahrer (*pl* **Taxifahrer**) *m* taxi driver
Taxistand (*pl* **Taxistände**) *m* taxi rank
Technik *f* ❶ technology ▷ *hoch entwickelte Technik* advanced technology; **die Gentechnik** genetic engineering ❷ technique ▷ *Sie beherrscht diese Technik des Hochsprungs noch nicht.* She hasn't mastered this high-jump technique yet.
Techniker (*pl* **Techniker**) *m* technician
technisch *adj* technical
Technologie *f* technology
Tee (*pl* **Tees**) *m* tea ▷ *Tee mit Milch und Zucker* tea with milk and sugar ▷ *Tee mit Zitrone* lemon tea ▷ *Kamillentee* camomile tea
Teebeutel (*pl* **Teebeutel**) *m* tea bag
Teekanne *f* teapot
Teelöffel (*pl* **Teelöffel**) *m* teaspoon; **ein Teelöffel Zucker** a teaspoonful of sugar

Teer *m* tar
Teich (*pl* **Teiche**) *m* pond
Teig (*pl* **Teige**) *m* dough
Teil (*pl* **Teile**) *m*
You can also say **das Teil**.
❶ part ▷ *der erste Teil des Buches* the first part of the book; **das Ersatzteil** the spare part ❷ share ▷ *Ich möchte meinen Teil am Gewinn.* I would like my share of the profit. ❸ component part ▷ *Er hat das Fahrrad in seine Teile zerlegt.* He dismantled the bike into its component parts.; **zum Teil** partly
teilen *vb* [38] to divide; **mit jemandem teilen** to share with somebody
teilnehmen (*pres* **nimmt teil**, *imperf* **nahm teil**, *perf* **hat teilgenommen**) *vb* [52] **an etwas teilnehmen** to take part in something
Teilnehmer (*pl* **Teilnehmer**) *m* participant
teils *adv* partly
teilweise *adv* in parts ▷ *Das Buch war teilweise sehr spannend.* The book was thrilling in parts.; **Sie waren teilweise beschädigt.** Some of them were damaged.
Teilzeitarbeit *f* part-time work
Telefax (*gen* **Telefax**, *pl* **Telefaxe**) *nt* fax
Telefon (*pl* **Telefone**) *nt* telephone
Telefonanruf (*pl* **Telefonanrufe**) *m* telephone call
Telefonat (*pl* **Telefonate**) *nt* phone call
Telefonbuch (*pl* **Telefonbücher**) *nt* phone book
Telefonhörer (*pl* **Telefonhörer**) *m* receiver ▷ *Er nahm den Telefonhörer ab.* He picked up the receiver.
telefonieren (*perf* **hat telefoniert**) *vb* [76] to telephone; **Ich habe gestern mit ihr telefoniert.** I talked to her on the phone yesterday.
telefonisch *adj* telephone ▷ *eine telefonische Nachricht* a telephone message; **Sie können mich telefonisch erreichen.** You can contact me by phone.
Telefonkarte *f* phonecard
Telefonnummer *f* telephone number
Telefonzelle *f* telephone box
Telegramm (*pl* **Telegramme**) *nt* telegram
Teleskop (*pl* **Teleskope**) *nt* telescope
Teller (*pl* **Teller**) *m* plate
Temperament (*pl* **Temperamente**) *nt* **Sie hat ein ziemlich lebhaftes Temperament.** She's quite a vivacious person.
temperamentvoll *adj* vivacious
Temperatur *f* temperature
Tempo (*pl* **Tempos**) *nt* ❶ speed ▷ *Er ist mit einem irren Tempo gefahren.* He drove at breakneck speed. ❷ rate ▷ *Wir müssen unser Arbeitstempo steigern.* We must increase our work rate.
tendieren (*perf* **hat tendiert**) *vb* [76] **zu etwas tendieren** to tend towards something
Tennis (*gen* **Tennis**) *nt* tennis
Tennisplatz (*gen* **Tennisplatzes**, *pl* **Tennisplätze**) *m* tennis court
Tennisschläger (*pl* **Tennisschläger**) *m* tennis racket
Tennisspieler (*pl* **Tennisspieler**) *m* tennis player
Teppich (*pl* **Teppiche**) *m* carpet
Teppichboden (*pl* **Teppichböden**) *m* wall-to-wall carpet
Termin (*pl* **Termine**) *m* ❶ date ▷ *Habt ihr schon einen Termin ausgemacht?* Have you already arranged a date? ❷ deadline ▷ *Ich muss den Aufsatz bis zu dem Termin fertig haben.* I must have the essay finished by that deadline. ❸ appointment ▷ *Ich habe einen Termin beim Zahnarzt.* I've got an appointment with the dentist.
Terminkalender (*pl* **Terminkalender**) *m* appointments diary
Terrasse *f* terrace
Terror *m* terror
Terrorismus (*gen* **Terrorismus**) *m* terrorism

Terrorist (*gen* **Terroristen**, *pl* **Terroristen**) *m* terrorist
Tesafilm® *m* Sellotape®
Test (*pl* **Tests**) *m* test
Testament (*pl* **Testamente**) *nt* will ▷ *sein Testament machen* to make one's will
testen *vb* [**2**] to test
teuer *adj* expensive
Teufel (*pl* **Teufel**) *m* devil
Text (*pl* **Texte**) *m* ❶ text ▷ *Lest den Text auf Seite zehn.* Read the text on page ten. ❷ lyrics *pl* ▷ *Kannst du mir den Text von dem Song übersetzen?* Can you translate the lyrics of the song for me?
Textilien *fpl* textiles *pl*
Textverarbeitung *f* word processing
Theater (*pl* **Theater**) *nt* ❶ theatre ▷ *Wir gehen ins Theater.* We're going to the theatre.; **Theater spielen** to act ❷ *(informal)* fuss ▷ *Mach nicht so ein Theater!* Don't make such a fuss.
Theaterstück (*pl* **Theaterstücke**) *nt* play
Theke *f* ❶ bar ▷ *Er stand an der Theke und trank ein Bier.* He stood at the bar drinking a beer. ❷ counter ▷ *Das bekommen Sie an der Käsetheke.* You'll get that at the cheese counter.
Thema (*pl* **Themen**) *nt* subject
theoretisch *adj* theoretical ▷ *Rein theoretisch betrachtet ist das richtig.* From a purely theoretical point of view, that's correct.
Theorie *f* theory
Therapie *f* therapy
Thermometer (*pl* **Thermometer**) *nt* thermometer
Thermosflasche *f* Thermos®
These *f* thesis
Thron (*pl* **Throne**) *m* throne
Thunfisch (*pl* **Thunfische**) *m* tuna
Thüringen *nt* Thuringia

Thüringen is one of the 16 **Länder**. Its capital is Erfurt. With its extensive forests, it is sometimes called 'Germany's green heartland'. It is not only rural, however: the Zeiss precision engineering company is based in Jena.

ticken *vb* [**48**] to tick ▷ *Die Uhr tickte.* The clock was ticking.; **Du tickst ja nicht richtig!** *(informal)* You're off your rocker!

Word for word, **Du tickst ja nicht richtig** means 'You're not ticking right'.

tief *adj* ❶ deep ▷ *Wie tief ist das Wasser?* How deep's the water? ❷ *(neckline, price, note)* low ▷ *ein tief ausgeschnittenes Kleid* a low-cut dress
Tief (*pl* **Tiefs**) *nt* depression ▷ *ein Tief über Norddeutschland* a depression over North Germany
Tiefdruck *m* low pressure
Tiefe *f* depth
tiefgekühlt *adj* frozen
Tiefkühltruhe *f* freezer
Tier (*pl* **Tiere**) *nt* animal
Tierarzt (*gen* **Tierarztes**, *pl* **Tierärzte**) *m* vet
Tiergarten (*pl* **Tiergärten**) *m* zoo
tierisch *adj* ❶ animal ▷ *tierische Fette* animal fats ❷ terrible ▷ *Du hast dich tierisch benommen.* You behaved terribly.
Tierkreis (*gen* **Tierkreises**) *m* zodiac

Word for word, **Tierkreis** means 'animal circle'.

Tierquälerei *f* cruelty to animals
Tiger (*pl* **Tiger**) *m* tiger
Tinte *f* ink
Tintenfisch (*pl* **Tintenfische**) *m* squid
Tipp (*pl* **Tipps**) *m* tip
tippen *vb* [**38**] ❶ to tap ▷ *Sie tippte leicht an die Statue.* She lightly tapped the statue. ❷ to type ▷ *Tippst du dein Referat?* Are you typing your assignment?; **im Lotto tippen** to play the lottery; **Auf wen tippst du bei den Wahlen?** Who're you tipping to win the elections?
Tippfehler (*pl* **Tippfehler**) *m* typing error

Tirol *nt* Tyrol
Tisch (*pl* **Tische**) *m* table ▷ *bei Tisch* at table
Tischdecke *f* tablecloth
Tischtennis *nt* table tennis
Tischtuch (*pl* **Tischtücher**) *nt* tablecloth
Titel (*pl* **Titel**) *m* title
Toast (*pl* **Toasts**) *m* toast
Toastbrot (*pl* **Toastbrote**) *nt* bread for toasting
Toaster (*pl* **Toaster**) *m* toaster
toben *vb* [**38**] ❶ to rage ▷ *Der Sturm tobte die ganze Nacht.* The storm raged all night long. ❷ to go mad ▷ *Wenn er das erfährt, wird er toben.* If he finds out he'll go mad. ❸ to romp about ▷ *Die Kinder toben im Garten.* The children are romping about in the garden.
Tochter (*pl* **Töchter**) *f* daughter
Tod (*pl* **Tode**) *m* death
todernst *adj, adv* ❶ grave ▷ *ein todernstes Gesicht* a grave face ❷ in deadly earnest ▷ *Er hat das todernst gesagt.* He said it in deadly earnest.
Todesstrafe *f* death penalty
todkrank *adj* critically ill
tödlich *adj* deadly ▷ *eine tödliche Waffe* a deadly weapon; **ein tödlicher Unfall** a fatal accident
todmüde *adj* exhausted
Toilette *f* toilet
Toilettenpapier *nt* toilet paper
tolerant *adj* tolerant
toll *adj (informal)* terrific
Tollwut *f* rabies *sg*
Tomate *f* tomato
Ton (*pl* **Töne**) *m* ❶ sound ▷ *Es war kein Ton zu hören.* Not a sound could be heard. ❷ note ▷ *Mit welchen Ton fängt das Lied an?* What note does the song start on? ❸ tone of voice ▷ *Sein Ton gefiel mir nicht.* I didn't like his tone of voice. ❹ shade ▷ *Pastelltöne sind in.* Pastel shades are in. ❺ stress ▷ *Bei Substantiven liegt der Ton meist auf der ersten Silbe.* Nouns are usually stressed on the first syllable.
Tonne *f* ton ▷ *Es wiegt drei Tonnen.* It weighs three tons.
Topf (*pl* **Töpfe**) *m* pot
toppen *vb* to do better than ▷ **einen Rekord toppen** to break a record
Tor (*pl* **Tore**) *nt* ❶ gate ▷ *Das Tor war offen.* The gate was open. ❷ goal ▷ *Wer hat das zweite Tor geschossen?* Who scored the second goal?
Torf *m* peat
Torte *f* ❶ gateau ❷ flan
Torwart (*pl* **Torwarte**) *m* goalkeeper
tot *adj* dead; **Er war sofort tot.** He was killed instantly.
total *adj, adv* ❶ complete ▷ *Das ist doch der totale Wahnsinn.* But that's complete madness. ❷ completely ▷ *Das ist total verrückt.* That's completely mad.
totalitär *adj* totalitarian
Tote (*gen* **Toten**, *pl* **Toten**) *mf* dead body ▷ *Auf der Straße lag ein Toter.* There was a dead body lying in the road.; **die Toten begraben** to bury the dead
töten *vb* [**2**] to kill
Tour (*pl* **Touren**) *f* trip ▷ *auf Tour gehen* to go on a trip; **auf vollen Touren** at full speed
Tourismus (*gen* **Tourismus**) *m* tourism
Tourist (*gen* **Touristen**, *pl* **Touristen**) *m* tourist
Tournee *f* tour ▷ *Bon Jovi auf Tournee* Bon Jovi on tour ▷ *auf Tournee gehen* to go on tour
Tracht *f* traditional costume ▷ *Im Schwarzwald tragen die Frauen noch Tracht.* Women still wear traditional costume in the Black Forest.; **eine Tracht Prügel** a sound beating
Tradition *f* tradition
traditionell *adj* traditional
traf *vb see* **treffen**
tragbar *adj* portable ▷ *ein tragbarer Fernseher* a portable TV
träge *adj* sluggish
tragen (*pres* **trägt**, *imperf* **trug**, *perf* **hat getragen**) *vb* [**77**] ❶ to carry ▷ *Kannst du meinen Koffer tragen?* Can you carry my case? ❷ to bear ▷ *die Verantwortung tragen* to bear responsibility ❸ *(clothes,*

glasses) to wear ▷ *Sie trug ein weißes Kleid und eine Sonnenbrille.* She was wearing a white dress and sunglasses.

Tragetasche *f* carrier bag

tragisch *adj* tragic

Tragödie *f* tragedy

Trainer (*pl* **Trainer**) *m* coach

trainieren (*perf* **hat trainiert**) *vb* **[76]** ❶ to train ▷ *Sie trainiert täglich für den Wettkampf.* She trains for the competition every day. ❷ to coach ▷ *Wer trainiert diese Tennisspielerin?* Who coaches this tennis player? ❸ to practise ▷ *Diese Übung muss ich noch mehr trainieren.* I need to practise this exercise more.

Training (*pl* **Trainings**) *nt* training

Trainingsanzug (*pl* **Trainingsanzüge**) *m* track suit

trampen *vb* **[38]** to hitchhike

Tramper (*pl* **Tramper**) *m* hitchhiker

Tramperin *f* hitchhiker

Träne *f* tear ▷ *in Tränen ausbrechen* to burst into tears

trank *vb see* **trinken**

Transport (*pl* **Transporte**) *m* transport

transportieren (*perf* **hat transportiert**) *vb* **[76]** to transport

Transportmittel (*pl* **Transportmittel**) *nt* means of transport *sg*

Traube *f* grape

trauen *vb* **[38] jemandem trauen** to trust somebody; **sich trauen** to dare

Traum (*pl* **Träume**) *m* dream

träumen *vb* **[38]** to dream ▷ *Ich habe von dir geträumt.* I dreamt about you.

traumhaft *adj* wonderful ▷ *Es waren traumhafte Ferien.* It was a wonderful holiday.

traurig *adj* sad

Traurigkeit *f* sadness

treffen (*pres* **trifft**, *imperf* **traf**, *perf* **hat getroffen**) *vb* **[78]** ❶ to hit ▷ *Er hat die Zielscheibe getroffen.* He hit the target. ▷ *Sie wurde am Kopf getroffen.* She was hit on the head.; **Du hast nicht getroffen.** You missed. ❷ to meet ▷ *Ich habe ihn gestern im Supermarkt getroffen.* I met him yesterday in the supermarket. ▷ *Wir sind in London auf ihn getroffen.* We met him in London.; **sich treffen** to meet ❸ to affect ▷ *Die Bemerkung hat sie sehr getroffen.* The remark affected her deeply.; **eine Entscheidung treffen** to make a decision; **Maßnahmen treffen** to take steps; **Es traf sich, dass ...** It so happened that ...; **Das trifft sich gut!** How very convenient!

Treffen (*pl* **Treffen**) *nt* meeting

Treffer (*pl* **Treffer**) *m* ❶ hit ▷ *Das Schiff musste einen Volltreffer hinnehmen.* The ship took a direct hit. ❷ goal ▷ *Klinsmann hat einen Treffer erzielt.* Klinsmann scored a goal. ▷ *Ich hatte vier Treffer im Lotto.* I got four numbers in the lottery.

Treffpunkt (*pl* **Treffpunkte**) *m* meeting place

treiben (*imperf* **trieb**, *perf* **hat/ist getrieben**) *vb*

> Use **haben** to form the perfect tense. Use **sein** to form the perfect tense for 'to drift'.

❶ to drive ▷ *Sie trieben die Kühe auf das Feld.* They drove the cows into the field.; **Sport treiben** to do sport; **Unsinn treiben** to fool around; **jemanden zu etwas treiben** to drive somebody to something; **Sie hat uns zur Eile getrieben.** She made us hurry up. ❷ to drift ▷ *Das Schiff ist aufs Meer getrieben.* The ship drifted out to sea.

Treibhaus (*gen* **Treibhauses**, *pl* **Treibhäuser**) *nt* greenhouse

Treibhauseffekt *m* greenhouse effect

Treibstoff (*pl* **Treibstoffe**) *m* fuel

trennen *vb* **[38]** ❶ to separate ▷ *Er hat die beiden Raufbolde getrennt.* He separated the two ruffians. ❷ to make a distinction between ▷ *Diese beiden Begriffe muss man sauber trennen.* You have to make a clear distinction between these two concepts. ❸ to

hyphenate ▷ *Wie wird dieses Wort getrennt?* Where do you hyphenate this word?; **sich trennen** to separate; **Du solltest dich von ihm trennen.** You ought to leave him.; **sich von etwas trennen** to part with something
Trennung *f* separation
Treppe *f* stairs *pl*
Treppenhaus (*gen* **Treppenhauses**, *pl* **Treppenhäuser**) *nt* staircase
treten (*pres* **tritt**, *imperf* **trat**, *perf* **hat/ist getreten**) *vb* [**79**]

> For the perfect tense use **haben** when the verb has an object and **sein** when there is no object.

❶ to step ▷ *Sie ist in die Pfütze getreten.* She stepped in the puddle. ▷ *Er trat auf die Bremse.* He stepped on the brakes. ▷ *Er trat ans Mikrofon.* He stepped up to the microphone.; **mit jemandem in Verbindung treten** to get in touch with somebody; **in Erscheinung treten** to appear ❷ to kick ▷ *Sie hat mich getreten.* She kicked me. ▷ *Sie trat nach dem Hund.* She kicked the dog. ❸ to tread ▷ *Er ist mir auf den Fuß getreten.* He trod on my foot.
treu *adj* faithful ▷ *Bist du mir auch treu gewesen?* Have you been faithful to me?
Treue *f* faithfulness
Tribüne *f* ❶ grandstand ▷ *Die Fans auf der Tribüne pfiffen.* The fans on the grandstand whistled. ❷ platform ▷ *Der Redner stand auf einer Tribüne.* The speaker stood on a platform.
Trichter (*pl* **Trichter**) *m* ❶ funnel ▷ *Sie hat das Öl mit einem Trichter in die Flasche gefüllt.* She used a funnel to fill the bottle with oil. ❷ crater ▷ *Das Gelände war von Bombentrichtern übersät.* The area was pitted with bomb craters.
Trick (*pl* **Tricks**) *m* trick ▷ *Das war ein fauler Trick.* That was a dirty trick.
Trickfilm (*pl* **Trickfilme**) *m* cartoon
trieb *vb see* **treiben**
trifft *vb see* **treffen**
Trimester (*pl* **Trimester**) *nt* term *(university)*
trinkbar *adj* drinkable
trinken (*imperf* **trank**, *perf* **hat getrunken**) *vb* [**80**] to drink; **Ich habe zu viel getrunken.** I've had too much to drink.
Trinkgeld (*pl* **Trinkgelder**) *nt* tip ▷ *Er gab dem Taxifahrer ein großzügiges Trinkgeld.* He gave the taxi driver a generous tip.
Trinkwasser (*pl* **Trinkwässer**) *nt* drinking water
trocken *adj* dry
trocknen *vb* [**53**] to dry
Trödel *m (informal)* junk
Trödelmarkt (*pl* **Trödelmärkte**) *m* flea market
trödeln *vb* [**88**] to dawdle
Trommel *f* drum ▷ *Er spielt Trommel.* He plays the drums.
Trommelfell (*pl* **Trommelfelle**) *nt* eardrum
trommeln *vb* [**34**] to drum
Trompete *f* trumpet ▷ *Sie spielt Trompete.* She plays the trumpet.
Tropen *pl* tropics *pl*
Tropfen (*pl* **Tropfen**) *m* drop
tropisch *adj* tropical
Trost *m* consolation
trösten *vb* [**2**] to console
trostlos *adj* bleak ▷ *eine trostlose Landschaft* a bleak landscape
Trostpreis (*gen* **Trostpreises**, *pl* **Trostpreise**) *m* consolation prize
Trottel (*pl* **Trottel**) *m (informal)* prat
trotz *prep*

> The preposition **trotz** takes the dative or genitive.

in spite of
Trotz (*gen* **Trotzes**) *m* defiance ▷ *ihm zum Trotz* in defiance of him; **etwas aus Trotz tun** to do something defiantly
trotzdem *adv* all the same ▷ *Ich gehe trotzdem.* I'm going all the same.
trotzig *adj* defiant

trüb *adj* ❶ dull ▷ *Es war ein trüber Tag.* It was a dull day. ❷ cloudy ▷ *Das Wasser war trüb.* The water was cloudy. ❸ gloomy ▷ *Die Zukunftsaussichten sind ziemlich trüb.* Prospects for the future are pretty gloomy.

Trubel *m* hurly-burly

trübsinnig *adj* gloomy

trug *vb see* **tragen**

trügen (*imperf* **trog**, *perf* **hat getrogen**) *vb* to be deceptive ▷ *Der Schein trügt.* Appearances are deceptive.

Trümmer *pl* ❶ wreckage *sg* ▷ *die Trümmer des Flugzeugs* the wreckage of the aeroplane ❷ ruins *pl* ▷ *Nach dem Bombenangriff war die Stadt voller Trümmer.* After the air raid the town was in ruins.

Trumpf (*pl* **Trümpfe**) *m* trump ▷ *Herz ist Trumpf.* Hearts is trumps.

Trunkenheit *f* drunkenness; **Trunkenheit am Steuer** drink-driving

> Word for word, **Trunkenheit am Steuer** means 'drunkenness at the steering wheel'.

Truppen *fpl* troops *pl*

Truthahn (*pl* **Truthähne**) *m* turkey

Tscheche (*gen* **Tschechen**, *pl* **Tschechen**) *m* Czech

Tschechin *f* Czech

tschechisch *adj* Czech

tschüs *excl* cheerio!

T-Shirt (*pl* **T-Shirts**) *nt* T-shirt

Tube *f* tube ▷ *eine Tube Zahnpasta* a tube of toothpaste

Tuch (*pl* **Tücher**) *nt* ❶ cloth ▷ *Mit welchem Tuch soll ich abstauben?* Which cloth should I use for dusting? ❷ towel ▷ *Nimm dir ein großes Tuch ins Schwimmbad mit.* Take a large towel with you to the swimming baths. ❸ scarf ▷ *Sie hatte ein seidenes Tuch um den Hals.* She wore a silk scarf around her neck.

tüchtig *adj* competent ▷ *Er ist ein sehr tüchtiger Mensch.* He's a very competent person.; **Er nahm einen tüchtigen Schluck aus der Flasche.** (*informal*) He took a hefty swig from the bottle.

Tulpe *f* tulip

tun (*imperf* **tat**, *perf* **hat getan**) *vb* **[81]** ❶ to do ▷ *Was sollen wir jetzt tun?* What shall we do now? ▷ *Er hat den ganzen Tag nichts getan.* He hasn't done anything all day. ▷ *Was kann ich für Sie tun?* What can I do for you? ❷ to put ▷ *Sie tat die Teller in den Schrank.* She put the plates in the cupboard. ❸ to act ▷ *Tu nicht so unschuldig!* Don't act so innocent. ❹ to pretend ▷ *Sie tat, als ob sie schliefe.* She pretended to be sleeping. ▷ *Er ist nicht krank, er tut nur so.* He isn't ill, he's only pretending.; **Der Hund tut dir bestimmt nichts.** The dog won't hurt you.; **Hoffentlich hast du dir bei dem Sturz nichts getan.** I hope you didn't hurt yourself when you fell.; **Es tut sich viel.** A lot's happening.; **mit etwas zu tun haben** to have something to do with something; **Das tut nichts zur Sache.** That's neither here nor there.

Tunfisch (*pl* **Tunfische**) *m* tuna

Tunnel (*pl* **Tunnel**) *m* tunnel

Tür *f* door

Türke (*gen* **Türken**, *pl* **Türken**) *m* Turk

Türkei *f* Turkey

Türkin *f* Turk

türkis *adj* turquoise

türkisch *adj* Turkish

Turm (*pl* **Türme**) *m* ❶ tower ▷ *die Türme der Burg* the castle towers ❷ steeple ▷ *Das Ulmer Münster hat den höchsten Kirchturm der Welt.* Ulm Cathedral has the world's highest steeple. ❸ rook ▷ *Er machte einen Zug mit dem Turm.* He moved his rook.

turnen *vb* **[38]** ❶ to do gymnastics ▷ *Sie turnt nicht gern.* She doesn't like doing gymnastics. ❷ to perform ▷ *Sie hat die Kür hervorragend geturnt.* She performed the free programme brilliantly.

Turnen *nt* ❶ gymnastics *sg* ▷ *Die Russinnen sind im Turnen gut.* The

Russian women are good at gymnastics. ❷ physical education ▷ *Wir haben in der vierten Stunde Turnen.* We have PE in the fourth period.

Turnhalle *f* gym

Turnhose *f* gym shorts *pl* ▷ *eine Turnhose* a pair of gym shorts

Turnier (*pl* **Turniere**) *nt* tournament

Turnschuh (*pl* **Turnschuhe**) *m* trainer ▷ *ein Paar Turnschuhe* a pair of trainers

Turnzeug *nt* gym things *pl* ▷ *Wo ist mein Turnzeug?* Where are my gym things?

Tüte *f* bag

Typ (*pl* **Typen**) *m* ❶ type ▷ *Er ist ein athletischer Typ.* He's an athletic type. ❷ *(informal)* bloke ▷ *der Typ da drüben* the bloke over there

typisch *adj* typical ▷ *typisch für* typical of

U

U-Bahn *f* underground ▷ *mit der U-Bahn fahren* to travel by underground

U-Bahn-Station *f* underground station

übel *adj* bad ▷ *ein übler Geruch* a bad smell ▷ *eine üble Lage* a bad situation ▷ *Nicht übel!* Not bad.; **jemandem ist übel** somebody feels sick; **Sie hat dir die Bemerkung übel genommen.** She was offended by your remark.

Übelkeit *f* nausea

übelnehmen *vb* [**52**] *see* **übel**

üben *vb* [**38**] to practise

über *prep, adv*

> Use the accusative to express movement or a change of place. Use the dative when there is no change of place.

❶ over ▷ *Über dem Tisch hängt eine Lampe.* There's a lamp hanging over the table. ▷ *Sie legten ein Brett über das Loch.* They put a board over the hole. ▷ *Flugzeuge dürfen nicht über dieses Gebiet fliegen.* Planes are not allowed to fly over this area. ▷ *Über Weihnachten bin ich zu Hause.* I'm at home over Christmas. ▷ *Kinder über zwölf Jahren* children over twelve years of age ▷ *Das hat über hundert Euro gekostet.* It cost over a hundred euros. ❷ above ▷ *Das Flugzeug flog hoch über der Stadt.* The plane flew high above the town.; **den ganzen Tag über** all day long; **zwei Grad über null** two degrees above zero; **ein Scheck über zweihundert Euro** a cheque for two hundred euros ❸ across ▷ *Er ging quer über das Feld.* He went across the field. ❹ via ▷ *nach Köln über Aachen* to Cologne via Aachen ▷ *über Satellit* via satellite ❺ about ▷ *Wir haben über das Wetter geredet.* We talked about the weather. ▷ *ein Buch über ...* a book about ... ❻ through ▷ *Ich habe den Job über einen Freund bekommen.* I got the job through a friend.; **über jemanden lachen** to laugh at somebody; **Sie liebt ihn über alles.** She loves him more than anything.; **über und über** over and over; **über kurz oder lang** sooner or later; **etwas über haben** *(informal)* to be fed up with something

überall *adv* everywhere

überbieten (*imperf* **überbot**, *perf* **hat überboten**) *vb* [**8**] to outbid ▷ *Er bot zweitausend Euro, aber wir haben ihn überboten.* He bid two thousand euros but we outbid him.; **einen Rekord überbieten** to break a record; **sich überbieten** to excel oneself

Überblick (*pl* **Überblicke**) *m* ❶ view ▷ *Von hier aus hat man einen guten Überblick über das Gelände.* You can get a good view of the area from here. ❷ overview ▷ *ein Überblick über die unregelmäßigen Verben* an overview of irregular verbs ❸ overall impression ▷ *Ich muss mir erst mal einen Überblick verschaffen.* I have to get an overall impression first.; **den Überblick verlieren** to lose track of things; **Sie hat den Überblick über ihre Arbeit verloren.** She has no idea where she is with her work.

überdenken (*imperf* **überdachte**, *perf* **hat überdacht**) *vb* [**14**] to think over

übereinander *adv* one on top of the other ▷ *Sie legte die Bücher übereinander.* She put one book on top of the other.; **übereinander sprechen** to talk about each other

überfahren (*pres* **überfährt**, *imperf* **überfuhr**, *perf* **hat überfahren**) *vb* [**21**] to run over ▷ *Die Katze wurde von einem Auto überfahren.* The cat was run over by a car.

Überfahrt *f* crossing

Überfall (*pl* **Überfälle**) *m* ❶ raid ▷ *ein Banküberfall* a bank raid ▷ *ein Überfall auf ein fremdes Land* a raid on a foreign country ❷ assault ▷ *Er wurde das Opfer eines Überfalls.* He was the victim of an assault.

überfallen (*pres* **überfällt**, *imperf* **überfiel**, *perf* **hat überfallen**) *vb* [**22**] ❶ to attack ▷ *Sie ist im Park überfallen worden.* She was attacked in the park.; **eine Bank überfallen** to raid a bank ❷ to descend on ▷ *Am Wochenende hat mich meine Freundin mit ihren Eltern überfallen.* My girlfriend and her parents descended on me at the weekend.

überfällig *adj* overdue

überflüssig *adj* superfluous

überfordern (*perf* **hat überfordert**) *vb* [**88**] to ask too much of ▷ *Unser Mathelehrer überfordert uns.* Our maths teacher asks too much of us.

überfüllt *adj* ❶ overcrowded ▷ *Die Gefängnisse sind völlig überfüllt.* The prisons are completely overcrowded. ❷ oversubscribed ▷ *Der Computerkurs ist überfüllt.* The computer course is oversubscribed.

Übergang (*pl* **Übergänge**) *m* ❶ crossing ▷ *ein Fußgängerübergang* a pedestrian crossing ❷ transition ▷ *der Übergang vom Sommer zum Herbst* the transition from summer to autumn

übergeben (*pres* **übergibt**, *imperf* **übergab**, *perf* **hat übergeben**) *vb* [**28**] to hand over ▷ *Sie hat uns die Schlüssel übergeben.* She handed the keys over to us.; **sich übergeben** to be sick

überhaupt *adv* ❶ at all ▷ *Kannst du überhaupt Auto fahren?* Can you drive a car at all? ▷ *Hast du überhaupt zugehört?* Have you been listening at all? ▷ *Ich habe überhaupt keine Lust.* I don't feel like it at all. ❷ in general ▷ *Die Engländer sind überhaupt sehr höflich.* In general the English are very polite.; **überhaupt nicht** not at all; **überhaupt nichts** nothing at all

überheblich *adj* arrogant

überholen (*perf* **hat überholt**) *vb* [**18**] ❶ to overtake ▷ *Er hat rechts überholt.* He overtook on the right. ❷ to check over ▷ *Ich muss mein Fahrrad überholen.* I have to check my bike over.

überholt *adj* out-of-date

Überholverbot (*pl* **Überholverbote**) *nt* restriction on overtaking

überlassen (*pres* **überlässt**, *imperf* **überließ**, *perf* **hat überlassen**) *vb* [**42**] **jemandem etwas überlassen** to leave something up to somebody

überlasten (*perf* **hat überlastet**) *vb* [**2**] to overload ▷ *Der Aufzug war überlastet.* The lift was overloaded.; **Ich fühle mich überlastet.** I feel overworked.

überleben (*perf* **hat überlebt**) *vb* [**18**] to survive

überlegen (*perf* **hat überlegt**) *vb* [**82**] to think about ▷ *Ich muss mir deinen Vorschlag überlegen.* I'll have to think about your suggestion. ▷ *Überleg doch mal.* Think about it.
▸ *adj* ❶ better ▷ *Er ist ihr in Englisch überlegen.* He's better at English than she is. ❷ convincingly ▷ *Unsere Mannschaft hat überlegen gewonnen.* Our team won convincingly.

überlisten (*perf* **hat überlistet**) *vb* [**2**] to outwit

überm = **über dem**

übermäßig *adj* excessive

übermorgen *adv* the day after tomorrow

übernächste *adj* next but one ▷ *An der übernächsten Haltestelle muss ich aussteigen.* I need to get off at the next stop but one.

übernachten (*perf* **hat übernachtet**) *vb* [**2**] **bei jemandem übernachten** to spend the night at somebody's house

Übernachtung *f* overnight stay; **Übernachtung mit Frühstück** bed and breakfast

übernehmen (*pres* **übernimmt**, *imperf* **übernahm**, *perf* **hat übernommen**) *vb* [**52**] to take over ▷ *Er hat das Geschäft seines Vaters übernommen.* He's taken over his father's business. ▷ *Er hat das Amt des Klassensprechers übernommen.* He took over as class representative.; **sich übernehmen** to take on too much

überprüfen (*perf* **hat überprüft**) *vb* [**18**] to check

überqueren (*perf* **hat überquert**) *vb* [**7**] to cross

überraschen (*perf* **hat überrascht**) *vb* [**18**] to surprise

überrascht *adj* surprised

Überraschung *f* surprise

überreden (*perf* **hat überredet**) *vb* [**54**] to persuade ▷ *Kannst du sie nicht überreden mitzukommen?* Can't you persuade her to come?

übers = **über das**

überschätzen (*perf* **hat überschätzt**) *vb* [**36**] to overestimate

überschlagen (*pres* **überschlägt**, *imperf* **überschlug**, *perf* **hat überschlagen**) *vb* [**59**] to estimate ▷ *Wir sollten die Kosten für das Fest überschlagen.* We should estimate how much the party will cost.; **eine Seite überschlagen** to miss a page; **Das Auto hat sich überschlagen.** The car rolled over.

Überschrift *f* heading

a b c d e f g h i j k l m n o p q r s t **u** v w x y z

Überschuss (*gen* **Überschusses**, *pl* **Überschüsse**) *m* surplus ▷ *ein Überschuss an* a surplus of

Überschwemmung *f* flood

übersehen (*pres* **übersieht**, *imperf* **übersah**, *perf* **hat übersehen**) *vb* [**64**] ❶ to overlook ▷ *Sie hat ein paar Fehler übersehen.* She overlooked a couple of mistakes. ❷ to see ▷ *Wir können die Folgen noch nicht übersehen.* We can't see the consequences yet.

übersetzen (*perf* **hat übersetzt**) *vb* [**36**] to translate ▷ *Übersetzt den Text ins Englische.* Translate the text into English.

Übersetzer (*pl* **Übersetzer**) *m* translator

Übersetzerin *f* translator

Übersetzung *f* translation ▷ *Das war eine schwierige Übersetzung.* That was a difficult translation.

Übersicht *f* ❶ view ▷ *Von hier aus hat man eine gute Übersicht.* You get a good view from here. ❷ overview ▷ *eine Übersicht über die unregelmäßigen Verben* an overview of irregular verbs

übersichtlich *adj* clear ▷ *Die Tabelle ist nicht besonders übersichtlich.* The table isn't particularly clear. ▷ *etwas übersichtlich gestalten* to arrange something clearly; **ein übersichtliches Gelände** open country

überspringen (*imperf* **übersprang**, *perf* **hat übersprungen**) *vb* [**71**] ❶ to jump over ▷ *Er hat die Hürde übersprungen.* He jumped over the hurdle. ❷ to skip ▷ *Das nächste Kapitel können wir überspringen.* We can skip the next chapter.

überstehen (*imperf* **überstand**, *perf* **hat überstanden**) *vb* [**72**] ❶ to get over ▷ *Wir haben das Schlimmste überstanden.* We've got over the worst. ❷ to survive ▷ *Die Pflanze hat den Winter nicht überstanden.* The plant didn't survive the winter.

übersteigen (*imperf* **überstieg**, *perf* **hat überstiegen**) *vb* [**74**] to exceed ▷ *Das übersteigt unsere Erwartungen.* That exceeds our expectations.

überstimmen (*perf* **hat überstimmt**) *vb* [**7**] to outvote

Überstunden *fpl* overtime *sg* ▷ *Er macht viele Überstunden.* He does a lot of overtime.

überstürzen (*perf* **hat überstürzt**) *vb* [**36**] to rush ▷ *Du solltest nichts überstürzen.* You shouldn't rush into things.; **sich überstürzen** to follow one another in rapid succession

überstürzt *adj* ❶ rash ▷ *eine überstürzte Entscheidung* a rash decision ❷ in a rush ▷ *Sie sind überstürzt abgereist.* They left in a rush.

übertragen (*pres* **überträgt**, *imperf* **übertrug**, *perf* **hat übertragen**) *vb* [**77**] ❶ to broadcast ▷ *Wir übertragen das Spiel live.* We're broadcasting the game live. ❷ to copy ▷ *Sie hat den Text in ihr Heft übertragen.* She copied the text into her exercise book. ❸ to transmit ▷ *eine Krankheit übertragen* to transmit an illness; **Sie hat mir diese Aufgabe übertragen.** She has assigned this task to me.; **sich übertragen auf** to spread to
▸ *adj* figurative ▷ *die übertragene Bedeutung eines Wortes* the figurative meaning of a word

übertreffen (*pres* **übertrifft**, *imperf* **übertraf**, *perf* **hat übertroffen**) *vb* [**78**] to surpass

übertreiben (*imperf* **übertrieb**, *perf* **hat übertrieben**) *vb* to exaggerate

Übertreibung *f* exaggeration

übertrieben *adj* excessive

überwachen (*perf* **hat überwacht**) *vb* [**18**] ❶ to supervise ▷ *Wer soll die Kinder überwachen?* Who will supervise the children? ❷ to keep under surveillance ▷ *Die Polizei überwacht ihn.* The police are keeping him under surveillance.

überweisen (*imperf* **überwies**, *perf* **hat überwiesen**) *vb* to transfer

überwinden (*imperf* **überwand**, *perf* **hat überwunden**) *vb* to overcome ▷ *Jetzt haben wir alle Schwierigkeiten überwunden.* Now we've overcome all difficulties.; **sich überwinden** to force oneself

überzeugen (*perf* **hat überzeugt**) *vb* [**18**] to convince

überzeugend *adj* convincing

Überzeugung *f* conviction ▷ *Er sagte es ohne große Überzeugung.* He said it without much conviction.

üblich *adj* usual

U-Boot (*pl* **U-Boote**) *nt* submarine

übrig *adj* remaining ▷ *Die übrigen Gäste sind auch bald gegangen.* The remaining guests left soon afterwards.; **Ist noch Kuchen übrig?** Is there any cake left?; **die übrigen** the others; **das Übrige** the rest; **im Übrigen** besides; **übrig bleiben** to be left; **übrig lassen** to leave

übrigens *adv* by the way ▷ *Übrigens, du schuldest mir noch zehn Euro.* By the way, you still owe me ten euros.

übrighaben (*pres* **hat übrig**, *imperf* **hatte übrig**, *perf* **hat übriggehabt**) *vb* [**32**] **für jemanden etwas übrighaben** to be fond of somebody

übriglassen *vb* [**42**] *see* **übrig**

Übung *f* ❶ practice ▷ *Mir fehlt die Übung.* I need more practice. ▷ *Übung macht den Meister.* Practice makes perfect. ❷ exercise ▷ *Bitte macht jetzt Übung dreizehn.* Please do exercise thirteen now. ▷ *eine Turnübung* a gym exercise

Ufer (*pl* **Ufer**) *nt* ❶ bank ▷ *Wir saßen am Ufer des Rheins.* We sat on the bank of the Rhine. ❷ shore ▷ *Treibholz, das ans Ufer gespült wurde* driftwood which was washed up onto the shore

Uhr *f* ❶ clock ▷ *Die Uhr am Bahnhof sollte richtig gehen.* The station clock should be right. ❷ watch ▷ *Er sah auf seine Uhr.* He looked at his watch.; **Wie viel Uhr ist es?** What time is it?; **ein Uhr** one o'clock; **zwanzig Uhr** eight o'clock in the evening; **um fünf Uhr** at five o'clock

Uhrzeigersinn *m* **im Uhrzeigersinn** clockwise; **entgegen dem Uhrzeigersinn** anticlockwise

Uhrzeit *f* time

Ultraschall *m* ultrasound

um *prep, conj, adv*

> The preposition **um** takes the accusative.

❶ round ▷ *Sie legte sich einen Schal um den Hals.* She wrapped a scarf round her neck. ▷ *Wir sind um die Stadt herumgefahren.* We drove round the town.; **um Weihnachten** around Christmas ❷ at ▷ *um acht Uhr* at eight o'clock ❸ by ▷ *etwas um vier Zentimeter kürzen* to shorten something by four centimetres; **um zehn Prozent teurer** ten per cent more expensive; **um vieles besser** better by far ❹ for ▷ *der Kampf um den Titel* the battle for the title ▷ *um Geld spielen* to play for money; **um ... willen** for the sake of ...

> **um ... willen** takes the genitive.

▷ *um meiner Mutter willen* for my mother's sake; **um ... zu** in order to ...

> **um ... zu** is used with the infinitive.

▷ *Ich gehe in die Schule, um etwas zu lernen.* I go to school in order to learn something.; **zu klug, um zu ...** too clever to ... ❺ about ▷ *um die dreißig Leute* about thirty people; **Die zwei Stunden sind um.** The two hours are up.

umarmen (*perf* **hat umarmt**) *vb* [**7**] to hug ▷ *Sie umarmten sich.* They hugged.

umbringen (*imperf* **brachte um**, *perf* **hat umgebracht**) *vb* [**13**] to kill

umdrehen (*perf* **hat umgedreht**) *vb* [**4**] to turn round ▷ *Dreh das Bild mal um.* Turn the picture round.; **sich umdrehen** to turn round

umfallen (*pres* **fällt um**, *imperf* **fiel um**, *perf* **ist umgefallen**) *vb* [**22**] to fall down

Umfang *m* ❶ extent ▷ *Der Umfang der Arbeiten war am Anfang nicht absehbar.* The extent of the work couldn't be seen at the beginning. ❷ circumference ▷ *Berechnet den Umfang des Kreises.* Calculate the circumference of the circle.

Umfrage *f* poll

Umgang *m* **erfahren im Umgang mit Kindern** experienced in dealing with children; **der Umgang mit dem Computer** working with computers

Umgangssprache *f* colloquial language

umgeben (*pres* **umgibt**, *imperf* **umgab**, *perf* **hat umgeben**) *vb* **[28]** to surround

Umgebung *f* ❶ surroundings *pl* ▷ *ein Haus in schöner Umgebung* a house in beautiful surroundings ❷ environment ▷ *Diese Pflanze wächst am besten in sonniger Umgebung.* This plant grows best in a sunny environment.

umgehen (1) (*imperf* **ging um**, *perf* **ist umgegangen**) *vb* **[29]**

Note that here the stress is on **um**.

mit jemandem grob umgehen to treat somebody roughly; **mit Geld sparsam umgehen** to be careful with one's money; **Sie kann nicht gut mit Geld umgehen.** She's not very good with money.

umgehen (2) (*imperf* **umging**, *perf* **hat umgangen**) *vb* **[29]**

Note that here the stress is on **gehen**.

to avoid ▷ *Dieses Problem sollten wir besser umgehen.* It would be better if we could avoid this problem.

umgehend *adj* immediate

Umgehungsstraße *f* bypass

umgekehrt *adj, adv* ❶ reverse ▷ *in umgekehrter Reihenfolge* in reverse order; **genau umgekehrt** exactly the opposite ❷ the other way around ▷ *Du musst das Bild umgekehrt hängen.* You'll have to hang the picture the other way round. ▷ *Mach das doch umgekehrt, und fang hiermit an.* Do it the other way round and start here.; **... und umgekehrt** ... and vice versa

umhauen (*perf* **hat umgehauen**) *vb* **[4]** ❶ to bowl over ▷ *Die Neuigkeit wird dich umhauen.* The news will bowl you over. ❷ to fell ▷ *Sie haben die alte Eiche umgehauen.* They've felled the old oak tree.

umkehren (*perf* **hat/ist umgekehrt**) *vb* **[4]**

For the perfect tense use **haben** when the verb has an object and **sein** when there is no object.

❶ to turn back ▷ *Wir sind auf halbem Weg umgekehrt.* We turned back halfway. ❷ to turn round ▷ *Warum hast du das Bild umgekehrt?* Why did you turn the picture round? ❸ to turn inside out ▷ *Sie hat ihre Tasche umgekehrt, den Schlüssel aber nicht gefunden.* She turned her bag inside out but couldn't find the key. ❹ to turn upside down ▷ *Kehr mal den Eimer um, dann kann ich mich draufstellen.* Turn the bucket upside down so that I can stand on it.

umkippen (*perf* **hat/ist umgekippt**) *vb* **[4]**

For the perfect tense use **haben** when the verb has an object and **sein** when there is no object.

❶ to tip over ▷ *Der Stuhl ist umgekippt.* The chair tipped over. ❷ to overturn ▷ *Sie haben das Boot umgekippt.* They overturned the boat. ❸ *(informal)* to keel over ▷ *Wenn ich Blut sehe, kippe ich immer um.* I keel over whenever I see blood.

Umkleidekabine *f* changing cubicle

Umkleideraum (*pl* **Umkleideräume**) *m* changing room

umkommen (*imperf* **kam um**, *perf* **ist umgekommen**) *vb* **[40]** to be killed ▷ *Alle Passagiere sind umgekommen.* All the passengers were killed.

Umkreis (*gen* **Umkreises**, *pl* **Umkreise**) *m* neighbourhood; **im Umkreis von** within a radius of

Umlaut (*pl* **Umlaute**) *m* umlaut

umlegen (*perf* **hat umgelegt**) *vb* [**4**] ❶ to put on ▷ *Du solltest dir eine Jacke umlegen.* You should put on a jacket.; **die Kosten für etwas umlegen** to divide the cost of something ❷ *(informal)* to bump off ▷ *Er ist von der Mafia umgelegt worden.* He was bumped off by the Mafia.

umleiten (*perf* **hat umgeleitet**) *vb* [**4**] to divert

Umleitung *f* diversion

umrechnen (*perf* **hat umgerechnet**) *vb* [**4**] to convert

Umrechnung *f* conversion

umrühren (*perf* **hat umgerührt**) *vb* [**4**] to stir

ums = **um das**

Umsatz (*gen* **Umsatzes**, *pl* **Umsätze**) *m* turnover

umschalten (*perf* **hat umgeschaltet**) *vb* [**4**] to switch ▷ *Schalt bitte ins zweite Programm um.* Please switch over to Channel two.; **Die Ampel hat auf Gelb umgeschaltet.** The traffic lights changed to amber.; **Wir schalten um ins Studio.** We'll now go back to the studio.

Umschlag (*pl* **Umschläge**) *m* ❶ cover ▷ *Alle meine Mathehefte haben einen schwarzen Umschlag.* All my maths exercise books have a black cover. ❷ jacket ▷ *Ich habe den Umschlag von dem Wörterbuch abgemacht.* I took the jacket off the dictionary. ❸ envelope ▷ *Sie steckte den Brief in den Umschlag.* She put the letter in the envelope.

sich **umsehen** (*pres* **sieht sich um**, *imperf* **sah sich um**, *perf* **hat sich umgesehen**) *vb* [**64**] to look around ▷ *Als sie Schritte hörte, sah sie sich um.* When she heard steps, she looked around.; **sich nach etwas umsehen** to look for something

umso *conj* so much ▷ *umso besser* so much the better ▷ *umso schlimmer* so much the worse; **Je mehr ich höre, umso weniger verstehe ich.** The more I hear the less I understand.

umsonst *adv* ❶ in vain ▷ *Wir haben umsonst gewartet.* We waited in vain. ❷ for nothing ▷ *Wir sind umsonst ins Museum gekommen.* We got into the museum for nothing. ❸ free of charge ▷ *Diese Broschüre gibt es umsonst.* This brochure is free of charge.

Umstand (*pl* **Umstände**) *m* circumstance ▷ *unter keinen Umständen* under no circumstances; **Wenn es keine Umstände macht.** If it's no trouble.; **unter Umständen** possibly; **in anderen Umständen sein** to be pregnant

> Word for word, **in anderen Umständen sein** means 'to be in different circumstances'.

umständlich *adj* ❶ complicated ▷ *Das ist aber umständlich, wie du das machst.* The way you do it is complicated. ❷ long-winded ▷ *eine umständliche Erklärung* a long-winded explanation

umsteigen (*imperf* **stieg um**, *perf* **ist umgestiegen**) *vb* [**74**] to change ▷ *Wir müssen in München umsteigen.* We have to change in Munich.

umstellen (1) (*perf* **hat umgestellt**) *vb* [**4**]

> Note that here the stress is on **um**.

to move ▷ *Ich werde meinen Schreibtisch umstellen.* I'm going to move my desk.; **auf metrische Maße umstellen** to go over to the metric system; **sich umstellen** to adapt

umstellen (2) (*perf* **hat umstellt**) *vb* [**7**]

> Note that here the stress is on **stellen**.

to surround ▷ *Die Polizei hat das Haus umstellt.* The police have surrounded the house.

umstritten *adj* controversial ▷ *ein umstrittenes Thema* a controversial subject

a b c d e f g h i j k l m n o p q r s t **u** v w x y z

Umtausch *m* exchange
umtauschen (*perf* **hat umgetauscht**) *vb* **[4]** to exchange
Umweg (*pl* **Umwege**) *m* detour ▷ *Wir haben einen Umweg gemacht.* We made a detour.
Umwelt *f* environment
umweltfreundlich *adj* environment-friendly
Umweltschützer (*pl* **Umweltschützer**) *m* environmentalist
Umweltverschmutzung *f* environmental pollution
umziehen (*imperf* **zog um**, *perf* **hat/ist umgezogen**) *vb* **[96]**

Use **haben** to form the perfect tense. Use **sein** to form the perfect tense for 'to move'.

❶ to change ▷ *Ich habe Carolin heute schon zweimal umgezogen.* I've already changed Carolin's clothes twice today.; **sich umziehen** to get changed ❷ to move ▷ *Mein Freund ist nach Bremen umgezogen.* My friend's moved to Bremen.
Umzug (*pl* **Umzüge**) *m* ❶ move ▷ *Alle meine Freunde haben beim Umzug geholfen.* All my friends helped with the move. ❷ procession ▷ *Zu Karneval finden überall Umzüge statt.* There are processions everywhere during the Carnival.
unabhängig *adj* independent
Unabhängigkeit *f* independence
unangebracht *adj* uncalled-for
unangenehm *adj* unpleasant
Unannehmlichkeiten *fpl* trouble *sg* ▷ *Das gibt Unannehmlichkeiten mit dem Klassenlehrer.* That'll cause trouble with the class teacher.
unanständig *adj* improper
unartig *adj* naughty
unaufmerksam *adj* inattentive
unausstehlich *adj* intolerable
unbeabsichtigt *adj* unintentional
unbedeutend *adj* unimportant
unbedingt *adj, adv* ❶ unconditional ▷ *Ich verlange unbedingten Gehorsam.* I demand unconditional obedience. ❷ really ▷ *Er wollte unbedingt nach Hause.* He really wanted to go home. ▷ *Den Film musst du dir unbedingt ansehen.* You really have to see that film.
unbegreiflich *adj* inconceivable
unbekannt *adj* unknown
unbeliebt *adj* unpopular
unbequem *adj* uncomfortable ▷ *Das Bett ist unbequem.* The bed's uncomfortable.
unbestimmt *adj* ❶ indefinite ▷ *der unbestimmte Artikel* the indefinite article ❷ uncertain ▷ *Es ist noch unbestimmt, wann wir Ferien machen.* It's still uncertain when we're going on holiday.
unbewusst *adj* unconscious
und *conj* and ▷ *und so weiter* and so on; **Na und?** So what?
undankbar *adj* ungrateful
undeutlich *adj* indistinct
unehrlich *adj* dishonest
unempfindlich *adj* practical ▷ *Wir brauchen für das Sofa einen unempfindlichen Bezug.* We need a practical cover for the sofa.; **Ich bin gegen Kälte unempfindlich.** I don't feel the cold.
unendlich *adj* infinite
unentschieden *adj* undecided; **unentschieden enden** to end in a draw
unerfahren *adj* inexperienced
unerfreulich *adj* unpleasant
unerträglich *adj* unbearable ▷ *Die Schmerzen sind unerträglich.* The pain's unbearable.
unerwünscht *adj* undesirable
unfähig *adj* incapable ▷ *zu etwas unfähig sein* to be incapable of something
unfair *adj* unfair
Unfall (*pl* **Unfälle**) *m* accident
unfreundlich *adj* unfriendly
Unfreundlichkeit *f* unfriendliness

Unfug *m* ❶ mischief ▷ *Die Kinder machen dauernd Unfug.* The children are always getting up to mischief. ❷ nonsense ▷ *Red nicht so einen Unfug.* Don't talk such nonsense.
Ungar (*gen* **Ungarn**, *pl* **Ungarn**) *m* Hungarian
Ungarin *f* Hungarian
ungarisch *adj* Hungarian
Ungarn *nt* Hungary
Ungeduld *f* impatience
ungeduldig *adj* impatient
ungeeignet *adj* unsuitable
ungefähr *adj* approximate ▷ *Kannst du mir eine ungefähre Zeit nennen?* Can you give me an approximate time? ▷ *um ungefähr zwei Uhr* at approximately two o'clock
ungefährlich *adj* harmless
Ungeheuer (*pl* **Ungeheuer**) *nt* monster ▷ *das Ungeheuer von Loch Ness* the Loch Ness monster
ungehörig *adj* impertinent
ungehorsam *adj* disobedient
ungeklärt *adj* unsolved ▷ *ein ungeklärtes Rätsel* an unsolved puzzle
ungelegen *adj* inconvenient ▷ *Ich hoffe, ich komme nicht ungelegen.* I hope I haven't come at an inconvenient time.
ungelernt *adj* unskilled ▷ *ein ungelernter Arbeiter* an unskilled worker
ungemütlich *adj* ❶ uncomfortable ▷ *ein ungemütlicher Stuhl* an uncomfortable chair ❷ disagreeable ▷ *Jetzt wird er ungemütlich.* Now he's going to get disagreeable.
ungenau *adj* inaccurate
ungenießbar *adj* ❶ inedible ▷ *Das Essen war ungenießbar.* The food was inedible. ❷ undrinkable ▷ *Diese Limonade ist ungenießbar.* This lemonade's undrinkable. ❸ unbearable ▷ *Du bist heute aber ungenießbar.* You're really unbearable today.
ungenügend *adj* ❶ insufficient ▷ *eine ungenügende Menge* an insufficient amount ❷ unsatisfactory
German marks range from one (**sehr gut**) to six (**ungenügend**).
ungepflegt *adj* **ein ungepflegter Garten** a neglected garden; **ungepflegte Hände** uncared-for hands
ungerade *adj* **eine ungerade Zahl** an odd number
ungerecht *adj* unjust
Ungerechtigkeit *f* injustice
ungern *adv* reluctantly
ungeschickt *adj* clumsy
ungestört *adj* undisturbed
ungesund *adj* unhealthy
ungewiss *adj* uncertain
Ungewissheit *f* uncertainty
ungewöhnlich *adj* unusual
ungewohnt *adj* unaccustomed
Ungeziefer *nt* vermin
ungezogen *adj* rude
unglaublich *adj* incredible
Unglück (*pl* **Unglücke**) *nt* ❶ accident ▷ *Er ist bei einem Unglück ums Leben gekommen.* He lost his life in an accident. ❷ misfortune ▷ *Lass sie in ihrem Unglück nicht allein.* Don't leave her alone in her misfortune. ❸ bad luck ▷ *Eine schwarze Katze bringt Unglück.* A black cat means bad luck.
unglücklich *adj* ❶ unhappy ▷ *Sie ist furchtbar unglücklich.* She's terribly unhappy. ❷ unfortunate ▷ *ein unglücklicher Zufall* an unfortunate coincidence ▷ *eine unglückliche Formulierung* an unfortunate choice of words; **Sie ist unglücklich gefallen.** She fell awkwardly.
ungültig *adj* invalid
ungünstig *adj* unfavourable
unheilbar *adj* incurable
unheimlich *adj, adv* ❶ weird ▷ *Das war ein unheimliches Geräusch.* That was a weird noise.; **Mir wird's etwas unheimlich.** I'm getting a bit scared. ❷ incredibly ▷ *Das hat mich unheimlich gefreut.* I was incredibly pleased about it.

a b c d e f g h i j k l m n o p q r s t u v w x y z

unhöflich *adj* impolite
Uni (*pl* **Unis**) *f (informal)* uni
Uniform *f* uniform
uninteressant *adj* uninteresting
Universität *f* university
unklar *adj* unclear; **über etwas im Unklaren sein** to be unclear about something; **jemanden über etwas im Unklaren lassen** to leave somebody in the dark about something
unklug *adj* unwise
Unkosten *pl* expenses *pl*
unlogisch *adj* illogical
unlösbar *adj* insoluble ▷ *ein unlösbares Problem* an insoluble problem
unmissverständlich *adj* unmistakeable
unmittelbar *adj* immediate
unmöglich *adj* impossible
unmoralisch *adj* immoral
unnötig *adj* unnecessary
unordentlich *adj* untidy
Unordnung *f* disorder
unparteiisch *adj* impartial
unpassend *adj* ❶ inappropriate ▷ *unpassende Kleidung* inappropriate clothes ❷ inopportune ▷ *zu einer unpassenden Zeit* at an inopportune time
unpersönlich *adj* impersonal ▷ *das unpersönliche Fürwort* the impersonal pronoun
unpraktisch *adj* unpractical
unpünktlich *adj* **Sie ist immer unpünktlich.** She's always late.
unrecht *adj* wrong ▷ *Du tust ihr unrecht.* You are wronging her.; **unrecht haben** to be wrong
Unrecht *nt* wrong ▷ *ein großes Unrecht* a great wrong; **zu Unrecht** wrongly
unregelmäßig *adj* irregular ▷ *ein unregelmäßiges Verb* an irregular verb
unreif *adj* ❶ not ripe ▷ *Der Apfel ist noch unreif.* The apple's not ripe yet. ❷ immature ▷ *Elisabeth ist noch furchtbar unreif.* Elisabeth's still terribly immature.
unrichtig *adj* incorrect
Unruhe *f* unrest
unruhig *adj* restless
uns *pron*

> **uns** is the accusative and dative of **wir**.

❶ us ▷ *Sie haben uns eingeladen.* They've invited us. ❷ to us ▷ *Sie haben es uns gegeben.* They gave it to us. ❸ ourselves ▷ *Wir fragen uns, ob das sein muss.* We're asking ourselves whether that is necessary. ❹ each other ▷ *Wir lieben uns.* We love each other.
unschlagbar *adj* invincible
Unschuld *f* innocence
unschuldig *adj* innocent
unser *adj* ❶ our ▷ *Unser Deutschlehrer ist nett.* Our German teacher's nice. ▷ *Unser Haus ist ganz in der Nähe der Schule.* Our house is very near the school. ▷ *Unsere Lehrer sind prima.* Our teachers are great. ❷ ours ▷ *Das ist nicht euer Lehrer, das ist unserer.* He's not your teacher, he's ours. ▷ *Seine Note war besser als unsere.* His mark was better than ours. ▷ *Deine Eltern sind netter als unsere.* Your parents are nicer than ours.
unseretwegen *adv* ❶ for our sake ▷ *Ihr braucht unseretwegen nicht zu warten.* You needn't wait for our sake. ❷ on our account ▷ *Hat sie sich unseretwegen so aufgeregt?* Did she get so upset on our account? ❸ as far as we're concerned ▷ *Unseretwegen kann man das gern anders machen.* As far as we're concerned you're welcome to do it differently.
unsicher *adj* ❶ uncertain ▷ *Es ist unsicher, ob wir kommen können.* It's uncertain whether we can come. ❷ insecure ▷ *Elisabeth ist sehr unsicher.* Elisabeth's very insecure.
unsichtbar *adj* invisible
Unsinn *m* nonsense ▷ *Unsinn erzählen* to talk nonsense; **Unsinn machen** to do silly things

unsympathisch *adj* unpleasant ▷ *ein unsympathischer Mensch* an unpleasant person; **Er ist mir unsympathisch.** I don't like him.

unten *adv* ❶ at the bottom ▷ *Das beste Buch lag unten auf dem Stapel.* The best book was at the bottom of the pile. ▷ *Er stand unten an der Treppe.* He was standing at the bottom of the stairs. ▷ *unten am Berg* at the bottom of the mountain ❷ downstairs ▷ *Mutter ist unten in der Küche.* Mother's downstairs in the kitchen.; **nach unten** down

unter *prep* ❶ under

> Use the accusative to express movement or a change of place. Use the dative when there is no change of place.

▷ *Die Katze lag unter dem Tisch.* The cat lay under the table. ▷ *Der Ball rollte unter den Tisch.* The ball rolled under the table. ▷ *unter achtzehn Jahren* under eighteen years of age ❷ below ▷ *Temperaturen unter null* below-zero temperatures ❸ among ▷ *Unter den Büchern war auch ein Atlas.* There was also an atlas among the books.; **Sie waren unter sich.** They were by themselves.; **einer unter ihnen** one of them; **unter anderem** among other things

unterbrechen (*pres* **unterbricht**, *imperf* **unterbrach**, *perf* **hat unterbrochen**) *vb* [11] to interrupt

Unterbrechung *f* interruption

unterdrücken (*perf* **hat unterdrückt**) *vb* [7] ❶ to suppress ▷ *Sie unterdrückte ein Lächeln.* She suppressed a smile. ❷ to oppress ▷ *Menschen unterdrücken* to oppress people

untere *adj* lower ▷ *die unteren Stockwerke* the lower floors

untergehen (*imperf* **ging unter**, *perf* **ist untergegangen**) *vb* [29] ❶ to sink ❷ to set ▷ *sobald die Sonne untergegangen ist ...* as soon as the sun has set ...; **Die Welt geht unter.** The world's coming to an end.; **Seine Rede ging im Lärm unter.** His speech was drowned out by the noise.

Untergeschoss *nt* basement

unterhalb *prep*

> The preposition **unterhalb** takes the genitive.

below ▷ *Ihr Haus befindet sich unterhalb der Kirche.* Her house is below the church.

unterhalten (*pres* **unterhält**, *imperf* **unterhielt**, *perf* **hat unterhalten**) *vb* [33] ❶ to entertain ▷ *Sie hat uns den ganzen Abend mit lustigen Geschichten unterhalten.* She entertained us with funny stories all evening. ❷ to run ▷ *Das Schwimmbad wird von der Stadt unterhalten.* The swimming pool is run by the town council.; **sich unterhalten** to talk

unterhaltsam *adj* entertaining

Unterhaltung *f* ❶ talk ▷ *Es war eine sehr aufschlussreiche Unterhaltung.* It was a very informative talk. ❷ entertainment ▷ *Zur Unterhaltung der Gäste spielt die örtliche Musikkapelle.* Entertainment will be provided by the local brass band.

Unterhemd (*pl* **Unterhemden**) *nt* vest

Unterhose *f* underpants *pl* ▷ *eine Unterhose* a pair of underpants

Unterkunft (*pl* **Unterkünfte**) *f* accommodation

Untermieter (*pl* **Untermieter**) *m* lodger

unternehmen (*pres* **unternimmt**, *imperf* **unternahm**, *perf* **hat unternommen**) *vb* [52] **Was sollen wir heute unternehmen?** What shall we do today?

Unternehmen (*pl* **Unternehmen**) *nt* enterprise

Unternehmer (*pl* **Unternehmer**) *m* entrepreneur

Unterricht *m* lessons *pl* ▷ *Nachmittags haben wir selten Unterricht.* We seldom have lessons in the afternoon.

unterrichten (*perf* **hat unterrichtet**) *vb* [**2**] ❶ to teach ▷ *Sie unterrichtet Englisch und Französisch.* She teaches English and French.; **Wer unterrichtet euch in Sport?** Who do you have for sport? ❷ to inform ▷ *Wir müssen deine Eltern davon unterrichten.* We'll have to inform your parents.
Unterrock (*pl* **Unterröcke**) *m* underskirt
untersagt *adj* forbidden
unterschätzen (*perf* **hat unterschätzt**) *vb* [**36**] to underestimate
unterscheiden (*imperf* **unterschied**, *perf* **hat unterschieden**) *vb* [**60**] to distinguish ▷ *Man muss zwischen Sachlichkeit und Unfreundlichkeit unterscheiden.* You have to distinguish between objectivity and unfriendliness.; **sich unterscheiden** to differ
Unterschied (*pl* **Unterschiede**) *m* difference; **im Unterschied zu** as distinct from
unterschiedlich *adj* different ▷ *Sie haben sehr unterschiedliche Begabungen.* They have very different talents. ▷ *Sie sind unterschiedlich groß.* They're different sizes.; **Das Wetter war sehr unterschiedlich.** The weather was mixed.
unterschreiben (*imperf* **unterschrieb**, *perf* **hat unterschrieben**) *vb* [**61**] to sign ▷ *Du musst das Zeugnis unterschreiben lassen.* You have to have the report signed.
Unterschrift *f* signature
unterste *adj* bottom ▷ *Es ist im untersten Fach.* It's on the bottom shelf.; **Sie ist in der untersten Klasse.** She's in the first form.
unterstreichen (*imperf* **unterstrich**, *perf* **hat unterstrichen**) *vb* to underline
unterstützen (*perf* **hat unterstützt**) *vb* [**36**] to support
Unterstützung *f* support
untersuchen (*perf* **hat untersucht**) *vb* [**18**] to examine
Untersuchung *f* examination
Untertasse *f* saucer ▷ *eine fliegende Untertasse* a flying saucer
unterteilen (*perf* **hat unterteilt**) *vb* [**7**] to divide up
Untertitel (*pl* **Untertitel**) *m* subtitle
Unterwäsche *f* underwear
unterwegs *adv* on the way
untreu *adj* unfaithful ▷ *Ich hoffe, du warst mir nicht untreu.* I hope you weren't unfaithful to me.
untröstlich *adj* inconsolable
unübersichtlich *adj* unclear ▷ *eine unübersichtliche Darstellung* an unclear presentation; **eine unübersichtliche Kurve** a blind corner
ununterbrochen *adj* uninterrupted
unveränderlich *adj* unchangeable
unverantwortlich *adj* irresponsible
unverbesserlich *adj* incorrigible
unverbleit *adj* unleaded ▷ *Ich fahre unverbleit.* I use unleaded.
unvergesslich *adj* unforgettable
unverkrampft *adj* relaxed
unvermeidlich *adj* unavoidable
unvernünftig *adj* foolish
unverschämt *adj* impudent
Unverschämtheit *f* impudence
unverzeihlich *adj* unpardonable
unvollständig *adj* incomplete
unvorsichtig *adj* careless
unvorstellbar *adj* inconceivable
unwahr *adj* untrue
unwahrscheinlich *adj, adv* ❶ unlikely ▷ *eine unwahrscheinliche Geschichte* an unlikely story ❷ incredibly ▷ *Ich habe mich unwahrscheinlich gefreut.* I was incredibly pleased.
unwichtig *adj* unimportant
unwirksam *adj* ineffective
unzählig *adj* countless
unzufrieden *adj* dissatisfied
unzutreffend *adj* incorrect

updaten *vb* [**38**] to update
uralt *adj* ancient
Ureinwohner (*pl* **Ureinwohner**) *m* original inhabitant
Urin (*pl* **Urine**) *m* urine
Urkunde *f* certificate
Urlaub (*pl* **Urlaube**) *m* holiday ▷ *Wir fahren morgen in Urlaub.* We're going on holiday tomorrow. ▷ *Wo warst du im Urlaub?* Where did you go on holiday?
Ursache *f* cause; **Keine Ursache!** That's all right.
ursprünglich *adj, adv* ❶ original ▷ *Wir mussten unsere ursprünglichen Pläne aufgeben.* We had to abandon our original plans. ❷ originally ▷ *Ursprünglich wollten wir nach Griechenland fahren.* We originally wanted to go to Greece.
Urteil (*pl* **Urteile**) *nt* ❶ opinion ▷ *Wie lautet dein Urteil?* What's your opinion? ❷ sentence ▷ *Die Richter haben das Urteil noch nicht verkündet.* The judges haven't passed sentence yet.
urteilen *vb* [**38**] to judge
Urwald (*pl* **Urwälder**) *m* jungle
USA *pl* USA *sg*; **aus den USA** from the USA; **in den USA** in the USA; **nach den USA** to the USA
usw. *abbr* (= *und so weiter*) etc

V

vage *adj* vague
Vanille *f* vanilla
Vase *f* vase
Vater (*pl* **Väter**) *m* father
Vati (*pl* **Vatis**) *m* (*informal*) daddy
Vegetarier (*pl* **Vegetarier**) *m* vegetarian
Vegetarierin *f* vegetarian
vegetarisch *adj* vegetarian
Veilchen (*pl* **Veilchen**) *nt* violet
Vene *f* vein
Ventil (*pl* **Ventile**) *nt* valve
verabreden (*perf* **hat verabredet**) *vb* [**54**] to arrange ▷ *Wir sollten Zeit und Ort des Treffens verabreden.* We ought to arrange when and where to meet.; **sich mit jemandem verabreden** to arrange to meet somebody; **mit jemandem verabredet sein** to have arranged to meet somebody
Verabredung *f* date
verabschieden (*perf* **hat verabschiedet**) *vb* [**54**] to say goodbye to ▷ *Wir verabschiedeten unsere*

Gäste. We said goodbye to our guests.; **sich verabschieden** to take one's leave

veralten (*perf* **ist veraltet**) *vb* [**2**] to become obsolete

veränderlich *adj* changeable

verändern (*perf* **hat verändert**) *vb* [**88**] to change; **sich verändern** to change

Veränderung *f* change

Veranlagung *f* disposition ▷ *eine nervöse Veranlagung* a nervous disposition

veranlassen (*perf* **hat veranlasst**) *vb* [**84**] **etwas veranlassen** to have something done; **sich veranlasst sehen, etwas zu tun** to be prompted to do something

veranstalten (*perf* **hat veranstaltet**) *vb* [**2**] to organize

Veranstalter (*pl* **Veranstalter**) *m* organizer

Veranstaltung *f* event

verantworten (*perf* **hat verantwortet**) *vb* [**2**] to take responsibility for ▷ *Wenn das nicht klappt, hast du das zu verantworten.* If it doesn't work, you'll have to take responsibility for it.; **Das kann ich nicht verantworten.** I couldn't possibly allow that.

verantwortlich *adj* responsible

Verantwortung *f* responsibility

verarbeiten (*perf* **hat verarbeitet**) *vb* [**2**] ❶ to process ▷ *In diesem Werk wird Metall verarbeitet.* Metal is processed in this factory.; **etwas zu etwas verarbeiten** to make something into something ❷ to digest ▷ *Ich muss die Reiseeindrücke erst noch verarbeiten.* I still have to digest my impressions from the journey.

verärgern (*perf* **hat verärgert**) *vb* [**88**] to annoy

Verb (*pl* **Verben**) *nt* verb

Verband (*pl* **Verbände**) *m* ❶ dressing; **Die Schwester hat ihm einen Verband angelegt.** The nurse dressed his wound. ❷ association ▷ *Die Bauern haben sich zu einem Verband zusammengeschlossen.* The farmers have formed an association.

Verbandskasten (*pl* **Verbandskästen**) *m* first-aid box

verbergen (*pres* **verbirgt**, *imperf* **verbarg**, *perf* **hat verborgen**) *vb* to hide; **sich vor jemandem verbergen** to hide from somebody

verbessern (*perf* **hat verbessert**) *vb* [**88**] ❶ to improve ▷ *Ich konnte meine Noten verbessern.* I was able to improve my marks. ❷ to correct ▷ *Meine Mutter hat meine Hausaufgaben verbessert.* My mother corrected my homework.; **sich verbessern** to improve

Verbesserung *f* ❶ improvement ▷ *eine Verbesserung seiner Leistungen* an improvement in his work ❷ correction ▷ *Schreibt bitte die Verbesserung ins Heft.* Please write the correction in your exercise book.

verbieten (*imperf* **verbot**, *perf* **hat verboten**) *vb* [**8**] to forbid ▷ *Meine Mutter hat mir verboten, mit Frank auszugehen.* My mother forbade me to go out with Frank.

verbinden (*imperf* **verband**, *perf* **hat verbunden**) *vb* ❶ to combine ▷ *Ich habe das Nützliche mit dem Angenehmen verbunden.* I was able to combine business with pleasure. ❷ to bandage ▷ *Die Wunde muss verbunden werden.* The wound has to be bandaged.; **jemandem die Augen verbinden** to blindfold somebody ❸ to connect ▷ *Ein Kanal verbindet die beiden Flüsse.* A canal connects the two rivers. ❹ to put through ▷ *Können Sie mich bitte mit Frau Karl verbinden?* Can you put me through to Mrs Karl, please? ▷ *Ich verbinde!* I'm putting you through.; **Sie sind falsch verbunden.** You've got the wrong number.

Verbindung (*pl* **Verbindungen**) *f* ❶ connection ▷ *Es gibt eine direkte*

Verbindungen nach München. There is a direct connection to Munich. ❷ communication ▷ *eine telefonische Verbindung* a telephone communication; **eine chemische Verbindung** a compound

verbleit *adj* leaded

verblüffen (*perf* **hat verblüfft**) *vb* [**84**] to amaze

verbluten (*perf* **ist verblutet**) *vb* [**2**] to bleed to death

verborgen *adj* hidden

Verbot (*pl* **Verbote**) *nt* ban ▷ *Die Regierung verhängte ein Verbot für Rindfleischimporte aus England.* The government imposed a ban on beef imports from England.

verboten *adj* forbidden; **Rauchen verboten!** No smoking

Verbrauch *m* consumption

verbrauchen (*perf* **hat verbraucht**) *vb* [**84**] to use up ▷ *Das Gerät verbraucht viel Strom.* The machine uses up a lot of electricity.

Verbraucher (*pl* **Verbraucher**) *m* consumer

Verbrauchermarkt (*pl* **Verbrauchermärkte**) *m* hypermarket

Verbrechen (*pl* **Verbrechen**) *nt* crime

Verbrecher (*pl* **Verbrecher**) *m* criminal

verbreiten (*perf* **hat verbreitet**) *vb* [**2**] ❶ to spread ▷ *eine Krankheit verbreiten* to spread a disease ❷ to broadcast ▷ *eine Nachricht verbreiten* to broadcast a message; **sich verbreiten** to spread

verbrennen (*imperf* **verbrannte**, *perf* **hat verbrannt**) *vb* [**12**] ❶ to burn ▷ *In dieser Anlage wird Müll verbrannt.* Waste is burnt in this plant. ❷ to cremate ▷ *Sie möchte nach ihrem Tod verbrannt werden.* She'd like to be cremated when she dies.

verbringen (*imperf* **verbrachte**, *perf* **hat verbracht**) *vb* [**13**] to spend ▷ *Wir haben das Wochenende im Schwarzwald verbracht.* We spent the weekend in the Black Forest.

Verdacht (*pl* **Verdachte**) *m* suspicion

verdächtig *adj* suspicious

verdächtigen (*perf* **hat verdächtigt**) *vb* [**84**] to suspect

verdammt *adj, adv (informal)* damned ▷ *Diese verdammten Fliegen!* These damned flies!; **Verdammt noch mal!** Damn it all!; **Verdammt!** Damn!

verdampfen (*perf* **ist verdampft**) *vb* [**7**] to evaporate

verdanken (*perf* **hat verdankt**) *vb* [**84**] **jemandem sein Leben verdanken** to owe one's life to somebody

verdauen (*perf* **hat verdaut**) *vb* [**84**] to digest

verdaulich *adj* **Das ist schwer verdaulich.** That's hard to digest.

Verdauung *f* digestion

verderben (*pres* **verdirbt**, *imperf* **verdarb**, *perf* **hat/ist verdorben**) *vb*

> Use **haben** to form the perfect tense. Use **sein** to form the perfect tense for 'to go bad'.

❶ to ruin ▷ *Du verdirbst dir bei dem schlechten Licht die Augen.* You'll ruin your eyes in this bad light. ▷ *Er hat mir den Urlaub verdorben.* He ruined my holiday. ❷ to corrupt ▷ *Geld verdirbt den Menschen.* Money corrupts people.; **es mit jemandem verderben** to get into somebody's bad books ❸ to go bad ▷ *Die Wurst ist verdorben.* The sausage has gone bad.

verdienen (*perf* **hat verdient**) *vb* [**84**] ❶ to earn ▷ *Wie viel verdient dein Vater?* How much does your father earn? ❷ to deserve ▷ *Du hast die Strafe verdient.* You deserved the punishment.

verdreifachen (*perf* **hat verdreifacht**) *vb* [**7**] to treble

verdünnen (*perf* **hat verdünnt**) *vb* [**7**] to dilute

verdunsten (*perf* **ist verdunstet**) *vb* [**2**] to evaporate

verdursten (*perf* **ist verdurstet**) *vb* [**2**] to die of thirst

Verein (*pl* **Vereine**) *m* club ▷ *ein Sportverein* a sports club
vereinbar *adj* compatible ▷ *mit etwas vereinbar* compatible with something
vereinbaren (*perf* **hat vereinbart**) *vb* [**84**] to agree on
Vereinbarung *f* agreement
vereinen (*perf* **hat vereint**) *vb* [**84**] ❶ to unite ▷ *Das geteilte Land wurde wieder vereint.* The divided country was reunited. ❷ to reconcile ▷ *Ich kann das nicht mit meinem Gewissen vereinen.* I can't reconcile that with my conscience.; **Mit vereinten Kräften schaffen wir das.** If we all pull together, we'll manage to do it.; **die Vereinten Nationen** the United Nations
vereinfachen (*perf* **hat vereinfacht**) *vb* [**84**] to simplify
vereinigen (*perf* **hat vereinigt**) *vb* [**84**] to unite
vereinzelt *adj* isolated ▷ *vereinzelte Schauer* isolated showers
vererben (*perf* **hat vererbt**) *vb* [**18**] to leave ▷ *Meine Oma hat mir all ihre Bücher vererbt.* My granny left me all her books.; **sich vererben** to be hereditary
verfahren (*pres* **verfährt**, *imperf* **verfuhr**, *perf* **hat/ist verfahren**) *vb* [**21**] ❶ to proceed ▷ *Wie sollen wir verfahren?* How shall we proceed? ❷ to use up ▷ *Wir haben 50 Liter Benzin verfahren.* We have used up 50 litres of petrol.; **Wir haben uns verfahren.** We have lost our way.
Verfahren (*pl* **Verfahren**) *nt* ❶ process ▷ *Das ist ein neuartiges Verfahren zum Recyceln von Plastik.* This is a new recycling process for plastic. ❷ proceedings *pl* ▷ *ein Verfahren gegen jemanden einleiten* to bring proceedings against somebody
Verfassung *f* ❶ constitution ▷ *Die Opposition hat eine Änderung der Verfassung beantragt.* The opposition's called for an amendment to the constitution. ❷ state ▷ *Ich bin nicht in der Verfassung, da mitzumachen.* I'm in no state to join in.
verfolgen (*perf* **hat verfolgt**) *vb* [**84**] ❶ to pursue ▷ *Die Polizei verfolgte die Täter.* The police pursued the culprits.; **Die Hunde verfolgten ihre Fährte.** The dogs tracked them. ❷ to persecute ▷ *In vielen Ländern werden Minderheiten verfolgt.* Minorities are persecuted in many countries.
Verfolgung *f* ❶ hunt ▷ *Die Verfolgung der Täter war erfolgreich.* The hunt for the culprits had a successful outcome. ❷ persecution ▷ *die Verfolgung von Minderheiten* the persecution of minorities
verfügbar *adj* available
verführen (*perf* **hat verführt**) *vb* [**84**] ❶ to tempt ▷ *Verführ mich nicht, ich habe schon zwei Stück Kuchen gegessen.* Don't tempt me, I've already had two pieces of cake. ❷ to seduce ▷ *Er hat versucht, sie zu verführen.* He tried to seduce her.
Vergangenheit *f* past ▷ *in der Vergangenheit* in the past
vergaß *vb see* **vergessen**
vergeben (*pres* **vergibt**, *imperf* **vergab**, *perf* **hat vergeben**) *vb* [**28**] to forgive ▷ *Kannst du mir noch einmal vergeben?* Can you forgive me one more time? ▷ *Diese Lüge werde ich dir nie vergeben.* I'll never forgive you for that lie.; **vergeben sein** to be taken; **Er ist schon vergeben.** He's already spoken for.

> Word for word, **Er ist schon vergeben** means 'He is already given away'.

vergeblich *adv, adj* in vain ▷ *Wir haben uns vergeblich bemüht.* We tried, but in vain. ▷ *All mein Reden war vergeblich.* All my words were in vain.
vergehen (*imperf* **verging**, *perf* **ist vergangen**) *vb* [**29**] to pass; **Wie schnell die Zeit doch vergeht!** How time flies!; **Mir ist der Appetit**

vergangen. I've lost my appetite.; **sich an jemandem vergehen** to indecently assault somebody

vergessen (*pres* **vergisst**, *imperf* **vergaß**, *perf* **hat vergessen**) *vb* **[83]** to forget ▷ *Ich habe seinen Namen vergessen.* I've forgotten his name.; **Vergiss nicht, die Blumen zu gießen.** Remember to water the flowers.

vergesslich *adj* forgetful

vergeuden (*perf* **hat vergeudet**) *vb* **[7]** to squander

vergewaltigen (*perf* **hat vergewaltigt**) *vb* **[7]** to rape ▷ *Er hat eine Frau vergewaltigt.* He raped a woman.

Vergewaltigung *f* rape

sich **vergewissern** (*perf* **hat sich vergewissert**) *vb* **[88]** to make sure

vergiften (*perf* **hat vergiftet**) *vb* **[2]** to poison

Vergiftung *f* poisoning

vergisst *vb see* **vergessen**

Vergleich (*pl* **Vergleiche**) *m* comparison; **im Vergleich zu** compared with

vergleichen (*imperf* **verglich**, *perf* **hat verglichen**) *vb* to compare ▷ *Er hat mein Wörterbuch mit seinem verglichen.* He compared my dictionary with his. ▷ *Man kann doch Äpfel und Birnen nicht vergleichen.* You can't compare apples and pears.

Vergnügen (*pl* **Vergnügen**) *nt* pleasure; **Viel Vergnügen!** Have fun!

vergnügt *adj* cheerful

vergraben (*pres* **vergräbt**, *imperf* **vergrub**, *perf* **hat vergraben**) *vb* to bury

vergrößern (*perf* **hat vergrößert**) *vb* **[88]** ❶ to enlarge ▷ *Ich habe das Foto vergrößern lassen.* I had the photo enlarged. ❷ to extend ▷ *Wir wollen das Haus vergrößern.* We want to extend the house.; **sich vergrößern** to grow larger

verhaften (*perf* **hat verhaftet**) *vb* **[2]** to arrest

sich **verhalten** (*pres* **verhält sich**, *imperf* **verhielt sich**, *perf* **hat sich verhalten**) *vb* **[33]** to behave ▷ *Er hat sich uns gegenüber sehr fair verhalten.* He behaved very fairly towards us.

Verhalten *nt* behaviour

Verhältnis (*gen* **Verhältnisses**, *pl* **Verhältnisse**) *nt* ❶ affair ▷ *Er hat ein Verhältnis mit einer verheirateten Frau.* He's having an affair with a married woman. ❷ proportion ▷ *Unser Gehalt steht in keinem Verhältnis zu unserer Leistung.* Our salary is not in proportion to our efforts.; **Verhältnisse (1)** conditions ▷ *Wenn die Verhältnisse anders wären, könnten wir die Arbeit schneller beenden.* If conditions were different we could get the work finished sooner. **(2)** background *sg* ▷ *Er kommt aus bescheidenen Verhältnissen.* He comes from a modest background.; **über seine Verhältnisse leben** to live beyond one's means

verhältnismäßig *adv* relatively

verhandeln (*perf* **hat verhandelt**) *vb* **[34]** to negotiate ▷ *Sie verhandeln einen Waffenstillstand.* They're negotiating a ceasefire.; **Mein Fall wird nächste Woche vor dem Arbeitsgericht verhandelt.** My case is being heard by the industrial tribunal next week.

Verhandlung *f* ❶ negotiation ▷ *die Friedensverhandlungen* peace negotiations ▷ *Wir sind mit der Firma noch in Verhandlung.* We're still involved in negotiations with the company. ❷ trial ▷ *Die Verhandlung gegen Klitt ist morgen.* Klitt's trial is tomorrow. ❸ hearing ▷ *die Verhandlung vor dem Arbeitsgericht* the hearing before the industrial tribunal

verharmlosen (*perf* **hat verharmlost**) *vb* **[7]** to play down

verhauen (*perf* **hat verhauen**) *vb* **[7]** to beat up

verheerend *adj* devastating

verheimlichen (*perf* **hat verheimlicht**) *vb* [**7**] **jemandem etwas verheimlichen** to keep something secret from somebody

verheiratet *adj* married

verhindern (*perf* **hat verhindert**) *vb* [**88**] to prevent; **verhindert sein** to be unable to make it

verhungern (*perf* **ist verhungert**) *vb* [**88**] to starve to death

Verhütungsmittel (*pl* **Verhütungsmittel**) *nt* contraceptive

sich **verirren** (*perf* **hat sich verirrt**) *vb* [**84**] to get lost ▷ *Wir hatten uns im Nebel verirrt.* We lost our way in the fog.

Verkauf (*pl* **Verkäufe**) *m* sale

verkaufen (*perf* **hat verkauft**) *vb* [**84**] to sell

Verkäufer (*pl* **Verkäufer**) *m* shop assistant ▷ *Der Verkäufer hat uns sehr gut beraten.* The shop assistant was extremely helpful.

Verkäuferin *f* shop assistant ▷ *Sie ist Verkäuferin in einer Modeboutique.* She's a shop assistant in a fashion boutique.

Verkehr *m* ❶ traffic ▷ *Heute war viel Verkehr auf den Straßen.* There was heavy traffic on the roads today. ❷ intercourse ▷ *Haben Sie mit der Frau Verkehr gehabt?* Did you have intercourse with this woman?

Verkehrsampel *f* traffic lights *pl*

Verkehrsmittel (*pl* **Verkehrsmittel**) *nt* means of transport *sg*

Verkehrsschild (*pl* **Verkehrsschilder**) *nt* road sign

Verkehrsunfall (*pl* **Verkehrsunfälle**) *m* traffic accident

Verkehrszeichen (*pl* **Verkehrszeichen**) *nt* traffic sign

verkehrt *adj* wrong ▷ *Das war die verkehrte Antwort.* That was the wrong answer.; **verkehrt herum** back to front

sich **verkleiden** (*perf* **hat sich verkleidet**) *vb* [**54**] to dress up ▷ *Sie verkleidete sich als Hexe.* She dressed up as a witch.

verkleinern (*perf* **hat verkleinert**) *vb* [**88**] to reduce ▷ *Wir sollten den Zeilenabstand verkleinern.* We should reduce the line spacing.; **sich verkleinern** to grow smaller

Verlag (*pl* **Verlage**) *m* publisher

verlangen (*perf* **hat verlangt**) *vb* [**84**] to ask for ▷ *Ich verlange etwas mehr Verständnis.* I'm asking for a bit more understanding. ▷ *Wie viel hat er dafür verlangt?* How much did he ask for it?; **etwas von jemandem verlangen** to expect something of somebody

verlängern (*perf* **hat verlängert**) *vb* [**88**] ❶ to extend ▷ *Wir haben die Ferien um eine Woche verlängert.* We've extended our holiday by a week. ❷ to lengthen ▷ *Wir müssen das Seil verlängern.* We'll have to lengthen the rope.

verlassen (*pres* **verlässt**, *imperf* **verließ**, *perf* **hat verlassen**) *vb* [**42**] to leave ▷ *Er hat seine Frau und Kinder verlassen.* He's left his wife and children.; **Verlassen Sie sofort das Gebäude!** Get out of the building immediately.; **sich verlassen auf** to depend on

▶ *adj* ❶ deserted ▷ *eine verlassene Gegend* a deserted area ▷ *die verlassene Ehefrau* the deserted wife ❷ empty ▷ *ein verlassenes Haus* an empty house

sich **verlaufen** (*pres* **verläuft sich**, *imperf* **verlief sich**, *perf* **hat sich verlaufen**) *vb* [**43**] ❶ to get lost ▷ *Wir haben uns im Wald verlaufen.* We got lost in the forest. ❷ to disperse ▷ *Nach Ende der Veranstaltung verlief sich die Menge.* After the event the crowd dispersed.

verlegen *adj* embarrassed; **nicht verlegen um** never at a loss for

verleihen (*imperf* **verlieh**, *perf* **hat verliehen**) *vb* ❶ to lend ▷ *Ich habe mein Wörterbuch an sie verliehen.* I've lent her my dictionary. ❷ to hire out ▷ *Ich suche jemanden, der Fahrräder verleiht.* I'm looking for somebody who hires out bikes. ❸ to award ▷ *Sie hat einen Preis verliehen bekommen.* She was awarded a prize.

verleiten (*perf* **hat verleitet**) *vb* [**2**] **jemanden dazu verleiten, etwas zu tun** to tempt somebody into doing something

verlernen (*perf* **hat verlernt**) *vb* [**84**] to forget

verletzen (*perf* **hat verletzt**) *vb* [**36**] ❶ to hurt ▷ *Deine Bemerkung hat mich verletzt.* Your remark hurt me. ❷ to injure ▷ *Sie ist schwer verletzt.* She's seriously injured.; **ein Gesetz verletzen** to violate a law

Verletzte (*gen* **Verletzten**, *pl* **Verletzten**) *mf* injured person ▷ *Auf der Straße lag ein Verletzter.* An injured person was lying in the street.

Verletzung *f* injury; **Er hatte schwere Verletzungen.** He was seriously injured.; **Das ist eine Verletzung der Spielregeln.** That's against the rules of the game.

sich **verlieben** (*perf* **hat sich verliebt**) *vb* [**84**] **sich in jemanden verlieben** to fall in love with somebody

verliebt *adj* in love ▷ *Ich bin in Anke verliebt.* I'm in love with Anke.

verlieren (*imperf* **verlor**, *perf* **hat verloren**) *vb* [**85**] to lose

Verlierer (*pl* **Verlierer**) *m* loser

sich **verloben** (*perf* **hat sich verlobt**) *vb* [**84**] **sich mit jemandem verloben** to get engaged to somebody

Verlobte (*gen* **Verlobten**, *pl* **Verlobten**) *m* fiancé ▷ *Mathias ist mein Verlobter.* Mathias is my fiancé.

Verlobte (*gen* **Verlobten**, *pl* **Verlobten**) *f* fiancée ▷ *Ingrid ist seine Verlobte.* Ingrid's his fiancée.

Verlobung *f* engagement

verloren *adj* lost ▷ *die verlorene Zeit wieder einholen* to make up for lost time; **verlorene Eier** poached eggs; **verloren gehen** to get lost

Verlosung *f* raffle

Verlust (*pl* **Verluste**) *m* loss

vermehren (*perf* **hat vermehrt**) *vb* [**7**] increase ▷ *Die Firma hat ihren Umsatz vermehrt.* The company has increased its turnover.; **sich vermehren** to reproduce

vermeiden (*imperf* **vermied**, *perf* **hat vermieden**) *vb* to avoid

vermieten (*perf* **hat vermietet**) *vb* [**2**] ❶ to let ▷ *'Zimmer zu vermieten'* 'Rooms to let' ❷ to rent ▷ *Sie vermietet Zimmer.* She rents rooms. ❸ to hire out ▷ *Wir vermieten Boote und Fahrräder.* We hire out boats and bikes.

Vermieter (*pl* **Vermieter**) *m* landlord

Vermieterin *f* landlady

vermissen (*perf* **hat vermisst**) *vb* [**7**] to miss ▷ *Ich habe dich vermisst.* I missed you.; **Ich vermisse eines meiner Bücher.** One of my books is missing.

Vermögen (*pl* **Vermögen**) *nt* wealth; **ein Vermögen kosten** to cost a fortune

vermuten (*perf* **hat vermutet**) *vb* [**2**] ❶ to guess ▷ *Ich kann nur vermuten, was er damit gemeint hat.* I can only guess what he meant by that.; **Man vermutet, dass er im Ausland ist.** He is thought to be abroad. ❷ to suspect ▷ *Die Polizei vermutet, dass er der Täter ist.* The police suspect that he's the culprit. ❸ to suppose ▷ *Ich vermute, dass er das noch nicht weiß.* I don't suppose that he knows that yet.

vermutlich *adj, adv* ❶ probable ▷ *die vermutliche Ursache* the probable cause ❷ probably ▷ *Sie ist vermutlich schon gegangen.* She has probably already left.

Vermutung *f* ❶ supposition ▷ *Das legt die Vermutung nahe, dass sie schon gegangen ist.* It seems a likely supposition that she's already gone. ❷ suspicion ▷ *Die Polizei hat eine*

Vermutung, wer der Täter gewesen sein könnte. The police have a suspicion as to who the culprit could have been.

vernachlässigen (*perf* **hat vernachlässigt**) *vb* [**84**] to neglect

vernichten (*perf* **hat vernichtet**) *vb* [**2**] to destroy; **Insekten vernichten** to exterminate insects; **Unkraut vernichten** to eradicate weeds

Vernunft *f* reason

vernünftig *adj* reasonable ▷ *Sei doch vernünftig!* Be reasonable! ▷ *ein vernünftiger Preis* a reasonable price; **etwas Vernünftiges essen** to eat something decent

veröffentlichen (*perf* **hat veröffentlicht**) *vb* [**84**] to publish

Verpackung *f* packing

verpassen (*perf* **hat verpasst**) *vb* [**7**] to miss; **jemandem eine Ohrfeige verpassen** to give somebody a clip round the ear

verpflegen (*perf* **hat verpflegt**) *vb* [**7**] to cater for ▷ *Die Flüchtlinge wurden vom Roten Kreuz verpflegt.* The Red Cross catered for the refugees.

Verpflegung *f* food ▷ *Für Ihre Verpflegung wird gesorgt.* Food will be laid on. ▷ *Die Verpflegung im Schullandheim war gut.* The food at the school camp was good.

verpflichten (*perf* **hat verpflichtet**) *vb* [**2**] to sign ▷ *Der VfB will Köpke verpflichten.* VfB want to sign Köpke.; **sich verpflichten, etwas zu tun** to promise to do something; **Sie haben sich verpflichtet, für Ersatz zu sorgen.** You undertook to find a replacement.; **verpflichtet sein, etwas zu tun** to be obliged to do something; **Er ist zum Stillschweigen verpflichtet.** He's sworn to silence.; **Das verpflichtet Sie zu nichts.** This doesn't commit you to anything.; **jemandem zu Dank verpflichtet sein** to be obliged to somebody

verprügeln (*perf* **hat verprügelt**) *vb* [**7**] to beat up

verraten (*pres* **verrät**, *imperf* **verriet**, *perf* **hat verraten**) *vb* ❶ to betray ▷ *Er hat seine Mittäter verraten.* He betrayed his accomplices. ❷ to report ▷ *Fritz hat uns beim Lehrer verraten.* Fritz reported us to the teacher. ❸ to tell ▷ *Verrate mir doch, wer es war.* Tell me who it was. ▷ *Ich habe dieses Geheimnis niemandem verraten.* I haven't told anyone the secret.; **sich verraten** to give oneself away

verreisen (*perf* **ist verreist**) *vb* [**84**] to go away ▷ *Ich möchte diesen Sommer verreisen.* I'd like to go away this summer.; **Wir wollen nach Israel verreisen.** We intend to go to Israel.

verrenken (*perf* **hat verrenkt**) *vb* [**7**] to sprain ▷ *Er hat sich den Knöchel verrenkt.* He sprained his ankle.

verrosten (*perf* **ist verrostet**) *vb* [**2**] to rust

verrückt *adj* crazy

Vers (*gen* **Verses**, *pl* **Verse**) *m* verse

Versager (*pl* **Versager**) *m* failure

versalzen (*perf* **hat versalzen**) *vb* to put too much salt in ▷ *Sie hat die Suppe versalzen.* She put too much salt in the soup.; **Die Suppe ist versalzen.** There's too much salt in the soup.

versammeln (*perf* **hat versammelt**) *vb* [**34**] to assemble

Versammlung *f* meeting

Versandhaus (*gen* **Versandhauses**, *pl* **Versandhäuser**) *nt* mail-order firm

versäumen (*perf* **hat versäumt**) *vb* [**84**] to miss ▷ *Ich habe wegen Krankheit drei Stunden versäumt.* I missed three lessons due to illness. ▷ *Sie sollten nicht versäumen, sich die Kathedrale anzusehen.* Don't miss a visit to the cathedral.; **es versäumen, etwas zu tun** to fail to do something

verschenken (*perf* **hat verschenkt**) *vb* [**7**] to give away

verschicken (*perf* **hat verschickt**) *vb* [**7**] to send away

verschieben (*imperf* **verschob**, *perf* **hat verschoben**) *vb* to postpone ▷ *Wir müssen das Fest verschieben.* We'll have to postpone the party.

verschieden *adj* different ▷ *Die zwei Brüder sind sehr verschieden.* The two brothers are very different. ▷ *Sie sind verschieden groß.* They are different sizes.; **verschiedene** various

verschlafen (*pres* **verschläft**, *imperf* **verschlief**, *perf* **hat verschlafen**) *vb* [**58**] ❶ to sleep in ▷ *Tut mir leid, ich habe verschlafen.* Sorry, I slept in. ❷ to sleep through ▷ *Er hat den ganzen Vormittag verschlafen.* He slept through the whole morning. ❸ to forget ▷ *Ich habe deinen Geburtstag total verschlafen.* I completely forgot your birthday.
▶ *adj* sleepy ▷ *Sie sah mich mit einem verschlafenen Blick an.* She gave me a sleepy look. ▷ *ein verschlafenes kleines Dorf* a sleepy little village

verschlechtern (*perf* **hat verschlechtert**) *vb* [**88**] to make worse ▷ *Das verschlechtert die Lage.* That makes the situation worse.; **sich verschlechtern (1)** to get worse ▷ *Die Lage hat sich verschlechtert.* The situation's got worse. ▷ *In Englisch habe ich mich verschlechtert.* My marks in English have got worse. **(2)** to deteriorate ▷ *Sein Gesundheitszustand hat sich noch weiter verschlechtert.* His condition has deteriorated even further.

verschlimmern (*perf* **hat verschlimmert**) *vb* [**88**] to make worse ▷ *Du verschlimmerst alles, wenn du weiter lügst.* You'll make everything worse if you go on lying.; **sich verschlimmern** to get worse

Verschluss (*gen* **Verschlusses**, *pl* **Verschlüsse**) *m* ❶ cap ▷ *Die Flasche hat einen kindersicheren Verschluss.* The bottle has a childproof cap. ❷ fastening ▷ *Kannst du mir den Verschluss an meinem Kleid aufmachen?* Can you undo the fastening of my dress? ❸ catch ▷ *der Verschluss der Tasche* the catch of the bag ▷ *der Verschluss an einer Halskette* the catch of a necklace

verschmutzen (*perf* **hat verschmutzt**) *vb* [**7**] ❶ to soil; **stark verschmutzt** very dirty ❷ to pollute ▷ *die Umwelt verschmutzen* to pollute the environment

verschneit *adj* snow-covered ▷ *eine verschneite Straße* a snow-covered road

verschonen (*perf* **hat verschont**) *vb* [**84**] **jemanden mit etwas verschonen** to spare somebody something

verschreiben (*imperf* **verschrieb**, *perf* **hat verschrieben**) *vb* [**61**] to prescribe ▷ *Der Arzt hat mir Antibiotika verschrieben.* The doctor prescribed me antibiotics.; **sich verschreiben** to make a spelling mistake

verschütten (*perf* **hat verschüttet**) *vb* [**7**] to spill ▷ *Sie hat den Kaffee verschüttet.* She spilt the coffee.; **verschüttet werden** to be buried

verschweigen (*imperf* **verschwieg**, *perf* **hat verschwiegen**) *vb* **jemandem etwas verschweigen** to keep something from somebody

verschwenden (*perf* **hat verschwendet**) *vb* [**7**] to waste ▷ *Zeit verschwenden* to waste time

Verschwendung *f* waste

verschwinden (*imperf* **verschwand**, *perf* **ist verschwunden**) *vb* [**86**] to disappear

verschwommen *adj* blurred

Versehen (*pl* **Versehen**) *nt* oversight ▷ *Das war ein Versehen.* It was an oversight.; **aus Versehen** by mistake

versehentlich *adv* by mistake

versenden (*imperf* **versendete** *or* **versandte**, *perf* **hat versendet** *or* **versandt**) *vb* to dispatch

a b c d e f g h i j k l m n o p q r s t u v w x y z

versetzen (*perf* **hat versetzt**) *vb* **[7]** to transfer ▷ *Mein Vater wird nach Berlin versetzt.* My father's being transferred to Berlin.; **jemanden in die nächste Klasse versetzen** to move somebody up into the next class

- In Germany, pupils do not automatically move up (**versetzt werden**) to the next class at the end of the school year. If their performance is not good enough, they have to repeat the school year. This is known as **sitzen bleiben**.

jemanden versetzen *(informal)* to stand somebody up; **sich in jemandes Lage versetzen** to put oneself in somebody's shoes; **jemandem einen Schlag versetzen** to hit somebody; **jemandem einen Tritt versetzen** to kick somebody; **jemanden in gute Laune versetzen** to put somebody in a good mood

verseuchen (*perf* **hat verseucht**) *vb* **[7]** to contaminate

versichern (*perf* **hat versichert**) *vb* **[88]** ❶ to assure ▷ *Er hat mir versichert, dass das stimmt.* He assured me that this is correct. ❷ to insure ▷ *Wir sind nicht gegen Diebstahl versichert.* We are not insured against theft.

Versicherung *f* insurance

sich **versöhnen** (*perf* **hat sich versöhnt**) *vb* **[84]** to make up ▷ *Na, habt ihr euch wieder versöhnt?* Well, have you two made up again?; **sich mit jemandem versöhnen** to make it up with somebody

versorgen (*perf* **hat versorgt**) *vb* **[7]** to supply ▷ *Von hier aus wird die Stadt mit Elektrizität versorgt.* The town is supplied with electricity from here.; **einen Kranken versorgen** to look after a patient; **eine Familie versorgen** to support a family

sich **verspäten** (*perf* **hat sich verspätet**) *vb* **[2]** to be late

verspätet *adj* late ▷ *die verspätete Ankunft* the late arrival; **der verspätete Flug** the delayed flight; **verspätete Glückwünsche** belated best wishes

Verspätung *f* delay; **Verspätung haben** to be late

versprechen (*pres* **verspricht**, *imperf* **versprach**, *perf* **hat versprochen**) *vb* **[70]** to promise ▷ *Du hast es versprochen.* You promised.; **Ich habe mir von dem Kurs mehr versprochen.** I expected more from this course.

Versprechen (*pl* **Versprechen**) *nt* promise ▷ *Sie hat ihr Versprechen gehalten.* She kept her promise.

Verstand *m* mind ▷ *den Verstand verlieren* to go out of one's mind; **über jemandes Verstand gehen** to be beyond somebody

verständigen (*perf* **hat verständigt**) *vb* **[7]** to inform ▷ *Wir müssen ihre Eltern verständigen.* We must inform her parents.; **sich verständigen** to communicate; **sich auf etwas verständigen** to agree on something

verständlich *adj* understandable; **sich verständlich ausdrücken** to express oneself clearly

verstärken (*perf* **hat verstärkt**) *vb* **[7]** ❶ to strengthen ▷ *Wir müssen den Karton verstärken.* We'll have to strengthen the box. ▷ *ein Team verstärken* to strengthen a team ❷ to amplify ▷ *den Ton verstärken* to amplify the sound; **Das verstärkt die Schmerzen.** That makes the pain worse.

Verstärker (*pl* **Verstärker**) *m* amplifier

Verstärkung *f* reinforcements *pl* ▷ *Wir brauchen Verstärkung.* We need reinforcements.

verstauchen (*perf* **hat verstaucht**) *vb* **[7]** to sprain ▷ *Ich habe mir den Knöchel verstaucht.* I've sprained my ankle.

Versteck (*pl* **Verstecke**) *nt* hiding place

verstecken (*perf* **hat versteckt**) *vb* [**7**] to hide

verstehen (*imperf* **verstand**, *perf* **hat verstanden**) *vb* [**72**] to understand ▷ *Ich habe die Frage nicht verstanden.* I didn't understand the question. ▷ *Ich verstehe nicht.* I don't understand.; **sich verstehen** to get on; **Das versteht sich von selbst.** That goes without saying.

verstopft *adj* ❶ blocked ▷ *ein verstopfter Abfluss* a blocked drain ❷ constipated ▷ *Ich bin seit gestern verstopft.* I've been constipated since yesterday.

verstreuen (*perf* **hat verstreut**) *vb* [**7**] to scatter

Versuch (*pl* **Versuche**) *m* ❶ attempt ▷ *Ich habe den Versuch gemacht, Spanisch zu lernen.* I made an attempt to learn Spanish. ▷ *Sie ist schon beim ersten Versuch gescheitert.* She failed at the very first attempt. ❷ experiment ▷ *Versuche mit Tieren lehnen wir ab.* We disapprove of experiments with animals.

versuchen (*perf* **hat versucht**) *vb* [**84**] to try ▷ *Ich versuche zu kommen.* I'll try to come. ▷ *Willst du mal die Soße versuchen?* Would you like to try the sauce?; **sich an etwas versuchen** to try one's hand at something

vertagen (*perf* **hat vertagt**) *vb* [**7**] to adjourn

vertauschen (*perf* **hat vertauscht**) *vb* [**7**] ❶ to mix up ▷ *Die Babys wurden im Krankenhaus vertauscht.* They mixed the babies up at the hospital. ▷ *Er hat offensichtlich seinen Mantel mit meinem vertauscht.* He must have got his coat and mine mixed up. ❷ to exchange ▷ *Er hat seinen Sportwagen mit einem Familienwagen vertauscht.* He exchanged his sports car for a family car.

verteidigen (*perf* **hat verteidigt**) *vb* [**84**] to defend

Verteidiger (*pl* **Verteidiger**) *m* ❶ defender ▷ *Der Verteidiger wurde gefoult.* The defender was fouled. ❷ defence counsel ▷ *Wer ist der Verteidiger des Angeklagten?* Who's counsel for the defence?

verteilen (*perf* **hat verteilt**) *vb* [**84**] ❶ to hand out ▷ *Sie verteilte die Hefte an die Schüler.* She handed the exercise books out to the pupils. ❷ to spread ▷ *Die Salbe sollte gleichmäßig auf der Haut verteilt werden.* The ointment should be spread evenly over the skin.

Vertrag (*pl* **Verträge**) *m* ❶ contract ▷ *ein Arbeitsvertrag* a contract of employment ❷ treaty ▷ *ein Friedensvertrag* a peace treaty

vertragen (*pres* **verträgt**, *imperf* **vertrug**, *perf* **hat vertragen**) *vb* [**77**] ❶ to be able to stand ▷ *Ich vertrage die Hitze nicht.* I can't stand the heat. ❷ to tolerate ▷ *Ich kann eine solche Behandlung nicht vertragen.* I can't tolerate such treatment.; **sich vertragen** to get along; **sich wieder vertragen** to patch things up

verträglich *adj* ❶ good-natured ▷ *ein verträglicher Mensch* a good-natured person ❷ easily digestible ▷ *Im Sommer sollte man nur leicht verträgliche Speisen zu sich nehmen.* In summer, you should only eat easily digestible food.; **Das Medikament ist gut verträglich.** The drug has no side effects.

vertrauen (*perf* **hat vertraut**) *vb* [**84**] **jemandem vertrauen** to trust somebody; **vertrauen auf** to rely on; **Ich vertraue auf mein Glück.** I'm trusting my luck.

Vertrauen *nt* trust ▷ *Vertrauen zu jemandem haben* to have trust in somebody

vertraulich *adj* ❶ confidential ▷ *ein vertrauliches Gespräch* a confidential talk ❷ familiar ▷ *Ich verbitte mir diesen vertraulichen Ton.* I'll not have you talking to me in such familiar way.

vertraut *adj* familiar ▷ *vertraute Gesichter* familiar faces
vertreiben (*imperf* **vertrieb**, *perf* **hat vertrieben**) *vb* ❶ to drive ▷ *Er hat uns von seinem Grundstück vertrieben.* He drove us off his land. ❷ to sell ▷ *Wir vertreiben Hardware und Software.* We sell hardware and software.; **sich die Zeit vertreiben** to pass the time
vertreten (*pres* **vertritt**, *imperf* **vertrat**, *perf* **hat vertreten**) *vb* **[79]** ❶ to stand in for ▷ *Während ich in Urlaub bin, vertritt mich Frau Wengel.* While I'm on holiday, Mrs Wengel's standing in for me. ❷ to represent ▷ *Die Lobby vertritt die Interessen der Wirtschaft.* The lobby represents business interests.; **eine Meinung vertreten** to hold an opinion; **sich den Fuß vertreten** to twist one's ankle; **sich die Beine vertreten** to stretch one's legs
Vertreter (*pl* **Vertreter**) *m* sales representative ▷ *Er ist Vertreter für Collins.* He's a sales representative for Collins.
Vertrieb (*pl* **Vertriebe**) *m* ❶ sale ▷ *Der Vertrieb von Raubkopien steht unter Strafe.* The sale of pirate copies is punishable by law. ❷ marketing department ▷ *Sie arbeitet im Vertrieb.* She works in the marketing department.
sich **vertun** (*imperf* **vertat sich**, *perf* **hat sich vertan**) *vb* **[81]** to make a mistake
verunglücken (*perf* **ist verunglückt**) *vb* **[84]** to have an accident ▷ *Sie sind mit dem Auto verunglückt.* They've had a car accident.
verursachen (*perf* **hat verursacht**) *vb* **[84]** to cause
verurteilen (*perf* **hat verurteilt**) *vb* **[84]** to condemn
Verwaltung *f* administration ▷ *Er arbeitet in der Verwaltung.* He works in administration.
verwandt *adj* **mit jemandem verwandt sein** to be related to somebody
Verwandte (*gen* **Verwandten**, *pl* **Verwandten**) *mf* relative ▷ *Ein Verwandter von mir ist gestern gestorben.* A relative of mine died yesterday.
Verwandtschaft *f* relations *pl* ▷ *Die ganze Verwandtschaft war eingeladen.* All my relations were invited.
verwechseln (*perf* **hat verwechselt**) *vb* **[34]** ❶ to confuse ▷ *Du darfst die beiden Begriffe nicht verwechseln.* You mustn't confuse the two ideas. ❷ to mix up ▷ *Sie haben offensichtlich die Mäntel verwechselt.* They must have got their coats mixed up.; **verwechseln mit (1)** to confuse with ▷ *Ich verwechsle 'akut' immer mit 'aktuell'.* I always confuse 'akut' with 'aktuell'. **(2)** to mistake for ▷ *Ich habe dich mit deiner Schwester verwechselt.* I mistook you for your sister.; **Sie sind zum Verwechseln ähnlich.** They're the spitting image of each other.
Verwechslung *f* mix-up
verweigern (*perf* **hat verweigert**) *vb* **[88]** **jemandem etwas verweigern** to refuse somebody something; **den Gehorsam verweigern** to refuse to obey; **die Aussage verweigern** to refuse to testify
Verweis (*gen* **Verweises**, *pl* **Verweise**) *m* reprimand ▷ *Er hat für sein Zuspätkommen einen schweren Verweis bekommen.* He was given a severe reprimand for being late.
verwelken (*perf* **ist verwelkt**) *vb* **[7]** to fade
verwenden (*imperf* **verwendete** *or* **verwandte**, *perf* **hat verwendet** *or* **verwandt**) *vb* ❶ to use ▷ *Verwenden Sie einen Computer?* Do you use a computer? ❷ (*effort, time, work*) to spend ▷ *Ich habe auf diesen Aufsatz viel Zeit verwendet.* I spent a lot of time on this essay.
verwerten (*perf* **hat verwertet**) *vb* **[2]** to utilize

verwirren (*perf* **hat verwirrt**) *vb* [**84**] ❶ to confuse ▷ *Jetzt hast du mich total verwirrt.* Now you've completely confused me. ❷ *(thread)* to tangle up ▷ *Die Katze hat die Wolle verwirrt.* The cat's tangled the wool up.

verwöhnen (*perf* **hat verwöhnt**) *vb* [**84**] to spoil

verwunden (*perf* **hat verwundet**) *vb* [**7**] to wound

Verwundete (*gen* **Verwundeten**, *pl* **Verwundeten**) *mf* injured person ▷ *Der Arzt versorgt gerade einen Verwundeten.* The doctor is just attending to an injured person.

Verwundung *f* injury

Verzeichnis (*gen* **Verzeichnisses**, *pl* **Verzeichnisse**) *nt* list ▷ *Am Ende des Buches ist ein Verzeichnis aller Fachbegriffe.* At the end of the book there's a list of all the technical terms.; **das Inhaltsverzeichnis** the table of contents

verzeihen (*imperf* **verzieh**, *perf* **hat verziehen**) *vb* to forgive ▷ *jemandem etwas verzeihen* to forgive somebody for something

Verzeihung *f* forgiveness; **Verzeihung! (1)** sorry ▷ *Verzeihung, ich wollte Sie nicht treten.* Sorry, I didn't mean to kick you. **(2)** excuse me ▷ *Verzeihung, aber können Sie mir sagen, wie spät es ist?* Excuse me, could you tell me what time it is?

verzichten (*perf* **hat verzichtet**) *vb* [**2**] **auf etwas verzichten (1)** to do without something ▷ *Ich werde heute wohl auf meinen Mittagsschlaf verzichten müssen.* It looks like I'll have to do without my afternoon nap today. ▷ *Ich verzichte auf deine Hilfe.* I can do without your help. **(2)** to forego something ▷ *Er hat auf eine Bezahlung verzichtet.* He forewent payment. ▷ *Ich verzichte nicht auf meine Rechte.* I won't forego my rights.

Verzierung *f* decoration

verzögern (*perf* **hat verzögert**) *vb* [**88**] to delay

Verzögerung *f* delay

verzweifeln (*perf* **ist verzweifelt**) *vb* [**7**] to despair

verzweifelt *adj* desperate

Verzweiflung *f* despair

Vetter (*pl* **Vettern**) *m* cousin

Videogerät (*pl* **Videogeräte**) *nt* video recorder

Videorekorder (*pl* **Videorekorder**) *m* video recorder

Vieh *nt* cattle *pl* ▷ *Das Vieh ist auf der Weide.* The cattle are out in the meadow.

viel *adj, adv* ❶ a lot of ▷ *Sie haben viel Arbeit.* They've got a lot of work. ❷ much ▷ *Wir haben nicht viel Geld.* We haven't got much money. ▷ *Wir haben nicht viel gelernt.* We didn't learn much.; **Vielen Dank!** Thank you very much. ❸ a lot ▷ *Wir haben viel gesehen.* We saw a lot.; **viel zu wenig** far too little; **Viel Glück!** Good luck.; **so viel** so much; **so viel wie** as much as; **wie viel?** how much?; **zu viel** too much

viele *pron pl* ❶ a lot of ▷ *Sie hat viele Bücher.* She's got a lot of books. ❷ many ▷ *Er hat nicht viele Fehler gemacht.* He didn't make many mistakes. ▷ *Viele Schüler mögen Chemie nicht.* Many pupils don't like chemistry.; **Viele wissen das nicht.** A lot of people don't know that.

vieles *pron* many things *pl* ▷ *Vieles war neu für mich.* Many things were new to me.

vielleicht *adv* perhaps

vielmals *adv* **Danke vielmals!** Many thanks!

vielseitig *adj* many-sided

vielversprechend *adj* promising

vier *num* four

Vier *f* ❶ four ❷ adequate
German marks range from one (**sehr gut**) to six (**ungenügend**).

Viereck (*pl* **Vierecke**) *nt* ❶ rectangle ❷ square

viereckig *adj* ❶ rectangular ❷ square
vierte *adj* fourth ▷ *Sie hat erst beim vierten Klingeln abgenommen.* She didn't answer until the fourth ring. ▷ *Er kam als Vierter.* He was the fourth to arrive.
Viertel (*pl* **Viertel**) *nt* quarter ▷ *Viertel vor zwei* quarter to two
Vierteljahr (*pl* **Vierteljahre**) *nt* quarter
vierteln *vb* [**88**] ❶ to divide by four ▷ *wenn man den Betrag viertelt ...* if you divide the amount by four ... ❷ to cut into quarters ▷ *Sie hat den Kuchen geviertelt.* She cut the cake into quarters.
Viertelstunde *f* quarter of an hour
vierzehn *num* fourteen; **in vierzehn Tagen** in a fortnight
vierzig *num* forty
Villa (*pl* **Villen**) *f* villa
virtuell *adj* virtual ▷ *die virtuelle Realität* virtual reality
Visitenkarte *f* business card
Visum (*pl* **Visa**) *nt* visa
Vitamin (*pl* **Vitamine**) *nt* vitamin
Vogel (*pl* **Vögel**) *m* bird; **einen Vogel haben** *(informal)* to have a screw loose; **jemandem den Vogel zeigen** to make a rude sign

> Word for word, **jemandem den Vogel zeigen** means 'to show somebody the bird'.

> In Germany you make a rude sign at somebody by tapping your forehead to show that you think they are stupid.

Vokabel *f* word
Vokabular (*pl* **Vokabulare**) *nt* vocabulary
Vokal (*pl* **Vokale**) *m* vowel
Volk (*pl* **Völker**) *nt* ❶ people ▷ *das einfache Volk* the simple people ❷ nation ▷ *das deutsche Volk* the German nation
Volksfest (*pl* **Volksfeste**) *nt* fair
Volkshochschule *f* adult education classes *pl*
Volkswirtschaft *f* economics *sg*
voll *adj* full; **voll und ganz** completely; **jemanden für voll nehmen** to take somebody seriously
völlig *adj, adv* ❶ complete ▷ *bis zur völligen Erschöpfung* to the point of complete exhaustion ❷ completely ▷ *Das ist völlig unmöglich.* That's completely impossible. ▷ *Ich bin völlig deiner Meinung.* I completely agree with you.
volljährig *adj* of age ▷ *volljährig werden* to come of age
vollkommen *adj* perfect ▷ *vollkommen richtig* perfectly right; **vollkommen unmöglich** completely impossible
Vollkornbrot (*pl* **Vollkornbrote**) *nt* wholemeal bread
vollmachen *vb* [**48**] to fill up
Vollmacht *f* power of attorney
Vollmond *m* full moon ▷ *bei Vollmond* at full moon
Vollpension *f* full board
vollständig *adj* complete
volltanken *vb* [**4**] to fill up *(car)*
vom = **von dem**
von *prep*

> **von** takes the dative.

❶ from ▷ *von Hamburg nach Kiel* from Hamburg to Kiel; **von ... bis** from ... to; **von ... an** from ...; **von ... aus** from ...; **etwas von sich aus tun** to do something of one's own accord; **von mir aus** I don't mind; **Von wo bist du?** Where are you from?; **Von wann ist der Brief?** When's the letter from? ❷ by ▷ *Ich bin von einem Hund gebissen worden.* I was bitten by a dog. ▷ *ein Gedicht von Schiller* a poem by Schiller; **von etwas kommen** to be caused by something ❸ of ▷ *ein Freund von mir* a friend of mine ▷ *Wie nett von dir!* How nice of you!; **jeweils zwei von zehn** two out of every ten ❹ about ▷ *Er erzählte vom Urlaub.* He talked about his holiday.; **Von wegen!** *(informal)* No way!

voneinander *adv* from each other

vor *prep, adv*

> Use the accusative to express movement or a change of place. Use the dative when there is no change of place.

❶ in front of ▷ *Er stand vor dem Spiegel.* He stood in front of the mirror. ▷ *Stell den Stuhl vor das Fenster.* Put the chair in front of the window. ❷ before ▷ *Der Artikel steht vor dem Substantiv.* The article goes before the noun. ▷ *Vor der Kirche links abbiegen.* Turn left just before you get to the church. ▷ *Ich war vor ihm da.* I was there before him. ❸ ago ▷ *vor zwei Tagen* two days ago ▷ *vor einem Jahr* a year ago; **Es ist fünf vor vier.** It's five to four.; **vor Kurzem** a little while ago ❹ with ▷ *vor Wut* with rage ▷ *vor Liebe* with love; **vor Hunger sterben** to die of hunger; **vor lauter Arbeit** because of work; **vor allem** above all; **vor und zurück** backwards and forwards

vorankommen (*imperf* **kam voran**, *perf* **ist vorangekommen**) *vb* [**40**] to make progress

voraus *adv* ahead ▷ *Fahr du schon mal voraus.* You go on ahead. ▷ *Er war seiner Zeit voraus.* He was ahead of his time.; **im Voraus** in advance

vorausgehen (*imperf* **ging voraus**, *perf* **ist vorausgegangen**) *vb* [**29**] ❶ to go on ahead ▷ *Geht ihr voraus, ich komme nach.* Go on ahead, I'll catch up with you. ❷ to precede ▷ *Der Schlägerei ging ein Streit voraus.* The fight was preceded by an argument.

voraussetzen (*perf* **hat vorausgesetzt**) *vb* [**15**] to assume ▷ *Ich setze voraus, dass du auch kommst.* I assume that you're coming too.; **vorausgesetzt, dass ...** provided that ...

Voraussetzung *f* prerequisite; **unter der Voraussetzung, dass ...** provided that ...

voraussichtlich *adv* probably

vorbei *adv* past ▷ *Fahren Sie am Rathaus vorbei.* Drive past the town hall.; **Ich sehe noch kurz bei ihr vorbei.** I'll just pop round to her place.; **vorbei sein** o be over

vorbeigehen (*imperf* **ging vorbei**, *perf* **ist vorbeigegangen**) *vb* [**29**] to go past ▷ *Er ging vorbei, ohne zu grüßen.* He went past without saying hello.; **an etwas vorbeigehen** to go past something; **bei jemandem vorbeigehen** to call in at somebody's

vorbeikommen (*imperf* **kam vorbei**, *perf* **ist vorbeigekommen**) *vb* [**40**] **bei jemandem vorbeikommen** to drop in on somebody

vorbereiten (*perf* **hat vorbereitet**) *vb* [**2**] to prepare

Vorbereitung *f* preparation

vorbeugen (*perf* **hat vorgebeugt**) *vb* [**4**] **sich vorbeugen** to lean forward; **einer Sache vorbeugen** to prevent something

Vorbild (*pl* **Vorbilder**) *nt* role model ▷ *Er ist mein Vorbild.* He's my role model.; **sich jemanden zum Vorbild nehmen** to follow somebody's example

vordere *adj* front ▷ *Das Haus hat einen vorderen und einen hinteren Eingang.* The house has a front door and a back door.

Vorderseite *f* front

vorderste *adj* front ▷ *die vorderste Reihe* the front row

voreilig *adj* hasty ▷ *Du solltest nicht voreilig urteilen.* You shouldn't make hasty judgements.

vorerst *adv* for the moment

Vorfahrt *f* right of way; **Vorfahrt achten!** Give way!

Vorfall (*pl* **Vorfälle**) *m* incident

vorführen (*perf* **hat vorgeführt**) *vb* [**4**] to show

vorgehen (*imperf* **ging vor**, *perf* **ist vorgegangen**) *vb* [**29**] ❶ to go on ahead ▷ *Geht ihr vor, ich komme nach.* Go on ahead, I'll catch up. ❷ to go up to

▷ *Sie ging ans Rednerpult vor.* She went up to the lectern. ❸ to proceed ▷ *Ich weiß nicht, wie wir vorgehen sollen.* I don't know how we should proceed.; **Die Uhr geht vor.** The clock is fast.; **Was geht hier vor?** What's going on here?

vorgestern *adv* the day before yesterday

vorhaben (*pres* **hat vor**, *imperf* **hatte vor**, *perf* **hat vorgehabt**) *vb* [**32**] to intend ▷ *Wir haben vor, nach Italien zu fahren.* We intend to go to Italy. ▷ *Was hast du vor?* What do you intend to do?; **Ich habe heute viel vor.** I've got a lot planned for today.; **Hast du schon was vor?** Have you got anything on?; **Was hast du heute Abend vor?** What are you doing this evening?

Vorhang (*pl* **Vorhänge**) *m* curtain

vorher *adv* beforehand

Vorhersage *f* forecast

vorhersehbar *adj* predictable

vorhersehen (*pres* **sieht vorher**, *imperf* **sah vorher**, *perf* **hat vorhergesehen**) *vb* [**64**] to foresee

vorhin *adv* just now

vorig *adj* previous

vorkommen (*imperf* **kam vor**, *perf* **ist vorgekommen**) *vb* [**40**] ❶ to happen ▷ *So ein Fehler sollte nicht vorkommen.* A mistake like that shouldn't happen.; **Es kommt vor, dass ich früh ins Bett gehe.** I sometimes go to bed early.; **jemandem vorkommen** to seem to somebody; **sich dumm vorkommen** to feel stupid ❷ to come out ▷ *Komm endlich hinter dem Schrank vor.* Come out from behind that cupboard, will you?

vorläufig *adj* provisional

vorlaut *adj* impertinent

vorlesen (*pres* **liest vor**, *imperf* **las vor**, *perf* **hat vorgelesen**) *vb* [**45**] to read out

vorletzte *adj* last but one ▷ *Ich wohne im vorletzten Haus.* My house is the last but one.

Vorliebe *f* partiality; **eine Vorliebe für etwas haben** to be partial to something

Vormittag (*pl* **Vormittage**) *m* morning ▷ *am Vormittag* in the morning

vormittags *adv* in the morning

vorn *adv* in front ▷ *Der deutsche Schwimmer liegt vorn.* The German swimmer is in front.; **Er stand ganz vorn in der Schlange.** He was right at the front of the queue.; **nach vorn** to the front; **von vorn anfangen** to start at the beginning; **wieder von vorn anfangen** to start again from the beginning

Vorname (*gen* **Vornamens**, *pl* **Vornamen**) *m* first name

vornehm *adj* ❶ distinguished ▷ *eine vornehme Familie* a distinguished family ❷ refined ▷ *sich vornehm ausdrücken* to use refined language ▷ *vornehme Manieren* refined manners ❸ posh ▷ *ein vornehmes Hotel* a posh hotel ❹ elegant ▷ *eine vornehme Dame* an elegant lady

vornehmen (*pres* **nimmt vor**, *imperf* **nahm vor**, *perf* **hat vorgenommen**) *vb* [**52**] **sich etwas vornehmen** to resolve to do something

vornherein *adv* **von vornherein** from the start

Vorort (*pl* **Vororte**) *m* suburb

Vorrat (*pl* **Vorräte**) *m* stock ▷ *solange der Vorrat reicht* while stocks last

vorrätig *adj* in stock

Vorschlag (*pl* **Vorschläge**) *m* suggestion

vorschlagen (*pres* **schlägt vor**, *imperf* **schlug vor**, *perf* **hat vorgeschlagen**) *vb* [**59**] to suggest

Vorschrift *f* rule ▷ *Das ist gegen die Vorschriften.* It's against the rules.

Vorsicht *f* caution; **Vorsicht! (1)** Look out! **(2)** Caution!; **Vorsicht, Stufe!** Mind the step!

vorsichtig *adj* careful

Vorspeise *f* starter

Vorsprung (*pl* **Vorsprünge**) *m* lead ▷ *Wir haben einen Vorsprung vor unseren Konkurrenten gewonnen.* We have gained a lead over our competitors.
Vorstadt (*pl* **Vorstädte**) *f* suburbs *pl*
vorstellbar *adj* conceivable
vorstellen (*perf* **hat vorgestellt**) *vb* [**4**] **sich etwas vorstellen** to imagine something; **jemanden jemandem vorstellen** to introduce somebody to somebody
Vorstellung *f* ❶ performance ▷ *Die Vorstellung endet gegen zehn Uhr.* The performance ends at about ten. ❷ idea ▷ *Hast du eine Vorstellung, wie wir das machen sollen?* Have you got any idea how we should do that? ▷ *Du hast ja keine Vorstellung, wie weh das tut.* You've no idea how much it hurts.
Vorstellungsgespräch (*pl* **Vorstellungsgespräche**) *nt* interview (*for job*)
Vorteil (*pl* **Vorteile**) *m* advantage; **im Vorteil sein** to have the advantage
Vortrag (*pl* **Vorträge**) *m* talk ▷ *einen Vortrag halten* to give a talk
vorüber *adv* over
vorübergehend *adj* ❶ passing ▷ *eine vorübergehende Phase* a passing phase ❷ temporarily ▷ *Das Geschäft ist vorübergehend geschlossen.* The shop's temporarily closed.
Vorurteil (*pl* **Vorurteile**) *nt* prejudice
Vorwahl *f* dialling code ▷ *Was ist die Vorwahl von Liverpool?* What's the dialling code for Liverpool?
Vorwand (*pl* **Vorwände**) *m* pretext
vorwärts *adv* forward
vorwerfen (*pres* **wirft vor**, *imperf* **warf vor**, *perf* **hat vorgeworfen**) *vb* [**92**] **jemandem etwas vorwerfen** to accuse somebody of something; **sich nichts vorzuwerfen haben** to have nothing to reproach oneself for
vorwiegend *adv* predominantly
Vorwort (*pl* **Vorworte**) *nt* preface
Vorwurf (*pl* **Vorwürfe**) *m* reproach; **jemandem Vorwürfe machen** to reproach somebody; **sich Vorwürfe machen** to reproach oneself
vorziehen (*imperf* **zog vor**, *perf* **hat vorgezogen**) *vb* [**96**] ❶ to prefer ▷ *Was ziehst du vor: Kaffee oder Tee?* Do you prefer coffee or tea? ❷ to pull forward ▷ *Du solltest den Stuhl etwas vorziehen.* You should pull your chair forward a bit.
vulgär *adj* vulgar ▷ *sich vulgär ausdrücken* to use vulgar language
Vulkan (*pl* **Vulkane**) *m* volcano

W

Waage *f* ❶ scales *pl* ▷ *Die Waage stimmt nicht genau.* The scales aren't accurate. ❷ Libra ▷ *Ulla ist Waage.* Ulla's Libra.

waagerecht *adj* horizontal

wach *adj* **wach sein** to be awake

Wache *f* guard ▷ *Wache stehen* to stand guard

Wachs (*gen* **Wachses**, *pl* **Wachse**) *nt* wax

wachsen (*pres* **wächst**, *imperf* **wuchs**, *perf* **ist gewachsen**) *vb* [**87**] to grow

Wachstum *nt* growth

wackelig *adj* wobbly

Wade *f* calf ▷ *Ich habe mich an der Wade verletzt.* I've hurt my calf.

Waffe *f* weapon

Waffel *f* ❶ waffle ▷ *Heute gab's zum Mittagessen Waffeln.* We had waffles for lunch today. ❷ wafer ▷ *Willst du eine Waffel zu deinem Eis?* Would you like a wafer with your ice?

wagen *vb* [**38**] **es wagen, etwas zu tun** to dare to do something; **sich irgendwohin wagen** to dare to go somewhere

Wagen (*pl* **Wagen**) *m* ❶ car ▷ *Seid ihr mit dem Wagen da?* Did you come by car? ❷ carriage ▷ *ein Eisenbahnwagen* a railway carriage; **ein Pferdewagen** a cart

Wagenheber (*pl* **Wagenheber**) *m* jack *(for car)*

Wahl (*pl* **Wahlen**) *f* ❶ choice ▷ *Du hast die Wahl.* It's your choice. ❷ election ▷ *Wann sind die nächsten Wahlen?* When are the next elections?

wählen *vb* [**38**] ❶ to choose ▷ *Du kannst wählen, entweder das rote oder das grüne.* You can choose, either the red one or the green one. ❷ to vote ▷ *Wer wurde zum Klassensprecher gewählt?* Who was voted class representative?; **Wählt Kowalski!** Vote for Kowalski.; **Nächsten Sonntag wird gewählt.** There are elections next Sunday. ❸ to dial ▷ *Sie wählte die Nummer ihrer Freundin.* She dialled her friend's number.

wählerisch *adj* particular

Wahlfach (*pl* **Wahlfächer**) *nt* optional subject

Wahnsinn *m* madness

wahnsinnig *adj, adv* ❶ mad ▷ *Wer hatte denn diese wahnsinnige Idee?* Whose mad idea was it? ❷ incredibly ▷ *Das Kleid war wahnsinnig schön.* The dress was incredibly pretty. ▷ *Das tut wahnsinnig weh.* It's incredibly sore.

wahr *adj* true ▷ *eine wahre Geschichte* a true story; **Sie ist verheiratet, nicht wahr?** She's married, isn't she?

während *prep, conj*

> The preposition **während** takes the genitive.

❶ during ▷ *Was hast du während der Ferien gemacht?* What did you do during the holidays? ❷ while ▷ *Sie sah fern, während sie ihre Hausaufgaben machte.* She was watching TV while she was doing her homework. ❸ whereas

▷ *Er ist ganz nett, während seine Frau unhöflich ist.* He's quite nice, whereas his wife's impolite.

Wahrheit *f* truth

wahrnehmen (*pres* **nimmt wahr**, *imperf* **nahm wahr**, *perf* **hat wahrgenommen**) *vb* **[52]** to perceive

Wahrsager (*pl* **Wahrsager**) *m* fortune teller

Wahrsagerin *f* fortune teller

wahrscheinlich *adj, adv* ❶ likely ▷ *Das ist nicht sehr wahrscheinlich.* That's not very likely. ❷ probably ▷ *Er kommt wahrscheinlich nicht.* He's probably not coming.

Währung *f* currency

Wal (*pl* **Wale**) *m* whale

Wald (*pl* **Wälder**) *m* ❶ wood ▷ *Hinter unserem Haus ist ein Wald.* There's a wood behind our house. ❷ forest ▷ *die Wälder Kanadas* the forests of Canada

Wales *nt* Wales

Walfisch (*pl* **Walfische**) *m* whale

Waliser (*pl* **Waliser**) *m* Welshman; **Er ist Waliser.** He's Welsh.; **die Waliser** the Welsh

Waliserin *f* Welshwoman; **Sie ist Waliserin.** She's Welsh.

walisisch *adj* Welsh

Walnuss (*pl* **Walnüsse**) *f* walnut

Wand (*pl* **Wände**) *f* wall

Wanderer (*pl* **Wanderer**) *m* rambler

Wanderin *f* rambler

wandern (*perf* **ist gewandert**) *vb* **[88]** to hike ▷ *Wir sind am Wochenende gewandert.* We went hiking at the weekend.

Wanderung *f* hike

Wandschrank (*pl* **Wandschränke**) *m* wall cupboard

wann *adv* when

war *vb see* **sein**

Ware *f* goods *pl*

Warenhaus (*gen* **Warenhauses**, *pl* **Warenhäuser**) *nt* department store

warf *vb see* **werfen**

warm *adj* warm ▷ *Heute ist es wärmer als gestern.* It's warmer today than yesterday.; **ein warmes Essen** a hot meal; **Mir ist warm.** I'm warm.

Wärme *f* warmth

Wärmflasche *f* hot-water bottle

warnen *vb* **[38]** to warn ▷ *jemanden vor etwas warnen* to warn somebody of something

Warnung *f* warning

warten *vb* **[2]** to wait ▷ *Ich habe eine Stunde gewartet.* I waited an hour.; **warten auf** to wait for; **auf sich warten lassen** to take a long time

Wartesaal (*pl* **Wartesäle**) *m* waiting room *(in station)*

Wartezimmer (*pl* **Wartezimmer**) *nt* waiting room

warum *adv* why

was *pron* ❶ what ▷ *Was hast du gesagt?* What did you say? ▷ *Was für eine Enttäuschung!* What a disappointment!; **Was für ein ...** What kind of ... ❷ something ▷ *Heute gibt's was Leckeres zum Mittagessen.* We're having something delicious for lunch today.

Waschbecken (*pl* **Waschbecken**) *nt* washbasin

Wäsche *f* washing ▷ *Wäsche waschen* to do the washing; **die Bettwäsche** bed linen; **die Unterwäsche** underwear

Wäscheklammer *f* clothes peg

waschen (*pres* **wäscht**, *imperf* **wusch**, *perf* **hat gewaschen**) *vb* **[89]** to wash; **sich waschen** to have a wash; **sich die Hände waschen** to wash one's hands

Waschmaschine *f* washing machine

Waschmittel (*pl* **Waschmittel**) *nt* detergent

Waschpulver (*pl* **Waschpulver**) *nt* washing powder

Waschsalon (*pl* **Waschsalons**) *m* launderette

Wasser (*pl* **Wasser** *or* **Wässer**) *nt* water

wasserdicht *adj* waterproof

Wasserfall (*pl* **Wasserfälle**) *m* waterfall

Wasserhahn (*pl* **Wasserhähne**) *m* tap

Wassermann *m* Aquarius ▷ *Gerda ist Wassermann.* Gerda's Aquarius.

Wassermelone *f* water melon

Wasserstoff *m* hydrogen

Watte *f* cotton wool

Webseite *f* web page

Wechsel (*pl* **Wechsel**) *m* change

Wechselkurs (*gen* **Wechselkurses**, *pl* **Wechselkurse**) *m* rate of exchange

wechseln *vb* [**34**] ❶ to change ▷ *Wir mussten einen Reifen wechseln.* We had to change a tyre. ▷ *Wie viel Geld wechselst du?* How much money are you changing?; **Blicke wechseln** to exchange glances ❷ to have change ▷ *Können Sie wechseln?* Do you have any change? ▷ *Kannst du mir zwanzig Euro in Münzen wechseln?* Have you got change for twenty euros?

Wechselstube *f* bureau de change

wecken *vb* [**38**] to wake up

Wecker (*pl* **Wecker**) *m* alarm clock

weder *conj* neither; **weder ... noch ...** neither ... nor ...

weg *adv* away ▷ *Geh weg!* Go away!; **Weg da!** Out of the way!; **Finger weg!** Hands off!; **Er war schon weg.** He'd already left.

Weg (*pl* **Wege**) *m* ❶ way ▷ *Es gibt sicher einen Weg, das zu reparieren.* There must be a way to repair it. ❷ path ▷ *Ein Weg führte zur Kapelle hinauf.* A path led up to the chapel. ❸ route ▷ *Welchen Weg habt ihr genommen?* Which route did you take?; **sich auf den Weg machen** to be on one's way; **jemandem aus dem Weg gehen** to keep out of somebody's way

wegen *prep*

> The preposition **wegen** takes the dative or sometimes the genitive.

because of ▷ *Wegen dir bin ich zu spät gekommen.* Because of you I arrived late. ▷ *Wegen des schlechten Wetters wurde die Veranstaltung abgesagt.* The event was cancelled because of the bad weather.

weggehen (*imperf* **ging weg**, *perf* **ist weggegangen**) *vb* [**29**] to go away

weglassen (*pres* **lässt weg**, *imperf* **ließ weg**, *perf* **hat weggelassen**) *vb* [**42**] to leave out

weglaufen (*pres* **läuft weg**, *imperf* **lief weg**, *perf* **ist weggelaufen**) *vb* [**43**] to run away

wegmachen (*perf* **hat weggemacht**) *vb* [**48**] to get rid of ▷ *einen Fleck wegmachen* to get rid of a stain

wegnehmen (*pres* **nimmt weg**, *imperf* **nahm weg**, *perf* **hat weggenommen**) *vb* [**52**] to take away

wegtun (*imperf* **tat weg**, *perf* **hat weggetan**) *vb* [**81**] to put away

Wegweiser (*pl* **Wegweiser**) *m* signpost

wegwerfen (*pres* **wirft weg**, *imperf* **warf weg**, *perf* **hat weggeworfen**) *vb* [**92**] to throw away

weh *adj see* **wehtun**

sich **wehren** *vb* [**38**] to defend oneself

wehtun (*imperf* **tat weh**, *perf* **hat wehgetan**) *vb* [**81**] ❶ to hurt ▷ *Mein Bein tut weh.* My leg hurts. ❷ to be sore ▷ *Mein Hals tut weh.* My throat's sore.; **sich wehtun** to hurt oneself; **jemandem wehtun** to hurt somebody

weiblich *adj* feminine ▷ *ein weibliches Substantiv* a feminine noun

weich *adj* soft ▷ *ein weiches Bett* a soft bed

sich **weigern** *vb* [**88**] to refuse

Weihnachten (*gen* **Weihnachten**) *nt* Christmas ▷ *an Weihnachten* at Christmas; **Frohe Weihnachten!** Merry Christmas.

Weihnachtsferien *pl* Christmas holidays *pl*

Weihnachtslied (*pl* **Weihnachtslieder**) *nt* Christmas carol
Weihnachtsmann (*pl* **Weihnachtsmänner**) *m* Father Christmas
Weihnachtsmarkt (*pl* **Weihnachtsmärkte**) *m* Christmas fair
Weihnachtstag (*pl* **Weihnachtstage**) *m* **der erste Weihnachtstag** Christmas Day

> Word for word, **der erste Weihnachtstag** means 'the first day of Christmas'.

der zweite Weihnachtstag Boxing Day

> Word for word, **der zweite Weihnachtstag** means 'the second day of Christmas'.

weil *conj* because
Weile *f* while ▷ *Es wird eine Weile dauern.* It'll take a while.
Wein (*pl* **Weine**) *m* wine
Weinberg (*pl* **Weinberge**) *m* vineyard

> Word for word, **Weinberg** means 'wine mountain'.

Weinbrand (*pl* **Weinbrände**) *m* brandy
weinen *vb* [**38**] to cry; **Das ist zum Weinen.** It's enough to make you cry.
Weinglas (*gen* **Weinglases**, *pl* **Weingläser**) *nt* wine glass
Weinkarte *f* wine list
Weinkeller (*pl* **Weinkeller**) *m* ❶ wine cellar ❷ wine bar
Weinstube *f* wine bar
Weintraube *f* grape
Weise *f* way ▷ *Die Art und Weise, wie er uns behandelt hat.* The way he treated us.; **auf diese Weise** in this way
Weisheit *f* wisdom
weiß *vb see* **wissen**
▶ *adj* white
Weißbrot (*pl* **Weißbrote**) *nt* white bread
Weißwein (*pl* **Weißweine**) *m* white wine
weit *adj, adv* ❶ long ▷ *Das ist eine weite Reise.* That's a long journey. ▷ *Das war sein weitester Wurf.* That was his longest throw. ❷ far ▷ *Wie weit ist es ...?* How far is it ...? ▷ *Nach Berlin ist es weiter als nach München.* It's further to Berlin than to Munich. ▷ *so weit wie möglich* as far as possible ▷ *Das geht zu weit.* That's going too far. ❸ baggy ▷ *Sie hatte einen weiten Pulli an.* She was wearing a baggy pullover.; **ein weiter Begriff** a broad idea; **so weit sein** to be ready; **Ich bin so weit zufrieden.** By and large I'm quite satisfied.
weitaus *adv* by far
weiter *adj, adv* further ▷ *Wenn du noch weitere Fragen hast ...* If you have any further questions ... ▷ *Alles Weitere besprechen wir morgen.* We can discuss any further details tomorrow.; **ohne weiteres** just like that; **weiter nichts** nothing else; **weiter niemand** nobody else
Weiterbildung *f* further education
weitergehen (*imperf* **ging weiter**, *perf* **ist weitergegangen**) *vb* [**29**] to go on
weiterhin *adv* **etwas weiterhin tun** to go on doing something
weiterleiten (*perf* **hat weitergeleitet**) *vb* [**4**] to pass on
weitermachen (*perf* **hat weitergemacht**) *vb* [**48**] to continue
Weitsprung *m* long jump
Weizen *m* wheat
welche *pron* ❶ which ▷ *Welcher Mann?* Which man? ▷ *Welche Frau?* Which woman? ▷ *Welches Mädchen?* Which girl? ▷ *Welcher von beiden?* Which of the two? ▷ *Welchen hast du genommen?* Which one did you take? ❷ what ▷ *Welch eine Überraschung!* What a surprise!; **Welche Freude!** What joy! ❸ some ▷ *Ich habe Kirschen, willst du welche?* I have some cherries, would you like some? ▷ *Ich habe welche.* I have some. ❹ any ▷ *Ich brauche Briefmarken, hast du welche?* I need stamps, have you got any? ▷ *Ich brauche Kleingeld, hast du welches?* I need change, have you got any?

Welle *f* wave
Wellenlänge *f* wavelength
Wellensittich (*pl* **Wellensittiche**) *m* budgie
Welt *f* world
Weltall *nt* universe
weltberühmt *adj* world-famous
Weltkrieg (*pl* **Weltkriege**) *m* world war
Weltmeister (*pl* **Weltmeister**) *m* world champion
Weltraum *m* space
weltweit *adj, adv* worldwide
wem *pron*
wem is the dative of **wer**.
to whom; **Mit wem bist du gekommen?** Who did you come with?
wen *pron*
wen is the accusative of **wer**.
whom; **Wen hast du gesehen?** Who did you see?
wenig *adj, adv* little; **so wenig wie** as little as; **zu wenig** too little
wenige *pron pl* few *pl* ▷ *Das wissen nur wenige.* Only a few people know that.
weniger *adj, adv* ❶ less ▷ *Ich habe weniger Geld als du.* I have less money than you. ❷ fewer ▷ *Ich habe weniger Fehler gemacht.* I've made fewer mistakes. ❸ minus ▷ *Zehn weniger drei ist sieben.* Ten minus three is seven.
wenigste *adj* least ▷ *Das ist das wenigste, was ich tun kann.* That's the least I can do.; **am wenigsten** the least
wenigstens *adv* at least
wenn *conj* ❶ if ▷ *Wenn er anruft, sag mir Bescheid.* If he calls, tell me.; **selbst wenn ...** even if ...; **wenn ich doch ...** if only I ... ❷ when ▷ *Wenn ich nach Hause komme, dusche ich erst mal.* When I get home, the first thing I'm going to do is have a shower.; **immer wenn** whenever
wer *pron* who
Be careful! **wer** does not mean **where**.
werben (*pres* **wirbt**, *imperf* **warb**, *perf* **hat geworben**) *vb* [**90**] to advertise ▷ *Im Fernsehen wird zu viel geworben.* There's too much advertising on TV.; **Mitglieder werben** to recruit members
Werbespot (*pl* **Werbespots**) *m* commercial
Werbung *f* ❶ advert ▷ *Hast du die Werbung für den neuen Schokoriegel gesehen?* Have you seen the advert for the new chocolate bar? ▷ *Wenn Werbung kommt, schalte ich um.* I switch over when the adverts come on. ❷ advertising ▷ *Er arbeitet in der Werbung.* He works in advertising.; **für etwas Werbung machen** to advertise something
werden *vb* [**91**] ❶ to become ▷ *Sie ist Lehrerin geworden.* She became a teacher. ▷ *Er ist reich geworden.* He became rich. ▷ *Was ist aus ihm geworden?* What became of him?; **Erster werden** to come first; **Was willst du einmal werden?** What do you want to be?; **rot werden** to turn red; **Es ist gut geworden.** It turned out well.; **Die Fotos sind gut geworden.** The photos have come out well.; **Es ist nichts geworden.** It came to nothing.; **Es wird Tag.** It's getting light.; **Es wird Nacht.** It's getting dark.; **Mir wird kalt.** I'm getting cold.; **Mir wird schlecht.** I feel sick. ❷ will
werden is used to form the future tense.
Das muss anders werden. That'll have to change. ▷ *Er wird es tun.* He'll do it. ▷ *Er wird das nicht tun.* He won't do it. ▷ *Sie wird in der Küche sein.* She'll be in the kitchen.; **Es wird gleich regnen.** It's going to rain. ❸ to be
werden is used to form the passive.
▷ *gebraucht werden* to be needed ▷ *Er ist erschossen worden.* He's been shot. ▷ *Mir wurde gesagt, dass ...* I was told that ...
werden is used to form the conditional tense.

Ich würde ... I would ...; **Er würde gern ...** He'd like to ...; **Ich würde lieber ...** I'd rather ...

werfen (*pres* **wirft**, *imperf* **warf**, *perf* **hat geworfen**) *vb* [**92**] to throw

Werkstatt (*pl* **Werkstätten**) *f* ❶ workshop ▷ *eine Werkstatt für Behinderte* a workshop for people with disabilities ❷ garage ▷ *Das Auto ist in der Werkstatt.* The car's in the garage.

Werktag (*pl* **Werktage**) *m* working day

werktags *adv* on working days

Werkzeug (*pl* **Werkzeuge**) *nt* tool

wert *adj* worth ▷ *Wie viel ist das Bild wert?* How much is that picture worth? ▷ *Das ist nichts wert.* It's not worth anything. ▷ *Das ist viel wert.* It's worth a lot.

Wert (*pl* **Werte**) *m* value; **Wert legen auf** to attach importance to; **Es hat doch keinen Wert.** There's no point.

wertlos *adj* worthless

wertvoll *adj* valuable

Wesen (*pl* **Wesen**) *nt* manner ▷ *Er hat ein freundliches Wesen.* He has a friendly manner.

wesentlich *adj* significant

weshalb *adv* why

Wespe *f* wasp

wessen *pron*

wessen is the genitive of **wer**.

whose

Weste *f* waistcoat

Westen *m* west

westlich *adj, prep, adv* westerly ▷ *in westlicher Richtung* in a westerly direction; **westlich einer Sache** to the west of something; **westlich von** west of

weswegen *adv* why

Wettbewerb (*pl* **Wettbewerbe**) *m* competition

Wette *f* bet

wetten *vb* [**2**] to bet ▷ *Ich wette, du fällst durchs Examen.* I bet you fail the exam.

Wetter *nt* weather

Wetterbericht (*pl* **Wetterberichte**) *m* weather report

Wetterlage (*pl* **Wetterlagen**) *f* weather situation

Wettervorhersage *f* weather forecast

Wettkampf (*pl* **Wettkämpfe**) *m* contest

Wettlauf (*pl* **Wettläufe**) *m* race

wichtig *adj* important

Widder (*pl* **Widder**) *m* ❶ ram ❷ Aries ▷ *Horst ist Widder.* Horst's Aries.

widerlich *adj* disgusting

widersprechen (*pres* **widerspricht**, *imperf* **widersprach**, *perf* **hat widersprochen**) *vb* [**70**] **jemandem widersprechen** to contradict somebody

Widerspruch (*pl* **Widersprüche**) *m* contradiction

Widerstand (*pl* **Widerstände**) *m* resistance

widerwillig *adj* unwilling

wie *adv* ❶ how ▷ *Wie groß?* How big? ▷ *Wie schnell?* How fast? ▷ *Wie schön!* How lovely! ▷ *Und wie!* And how! ▷ *Wie wär's?* How about it? ▷ *Wie geht's dir?* How are you?; **Wie bitte?** (1) Pardon? ▷ *Wie bitte, was haben Sie gesagt?* Pardon, what did you say? (2) What? ▷ *Wie bitte, du willst zweitausend Euro von mir haben?* What? You want me to give you two thousand euros?; **so schön wie ...** as beautiful as ...; **wie ich schon sagte** as I said ❷ like ▷ *wie du* like you ▷ *singen wie ein ...* to sing like a ...; **wie zum Beispiel** such as

wieder *adv* again ▷ *wieder da sein* to be back again ▷ *Gehst du schon wieder?* Are you off again?; **wieder ein ...** another ...

wiederaufbereiten (*perf* **hat wiederaufbereitet**) *vb* [**2**] to recycle

wiederbekommen (*imperf* **bekam wieder**, *perf* **hat wiederbekommen**) *vb* [**40**] to get back

wiedererkennen (*imperf* **erkannte wieder**, *perf* **hat wiedererkannt**) *vb* [**39**] to recognize

wiederholen (*perf* **hat wiederholt**) *vb* [**4**] to repeat
Wiederholung *f* ❶ repetition ▷ *Es darf keine Wiederholung dieses Vorfalls geben.* There must be no repetition of this incident. ❷ repeat ▷ *Im Fernsehen kommen zu viele Wiederholungen.* There are too many repeats on TV.
Wiederhören *nt* **Auf Wiederhören!** Goodbye! *(on telephone, radio)*
wiedersehen (*pres* **sieht wieder**, *imperf* **sah wieder**, *perf* **hat wiedergesehen**) *vb* [**64**] to see again; **Auf Wiedersehen!** Goodbye.
wiederverwerten (*perf* **hat wiederverwertet**) *vb* [**7**] to recycle
Wiege *f* cradle
wiegen (*imperf* **wog**, *perf* **hat gewogen**) *vb* to weigh ▷ *Ich habe mich heute früh gewogen.* I weighed myself this morning.
Wien *nt* Vienna
Wiese *f* meadow
wieso *adv* why
wie viel *adj* how much ▷ *Wie viel hat das gekostet?* How much did it cost?; **wie viel Menschen** how many people
wievielte *adj* **Zum wievielten Mal?** How many times?; **Den Wievielten haben wir?** What's the date?
Wi-Fi *nt* Wi-Fi
wild *adj* wild
will *vb see* **wollen**
Wille (*gen* **Willens**, *pl* **Willen**) *m* will ▷ *Ich habe es aus freiem Willen getan.* I did it of my own free will.
willkommen *adj* welcome ▷ *Herzlich willkommen!* Welcome!; **jemanden willkommen heißen** to welcome somebody
wimmeln *vb* [**88**] **Es wimmelt von ...** It's teeming with ...
Wimper *f* eyelash
Wimperntusche *f* mascara
Wind (*pl* **Winde**) *m* wind
Windel *f* nappy ▷ *Kannst du dem Baby die Windeln wechseln?* Can you change the baby's nappy?
Windenergie *f* wind energy
windig *adj* windy ▷ *Es ist windig.* It's windy.
Windmühle *f* windmill
Windpark *m* wind farm
Windpocken *pl* chickenpox *sg* ▷ *Windpocken sind ansteckend.* Chickenpox is catching.
Windschutzscheibe *f* windscreen
Windsurfen *nt* windsurfing
Winkel (*pl* **Winkel**) *m* ❶ angle ▷ *ein spitzer Winkel* an acute angle ❷ corner ▷ *Ich habe jeden Winkel des Zimmers durchsucht.* I've searched every corner of the room.
winken *vb* [**38**] to wave ▷ *jemandem winken* to wave to somebody
Winter (*pl* **Winter**) *m* winter ▷ *im Winter* in winter
winzig *adj* tiny
wir *pron* we ▷ *Wir kommen.* We're coming.; **wir alle** all of us; **Wir sind's.** It's us.
Wirbelsäule *f* spine
wird *vb see* **werden**
wirft *vb see* **werfen**
wirken *vb* [**38**] ❶ to have an effect ▷ *Die Tablette wirkt schon.* The pill's already having an effect. ❷ to seem ▷ *Er wirkte traurig.* He seemed sad.
wirklich *adj, adv* ❶ real ▷ *Er ist ein wirklicher Freund.* He's a real friend. ❷ really ▷ *Das ist wirklich passiert.* That really happened. ▷ *Ich weiß es wirklich nicht.* I really don't know.
Wirklichkeit *f* reality
wirksam *adj* effective
Wirkung *f* effect ▷ *Wirkung auf etwas haben* to have an effect on something
wirr *adj* confused
Wirsing *m* savoy cabbage
wirst *vb see* **werden**
Wirt (*pl* **Wirte**) *m* landlord
Wirtin *f* landlady

Wirtschaft *f* ❶ pub ▷ *Wir sind in einer Wirtschaft eingekehrt.* We stopped at a pub. ❷ economy ▷ *Die Wirtschaft leidet unter der Rezession.* The economy's suffering because of the recession.
wirtschaftlich *adj* ❶ economical ▷ *Die große Packung ist wirtschaftlicher.* The large packet's more economical. ❷ economic ▷ *ein wirtschaftlicher Aufschwung* an economic upswing
Wirtschaftslehre *f* economics *sg*
Wirtshaus (*gen* **Wirtshauses**, *pl* **Wirtshäuser**) *nt* inn
wischen *vb* [**48**] to wipe
wissen (*pres* **weiß**, *imperf* **wusste**, *perf* **hat gewusst**) *vb* [**93**] to know ▷ *Sie weiß sehr viel.* She knows a lot. ▷ *Weißt du, wie die Hauptstadt von Deutschland heißt?* Do you know what the capital of Germany is called? ▷ *Ich weiß es nicht.* I don't know.; **Was weiß ich!** How should I know?
Wissen *nt* knowledge
Wissenschaft *f* science
Wissenschaftler (*pl* **Wissenschaftler**) *m* scientist
wissenschaftlich *adj* scientific
Witwe *f* widow ▷ *Sie ist Witwe.* She's a widow.
Witwer (*pl* **Witwer**) *m* widower ▷ *Er ist Witwer.* He's a widower.
Witz (*gen* **Witzes**, *pl* **Witze**) *m* joke ▷ *einen Witz erzählen* to tell a joke
witzig *adj* funny
wo *adv* where ▷ *Wo warst du?* Where were you?

> Be careful! **wo** does not mean **who**.

woanders *adv* elsewhere
Woche *f* week ▷ *nächste Woche* next week
Wochenende (*pl* **Wochenenden**) *nt* weekend ▷ *am Wochenende* at the weekend
wochenlang *adj, adv* for weeks
Wochentag (*pl* **Wochentage**) *m* weekday
wöchentlich *adj, adv* weekly
wofür *adv* what ... for ▷ *Wofür brauchst du das Geld?* What do you need the money for?
wog *vb see* **wiegen**
woher *adv* where ... from ▷ *Woher sind Sie?* Where do you come from?
wohin *adv* ❶ where ... to ▷ *Wohin zieht ihr um?* Where are you moving to? ❷ where ▷ *Wohin gehst du?* Where are you going?
wohl *adv* probably ▷ *Das hat er wohl vergessen.* He's probably forgotten.; **Es ist wohl gestohlen worden.** It must have been stolen.; **Das ist doch wohl nicht dein Ernst!** Surely you're not being serious!; **Das mag wohl sein.** That may well be.; **Ob das wohl stimmt?** I wonder if that's true.; **Er weiß das sehr wohl.** He knows that perfectly well.; **Ich muss wohl oder übel hingehen.** I have to go whether I like it or not.
Wohl *nt* benefit ▷ *zu eurem Wohl* for your benefit; **Zum Wohl!** Cheers!
sich **wohlfühlen** *vb* [**4**] ❶ to be happy ▷ *Ich fühle mich in diesem Haus sehr wohl.* I'm very happy in this house. ❷ to feel well ▷ *Sie fühlte sich nicht wohl.* She didn't feel well.
Wohnblock (*pl* **Wohnblocks**) *m* block of flats
wohnen *vb* [**38**] to live ▷ *Ich wohne in Bremen.* I live in Bremen.
Wohngemeinschaft *f* **Ich wohne in einer Wohngemeinschaft.** I share a flat.
Wohnheim (*pl* **Wohnheime**) *nt* ❶ home ▷ *ein Wohnheim für ältere Menschen* a home for senior citizens; **ein Studentenwohnheim** a hall of residence ❷ hostel
Wohnort (*pl* **Wohnorte**) *m* place of residence
Wohnsitz (*gen* **Wohnsitzes**, *pl* **Wohnsitze**) *m* place of residence
Wohnung *f* flat

a b c d e f g h i j k l m n o p q r s t u v w x y z

Wohnwagen (*pl* **Wohnwagen**) *m* caravan
Wohnzimmer (*pl* **Wohnzimmer**) *nt* living room
Wolf (*pl* **Wölfe**) *m* wolf
Wolke *f* cloud
Wolkenkratzer (*pl* **Wolkenkratzer**) *m* skyscraper
wolkig *adj* cloudy
Wolle *f* wool
wollen (*pres* **will**, *imperf* **wollte**, *perf* **hat gewollt** *or* **wollen**) *vb* [**94**]

> The past participle **wollen** is used when **wollen** is a modal auxiliary.

to want ▷ *Er hat nicht gewollt.* He didn't want to. ▷ *Er wollte das nicht.* He didn't want it. ▷ *Ich will nach Hause.* I want to go home. ▷ *Ich will, dass du mir zuhörst.* I want you to listen to me.; **Wenn du willst.** If you like.; **etwas tun wollen** to want to do something; **etwas gerade tun wollen** to be on the point of doing something; **Ich wollte, ich wäre ...** I wish I were ...
womit *adv* ❶ with which ▷ *Das ist der Gegenstand, womit er erschlagen wurde.* This is the instrument with which he was killed. ❷ what ... with ▷ *Womit hast du das repariert?* What did you repair it with?
wonach *adv* ❶ what ... for ▷ *Das war genau, wonach er gesucht hatte.* That was just what he had been looking for. ❷ what ... by ▷ *Wonach sollen wir die Uhr stellen?* What shall we set the clock by?; **der Tag, wonach er verunglückte** the day before his accident
woran *adv* **das Paket, woran dieser Zettel hing** the parcel the note was attached to; **Woran war dieser Zettel befestigt?** What was this note attached to?; **Woran ist er gestorben?** What did he die of?
worauf *adv* what ... on ▷ *Worauf soll ich den Computer stellen?* What shall I put the computer on?; **der Tisch, worauf der Computer steht** the table the computer is on
woraus *adv* **das Material, woraus es hergestellt ist** the material it is made of; **das Leck, woraus Gas strömte** the hole gas was pouring out of
worin *adv* what ... in ▷ *Worin war das versteckt?* What was it hidden in?; **die Schublade, worin der Schlüssel ist** the drawer the key is in; **Worin besteht der Unterschied?** What's the difference?
Wort (*pl* **Wörter** *or* **Worte**) *nt* word ▷ *Sie sprach ein paar bewegende Worte.* She said a few moving words. ▷ *Manche Wörter werden wie im Französischen ausgesprochen.* Some words are pronounced as in French.; **jemanden beim Wort nehmen** to take somebody at his word; **mit anderen Worten** in other words
Wörterbuch (*pl* **Wörterbücher**) *nt* dictionary

> Word for word, **Wörterbuch** means 'word book'.

wörtlich *adj* literal
Wortschatz (*gen* **Wortschatzes**) *m* vocabulary
Wortspiel (*pl* **Wortspiele**) *nt* pun
worüber *adv* **das Thema, worüber wir reden** the subject we're talking about; **der Tisch, worüber eine Lampe hing** the table a lamp was hanging over; **Worüber kann ich meinen Mantel legen?** Where can I put my coat?
worunter *adv* what ... under ▷ *Worunter hat sich die Katze verkrochen?* What did the cat crawl under?; **der Tisch, worunter die Katze lag** the table the cat was lying under
wovon *adv* **Das war es, wovon wir sprachen.** That was what we were talking about.; **das Essen, wovon ihm schlecht wurde** the food which made him ill
wovor *adv* **das Haus, wovor du stehst** the house you're standing in front of;

die Arbeit, wovor sie am meisten Angst hat the test which she's most afraid of
wozu *adv* ❶ why ▷ *Wozu willst du das wissen?* Why do you want to know that? ❷ what ... for ▷ *Wozu dient dieser Schalter?* What's this switch for? ▷ *Wozu brauchst du einen Computer?* What do you need a computer for?
Wrack (*pl* **Wracks**) *nt* wreck
Wucher *m* **Das ist Wucher!** (*informal*) That's daylight robbery!
wund *adj* sore ▷ *Ich habe mir die Füße beim Einkaufen wund gelaufen.* My feet are sore from going round the shops.
Wunde *f* wound
Wunder (*pl* **Wunder**) *nt* miracle; **es ist kein Wunder** it's no wonder
wunderbar *adj* wonderful
wundern *vb* [**88**] to surprise ▷ *Diese Frage hat mich sehr gewundert.* This question really surprised me.; **sich wundern über** to be surprised at; **Ich muss mich schon über dich wundern.** I must say you surprise me.; **Es wundert mich, dass du das fragst.** I'm surprised you ask.; **Er wird sich noch wundern!** He's in for a surprise!
wunderschön *adj* beautiful
wundervoll *adj* wonderful
Wunsch (*pl* **Wünsche**) *m* wish
wünschen *vb* [**48**] to wish ▷ *Ich wünsche dir viel Erfolg!* I wish you every success.; **sich etwas wünschen** to want something
wurde *vb see* **werden**
Wurf (*pl* **Würfe**) *m* throw
Würfel (*pl* **Würfel**) *m* ❶ dice ▷ *zwei Würfel* two dice ▷ *Wir haben Würfel gespielt.* We played dice. ❷ cube ▷ *Ein Würfel hat sechs gleich große Flächen.* A cube has six equal surfaces.
würfeln *vb* [**34**] ❶ to throw a dice ▷ *Ich bin dran mit Würfeln.* It's my turn to throw the dice. ▷ *Wir haben darum gewürfelt, wer abwaschen muss.* We threw a dice to see who was going to wash up. ❷ to dice ▷ *den Speck würfeln* to dice the bacon
Wurm (*pl* **Würmer**) *m* worm
Wurst (*pl* **Würste**) *f* ❶ sausage ▷ *Leberwurst* liver sausage ❷ cold meat; **eine Wurstplatte** a platter of cold meat; **Das ist mir Wurst.** (*informal*) I don't give a toss.
Würstchen (*pl* **Würstchen**) *nt* sausage
Würze *f* seasoning
Wurzel *f* root
wusch *vb see* **waschen**
wusste *vb see* **wissen**
Wüste *f* desert
Wut *f* rage; **eine Wut haben** to be furious
wütend *adj* furious ▷ *Ich bin wütend auf ihn.* I'm furious with him.

X

x-beliebig *adj* any ... whatever ▷ *Wähle eine x-beliebige Zahl*. Choose any number whatever.

x-mal *adv* any number of times ▷ *Ich habe es ihm x-mal gesagt*. I've told him any number of times.

Xylofon (*pl* **Xylofone**) *nt* xylophone

Y

Yoga (*gen* **Yoga** *or* **Yogas**) *nt* yoga

Ypsilon (*gen* **Ypsilon** *or* **Ypsilons**, *pl* **Ypsilons**) *nt* the letter Y

Z

zäh *adj* ❶ tough ▷ *Das Steak ist zäh.* The steak's tough. ▷ *Ich bin zäh, ich halte es noch eine Weile aus.* I'm tough, I can stand it for a bit yet. ❷ slow-moving ▷ *Der Verkehr war zäh.* Traffic was slow-moving.

Zahl *f* number

zahlen *vb* [**38**] to pay ▷ *Wie viel hast du dafür gezahlt?* How much did you pay for it?; **Zahlen bitte!** The bill, please!

zählen *vb* [**38**] to count ▷ *Ich zähle bis drei.* I'll count to three. ▷ *Ich habe die Hefte gezählt.* I've counted the exercise books.; **zählen auf** to count on; **zählen zu** to be one of

zahlreich *adj* numerous

Zahlung *f* payment

Zahlwort (*pl* **Zahlwörter**) *nt* numeral

zahm *adj* tame

Zahn (*pl* **Zähne**) *m* tooth

Zahnarzt (*gen* **Zahnarztes**, *pl* **Zahnärzte**) *m* dentist

Zahnbürste *f* toothbrush

Zahncreme (*pl* **Zahncremes**) *f* toothpaste

Zahnpasta (*pl* **Zahnpasten**) *f* toothpaste

Zahnschmerzen *pl* toothache *sg* ▷ *Zahnschmerzen sind sehr unangenehm.* Toothache is very unpleasant.

Zange *f* ❶ pliers *pl* ▷ *Ich brauche eine isolierte Zange.* I need a pair of insulated pliers. ❷ pincers *pl* ▷ *die Zangen eines Hummers* a lobster's pincers

zappeln *vb* [**34**] ❶ to wriggle ▷ *Der Fisch zappelt noch.* The fish is still wriggling. ❷ to fidget ▷ *Hör auf zu zappeln.* Stop fidgeting.

zart *adj* ❶ soft ▷ *zarte Haut* soft skin ❷ gentle ▷ *eine zarte Berührung* a gentle touch ❸ delicate ▷ *zarte Farben* delicate colours ▷ *Sie ist ein sehr zartes Kind.* She's a very delicate child.; **zartes Fleisch** tender meat

zärtlich *adj* loving ▷ *Mein Freund ist sehr zärtlich.* My boyfriend's very loving. ▷ *ein zärtlicher Kuss* a loving kiss ▷ *eine zärtliche Berührung* a loving touch

Zauberei *f* magic

Zaun (*pl* **Zäune**) *m* fence

z. B. *abbr* (*= zum Beispiel*) e.g.

Zebrastreifen (*pl* **Zebrastreifen**) *m* zebra crossing

Zehe *f* toe ▷ *die große Zehe* the big toe; **eine Knoblauchzehe** a clove of garlic

zehn *num* ten

zehnte *adj* tenth

Zeichen (*pl* **Zeichen**) *nt* sign

Zeichentrickfilm (*pl* **Zeichentrickfilme**) *m* animated cartoon

zeichnen *vb* [**53**] to draw ▷ *Marek kann gut zeichnen.* Marek's good at drawing. ▷ *Sie hat eine Maus gezeichnet.* She's drawn a mouse.

Zeichnung *f* drawing

Zeigefinger (*pl* **Zeigefinger**) *m* index finger

zeigen *vb* [**38**] ❶ to show ▷ *Sie hat mir ihre Fotos gezeigt.* She showed me her photos. ▷ *Zeig mal, was du da hast.* Show us what you've got there. ❷ to point ▷ *Sie zeigte an die Tafel.* She pointed to the blackboard.; **zeigen auf** to point at; **es wird sich zeigen** time will tell; **Es zeigte sich, dass ...** It turned out that ...

Zeiger (*pl* **Zeiger**) *m* ❶ hand ▷ *der große und der kleine Zeiger der Uhr* the big hand and the little hand of the clock ❷ pointer ▷ *der Zeiger der Waage* the pointer of the scales

Zeile *f* line ▷ *Ich schreibe ihr ein paar Zeilen.* I'm going to write her a few lines.

Zeit *f* ❶ time ▷ *Wir haben keine Zeit mehr.* We haven't got any more time. ▷ *Um welche Zeit seid ihr nach Hause gekommen?* What time did you get home? ❷ tense ▷ *die Zeiten der Vergangenheit* the past tenses; **sich Zeit lassen** to take one's time; **von Zeit zu Zeit** from time to time; **Zeit raubend** *see* **zeitraubend**

zeitlich *adj* chronological

zeitnah *adj, adv* ❶ prompt ▷ *eine zeitnahe Antwort* a prompt reply ❷ promptly ▷ *Der Aufzug wurde zeitnah repariert.* The lift was repaired promptly.

Zeitlupe *f* slow motion ▷ *in Zeitlupe* in slow motion

zeitraubend *adj* time-consuming

Zeitraum (*pl* **Zeiträume**) *m* period ▷ *innerhalb dieses Zeitraums* within this period

Zeitschrift *f* magazine

Zeitung *f* newspaper

Zelle *f* ❶ cell ▷ *Im Alter sterben die Zellen ab.* Cells die off in old age. ❷ call box ▷ *Ich rufe aus einer Zelle an.* I'm phoning from a call box.

Zelt (*pl* **Zelte**) *nt* tent

zelten *vb* [**2**] to camp

Zeltplatz (*gen* **Zeltplatzes**, *pl* **Zeltplätze**) *m* camp site

Zement (*pl* **Zemente**) *m* cement

zensieren (*perf* **hat zensiert**) *vb* [**76**] ❶ to censor ▷ *Der Film wurde zensiert.* The film was censored. ❷ to give a mark ▷ *Wie hat deine Deutschlehrerin den Aufsatz zensiert?* What mark did your German teacher give you for your essay?

Zensur *f* mark ▷ *Ich habe durchweg gute Zensuren.* I've got good marks in everything.

Zentimeter (*pl* **Zentimeter**) *m* centimetre

Zentner (*pl* **Zentner**) *m* hundredweight ▷ *drei Zentner* three hundredweight

zentral *adj* central

Zentrale *f* ❶ head office ▷ *Das Gerät müssen wir in der Zentrale anfordern.* We'll have to order the appliance from the head office. ❷ switchboard ▷ *Du musst dich über die Zentrale verbinden lassen.* You have to go through the switchboard.

Zentralheizung *f* central heating

Zentrum (*pl* **Zentren**) *nt* centre

zerbrechen (*pres* **zerbricht**, *imperf* **zerbrach**, *perf* **hat/ist zerbrochen**) *vb* [**11**]

> For the perfect tense use **haben** when the verb has an object and **sein** when there is no object.

to break ▷ *Sie hat den Teller zerbrochen.* She's broken the plate. ▷ *Der Teller ist zerbrochen.* The plate broke.

zerbrechlich *adj* fragile

zerreißen (*imperf* **zerriss**, *perf* **hat/ist zerrissen**) *vb*

> For the perfect tense use **haben** when the verb has an object and **sein** when there is no object.

❶ to tear to pieces ▷ *Sie hat seinen Brief zerrissen.* She tore his letter to pieces. ❷ to tear ▷ *Der Umschlag ist unterwegs zerrissen.* The envelope got torn in the post.

zerren *vb* [**38**] to drag ▷ *Er zerrte sie in die Büsche.* He dragged her into the bushes.; **zerren an** to tug at

zerrissen *vb see* **zerreißen**

zerschlagen (*pres* **zerschlägt**, *imperf* **zerschlug**, *perf* **hat zerschlagen**) *vb* [**59**] to smash ▷ *Sie haben alles Porzellan zerschlagen.* They smashed all the china.; **sich zerschlagen** to fall through

zerstören (*pres* **hat zerstört**) *vb* [**95**] to destroy

Zerstörung *f* destruction

zerstreut *adj* ❶ absent-minded ▷ *Er ist furchtbar zerstreut.* He's terribly absent-minded. ❷ scattered ▷ *Sie sammelte die zerstreuten Seiten auf.* She picked up the scattered pages.

Zettel (*pl* **Zettel**) *m* ❶ note ▷ *Auf dem Küchentisch liegt ein Zettel für dich.* There's a note on the kitchen table for you. ❷ piece of paper ▷ *Sie schrieb seine Telefonnummer auf einen Zettel.* She wrote his telephone number on a piece of paper. ❸ form ▷ *Wenn du dem Klub beitreten willst, musst du diesen Zettel ausfüllen.* If you want to join the club you'll have to fill in this form.

Zeug *nt* ❶ *(informal)* stuff ▷ *Was ist das für ein Zeug?* What's this stuff? ▷ *mein Sportzeug* my sports stuff ❷ gear ▷ *mein Angelzeug* my fishing gear; **dummes Zeug** nonsense; **das Zeug haben zu** to have the makings of

Zeuge (*gen* **Zeugen**, *pl* **Zeugen**) *m* witness

Zeugin *f* witness

Zeugnis (*gen* **Zeugnisses**, *pl* **Zeugnisse**) *nt* report ▷ *Oliver hat ein sehr gutes Zeugnis.* Oliver's got a very good report.

Ziege *f* goat

Ziegel (*pl* **Ziegel**) *m* ❶ brick ▷ *eine Mauer aus Ziegeln* a brick wall ❷ tile ▷ *Deutsche Dächer sind meist mit roten Ziegeln gedeckt.* German roofs are usually covered with red tiles.

ziehen (*imperf* **zog**, *perf* **hat/ist gezogen**) *vb* [**96**]

> Use **sein** to form the perfect tense for 'to move' (house) and 'to roam'. Use **haben** for 'to move' (in chess), 'to draw' and 'to pull'.

❶ to draw ▷ *Er hat eine Niete gezogen.* He drew a blank. ❷ to pull ▷ *Sie zog mich am Ärmel.* She pulled at my sleeve. ❸ to move ▷ *Sie sind nach Wuppertal gezogen.* They've moved to Wuppertal. ▷ *Er zog mit seinem Turm.* He moved his rook. ❹ to roam ▷ *Früher zogen die Zigeuner durchs Land.* In the old days, gypsies used to roam the countryside.; **Es zieht.** There's a draught.; **sich in die Länge ziehen** to be drawn out

Ziel (*pl* **Ziele**) *nt* ❶ destination ▷ *Unser heutiges Ziel ist Bonn.* Our destination today is Bonn. ❷ finishing line ▷ *Er ging als Erster durchs Ziel.* He was the first to cross the finishing line. ❸ target ▷ *Ulm war das Ziel eines Bombenangriffs.* Ulm was the target of an air raid. ❹ goal ▷ *Es ist nicht mein Ziel im Leben, reich zu werden.* Getting rich is not my goal in life.

zielen *vb* [**38**] to aim ▷ *Er hat auf seine Beine gezielt.* He aimed at his legs.

ziemlich *adj, adv* ❶ quite ▷ *Das war eine ziemliche Katastrophe.* That was quite a disaster. ❷ fair ▷ *eine ziemliche Menge Fehler* a fair number of mistakes ❸ rather ▷ *Er war ziemlich sauer.* He was rather cross.; **ziemlich viel** quite a bit

zierlich *adj* dainty

Ziffer *f* figure

zig *adj (informal)* umpteen

Zigarette *f* cigarette

Zigarettenschachtel *f* cigarette packet

Zigarre *f* cigar

Zigeuner (*pl* **Zigeuner**) *m* gypsy

Zigeunerin *f* gypsy

Zimmer (*pl* **Zimmer**) *nt* room; **'Zimmer frei'** 'Vacancies'

Zimmermädchen (*pl* **Zimmermädchen**) *nt* chambermaid

Zimt *m* cinnamon

Zinn *nt* ❶ tin ▷ *In Cornwall wurde früher Zinn abgebaut.* They used to mine tin in Cornwall. ❷ pewter ▷ *Mein Bruder sammelt Zinn.* My brother collects pewter.

a b c d e f g h i j k l m n o p q r s t u v w x y z

Zins (*gen* **Zinses**, *pl* **Zinsen**) *m* interest ▷ *acht Prozent Zinsen* eight per cent interest

zirka *adv* approximately

Zirkus (*gen* **Zirkus**, *pl* **Zirkusse**) *m* circus

Zitat (*pl* **Zitate**) *nt* quotation

zitieren (*perf* **hat zitiert**) *vb* [**76**] to quote

Zitrone *f* lemon

Zitronensaft (*pl* **Zitronensäfte**) *m* lemon juice

zittern *vb* [**88**] to tremble ▷ *vor Angst zittern* to tremble with fear; **Sie zitterte vor Kälte.** She was shivering.

Zivildienst *m* community service

Until the abolition of compulsory military service in 2011, those young men who opted out of this could choose to do **Zivildienst** or community service instead, for example with the Red Cross.

zögern *vb* [**88**] to hesitate

Zoll (*pl* **Zölle**) *m* ❶ customs *pl* ▷ *Wir mussten am Zoll lange warten.* We had to wait a long time at customs. ❷ duty ▷ *Darauf musst du Zoll bezahlen.* You have to pay duty on that.

Zollbeamte (*gen* **Zollbeamten**, *pl* **Zollbeamten**) *m* customs official ▷ *Ein Zollbeamter hat unser Auto durchsucht.* A customs official searched our car.

Zollkontrolle *f* customs check

Zone *f* zone

Zoo (*pl* **Zoos**) *m* zoo

Zopf (*pl* **Zöpfe**) *m* ❶ plait ▷ *zwei blonde Zöpfe* two blonde plaits ❷ pigtail ▷ *Sie hatte ihre Haare zu einem Zopf zusammengebunden.* She had put her hair into a pigtail.

Zorn *m* anger

zornig *adj* angry

zu *prep, conj, adv*

The preposition **zu** takes the dative.

❶ to ▷ *zum Bahnhof gehen* to go to the station ▷ *zum Arzt gehen* to go to the doctor ▷ *zur Schule gehen* to go to school ▷ *zur Kirche gehen* to go to church ▷ *Sollen wir zu euch gehen?* Shall we go to your place?; **Sie sah zu ihm hin.** She looked towards him.; **zum Fenster herein** through the window; **zu meiner Linken** on my left

zu is used with the infinitive.

▷ *etwas zu essen* something to eat ▷ *ohne es zu wissen* without knowing it ❷ at ▷ *zu Ostern* at Easter; **zu Hause** at home; **bis zum ersten Mai (1)** until the first of May ▷ *Das Sonderangebot gilt bis zum ersten Mai.* The special offer is valid until the first of May. **(2)** by the first of May ▷ *Bis zum ersten Mai muss mein Referat fertig sein.* My assignment has to be finished by the first of May.; **zu meinem Geburtstag** for my birthday; **zu meiner Zeit** in my time ❸ with ▷ *Wein zum Essen trinken* to drink wine with one's meal; **sich zu jemandem setzen** to sit down beside somebody ❹ on ▷ *Anmerkungen zu etwas* notes on something ❺ for ▷ *Wasser zum Waschen* water for washing; **Papier zum Schreiben** paper to write on; **zu etwas werden** to develop into something; **jemanden zu etwas machen** to make somebody something; **drei zu zwei** three two; **das Stück zu drei Euro** at three euros each; **zum ersten Mal** for the first time; **zu meiner Freude** to my delight; **zum Scherz** as a joke; **zu Fuß** on foot; **Es ist zum Weinen.** It's enough to make you cry. ❻ too ▷ *zu schnell* too fast ▷ *zu sehr* too much ❼ closed ▷ *Die Geschäfte haben zu.* The shops are closed.; **zu sein** to be shut

Zubehör (*pl* **Zubehöre**) *nt* accessories *pl* ▷ *Das Zubehör kostet extra.* You pay extra for the accessories.

zubereiten (*perf* **hat zubereitet**) *vb* [**2**] to prepare

Zucchini *pl* courgette *sg*

züchten *vb* [**2**] ❶ to breed ▷ *Er züchtet Tauben.* He breeds pigeons. ❷ to grow

▷ *Mein Vater züchtet Rosen.* My father grows roses.

zucken *vb* [**38**] ❶ to twitch ▷ *Seine Mundwinkel zuckten.* The corners of his mouth twitched. ❷ to flash ▷ *Ein Blitz zuckte durch die Nacht.* Lightning flashed across the night sky.; **mit den Schultern zucken** to shrug one's shoulders

Zucker *m* ❶ sugar ▷ *Ich nehme keinen Zucker in den Tee.* I don't take sugar in my tea. ❷ diabetes ▷ *Meine Tante hat Zucker.* My aunt's got diabetes.

zudecken (*perf* **hat zugedeckt**) *vb* [**4**] ❶ to cover up ▷ *Man sollte das Loch zudecken.* They ought to cover up the hole. ❷ to tuck up ▷ *Sie deckte die Kinder zu.* She tucked the children up.

zueinander *adv* ❶ to one another ▷ *Seid nett zueinander.* Be nice to one another.; **Wir haben viel Vertrauen zueinander.** We trust each other. ❷ together ▷ *Wir halten zueinander, egal, was kommt.* Whatever happens, we'll stick together.

zuerst *adv* ❶ first ▷ *Was soll ich zuerst machen?* What shall I do first? ▷ *Er ist zuerst gekommen, dann kam seine Schwester.* He arrived first, then his sister. ❷ at first ▷ *Zuerst war sie noch etwas schüchtern.* At first, she was still a bit shy.; **zuerst einmal** first of all

Zufahrt *f* approach road; **'keine Zufahrt'** 'no access'

Zufall (*pl* **Zufälle**) *m* ❶ chance ▷ *Wie es der Zufall so wollte ...* As chance would have it ...; **durch Zufall** by chance ❷ coincidence ▷ *Es war schon ein Zufall, dass ich ihm in London begegnet bin.* It was quite a coincidence that I met him in London. ▷ *Was für ein glücklicher Zufall!* What a happy coincidence! ▷ *So ein Zufall!* What a coincidence!

zufällig *adj, adv* ❶ chance ▷ *eine zufällige Begegnung* a chance meeting ❷ by chance ▷ *Ich habe das Restaurant ganz zufällig gefunden.* I found the restaurant quite by chance.; **Ich habe zufällig Zeit.** I happen to have time. ❸ by any chance ▷ *Hast du zufällig mein Heft gesehen?* Have you seen my exercise book by any chance?

zufrieden *adj* satisfied ▷ *Ich bin mit deinen Leistungen nicht zufrieden.* I'm not satisfied with your work. ▷ *Bist du jetzt zufrieden?* Are you satisfied now? ▷ *ein zufriedener Gesichtsausdruck* a satisfied expression

zufrieren (*imperf* **fror zu**, *perf* **ist zugefroren**) *vb* to freeze over ▷ *Der See ist zugefroren.* The lake's frozen over.

Zug (*pl* **Züge**) *m* ❶ train ▷ *Wir sind mit dem Zug gefahren.* We went by train. ❷ draught ▷ *Hier ist ein furchtbarer Zug.* There's a terrible draught in here. ❸ move ▷ *Du bist am Zug.* It's your move. ❹ gulp ▷ *Er trank das Glas auf einen Zug leer.* He emptied the glass in one gulp. ❺ trait ▷ *Sein Geiz ist ein unangenehmer Zug an ihm.* His meanness is an unpleasant trait.; **etwas in vollen Zügen genießen** to enjoy something to the full

Zugabe *f* ❶ free gift ▷ *ein Handy als Zugabe.* a mobile as a free gift ❷ encore ▷ *Die Zuhörer brüllten: 'Zugabe, Zugabe'.* The audience roared: 'encore, encore'.

zugeben (*pres* **gibt zu**, *imperf* **gab zu**, *perf* **hat zugegeben**) *vb* [**28**] to admit ▷ *Gib doch zu, dass du dich getäuscht hast.* Admit you were wrong. ▷ *Sie wollte ihren Irrtum nicht zugeben.* She didn't want to admit her mistake.

zugehen (*imperf* **ging zu**, *perf* **ist zugegangen**) *vb* [**29**] to shut ▷ *Die Tür geht nicht zu.* The door won't shut.; **auf jemanden zugehen** to walk up to somebody; **auf etwas zugehen** to walk towards something; **Es geht dort seltsam zu.** There are strange goings-on there.; **dem Ende zugehen** to be nearing the end

Zugführer (*pl* **Zugführer**) *m* chief guard (*on train*)

zügig *adj* swift ▷ *eine zügige Entscheidung* a swift decision

zugreifen (*imperf* **griff zu**, *perf* **hat zugegriffen**) *vb* ❶ to help oneself ▷ *Greift ungeniert zu, es ist genügend Kuchen da!* Feel free to help yourselves, there's plenty of cake. ❷ to seize ▷ *Er sah das Seil und griff zu.* He saw the rope and seized it. ❸ to lend a hand ▷ *Du könntest ruhig ein bisschen zugreifen und mich nicht alles allein machen lassen.* You could at least lend a hand a bit instead of letting me do everything.

zugrunde *adv* **elend zugrunde gehen** to come to a wretched end; **zugrunde richten** to destroy; **einer Sache etwas zugrunde legen** to base something on something

zugunsten *prep*

The preposition **zugunsten** takes the dative or the genitive.

in favour of ▷ *Das Gericht entschied zugunsten des Angeklagten.* The court decided in favour of the accused.

Zuhause (*gen* **Zuhause**) *nt* home

zuhören (*perf* **hat zugehört**) *vb* [**4**] to listen ▷ *Du hörst mir ja gar nicht zu.* You're not listening to me at all.

Zuhörer (*pl* **Zuhörer**) *m* listener

zukommen (*imperf* **kam zu**, *perf* **ist zugekommen**) *vb* [**40**] **auf jemanden zukommen** to come up to somebody; **jemandem etwas zukommen lassen** to give somebody something; **etwas auf sich zukommen lassen** to take something as it comes

Zukunft *f* future ▷ *in Zukunft* in the future

zulassen (*pres* **lässt zu**, *imperf* **ließ zu**, *perf* **hat zugelassen**) *vb* [**42**] ❶ to allow ▷ *Ich kann es nicht zulassen, dass du so spät noch fernsiehst.* I can't allow you to watch TV so late. ❷ to register ▷ *Hast du dein Moped schon zugelassen?* Have you registered your moped yet? ❸ to leave closed ▷ *Bitte lass das Fenster zu.* Please leave the window closed.

zulässig *adj* permissible

zuletzt *adv* ❶ last ▷ *Er wurde zuletzt in Begleitung einer Dame gesehen.* He was last seen in the company of a lady. ▷ *Wir sollten das zuletzt machen.* We should do that last. ❷ in the end ▷ *Zuletzt hat sie es dann doch verstanden.* In the end she understood.

zuliebe *adv* **jemandem zuliebe** to please somebody

zum = **zu dem**

zumachen (*perf* **hat zugemacht**) *vb* [**4**] ❶ to shut ▷ *Mach bitte die Tür zu.* Please shut the door. ▷ *Wann machen die Geschäfte zu?* When do the shops shut? ❷ to fasten ▷ *Kannst du mal bitte mein Kleid zumachen?* Can you fasten my dress, please?

zumindest *adv* at least

zumute *adv* **Wie ist ihm zumute?** How does he feel?

zumuten (*perf* **hat zugemutet**) *vb* [**2**] **jemandem etwas zumuten** to ask something of somebody

zunächst *adv* first of all ▷ *Wir sollten zunächst diese Frage klären.* We ought to clear this issue up first of all.; **zunächst einmal** to start with

zunehmen (*pres* **nimmt zu**, *imperf* **nahm zu**, *perf* **hat zugenommen**) *vb* [**52**] ❶ to increase ▷ *Der Lärm nahm zu.* The noise increased. ❷ to put on weight ▷ *Ich habe schon wieder zugenommen.* I've put on weight yet again.; **Er hat fünf Kilo zugenommen.** He's put on five kilos.

Zuneigung *f* affection

Zunge *f* tongue

zur = **zu der**

zurechtkommen (*imperf* **kam zurecht**, *perf* **ist zurechtgekommen**) *vb* [**40**] to manage

zurechtlegen (*perf* **hat zurechtgelegt**) *vb* [**4**] to sort out ▷ *Ich habe die Sachen für die Ferien schon zurechtgelegt.* I've already sorted out my things for my holiday.; **sich eine**

Ausrede zurechtlegen to think up an excuse

zurück *adv* back

zurückbekommen (*imperf* **bekam zurück**, *perf* **hat zurückbekommen**) *vb* [**40**] to get back

zurückbringen (*imperf* **brachte zurück**, *perf* **hat zurückgebracht**) *vb* [**13**] to bring back

zurückfahren (*pres* **fährt zurück**, *imperf* **fuhr zurück**, *perf* **ist/hat zurückgefahren**) *vb* [**21**]

> For the perfect tense use **haben** when the verb has an object and **sein** when there is no object.

to return ▷ *Wann fahrt ihr zurück?* When do you return?; **jemanden zurückfahren** to drive somebody back

zurückgeben (*pres* **gibt zurück**, *imperf* **gab zurück**, *perf* **hat zurückgegeben**) *vb* [**28**] to give back ▷ *Gib mir bitte mein Buch zurück.* Please give me my book back.

zurückgehen (*imperf* **ging zurück**, *perf* **ist zurückgegangen**) *vb* [**29**] ❶ to go back ▷ *Wir sollten zurückgehen, bevor es zu spät wird.* We should go back before it gets too late. ❷ to recede ▷ *Das Hochwasser ist zurückgegangen.* The floodwater receded. ❸ to fall ▷ *Die Nachfrage geht zurück.* Demand is falling.; **zurückgehen auf** to date back to

zurückhaltend *adj* reserved ▷ *Er ist sehr zurückhaltend.* He is very reserved.

zurückkehren (*perf* **ist zurückgekehrt**) *vb* [**15**] to return

zurückkommen (*imperf* **kam zurück**, *perf* **ist zurückgekommen**) *vb* [**40**] to come back ▷ *Er kam nach dem Film zurück.* He came back after the film. ▷ *Darf ich auf das zurückkommen, was Sie vorhin gesagt haben?* May I come back to what you were saying earlier?; **Komm nicht zu spät zurück.** Don't be too late back.

zurücklegen (*perf* **hat zurückgelegt**) *vb* [**15**] ❶ to put back ▷ *Leg das Buch bitte an seinen Platz zurück.* Please put the book back in its place. ❷ to put by ▷ *Wir haben für die Ferien etwas Geld zurückgelegt.* We've put some money by for the holidays. ❸ to put aside ▷ *Können Sie mir diesen Pulli bitte zurücklegen?* Could you put this pullover aside for me, please? ❹ to cover ▷ *Wir haben heute zweihundert Kilometer zurückgelegt.* We've covered two hundred kilometres today.

zurücknehmen (*pres* **nimmt zurück**, *imperf* **nahm zurück**, *perf* **hat zurückgenommen**) *vb* [**52**] to take back

zurücktreten (*pres* **tritt zurück**, *imperf* **trat zurück**, *perf* **ist zurückgetreten**) *vb* [**79**] ❶ to step back ▷ *Treten Sie etwas zurück bitte!* Step back a bit, please. ❷ to resign ▷ *Warum ist er zurückgetreten?* Why did he resign?

zurückzahlen (*perf* **hat zurückgezahlt**) *vb* [**15**] to repay ▷ *Du solltest endlich das geliehene Geld zurückzahlen.* It's high time you repaid the money you borrowed.

zurzeit *adv* at the moment

zusagen (*perf* **hat zugesagt**) *vb* [**4**] ❶ to promise ▷ *Er hat mir seine Hilfe zugesagt.* He promised to help me. ❷ to accept an invitation ▷ *Die meisten Gäste haben zugesagt.* Most of the guests have accepted the invitation.; **jemandem zusagen** to appeal to somebody

zusammen *adv* together

zusammenbleiben (*imperf* **blieb zusammen**, *perf* **sind zusammengeblieben**) *vb* [**10**] to stay together

zusammenbrechen (*pres* **bricht zusammen**, *imperf* **brach zusammen**, *perf* **ist zusammengebrochen**) *vb* [**11**] ❶ to collapse ▷ *Das Gebäude ist zusammengebrochen.* The building collapsed. ❷ to break down ▷ *Als sie von seinem Tod erfuhr, ist sie zusammengebrochen.* When she heard of his death she broke down.

zusammenfassen (*perf* **hat zusammengefasst**) *vb* [15] to summarize ▷ *Sie fasste das Gesagte noch einmal kurz zusammen.* She briefly summarized once again what had been said.

Zusammenfassung *f* summary

Zusammenhang (*pl* **Zusammenhänge**) *m* connection ▷ *Gibt es einen Zusammenhang zwischen diesen Ereignissen?* Is there a connection between these events?; **im Zusammenhang mit** in connection with; **aus dem Zusammenhang** out of context

zusammenhängen (*imperf* **hing zusammen**, *perf* **hat zusammengehangen**) *vb* [69] to be connected ▷ *Die beiden Ereignisse hängen miteinander zusammen.* The two events are connected.

zusammenkommen (*imperf* **kam zusammen**, *perf* **ist zusammengekommen**) *vb* [40] ❶ to meet up ▷ *Früher sind wir öfter zusammengekommen.* We used to meet up more often. ❷ to come together ▷ *Es ist alles zusammengekommen.* Everything came together.

zusammennehmen (*pres* **nimmt zusammen**, *imperf* **nahm zusammen**, *perf* **hat zusammengenommen**) *vb* [52] to summon up ▷ *Ich musste meinen ganzen Mut zusammennehmen.* I had to summon up all my courage.; **alles zusammengenommen** all in all; **sich zusammennehmen** to pull oneself together

zusammenpassen (*perf* **hat zusammengepasst**) *vb* [4] ❶ to be well suited ▷ *Die beiden passen gut zusammen.* The two are well suited. ❷ to go together ▷ *Der Pulli und die Hose passen nicht zusammen.* The pullover and the trousers don't go together.

Zusammensein *nt* get-together ▷ *ein gemütliches Zusammensein* a cosy get-together

zusammenstellen (*perf* **hat zusammengestellt**) *vb* [15] ❶ to put together ▷ *Stellt alle Stühle zusammen.* Put all the chairs together. ❷ to compile ▷ *Ich habe eine Wunschliste zusammengestellt.* I've compiled a list of presents I'd like.

Zusammenstoß (*gen* **Zusammenstoßes**, *pl* **Zusammenstöße**) *m* collision

zusammenstoßen (*pres* **stößt zusammen**, *imperf* **stieß zusammen**, *perf* **sind zusammengestoßen**) *vb* to collide

zusammenzählen (*perf* **hat zusammengezählt**) *vb* [4] to add up

zusätzlich *adj, adv* ❶ additional ▷ *Wir sollen eine zusätzliche Englischstunde bekommen.* We're to get an additional English lesson. ❷ in addition ▷ *Zusätzlich zu den Matheaufgaben muss ich noch Physik machen.* I still have some physics to do in addition to my maths homework.

zuschauen (*perf* **hat zugeschaut**) *vb* [4] to watch ▷ *Habt ihr beim Match zugeschaut?* Did you watch the match?

Zuschauer *pl* audience *sg* ▷ *Die Zuschauer haben geklatscht.* The audience clapped.

Zuschlag (*pl* **Zuschläge**) *m* surcharge ▷ *Für den ICE brauchst du einen Zuschlag.* You have to pay a surcharge if you go by Intercity Express.

zusehen (*pres* **sieht zu**, *imperf* **sah zu**, *perf* **hat zugesehen**) *vb* [64] to watch ▷ *Wir haben beim Match zugesehen.* We watched the match. ▷ *Er stand nur dabei und sah zu.* He just stood there watching.; **jemandem zusehen** to watch somebody; **zusehen, dass**

etwas gemacht wird to make sure something is done

zusenden (*imperf* **sendete** *or* **sandte zu**, *perf* **hat zugesendet** *or* **zugesandt**) *vb* to send ▷ *Wir werden Ihnen unseren Prospekt zusenden.* We'll send you our brochure.

Zustand (*pl* **Zustände**) *m* ❶ state ▷ *Das Haus war in einem furchtbaren Zustand.* The house was in an awful state. ▷ *Das sind hier ja schreckliche Zustände.* This is a terrible state of affairs. ❷ condition ▷ *Das Auto ist noch in gutem Zustand.* The car's still in good condition.

zustande *adv* **zustande bringen** to bring about; **zustande kommen** to come about

zuständig *adj* **Dafür bin ich nicht zuständig.** That's not my responsibility.; **der zuständige Beamte** the official in charge

zustimmen (*perf* **hat zugestimmt**) *vb* [4] to agree ▷ *Ich stimme dir zu.* I agree with you.

Zustimmung *f* ❶ consent ▷ *Du brauchst die Zustimmung deiner Eltern.* You need your parents' consent. ❷ approval ▷ *wenn das deine Zustimmung findet* if that meets with your approval

zustoßen (*pres* **stößt zu**, *imperf* **stieß zu**, *perf* **ist zugestoßen**) *vb* to happen ▷ *Ihm ist doch hoffentlich nichts zugestoßen.* Let's hope nothing's happened to him.

Zutaten *fpl* ingredients *pl*

zutreffen (*pres* **trifft zu**, *imperf* **traf zu**, *perf* **hat zugetroffen**) *vb* [78] ❶ to be true ▷ *Es trifft nicht zu, dass ich das Buch mitgenommen habe.* It's not true that I took the book with me. ❷ to apply ▷ *Diese Beschreibung trifft nicht auf sie zu.* This description doesn't apply to her.

zutreffend *adj* **Zutreffendes bitte unterstreichen.** Please underline where applicable.

zuverlässig *adj* reliable

zuversichtlich *adj* confident

zuviel *adv see* **viel**

zuvor *adv* before ▷ *der Tag zuvor* the day before

zuwenig *adv see* **wenig**

zuziehen (*imperf* **zog zu**, *perf* **hat zugezogen**) *vb* [96] ❶ to draw ▷ *Es wird dunkel, zieh bitte die Vorhänge zu.* It's getting dark, please draw the curtains. ❷ to call in ▷ *Wir sollten einen Fachmann zuziehen.* We should call in an expert.; **sich etwas zuziehen** to catch something

Zwang (*pl* **Zwänge**) *m* compulsion

zwängen *vb* [38] to squeeze

zwanglos *adj* informal ▷ *ein zwangloses Gespräch* an informal talk

zwanzig *num* twenty

zwar *adv* although ▷ *Ich habe das zwar gesagt, aber es war nicht so gemeint.* Although I said it, it wasn't meant like that.; **das ist zwar ..., aber ...** that may be ... but ... ▷ *Das ist zwar viel, aber mir reicht es nicht.* That may be a lot, but it's not enough for me.; **und zwar (1)** to be precise ▷ *und zwar am Sonntag* on Sunday to be precise **(2)** in fact ▷ *und zwar so schnell, dass ...* in fact, so quickly that ...

Zweck (*pl* **Zwecke**) *m* ❶ purpose ▷ *Was ist der Zweck Ihres Besuchs?* What's the purpose of your visit? ❷ point ▷ *Was ist der Zweck dieser Übung?* What's the point of this exercise? ▷ *Es hat keinen Zweck.* There's no point.

zwecklos *adj* pointless

zwei *num* two

Zwei *f* ❶ two ❷ good

German marks range from one (**sehr gut**) to six (**ungenügend**).

zweideutig *adj* ❶ ambiguous ▷ *Sie hat sich zweideutig ausgedrückt.* She expressed herself very ambiguously. ❷ suggestive ▷ *Er macht immer so zweideutige Witze.* He's always making such suggestive jokes.

zweierlei *adj* two different ▷ *zweierlei Stoff* two different kinds of material

▷ *Das sind doch zweierlei Dinge.* They're two different things.; **zweierlei Meinung** of differing opinions

zweifach *adj, adv* ❶ double ▷ *die zweifache Menge* double the quantity ❷ twice ▷ *Der Brief war zweifach gefaltet.* The letter had been folded twice.

Zweifel (*pl* **Zweifel**) *m* doubt ▷ *ohne Zweifel* without doubt

zweifelhaft *adj* ❶ doubtful ▷ *Es ist noch zweifelhaft, ob wir kommen.* It's still doubtful whether we're coming. ❷ dubious ▷ *eine zweifelhafte Lösung* a dubious solution; **ein zweifelhaftes Kompliment** a backhanded compliment

zweifellos *adv* doubtless; **Sie hat sich zweifellos bemüht.** There's no doubt that she tried.

zweifeln *vb* [**34**] **an etwas zweifeln** to doubt something; **zweifeln, ob** to doubt whether

Zweig (*pl* **Zweige**) *m* branch

Zweigstelle *f* branch ▷ *Die nächste Zweigstelle ist in Villach.* The nearest branch is in Villach.

zweihundert *num* two hundred

zweimal *adv* twice

zweit *adv* **zu zweit (1)** together ▷ *Wir fahren zu zweit in die Ferien.* We're going on holiday together. **(2)** in twos ▷ *Stellt euch zu zweit auf.* Line up in twos.

zweitbeste *adj* second best

zweite *adj* second ▷ *Er kam als Zweiter.* He was the second to arrive.

zweitens *adv* secondly

Zwetschge *f* damson

Zwieback (*pl* **Zwiebacke**) *m* rusk

Zwiebel *f* onion ▷ *Sebastian mag keine Zwiebeln.* Sebastian doesn't like onions.

Zwilling (*pl* **Zwillinge**) *m* twin ▷ *Diese Zwillinge sehen sich zum Verwechseln ähnlich.* The twins are the spitting image of each other.; **Zwillinge** Gemini

zwingen (*imperf* **zwang**, *perf* **hat gezwungen**) *vb* [**97**] to force

zwischen *prep*

> Use the accusative to express movement or a change of place. Use the dative when there is no change of place.

between ▷ *Er stand zwischen den beiden Mädchen.* He was standing between the two girls. ▷ *Stell deinen Stuhl zwischen unsere.* Put your chair between ours.

Zwischending *nt* cross ▷ *Das ist ein Zwischending zwischen Schreibmaschine und Computer.* It's a cross between a typewriter and a computer.

zwischendurch *adv* in between ▷ *Wir haben zwischendurch eine Pause gemacht.* We had a break in between.

Zwischenfall (*pl* **Zwischenfälle**) *m* incident

Zwischenfrage *f* question

zwölf *num* twelve

Zypern *nt* Cyprus

ENGLISH - GERMAN | ENGLISCH - DEUTSCH

a

A *n (school mark)* Eins *f (pl* Einsen) ▷ *I got an A for my essay.* Ich habe für meinen Aufsatz eine Eins bekommen.

a *art*

> In the nominative use **ein** for masculine and neuter nouns, **eine** for feminine nouns.

❶ ein ▷ *a man* ein Mann ▷ *I saw a man.* Ich habe einen Mann gesehen. ▷ *a child* ein Kind ▷ *an apple* ein Apfel ❷ eine ▷ *a woman* eine Frau ▷ *He gave it to a woman.* Er hat es einer Frau gegeben.

> You do not translate 'a' when you want to describe what somebody does for a living.

▷ *He's a butcher.* Er ist Metzger. ▷ *She's a doctor.* Sie ist Ärztin.; **once a week** einmal pro Woche; **thirty kilometres an hour** dreißig Kilometer in der Stunde; **thirty pence a kilo** dreißig Pence das Kilo; **a hundred pounds** einhundert Pfund

abandon *vb* ❶ *(place)* verlassen [**42**] ❷ *(plan, idea)* aufgeben [**28**]

abbey *n* Kloster *nt (pl* Klöster)

abbreviation *n* Abkürzung *f*

ability *n* Fähigkeit *f*; **to have the ability to do something** fähig sein [**65**], etwas zu tun

able *adj* **to be able to do something** etwas tun können [**41**]

abolish *vb* abschaffen [**4**]

abortion *n* Abtreibung *f*; **She had an abortion.** Sie hat abgetrieben.

about *prep, adv* ❶ *(concerning)* wegen ▷ *I'm phoning about tomorrow's meeting.* Ich rufe wegen des morgigen Treffens an. ❷ *(approximately)* etwa ▷ *It takes about ten hours.* Es dauert etwa zehn Stunden. ▷ *about a hundred pounds* etwa hundert Pfund ▷ *at about eleven o'clock* um etwa elf Uhr ❸ *(around)* in ... herum ▷ *to walk about the town* in der Stadt herumlaufen ❹ über ▷ *a book about London* ein Buch über London; **to be about to do something** gerade etwas tun wollen [**94**]; **to talk about something** über etwas reden [**54**]; **What's the film about?** Wovon handelt der Film?; **How about going to the cinema?** Wie wär's, wenn wir ins Kino gingen?

above *prep, adv* über ▷ *above forty degrees* über vierzig Grad

> Use the accusative to express movement or a change of place. Use the dative when there is no change of place.

▷ *He put his hands above his head.* Er hielt die Hände über den Kopf. ▷ *It's in the cupboard above the sink.* Es ist im Schrank über der Spüle.; **the flat above** die Wohnung darüber; **mentioned above** oben erwähnt; **above all** vor allem

abroad *adv* ❶ im Ausland ▷ *She lives abroad.* Sie lebt im Ausland. ❷ ins Ausland ▷ *to go abroad* ins Ausland gehen

absence *n* Abwesenheit *f*

absent *adj* abwesend

absent-minded *adj* zerstreut ▷ *She's a bit absent-minded.* Sie ist etwas zerstreut.

absolutely *adv* ❶ *(completely)* völlig ▷ *Beate's absolutely right.* Beate hat völlig recht. ❷ ganz sicher ▷ *Do you think it's a good idea? — Absolutely!* Meinst du, das ist eine gute Idee? — Ganz sicher!

abuse *n (of power, drugs)* Missbrauch *m*; **child abuse** die Kindesmisshandlung; **to shout abuse at somebody** jemanden beschimpfen [**18**] ▶ *vb* missbrauchen [**49**]; **to abuse drugs** Drogen missbrauchen [**49**]; **abused children** misshandelte Kinder

academic *adj* **the academic year** das Studienjahr

academy *n* Akademie *f* ▷ *a military academy* eine Militärakademie

accelerate *vb* beschleunigen [**7**]

accelerator *n* Gaspedal *nt (pl* Gaspedale)

accent *n* Akzent *m (pl* Akzente) ▷ *He's got a German accent.* Er hat einen deutschen Akzent.

accept *vb* annehmen [**1**]

acceptable *adj* annehmbar

access *n* ❶ Zugang *m* ▷ *He has access to confidential information.* Er hat Zugang zu vertraulichen Informationen. ❷ Besuchsrecht *nt* ▷ *The father has access to the children.* Der Vater hat ein Besuchsrecht.

accessory *n* **fashion accessories** die Modeartikel *mpl*

accident *n* Unfall *m (pl* Unfälle) ▷ *to have an accident* einen Unfall haben; **by accident (1)** *(by mistake)* versehentlich ▷ *The burglar killed him by accident.* Der Einbrecher hat ihn versehentlich getötet. **(2)** *(by chance)* zufällig ▷ *She met him by accident.* Sie ist ihm zufällig begegnet.

accidental *adj* zufällig

accommodation *n* Unterkunft *f (pl* Unterkünfte)

accompany *vb* begleiten [**2**]

according to *prep* laut ▷ *According to him, everyone had gone.* Laut ihm waren alle weggegangen.

account *n* ❶ Konto *nt (pl* Konten) ▷ *a bank account* ein Bankkonto; **to do the accounts** die Buchführung machen [**48**] ❷ *(report)* Bericht *m (pl* Berichte); **He gave a detailed account of what happened.** Er berichtete genau, was passiert war.; **to take something into account** etwas berücksichtigen [**7**]; **on account of** wegen; **to account for** erklären [**19**]

accountant *n* ❶ *(bookkeeper)* Buchhalter *m (pl* Buchhalter), Buchhalterin *f* ▷ *She's an accountant.* Sie ist Buchhalterin. ❷ *(tax consultant)* Steuerberater *m (pl* Steuerberater), Steuerberaterin *f*

accuracy *n* Genauigkeit *f*

accurate *adj* genau ▷ *accurate information* genaue Information

accurately *adv* genau

accuse *vb* **to accuse somebody (1)** jemanden beschuldigen [**84**] ▷ *She accused me of lying.* Sie beschuldigte mich, ich würde lügen. **(2)** *(police)* jemanden anklagen [**4**] ▷ *The police are accusing her of murder.* Die Polizei klagt sie wegen Mordes an.

ace *n* Ass *nt (gen* Asses, *pl* Asse) ▷ *the ace of hearts* das Herzass

ache *n* Schmerz *m (gen* Schmerzes, *pl* Schmerzen) ▷ *I have an ache in my side.* Ich habe Schmerzen in der Seite. ▶ *vb* wehtun [**81**] ▷ *My leg's aching.* Mein Bein tut weh.

achieve *vb* ❶ *(an aim)* erreichen [**19**] ❷ *(victory)* erringen *(imperf* errang, *perf* hat errungen)

achievement *n* Leistung *f* ▷ *That was quite an achievement.* Das war eine Leistung.

acid *n* Säure *f*; **acid rain** saurer Regen *m*

acne *n* Akne *f* ▷ *She's got acne.* Sie hat Akne.

acquit *vb* **to be acquitted** freigesprochen werden [**91**]

acrobat *n* Akrobat *m (gen* Akrobaten, *pl* Akrobaten), Akrobatin *f* ▷ *He's an acrobat.* Er ist Akrobat.

across *prep, adv* über

> Use the accusative to express movement or a change of place. Use the dative when there is no change of place.

▷ *the shop across the road* der Laden über der Straße ▷ *to walk across the road* über die Straße gehen; **across from** *(opposite)* gegenüber

act *vb* ❶ *(in play, film)* spielen [**38**] ▷ *He acts well.* Er spielt gut. ▷ *She's acting the part of Juliet.* Sie spielt die Rolle der Julia. ❷ *(take action)* handeln [**34**] ▷ *The police acted quickly.* Die Polizei hat schnell gehandelt.; **She acts as his interpreter.** Sie übersetzt für ihn.
▶ *n (in play)* Akt *m (pl* Akte) ▷ *in the first act* im ersten Akt

action *n* Handlung *f*; **The film was full of action.** In dem Film gab es viel Action.; **to take firm action against somebody** hart gegen jemanden vorgehen [**29**]

active *adj* aktiv ▷ *He's a very active person.* Er ist ein sehr aktiver Mensch. ▷ *an active volcano* ein aktiver Vulkan

activity *n* Tätigkeit *f*; **outdoor activities** die Betätigung im Freien *sg*

actor *n* Schauspieler *m (pl* Schauspieler) ▷ *His father is a well-known actor.* Sein Vater ist ein bekannter Schauspieler.

actress *n* Schauspielerin *f* ▷ *Her sister is a well-known actress.* Ihre Schwester ist eine bekannte Schauspielerin.

actual *adj* wirklich ▷ *The film is based on actual events.* Der Film basiert auf wirklichen Begebenheiten.

> Be careful not to translate **actual** by **aktuell**.

actually *adv* ❶ *(really)* wirklich ▷ *Did it actually happen?* Ist das wirklich passiert? ❷ *(in fact)* eigentlich ▷ *Actually, I don't know him at all.* Eigentlich kenne ich ihn überhaupt nicht.

AD *abbr* n. Chr. *(= nach Christus)* ▷ *in 800 AD* im Jahre 800 n. Chr.

ad *n* ❶ *(in paper)* Anzeige *f* ❷ *(on TV, radio)* Werbung *f*

adapt *vb* bearbeiten [**2**] ▷ *His novel was adapted for television.* Sein Roman wurde fürs Fernsehen bearbeitet.; **to adapt to something** *(get used to)* sich in etwas eingewöhnen [**7**]

adaptor *n* Adapter *m (pl* Adapter)

add *vb* hinzufügen [**15**] ▷ *Add two eggs to the mixture.* Fügen Sie dem Teig zwei Eier hinzu.; **to add up** zusammenzählen [**4**]

addict *n (drug addict)* Süchtige *m (gen* Süchtigen, *pl* Süchtigen), Süchtige *f (gen* Süchtigen) ▷ *an addict (man)* ein Süchtiger; **Martin's a football addict.** Martin ist ein Fußballnarr.

addicted *adj* süchtig ▷ *She's addicted to heroin.* Sie ist heroinsüchtig. ▷ *She's addicted to soap operas.* Sie ist süchtig nach Seifenopern.

addition *n* **in addition** außerdem; **in addition to** zusätzlich zu

address *n* Adresse *f* ▷ *What's your address?* Wie ist Ihre Adresse?
▶ *vb* ❶ *(envelope, letter)* adressieren [**76**] ❷ *(speak to)* sprechen [**70**] zu ▷ *She addressed the audience.* Sie sprach zum Publikum.

adjective *n* Adjektiv *nt (pl* Adjektive)

adjust *vb* einstellen [**4**] ▷ *He adjusted the seat to the right height.* Er stellte den Stuhl auf die richtige Höhe ein.; **to adjust to something** *(get used to)* sich in etwas eingewöhnen [**7**]

adjustable *adj* verstellbar

administration *n* Verwaltung *f*

admiral *n* Admiral *m (pl* Admirale)

admire *vb* bewundern [**88**]

admission *n* Eintritt *m* ▷ *'admission free'* 'Eintritt frei'

admit *vb* zugeben [**28**] ▷ *I must admit that ...* Ich muss zugeben, dass ... ▷ *He admitted that he'd done it.* Er gab zu, dass er es getan hat.
adolescent *n* Jugendliche *m* (*gen* Jugendlichen, *pl* Jugendlichen), Jugendliche *f* (*gen* Jugendlichen) ▷ *an adolescent (male)* ein Jugendlicher
adopt *vb* ❶ *(child)* adoptieren [**76**] ▷ *Phil was adopted.* Phil wurde adoptiert. ❷ *(idea)* annehmen [**1**] ▷ *Her suggestion was adopted.* Ihr Vorschlag wurde angenommen.
adopted *adj* adoptiert; **an adopted son** ein Adoptivsohn
adoption *n* Adoption *f*
adore *vb* bewundern [**88**]
Adriatic Sea *n* Adria *f*
adult *n* Erwachsene *m* (*gen* Erwachsenen, *pl* Erwachsenen), Erwachsene *f* (*gen* Erwachsenen) ▷ *an adult (man)* ein Erwachsener; **adult education** die Erwachsenenbildung
advance *vb* ❶ *(move forward)* vorrücken [**4**] (*perf* ist vorgerückt) ▷ *The troops are advancing.* Die Truppen rücken vor. ❷ *(progress)* Fortschritte machen [**48**] ▷ *Technology has advanced a lot.* Die Technik hat große Fortschritte gemacht.
▸ *n* **in advance** vorher
advanced *adj* fortgeschritten
advantage *n* Vorteil *m* (*pl* Vorteile) ▷ *Going to university has many advantages.* Das Studium hat viele Vorteile.; **to take advantage of something** etwas ausnutzen [**4**]; **to take advantage of somebody** jemanden ausnutzen [**4**]
adventure *n* Abenteuer *nt* (*pl* Abenteuer)
adverb *n* Adverb *nt* (*pl* Adverbien)
advert *n* *see* **advertisement**
advertise *vb* annoncieren [**76**] ▷ *Jobs are advertised in the paper.* Stellenangebote werden in der Zeitung annonciert.
advertisement *n* ❶ *(in paper)* Anzeige *f* ❷ *(on TV, radio)* Werbung *f*
advertising *n* Werbung *f* ▷ *She works in advertising.* Sie ist in der Werbung tätig. ▷ *They've increased spending on advertising.* Sie geben mehr Geld für Werbung aus.
advice *n* Rat *m* ▷ *to give somebody advice* jemandem einen Rat geben; **a piece of advice** ein Rat
advise *vb* raten (*pres* rät, *imperf* riet, *perf* hat geraten) ▷ *He advised me to wait.* Er riet mir zu warten. ▷ *He advised me not to go.* Er hat mir geraten, nicht zu gehen.
aerial *n* Antenne *f*
aerobics *npl* Aerobic *nt* ▷ *I'm going to aerobics tonight.* Ich mache heute Abend Aerobic.
aeroplane *n* Flugzeug *nt* (*pl* Flugzeuge)
aerosol *n* Spray *m* (*pl* Sprays)
affair *n* ❶ *(romantic)* Verhältnis *nt* (*gen* Verhältnisses, *pl* Verhältnisse) ▷ *to have an affair with somebody* mit jemandem ein Verhältnis haben ❷ *(event)* Angelegenheit *f*
affect *vb* ❶ *(influence)* beeinflussen [**7**] ▷ *Does junk food affect children's behaviour?* Beeinflusst Junkfood das Verhalten von Kindern? ❷ *(have effect on)* beeinträchtigen [**84**] ▷ *The weather has affected sales.* Das Wetter hat den Absatz beeinträchtigt.
affectionate *adj* liebevoll
afford *vb* sich leisten [**2**] ▷ *I can't afford a new pair of jeans.* Ich kann mir keine neue Jeans leisten. ▷ *We can't afford to go on holiday.* Wir können es uns nicht leisten, in Urlaub zu fahren.
afraid *adj* **to be afraid of something** vor etwas Angst haben [**32**]; **I'm afraid I can't come.** Ich kann leider nicht kommen.; **I'm afraid so.** Ja, leider.; **I'm afraid not.** Leider nicht.
Africa *n* Afrika *nt*; **from Africa** aus Afrika; **to Africa** nach Afrika

African *adj* afrikanisch
▶ *n* Afrikaner *m* (*pl* Afrikaner), Afrikanerin *f*

after *prep, adv, conj* nach ▷ *after dinner* nach dem Abendessen ▷ *He ran after me.* Er rannte mir nach.; **soon after** kurz danach; **after I'd had a rest** nachdem ich mich ausgeruht hatte; **After eating I left.** Nachdem ich gegessen hatte, ging ich.; **after all** schließlich

afternoon *n* Nachmittag *m* (*pl* Nachmittage) ▷ *three o'clock in the afternoon* drei Uhr nachmittags ▷ *this afternoon* heute Nachmittag ▷ *on Saturday afternoon* Samstag Nachmittag

afters *npl* Nachtisch *msg* (*pl* Nachtische)

aftershave *n* Aftershave *nt* (*pl* Aftershaves)

afterwards *adv* danach ▷ *She left not long afterwards.* Sie ging kurz danach.

again *adv* ❶ *(once more)* wieder ▷ *They're friends again.* Sie sind wieder Freunde. ❷ *(one more time)* noch einmal ▷ *Can you tell me again?* Kannst du mir das noch einmal sagen?; **not ... again** nie mehr; **Do it again!** Mach's noch mal!; **again and again** immer wieder

against *prep* gegen ▷ *He leant against the wall.* Er lehnte gegen die Wand. ▷ *I'm against animal testing.* Ich bin gegen Tierversuche.

age *n* Alter *nt* (*pl* Alter) ▷ *an age limit* eine Altersgrenze; **at the age of sixteen** mit sechzehn; **I haven't seen her for ages.** Ich habe sie schon ewig nicht mehr gesehen.

agenda *n* Tagesordnung *f*

agent *n* Agent *m* (*gen* Agenten, *pl* Agenten), Agentin *f*; **an estate agent** ein Immobilienmakler; **a travel agent** ein Reisebüro

aggressive *adj* aggressiv

ago *adv* **two days ago** vor zwei Tagen; **two years ago** vor zwei Jahren; **not long ago** vor Kurzem; **How long ago did it happen?** Wie lange ist das her?

agony *n* **He was in agony.** Er hatte furchtbare Schmerzen.

agree *vb* **to agree with somebody** jemandem zustimmen [**4**]; **to agree to do something** bereit sein [**65**], etwas zu tun; **to agree that ...** *(admit)* zugeben [**28**], dass ...; **Garlic doesn't agree with me.** Ich vertrage Knoblauch nicht.

agreement *n* Abmachung *f*; **to be in agreement** übereinstimmen [**4**]

agricultural *adj* landwirtschaftlich

agriculture *n* Landwirtschaft *f*

ahead *adv* voraus ▷ *We sent him on ahead.* Wir schickten ihn voraus.; **The Germans are five points ahead.** Die Deutschen führen mit fünf Punkten.; **She looked straight ahead.** Sie sah geradeaus.; **ahead of time** vorzeitig; **to plan ahead** vorausplanen [**15**]; **Go ahead!** Ja bitte!

aid *n* **in aid of charity** für wohltätige Zwecke

AIDS *n* Aids *nt* (*gen* Aids) ▷ *He died of AIDS.* Er starb an Aids.

aim *vb* **to aim at** zielen [**38**] auf; **The film is aimed at children.** Der Film ist für Kinder gedacht.; **to aim to do something** beabsichtigen [**84**], etwas zu tun
▶ *n* Ziel *nt* (*pl* Ziele) ▷ *The aim of the festival is to raise money.* Ziel des Festivals ist, Geld aufzutreiben.

air *n* Luft *f* (*pl* Lüfte); **to get some fresh air** frische Luft schnappen [**48**]; **by air** mit dem Flugzeug

air-conditioned *adj* mit Klimaanlage

air conditioning *n* Klimaanlage *f*

Air Force *n* Luftwaffe *f*

air hostess *n* Stewardess *f* (*pl* Stewardessen) ▷ *She's an air hostess.* Sie ist Stewardess.

airline *n* Fluggesellschaft *f*

airmail *n* **by airmail** mit Luftpost

a b c d e f g h i j k l m n o p q r s t u v w x y z

airplane *n (US)* Flugzeug *nt (pl* Flugzeuge)
airport *n* Flughafen *m (pl* Flughäfen)
aisle *n* ❶ *(in church)* Mittelgang *m (pl* Mittelgänge) ❷ *(in plane)* Gang *m (pl* Gänge) ▷ *an aisle seat* ein Platz am Gang
alarm *n (warning)* Alarm *m (pl* Alarme); **a fire alarm** ein Feueralarm
alarm clock *n* Wecker *m (pl* Wecker)
album *n* Album *nt (pl* Alben)
alcohol *n* Alkohol *m*
alcoholic *n* Alkoholiker *m (pl* Alkoholiker), Akoholikerin *f* ▷ *He's an alcoholic.* Er ist Alkoholiker. ▶ *adj* alkoholisch ▷ *alcoholic drinks* alkoholische Getränke
alert *adj* ❶ *(bright)* aufgeweckt ▷ *He's a very alert baby.* Er ist ein sehr aufgewecktes Baby. ❷ *(paying attention)* wachsam ▷ *We must stay alert.* Wir müssen wachsam bleiben.
A levels *npl* Abitur *nt sg*

- Germans take their **Abitur** at the age of 19. The students sit examinations in a variety of subjects to attain an overall grade. If you pass, you have the right to a place at university.

alike *adv* **to look alike** sich ähnlich sehen [**64**]
alive *adj* am Leben
all *adj, pron, adv* ❶ alle ▷ *all the books* alle Bücher; **all the time** die ganze Zeit; **all day** den ganzen Tag ❷ alles ▷ *He ate it all.* Er hat alles gegessen. ▷ *I ate all of it.* Ich habe alles gegessen.; **All of us went.** Wir sind alle hingegangen.; **after all** schließlich; **all alone** ganz allein; **not at all** überhaupt nicht; **The score is five all.** Es steht fünf zu fünf.
allergic *adj* allergisch; **to be allergic to something** allergisch gegen etwas sein [**65**]
allergy *n* Allergie *f (pl* Allergien) ▷ *Have you got any allergies?* Hast du Allergien?
allow *vb* **to be allowed to do something** etwas tun dürfen [**16**]; **to allow somebody to do something** jemandem erlauben [**19**], etwas zu tun
all right *adv* ❶ *(okay)* gut ▷ *Everything turned out all right.* Alles ist gut gegangen.; **Are you all right?** Bist du in Ordnung? ❷ *(not bad)* okay ▷ *The film was all right.* Der Film war okay. ❸ *(when agreeing)* einverstanden ▷ *We'll talk about it later. — All right.* Wir reden später darüber. — Einverstanden.; **Is that all right with you?** Ist das okay?
almond *n* Mandel *f (pl* Mandeln)
almost *adv* fast ▷ *I've almost finished.* Ich bin fast fertig.
alone *adj, adv* allein ▷ *She lives alone.* Sie lebt allein.; **to leave somebody alone** jemanden in Ruhe lassen [**42**]; **to leave something alone** etwas nicht anfassen [**31**]
along *prep, adv* entlang ▷ *Chris was walking along the beach.* Chris ging am Strand entlang.; **all along** die ganze Zeit
aloud *adv* laut ▷ *He read the poem aloud.* Er las das Gedicht vor.
alphabet *n* Alphabet *nt (pl* Alphabete)
Alps *npl* Alpen *fpl*
already *adv* schon ▷ *Liz had already gone.* Liz war schon weg.
also *adv* auch

Be careful not to translate **also** by the German word **also**.

alter *vb* verändern [**88**]
alternate *adj* **on alternate days** abwechselnd jeden zweiten Tag
alternative *n* Alternative *f* ▷ *Fruit is a healthy alternative to chocolate.* Obst ist eine gesunde Alternative zu Schokolade.; **You have no alternative.** Du hast keine andere Wahl.; **There are several alternatives.** Es gibt mehrere Möglichkeiten. ▶ *adj* andere ▷ *an alternative solution*

eine andere Lösung ▷ *an alternative suggestion* ein anderer Vorschlag; **alternative medicine** die alternative Medizin

alternatively *adv* **Alternatively, we could just stay at home.** Wir könnten auch zu Hause bleiben.

although *conj* obwohl ▷ *Although she was tired, she stayed up late.* Obwohl sie müde war, blieb sie lange auf.

altogether *adv* ❶ *(in total)* insgesamt ▷ *You owe me twenty pounds altogether.* Du schuldest mir insgesamt zwanzig Pfund. ❷ *(completely)* ganz ▷ *I'm not altogether happy with your work.* Ich bin mit Ihrer Arbeit nicht ganz zufrieden.

aluminium (*US* **aluminum**) *n* Aluminium *nt*

always *adv* immer ▷ *He's always moaning.* Er beklagt sich immer.

am *vb see* **be**

a.m. *abbr* morgens ▷ *at four a.m.* um vier Uhr morgens

amateur *n* Amateur *m* (*pl* Amateure), Amateurin *f* ▷ *He's an amateur.* Er ist Amateur.

amaze *vb* **to be amazed** erstaunt sein [**65**]

amazing *adj* ❶ *(surprising)* erstaunlich ▷ *That's amazing news!* Das sind erstaunliche Neuigkeiten! ❷ *(excellent)* ausgezeichnet ▷ *Vivian's an amazing cook.* Vivian ist eine ausgezeichnete Köchin.

ambassador *n* Botschafter *m* (*pl* Botschafter), Botschafterin *f*

ambition *n* Ehrgeiz *m* (*gen* Ehrgeizes)

ambitious *adj* ehrgeizig ▷ *She's very ambitious.* Sie ist sehr ehrgeizig.

ambulance *n* Krankenwagen *m* (*pl* Krankenwagen)

amenities *npl* **The hotel has very good amenities.** Das Hotel hat viel zu bieten.

America *n* Amerika *nt*; **from America** aus Amerika; **in America** in Amerika; **to America** nach Amerika

American *adj* amerikanisch ▷ *He's American.* Er ist Amerikaner. ▷ *She's American.* Sie ist Amerikanerin.
▶ *n* Amerikaner *m* (*pl* Amerikaner), Amerikanerin *f*; **the Americans** die Amerikaner

among *prep* unter ▷ *I was among friends.* Ich war unter Freunden.; **among other things** unter anderem

amount *n* ❶ Betrag *m* (*pl* Beträge) ▷ *a large amount of money* ein großer Geldbetrag ❷ Menge *f* ▷ *a huge amount of rice* eine enorme Menge Reis

amp *n* ❶ *(of electricity)* Ampere *nt* (*gen* Ampere, *pl* Ampere) ❷ *(for hi-fi)* Verstärker *m* (*pl* Verstärker)

amplifier *n* *(for hi-fi)* Verstärker *m* (*pl* Verstärker)

amuse *vb* belustigen [**7**]; **He was most amused by the story.** Er fand die Geschichte sehr lustig.

amusement *n* *(enjoyment)* Vergnügen *nt* (*pl* Vergnügen); **amusement arcade** die Spielhalle

an *art see* **a**

analyse *vb* analysieren [**76**]

analysis *n* Analyse *f*

ancestor *n* Vorfahr *m* (*gen* Vorfahren, *pl* Vorfahren), Vorfahrin *f*

anchor *n* Anker *m* (*pl* Anker)

ancient *adj* alt ▷ *This is an ancient custom.* Das ist ein alter Brauch.; **ancient Greece** das antike Griechenland; **an ancient monument** ein historisches Denkmal

and *conj* und ▷ *you and me* du und ich ▷ *Two and two are four.* Zwei und zwei gibt vier. ▷ *He talked and talked.* Er redete und redete.; **Please try and come!** Versuche bitte zu kommen!; **better and better** immer besser

angel *n* Engel *m* (*pl* Engel)

> Be careful not to translate **angel** by the German word **Angel**.

anger *n* Wut *f*

angle *n* Winkel *m* (*pl* Winkel)

a b c d e f g h i j k l m n o p q r s t u v w x y z

angry *adj* böse ▷ *Dad looks very angry.* Papa sieht sehr böse aus.; **to be angry with somebody** mit jemandem böse sein [**65**]; **to get angry** wütend werden [**91**]
animal *n* Tier *nt* (*pl* Tiere)
ankle *n* Fußknöchel *m* (*pl* Fußknöchel)
anniversary *n* Jahrestag *m* (*pl* Jahrestage); **wedding anniversary** der Hochzeitstag
announce *vb* ankündigen [**4**]
announcement *n* Ankündigung *f*
annoy *vb* ärgern [**88**] ▷ *He's really annoying me.* Er ärgert mich echt.; **to get annoyed** wütend werden [**91**]
annoying *adj* ärgerlich ▷ *It's really annoying.* Es ist wirklich ärgerlich.
annual *adj* jährlich ▷ *an annual meeting* ein jährliches Treffen
anonymous *adj* anonym
anorak *n* Anorak *m* (*pl* Anoraks)
another *adj*

Use **noch ein** for masculine and neuter nouns, **noch eine** for feminine nouns.

❶ noch ein ▷ *I bought another hat.* Ich habe noch einen Hut gekauft. ▷ *Would you like another piece of cake?* Möchtest du noch ein Stück Kuchen?
noch eine ▷ *Would you like another cup of tea?* Möchten Sie noch eine Tasse Tee?

Use **ein anderer** for masculine, **eine andere** for feminine and **ein anderes** for neuter nouns.

❷ (*different*) ein anderer ▷ *Could you show me another hat?* Könnten Sie mir einen anderen Hut zeigen?
eine andere ▷ *My girlfriend goes to another school.* Meine Freundin besucht eine andere Schule.
ein anderes ▷ *Have you got another shirt?* Haben Sie noch ein anderes Hemd?; **another time** ein andermal
answer *vb* beantworten [**2**] ▷ *Can you answer my question?* Kannst du meine Frage beantworten?; **to answer the phone** ans Telefon gehen [**29**]; **to answer the door** aufmachen [**4**]
▶ *n* ❶ (*to question*) Antwort *f* ❷ (*to problem*) Lösung *f*
answering machine *n* Anrufbeantworter *m* (*pl* Anrufbeantworter)
ant *n* Ameise *f*
Antarctic *n* Antarktis *f*
anthem *n* **the national anthem** die Nationalhymne
antibiotic *n* Antibiotikum *nt* (*pl* Antibiotika)
antique *n* (*furniture*) Antiquität *f*
antique shop *n* Antiquitätenladen *m* (*pl* Antiquitätenläden)
antiseptic *n* Antiseptikum *nt* (*pl* Antiseptika)
any *adj, pron, adv*

In most cases 'any' is not translated.

▷ *Would you like any bread?* Möchten Sie Brot? ▷ *Have you got any mineral water?* Haben Sie Mineralwasser?

Use **kein** for 'not any'.

▷ *We haven't got any milk left.* Wir haben keine Milch mehr. ▷ *I haven't got any money.* Ich habe kein Geld. ▷ *I haven't got any books.* Ich habe keine Bücher. ▷ *Sorry, we haven't got any.* Tut mir leid, wir haben keine.; **any more** (**1**) (*additional*) noch etwas ▷ *Would you like any more coffee?* Möchten Sie noch etwas Kaffee? (**2**) (*no longer*) nicht mehr ▷ *I don't love him any more.* Ich liebe ihn nicht mehr.
anybody *pron* ❶ (*in question*) jemand ▷ *Has anybody got a pen?* Hat jemand etwas zum Schreiben? ❷ (*no matter who*) jeder ▷ *Anybody can learn to swim.* Jeder kann schwimmen lernen.

Use **niemand** for 'not ... anybody'.

▷ *I can't see anybody.* Ich kann niemanden sehen.
anyhow *adv* sowieso
anyone *pron* ❶ (*in question*) jemand ❷ (*no matter who*) jeder

anything *pron* ❶ *(in question)* etwas ▷ *Would you like anything to eat?* Möchtest du etwas zu essen? ❷ *(no matter what)* alles ▷ *Anything could happen.* Alles könnte passieren.

Use **nichts** for 'not ... anything'.

▷ *I can't hear anything.* Ich kann nichts hören.

anyway *adv* sowieso ▷ *He doesn't want to go out and anyway he's not allowed.* Er will nicht ausgehen, und er darf es sowieso auch nicht.

anywhere *adv* ❶ *(in question)* irgendwo ▷ *Have you seen my coat anywhere?* Hast du irgendwo meinen Mantel gesehen? ❷ überall ▷ *You can buy stamps almost anywhere.* Man kann fast überall Briefmarken kaufen.

Use **nirgends** for 'not ... anywhere'.

❸ nirgends ▷ *I can't find it anywhere.* Ich kann es nirgends finden.

apart *adv* **The two towns are ten kilometres apart.** Die zwei Städte liegen zehn Kilometer voneinander entfernt.; **apart from** abgesehen von

apartment *n* Wohnung *f*

apologize *vb* sich entschuldigen **[18]** ▷ *He apologized for being late.* Er entschuldigte sich für sein Zuspätkommen.; **I apologize!** Ich bitte um Entschuldigung!

apology *n* Entschuldigung *f*

apostrophe *n* Apostroph *m* (*pl* Apostrophe)

app *n* (= *application*) App *f* (*pl* Apps)

apparent *adj* offensichtlich

apparently *adv* offensichtlich

appeal *vb* bitten **[9]** ▷ *They appealed for help.* Sie baten um Hilfe.; **to appeal to somebody** *(attract)* jemanden reizen **[36]**

▶ *n* Aufruf *m* (*pl* Aufrufe)

appear *vb* ❶ *(come into view)* kommen **[40]** ▷ *The bus appeared around the corner.* Der Bus kam um die Ecke.; **to appear on TV** im Fernsehen auftreten **[79]** ❷ *(seem)* scheinen **[57]** ▷ *She appeared to be asleep.* Sie schien zu schlafen.

appendicitis *n* Blinddarmentzündung *f*

appetite *n* Appetit *m*

applaud *vb* klatschen **[48]**

applause *n* Beifall *m*

apple *n* Apfel *m* (*pl* Äpfel); **an apple tree** ein Apfelbaum *m*

applicant *n* Bewerber *m* (*pl* Bewerber), Bewerberin *f* ▷ *There were a hundred applicants for the job.* Es gab hundert Bewerber für die Stelle.

application *n* **a job application** eine Bewerbung

application form *n* ❶ *(for job)* Bewerbungsformular *nt* (*pl* Bewerbungsformulare) ❷ *(for university)* Anmeldeformular *nt* (*pl* Anmeldeformulare)

apply *vb* **to apply for a job** sich für eine Stelle bewerben **[90]**; **to apply to** *(be relevant)* zutreffen **[78]** auf

appointment *n* Termin *m* (*pl* Termine) ▷ *I've got a dental appointment.* Ich habe einen Zahnarzttermin.

appreciate *vb* zu schätzen wissen **[93]** ▷ *I really appreciate your help.* Ich weiß deine Hilfe wirklich zu schätzen.

apprentice *n* Lehrling *m* (*pl* Lehrlinge)

der Lehrling is also used for women.

▷ *She is an apprentice.* Sie ist Lehrling.

approach *vb* ❶ *(get nearer to)* sich nähern **[88]** ▷ *He approached the house.* Er näherte sich dem Haus. ❷ *(tackle)* angehen **[29]** ▷ *to approach a problem* ein Problem angehen

appropriate *adj* passend ▷ *That dress isn't very appropriate for an interview.* Dieses Kleid ist für ein Vorstellungsgespräch nicht sehr passend.

approval *n* Zustimmung *f*

approve *vb* **to approve of** gutheißen; **They didn't approve of his girlfriend.** Sie hatten etwas gegen seine Freundin.

approximate *adj* ungefähr

apricot *n* Aprikose *f*

April *n* April *m* ▷ *in April* im April; **April Fool's Day** der erste April; **April Fool!** April, April!

apron *n* Schürze *f*

Aquarius *n* Wassermann *m* ▷ *I'm Aquarius.* Ich bin Wassermann.

Arab *adj* arabisch ▷ *the Arab countries* die arabischen Länder
▶ *n* Araber *m* (*pl* Araber), Araberin *f*

Arabic *adj* arabisch

arch *n* Bogen *m* (*pl* Bögen)

archaeologist (*US* **archeologist**) *n* Archäologe *m* (*gen* Archäologen, *pl* Archäologen), Archäologin *f* ▷ *She's an archaeologist.* Sie ist Archäologin.

archaeology (*US* **archeology**) *n* Archäologie *f*

archbishop *n* Erzbischof *m* (*pl* Erzbischöfe)

archeologist *n (US)* Archäologe *m* (*gen* Archäologen, *pl* Archäologen), Archäologin *f*

archeology *n (US)* Archäologie *f*

architect *n* Architekt *m* (*gen* Architekten, *pl* Architekten), Architektin *f* ▷ *She's an architect.* Sie ist Architektin.

architecture *n* Architektur *f*

Arctic *n* Arktis *f*

are *vb see* **be**

area *n* ❶ Gegend *f* ▷ *She lives in the London area.* Sie lebt in der Gegend von London. ❷ Viertel *nt* (*pl* Viertel) ▷ *my favourite area of London* mein Lieblingsviertel von London ❸ Fläche *f* ▷ *an area of one thousand square metres* eine Fläche von eintausend Quadratmetern

Argentina *n* Argentinien *nt*; **from Argentina** aus Argentinien

Argentinian *adj* argentinisch

argue *vb* streiten (*imperf* stritt, *perf* hat gestritten) ▷ *They never stop arguing.* Sie streiten dauernd.

argument *n* Streit *m* (*pl* Streite); **to have an argument** Streit haben [**32**]

Aries *n* Widder *m* ▷ *I'm Aries.* Ich bin Widder.

arm *n* Arm *m* (*pl* Arme)

armchair *n* Sessel *m* (*pl* Sessel)

army *n* Armee *f* (*pl* Armeen)

around *prep, adv* ❶ um ▷ *around the corner* um die Ecke ❷ *(approximately)* etwa ▷ *around a hundred pounds* etwa einhundert Pfund ❸ *(date, time)* gegen ▷ *around eight p.m.* gegen acht Uhr abends; **around here (1)** *(nearby)* hier in der Nähe ▷ *Is there a chemist's around here?* Gibt es hier in der Nähe eine Apotheke? **(2)** *(in this area)* hier in der Gegend ▷ *He lives around here.* Er wohnt hier in der Gegend.

arrange *vb* **to arrange to do something** verabreden [**84**], etwas zu tun; **to arrange a meeting** ein Treffen ausmachen [**48**]; **to arrange a party** eine Party vorbereiten [**2**]

arrangement *n (plan)* Plan *m* (*pl* Pläne); **They made arrangements to go out on Friday night.** Sie haben verabredet, am Freitagabend auszugehen.

arrest *vb* verhaften [**2**] ▷ *The police have arrested five people.* Die Polizei hat fünf Leute verhaftet.
▶ *n* Verhaftung *f*; **You're under arrest!** Sie sind verhaftet!

arrival *n* Ankunft *f* (*pl* Ankünfte)

arrive *vb* ankommen [**40**] ▷ *I arrived at five o'clock.* Ich bin um fünf Uhr angekommen.

arrogant *adj* arrogant

arrow *n* Pfeil *m* (*pl* Pfeile)

art *n* Kunst *f* (*pl* Künste)

artery *n* Arterie *f*

art gallery *n* Kunstgalerie *f*

article *n* Artikel *m* (*pl* Artikel) ▷ *a newspaper article* ein Zeitungsartikel

artificial *adj* künstlich

artist *n* Künstler *m* (*pl* Künstler), Künstlerin *f* ▷ *She's an artist.* Sie ist Künstlerin.
artistic *adj* künstlerisch
as *conj, adv* ❶ *(while)* als ▷ *He came in as I was leaving.* Er kam herein, als ich gehen wollte.; **He works as a waiter in the holidays.** In den Ferien jobbt er als Kellner. ❷ *(since)* da ▷ *As it's Sunday, you can have a lie-in.* Da es Sonntag ist, kannst du ausschlafen.; **as ... as** so ... wie; **as much ... as** so viel ... wie; **as soon as possible** sobald wie möglich; **as from tomorrow** ab morgen; **as if** als ob; **as though** als ob

Note that **als ob** is followed by the subjunctive.

▷ *She acted as though she hadn't seen me.* Sie tat so, als ob sie mich nicht sähe.
ash *n* Asche *f*
ashamed *adj* **to be ashamed** sich schämen [**38**]
ashtray *n* Aschenbecher *m* (*pl* Aschenbecher)
Asia *n* Asien *nt*; **from Asia** aus Asien
Asian *adj* asiatisch ▷ *He's Asian.* Er ist Asiate. ▷ *She's Asian.* Sie ist Asiatin. ▶ *n* Asiate *m* (*gen* Asiaten, *pl* Asiaten), Asiatin *f*
ask *vb* ❶ *(inquire, request)* fragen [**38**] ▷ *'Have you finished?' she asked.* 'Bist du fertig?' fragte sie.; **to ask somebody something** jemanden etwas fragen [**38**]; **to ask for something** um etwas bitten [**9**]; **to ask somebody to do something** jemanden bitten [**9**], etwas zu tun; **to ask about something** sich nach etwas erkundigen [**19**]; **to ask somebody a question** jemanden etwas fragen [**38**] ❷ *(invite)* einladen (*pres* lädt ein, *imperf* lud ein, *perf* hat eingeladen) ▷ *Have you asked Matthew to the party?* Hast du Matthew zur Party eingeladen?; **He asked her out.** *(on a date)* Er hat sie um ein Rendezvous gebeten.
asleep *adj* **to be asleep** schlafen [**58**]; **to fall asleep** einschlafen [**58**]
asparagus *n* Spargel *m* (*pl* Spargel)
aspirin *n* Schmerztablette *f*
assignment *n (in school)* Referat *nt* (*pl* Referate)
assistance *n* Hilfe *f*
assistant *n* ❶ *(in shop)* Verkäufer *m* (*pl* Verkäufer), Verkäuferin *f* ❷ *(helper)* Assistent *m* (*gen* Assistenten, *pl* Assistenten), Assistentin *f*
association *n* Verband *m* (*pl* Verbände)
assortment *n* ❶ *(choice)* Auswahl *f* ▷ *a large assortment of cheeses* eine große Auswahl an Käse ❷ *(mixture)* Mischung *f* ▷ *an assortment of biscuits* eine Keksmischung
assume *vb* annehmen [**1**] ▷ *I assume she won't be coming.* Ich nehme an, dass sie nicht kommt.
assure *vb* versichern [**88**] ▷ *He assured me he was coming.* Er versicherte mir, dass er kommt.
asthma *n* Asthma *nt* ▷ *I've got asthma.* Ich habe Asthma.
astonishing *adj* erstaunlich
astrology *n* Astrologie *f*
astronaut *n* Astronaut *m* (*gen* Astronauten, *pl* Astronauten), Astronautin *f*
astronomy *n* Astronomie *f*
asylum *n* Asyl *nt* ▷ *to ask for asylum* um Asyl bitten
asylum-seeker *n* Asylbewerber *m* (*pl* Asylbewerber), Asylbewerberin *f*
at *prep* ❶ um ▷ *at four o'clock* um vier Uhr ❷ an ▷ *at Christmas* an Weihnachten ▷ *What are you doing at the weekend?* Was machst du am Wochenende?; **at night** nachts ❸ mit ▷ *at fifty kilometres per hour* mit fünfzig Stundenkilometern ❹ in ▷ *at school* in der Schule ▷ *at the office* im Büro; **at home** zu Hause; **two at a time** jeweils zwei; **at the races** beim Pferderennen ▶ *n (@ symbol)* At-Zeichen *nt* (*pl* At-Zeichen)

ate *vb see* **eat**
Athens *n* Athen *nt*
athlete *n* Athlet *m* (*gen* Athleten, *pl* Athleten), Athletin *f*
athletic *adj* athletisch
athletics *n* Leichtathletik *f* ▷ *I like watching the athletics on TV.* Ich sehe mir im Fernsehen gern Leichtathletik an.
Atlantic *n* Atlantik *m*
atlas *n* Atlas *m* (*gen* Atlasses, *pl* Atlanten)
atmosphere *n* Atmosphäre *f*
atom *n* Atom *nt* (*pl* Atome)
atomic *adj* **an atomic bomb** eine Atombombe
attach *vb* festbinden (*imperf* band fest, *perf* hat festgebunden) ▷ *They attached a rope to the car.* Sie banden ein Seil am Auto fest.; **Please find attached ...** Anbei erhalten Sie ...
attached *adj* **to be attached to somebody** an jemandem hängen [**35**]
attack *vb* angreifen (*imperf* griff an, *perf* hat angegriffen) ▷ *The dog attacked me.* Der Hund hat mich angegriffen.
▶ *n* Angriff *m* (*pl* Angriffe)
attempt *n* Versuch *m* (*pl* Versuche) ▷ *She gave up after several attempts.* Sie gab nach mehreren Versuchen auf.
▶ *vb* versuchen [**84**]; **to attempt to do something** versuchen [**84**], etwas zu tun
attend *vb* teilnehmen [**52**] ▷ *to attend a meeting* an einem Treffen teilnehmen
attention *n* Aufmerksamkeit *f*; **to pay attention to something** auf etwas achten [**2**]
attic *n* Speicher *m* (*pl* Speicher)
attitude *n* Einstellung *f* ▷ *I really don't like your attitude!* Mir gefällt deine Einstellung nicht!
attorney *n* (*US*) Rechtsanwalt *m* (*pl* Rechtsanwälte), Rechtsanwältin *f* ▷ *My mother's an attorney.* Meine Mutter ist Rechtsanwältin.
attract *vb* anziehen [**96**] ▷ *The Lake District attracts lots of tourists.* Der Lake District zieht viele Touristen an.
attraction *n* Attraktion *f* ▷ *a tourist attraction* eine Touristenattraktion
attractive *adj* attraktiv ▷ *She's very attractive.* Sie ist sehr attraktiv.
aubergine *n* Aubergine *f*
auction *n* Auktion *f*
audience *n* (*in theatre*) Zuschauer *mpl* ▷ *The audience clapped.* Die Zuschauer klatschten.
August *n* August *m* ▷ *in August* im August
aunt *n* Tante *f* ▷ *my aunt* meine Tante
aunty *n* Tante *f* ▷ *my aunty* meine Tante
au pair *n* Au-pair-Mädchen *nt* (*pl* Au-pair-Mädchen) ▷ *She's an au pair.* Sie ist Au-pair-Mädchen.
Australia *n* Australien *nt*
Australian *adj* australisch ▷ *He's Australian.* Er ist Australier. ▷ *She's Australian.* Sie ist Australierin.
▶ *n* Australier *m* (*pl* Australier), Australierin *f*; **the Australians** die Australier
Austria *n* Österreich *nt*; **from Austria** aus Österreich; **in Austria** in Österreich; **to Austria** nach Österreich
Austrian *adj* österreichisch ▷ *He's Austrian.* Er ist Österreicher. ▷ *She's Austrian.* Sie ist Österreicherin.
▶ *n* Österreicher *m* (*pl* Österreicher), Österreicherin *f*; **the Austrians** die Österreicher
author *n* Autor *m* (*pl* Autoren), Autorin *f* ▷ *She's a famous author.* Sie ist eine berühmte Autorin.
autobiography *n* Autobiografie *f*
autograph *n* Autogramm *nt* (*pl* Autogramme) ▷ *May I have your autograph?* Kann ich Ihr Autogramm haben?
automatic *adj* automatisch ▷ *an automatic door* eine automatische Tür
automatically *adv* automatisch

autumn *n* Herbst *m* (*pl* Herbste) ▷ *in autumn* im Herbst
availability *n (of goods)* Erhältlichkeit *f*; **subject to availability** falls vorrätig
available *adj* erhältlich ▷ *Brochures are available on request.* Prospekte sind auf Anfrage erhältlich.; **Is Mr Cooke available today?** Ist Herr Cooke heute zu sprechen?
avalanche *n* Lawine *f*
avatar *n* Avatar *m* (*pl* Avatars)
avenue *n* Allee *f*
average *n* Durchschnitt *m* (*pl* Durchschnitte) ▷ *on average* im Durchschnitt
▶ *adj* durchschnittlich ▷ *the average price* der durchschnittliche Preis
avocado *n* Avocado *f* (*pl* Avocados)
avoid *vb* ❶ meiden (*imperf* mied, *perf* hat gemieden) ▷ *He avoids her when she's in a bad mood.* Er meidet sie, wenn sie schlechte Laune hat. ❷ vermeiden ▷ *You should avoid going out on your own at night.* Du solltest vermeiden, nachts allein auszugehen.
awake *adj* **to be awake** wach sein [**65**]
award *n* Preis *m* (*pl* Preise) ▷ *He's won an award.* Er hat einen Preis bekommen. ▷ *the award for the best actor* der Preis für den besten Schauspieler
aware *adj* **to be aware that ...** sich bewusst sein [**65**], dass ...; **to be aware of something** etwas merken [**38**]; **not that I am aware of** nicht dass ich wüsste
away *adj, adv (not here)* weg ▷ *Felix is away today.* Felix ist heute weg. ▷ *He's away for a week.* Er ist eine Woche lang weg.; **The town's two kilometres away.** Die Stadt ist zwei Kilometer entfernt.; **The coast is two hours away by car.** Zur Küste sind es mit dem Auto zwei Stunden.; **Go away!** Geh weg!
away match *n* Auswärtsspiel *nt* (*pl* Auswärtsspiele) ▷ *Our team has an away match this week.* Unsere Mannschaft hat diese Woche ein Auswärtsspiel.
awful *adj* schrecklich ▷ *That's awful!* Das ist schrecklich!; **an awful lot of ...** furchtbar viel ...
awkward *adj* ❶ *(difficult)* schwierig ▷ *an awkward situation* eine schwierige Situation ▷ *It's a bit awkward for me to come and see you.* Es ist für mich etwas schwierig, dich zu besuchen.
❷ *(embarrassing)* unangenehm ▷ *an awkward question* eine unangenehme Frage
axe *n* Axt *f* (*pl* Äxte)

b

baby *n* Baby *nt* (*pl* Babys)

babysit *vb* babysitten [**2**] ▷ *Veronika is babysitting for her friend.* Veronika babysittet bei ihrer Freundin.

babysitter *n* Babysitter *m* (*pl* Babysitter), Babysitterin *f*

babysitting *n* Babysitten *nt*

bachelor *n* Junggeselle *m* (*gen* Junggesellen, *pl* Junggesellen) ▷ *He's a bachelor.* Er ist Junggeselle.

back *n* ❶ *(of person, horse, book)* Rücken *m* (*pl* Rücken) ❷ *(of page, house)* Rückseite *f* ▷ *Write your name on the back.* Schreiben Sie Ihren Namen auf die Rückseite.; **in the back of the car** hinten im Auto; **at the back** hinten ▶ *adj, adv* hintere ▷ *the back wheel of my bike* das hintere Rad meines Fahrrads; **the back seat** der Rücksitz; **the back door** die Hintertür; **to get back** zurückkommen [**40**]; **We went there by bus and walked back.** Wir sind mit dem Bus hingefahren und zu Fuß zurückgegangen.; **He's not back yet.** Er ist noch nicht zurück.; **to call somebody back** jemanden zurückrufen [**56**] ▶ *vb* **to back somebody** für jemanden sein [**65**]; **to back a horse** auf ein Pferd setzen [**36**]; **to back out** einen Rückzieher machen [**48**]; **to back somebody up** jemanden unterstützen [**36**]

backache *n* Rückenschmerzen *mpl* ▷ *to have backache* Rückenschmerzen haben

backbone *n* Rückgrat *nt* (*pl* Rückgrate)

backfire *vb* *(go wrong)* schiefgehen [**29**] (*imperf* ging schief, *perf* ist schiefgegangen)

background *n* Hintergrund *m* (*pl* Hintergründe) ▷ *a house in the background* ein Haus im Hintergrund ▷ *his family background* sein familiärer Hintergrund; **background noise** die Hintergrundgeräusche *ntpl*

backhand *n* Rückhand *f* (*pl* Rückhände)

backing *n* *(support)* Unterstützung *f*

backpack *n* Rucksack *m* (*pl* Rucksäcke)

backpacker *n* Wanderer *m* (*pl* Wanderer), Wanderin *f*

backside *n* Hintern *m* (*pl* Hintern)

backstroke *n* Rückenschwimmen *nt*

backup *n* *(support)* Unterstützung *f*; **a backup file** eine Sicherungsdatei

backwards *adv* zurück ▷ *to take a step backwards* einen Schritt zurück machen; **to fall backwards** nach hinten fallen [**22**]

bacon *n* Speck *m* ▷ *bacon and eggs* Eier mit Speck

bad *adj* ❶ schlecht ▷ *a bad film* ein schlechter Film ▷ *the bad weather* das schlechte Wetter ▷ *to be in a bad mood* schlechte Laune haben ▷ *not bad* nicht schlecht ▷ *That's not bad at all.* Das ist gar nicht schlecht.; **to be bad at something** in etwas schlecht sein [**65**] ❷ *(serious)* schlimm ▷ *a bad accident* ein schlimmer Unfall ❸ *(naughty)* böse

▷ *You bad boy!* Du böser Junge!; **to go bad** *(food)* schlecht werden [**91**]; **I feel bad about it.** Das tut mir echt leid.

badge *n* ❶ *(metal)* Button *m* (*pl* Buttons) ❷ *(sticker)* Aufkleber *m* (*pl* Aufkleber)

badly *adv* schlecht ▷ *badly paid* schlecht bezahlt; **badly wounded** schwer verletzt; **He's badly in need of some money.** Er braucht dringend Geld.

badminton *n* Badminton *nt* ▷ *to play badminton* Badminton spielen

bad-tempered *adj* **to be bad-tempered (1)** *(by nature)* griesgrämig sein [**65**] ▷ *He's a really bad-tempered person.* Er ist wirklich ein griesgrämiger Mensch. **(2)** *(temporarily)* schlechte Laune haben [**32**] ▷ *He was really bad-tempered yesterday.* Er hatte gestern wirklich schlechte Laune.

baffle *vb* verblüffen [**84**] (*perf* hat verblüfft) ▷ *She was baffled.* Sie war verblüfft.

bag *n* Tasche *f*; **an old bag** *(person)* eine alte Schachtel

baggage *n* Gepäck *nt*

baggage reclaim *n* Gepäckausgabe *f*

bagpipes *npl* Dudelsack *m* (*pl* Dudelsäcke) ▷ *Ed plays the bagpipes.* Ed spielt Dudelsack.

bake *vb* backen (*pres* bäckt, *imperf* backte, *perf* hat gebacken) ▷ *to bake a cake* einen Kuchen backen

baker *n* Bäcker *m* (*pl* Bäcker), Bäckerin *f* ▷ *He's a baker.* Er ist Bäcker.

bakery *n* Bäckerei *f*

balance *n* Gleichgewicht *nt* ▷ *to lose one's balance* das Gleichgewicht verlieren
▶ *vb* balancieren [**76**] (*perf* ist balanciert) ▷ *I balanced on the window ledge.* Ich balancierte auf dem Fensterbrett.; **The boxes were carefully balanced.** Die Kartons befanden sich genau im Gleichgewicht.

balanced *adj* ausgewogen ▷ *a balanced diet* eine ausgewogene Ernährung

balcony *n* Balkon *m* (*pl* Balkone)

bald *adj* glatzköpfig; **to be bald** eine Glatze haben [**32**]

ball *n* Ball *m* (*pl* Bälle)

ballet *n* Ballett *nt* (*pl* Ballette)

> Note that you pronounce the 'tt' in German.

▷ *We went to a ballet.* Wir sind ins Ballett gegangen.; **ballet lessons** Ballettstunden

ballet dancer *n* Balletttänzer *m* (*pl* Balletttänzer), Balletttänzerin *f*

ballet shoes *npl* Ballettschuhe *mpl*

balloon *n (at parties)* Luftballon *m* (*pl* Luftballone); **a hot-air balloon** ein Heißluftballon

ballpoint pen *n* Kugelschreiber *m* (*pl* Kugelschreiber)

ban *n* Verbot *nt* (*pl* Verbote)
▶ *vb* verbieten [**8**] (*imperf* verbot, *perf* hat verboten) ▷ *to ban somebody from doing something* jemandem verbieten, etwas zu tun; **She was banned from driving.** Sie bekam Fahrverbot.

banana *n* Banane *f* ▷ *a banana skin* eine Bananenschale

band *n* ❶ *(rock band)* Band *f* (*pl* Bands) ❷ *(brass band)* Kapelle *f*

bandage *n* Verband *m* (*pl* Verbände)
▶ *vb* verbinden (*imperf* verband, *perf* hat verbunden) ▷ *She bandaged his arm.* Sie verband ihm den Arm.

Band-Aid® *n (US)* Heftpflaster *nt* (*pl* Heftpflaster)

bang *n* ❶ Knall *m* (*pl* Knalle) ▷ *I heard a loud bang.* Ich habe einen lauten Knall gehört. ❷ Schlag *m* (*pl* Schläge) ▷ *a bang on the head* ein Schlag auf den Kopf; **Bang!** Peng!
▶ *vb (part of body)* anschlagen [**59**] (*pres* schlägt an, *imperf* schlug an, *perf* hat angeschlagen) ▷ *I banged my head.* Ich habe mir den Kopf angeschlagen.; **to bang the door** die Tür zuknallen [**4**]; **to bang on the door** gegen die Tür hämmern [**34**]

bank *n* ① *(financial)* Bank *f* (*pl* Banken) ② *(of river, lake)* Ufer *nt* (*pl* Ufer)

bank on *vb* sich verlassen **[42]** auf (*pres* verlässt, *imperf* verließ, *perf* hat verlassen)

bank account *n* Bankkonto *nt* (*pl* Bankkonten)

banker *n* Banker *m* (*pl* Banker), Bankerin *f*

bank holiday *n* Feiertag *m* (*pl* Feiertage)

banknote *n* Banknote *f*

bankrupt *adj* bankrott

bar *n* ① *(pub)* Bar *f* (*pl* Bars) ② *(counter)* Theke *f*; **a bar of chocolate** eine Tafel Schokolade; **a bar of soap** ein Stück Seife

barbecue *n* Barbecue *nt* (*pl* Barbecues); **We could have a barbecue this evening.** Wir könnten heute Abend grillen.

bare *adj* nackt

barefoot *adj, adv* barfuß ▷ *They go around barefoot.* Sie laufen barfuß herum.

barely *adv* kaum ▷ *I could barely hear her.* Ich konnte sie kaum hören.

bargain *n* Schnäppchen *nt* (*pl* Schnäppchen) ▷ *It was a bargain!* Das war ein Schnäppchen!

barge *n* Kahn *m* (*pl* Kähne)

bark *vb* bellen **[38]**

barmaid *n* Bardame *f* ▷ *She's a barmaid.* Sie ist Bardame.

barman *n* Barkeeper *m* (*pl* Barkeeper) ▷ *He's a barman.* Er ist Barkeeper.

barn *n* Scheune *f*

barrel *n* Fass *nt* (*gen* Fasses, *pl* Fässer)

barrier *n* Schranke *f*

base *n* ① *(basis)* Basis *f* (*pl* Basen) ▷ *a good base for a successful career* eine gute Basis für eine erfolgreiche Karriere ② *(of lamp, mountain)* Fuß *m* (*gen* Fußes, *pl* Füße) ③ *(of container)* Boden *m* (*pl* Böden) ④ *(for paint, make-up)* Grundlage *f* ⑤ *(military)* Stützpunkt *m* (*pl* Stützpunkte)

baseball *n* Baseball *m* ▷ *a baseball cap* eine Baseballmütze

based *adj* **based on** basierend auf

basement *n* Untergeschoss *nt* (*gen* Untergeschosses, *pl* Untergeschosse)

bash *vb* **to bash something in** etwas einschlagen **[59]**
▶ *n* **I'll have a bash.** Ich versuch's mal.

basic *adj* ① *(knowledge, education)* elementar; **basic vocabulary** der Grundwortschatz; **It's a basic model.** Es ist ein Grundmodell. ② einfach ▷ *The accommodation is pretty basic.* Die Unterkunft ist sehr einfach.

basically *adv* eigentlich ▷ *Basically, I just don't like him.* Eigentlich mag ich ihn nicht.

basics *npl* Grundlagen *fpl*

basin *n (washbasin)* Waschbecken *nt* (*pl* Waschbecken)

basis *n* **on a daily basis** täglich; **on a regular basis** regelmäßig

basket *n* Korb *m* (*pl* Körbe)

basketball *n* Basketball *m*

bass *n* Bass *m* (*gen* Basses, *pl* Bässe) ▷ *He plays bass.* Er spielt Bass. ▷ *He's a bass.* Er singt Bass.; **a bass drum** eine Basstrommel; **a bass guitar** eine Bassgitarre

bassoon *n* Fagott *nt* (*pl* Fagotte) ▷ *I play the bassoon.* Ich spiele Fagott.

bat *n* ① *(for cricket, rounders, table tennis)* Schläger *m* (*pl* Schläger) ② *(animal)* Fledermaus *f* (*pl* Fledermäuse)

bath *n* ① Bad *nt* (*pl* Bäder) ▷ *a hot bath* ein heißes Bad; **to have a bath** baden **[54]** ② *(bathtub)* Badewanne *f* ▷ *There's a spider in the bath.* In der Badewanne ist eine Spinne.

bathe *vb* baden **[54]**

bathroom *n* Badezimmer *nt* (*pl* Badezimmer)

bath towel *n* Badetuch *nt* (*pl* Badetücher)

batter *n* Pfannkuchenteig *m*

battery *n* Batterie *f*

battle *n* Schlacht *f* ▷ *the Battle of Hastings* die Schlacht von Hastings; **It was a battle, but we managed in the end.** Es war ein Kampf, aber wir haben es schließlich geschafft.

bay *n* Bucht *f*

BC *abbr* (= *before Christ*) v. Chr. (= *vor Christus*) ▷ *in 200 BC* im Jahre 200 v. Chr.

be *vb* sein [**65**] (*pres* ist, *imperf* war, *perf* ist gewesen) ▷ *I'm tired.* Ich bin müde. ▷ *You're late.* Du bist spät dran. ▷ *She's English.* Sie ist Engländerin. ▷ *It's cold.* Es ist kalt. ▷ *It's a nice day.* Es ist ein schöner Tag. ▷ *It's four o'clock.* Es ist vier Uhr. ▷ *I'm fourteen.* Ich bin vierzehn. ▷ *We are all happy.* Wir sind alle glücklich. ▷ *I've been ill.* Ich war krank. ▷ *I've never been to Dresden.* Ich war noch nie in Dresden.; **to be beaten** geschlagen werden [**91**]

> Questions like 'isn't it?' don't exist in German.

▷ *The film was good, wasn't it?* Der Film war gut, nicht wahr?

> You do not translate 'a' when you want to describe somebody's occupation.

▷ *She's a doctor.* Sie ist Ärztin.; **I'm cold.** Mir ist kalt.; **I'm hungry.** Ich habe Hunger.

beach *n* Strand *m* (*pl* Strände)

bead *n* Perle *f*

beak *n* Schnabel *m* (*pl* Schnäbel)

beam *n* Strahl *m* (*pl* Strahlen)

beans *npl* Bohnen *fpl*; **baked beans** gebackene Bohnen

> Few Germans eat baked beans and not many shops sell them.

broad beans dicke Bohnen; **green beans** grüne Bohnen; **kidney beans** Kidneybohnen

bean sprouts *npl* Sojasprossen *mpl*

bear *n* Bär *m* (*gen* Bären, *pl* Bären)
▶ *vb* (*endure*) ertragen [**77**] (*pres* erträgt, *imperf* ertrug, *perf* hat ertragen) ▷ *I can't bear it.* Ich kann es nicht ertragen.; **to bear up** sich halten [**33**]; **Bear up!** Kopf hoch!; **If you would bear with me for a moment ...** Wenn Sie sich bitte einen Moment gedulden könnten ...

beard *n* Bart *m* (*pl* Bärte) ▷ *He's got a beard.* Er hat einen Bart.; **a man with a beard** ein bärtiger Mann

bearded *adj* bärtig

beat *n* Rhythmus *m* (*gen* Rhythmus, *pl* Rhythmen)
▶ *vb* schlagen [**59**] (*pres* schlägt, *imperf* schlug, *perf* hat geschlagen) ▷ *We beat them three nil.* Wir haben sie drei zu null geschlagen.; **Beat it!** (*informal*) Hau ab!; **to beat somebody up** jemanden zusammenschlagen [**59**]

beautiful *adj* schön

beautifully *adv* schön

beauty *n* Schönheit *f*

became *vb see* **become**

because *conj* weil ▷ *I did it because ...* Ich habe es getan, weil ...; **because of** wegen

become *vb* werden [**91**] (*pres* wird, *imperf* wurde, *perf* ist geworden) ▷ *He became famous.* Er wurde berühmt.

> Be careful not to translate **to become** by **bekommen**.

bed *n* Bett *nt* (*pl* Betten) ▷ *in bed* im Bett; **to go to bed** ins Bett gehen [**29**]; **bed and breakfast** Zimmer mit Frühstück *nt* ▷ *How much is it for bed and breakfast?* Wie viel kostet das Zimmer mit Frühstück?; **We stayed in a bed and breakfast.** Wir waren in einer Frühstückspension.

bedclothes *npl* Bettwäsche *fsg*

bedding *n* Bettzeug *nt*

bedroom *n* Schlafzimmer *nt* (*pl* Schlafzimmer)

bedsit *n* **She lives in a bedsit.** Sie wohnt in einem möblierten Zimmer *nt*.

bedspread *n* Tagesdecke *f*

bedtime *n* **Ten o'clock is my usual bedtime.** Ich gehe normalerweise um zehn Uhr ins Bett.; **Bedtime!** Ab ins Bett!

bee *n* Biene *f*
beef *n* Rindfleisch *nt*; **roast beef** das Roastbeef
beefburger *n* Frikadelle *f*
been *vb see* **be**
beer *n* Bier *nt* (*pl* Biere *or* Bier)
When ordering more than one beer use the plural form **Bier**.
▷ *Two beers, please!* Zwei Bier bitte!
beetle *n* Käfer *m* (*pl* Käfer)
beetroot *n* Rote Bete *f*
before *prep, conj, adv* ❶ vor ▷ *before Tuesday* vor Dienstag ❷ bevor ▷ *Wash your hands before eating.* Wasch die Hände bevor du isst. ▷ *I'll phone before I leave.* Ich rufe an, bevor ich gehe. ❸ *(already)* schon ▷ *I've seen this film before.* Ich habe diesen Film schon gesehen. ▷ *Have you been to Scotland before?* Warst du schon einmal in Schottland?; **the day before** am Tag davor; **the week before** die Woche davor
beforehand *adv* vorher
beg *vb* ❶ *(for money)* betteln [34] ❷ anflehen [4] (*perf* hat angefleht) ▷ *He begged me to stop.* Er flehte mich an aufzuhören.
began *vb see* **begin**
beggar *n* Bettler *m* (*pl* Bettler), Bettlerin *f*
begin *vb* anfangen [23] (*pres* fängt an, *imperf* fing an, *perf* hat angefangen); **to begin doing something** anfangen [23], etwas zu tun
beginner *n* Anfänger *m* (*pl* Anfänger), Anfängerin *f* ▷ *I'm just a beginner.* Ich bin noch Anfänger.
beginning *n* Anfang *m* (*pl* Anfänge) ▷ *in the beginning* am Anfang
begun *vb see* **begin**
behalf *n* **on behalf of somebody** für jemanden
behave *vb* sich benehmen [52] (*pres* benimmt sich, *imperf* benahm sich, *perf* hat sich benommen) ▷ *He behaved like an idiot.* Er hat sich wie ein Idiot benommen. ▷ *She behaved very badly.* Sie hat sich sehr schlecht benommen.; **to behave oneself** sich anständig benehmen [52]; **Behave!** Sei brav!
behaviour (*US* **behavior**) *n* Benehmen *nt*
behind *prep, adv* hinter
Use the accusative to express movement or a change of place. Use the dative when there is no change of place.
▷ *the wall behind the television* die Wand hinter dem Fernseher ▷ *The book fell behind the television.* Das Buch fiel hinter den Fernseher.; **to be behind** *(late)* im Rückstand sein [65]
▶ *n* Hintern *m* (*gen* Hintern, *pl* Hintern)
beige *adj* beige
Belgian *adj* belgisch; **He's Belgian.** Er ist Belgier.; **She's Belgian.** Sie ist Belgierin.
▶ *n* Belgier *m* (*pl* Belgier), Belgierin *f*; **the Belgians** die Belgier
Belgium *n* Belgien *nt*; **from Belgium** aus Belgien; **in Belgium** in Belgien
believe *vb* glauben [38] ▷ *I don't believe you.* Ich glaube dir nicht.; **to believe in something** an etwas glauben [38]
bell *n* ❶ *(doorbell, in school)* Klingel *f*; **to ring the bell** klingeln [34]; **When the bell rings the children go out into the playground.** Wenn es klingelt, gehen die Kinder auf den Schulhof. ❷ *(in church)* Glocke *f* ❸ Glöckchen *nt* (*pl* Glöckchen) ▷ *Our cat has a bell on its neck.* Unsere Katze hat ein Glöckchen um den Hals.
belong *vb* gehören [38] (*perf* hat gehört); **to belong to somebody** jemandem gehören [38]; **Do you belong to the club?** Bist du Mitglied im Klub?; **Where does this belong?** Wo gehört das hin?
belongings *npl* Sachen *fpl*
below *prep, adv* ❶ unterhalb ▷ *below the castle* unterhalb der Burg ❷ unter

Use the accusative to express movement or a change of place. Use the dative when there is no change of place.

▷ *The sun sank below the horizon.* Die Sonne sank unter den Horizont. ▷ *We were below the clouds.* Wir waren unter den Wolken. ❸ darunter ▷ *on the floor below* im Stock darunter; **ten degrees below freezing** zehn Grad unter null

belt *n* Gürtel *m* (*pl* Gürtel)

bench *n* ❶ *(seat)* Bank *f* (*pl* Bänke) ❷ *(for woodwork)* Werkbank *f* (*pl* Werkbänke)

benchmark *n* Maßstab *m* (*pl* Maßstäbe)

bend *n* ❶ *(in road)* Kurve *f* ❷ *(in river)* Biegung *f*

▸ *vb* ❶ *(leg, arm)* beugen [**38**] ▷ *I can't bend my arm.* Ich kann den Arm nicht beugen.; **to bend down** sich bücken [**48**]; **to bend over** sich nach vorne beugen [**38**] ❷ *(object)* verbiegen (*imperf* verbog, *perf* hat verbogen) ▷ *You've bent it.* Du hast es verbogen.; **It bends easily.** Das lässt sich leicht biegen.; **'do not bend'** 'nicht knicken'

beneath *prep* unter

Use the accusative to express movement or a change of place. Use the dative when there is no change of place.

▷ *He placed his boots beneath the chair.* Er stellte seine Stiefel unter den Stuhl. ▷ *She found his jumper beneath the bed.* Sie fand seinen Pullover unter dem Bett.

benefit *n (advantage)* Vorteil *m* (*pl* Vorteile); **unemployment benefit** die Arbeitslosenunterstützung

▸ *vb* profitieren [**76**] ▷ *You'll benefit from that experience.* Du wirst von dieser Erfahrung profitieren.; **He benefited from the change.** Die Veränderung hat ihm gutgetan.

bent *vb see* **bend**

▸ *adj* verbogen ▷ *a bent fork* eine verbogene Gabel

berth *n* ❶ *(on ship)* Koje *f* ❷ *(on train)* Schlafwagenplatz *m* (*pl* Schlafwagenplätze)

beside *prep* neben

Use the accusative to express movement or a change of place. Use the dative when there is no change of place.

▷ *the lamp beside the television* die Lampe neben dem Fernseher ▷ *Put that chair beside the television.* Stell den Stuhl neben den Fernseher.; **I was beside myself.** Ich war außer mir.; **That's beside the point.** Das tut hier nichts zur Sache.

besides *adv* außerdem ▷ *Besides, it's too expensive.* Und außerdem ist es zu teuer.

best *adj, adv* ❶ beste ▷ *He's the best player in the team.* Er ist der beste Spieler der Mannschaft. ▷ *Janet's the best at maths.* Janet ist in Mathe die Beste. ❷ am besten ▷ *Emma sings best.* Emma singt am besten.; **to do one's best** sein Bestes tun [**81**]; **to make the best of it** das Beste daraus machen [**48**]

best man *n* Trauzeuge *m* (*gen* Trauzeugen, *pl* Trauzeugen)

There is no real equivalent in Germany to 'best man'. A **Trauzeuge** is merely an official witness to the wedding ceremony.

bet *n* Wette *f* ▷ *to make a bet* eine Wette machen

▸ *vb* wetten [**2**]; **I bet you he won't come.** Wetten, dass er nicht kommt.; **I bet he forgot.** Wetten, dass er es vergessen hat.

better *adj, adv* besser ▷ *This one's better than that one.* Dieses hier ist besser als das da. ▷ *a better way to do it* eine bessere Methode ▷ *You'd better do it straight away.* Das machst du besser sofort. ▷ *I'd better go home.* Ich gehe besser nach Hause. ▷ *That's better!* Das ist schon besser!; **better still** noch besser; **to get better** (1) *(improve)* besser werden [**91**] ▷ *I hope the weather gets better soon.* Ich hoffe, das Wetter wird bald besser. ▷ *My German is getting* *better.* Mein Deutsch wird besser. **(2)** *(from illness)* sich erholen [**19**]; **I hope you get better soon.** Gute Besserung!; **to feel better** sich besser fühlen [**38**]

between *prep* zwischen

> Use the accusative to express movement or a change of place. Use the dative when there is no change of place.

▷ *The cathedral is between the town hall and the river.* Der Dom liegt zwischen dem Rathaus und dem Fluss. ▷ *He sat down between the two girls.* Er setzte sich zwischen die beiden Mädchen. ▷ *between fifteen and twenty minutes* zwischen fünfzehn und zwanzig Minuten

beware *vb* **'Beware of the dog!'** 'Vorsicht bissiger Hund!'

bewilder *vb* verwirren [**84**] ▷ *She was bewildered.* Sie war verwirrt.

beyond *prep* hinter ▷ *There was a lake beyond the mountain.* Hinter dem Berg war ein See.; **beyond belief** nicht zu glauben; **beyond repair** nicht mehr zu reparieren

Bible *n* Bibel *f*

bicycle *n* Fahrrad *nt* (*pl* Fahrräder)

big *adj* groß ▷ *a big house* ein großes Haus ▷ *a bigger house* ein größeres Haus ▷ *my big brother* mein großer Bruder ▷ *her big sister* ihre große Schwester; **He's a big guy.** Er ist kräftig gebaut.

bigheaded *adj* eingebildet

bike *n* Fahrrad *nt* (*pl* Fahrräder) ▷ *by bike* mit dem Fahrrad

bikini *n* Bikini *m* (*pl* Bikinis)

bilingual *adj* zweisprachig

bill *n* ❶ Rechnung *f* ▷ *the gas bill* die Gasrechnung; **Can we have the bill, please?** Können wir bitte zahlen? ❷ *(banknote)* Geldschein *m* (*pl* Geldscheine) ▷ *a dollar bill* ein Dollarschein

billiards *nsg* Billard *nt* ▷ *to play billiards* Billard spielen

billion *n* Milliarde *f*

bin *n* ❶ *(indoors)* Abfalleimer *m* (*pl* Abfalleimer) ❷ *(outside)* Mülleimer *m* (*pl* Mülleimer)

binoculars *npl* Fernglas *nt* (*pl* Ferngläser) ▷ *a pair of binoculars* ein Fernglas

biochemistry *n* Biochemie *f*

biography *n* Biografie *f*

biology *n* Biologie *f*

bird *n* Vogel *m* (*pl* Vögel)

bird-watching *n* **My hobby's bird-watching.** Mein Hobby ist das Beobachten von Vögeln.

Biro® *n* Kuli *m* (*pl* Kulis)

birth *n* Geburt *f* ▷ *date of birth* das Geburtsdatum

birth certificate *n* Geburtsurkunde *f*

birth control *n* Empfängnisverhütung *f*

birthday *n* Geburtstag *m* (*pl* Geburtstage) ▷ *When's your birthday?* Wann hast du Geburtstag? ▷ *a birthday cake* ein Geburtstagskuchen ▷ *I'm going to have a birthday party.* Ich gebe eine Geburtstagsparty.

biscuit *n* Keks *m* (*pl* Kekse)

bishop *n* Bischof *m* (*pl* Bischöfe)

bit *vb see* **bite**

▸ *n (piece)* Stück *nt* (*pl* Stücke) ▷ *Would you like another bit?* Möchtest du noch ein Stück? ▷ *a bit of cake* ein Stück Kuchen; **a bit (1)** etwas ▷ *He's a bit mad.* Er ist etwas verrückt. ▷ *a bit too hot* etwas zu heiß **(2)** ein bisschen ▷ *Wait a bit!* Warte ein bisschen! ▷ *Do you play football? — A bit.* Spielst du Fußball? — Ein bisschen.; **a bit of** *(a little)* etwas ▷ *a bit of music* etwas Musik ▷ *It's a bit of a nuisance.* Das ist schon etwas ärgerlich.; **to fall to bits** kaputtgehen [**29**]; **to take something to bits** etwas auseinandernehmen [**52**]; **bit by bit** nach und nach

bite *vb* ❶ *(person, dog)* beißen [**6**] (*imperf* biss, *perf* hat gebissen) ❷ *(insect)* stechen (*pres* sticht, *imperf* stach, *perf*

hat gestochen) ▷ *I got bitten by mosquitoes.* Ich bin von Mücken gestochen worden.; **to bite one's nails** an den Nägeln kauen [**38**]
▶ *n* ❶ *(insect bite)* Stich *m* (*pl* Stiche) ❷ *(animal bite)* Biss *m* (*gen* Bisses, *pl* Bisse); **to have a bite to eat** eine Kleinigkeit essen [**20**]

bitter *adj* ❶ bitter ❷ *(weather, wind)* bitterkalt ▷ *It's bitter today.* Heute ist es bitterkalt.

black *adj* schwarz ▷ *a black jacket* eine schwarze Jacke; **She's black.** Sie ist eine Schwarze.

blackberry *n* Brombeere *f*

blackbird *n* Amsel *f*

blackboard *n* Tafel *f*

blackcurrant *n* Schwarze Johannisbeere *f*

blackmail *n* Erpressung *f* ▷ *That's blackmail!* Das ist Erpressung!
▶ *vb* erpressen [**7**] (*perf* hat erpresst) ▷ *He blackmailed her.* Er erpresste sie.

black pudding *n* Blutwurst *f* (*pl* Blutwürste)

blacksmith *n* Schmied *m* ▷ *He's a blacksmith.* Er ist Schmied.

blade *n* Klinge *f*

blame *vb* **Don't blame me!** Ich bin nicht schuld!; **I blame him.** Ich gebe ihm die Schuld.; **He blamed it on my sister.** Er gab meiner Schwester die Schuld.

blank *adj* leer; **My mind went blank.** Ich hatte ein Brett vor dem Kopf.
▶ *n* Lücke *f* ▷ *Fill in the blanks.* Füllt die Lücken aus.

blanket *n* Decke *f*

blast *n* **a bomb blast** eine Bombenexplosion

blaze *n* Feuer *nt* (*pl* Feuer)

blazer *n* Blazer *m* (*pl* Blazer)

bleach *n* Bleichmittel *nt* (*pl* Bleichmittel)

bleed *vb* bluten [**2**] ▷ *My nose is bleeding.* Ich blute aus der Nase.

blender *n* Mixer *m* (*pl* Mixer)

bless *vb* *(religiously)* segnen [**53**]; **Bless you!** *(after sneezing)* Gesundheit!

blew *vb see* **blow**

blind *adj* blind
▶ *n (fabric)* Rollo *nt* (*pl* Rollos)

blink *vb* zwinkern [**88**]

blister *n* Blase *f*

blizzard *n* Schneesturm *m* (*pl* Schneestürme)

block *n* Block *m* (*pl* Blöcke) ▷ *He lives in our block.* Er lebt in unserem Block.; **a block of flats** ein Wohnblock *m*
▶ *vb* blockieren [**76**] (*perf* hat blockiert)

blog *n (internet)* Blog *nt*
▶ *vb* bloggen [**48**]

blogger *n* Blogger *m* (*pl* Blogger), Bloggerin *f*

blogpost *n* Blogpost *m* (*pl* Blogposts)

blonde *adj* blond ▷ *She's got blonde hair.* Sie hat blondes Haar.

blood *n* Blut *nt*

blood pressure *n* Blutdruck *m* ▷ *to have high blood pressure* hohen Blutdruck haben

blood test *n* Blutuntersuchung *f*

blouse *n* Bluse *f*

blow *n* Schlag *m* (*pl* Schläge)
▶ *vb* ❶ *(person)* blasen (*pres* bläst, *imperf* blies, *perf* hat geblasen) ❷ *(wind)* wehen [**38**]; **to blow one's nose** sich die Nase putzen [**36**] ▷ *Blow your nose!* Putz dir die Nase!; **to blow a whistle** pfeifen; **to blow out a candle** eine Kerze ausblasen; **to blow up (1)** in die Luft jagen [**38**] ▷ *The terrorists blew up a police station.* Die Terroristen haben ein Polizeirevier in die Luft gejagt. **(2)** aufblasen ▷ *to blow up a balloon* einen Luftballon aufblasen; **The house blew up.** Das Haus flog in die Luft.

blow-dry *n* Föhnen *nt* ▷ *A cut and blow-dry, please.* Schneiden und Föhnen bitte.

blown *vb see* **blow**

blue *adj* blau ▷ *a blue dress* ein blaues Kleid; **a blue film** ein Pornofilm *m*; **It came out of the blue.** Das kam aus heiterem Himmel.

blues *npl (music)* Blues *msg (gen* Blues)
blunder *n* Schnitzer *m (pl* Schnitzer)
blunt *adj* ❶ *(person)* unverblümt ❷ *(knife)* stumpf
blush *vb* rot werden [**91**] *(pres* wird rot, *imperf* wurde rot, *perf* ist rot geworden)
board *n* ❶ Brett *nt (pl* Bretter) ❷ *(blackboard)* Tafel *f* ▷ *Write it on the board.* Schreib es an die Tafel.; **It's on the board in the office.** *(noticeboard)* Es hängt am schwarzen Brett im Büro.; **on board** an Bord; **full board** die Vollpension
boarder *n* Internatsschüler *m (pl* Internatsschüler), Internatsschülerin *f*
board game *n* Brettspiel *nt (pl* Brettspiele)
boarding card *n* Bordkarte *f*
boarding school *n* Internat *nt (pl* Internate) ▷ *I go to boarding school.* Ich gehe in ein Internat.
boast *vb* prahlen [**38**] ▷ *to boast about something* mit etwas prahlen
boat *n* Boot *nt (pl* Boote)
body *n* Körper *m (pl* Körper)
bodybuilding *n* Bodybuilding *nt* ▷ *He does bodybuilding.* Er macht Bodybuilding.
bodyguard *n* Leibwächter *m (pl* Leibwächter)
boil *n* Furunkel *m (pl* Furunkel)
▸ *vb* kochen [**48**] ▷ *to boil some water* Wasser kochen ▷ *to boil an egg* ein Ei kochen ▷ *The water's boiling.* Das Wasser kocht.; **to boil over** überkochen [**4**]
boiled *adj* **a soft-boiled egg** ein weich gekochtes Ei *nt*; **boiled potatoes** Salzkartoffeln *fpl*
boiling *adj* **It's boiling in here!** Hier ist eine Bruthitze!; **boiling hot** brütend heiß
bolt *n* ❶ *(on door)* Riegel *m (pl* Riegel) ❷ *(with nut)* Bolzen *m (pl* Bolzen)
bomb *n* Bombe *f*

> Note that you pronounce the second 'b' in German.

▸ *vb* bombardieren [**76**] *(perf* hat bombardiert)
bomber *n* Bomber *m (pl* Bomber)

> Note that you pronounce the second 'b' in German.

bombing *n* Bombenangriff *m (pl* Bombenangriffe)
bone *n* ❶ *(of human, animal)* Knochen *m (pl* Knochen) ❷ *(of fish)* Gräte *f*
bonfire *n* Feuer *nt (pl* Feuer)
bonnet *n (of car)* Motorhaube *f*
bonus *n* ❶ *(extra payment)* Bonus *m (pl* Bonusse) ❷ *(added advantage)* Vorteil *m*
book *n* Buch *nt (pl* Bücher)
▸ *vb* buchen [**48**] ▷ *We haven't booked.* Wir haben nicht gebucht.
bookcase *n* ❶ *(open)* Bücherregal *nt (pl* Bücherregale) ❷ *(with doors)* Bücherschrank *m (pl* Bücherschränke)
booklet *n* Broschüre *f*
bookshelf *n* Bücherbrett *nt (pl* Bücherbretter); **bookshelves** das Bücherregal *sg*
bookshop *n* Buchhandlung *f*
boot *n* ❶ *(of car)* Kofferraum *m (pl* Kofferräume) ❷ *(footwear)* Stiefel *m (pl* Stiefel); **football boots** die Fußballschuhe *mpl*
border *n* Grenze *f*
bore *vb see* **bear**
bored *adj* **to be bored** sich langweilen [**38**]; **She gets bored easily.** Ihr wird schnell langweilig.
boring *adj* langweilig
born *adj* **to be born** geboren werden [**91**]
borne *vb see* **bear**
borrow *vb* ausleihen *(imperf* lieh aus, *perf* hat ausgeliehen) ▷ *Can I borrow your pen?* Kann ich deinen Schreiber ausleihen?; **to borrow something from somebody** sich etwas von jemandem leihen
Bosnia *n* Bosnien *nt*; **from Bosnia** aus Bosnien; **to Bosnia** nach Bosnien
Bosnian *adj* bosnisch
boss *n* Chef *m (pl* Chefs), Chefin *f*

boss around *vb* **to boss somebody around** jemanden herumkommandieren [**76**]

bossy *adj* herrisch

both *adj, pron* beide ▷ *We both went.* Wir sind beide gegangen. ▷ *Emma and Jane both went.* Emma und Jane sind beide gegangen. ▷ *Both of your answers are wrong.* Beide Antworten sind falsch. ▷ *Both of them have left.* Beide sind gegangen. ▷ *Both of us went.* Wir sind beide gegangen.; **both ... and** sowohl ... als auch

bother *n* Ärger *m* ▷ *We had a spot of bother with the car.* Wir hatten Ärger mit dem Auto.; **No bother!** Kein Problem!
▶ *vb* ❶ *(worry)* beunruhigen [**7**] *(perf* hat beunruhigt) ▷ *Is something bothering you?* Beunruhigt dich etwas? ❷ *(disturb)* stören [**38**] ▷ *I'm sorry to bother you.* Es tut mir leid, dass ich dich störe.; **Don't bother!** Nicht nötig!; **to bother to do something** es für nötig finden [**24**], etwas zu tun ▷ *He didn't bother to tell me about it.* Er hat es nicht für nötig gefunden, es mir zu sagen.

bottle *n* Flasche *f*

bottle bank *n* Altglascontainer *m (pl* Altglascontainer)

bottle-opener *n* Flaschenöffner *m (pl* Flaschenöffner)

bottom *n* ❶ *(of container, bag, sea)* Boden *m (pl* Böden) ❷ *(buttocks)* Hintern *m (gen* Hintern, *pl* Hintern) ❸ *(of list)* Ende *nt (pl* Enden); **at the bottom of page two** unten auf Seite zwei
▶ *adj* unterste ▷ *the bottom shelf* das unterste Regalbrett; **the bottom sheet** das Bettlaken

bought *vb see* **buy**

bounce *vb* hüpfen [**38**] *(perf* ist gehüpft)

bouncer *n* Rausschmeißer *m (pl* Rausschmeißer)

bound *adj* **He's bound to say that.** Er muss das ja sagen.; **She's bound to come.** Sie kommt sicher.

boundary *n* Grenze *f*

bow *n* ❶ *(knot)* Schleife *f* ▷ *to tie a bow* eine Schleife machen ❷ Bogen *m (pl* Bogen) ▷ *a bow and arrow* ein Pfeil und Bogen
▶ *vb* sich verneigen [**84**] *(perf* hat sich verneigt)

bowl *n (for soup, cereal)* Schale *f*
▶ *vb (in cricket)* werfen [**92**] *(pres* wirft, *imperf* warf, *perf* hat geworfen)

bowling *n* Bowling *nt*; **to go bowling** Bowling spielen [**38**]; **a bowling alley** eine Bowlingbahn

bow tie *n* Fliege *f*

box *n* Schachtel *f* ▷ *a box of matches* eine Schachtel Streichhölzer; **a cardboard box** ein Karton *m*

boxer *n* Boxer *m (pl* Boxer)

boxer shorts *npl* Boxershorts *pl* ▷ *He was wearing a pair of boxer shorts.* Er trug Boxershorts.

boxing *n* Boxen *nt*

Boxing Day *n* **It was Boxing Day.** Es war der zweite Weihnachtstag.

boy *n* Junge *m (gen* Jungen, *pl* Jungen)

boyfriend *n* Freund *m (pl* Freunde) ▷ *Have you got a boyfriend?* Hast du einen Freund?

bra *n* BH *m (pl* BHs)

brace *n (on teeth)* Zahnspange *f* ▷ *She wears a brace.* Sie hat eine Zahnspange.

bracelet *n* Armband *nt (pl* Armbänder)

brackets *npl* Klammern *fpl* ▷ *in brackets* in Klammern

brain *n* Gehirn *nt (pl* Gehirne)

brainy *adj* gescheit

brake *n* Bremse *f*
▶ *vb* bremsen [**36**]

branch *n* ❶ *(of tree)* Zweig *m (pl* Zweige) ❷ *(of bank)* Filiale *f*

brand *n* Marke *f* ▷ *a well-known brand of coffee* eine bekannte Kaffeemarke

brand-new *adj* brandneu

brandy *n* Weinbrand *m (pl* Weinbrände)

brass *n (metal)* Messing *nt*; **the brass section** die Blechbläser *mpl*

brass band *n* Blaskapelle *f*

brave *adj* mutig

Be careful not to translate **brave** by **brav**.

Brazil *n* Brasilien *nt*; **from Brazil** aus Brasilien; **to Brazil** nach Brasilien

bread *n* Brot *nt* (*pl* Brote) ▷ *bread and butter* Brot mit Butter; **brown bread** das Graubrot; **white bread** das Weißbrot

There is a huge variety of types of bread in Germany which can't simply be divided into brown and white.

break *n* (*rest*) Pause *f* ▷ *to take a break* eine Pause machen ▷ *during morning break* während der Vormittagspause; **the Christmas break** die Weihnachtsfeiertage *mpl*; **Give me a break!** Mach mal halblang!
▶ *vb* ❶ kaputt machen [**48**] (*perf* hat kaputt gemacht) ▷ *Careful, you'll break something!* Vorsicht, du machst sonst was kaputt! ❷ (*record, law*) brechen [**11**] (*pres* bricht, *imperf* brach, *perf* hat gebrochen) ▷ *to break a promise* sein Versprechen brechen; **to break one's leg** sich das Bein brechen [**11**]; **He broke his arm.** Er hat sich den Arm gebrochen. ❸ (*get broken*) brechen [**11**] ▷ *Careful, it'll break!* Vorsicht, es bricht!

break down *vb* eine Panne haben [**32**] (*pres* hat eine Panne, *imperf* hatte eine Panne, *perf* hat eine Panne gehabt)

break in *vb* einbrechen [**11**] (*pres* bricht ein, *imperf* brach ein, *perf* hat eingebrochen)

break into *vb* einbrechen [**11**] in (*pres* bricht ein, *imperf* brach ein, *perf* ist eingebrochen)

break off *vb* abbrechen [**11**] (*pres* bricht ab, *imperf* brach ab, *perf* hat abgebrochen)

break open *vb* (*door, cupboard*) aufbrechen [**11**] (*pres* bricht auf, *imperf* brach auf, *perf* hat aufgebrochen)

break out *vb* ausbrechen [**11**] (*pres* bricht aus, *imperf* brach aus, *perf* ist ausgebrochen)

break up *vb* ❶ (*crowd*) sich auflösen [**4**] (*perf* hat sich aufgelöst) ❷ (*meeting, party*) zu Ende gehen [**29**] (*imperf* ging zu Ende, *perf* ist zu Ende gegangen) ❸ (*couple*) sich trennen [**38**]

breakdown *n* ❶ (*in vehicle*) Panne *f* ▷ *to have a breakdown* eine Panne haben ❷ (*mental*) Nervenzusammenbruch *m* (*pl* Nervenzusammenbrüche) ▷ *to have a breakdown* einen Nervenzusammenbruch haben

breakfast *n* Frühstück *nt* (*pl* Frühstücke) ▷ *What would you like for breakfast?* Was möchtest du zum Frühstück?; **to have breakfast** frühstücken [**38**]

break-in *n* Einbruch *m* (*pl* Einbrüche)

breast *n* Brust *f* (*pl* Brüste); **chicken breast** die Hähnchenbrust

breaststroke *n* Brustschwimmen *nt*

breath *n* Atem *m* ▷ *to be out of breath* außer Atem sein; **to have bad breath** Mundgeruch haben [**32**]; **to get one's breath back** verschnaufen [**84**]

breathe *vb* atmen [**3**]; **to breathe in** einatmen [**4**]; **to breathe out** ausatmen [**4**]

breed *vb* züchten [**2**] ▷ *to breed dogs* Hunde züchten
▶ *n* Rasse *f*

breeze *n* Brise *f*

brewery *n* Brauerei *f*

bribe *n* Bestechung *f*
▶ *vb* bestechen (*pres* besticht, *imperf* bestach, *perf* hat bestochen)

brick *n* Backstein *m* (*pl* Backsteine) ▷ *a brick wall* eine Backsteinmauer

bride *n* Braut *f* (*pl* Bräute)

bridegroom *n* Bräutigam *m* (*pl* Bräutigame)

bridesmaid *n* Brautjungfer *f*

bridge *n* ❶ Brücke *f* ▷ *a suspension bridge* eine Hängebrücke ❷ Bridge *nt* (*gen* Bridge) ▷ *to play bridge* Bridge spielen

brief *adj* kurz

briefcase *n* Aktentasche *f*

briefly *adv* kurz
briefs *npl* Unterhose *f* ▷ *a pair of briefs* eine Unterhose
bright *adj* ❶ *(light)* hell ❷ *(colour)* leuchtend ▷ *a brighter colour* eine leuchtendere Farbe; **bright blue** hellblau ❸ intelligent ▷ *He's not very bright.* Er ist nicht besonders intelligent.
brilliant *adj* ❶ *(wonderful)* prima ▷ *Brilliant!* Prima! ❷ *(clever)* glänzend ▷ *a brilliant scientist* ein glänzender Wissenschaftler
bring *vb* ❶ bringen [**13**] (*imperf* brachte, *perf* hat gebracht) ▷ *Could you bring me my trainers?* Könntest du mir meine Sportschuhe bringen? ❷ *(bring along)* mitbringen [**13**] ▷ *Bring warm clothes.* Bringt warme Kleidung mit! ▷ *Can I bring a friend?* Darf ich einen Freund mitbringen?; **to bring about** herbeiführen [**4**]; **to bring back** zurückbringen [**13**]; **to bring forward** vorverlegen [**84**]; **to bring up** aufziehen [**96**]
Britain *n* Großbritannien *nt*; **from Britain** aus Großbritannien; **in Britain** in Großbritannien; **to Britain** nach Großbritannien; **Great Britain** Großbritannien
British *adj* britisch; **He's British.** Er ist Brite.; **She's British.** Sie ist Britin.; **the British** die Briten *mpl*; **the British Isles** die Britischen Inseln
Brittany *n* Bretagne *f*; **in Brittany** in der Bretagne
broad *adj (wide)* breit; **in broad daylight** am helllichten Tag
broadcast *n* Sendung *f*
▶ *vb* senden ▷ *The interview was broadcast all over the world.* Das Interview wurde in der ganzen Welt gesendet.
broccoli *nsg* Brokkoli *mpl* ▷ *Broccoli is her favourite vegetable.* Ihr Lieblingsgemüse ist Brokkoli.
brochure *n* Broschüre *f*
broke *vb see* **break**
▶ *adj* **to be broke** *(without money)* pleite sein [**65**]
broken *vb see* **break**
▶ *adj* ❶ kaputt ▷ *It's broken.* Es ist kaputt. ❷ *(limb)* gebrochen ▷ *He's got a broken arm.* Er hat einen gebrochenen Arm.
bronchitis *n* Bronchitis *f*
bronze *n* Bronze *f* ▷ *the bronze medal* die Bronzemedaille
brooch *n* Brosche *f*
broom *n* Besen *m* (*pl* Besen)
brother *n* Bruder *m* (*pl* Brüder) ▷ *my brother* mein Bruder ▷ *my big brother* mein großer Bruder
brother-in-law *n* Schwager *m* (*pl* Schwäger)
brought *vb see* **bring**
brown *adj* braun; **brown bread** das Graubrot
browse *vb (computer)* browsen [**38**] (*perf* hat gebrowst); **to browse in a shop** sich in einem Geschäft umsehen [**64**]
brush *n* ❶ Bürste *f* ❷ *(paintbrush)* Pinsel *m* (*pl* Pinsel)
▶ *vb* bürsten [**2**]; **to brush one's hair** sich die Haare bürsten [**2**]; **to brush one's teeth** die Zähne putzen [**36**]
Brussels *n* Brüssel *nt*; **to Brussels** nach Brüssel
Brussels sprouts *npl* Rosenkohl *msg* ▷ *Do you like Brussels sprouts?* Magst du Rosenkohl?
bubble *n* Blase *f*
bubble bath *n* Schaumbad *nt* (*pl* Schaumbäder)
bubble gum *n* Bubblegum *m* (*pl* Bubblegums)
bucket *n* Eimer *m* (*pl* Eimer)
buckle *n (on belt, watch, shoe)* Schnalle *f*
Buddhism *n* Buddhismus *m* (*gen* Buddhismus) ▷ *Buddhism and Hinduism* Buddhismus und Hinduismus
Buddhist *adj* buddhistisch
budgie *n* Wellensittich *m* (*pl* Wellensittiche)

buffet *n* Büfett *nt* (*pl* Büfetts)
buffet car *n* Speisewagen *m* (*pl* Speisewagen)
bug *n* ❶ *(insect)* Wanze *f*; **There are many bugs there.** Dort gibt es viel Ungeziefer.; **a stomach bug** eine Magen-Darm-Infektion; **There's a bug going round.** Da geht etwas herum. ❷ *(in computer)* Programmfehler *m* (*pl* Programmfehler)
buggy *n* Kinderwagen *m* (*pl* Kinderwagen)
build *vb* bauen [**38**] ▷ *They're going to build houses here.* Hier werden Häuser gebaut.; **to build up** *(increase)* zunehmen [**52**]
builder *n* ❶ *(owner of firm)* Bauunternehmer *m* (*pl* Bauunternehmer), Bauunternehmerin *f* ❷ *(worker)* Bauarbeiter *m* (*pl* Bauarbeiter), Bauarbeiterin *f*
building *n* Gebäude *nt* (*pl* Gebäude)
built *vb see* **build**
bulb *n (electric)* Glühbirne *f*
Bulgaria *n* Bulgarien *nt*; **from Bulgaria** aus Bulgarien; **to Bulgaria** nach Bulgarien
bull *n* Stier *m* (*pl* Stiere)
bullet *n* Kugel *f*
bullfighting *n* Stierkampf *m* (*pl* Stierkämpfe)
bully *n* **He's a big bully.** Er tyrannisiert andere gern.
▶ *vb* tyrannisieren [**76**] (*perf* hat tyrannisiert)
bum *n (informal: bottom)* Po *m* (*pl* Pos)
bum bag *n* Gürteltasche *f*
bump *n* ❶ *(lump)* Beule *f* ❷ *(minor accident)* Zusammenstoß *m* (*gen* Zusammenstoßes, *pl* Zusammenstöße); **We had a bump.** Es hat gebumst.
▶ *vb* **to bump into something** gegen etwas laufen [**43**]; **We bumped into his car.** Wir sind in sein Auto gefahren.; **I bumped into an old friend.** Ich bin zufällig einem alten Freund begegnet.
bumper *n* Stoßstange *f*
bumpy *adj* holperig
bun *n* Brötchen *nt* (*pl* Brötchen)
bunch *n* **a bunch of flowers** ein Blumenstrauß *m*; **a bunch of grapes** eine Traube; **a bunch of keys** ein Schlüsselbund *m*
bunches *npl* Rattenschwänze *mpl* ▷ *She has her hair in bunches.* Sie hat Rattenschwänze.
bungalow *n* Bungalow *m* (*pl* Bungalows)
bunk *n* ❶ Bett *nt* (*pl* Betten) ❷ *(on ship)* Koje *f*
burger *n* Hamburger *m* (*pl* Hamburger)
burglar *n* Einbrecher *m* (*pl* Einbrecher), Einbrecherin *f*
burglary *n* Einbruch *m* (*pl* Einbrüche)
burgle *vb* einbrechen [**11**] in (*pres* bricht ein, *imperf* brach ein, *perf* ist eingebrochen) ▷ *Her house was burgled.* Bei ihr wurde eingebrochen.
burn *n* Verbrennung *f*
▶ *vb* ❶ *(rubbish, documents)* verbrennen [**12**] ❷ *(food)* anbrennen lassen [**42**] ▷ *I burned the cake.* Ich habe den Kuchen anbrennen lassen. ❸ *(CD, DVD)* brennen [**12**]; **to burn oneself** sich verbrennen [**12**]; **I've burned my hand.** Ich habe mir die Hand verbrannt.; **to burn down** abbrennen [**12**]
burst *vb* platzen [**36**] (*perf* ist geplatzt) ▷ *The balloon burst.* Der Luftballon ist geplatzt.; **to burst a balloon** einen Luftballon platzen lassen [**42**]; **to burst out laughing** laut loslachen [**4**]; **to burst into flames** in Flammen aufgehen [**29**]; **to burst into tears** in Tränen ausbrechen [**11**]
bury *vb* ❶ *(dead people, animals)* begraben (*pres* begräbt, *imperf* begrub, *perf* hat begraben) ▷ *We buried my guinea pig in the garden.* Wir haben mein Meerschweinchen im Garten begraben. ❷ *(things)* vergraben ▷ *My dog buries his bones.* Mein Hund vergräbt seine Knochen.

bus *n* Bus *m* (*gen* Busses, *pl* Busse) ▷ *the bus driver* der Busfahrer ▷ *the school bus* der Schulbus; **a bus pass** (*monthly*) eine Monatskarte für den Bus

Almost all German cities operate an integrated public transport system; you can buy a weekly (**Wochenkarte**), monthly (**Monatskarte**) or yearly (**Jahreskarte**) pass which is valid for that period on all buses, trams and light railway vehicles in a particular zone.

a bus station ein Busbahnhof *m*; **a bus ticket** eine Busfahrkarte

bush *n* Busch *m* (*pl* Büsche)

business *n* ❶ (*firm*) Firma *f* (*pl* Firmen) ▷ *He's got his own business.* Er hat seine eigene Firma. ❷ (*commerce*) Geschäft *nt* (*pl* Geschäfte) ▷ *a business trip* eine Geschäftsreise; **He's away on business.** Er ist geschäftlich unterwegs.; **It's none of my business.** Das geht mich nichts an.

businessman *n* Geschäftsmann *m* (*pl* Geschäftsleute)

businesswoman *n* Geschäftsfrau *f*

bus stop *n* Bushaltestelle *f*

bust *n* (*chest*) Busen *m* (*pl* Busen); **bust measurement** die Oberweite

busy *adj* ❶ (*person*) beschäftigt ❷ (*shop, street*) belebt ❸ (*phone line*) besetzt; **It's been a busy day.** Es war viel los heute.

but *conj* aber ▷ *I'd like to come, but I'm busy.* Ich würde gerne kommen, aber ich habe zu tun.

butcher *n* Metzger *m* (*pl* Metzger), Metzgerin *f* ▷ *He's a butcher.* Er ist Metzger.

butcher's *n* Metzgerei *f*

butter *n* Butter *f*

butterfly *n* Schmetterling *m* (*pl* Schmetterlinge)

button *n* Knopf *m* (*pl* Knöpfe)

buy *vb* kaufen [**38**] ▷ *He bought me an ice cream.* Er hat mir ein Eis gekauft.; **to buy something from somebody** etwas von jemandem kaufen [**38**]
▶ *n* Kauf *m* (*pl* Käufe) ▷ *It was a good buy.* Es war ein guter Kauf.

by *prep* ❶ von ▷ *They were caught by the police.* Sie wurden von der Polizei erwischt. ▷ *a painting by Picasso* ein Gemälde von Picasso ❷ mit ▷ *by car* mit dem Auto ▷ *by train* mit dem Zug ▷ *by bus* mit dem Bus ❸ (*close to*) bei ▷ *Where's the bank? — It's by the post office.* Wo ist die Bank? — Sie ist bei der Post.; **by day** bei Tag; **by night** bei Nacht ❹ (*not later than*) bis ▷ *We have to be there by four o'clock.* Wir müssen bis vier Uhr dort sein.; **by the time ...** bis ... ▷ *By the time I got there it was too late.* Bis ich dort war, war es zu spät.; **That's fine by me.** Ist in Ordnung!; **all by himself** ganz allein; **all by herself** ganz allein; **I did it all by myself.** Ich habe es ganz allein gemacht.; **by the way** übrigens

bye *excl* tschüs!

bypass *n* (*road*) Umgehungsstraße *f*

C

cab *n* Taxi *nt* (*pl* Taxis)
cabbage *n* Kohl *m*
cabin *n* (*on ship*) Kabine *f*
cable *n* Kabel *nt* (*pl* Kabel)
cable car *n* Drahtseilbahn *f*
cable television *n* Kabelfernsehen *nt*
cactus *n* Kaktus *m* (*gen* Kaktus, *pl* Kakteen)
café *n* Imbissstube *f*
cage *n* Käfig *m* (*pl* Käfige)
cagoule *n* Windjacke *f*
cake *n* Kuchen *m* (*pl* Kuchen)
calculate *vb* rechnen **[53]**
calculation *n* Rechnung *f*
calculator *n* Taschenrechner *m* (*pl* Taschenrechner)
calendar *n* Kalender *m* (*pl* Kalender)
calf *n* ❶ (*of cow*) Kalb *nt* (*pl* Kälber) ❷ (*of leg*) Wade *f*
call *n* (*by phone*) Anruf *m* (*pl* Anrufe) ▷ *Thanks for your call.* Danke für Ihren Anruf.; **a phone call** ein Telefongespräch *nt*; **to be on call** (*doctor*) Bereitschaftsdienst haben **[32]**
▶ *vb* ❶ (*by phone*) anrufen **[56]** (*imperf* rief an, *perf* hat angerufen) ▷ *I'll tell him you called.* Ich sage ihm, dass du angerufen hast. ▷ *This is the number to call.* Das ist die Nummer, die du anrufen musst.; **to call back** (*phone again*) zurückrufen **[56]** ❷ (*fetch*) rufen **[56]** ▷ *We called the police.* Wir haben die Polizei gerufen. ❸ (*by name*) nennen (*imperf* nannte, *perf* hat genannt) ▷ *Everyone calls him Jimmy.* Alle nennen ihn Jimmy.; **to be called** heißen; **to call somebody names** jemanden beschimpfen **[18]**; **to call for** abholen **[4]**; **to call off** absagen **[4]**
call box *n* Telefonzelle *f*
call centre *n* Callcenter *nt* (*pl* Callcenters)
calm *adj* ruhig
calm down *vb* sich beruhigen **[18]** (*perf* hat sich beruhigt)
Calor gas® *n* Butangas *nt*
calorie *n* Kalorie *f*
calves *npl see* **calf**
camcorder *n* Camcorder *m* (*pl* Camcorder)
came *vb see* **come**
camel *n* Kamel *nt* (*pl* Kamele)
camera *n* ❶ (*for photos*) Fotoapparat *m* (*pl* Fotoapparate) ❷ (*for filming, TV*) Kamera *f* (*pl* Kameras)
cameraman *n* Kameramann *m* (*pl* Kameramänner)
cameraphone *n* Fotohandy *nt* (*pl* Fotohandys)
camp *vb* zelten **[2]**
▶ *n* Lager *nt* (*pl* Lager); **a camp bed** eine Campingliege
campaign *n* Kampagne *f*
▶ *vb* sich einsetzen **[36]** (*perf* hat sich eingesetzt) ▷ *They are campaigning for a change in the law.* Sie setzen sich für eine Gesetzesänderung ein.
camper *n* ❶ (*person*) Camper *m* (*pl* Camper), Camperin *f* ❷ (*van*) Wohnmobil *nt* (*pl* Wohnmobile)
camping *n* Camping *nt*; **to go camping** zelten **[2]**

camping gas *n* Campinggas *nt*
campsite *n* Zeltplatz *m* (*pl* Zeltplätze)
can *vb* können [41] (*pres* kann, *imperf* konnte, *perf* hat können) ▷ *I can't come.* Ich kann nicht kommen. ▷ *Can I help you?* Kann ich dir helfen? ▷ *You could hire a bike.* Du könntest dir ein Fahrrad mieten. ▷ *I couldn't sleep.* Ich konnte nicht schlafen. ▷ *I can swim.* Ich kann schwimmen. ▷ *He can't drive.* Er kann nicht Auto fahren. ▷ *Can you speak German?* Können Sie Deutsch?; **That can't be true!** Das darf nicht wahr sein!; **You could be right.** Da könntest du recht haben.
▶ *n* ❶ *(tin)* Dose *f* ▷ *a can of sweetcorn* eine Dose Mais ▷ *a can of beer* eine Dose Bier ❷ *(jerry can)* Kanister *m* (*pl* Kanister) ▷ *a can of petrol* ein Benzinkanister
Canada *n* Kanada *nt*; **from Canada** aus Kanada; **in Canada** in Kanada; **to Canada** nach Kanada
Canadian *adj* kanadisch ▷ *He's Canadian.* Er ist Kanadier. ▷ *She's Canadian.* Sie ist Kanadierin.
▶ *n* Kanadier *m* (*pl* Kanadier), Kanadierin *f*
canal *n* Kanal *m* (*pl* Kanäle)
Canaries *n* **the Canaries** die Kanarischen Inseln *pl*
canary *n* Kanarienvogel *m* (*pl* Kanarienvögel)
cancel *vb* ❶ absagen [4] (*perf* hat abgesagt) ▷ *The match was cancelled.* Das Spiel wurde abgesagt.
❷ *(booking)* stornieren [76] (*perf* hat storniert) ▷ *He cancelled his hotel booking.* Er hat seine Hotelreservierung storniert.
cancer *n* Krebs *m* (*gen* Krebses) ▷ *He's got cancer.* Er hat Krebs.; **I'm Cancer.** Ich bin Krebs.
candidate *n* Kandidat *m* (*gen* Kandidaten, *pl* Kandidaten), Kandidatin *f*
candle *n* Kerze *f*
candy *n (US)* ❶ *(sweet)* Bonbon *nt* (*pl* Bonbons) ❷ *(sweets)* Süßigkeit *f*
candyfloss *n* Zuckerwatte *f*
canned *adj (food)* in Dosen ▷ *canned soup* Suppe in Dosen
cannot *vb see* **can**
canoe *n* Kanu *nt* (*pl* Kanus)
canoeing *n* **to go canoeing** Kanu fahren [21]
can-opener *n* Dosenöffner *m* (*pl* Dosenöffner)
can't *vb see* **can**
canteen *n* Kantine *f*
canvas *n* Leinwand *f* (*pl* Leinwände)
cap *n* ❶ *(hat)* Mütze *f* ❷ *(of bottle, tube)* Verschluss *m* (*gen* Verschlusses, *pl* Verschlüsse)
capable *adj* fähig; **to be capable of doing something** etwas tun können [41]
capacity *n* ❶ Fähigkeit *f* ▷ *He has the capacity to succeed.* Er hat die Fähigkeit, Erfolg zu haben. ❷ *(quantity)* Fassungsvermögen *nt* ▷ *a capacity of fifty litres* ein Fassungsvermögen von fünfzig Litern
cape *n* Kap *nt* (*pl* Kaps) ▷ *Cape Horn* Kap Hoorn
capital *n* ❶ Hauptstadt *f* (*pl* Hauptstädte) ▷ *Cardiff is the capital of Wales.* Cardiff ist die Hauptstadt von Wales. ❷ *(letter)* Großbuchstabe *m* (*gen* Großbuchstaben, *pl* Großbuchstaben) ▷ *Write your address in capitals.* Schreib deine Adresse in Großbuchstaben.
capitalism *n* Kapitalismus *m* (*gen* Kapitalismus)
Capricorn *n* Steinbock *m* ▷ *I'm Capricorn.* Ich bin Steinbock.
captain *n* Kapitän *m* (*pl* Kapitäne), Kapitänin *f* ▷ *She's captain of the hockey team.* Sie ist die Kapitänin der Hockeymannschaft.
capture *vb* ❶ *(person)* gefangen nehmen [52] (*pres* nimmt gefangen, *imperf* nahm gefangen, *perf* hat gefangen genommen) ▷ *He was*

captured by the enemy. Er wurde vom Feind gefangen genommen. ❷ *(animal)* fangen [**23**] (*pres* fängt, *imperf* fing, *perf* hat gefangen) ▷ *They managed to capture the lion.* Sie konnten den Löwen fangen.

car *n* Auto *nt* (*pl* Autos); **to go by car** mit dem Auto fahren [**21**]; **a car crash** ein Autounfall *m*

caramel *n (sweet)* Karamellbonbon *nt* (*pl* Karamellbonbons)

caravan *n* Wohnwagen *m* (*pl* Wohnwagen) ▷ *a caravan site* ein Campingplatz für Wohnwagen

car boot sale *n* Flohmarkt *m* (*pl* Flohmärkte)

card *n* Karte *f*; **a card game** ein Kartenspiel *nt*

cardboard *n* Karton *m* (*pl* Kartons)

cardigan *n* Strickjacke *f*

card phone *n* Kartentelefon *nt* (*pl* Kartentelefone)

care *n* Vorsicht *f*; **with care** vorsichtig; **to take care of** aufpassen [**4**] auf; **Take care! (1)** *(Be careful!)* Sei vorsichtig! **(2)** *(Look after yourself!)* Pass auf dich auf!
▶ *vb* **to care about** achten [**2**] auf; **I don't care!** Das ist mir egal!; **to care for somebody** *(patients, old people)* jemanden pflegen [**38**]

career *n* Karriere *f*

careful *adj* vorsichtig ▷ *Be careful!* Sei vorsichtig!

carefully *adv* ❶ sorgsam ▷ *She carefully avoided the subject.* Sie vermied das Thema sorgsam. ❷ *(safely)* vorsichtig ▷ *Drive carefully!* Fahr vorsichtig!; **Think carefully!** Denk gut nach!

careless *adj* ❶ *(work)* schluderig; **a careless mistake** ein Flüchtigkeitsfehler *m* ❷ *(person)* nachlässig ▷ *She's very careless.* Sie ist sehr nachlässig. ❸ unvorsichtig ▷ *a careless driver* ein unvorsichtiger Fahrer

caretaker *n* Hausmeister *m* (*pl* Hausmeister), Hausmeisterin *f*

car ferry *n* Autofähre *f*

cargo *n* Fracht *f*

car hire *n* Autoverleih *m* (*pl* Autoverleihe)

Caribbean *adj* karibisch
▶ *n (islands)* Karibik *f* ▷ *We're going to the Caribbean.* Wir fahren in die Karibik. ▷ *He's from the Caribbean.* Er kommt aus der Karibik.

carnation *n* Nelke *f*

carnival *n* Karneval *m* (*pl* Karnevale)

carol *n* **a Christmas carol** ein Weihnachtslied *nt*

car park *n* Parkplatz *m* (*pl* Parkplätze)

carpenter *n* Schreiner *m* (*pl* Schreiner), Schreinerin *f* ▷ *He's a carpenter.* Er ist Schreiner.

carpentry *n* Schreinerei *f*

carpet *n* Teppich *m* (*pl* Teppiche) ▷ *a Persian carpet* ein Perserteppich

carriage *n* Eisenbahnwagen *m* (*pl* Eisenbahnwagen)

carrier bag *n* Tragetasche *f*

carrot *n* Karotte *f*

carry *vb* tragen [**77**] (*pres* trägt, *imperf* trug, *perf* hat getragen) ▷ *He carried her bag.* Er trug ihre Tasche.; **a plane carrying a hundred passengers** ein Flugzeug mit hundert Passagieren an Bord; **to carry on** weitermachen [**48**]; **She carried on talking.** Sie redete weiter.; **to carry out** *(orders)* ausführen [**4**]

carrycot *n* Babytragetasche *f*

cart *n* Karren *m* (*pl* Karren)

carton *n (of milk, juice)* Tüte *f*

cartoon *n* ❶ *(film)* Zeichentrickfilm *m* (*pl* Zeichentrickfilme) ❷ *(in newspaper)* Cartoon *m* (*pl* Cartoons); **a strip cartoon** ein Comic *m*

cartridge *n* Patrone *f*

carve *vb (meat)* aufschneiden [**60**] (*imperf* schnitt auf, *perf* hat aufgeschnitten)

case *n* ❶ Koffer *m* (*pl* Koffer) ▷ *I've packed my case.* Ich habe meinen Koffer gepackt. ❷ Fall *m* (*pl* Fälle) ▷ *in some* *cases* in manchen Fällen ▷ *Which case does 'außer' take?* Welcher Fall steht nach 'außer'?; **in that case** in dem Fall; **in case** für den Fall; **just in case** für alle Fälle

cash *n* Bargeld *nt* ▷ *I desperately need some cash.* Ich brauche dringend Bargeld.; **in cash** in bar ▷ *two thousand pounds in cash* zweitausend Pfund in bar; **to pay cash** bar bezahlen [7]; **I'm a bit short of cash.** Ich bin etwas knapp bei Kasse.; **a cash card** eine Geldautomatenkarte; **the cash desk** die Kasse; **a cash machine** ein Geldautomat *m*; **a cash register** eine Registrierkasse

cashew nut *n* Cashewnuss *f* (*pl* Cashewnüsse)

cashier *n* Kassierer *m* (*pl* Kassierer), Kassiererin *f*

cashmere *n* Kaschmir *m* ▷ *a cashmere sweater* ein Kaschmirpullover

casino *n* Kasino *nt* (*pl* Kasinos)

cassette *n* Kassette *f*; **cassette recorder** der Kassettenrekorder; **cassette player** der Kassettenspieler

cast *n* Besetzung *f* ▷ *After the play, we met the cast.* Nach dem Stück haben wir die Besetzung kennengelernt.

castle *n* Burg *f*

casual *adj* ❶ leger ▷ *casual clothes* legere Kleidung ❷ lässig ▷ *a casual attitude* eine lässige Haltung ❸ beiläufig ▷ *It was just a casual remark.* Es war nur eine beiläufige Bemerkung.

casualty *n* (*hospital department*) Unfallstation *f*

cat *n* Katze *f* ▷ *Have you got a cat?* Hast du eine Katze?

catalogue *n* Katalog *m* (*pl* Kataloge)

catastrophe *n* Katastrophe *f*

catch *vb* ❶ fangen [23] (*pres* fängt, *imperf* fing, *perf* hat gefangen) ▷ *My cat catches birds.* Meine Katze fängt Vögel.; **to catch a thief** einen Dieb fassen [31]; **to catch somebody doing something** jemanden dabei erwischen [48], wie er etwas tut ❷ (*bus, train*) nehmen [52] (*pres* nimmt, *imperf* nahm, *perf* hat genommen) ▷ *We caught the last bus.* Wir haben den letzten Bus genommen. ❸ (*hear*) mitbekommen [40] (*imperf* bekam mit, *perf* hat mitbekommen) ▷ *I didn't catch his name.* Ich habe seinen Namen nicht mitbekommen.; **to catch up** aufholen [38]; **to catch a cold** einen Schnupfen bekommen [40]

catering *n* **Who did the catering?** Wer hat das Essen und die Getränke geliefert?

cathedral *n* Kathedrale *f*

Catholic *adj* katholisch
▶ *n* Katholik *m* (*gen* Katholiken, *pl* Katholiken), Katholikin *f*; **I'm a Catholic.** Ich bin katholisch.

cattle *npl* Vieh *nt sg*

caught *vb see* **catch**

cauliflower *n* Blumenkohl *m* (*pl* Blumenkohle)

cause *n* Ursache *f* ▷ *the cause of the fire* die Ursache des Feuers
▶ *vb* verursachen [84] (*perf* hat verursacht) ▷ *to cause an accident* einen Unfall verursachen

cautious *adj* vorsichtig

cave *n* Höhle *f*

caviar *n* Kaviar *m*

CD *n* (= *compact disc*) CD *f* (*pl* CDs)

CD player *n* CD-Spieler *m* (*pl* CD-Spieler)

CD-ROM *n* CD-ROM *f* (*pl* CD-ROMs)

CDT *n* (= *Craft, Design and Technology*) Arbeitslehre *f*

ceiling *n* Decke *f*

celebrate *vb* (*birthday*) feiern [88]

celebration *n* Feier *f*

celebrity *n* Berühmtheit *f*

celery *n* Stangensellerie *m* (*gen* Stangensellerie, *pl* Stangenselleries)

cell *n* Zelle *f*

cellar *n* Keller *m* (*pl* Keller) ▷ *a wine cellar* ein Weinkeller

cello *n* Cello *nt* (*pl* Celli) ▷ *I play the cello.* Ich spiele Cello.

cell phone *n (US)* Handy *nt (pl* Handys)
cement *n* Zement *m*
cemetery *n* Friedhof *m (pl* Friedhöfe)
cent *n* Cent *m (pl* Cents *or* Cent)
When talking about amounts of money use the plural form **Cent**.
▷ *twenty cents* zwanzig Cent
center *n (US)* Zentrum *nt (pl* Zentren)
centigrade *adj* **twenty degrees centigrade** zwanzig Grad Celsius
centimetre (*US* **centimeter**) *n* Zentimeter *m (pl* Zentimeter) ▷ *twenty centimetres* zwanzig Zentimeter
central *adj* zentral
central heating *n* Zentralheizung *f*
centre (*US* **center**) *n* Zentrum *nt (pl* Zentren) ▷ *a sports centre* ein Sportzentrum
century *n* Jahrhundert *nt (pl* Jahrhunderte) ▷ *the twentieth century* das zwanzigste Jahrhundert ▷ *the twenty-first century* das einundzwanzigste Jahrhundert
cereal *n* Getreideflocken *fpl* ▷ *I have cereal for breakfast.* Zum Frühstück esse ich Getreideflocken.
ceremony *n* Zeremonie *f*
certain *adj* ❶ sicher ▷ *I'm absolutely certain it was him.* Ich bin ganz sicher, dass er es war.; **I don't know for certain.** Ich bin mir nicht sicher.; **to make certain** sich vergewissern [**88**] ❷ bestimmt ▷ *a certain person* eine bestimmte Person
certainly *adv* natürlich ▷ *I certainly expected something better.* Ich habe natürlich etwas Besseres erwartet.; **Certainly not!** Sicher nicht!; **So it was a surprise? — It certainly was!** Also war's eine Überraschung? — Und ob!
certificate *n* Urkunde *f*
CFC *n (= chlorofluorocarbon)* FCKW *m (= Fluorchlorkohlenwasserstoff)*
chain *n* Kette *f*
chair *n* ❶ Stuhl *m (pl* Stühle) ▷ *a table and four chairs* ein Tisch und vier Stühle ❷ *(armchair)* Sessel *m (pl* Sessel)
chairlift *n* Sessellift *m (pl* Sessellifte)
chairman *n* Vorsitzende *m (gen* Vorsitzenden, *pl* Vorsitzenden) ▷ *a chairman* ein Vorsitzender
chalet *n* Ferienhaus *nt (pl* Ferienhäuser)
chalk *n* Kreide *f*
challenge *n* Herausforderung *f* ▶ *vb* **She challenged me to a race.** Sie wollte mit mir um die Wette laufen.
champagne *n* Champagner *m (pl* Champagner)
champion *n* Meister *m (pl* Meister), Meisterin *f*
championship *n* Meisterschaft *f*
chance *n* ❶ Chance *f* ▷ *Do you think I've got any chance?* Meinst du, ich habe eine Chance? ▷ *Their chances of winning are very good.* Ihre Gewinnchancen sind sehr gut. ❷ Möglichkeit *f* ▷ *a chance to travel* eine Möglichkeit, auf Reisen zu gehen; **I'll write when I get the chance.** Ich schreibe, sobald ich dazu komme.; **by chance** zufällig; **to take a chance** ein Risiko eingehen [**29**]; **No chance!** Denkste!
chandelier *n* Kronleuchter *m (pl* Kronleuchter)
change *vb* ❶ sich verändern [**88**] *(perf* hat sich verändert) ▷ *The town has changed a lot.* Die Stadt hat sich sehr verändert. ❷ *(money, job)* wechseln [**34**] ▷ *I'd like to change fifty pounds.* Ich würde gern fünfzig Pfund wechseln. ▷ *He wants to change his job.* Er möchte den Job wechseln.; **You have to change trains in Stuttgart.** Sie müssen in Stuttgart umsteigen.; **I'm going to change my shoes.** Ich ziehe andere Schuhe an.; **to change one's mind** es sich anders überlegen [**82**]; **to change gear** schalten [**2**] ❸ sich umziehen [**96**] *(imperf* zog sich um, *perf* hat sich umgezogen) ▷ *She's changing to go out.* Sie zieht sich zum Ausgehen um.; **to get changed** sich umziehen [**96**] ❹ *(swap)* umtauschen [**4**] *(perf* hat umgetauscht) ▷ *Can I change this*

sweater? It's too small. Kann ich diesen Pullover umtauschen? Er ist zu klein.
▸ *n* ❶ Änderung *f*; **There's been a change of plan.** Die Pläne haben sich geändert.; **a change of clothes** Kleidung zum Wechseln; **for a change** zur Abwechslung ❷ *(money)* Kleingeld *nt* ▹ *I haven't got any change.* Ich habe kein Kleingeld.

changing room *n* Umkleideraum *m* (*pl* Umkleideräume)

channel *n (TV)* Programm *nt* (*pl* Programme) ▹ *There's football on the other channel.* Im anderen Programm gibt es Fußball.; **the English Channel** der Ärmelkanal; **the Channel Islands** die Kanalinseln; **the Channel Tunnel** der Kanaltunnel

chaos *n* Chaos *nt* (*gen* Chaos)

chapel *n (part of church)* Kapelle *f*

chapter *n* Kapitel *nt* (*pl* Kapitel)

character *n* ❶ Charakter *m* (*pl* Charaktere) ▹ *Give me some idea of his character.* Beschreiben Sie mir seinen Charakter.; **She's quite a character.** Sie ist ein Unikum. ❷ *(in play, film)* Figur *f* ▹ *the character played by Tom Cruise* die Figur, die Tom Cruise spielt

characteristic *n* Merkmal *nt* (*pl* Merkmale)

charcoal *n* Holzkohle *f*

charge *n* Gebühr *f* ▹ *Is there a charge for delivery?* Wird für die Zustellung eine Gebühr erhoben? ▹ *an extra charge* eine Extragebühr; **free of charge** kostenlos; **to reverse the charges** ein R-Gespräch führen [**38**]; **to be on a charge** angeklagt sein [**65**]; **to be in charge** die Verantwortung haben [**32**]
▸ *vb* ❶ *(money)* verlangen [**84**] (*perf* hat verlangt) ▹ *How much did he charge you?* Wie viel hat er verlangt? ▹ *They charge ten pounds an hour.* Sie verlangen zehn Pfund die Stunde. ❷ *(with crime)* anklagen [**4**] (*perf* hat angeklagt) ▹ *The police have charged him with murder.* Die Polizei hat ihn des Mordes angeklagt.

charity *n* Wohlfahrt *f* ▹ *She does a lot of work for charity.* Sie arbeitet viel für die Wohlfahrt.; **He gave the money to charity.** Er hat das Geld für wohltätige Zwecke gespendet.

charm *n* Charme *m*

> Note that the 'e' in **Charme** is silent.

▹ *He's got a lot of charm.* Er hat viel Charme.

charming *adj* bezaubernd

chart *n* Grafik *f* ▹ *The chart shows the rise of unemployment.* Die Grafik stellt den Anstieg der Arbeitslosigkeit dar.; **the charts** die Hitparade *sg*

charter flight *n* Charterflug *m* (*pl* Charterflüge)

chase *vb* verfolgen [**84**] (*perf* hat verfolgt)
▸ *n* Verfolgung *f*; **a car chase** eine Verfolgungsjagd im Auto

chat *n* Schwätzchen *nt* (*pl* Schwätzchen) ▹ *to have a chat* ein Schwätzchen halten

chat room *n* Chatroom *m* (*pl* Chatrooms)

chat show *n* Talkshow *f* (*pl* Talkshows)

chauvinist *n* **male chauvinist** der Chauvi

cheap *adj* billig ▹ *a cheap T-shirt* ein billiges T-Shirt ▹ *It's cheaper by bus.* Mit dem Bus ist es billiger.

cheat *vb* betrügen (*imperf* betrog, *perf* hat betrogen) ▹ *He cheated me.* Er hat mich betrogen.; **You're cheating!** *(in games, at school)* Du schummelst!
▸ *n* Betrüger *m* (*pl* Betrüger), Betrügerin *f*

check *n* ❶ Kontrolle *f* ▹ *a security check* eine Sicherheitskontrolle ❷ *(US: bill)* Rechnung *f* ▹ *The waiter brought us the check.* Der Kellner brachte uns die Rechnung. ❸ *(US)* Scheck *m* (*pl* Schecks) ▹ *to write a check* einen Scheck ausstellen
▸ *vb* nachsehen [**64**] (*pres* sieht nach, *imperf* sah nach, *perf* hat nachgesehen)

▷ *I'll check the time of the train.* Ich sehe die Abfahrtszeiten des Zuges nach. ▷ *Could you check the oil, please?* Könnten Sie bitte das Öl nachsehen?; **to check in** einchecken [4]; **to check out** *(from hotel)* sich auschecken [4]

checked *adj* kariert ▷ *a checked shirt* ein kariertes Hemd

checkers *nsg (US)* Dame *f* ▷ *Checkers is her favourite game.* Dame ist ihr Lieblingsspiel.

check-in *n* Check-in *m (pl* Check-ins)

checkout *n* Kasse *f*

check-up *n* Check-up *m (pl* Check-ups)

cheddar *n* Cheddar *m (pl* Cheddars)

cheek *n* ❶ Wange *f* ▷ *He kissed her on the cheek.* Er küsste sie auf die Wange. ❷ Frechheit *f* ▷ *What a cheek!* So eine Frechheit!

cheeky *adj* frech ▷ *Don't be cheeky!* Sei nicht so frech! ▷ *a cheeky smile* ein freches Lächeln

cheer *n* Hurraruf *m (pl* Hurrarufe); **to give a cheer** Hurra rufen [56]; **Cheers!** **(1)** *(good health)* Prost! **(2)** *(thanks)* Danke schön!
▶ *vb* ❶ *(team)* anfeuern [4] *(perf* hat angefeuert) ❷ *(speaker)* zujubeln [4] *(perf* hat zugejubelt) ▷ *The speaker was cheered.* Dem Redner wurde zugejubelt.; **to cheer somebody up** jemanden aufheitern [88] ▷ *I was trying to cheer him up.* Ich habe versucht, ihn aufzuheitern.; **Cheer up!** Kopf hoch!

cheerful *adj* fröhlich

cheese *n* Käse *m (pl* Käse)

chef *n* Küchenchef *m (pl* Küchenchefs)

chemical *n* Chemikalie *f*

chemist *n* ❶ *(pharmacist)* Apotheker *m (pl* Apotheker), Apothekerin *f* ❷ *(pharmacy)* Apotheke *f* ▷ *You get it from the chemist.* Du bekommst das in der Apotheke. ❸ *(shop selling toiletries)* Drogerie *f* ❹ *(scientist)* Chemiker *m (pl* Chemiker), Chemikerin *f*

chemistry *n* Chemie *f* ▷ *the chemistry lab* das Chemielabor

cheque *n* Scheck *m (pl* Schecks) ▷ *to write a cheque* einen Scheck ausstellen ▷ *to pay by cheque* mit Scheck bezahlen

chequebook *n* Scheckheft *nt (pl* Scheckhefte)

German banks provide customers with cheques in an envelope or wallet, usually ten at a time, rather than chequebooks.

cherry *n* Kirsche *f*

chess *n* Schach *nt* ▷ *to play chess* Schach spielen

chessboard *n* Schachbrett *nt (pl* Schachbretter)

chest *n (of person)* Brust *f (pl* Brüste); **his chest measurement** seine Oberweite; **a chest of drawers** eine Kommode

chestnut *n* Kastanie *f*

chew *vb* kauen [38]

chewing gum *n* Kaugummi *m (pl* Kaugummis)

chick *n* Küken *nt (pl* Küken) ▷ *a hen and her chicks* eine Henne mit ihren Küken

chicken *n* ❶ *(food)* Hähnchen *nt (pl* Hähnchen) ▷ *I bought a chicken in the supermarket.* Ich habe im Supermarkt ein Hähnchen gekauft. ❷ *(live)* Huhn *nt (pl* Hühner) ▷ *They keep chickens.* Sie halten Hühner.

chickenpox *nsg* Windpocken *pl* ▷ *My sister has chickenpox.* Meine Schwester hat Windpocken.

chickpeas *npl* Kichererbsen *fpl*

chief *n* Chef *m (pl* Chefs) ▷ *the chief of security* der Sicherheitschef
▶ *adj* hauptsächlich ▷ *the chief reason* der hauptsächliche Grund

child *n* Kind *nt (pl* Kinder) ▷ *all the children* alle Kinder

childish *adj* kindisch

child minder *n* Tagesmutter *f (pl* Tagesmütter)

children *npl see* **child**

Chile *n* Chile *nt*; **from Chile** aus Chile; **to Chile** nach Chile

chill *vb* kalt stellen [38] ▷ *Put the wine in the fridge to chill.* Stell den Wein kalt.

chilli *n* Chili *m* (*pl* Chilis); **chilli peppers** die Peperoni *pl*
chilly *adj* kühl
chimney *n* Schornstein *m* (*pl* Schornsteine)
chin *n* Kinn *nt* (*pl* Kinne)
China *n* China *nt*
china *n* Porzellan *nt* ▷ *a china plate* ein Porzellanteller *m*
Chinese *adj* chinesisch ▷ *a Chinese restaurant* ein chinesisches Restaurant; **a Chinese man** ein Chinese; **a Chinese woman** eine Chinesin
▶ *n (language)* Chinesisch *nt* (*gen* Chinesischen); **the Chinese** *(people)* die Chinesen
chip *n (in computer)* Chip *m* (*pl* Chips)
chips *npl* ❶ *(fried potatoes)* Pommes frites *fpl* ▷ *We bought some chips.* Wir haben Pommes frites gekauft.
❷ *(crisps)* die Kartoffelchips *mpl*
Be careful not to translate **chips** by the German word **Chips**.
chiropodist *n* Fußpfleger *m* (*pl* Fußpfleger), Fußpflegerin *f* ▷ *He's a chiropodist.* Er ist Fußpfleger.
chives *npl* Schnittlauch *m*
chocolate *n* Schokolade *f* ▷ *a chocolate cake* ein Schokoladenkuchen ▷ *hot chocolate* heiße Schokolade
choice *n* Wahl *f* ▷ *I had no choice.* Ich hatte keine andere Wahl.
choir *n* Chor *m* (*pl* Chöre) ▷ *I sing in the school choir.* Ich singe im Schulchor.
choke *vb* ersticken [**19**] (*perf* ist erstickt) ▷ *He's choking!* Er erstickt!
choose *vb* auswählen [**4**] (*perf* hat ausgewählt) ▷ *She chose the red shirt.* Sie hat das rote Hemd ausgewählt.
chop *vb* klein hacken [**48**] (*perf* hat klein gehackt) ▷ *She chopped the onions.* Sie hackte die Zwiebeln klein.
▶ *n* Kotelett *nt* (*pl* Koteletts) ▷ *a pork chop* ein Schweinekotelett
chopsticks *npl* Stäbchen *ntpl*
chose *vb see* **choose**
chosen *vb see* **choose**
Christ *n* Christus (*gen* Christi) ▷ *the birth of Christ* die Geburt Christi
christening *n* Taufe *f*
Christian *n* Christ *m* (*gen* Christen, *pl* Christen), Christin *f*
▶ *adj* christlich
Christian name *n* Vorname *m* (*gen* Vornamens, *pl* Vornamen)
Christmas *n* Weihnachten *nt* ▷ *Happy Christmas!* Fröhliche Weihnachten!; **Christmas Day** der erste Weihnachtsfeiertag; **Christmas Eve** Heiligabend
Traditionally, in Germany gifts are exchanged on Christmas Eve.
a Christmas tree ein Weihnachtsbaum *m*; **a Christmas card** eine Weihnachtskarte
Most Germans send very few Christmas cards.
Christmas dinner das Weihnachtsessen
Germans traditionally eat goose at Christmas rather than turkey.
Christmas pudding
Germans don't have any traditional dessert at Christmas. Most know what Christmas pudding is, but almost always refer to it as **Plumpudding**.
chuck out *vb* rauswerfen [**92**] (*pres* wirft raus, *imperf* warf raus, *perf* hat rausgeworfen) ▷ *Chuck out those old magazines.* Wirf diese alten Zeitschriften raus.
chunk *n* Stück *nt* (*pl* Stücke) ▷ *Cut the meat into chunks.* Schneiden Sie das Fleisch in Stücke.
church *n* Kirche *f* ▷ *I don't go to church.* Ich gehe nicht in die Kirche.; **the Church of England** die anglikanische Kirche
cider *n* Apfelwein *m*
cigar *n* Zigarre *f*
cigarette *n* Zigarette *f*
cigarette lighter *n* Zigarettenanzünder *m* (*pl* Zigarettenanzünder)

cinema *n* Kino *nt* (*pl* Kinos) ▷ *I'm going to the cinema this evening.* Ich gehe heute Abend ins Kino.
cinnamon *n* Zimt *m*
circle *n* Kreis *m* (*pl* Kreise)
circular *adj* rund
circumstances *npl* Umstände *mpl*
circus *n* Zirkus *m* (*gen* Zirkus, *pl* Zirkusse)
citizen *n* Bürger *m* (*pl* Bürger), Bürgerin *f*; **a German citizen** ein deutscher Staatsbürger
city *n* Stadt *f* (*pl* Städte); **the city centre** die Innenstadt; **the City** die Londoner City
civilization *n* Zivilisation *f*
civil servant *n* Beamte *m* (*gen* Beamten, *pl* Beamten), Beamtin *f*
In Germany most teachers are **Beamte**.
▷ *He's a civil servant.* Er ist Beamter.
civil war *n* Bürgerkrieg *m* (*pl* Bürgerkriege)
claim *vb* ❶ behaupten [**2**] (*perf* hat behauptet) ▷ *He claims to have found the money.* Er behauptet, er habe das Geld gefunden.
Note the use of the subjunctive.
❷ (*receive*) bekommen [**40**] (*imperf* bekam, *perf* hat bekommen) ▷ *She's claiming unemployment benefit.* Sie bekommt Arbeitslosenunterstützung.; **to claim on one's insurance** seine Versicherung in Anspruch nehmen [**52**]
▶ *n* (*on insurance policy*) Anspruch *m* (*pl* Ansprüche); **to make a claim for damages** Schadenersatz beanspruchen [**7**]
clap *vb* (*applaud*) klatschen [**48**] ▷ *The audience clapped.* Das Publikum klatschte.; **to clap one's hands** klatschen [**48**]
clarinet *n* Klarinette *f* ▷ *I play the clarinet.* Ich spiele Klarinette.
clash *vb* ❶ (*colours*) sich beißen [**6**] (*imperf* bissen sich, *perf* haben sich gebissen) ▷ *These colours clash.* Diese Farben beißen sich. ❷ (*events*) sich überschneiden [**60**] (*imperf* überschnitt sich, *perf* hat sich überschnitten) ▷ *The concert clashes with Ann's party.* Das Konzert überschneidet sich mit Anns Party.
clasp *n* (*of necklace*) Verschluss *m* (*gen* Verschlusses, *pl* Verschlüsse)
class *n* ❶ (*group*) Klasse *f* ▷ *We're in the same class.* Wir sind in derselben Klasse. ❷ (*lesson*) Stunde *f* ▷ *I go to dancing classes.* Ich nehme Tanzstunden.
classic *adj* klassisch ▷ *a classic example* ein klassisches Beispiel
▶ *n* (*book, film*) Klassiker *m* (*pl* Klassiker)
classical *adj* klassisch ▷ *I like classical music.* Ich mag klassische Musik.
classmate *n* Klassenkamerad *m* (*gen* Klassenkameraden, *pl* Klassenkameraden), Klassenkameradin *f*
classroom *n* Klassenzimmer *f* (*pl* Klassenzimmer)
classroom assistant *n* Assistenzlehrkraft *f* (*pl* Assistenzlehrkräfte)
clause *n* ❶ (*in legal document*) Klausel *f* ❷ (*in grammar*) Satz *m* (*gen* Satzes, *pl* Sätze)
claw *n* ❶ (*of cat, dog*) Kralle *f* ❷ (*of bird*) Klaue *f* ❸ (*of crab, lobster*) Schere *f*
clean *adj* sauber ▷ *a clean shirt* ein sauberes Hemd
▶ *vb* sauber machen [**48**] (*perf* hat sauber gemacht)
cleaner *n* Putzmann *m* (*pl* Putzmänner), Putzfrau *f* ▷ *She's a cleaner.* Sie ist Putzfrau.
cleaner's *n* Reinigung *f*
cleansing lotion *n* Reinigungslotion *f*
clear *adj* ❶ klar ▷ *It's clear you don't believe me.* Es ist klar, dass du mir nicht glaubst. ❷ (*road, way*) frei ▷ *The road's clear now.* Die Straße ist jetzt frei.
▶ *vb* ❶ räumen [**38**] ▷ *The police are clearing the road after the accident.* Die Polizei räumt die Straße nach dem Unfall. ❷ (*fog, mist*) sich auflösen [**4**]

(*perf* hat sich aufgelöst) ▷ *The mist soon cleared.* Der Nebel löste sich bald auf.; **to be cleared of a crime** von einem Verbrechen freigesprochen werden [91]; **to clear the table** den Tisch abräumen [4]; **to clear up** aufräumen [4]; **I think it's going to clear up.** (*weather*) Ich glaube, es hellt sich auf.

clearly *adv* klar ▷ *She explained it very clearly.* Sie hat es sehr klar erklärt. ▷ *The English coast was clearly visible.* Die englische Küste war klar zu sehen.; **to speak clearly** deutlich sprechen [70]

clementine *n* Klementine *f*

clench *vb* **She clenched her fists.** Sie ballte die Fäuste.

clerk *n* Büroangestellte *m* (*gen* Büroangestellten, *pl* Büroangestellten), Büroangestellte *f* (*gen* Büroangestellten) ▷ *She's a clerk.* Sie ist Büroangestellte.

clever *adj* ❶ klug ▷ *She's very clever.* Sie ist sehr klug. ❷ (*ingenious*) genial ▷ *a clever system* ein geniales System ▷ *What a clever idea!* Das ist eine geniale Idee!

click on *vb* (*computer*) anklicken [4] (*perf* hat angeklickt) ▷ *to click on an icon* ein Icon anklicken; **to click on the mouse** mit der Maus klicken [48]

client *n* Klient *m* (*gen* Klienten, *pl* Klienten), Klientin *f*

cliff *n* Klippe *f*

climate *n* Klima *nt* (*pl* Klimas)

climate change *n* Klimawandel *m*

climb *vb* ❶ steigen [74] auf (*imperf* stieg, *perf* ist gestiegen) ▷ *We're going to climb Snowdon.* Wir steigen auf den Snowdon. ❷ (*stairs*) hinaufgehen [29] (*imperf* ging hinauf, *perf* ist hinaufgegangen) ▷ *I watched him climb the stairs.* Ich sah ihn die Treppe hinaufgehen.; **She finds it difficult to climb the stairs.** Das Treppensteigen fällt ihr schwer.

climber *n* Kletterer *m* (*pl* Kletterer), Kletterin *f*

climbing *n* Klettern *nt*; **to go climbing** klettern gehen [29]

clingfilm *n* Frischhaltefolie *f*

clinic *n* Klinik *f*

cloakroom *n* ❶ (*for coats*) Garderobe *f* ❷ (*toilet*) Toilette *f*

clock *n* Uhr *f*; **a grandfather clock** eine Standuhr; **an alarm clock** ein Wecker *m*; **a clock radio** ein Radiowecker *m*

close *adj, adv* ❶ (*near*) nahe ▷ *close relations* nahe Verwandte ▷ *I'm very close to my sister.* Ich stehe meiner Schwester sehr nahe.; **The shops are very close.** Die Geschäfte sind ganz in der Nähe.; **She's a close friend of mine.** Sie ist eine gute Freundin von mir.; **Come closer!** Komm näher!; **close to** in der Nähe ❷ (*contest*) knapp ▷ *It's going to be very close.* Das wird sehr knapp. ❸ (*weather*) schwül ▷ *It's close today.* Es ist schwül heute.
▶ *vb* schließen (*imperf* schloss, *perf* hat geschlossen) ▷ *What time does the pool close?* Wann schließt das Schwimmbad? ▷ *The doors close automatically.* Die Türen schließen automatisch.; **Please close the door.** Bitte mach die Tür zu.

closed *adj* geschlossen ▷ *The bank's closed.* Die Bank ist geschlossen.

closely *adv* (*look, examine*) genau

cloth *n* (*material*) Stoff *m* (*pl* Stoffe); **a cloth** ein Lappen *m*

clothes *npl* Kleider *ntpl* ▷ *new clothes* neue Kleider; **a clothes line** eine Wäscheleine; **a clothes peg** eine Wäscheklammer

cloud *n* ❶ (*in sky, of dust*) Wolke *f* ❷ (*internet*) Cloud *f*

cloudy *adj* bewölkt

clove *n* **a clove of garlic** eine Knoblauchzehe

clown *n* Clown *m* (*pl* Clowns)

club *n* Klub *m* (*pl* Klubs) ▷ *a tennis club* ein Tennisklub ▷ *the youth club* der Jugendklub; **clubs** (*in cards*) Kreuz *nt*

club together *vb* zusammenlegen [**15**] (*perf* hat zusammengelegt)
clubbing *n* **to go clubbing** in Klubs gehen [**29**]
clue *n* Hinweis *m* (*pl* Hinweise) ▷ *an important clue* ein wichtiger Hinweis; **I haven't a clue.** Ich habe keine Ahnung.
clumsy *adj* tollpatschig ▷ *Toby is even clumsier than his sister.* Toby ist noch tollpatschiger als seine Schwester.
clutch *n* (*of car*) Kupplung *f*
▶ *vb* umklammern [**34**] (*perf* hat umklammert) ▷ *She clutched my arm.* Sie umklammerte meinen Arm.
clutter *n* Kram *m* ▷ *There's so much clutter in here.* Hier liegt so viel Kram herum.
coach *n* ❶ Reisebus *m* (*gen* Reisebusses, *pl* Reisebusse); **by coach** mit dem Bus; **the coach station** der Busbahnhof; **a coach trip** eine Busreise ❷ (*trainer*) Trainer *m* (*pl* Trainer), Trainerin *f* ▷ *the German coach* der deutsche Trainer
coal *n* Kohle *f* ▷ *a coal mine* eine Kohlezeche; **a coal miner** ein Bergarbeiter *m*
coarse *adj* ❶ grob ▷ *coarse black cloth* grober schwarzer Stoff ❷ grobkörnig ▷ *The sand is very coarse on that beach.* Der Sand an diesem Strand ist sehr grobkörnig.
coast *n* Küste *f* ▷ *It's on the west coast of Scotland.* Es liegt an der Westküste Schottlands.
coastguard *n* Küstenwache *f*
coat *n* Mantel *m* (*pl* Mäntel) ▷ *a warm coat* ein warmer Mantel; **a coat of paint** ein Anstrich *m*
coat hanger *n* Kleiderbügel *m* (*pl* Kleiderbügel)
cobweb *n* Spinnennetz *nt*
cocaine *n* Kokain *nt*
cockerel *n* Hahn *m* (*pl* Hähne)
cocoa *n* Kakao *m* (*pl* Kakaos *or* Kakao) ▷ *a cup of cocoa* eine Tasse Kakao

> When ordering more than one cup of cocoa use the plural form **Kakao**.

▷ *Two cocoas, please.* Zwei Kakao bitte.
coconut *n* Kokosnuss *f* (*pl* Kokosnüsse)
code *n* Code *m* (*pl* Codes)
▶ *vb* codieren [**76**]
coffee *n* Kaffee *m* (*pl* Kaffees *or* Kaffee) ▷ *A cup of coffee, please.* Eine Tasse Kaffee, bitte.

> When ordering more than one coffee use the plural form **Kaffee**.

▷ *Two coffees, please.* Zwei Kaffee bitte.
coffee table *n* Couchtisch *m* (*pl* Couchtische)
coffin *n* Sarg *m* (*pl* Särge)
coin *n* Münze *f*; **a five-mark coin** ein Fünfmarkstück *nt*
coincidence *n* Zufall *m* (*pl* Zufälle)
coin phone *n* Münztelefon *nt*
Coke® *n* Cola *f* (*pl* Colas) ▷ *a can of Coke®* eine Dose Cola
colander *n* Seiher *m* (*pl* Seiher)
cold *adj* kalt ▷ *The water's cold.* Das Wasser ist kalt. ▷ *It's cold today.* Heute ist es kalt.

> When you talk about a person being 'cold', you use the impersonal construction.

▷ *I'm cold.* Mir ist kalt. ▷ *Are you cold?* Ist dir kalt?
▶ *n* ❶ Kälte *f* ▷ *I can't stand the cold.* Ich kann Kälte nicht ausstehen.
❷ Schnupfen *m* (*pl* Schnupfen) ▷ *to catch a cold* einen Schnupfen bekommen ▷ *to have a cold* einen Schnupfen haben ▷ *I've got a bad cold.* Ich habe einen üblen Schnupfen.; **a cold sore** ein Fieberbläschen *nt*
coleslaw *n* Krautsalat *m* (*pl* Krautsalate)
collapse *vb* zusammenbrechen [**11**] (*pres* bricht zusammen, *imperf* brach zusammen, *perf* ist zusammengebrochen) ▷ *He collapsed.* Er brach zusammen.
collar *n* ❶ (*of coat, shirt*) Kragen *m* (*pl* Kragen) ❷ (*for animal*) Halsband *nt* (*pl* Halsbänder)
collarbone *n* Schlüsselbein *nt* (*pl* Schlüsselbeine) ▷ *I broke my collarbone.* Ich habe mir das Schlüsselbein gebrochen.

colleague *n* Kollege *m* (*gen* Kollegen, *pl* Kollegen), Kollegin *f*

collect *vb* ❶ einsammeln **[4]** (*perf* hat eingesammelt) ▷ *The teacher collected the exercise books.* Der Lehrer hat die Hefte eingesammelt. ❷ sammeln **[34]** ▷ *I collect stamps.* Ich sammle Briefmarken. ▷ *They're collecting for charity.* Sie sammeln für wohltätige Zwecke. ❸ (*come to fetch*) abholen **[4]** (*perf* hat abgeholt) ▷ *Their mother collects them from school.* Ihre Mutter holt sie von der Schule ab. ▷ *They collect the rubbish twice a week.* Der Müll wird zweimal pro Woche abgeholt.

collection *n* Sammlung *f* ▷ *my CD collection* meine CD-Sammlung ▷ *a collection for charity* eine Spendensammlung

collector *n* Sammler *m* (*pl* Sammler), Sammlerin *f*

college *n* Fachhochschule *f*

A **Fachhochschule** is an institute of higher education for pupils aged over 18, which combines academic studies with work experience. It is oriented towards the needs of industry and commerce.

collide *vb* zusammenstoßen (*pres* stößt zusammen, *imperf* stieß zusammen, *perf* ist zusammengestoßen)

collie *n* Collie *m* (*pl* Collies)

collision *n* Zusammenstoß *m* (*gen* Zusammenstoßes, *pl* Zusammenstöße)

colon *n* (*punctuation mark*) Doppelpunkt *m*

colonel *n* Oberst *m* (*gen* Obersten, *pl* Obersten)

colour (*US* **color**) *n* Farbe *f* ▷ *What colour is it?* Welche Farbe hat es?; **a colour film** (*for camera*) ein Farbfilm *m*

colourful (*US* **colorful**) *adj* farbig

comb *n* Kamm *m* (*pl* Kämme)
▶ *vb* **to comb one's hair** sich kämmen **[38]**

combination *n* Kombination *f*

combine *vb* vereinen **[84]** (*perf* hat vereint) ▷ *The film combines humour with suspense.* Der Film vereint Humor und Spannung.

come *vb* kommen **[40]** (*imperf* kam, *perf* ist gekommen) ▷ *I'm coming!* Ich komme! ▷ *The letter came this morning.* Der Brief kam heute früh. ▷ *Can I come too?* Kann ich mitkommen? ▷ *Some friends came to see us.* Einige Freunde sind zu Besuch gekommen. ▷ *I'll come with you.* Ich komme mit dir.; **to come across** zufällig finden **[24]**; **She comes across as a nice girl.** Sie scheint ein nettes Mädchen zu sein.; **to come back** zurückkommen **[40]**; **to come down (1)** (*person, lift*) herunterkommen **[40] (2)** (*prices*) fallen **[22]**; **to come from** kommen **[40]** aus; **to come in** hereinkommen **[40]**; **Come on!** Na komm!; **to come out** herauskommen **[40]**; **to come round** (*after faint, operation*) wieder zu sich kommen **[40]**; **to come up** heraufkommen **[40]**; **to come up to somebody** auf jemanden zukommen **[40]**

comedian *n* Komiker *m* (*pl* Komiker), Komikerin *f*

comedy *n* Komödie *f*

comfortable *adj* bequem; **I'm very comfortable, thanks.** Danke, ich fühle mich sehr wohl.

comic *n* (*magazine*) Comicheft *nt* (*pl* Comichefte)

comic strip *n* Comicstrip *m* (*pl* Comicstrips)

comma *n* Komma *nt* (*pl* Kommas)

command *n* Befehl *m* (*pl* Befehle)

comment *n* Kommentar *m* (*pl* Kommentare) ▷ *He made no comment.* Er gab keinen Kommentar ab. ▷ *No comment!* Kein Kommentar!
▶ *vb* **to comment on something** eine Bemerkung zu etwas machen **[48]**

commentary *n* (*on TV, radio*) Kommentar *m* (*pl* Kommentare)

commentator *n (sports)* Sportreporter *m (pl* Sportreporter), Sportreporterin *f*
commercial *n* Werbespot *m (pl* Werbespots)
commit *vb* **to commit a crime** ein Verbrechen begehen [**29**]; **to commit oneself** sich festlegen [**4**]; **to commit suicide** Selbstmord begehen [**29**]
committee *n* Ausschuss *m (gen* Ausschusses, *pl* Ausschüsse)
common *adj* gebräuchlich ▷ *'Smith' is a very common surname.* 'Smith' ist ein sehr gebräuchlicher Nachname.; **in common** gemein
▶ *n* Gemeindewiese *f* ▷ *We went for a walk on the common.* Wir sind auf der Gemeindewiese spazieren gegangen.
Commons *npl* **the House of Commons** das britische Unterhaus
communicate *vb* kommunizieren [**76**] (*perf* hat kommuniziert)
communication *n* Kommunikation *f*
communion *n* Kommunion *f* ▷ *my First Communion* meine Erstkommunion
communism *n* Kommunismus *m (gen* Kommunismus)
community *n* Gemeinschaft *f*; **the local community** die Gemeinde
commute *vb* pendeln [**34**] (*perf* ist gependelt) ▷ *She commutes between Liss and London.* Sie pendelt zwischen Liss und London.
compact disc *n* Compact Disc *f (pl* Compact Discs); **compact disc player** der CD-Spieler
company *n* ❶ Unternehmen *nt (pl* Unternehmen) ▷ *He works for a big company.* Er arbeitet für ein großes Unternehmen. ❷ Gesellschaft *f* ▷ *an insurance company* eine Versicherungsgesellschaft; **a theatre company** ein Theaterensemble *nt*; **to keep somebody company** jemandem Gesellschaft leisten [**2**]
comparatively *adv* relativ
compare *vb* vergleichen (*imperf* verglich, *perf* hat verglichen) ▷ *People always compare him with his brother.* Die Leute vergleichen ihn immer mit seinem Bruder.; **compared with** im Vergleich zu
comparison *n* Vergleich *m (pl* Vergleiche)
compartment *n* Abteil *nt (pl* Abteile)
compass *n* Kompass *m (gen* Kompasses, *pl* Kompasse)
compensation *n* Schadenersatz *m* ▷ *I got a thousand pounds compensation.* Ich bekam tausend Pfund Schadenersatz.
compete *vb* teilnehmen [**52**] (*pres* nimmt teil, *imperf* nahm teil, *perf* hat teilgenommen) ▷ *I'm competing in the marathon.* Ich nehme am Marathon teil.; **to compete for something** um etwas kämpfen [**38**]; **There are fifty students competing for six places.** Fünfzig Studenten bewerben sich auf sechs Studienplätze.
competent *adj* kompetent
competition *n (organized event)* Wettbewerb *m (pl* Wettbewerbe) ▷ *a singing competition* ein Gesangswettbewerb
competitive *adj* **I'm a very competitive person.** Ich bin ein sehr ehrgeiziger Mensch.
competitor *n (participant)* Teilnehmer *m (pl* Teilnehmer), Teilnehmerin *f*
complain *vb* sich beschweren [**18**] (*perf* hat sich beschwert) ▷ *I'm going to complain to the manager.* Ich werde mich beim Geschäftsführer beschweren. ▷ *We complained about the noise.* Wir haben uns über den Lärm beschwert.
complaint *n* Beschwerde *f* ▷ *There were lots of complaints about the food.* Es gab viele Beschwerden über das Essen.
complete *adj* vollständig
completely *adv* völlig
complexion *n* Teint *m (pl* Teints)
complicated *adj* kompliziert
compliment *n* Kompliment *nt (pl* Komplimente)
▶ *vb* **They complimented me on my**

German. Sie haben mir Komplimente zu meinem Deutsch gemacht.

compose *vb (music)* komponieren [**76**] (*perf* hat komponiert); **to be composed of something** aus etwas bestehen [**72**]

composer *n* Komponist *m (gen* Komponisten, *pl* Komponisten), Komponistin *f*

comprehension *n (school exercise)* Verständnis *nt*

comprehensive *adj* umfassend ▷ *a comprehensive guide* ein umfassender Reiseführer

comprehensive school *n* Gesamtschule *f*

Gesamtschulen are the exception rather than the rule in Germany.

compulsory *adj* obligatorisch

computer *n* Computer *m (pl* Computer)

computer game *n* Computerspiel *nt (pl* Computerspiele)

computer programmer *n* Programmierer *m (pl* Programmierer), Programmiererin *f* ▷ *She's a computer programmer.* Sie ist Programmiererin.

computer science *n* Informatik *f*

computing *n* Informatik *f*

concentrate *vb* sich konzentrieren [**76**] (*perf* hat sich konzentriert) ▷ *I couldn't concentrate.* Ich konnte mich nicht konzentrieren.

concentration *n* Konzentration *f*

concern *n* Sorge *f* ▷ *to express concern about something* Sorge über etwas ausdrücken

▶ *vb* betreffen [**78**] (*pres* betrifft, *imperf* betraf, *perf* hat betroffen) ▷ *It concerns all of us.* Es betrifft uns alle.

concerned *adj* **to be concerned** sich Sorgen machen [**48**]; **as far as I'm concerned** was mich betrifft

concerning *prep* bezüglich ▷ *For further information concerning the job, contact Mr Ross.* Für weitere Informationen bezüglich der Stelle wenden Sie sich an Herrn Ross.

concert *n* Konzert *nt (pl* Konzerte)

concrete *n* Beton *m (pl* Betons)

condemn *vb* verurteilen [**84**] (*perf* hat verurteilt)

condition *n* ❶ Bedingung *f* ▷ *I'll do it, on one condition ...* Ich mache es unter einer Bedingung ... ❷ Zustand *m (pl* Zustände) ▷ *in good condition* in gutem Zustand

conditional *n* Konditional *m*

conditioner *n (for hair)* Spülung *f*

condom *n* Kondom *nt (pl* Kondome)

conduct *vb (orchestra)* dirigieren [**76**] (*perf* hat dirigiert)

conductor *n* Dirigent *m (gen* Dirigenten, *pl* Dirigenten), Dirigentin *f*

cone *n* ❶ Eistüte *f* ▷ *an ice-cream cone* eine Eistüte ❷ *(geometric shape)* Kegel *m (pl* Kegel); **a traffic cone** ein Pylon *m*

conference *n* Konferenz *f*

confess *vb* gestehen [**72**] (*imperf* gestand, *perf* hat gestanden) ▷ *He finally confessed.* Er hat schließlich gestanden. ▷ *He confessed to the murder.* Er hat den Mord gestanden.

confession *n* ❶ Geständnis *nt (gen* Geständnisses, *pl* Geständnisse) ▷ *He signed a confession.* Er unterschrieb ein Geständnis. ❷ *(in church)* Beichte *f* ▷ *to go to confession* zur Beichte gehen

confidence *n* ❶ Vertrauen *nt* ▷ *I've got confidence in you.* Ich habe Vertrauen in dich. ❷ Selbstvertrauen *nt* ▷ *She lacks confidence.* Sie hat zu wenig Selbstvertrauen.

confident *adj* ❶ *(sure of something)* zuversichtlich ▷ *I'm confident everything will be okay.* Ich bin zuversichtlich, dass alles gut gehen wird. ❷ *(self-assured)* selbstbewusst ▷ *She seems to be a confident person.* Sie scheint eine selbstbewusste Frau zu sein.

confidential *adj* vertraulich

confirm *vb (booking)* bestätigen [**18**] (*perf* hat bestätigt)

confuse *vb* durcheinanderbringen [**13**] (*imperf* brachte durcheinander, *perf* hat

durcheinandergebracht) ▷ *Don't confuse me!* Bring mich nicht durcheinander!
confused *adj* durcheinander
confusing *adj* verwirrend
confusion *n* Durcheinander *nt*
congratulate *vb* beglückwünschen [**7**] (*perf* hat beglückwünscht) ▷ *All my friends congratulated me.* Alle meine Freunde haben mich beglückwünscht.
congratulations *npl* Glückwunsch *m* (*pl* Glückwünsche) ▷ *Congratulations on your new job!* Herzlichen Glückwunsch zum neuen Job!
conjunction *n* Konjunktion *f*
conjurer *n* Zauberkünstler *m* (*pl* Zauberkünstler), Zauberkünstlerin *f*
connection *n* ❶ Zusammenhang *m* (*pl* Zusammenhänge) ▷ *There's no connection between the two events.* Es besteht kein Zusammenhang zwischen den beiden Ereignissen. ❷ *(electrical)* Kontakt *m* (*pl* Kontakte) ▷ *There's a loose connection.* Da ist ein Wackelkontakt. ❸ *(of trains, planes)* Anschluss *m* (*gen* Anschlusses, *pl* Anschlüsse) ▷ *We missed our connection.* Wir haben unseren Anschluss verpasst.
conscience *n* Gewissen *nt* ▷ *I have a guilty conscience.* Ich habe ein schlechtes Gewissen.
conscious *adj* bewusst ▷ *politically conscious* politisch bewusst ▷ *a conscious effort* eine bewusste Anstrengung; **to be conscious of something (1)** *(know)* sich einer Sache bewusst sein [**65**] ▷ *I was conscious of his disapproval.* Ich war mir seiner Missbilligung bewusst. **(2)** *(notice)* etwas bemerken [**7**] ▷ *She was conscious of Max looking at her.* Sie hatte bemerkt, dass Max sie ansah.
consciousness *n* Bewusstsein *nt*; **to lose consciousness** bewusstlos werden [**91**]
consequence *n* Folge *f*
consequently *adv* folglich
conservation *n* Schutz *m* ▷ *nature conservation* der Naturschutz
conservative *adj* konservativ; **the Conservative Party** die Konservative Partei
conservatory *n* Wintergarten *m* (*pl* Wintergärten)
consider *vb* in Erwägung ziehen [**96**] (*imperf* zog in Erwägung, *perf* hat in Erwägung gezogen) ▷ *We considered cancelling our holiday.* Wir zogen in Erwägung, den Urlaub abzusagen.; **I'm considering the idea.** Ich denke darüber nach.; **He considered it a waste of time.** Er hielt es für Zeitverschwendung.
considerate *adj* aufmerksam ▷ *That was very considerate of you.* Das war sehr aufmerksam von dir.; **not very considerate** nicht sehr rücksichtsvoll
considering *prep* ❶ dafür, dass ▷ *Considering we were there for a month ...* Dafür, dass wir einen Monat da waren ... ❷ unter den Umständen ▷ *I got a good mark, considering.* Unter den Umständen bekam ich eine gute Note.
consist *vb* **to consist of** bestehen [**72**] aus
consistent *adj* beständig ▷ *He's our most consistent player.* Er ist unser beständigster Spieler.
consonant *n* Konsonant *m* (*gen* Konsonanten, *pl* Konsonanten)
constant *adj* beständig
constantly *adv* dauernd
constipated *adj* verstopft
construct *vb* bauen [**38**]
construction *n* Bau *m*
consult *vb* ❶ *(solicitor, doctor)* um Rat fragen [**38**] ❷ *(book)* nachsehen [**64**] in (*pres* sieht nach, *imperf* sah nach, *perf* hat nachgesehen) ▷ *Consult the dictionary!* Sieh im Wörterbuch nach!
consumer *n* Verbraucher *m* (*pl* Verbraucher), Verbraucherin *f*
contact *n* Kontakt *m* (*pl* Kontakte) ▷ *I'm in contact with her.* Ich bin in Kontakt mit ihr.

▶ *vb* sich in Verbindung setzen [**36**] mit ▷ *Please contact us immediately.* Bitte setzen Sie sich sofort mit uns in Verbindung.; **Where can we contact you?** Wo können wir Sie erreichen?

contact lenses *npl* Kontaktlinsen *fpl*

contactless *adj (payment)* kontaktlos

contain *vb* enthalten [**33**] (*pres* enthält, *imperf* enthielt, *perf* hat enthalten)

container *n* Behälter *m* (*pl* Behälter)

contents *npl* Inhalt *m*; **table of contents** das Inhaltsverzeichnis

contest *n* Wettbewerb *m* (*pl* Wettbewerbe)

contestant *n* Teilnehmer *m* (*pl* Teilnehmer), Teilnehmerin *f*

context *n* Zusammenhang *m* (*pl* Zusammenhänge)

continent *n* Kontinent *m* (*pl* Kontinente) ▷ *How many continents are there?* Wie viele Kontinente gibt es?; **the Continent** Kontinentaleuropa *nt*; **I've never been to the Continent.** Ich war noch nie auf dem Kontinent.

continental quilt *n* Steppdecke *f*

continue *vb* weitermachen [**48**] (*perf* hat weitergemacht) ▷ *We'll continue tomorrow.* Wir machen morgen weiter.; **Please continue!** Bitte fahren Sie fort!; **She continued talking to her friend.** Sie redete weiter mit ihrer Freundin.

continuous *adj* laufend; **continuous assessment** laufende Leistungskontrolle

contraceptive *n* Verhütungsmittel *nt* (*pl* Verhütungsmittel)

contract *n* Vertrag *m* (*pl* Verträge)

contradict *vb* widersprechen [**70**] (*pres* widerspricht, *imperf* widersprach, *perf* hat widersprochen) ▷ *Don't contradict me!* Widersprich mir nicht!

contrary *n* Gegenteil *nt*; **on the contrary** im Gegenteil

contrast *n* Kontrast *m* (*pl* Kontraste)

contribute *vb* ❶ beitragen [**77**] (*pres* trägt bei, *imperf* trug bei, *perf* hat beigetragen) ▷ *The treaty will contribute to world peace.* Der Vertrag wird zum Weltfrieden beitragen. ❷ *(donate)* spenden [**54**] ▷ *She contributed ten pounds.* Sie hat zehn Pfund gespendet.

contribution *n* Beitrag *m* (*pl* Beiträge)

control *n* Kontrolle *f*; **to lose control** *(of vehicle)* die Kontrolle verlieren [**85**]; **the controls** *(of machine)* die Bedienelemente *ntpl*; **to be in control** das Sagen haben [**32**]; **to keep control** *(of people)* Disziplin halten [**33**]; **out of control** *(child, class)* außer Rand und Band

▶ *vb* ❶ *(country, organization)* unter Kontrolle haben [**32**] (*pres* hat unter Kontrolle, *imperf* hatte unter Kontrolle, *perf* hat unter Kontrolle gehabt) ❷ Disziplin halten [**33**] in (*pres* hält Disziplin in, *imperf* hielt Disziplin in, *perf* hat Disziplin gehalten in) ▷ *He can't control the class.* Er kann in der Klasse keine Disziplin halten. ❸ unter Kontrolle halten [**33**] ▷ *I couldn't control the horse.* Ich konnte das Pferd nicht mehr unter Kontrolle halten. ❹ *(regulate)* regeln [**34**] ▷ *You can control the volume.* Sie können die Lautstärke regeln.; **to control oneself** sich beherrschen [**7**]

controversial *adj* umstritten ▷ *a controversial book* ein umstrittenes Buch

convenient *adj (place)* günstig ▷ *The hotel's convenient for the airport.* Das Hotel ist in günstiger Lage zum Flughafen. ▷ *It's not convenient for me right now.* Es ist gerade ungünstig.; **Would Monday be convenient for you?** Würde dir Montag passen?

conventional *adj* konventionell

conversation *n* Unterhaltung *f*; **a German conversation class** deutsche Konversation

convert *vb* umbauen [**4**] (*perf* hat umgebaut) ▷ *We've converted the loft into a spare room.* Wir haben den Speicher zu einem Gästezimmer umgebaut.

conviction *n* Überzeugung *f* ▷ *She spoke with great conviction.* Sie sprach mit großer Überzeugung.; **He has three previous convictions for robbery.** Er ist bereits dreimal wegen Raubes vorbestraft.

convince *vb* überzeugen [**18**] (*perf* hat überzeugt) ▷ *I'm not convinced.* Ich bin nicht überzeugt.

cook *vb* kochen [**48**] ▷ *I can't cook.* Ich kann nicht kochen. ▷ *She's cooking lunch.* Sie kocht das Mittagessen.; **to be cooked** fertig sein [**65**]
▶ *n* Koch *m* (*pl* Köche), Köchin *f* ▷ *Werner's an excellent cook.* Werner ist ein ausgezeichneter Koch.

cooker *n* Herd *m* (*pl* Herde) ▷ *a gas cooker* ein Gasherd

cookery *n* Kochen *nt*; **a cookery class** ein Kochkurs *m*

cookie *n* (*US*) Keks *m* (*gen* Kekses, *pl* Kekse)

cooking *n* Kochen *nt*; **I like cooking.** Ich koche gern.

cool *adj* ❶ kühl ▷ *a cooler place* ein kühlerer Ort ❷ (*great*) cool ▷ *That's really cool!* Das ist echt cool!; **to stay cool** (*keep calm*) ruhig bleiben [**10**]
▶ *vb* kühlen [**38**]; **Just cool it!** (*informal*) Immer mit der Ruhe!

cooperation *n* Zusammenarbeit *f*

cop *n* Polizist *m* (*gen* Polizisten, *pl* Polizisten), Polizistin *f*

co-parent *vb* eine gemeinsame Elternschaft eingehen [**29**]

cope *vb* es schaffen [**48**] ▷ *It was hard, but we coped.* Es war schwer, aber wir haben es geschafft.; **to cope with** bewältigen [**84**]

copper *n* ❶ Kupfer *nt* ▷ *a copper bracelet* ein Kupferarmband ❷ (*police officer*) Polizist *m* (*gen* Polizisten, *pl* Polizisten), Polizistin *f*

copy *n* ❶ (*of letter, document*) Kopie *f* ❷ (*of book*) Exemplar *nt* (*pl* Exemplare)
▶ *vb* ❶ (*write down*) abschreiben [**61**] (*imperf* schrieb ab, *perf* hat abgeschrieben) ▷ *She copied the sentence.* Sie schrieb den Satz ab. ▷ *The teacher accused him of copying.* Der Lehrer warf ihm vor, abgeschrieben zu haben. ❷ (*person*) nachmachen [**4**] (*perf* hat nachgemacht) ▷ *She always copies her sister.* Sie macht ihrer Schwester alles nach. ❸ (*computer*) kopieren [**76**] (*perf* hat kopiert) ▷ *to copy and paste* kopieren und einfügen

core *n* (*of fruit*) Stein *m*

cork *n* ❶ (*of bottle*) Korken *m* (*pl* Korken) ❷ (*material*) Kork *m* ▷ *a cork table mat* ein Korkuntersetzer *m*

corkscrew *n* Korkenzieher *m* (*pl* Korkenzieher)

corn *n* ❶ (*wheat*) Getreide *nt* (*pl* Getreide) ❷ (*sweetcorn*) Mais *m*; **corn on the cob** der Maiskolben

corner *n* ❶ Ecke *f* ▷ *in a corner of the room* in einer Ecke des Zimmers ▷ *the shop on the corner* das Geschäft an der Ecke ▷ *He lives just round the corner.* Er wohnt gleich um die Ecke. ❷ (*in football*) Eckball *m* (*pl* Eckbälle)

cornflakes *npl* Cornflakes *pl*

Cornwall *n* Cornwall *nt*; **in Cornwall** in Cornwall

corpse *n* Leiche *f*

correct *adj* richtig ▷ *That's correct.* Das ist richtig. ▷ *the correct answer* die richtige Antwort
▶ *vb* korrigieren [**76**] (*perf* hat korrigiert)

correction *n* Verbesserung *f*

correctly *adv* richtig

corridor *n* Korridor *m* (*pl* Korridore)

corruption *n* Korruption *f*

Corsica *n* Korsika *nt*; **from Corsica** aus Korsika; **to Corsica** nach Korsika

cosmetics *npl* Kosmetika *ntpl*

cosmetic surgery *n* Schönheitschirurgie *f*

cost *vb* kosten [**2**] ▷ *The meal cost seventy euros.* Das Essen hat siebzig Euro gekostet. ▷ *How much does it cost?* Wie viel kostet das? ▷ *It costs too much.* Das kostet zu viel.
▶ *n* Kosten *pl* ▷ *the cost of living* die

Lebenshaltungskosten; **at all costs** um jeden Preis

costume *n* Kostüm *nt* (*pl* Kostüme)

cosy *adj* gemütlich

cot *n* ❶ *(for children)* Kinderbett *nt* (*pl* Kinderbetten) ❷ *(camp bed)* Campingliege *f*

cotton *n* Baumwolle *f* ▷ *a cotton shirt* ein Baumwollhemd *nt*; **cotton candy** die Zuckerwatte; **cotton wool** die Watte

couch *n* Couch *f* (*pl* Couchs)

cough *vb* husten [**2**]
▶ *n* Husten *m* ▷ *a bad cough* ein schlimmer Husten ▷ *I've got a cough*. Ich habe Husten.

could *vb see* **can**

council *n* Gemeinderat *m* (*pl* Gemeinderäte) ▷ *He's on the council*. Er ist im Gemeinderat.; **a council estate** eine Siedlung des sozialen Wohnungsbaus; **a council house** eine Sozialwohnung

In Germany the council provides flats rather than houses.

councillor *n* Gemeinderat *m* (*pl* Gemeinderäte), Gemeinderätin *f* ▷ *She's a local councillor*. Sie ist Gemeinderätin.

count *vb* zählen [**38**]; **to count on** zählen [**38**] auf

counter *n* ❶ *(in shop)* Ladentisch *m* (*pl* Ladentische) ❷ *(in post office, bank)* Schalter *m* (*pl* Schalter) ❸ *(in game)* Spielmarke *f*

country *n* Land *nt* (*pl* Länder) ▷ *the border between the two countries* die Grenze zwischen den beiden Ländern; **in the country** auf dem Land; **country dancing** der Volkstanz

countryside *n* Landschaft *f*

county *n* Grafschaft *f*

The nearest German equivalent of a county would be a **Bundesland**.

the county council der Grafschaftsrat

The nearest German equivalent of a county council would be the **Landtag**.

couple *n* Paar *nt* (*pl* Paare) ▷ *the couple who live next door* das Paar von nebenan; **a couple** ein paar

Note that in this sense **paar** is spelt with a small 'p'.

▷ *a couple of hours* ein paar Stunden

courage *n* Mut *m*

courgette *n* Zucchini *f* (*pl* Zucchini)

courier *n* ❶ *(for tourists)* Reiseleiter *m* (*pl* Reiseleiter), Reiseleiterin *f* ❷ *(delivery service)* Kurier *m* (*pl* Kuriere) ▷ *They sent it by courier*. Sie haben es mit Kurier geschickt.

course *n* ❶ Kurs *m* (*pl* Kurse) ▷ *a German course* ein Deutschkurs ▷ *to go on a course* einen Kurs machen ❷ Gang *m* (*pl* Gänge) ▷ *the first course* der erste Gang; **the main course** das Hauptgericht ❸ Platz *m* (*pl* Plätze) ▷ *a golf course* ein Golfplatz; **of course** natürlich

court *n* ❶ *(of law)* Gericht *nt* (*pl* Gerichte) ▷ *He was in court last week*. Er war letzte Woche vor Gericht. ❷ *(tennis)* Platz *m* (*pl* Plätze) ▷ *There are tennis and squash courts*. Es gibt Tennis- und Squashplätze.

courtyard *n* Hof *m* (*pl* Höfe)

cousin *n* ❶ *(man)* Vetter *m* (*pl* Vettern) ❷ *(woman)* Cousine *f*

cover *n* ❶ *(of book)* Umschlag *m* (*pl* Umschläge) ❷ *(of duvet)* Bezug *m* (*pl* Bezüge)
▶ *vb* ❶ bedecken [**18**] (*perf* hat bedeckt) ▷ *Cover the dough with a cloth*. Bedecke den Teig mit einem Tuch.; **My face was covered with mosquito bites.** Mein Gesicht war voller Mückenstiche. ❷ decken [**38**] ▷ *Our insurance didn't cover it*. Unsere Versicherung hat das nicht gedeckt.; **to cover up a scandal** einen Skandal vertuschen [**7**]

cow *n* Kuh *f* (*pl* Kühe)

coward *n* Feigling *m* (*pl* Feiglinge)

der Feigling is also used for women.

▷ *She's a coward*. Sie ist ein Feigling.

cowboy *n* Cowboy *m* (*pl* Cowboys)

a b c d e f g h i j k l m n o p q r s t u v w x y z

crab *n* Krabbe *f*

crack *n* ❶ *(in wall)* Riss *m* (*gen* Risses, *pl* Risse) ❷ *(in cup, window)* Sprung *m* (*pl* Sprünge) ❸ *(drug)* Crack *nt*; **I'll have a crack at it.** Ich werd's mal versuchen.
▸ *vb* ❶ *(nut)* knacken [**48**] ❷ *(egg)* aufschlagen [**59**] (*pres* schlägt auf, *imperf* schlug auf, *perf* hat aufgeschlagen); **to crack a joke** einen Witz reißen; **to crack down on** hart durchgreifen gegen

cracked *adj (cup, window)* kaputt

cracker *n* ❶ *(biscuit)* Cracker *m* (*pl* Cracker) ❷ *(Christmas cracker)* Knallbonbon *nt* (*pl* Knallbonbons)

craft *n* Werken *nt* ▷ *We do craft at school.* Wir haben Werken in der Schule.; **a craft centre** ein Kunstgewerbezentrum *nt*

crane *n (machine)* Kran *m*

crash *vb* kaputt fahren [**21**] (*pres* fährt kaputt, *imperf* fuhr kaputt, *perf* hat kaputt gefahren) ▷ *He's crashed his car.* Er hat sein Auto kaputt gefahren.; **The plane crashed.** Das Flugzeug stürzte ab.; **to crash into something** auf etwas fahren [**21**]
▸ *n* ❶ *(of car)* Unfall *m* (*pl* Unfälle) ❷ *(of plane)* Unglück *nt* (*pl* Unglücke); **a crash helmet** ein Sturzhelm *m*; **a crash course** ein Crashkurs *m*

crawl *vb (baby)* krabbeln [**88**] (*perf* ist gekrabbelt)
▸ *n* Kraulen *nt*; **to do the crawl** kraulen [**38**]

crazy *adj* verrückt

cream *adj (colour)* cremefarben
▸ *n* Sahne *f* ▷ *strawberries and cream* Erdbeeren mit Sahne ▷ *a cream cake* eine Sahnetorte; **cream cheese** der Frischkäse; **sun cream** die Sonnencreme

crease *n* Falte *f*

creased *adj* zerknittert

create *vb* schaffen (*imperf* schuf, *perf* hat geschaffen)

creative *adj* kreativ

creature *n* Lebewesen *nt* (*pl* Lebewesen)

crèche *n* Kinderkrippe *f*

credit *n* Kredit *m* (*pl* Kredite) ▷ *on credit* auf Kredit

credit card *n* Kreditkarte *f*

creep *n* **It gives me the creeps.** Es ist mir nicht geheuer.
▸ *vb* kriechen (*imperf* kroch, *perf* ist gekrochen)

crew *n* Mannschaft *f*

crew cut *n* Bürstenhaarschnitt *m* (*pl* Bürstenhaarschnitte)

cricket *n* ❶ Cricket *nt*
Cricket is practically never played in Germany.
▷ *I play cricket.* Ich spiele Cricket.; **a cricket bat** ein Cricketschläger *m*
❷ *(insect)* Grille *f*

crime *n* ❶ Verbrechen *nt* (*pl* Verbrechen) ▷ *Murder is a crime.* Mord ist ein Verbrechen.
❷ *(lawlessness)* Kriminalität *f* ▷ *Crime is rising.* Die Kriminalität nimmt zu.

criminal *n* Verbrecher *m* (*pl* Verbrecher), Verbrecherin *f*
▸ *adj* kriminell ▷ *It's criminal!* Das ist kriminell!; **It's a criminal offence.** Das ist eine strafbare Handlung.; **to have a criminal record** vorbestraft sein [**65**]

crippled *adj* gelähmt ▷ *He was crippled in an accident.* Er ist seit einem Unfall gelähmt.

crisis *n* Krise *f*

crisp *adj (food)* knusprig

crisps *npl* Chips *mpl* ▷ *a bag of crisps* eine Tüte Chips

critical *adj* kritisch

criticism *n* Kritik *f*

criticize *vb* kritisieren [**76**] (*perf* hat kritisiert)

Croatia *n* Kroatien *nt*; **from Croatia** aus Kroatien; **to Croatia** nach Kroatien

crochet *vb* häkeln [**34**]

crocodile *n* Krokodil *nt* (*pl* Krokodile)

crook *n (criminal)* Verbrecher *m* (*pl* Verbrecher)

crop *n* Ernte *f* ▷ *a good crop of apples* eine gute Apfelernte

cross *n* Kreuz *nt* (*pl* Kreuze)
▶ *adj* böse ▷ *to be cross about something* wegen etwas böse sein
▶ *vb (street, bridge)* überqueren [**7**] (*perf* hat überquert); **to cross out** durchstreichen; **to cross over** hinübergehen [**29**]

cross-country *n (race)* Querfeldeinrennen *nt* (*pl* Querfeldeinrennen); **cross-country skiing** der Langlauf

crossing *n* ❶ *(by boat)* Überfahrt *f* ▷ *the crossing from Dover to Calais* die Überfahrt von Dover nach Calais ❷ *(for pedestrians)* Fußgängerüberweg *m* (*pl* Fußgängerüberwege)

crossroads *nsg* Kreuzung *f*

crossword *n* Kreuzworträtsel *nt* (*pl* Kreuzworträtsel) ▷ *I like doing crosswords.* Ich mache gern Kreuzworträtsel.

crouch down *vb* sich niederkauern [**15**] (*perf* hat sich niedergekauert)

crow *n* Krähe *f*

crowd *n* Menge *f*; **the crowd** *(at sports match)* die Zuschauer *mpl*
▶ *vb* sich drängen [**38**] ▷ *The children crowded round the model.* Die Kinder drängten sich um das Modell.

crowded *adj* voll

crown *n* Krone *f*

crude *adj (vulgar)* ordinär

cruel *adj* grausam

cruise *n* Kreuzfahrt *f* ▷ *to go on a cruise* eine Kreuzfahrt machen

crumb *n* Krümel *m* (*pl* Krümel)

crush *vb* ❶ zerquetschen [**95**] (*perf* hat zerquetscht) ▷ *The tomatoes got crushed.* Die Tomaten wurden zerquetscht. ❷ *(finger)* quetschen [**48**] ▷ *I crushed my finger in the car door.* Ich habe mir den Finger in der Autotür gequetscht.
▶ *n* **to have a crush on somebody** für jemanden schwärmen [**38**]

crutch *n* Krücke *f*

cry *n* Schrei *m* ▷ *a cry of fear* ein Angstschrei; **to have a good cry** sich ausweinen [**4**]
▶ *vb* weinen [**38**] ▷ *The baby's crying.* Das Baby weint.

crystal *n* Kristall *m* (*pl* Kristalle)

cub *n* ❶ Junge *nt* (*gen* Jungen, *pl* Jungen) ▷ *the lioness and her cub* die Löwin und ihr Junges ❷ *(scout)* Wölfling *m* (*pl* Wölflinge)

cube *n* Würfel *m* (*pl* Würfel)

cubic *adj* **a cubic metre** ein Kubikmeter *m*

cucumber *n* Gurke *f*

cuddle *n* **Come and give me a cuddle.** Komm und nimm mich in den Arm.
▶ *vb* **to cuddle somebody** jemanden in den Arm nehmen [**52**]

cue *n (for snooker, pool)* Queue *nt* (*pl* Queues)

> **Queue** is pronounced as if spelt 'Kö'.

culture *n* Kultur *f*

cunning *adj* schlau

cup *n* ❶ Tasse *f* ▷ *a china cup* eine Porzellantasse ▷ *a cup of coffee* eine Tasse Kaffee ❷ *(trophy)* Pokal *m* (*pl* Pokale)

cupboard *n* Schrank *m* (*pl* Schränke)

cure *vb* heilen [**38**]
▶ *n* Mittel *nt* (*pl* Mittel) ▷ *a cure for a cold* ein Mittel gegen Schnupfen

curious *adj* neugierig

curl *n* Locke *f*
▶ *vb (hair)* in Locken legen [**38**]

curly *adj* lockig ▷ *When I was young my hair was curlier.* Als ich jung war, waren meine Haare lockiger.

currant *n (dried fruit)* Korinthe *f*

currency *n* Währung *f* ▷ *foreign currency* ausländische Währung

current *n* Strömung *f* ▷ *The current is very strong.* Die Strömung ist sehr stark.
▶ *adj* aktuell ▷ *the current situation* die aktuelle Lage

current affairs *npl* Tagespolitik *fsg*

curriculum *n* Lehrplan *m* (*pl* Lehrpläne)

a b **c** d e f g h i j k l m n o p q r s t u v w x y z

curriculum vitae *n* Lebenslauf *m* (*pl* Lebensläufe)
curry *n* Curry *nt* (*pl* Currys)
curtain *n* Vorhang *m* (*pl* Vorhänge)
cushion *n* Kissen *nt* (*pl* Kissen)
custard *n* *(for pouring)* Vanillesoße *f*
custody *n* *(of child)* Sorgerecht *nt* ▷ *He got custody of his son.* Er bekam das Sorgerecht für seinen Sohn.; **to be remanded in custody** inhaftiert werden [**91**]
custom *n* Brauch *m* (*pl* Bräuche) ▷ *It's an old custom.* Es ist ein alter Brauch.
customer *n* Kunde *m* (*gen* Kunden, *pl* Kunden), Kundin *f*
customs *npl* Zoll *m* (*pl* Zölle)
customs officer *n* Zollbeamte *m* (*gen* Zollbeamten, *pl* Zollbeamten), Zollbeamtin *f* ▷ *a customs officer (man)* ein Zollbeamter
cut *n* ❶ Schnittwunde *f* ▷ *He's got a cut on his forehead.* Er hat eine Schnittwunde an der Stirn. ❷ *(in price)* Senkung *f* ❸ *(in spending)* Kürzung *f*; **a cut and blow-dry** Schneiden und Föhnen
▶ *vb* ❶ schneiden [**60**] (*imperf* schnitt, *perf* hat geschnitten) ▷ *I'll cut some bread.* Ich schneide Brot.; **I cut my foot on a piece of glass.** Ich habe mir den Fuß an einer Glasscherbe verletzt.; **to cut oneself** sich schneiden [**60**] ▷ *Watch you don't cut yourself!* Pass auf, dass du dich nicht schneidest! ❷ *(price)* senken [**38**] ❸ *(spending)* kürzen [**36**]; **to cut down (1)** *(tree)* fällen [**38**] **(2)** einschränken [**4**] ▷ *I'm cutting down on chocolate.* Ich bin dabei, meinen Schokoladenkonsum einzuschränken.; **The electricity was cut off.** Der Strom wurde abgestellt.; **to cut up** *(vegetables, meat)* klein schneiden [**60**]
cute *adj* niedlich
cutlery *n* Besteck *nt* (*pl* Bestecke)
CV *n* (= *curriculum vitae*) Lebenslauf *m* (*pl* Lebensläufe)
cyberbully *n* Cybermobber *m* (*pl* Cybermobber), Cybermobberin *f* (*pl* Cybermobberinnen)
cyberbullying *n* Cybermobbing *nt*
cybercafé *n* Internet-Café *nt* (*pl* Internet-Cafés)
cycle *vb* Rad fahren [**21**] (*pres* fährt Rad, *imperf* fuhr Rad, *perf* ist Rad gefahren) ▷ *I like cycling.* Ich fahre gern Rad.; **I cycle to school.** Ich fahre mit dem Rad zur Schule.
▶ *n* Fahrrad *nt* (*pl* Fahrräder) ▷ *a cycle ride* eine Fahrradfahrt
cycling *n* Radfahren *nt* ▷ *My hobby is cycling.* Radfahren ist mein Hobby.
cyclist *n* Radfahrer *m* (*pl* Radfahrer), Radfahrerin *f*
cylinder *n* Zylinder *m* (*pl* Zylinder)
Cyprus *n* Zypern *nt*; **from Cyprus** aus Zypern; **in Cyprus** auf Zypern; **to Cyprus** nach Zypern
Czech *adj* tschechisch; **the Czech Republic** die Tschechische Republik
▶ *n* ❶ *(person)* Tscheche *m* (*gen* Tschechen, *pl* Tschechen), Tschechin *f* ❷ *(language)* Tschechisch *nt* (*gen* Tschechischen)

d

dad *n* Papa *m* (*pl* Papas) ▷ *his dad* sein Papa ▷ *I'll ask Dad.* Ich werde Papa fragen.
daffodil *n* Osterglocke *f*
daft *adj* verrückt
daily *adj, adv* täglich ▷ *It's part of my daily routine.* Es gehört zu meiner täglichen Routine. ▷ *The pool is open daily from nine a.m. to six p.m.* Das Schwimmbad ist täglich von neun bis achtzehn Uhr geöffnet.
dairy products *npl* Milchprodukte *ntpl*
daisy *n* Gänseblümchen *nt* (*pl* Gänseblümchen)
dam *n* Damm *m* (*pl* Dämme)
damage *n* Schaden *m* (*pl* Schäden) ▷ *The storm did a lot of damage.* Der Sturm hat viel Schaden angerichtet.
▶ *vb* beschädigen [**7**] (*perf* hat beschädigt)
damp *adj* feucht
dance *n* Tanz *m* (*pl* Tänze) ▷ *The last dance was a waltz.* Der letzte Tanz war ein Walzer. ▷ *Are you going to the dance tonight?* Gehst du heute Abend zum Tanz?
▶ *vb* tanzen [**36**]
dancer *n* Tänzer *m* (*pl* Tänzer), Tänzerin *f*
dancing *n* Tanzen *nt*; **to go dancing** tanzen gehen [**29**]
dandruff *n* Schuppen *fpl*
Dane *n* Däne *m* (*gen* Dänen, *pl* Dänen), Dänin *f*
danger *n* Gefahr *f*; **in danger** in Gefahr; **I'm in danger of failing maths.** Es könnte durchaus sein, dass ich in Mathe durchfalle.
dangerous *adj* gefährlich
Danish *adj* dänisch
▶ *n (language)* Dänisch *nt* (*gen* Dänischen)
Danube *n* Donau *f*
dare *vb* sich trauen [**38**]; **to dare to do something** sich trauen [**38**], etwas zu tun; **I dare say it'll be okay.** Ich denke, dass das in Ordnung ist.
daring *adj* mutig
dark *adj* dunkel ▷ *It's dark.* Es ist dunkel. ▷ *It's getting dark.* Es wird dunkel. ▷ *She's got dark hair.* Sie hat dunkle Haare. ▷ *a dark green sweater* ein dunkelgrüner Pullover
▶ *n* Dunkelheit *f* ▷ *after dark* nach Einbruch der Dunkelheit; **in the dark** im Dunkeln; **I'm afraid of the dark.** Ich habe Angst im Dunkeln.
darkness *n* Dunkelheit *f*; **The room was in darkness.** Das Zimmer war dunkel.
darling *n* Liebling *m* (*pl* Lieblinge)

> **der Liebling** is also used for women.

▷ *Thank you, darling!* Danke, Liebling!
dart *n* Pfeil *m* (*pl* Pfeile); **to play darts** Darts spielen [**38**]
dashboard *n* Armaturenbrett *nt* (*pl* Armaturenbretter)
data *npl* Daten *pl*
database *n (on computer)* Datenbank *f* (*pl* Datenbanken)
date *n* ❶ Datum *nt* (*pl* Daten) ▷ *my date of birth* mein Geburtsdatum; **What's**

the date today? Der Wievielte ist heute?; **to have a date with somebody** mit jemandem eine Verabredung haben [**32**] ▷ *She's got a date with Ian tonight.* Sie hat heute Abend eine Verabredung mit Ian.; **out of date (1)** *(passport)* abgelaufen **(2)** *(technology)* veraltet **(3)** *(clothes)* altmodisch ❷ *(fruit)* Dattel *f*

daughter *n* Tochter *f* (*pl* Töchter)

daughter-in-law *n* Schwiegertochter *f* (*pl* Schwiegertöchter)

dawn *n* Morgengrauen *nt* ▷ *at dawn* im Morgengrauen

day *n* Tag *m* (*pl* Tage) ▷ *We stayed in Vienna for three days.* Wir sind drei Tage in Wien geblieben. ▷ *I stayed at home all day.* Ich war den ganzen Tag zu Hause.; **every day** jeden Tag; **during the day** tagsüber; **the day before** der Tag davor; **the day before my birthday** der Tag vor meinem Geburtstag; **the day after** der Tag danach; **the day after my birthday** der Tag nach meinem Geburtstag; **the day before yesterday** vorgestern; **the day after tomorrow** übermorgen

dead *adj, adv* ❶ tot ▷ *He was already dead.* Er war schon tot.; **He was shot dead.** Er wurde erschossen. ❷ *(totally)* völlig ▷ *You're dead right!* Du hast völlig recht!; **dead on time** ganz pünktlich

dead end *n* Sackgasse *f*

deadline *n* Termin *m* (*pl* Termine) ▷ *We'll never meet the deadline.* Den Termin schaffen wir nie.

dead spot *n* *(mobile)* Funkloch *nt* (*pl* Funklöcher)

deaf *adj* taub

deafening *adj* ohrenbetäubend

deal *n* Geschäft *nt* (*pl* Geschäfte); **It's a deal!** Abgemacht!; **a great deal** viel
▶ *vb* *(cards)* geben [**28**] (*pres* gibt, *imperf* gab, *perf* hat gegeben) ▷ *It's your turn to deal.* Du gibst!; **to deal with something** sich um etwas kümmern [**38**]

dealer *n* Händler *m* (*pl* Händler), Händlerin *f* ▷ *a drug dealer* ein Drogenhändler ▷ *an antique dealer* ein Antiquitätenhändler

dear *adj* ❶ lieb; **Dear Mrs Sinclair (1)** Liebe Frau Sinclair **(2)** *(more formal)* Sehr geehrte Frau Sinclair; **Dear Sir/Madam** *(in a circular)* Sehr geehrte Damen und Herren ❷ *(expensive)* teuer

death *n* Tod *m* (*pl* Tode) ▷ *after her death* nach ihrem Tod ▷ *I was bored to death.* Ich habe mich zu Tode gelangweilt.

debate *n* Debatte *f*
▶ *vb* debattieren [**76**] (*perf* hat debattiert) ▷ *We debated the issue.* Wir haben die Frage debattiert.

debt *n* Schulden *fpl* ▷ *He's got a lot of debts.* Er hat viele Schulden.; **to be in debt** verschuldet sein [**65**]

decade *n* Jahrzehnt *nt* (*pl* Jahrzehnte)

decaffeinated *adj* entkoffeiniert

deceive *vb* täuschen [**48**]

December *n* Dezember *m* ▷ *in December* im Dezember

decent *adj* ordentlich ▷ *a decent education* eine ordentliche Ausbildung

decide *vb* ❶ beschließen (*imperf* beschloss, *perf* hat beschlossen) ▷ *I decided to write to her.* Ich habe beschlossen, ihr zu schreiben. ▷ *I decided not to go.* Ich habe beschlossen, nicht hinzugehen. ❷ sich entscheiden (*imperf* entschied sich, *perf* hat sich entschieden) ▷ *I can't decide.* Ich kann mich nicht entscheiden. ▷ *Haven't you decided yet?* Hast du dich noch nicht entschieden?; **to decide on something** über etwas entscheiden

decimal *adj* dezimal ▷ *the decimal system* das Dezimalsystem

decision *n* Entscheidung *f* ▷ *to make a decision* eine Entscheidung treffen

deck *n* ❶ *(of ship)* Deck *nt* (*pl* Decks) ▷ *on deck* an Deck ❷ *(of cards)* Spiel *nt* (*pl* Spiele)

deckchair *n* Liegestuhl *m* (*pl* Liegestühle)

declare *vb* erklären [**19**] (*perf* hat erklärt)

decline *vb* ❶ ablehnen [**4**] (*perf* hat abgelehnt) ▷ *He declined to comment.* Er lehnte einen Kommentar ab. ❷ zurückgehen [**29**] (*imperf* ging zurück, *perf* ist zurückgegangen) ▷ *The birth rate is declining.* Die Geburtenrate geht zurück.

decorate *vb* ❶ dekorieren [**76**] (*perf* hat dekoriert) ▷ *I decorated the cake with glacé cherries.* Ich habe den Kuchen mit glasierten Kirschen dekoriert. ❷ *(paint)* streichen (*imperf* strich, *perf* hat gestrichen) ❸ *(wallpaper)* tapezieren [**76**] (*perf* hat tapeziert)

decorations *npl* Schmuck *m* ▷ *Christmas decorations* der Weihnachtsschmuck

decrease *n* Abnahme *f* ▷ *a decrease in the number of unemployed people* eine Abnahme der Arbeitslosenzahl
▶ *vb* abnehmen [**52**] (*pres* nimmt ab, *imperf* nahm ab, *perf* hat abgenommen)

deduct *vb* abziehen [**96**] (*imperf* zog ab, *perf* hat abgezogen)

deep *adj (water, hole, cut)* tief ▷ *How deep is the lake?* Wie tief ist der See? ▷ *a hole four metres deep* ein vier Meter tiefes Loch ▷ *He's got a deep voice.* Er hat eine tiefe Stimme.; **to take a deep breath** tief einatmen [**3**]; **The snow was really deep.** Es lag sehr viel Schnee.

deeply *adv (depressed)* zutiefst

deer *n* Reh *nt* (*pl* Rehe)

defeat *n* Niederlage *f*
▶ *vb* besiegen [**7**] (*perf* hat besiegt)

defect *n* Defekt *m* (*pl* Defekte)

defence (*US* **defense**) *n* Verteidigung *f*

defend *vb* verteidigen [**84**] (*perf* hat verteidigt)

defender *n* Verteidiger *m* (*pl* Verteidiger), Verteidigerin *f*

defense *n (US)* Verteidigung *f*

define *vb* definieren [**76**] (*perf* hat definiert)

definite *adj* ❶ genau ▷ *I haven't got any definite plans.* Ich habe noch keine genauen Pläne. ❷ eindeutig ▷ *It's a definite improvement.* Es ist eine eindeutige Verbesserung. ❸ sicher ▷ *Perhaps we'll go to Spain, but it's not definite.* Vielleicht fahren wir nach Spanien, aber es ist noch nicht sicher.; **He was definite about it.** Er war sich sehr sicher.

definitely *adv* eindeutig ▷ *He's definitely the best.* Er ist eindeutig der Beste.; **He's the best player. — Definitely!** Er ist der beste Spieler. — Absolut!; **I definitely think he'll come.** Ich bin sicher, dass er kommt.

definition *n* Definition *f*

degree *n* ❶ Grad *m* (*pl* Grade) ▷ *a temperature of thirty degrees* eine Temperatur von dreißig Grad ❷ Universitätsabschluss *m* (*gen* Universitätsabschlusses, *pl* Universitätsabschlüsse) ▷ *a degree in English* ein Universitätsabschluss in Englisch

delay *vb* verschieben (*imperf* verschob, *perf* hat verschoben) ▷ *We delayed our departure.* Wir haben unsere Abreise verschoben.; **to be delayed** Verspätung haben [**32**]
▶ *n* Verzögerung *f*; **without delay** unverzüglich

delete *vb (on computer, tape)* löschen [**48**]

deliberate *adj* absichtlich

deliberately *adv* absichtlich ▷ *She did it deliberately.* Sie hat es absichtlich getan.

delicate *adj* ❶ zierlich ▷ *She has very delicate hands.* Sie hat sehr zierliche Hände. ❷ *(object)* zerbrechlich ▷ *That vase is very delicate.* Die Vase ist sehr zerbrechlich. ❸ *(often ill)* anfällig ▷ *a delicate child* ein anfälliges Kind ❹ *(situation)* heikel ▷ *The situation is rather delicate.* Die Lage ist ziemlich heikel.

delicatessen *nsg* Feinkostgeschäft *nt* (*pl* Feinkostgeschäfte)
delicious *adj* köstlich
delight *n* Freude *f*
delighted *adj* hocherfreut ▷ *He'll be delighted.* Er wird hocherfreut sein.
deliver *vb* ❶ austragen [**77**] (*pres* trägt aus, *imperf* trug aus, *perf* hat ausgetragen) ▷ *I deliver newspapers.* Ich trage Zeitungen aus. ❷ *(mail)* ausliefern [**4**] (*perf* hat ausgeliefert)
delivery *n* Lieferung *f*
demand *vb* fordern [**88**]
▶ *n (for product)* Nachfrage *f*
democracy *n* Demokratie *f*
democratic *adj* demokratisch
demolish *vb (building)* abreißen (*imperf* riss ab, *perf* hat abgerissen)
demonstrate *vb* ❶ *(show)* vorführen [**4**] (*perf* hat vorgeführt) ▷ *She demonstrated the technique.* Sie hat die Methode vorgeführt. ❷ *(protest)* demonstrieren [**76**] (*perf* hat demonstriert) ▷ *to demonstrate against something* gegen etwas demonstrieren
demonstration *n* ❶ *(of method, technique)* Vorführung *f* ❷ *(protest)* Demonstration *f*
demonstrator *n (protester)* Demonstrant *m* (*gen* Demonstranten, *pl* Demonstranten), Demonstrantin *f*
denim *n* Jeansstoff *m*; **a denim jacket** eine Jeansjacke
Denmark *n* Dänemark *nt*; **from Denmark** aus Dänemark; **to Denmark** nach Dänemark
dense *adj* ❶ *(crowd, fog)* dicht ❷ *(smoke)* dick; **He's so dense!** *(informal)* Er ist furchtbar blöd!
dent *n* Delle *f*
▶ *vb* eindellen [**4**] (*perf* hat eingedellt)
dental *adj* **dental treatment** die Zahnbehandlung; **dental floss** die Zahnseide; **dental surgeon** der Zahnarzt
dentist *n* Zahnarzt *m* (*pl* Zahnärzte), Zahnärztin *f* ▷ *Catherine is a dentist.* Catherine ist Zahnärztin.
deny *vb* leugnen [**53**] ▷ *She denied everything.* Sie hat alles geleugnet.
deodorant *n* Deo *nt* (*pl* Deos)
depart *vb* ❶ *(person)* abreisen [**4**] (*perf* ist abgereist) ❷ *(train)* abfahren [**21**] (*pres* fährt ab, *imperf* fuhr ab, *perf* ist abgefahren)
department *n* ❶ *(in shop)* Abteilung *f* ▷ *the shoe department* die Schuhabteilung ❷ *(university, school)* Fachbereich *m* (*pl* Fachbereiche) ▷ *the English department* der Fachbereich Englisch
department store *n* Kaufhaus *nt* (*gen* Kaufhauses, *pl* Kaufhäuser)
departure *n* Abfahrt *f*
departure lounge *n* Abflughalle *f*
depend *vb* **to depend on** abhängen [**35**] von; **depending on the weather** je nach Wetterlage; **It depends.** Das kommt drauf an.
deposit *n* ❶ *(part payment)* Anzahlung *f* ▷ *You have to pay a deposit when you book.* Sie müssen eine Anzahlung leisten, wenn Sie buchen. ❷ *(when hiring something)* Kaution *f* ▷ *You get the deposit back when you return the bike.* Sie bekommen die Kaution zurück, wenn Sie das Fahrrad zurückbringen. ❸ *(on bottle)* Pfand *nt* (*pl* Pfänder)
depressed *adj* deprimiert ▷ *I'm feeling depressed.* Ich bin deprimiert.
depressing *adj* deprimierend
depth *n* Tiefe *f*
deputy head *n* Konrektor *m* (*pl* Konrektoren), Konrektorin *f*
descend *vb* hinuntersteigen [**74**] (*imperf* stieg hinunter, *perf* ist hinuntergestiegen)
describe *vb* beschreiben [**61**] (*imperf* beschrieb, *perf* hat beschrieben)
description *n* Beschreibung *f*
desert *n* Wüste *f*
desert island *n* einsame Insel *f*
deserve *vb* verdienen [**84**] (*perf* hat verdient) ▷ *He deserves a holiday.* Er hat einen Urlaub verdient.; **She deserves to be punished.** Sie gehört bestraft.

design *n* ❶ Design *nt* (*pl* Designs) ▷ *fashion design* das Modedesign; **It's a completely new design.** Es ist eine völlig neue Konstruktion. ❷ *(pattern)* Muster *nt* (*pl* Muster) ▷ *a geometric design* ein geometrisches Muster ▶ *vb (clothes, furniture)* entwerfen [**92**] (*pres* entwirft, *imperf* entwarf, *perf* hat entworfen)

designer *n (of clothes)* Modeschöpfer *m* (*pl* Modeschöpfer), Modeschöpferin *f*; **designer clothes** die Designerkleidung *sg*

desire *n* Verlangen *nt* (*pl* Verlangen) ▶ *vb* wünschen [**48**] ▷ *if desired* falls gewünscht

desk *n* ❶ *(in office)* Schreibtisch *m* (*pl* Schreibtische) ❷ *(in school)* Bank *f* (*pl* Bänke) ❸ *(in hotel)* Rezeption *f* ❹ *(at airport)* Schalter *m* (*pl* Schalter)

desktop *n* Desktop *m* (*pl* Desktops)

despair *n* Verzweiflung *f*; **I was in despair.** Ich war verzweifelt.

desperate *adj* verzweifelt ▷ *a desperate situation* eine verzweifelte Lage; **to get desperate** fast verzweifeln [**7**]; **I'm desperate for a drink.** Ich brauche dringend etwas zu trinken.

desperately *adv* ❶ äußerst ▷ *We're desperately worried.* Wir sind äußerst besorgt. ❷ verzweifelt ▷ *He was desperately trying to persuade her.* Er versuchte verzweifelt, sie zu überzeugen.

despise *vb* verachten [**18**] (*perf* hat verachtet)

despite *prep* trotz ▷ *despite the bad weather* trotz des schlechten Wetters

dessert *n* Nachtisch *m* ▷ *for dessert* zum Nachtisch

destination *n* Ziel *nt* (*pl* Ziele)

destroy *vb* zerstören [**95**] (*perf* hat zerstört)

destruction *n* Zerstörung *f*

detached house *n* Einzelhaus *nt* (*gen* Einzelhauses, *pl* Einzelhäuser)

detail *n* Detail *nt* (*pl* Details); **in detail** ganz genau

detailed *adj* ausführlich

detective *n* Detektiv *m* (*pl* Detektive), Detektivin *f*; **a private detective** ein Privatdetektiv; **a detective story** eine Detektivgeschichte

detention *n* **to get a detention** nachsitzen müssen [**51**]

detergent *n* Waschmittel *nt* (*pl* Waschmittel)

determined *adj* entschlossen; **to be determined to do something** entschlossen sein [**65**], etwas zu tun

detour *n* Umweg *m* (*pl* Umwege)

devastated *adj* am Boden zerstört ▷ *I was devastated.* Ich war am Boden zerstört.

develop *vb* ❶ entwickeln [**34**] (*perf* hat entwickelt) ▷ *to get a film developed* einen Film entwickeln lassen ❷ sich entwickeln [**34**] (*perf* hat sich entwickelt) ▷ *Girls develop faster.* Mädchen entwickeln sich schneller. ▷ *The argument developed into a fight.* Der Streit entwickelte sich zu einer Schlägerei.; **a developing country** ein Entwicklungsland *nt*

development *n* Entwicklung *f* ▷ *the latest developments* die neuesten Entwicklungen

devil *n* Teufel *m* (*pl* Teufel) ▷ *Poor devil!* Armer Teufel!

devoted *adj* **He's completely devoted to her.** Er liebt sie über alles.

diabetes *n* Zucker *m* ▷ *She's got diabetes.* Sie hat Zucker.

diabetic *n* Zuckerkranke *m* (*gen* Zuckerkranken, *pl* Zuckerkranken), Zuckerkranke *f* (*gen* Zuckerkranken); **I'm a diabetic.** Ich habe Zucker.

diagonal *adj* diagonal

diagram *n* Diagramm *nt* (*pl* Diagramme)

dial *vb (number)* wählen [**38**]; **He dialled the wrong number.** Er hat sich verwählt.

dialling tone *n* Amtszeichen *nt* (*pl* Amtszeichen)
dialogue *n* Dialog *m* (*pl* Dialoge)
diamond *n* Diamant *m* (*gen* Diamanten, *pl* Diamanten) ▷ *a diamond ring* ein Diamantring *m*; **diamonds** *(in cards)* das Karo
diaper *n (US)* Windel *f*
diarrhoea *n* Durchfall *m* (*pl* Durchfälle) ▷ *I've got diarrhoea.* Ich habe Durchfall.
diary *n* ❶ Kalender *m* (*pl* Kalender) ▷ *I've got her address in my diary.* Ich habe ihre Adresse in meinem Kalender. ❷ Tagebuch *nt* (*pl* Tagebücher) ▷ *I keep a diary.* Ich führe ein Tagebuch.
dice *n* Würfel *m* (*pl* Würfel)
dictation *n* Diktat *nt* (*pl* Diktate)
dictator *n* Diktator *m* (*pl* Diktatoren)
dictionary *n* Wörterbuch *nt* (*pl* Wörterbücher)
did *vb see* **do**
die *vb* sterben **[75]** (*pres* stirbt, *imperf* starb, *perf* ist gestorben) ▷ *She's dying.* Sie stirbt. ▷ *He died last year.* Er ist letztes Jahr gestorben.; **to be dying to do something** es kaum erwarten können **[41]**, etwas zu tun
die down *vb* nachlassen **[42]** (*pres* lässt nach, *imperf* ließ nach, *perf* hat nachgelassen)
diesel *n* ❶ *(fuel)* Diesel *m* ▷ *Thirty litres of diesel, please.* Dreißig Liter Diesel, bitte. ❷ *(car)* Diesel *m* (*pl* Diesel) ▷ *Our car's a diesel.* Unser Auto ist ein Diesel.
diet *n* ❶ Nahrung *f* ▷ *a healthy diet* gesunde Nahrung ❷ *(for slimming)* Diät *f*; **I'm on a diet.** Ich mache eine Diät.
▶ *vb* eine Diät machen **[48]** ▷ *I've been dieting for two months.* Ich mache seit zwei Monaten eine Diät.
difference *n* Unterschied *m* (*pl* Unterschiede) ▷ *There's not much difference in age between us.* Es besteht kein großer Altersunterschied zwischen uns.; **It makes no difference.** Das ist egal.
different *adj* verschieden ▷ *We are very different.* Wir sind sehr verschieden.; **Berlin is different from London.** Berlin ist anders als London.
difficult *adj* schwierig ▷ *It's difficult to choose.* Es ist schwierig, sich zu entscheiden.
difficulty *n* Schwierigkeit *f* ▷ *to have difficulty doing something* Schwierigkeiten haben, etwas zu tun; **without difficulty** problemlos
dig *vb* ❶ *(hole)* graben (*pres* gräbt, *imperf* grub, *perf* hat gegraben) ❷ *(garden)* umgraben (*perf* hat umgegraben); **to dig something up** etwas ausgraben
digestion *n* Verdauung *f*
digital *adj* digital ▷ *the digital revolution* die digitale Revolution; **a digital camera** eine Digitalkamera; **a digital radio** ein DAB-Radio *nt*; **a digital watch** eine Digitaluhr; **digital TV** das Digitalfernsehen
dim *adj* ❶ *(light)* schwach ❷ *(stupid)* beschränkt
dimension *n (measurement)* Maß *nt* (*gen* Maßes, *pl* Maße)
din *n* Krach *m* (*pl* Kräche)
diner *n (US)* Gaststätte *f*
dinghy *n* **a rubber dinghy** ein Gummiboot *nt*; **a sailing dinghy** ein Segelboot *nt*
dining room *n* Esszimmer *nt* (*pl* Esszimmer)
dinner *n* ❶ *(at midday)* Mittagessen *nt* (*pl* Mittagessen) ❷ *(in the evening)* Abendessen *nt* (*pl* Abendessen)
dinner party *n* Abendgesellschaft *f*; **We're having a dinner party on Saturday.** Wir haben am Samstag Leute zum Essen eingeladen.
dinner time *n* Essenszeit *f*
dinosaur *n* Dinosaurier *m* (*pl* Dinosaurier)
diploma *n* Diplom *nt* (*pl* Diplome); **She has a diploma in social work.** Sie hat Sozialarbeiterin gelernt.

direct *adj, adv* direkt ▷ *the most direct route* der direkteste Weg ▷ *You can't fly to Stuttgart direct from Glasgow.* Sie können von Glasgow nicht direkt nach Stuttgart fliegen.
▶ *vb (film, play)* Regie führen **[38]** bei ▷ *Who directed the film?* Wer hat bei dem Film Regie geführt?

direction *n* Richtung *f* ▷ *We're going in the wrong direction.* Wir fahren in die falsche Richtung.; **to ask somebody for directions** jemanden nach dem Weg fragen **[38]**

director *n* ❶ *(of company)* Direktor *m (pl* Direktoren), Direktorin *f* ❷ *(of play, film)* Regisseur *m (pl* Regisseure), Regisseurin *f* ❸ *(of programme)* Leiter *m (pl* Leiter), Leiterin *f*

directory *n* ❶ Verzeichnis *nt (gen* Verzeichnisses, *pl* Verzeichnisse) ▷ *file directory* das Dateiverzeichnis ❷ *(telephone book)* Telefonbuch *nt (pl* Telefonbücher)

dirt *n* Schmutz *m*

dirty *adj* schmutzig ▷ *to get dirty* sich schmutzig machen ▷ *to get something dirty* etwas schmutzig machen ▷ *a dirty joke* ein schmutziger Witz

disabled *adj* behindert

disadvantage *n* Nachteil *m (pl* Nachteile)

disagree *vb* **We always disagree.** Wir sind nie einer Meinung.; **I disagree!** Ich bin anderer Meinung.; **He disagreed with me.** Er war anderer Meinung als ich.

disagreement *n* Meinungsverschiedenheit *f*

disappear *vb* verschwinden **[86]** *(imperf* verschwand, *perf* ist verschwunden)

disappearance *n* Verschwinden *nt*

disappointed *adj* enttäuscht

disappointment *n* Enttäuschung *f*

disaster *n* Katastrophe *f*

disastrous *adj* katastrophal

disc *n* Platte *f*

discipline *n* Disziplin *f*

disc jockey *n* Diskjockey *m (pl* Diskjockeys)

disco *n* Disco *f (pl* Discos) ▷ *There's a disco at the school tonight.* Heute Abend gibt es in der Schule eine Disco.

disconnect *vb* ❶ *(electrical equipment)* ausstecken **[4]** *(perf* hat ausgesteckt) ❷ *(telephone, water supply)* abstellen **[4]** *(perf* hat abgestellt)

discount *n* Rabatt *m (pl* Rabatte) ▷ *a discount of twenty per cent* zwanzig Prozent Rabatt; **a discount for students** eine Studentenermäßigung

discourage *vb* entmutigen **[18]** *(perf* hat entmutigt); **to get discouraged** sich entmutigen lassen **[42]**

discover *vb* entdecken **[18]** *(perf* hat entdeckt)

discovery *n* Entdeckung *f*

discrimination *n* Diskriminierung *f* ▷ *racial discrimination* die Rassendiskriminierung

discuss *vb* ❶ besprechen **[70]** *(pres* bespricht, *imperf* besprach, *perf* hat besprochen) ▷ *I'll discuss it with my parents.* Ich werde es mit meinen Eltern besprechen. ❷ *(topic)* diskutieren **[76]** über *(perf* hat diskutiert) ▷ *We discussed the problem.* Wir haben über das Problem diskutiert.

discussion *n* Diskussion *f*

disease *n* Krankheit *f*

disgraceful *adj* schändlich

disguise *vb* verkleiden **[54]** *(perf* hat verkleidet) ▷ *He was disguised as a police officer.* Er war als Polizist verkleidet.

disgusted *adj* angewidert ▷ *I was absolutely disgusted.* Ich war total angewidert.

disgusting *adj* ❶ *(food, smell)* widerlich ▷ *It looks disgusting.* Es sieht widerlich aus. ❷ *(disgraceful)* abscheulich ▷ *That's disgusting!* Das ist abscheulich!

dish *n* ❶ Schüssel *f* ▷ *a china dish* eine Porzellanschüssel; **the dishes** das

Geschirr *sg*; **to do the dishes** abwaschen **[89]** ❷ *(food)* Gericht *nt* (*pl* Gerichte) ▷ *a vegetarian dish* ein vegetarisches Gericht
dishonest *adj* unehrlich
dishwasher *n* Geschirrspülmaschine *f*
disinfectant *n* Desinfektionsmittel *nt* (*pl* Desinfektionsmittel)
disk *n* Platte *f*; **the hard disk** die Festplatte; **a floppy disk** eine Diskette
dismal *adj* kläglich ▷ *a dismal failure* ein kläglicher Fehlschlag
dismiss *vb (employee)* entlassen **[42]** (*pres* entlässt, *imperf* entließ, *perf* hat entlassen)
disobedient *adj* ungehorsam
display *n (of goods)* Auslage *f*; **to be on display** ausgestellt sein **[65]**; **a firework display** ein Feuerwerk *nt*
▶ *vb* ❶ zeigen **[38]** ▷ *She proudly displayed her medal.* Sie zeigte stolz ihre Medaille. ❷ *(in shop window)* ausstellen **[4]** (*perf* hat ausgestellt) ▷ *the fruit displayed in the shop window ...* das Obst, das im Schaufenster ausgestellt war ...
disposable *adj* zum Wegwerfen; **disposable nappies** die Wegwerfwindeln *fpl*
disqualify *vb* disqualifizieren **[76]** (*perf* hat disqualifiziert); **to be disqualified** disqualifiziert werden **[91]**
disrupt *vb* ❶ stören **[38]** ▷ *Protesters disrupted the meeting.* Protestierende haben die Versammlung gestört. ❷ *(service)* unterbrechen **[11]** (*pres* unterbricht, *imperf* unterbrach, *perf* hat unterbrochen) ▷ *Train services were disrupted.* Der Zugverkehr wurde unterbrochen.
dissolve *vb* ❶ auflösen **[4]** (*perf* hat aufgelöst) ▷ *Dissolve the crystals in water.* Löse die Kristalle in Wasser auf. ❷ sich auflösen **[4]** ▷ *Sugar dissolves quickly in hot tea.* Zucker löst sich in heißem Tee schnell auf.
distance *n* Entfernung *f* ▷ *a distance of forty kilometres* eine Entfernung von vierzig Kilometern; **It's within walking distance.** Man kann zu Fuß hingehen.; **in the distance** in der Ferne
distant *adj* weit ▷ *in the distant future* in weiter Zukunft
distract *vb* ablenken **[4]** (*perf* hat abgelenkt)
distribute *vb* verteilen **[84]** (*perf* hat verteilt)
district *n* ❶ *(of town)* Viertel *nt* (*pl* Viertel) ❷ *(of country)* Gegend *f*
disturb *vb* stören **[38]**; **I'm sorry to disturb you.** Verzeihen Sie die Störung.
ditch *n* Graben *m* (*pl* Gräben)
▶ *vb (informal)* Schluss machen **[48]** mit ▷ *She's just ditched her boyfriend.* Sie hat gerade mit ihrem Freund Schluss gemacht.
dive *n* Kopfsprung *m* (*pl* Kopfsprünge)
▶ *vb* ❶ *(under water)* tauchen **[48]** ▷ *They are diving for pearls.* Sie tauchen nach Perlen. ❷ *(into water)* einen Kopfsprung machen **[48]** ▷ *She dived into the water.* Sie machte einen Kopfsprung ins Wasser.
diver *n (with breathing apparatus)* Taucher *m* (*pl* Taucher), Taucherin *f*
diversion *n (for traffic)* Umleitung *f*
divide *vb* ❶ teilen **[38]** ▷ *Divide the pastry in half.* Teilen Sie den Teig in zwei Teile. ▷ *Twelve divided by three is four.* Zwölf geteilt durch drei macht vier. ❷ sich aufteilen **[4]** (*perf* hat sich aufgeteilt) ▷ *We divided into two groups.* Wir haben uns in zwei Gruppen aufgeteilt.
diving *n* ❶ *(under water)* Tauchen *nt* ❷ *(into water)* Springen *nt*; **diving board** das Sprungbrett
division *n* ❶ Division *f* ▷ *division and multiplication* Division und Multiplikation; **the division of labour** die Arbeitsteilung ❷ *(in football)* Liga *f* (*pl* Ligen)
divorce *n* Scheidung *f*
divorced *adj* geschieden ▷ *My parents are divorced.* Meine Eltern sind geschieden.

Diwali *n* Diwali *nt*

DIY *n (= do-it-yourself)* Heimwerken *nt*; **to do DIY** Heimwerker sein [**65**]; **a DIY shop** ein Geschäft für Heimwerker; **DIY superstore** der Baumarkt

dizzy *adj* **I feel dizzy.** Mir ist schwindlig.

DJ *n (= disc jockey)* Diskjockey *m (pl* Diskjockeys)

do *vb* ❶ machen [**48**] ▷ *What are you doing this evening?* Was macht ihr heute Abend? ▷ *I haven't done my homework.* Ich habe meine Hausaufgaben noch nicht gemacht. ▷ *She did it by herself.* Sie hat es allein gemacht. ❷ tun [**81**] ▷ *What shall I do?* Was soll ich tun? ▷ *I'll do my best.* Ich werde mein Bestes tun. ▷ *I'll tell you what to do.* Ich sage dir, was du tun sollst.

> In combination with certain nouns and verbs 'do' is not translated.

▷ *I do a lot of cycling.* Ich fahre viel Rad. ▷ *She was doing her knitting.* Sie strickte. ▷ *to do the ironing* bügeln; **to do well** erfolgreich sein [**65**] ▷ *The firm is doing well.* Die Firma ist sehr erfolgreich.; **She's doing well at school.** Sie ist gut in der Schule. ❸ *(be enough)* reichen [**48**] ▷ *It's not very good, but it'll do.* Es ist nicht besonders gut, aber es wird reichen. ▷ *That'll do, thanks.* Danke, das reicht.

> In English 'do' is used to make questions. In German, questions are expressed by reversing the order of verb and subject.

▷ *Do you like German food?* Magst du deutsches Essen? ▷ *Where does he live?* Wo wohnt er? ▷ *Do you speak English?* Sprechen Sie Englisch? ▷ *What do you do in your spare time?* Was machen Sie in Ihrer Freizeit? ▷ *Where did you go for your holidays?* Wohin seid ihr in den Ferien gefahren?

> Use **nicht** in negative sentences for 'don't'.

▷ *I don't understand.* Ich verstehe nicht. ▷ *Why didn't you come?* Warum bist du nicht gekommen?

> 'do' is not translated when it is used in place of another verb.

▷ *I hate maths. — So do I.* Ich hasse Mathe. — Ich auch. ▷ *I didn't like the film. — Neither did I.* Ich mochte den Film nicht. — Ich auch nicht. ▷ *Do you like horses? — No, I don't.* Magst du Pferde? — Nein.

> Questions like 'doesn't it?' don't exist in German.

▷ *The bus stops at the youth hostel, doesn't it?* Der Bus hält an der Jugendherberge, nicht wahr? ▷ *You go swimming on Fridays, don't you?* Du gehst freitags schwimmen, nicht wahr?; **How do you do?** Guten Tag!; **I could do with a holiday.** Ich könnte einen Urlaub gebrauchen.

do up *vb* ❶ *(shoes, shirt, cardigan)* zumachen [**4**] ▷ *Do up your shoes!* Mach deine Schuhe zu! ❷ *(renovate)* renovieren [**76**] ▷ *They're doing up an old cottage.* Sie renovieren ein altes Haus.

do without *vb* ohne etwas auskommen[**40**] ▷ *I couldn't do without my computer.* Ich käme nicht ohne meinen Computer aus.

doctor *n* Arzt *m (pl* Ärzte), Ärztin *f* ▷ *She's a doctor.* Sie ist Ärztin. ▷ *She'd like to be a doctor.* Sie möchte gerne Ärztin werden.

document *n* Dokument *nt (pl* Dokumente)

documentary *n* Dokumentarfilm *m (pl* Dokumentarfilme)

dodge *vb (attacker)* ausweichen *(imperf* wich aus, *perf* ist ausgewichen) ▷ *to dodge something* einer Sache ausweichen

Dodgems® *npl* Autoskooter *msg (pl* Autoskooter) ▷ *to go on the Dodgems* Autoskooter fahren

does *vb see* **do**

doesn't = **does not**

dog *n* Hund *m (pl* Hunde) ▷ *Have you got a dog?* Hast du einen Hund?

a b c d e f g h i j k l m n o p q r s t u v w x y z

do-it-yourself *n* Heimwerken *nt*
dole *n* Arbeitslosenunterstützung *f*; **to be on the dole** stempeln gehen [**29**]; **to go on the dole** sich arbeitslos melden [**54**]
doll *n* Puppe *f*
dollar *n* Dollar *m* (*pl* Dollars *or* Dollar)
When talking about amounts of money use the plural form **Dollar**.
▷ *That costs fifty dollars.* Das kostet fünfzig Dollar.
dolphin *n* Delfin *m* (*pl* Delfine)
dominoes *nsg* **to have a game of dominoes** Domino spielen [**38**]
donate *vb* spenden [**54**]
done *vb see* **do**
donkey *n* Esel *m* (*pl* Esel)
don't = **do not**
door *n* Tür *f*
doorbell *n* Klingel *f*; **to ring the doorbell** klingeln [**34**]; **Suddenly the doorbell rang.** Es klingelte plötzlich.
doorstep *n* Eingangsstufe *f*
dormitory *n* Schlafsaal *m* (*pl* Schlafsäle)
dot *n* (*on letter 'i', in email address*) Punkt *m* (*pl* Punkte); **on the dot** genau
double *vb* sich verdoppeln [**34**] (*perf* hat sich verdoppelt) ▷ *The number of attacks has doubled.* Die Zahl der Überfälle hat sich verdoppelt.
▶ *adj, adv* doppelt ▷ *a double helping* eine doppelte Portion; **to cost double** doppelt so viel kosten [**2**]; **a double bed** ein Doppelbett *nt*; **a double room** ein Doppelzimmer *nt*; **a double-decker bus** ein Doppeldeckerbus *m*
double bass *n* Kontrabass *m* (*gen* Kontrabasses, *pl* Kontrabässe) ▷ *I play the double bass.* Ich spiele Kontrabass.
double-click *vb* (*computer*) doppelklicken [**15**] (*perf* hat doppelgeklickt)
double glazing *n* Doppelfenster *nt* (*pl* Doppelfenster)
doubles *npl* (*in tennis*) Doppel *nt* (*pl* Doppel) ▷ *to play mixed doubles* gemischtes Doppel spielen
doubt *n* Zweifel *m* (*pl* Zweifel) ▷ *I have my doubts.* Ich habe meine Zweifel.
▶ *vb* bezweifeln [**34**] (*perf* hat bezweifelt) ▷ *I doubt it.* Das bezweifle ich.; **to doubt that** bezweifeln [**34**], dass
doubtful *adj* **to be doubtful about doing something** nicht wissen [**93**], ob man etwas tun soll; **It's doubtful.** Es ist fraglich.; **You sound doubtful.** Du scheinst nicht sicher zu sein.
dough *n* Teig *m* (*pl* Teige)
doughnut *n* Berliner *m* (*pl* Berliner) ▷ *a jam doughnut* ein gefüllter Berliner
Dover *n* Dover *nt* ▷ *We went from Dover to Boulogne.* Wir sind von Dover nach Boulogne gefahren.
down *adv, adj, prep* ❶ (*below*) unten ▷ *down on the first floor* unten im ersten Stock ▷ *It's down there.* Es ist da unten. ❷ (*to the ground*) auf den Boden ▷ *He threw down his racket.* Er warf seinen Schläger auf den Boden.; **They live just down the road.** Sie wohnen etwas weiter unten.; **to come down** herunterkommen [**40**]; **to go down** hinuntergehen [**29**]; **to sit down** sich hinsetzen [**15**]; **to feel down** niedergeschlagen sein [**65**]; **The computer's down.** Der Computer ist abgestürzt.
download *vb* (*computer*) runterladen (*pres* lädt runter, *imperf* lud runter, *perf* hat runtergeladen) ▷ *to download a file* eine Datei runterladen
▶ *n* Download *m* (*pl* Downloads) ▷ *a free download* ein Gratis-Download
downstairs *adv, adj* ❶ unten ▷ *The bathroom's downstairs.* Das Badezimmer ist unten.; **the people downstairs** die Leute von unten; **to go downstairs** nach unten gehen [**29**] ❷ untere ▷ *the downstairs bathroom* das untere Badezimmer

downtown *adv (US)* im Stadtzentrum
doze *vb* dösen **[38]**; **to doze off** einnicken **[4]**
dozen *n* Dutzend *nt (pl* Dutzende *or* Dutzend)

When talking about more than one dozen use the plural form **Dutzend**.

▷ *two dozen* zwei Dutzend ▷ *a dozen eggs* ein Dutzend Eier; **I've told you that dozens of times.** Ich habe dir das schon x-mal gesagt.
draft *n (US)* Luftzug *m (pl* Luftzüge)
drag *vb (thing, person)* schleppen **[48]**
▶ *n* **It's a real drag!** *(informal)* Das ist echt öde!; **in drag** in Frauenkleidern
dragon *n* Drache *m (gen* Drachen, *pl* Drachen)
drain *n* Abfluss *m (gen* Abflusses, *pl* Abflüsse) ▷ *The drains are blocked.* Der Abfluss ist verstopft.
▶ *vb (vegetables, pasta)* abtropfen lassen **[42]** *(pres* lässt abtropfen, *imperf* ließ abtropfen, *perf* hat abtropfen lassen)
drama *n* Drama *nt (pl* Dramen) ▷ *Drama is my favourite subject.* Drama ist mein Lieblingsfach.; **drama school** die Schauspielschule
dramatic *adj* dramatisch ▷ *It was really dramatic!* Es war wirklich dramatisch! ▷ *a dramatic improvement* eine dramatische Besserung
drank *vb see* **drink**
drapes *npl (US)* Vorhänge *mpl*
draught *n* Luftzug *m(pl* Luftzüge); **There's a draught!** Es zieht!
draughts *nsg* Dame *f* ▷ *to play draughts* Dame spielen
draw *n* ❶ *(sport)* Unentschieden *nt (pl* Unentschieden) ▷ *The game ended in a draw.* Das Spiel endete mit einem Unentschieden. ❷ *(in lottery)* Ziehung *f* ▷ *The draw takes place on Saturday.* Die Ziehung findet am Samstag statt.
▶ *vb* ❶ malen **[38]** ▷ *He's good at drawing.* Er kann gut malen. ▷ *to draw a picture* ein Bild malen; **to draw a line** einen Strich machen **[48]** ❷ *(sport)* unentschieden spielen **[38]** ▷ *We drew two all.* Wir haben zwei zu zwei gespielt.; **to draw the curtains** die Vorhänge zuziehen **[96]**; **to draw lots** losen **[38]**
draw on *vb* zurückgreifen auf *(imperf* griff zurück, *perf* hat zurückgegriffen)
draw up *vb* halten **[33]** *(pres* hält, *imperf* hielt, *perf* hat gehalten)
drawback *n* Nachteil *m (pl* Nachteile)
drawer *n* Schublade *f*
drawing *n* Zeichnung *f*
drawing pin *n* Reißzwecke *f*
drawn *vb see* **draw**
dreadful *adj* ❶ furchtbar ▷ *a dreadful mistake* ein furchtbarer Fehler ▷ *You look dreadful. (ill)* Du siehst furchtbar aus. ▷ *I feel dreadful.* Ich fühle mich furchtbar. ❷ schrecklich ▷ *The weather was dreadful.* Das Wetter war schrecklich.
dream *vb* träumen **[38]** ▷ *I dreamt I was in Belgium.* Ich habe geträumt, ich sei in Belgien.

Note the use of the subjunctive.

▶ *n* Traum *m (pl* Träume) ▷ *It was just a dream.* Es war nur ein Traum. ▷ *a bad dream* ein böser Traum
drench *vb* **to get drenched** klatschnass werden **[91]**
dress *n* Kleid *nt (pl* Kleider)
▶ *vb* sich anziehen **[96]** *(imperf* zog sich an, *perf* hat sich angezogen) ▷ *I got up, dressed, and went downstairs.* Ich stand auf, zog mich an und ging hinunter.; **to dress somebody** jemanden anziehen **[96]**; **to get dressed** sich anziehen **[96]**; **to dress up** sich verkleiden **[54]**
dressed *adj* angezogen ▷ *I'm not dressed yet.* Ich bin noch nicht angezogen. ▷ *How was she dressed?* Wie war sie angezogen?; **She was dressed in a green sweater and jeans.** Sie hatte einen grünen Pullover und Jeans an.
dresser *n (furniture)* Kommode *f*
dressing *n (for salad)* Dressing *nt (pl* Dressings)

dressing gown *n* Morgenmantel *m* (*pl* Morgenmäntel)

dressing table *n* Frisiertisch *m* (*pl* Frisiertische)

drew *vb see* **draw**

drier *n* ❶ (*for washing*) Wäschetrockner *m* (*pl* Wäschetrockner) ❷ (*for hair*) Haartrockner *m* (*pl* Haartrockner)

drift *n* **a snow drift** eine Schneeverwehung
▸ *vb* (*boat, snow*) treiben (*imperf* trieb, *perf* ist getrieben)

drill *n* Bohrer *m* (*pl* Bohrer)
▸ *vb* bohren [**38**]

drink *vb* trinken [**80**] (*imperf* trank, *perf* hat getrunken) ▷ *What would you like to drink?* Was möchtest du trinken? ▷ *She drank three cups of tea.* Sie trank drei Tassen Tee. ▷ *He'd been drinking.* Er hatte getrunken. ▷ *I don't drink.* Ich trinke nicht.
▸ *n* ❶ Getränk *nt* (*pl* Getränke) ▷ *a cold drink* ein kaltes Getränk ▷ *a hot drink* ein heißes Getränk ❷ (*alcoholic*) Drink *m* (*pl* Drinks); **They've gone out for a drink.** Sie sind etwas trinken gegangen.; **to have a drink** etwas trinken [**80**]

drive *n* ❶ Fahrt *f* ▷ *It's a long drive.* Es ist eine lange Fahrt.; **to go for a drive** fahren [**21**] ▷ *We went for a drive in the country.* Wir sind aufs Land gefahren. ❷ (*of house*) Auffahrt *f* ▷ *He parked his car in the drive.* Er parkte sein Auto in der Auffahrt.
▸ *vb* ❶ fahren [**21**] (*pres* fährt, *imperf* fuhr, *perf* ist/hat gefahren) ▷ *My mother drives me to school.* Meine Mutter fährt mich in die Schule. ▷ *I drove down to London.* Ich bin nach London gefahren.

> When **fahren** is used with an object it takes **haben** not **sein**.

▷ *He drove me home.* Er hat mich nach Hause gefahren. ❷ (*operate a car*) Auto fahren [**21**] (*pres* fährt Auto, *imperf* fuhr Auto, *perf* ist Auto gefahren) ▷ *Can you drive?* Kannst du Auto fahren?; **She's learning to drive.** Sie macht den Führerschein. ❸ (*go by car*) mit dem Auto fahren [**21**] ▷ *Did you go by train? — No, we drove.* Seid ihr mit dem Zug gefahren? — Nein, wir sind mit dem Auto gefahren.; **to drive somebody mad** jemanden wahnsinnig machen [**48**] ▷ *He drives her mad.* Er macht sie wahnsinnig.

driver *n* Fahrer *m* (*pl* Fahrer), Fahrerin *f* ▷ *She's an excellent driver.* Sie ist eine ausgezeichnete Fahrerin. ▷ *He's a bus driver.* Er ist Busfahrer.

driver's license *n* (*US*) Führerschein *m* (*pl* Führerscheine)

driving instructor *n* Fahrlehrer *m* (*pl* Fahrlehrer), Fahrlehrerin *f* ▷ *He's a driving instructor.* Er ist Fahrlehrer.

driving lesson *n* Fahrstunde *f*

driving licence *n* Führerschein *m* (*pl* Führerscheine)

driving test *n* Fahrprüfung *f*; **to take one's driving test** die Fahrprüfung machen [**48**]; **She's just passed her driving test.** Sie hat gerade ihren Führerschein gemacht.

drop *n* Tropfen *m* (*pl* Tropfen) ▷ *a drop of water* ein Wassertropfen
▸ *vb* ❶ fallen lassen [**42**] (*pres* lässt fallen, *imperf* ließ fallen, *perf* hat fallen lassen) ▷ *I dropped the glass.* Ich habe das Glas fallen lassen. ❷ (*abandon*) aufgeben [**28**] (*pres* gibt auf, *imperf* gab auf, *perf* hat aufgegeben) ▷ *I'm going to drop chemistry.* Ich gebe Chemie auf. ❸ absetzen [**36**] (*perf* hat abgesetzt) ▷ *Could you drop me at the station?* Könntest du mich am Bahnhof absetzen?

drought *n* Dürre *f*

drove *vb see* **drive**

drown *vb* ertrinken [**80**] (*imperf* ertrank, *perf* ist ertrunken) ▷ *A boy drowned here yesterday.* Hier ist gestern ein Junge ertrunken.

drug *n* ❶ (*medicine*) Medikament *nt* (*pl* Medikamente) ▷ *They need food and drugs.* Sie brauchen Nahrung und

Medikamente. ❷ *(illegal)* Droge *f* ▷ *hard drugs* harte Drogen ▷ *soft drugs* weiche Drogen ▷ *to take drugs* Drogen nehmen; **a drug addict** *(man)* ein Drogensüchtiger; **She's a drug addict.** Sie ist drogensüchtig.; **a drug pusher** ein Dealer *m*; **a drug smuggler** ein Drogenschmuggler *m*; **the drugs squad** das Rauschgiftdezernat

drugstore *n (US)* Drugstore *m (pl* Drugstores)

drum *n* Trommel *f* ▷ *an African drum* eine afrikanische Trommel; **a drum kit** ein Schlagzeug *nt*; **drums** das Schlagzeug *sg*

drummer *n (in rock group)* Schlagzeuger *m (pl* Schlagzeuger), Schlagzeugerin *f*

drunk *vb see* **drink**

▶ *adj* betrunken ▷ *He was drunk.* Er war betrunken.

▶ *n* Betrunkene *m (gen* Betrunkenen, *pl* Betrunkenen), Betrunkene *f (gen* Betrunkenen) ▷ *a drunk (man)* ein Betrunkener ▷ *The streets were full of drunks.* Die Straßen waren voll von Betrunkenen.

dry *adj* trocken ▷ *The paint isn't dry yet.* Die Farbe ist noch nicht trocken.; **a long dry period** eine lange Trockenzeit

▶ *vb* ❶ trocknen [**53**] ▷ *The washing will dry quickly in the sun.* Die Wäsche wird in der Sonne schnell trocknen. ▷ *some dried flowers* getrocknete Blumen; **to dry one's hair** sich die Haare föhnen [**38**] ❷ *(clothes)* trocknen lassen [**42**] *(pres* lässt trocknen, *imperf* ließ trocknen, *perf* hat trocknen lassen) ▷ *There's nowhere to dry clothes here.* Hier kann man nirgends Kleider trocknen lassen.; **to dry the dishes** das Geschirr abtrocknen [**53**]

dry-cleaner's *n* Reinigung *f*

dryer *n (for clothes)* Wäschetrockner *m (pl* Wäschetrockner); **a tumble dryer** ein Wäschetrockner; **a hair dryer** ein Föhn *m*

dubbed *adj* synchronisiert ▷ *The film was dubbed into German.* Der Film war deutsch synchronisiert.

duck *n* Ente *f*

due *adj, adv* **to be due to do something** etwas tun sollen [**69**]; **The plane's due in half an hour.** Das Flugzeug sollte in einer halben Stunde ankommen.; **When's the baby due?** Wann kommt das Baby?; **due to** wegen

dug *vb see* **dig**

dull *adj* ❶ langweilig ▷ *He's nice, but a bit dull.* Er ist nett, aber ein bisschen langweilig. ❷ *(weather, day)* trüb

dumb *adj (stupid)* blöd ▷ *That was a really dumb thing I did!* Da habe ich etwas echt Blödes gemacht!

dummy *n (for baby)* Schnuller *m (pl* Schnuller)

dump *n* **It's a real dump!** *(informal)* Das ist ein Dreckloch!; **a rubbish dump** eine Müllkippe

▶ *vb* ❶ *(waste)* abladen *(pres* lädt ab, *imperf* lud ab, *perf* hat abgeladen); **'no dumping'** 'Schutt abladen verboten' ❷ *(informal: get rid of)* Schluss machen [**48**] mit ▷ *He's just dumped his girlfriend.* Er hat gerade mit seiner Freundin Schluss gemacht.

dungarees *npl* Latzhose *f* ▷ *a pair of dungarees* eine Latzhose

dungeon *n* Verlies *nt (pl* Verliese)

during *prep* während ▷ *during the holidays* während der Ferien; **during the day** tagsüber

dusk *n* Dämmerung *f* ▷ *at dusk* bei Dämmerung

dust *n* Staub *m*

▶ *vb* abstauben [**4**] *(perf* hat abgestaubt) ▷ *I dusted the shelves.* Ich habe das Regal abgestaubt.; **I hate dusting!** Ich hasse Staubwischen!

dustbin *n* Mülleimer *m (pl* Mülleimer)

dustman *n* Müllmann *m (pl* Müllmänner); **He's a dustman.** Er arbeitet bei der Müllabfuhr.

dusty *adj* staubig

Dutch *adj* holländisch ▷ *She's Dutch.* Sie ist Holländerin.
▶ *n (language)* Holländisch *nt (gen* Holländischen); **the Dutch** die Holländer *mpl*
Dutchman *n* Holländer *m (pl* Holländer)
Dutchwoman *n* Holländerin *f*
duty *n* Pflicht *f* ▷ *It was his duty to tell the police.* Es war seine Pflicht, die Polizei zu informieren.; **to be on duty** Dienst haben [**32**]
duty-free *adj* zollfrei; **the duty-free shop** der Duty-free-Laden
duvet *n* Deckbett *nt (pl* Deckbetten)
DVD *n (= digital video disc)* DVD *f (pl* DVDs)
DVD player *n* DVD-Player *m (pl* DVD-Player)
dye *n* Farbstoff *m*; **hair dye** das Haarfärbemittel
▶ *vb* färben [**38**] ▷ *to dye something red* etwas rot färben ▷ *She has dyed her hair blonde.* Sie hat blond gefärbte Haare.
dynamic *adj* dynamisch
dyslexia *n* Legasthenie *f*; **She has dyslexia.** Sie ist Legasthenikerin.
dyspraxia *n* Dyspraxie *f*; **She has dyspraxia.** Sie leidet an Dyspraxie.

e

each *adj, pron* jeder ▷ *Each person has their own desk.* Jeder hat seinen eigenen Schreibtisch. ▷ *They have ten points each.* Jeder hat zehn Punkte. ▷ *He gave each of us ten pounds.* Er gab jedem von uns zehn Pfund. ▷ *each day* jeder Tag
jede ▷ *Each dancer wore a different costume.* Jede Tänzerin trug ein anderes Kostüm. ▷ *He gave each of the dancers a red rose.* Er gab jeder Tänzerin eine rote Rose.
jedes ▷ *Each house has a garden.* Jedes Haus hat einen Garten. ▷ *The girls each have their own bedroom.* Jedes der Mädchen hat sein eigenes Zimmer.; **each other** einander; **They don't know each other.** Sie kennen sich nicht.
eagle *n* Adler *m (pl* Adler)
ear *n* Ohr *nt (pl* Ohren)
earache *n* Ohrenschmerzen *mpl* ▷ *to have earache* Ohrenschmerzen haben
earlier *adv* ❶ vorher ▷ *I saw him earlier.* Ich habe ihn vorher gesehen. ❷ *(in the*

morning) früher ▷ *I ought to get up earlier.* Ich sollte früher aufstehen.
early *adv, adj* früh ▷ *I have to get up early.* Ich muss früh aufstehen. ▷ *I came early to get a good seat.* Ich bin früh gekommen, um einen guten Platz zu bekommen.; **to have an early night** früh ins Bett gehen [**29**]
earn *vb* verdienen [**84**] (*perf* hat verdient) ▷ *She earns five pounds an hour.* Sie verdient fünf Pfund in der Stunde.
earnings *npl* Verdienst *m* (*pl* Verdienste)
earring *n* Ohrring *m* (*pl* Ohrringe)
earth *n* Erde *f*
earthquake *n* Erdbeben *nt* (*pl* Erdbeben)
easily *adv* leicht
east *adj, adv* nach Osten ▷ *We were travelling east.* Wir sind nach Osten gefahren.; **the east coast** die Ostküste; **an east wind** ein Ostwind *m*; **east of** östlich von
▶ *n* Osten *m* ▷ *in the east* im Osten
Easter *n* Ostern *nt* ▷ *at Easter* an Ostern ▷ *We went to Spain for Easter.* Wir waren über Ostern in Spanien.
Easter egg *n* Osterei *nt* (*pl* Ostereier)
eastern *adj* östlich ▷ *the eastern part of the island* der östliche Teil der Insel; **Eastern Europe** Osteuropa *nt*
easy *adj* einfach
eat *vb* essen [**20**] (*pres* isst, *imperf* aß, *perf* hat gegessen) ▷ *Would you like something to eat?* Möchtest du etwas essen?
e-book *n* E-Book *nt* (*pl* E-Books)
echo *n* Echo *nt* (*pl* Echos)
ecology *n* Ökologie *f*
economic *adj (profitable)* rentabel
economical *adj* sparsam
economics *nsg* Volkswirtschaft *f* ▷ *He's studying economics.* Er studiert Volkswirtschaft.
economy *n* Wirtschaft *f* ▷ *the German economy* die deutsche Wirtschaft
ecstasy *n (drug)* Ecstasy *nt* (*gen* Ecstasy); **to be in ecstasy** entzückt sein [**65**]
eczema *n* Hautausschlag *m* (*pl* Hautausschläge)
edge *n* ❶ Rand *m* (*pl* Ränder) ▷ *They live on the edge of the moors.* Sie leben am Rand des Moors. ❷ *(of table)* Kante *f* ❸ *(of lake)* Ufer *nt* (*pl* Ufer)
Edinburgh *n* Edinburgh *nt*
editor *n (of newspaper)* Redakteur *m* (*pl* Redakteure), Redakteurin *f*
education *n* ❶ Bildungswesen *nt* ▷ *There should be more investment in education.* Es sollte mehr Geld ins Bildungswesen investiert werden. ❷ *(teaching)* Lehramt *nt* ▷ *She works in education.* Sie ist im Lehramt tätig.
educational *adj (experience)* lehrreich ▷ *It was very educational.* Das was sehr lehrreich.
effect *n* Effekt *m* (*pl* Effekte) ▷ *special effects* Spezialeffekte
effective *adj* effektiv
efficient *adj* effizient
effort *n* Bemühung *f*; **to make an effort to do something** sich bemühen [**7**], etwas zu tun
e.g. *abbr* z. B. (= *zum Beispiel*)
egg *n* Ei *nt* (*pl* Eier) ▷ *a hard-boiled egg* ein hart gekochtes Ei ▷ *a soft-boiled egg* ein weich gekochtes Ei; **a fried egg** ein Spiegelei; **scrambled eggs** die Rühreier *ntpl*
egg cup *n* Eierbecher *m* (*pl* Eierbecher)
eggplant *n (US)* Aubergine *f*
Egypt *n* Ägypten *nt* ▷ *to Egypt* nach Ägypten
eight *num* acht ▷ *She's eight.* Sie ist acht.
eighteen *num* achtzehn ▷ *She's eighteen.* Sie ist achtzehn.
eighteenth *adj* achtzehnte ▷ *the eighteenth of August* der achtzehnte August
eighth *adj* achte ▷ *the eighth floor* der achte Stock ▷ *the eighth of August* der achte August
eighty *num* achtzig ▷ *She's eighty.* Sie ist achtzig.

Eire *n* Irland *nt*; **from Eire** aus Irland; **in Eire** in Irland; **to Eire** nach Irland

either *adv, conj, pron* ❶ auch kein ▷ *I don't like milk, and I don't like eggs either.* Ich mag keine Milch und ich mag auch keine Eier. ❷ auch nicht ▷ *I've never been to Spain. — I haven't either.* Ich war noch nie in Spanien. — Ich auch nicht.; **either ... or ...** entweder ... oder ... ▷ *You can have either ice cream or yoghurt.* Du kannst entweder Eis oder Joghurt haben.; **either of them** einer von beiden ▷ *Take either of them.* Nimm einen von beiden.; **I don't like either of them.** Ich mag keinen von beiden.

elastic *n* Gummiband *nt* (*pl* Gummibänder)

elastic band *n* Gummiband *nt* (*pl* Gummibänder)

elbow *n* Ellbogen *m* (*pl* Ellbogen)

elder *adj* älter ▷ *my elder sister* meine ältere Schwester

elderly *adj* älter ▷ *an elderly lady* eine ältere Dame

eldest *adj* älteste ▷ *my eldest brother* mein ältester Bruder ▷ *my eldest sister* meine älteste Schwester ▷ *He's the eldest.* Er ist der Älteste.

elect *vb* wählen [**38**]

election *n* Wahl *f* ▷ *The general election takes place tomorrow.* Morgen finden die allgemeinen Wahlen statt.

electric *adj* elektrisch ▷ *an electric fire* ein elektrischer Ofen ▷ *an electric guitar* eine elektrische Gitarre; **an electric blanket** eine Heizdecke

electrical *adj* elektrisch; **an electrical engineer** ein Elektrotechniker

electrician *n* Elektriker *m* (*pl* Elektriker), Elektrikerin *f* ▷ *He's an electrician.* Er ist Elektriker.

electricity *n* Strom *m* ▷ *They cut off our electricity.* Sie haben den Strom abgestellt.

electronic *adj* elektronisch

electronics *nsg* Elektronik *f* ▷ *My hobby is electronics.* Elektronik ist mein Hobby.

elegant *adj* elegant

elementary school *n* (*US*) Grundschule *f*

elephant *n* Elefant *m* (*gen* Elefanten, *pl* Elefanten)

elevator *n* (*US*) Aufzug *m* (*pl* Aufzüge)

eleven *num* elf ▷ *She's eleven.* Sie ist elf.

eleventh *adj* elfte ▷ *the eleventh floor* der elfte Stock ▷ *the eleventh of August* der elfte August

else *adv* ❶ anders ▷ *somebody else* jemand anders ▷ *nobody else* niemand anders ▷ *somewhere else* irgendwo anders ▷ *anywhere else* irgendwo anders ❷ anderes ▷ *nothing else* nichts anderes ▷ *something else* etwas anderes ▷ *anything else* etwas anderes; **Would you like anything else?** Möchtest du noch etwas?; **I don't want anything else.** Ich will nichts anderes.; **Give me the money, or else!** Gib mir das Geld, sonst gibt's was!

email *n* E-Mail *f* (*pl* E-Mails) ▷ *My email address is ...* Meine E-Mail-Adresse ist ... ▶ *vb* mailen [**38**] (*perf* hat gemailt) ▷ *Did you email it?* Hast du es gemailt?; **to email somebody** jemandem eine E-Mail senden

embankment *n* Böschung *f*

embarrassed *adj* verlegen ▷ *He seemed to be pretty embarrassed.* Er schien sehr verlegen.; **I was really embarrassed.** Es war mir wirklich peinlich.

embarrassing *adj* peinlich ▷ *It was so embarrassing.* Es war so peinlich.

embassy *n* Botschaft *f*

embroider *vb* besticken [**7**] (*perf* hat bestickt)

embroidery *n* Stickerei *f*; **I do embroidery.** Ich sticke.

emergency *n* Notfall *m* (*pl* Notfälle) ▷ *This is an emergency!* Dies ist ein Notfall! ▷ *in an emergency* in einem Notfall; **an emergency exit** ein Notausgang *m*; **an emergency**

landing eine Notlandung; **the emergency services** die Rettungsdienste *mpl*
emigrate *vb* auswandern [**88**] (*perf* ist ausgewandert)
emoji *n* Emoji *nt* (*pl* Emojis)
emotion *n* Gefühl *nt* (*pl* Gefühle)
emotional *adj* (*person*) emotional
emperor *n* Kaiser *m* (*pl* Kaiser)
emphasize *vb* betonen [**7**] (*perf* hat betont)
empire *n* Reich *nt* (*pl* Reiche)
employ *vb* beschäftigen [**18**] (*perf* hat beschäftigt) ▷ *The factory employs six hundred people.* Die Fabrik beschäftigt sechshundert Leute.
employee *n* Angestellte *m* (*gen* Angestellten, *pl* Angestellten), Angestellte *f* (*gen* Angestellten) ▷ *He's an employee.* Er ist Angestellter.
employer *n* Arbeitgeber *m* (*pl* Arbeitgeber), Arbeitgeberin *f*
employment *n* Beschäftigung *f*
empty *adj* leer
▶ *vb* leeren [**38**]; **to empty something out** etwas ausleeren [**4**]
encourage *vb* ermutigen [**7**] (*perf* hat ermutigt); **to encourage somebody to do something** jemanden ermutigen [**7**], etwas zu tun
encouragement *n* Ermutigung *f*
encyclopedia *n* Lexikon *nt* (*pl* Lexika)
end *n* Ende *nt* (*pl* Enden) ▷ *the end of the holidays* das Ende der Ferien ▷ *at the end of the street* am Ende der Straße ▷ *at the other end of the table* am anderen Ende des Tisches; **the end of the film** der Schluss des Films; **in the end** schließlich; **for hours on end** stundenlang
▶ *vb* zu Ende sein [**65**] (*pres* ist zu Ende, *imperf* war zu Ende, *perf* ist zu Ende gewesen) ▷ *What time does the film end?* Wann ist der Film zu Ende?; **to end up doing something** schließlich etwas tun [**81**]
ending *n* Schluss *m* (*gen* Schlusses, *pl* Schlüsse) ▷ *It was an exciting film, especially the ending.* Es war ein spannender Film, besonders am Schluss.
endless *adj* endlos ▷ *The journey seemed endless.* Die Reise erschien endlos.
enemy *n* Feind *m* (*pl* Feinde), Feindin *f*
energetic *adj* (*person*) voller Energie
energy *n* Energie *f*
engaged *adj* ❶ (*busy, in use*) besetzt ▷ *I phoned, but it was engaged.* Ich habe angerufen, aber es war besetzt. ❷ (*to be married*) verlobt ▷ *She's engaged to Brian.* Sie ist mit Brian verlobt.; **to get engaged** sich verloben [**84**]
engagement *n* Verlobung *f* ▷ *an engagement ring* ein Verlobungsring *m*
engine *n* Motor *m* (*pl* Motoren)
engineer *n* ❶ Ingenieur *m* (*pl* Ingenieure), Ingenieurin *f* ▷ *He's an engineer.* Er ist Ingenieur. ❷ (*train driver*) Lokomotivführer *m* (*pl* Lokomotivführer)
engineering *n* Technik *f* ▷ *genetic engineering* die Gentechnik; **mechanical engineering** der Maschinenbau
England *n* England *nt*; **from England** aus England; **in England** in England; **to England** nach England
- Germans frequently use **England** to mean Great Britain or the United Kingdom.

English *adj* englisch; **He's English.** Er ist Engländer.; **She's English.** Sie ist Engländerin.; **English people** die Engländer *mpl*
▶ *n* (*language*) Englisch *nt* (*gen* Englischen) ▷ *Do you speak English?* Sprechen Sie Englisch?; **the English** (*people*) die Engländer *mpl*
Englishman *n* Engländer *m* (*pl* Engländer)
Englishwoman *n* Engländerin *f*
enjoy *vb* genießen (*imperf* genoss, *perf* hat genossen) ▷ *I enjoyed my holiday.* Ich habe meinen Urlaub genossen.; **Did you enjoy the film?** Hat dir der Film

a b c d e f g h i j k l m n o p q r s t u v w x y z

gefallen?; **Did you enjoy your meal?** Hat es Ihnen geschmeckt?; **to enjoy oneself** sich amüsieren **[76]**

enjoyable *adj* nett

enlargement *n (of photo)* Vergrößerung *f*

enormous *adj* riesig

enough *pron, adj* genug ▷ *enough time* genug Zeit ▷ *I didn't have enough money.* Ich hatte nicht genug Geld. ▷ *big enough* groß genug ▷ *warm enough* warm genug; **Have you got enough?** Reicht dir das?; **I've had enough!** Mir reicht's!; **That's enough.** Das reicht.

enquire *vb* sich erkundigen **[19]** *(perf* hat sich erkundigt); **to enquire about something** sich nach etwas erkundigen **[19]**

enquiry *n (official investigation)* Untersuchung *f*; **to make an enquiry** sich erkundigen **[19]**

enter *vb (room)* betreten **[79]** *(pres* betritt, *imperf* betrat, *perf* hat betreten); **to enter a competition** an einem Wettbewerb teilnehmen **[52]**

entertain *vb (guests)* unterhalten **[33]** *(pres* unterhält, *imperf* unterhielt, *perf* hat unterhalten)

entertaining *adj* unterhaltsam

enthusiasm *n* Begeisterung *f*

enthusiast *n* **a railway enthusiast** ein Eisenbahnfan *m*; **She's a DIY enthusiast.** Sie ist begeisterte Heimwerkerin.

enthusiastic *adj* begeistert

entire *adj* ganz ▷ *the entire world* die ganze Welt

entirely *adv* ganz

entrance *n* Eingang *m (pl* Eingänge); **an entrance exam** eine Aufnahmeprüfung; **entrance fee** der Eintritt

entry *n (way in)* Eingang *m (pl* Eingänge); **'no entry' (1)** *(on door)* 'kein Zutritt' **(2)** *(on road sign)* 'Einfahrt verboten'; **an entry form** ein Teilnahmeformular *nt*

entry phone *n* Gegensprechanlage *f*

envelope *n* Umschlag *m (pl* Umschläge)

envious *adj* neidisch

environment *n* Umwelt *f*

environmental *adj* **environmental pollution** die Umweltverschmutzung; **environmental protection** der Umweltschutz

environment-friendly *adj* umweltfreundlich

envy *n* Neid *m*
▶ *vb* beneiden **[54]** *(perf* hat beneidet) ▷ *I don't envy you!* Ich beneide dich nicht!

epileptic *n* Epileptiker *m (pl* Epileptiker), Epileptikerin *f*

episode *n (of TV programme, story)* Folge *f*

equal *adj* gleich
▶ *vb* **Ten times two equals twenty.** Zehn mal zwei ist gleich zwanzig.

equality *n* Gleichheit *f*

equalize *vb (in sport)* ausgleichen *(imperf* glich aus, *perf* hat ausgeglichen)

equator *n* Äquator *m*

equipment *n* Ausrüstung *f* ▷ *fishing equipment* die Anglerausrüstung ▷ *skiing equipment* die Skiausrüstung

equipped *adj* **equipped with** ausgerüstet mit; **to be well equipped** gut ausgestattet sein **[65]**

error *n* Fehler *m (pl* Fehler)

escalator *n* Rolltreppe *f*

escape *n (from prison)* Ausbruch *m (pl* Ausbrüche)
▶ *vb* ausbrechen **[11]** *(pres* bricht aus, *imperf* brach aus, *perf* ist ausgebrochen) ▷ *A lion has escaped.* Ein Löwe ist ausgebrochen. ▷ *to escape from prison* aus dem Gefängnis ausbrechen

escort *n* Eskorte *f* ▷ *a police escort* eine Polizeieskorte

especially *adv* besonders ▷ *It's very hot there, especially in the summer.* Dort ist es sehr heiß, besonders im Sommer.

essay *n* Aufsatz *m (pl* Aufsätze) ▷ *a history essay* ein Aufsatz in Geschichte

essential *adj* wichtig ▷ *It's essential to bring warm clothes.* Es ist ganz wichtig, warme Kleidung mitzubringen.
estate *n (housing estate)* Siedlung *f* ▷ *I live on an estate.* Ich wohne in einer Siedlung.
estate agent *n* Immobilienmakler *m* (*pl* Immobilienmakler), Immobilienmaklerin *f*
estate car *n* Kombiwagen *m* (*pl* Kombiwagen)
estimate *vb* schätzen [**36**] ▷ *They estimated it would take three weeks.* Sie schätzten, dass es drei Wochen dauern würde.
etc *abbr (= et cetera)* usw. *(= und so weiter)*
Ethiopia *n* Äthiopien *nt*; **in Ethiopia** in Äthiopien
ethnic *adj* ❶ *(racial)* ethnisch ▷ *an ethnic minority* eine ethnische Minderheit ❷ *(clothes, music)* folkloristisch
e-ticket *n* E-Ticket *nt* (*pl* E-Tickets)
EU *n (= European Union)* EU *f (= Europäische Union)*
euro *n* Euro *m* (*pl* Euros *or* Euro)

When talking about amounts of money use the plural form **Euro**.

▷ *fifty euros* fünfzig Euro
Europe *n* Europa *nt*; **from Europe** aus Europa; **in Europe** in Europa; **to Europe** nach Europa
European *adj* europäisch; **He's European.** Er ist Europäer.
▶ *n (person)* Europäer *m* (*pl* Europäer), Europäerin *f*
eve *n* **Christmas Eve** der Heilige Abend; **New Year's Eve** Silvester *nt*
even *adv* sogar ▷ *I like all animals, even snakes.* Ich mag alle Tiere, sogar Schlangen.; **even if** selbst wenn; **not even** nicht einmal; **even though** obwohl; **I liked Hamburg even more than Munich.** Hamburg hat mir noch besser gefallen als München.
▶ *adj* gleichmäßig ▷ *an even layer of snow* eine gleichmäßige Schneeschicht; **an even number** eine gerade Zahl; **to get even with somebody** es jemandem heimzahlen [**4**]
evening *n* Abend *m* (*pl* Abende) ▷ *in the evening* am Abend ▷ *all evening* den ganzen Abend ▷ *yesterday evening* gestern Abend ▷ *tomorrow evening* morgen Abend; **Good evening!** Guten Abend!
evening class *n* Abendkurs *m* (*pl* Abendkurse)
event *n* Ereignis *nt* (*gen* Ereignisses, *pl* Ereignisse); **a sporting event** eine Sportveranstaltung
eventful *adj* ereignisreich
eventual *adj* schließlich; **the eventual outcome** das Endergebnis

Be careful not to translate **eventual** by **eventuell**.

eventually *adv* schließlich
ever *adv* ❶ schon einmal ▷ *Have you ever been to America?* Warst du schon einmal in Amerika? ▷ *Have you ever seen her?* Hast du sie schon einmal gesehen? ❷ je ▷ *the best I've ever seen* das Beste, was ich je gesehen habe; **for the first time ever** das allererste Mal; **ever since** seit; **ever since then** seither
every *adj* jeder ▷ *every student* jeder Student ▷ *every day* jeden Tag
jede ▷ *every mother* jede Mutter ▷ *every week* jede Woche
jedes ▷ *every child* jedes Kind ▷ *every year* jedes Jahr; **every time** jedes Mal; **every now and then** ab und zu
everybody *pron* ❶ alle ▷ *Everybody had a good time.* Alle hatten ihren Spaß. ❷ jeder ▷ *Everybody makes mistakes.* Jeder macht mal Fehler.
everyone *pron* ❶ alle ❷ jeder
everything *pron* alles ▷ *You've thought of everything!* Du hast an alles gedacht! ▷ *Money isn't everything.* Geld ist nicht alles.
everywhere *adv* überall ▷ *I've looked everywhere.* Ich habe überall gesucht. ▷ *There were policemen everywhere.* Überall waren Polizisten.

a b c d e f g h i j k l m n o p q r s t u v w x y z

evil *adj* böse
exact *adj* genau
exactly *adv* genau ▷ *exactly the same* genau das gleiche ▷ *It's exactly ten o'clock.* Es ist genau zehn Uhr.
exaggerate *vb* übertreiben (*imperf* übertrieb, *perf* hat übertrieben)
exaggeration *n* Übertreibung *f*
exam *n* Prüfung *f* ▷ *a German exam* eine Deutschprüfung ▷ *the exam results* die Prüfungsergebnisse
examination *n* Prüfung *f*; **a medical examination** eine ärztliche Untersuchung
examine *vb* untersuchen [**18**] (*perf* hat untersucht) ▷ *The doctor examined him.* Der Arzt untersuchte ihn.; **He examined her passport.** Er prüfte ihren Pass.
examiner *n* Prüfer *m* (*pl* Prüfer), Prüferin *f*
example *n* Beispiel *nt* (*pl* Beispiele); **for example** zum Beispiel
excellent *adj* ausgezeichnet ▷ *Her results were excellent.* Ihre Noten waren ausgezeichnet.
except *prep* außer ▷ *everyone except me* alle außer mir; **except for** abgesehen von; **except that** außer, dass
exception *n* Ausnahme *f* ▷ *to make an exception* eine Ausnahme machen
exchange *vb* tauschen [**48**] ▷ *I exchanged the book for a DVD.* Ich habe das Buch gegen eine DVD getauscht.
exchange rate *n* Wechselkurs *m* (*pl* Wechselkurse)
excited *adj* aufgeregt
exciting *adj* aufregend
exclamation mark *n* Ausrufezeichen *nt* (*pl* Ausrufezeichen)
excuse *n* Entschuldigung *f*
▶ *vb* **Excuse me!** Entschuldigung!
exercise *n* ❶ Übung *f* ▷ *an exercise book* ein Übungsheft ❷ Bewegung *f* ▷ *You need more exercise.* Sie brauchen mehr Bewegung.; **an exercise bike** ein Heimtrainer *m*; **She does her exercises every morning.** Sie macht jeden Morgen ihre Gymnastik.
exhaust *n* Auspuff *m*; **exhaust fumes** die Abgase *ntpl*
exhausted *adj* erschöpft
exhaust pipe *n* Auspuffrohr *nt* (*pl* Auspuffrohre)
exhibition *n* Ausstellung *f*
exist *vb* existieren [**76**] (*perf* hat existiert); **It doesn't exist.** Das gibt es nicht.
exit *n* (*way out*) Ausgang *m* (*pl* Ausgänge)
expect *vb* ❶ erwarten [**2**] (*perf* hat erwartet) ▷ *I'm expecting him for dinner.* Ich erwarte ihn zum Abendessen. ▷ *She's expecting a baby.* Sie erwartet ein Kind. ▷ *I didn't expect that from him.* Das habe ich von ihm nicht erwartet. ❷ annehmen [**1**] (*pres* nimmt an, *imperf* nahm an, *perf* hat angenommen) ▷ *I expect he'll be late.* Ich nehme an, dass er sich verspäten wird. ▷ *I expect so.* Das nehme ich mal an.
expedition *n* Expedition *f*
expel *vb* **to get expelled** (*from school*) von der Schule verwiesen werden [**91**]
expenses *npl* Kosten *pl*
expensive *adj* teuer
experience *n* Erfahrung *f*
▶ *vb* ❶ haben [**32**] (*pres* hat, *imperf* hatte, *perf* hat gehabt) ▷ *They're experiencing some problems.* Sie haben einige Probleme. ❷ (*feel*) empfinden [**24**] (*imperf* empfand, *perf* hat empfunden) ▷ *He experienced fear and excitement.* Er empfand Angst und Aufregung.
experienced *adj* erfahren
experiment *n* Experiment *nt* (*pl* Experimente)
expert *n* Fachmann *m* (*pl* Fachleute), Fachfrau *f* ▷ *He's a computer expert.* Er ist Computerfachmann.; **He's an expert cook.** Er kocht ausgezeichnet.

expire *vb (passport)* ablaufen **[43]** *(pres* läuft ab, *imperf* lief ab, *perf* ist abgelaufen)
explain *vb* erklären **[19]** *(perf* hat erklärt)
explanation *n* Erklärung *f*
explode *vb* explodieren **[76]** *(perf* ist explodiert)
explore *vb (place)* erkunden **[18]** *(perf* hat erkundet)
explosion *n* Explosion *f*
export *vb* exportieren **[76]** *(perf* hat exportiert)
express *vb* ausdrücken **[4]** *(perf* hat ausgedrückt); **to express oneself** sich ausdrücken **[4]**
expression *n* Ausdruck *m (pl* Ausdrücke); **It's an English expression.** Das ist eine englische Redewendung.
expressway *n (US)* Schnellstraße *f*
extension *n* ❶ *(of building)* Anbau *m (pl* Anbauten) ❷ *(telephone)* Apparat *m (pl* Apparate) ▷ *Extension 3137, please.* Apparat 3137, bitte.
extent *n* **to some extent** in gewisser Weise
exterior *adj* äußere ▷ *the exterior walls* die äußeren Wände
extinct *adj* **to become extinct** aussterben **[75]**; **to be extinct** ausgestorben sein **[65]**
extinguisher *n (fire extinguisher)* Feuerlöscher *m (pl* Feuerlöscher)
extra *adj, adv* zusätzlich ▷ *an extra blanket* eine zusätzliche Decke; **to pay extra** extra bezahlen **[7]**; **Breakfast is extra.** Frühstück wird extra berechnet.; **It costs extra.** Das kostet extra.
extraordinary *adj* außergewöhnlich
extravagant *adj (person)* verschwenderisch
extreme *adj* extrem
extremely *adv* äußerst
extremist *n* Extremist *m (gen* Extremisten, *pl* Extremisten), Extremistin *f*
eye *n* Auge *nt (pl* Augen) ▷ *I've got green eyes.* Ich habe grüne Augen.; **to keep an eye on something** auf etwas aufpassen **[31]**
eyebrow *n* Augenbraue *f*
eyelash *n* Wimper *f*
eyelid *n* Augenlid *nt (pl* Augenlider)
eyeliner *n* Eyeliner *m (pl* Eyeliner)
eye shadow *n* Lidschatten *m (pl* Lidschatten)
eyesight *n* Sehvermögen *nt* ▷ *Her eyesight is deteriorating.* Ihr Sehvermögen lässt nach.; **to have good eyesight** gute Augen haben **[32]**

a b c d e f g h i j k l m n o p q r s t u v w x y z

f

fabric *n* Stoff *m* (*pl* Stoffe)
fabulous *adj* traumhaft ▷ *The show was fabulous.* Die Show war traumhaft.
face *n* ❶ *(of person)* Gesicht *nt* (*pl* Gesichter) ❷ *(of clock)* Zifferblatt *nt* (*pl* Zifferblätter) ❸ *(of cliff)* Wand *f* (*pl* Wände); **on the face of it** auf den ersten Blick; **in the face of these difficulties** angesichts dieser Schwierigkeiten; **face to face** Auge in Auge; **a face cloth** ein Waschlappen *m*
▶ *vb (place, problem)* konfrontiert sein [**65**] mit (*pres* ist konfrontiert mit, *imperf* war konfrontiert mit, *perf* ist konfrontiert gewesen mit); **to face up to something** sich einer Sache stellen [**38**]
Facebook® *n* Facebook®
facilities *npl* Einrichtungen *fpl*; **This school has excellent facilities.** Diese Schule ist ausgezeichnet ausgestattet.; **toilet facilities** Toiletten *fpl*; **cooking facilities** die Kochgelegenheit *sg*
fact *n* Tatsache *f*; **in fact** tatsächlich
factory *n* Fabrik *f*
fail *vb* ❶ durchfallen [**22**] in (*pres* fällt durch, *imperf* fiel durch, *perf* ist durchgefallen) ▷ *I failed the history exam.* Ich bin in der Geschichtsprüfung durchgefallen. ❷ durchfallen [**22**] ▷ *In our class, no one failed.* In unserer Klasse ist niemand durchgefallen. ❸ versagen [**84**] (*perf* hat versagt) ▷ *My brakes failed.* Meine Bremsen haben versagt.; **to fail to do something** etwas nicht tun [**81**]
▶ *n* **without fail** ganz bestimmt
failure *n* ❶ Versagen *nt* ▷ *a mechanical failure* ein mechanisches Versagen; **feelings of failure** das Gefühl zu versagen ❷ Versager *m* (*pl* Versager), Versagerin *f* ▷ *He's a failure.* Er ist ein Versager.
faint *adj* schwach ▷ *His voice was very faint.* Seine Stimme war sehr schwach.; **I feel faint.** Mir ist schwindlig.
▶ *vb* ohnmächtig werden [**91**] (*pres* wird ohnmächtig, *imperf* wurde ohnmächtig, *perf* ist ohnmächtig geworden) ▷ *All of a sudden she fainted.* Plötzlich wurde sie ohnmächtig.
fair *adj* ❶ fair ▷ *That's not fair.* Das ist nicht fair. ❷ *(hair)* blond ▷ *He's got fair hair.* Er hat blonde Haare. ❸ *(skin)* hell ▷ *people with fair skin* Menschen mit heller Haut ❹ *(weather)* schön ▷ *The weather was fair.* Das Wetter war schön. ❺ *(good enough)* gut ▷ *I have a fair chance of winning.* Ich habe gute Gewinnchancen. ❻ *(sizeable)* ordentlich ▷ *That's a fair distance.* Das ist eine ordentliche Entfernung.
▶ *n* Volksfest *nt* (*pl* Volksfeste) ▷ *They went to the fair.* Sie sind aufs Volksfest gegangen.; **a trade fair** eine Handelsmesse
fairground *n* Rummelplatz *m* (*pl* Rummelplätze)
fairly *adv* ❶ gerecht ▷ *The cake was divided fairly.* Der Kuchen wurde

gerecht verteilt. ❷ *(quite)* ziemlich ▷ *That's fairly good.* Das ist ziemlich gut.

fairy *n* Fee *f*

fairy tale *n* Märchen *nt* (*pl* Märchen)

faith *n* ❶ Glaube *m* (*gen* Glaubens) ▷ *the Catholic faith* der katholische Glaube ❷ Vertrauen *nt* ▷ *People have lost faith in the government.* Die Menschen haben das Vertrauen in die Regierung verloren.

faithful *adj* treu

faithfully *adv* **Yours faithfully ...** *(in letter)* Hochachtungsvoll ...

fake *n* Fälschung *f* ▷ *The painting was a fake.* Das Gemälde war eine Fälschung. ▶ *adj* gefälscht ▷ *a fake certificate* eine gefälschte Urkunde; **She wore fake fur.** Sie trug eine Pelzimitation.

fall *n* ❶ Sturz *m* (*gen* Sturzes, *pl* Stürze); **She had a nasty fall.** Sie ist übel gestürzt.; **a fall of snow** ein Schneefall *m*; **the Niagara Falls** die Niagarafälle ❷ *(US: autumn)* Herbst *m* (*pl* Herbste) ▷ *in fall* im Herbst ▶ *vb* ❶ hinfallen **[22]** (*perf* ist hingefallen) ▷ *He tripped and fell.* Er ist gestolpert und hingefallen. ❷ fallen **[22]** ▷ *Prices are falling.* Die Preise fallen.; **to fall apart** auseinanderfallen **[22]**; **to fall down (1)** *(person)* hinfallen **[22]** ▷ *She's fallen down.* Sie ist hingefallen. **(2)** *(building)* einfallen **[22]** ▷ *The wall fell down.* Die Mauer ist eingefallen.; **to fall for (1)** hereinfallen **[22]** auf ▷ *They fell for it.* Sie sind darauf hereingefallen. **(2)** sich verlieben **[84]** in ▷ *She's falling for him.* Sie ist dabei, sich in ihn zu verlieben.; **to fall off** herunterfallen **[22]** von; **to fall out** sich zerstreiten; **to fall through** ins Wasser fallen **[22]**

false *adj* falsch; **a false alarm** ein falscher Alarm; **false teeth** das Gebiss

fame *n* Ruhm *m*

familiar *adj* vertraut ▷ *a familiar face* ein vertrautes Gesicht; **to be familiar with something** mit etwas vertraut sein **[65]**

family *n* Familie *f* ▷ *the Airlie family* die Familie Airlie

famine *n* Hungersnot *f* (*pl* Hungersnöte)

famous *adj* berühmt

fan *n* ❶ *(hand-held)* Fächer *m* (*pl* Fächer) ❷ *(electric)* Ventilator *m* (*pl* Ventilatoren) ❸ *(of person, band, sport)* Fan *m* (*pl* Fans)

der Fan is also used for women.

▷ *I'm a fan of theirs.* Ich bin ein Fan von ihnen. ▷ *football fans* Fußballfans

fanatic *n* Fanatiker *m* (*pl* Fanatiker), Fanatikerin *f*

fancy *vb* **to fancy something** Lust auf etwas haben **[32]**; **to fancy doing something** Lust haben **[32]**, etwas zu tun; **He fancies her.** Er steht auf sie.

fancy dress *n* Kostüm *nt* (*pl* Kostüme); **He was wearing fancy dress.** Er war kostümiert.; **a fancy-dress ball** ein Kostümball *m*

fantastic *adj* fantastisch

far *adj, adv* weit ▷ *Is it far?* Ist es weit? ▷ *How far is it?* Wie weit ist es? ▷ *How far is it to Geneva?* Wie weit ist es nach Genf?; **far from (1)** weit entfernt von ▷ *It's not far from London.* Es ist nicht weit von London entfernt. **(2)** überhaupt nicht ▷ *It's far from easy.* Es ist überhaupt nicht einfach.; **How far have you got?** *(with a task)* Wie weit bist du gekommen?; **at the far end** am anderen Ende ▷ *at the far end of the room* am anderen Ende des Zimmers; **far better** viel besser; **as far as I know** soviel ich weiß; **the Far East** der Ferne Osten

fare *n* Fahrpreis *m* (*pl* Fahrpreise); **half fare** halber Preis; **full fare** voller Preis

farm *n* Bauernhof *m* (*pl* Bauernhöfe)

farmer *n* Bauer *m* (*gen* Bauern, *pl* Bauern), Bäuerin *f* ▷ *He's a farmer.* Er ist Bauer.; **a farmers' market** ein Bauernmarkt *m*

farmhouse *n* Bauernhaus *nt* (*gen* Bauernhauses, *pl* Bauernhäuser)

farming *n* Landwirtschaft *f*; **dairy farming** die Milchwirtschaft
fascinating *adj* faszinierend
fashion *n* Mode *f*; **in fashion** in Mode
fashionable *adj* modisch ▷ *Jane wears very fashionable clothes.* Jane trägt sehr modische Kleidung.; **a fashionable restaurant** ein Restaurant, das in Mode ist
fast *adj, adv* schnell ▷ *He can run fast.* Er kann schnell laufen. ▷ *a fast car* ein schnelles Auto; **That clock's fast.** Die Uhr geht vor.; **He's fast asleep.** Er schläft fest.

Be careful not to translate **fast** by the German word **fast**.

fat *adj (person)* dick
▶ *n* Fett *nt* (*pl* Fette); **It's very high in fat.** Es ist sehr fett.
fatal *adj* ❶ *(causing death)* tödlich ▷ *a fatal accident* ein tödlicher Unfall ❷ *(disastrous)* fatal ▷ *He made a fatal mistake.* Er machte einen fatalen Fehler.
father *n* Vater *m* (*pl* Väter) ▷ *my father* mein Vater; **Father Christmas** der Weihnachtsmann
father-in-law *n* Schwiegervater *m* (*pl* Schwiegerväter)
faucet *n (US)* Wasserhahn *m* (*pl* Wasserhähne)
fault *n* ❶ *(mistake)* Schuld *f* ▷ *It's my fault.* Es ist meine Schuld. ❷ *(defect)* Fehler *m* (*pl* Fehler) ▷ *a mechanical fault* ein mechanischer Fehler
favour (*US* **favor**) *n* Gefallen *m* (*pl* Gefallen); **to do somebody a favour** jemandem einen Gefallen tun [81]; **to be in favour of something** für etwas sein [65]
favourite (*US* **favorite**) *adj* **Blue's my favourite colour.** Blau ist meine Lieblingsfarbe.
▶ *n* ❶ Liebling *m* (*pl* Lieblinge)

der Liebling is also used for women.

▷ *She's his favourite.* Sie ist sein Liebling. ❷ Favorit *m* (*pl* Favoriten), Favoritin *f* ▷ *Liverpool are favourites to win the Cup.* Der FC Liverpool ist Favorit für den Pokal.
fax *n* Fax *nt* (*gen* Fax, *pl* Faxe)
▶ *vb* faxen [36]
fear *n* Furcht *f*
▶ *vb* befürchten [2] (*perf* hat befürchtet) ▷ *You have nothing to fear.* Sie haben nichts zu befürchten.
feather *n* Feder *f*
feature *n (of person, object)* Eigenschaft *f* ▷ *an important feature* eine wichtige Eigenschaft
February *n* Februar *m* ▷ *in February* im Februar
fed *vb see* **feed**
fed up *adj* **to be fed up with something** etwas satthaben [32]
feed *vb* füttern [88] ▷ *Have you fed the cat?* Hast du die Katze gefüttert?; **He worked hard to feed his family.** Er arbeitete hart, um seine Familie zu ernähren.
feel *vb* ❶ sich fühlen [38] ▷ *I don't feel well.* Ich fühle mich nicht wohl. ▷ *I feel a bit lonely.* Ich fühle mich etwas einsam. ❷ spüren [38] ▷ *I didn't feel much pain.* Ich habe keine großen Schmerzen gespürt. ❸ befühlen [7] (*perf* hat befühlt) ▷ *The doctor felt his forehead.* Der Arzt hat ihm die Stirn befühlt.; **I was feeling hungry.** Ich hatte Hunger.; **I felt very cold.** Mir war sehr kalt.; **I feel like ...** *(want)* Ich habe Lust auf ...
feeling *n* Gefühl *nt* (*pl* Gefühle) ▷ *a feeling of satisfaction* ein Gefühl der Befriedigung; **an itchy feeling** ein Jucken *nt*
feet *npl see* **foot**
fell *vb see* **fall**
felt *vb see* **feel**
felt-tip pen *n* Filzschreiber *m* (*pl* Filzschreiber)
female *adj* weiblich ▷ *a female animal* ein weibliches Tier ▷ *the female sex* das weibliche Geschlecht

In many cases, the ending indicates clearly whether the noun refers to a man or a woman and there is therefore no need for the word 'female'.

▷ *male and female students* Studenten und Studentinnen
▶ *n (animal)* Weibchen *nt (pl* Weibchen)

feminine *adj* feminin

feminist *n* Feminist *m (gen* Feministen, *pl* Feministen), Feministin *f*

fence *n* Zaun *m (pl* Zäune)

fern *n* Farn *m (pl* Farne)

ferocious *adj* wild

ferry *n* Fähre *f*

festival *n* Festival *nt (pl* Festivals) ▷ *a jazz festival* ein Jazzfestival

fetch *vb* ❶ holen **[38]** ▷ *Fetch the bucket.* Hol den Eimer. ❷ *(sell for)* einbringen **[13]** *(imperf* brachte ein, *perf* hat eingebracht) ▷ *His painting fetched five thousand pounds.* Sein Bild hat fünftausend Pfund eingebracht.

fever *n (temperature)* Fieber *nt*

few *adj, pron (not many)* wenige ▷ *few books* wenige Bücher; **a few** ein paar; **quite a few people** einige Leute

fewer *adj* weniger ▷ *There are fewer people than there were yesterday.* Es sind weniger Leute da als gestern. ▷ *There are fewer students in this class.* In dieser Klasse sind weniger Schüler.

fiancé *n* Verlobte *m (gen* Verlobten, *pl* Verlobten) ▷ *He's my fiancé.* Er ist mein Verlobter.

fiancée *n* Verlobte *f (gen* Verlobten, *pl* Verlobten) ▷ *She's my fiancée.* Sie ist meine Verlobte.

fiction *n (novels)* Romane *mpl*

field *n* ❶ *(in countryside)* Feld *nt (pl* Felder) ▷ *a field of wheat* ein Weizenfeld ❷ *(for sport)* Platz *m (gen* Platzes, *pl* Plätze) ▷ *a football field* ein Fußballplatz ❸ *(subject)* Gebiet *nt (pl* Gebiete) ▷ *He's an expert in his field.* Er ist Fachmann auf seinem Gebiet.

fierce *adj* ❶ gefährlich ▷ *The dog looked very fierce.* Der Hund sah sehr gefährlich aus. ❷ heftig ▷ *a fierce attack* ein heftiger Angriff; **The wind was very fierce.** Es wehte ein sehr scharfer Wind.

fifteen *num* fünfzehn ▷ *I'm fifteen.* Ich bin fünfzehn.

fifteenth *adj* fünfzehnte ▷ *the fifteenth of August* der fünfzehnte August

fifth *adj* fünfte ▷ *the fifth floor* der fünfte Stock ▷ *the fifth of August* der fünfte August

fifty *num* fünfzig ▷ *He's fifty.* Er ist fünfzig.

fight *n* ❶ Schlägerei *f* ▷ *There was a fight in the pub.* In der Kneipe gab es eine Schlägerei. ❷ Kampf *m (pl* Kämpfe) ▷ *the fight against cancer* der Kampf gegen Krebs
▶ *vb* ❶ *(physically)* sich prügeln **[34]** ▷ *They were fighting.* Sie haben sich geprügelt. ❷ *(quarrel)* streiten *(imperf* stritt, *perf* hat gestritten) ▷ *He's always fighting with his wife.* Er streitet dauernd mit seiner Frau. ❸ *(combat)* bekämpfen **[7]** *(perf* hat bekämpft) ▷ *Doctors fought the disease.* Die Ärzte bekämpften die Krankheit.

fight back *vb* sich wehren **[38]**

figure *n* ❶ *(number)* Zahl *f* ▷ *Can you give me the exact figures?* Können Sie mir genaue Zahlen nennen? ❷ *(outline of person)* Gestalt *f* ▷ *Mary saw the figure of a man on the bridge.* Mary sah die Gestalt eines Mannes auf der Brücke. ❸ *(shape)* Figur *f* ▷ *She's got a good figure.* Sie hat eine gute Figur. ▷ *I have to watch my figure.* Ich muss auf meine Figur achten. ❹ *(personality)* Persönlichkeit *f* ▷ *She's an important political figure.* Sie ist eine wichtige politische Persönlichkeit.

figure out *vb* ❶ ausrechnen **[4]** *(perf* hat ausgerechnet) ❷ herausfinden **[24]** *(imperf* fand heraus, *perf* hat herausgefunden) ❸ schlau werden **[91]**

a b c d e f g h i j k l m n o p q r s t u v w x y z

aus (*pres* wird schlau, *imperf* wurde schlau, *perf* ist schlau geworden)

file *n* ❶ *(document)* Akte *f* ▷ *Have we got a file on the suspect?* Haben wir über den Verdächtigen eine Akte? ❷ *(folder)* Aktenmappe *f* ▷ *She keeps all her letters in a cardboard file.* Sie bewahrt all ihre Briefe in einer Aktenmappe auf. ❸ *(ring binder)* Aktenordner *m* (*pl* Aktenordner) ❹ *(on computer)* Datei *f* ❺ *(for nails, metal)* Feile *f*
▸ *vb* ❶ *(papers)* abheften [2] (*perf* hat abgeheftet) ❷ *(nails, metal)* feilen [38] ▷ *I'll have to file my nails.* Ich muss mir die Nägel feilen.

fill *vb* füllen [38] ▷ *She filled the glass with water.* Sie füllte das Glas mit Wasser.; **to fill in (1)** ausfüllen [4] ▷ *Can you fill this form in, please?* Können Sie bitte dieses Formular ausfüllen? **(2)** auffüllen [4] ▷ *He filled the hole in with soil.* Er füllte das Loch mit Erde auf.; **to fill up** vollmachen [48] ▷ *He filled the cup up to the brim.* Er machte die Tasse bis zum Rand voll.; **Fill it up, please.** *(at petrol station)* Volltanken, bitte.

film *n* Film *m* (*pl* Filme)

film star *n* Filmstar *m* (*pl* Filmstars)
der Filmstar is also used for women.
▷ *She's a film star.* Sie ist ein Filmstar.

filthy *adj* schmutzig

final *adj* ❶ *(last)* letzte ▷ *our final match of the season* unser letztes Spiel der Saison ❷ *(definite)* endgültig ▷ *a final decision* eine endgültige Entscheidung; **I'm not going and that's final.** Ich gehe nicht, und damit basta.
▸ *n* Finale *nt* (*pl* Finale) ▷ *Murray is in the final.* Murray ist im Finale.

finally *adv* ❶ *(lastly)* schließlich ▷ *Finally, I would like to say ...* Und schließlich möchte ich sagen ... ❷ *(eventually)* letztendlich ▷ *They finally decided to leave on Saturday.* Sie haben letztendlich beschlossen, am Samstag zu fahren.

financial *adj* finanziell

find *vb* finden [24] (*imperf* fand, *perf* hat gefunden) ▷ *I can't find the exit.* Ich kann den Ausgang nicht finden. ▷ *Did you find your pen?* Hast du deinen Schreiber gefunden?; **to find something out** etwas herausfinden [24] ▷ *I'm determined to find out the truth.* Ich bin entschlossen, die Wahrheit herauszufinden.; **to find out about (1)** *(make enquiries)* sich erkundigen [19] nach ▷ *Try to find out about the cost of a hotel.* Versuche, dich nach dem Preis für ein Hotel zu erkundigen. **(2)** *(by chance)* erfahren [21] ▷ *I found out about their affair.* Ich habe von ihrem Verhältnis erfahren.

fine *adj, adv* ❶ *(very good)* ausgezeichnet ▷ *He's a fine musician.* Er ist ein ausgezeichneter Musiker.; **How are you? — I'm fine.** Wie geht's? — Gut!; **I feel fine.** Mir geht's gut.; **The weather is fine today.** Das Wetter ist heute schön. ❷ *(not coarse)* fein ▷ *She's got very fine hair.* Sie hat sehr feine Haare.
▸ *n* ❶ Geldbuße *f* ▷ *She got a fine.* Sie hat eine Geldbuße bekommen. ❷ *(for traffic offence)* Strafzettel *m* (*pl* Strafzettel) ▷ *I got a fine for speeding.* Ich habe einen Strafzettel bekommen, weil ich zu schnell gefahren bin.

finger *n* Finger *m* (*pl* Finger) ▷ *my little finger* mein kleiner Finger

fingernail *n* Fingernagel *m* (*pl* Fingernägel)

finish *n* *(of race)* Finish *nt* (*pl* Finishs) ▷ *We saw the finish of the London Marathon.* Wir sahen das Finish des Londoner Marathonlaufs.
▸ *vb* ❶ fertig sein [65] (*pres* ist fertig, *imperf* war fertig, *perf* ist fertig gewesen) ▷ *I've finished!* Ich bin fertig! ❷ zu Ende sein [65] (*pres* ist zu Ende, *imperf* war zu Ende, *perf* ist zu Ende gewesen) ▷ *The film has finished.* Der Film ist zu Ende.; **I've finished the book.** Ich habe das Buch zu Ende

gelesen.; **to finish doing something** etwas zu Ende machen [**48**]

Finland *n* Finnland *nt*; **from Finland** aus Finnland; **to Finland** nach Finnland

Finn *n* Finne *m* (*gen* Finnen, *pl* Finnen), Finnin *f*

Finnish *adj* finnisch; **She's Finnish.** Sie ist Finnin.
▸ *n (language)* Finnisch *nt* (*gen* Finnischen)

fir *n* Tanne *f*; **fir cone** der Tannenzapfen; **fir tree** der Tannenbaum

fire *n* ❶ Feuer *nt* (*pl* Feuer) ▹ *He made a fire to warm himself up.* Er machte ein Feuer, um sich aufzuwärmen.; **to be on fire** brennen [**12**] ❷ *(accidental)* Brand *m* (*pl* Brände); **The house was destroyed by fire.** Das Haus ist abgebrannt. ❸ *(heater)* Heizung *f* ▹ *Turn the fire on.* Mach die Heizung an.; **the fire brigade** die Feuerwehr; **a fire alarm** ein Feueralarm *m*; **a fire engine** ein Feuerwehrauto *nt*; **a fire escape** *(stairs)* eine Feuertreppe; **a fire extinguisher** ein Feuerlöscher *m*; **a fire station** eine Feuerwehrstation
▸ *vb (shoot)* schießen (*imperf* schoss, *perf* hat geschossen) ▹ *She fired twice.* Sie hat zweimal geschossen.; **to fire at somebody** auf jemanden schießen; **to fire a gun** einen Schuss abgeben [**28**]; **to fire somebody** jemanden feuern [**34**]

firefighter *n* Feuerwehrmann *m* (*pl* Feuerwehrleute), Feuerwehrfrau *f* ▹ *She's a firefighter.* Sie ist Feuerwehrfrau.

fireworks *npl* Feuerwerk *nt* (*pl* Feuerwerke) ▹ *Are you going to see the fireworks?* Seht ihr euch das Feuerwerk an?

firm *adj* streng ▹ *to be firm with somebody* streng mit jemandem sein
▸ *n* Firma *f* (*pl* Firmen) ▹ *He works for a large firm in London.* Er arbeitet für eine große Firma in London.

first *adj, adv* ❶ erste ▹ *my first boyfriend* mein erster Freund ▹ *the first time* das erste Mal ▹ *the first of August* der erste August; **Rachel came first.** *(in exam, race)* Rachel war Erste.; **John came first.** *(in exam, race)* John war Erster. ❷ zuerst ▹ *I want to get a job, but first I have to pass my exams.* Ich will mir einen Job suchen, aber zuerst muss ich meine Prüfung bestehen.; **first of all** zuallererst
▸ *n* Erste *m* (*gen* Ersten, *pl* Ersten), Erste *f* (*gen* Ersten) ▹ *She was the first to arrive.* Sie ist als Erste angekommen.; **at first** zuerst

first aid *n* Erste Hilfe *f*; **a first aid kit** ein Verbandszeug *nt*

first-class *adj* ❶ erster Klasse ▹ *a first-class ticket* ein Ticket erster Klasse ❷ erstklassig ▹ *a first-class meal* ein erstklassiges Essen

In Germany there is no first-class or second-class post. However, letters cost more to send than postcards, so you have to remember to say what you are sending when buying stamps. There is also an express service.

firstly *adv* ❶ zuerst ▹ *Firstly, let's see what the book is about.* Wir wollen erst mal sehen, wovon das Buch handelt. ❷ erstens ▹ *firstly ... secondly ...* erstens ... zweitens ...

fish *n* Fisch *m* (*pl* Fische) ▹ *I caught three fish.* Ich habe drei Fische gefangen. ▹ *I don't like fish.* Ich mag Fisch nicht.
▸ *vb* fischen [**48**]; **to go fishing** fischen gehen [**29**]

fisherman *n* Fischer *m* (*pl* Fischer) ▹ *He's a fisherman.* Er ist Fischer.

fish finger *n* Fischstäbchen *nt* (*pl* Fischstäbchen)

fishing *n* Angeln *nt* ▹ *My hobby is fishing.* Angeln ist mein Hobby.

fishing boat *n* Fischerboot *nt* (*pl* Fischerboote)

fishing rod *n* Angel *f*

fishing tackle *n* Angelzeug *nt*
fishmonger's *n* Fischladen *m* (*pl* Fischläden)
fist *n* Faust *f* (*pl* Fäuste)
fit *vb* ❶ *(be the right size)* passen [**31**] (*perf* hat gepasst) ▷ *Does it fit?* Passt es? ▷ *These trousers don't fit me. (wrong size)* Diese Hose passt mir nicht. ❷ *(fix up)* einbauen [**4**] (*perf* hat eingebaut) ▷ *He fitted an alarm in his car.* Er hat eine Alarmanlage in sein Auto eingebaut. ❸ *(attach)* anbringen [**13**] (*imperf* brachte an, *perf* hat angebracht) ▷ *She fitted a plug to the hair dryer.* Sie brachte am Föhn einen Stecker an.; **to fit in (1)** *(match up)* passen [**31**] zu ▷ *That story doesn't fit in with what he told us.* Diese Geschichte passt nicht zu dem, was er uns gesagt hat. **(2)** *(person)* sich einpassen [**4**] ▷ *She fitted in well at her new school.* Sie hat sich in ihrer neuen Schule gut eingepasst.
▶ *adj (healthy)* fit ▷ *He felt relaxed and fit after his holiday.* Nach seinem Urlaub fühlte er sich entspannt und fit.
▶ *n* **to have a fit (1)** *(epileptic)* einen Anfall haben [**32**] **(2)** *(be angry)* Zustände bekommen [**40**] ▷ *My Mum will have a fit!* Meine Mutter bekommt Zustände!
fitted carpet *n* Teppichboden *m* (*pl* Teppichböden)
five *num* fünf ▷ *He's five.* Er ist fünf.
fix *vb* ❶ *(mend)* reparieren [**76**] (*perf* hat repariert) ▷ *Can you fix my bike?* Kannst du mein Fahrrad reparieren? ❷ *(decide)* festlegen [**4**] (*perf* hat festgelegt) ▷ *Let's fix a date for the party.* Lass uns einen Tag für die Party festlegen. ▷ *They fixed a price for the car.* Sie haben einen Preis für das Auto festgelegt. ❸ machen [**48**] ▷ *Janice fixed some food for us.* Janice hat uns etwas zum Essen gemacht.
fizzy *adj* mit Kohlensäure ▷ *I don't like fizzy drinks.* Ich mag keine Getränke mit Kohlensäure.
flag *n* Fahne *f*
flame *n* Flamme *f*
flan *n* ❶ *(sweet)* Kuchen *m* (*pl* Kuchen) ▷ *a raspberry flan* ein Himbeerkuchen ❷ *(savoury)* Quiche *f* (*pl* Quiches) ▷ *a cheese and onion flan* eine Käse-Zwiebel-Quiche
flap *vb* flattern [**34**] mit ▷ *The bird flapped its wings.* Der Vogel flatterte mit den Flügeln.
flash *n* Blitzlicht *nt* (*pl* Blitzlichter) ▷ *Has your camera got a flash?* Hat dein Fotoapparat ein Blitzlicht?; **a flash of lightning** ein Blitz *m*; **in a flash** blitzschnell
▶ *vb* ❶ blinken [**38**] ▷ *The police car's blue light was flashing.* Das Blaulicht des Polizeiautos blinkte. ❷ leuchten [**2**] mit ▷ *They flashed a torch in his face.* Sie leuchteten ihm mit einer Taschenlampe ins Gesicht.; **She flashed her headlights.** Sie betätigte die Lichthupe.
flask *n* Thermosflasche® *f*
flat *adj* ❶ flach ▷ *flat shoes* flache Schuhe; **a flat roof** ein Flachdach *nt* ❷ *(tyre)* platt ▷ *I've got a flat tyre.* Ich habe einen platten Reifen.
▶ *n* Wohnung *f* ▷ *She lives in a flat.* Sie wohnt in einer Wohnung.
flatscreen *n* Flachbildschirm *m* (*pl* Flachbildschirme) ▷ *a flatscreen TV* ein Flachbildschirm-Fernseher *m*
flatter *vb* schmeicheln [**38**] ▷ *Are you trying to flatter me?* Willst du mir schmeicheln? ▷ *I feel flattered.* Ich fühle mich geschmeichelt.
flavour (*US* **flavor**) *n* Geschmack *m* (*pl* Geschmäcke) ▷ *This cheese has a very strong flavour.* Dieser Käse hat einen sehr pikanten Geschmack.; **Which flavour of ice cream would you like?** Was für ein Eis möchtest du?
flea *n* Floh *m* (*pl* Flöhe)
flew *vb see* **fly**
flexible *adj* flexibel; **flexible working hours** gleitende Arbeitszeit

flick *vb* schnipsen [**48**] ▷ *She flicked the ash off her jumper.* Sie schnipste die Asche von ihrem Pullover.; **to flick through a book** ein Buch durchblättern [**15**]

flight *n* Flug *m* (*pl* Flüge) ▷ *What time is the flight to Munich?* Um wie viel Uhr geht der Flug nach München?; **a flight of stairs** eine Treppe

flight attendant *n* Flugbegleiter *m* (*pl* Flugbegleiter), Flugbegleiterin *f*

fling *vb* schmeißen (*imperf* schmiss, *perf* hat geschmissen) ▷ *He flung the dictionary onto the floor.* Er schmiss das Wörterbuch auf den Boden.

float *vb* schwimmen [**63**] (*imperf* schwamm, *perf* ist geschwommen) ▷ *A leaf was floating on the water.* Auf dem Wasser schwamm ein Blatt.

flood *n* ❶ Überschwemmung *f* ▷ *The rain has caused many floods.* Der Regen hat zu vielen Überschwemmungen geführt. ❷ Flut *f* ▷ *He received a flood of letters.* Er erhielt eine Flut von Briefen.
▸ *vb* überschwemmen [**18**] (*perf* hat überschwemmt) ▷ *The river has flooded the village.* Der Fluss hat das Dorf überschwemmt.

floor *n* ❶ Fußboden *m* (*pl* Fußböden); **a tiled floor** ein Fliesenboden; **on the floor** auf dem Boden ❷ (*storey*) Stock *m* (*pl* Stock); **the first floor** der erste Stock; **the ground floor** das Erdgeschoss

> Be careful not to translate **floor** by **Flur**.

floppy disk *n* Diskette *f*

florist *n* Florist *m* (*gen* Floristen, *pl* Floristen), Floristin *f*

flour *n* Mehl *nt* (*pl* Mehle)

flow *vb* fließen [**27**] (*imperf* floss, *perf* ist geflossen) ▷ *Water was flowing from the pipe.* Aus dem Rohr floss Wasser.

flower *n* Blume *f*
▸ *vb* blühen [**38**]

flown *vb see* **fly**

flu *n* Grippe *f* ▷ *She's got flu.* Sie hat Grippe.

fluent *adj* **He speaks fluent German.** Er spricht fließend Deutsch.

flung *vb see* **fling**

flush *n* (*of toilet*) Spülung *f*
▸ *vb* **to flush the toilet** spülen [**38**]

flute *n* Querflöte *f* ▷ *I play the flute.* Ich spiele Querflöte.

fly *n* (*insect*) Fliege *f*
▸ *vb* fliegen [**25**] (*imperf* flog, *perf* ist geflogen) ▷ *He flew from Berlin to New York.* Er flog von Berlin nach New York.; **to fly away** wegfliegen [**25**]

focus *n* **to be out of focus** unscharf sein [**65**] ▷ *The house is out of focus in this photo.* Das Haus ist auf diesem Foto unscharf.
▸ *vb* scharf einstellen [**4**] (*perf* hat scharf eingestellt) ▷ *Try to focus the binoculars.* Versuch, das Fernglas scharf einzustellen.; **to focus on something** (**1**) (*with camera*) die Kamera auf etwas einstellen [**4**] ▷ *The cameraman focused on the bird.* Der Kameramann stellte die Kamera auf den Vogel ein. (**2**) (*concentrate*) sich auf etwas konzentrieren [**76**] ▷ *Let's focus on the plot.* Wir wollen uns auf die Handlung konzentrieren.

fog *n* Nebel *m* (*pl* Nebel)

foggy *adj* neblig ▷ *a foggy day* ein nebliger Tag

foil *n* (*kitchen foil*) Alufolie *f* ▷ *She wrapped the meat in foil.* Sie wickelte das Fleisch in Alufolie.

fold *n* Falte *f*
▸ *vb* falten [**2**] ▷ *He folded the newspaper in half.* Er faltete die Zeitung in der Mitte zusammen.; **to fold up** (**1**) (*paper*) zusammenfalten [**2**] (**2**) (*chair*) zusammenklappen [**4**]; **to fold one's arms** die Arme verschränken [**7**] ▷ *She folded her arms.* Sie verschränkte die Arme.

folder *n* ❶ Mappe *f* ▷ *She kept all her letters in a folder.* Sie bewahrte all ihre Briefe in einer Mappe auf. ❷ (*ring binder*) Ordner *m* (*pl* Ordner)

follow *vb* ❶ folgen [**38**] (*perf* ist gefolgt) ▷ *She followed him.* Sie folgte ihm.; **You go first and I'll follow.** Geh du vor, ich komme nach. ❷ followen [**38**]

following *adj* folgend ▷ *the following day* am folgenden Tag

fond *adj* **to be fond of somebody** jemanden gernhaben [**32**]

food *n* Nahrung *f*; **We need to buy some food.** Wir müssen etwas zum Essen kaufen.; **cat food** das Katzenfutter; **dog food** das Hundefutter

fool *n* Idiot *m* (*gen* Idioten, *pl* Idioten), Idiotin *f*

foot *n* ❶ (*of person*) Fuß *m* (*gen* Fußes, *pl* Füße) ▷ *My feet are aching.* Mir tun die Füße weh.; **on foot** zu Fuß ❷ (*12 inches*) Fuß *m* (*pl* Fuß)

In Germany measurements are in metres and centimetres rather than feet and inches. A foot is about 30 centimetres.

▷ *Dave is six foot tall.* Dave ist ein Meter achtzig groß. ▷ *That mountain is five thousand feet high.* Dieser Berg ist eintausendsechshundert Meter hoch.

football *n* Fußball *m* (*pl* Fußbälle) ▷ *I like playing football.* Ich spiele gern Fußball. ▷ *Paul threw the football over the fence.* Paul warf den Fußball über den Zaun.

footballer *n* Fußballer *m* (*pl* Fußballer), Fußballerin *f*

footpath *n* Fußweg *m* (*pl* Fußwege) ▷ *the footpath through the forest* der Fußweg durch den Wald

for *prep*

There are several ways of translating 'for'. Scan the examples to find one that is similar to what you want to say.

❶ für ▷ *a present for me* ein Geschenk für mich ▷ *He works for the government.* Er arbeitet für die Regierung. ▷ *I'll do it for you.* Ich mache es für dich. ▷ *Are you for or against the idea?* Bist du für oder gegen die Idee? ▷ *Oxford is famous for its university.* Oxford ist für seine Universität berühmt. ▷ *I sold it for five pounds.* Ich habe es für fünf Pfund verkauft.; **What for?** Wofür?

When referring to periods of time, use **lang** for the future and completed action in the past, and **seit** (with the German verb in the present tense) for something that started in the past and is still going on.

❷ lang ▷ *He worked in Germany for two years.* Er hat zwei Jahre lang in Deutschland gearbeitet. ▷ *She will be away for a month.* Sie wird einen Monat lang weg sein.; **There are road works for three kilometres.** Es gibt dort über drei Kilometer Bauarbeiten. ❸ seit ▷ *He's been learning German for two years.* Er lernt seit zwei Jahren Deutsch. ▷ *She's been away for a month.* Sie ist seit einem Monat weg.; **What's the German for 'lion'?** Wie sagt man 'lion' auf Deutsch?; **It's time for lunch.** Es ist Zeit zum Mittagessen.; **the train for London** der Zug nach London; **for sale** zu verkaufen

forbid *vb* verbieten [**8**] (*imperf* verbot, *perf* hat verboten); **to forbid somebody to do something** jemandem verbieten, etwas zu tun [**81**]

forbidden *adj* verboten ▷ *Smoking is strictly forbidden.* Rauchen ist streng verboten.

force *n* Gewalt *f* ▷ *the forces of nature* die Naturgewalten; **The force of the explosion blew out all the windows.** Die Explosion war so stark, dass alle Fenster kaputtgingen.; **in force** in Kraft

▶ *vb* zwingen [**97**] (*imperf* zwang, *perf* hat gezwungen) ▷ *They forced him to open the safe.* Sie zwangen ihn, den Safe aufzumachen.

forecast *n* **the weather forecast** die Wettervorhersage

forehead *n* Stirn *f*

foreign *adj* ausländisch

foreigner *n* Ausländer *m* (*pl* Ausländer), Ausländerin *f*
forest *n* Wald *m* (*pl* Wälder)
forever *adv* ❶ für immer ▷ *He's gone forever.* Er ist für immer weg. ❷ *(always)* dauernd ▷ *She's forever complaining.* Sie beklagt sich dauernd.
forgave *vb see* **forgive**
forge *vb* fälschen [**38**] ▷ *She tried to forge his signature.* Sie versuchte, seine Unterschrift zu fälschen.
forged *adj* gefälscht ▷ *forged banknotes* gefälschte Banknoten
forget *vb* vergessen [**83**] (*pres* vergisst, *imperf* vergaß, *perf* hat vergessen) ▷ *I've forgotten his name.* Ich habe seinen Namen vergessen. ▷ *I'm sorry, I completely forgot!* Tut mir leid, das habe ich total vergessen!
forgetful *adj* vergesslich
forgive *vb* **to forgive somebody** jemandem verzeihen; **to forgive somebody for doing something** jemandem verzeihen, etwas getan zu haben
fork *n* ❶ *(for eating, gardening)* Gabel *f* ▷ *He ate his chips with a fork.* Er aß seine Pommes frites mit einer Gabel. ❷ *(in road)* Gabelung *f*; **There was a fork in the road.** Die Straße gabelte sich.
form *n* ❶ *(paper)* Formular *nt* (*pl* Formulare) ▷ *to fill in a form* ein Formular ausfüllen ❷ *(type)* Form *f* ▷ *I'm against hunting in any form.* Ich bin gegen die Jagd in jeglicher Form.; **in top form** in Topform
formal *adj* ❶ *(occasion)* formell ▷ *a formal dinner* ein formelles Abendessen ❷ *(person)* förmlich ❸ *(language)* gehoben ▷ *a formal word* ein gehobener Ausdruck; **formal clothes** die Gesellschaftskleidung *sg*; **He's got no formal qualifications.** Er hat keinen offiziellen Abschluss.
former *adj* früher ▷ *a former pupil* ein früherer Schüler ▷ *the former Prime Minister* der frühere Premierminister
forthcoming *adj* kommend ▷ *the forthcoming meeting* die kommende Besprechung
fortnight *n* **a fortnight** vierzehn Tage
fortunate *adj* **to be fortunate** Glück haben [**32**]; **It's fortunate that I remembered the map.** Zum Glück habe ich an die Landkarte gedacht.
fortunately *adv* zum Glück ▷ *Fortunately, it didn't rain.* Zum Glück hat es nicht geregnet.
fortune *n* Vermögen *nt* (*pl* Vermögen) ▷ *Kate earns a fortune!* Kate verdient ein Vermögen!; **to tell somebody's fortune** jemandem wahrsagen [**15**]
forty *num* vierzig ▷ *He's forty.* Er ist vierzig.
forward *adv* **to move forward** sich vorwärtsbewegen [**4**]
▶ *vb* nachsenden (*imperf* sandte nach, *perf* hat nachgesandt) ▷ *He forwarded all her letters.* Er sandte alle ihre Briefe nach.
foster child *n* Pflegekind *nt* (*pl* Pflegekinder) ▷ *She's their foster child.* Sie ist ihr Pflegekind.
fought *vb see* **fight**
foul *adj* furchtbar ▷ *The weather was foul.* Das Wetter war furchtbar. ▷ *What a foul smell!* Was für ein furchtbarer Gestank!
▶ *n* Foul *nt* (*pl* Fouls) ▷ *Ferguson committed a foul.* Ferguson hat ein Foul begangen.
fountain *n* Brunnen *m* (*pl* Brunnen)
fountain pen *n* Füllfederhalter *m* (*pl* Füllfederhalter)
four *num* vier ▷ *She's four.* Sie ist vier.
fourteen *num* vierzehn ▷ *I'm fourteen.* Ich bin vierzehn.
fourteenth *adj* vierzehnte ▷ *the fourteenth of August* der vierzehnte August
fourth *adj* vierte ▷ *the fourth floor* der vierte Stock ▷ *the fourth of August* der vierte August
fox *n* Fuchs *m* (*gen* Fuchses, *pl* Füchse)
fragile *adj* zerbrechlich

frame *n (for picture)* Rahmen *m (pl* Rahmen)

France *n* Frankreich *nt*; **from France** aus Frankreich; **in France** in Frankreich; **to France** nach Frankreich

frantic *adj* **I was going frantic.** Ich bin fast durchgedreht.; **I was frantic with worry.** Ich habe mir furchtbare Sorgen gemacht.

fraud *n* ❶ *(crime)* Betrug *m* ▷ *He was jailed for fraud.* Er kam wegen Betrugs ins Gefängnis. ❷ *(person)* Betrüger *m (pl* Betrüger), Betrügerin *f* ▷ *He's not a real doctor, he's a fraud.* Er ist kein echter Arzt, er ist ein Betrüger.

freckles *npl* Sommersprossen *fpl*

free *adj* ❶ *(free of charge)* kostenlos ▷ *a free brochure* eine kostenlose Broschüre ❷ *(not busy, not taken)* frei ▷ *Is this seat free?* Ist dieser Platz frei?; **'admission free'** 'Eintritt frei'; **Are you free after school?** Hast du nach der Schule Zeit?
▶ *vb* befreien **[7]** *(perf* hat befreit)

freedom *n* Freiheit *f*

freeway *n (US)* Autobahn *f*

freeze *vb* ❶ gefrieren *(imperf* gefror, *perf* ist gefroren) ▷ *The water had frozen.* Das Wasser war gefroren. ❷ *(food)* einfrieren ▷ *She froze the rest of the raspberries.* Sie hat die restlichen Himbeeren eingefroren.

freezer *n* Gefrierschrank *m (pl* Gefrierschränke)

freezing *adj* **It's freezing!** *(informal)* Es ist eiskalt!; **I'm freezing!** *(informal)* Mir ist eiskalt!; **three degrees below freezing** drei Grad minus

French *adj* französisch ▷ *He's French.* Er ist Franzose. ▷ *She's French.* Sie ist Französin.
▶ *n (language)* Französisch *nt (gen* Französischen) ▷ *Do you speak French?* Sprechen Sie Französisch?; **the French** *(people)* die Franzosen *mpl*

French fries *npl* Pommes frites *fpl*

French kiss *n* Zungenkuss *m (gen* Zungenkusses, *pl* Zungenküsse)

Frenchman *n* Franzose *m (gen* Franzosen, *pl* Franzosen)

French windows *npl* Verandatür *f*

Frenchwoman *n* Französin *f*

frequent *adj* häufig ▷ *frequent showers* häufige Niederschläge; **There are frequent buses to the town centre.** Es gehen häufig Busse ins Stadtzentrum.

fresh *adj* frisch ▷ *I need some fresh air.* Ich brauche frische Luft.

Friday *n* Freitag *m (pl* Freitage) ▷ *on Friday* am Freitag ▷ *every Friday* jeden Freitag ▷ *last Friday* letzten Freitag ▷ *next Friday* nächsten Freitag; **on Fridays** freitags

fridge *n* Kühlschrank *m (pl* Kühlschränke)

fried *adj* gebraten ▷ *fried onions* gebratene Zwiebeln; **a fried egg** ein Spiegelei *nt*

friend *n* Freund *m (pl* Freunde), Freundin *f*
▶ *vb* sich befreunden **[54]** mit

friendly *adj* freundlich ▷ *She's really friendly.* Sie ist wirklich freundlich. ▷ *Liverpool is a very friendly city.* Liverpool ist eine sehr freundliche Stadt.

friendship *n* Freundschaft *f*

fright *n* Schrecken *m (pl* Schrecken) ▷ *I got a terrible fright!* Ich habe einen furchtbaren Schrecken bekommen!

frighten *vb* Angst machen **[48]** ▷ *Horror films frighten him.* Horrorfilme machen ihm Angst.

frightened *adj* **to be frightened** Angst haben **[32]**; **to be frightened of something** vor etwas Angst haben **[32]**

frightening *adj* beängstigend

fringe *n (of hair)* Pony *m (pl* Ponys) ▷ *She's got a fringe.* Sie hat einen Pony.

Frisbee® *n* Frisbee® *nt (pl* Frisbees) ▷ *to play Frisbee* Frisbee spielen

frog *n* Frosch *m (pl* Frösche)

from *prep* ❶ *(from country, town)* aus ▷ *I'm from Yorkshire.* Ich bin aus

Yorkshire. ▷ *I come from Perth.* Ich bin aus Perth.; **Where do you come from?** Woher sind Sie? ❷ *(from person)* von ▷ *a letter from my sister* ein Brief von meiner Schwester; **The hotel is one kilometre from the beach.** Das Hotel ist einen Kilometer vom Strand entfernt. ❸ *(number)* ab ▷ *from ten pounds* ab zehn Pfund ▷ *from the age of fourteen* ab vierzehn; **from ... to ...** **(1)** *(distance)* von ... nach ... ▷ *He flew from London to Paris.* Er flog von London nach Paris. **(2)** *(time)* von ... bis ... ▷ *from one o'clock to two* von eins bis zwei; **The price was reduced from ten pounds to five.** Der Preis war von zehn auf fünf Pfund herabgesetzt.; **from ... onwards** ab ... ▷ *We'll be at home from seven o'clock onwards.* Wir werden ab sieben Uhr zu Hause sein.

front *n* Vorderseite *f* ▷ *the front of the house* die Vorderseite des Hauses; **in front** davor; **in front of** vor

> Use the accusative to express movement or a change of place. Use the dative when there is no change of place.

▷ *He stood in front of the house.* Er stand vor dem Haus. ▷ *He ran in front of a bus.* Er lief vor einen Bus.; **in the front** *(of car)* vorn; **at the front of the train** vorn im Zug
▶ *adj* vordere ▷ *the front row* die vordere Reihe ▷ *the front seats of the car* die vorderen Sitze des Autos; **the front door** die Haustür

frontier *n* Grenze *f*

frost *n* Frost *m* (*pl* Fröste)

frosty *adj* frostig ▷ *It's frosty today.* Heute ist es frostig.

frown *vb* die Stirn runzeln **[34]** ▷ *He frowned.* Er runzelte die Stirn.

frozen *adj (food)* tiefgefroren ▷ *frozen chips* tiefgefrorene Pommes frites

fruit *n* ❶ Frucht *f* (*pl* Früchte) ▷ *an exotic fruit* eine exotische Frucht ❷ Obst *nt* ▷ *Fruit is very healthy.* Obst ist sehr gesund.; **fruit juice** der Fruchtsaft; **a fruit salad** ein Obstsalat *m*

fruit machine *n* Spielautomat *m* (*gen* Spielautomaten, *pl* Spielautomaten)

frustrated *adj* frustriert

fry *vb* braten (*pres* brät, *imperf* briet, *perf* hat gebraten) ▷ *Fry the onions for five minutes.* Braten Sie die Zwiebeln fünf Minuten lang.

frying pan *n* Bratpfanne *f*

fuel *n (for car, aeroplane)* Benzin *nt* (*pl* Benzine) ▷ *to run out of fuel* kein Benzin mehr haben

full *adj, adv* ❶ voll ▷ *The tank's full.* Der Tank ist voll. ❷ ausführlich ▷ *He asked for full information on the job.* Er bat um ausführliche Informationen über die Stelle.; **your full name** Name und Vornamen; **My full name is Ian John Marr.** Ich heiße Ian John Marr.; **I'm full.** *(after meal)* Ich bin satt.; **at full speed** mit Höchstgeschwindigkeit; **There was a full moon.** Es war Vollmond.

full stop *n* Punkt *m* (*pl* Punkte)

full-time *adj, adv* ganztags ▷ *She works full-time.* Sie arbeitet ganztags.; **She's got a full-time job.** Sie hat einen Ganztagsjob.

fully *adv* ganz ▷ *He hasn't yet fully recovered.* Er hat sich noch nicht ganz erholt.

fumes *npl* Abgase *ntpl* ▷ *dangerous fumes* gefährliche Abgase; **exhaust fumes** Autoabgase

fun *adj* lustig ▷ *She's a fun person.* Sie ist ein lustiger Mensch.
▶ *n* **to have fun** Spaß haben **[32]**; **for fun** zum Spaß; **to make fun of somebody** sich über jemanden lustig machen **[48]**; **It's fun!** Das macht Spaß!; **Have fun!** Viel Spaß!

funds *npl* **to raise funds** Spenden sammeln **[34]**

funeral *n* Beerdigung *f*

funfair *n* Volksfest *nt* (*pl* Volksfeste)

funny *adj* ❶ *(amusing)* lustig ▷ *It was really funny.* Es war wirklich lustig.

❷ *(strange)* komisch ▷ *There's something funny about him.* Er hat etwas Komisches an sich.

fur *n* ❶ Pelz *m (gen* Pelzes, *pl* Pelze) ▷ *a fur coat* ein Pelzmantel *m* ❷ Fell *nt (pl* Felle) ▷ *the dog's fur* das Fell des Hundes

furious *adj* wütend ▷ *Dad was furious with me.* Papa war wütend auf mich.

furniture *n* Möbel *ntpl* ▷ *a piece of furniture* ein Möbelstück *nt*

further *adv, adj* weiter entfernt ▷ *London is further from Manchester than Leeds is.* London ist weiter von Manchester entfernt als Leeds.; **How much further is it?** Wie weit ist es noch?

further education *n* Weiterbildung *f*

fuse *n* Sicherung *f* ▷ *The fuse has blown.* Die Sicherung ist durchgebrannt.

fuss *n* Aufregung *f* ▷ *What's all the fuss about?* Was soll die ganze Aufregung?; **to make a fuss** Theater machen **[48]**

fussy *adj* pingelig ▷ *She is very fussy about her food.* Sie ist mit dem Essen sehr pingelig.

future *n* ❶ Zukunft *f*; **in future** in Zukunft; **What are your plans for the future?** Was für Zukunftspläne haben Sie? ❷ *(in grammar)* Futur *nt* ▷ *Put this sentence into the future.* Setzt diesen Satz ins Futur.

g

gain *vb* **to gain weight** zunehmen **[52]**; **to gain speed** schneller werden **[91]**

gallery *n* Galerie *f* ▷ *an art gallery* eine Kunstgalerie

gamble *vb* spielen **[38]**

gambling *n* Glücksspiel *nt (pl* Glücksspiele); **He likes gambling.** Er spielt gern.

game *n* Spiel *nt (pl* Spiele) ▷ *The children were playing a game.* Die Kinder spielten ein Spiel. ▷ *a game of football* ein Fußballspiel ▷ *a game of cards* ein Kartenspiel

gamer *n (on computer)* Gamer *m (pl* Gamer), Gamerin *f*

gang *n* Gang *f (pl* Gangs)

gangster *n* Gangster *m (pl* Gangster)

gap *n* ❶ Lücke *f* ▷ *There's a gap in the hedge.* In der Hecke ist eine Lücke. ❷ Pause *f* ▷ *a gap of four years* eine Pause von vier Jahren

garage *n* ❶ *(for parking cars)* Garage *f* ❷ *(for repairs)* Werkstatt *f (pl* Werkstätten)

garbage *n* Müll *m* ▷ *the garbage can* die Mülltonne; **That's garbage!** Das ist Blödsinn!
garden *n* Garten *m* (*pl* Gärten)
garden centre *n* Gartencenter *nt* (*pl* Gartencenter)
gardener *n* Gärtner *m* (*pl* Gärtner), Gärtnerin *f* ▷ *He's a gardener.* Er ist Gärtner.
gardening *n* Gartenarbeit *f* ▷ *Margaret loves gardening.* Margaret liebt Gartenarbeit.
garlic *n* Knoblauch *m*
garment *n* Kleidungsstück *nt* (*pl* Kleidungsstücke)
gas *n* ❶ Gas *nt* (*pl* Gase); **a gas cooker** ein Gasherd *m*; **a gas cylinder** eine Gasflasche; **a gas fire** ein Gasofen *m*; **a gas leak** eine undichte Stelle in der Gasleitung ❷ *(US)* Benzin *nt*; **a gas station** eine Tankstelle
gasoline *n (US)* Benzin *nt*
gate *n* ❶ *(of garden)* Tor *nt* (*pl* Tore) ❷ *(of field)* Gatter *nt* (*pl* Gatter) ❸ *(at airport)* Flugsteig *m* (*pl* Flugsteige)
gather *vb (assemble)* sich versammeln [**34**] (*perf* haben sich versammelt) ▷ *People gathered in front of the church.* Menschen versammelten sich vor der Kirche.; **to gather speed** schneller werden [**91**]
gave *vb see* **give**
gay *adj (homosexual)* schwul
GCSE *n (= General Certificate of Secondary Education)* mittlere Reife *f*
gear *n* ❶ *(in car)* Gang *m* (*pl* Gänge) ▷ *in first gear* im ersten Gang; **to change gear** schalten [**2**] ❷ Ausrüstung *f* ▷ *camping gear* die Campingausrüstung; **your sports gear** *(clothes)* dein Sportzeug *nt*
gear lever *n* Schalthebel *m* (*pl* Schalthebel)
gearshift *n (US)* Schaltknüppel *m* (*pl* Schaltknüppel)
geese *npl see* **goose**
gel *n* Gel *nt* (*pl* Gele)

> Note that in German the 'g' in **Gel** is pronounced like the 'g' in girl.

▷ *hair gel* das Haargel
Gemini *nsg* Zwillinge *mpl* ▷ *I'm Gemini.* Ich bin Zwilling.
gender *n* Geschlecht *nt* (*pl* Geschlechter)
general *n* General *m* (*pl* Generäle) ▶ *adj* allgemein; **in general** im Allgemeinen
general knowledge *n* Allgemeinbildung *f*
generally *adv* normalerweise ▷ *I generally go shopping on Saturday.* Ich gehe normalerweise samstags einkaufen.
generation *n* Generation *f* ▷ *the younger generation* die jüngere Generation
generous *adj* großzügig ▷ *That's very generous of you.* Das ist sehr großzügig von Ihnen.
genetically *adv* genetisch; **genetically modified** genmanipuliert
Geneva *n* Genf *nt*; **to Geneva** nach Genf; **Lake Geneva** der Genfer See
genius *n* Genie *nt* (*pl* Genies) ▷ *She's a genius!* Sie ist ein Genie!
gentle *adj* sanft
gentleman *n* Gentleman *m* (*pl* Gentlemen); **Good morning, gentlemen.** Guten Morgen, meine Herren.
gently *adv* sanft
gents *nsg* Herrentoilette *f*; **'gents'** *(on sign)* 'Herren'
genuine *adj* ❶ *(real)* echt ▷ *These are genuine diamonds.* Das sind echte Diamanten. ❷ *(sincere)* geradlinig ▷ *She's a very genuine person.* Sie ist ein sehr geradliniger Mensch.
geography *n* Geografie *f*
gerbil *n* Wüstenrennmaus *f* (*pl* Wüstenrennmäuse)
germ *n* Bazille *f*
German *adj* deutsch ▷ *He is German.* Er ist Deutscher. ▷ *She is German.* Sie ist

Deutsche.; **German shepherd** der Schäferhund
▶ *n* ❶ *(person)* Deutsche *m (gen* Deutschen, *pl* Deutschen), Deutsche *f (gen* Deutschen) ▷ *a German (man)* ein Deutscher; **the Germans** die Deutschen ❷ *(language)* Deutsch *nt (gen* Deutschen) ▷ *Do you speak German?* Sprechen sie Deutsch?

Germany *n* Deutschland *nt*; **from Germany** aus Deutschland; **in Germany** in Deutschland; **to Germany** nach Deutschland

get *vb* ❶ *(receive)* bekommen [**40**] *(imperf* bekam, *perf* hat bekommen) ▷ *I got lots of presents.* Ich habe viele Geschenke bekommen. ▷ *He got first prize.* Er hat den ersten Preis bekommen. ▷ *Jackie got good exam results.* Jackie hat gute Noten bekommen.; **have got** haben ▷ *How many have you got?* Wie viele hast du? ❷ *(fetch)* holen [**38**] ▷ *Get help!* Hol Hilfe! ❸ *(catch)* fassen [**31**] ▷ *They've got the thief.* Sie haben den Dieb gefasst. ❹ *(train, bus)* nehmen [**52**] *(pres* nimmt, *imperf* nahm, *perf* hat genommen) ▷ *I'm getting the bus into town.* Ich nehme den Bus in die Stadt. ❺ *(understand)* verstehen [**72**] *(imperf* verstand, *perf* hat verstanden) ▷ *I don't get the joke.* Ich verstehe den Witz nicht. ❻ *(go)* kommen [**40**] *(imperf* kam, *perf* ist gekommen) ▷ *How do you get to the castle?* Wie kommt man zur Burg? ❼ *(become)* werden [**91**] *(pres* wird, *imperf* wurde, *perf* ist geworden) ▷ *to get old* alt werden; **to get something done** etwas machen lassen [**42**]; **to get something for somebody** jemandem etwas holen [**38**]; **to have got to do something** etwas tun müssen [**51**]; **to get away** entkommen [**40**]; **You'll never get away with it.** Das wird man dir niemals durchgehen lassen.; **to get back (1)** zurückkommen [**40**] ▷ *What time did you get back?* Wann seid ihr zurückgekommen? **(2)** zurückbekommen [**40**] ▷ *He got his money back.* Er hat sein Geld zurückbekommen.; **to get down** herunterkommen [**40**]; **to get in** nach Hause kommen [**40**]; **to get into** einsteigen [**74**] in; **to get off (1)** *(vehicle)* aussteigen [**74**] aus ▷ *Isobel got off the train.* Isobel stieg aus dem Zug aus. **(2)** *(bike)* absteigen [**74**] von ▷ *He got off his bike.* Er stieg vom Fahrrad ab.; **to get on (1)** *(vehicle)* einsteigen [**74**] in ▷ *Phyllis got on the bus.* Phyllis stieg in den Bus ein. **(2)** *(bike)* steigen [**74**] auf ▷ *Carol got on her bike.* Carol stieg auf ihr Fahrrad.; **to get on with somebody** sich mit jemandem verstehen [**72**]; **to get out** aussteigen [**74**] aus; **Get out!** Raus!; **to get something out** etwas hervorholen [**4**]; **to get over something (1)** sich von etwas erholen [**19**] ▷ *It took her a long time to get over the illness.* Sie brauchte lange Zeit, um sich von der Krankheit zu erholen. **(2)** etwas überwinden [**86**] ▷ *He managed to get over the problem.* Er konnte das Problem überwinden.; **to get round to something** zu etwas kommen [**40**]; **to get together** sich treffen [**78**]; **to get up** aufstehen [**72**]

ghost *n* Gespenst *nt (pl* Gespenster)

giant *adj* riesig ▷ *They ate a giant meal.* Sie haben ein riesiges Essen vertilgt.
▶ *n* Riese *m (gen* Riesen, *pl* Riesen), Riesin *f*

gift *n* ❶ *(present)* Geschenk *nt (pl* Geschenke) ❷ *(talent)* Begabung *f*; **to have a gift for something** für etwas begabt sein [**65**]

> Be careful not to translate **gift** by the German word **Gift**.

giggle *vb* kichern [**88**]

gin *n* Gin *m (pl* Gins *or* Gin)

> When ordering more than one gin use the plural form **Gin**.

▷ *Three gins, please.* Drei Gin bitte.; **a gin and tonic** ein Gin Tonic

ginger *n* Ingwer *m* ▷ *Add a teaspoon of ginger.* Fügen Sie einen Teelöffel Ingwer zu.
▶ *adj* rot ▷ *David has ginger hair.* David hat rote Haare.

gipsy *n* Zigeuner *m* (*pl* Zigeuner), Zigeunerin *f*

giraffe *n* Giraffe *f*

girl *n* Mädchen *nt* (*pl* Mädchen) ▷ *They've got a girl and two boys.* Sie haben ein Mädchen und zwei Jungen. ▷ *a five-year-old girl* ein fünfjähriges Mädchen; **an English girl** eine junge Engländerin

girlfriend *n* Freundin *f* ▷ *Damon's girlfriend is called Justine.* Damons Freundin heißt Justine. ▷ *She often went out with her girlfriends.* Sie ging oft mit ihren Freundinnen aus.

give *vb* geben **[28]** (*pres* gibt, *imperf* gab, *perf* hat gegeben); **to give something to somebody** jemandem etwas geben **[28]**; **to give something back to somebody** jemandem etwas zurückgeben **[28]**; **to give in** nachgeben **[28]**; **to give out** austeilen **[4]**; **to give up** aufgeben **[28]**; **to give up doing something** etwas aufgeben **[28]**; **to give oneself up** sich ergeben **[28]**; **to give way** *(in traffic)* die Vorfahrt achten **[2]**

glad *adj* froh ▷ *She's glad she's done it.* Sie ist froh, dass sie es getan hat.

glamorous *adj (person)* glamourös

glass *n* Glas *nt* (*gen* Glases, *pl* Gläser) ▷ *a glass of milk* ein Glas Milch

glasses *npl* Brille *f* ▷ *Veronika wears glasses.* Veronika trägt eine Brille.

gleam *vb* funkeln **[88]** ▷ *Her eyes gleamed with excitement.* Ihre Augen funkelten vor Aufregung.

glider *n* Segelflugzeug *nt* (*pl* Segelflugzeuge)

glimpse *n* **to catch a glimpse of somebody** jemanden kurz zu sehen bekommen **[40]**

glitter *vb* glitzern **[88]**

global *adj* weltweit; **on a global scale** weltweit

global warming *n* Erwärmung der Erdatmosphäre *f*

globe *n* Globus *m* (*gen* Globus, *pl* Globen)

gloomy *adj* ❶ düster ▷ *a small gloomy flat* eine kleine, düstere Wohnung ❷ niedergeschlagen ▷ *She's been feeling very gloomy recently.* Sie fühlt sich in letzter Zeit sehr niedergeschlagen.

glorious *adj* herrlich

glove *n* Handschuh *m* (*pl* Handschuhe)

glow *vb* leuchten **[2]** ▷ *Her watch glows in the dark.* Ihre Uhr leuchtet im Dunkeln.

glue *n* Klebstoff *m* (*pl* Klebstoffe)
▶ *vb* kleben **[38]** ▷ *to glue something together* etwas zusammenkleben

GM *abbr* (= *genetically modified*) genmanipuliert ▷ *GM food* genmanipulierte Lebensmittel *pl*

go *n* **to have a go at doing something** etwas versuchen **[84]** ▷ *He had a go at making a cake.* Er hat versucht, einen Kuchen zu backen.; **Whose go is it?** Wer ist dran?
▶ *vb* ❶ gehen **[29]** (*imperf* ging, *perf* ist gegangen) ▷ *I'm going to the cinema tonight.* Ich gehe heute Abend ins Kino. ▷ *I'm going now.* Ich gehe jetzt. ❷ *(leave)* weggehen **[29]** ▷ *Where's Thomas? — He's gone.* Wo ist Thomas? — Er ist weggegangen. ❸ *(vehicle)* fahren **[21]** (*pres* fährt, *imperf* fuhr, *perf* ist gefahren) ▷ *My car won't go.* Mein Auto fährt nicht.; **to go home** nach Hause gehen **[29]** ▷ *I go home at about four o'clock.* Ich gehe um etwa vier Uhr nach Hause.; **to go for a walk** einen Spaziergang machen **[48]** ▷ *Shall we go for a walk?* Sollen wir einen Spaziergang machen?; **How did it go?** Wie ist es gelaufen?; **I'm going to do it tomorrow.** Ich werde es morgen tun.; **It's going to be difficult.** Es wird schwierig werden.

go after *vb (follow)* nachgehen [**29**] (*imperf* ging nach, *perf* ist nachgegangen) ▷ *I went after him.* Ich ging ihm nach.; **Quick, go after them!** Schnell, ihnen nach!

go ahead *vb* vorangehen [**29**] (*imperf* ging voran, *perf* ist vorangegangen); **to go ahead with something** etwas durchführen [**4**]

go around *vb* herumgehen [**29**] (*imperf* ging herum, *perf* ist herumgegangen) ▷ *There's a rumour going around that they're getting married.* Es geht das Gerücht herum, sie würden heiraten.

go away *vb* weggehen [**29**] (*imperf* ging weg, *perf* ist weggegangen) ▷ *Go away!* Geh weg!

go back *vb* zurückgehen [**29**] (*imperf* ging zurück, *perf* ist zurückgegangen) ▷ *We went back to the same place.* Wir sind an denselben Ort zurückgegangen.; **Is he still here? — No, he's gone back home.** Ist er noch hier? — Nein, er ist nach Hause gegangen.

go by *vb* vorbeigehen [**29**] (*imperf* ging vorbei, *perf* ist vorbeigegangen) ▷ *Two policemen went by.* Zwei Polizisten gingen vorbei.

go down *vb* ❶ *(person)* hinuntergehen [**29**] (*imperf* ging hinunter, *perf* ist hinuntergegangen) ▷ *to go down the stairs* die Treppe hinuntergehen ❷ *(decrease)* sinken [**67**] (*imperf* sank, *perf* ist gesunken) ▷ *The price of computers has gone down.* Die Preise für Computer sind gesunken. ❸ *(deflate)* Luft verlieren [**85**] (*imperf* verlor Luft, *perf* hat Luft verloren) ▷ *My airbed kept going down.* Meine Luftmatratze verlor dauernd Luft.; **My brother's gone down with flu.** Mein Bruder hat die Grippe bekommen.

go for *vb (attack)* angreifen (*imperf* griff an, *perf* hat angegriffen) ▷ *The dog went for me.* Der Hund griff mich an.; **Go for it!** *(go on!)* Na los!

go in *vb* hineingehen [**29**] (*imperf* ging hinein, *perf* ist hineingegangen) ▷ *He knocked and went in.* Er klopfte und ging hinein.

go off *vb* ❶ losgehen [**29**] (*imperf* ging los, *perf* ist losgegangen) ▷ *The bomb went off.* Die Bombe ging los. ▷ *The fire alarm went off.* Der Feueralarm ging los. ❷ klingeln [**34**] ▷ *My alarm clock goes off at seven every morning.* Mein Wecker klingelt jeden Morgen um sieben Uhr. ❸ schlecht werden [**91**] (*pres* wird schlecht, *imperf* wurde schlecht, *perf* ist schlecht geworden); **The milk's gone off.** Die Milch ist sauer geworden. ❹ *(go away)* weggehen [**29**] ▷ *He went off in a huff.* Er ist beleidigt weggegangen.

go on *vb* ❶ *(happen)* los sein [**65**] (*pres* ist los, *imperf* war los, *perf* ist los gewesen) ▷ *What's going on?* Was ist los? ❷ *(carry on)* dauern [**88**] ▷ *The concert went on until eleven o'clock at night.* Das Konzert hat bis nach elf Uhr nachts gedauert.; **to go on doing something** etwas weiter tun [**81**] ▷ *He went on reading.* Er las weiter.; **to go on at somebody** an jemandem herumkritisieren [**76**] ▷ *My parents always go on at me.* Meine Eltern kritisieren dauernd an mir herum.; **Go on!** Na los! ▷ *Go on, tell us!* Na los, sag schon!

go out *vb* ausgehen [**29**] (*imperf* ging aus, *perf* ist ausgegangen) ▷ *Are you going out tonight?* Gehst du heute Abend aus? ▷ *Suddenly the lights went out.* Plötzlich ging das Licht aus.; **to go out with somebody** mit jemandem ausgehen [**29**] ▷ *Are you going out with him?* Gehst du mit ihm aus?

go past *vb* **to go past something** an etwas vorbeigehen [**29**] ▷ *He went past the shop.* Er ging an dem Geschäft vorbei.

go round *vb* **to go round a corner** um die Ecke biegen; **to go round to somebody's house** jemanden besuchen [**7**]; **to go round a museum**

sich ein Museum ansehen [**64**]; **to go round the shops** einen Einkaufsbummel machen [**48**]

go through *vb (by car)* fahren [**21**] durch (*pres* fährt, *imperf* fuhr, *perf* ist gefahren); **We went through London to get to Birmingham.** Wir sind über London nach Birmingham gefahren.

go up *vb* ❶ *(person)* hinaufgehen [**29**] (*imperf* ging hinauf, *perf* ist hinaufgegangen) ▷ *to go up the stairs* die Treppe hinaufgehen ❷ *(increase)* steigen [**74**] (*imperf* stieg, *perf* ist gestiegen) ▷ *The price has gone up.* Der Preis ist gestiegen.; **to go up in flames** in Flammen aufgehen [**29**] ▷ *The factory went up in flames.* Die Fabrik ist in Flammen aufgegangen.

go with *vb* passen [**31**] zu ▷ *Does this blouse go with that skirt?* Passt diese Bluse zu dem Rock?

goal *n* ❶ *(sport)* Tor *nt* (*pl* Tore) ▷ *to score a goal* ein Tor schießen ❷ *(aim)* Ziel *nt* (*pl* Ziele) ▷ *His goal is to become the world champion.* Sein Ziel ist es, Weltmeister zu werden.

goalkeeper *n* Torwart *m* (*pl* Torwarte)

goat *n* Ziege *f*; **goat's cheese** der Ziegenkäse

god *n* Gott *m* (*pl* Götter) ▷ *I believe in God.* Ich glaube an Gott.

goddaughter *n* Patentochter *f* (*pl* Patentöchter)

godfather *n* Patenonkel *m* (*pl* Patenonkel) ▷ *my godfather* mein Patenonkel

godmother *n* Patentante *f* ▷ *my godmother* meine Patentante

godson *n* Patensohn *m* (*pl* Patensöhne)

goes *vb see* **go**

goggles *npl* Schutzbrille *f*

gold *n* Gold *nt* ▷ *They found some gold.* Sie haben Gold gefunden.; **a gold necklace** eine goldene Halskette

goldfish *n* Goldfisch *m* (*pl* Goldfische) ▷ *I've got five goldfish.* Ich habe fünf Goldfische.

golf *n* Golf *nt* ▷ *My dad plays golf.* Mein Papa spielt Golf.; **a golf club (1)** *(stick)* ein Golfschläger *m* **(2)** *(place)* ein Golfklub *m*

golf course *n* Golfplatz *m* (*gen* Golfplatzes, *pl* Golfplätze)

gone *vb see* **go**

good *adj* ❶ gut ▷ *It's a very good film.* Das ist ein sehr guter Film.; **Vegetables are good for you.** Gemüse ist gesund.; **to be good at something** gut in etwas sein [**65**] ❷ *(kind)* freundlich ▷ *They were very good to me.* Sie waren sehr freundlich zu mir. ▷ *That's very good of you.* Das ist sehr freundlich von Ihnen. ❸ *(not naughty)* artig ▷ *Be good!* Sei artig!; **for good** für immer; **Good morning!** Guten Morgen!; **Good afternoon!** Guten Tag!; **Good evening!** Guten Abend!; **Good night!** Gute Nacht!; **It's no good complaining.** Es hat keinen Wert, sich zu beklagen.

goodbye *excl* auf Wiedersehen

Good Friday *n* Karfreitag *m* (*pl* Karfreitage)

good-looking *adj* gut aussehend; **Andrew's very good-looking.** Andrew sieht sehr gut aus.

goods *npl (in shop)* Ware *f*; **a goods train** ein Güterzug *m*

google *vb* googeln [**88**]

goose *n* Gans *f* (*pl* Gänse)

gorgeous *adj* ❶ hinreißend ▷ *She's gorgeous!* Sie sieht hinreißend aus! ❷ herrlich ▷ *The weather was gorgeous.* Das Wetter war herrlich.

gorilla *n* Gorilla *m* (*pl* Gorillas)

gossip *n* ❶ *(rumours)* Tratsch *m* ▷ *Tell me the gossip!* Erzähl mir den neuesten Tratsch! ❷ *(woman)* Klatschtante *f* ▷ *She's such a gossip!* Sie ist eine furchtbare Klatschtante! ❸ *(man)* Klatschweib *nt* (*pl* Klatschweiber) ▷ *What a gossip!* So ein Klatschweib! ▸ *vb* ❶ *(chat)* schwatzen [**48**] ▷ *They were always gossiping.* Sie haben dauernd geschwatzt. ❷ *(about somebody)* tratschen [**48**] ▷ *They gossiped about her.* Sie haben über sie getratscht.

got *vb see* **get**

gotten *vb see* **get**

government *n* Regierung *f*

GP *n* **My sister is a GP in Glasgow.** Meine Schwester ist praktische Ärztin in Glasgow.

GPS *n (= global positioning system)* GPS *nt (pl* GPS)

grab *vb* packen [**38**] ▷ *She grabbed her umbrella and ran out of the door.* Sie packte ihren Schirm und lief zur Tür hinaus.

graceful *adj* anmutig

grade *n* ❶ *(mark)* Note *f* ▷ *He got good grades.* Er hat gute Noten bekommen. ❷ *(class)* Klasse *f* ▷ *Which grade are you in?* In welcher Klasse bist du?

grade school *n (US)* Grundschule *f*

gradual *adj* allmählich

gradually *adv* allmählich ▷ *We gradually got used to it.* Wir haben uns allmählich daran gewöhnt.

graffiti *npl* Graffiti *pl*

grain *n* Korn *nt (pl* Körner)

gram *n* Gramm *nt (pl* Gramme *or* Gramm)

> When specifying a quantity of something use the plural form **Gramm**.

▷ *five hundred grams of cheese* fünfhundert Gramm Käse

grammar *n* Grammatik *f*

grammar school *n* Gymnasium *nt (pl* Gymnasien)

> **Gymnasium** education begins after year 4 of the **Grundschule** and lasts until year 13. (However, pupils can leave after year 10.) It mainly prepares children for university education.

grammatical *adj* grammatisch

gramme *n* Gramm *nt (pl* Gramme *or* Gramm)

> When specifying a quantity of something use the plural form **Gramm**.

▷ *five hundred grammes of cheese* fünfhundert Gramm Käse

grand *adj* prachtvoll ▷ *She lives in a very grand house.* Sie wohnt in einem prachtvollen Haus.

grandchild *n* Enkel *m (pl* Enkel)

granddad *n* Opa *m (pl* Opas) ▷ *my granddad* mein Opa

granddaughter *n* Enkelin *f*

grandfather *n* Großvater *m (pl* Großväter) ▷ *my grandfather* mein Großvater

grandma *n* Oma *f (pl* Omas) ▷ *my grandma* meine Oma

grandmother *n* Großmutter *f (pl* Großmütter) ▷ *my grandmother* meine Großmutter

grandpa *n* Opa *m (pl* Opas) ▷ *my grandpa* mein Opa

grandparents *npl* Großeltern *pl* ▷ *my grandparents* meine Großeltern

grandson *n* Enkel *m (pl* Enkel)

granny *n* Oma *f (pl* Omas) ▷ *my granny* meine Oma

grape *n* Traube *f*

grapefruit *n* Grapefruit *f (pl* Grapefruits)

graph *n* grafische Darstellung *f*

graphics *npl* Grafik *fsg*

grass *n* Gras *nt (gen* Grases) ▷ *The grass is long.* Das Gras ist hoch.; **to cut the grass** den Rasen mähen [**48**]

grasshopper *n* Heuschrecke *f*

grate *vb* reiben *(imperf* rieb, *perf* hat gerieben) ▷ *to grate some cheese* Käse reiben

grateful *adj* dankbar

grave *n* Grab *nt (pl* Gräber)

gravel *n* Kies *m*

graveyard *n* Friedhof *m (pl* Friedhöfe)

gravy *n* Bratensoße *f*

grease *n* Fett *nt (pl* Fette)

greasy *adj* fettig ▷ *He has greasy hair.* Er hat fettige Haare.; **The food was very greasy.** Das Essen war sehr fett.

great *adj* ❶ toll ▷ *That's great!* Das ist toll! ❷ *(big)* groß ▷ *a great mansion* eine große Villa
Great Britain *n* Großbritannien *nt*; **from Great Britain** aus Großbritannien; **in Great Britain** in Großbritannien; **to Great Britain** nach Großbritannien
great-grandfather *n* Urgroßvater *m* (*pl* Urgroßväter)
great-grandmother *n* Urgroßmutter *f* (*pl* Urgroßmütter)
Greece *n* Griechenland *nt*; **from Greece** aus Griechenland; **to Greece** nach Griechenland
greedy *adj* gierig ▷ *Don't be so greedy!* Sei nicht so gierig!
Greek *adj* griechisch ▷ *I love Greek food.* Ich mag griechisches Essen sehr gern. ▷ *Dionysis is Greek.* Dionysis ist Grieche. ▷ *She's Greek.* Sie ist Griechin.
▶ *n* ❶ *(person)* Grieche *m* (*gen* Griechen, *pl* Griechen), Griechin *f* ❷ *(language)* Griechisch *nt* (*gen* Griechischen)
green *adj* grün ▷ *a green car* ein grünes Auto ▷ *a green salad* ein grüner Salat; **the Green Party** die Grünen *mpl*
▶ *n* Grün *nt* ▷ *a dark green* ein dunkles Grün; **greens** *(vegetables)* das Grüngemüse *sg*; **the Greens** *(party)* die Grünen *mpl*
greenhouse *n* Treibhaus *nt* (*gen* Treibhauses, *pl* Treibhäuser); **the greenhouse effect** der Treibhauseffekt
Greenland *n* Grönland *nt*
greetings card *n* Grußkarte *f*
grew *vb see* **grow**
grey *adj* grau ▷ *She's got grey hair.* Sie hat graue Haare. ▷ *He's going grey.* Er wird grau.
grey-haired *adj* grauhaarig
grid *n* ❶ *(on map)* Gitter *nt* (*pl* Gitter) ❷ *(of electricity)* Netz *nt* (*gen* Netzes, *pl* Netze)
grief *n* Kummer *m*
grill *n (of cooker)* Grill *m* (*pl* Grills); **a mixed grill** ein Grillteller *m*
▶ *vb* grillen **[48]**
grin *vb* grinsen **[38]** ▷ *Dave grinned at me.* Dave grinste mich an.
▶ *n* Grinsen *nt*
grip *vb* packen **[38]** ▷ *He gripped my arm tightly.* Er packte mich fest am Arm.
grit *n* Splitt *m* (*pl* Splitte)
groan *vb* stöhnen **[38]** ▷ *He groaned with pain.* Er stöhnte vor Schmerzen.
▶ *n (of pain)* Stöhnen *nt*
grocer *n* Lebensmittelhändler *m* (*pl* Lebensmittelhändler), Lebensmittelhändlerin *f* ▷ *He's a grocer.* Er ist Lebensmittelhändler.
groceries *npl* Einkäufe *mpl*
grocery store *n (US)* Lebensmittelgeschäft *nt* (*pl* Lebensmittelgeschäfte)
groom *n (bridegroom)* Bräutigam *m* (*pl* Bräutigame) ▷ *the groom and his best man* der Bräutigam und sein Trauzeuge
gross *adj (revolting)* abscheulich ▷ *It was really gross!* Es war wirklich abscheulich!
ground *n* ❶ *(earth)* Boden *m* (*pl* Böden) ▷ *The ground's wet.* Der Boden ist nass. ❷ *(for sport)* Platz *m* (*gen* Platzes, *pl* Plätze) ▷ *a football ground* ein Fußballplatz ❸ *(reason)* Grund *m* (*pl* Gründe) ▷ *We've got grounds for complaint.* Wir haben Grund zur Klage.; **on the ground** auf dem Boden
group *n* Gruppe *f*
grow *vb* ❶ *(plant, person, animal)* wachsen **[87]** (*pres* wächst, *imperf* wuchs, *perf* ist gewachsen) ▷ *Grass grows quickly.* Gras wächst schnell. ▷ *Haven't you grown!* Bist du aber gewachsen!; **to grow a beard** sich einen Bart wachsen lassen **[42]**; **He's grown out of his jacket.** Er ist aus der Jacke herausgewachsen. ❷ *(increase)* zunehmen **[52]** (*pres* nimmt zu, *imperf* nahm zu, *perf* hat zugenommen) ▷ *The number of unemployed has grown.* Die Zahl der Arbeitslosen hat zugenommen. ❸ *(cultivate)* anbauen **[4]** (*perf* hat angebaut) ▷ *My Dad grows*

potatoes. Mein Papa baut Kartoffeln an.; **to grow up** erwachsen werden [**91**]

growl *vb* knurren [**38**]

grown *vb see* **grow**

growth *n* Wachstum *nt* ▷ *economic growth* das Wirtschaftswachstum

grudge *n* **to bear a grudge against somebody** einen Groll gegen jemanden haben [**32**]

gruesome *adj* furchtbar

guarantee *n* Garantie *f* ▷ *a five-year guarantee* eine Garantie von fünf Jahren ▶ *vb* garantieren [**76**] (*perf* hat garantiert) ▷ *I can't guarantee he'll come.* Ich kann nicht garantieren, dass er kommt.

guard *vb* bewachen [**7**] (*perf* hat bewacht) ▷ *They guarded the palace.* Sie bewachten den Palast.; **to guard against something** gegen etwas Vorsichtsmaßnahmen ergreifen ▶ *n (of train)* Zugbegleiter *m (pl* Zugbegleiter), Zugbegleiterin *f*; **a security guard** ein Wachmann *m*; **a guard dog** ein Wachhund *m*

guess *vb* raten (*pres* rät, *imperf* riet, *perf* hat geraten) ▷ *Can you guess what it is?* Rate mal, was das ist. ▷ *to guess wrong* falsch raten ▶ *n* Vermutung *f* ▷ *It's just a guess.* Es ist nur eine Vermutung.; **Have a guess!** Rate mal!

guest *n* Gast *m (pl* Gäste) **der Gast** is also used for women. ▷ *She is our guest.* Sie ist unser Gast. ▷ *We have guests staying with us.* Wir haben Gäste.

guesthouse *n* Pension *f* ▷ *We stayed in a guesthouse.* Wir haben in einer Pension gewohnt.

guide *n* ❶ *(book)* Führer *m (pl* Führer) ▷ *We bought a guide to Cologne.* Wir haben einen Führer von Köln gekauft. ❷ *(person)* Führer *m (pl* Führer), Führerin *f* ▷ *The guide showed us round the castle.* Unser Führer hat uns die Burg gezeigt. ❸ *(Girl Guide)* Pfadfinderin *f*; **the Guides** die Pfadfinderinnen

guidebook *n* Führer *m (pl* Führer)

guide dog *n* Blindenhund *m (pl* Blindenhunde)

guilty *adj* schuldig ▷ *to feel guilty* sich schuldig fühlen ▷ *She was found guilty.* Sie wurde schuldig gesprochen.

guinea pig *n* Meerschweinchen *nt (pl* Meerschweinchen)

guitar *n* Gitarre *f* ▷ *I play the guitar.* Ich spiele Gitarre.

gum *n (chewing gum)* Kaugummi *m (pl* Kaugummis); **gums** *(in mouth)* das Zahnfleisch *sg*

gun *n* ❶ *(small)* Pistole *f* ❷ *(rifle)* Gewehr *nt (pl* Gewehre)

gunpoint *n* **at gunpoint** mit Waffengewalt

guts *npl (informal: courage)* Mumm *m* ▷ *He's certainly got guts.* Er hat wirklich Mumm.; **I hate his guts.** Ich kann ihn nicht ausstehen.

guy *n* Typ *m (pl* Typen) ▷ *Who's that guy?* Wer ist der Typ?; **He's a nice guy.** Er ist ein netter Kerl.

gym *n* Turnhalle *f*; **gym classes** die Turnstunden

gymnast *n* Turner *m (pl* Turner), Turnerin *f* ▷ *She's a gymnast.* Sie ist Turnerin.

gymnastics *n* Turnen *nt*; **to do gymnastics** turnen [**38**]

gypsy *n* Zigeuner *m (pl* Zigeuner), Zigeunerin *f*

h

habit *n* Angewohnheit *f* ▷ *a bad habit* eine schlechte Angewohnheit
had *vb see* **have**
hadn't = **had not**
hail *n* Hagel *m*
▶ *vb* hageln [**88**] ▷ *It's hailing.* Es hagelt.
hair *n* Haare *ntpl* ▷ *She's got long hair.* Sie hat lange Haare. ▷ *He's got black hair.* Er hat schwarze Haare. ▷ *He's losing his hair.* Ihm gehen die Haare aus.; **to brush one's hair** sich die Haare bürsten [**2**]; **to wash one's hair** sich die Haare waschen [**89**]; **to have one's hair cut** sich die Haare schneiden lassen [**42**]; **a hair** ein Haar *nt*
hairbrush *n* Haarbürste *f*
hair clip *n* Haarspange *f*
haircut *n* Haarschnitt *m* (*pl* Haarschnitte); **to have a haircut** sich die Haare schneiden lassen [**42**]
hairdresser *n* Friseur *m* (*pl* Friseure), Friseuse *f* ▷ *He's a hairdresser.* Er ist Friseur.
hairdresser's *n* Friseur *m* (*pl* Friseure) ▷ *at the hairdresser's* beim Friseur
hair dryer *n* Haartrockner *m* (*pl* Haartrockner)
hair gel *n* Haargel *nt* (*pl* Haargele)
In German the 'g' in **Haargel** is pronounced like the 'g' in girl.
hairgrip *n* Haarklemme *f*
hair spray *n* Haarspray *m* (*pl* Haarsprays)
hairstyle *n* Frisur *f*
half *n* ❶ Hälfte *f* ▷ *half of the cake* die Hälfte des Kuchens ❷ *(ticket)* Kinderfahrkarte *f* ▷ *A half to York, please.* Ein Kinderfahrkarte nach York bitte.; **two and a half** zweieinhalb; **half an hour** eine halbe Stunde; **half past ten** halb elf; **half a kilo** ein halbes Kilo; **to cut something in half** etwas in zwei Teile schneiden [**60**]
▶ *adj, adv* ❶ halb ▷ *a half chicken* ein halbes Hähnchen ❷ fast ▷ *He was half asleep.* Er schlief fast.
half-hour *n* halbe Stunde *f*
half-price *adj, adv* zum halben Preis
half-time *n* Halbzeit *f*
halfway *adv* ❶ auf halber Strecke ▷ *halfway between Oxford and London* auf halber Strecke zwischen Oxford und London ❷ in der Mitte ▷ *halfway through the chapter* in der Mitte des Kapitels
hall *n* ❶ *(in house)* Flur *m* (*pl* Flure) ❷ Saal *m* (*pl* Säle) ▷ *the village hall* der Gemeindesaal; **hall of residence** das Wohnheim
hallway *n* Flur *m* (*pl* Flure)
ham *n* Schinken *m* (*pl* Schinken) ▷ *a ham sandwich* ein Schinkensandwich *nt*
hamburger *n* Hamburger *m* (*pl* Hamburger)
hammer *n* Hammer *m* (*pl* Hämmer)
hamster *n* Hamster *m* (*pl* Hamster)
hand *n* ❶ *(of person)* Hand *f* (*pl* Hände); **to give somebody a hand** jemandem helfen [**37**]; **on the one hand ..., on the other hand ...** einerseits ...,

anderseits ... ❷ *(of clock)* Zeiger *m* (*pl* Zeiger)
▸ *vb* reichen [**48**] ▷ *He handed me the book.* Er reichte mir das Buch.; **to hand something in** etwas abgeben [**28**]; **to hand something out** etwas austeilen [**4**]; **to hand something over** etwas übergeben [**28**]

handbag *n* Handtasche *f*

handcuffs *npl* Handschellen *fpl*

handkerchief *n* Taschentuch *nt* (*pl* Taschentücher)

handle *n* ❶ *(of door)* Klinke *f* ❷ *(of cup)* Henkel *m* (*pl* Henkel) ❸ *(of knife)* Griff *m* (*pl* Griffe) ❹ *(of saucepan)* Stiel *m* (*pl* Stiele)
▸ *vb* **He handled it well.** Er hat das gut gemacht.; **Kath handled the travel arrangements.** Kath hat sich um die Reisevorbereitungen gekümmert.; **She's good at handling children.** Sie kann gut mit Kindern umgehen.

handlebars *npl* Lenkstange *fsg*

handmade *adj* handgemacht

handsome *adj* gut aussehend ▷ *a handsome man* ein gut aussehender Mann; **He's very handsome.** Er sieht sehr gut aus.

handwriting *n* Handschrift *f*

handy *adj* ❶ praktisch ▷ *This knife's very handy.* Dieses Messer ist sehr praktisch. ❷ zur Hand ▷ *Have you got a pen handy?* Hast du einen Schreiber zur Hand?

hang *vb* ❶ aufhängen [**35**] (*perf* hat aufgehängt) ▷ *Mike hung the painting on the wall.* Mike hängte das Bild an der Wand auf. ❷ hängen [**35**] ▷ *They hanged the criminal.* Sie hängten den Verbrecher.; **to hang around** rumhängen [**35**]; **to hang on** warten [**2**]; **to hang up (1)** *(clothes)* aufhängen [**35**] ▷ *Hang your jacket up on the hook.* Häng deine Jacke am Haken auf. **(2)** *(phone)* auflegen [**4**] ▷ *I tried to phone him but he hung up on me.* Ich habe versucht, mit ihm zu telefonieren, aber er hat einfach aufgelegt.

hanger *n* *(for clothes)* Bügel *m* (*pl* Bügel)

hangover *n* Kater *m* (*pl* Kater) ▷ *to have a hangover* einen Kater haben

happen *vb* passieren [**76**] (*perf* ist passiert) ▷ *What's happened?* Was ist passiert?; **as it happens** zufälligerweise

happily *adv* ❶ fröhlich ▷ *'Don't worry!' he said happily.* 'Mach dir keine Sorgen!' sagte er fröhlich. ❷ *(fortunately)* zum Glück ▷ *Happily, everything went well.* Zum Glück ging alles gut.

happiness *n* Glück *nt*

happy *adj* glücklich ▷ *Janet looks happy.* Janet sieht glücklich aus.; **I'm very happy with your work.** Ich bin sehr zufrieden mit Ihrer Arbeit.; **Happy birthday!** Herzlichen Glückwunsch zum Geburtstag!

harbour (*US* **harbor**) *n* Hafen *m* (*pl* Häfen)

hard *adj, adv* ❶ hart ▷ *This cheese is very hard.* Dieser Käse ist sehr hart. ▷ *He's worked very hard.* Er hat sehr hart gearbeitet. ❷ schwierig ▷ *This question's too hard for me.* Diese Frage ist für mich zu schwierig.

hard disk *n* *(of computer)* Festplatte *f*

hardly *adv* kaum ▷ *I've hardly got any money.* Ich habe kaum Geld. ▷ *I hardly know you.* Ich kenne Sie kaum.; **hardly ever** fast nie

hard up *adj* pleite

harm *vb* **to harm somebody** jemandem wehtun [**81**]; **to harm something** einer Sache schaden [**54**]

harmful *adj* schädlich ▷ *harmful chemicals* schädliche Chemikalien

harmless *adj* harmlos ▷ *Most spiders are harmless.* Die meisten Spinnen sind harmlos.

harvest *n* Ernte *f*

has *vb* *see* **have**

hasn't = **has not**

hat *n* Hut *m* (*pl* Hüte)

hate *vb* hassen [**31**] ▷ *I hate maths.* Ich hasse Mathe.

hatred *n* Hass *m* (*gen* Hasses)

haunted *adj* verwunschen ▷ *a haunted house* ein verwunschenes Haus

have *vb* ❶ haben [**32**] (*pres* hat, *imperf* hatte, *perf* hat gehabt) ▷ *Have you got a sister?* Hast du eine Schwester? ▷ *He has blue eyes.* Er hat blaue Augen. ▷ *I've got a cold.* Ich habe eine Erkältung.

The perfect tense of most verbs is formed with **haben**.

▷ *They have eaten.* Sie haben gegessen. ▷ *Have you done your homework?* Hast du deine Hausaufgaben gemacht?

Questions like 'hasn't he?' don't exist in German.

▷ *He's done it, hasn't he?* Er hat es getan, nicht wahr?

'have' is not translated when it is used in place of another verb.

▷ *Have you got any money? — No, I haven't.* Hast du Geld? — Nein. ▷ *Does she have any pets? — Yes, she has.* Hat sie Haustiere? — Ja. ▷ *He hasn't done his homework. — Yes, he has.* Er hat seine Hausaufgaben nicht gemacht. — Doch. ❷ sein [**65**] (*pres* ist, *imperf* war, *perf* ist gewesen)

The perfect tense of some verbs is formed with **sein**.

▷ *They have arrived.* Sie sind angekommen. ▷ *Has he gone?* Ist er gegangen?

'have' plus noun is sometimes translated by a German verb.

▷ *He had his breakfast.* Er hat gefrühstückt. ▷ *to have a shower* duschen ▷ *to have a bath* baden; **to have got to do something** etwas tun müssen [**51**] ▷ *She's got to do it.* Sie muss es tun.; **to have a party** eine Party machen [**48**]; **I had my hair cut yesterday.** Ich habe mir gestern die Haare schneiden lassen [**42**].

haven't = **have not**

hay *n* Heu *nt*

hay fever *n* Heuschnupfen *m* ▷ *Do you get hay fever?* Hast du manchmal Heuschnupfen?

hazelnut *n* Haselnuss *f* (*pl* Haselnüsse)

he *pron* er ▷ *He loves dogs.* Er liebt Hunde.

head *n* ❶ (*of person*) Kopf *m* (*pl* Köpfe) ▷ *The wine went to my head.* Der Wein ist mir in den Kopf gestiegen. ❷ (*of private or primary school*) Rektor *m* (*pl* Rektoren), Rektorin *f* ❸ (*of state secondary school*) Direktor *m* (*pl* Direktoren), Direktorin *f* ❹ (*leader*) Oberhaupt *nt* (*pl* Oberhäupter) ▷ *a head of state* ein Staatsoberhaupt; **to have a head for figures** gut mit Zahlen umgehen können [**41**]; **Heads or tails? — Heads.** Kopf oder Zahl? — Kopf.
▶ *vb* **to head for something** auf etwas zugehen [**29**] ▷ *He headed straight for the bar.* Er ging direkt auf die Theke zu.

headache *n* Kopfschmerzen *mpl* ▷ *I've got a headache.* Ich habe Kopfschmerzen.

headlight *n* Scheinwerfer *m* (*pl* Scheinwerfer)

headline *n* Schlagzeile *f*

headmaster *n* ❶ (*of private or primary school*) Rektor *m* (*pl* Rektoren) ❷ (*of state secondary school*) Direktor *m* (*pl* Direktoren)

headmistress *n* ❶ (*of private or primary school*) Rektorin *f* ❷ (*of state secondary school*) Direktorin *f*

headphones *npl* Kopfhörer *m* (*pl* Kopfhörer) ▷ *a set of headphones* ein Kopfhörer

headquarters *npl* Hauptquartier *nt* ▷ *The bank's headquarters are in London.* Das Hauptquartier der Bank ist in London.

headteacher *n* ❶ (*of private or primary school*) Rektor *m* (*pl* Rektoren), Rektorin *f* ❷ (*of state secondary school*) Direktor *m* (*pl* Direktoren), Direktorin *f*

heal *vb* heilen [**38**]

health *n* Gesundheit *f*

healthy *adj* gesund ▷ *She's a healthy person.* Sie ist gesund. ▷ *a healthy diet* eine gesunde Ernährung

heap *n* Haufen *m* (*pl* Haufen) ▷ *a rubbish heap* ein Müllhaufen

hear *vb* hören [**38**] ▷ *He heard the dog bark.* Er hörte den Hund bellen. ▷ *She can't hear very well.* Sie hört nicht gut. ▷ *I heard that she was ill.* Ich habe gehört, dass sie krank war. ▷ *Did you hear the good news?* Hast du die gute Nachricht gehört?; **to hear about something** von etwas hören [**38**]; **to hear from somebody** von jemandem hören [**38**]

heart *n* Herz *nt* (*gen* Herzens, *pl* Herzen); **to learn something by heart** etwas auswendig lernen [**38**]; **the ace of hearts** das Herzass

heart attack *n* Herzinfarkt *m* (*pl* Herzinfarkte)

heartbroken *adj* zutiefst betrübt

heat *n* Hitze *f*
▶ *vb* erhitzen [**7**] (*perf* hat erhitzt) ▷ *Heat gently for five minutes.* Erhitzen Sie es bei schwacher Hitze fünf Minuten lang.; **to heat up (1)** *(cooked food)* aufwärmen [**4**] ▷ *He heated the soup up.* Er hat die Suppe aufgewärmt. **(2)** *(water, oven)* heiß werden [**91**] ▷ *The water is heating up.* Das Wasser wird heiß.

heater *n* Heizofen *m* (*pl* Heizöfen) ▷ *an electric heater* ein elektrischer Heizofen

heather *n* Heidekraut *nt* (*pl* Heidekräuter)

heating *n* Heizung *f*

heaven *n* Himmel *m* (*pl* Himmel)

heavy *adj* ❶ schwer ▷ *This bag's very heavy.* Diese Tasche ist sehr schwer.; **heavy rain** starker Regen ❷ *(busy)* anstrengend ▷ *I've got a very heavy week ahead.* Ich habe eine anstrengende Woche vor mir.; **to be a heavy drinker** viel trinken [**80**]

he'd = **he would**; **he had**

hedge *n* Hecke *f*

hedgehog *n* Igel *m* (*pl* Igel)

heel *n* Absatz *m* (*gen* Absatzes, *pl* Absätze)

height *n* ❶ *(of person)* Größe *f* ❷ *(of object, mountain)* Höhe *f*

held *vb see* **hold**

helicopter *n* Hubschrauber *m* (*pl* Hubschrauber)

hell *n* Hölle *f*; **Hell!** *(informal)* Mist!

he'll = **he will**; **he shall**

hello *excl* hallo

helmet *n* Helm *m* (*pl* Helme)

help *vb* helfen [**37**] (*pres* hilft, *imperf* half, *perf* hat geholfen); **to help somebody** jemandem helfen [**37**]; **Help!** Hilfe!; **Help yourself!** Bedienen Sie sich!; **He can't help it.** Er kann nichts dafür.
▶ *n* Hilfe *f* ▷ *Do you need any help?* Brauchst du Hilfe?

helpful *adj* hilfreich ▷ *a helpful suggestion* ein hilfreicher Vorschlag; **He was very helpful.** Er war eine große Hilfe.

help menu *n* Hilfemenü *nt* (*pl* Hilfemenüs)

hen *n* Henne *f*

her *adj* ihr ▷ *her father* ihr Vater ▷ *her mother* ihre Mutter ▷ *her child* ihr Kind ▷ *her parents* ihre Eltern

> Do not use **ihr** with parts of the body.

▷ *She's going to wash her hair.* Sie wäscht sich die Haare. ▷ *She's cleaning her teeth.* Sie putzt sich die Zähne. ▷ *She's hurt her foot.* Sie hat sich am Fuß verletzt.
▶ *pron* ❶ sie ▷ *I can see her.* Ich kann sie sehen. ▷ *Look at her!* Sieh sie an! ▷ *It's her again.* Sie ist es schon wieder. ▷ *I'm older than her.* Ich bin älter als sie.

> Use **sie** after prepositions which take the accusative.

▷ *I was thinking of her.* Ich habe an sie gedacht. ❷ ihr

> Use **ihr** after prepositions which take the dative.

▷ *I'm going with her.* Ich gehe mit ihr mit. ▷ *He sat next to her.* Er saß neben ihr.

> Use **ihr** when 'her' means 'to her'.

▷ *I gave her a book.* Ich gab ihr ein Buch. ▷ *I told her the truth.* Ich habe ihr die Wahrheit gesagt.

herb *n* Kraut *nt* (*pl* Kräuter)

here *adv* hier ▷ *I live here.* Ich wohne hier. ▷ *Here's Helen.* Hier ist Helen. ▷ *Here are the books.* Hier sind die Bücher. ▷ *Here he is!* Da ist er ja!

hero *n* Held *m* (*gen* Helden, *pl* Helden) ▷ *He's a real hero!* Er ist ein echter Held!

heroin *n* Heroin *nt* ▷ *Heroin is a hard drug.* Heroin ist eine harte Droge.; **a heroin addict** *(man)* ein Heroinsüchtiger; **She's a heroin addict.** Sie ist heroinsüchtig.

heroine *n* Heldin *f* ▷ *the heroine of the novel* die Heldin des Romans

hers *pron* ❶ ihrer ▷ *Is this her coat? — No, hers is black.* Ist das ihr Mantel? — Nein, ihrer ist schwarz.
ihre ▷ *Is this her cup? — No, hers is red.* Ist das ihre Tasse? — Nein, ihre ist rot.
ihres ▷ *Is this her car? — No, hers is white.* Ist das ihr Auto? — Nein, ihres ist weiß.
❷ ihre ▷ *my parents and hers* meine Eltern und ihre ▷ *I have my reasons and she has hers.* Ich habe meine Gründe und sie hat ihre.; **Is this hers?** Gehört das ihr? ▷ *This book is hers.* Dieses Buch gehört ihr. ▷ *Whose is this? — It's hers.* Wem gehört das? — Es gehört ihr.

herself *pron* ❶ sich ▷ *She's hurt herself.* Sie hat sich verletzt. ▷ *She talked mainly about herself.* Sie redete hauptsächlich über sich selbst. ❷ selbst ▷ *She did it herself.* Sie hat es selbst gemacht.; **by herself** allein

he's = **he is**; **he has**

hesitate *vb* zögern [**88**]

heterosexual *adj* heterosexuell

hi *excl* hallo

hiccups *npl* Schluckauf *msg* ▷ *He had the hiccups.* Er hatte einen Schluckauf.

hide *vb* sich verstecken [**7**] (*perf* hat sich versteckt) ▷ *He hid behind a bush.* Er versteckte sich hinter einem Busch.; **to hide something** etwas verstecken [**7**]

hide-and-seek *n* **to play hide-and-seek** Verstecken spielen [**38**]

hi-fi *n* Hi-Fi-Anlage *f*

high *adj, adv* hoch ▷ *It's too high.* Es ist zu hoch. ▷ *How high is the wall?* Wie hoch ist die Mauer? ▷ *The wall's two metres high.* Die Mauer ist zwei Meter hoch.

> Before a noun or after an article, use **hohe**.

▷ *She's got a very high voice.* Sie hat eine sehr hohe Stimme. ▷ *a high price* ein hoher Preis ▷ *a high temperature* eine hohe Temperatur ▷ *at high speed* mit hoher Geschwindigkeit; **It's very high in fat.** Es ist sehr fetthaltig.; **to be high** *(informal: on drugs)* high sein [**65**]; **to get high** *(informal: on drugs)* high werden [**91**]

higher education *n* Hochschulbildung *f*

high-heeled *adj* **high-heeled shoes** hochhackige Schuhe

high jump *n (sport)* Hochsprung *m* (*pl* Hochsprünge)

high-rise *n* Hochhaus *nt* (*gen* Hochhauses, *pl* Hochhäuser) ▷ *I live in a high-rise.* Ich wohne in einem Hochhaus.

high school *n* Gymnasium *nt* (*pl* Gymnasien)

hijack *vb* entführen [**18**] (*perf* hat entführt)

hijacker *n* Entführer *m* (*pl* Entführer), Entführerin *f*

hiking *n* **to go hiking** wandern gehen [**29**]

hilarious *adj* urkomisch ▷ *It was hilarious!* Es war urkomisch!

hill *n* Hügel *m* (*pl* Hügel) ▷ *She walked up the hill.* Sie ging den Hügel hinauf.

hill-walking *n* Bergwandern *nt*; **to go hill-walking** Bergwanderungen machen [**48**]

him *pron* ❶ ihn ▷ *I can see him.* Ich kann ihn sehen. ▷ *Look at him!* Sieh ihn an!

> Use **ihn** after prepositions which take the accusative.

▷ *I did it for him.* Ich habe es für ihn getan. ❷ ihm

> Use **ihm** after prepositions which take the dative.

▷ *I travelled with him.* Ich bin mit ihm gereist. ▷ *I haven't heard from him.* Ich habe nichts von ihm gehört.

Use **ihm** when 'him' means 'to him'.

▷ *I gave him a book.* Ich gab ihm ein Buch. ▷ *I told him the truth.* Ich habe ihm die Wahrheit gesagt. ❸ er ▷ *It's him again.* Er ist es schon wieder. ▷ *I'm older than him.* Ich bin älter als er.

himself *pron* ❶ sich ▷ *He's hurt himself.* Er hat sich verletzt. ▷ *He talked mainly about himself.* Er redete hauptsächlich über sich selbst. ❷ selbst ▷ *He did it himself.* Er hat es selbst gemacht.; **by himself** allein

Hindu *adj* hinduistisch; **a Hindu temple** ein Hindutempel *m*

hip *n* Hüfte *f*

hippie *n* Hippie *m* (*pl* Hippies)

der Hippie is also used for women.

▷ *She was a hippie.* Sie war ein Hippie.

hippo *n* Nilpferd *nt* (*pl* Nilpferde)

hipster *n* Hipster *m* (*pl* Hipsters)

hire *vb* ❶ mieten [**2**] ▷ *to hire a car* ein Auto mieten ❷ *(person)* anstellen [**4**] (*perf* hat angestellt) ▷ *They hired a cleaner.* Sie haben eine Putzfrau angestellt.
▶ *n* Verleih *m* (*pl* Verleihe); **car hire** der Autoverleih; **for hire** zu vermieten

his *adj* sein ▷ *his father* sein Vater ▷ *his mother* seine Mutter ▷ *his child* sein Kind ▷ *his parents* seine Eltern

Do not use **sein** with parts of the body.

▷ *He's going to wash his hair.* Er wäscht sich die Haare. ▷ *He's cleaning his teeth.* Er putzt sich die Zähne. ▷ *He's hurt his foot.* Er hat sich am Fuß verletzt.
▶ *pron* ❶ seiner ▷ *Is this his coat? — No, his is black.* Ist das sein Mantel? — Nein, seiner ist schwarz.; seine ▷ *Is this his cup? — No, his is red.* Ist das seine Tasse? — Nein, seine ist rot.; seines ▷ *Is this his car? — No, his is white.* Ist das sein Auto? — Nein, seines ist weiß. ❷ seine ▷ *my parents and his* meine Eltern und seine ▷ *I have my reasons and he has his.* Ich habe meine Gründe und er hat seine.; **Is this his?** Gehört das ihm? ▷ *This book is his.* Dieses Buch gehört ihm. ▷ *Whose is this? — It's his.* Wem gehört das? — Das gehört ihm.

history *n* Geschichte *f*

hit *vb* ❶ schlagen [**59**] (*pres* schlägt, *imperf* schlug, *perf* hat geschlagen) ▷ *Andrew hit him.* Andrew hat ihn geschlagen. ❷ anfahren [**21**] (*pres* fährt an, *imperf* fuhr an, *perf* hat angefahren) ▷ *He was hit by a car.* Er wurde von einem Auto angefahren. ❸ treffen [**78**] (*pres* trifft, *imperf* traf, *perf* hat getroffen) ▷ *The arrow hit the target.* Der Pfeil traf sein Ziel.; **to hit it off with somebody** sich gut mit jemandem verstehen [**72**]
▶ *n* ❶ *(song)* Hit *m* (*pl* Hits) ▷ *their latest hit* ihr neuester Hit ❷ *(success)* Erfolg *m* (*pl* Erfolge) ▷ *The film was a massive hit.* Der Film war ein enormer Erfolg.

hitch *n* Problem *nt* (*pl* Probleme) ▷ *a slight hitch* ein kleines Problem

hitchhike *vb* per Anhalter fahren [**21**] (*pres* fährt, *imperf* fuhr, *perf* ist gefahren)

hitchhiker *n* Anhalter *m* (*pl* Anhalter), Anhalterin *f*

hitchhiking *n* Trampen *nt* ▷ *Hitchhiking is dangerous.* Trampen ist gefährlich.

HIV-negative *adj* HIV-negativ

HIV-positive *adj* HIV-positiv

hobby *n* Hobby *nt* (*pl* Hobbys) ▷ *What are your hobbies?* Welche Hobbys haben Sie?

hockey *n* Hockey *nt* ▷ *I play hockey.* Ich spiele Hockey.

hold *vb* ❶ *(hold on to)* halten [**33**] (*pres* hält, *imperf* hielt, *perf* hat gehalten) ▷ *Hold this end of the rope, please.* Halt bitte dieses Ende des Seils.; **She held a bottle in her hand.** Sie hatte eine Flasche in der Hand. ❷ *(contain)* fassen [**31**] ▷ *This bottle holds two litres.* Diese Flasche fasst zwei Liter.; **to hold a**

meeting eine Versammlung abhalten [**33**]; **Hold the line!** *(on telephone)* Bleiben Sie am Apparat!; **Hold it!** *(wait)* Sekunde!; **to get hold of something** *(obtain)* etwas bekommen [**40**]

hold on *vb* ❶ *(keep hold)* sich festhalten [**33**] *(pres* hält sich fest, *imperf* hielt sich fest, *perf* hat sich festgehalten) ❷ *(wait)* warten [**2**]

hold up *vb* **to hold up one's hand** die Hand heben ▷ *I held up my hand.* Ich hob die Hand.; **to hold somebody up** *(delay)* jemanden aufhalten [**33**]; **to hold up a bank** *(rob)* eine Bank überfallen [**22**]

hold-up *n* ❶ *(at bank)* Überfall *m (pl* Überfälle) ❷ *(delay)* Verzögerung *f* ❸ *(traffic jam)* Stau *m (pl* Staus)

hole *n* Loch *nt (pl* Löcher)

holiday *n* ❶ *(from school)* Ferien *pl* ▷ *Did you have a good holiday?* Hattet ihr schöne Ferien?; **on holiday** in den Ferien; **the school holidays** die Schulferien ❷ *(from work)* Urlaub *m (pl* Urlaube) ▷ *Did you have a good holiday?* Hattet ihr einen schönen Urlaub?; **on holiday** im Urlaub ❸ *(public holiday)* Feiertag *m (pl* Feiertage) ▷ *Next Wednesday is a holiday.* Nächsten Mittwoch ist ein Feiertag. ❹ *(day off)* **He took a day's holiday.** Er nahm einen Tag frei.; **a holiday camp** ein Ferienlager *nt*; **a holiday home** eine Ferienwohnung *f*

Holland *n* Holland *nt*; **from Holland** aus Holland; **in Holland** in Holland; **to Holland** nach Holland

hollow *adj* hohl

holly *n* Stechpalme *f*

holy *adj* heilig

home *n* Zuhause *nt (gen* Zuhause); **at home** zu Hause; **Make yourself at home.** Machen Sie es sich bequem. ▸ *adv* ❶ zu Hause ▷ *to be at home* zu Hause sein ❷ nach Hause ▷ *to go home* nach Hause gehen; **to get home** nach Hause kommen [**40**]

homeland *n* Heimatland *nt (pl* Heimatländer)

homeless *adj* obdachlos; **the homeless** die Obdachlosen *mpl*

home match *n* Heimspiel *nt (pl* Heimspiele)

home page *n (internet)* Homepage *f (pl* Homepages)

homesick *adj* **to be homesick** Heimweh haben [**32**]

homework *n* Hausaufgaben *fpl* ▷ *Have you done your homework?* Hast du deine Hausaufgaben gemacht? ▷ *my geography homework* meine Erdkundeaufgaben

homosexual *adj* homosexuell ▸ *n* Homosexuelle *m (gen* Homosexuellen, *pl* Homosexuellen) ▷ *a homosexual (man)* ein Homosexueller

honest *adj* ehrlich ▷ *She's an honest person.* Sie ist ein ehrlicher Mensch. ▷ *He was honest with her.* Er war ehrlich zu ihr.

honestly *adv* ehrlich ▷ *I honestly don't know.* Ich weiß es ehrlich nicht.

honesty *n* Ehrlichkeit *f*

honey *n* Honig *m*

honeymoon *n* Flitterwochen *fpl*

honour (*US* **honor**) *n* Ehre *f*

hood *n* ❶ Kapuze *f* ▷ *a coat with a hood* ein Mantel mit Kapuze ❷ *(of car)* Motorhaube *f*

hook *n* Haken *m (pl* Haken) ▷ *He hung the painting on the hook.* Er hängte das Bild an den Haken.; **to take the phone off the hook** das Telefon aushängen [**35**]; **a fish-hook** ein Angelhaken

hooligan *n* Rowdy *m (pl* Rowdys)

hooray *excl* hurra

Hoover® *n* Staubsauger *m (pl* Staubsauger)

hoover *vb* staubsaugen [**38**] ▷ *She hoovered the lounge.* Sie hat im Wohnzimmer gestaubsaugt.

hop *vb* hüpfen [**38**] *(perf* ist gehüpft)

hope *vb* hoffen [**38**] ▷ *I hope he comes.* Ich hoffe, er kommt. ▷ *I'm hoping for good*

results. Ich hoffe, dass ich gute Noten bekomme.; **I hope so.** Hoffentlich.; **I hope not.** Hoffentlich nicht.
▸ *n* Hoffnung *f*; **to give up hope** die Hoffnung aufgeben [**28**]

hopefully *adv* hoffentlich ▹ *Hopefully he'll make it in time.* Hoffentlich schafft er es noch.

hopeless *adj* hoffnungslos ▹ *I'm hopeless at maths.* In Mathe bin ich ein hoffnungsloser Fall.

horizon *n* Horizont *m* (*pl* Horizonte)

horizontal *adj* horizontal

horn *n* ❶ *(of car)* Hupe *f*; **He sounded his horn.** Er hat gehupt. ❷ Horn *nt* (*pl* Hörner) ▹ *I play the horn.* Ich spiele Horn.

horoscope *n* Horoskop *nt* (*pl* Horoskope)

horrible *adj* furchtbar ▹ *What a horrible dress!* Was für ein furchtbares Kleid!

horrify *vb* entsetzen [**18**] ▹ *I was horrified by the news.* Ich war über die Neuigkeiten entsetzt.

horrifying *adj* schrecklich ▹ *a horrifying accident* ein schrecklicher Unfall

horror *n* Horror *m*

horror film *n* Horrorfilm *m* (*pl* Horrorfilme)

horse *n* Pferd *nt* (*pl* Pferde)

horse-racing *n* Pferderennen *nt* (*pl* Pferderennen)

hose *n* Schlauch *m* (*pl* Schläuche) ▹ *a garden hose* ein Gartenschlauch

> Be careful not to translate **hose** by the German word **Hose**.

hospital *n* Krankenhaus *nt* (*gen* Krankenhauses, *pl* Krankenhäuser) ▹ *Take me to the hospital!* Bringen Sie mich ins Krankenhaus! ▹ *in hospital* im Krankenhaus

hospitality *n* Gastfreundschaft *f*

host *n* ❶ Gastgeber *m* (*pl* Gastgeber), Gastgeberin *f* ❷ *(television)* Moderator *m* (*pl* Moderatoren), Moderatorin *f*

hostage *n* Geisel *f* ▹ *to take somebody hostage* jemanden als Geisel nehmen

hostel *n* Herberge *f*

hot *adj* ❶ *(warm)* heiß ▹ *a hot bath* ein heißes Bad ▹ *a hot country* ein heißes Land ▹ *It's hot.* Es ist heiß. ▹ *It's very hot today.* Heute ist es sehr heiß.

> When you talk about a person being 'hot', you use the impersonal construction.

▹ *I'm hot.* Mir ist heiß. ▹ *I'm too hot.* Mir ist es zu heiß. ❷ *(spicy)* scharf ▹ *a very hot curry* ein sehr scharfes Curry

hot dog *n* Hotdog *m* (*pl* Hotdogs)

hotel *n* Hotel *nt* (*pl* Hotels) ▹ *We stayed in a hotel.* Wir haben in einem Hotel übernachtet.

hour *n* Stunde *f* ▹ *She always takes hours to get ready.* Sie braucht immer Stunden, bis sie fertig ist.; **a quarter of an hour** eine Viertelstunde; **half an hour** eine halbe Stunde; **two and a half hours** zweieinhalb Stunden

hourly *adj, adv* stündlich ▹ *There are hourly buses.* Der Bus verkehrt stündlich.; **to be paid hourly** stundenweise bezahlt werden [**91**]

house *n* Haus *nt* (*gen* Hauses, *pl* Häuser); **at his house** bei ihm zu Hause; **We stayed at their house.** Wir haben bei ihnen übernachtet.

housewife *n* Hausfrau *f* ▹ *She's a housewife.* Sie ist Hausfrau.

housework *n* Hausarbeit *f* ▹ *to do the housework* die Hausarbeit machen

hovercraft *n* Luftkissenfahrzeug *nt* (*pl* Luftkissenfahrzeuge)

how *adv* wie ▹ *How old are you?* Wie alt bist du? ▹ *How far is it to Edinburgh?* Wie weit ist es nach Edinburgh? ▹ *How long have you been here?* Wie lange sind Sie schon hier? ▹ *How are you?* Wie geht's?; **How much?** Wie viel?; **How many?** Wie viele?

however *conj* aber ▹ *This, however, isn't true.* Das ist aber nicht wahr.

hug *vb* umarmen [**7**] (*perf* hat umarmt) ▹ *He hugged her.* Er umarmte sie.
▸ *n* **to give somebody a hug** jemanden umarmen [**7**]

huge *adj* riesig
hum *vb* summen **[38]** ▷ *She hummed to herself.* Sie summte vor sich hin.
human *adj* menschlich ▷ *the human body* der menschliche Körper
human being *n* Mensch *m* (*gen* Menschen, *pl* Menschen)
humour (*US* **humor**) *n* Humor *m*; **to have a sense of humour** Humor haben **[32]**
hundred *num* **a hundred** einhundert; **five hundred** fünfhundert; **five hundred and one** fünfhundertundeins; **hundreds of people** Hunderte von Menschen
hung *vb see* **hang**
Hungarian *adj* ungarisch
Hungary *n* Ungarn *nt*; **from Hungary** aus Ungarn; **to Hungary** nach Ungarn
hunger *n* Hunger *m*
hungry *adj* **to be hungry** Hunger haben **[32]**
hunt *vb* jagen **[38]** ▷ *People used to hunt wild boar.* Menschen haben früher Wildschweine gejagt.; **to go hunting** auf die Jagd gehen **[29]**; **The police are hunting the killer.** Die Polizei sucht den Mörder.; **to hunt for something** (*search*) nach etwas suchen **[48]**
hunting *n* Jagen *nt* ▷ *I'm against hunting.* Ich bin gegen Jagen.; **fox-hunting** die Fuchsjagd
hurdle *n* Hürde *f* ▷ *the 100 metres hurdles* die 100 Meter Hürden
hurricane *n* Orkan *m* (*pl* Orkane)
hurry *vb* eilen **[38]** (*perf* ist geeilt) ▷ *Sharon hurried back home.* Sharon eilte nach Hause.; **Hurry up!** Beeil dich! ▶ *n* **to be in a hurry** in Eile sein **[65]**; **to do something in a hurry** etwas auf die Schnelle machen **[48]**; **There's no hurry.** Das eilt nicht.
hurt *vb* wehtun **[81]** (*imperf* tat weh, *perf* hat wehgetan) ▷ *That hurts.* Das tut weh. ▷ *My leg hurts.* Mein Bein tut weh. ▷ *It hurts to have a tooth out.* Es tut weh, wenn einem ein Zahn gezogen wird.; **to hurt somebody (1)** jemandem wehtun **[81]** ▷ *You're hurting me!* Du tust mir weh! **(2)** (*offend*) jemanden verletzen **[36]** ▷ *His remarks hurt me.* Seine Bemerkungen haben mich verletzt.; **to hurt oneself** sich wehtun **[81]** ▷ *I fell over and hurt myself.* Ich bin hingefallen und habe mir wehgetan. ▶ *adj* verletzt ▷ *Is he badly hurt?* Ist er schlimm verletzt? ▷ *He was hurt in the leg.* Er hatte ein verletztes Bein. ▷ *Luckily, nobody got hurt.* Zum Glück wurde niemand verletzt. ▷ *I was hurt by what he said.* Was er sagte hat mich verletzt.
husband *n* Ehemann *m* (*pl* Ehemänner)
hut *n* Hütte *f*
hymn *n* Kirchenlied *nt* (*pl* Kirchenlieder)
hypermarket *n* Verbrauchermarkt *m* (*pl* Verbrauchermärkte)
hyphen *n* Bindestrich *m* (*pl* Bindestriche)

a b c d e f g h i j k l m n o p q r s t u v w x y z

i

I *pron* ich ▷ *I speak German.* Ich spreche Deutsch. ▷ *Ann and I* Ann und ich

ice *n* ❶ Eis *nt*; **There was ice on the lake.** Der See war gefroren. ❷ *(on road)* Glatteis *nt*

iceberg *n* Eisberg *m* (*pl* Eisberge)

ice cream *n* Eis *nt* (*pl* Eis) ▷ *vanilla ice cream* das Vanilleeis

ice cube *n* Eiswürfel *m* (*pl* Eiswürfel)

ice hockey *n* Eishockey *nt*

Iceland *n* Island *nt*; **from Iceland** aus Island; **to Iceland** nach Island

ice rink *n* Eisbahn *f*

ice-skating *n* Schlittschuhlaufen *nt*; **I like ice-skating.** Ich laufe gern Schlittschuh.; **to go ice-skating** Schlittschuh laufen gehen **[29]**

icing *n (on cake)* Zuckerguss *m* (*gen* Zuckergusses); **icing sugar** der Puderzucker

icon *n (computer)* Icon *nt* (*pl* Icons) ▷ *to click on an icon* ein Icon anklicken

ICT *n (= Information and Communications Technology)* die IuK *(= Informations- und Kommunikationstechnik)*

icy *adj* eiskalt ▷ *There was an icy wind.* Es wehte ein eiskalter Wind.; **The roads are icy.** Die Straßen sind vereist.

I'd = **I had**; **I would**

idea *n* Idee *f* ▷ *Good idea!* Gute Idee!

ideal *adj* ideal

identical *adj* identisch ▷ *identical to* identisch mit

identification *n* Identifikation *f*; **Have you got any identification?** Können Sie sich ausweisen?

identify *vb* identifizieren **[76]** (*perf* hat identifiziert)

identity card *n* Personalausweis *m* (*pl* Personalausweise)

idiom *n* Redewendung *f*

idiot *n* Idiot *m* (*gen* Idioten, *pl* Idioten), Idiotin *f*

idiotic *adj* idiotisch

i.e. *abbr* d. h. *(= das heißt)*

if *conj* ❶ wenn ▷ *You can have it if you like.* Wenn du willst, kannst du es haben. ❷ *(whether)* ob ▷ *Do you know if he's there?* Weißt du, ob er da ist?; **if only** wenn doch nur; **if not** falls nicht

ignore *vb* ❶ nicht beachten **[2]** (*perf* hat nicht beachtet) ▷ *She ignored my advice.* Sie hat meinen Rat nicht beachtet. ❷ ignorieren **[76]** (*perf* hat ignoriert) ▷ *She saw me, but she ignored me.* Sie sah mich, hat mich aber ignoriert.; **Just ignore him!** Beachte ihn einfach nicht!

ill *adj (sick)* krank; **to be taken ill** krank werden **[91]**

I'll = **I will**

illegal *adj* illegal

illness *n* Krankheit *f*

illusion *n* Illusion *f*

illustration *n* Illustration *f*

I'm = **I am**

image *n (public image)* Image *nt* (*gen* Image, *pl* Images) ▷ *the company's image* das Image der Firma

imagination *n* Fantasie *f* ▷ *You need a lot of imagination to be a writer.* Als Schriftsteller braucht man viel Fantasie.; **It's just your imagination!** Das bildest du dir nur ein!

imagine *vb* sich vorstellen [**4**] (*perf* hat sich vorgestellt) ▷ *Imagine how I felt!* Stell dir vor, wie mir zumute war!; **Is he angry? — I imagine so.** Ist er böse? — Ich denke schon.

imitate *vb* nachmachen [**4**] (*perf* hat nachgemacht)

imitation *n* Imitation *f*

immediate *adj* sofortig ▷ *We need an immediate answer.* Wir brauchen eine sofortige Antwort.; **in the immediate future** in unmittelbarer Zukunft

immediately *adv* sofort ▷ *I'll do it immediately.* Ich mache es sofort.

immigrant *n* Einwanderer *m* (*pl* Einwanderer), Einwanderin *f*

immigration *n* Einwanderung *f*

immune *adj* **to be immune to something** gegen etwas immun sein [**65**]

impatience *n* Ungeduld *f*

impatient *adj* ungeduldig ▷ *People are getting impatient.* Die Leute werden ungeduldig.

implement *vb* ausführen [**4**] (*perf* hat ausgeführt) ▷ *Chris will implement the plan.* Chris wird den Plan ausführen.

imply *vb* andeuten [**2**] (*perf* hat angedeutet) ▷ *Are you implying I stole it?* Wollen Sie andeuten, ich hätte es gestohlen?

import *vb* importieren [**76**] (*perf* hat importiert)

importance *n* Wichtigkeit *f* ▷ *the importance of a good knowledge of German* die Wichtigkeit guter Deutschkenntnisse

important *adj* wichtig

impose *vb* auferlegen [**4**] (*perf* hat auferlegt) ▷ *to impose a penalty* eine Strafe auferlegen

impossible *adj* unmöglich

impress *vb* beeindrucken [**7**] (*perf* hat beeindruckt) ▷ *She's trying to impress you.* Sie will dich beeindrucken.

impressed *adj* beeindruckt ▷ *I'm very impressed!* Ich bin sehr beeindruckt!

impression *n* Eindruck *m* (*pl* Eindrücke) ▷ *I was under the impression that ...* Ich hatte den Eindruck, dass ...

impressive *adj* beeindruckend

improve *vb* ❶ (*make better*) verbessern [**88**] (*perf* hat verbessert) ▷ *The hotel has improved its service.* Das Hotel hat den Service verbessert. ❷ (*get better*) besser werden [**91**] (*pres* wird besser, *imperf* wurde besser, *perf* ist besser geworden) ▷ *The weather is improving.* Das Wetter wird besser. ▷ *My German has improved.* Mein Deutsch ist besser geworden.

improvement *n* ❶ (*of condition*) Verbesserung *f* ▷ *It's a great improvement.* Das ist eine gewaltige Verbesserung. ❷ (*of learner*) Fortschritt *m* (*pl* Fortschritte) ▷ *There's been an improvement in his German.* Er hat in Deutsch Fortschritte gemacht.

in *prep, adv*

> Use the accusative to express movement or a change of place. Use the dative when there is no change of place.

❶ in ▷ *It's in my bag.* Es ist in meiner Tasche. ▷ *Put it in my bag.* Tu es in meine Tasche. ▷ *I read it in this book.* Ich habe es in diesem Buch gelesen. ▷ *Write it in your address book.* Schreib es in dein Adressbuch. ▷ *in hospital* im Krankenhaus ▷ *in school* in der Schule ▷ *in London* in London ▷ *in Germany* in Deutschland ▷ *in Switzerland* in der Schweiz ▷ *in May* im Mai ▷ *in spring* im Frühling ▷ *in the rain* im Regen ▷ *I'll see you in three weeks.* Ich sehe dich in drei Wochen.

> Sometimes 'in' is not translated.

▷ *It happened in 1996.* Es geschah 1996. ▷ *in the morning* morgens ▷ *in the afternoon* nachmittags ▷ *at six in the evening* um sechs Uhr abends ❷ mit ▷ *the boy in the blue shirt* der Junge mit dem blauen Hemd ▷ *It was written in pencil.* Es war mit Bleistift geschrieben. ▷ *in a loud voice* mit lauter Stimme ▷ *She paid in dollars.* Sie hat mit Dollar bezahlt. ❸ auf ▷ *in German* auf Deutsch ▷ *in English* auf Englisch

'in' is sometimes translated using the genitive.

▷ *the best pupil in the class* der beste Schüler der Klasse ▷ *the tallest person in the family* der Größte der Familie; **in the beginning** am Anfang; **in the country** auf dem Land; **in time** rechtzeitig; **in here** hier drin; **one person in ten** einer von zehn; **to be in** *(at home, work)* da sein [**65**]; **to ask somebody in** jemanden hereinbitten [**9**]

inadequate *adj* unzulänglich

include *vb* einschließen (*imperf* schloss ein, *perf* hat eingeschlossen) ▷ *Service is not included.* Bedienung ist nicht eingeschlossen.

including *prep* inklusive ▷ *That will be two hundred euros, including VAT.* Das macht zweihundert Euro, inklusive Mehrwertsteuer.

income *n* Einkommen *nt* (*pl* Einkommen)

income tax *n* Einkommensteuer *f*

inconsistent *adj* ❶ widersprüchlich; **to be inconsistent with ...** im Widerspruch stehen [**72**] zu ... ❷ unbeständig ▷ *Your work is very inconsistent.* Die Qualität deiner Arbeit ist sehr unbeständig.

inconvenient *adj* **That's very inconvenient for me.** Das passt mir gar nicht.

incorrect *adj* unrichtig

increase *n* Zunahme *f* ▷ *an increase in road accidents* eine Zunahme an Verkehrsunfällen
▶ *vb* ❶ *(traffic, number)* zunehmen [**52**] (*pres* nimmt zu, *imperf* nahm zu, *perf* hat zugenommen) ▷ *Traffic on motorways has increased.* Der Verkehr auf den Autobahnen hat zugenommen. ❷ *(price, demand)* steigen [**74**] (*imperf* stieg, *perf* ist gestiegen) ▷ *with increasing demand* bei steigender Nachfrage ❸ *(pain, wind)* stärker werden [**91**] (*pres* wird stärker, *imperf* wurde stärker, *perf* ist stärker geworden); **to increase in size** größer werden [**91**]; **to increase something** etwas erhöhen [**19**]; **increased cost of living** höhere Lebenshaltungskosten

incredible *adj* unglaublich

indeed *adv* wirklich ▷ *It's very hard indeed.* Es ist wirklich schwer.; **Know what I mean? — Indeed I do.** Weißt du, was ich meine? — Ja, ganz genau.; **Thank you very much indeed!** Ganz herzlichen Dank!

independence *n* Unabhängigkeit *f*

independent *adj* unabhängig; **an independent school** eine Privatschule

index *n (in book)* Verzeichnis *nt* (*gen* Verzeichnisses, *pl* Verzeichnisse)

India *n* Indien *nt*; **from India** aus Indien; **to India** nach Indien

Indian *adj* ❶ indisch ❷ *(American Indian)* indianisch
▶ *n (person)* Inder *m* (*pl* Inder), Inderin *f*; **an American Indian** ein Indianer *m*

indicate *vb* ❶ zeigen [**38**] ▷ *His reaction indicates how he feels about it.* Seine Reaktion zeigt, was er davon hält. ❷ *(make known)* andeuten [**2**] (*perf* hat angedeutet) ▷ *He indicated that he may resign.* Er hat angedeutet, dass er vielleicht zurücktritt. ❸ *(technical device)* anzeigen [**4**] (*perf* hat angezeigt) ▷ *The gauge indicated a very high temperature.* Das Messgerät zeigte eine sehr hohe Temperatur an.; **to indicate left** links blinken [**38**]

indicator *n (in car)* Blinker *m* (*pl* Blinker)

indigestion *n* Magenverstimmung *f*; **I've got indigestion.** Ich habe eine Magenverstimmung.

individual *n* Individuum *nt* (*pl* Individuen) ▶ *adj* individuell
indoor *adj* **an indoor swimming pool** ein Hallenbad *nt*
indoors *adv* im Haus ▷ *They're indoors.* Sie sind im Haus.; **to go indoors** hineingehen [**29**]
industrial *adj* industriell
industrial estate *n* Industriegebiet *nt* (*pl* Industriegebiete)
industry *n* Industrie *f* ▷ *the tourist industry* die Tourismusindustrie ▷ *the oil industry* die Erdölindustrie; **I'd like to work in industry.** Ich würde gern in der freien Wirtschaft arbeiten.
inevitable *adj* unvermeidlich
inexperienced *adj* unerfahren
infant school *n* Grundschule *f*

The **Grundschule** is a primary school which children attend from the age of 6 to 10. Many children attend **Kindergarten** before going to the **Grundschule**.

infection *n* Entzündung *f* ▷ *an ear infection* eine Ohrenentzündung ▷ *a throat infection* eine Halsentzündung
infectious *adj* ansteckend ▷ *It's not infectious.* Es ist nicht ansteckend.
infinitive *n* Infinitiv *m* (*pl* Infinitive)
inflation *n* Inflation *f*
inform *vb* informieren [**76**] (*perf* hat informiert); **to inform somebody of something** jemanden über etwas informieren [**76**]
informal *adj* ❶ *(person)* locker ❷ *(party)* zwanglos ▷ *'informal dress'* 'zwanglose Kleidung' ❸ *(colloquial)* umgangssprachlich; **informal language** die Umgangssprache; **an informal visit** ein inoffizieller Besuch
information *n* Information *f* ▷ *important information* wichtige Informationen; **a piece of information** eine Information; **Could you give me some information about Berlin?** Können Sie mir einige Informationen über Berlin geben?
information office *n* Auskunft *f* (*pl* Auskünfte)
information technology *n* Informationstechnik *f*
infuriating *adj* äußerst ärgerlich
ingredient *n* Zutat *f*
inhaler *n* Inhalator *m* (*pl* Inhalatoren)
inherit *vb* erben [**38**] ▷ *She inherited her father's house.* Sie erbte das Haus ihres Vaters.
initials *npl* Initialen *fpl* ▷ *Her initials are CDT.* Ihre Initialen sind CDT.
injection *n* Spritze *f*
injure *vb* verletzen [**36**] (*perf* hat verletzt)
injured *adj* verletzt
injury *n* Verletzung *f*
ink *n* Tinte *f*
in-laws *npl* Schwiegereltern *pl*
innocent *adj* unschuldig
insane *adj* wahnsinnig
inscription *n* Inschrift *f*
insect *n* Insekt *nt* (*pl* Insekten)
insect repellent *n* Insektenschutzmittel *nt* (*pl* Insektenschutzmittel)
insert *vb* einwerfen [**92**] (*pres* wirft ein, *imperf* warf ein, *perf* hat eingeworfen) ▷ *I inserted a coin.* Ich warf eine Münze ein.
inside *n* Innere *nt* (*gen* Inneren) ▶ *adv, prep* innen ▷ *inside and outside* innen und außen; **They're inside.** Sie sind drinnen.; **to go inside** hineingehen [**29**]; **Come inside!** Kommt herein!

Use the accusative to express movement or a change of place. Use the dative when there is no change of place.

inside the house (1) im Haus ▷ *She was inside the house.* Sie war im Haus. **(2)** ins Haus ▷ *She went inside the house.* Sie ging ins Haus.
insist *vb* darauf bestehen [**72**] (*imperf* bestand darauf, *perf* hat darauf bestanden) ▷ *I didn't want to, but he*

a b c d e f g h i j k l m n o p q r s t u v w x y z

insisted. Ich wollte nicht, aber er hat darauf bestanden.; **to insist on doing something** darauf bestehen [**72**], etwas zu tun; **He insisted he was innocent.** Er beteuerte seine Unschuld.

inspect *vb* kontrollieren [**76**] (*perf* hat kontrolliert)

inspector *n (police)* Kommissar *m* (*pl* Kommissare), Kommissarin *f* ▷ *Inspector Jill Brown* Kommissarin Jill Brown

install *vb* installieren [**76**] (*perf* hat installiert)

instalment (*US* **installment**) *n* ❶ Rate *f* ▷ *to pay in instalments* in Raten zahlen ❷ *(of TV, radio serial)* Folge *f* ❸ *(of publication)* Teil *m*

instance *n* **for instance** zum Beispiel

instant *adj* sofortig ▷ *It was an instant success.* Es war ein sofortiger Erfolg.; **instant coffee** der Pulverkaffee

instantly *adv* sofort

instead *adv* **instead of (1)** *(followed by noun)* anstelle von ▷ *Use honey instead of sugar.* Nehmen Sie Honig anstelle von Zucker. **(2)** *(followed by verb)* statt ▷ *We played tennis instead of going swimming.* Wir spielten Tennis statt schwimmen zu gehen.; **The pool was closed, so we played tennis instead.** Das Schwimmbad war zu, also spielten wir stattdessen Tennis.

instinct *n* Instinkt *m* (*pl* Instinkte)

instruct *vb* anweisen (*imperf* wies an, *perf* hat angewiesen); **to instruct somebody to do something** jemanden anweisen, etwas zu tun

instructions *npl* ❶ Anweisungen *fpl* ▷ *Follow the instructions carefully.* Befolgen Sie die Anweisungen genau. ❷ *(manual)* Gebrauchsanweisung *f* ▷ *Where are the instructions?* Wo ist die Gebrauchsanweisung?

instructor *n* Lehrer *m* (*pl* Lehrer), Lehrerin *f* ▷ *a skiing instructor* ein Skilehrer ▷ *a driving instructor* ein Fahrlehrer

instrument *n* Instrument *nt* (*pl* Instrumente) ▷ *Do you play an instrument?* Spielst du ein Instrument?

insulin *n* Insulin *nt*

insult *n* Beleidigung *f*
▶ *vb* beleidigen [**7**] (*perf* hat beleidigt)

insurance *n* Versicherung *f* ▷ *his car insurance* seine Kraftfahrzeugversicherung; **an insurance policy** eine Versicherungspolice

intelligent *adj* intelligent

intend *vb* **to intend to do something** beabsichtigen [**7**], etwas zu tun

intensive *adj* intensiv

intention *n* Absicht *f*

interest *n* Interesse *nt* (*pl* Interessen) ▷ *to show an interest in something* Interesse an etwas zeigen ▷ *What interests do you have?* Welche Interessen hast du?; **My main interest is music.** Ich interessiere mich hauptsächlich für Musik.
▶ *vb* interessieren [**76**] (*perf* hat interessiert) ▷ *It doesn't interest me.* Das interessiert mich nicht.; **to be interested in something** sich für etwas interessieren [**76**]

interesting *adj* interessant

interior *n* Innere *nt* (*gen* Inneren)

interior designer *n* Innenarchitekt *m* (*gen* Innenarchitekten, *pl* Innenarchitekten), Innenarchitektin *f*

international *adj* international

internet *n* Internet *nt* ▷ *on the internet* im Internet

internet café *n* Internet-Café *nt* (*pl* Internet-Cafés)

internet user *n* Internetbenutzer *m* (*pl* Internetbenutzer), Internetbenutzerin *f*

interpreter *n* Dolmetscher *m* (*pl* Dolmetscher), Dolmetscherin *f*

interrupt *vb* unterbrechen [**11**] (*pres* unterbricht, *imperf* unterbrach, *perf* hat unterbrochen)

interruption *n* Unterbrechung *f*

interval *n (in play, concert)* Pause *f*
interview *n* ❶ *(on TV, radio)* Interview *nt* (*pl* Interviews) ❷ *(for job)* Vorstellungsgespräch *nt* (*pl* Vorstellungsgespräche)
▶ *vb (on TV, radio)* interviewen **[84]** (*perf* hat interviewt) ▷ *I was interviewed on the radio.* Ich wurde im Radio interviewt.
interviewer *n (on TV, radio)* Moderator *m* (*pl* Moderatoren), Moderatorin *f*
into *prep* in
In this sense **in** is followed by the accusative.
▷ *He got into the car.* Er stieg ins Auto. ▷ *I'm going into town.* Ich gehe in die Stadt. ▷ *Translate it into German.* Übersetze das ins Deutsche. ▷ *Divide into two groups.* Teilt euch in zwei Gruppen.
intranet *n* Intranet *nt* (*pl* Intranets)
introduce *vb* vorstellen **[4]** (*perf* hat vorgestellt) ▷ *He introduced me to his parents.* Er stellte mich seinen Eltern vor.
introduction *n (in book)* Einleitung *f*
invade *vb* eindringen in (*imperf* drang ein, *perf* ist eingedrungen) ▷ *to invade a country* in ein Land eindringen
invalid *n* Kranke *m* (*gen* Kranken, *pl* Kranken), Kranke *f* (*gen* Kranken) ▷ *an invalid (man)* ein Kranker
invent *vb* erfinden **[24]** (*imperf* erfand, *perf* hat erfunden)
invention *n* Erfindung *f*
invest *vb* investieren **[76]** (*perf* hat investiert)
investigation *n (police)* Untersuchung *f*
invisible *adj* unsichtbar
invitation *n* Einladung *f*
invite *vb* einladen (*pres* lädt ein, *imperf* lud ein, *perf* hat eingeladen) ▷ *He's not invited.* Er ist nicht eingeladen.; **to invite somebody to a party** jemanden zu einer Party einladen
involve *vb* mit sich bringen **[13]** (*imperf* brachte mit sich, *perf* hat mit sich gebracht) ▷ *This will involve a lot of work.* Das wird viel Arbeit mit sich bringen.; **His job involves a lot of travelling.** Er muss in seinem Job viel reisen.; **to be involved in something** *(crime, drugs)* in etwas verwickelt sein **[65]**; **to be involved with somebody** *(in relationship)* mit jemandem eine Beziehung haben **[32]**; **I don't want to get involved.** Ich will damit nichts zu tun haben.
iPad® *n* iPad® *nt* (*pl* iPads)
iPhone® *n* iPhone® *nt* (*pl* iPhones)
iPod® *n* iPod® *m* (*pl* iPods)
Iran *n* Iran *m*
Note that the definite article is used in German for countries which are masculine.
from Iran aus dem Iran; **in Iran** im Iran; **to Iran** in den Iran
Iraq *n* Irak *m*
Note that the definite article is used in German for countries which are masculine.
from Iraq aus dem Irak; **in Iraq** im Irak; **to Iraq** in den Irak
Iraqi *n* Iraker *m* (*pl* Iraker), Irakerin *f*
▶ *adj* irakisch
Ireland *n* Irland *nt*; **from Ireland** aus Irland; **in Ireland** in Irland; **to Ireland** nach Irland
Irish *adj* irisch ▷ *Irish music* irische Musik; **He's Irish.** Er ist Ire.; **She's Irish.** Sie ist Irin.
▶ *n (language)* Irisch *nt* (*gen* Irischen); **the Irish** *(people)* die Iren *mpl*
Irishman *n* Ire *m* (*gen* Iren, *pl* Iren)
Irishwoman *n* Irin *f*
iron *n* ❶ *(metal)* Eisen *nt* ❷ *(for clothes)* Bügeleisen *nt* (*pl* Bügeleisen)
▶ *vb* bügeln **[34]**
ironing *n* Bügeln *nt*; **to do the ironing** bügeln **[34]**
ironing board *n* Bügelbrett *nt* (*pl* Bügelbretter)
irresponsible *adj (person)* verantwortungslos; **That was**

irresponsible of him. Das war unverantwortlich von ihm.

irritating *adj* nervend

is *vb see* **be**

Islam *n* Islam *m*

Islamic *adj* islamisch ▷ *Islamic fundamentalists* islamische Fundamentalisten; **Islamic law** das Recht des Islams

island *n* Insel *f*

isle *n* **the Isle of Man** die Insel Man; **the Isle of Wight** die Insel Wight

isolated *adj (place)* abgelegen; **She feels very isolated.** Sie fühlt sich sehr isoliert.; **an isolated case** ein Einzelfall *m*

Israel *n* Israel *nt*; **from Israel** aus Israel; **to Israel** nach Israel

Israeli *n* Israeli *m* (*gen* Israeli, *pl* Israeli), Israeli *f* (*gen* Israeli)
▶ *adj* israelisch; **He's Israeli.** Er ist Israeli.

issue *n* ❶ *(matter)* Frage *f* ▷ *a controversial issue* eine umstrittene Frage ❷ *(of magazine)* Ausgabe *f*
▶ *vb (equipment, supplies)* ausgeben **[28]** (*pres* gibt aus, *imperf* gab aus, *perf* hat ausgegeben)

it *pron*

> Remember to check if 'it' stands for a masculine, feminine or neuter noun, and use the appropriate gender and case.

❶ er ▷ *Your hat? — It's on the table.* Dein Hut? — Er ist auf dem Tisch.; sie ▷ *Where's your watch? — It's broken.* Wo ist deine Uhr? — Sie ist kaputt.; es ▷ *Have you seen her new dress, it's very pretty.* Hast du ihr neues Kleid gesehen, es ist sehr hübsch. ❷ ihn ▷ *Where's my hat? — I haven't seen it.* Wo ist mein Hut? — Ich habe ihn nicht gesehen.; sie ▷ *Where's your jacket? — I've lost it.* Wo ist deine Jacke? — Ich habe sie verloren. es ▷ *Take my ruler, I don't need it.* Nimm mein Lineal, ich brauche es nicht.; **It's raining.** Es regnet.; **It's six o'clock.** Es ist sechs Uhr.; **It's Friday tomorrow.** Morgen ist Freitag.; **Who is it? — It's me.** Wer ist's? — Ich bin's.; **It's expensive.** Das ist teuer.

Italian *adj* italienisch; **She's Italian.** Sie ist Italienerin.
▶ *n* ❶ *(person)* Italiener *m* (*pl* Italiener), Italienerin *f* ❷ *(language)* Italienisch *nt* (*gen* Italienischen)

italics *npl* Kursivschrift *f*; **in italics** kursiv

Italy *n* Italien *nt*; **from Italy** aus Italien; **in Italy** in Italien; **to Italy** nach Italien

itch *vb* jucken **[38]** ▷ *It itches.* Es juckt. ▷ *My head's itching.* Mein Kopf juckt.

itchy *adj* **My arm is itchy.** Mein Arm juckt.

it'd = **it had**; **it would**

item *n (object)* Artikel *m* (*pl* Artikel)

it'll = **it will**

its *adj*

> Remember to check if 'its' refers back to a masculine, feminine or neuter noun, and use the appropriate gender and case.

sein ▷ *The dog is in its kennel.* Der Hund ist in seiner Hütte.; ihr ▷ *The cup is in its usual place.* Die Tasse ist an ihrem üblichen Platz.; sein ▷ *The baby is in its cot.* Das Baby ist in seinem Bett.

it's = **it is**; **it has**

itself *pron* ❶ sich ▷ *The dog scratched itself.* Der Hund kratzte sich. ❷ selbst ▷ *The heating switches itself off.* Die Heizung schaltet von selbst aus.

I've = **I have**

J

jack *n* ❶ *(for car)* Wagenheber *m* (*pl* Wagenheber) ❷ *(playing card)* Bube *m* (*gen* Buben, *pl* Buben)
jacket *n* Jacke *f*; **jacket potatoes** gebackene Kartoffeln
jail *n* Gefängnis *nt* (*gen* Gefängnisses, *pl* Gefängnisse); **She was sent to jail.** Sie musste ins Gefängnis.
▶ *vb* einsperren [**4**] (*perf* hat eingesperrt); **He was jailed for ten years.** Er hat zehn Jahre Gefängnis bekommen.
jam *n* Marmelade *f* ▷ *strawberry jam* Erdbeermarmelade; **a traffic jam** ein Verkehrsstau *m*
jammed *adj* **The window's jammed.** Das Fenster klemmt.
janitor *n* Hausmeister *m* (*pl* Hausmeister), Hausmeisterin *f* ▷ *He's a janitor.* Er ist Hausmeister.
January *n* Januar *m* ▷ *in January* im Januar
Japan *n* Japan *nt*
Japanese *adj* japanisch
▶ *n* ❶ *(person)* Japaner *m* (*pl* Japaner), Japanerin *f*; **the Japanese** die Japaner *mpl* ❷ *(language)* Japanisch *nt* (*gen* Japanischen)
jar *n* Glas *nt* (*gen* Glases, *pl* Gläser) ▷ *an empty jar* ein leeres Glas ▷ *a jar of honey* ein Glas Honig
javelin *n* Speer *m* (*pl* Speere)
jaw *n* Kiefer *m* (*pl* Kiefer)
jazz *n* Jazz *m* (*gen* Jazz)
jealous *adj* eifersüchtig
jeans *npl* Jeans *fpl* ▷ *a pair of jeans* eine Jeans
Jello® *n (US)* Wackelpudding *m*
jelly *n* ❶ *(dessert)* Wackelpudding *m* ❷ *(jam)* Marmelade *f*
jellyfish *n* Qualle *f*
jersey *n* Pullover *m* (*pl* Pullover)
Jesus *n* Jesus *m* (*gen* Jesus)
jet *n (plane)* Düsenflugzeug *nt* (*pl* Düsenflugzeuge)
jetlag *n* **to be suffering from jetlag** unter der Zeitverschiebung leiden [**44**]
Jew *n* Jude *m* (*gen* Juden, *pl* Juden), Jüdin *f*
jewel *n (stone)* Edelstein *m* (*pl* Edelsteine)
jeweller *n* Juwelier *m* (*pl* Juweliere), Juwelierin *f* ▷ *He's a jeweller.* Er ist Juwelier.
jeweller's shop *n* Juweliergeschäft *nt* (*pl* Juweliergeschäfte)
jewellery *n* Schmuck *m*
Jewish *adj* jüdisch
jigsaw *n* Puzzle *nt* (*pl* Puzzles)
job *n* ❶ Job *m* (*pl* Jobs) ▷ *He's lost his job.* Er hat seinen Job verloren. ▷ *I've got a Saturday job.* Ich habe einen Samstagsjob. ❷ *(chore, task)* Arbeit *f* ▷ *That was a difficult job.* Das war eine schwierige Arbeit.
jobless *adj* arbeitslos
jockey *n* Jockey *m* (*pl* Jockeys)
jog *vb* joggen [**48**]
jogging *n* Jogging *nt* ▷ *I like jogging.* Ich mag Jogging.; **to go jogging** joggen [**48**]
join *vb* ❶ *(become member of)* beitreten [**79**] (*pres* tritt bei, *imperf* trat bei, *perf* ist

beigetreten) ▷ *I'm going to join the tennis club.* Ich trete dem Tennisklub bei. ❷ *(accompany)* sich anschließen (*imperf* schloss sich an, *perf* hat sich angeschlossen) ▷ *Do you mind if I join you?* Macht es dir etwas aus, wenn ich mich dir anschließe?

join in *vb* ❶ mitmachen [**48**] (*perf* hat mitgemacht) ▷ *He doesn't join in with what we do.* Er macht nicht mit bei den Dingen, die wir tun. ❷ einstimmen [**4**] (*perf* hat eingestimmt)

joiner *n* Schreiner *m* (*pl* Schreiner), Schreinerin *f* ▷ *She's a joiner.* Sie ist Schreinerin.

joint *n* ❶ *(in body)* Gelenk *nt* (*pl* Gelenke) ❷ *(of meat)* Braten *m* (*pl* Braten) ❸ *(drugs)* Joint *m* (*pl* Joints)

joke *n* Witz *m* (*gen* Witzes, *pl* Witze) ▷ *to tell a joke* einen Witz erzählen
▸ *vb* Spaß machen [**48**] ▷ *I'm only joking.* Ich mache nur Spaß.

Jordan *n (country)* Jordanien *nt*

jotter *n (pad)* Notizblock *m* (*pl* Notizblöcke)

journalism *n* Journalismus *m* (*gen* Journalismus)

journalist *n* Journalist *m* (*gen* Journalisten, *pl* Journalisten), Journalistin *f* ▷ *She's a journalist.* Sie ist Journalistin.

journey *n* ❶ Reise *f* ▷ *I don't like long journeys.* Ich mag lange Reisen nicht.; **to go on a journey** eine Reise machen [**48**] ❷ *(to school, work)* Fahrt *f* ▷ *the journey to school* die Fahrt zur Schule; **a bus journey** eine Busfahrt

joy *n* Freude *f*

joystick *n (for computer game)* Joystick *m* (*pl* Joysticks)

judge *n* Richter *m* (*pl* Richter), Richterin *f* ▷ *She's a judge.* Sie ist Richterin.
▸ *vb (assess)* beurteilen [**7**] (*perf* hat beurteilt) ▷ *You can judge for yourself which is better.* Du kannst das selbst beurteilen, welches besser ist.

judo *n* Judo *nt* (*gen* Judo)

jug *n* Krug *m* (*pl* Krüge)

juggler *n* Jongleur *m*, Jongleurin *f*

juice *n* Saft *m* (*pl* Säfte) ▷ *orange juice* der Orangensaft

July *n* Juli *m* ▷ *in July* im Juli

jumble sale *n* Flohmarkt *m* (*pl* Flohmärkte)

jump *vb* springen [**71**] (*imperf* sprang, *perf* ist gesprungen) ▷ *to jump out of the window* aus dem Fenster springen ▷ *to jump off the roof* vom Dach springen; **to jump over something** über etwas springen [**71**]

jumper *n* ❶ Pullover *m* (*pl* Pullover) ❷ *(US: dress)* Trägerkleid *nt* (*pl* Trägerkleider)

junction *n* ❶ *(of roads)* Kreuzung *f* ❷ *(motorway exit)* Ausfahrt *f*

June *n* Juni *m* ▷ *in June* im Juni

jungle *n* Dschungel *m* (*pl* Dschungel)

junior *n* **the juniors** die Grundschüler *mpl*

junior school *n* Grundschule *f*

The **Grundschule** is a primary school which children attend from the age of 6 to 10.

junk *n (old things)* Krempel *m* ▷ *The attic's full of junk.* Der Speicher ist voller Krempel.; **to eat junk food** Junkfood essen [**20**]; **a junk shop** ein Trödelladen *m*

jury *n (in court)* Geschworenen *mpl*

just *adv* ❶ *(barely)* gerade ▷ *We had just enough money.* Wir hatten gerade genug Geld. ▷ *just in time* gerade noch rechtzeitig ❷ *(shortly)* kurz ▷ *just after Christmas* kurz nach Weihnachten ❸ *(exactly)* genau ▷ *just here* genau hier ❹ *(this minute)* eben ▷ *I did it just now.* Ich habe es eben gemacht. ▷ *He's just arrived.* Er ist eben angekommen.; **I'm rather busy just now.** Ich bin gerade ziemlich beschäftigt.; **I'm just coming!** Ich komme schon! ❺ *(only)* nur ▷ *It's just a suggestion.* Es ist nur ein Vorschlag.

justice *n* Gerechtigkeit *f*

K

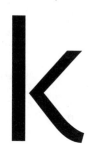

kangaroo *n* Känguru *nt* (*pl* Kängurus)
karate *n* Karate *nt* (*gen* Karate) ▷ *I like karate.* Ich mag Karate.
kebab *n* Kebab *m* (*pl* Kebabs)
keen *adj* ❶ *(enthusiastic)* begeistert ▷ *He doesn't seem very keen.* Er scheint nicht gerade begeistert. ❷ *(hardworking)* eifrig ▷ *She's a keen student.* Sie ist eine eifrige Studentin.; **to be keen on something** etwas mögen [50]; **to be keen on somebody** *(fancy them)* auf jemanden stehen [72]; **to be keen on doing something** Lust haben [32], etwas zu tun
keep *vb* ❶ *(retain)* behalten [33] ▷ *You can keep it.* Das kannst du behalten. ❷ *(remain)* sein [65] ▷ *Keep quiet!* Sei still!; **Keep still!** Halt still!; **I keep forgetting my keys.** Ich vergesse dauernd meine Schlüssel.; **to keep on doing something (1)** *(continue)* etwas weiter tun [81] ▷ *He kept on reading.* Er las weiter. **(2)** *(repeatedly)* etwas dauernd tun [81] ▷ *The car keeps on breaking down.* Das Auto ist dauernd kaputt.; **'keep out'** 'Kein Zutritt'; **to keep up** mithalten [33] ▷ *Matthew walks so fast I can't keep up.* Matthew geht so schnell, da kann ich nicht mithalten.
keep-fit *n* Gymnastik *f* ▷ *I like keep-fit.* Ich mache gern Gymnastik.; **I go to keep-fit classes.** Ich gehe zur Gymnastik.
kept *vb see* **keep**
kettle *n* Wasserkessel *m* (*pl* Wasserkessel)
key *n* Schlüssel *m* (*pl* Schlüssel)
keyboard *n* ❶ *(of piano, computer)* Tastatur *f* ❷ *(of electric organ)* Keyboard *nt* (*pl* Keyboards) ▷ *... with Mike Moran on keyboards ...* mit Mike Moran am Keyboard
kick *n* Tritt *m* (*pl* Tritte)
▶ *vb* treten [79] (*pres* tritt, *imperf* trat, *perf* hat getreten) ▷ *He kicked me.* Er hat mich getreten. ▷ *He kicked the ball hard.* Er trat kräftig gegen den Ball.; **to kick off** *(in football)* anfangen [23]
kick-off *n* Anstoß *m* (*gen* Anstoßes, *pl* Anstöße) ▷ *Kick-off is at ten o'clock.* Um zehn Uhr ist Anstoß.
kid *n* *(child)* Kind *nt* (*pl* Kinder)
▶ *vb* Spaß machen [48] ▷ *I'm just kidding.* Ich mache nur Spaß.
kidnap *vb* entführen [18] (*perf* hat entführt)
kidney *n* Niere *f* ▷ *He's got kidney trouble.* Er hat Nierenprobleme. ▷ *I don't like kidneys.* Ich mag Nieren nicht.
kill *vb* töten [2]; **to be killed** umkommen [40]; **to kill oneself** sich umbringen [13]
killer *n* ❶ *(murderer)* Mörder *m* (*pl* Mörder), Mörderin *f* ▷ *The police are searching for the killer.* Die Polizei sucht nach dem Mörder. ❷ *(hitman)* Killer *m* (*pl* Killer) ▷ *a hired killer* ein Auftragskiller; **Meningitis can be a killer.** Hirnhautentzündung kann tödlich sein.

kilo *n* Kilo *nt* (*pl* Kilos *or* Kilo) ▷ *twenty euros a kilo* zwanzig Euro das Kilo

When specifying a quantity of something use the plural form **Kilo**.

▷ *three kilos of tomatoes* drei Kilo Tomaten

kilometre *n* Kilometer *m* (*pl* Kilometer) ▷ *a hundred kilometres* hundert Kilometer

kilt *n* Kilt *m* (*pl* Kilts)

kind *adj* nett ▷ *Thank you for being so kind.* Vielen Dank, dass Sie so nett waren.; **to be kind to somebody** zu jemandem nett sein [**65**]

▶ *n* Art *f* ▷ *It's a kind of sausage.* Es ist eine Art Wurst.; **a new kind of dictionary** ein neuartiges Wörterbuch

kindness *n* Freundlichkeit *f*

king *n* König *m* (*pl* Könige)

kingdom *n* Königreich *nt* (*pl* Königreiche)

kiosk *n* ❶ *(phone box)* Telefonzelle *f* ❷ Kiosk *m* (*pl* Kioske) ▷ *a newspaper kiosk* ein Zeitungskiosk

kiss *n* Kuss *m* (*gen* Kusses, *pl* Küsse) ▷ *a passionate kiss* ein leidenschaftlicher Kuss

▶ *vb* ❶ küssen [**48**] ▷ *He kissed me.* Er küsste mich. ❷ sich küssen [**48**] ▷ *They kissed.* Sie küssten sich.

kit *n* ❶ *(clothes for sport)* Zeug *nt* ▷ *I've forgotten my gym kit.* Ich habe mein Sportzeug vergessen. ❷ Kasten *m* (*pl* Kästen) ▷ *a tool kit* ein Werkzeugkasten ▷ *a first-aid kit* ein Erste-Hilfe-Kasten; **puncture repair kit** das Flickzeug; **sewing kit** das Nähzeug

kitchen *n* Küche *f* ▷ *a fitted kitchen* eine Einbauküche; **the kitchen units** die Küchenschränke; **a kitchen knife** ein Küchenmesser *nt*

kite *n* Drachen *m* (*pl* Drachen)

kitten *n* Kätzchen *nt* (*pl* Kätzchen)

knee *n* Knie *nt* (*pl* Knie) ▷ *He was on his knees.* Er lag auf den Knien.

knew *vb see* **know**

knickers *npl* Unterhose *f* ▷ *a pair of knickers* eine Unterhose

knife *n* Messer *nt* (*pl* Messer); **a sheath knife** ein Fahrtenmesser; **a penknife** ein Taschenmesser

knit *vb* stricken [**48**]

knitting *n* Stricken *nt*; **I like knitting.** Ich stricke gern.

knives *npl see* **knife**

knob *n* ❶ *(on door)* Griff *m* ❷ *(on radio, TV)* Knopf *m* (*pl* Knöpfe)

knock *vb* klopfen [**38**] ▷ *to knock on the door* an die Tür klopfen; **Someone's knocking at the door.** Es klopft.; **She was knocked down by a car.** Ein Auto hat sie umgefahren.; **He was knocked out.** *(stunned)* Er wurde bewusstlos geschlagen.; **to knock somebody out** *(defeat)* jemanden schlagen [**59**]; **They were knocked out early in the tournament.** Sie schieden beim Turnier früh aus.; **to knock something over** etwas umstoßen

▶ *n* **There was a knock on the door.** Es hat geklopft.

knot *n* Knoten *m* (*pl* Knoten)

know *vb*

Use **wissen** for knowing facts, **kennen** for knowing people and places.

❶ wissen [**93**] (*pres* weiß, *imperf* wusste, *perf* hat gewusst) ▷ *It's a long way. — Yes, I know.* Es ist weit. — Ja, ich weiß. ▷ *I don't know.* Ich weiß nicht. ▷ *I don't know what to do.* Ich weiß nicht, was ich tun soll. ▷ *I don't know how to do it.* Ich weiß nicht, wie ich es machen soll. ❷ kennen [**39**] (*imperf* kannte, *perf* hat gekannt) ▷ *I know her.* Ich kenne sie. ▷ *I know Berlin well.* Ich kenne Berlin gut.; **I don't know any French.** Ich kann kein Französisch.; **to know that ...** wissen [**93**], dass ... ▷ *I know that you like chocolate.* Ich weiß, dass du Schokolade magst. ▷ *I didn't know that your dad was a policeman.* Ich wusste nicht, dass dein Vater Polizist

ist.; **to know about something (1)** *(be aware of)* von etwas wissen [**93**] ▷ *Do you know about the meeting this afternoon?* Weißt du von dem Treffen heute Nachmittag? **(2)** *(be knowledgeable about)* sich mit etwas auskennen [**39**] ▷ *He knows a lot about cars.* Er kennt sich mit Autos aus. ▷ *I don't know much about computers.* Mit Computern kenne ich mich nicht besonders aus.; **to get to know somebody** jemanden kennenlernen [**4**]; **How should I know?** *(I don't know!)* Wie soll ich das wissen?; **You never know!** Man kann nie wissen!

knowledge *n* ❶ *(general knowledge)* Wissen *nt* ▷ *Our knowledge of the universe is limited.* Unser Wissen über das Universum ist begrenzt. ❷ *(things learnt)* Kenntnisse *fpl* ▷ *my knowledge of German* meine Deutschkenntnisse

known *vb see* **know**

Koran *n* Koran *m*

Korea *n* Korea *nt*; **from Korea** aus Korea; **to Korea** nach Korea

kosher *adj* koscher

l

lab *n (= laboratory)* Labor *nt* (*pl* Labors); **a lab technician** ein Laborant *m*

label *n* ❶ *(sticker)* Aufkleber *m* (*pl* Aufkleber) ❷ *(on clothes)* Etikett *nt* (*pl* Etiketts) ❸ *(for luggage)* Anhänger *m* (*pl* Anhänger)

laboratory *n* Labor *nt* (*pl* Labors)

labor union *n (US)* Gewerkschaft *f*

lace *n* ❶ *(of shoe)* Schnürsenkel *m* (*pl* Schnürsenkel) ❷ Spitze *f* ▷ *a lace collar* ein Spitzenkragen

lad *n* Junge *m* (*gen* Jungen, *pl* Jungen)

ladder *n* ❶ Leiter *f* ❷ *(in tights)* Laufmasche *f*

lady *n* Dame *f* ▷ *a young lady* eine junge Dame; **Ladies and gentlemen ...** Meine Damen und Herren ...; **the ladies'** die Damentoilette

ladybird *n* Marienkäfer *m* (*pl* Marienkäfer)

laid *vb see* **lay**

laid-back *adj* locker

lain *vb see* **lie**

lake *n* See *m* (*pl* Seen); **Lake Geneva** der Genfer See; **Lake Constance** der Bodensee

lamb *n* Lamm *nt* (*pl* Lämmer); **a lamb chop** ein Lammkotelett *nt*

lamp *n* Lampe *f*

lamppost *n* Laternenpfahl *m* (*pl* Laternenpfähle)

lampshade *n* Lampenschirm *m*

land *n* Land *nt* (*pl* Länder) ▷ *a piece of land* ein Stück Land
▸ *vb (plane, passenger)* landen [**54**] (*perf* ist gelandet)

landing *n* ❶ *(of plane)* Landung *f* ❷ *(of staircase)* Treppenabsatz *m* (*gen* Treppenabsatzes, *pl* Treppenabsätze)

landlady *n* Vermieterin *f*

landlord *n* Vermieter *m* (*pl* Vermieter)

landscape *n* Landschaft *f*

lane *n* ❶ *(in country)* Sträßchen *nt* (*pl* Sträßchen) ❷ *(on motorway)* Spur *f*

language *n* Sprache *f* ▷ *a difficult language* eine schwierige Sprache; **to use bad language** Kraftausdrücke benutzen [**36**]

language laboratory *n* Sprachlabor *nt* (*pl* Sprachlabors)

lap *n (sport)* Runde *f* ▷ *I ran ten laps.* Ich bin zehn Runden gelaufen.; **on my lap** auf meinem Schoß

laptop *n (computer)* Laptop *m* (*pl* Laptops)

large *adj* groß ▷ *a large house* ein großes Haus ▷ *a large dog* ein großer Hund

laser *n* Laser *m* (*pl* Laser)

last *adj, adv* ❶ letzte ▷ *one last time* ein letztes Mal ▷ *the last question* die letzte Frage ▷ *last Friday* letzten Freitag ▷ *last week* letzte Woche ❷ als Letzte ▷ *He arrived last.* Er kam als Letzter an. ❸ zuletzt ▷ *I've lost my bag. — When did you see it last?* Ich habe meine Tasche verloren. — Wann hast du sie zuletzt gesehen?; **When I last saw him, he was okay.** Als ich ihn das letzte Mal sah, war er in Ordnung.; **the last time** das letzte Mal ▷ *the last time I saw her* als ich sie das letzte Mal sah ▷ *That's the last time I take your advice!* Das ist das letzte Mal, dass ich auf deinen Rat höre!; **last night (1)** *(evening)* gestern Abend ▷ *I got home at midnight last night.* Ich bin gestern Abend um Mitternacht nach Hause gekommen. **(2)** *(sleeping hours)* heute Nacht ▷ *I couldn't sleep last night.* Ich konnte heute Nacht nicht schlafen.; **at last** endlich
▸ *vb* dauern [**88**] ▷ *The concert lasts two hours.* Das Konzert dauert zwei Stunden.

lastly *adv* schließlich ▷ *Lastly I'd like to mention that ...* Und schließlich möchte ich erwähnen, dass ...

late *adj, adv* ❶ zu spät ▷ *Hurry up or you'll be late!* Beeil dich, du kommst sonst zu spät! ▷ *I'm often late for school.* Ich komme oft zu spät zur Schule.; **to arrive late** zu spät kommen [**40**] ❷ spät ▷ *I went to bed late.* Ich bin spät ins Bett gegangen. ▷ *in the late afternoon* am späten Nachmittag; **in late May** Ende Mai

lately *adv* in letzter Zeit ▷ *I haven't seen him lately.* Ich habe ihn in letzter Zeit nicht gesehen.

later *adv* später ▷ *I'll do it later.* Ich mache es später.; **See you later!** Bis später!

latest *adj* neueste ▷ *the latest news* die neuesten Nachrichten ▷ *their latest album* ihr neuestes Album; **at the latest** spätestens

Latin *n* Latein *nt* ▷ *I do Latin.* Ich lerne Latein.

Latin America *n* Lateinamerika *nt*; **from Latin America** aus Lateinamerika; **to Latin America** nach Lateinamerika

Latin American *adj* lateinamerikanisch

laugh *n* Lachen *nt*; **It was a good laugh.** *(it was fun)* Es war lustig.
▸ *vb* lachen [**48**]; **to laugh at**

something über etwas lachen [48]; **to laugh at somebody** jemanden auslachen [4]

launch *vb* ❶ *(product)* auf den Markt bringen [13] *(imperf* brachte, *perf* hat gebracht) ❷ *(rocket)* abschießen *(imperf* schoss ab, *perf* hat abgeschossen)

Launderette® *n* Waschsalon *m (pl* Waschsalons)

Laundromat® *n (US)* Waschsalon *m (pl* Waschsalons)

laundry *n (clothes)* Wäsche *f*

lavatory *n* Toilette *f*

lavender *n* Lavendel *m*

law *n* ❶ Gesetz *nt (gen* Gesetzes, *pl* Gesetze) ▷ *It's against the law.* Das ist gegen das Gesetz. ❷ *(subject)* Jura ▷ *She's studying law.* Sie studiert Jura.

lawn *n* Rasen *m (pl* Rasen)

lawnmower *n* Rasenmäher *m (pl* Rasenmäher)

lawyer *n* Rechtsanwalt *m (pl* Rechtsanwälte), Rechtsanwältin *f* ▷ *My mother's a lawyer.* Meine Mutter ist Rechtsanwältin.

lay *vb*

'lay' is also a form of 'lie (2)' **verb**

legen [38] ▷ *She laid the baby in her cot.* Sie legte das Baby ins Bettchen.; **to lay the table** den Tisch decken [38]; **to lay something on (1)** *(provide)* etwas bereitstellen [15] ▷ *They laid on extra buses.* Sie stellten zusätzliche Busse bereit. **(2)** *(prepare)* etwas vorbereiten [2] ▷ *They had laid on a special meal.* Sie hatten ein besonderes Essen vorbereitet.; **to lay off** entlassen [42] ▷ *My father's been laid off.* Mein Vater ist entlassen worden.

lay-by *n* Rastplatz *m (gen* Rastplatzes, *pl* Rastplätze)

layer *n* Schicht *f*

layout *n (of house, garden)* Design *nt (pl* Designs)

lazy *adj* faul

lb. *abbr (= pound)* Pfund

lead (1) *n* ❶ *(cable)* Kabel *nt (pl* Kabel) ❷ *(for dog)* Hundeleine *f*; **to be in the lead** in Führung sein [65]

lead (2) *n (metal)* Blei *nt*

lead *vb* führen [38] ▷ *the street that leads to the station* die Straße, die zum Bahnhof führt; **to lead the way** vorangehen [29]; **to lead somebody away** jemanden abführen [4]

leader *n* ❶ *(of expedition, gang)* Führer *m (pl* Führer), Führerin *f* ❷ *(of political party)* Anführer *m (pl* Anführer), Anführerin *f*

lead-free *adj* **lead-free petrol** das bleifreie Benzin

lead singer *n* Leadsinger *m (pl* Leadsinger), Leadsingerin *f*

leaf *n* Blatt *nt (pl* Blätter)

leaflet *n (advertising)* Prospekt *m (pl* Prospekte) ▷ *a leaflet about their products* einen Prospekt über ihre Produkte

league *n* Liga *f (gen* Liga, *pl* Ligen) ▷ *the Premier League* die erste Liga

The 'Premier League' is similar to the German **Bundesliga**.

They are at the top of the league. Sie sind Tabellenführer.

leak *n* undichte Stelle *f* ▷ *a gas leak* eine undichte Stelle in der Gasleitung ▶ *vb* ❶ *(pipe)* undicht sein [65] *(pres* ist undicht, *imperf* war undicht, *perf* ist undicht gewesen) ❷ *(water)* auslaufen [43] *(pres* läuft aus, *imperf* lief aus, *perf* ist ausgelaufen) ❸ *(gas)* austreten [79] *(pres* tritt aus, *imperf* trat aus, *perf* ist ausgetreten)

lean *vb* sich lehnen [38] ▷ *Don't lean over too far.* Lehn dich nicht zu weit vor. ▷ *She leant out of the window.* Sie lehnte sich zum Fenster hinaus.; **to lean forward** sich nach vorn beugen [38]; **to lean on something** sich auf etwas stützen [48]; **to be leaning against something** gegen etwas gelehnt sein [65]; **to lean something against a wall** etwas an einer Mauer anlehnen [4]

leap *vb* springen [71] (*imperf* sprang, *perf* ist gesprungen) ▷ *He leapt out of his chair when his team scored.* Er sprang vom Stuhl auf, als seine Mannschaft ein Tor schoss.

leap year *n* Schaltjahr *nt* (*pl* Schaltjahre)

learn *vb* lernen [38] ▷ *I'm learning to ski.* Ich lerne Ski fahren.

learner *n* **She's a quick learner.** Sie lernt schnell.; **German learners** *(people learning German)* Deutschschüler *mpl*

learner driver *n* Fahrschüler *m* (*pl* Fahrschüler), Fahrschülerin *f*

learnt *vb see* **learn**

least *adv, adj, pron* **the least (1)** *(followed by noun)* wenigste ▷ *the least time* die wenigste Zeit ▷ *She has the least money.* Sie hat das wenigste Geld. **(2)** *(followed by adjective)* am wenigsten ... ▷ *the least intelligent pupil* der am wenigsten intelligente Schüler ▷ *the least attractive woman* die am wenigsten attraktive Frau ▷ *the least interesting book* das am wenigsten interessante Buch **(3)** *(after a verb)* am wenigsten ▷ *Maths is the subject I like the least.* Mathe ist das Fach, das ich am wenigsten mag.; **It's the least I can do.** Das ist das wenigste, was ich tun kann.; **at least (1)** mindestens ▷ *It'll cost at least two hundred pounds.* Das kostet mindestens zweihundert Pfund. **(2)** wenigstens ▷ *... but at least nobody was hurt.* ... aber wenigstens wurde niemand verletzt.; **It's totally unfair – at least, that's my opinion.** Das ist total ungerecht – zumindest meiner Meinung nach.

leather *n* Leder *nt* (*pl* Leder) ▷ *a black leather jacket* eine schwarze Lederjacke

leave *vb* ❶ *(deliberately)* lassen [42] (*pres* lässt, *imperf* ließ, *perf* hat gelassen) ▷ *He always leaves his camera in the car.* Er lässt immer seinen Fotoapparat im Auto. ❷ *(by mistake)* vergessen [83] (*pres* vergisst, *imperf* vergaß, *perf* hat vergessen) ▷ *I've left my book at home.* Ich habe mein Buch zu Hause vergessen.; **Don't leave anything behind.** Lassen Sie nichts liegen. ❸ *(bus, train)* abfahren [21] (*pres* fährt ab, *imperf* fuhr ab, *perf* ist abgefahren) ▷ *The bus leaves at eight.* Der Bus fährt um acht ab. ❹ *(plane)* abfliegen [25] (*imperf* flog ab, *perf* ist abgeflogen) ▷ *The plane leaves at six.* Das Flugzeug fliegt um sechs ab. ❺ *(person)* weggehen [29] (*imperf* ging weg, *perf* ist weggegangen) ▷ *She's just left.* Sie ist eben weggegangen.; **She left home last year.** Sie ist letztes Jahr von zu Hause weggezogen. ❻ *(abandon)* verlassen [42] (*pres* verlässt, *imperf* verließ, *perf* hat verlassen) ▷ *She left her husband.* Sie hat ihren Mann verlassen.; **to leave somebody alone** jemanden in Ruhe lassen [42]; **to leave out** auslassen [42]; **I felt really left out.** Ich fühlte mich richtig ausgeschlossen.
▶ *n (from job, army)* Urlaub *m* (*pl* Urlaube) ▷ *a week's leave* eine Woche Urlaub

leaves *npl see* **leaf**

Lebanon *n* Libanon *m*

> Note that the definite article is used in German for countries which are masculine.

from Lebanon aus dem Libanon; **in Lebanon** im Libanon; **to Lebanon** in den Libanon

lecture *n* ❶ *(public)* Vortrag *m* (*pl* Vorträge) ❷ *(at university)* Vorlesung *f*

> Be careful not to translate **lecture** by **Lektüre**.

▶ *vb* ❶ unterrichten [2] (*perf* hat unterrichtet) ▷ *She lectures at the technical college.* Sie unterrichtet an der Fachschule. ❷ *(tell off)* belehren [7] (*perf* hat belehrt) ▷ *He's always lecturing us.* Er belehrt uns andauernd.

lecturer *n* Dozent *m* (*gen* Dozenten, *pl* Dozenten), Dozentin *f* ▷ *She's a lecturer.* Sie ist Dozentin.

led *vb see* **lead** *vb*

leek *n* Lauch *m* (*pl* Lauche)

left *vb see* **leave**

▶ *adj, adv* ❶ linke ▷ *the left foot* der linke Fuß ▷ *my left arm* mein linker Arm ▷ *your left hand* deine linke Hand ▷ *her left eye* ihr linkes Auge ❷ links ▷ *Turn left at the traffic lights.* Biegen Sie an der Ampel links ab.; **Look left!** Sehen Sie nach links!; **I haven't got any money left.** Ich habe kein Geld mehr.

▶ *n* linke Seite *f*; **on the left** links

left-hand *adj* **the left-hand side** die linke Seite; **It's on the left-hand side.** Es liegt links.

left-handed *adj* linkshändig

left-luggage office *n* Gepäckaufbewahrung *f*

leg *n* Bein *nt* (*pl* Beine) ▷ *I've broken my leg.* Ich habe mir das Bein gebrochen.; **a chicken leg** eine Hähnchenkeule; **a leg of lamb** eine Lammkeule

legal *adj* legal

leggings *npl* Leggings *pl*

leisure *n* Freizeit *f* ▷ *What do you do in your leisure time?* Was machen Sie in Ihrer Freizeit?

leisure centre *n* Freizeitzentrum *nt* (*pl* Freizeitzentren)

lemon *n* Zitrone *f*

lemonade *n* Limonade *f*

lend *vb* leihen (*imperf* lieh, *perf* hat geliehen) ▷ *I can lend you some money.* Ich kann dir Geld leihen.

length *n* Länge *f*; **It's about a metre in length.** Es ist etwa einen Meter lang.

lens *n* ❶ (*contact lens*) Kontaktlinse *f* ❷ (*of spectacles*) Glas *nt* (*gen* Glases, *pl* Gläser) ❸ (*of camera*) Objektiv *nt* (*pl* Objektive)

Lent *n* Fastenzeit *f* ▷ *during Lent* während der Fastenzeit

lent *vb see* **lend**

lentil *n* Linse *f*

Leo *n* Löwe *m* (*gen* Löwen) ▷ *I'm Leo.* Ich bin Löwe.

leotard *n* Gymnastikanzug *m* (*pl* Gymnastikanzüge)

lesbian *n* Lesbierin *f*; **She's a lesbian.** Sie ist lesbisch.

less *pron, adv, adj* weniger ▷ *A bit less, please.* Etwas weniger, bitte. ▷ *I've got less time for hobbies now.* Ich habe jetzt weniger Zeit für Hobbys.; **He's less intelligent than his brother.** Er ist nicht so intelligent wie sein Bruder.; **less than** weniger als

lesson *n* ❶ Lektion *f* ▷ *'Lesson Sixteen' (in textbook)* 'Lektion sechzehn' ❷ (*class*) Stunde *f* ▷ *A lesson lasts forty minutes.* Eine Stunde dauert vierzig Minuten.

let *vb* ❶ (*allow*) lassen [**42**] (*pres* lässt, *imperf* ließ, *perf* hat gelassen); **to let somebody do something** jemanden etwas tun lassen [**42**]; **to let somebody down** jemanden enttäuschen [**18**]; **to let somebody know** jemandem Bescheid sagen [**38**]; **to let go** (*release*) loslassen [**42**]; **to let in** hineinlassen [**42**]; **Let's go to the cinema!** Lass uns ins Kino gehen!; **Let's go!** Gehen wir! ❷ (*hire out*) vermieten [**2**] (*perf* hat vermietet); **'to let'** 'zu vermieten'

letter *n* ❶ Brief *m* (*pl* Briefe) ▷ *She wrote me a long letter.* Sie hat mir einen langen Brief geschrieben. ❷ (*of alphabet*) Buchstabe *m* (*gen* Buchstaben, *pl* Buchstaben) ▷ *the letters of the alphabet* die Buchstaben des Alphabets

letterbox *n* Briefkasten *m* (*pl* Briefkästen)

lettuce *n* Kopfsalat *m* (*pl* Kopfsalate)

leukaemia *n* Leukämie *f* ▷ *He suffers from leukaemia.* Er leidet an Leukämie.

level *adj* eben ▷ *A snooker table must be perfectly level.* Ein Snookertisch muss ganz eben sein.

▶ *n* ❶ (*of river, lake*) Wasserstand *m* (*pl* Wasserstände) ▷ *The level of the river is rising.* Der Wasserstand des Flusses steigt. ❷ (*height*) Höhe *f* ▷ *at eye level* in Augenhöhe; **A levels** das Abitur

- Germans take their **Abitur** at the age of 19. The students sit examinations in a variety of subjects to attain an overall grade. If you pass, you have the right to a place at university.

level crossing *n* Bahnübergang *m* (*pl* Bahnübergänge)
lever *n* Hebel *m* (*pl* Hebel)
liar *n* Lügner *m* (*pl* Lügner), Lügnerin *f*
liberal *adj* (*opinions*) liberal; **the Liberal Democrats** die Liberaldemokraten
Libra *n* Waage *f* ▷ *I'm Libra.* Ich bin Waage.
librarian *n* Bibliothekar *m* (*pl* Bibliothekare), Bibliothekarin *f* ▷ *She's a librarian.* Sie ist Bibliothekarin.
library *n* ❶ (*public lending library*) Bücherei *f* ❷ (*of school, university*) Bibliothek *f*
licence *n* Schein *m* (*pl* Scheine); **a driving licence** ein Führerschein *m*
lick *vb* lecken [**48**]
lid *n* Deckel *m* (*pl* Deckel)
lie *n* Lüge *f* ▷ *That's a lie!* Das ist eine Lüge!; **to tell a lie** lügen [**47**]
lie (1) *vb* (*not tell the truth*) lügen [**47**] (*imperf* log, *perf* hat gelogen) ▷ *I know she's lying.* Ich weiß, dass sie lügt.
lie (2) *vb* liegen [**46**] (*imperf* lag, *perf* hat gelegen) ▷ *He was lying on the sofa.* Er lag auf dem Sofa. ▷ *When I'm on holiday I lie on the beach all day.* In den Ferien liege ich den ganzen Tag am Strand.; **to lie down** sich hinlegen [**4**]; **to be lying down** liegen [**46**]
lie-in *n* **to have a lie-in** ausschlafen [**58**]
lieutenant *n* Leutnant *m* (*pl* Leutnants)
life *n* Leben *nt* (*pl* Leben)
lifebelt *n* Rettungsring *m* (*pl* Rettungsringe)
lifeboat *n* Rettungsboot *nt* (*pl* Rettungsboote)
lifeguard *n* ❶ (*at beach*) Rettungsschwimmer *m* (*pl* Rettungsschwimmer), Rettungsschwimmerin *f* ❷ (*at swimming pool*) Bademeister *m* (*pl* Bademeister), Bademeisterin *f*
life jacket *n* Schwimmweste *f*
lifestyle *n* Lebensstil *m* (*pl* Lebensstile)
lift *vb* hochheben (*imperf* hob hoch, *perf* hat hochgehoben) ▷ *I can't lift it.* Ich kann es nicht hochheben.
▸ *n* Aufzug *m* (*pl* Aufzüge) ▷ *The lift isn't working.* Der Aufzug geht nicht.; **He gave me a lift to the cinema.** Er hat mich zum Kino gefahren.; **Would you like a lift?** Wollen Sie mitfahren?
light *adj* ❶ (*not heavy*) leicht ▷ *a light jacket* eine leichte Jacke ▷ *a light meal* ein leichtes Essen ❷ (*colour*) hell ▷ *a light blue sweater* ein hellblauer Pullover
▸ *n* ❶ Licht *nt* (*pl* Lichter) ▷ *to switch on the light* das Licht anmachen ▷ *to switch off the light* das Licht ausmachen
❷ Lampe *f* ▷ *There's a light by my bed.* Ich habe am Bett eine Lampe.; **the traffic lights** die Ampel *sg*; **Have you got a light?** (*for cigarette*) Haben Sie Feuer?
▸ *vb* (*candle, cigarette, fire*) anzünden [**54**] (*perf* hat angezündet)
light bulb *n* Glühbirne *f*
lighter *n* (*for cigarettes*) Feuerzeug *nt* (*pl* Feuerzeuge)
lighthouse *n* Leuchtturm *m* (*pl* Leuchttürme)
lightning *n* Blitz *m* (*gen* Blitzes, *pl* Blitze); **a flash of lightning** ein Blitz; **There was a flash of lightning.** Es hat geblitzt.
like *vb* mögen [**50**] (*pres* mag, *imperf* mochte, *perf* hat gemocht) ▷ *I don't like mustard.* Ich mag Senf nicht. ▷ *I like Paul, but I don't want to go out with him.* Ich mag Paul, aber ich will nicht mit ihm ausgehen.; **I like riding.** Ich reite gern.; **Would you like ...?** Möchtest du ...?; **I'd like ...** Ich hätte gern ...; **I'd like to ...** Ich würde gern ...; **... if you like** ... wenn du möchtest
▸ *prep* ❶ (*this way*) so ▷ *It's fine like that.* So ist es gut. ▷ *Do it like this.* Mach das so. ❷ (*similar to*) wie ▷ *a city like Munich* eine Stadt wie München ▷ *It's a bit like*

salmon. Es ist ein bisschen wie Lachs.; **What's the weather like?** Wie ist das Wetter?; **to look like somebody** jemandem ähnlich sehen [**64**]

likely *adj* wahrscheinlich ▷ *That's not very likely.* Das ist nicht sehr wahrscheinlich.; **She's likely to come.** Sie kommt wahrscheinlich.; **She's not likely to come.** Sie kommt wahrscheinlich nicht.

Lilo® *n* Luftmatratze *f*

lime *n (fruit)* Limone *f*

limit *n* Grenze *f*; **the speed limit** die Geschwindigkeitsbegrenzung

limp *vb* hinken [**38**]

line *n* ❶ Linie *f* ▷ *a straight line* eine gerade Linie ❷ *(to divide, cancel)* Strich *m (pl* Striche) ▷ *Draw a line under each answer.* Machen Sie unter jede Antwort einen Strich. ❸ *(railway track)* Gleis *nt (gen* Gleises, *pl* Gleise) ❹ Schlange *f* ▷ *to stand in line* Schlange stehen; **Hold the line, please.** *(on telephone)* Bleiben Sie bitte am Apparat.; **It's a very bad line.** *(on telephone)* Die Verbindung ist sehr schlecht.

linen *n* Leinen *nt* ▷ *a linen jacket* eine Leinenjacke

lining *n (of clothes)* Futter *nt (pl* Futter)

link *n* ❶ Zusammenhang *m (pl* Zusammenhänge) ▷ *the link between smoking and cancer* der Zusammenhang zwischen Rauchen und Krebs ❷ *(computer)* Link *m (pl* Links)
▶ *vb* verbinden *(imperf* verband, *perf* hat verbunden)

lion *n* Löwe *m (gen* Löwen, *pl* Löwen)

lip *n* Lippe *f*

lip-read *vb* von den Lippen ablesen [**4**] *(pres* liest von den Lippen ab, *imperf* las von den Lippen ab, *perf* hat von den Lippen abgelesen); **I'm learning to lip-read.** Ich lerne gerade Lippenlesen.

lipstick *n* Lippenstift *m (pl* Lippenstifte)

liquid *n* Flüssigkeit *f*

liquidizer *n* Mixer *m (pl* Mixer)

list *n* Liste *f*
▶ *vb* aufzählen [**4**] *(perf* hat aufgezählt) ▷ *List your hobbies.* Zählen Sie Ihre Hobbys auf.

listen *vb* zuhören [**4**] *(perf* hat zugehört) ▷ *Listen to me!* Hör mir zu!; **Listen to this!** Hör dir das an!

lit *vb see* **light**

liter *n (US)* Liter *m (pl* Liter)

literature *n* Literatur *f* ▷ *I'm studying English Literature.* Ich studiere englische Literatur.

litre *n* Liter *m (pl* Liter) ▷ *three litres* drei Liter

litter *n* Abfall *m (pl* Abfälle)

litter bin *n* Abfallkorb *m (pl* Abfallkörbe)

little *adj* klein ▷ *a little girl* ein kleines Mädchen; **a little** ein bisschen; **very little** sehr wenig; **little by little** nach und nach

live *adj* ❶ *(animal)* lebendig ❷ *(broadcast)* live; **There's live music on Fridays.** Freitags gibt es Livemusik.
▶ *vb* ❶ leben [**38**] ▷ *I live with my grandmother.* Ich lebe bei meiner Großmutter. ▷ *They're living together.* Sie leben zusammen.; **to live on something** von etwas leben [**38**] ❷ *(in house, town)* wohnen [**38**] ▷ *Where do you live?* Wo wohnst du? ▷ *I live in Edinburgh.* Ich wohne in Edinburgh.

lively *adj* lebhaft ▷ *She's got a lively personality.* Sie ist ein lebhafter Typ.

liver *n* Leber *f*; **liver sausage** die Leberwurst

livestream *n* Livestream *m (pl* Livestreams)
▶ *vb* livestreamen [**76**]

lives *npl see* **life**

living *n* **to make a living** sich seinen Lebensunterhalt verdienen [**84**]; **What does she do for a living?** Was macht sie beruflich?

living room *n* Wohnzimmer *nt (pl* Wohnzimmer)

lizard *n* Echse *f*

load *n* **loads of** eine Menge; **You're talking a load of rubbish!** Du redest vielleicht einen Unsinn!
▶ *vb* beladen *(pres* belädt, *imperf* belud,

perf hat beladen) ▷ *He's loading the van right now.* Er belädt gerade den Lieferwagen.

loaf *n* Laib *m* (*pl* Laibe); **a loaf of bread** ein Brot *nt*

loan *n* (*money*) Darlehen *nt* (*pl* Darlehen)
▸ *vb* ausleihen (*imperf* lieh aus, *perf* hat ausgeliehen)

loaves *npl see* **loaf**

lobster *n* Hummer *m* (*pl* Hummer)

local *adj* örtlich ▷ *the local police* die örtliche Polizei; **the local paper** das Lokalblatt; **a local call** ein Ortsgespräch *nt*

loch *n* See *m* (*pl* Seen)

lock *n* Schloss *nt* (*gen* Schlosses, *pl* Schlösser) ▷ *The lock is broken.* Das Schloss ist kaputt.
▸ *vb* abschließen (*imperf* schloss ab, *perf* hat abgeschlossen) ▷ *Make sure you lock your door.* Schließen Sie die Tür ab.; **to be locked out** ausgesperrt sein [**65**]

locker *n* Schließfach *nt* (*pl* Schließfächer); **the locker room** der Umkleideraum; **the left-luggage lockers** die Gepäckschließfächer

lodger *n* Untermieter *m* (*pl* Untermieter), Untermieterin *f*

loft *n* Speicher *m* (*pl* Speicher)

log *n* (*of wood*) Scheit *nt* (*pl* Scheite)

log in *vb* (*computer*) einloggen [**4**] (*perf* hat eingeloggt)

log off *vb* (*computer*) ausloggen [**4**] (*perf* hat ausgeloggt)

log on *vb* (*computer*) einloggen [**4**] (*perf* hat eingeloggt)

log out *vb* (*computer*) ausloggen [**4**] (*perf* hat ausgeloggt)

logical *adj* logisch

lollipop *n* Lutscher *m* (*pl* Lutscher)

London *n* London *nt*; **from London** aus London; **to London** nach London

Londoner *n* Londoner *m* (*pl* Londoner), Londonerin *f*

loneliness *n* Einsamkeit *f*

lonely *adj* einsam; **to feel lonely** sich einsam fühlen [**38**]

long *adj, adv* lang ▷ *She's got long hair.* Sie hat lange Haare. ▷ *The room is six metres long.* Das Zimmer ist sechs Meter lang.; **how long?** (*time*) wie lange?

> When you want to say how long you 'have been' doing something, use the present tense in German.

▷ *How long have you been here?* Wie lange bist du schon da?; **It takes a long time.** Das dauert lange.; **as long as** solange
▸ *vb* **to long to do something** es kaum erwarten können [**41**], etwas zu tun

longer *adv* **They're no longer going out together.** Sie gehen nicht mehr miteinander.; **I can't stand it any longer.** Ich halte das nicht länger aus.

long jump *n* Weitsprung *m* (*pl* Weitsprünge)

loo *n* (*informal*) Klo *nt* (*pl* Klos) ▷ *Where's the loo?* Wo ist das Klo?; **I need the loo.** (*informal*) Ich muss mal.

look *n* **to have a look** ansehen [**64**]; **I don't like the look of it.** Das gefällt mir nicht.
▸ *vb* ❶ sehen [**64**] (*pres* sieht, *imperf* sah, *perf* hat gesehen); **Look!** Sieh mal!; **to look at something** etwas ansehen [**64**] ❷ (*seem*) aussehen [**64**] (*perf* hat ausgesehen) ▷ *She looks surprised.* Sie sieht überrascht aus. ▷ *That cake looks nice.* Der Kuchen sieht gut aus. ▷ *It looks fine.* Es sieht gut aus.; **to look like somebody** jemandem ähnlich sehen [**64**]; **What does she look like?** Wie sieht sie aus?; **Look out!** Pass auf!; **to look after** sich kümmern [**34**] um; **to look for** suchen [**48**]; **to look forward to something** sich auf etwas freuen [**38**]; **Looking forward to hearing from you ...** In der Hoffnung, bald etwas von dir zu hören, ...; **to look round** sich umsehen [**64**]; **to look round a museum** ein Museum ansehen [**64**]; **to look up** (*word, name*) nachschlagen [**59**]

loose *adj (clothes)* weit; **loose change** das Kleingeld
lord *n (feudal)* Lord *m (pl* Lords); **the House of Lords** das Oberhaus; **the Lord** *(god)* Gott; **Good Lord!** Großer Gott!
lorry *n* Lastwagen *m (pl* Lastwagen)
lorry driver *n* Lastwagenfahrer *m (pl* Lastwagenfahrer), Lastwagenfahrerin *f* ▷ *He's a lorry driver.* Er ist Lastwagenfahrer.
lose *vb* verlieren [**85**] *(imperf* verlor, *perf* hat verloren) ▷ *I've lost my purse.* Ich habe meinen Geldbeutel verloren.; **to get lost** sich verlaufen [**43**]
loss *n* Verlust *m (pl* Verluste)
lost *vb see* **lose**
▶ *adj* verloren
lost-and-found *n (US)* Fundbüro *nt (pl* Fundbüros)
lost property office *n* Fundbüro *nt (pl* Fundbüros)
lot *n* **a lot** viel; **a lot of (1)** viel ▷ *He earns a lot of money.* Er verdient viel Geld. **(2)** viele ▷ *We saw a lot of interesting things.* Wir haben viele interessante Dinge gesehen.; **lots of** eine Menge ▷ *lots of money* eine Menge Geld ▷ *lots of friends* eine Menge Freunde; **What did you do at the weekend? — Not a lot.** Was hast du am Wochenende gemacht? — Nicht viel.; **Do you like football? — Not a lot.** Magst du Fußball? — Nicht besonders.; **That's the lot.** Das ist alles.
lottery *n* Lotto *nt*; **to win the lottery** im Lotto gewinnen [**30**]
loud *adj* laut ▷ *The television is too loud.* Der Fernseher ist zu laut.
loudly *adv* laut
loudspeaker *n* Lautsprecher *m (pl* Lautsprecher)
lounge *n* Wohnzimmer *nt (pl* Wohnzimmer)
love *n* Liebe *f*; **to be in love** verliebt sein [**65**]; **to make love** sich lieben [**38**]; **Give Heike my love.** Grüß Heike von mir.; **Love, Rosemary.** Alles Liebe, Rosemary.
▶ *vb* ❶ *(person, thing)* lieben [**38**] ▷ *I love you.* Ich liebe dich. ▷ *I love chocolate.* Ich liebe Schokolade. ❷ *(like a lot)* mögen [**50**] *(pres* mag, *imperf* mochte, *perf* hat gemocht) ▷ *Everybody loves her.* Alle mögen sie.; **I'd love to come.** Ich würde liebend gern kommen.; **I love skiing.** Ich fahre unheimlich gern Ski.
lovely *adj* ❶ wunderbar ▷ *What a lovely surprise!* Was für eine wunderbare Überraschung! ❷ *(pretty)* schön ▷ *They've got a lovely house.* Sie haben ein schönes Haus.; **It's a lovely day.** Es ist ein herrlicher Tag.; **She's a lovely person.** Sie ist ein sehr netter Mensch.; **Is your meal OK? — Yes, it's lovely.** Schmeckt dein Essen? — Ja, prima.; **Have a lovely time!** Viel Spaß!
lover *n* Liebhaber *m (pl* Liebhaber), Liebhaberin *f*
low *adj, adv* niedrig ▷ *low prices* niedrige Preise; **That plane is flying very low.** Das Flugzeug fliegt sehr tief.; **the low season** die Nebensaison
lower sixth *n* zwölfte Klasse *f* ▷ *He's in the lower sixth.* Er ist in der zwölften Klasse.
loyalty *n* Treue *f*
loyalty card *n* Kundenkarte *f*
luck *n* Glück *nt* ▷ *She hasn't had much luck.* Sie hat nicht viel Glück gehabt.; **Good luck!** Viel Glück!; **Bad luck!** So ein Pech!
luckily *adv* zum Glück
lucky *adj* **to be lucky (1)** *(be fortunate)* Glück haben [**32**] ▷ *He's lucky, he's got a job.* Er hat Glück, er hat Arbeit. **(2)** *(bring luck)* Glück bringen [**13**] ▷ *Black cats are lucky.* Schwarze Katzen bringen Glück.; **He wasn't hurt. — That was lucky!** Er wurde nicht verletzt. — Das war Glück!; **a lucky horseshoe** ein Glückshufeisen *nt*
luggage *n* Gepäck *nt*
lump *n* ❶ Stück *nt (pl* Stücke) ▷ *a lump of*

coal ein Stück Kohle ❷ *(swelling)* Beule *f* ▷ *He's got a lump on his forehead.* Er hat eine Beule an der Stirn.

lunch *n* Mittagessen *nt* (*pl* Mittagessen); **to have lunch** zu Mittag essen [**20**]

lung *n* Lunge *f* ▷ *lung cancer* der Lungenkrebs

Luxembourg *n (country, city)* Luxemburg *nt*; **from Luxembourg** aus Luxemburg; **to Luxembourg** nach Luxemburg

luxurious *adj* luxuriös

luxury *n* Luxus *m* (*gen* Luxus) ▷ *It was luxury!* Das war wirklich ein Luxus!; **a luxury hotel** ein Luxushotel *nt*

lying *vb see* **lie**

lyrics *npl (of song)* Text *msg* (*pl* Texte)

m

macaroni *nsg* Makkaroni *pl*

machine *n* Maschine *f*

machine gun *n* Maschinengewehr *nt*

machinery *n* Maschinen *fpl*

mad *adj* ❶ *(insane)* verrückt ▷ *You're mad!* Du bist verrückt!; **to be mad about** verrückt sein [**65**] nach ❷ *(angry)* wütend ▷ *She'll be mad when she finds out.* Wenn sie das erfährt, wird sie wütend sein.; **to be mad at somebody** wütend auf jemanden sein [**65**]

madam *n*

> In German no form of address is normally used apart from **Sie**.

▷ *Would you like to order, Madam?* Möchten Sie bestellen?

made *vb see* **make**

madness *n* Wahnsinn *m* ▷ *It's absolute madness.* Das ist totaler Wahnsinn.

magazine *n* Zeitschrift *f*

maggot *n* Made *f*

magic *adj* ❶ *(magical)* magisch ▷ *magic powers* magische Kräfte; **a magic trick**

ein Zaubertrick *m*; **a magic wand** ein Zauberstab *m* ❷ *(brilliant)* echt toll ▷ *It was magic!* Es war echt toll!
▶ *n* Zaubern *nt* ▷ *My hobby is magic.* Zaubern ist mein Hobby.

magician *n (conjurer)* Zauberkünstler *m* (*pl* Zauberkünstler), Zauberkünstlerin *f*

magnet *n* Magnet *m*

magnifying glass *n* Lupe *f*

maid *n (servant)* Hausangestellte *f* (*gen* Hausangestellten); **an old maid** *(spinster)* eine alte Jungfer

maiden name *n* Mädchenname *m* (*gen* Mädchennamens, *pl* Mädchennamen)

mail *n* ❶ Post *f* ▷ *Here's your mail.* Hier ist deine Post.; **by mail** per Post
❷ *(electronic mail)* E-Mail *f* (*pl* E-Mails)

mailbox *n (US)* Briefkasten *m* (*pl* Briefkästen)

mailman *n (US)* Briefträger *m* (*pl* Briefträger)

main *adj* **the main problem** das Hauptproblem; **the main thing** die Hauptsache

mainly *adv* hauptsächlich

main road *n* Hauptstraße *f* ▷ *I don't like cycling on main roads.* Ich fahre nicht gern auf Hauptstraßen Rad.

majesty *n* Majestät *f*; **Your Majesty** Eure Majestät

major *adj* groß ▷ *a major problem* ein großes Problem; **in C major** in C-Dur

Majorca *n* Mallorca *nt*; **to Majorca** nach Mallorca

majority *n* Mehrheit *f*

make *n* Marke *f* ▷ *What make is that car?* Welche Marke ist das Auto?
▶ *vb* ❶ machen [**48**] ▷ *He made it himself.* Er hat es selbst gemacht. ▷ *I make my bed every morning.* Ich mache jeden Morgen mein Bett. ▷ *Two and two make four.* Zwei und zwei macht vier.; **to make lunch** das Mittagessen machen [**48**]; **I'm going to make a cake.** Ich werde einen Kuchen backen.
❷ *(manufacture)* herstellen [**4**] (*perf* hat hergestellt) ▷ *made in Germany* in Deutschland hergestellt ❸ *(earn)* verdienen [**84**] (*perf* hat verdient) ▷ *He makes a lot of money.* Er verdient viel Geld.; **to make somebody do something** jemanden zwingen [**97**], etwas zu tun; **to make a phone call** telefonieren [**76**]; **to make fun of somebody** sich über jemanden lustig machen [**48**]; **What time do you make it?** Wie viel Uhr hast du?

make out *vb* ❶ entziffern [**34**] (*perf* hat entziffert) ❷ verstehen [**72**] (*imperf* verstand, *perf* hat verstanden)
❸ behaupten [**2**] (*perf* hat behauptet)

make up *vb* ❶ *(invent)* erfinden [**24**] (*imperf* erfand, *perf* hat erfunden)
❷ *(after argument)* sich versöhnen [**84**] (*perf* haben sich versöhnt)

make-up *n* Make-up *nt* (*pl* Make-ups)

Malaysia *n* Malaysia *nt*; **to Malaysia** nach Malaysia

male *adj* männlich ▷ *a male kitten* ein männliches Katzenjunges ▷ *Sex: male* Geschlecht: männlich

> In many cases, the ending in German indicates clearly whether the noun refers to a man or a woman and there is therefore no need for the word 'male'.

▷ *male and female students* Studenten und Studentinnen; **a male chauvinist** ein Macho *m*; **a male nurse** ein Krankenpfleger *m*

mall *n* Einkaufszentrum *nt* (*pl* Einkaufszentren)

Malta *n* Malta *nt*; **from Malta** aus Malta; **to Malta** nach Malta

man *n* Mann *m* (*pl* Männer) ▷ *an old man* ein alter Mann

manage *vb* ❶ *(be in charge of)* leiten [**2**] ▷ *She manages a big store.* Sie leitet ein großes Geschäft. ❷ *(band, football team)* managen [**48**] ▷ *He manages the team.* Er managt die Mannschaft.
❸ *(get by)* klarkommen [**40**] (*imperf* kam klar, *perf* ist klargekommen) ▷ *We*

haven't got much money, but we manage. Wir haben nicht viel Geld, aber wir kommen klar. ▷ *It's okay, I can manage.* Das ist okay, ich komme klar. ❹ schaffen [**48**] ▷ *Can you manage okay?* Schaffst du es? ▷ *I can't manage all that.* *(food)* Das schaffe ich nicht alles.; **to manage to do something** es schaffen [**48**], etwas zu tun

management *n (organization)* Leitung *f* ▷ *the management of the company* die Leitung des Unternehmens ▷ *'under new management'* 'unter neuer Leitung'

manager *n* ❶ *(of company, shop, restaurant)* Geschäftsführer *m (pl* Geschäftsführer), Geschäftsführerin *f* ❷ *(of performer, football team)* Manager *m (pl* Manager), Managerin *f*

manageress *n* Geschäftsführerin *f*

mandarin *n (fruit)* Mandarine *f*

mango *n* Mango *f (pl* Mangos)

mania *n* Manie *f*

maniac *n* Verrückte *m (gen* Verrückten, *pl* Verrückten), Verrückte *f (gen* Verrückten) ▷ *He drives like a maniac.* Er fährt wie ein Verrückter.

mankind *n* Menschheit *f*

manner *n* Art und Weise *f* ▷ *in this manner* auf diese Art und Weise; **She behaves in an odd manner.** Sie benimmt sich eigenartig.; **He has a confident manner.** Er wirkt selbstsicher.

manners *npl* Benehmen *nt sg* ▷ *good manners* gutes Benehmen; **Her manners are appalling.** Sie benimmt sich schrecklich.; **It's bad manners to speak with your mouth full.** Es gehört sich nicht, mit vollem Mund zu sprechen.

mansion *n* Villa *f (pl* Villen)

mantelpiece *n* Kaminsims *m (gen* Kaminsimses, *pl* Kaminsimse)

manual *n* Handbuch *nt (pl* Handbücher)

manufacture *vb* herstellen [**4**] *(perf* hat hergestellt)

manufacturer *n* Hersteller *m (pl* Hersteller)

many *adj, pron* viele ▷ *The film has many special effects.* In dem Film gibt es viele Spezialeffekte. ▷ *He hasn't got many friends.* Er hat nicht viele Freunde. ▷ *Were there many people at the concert?* Waren viele Leute in dem Konzert?; **very many** sehr viele; **Not many.** Nicht viele.; **How many?** Wie viele?; **How many euros do you get for one pound?** Wie viel Euro bekommt man für ein Pfund?; **too many** zu viele; **so many** so viele

map *n* ❶ *(of country, area)* Landkarte *f* ❷ *(of town)* Stadtplan *m (pl* Stadtpläne)

> Be careful not to translate **map** by **Mappe**.

marathon *n* Marathonlauf *m (pl* Marathonläufe) ▷ *the London marathon* der Londoner Marathonlauf

marble *n* Marmor *m* ▷ *a marble statue* eine Marmorstatue; **to play marbles** Murmeln spielen [**38**]

March *n* März *m* ▷ *in March* im März

march *n (demonstration)* Protestmarsch *m (gen* Protestmarsches, *pl* Protestmärsche)
▸ *vb* ❶ *(soldiers)* marschieren [**76**] *(perf* ist marschiert) ❷ *(protesters)* aufmarschieren [**76**] *(perf* ist aufmarschiert)

mare *n* Stute *f*

margarine *n* Margarine *f*

margin *n* Rand *m (pl* Ränder) ▷ *I wrote notes in the margin.* Ich schrieb Notizen an den Rand.

marijuana *n* Marihuana *nt*

mark *n* ❶ *(in school)* Note *f* ▷ *I get good marks for German.* Ich habe in Deutsch gute Noten. ❷ *(stain)* Fleck *m (pl* Flecken) ▷ *You've got a mark on your shirt.* Du hast einen Fleck auf dem Hemd. ❸ *(old German currency)* Mark *f (pl* Mark)
▸ *vb* korrigieren [**76**] *(perf* hat korrigiert) ▷ *The teacher hasn't marked*

my homework yet. Der Lehrer hat meine Hausarbeit noch nicht korrigiert.

market *n* Markt *m* (*pl* Märkte)

marketing *n* Marketing *nt* (*gen* Marketing)

marmalade *n* Orangenmarmelade *f*

marriage *n* Ehe *f*

married *adj* verheiratet ▷ *They are not married*. Sie sind nicht verheiratet. ▷ *They have been married for fifteen years*. Sie sind seit fünfzehn Jahren verheiratet.; **a married couple** ein Ehepaar *nt*

marry *vb* heiraten [2] ▷ *He wants to marry her*. Er will sie heiraten.; **to get married** heiraten [2]

marvellous *adj* wunderbar ▷ *She's a marvellous cook*. Sie ist eine wunderbare Köchin. ▷ *The weather was marvellous*. Das Wetter war wunderbar.

marzipan *n* Marzipan *m* (*pl* Marzipane)

mascara *n* Wimperntusche *f*

masculine *adj* männlich

mashed potatoes *npl* Kartoffelbrei *m* ▷ *sausages and mashed potatoes* Würstchen mit Kartoffelbrei

mask *n* Maske *f*

mass *n* ❶ Haufen *m* (*pl* Haufen) ▷ *a mass of books and papers* ein Haufen Bücher und Papiere ❷ (*in church*) Messe *f* ▷ *We go to mass on Sunday*. Wir gehen am Sonntag zur Messe.; **the mass media** die Massenmedien

massage *n* Massage *f*

massive *adj* enorm

master *vb* beherrschen [7] (*perf* hat beherrscht) ▷ *to master a language* eine Sprache beherrschen

masterpiece *n* Meisterstück *nt* (*pl* Meisterstücke)

mat *n* (*doormat*) Vorleger *m* (*pl* Vorleger); **a table mat** ein Untersetzer *m*; **a place mat** ein Set *nt*

match *n* ❶ Streichholz *nt* (*gen* Streichholzes, *pl* Streichhölzer) ▷ *a box of matches* eine Schachtel Streichhölzer ❷ (*sport*) Spiel *nt* (*pl* Spiele) ▷ *a football match* ein Fußballspiel
▶ *vb* passen [31] zu ▷ *The jacket matches the trousers*. Die Jacke passt zu der Hose. ▷ *These colours don't match*. Diese Farben passen nicht zueinander.

mate *n* (*informal*) Kumpel *m* (*pl* Kumpel)

> **der Kumpel** is also used for women.

▷ *On Friday night I go out with my mates*. Freitag Abend gehe ich mit meinen Kumpels aus.

material *n* ❶ (*cloth*) Stoff *m* (*pl* Stoffe) ❷ (*information, data*) Material *nt* (*pl* Materialien) ▷ *I'm collecting material for my project*. Ich sammle Material für mein Referat.; **raw materials** die Rohstoffe

mathematics *nsg* Mathematik *f*

maths *nsg* Mathe *f*

matter *n* Angelegenheit *f* ▷ *It's a serious matter*. Das ist eine ernste Angelegenheit.; **It's a matter of life and death.** Es geht um Leben und Tod.; **What's the matter?** Was ist los?; **as a matter of fact** tatsächlich
▶ *vb* **it doesn't matter (1)** (*I don't mind*) das macht nichts ▷ *I can't give you the money today. — It doesn't matter*. Ich kann dir das Geld heute nicht geben. — Das macht nichts. **(2)** (*makes no difference*) das ist egal ▷ *Shall I phone today or tomorrow? — Whenever, it doesn't matter*. Soll ich heute oder morgen anrufen? — Wann du willst, das ist egal.; **It matters a lot to me.** Das ist mir sehr wichtig.

mattress *n* Matratze *f*

mature *adj* reif ▷ *She's very mature for her age*. Sie ist sehr reif für ihr Alter.

maximum *n* Maximum *nt* (*pl* Maxima)
▶ *adj* **the maximum speed** die Höchstgeschwindigkeit; **the maximum amount** der Höchstbetrag

May *n* Mai *m* ▷ *in May* im Mai; **May Day** der Erste Mai

may *vb* **He may come.** Er kommt vielleicht. ▷ *It may rain.* Es regnet vielleicht.; **Are you going to the party? — I don't know, I may.** Gehst du zur Party? — Ich weiß nicht, vielleicht.; **May I smoke?** Darf ich rauchen?

maybe *adv* vielleicht ▷ *maybe not* vielleicht nicht ▷ *a bit boring, maybe* vielleicht etwas langweilig ▷ *Maybe she's at home.* Vielleicht ist sie zu Hause. ▷ *Maybe he'll change his mind.* Vielleicht überlegt er es sich anders.

mayonnaise *n* Mayonnaise *f*

mayor *n* Bürgermeister *m (pl* Bürgermeister), Bürgermeisterin *f*

me *pron* ❶ mich ▷ *Can you hear me?* Kannst du mich hören? ▷ *Look at me!* Sieh mich an!

> Use **mich** after prepositions which take the accusative.

▷ *Is this present for me?* Ist das Geschenk für mich? ▷ *Wait for me!* Warte auf mich! ❷ mir

> Use **mir** after prepositions which take the dative.

▷ *Will you come with me?* Kommst du mit mir mit? ▷ *He sat next to me.* Er saß neben mir.

> Use **mir** when 'me' means 'to me'.

▷ *Give me the book, please!* Gib mir bitte das Buch! ▷ *She told me the truth.* Sie hat mir die Wahrheit erzählt. ❸ ich ▷ *It's me!* Ich bin's! ▷ *Me too!* Ich auch! ▷ *She's older than me.* Sie ist älter als ich.

meal *n* Essen *nt (pl* Essen)

mean *vb* ❶ *(signify)* bedeuten [**2**] *(perf* hat bedeutet) ▷ *What does 'besetzt' mean?* Was bedeutet 'besetzt'? ▷ *I don't know what it means.* Ich weiß nicht, was es bedeutet. ❷ *(mean to say)* meinen [**38**] ▷ *What do you mean?* Was meinst du damit? ▷ *That's not what I meant.* Das habe ich nicht gemeint. ▷ *Which one do you mean?* Welchen meinst du? ▷ *Do you really mean it?* Meinst du das wirklich?; **to mean to do something** etwas tun wollen [**94**]
▶ *adj* ❶ *(with money)* geizig ▷ *He's too mean to buy Christmas presents.* Er ist zu geizig, um Weihnachtsgeschenke zu kaufen. ❷ *(unkind)* gemein ▷ *You're being mean to me.* Du bist gemein zu mir. ▷ *That's a really mean thing to say!* Das ist gemein, so etwas zu sagen!

meaning *n* Bedeutung *f*

> Be careful not to translate **meaning** by **Meinung**.

meant *vb see* **mean**

meanwhile *adv* inzwischen

measles *nsg* Masern *pl* ▷ *She's got measles.* Sie hat Masern.

measure *vb* ❶ ausmessen *(pres* misst aus, *imperf* maß aus, *perf* hat ausgemessen) ▷ *I measured the page.* Ich habe die Seite ausgemessen. ❷ messen ▷ *The room measures three metres by four.* Das Zimmer misst drei auf vier Meter.

measurement *n (of object)* Maß *nt (pl* Maße) ▷ *What are the measurements of the room?* Wie sind die Maße des Zimmers? ▷ *What are your measurements?* Was sind Ihre Maße?; **my waist measurement** meine Taillenweite; **What's your neck measurement?** Welche Kragenweite haben Sie?

meat *n* Fleisch *nt* ▷ *I don't eat meat.* Ich esse kein Fleisch.

Mecca *n* Mekka *nt*

mechanic *n* Mechaniker *m (pl* Mechaniker), Mechanikerin *f* ▷ *He's a mechanic.* Er ist Mechaniker.

medal *n* Medaille *f*; **the gold medal** die Goldmedaille

media *npl* Medien *ntpl*

medical *adj* medizinisch ▷ *medical treatment* die medizinische Behandlung; **medical insurance** die Krankenversicherung; **to have medical problems** gesundheitliche Probleme haben [**32**]; **She's a medical**

student. Sie ist Medizinstudentin. ▶ *n* **to have a medical** sich ärztlich untersuchen lassen [**42**]

medicine *n* Medizin *f* ▷ *I want to study medicine.* Ich möchte Medizin studieren. ▷ *I need some medicine.* Ich brauche Medizin.; **alternative medicine** die alternative Medizin

Mediterranean *adj (person, character, scenery)* südländisch

Mediterranean *n* **the Mediterranean** das Mittelmeer

medium *adj* mittlere ▷ *a man of medium height* ein Mann von mittlerer Größe

medium-sized *adj* mittelgroß ▷ *a medium-sized town* eine mittelgroße Stadt

meet *vb* ❶ *(by chance)* treffen [**78**] (*pres* trifft, *imperf* traf, *perf* hat getroffen) ▷ *I met Paul when I was walking the dog.* Ich habe Paul getroffen, als ich mit dem Hund spazieren war. ❷ *(by arrangement)* sich treffen [**78**] ▷ *Let's meet in front of the tourist office.* Treffen wir uns doch vor dem Verkehrsbüro. ▷ *I'm going to meet my friends.* Ich treffe mich mit meinen Freunden. ❸ *(get to know)* kennenlernen [**4**] (*perf* hat kennengelernt) ▷ *I like meeting new people.* Ich lerne gerne neue Leute kennen.; **Have you met him before?** Kennen Sie ihn? ❹ *(pick up)* abholen [**4**] (*perf* hat abgeholt) ▷ *I'll meet you at the station.* Ich hole dich am Bahnhof ab.

meeting *n* ❶ *(for work)* Besprechung *f* ▷ *a business meeting* eine geschäftliche Besprechung ❷ *(socially)* Treffen *nt* (*pl* Treffen) ▷ *their first meeting* ihr erstes Treffen

mega *adj* **He's mega rich.** *(informal)* Er ist superreich.

melon *n* Melone *f*

melt *vb* schmelzen (*pres* schmilzt, *imperf* schmolz, *perf* ist geschmolzen) ▷ *The snow is melting.* Der Schnee schmilzt.

member *n* Mitglied *nt* (*pl* Mitglieder); **a Member of Parliament (1)** *(man)* ein Abgeordneter **(2)** *(woman)* eine Abgeordnete

meme *n (internet)* Meme *m* (*pl* Memes)

memorial *n* Denkmal *nt* (*pl* Denkmäler); **a war memorial** ein Kriegerdenkmal

memorize *vb* auswendig lernen [**38**]

memory *n* ❶ Gedächtnis *nt* (*gen* Gedächtnisses) ▷ *I haven't got a good memory.* Ich habe kein gutes Gedächtnis. ❷ *(recollection)* Erinnerung *f* ▷ *to bring back memories* Erinnerungen wachrufen ❸ *(computer)* Speicher *m* (*gen* Speicher)

memory stick *n (for computer)* Memorystick® *m* (*pl* Memorysticks)

men *npl see* **man**

mend *vb* flicken [**48**]

mental *adj* ❶ geistig; **a mental illness** eine Geisteskrankheit ❷ *(mad)* wahnsinnig ▷ *You're mental!* Du bist wahnsinnig!

mention *vb* erwähnen [**19**] (*perf* hat erwähnt); **Thank you! — Don't mention it!** Danke! — Bitte!

mentor *n* Mentor *m* (*pl* Mentoren)

menu *n* ❶ Speisekarte *f* ▷ *Could I have the menu please?* Könnte ich bitte die Speisekarte haben? ❷ *(on computer)* Menü *nt* (*pl* Menüs)

meringue *n* Meringe *f*

merry *adj* **Merry Christmas!** Fröhliche Weihnachten!

merry-go-round *n* Karussell *nt* (*pl* Karussells)

mess *n* Unordnung *f* ▷ *His bedroom's always in a mess.* In seinem Schlafzimmer herrscht ständig Unordnung.

mess about *vb* **to mess about with something** *(interfere with)* an etwas herumfummeln [**4**] ▷ *Stop messing about with my computer!* Hör auf, an meinem Computer herumzufummeln!; **Don't mess about with my things!** Lass meine Sachen in Ruhe!

mess up *vb* **to mess something up** etwas durcheinanderbringen [**13**]

message *n* Nachricht *f*
▸ *vb* **She messaged me on Facebook.** Sie schickte mir eine Nachricht auf Facebook.
messenger *n* Bote *m* (*gen* Boten, *pl* Boten), Botin *f*
messy *adj* ❶ (*dirty*) schmutzig ▷ *a messy job* eine schmutzige Arbeit ❷ (*untidy*) unordentlich ▷ *Your room's really messy.* Dein Zimmer ist wirklich unordentlich. ▷ *She's so messy!* Sie ist so unordentlich!; **My writing is terribly messy.** Ich habe eine schreckliche Schrift.
met *vb see* **meet**
metal *n* Metall *nt* (*pl* Metalle)
meter *n* ❶ (*for gas, electricity, taxi*) Zähler *m* (*pl* Zähler) ❷ (*parking meter*) Parkuhr *f*
method *n* Methode *f*
Methodist *n* Methodist *m* (*gen* Methodisten, *pl* Methodisten), Methodistin *f* ▷ *She's a Methodist.* Sie ist Methodistin.
metre *n* Meter *m* (*pl* Meter)
metric *adj* metrisch
Mexico *n* Mexiko *nt*; **from Mexico** aus Mexiko; **to Mexico** nach Mexiko
mice *npl see* **mouse**
microchip *n* Mikrochip *m* (*pl* Mikrochips)
microphone *n* Mikrofon *nt* (*pl* Mikrofone)
microscope *n* Mikroskop *nt* (*pl* Mikroskope)
microwave *n* Mikrowelle *f*
microwave oven *n* Mikrowellenherd *m* (*pl* Mikrowellenherde)
midday *n* Mittag *m* (*pl* Mittage); **at midday** mittags
middle *n* Mitte *f*; **in the middle of the road** mitten auf der Straße; **in the middle of the night** mitten in der Nacht; **the middle seat** der mittlere Sitz; **the Middle East** der Nahe Osten
middle-aged *adj* mittleren Alters ▷ *a middle-aged man* ein Mann mittleren Alters ▷ *She's middle-aged.* Sie ist mittleren Alters.
middle-class *adj* **a middle-class family** eine Familie der Mittelschicht
midge *n* Mücke *f*
midnight *n* Mitternacht *f*; **at midnight** um Mitternacht
midwife *n* Hebamme *f* ▷ *She's a midwife.* Sie ist Hebamme.
might *vb*

> Use **vielleicht** to express possibility.

▷ *He might come later.* Er kommt vielleicht später. ▷ *We might go to Spain next year.* Wir fahren nächstes Jahr vielleicht nach Spanien. ▷ *She might not have understood.* Sie hat es vielleicht nicht verstanden.
migraine *n* Migräne *f* ▷ *I've got a migraine.* Ich habe Migräne.
mike *n* Mikro *nt* (*pl* Mikros)
mild *adj* mild ▷ *The winters are quite mild.* Die Winter sind ziemlich mild.
mile *n* Meile *f*

> In Germany distances and speeds are expressed in kilometres. A mile is about 1.6 kilometres.

▷ *It's five miles from here.* Es ist acht Kilometer von hier. ▷ *at fifty miles per hour* mit achtzig Kilometern pro Stunde; **We walked miles!** Wir sind meilenweit gegangen!
military *adj* militärisch
milk *n* Milch *f* ▷ *tea with milk* der Tee mit Milch
▸ *vb* melken (*perf* hat gemolken)
milk chocolate *n* Milchschokolade *f*
milkman *n* Milchmann *m* (*pl* Milchmänner) ▷ *He's a milkman.* Er ist Milchmann.
milk shake *n* Milchshake *m* (*pl* Milchshakes)
millennium *n* Jahrtausend *nt*
millimetre *n* Millimeter *m* (*pl* Millimeter)
million *n* Million *f*
millionaire *n* Millionär *m* (*pl* Millionäre), Millionärin *f*
mince *n* Hackfleisch *nt*

mind *vb* aufpassen [**31**] auf (*perf* hat aufgepasst) ▷ *Could you mind the baby this afternoon?* Kannst du heute Nachmittag auf das Baby aufpassen? ▷ *Could you mind my bags?* Können Sie auf mein Gepäck aufpassen?; **Do you mind if I open the window?** Macht es Ihnen etwas aus, wenn ich das Fenster aufmache?; **I don't mind.** Es macht mir nichts aus.; **Never mind!** Macht nichts!; **Mind that bike!** Pass auf das Fahrrad auf!; **Mind the step!** Vorsicht Stufe!
▶ *n* **to make up one's mind** sich entscheiden; **to change one's mind** es sich anders überlegen [**82**]; **Are you out of your mind?** Bist du wahnsinnig?

mindfulness *n* Achtsamkeit *f*

mine *pron* ❶ meiner ▷ *Is this your coat? — No, mine's black.* Ist das dein Mantel? — Nein, meiner ist schwarz.
meine ▷ *Is this your cup? — No, mine's red.* Ist das deine Tasse? — Nein, meine ist rot.
meines ▷ *Is this your car? — No, mine's green.* Ist das dein Auto? — Nein, meines ist grün. ❷ meine ▷ *her parents and mine* ihre Eltern und meine ▷ *Your hands are dirty, mine are clean.* Deine Hände sind schmutzig, meine sind sauber.; **It's mine.** Das gehört mir. ▷ *This book is mine.* Dieses Buch gehört mir. ▷ *Whose is this? — It's mine.* Wem gehört das? — Es gehört mir.
▶ *n* Mine *f*; **a land mine** eine Landmine; **a coal mine** ein Kohlebergwerk *nt*

miner *n* Bergarbeiter *m* (*pl* Bergarbeiter)

mineral water *n* Mineralwasser *nt* (*pl* Mineralwasser)

miniature *n* Miniatur *f*

minibus *n* Minibus *m* (*gen* Minibusses, *pl* Minibusse)

minimum *n* Mininum *nt* (*pl* Minima)
▶ *adj* **minimum age** das Mindestalter; **minimum amount** der Mindestbetrag; **minimum wage** der Mindestlohn

miniskirt *n* Minirock *m* (*pl* Miniröcke)

minister *n* ❶ (*in government*) Minister *m* (*pl* Minister), Ministerin *f* ❷ (*of church*) Pfarrer *m* (*pl* Pfarrer), Pfarrerin *f*

minor *adj* kleiner ▷ *a minor problem* ein kleineres Problem ▷ *a minor operation* eine kleinere Operation; **in D minor** in d-Moll

minority *n* Minderheit *f*

mint *n* ❶ (*plant*) Pfefferminze *f*; **mint sauce** die Pfefferminzsoße ❷ (*sweet*) Pfefferminzbonbon *nt* (*pl* Pfefferminzbonbons)

minus *prep* minus ▷ *Sixteen minus three is thirteen.* Sechzehn minus drei ist dreizehn. ▷ *It's minus two degrees outside.* Draußen hat es zwei Grad minus. ▷ *I got a B minus.* Ich habe eine Zwei minus bekommen.

In Germany, grades are given from 1 to 6, with 1 being the best.

minute *n* Minute *f*; **Wait a minute!** Einen Augenblick!
▶ *adj* winzig ▷ *Her flat is minute.* Ihre Wohnung ist winzig.

miracle *n* Wunder *nt* (*pl* Wunder)

mirror *n* Spiegel *m* (*pl* Spiegel)

misbehave *vb* sich schlecht benehmen [**52**] (*pres* benimmt sich schlecht, *imperf* benahm sich schlecht, *perf* hat sich schlecht benommen)

miscellaneous *adj* verschieden ▷ *miscellaneous items* verschiedene Artikel

mischief *n* Dummheiten *fpl* ▷ *She's always up to mischief.* Sie macht dauernd Dummheiten.

mischievous *adj* verschmitzt

miser *n* Geizhals *m* (*gen* Geizhalses, *pl* Geizhälse)

miserable *adj* ❶ (*person*) unglücklich ▷ *You're looking miserable.* Du siehst richtig unglücklich aus. ❷ (*weather*) schrecklich ▷ *The weather was miserable.* Das Wetter war schrecklich.; **to feel miserable** sich miserabel fühlen [**38**]

misery *n* ❶ Elend *nt* ▷ *All that money brought nothing but misery.* All das Geld hat nichts als Elend gebracht. ❷ *(informal)* Miesepeter *m (pl* Miesepeter) ▷ *She's a real misery.* Sie ist ein richtiger Miesepeter.
mislead *vb* irreführen [**4**] (*perf* hat irregeführt)
misprint *n* Druckfehler *m (pl* Druckfehler)
Miss *n* Fräulein *nt*
Nowadays it is regarded as old-fashioned to call somebody **Fräulein** and **Frau** is used instead.
▷ *Miss Jones* Frau Jones
miss *vb* verpassen [**7**] ▷ *Hurry or you'll miss the bus.* Beeil dich, sonst ver passt du den Bus! ▷ *to miss an opportunity* eine Gelegenheit verpassen; **I miss you.** Du fehlst mir.; **He missed the target.** Er hat nicht getroffen.
missing *adj* fehlend ▷ *the missing part* das fehlende Teil; **to be missing** fehlen [**38**]
mist *n* Nebel *m (pl* Nebel)
Be careful not to translate **mist** by the German word **Mist**.
mistake *n* Fehler *m (pl* Fehler) ▷ *It was a mistake to buy those yellow shoes.* Es war ein Fehler, diese gelben Schuhe zu kaufen.; **a spelling mistake** ein Rechtschreibfehler; **to make a mistake (1)** *(in writing, speaking)* einen Fehler machen [**48**] **(2)** *(get mixed up)* sich vertun [**81**] ▷ *I'm sorry, I made a mistake.* Tut mir leid, ich habe mich vertan.; **by mistake** aus Versehen ▷ *I took his bag by mistake.* Ich habe aus Versehen seine Tasche genommen.
▸ *vb* **He mistook me for my sister.** Er hat mich mit meiner Schwester verwechselt.
mistaken *adj* **to be mistaken** sich irren [**38**]
mistletoe *n* Mistel *f*
mistook *vb see* **mistake**
misty *adj* neblig ▷ *a misty morning* ein nebliger Morgen
misunderstand *vb* missverstehen [**72**] (*imperf* missverstand, *perf* hat missverstanden) ▷ *Sorry, I misunderstood you.* Entschuldigung, ich habe Sie missverstanden.
misunderstanding *n* Missverständnis *nt (gen* Missverständnisses, *pl* Missverständnisse)
misunderstood *vb see* **misunderstand**
mix *n* Mischung *f* ▷ *It's a mix of science fiction and comedy.* Es ist eine Mischung aus Science-Fiction und Komödie.; **a cake mix** eine Backmischung
▸ *vb* ❶ vermischen [**7**] (*perf* hat vermischt) ▷ *Mix the flour with the sugar.* Vermischen Sie das Mehl mit dem Zucker. ❷ verbinden (*imperf* verband, *perf* hat verbunden) ▷ *He's mixing business with pleasure.* Er verbindet das Geschäftliche mit dem Vergnügen.; **to mix with somebody** *(associate)* mit jemandem verkehren [**7**]; **He doesn't mix much.** Er geht nicht viel unter Menschen.; **to mix up** verwechseln [**34**]; **I'm getting mixed up.** Ich werde ganz konfus.
mixed *adj* gemischt ▷ *a mixed salad* ein gemischter Salat ▷ *a mixed school* eine gemischte Schule; **a mixed grill** ein Grillteller *m*
mixer *n (for food)* Mixer *m (pl* Mixer)
mixture *n* Mischung *f* ▷ *a mixture of spices* eine Gewürzmischung; **cough mixture** der Hustensaft
mix-up *n* Verwechslung *f*
MMS *n (= multimedia messaging service)* MMS® *m*
moan *vb* sich beklagen [**7**] (*perf* hat sich beklagt) ▷ *She's always moaning.* Sie beklagt sich dauernd.
mobile *n (phone)* Handy *nt (pl* Handys)
mobile home *n* Wohnmobil *nt (pl* Wohnmobile)
mobile phone *n* Handy *nt (pl* Handys)

mock *vb* sich lustig machen [**48**] über ▷ *Stop mocking him!* Mach dich nicht über ihn lustig!
▶ *adj* **a mock exam** eine Übungsprüfung
model *n* ❶ Modell *nt* (*pl* Modelle) ▷ *the latest model* das neueste Modell ▷ *a model of the castle* ein Modell der Burg ❷ *(fashion)* Mannequin *nt* (*pl* Mannequins) ▷ *She's a famous model*. Sie ist ein berühmtes Mannequin.
▶ *adj* **a model plane** ein Modellflugzeug *nt*; **a model railway** eine Modelleisenbahn; **He's a model pupil.** Er ist ein vorbildlicher Schüler.
▶ *vb* als Model arbeiten [**2**] ▷ *She was modelling in New York*. Sie arbeitete in New York als Model.; **She was modelling a Paul Costello outfit.** Sie führte ein Outfit von Paul Costello vor.
modem *n* Modem *nt* (*pl* Modems)
moderate *adj* gemäßigt ▷ *His views are quite moderate*. Er hat sehr gemäßigte Ansichten.; **a moderate amount of alcohol** wenig Alkohol; **a moderate price** ein annehmbarer Preis
modern *adj* modern
modernize *vb* modernisieren [**76**] (*perf* hat modernisiert)
modest *adj* bescheiden
moisturizer *n* ❶ *(cream)* Feuchtigkeitscreme *f* (*pl* Feuchtigkeitscremes) ❷ *(lotion)* Feuchtigkeitslotion *f*
moldy *adj (US)* schimmlig
mole *n* ❶ *(animal)* Maulwurf *m* (*pl* Maulwürfe) ❷ *(on skin)* Leberfleck *m* (*pl* Leberflecke)
moment *n* Augenblick *m* (*pl* Augenblicke) ▷ *Could you wait a moment?* Können Sie einen Augenblick warten? ▷ *in a moment* in einem Augenblick ▷ *Just a moment!* Einen Augenblick!; **at the moment** momentan; **any moment now** jeden Moment
monarchy *n* Monarchie *f*
Monday *n* Montag *m* (*pl* Montage) ▷ *on Monday* am Montag ▷ *every Monday* jeden Montag ▷ *last Monday* letzten Montag ▷ *next Monday* nächsten Montag; **on Mondays** montags
monetize *vb* monetarisieren [**76**]
money *n* Geld *nt* (*pl* Gelder) ▷ *I need to change some money*. Ich muss Geld wechseln.; **to make money** Geld verdienen [**84**]
mongrel *n* Promenadenmischung *f* ▷ *My dog's a mongrel*. Mein Hund ist eine Promenadenmischung.
monitor *n (of computer)* Monitor *m* (*pl* Monitore)
monkey *n* Affe *m* (*gen* Affen, *pl* Affen)
monopoly *n* Monopol *nt*; **to play Monopoly®** Monopoly spielen [**38**]
monotonous *adj* monoton
monster *n* Monster *nt* (*pl* Monster)
month *n* Monat *m* (*pl* Monate) ▷ *this month* diesen Monat ▷ *next month* nächsten Monat ▷ *last month* letzten Monat ▷ *every month* jeden Monat ▷ *at the end of the month* Ende des Monats
monthly *adj* monatlich
monument *n* Denkmal *nt* (*pl* Denkmäler)
mood *n* Laune *f* ▷ *to be in a bad mood* schlechte Laune haben ▷ *to be in a good mood* gute Laune haben
moody *adj* ❶ *(temperamental)* launisch ❷ *(in a bad mood)* schlecht gelaunt
moon *n* Mond *m* (*pl* Monde); **There's a full moon tonight.** Heute ist Vollmond.; **to be over the moon** *(happy)* überglücklich sein [**65**]
moped *n* Moped *nt* (*pl* Mopeds)
moral *adj* moralisch
▶ *n* Moral *f* ▷ *the moral of the story* die Moral der Geschichte; **morals** die Moral *sg*
more *adj, pron, adv* mehr ▷ *a bit more* etwas mehr ▷ *There are more girls in the class*. In der Klasse sind mehr Mädchen.; **more than** mehr als

In comparisons you usually add **-er** to the adjective.

▷ *Could you speak more slowly?* Könnten Sie langsamer sprechen?

> When referring to an additional amount, over and above what there already is, you usually use **noch**.

▷ *Is there any more?* Gibt es noch mehr?; **There isn't any more.** Es ist nichts mehr da.; **more or less** mehr oder weniger; **more than ever** mehr denn je

morning *n* Morgen *m* (*pl* Morgen) ▷ *every morning* jeden Morgen; **this morning** heute Morgen; **tomorrow morning** morgen früh; **in the morning** morgens; **a morning paper** eine Morgenzeitung

Morocco *n* Marokko *nt*; **from Morocco** auf Marokko; **to Morocco** nach Marokko

mortgage *n* Hypothek *f* (*pl* Hypotheken)

Moscow *n* Moskau *nt*; **to Moscow** nach Moskau

Moslem *n* Moslem *m* (*pl* Moslems), Moslime *f* ▷ *He's a Moslem.* Er ist Moslem.

mosque *n* Moschee *f*

mosquito *n* Stechmücke *f*; **a mosquito bite** ein Mückenstich *m*

most *adv, adj, pron* ❶ die meisten ▷ *most of my friends* die meisten meiner Freunde ▷ *most of them* die meisten von ihnen ▷ *most people* die meisten Menschen ▷ *Most cats are affectionate.* Die meisten Katzen sind anhänglich. ❷ am meisten ▷ *what I hate most* was ich am meisten hasse; **most of the time** meist; **most of the evening** fast den ganzen Abend; **most of the money** fast das ganze Geld; **the most** am meisten; **to make the most of something** das Beste aus etwas machen [**48**]; **at the most** höchstens

> For the superlative you usually add **-ste** to the adjective.

▷ *the most expensive restaurant* das teuerste Restaurant

moth *n* Motte *f*

mother *n* Mutter *f* (*pl* Mütter) ▷ *my mother* meine Mutter; **mother tongue** die Muttersprache

mother-in-law *n* Schwiegermutter *f* (*pl* Schwiegermütter)

Mother's Day *n* Muttertag *m* (*pl* Muttertage)

> In Germany **Muttertag** is on the second Sunday in May.

motivated *adj* motiviert ▷ *He is highly motivated.* Er ist höchst motiviert.

motivation *n* Motivation *f*

motor *n* Motor *m* (*pl* Motoren) ▷ *The boat has a motor.* Das Boot hat einen Motor.

motorbike *n* Motorrad *nt* (*pl* Motorräder)

motorboat *n* Motorboot *nt* (*pl* Motorboote)

motorcycle *n* Motorrad *nt* (*pl* Motorräder)

motorcyclist *n* Motorradfahrer *m* (*pl* Motorradfahrer), Motorradfahrerin *f*

motorist *n* Autofahrer *m* (*pl* Autofahrer), Autofahrerin *f*

motor racing *n* Autorennen *nt* (*pl* Autorennen)

motorway *n* Autobahn *f* ▷ *on the motorway* auf der Autobahn

mouldy *adj* schimmlig

mountain *n* Berg *m* (*pl* Berge); **a mountain bike** ein Mountainbike *nt*

mountaineer *n* Bergsteiger *m* (*pl* Bergsteiger), Bergsteigerin *f*

mountaineering *n* Bergsteigen *nt*; **I go mountaineering.** Ich gehe bergsteigen.

mountainous *adj* bergig

mouse *n* (*also for computer*) Maus *f* (*pl* Mäuse) ▷ *white mice* weiße Mäuse

mouse mat *n* (*computer*) Mousepad *nt* (*pl* Mousepads)

mousse *n* ❶ (*food*) Creme *f* (*pl* Cremes); **chocolate mousse** die

Schokoladencreme ❷ *(for hair)* Schaumfestiger *m* (*pl* Schaumfestiger)

moustache *n* Schnurrbart *m* (*pl* Schnurrbärte) ▷ *He's got a moustache.* Er hat einen Schnurrbart.

mouth *n* Mund *m* (*pl* Münder)

mouthful *n* Bissen *m* (*pl* Bissen)

mouth organ *n* Mundharmonika *f* (*pl* Mundharmonikas) ▷ *I play the mouth organ.* Ich spiele Mundharmonika.

move *n* ❶ Zug *m* (*pl* Züge) ▷ *That was a good move.* Das war ein guter Zug.; **It's your move.** Du bist dran. ❷ Umzug *m* (*pl* Umzüge) ▷ *our move from Oxford to Luton* unser Umzug von Oxford nach Luton; **to get a move on** schneller machen [**48**]; **Get a move on!** Nun mach schon!

▸ *vb* ❶ bewegen [**7**] (*perf* hat bewegt) ▷ *I can't move my arm.* Ich kann den Arm nicht bewegen. ▷ *I was very moved by the film.* Der Film hat mich sehr bewegt.; **Could you move your stuff?** Könntest du dein Zeug wegtun?; **Could you move your car?** Könnten Sie Ihr Auto wegfahren? ❷ sich bewegen [**7**] ▷ *Try not to move.* Versuche, dich nicht zu bewegen.; **Don't move!** Keine Bewegung! ❸ *(vehicle)* fahren [**21**] (*pres* fährt, *imperf* fuhr, *perf* ist gefahren) ▷ *The car was moving very slowly.* Das Auto fuhr sehr langsam.; **to move house** umziehen [**96**]; **to move forward** sich vorwärtsbewegen [**15**]; **to move in** einziehen [**96**]; **to move over** rücken [**38**]

movement *n* Bewegung *f*

movie *n* Film *m* (*pl* Filme); **the movies** das Kino *sg*

moving *adj* ❶ *(not stationary)* fahrend ▷ *a moving bus* ein fahrender Bus ❷ *(touching)* ergreifend ▷ *a moving story* eine ergreifende Geschichte

MP *n* (= *Member of Parliament*) Abgeordnete *m* (*gen* Abgeordneten, *pl* Abgeordneten), Abgeordnete *f* (*gen* Abgeordneten) ▷ *an MP (man)* ein Abgeordneter ▷ *She's an MP.* Sie ist Abgeordnete.

MP3 player *n* MP3-Spieler *m* (*pl* MP3-Spieler)

mph *abbr* (= *miles per hour*) Meilen pro Stunde

Mr *n* (= *Mister*) Herr

Mrs *n* Frau

MS *n* (= *multiple sclerosis*) MS ▷ *She's got MS.* Sie hat MS.

Ms *n* Frau

Generally **Frau** is used to address all women whether married or not.

much *adj, adv, pron* ❶ viel ▷ *I haven't got much money.* Ich habe nicht viel Geld. ▷ *I haven't got very much money.* Ich habe nicht sehr viel Geld. ▷ *This is much better.* Das ist viel besser. ▷ *I feel much better now.* Ich fühle mich jetzt viel besser. ❷ sehr

Use **sehr** with most verbs.

▷ *I didn't like it much.* Es hat mir nicht sehr gefallen. ▷ *I enjoyed the film very much.* Der Film hat mir sehr gefallen. ❸ viel

Use **viel** with verbs implying physical activity.

▷ *She doesn't travel much.* Sie reist nicht viel. ▷ *We didn't laugh much.* Wir haben nicht viel gelacht.; **Do you go out much?** Gehst du oft aus?; **Thank you very much.** Vielen Dank!; **not much** nicht viel; **How much?** Wie viel?; **too much** zu viel; **so much** so viel

mud *n* Schlamm *m*

muddle *n* Durcheinander *nt*; **to be in a muddle** durcheinander sein [**65**]

muddle up *vb (people)* verwechseln [**34**] (*perf* hat verwechselt)

muddy *adj* schlammig

muesli *n* Müsli *nt* (*pl* Müsli)

mug *n* Becher *m* (*pl* Becher) ▷ *Do you want a cup or a mug?* Möchtest du eine Tasse oder einen Becher?; **a beer mug** ein Bierkrug *m*

▸ *vb* überfallen [**22**] (*pres* überfällt, *imperf* überfiel, *perf* hat überfallen)

▷ *He was mugged in the city centre.* Er wurde in der Innenstadt überfallen.
mugging *n* Überfall *m* (*pl* Überfälle) ▷ *Mugging has increased in recent years.* Die Zahl der Überfälle hat in den letzten Jahren zugenommen.
multiple choice test *n* Multiple-Choice-Test *m* (*pl* Multiple-Choice-Tests)
multiplication *n* Multiplikation *f*
multiply *vb* multiplizieren [**76**] (*perf* hat multipliziert) ▷ *to multiply six by three* sechs mit drei multiplizieren
mum *n* Mama *f* (*pl* Mamas) ▷ *my mum* meine Mama ▷ *I'll ask Mum.* Ich frage Mama.
mummy *n* ❶ *(mum)* Mutti *f* (*pl* Muttis) ▷ *Mummy says I can go.* Mutti sagt, ich kann gehen. ❷ *(Egyptian)* Mumie *f*
mumps *nsg* Mumps *m* ▷ *My brother's got mumps.* Mein Bruder hat Mumps.
Munich *n* München *nt*; **to Munich** nach München
murder *n* Mord *m* (*pl* Morde)

> Be careful not to translate **murder** by **Mörder**.

▸ *vb* ermorden [**53**] (*perf* hat ermordet) ▷ *He was murdered.* Er wurde ermordet.
murderer *n* Mörder *m* (*pl* Mörder), Mörderin *f*
muscle *n* Muskel *m* (*pl* Muskeln)
museum *n* Museum *nt* (*pl* Museen)
mushroom *n* ❶ Pilz *m* (*pl* Pilze) ❷ *(button mushroom)* Champignon *m* (*pl* Champignons) ▷ *mushroom omelette* das Champignonomelett
music *n* Musik *f*
musical *adj* musikalisch ▷ *I'm not musical.* Ich bin nicht musikalisch.; **a musical instrument** ein Musikinstrument *nt*
▸ *n* Musical *nt* (*pl* Musicals)
musician *n* Musiker *m* (*pl* Musiker), Musikerin *f*
Muslim *n* Moslem *m* (*pl* Moslems), Moslime *f* ▷ *He's a Muslim.* Er ist Moslem.
mussel *n* Miesmuschel *f*
must *vb* ❶ müssen [**51**] (*pres* muss, *imperf* musste, *perf* hat gemusst) ▷ *I must buy some presents.* Ich muss Geschenke kaufen. ▷ *I really must go now.* Ich muss jetzt wirklich gehen. ▷ *You must be tired.* Du musst müde sein. ▷ *They must have plenty of money.* Sie müssen viel Geld haben. ▷ *You must come and see us.* Sie müssen uns besuchen. ❷ dürfen [**16**] (*pres* darf, *imperf* durfte, *perf* hat gedurft)

> Use **dürfen** in negative sentences.

▷ *You mustn't say things like that.* So was darfst du nicht sagen.; **You mustn't forget to send her a card.** Vergiss nicht, ihr eine Karte zu schicken.
mustard *n* Senf *m* (*pl* Senfe)
mutual *adj* gegenseitig ▷ *The feeling was mutual.* Das Gefühl war gegenseitig.; **a mutual friend** ein gemeinsamer Freund
my *adj* mein ▷ *my father* mein Vater ▷ *my aunt* meine Tante ▷ *my car* mein Auto ▷ *my parents* meine Eltern; **my friend** **(1)** *(male)* mein Freund **(2)** *(female)* meine Freundin

> Do not use **mein** with parts of the body.

▷ *I want to wash my hair.* Ich will mir die Haare waschen. ▷ *I'm going to clean my teeth.* Ich putze mir die Zähne. ▷ *I've hurt my foot.* Ich habe mich am Fuß verletzt.
myself *pron* ❶ mich ▷ *I've hurt myself.* Ich habe mich verletzt. ▷ *When I look at myself in the mirror ...* Wenn ich mich im Spiegel ansehe ... ▷ *I don't like talking about myself.* Ich rede nicht gern über mich selbst. ❷ mir ▷ *I said to myself ...* Ich sagte mir ... ▷ *I am not very pleased with myself.* Ich bin mit mir selbst nicht sehr zufrieden. ❸ selbst ▷ *I made it myself.* Ich habe es selbst gemacht.; **by myself** allein
mysterious *adj* rätselhaft

mystery *n* Rätsel *nt* (*pl* Rätsel); **a murder mystery** *(novel)* ein Krimi *m*

myth *n* ❶ *(legend)* Mythos *m* (*gen* Mythos, *pl* Mythen) ▷ *a Greek myth* ein griechischer Mythos ❷ *(untrue idea)* Märchen *nt* (*pl* Märchen) ▷ *That's a myth.* Das ist ein Märchen.

n

nag *vb (scold)* herumnörgeln [15] an (*perf* hat herumgenörgelt) ▷ *She's always nagging me.* Sie nörgelt dauernd an mir herum.

nail *n* Nagel *m* (*pl* Nägel) ▷ *Don't bite your nails!* Kau nicht an den Nägeln!

nailbrush *n* Nagelbürste *f*

nailfile *n* Nagelfeile *f*

nail scissors *npl* Nagelschere *f* ▷ *a pair of nail scissors* eine Nagelschere

nail varnish *n* Nagellack *m* (*pl* Nagellacke); **nail varnish remover** der Nagellackentferner

naked *adj* nackt

name *n* Name *m* (*gen* Namens, *pl* Namen); **What's your name?** Wie heißt du?

nanny *n* Kindermädchen *nt* (*pl* Kindermädchen) ▷ *She's a nanny.* Sie ist Kindermädchen.

napkin *n* Serviette *f*

nappy *n* Windel *f*

narrow *adj* eng

nasty *adj* ❶ *(bad)* übel ▷ *a nasty cold* eine üble Erkältung ▷ *a nasty smell* ein übler

Geruch ❷ *(unfriendly)* böse ▷ *He gave me a nasty look.* Er warf mir einen bösen Blick zu.

nation *n* Nation *f*

national *adj* national; **a national newspaper** eine überregionale Zeitung; **the national elections** die Parlamentswahlen

In Germany the national elections are called **Bundestagswahlen**.

national anthem *n* Nationalhymne *f*

nationality *n* Staatsangehörigkeit *f*

National Lottery *n* Lotto *nt*

national park *n* Nationalpark *m* (*pl* Nationalparks)

natural *adj* natürlich

naturally *adv* natürlich ▷ *Naturally, we were very disappointed.* Natürlich waren wir sehr enttäuscht.

nature *n* Natur *f*

naughty *adj* böse ▷ *Naughty girl!* Böses Mädchen!; **Don't be naughty!** Sei nicht ungezogen!

navy *n* Marine *f* ▷ *He's in the navy.* Er ist bei der Marine.

navy-blue *adj* marineblau ▷ *a navy-blue shirt* ein marineblaues Hemd

near *adj* nah ▷ *It's fairly near.* Es ist ziemlich nah. ▷ *It's near enough to walk.* Es ist nah genug, um zu Fuß zu gehen.; **nearest** nächste

▶ *prep, adv* in der Nähe von ▷ *I live near Liverpool.* Ich wohne in der Nähe von Liverpool. ▷ *near my house* in der Nähe meines Hauses; **near here** hier in der Nähe; **near to** in der Nähe

nearby *adv, adj* ❶ in der Nähe ▷ *There's a supermarket nearby.* Es gibt einen Supermarkt in der Nähe. ❷ *(close)* nahe gelegen ▷ *a nearby garage* eine nahe gelegene Tankstelle

nearly *adv* fast ▷ *Dinner's nearly ready.* Das Essen ist fast fertig. ▷ *I'm nearly fifteen.* Ich bin fast fünfzehn. ▷ *I nearly missed the train.* Ich habe fast meinen Zug verpasst.

neat *adj* ordentlich ▷ *She has very neat writing.* Sie hat eine sehr ordentliche Schrift.; **a neat whisky** ein Whisky pur

neatly *adv* ordentlich ▷ *neatly folded* ordentlich gefaltet ▷ *neatly dressed* ordentlich gekleidet

necessarily *adv* **not necessarily** nicht unbedingt

necessary *adj* nötig

neck *n* ❶ *(of body)* Hals *m* (*gen* Halses, *pl* Hälse) ❷ *(of garment)* Ausschnitt *m* (*pl* Ausschnitte) ▷ *a V-neck sweater* ein Pullover mit V-Ausschnitt

necklace *n* Halskette *f*

need *vb* brauchen [**48**] ▷ *I need a bigger size.* Ich brauche eine größere Größe.; **to need to do something** etwas tun müssen [**51**]

▶ *n* **There's no need to book.** Man braucht nicht zu buchen.

needle *n* Nadel *f*

negative *n (photo)* Negativ *nt* (*pl* Negative)

▶ *adj* negativ ▷ *He's got a very negative attitude.* Er hat eine sehr negative Einstellung.

neglected *adj (untidy)* ungepflegt ▷ *The garden is neglected.* Der Garten ist ungepflegt.

negotiate *vb* verhandeln [**34**]

neighbour *n* Nachbar *m* (*gen* Nachbarn, *pl* Nachbarn), Nachbarin *f* ▷ *the neighbours' garden* der Garten der Nachbarn

neighbourhood *n* Nachbarschaft *f*

neither *pron, conj, adv* weder noch ▷ *Carrots or peas? — Neither, thanks.* Karotten oder Erbsen? — Weder noch, danke.; **Neither of them is coming.** Keiner von beiden kommt.; **neither ... nor ...** weder ... noch ... ▷ *Neither Sarah nor Tamsin is coming to the party.* Weder Sarah noch Tamsin kommen zur Party.; **Neither do I.** Ich auch nicht. ▷ *I don't like him. — Neither do I!* Ich mag ihn nicht. — Ich auch nicht!; **Neither have I.** Ich auch nicht. ▷ *I've never been* *to Spain. — Neither have I.* Ich war noch nie in Spanien. — Ich auch nicht.

nephew *n* Neffe *m (gen* Neffen, *pl* Neffen) ▷ *my nephew* mein Neffe

nerve *n* Nerv *m (pl* Nerven) ▷ *She gets on my nerves.* Sie geht mir auf die Nerven.; **He's got a nerve!** Der hat vielleicht Nerven!

nervous *adj (tense)* nervös ▷ *I bite my nails when I'm nervous.* Wenn ich nervös bin, kaue ich an den Nägeln.; **to be nervous about something** vor etwas Angst haben [**32**]

nest *n* Nest *nt (pl* Nester)

Net *n* **the Net** das Internet

net *n* Netz *nt (gen* Netzes, *pl* Netze) ▷ *a fishing net* ein Fischnetz

netball *n* Netzball *m*

Netherlands *npl* Niederlande *pl*

> Note that the definite article is used in German for countries which are plural.

from the Netherlands aus den Niederlanden; **in the Netherlands** in den Niederlanden; **to the Netherlands** in die Niederlande

network *n* ❶ Netz *nt (gen* Netzes, *pl* Netze) ❷ *(for computers)* Netzwerk *nt (pl* Netzwerke)

never *adv* nie ▷ *Have you ever been to Germany? — No, never.* Waren Sie schon mal in Deutschland? — Nein, nie. ▷ *I never write letters.* Ich schreibe nie Briefe. ▷ *Never again!* Nie wieder!; **Never mind.** Macht nichts!

new *adj* neu ▷ *her new boyfriend* ihr neuer Freund ▷ *I need a new dress.* Ich brauche ein neues Kleid.

news *nsg*

> **Nachricht** is a piece of news; **Nachrichten** is the news, for example on TV.

❶ Nachrichten *fpl* ▷ *good news* gute Nachrichten ▷ *I've had some bad news.* Ich habe schlechte Nachrichten bekommen. ▷ *I watch the news every evening.* Ich sehe mir jeden Abend die Nachrichten an. ▷ *I listen to the news every morning.* Ich höre jeden Morgen die Nachrichten. ❷ Nachricht *f* ▷ *That's wonderful news!* Das ist eine wunderbare Nachricht!

newsagent *n* Zeitungshändler *m (pl* Zeitungshändler), Zeitungshändlerin *f*

news dealer *n (US)* Zeitungshändler *m (pl* Zeitungshändler), Zeitungshändlerin *f*

newspaper *n* Zeitung *f* ▷ *I deliver newspapers.* Ich trage Zeitungen aus.

newsreader *n* Nachrichtensprecher *m (pl* Nachrichtensprecher), Nachrichtensprecherin *f*

New Year *n* Neujahr *nt* ▷ *to celebrate New Year* Neujahr feiern; **Happy New Year!** Ein gutes neues Jahr!; **New Year's Day** das Neujahr; **New Year's Eve** das Silvester

New Zealand *n* Neuseeland *nt*; **from New Zealand** aus Neuseeland; **in New Zealand** in Neuseeland; **to New Zealand** nach Neuseeland

New Zealander *n* Neuseeländer *m (pl* Neuseeländer), Neuseeländerin *f*

next *adj, adv, prep* ❶ nächste ▷ *next Saturday* nächsten Samstag ▷ *next week* nächste Woche ▷ *next year* nächstes Jahr ▷ *the next train* der nächste Zug; **Next please!** der Nächste, bitte! ❷ *(afterwards)* danach ▷ *What happened next?* Was ist danach passiert?; **What shall I do next?** Was soll ich als Nächstes machen?; **next to** neben

> Use the accusative to express movement or a change of place. Use the dative when there is no change of place.

▷ *I sat down next to my sister.* Ich setzte mich neben meine Schwester. ▷ *The post office is next to the bank.* Die Post ist neben der Bank.; **the next day** am nächsten Tag; **the next time** das nächste Mal; **next door** nebenan; **the next room** das Nebenzimmer

a b c d e f g h i j k l m **n** o p q r s t u v w x y z

NHS *n* **The NHS is very important.** Der staatliche Gesundheitsdienst ist sehr wichtig.
- In Germany there are a large number of health schemes, not just a single service.

nice *adj* ❶ *(kind)* nett ▷ *Your parents are nice.* Deine Eltern sind nett. ▷ *It was nice of you to remember my birthday.* Es war nett, dass du an meinen Geburtstag gedacht hast. ▷ *to be nice to somebody* nett zu jemandem sein ❷ *(pretty)* hübsch ▷ *That's a nice dress!* Das ist ein hübsches Kleid! ▷ *Ulm is a nice town.* Ulm ist eine hübsche Stadt. ❸ schön ▷ *nice weather* schönes Wetter ▷ *It's a nice day.* Es ist ein schöner Tag. ❹ *(food)* lecker ▷ *This pizza's very nice.* Diese Pizza ist sehr lecker.; **Have a nice time!** Viel Spaß!

nickname *n* Spitzname *m (gen* Spitznamens, *pl* Spitznamen)

niece *n* Nichte *f* ▷ *my niece* meine Nichte

Nigeria *n* Nigeria *nt* ▷ *in Nigeria* in Nigeria

night *n* ❶ Nacht *f (pl* Nächte) ▷ *I want a single room for two nights.* Ich möchte ein Einzelzimmer für zwei Nächte.; **at night** nachts; **Good night!** Gute Nacht!; **a night club** ein Nachtklub *m* ❷ *(evening)* Abend *m (pl* Abende) ▷ *last night* gestern Abend

nightie *n* Nachthemd *nt (pl* Nachthemden)

nightmare *n* Albtraum *m (pl* Albträume) ▷ *I had a nightmare.* Ich hatte einen Albtraum. ▷ *It was a real nightmare!* Es war ein Albtraum!

nil *n* null ▷ *We won one nil.* Wir haben eins zu null gewonnen.

nine *num* neun ▷ *She's nine.* Sie ist neun.

nineteen *num* neunzehn ▷ *She's nineteen.* Sie ist neunzehn.

nineteenth *adj* neunzehnte ▷ *the nineteenth of August* der neunzehnte August

ninety *num* neunzig ▷ *She's ninety.* Sie ist neunzig.

ninth *adj* neunte ▷ *the ninth floor* der neunte Stock ▷ *the ninth of August* der neunte August

no *adv, adj* ❶ nein ▷ *Are you coming? — No.* Kommst du? — Nein. ▷ *Would you like some more? — No thank you.* Möchten Sie noch etwas? — Nein danke. ❷ *(not any)* kein ▷ *There's no hot water.* Es gibt kein heißes Wasser. ▷ *There are no trains on Sundays.* Sonntags verkehren keine Züge. ▷ *No problem.* Kein Problem. ▷ *I've got no idea.* Ich habe keine Ahnung.; **No way!** Auf keinen Fall!; **'no smoking'** 'Rauchen verboten'

nobody *pron* niemand ▷ *Who's going with you? — Nobody.* Wer geht mit dir mit? — Niemand. ▷ *There was nobody in the office.* Es war niemand im Büro.

nod *vb* nicken **[48]**

noise *n* Lärm *m* ▷ *Please make less noise.* Macht bitte weniger Lärm.

noisy *adj* laut ▷ *It's too noisy here.* Hier ist es zu laut.

nominate *vb* nominieren **[76]** *(perf* hat nominiert) ▷ *She was nominated for an Oscar.* Sie war für einen Oscar nominiert.

none *pron* keiner ▷ *None of my friends wanted to come.* Keiner meiner Freunde wollte kommen. ▷ *How many brothers have you got? — None.* Wie viele Brüder hast du? — Keinen.
keine ▷ *Milk? There's none left.* Milch? Es ist keine mehr da.
keines ▷ *Which of the books have you read? — None.* Welches der Bücher hast du gelesen? — Keines.; **There are none left.** Es sind keine mehr da.

nonsense *n* Unsinn *m* ▷ *She talks a lot of nonsense.* Sie redet viel Unsinn. ▷ *Nonsense!* Unsinn!

nonsmoker *n* Nichtraucher *m (pl* Nichtraucher), Nichtraucherin *f* ▷ *She's a nonsmoker.* Sie ist Nichtraucherin.

nonsmoking *adj* **a nonsmoking area** ein Nichtraucherbereich *m*
nonstop *adj, adv* ❶ nonstop ▷ *We flew nonstop.* Wir sind nonstop geflogen.; **a nonstop flight** ein Nonstop-Flug *m* ❷ ununterbrochen ▷ *Liz talks nonstop.* Liz redet ununterbrochen.
noodles *npl* Nudeln *fpl*
noon *n* Mittag *m* (*pl* Mittage); **at noon** um zwölf Uhr mittags
no one *pron* niemand
nor *conj* **neither ... nor** weder ... noch; **Nor do I.** Ich auch nicht.; **Nor have I.** Ich auch nicht.
normal *adj* normal ▷ *at the normal time* zur normalen Zeit ▷ *a normal car* ein normales Auto
normally *adv* ❶ *(usually)* normalerweise ▷ *I normally arrive at nine o'clock.* Normalerweise komme ich um neun Uhr. ❷ *(as normal)* normal ▷ *In spite of the strike, the airports are working normally.* Trotz des Streiks arbeiten die Flughäfen normal.
Normandy *n* Normandie *f*; **in Normandy** in der Normandie
north *adj, adv* nach Norden ▷ *We were travelling north.* Wir sind nach Norden gefahren.; **the north coast** die Nordküste; **a north wind** ein Nordwind *m*; **north of** nördlich von
▶ *n* Norden *m* ▷ *in the north* im Norden
North America *n* Nordamerika *nt*; **from North America** aus Nordamerika; **to North America** nach Nordamerika
northeast *n* Nordosten *m* ▷ *in the northeast* im Nordosten
northern *adj* nördlich ▷ *the northern part of the island* der nördliche Teil der Insel; **Northern Europe** Nordeuropa *nt*
Northern Ireland *n* Nordirland *nt*; **from Northern Ireland** aus Nordirland; **in Northern Ireland** in Nordirland; **to Northern Ireland** nach Nordirland
North Pole *n* Nordpol *m*
North Sea *n* Nordsee *f*
northwest *n* Nordwesten *m* ▷ *in the northwest* im Nordwesten
Norway *n* Norwegen *nt*; **from Norway** aus Norwegen; **to Norway** nach Norwegen
Norwegian *adj* norwegisch; **He's Norwegian.** Er ist Norweger.
▶ *n* ❶ *(person)* Norweger *m* (*pl* Norweger), Norwegerin *f* ❷ *(language)* Norwegisch *nt* (*gen* Norwegischen)
nose *n* Nase *f*
nosebleed *n* Nasenbluten *nt* ▷ *I often get nosebleeds.* Ich habe oft Nasenbluten.
nosey *adj* neugierig ▷ *She's very nosey.* Sie ist sehr neugierig.
not *adv* ❶ nicht ▷ *Are you coming or not?* Kommst du oder nicht? ▷ *I'm not sure.* Ich bin nicht sicher. ▷ *It's not raining.* Es regnet nicht.; **not really** eigentlich nicht; **not at all** überhaupt nicht; **not yet** noch nicht ▷ *Have you finished? — Not yet.* Bist du fertig? — Noch nicht. ▷ *They haven't arrived yet.* Sie sind noch nicht angekommen. ❷ nein ▷ *Can you lend me ten pounds? — I'm afraid not.* Können Sie mir zehn Pfund leihen? — Leider nein.
note *n* ❶ Notiz *f*; **to take notes** sich Notizen machen [**48**] ❷ *(letter)* Brief *m* (*pl* Briefe); **I'll write her a note.** Ich werde ihr schreiben. ❸ *(banknote)* Schein *m* (*pl* Scheine) ▷ *a five-pound note* ein Fünfpfundschein
note down *vb* aufschreiben [**61**] (*imperf* schrieb auf, *perf* hat aufgeschrieben)
notebook *n* ❶ Notizbuch *nt* (*pl* Notizbücher) ❷ *(computer)* Notebookcomputer *m* (*pl* Notebookcomputer)
notepad *n* Notizblock *m* (*pl* Notizblöcke)
nothing *n* nichts ▷ *What's wrong? — Nothing.* Was ist los? — Nichts. ▷ *nothing special* nichts Besonderes ▷ *He does nothing.* Er tut

nichts. ▷ *He ate nothing for breakfast.* Er hat nichts zum Frühstück gegessen.

notice *n (sign)* Notiz *f* ▷ *to put up a notice* eine Notiz aushängen ▷ *Don't take any notice of him!* Nimm keine Notiz von ihm!; **a warning notice** ein Warnschild *nt*
▸ *vb* bemerken [7] (*perf* hat bemerkt)

notice board *n* Anschlagbrett *nt* (*pl* Anschlagbretter)

nought *n* Null *f*

noun *n* Substantiv *nt* (*pl* Substantive)

novel *n* Roman *m* (*pl* Romane)

novelist *n* Romanautor *m* (*pl* Romanautoren), Romanautorin *f*

November *n* November *m* ▷ *in November* im November

now *adv, conj* jetzt ▷ *What are you doing now?* Was tust du jetzt?; **just now** gerade; **by now** inzwischen; **now and then** ab und zu

nowhere *adv* nirgends ▷ *nowhere else* sonst nirgends

nuclear *adj* nuklear; **nuclear power** die Kernkraft; **a nuclear power station** ein Kernkraftwerk *nt*

nuisance *n* **It's a nuisance.** Es ist sehr lästig.; **Sorry to be a nuisance.** Tut mir leid, dass ich schon wieder ankomme.

numb *adj* taub ▷ *numb with cold* taub vor Kälte

number *n* ❶ *(total amount)* Anzahl *f* ▷ *a large number of people* eine große Anzahl von Menschen ❷ *(of house, telephone, bank account)* Nummer *f* ▷ *They live at number five.* Sie wohnen in der Nummer fünf. ▷ *What's your phone number?* Wie ist Ihre Telefonnummer?; **You've got the wrong number.** Sie sind falsch verbunden. ❸ *(figure, digit)* Zahl *f* ▷ *I can't read the second number.* Ich kann die zweite Zahl nicht lesen.

number plate *n* Nummernschild *nt* (*pl* Nummernschilder)

- The first letters of a German number plate allow you to tell where the car's owner lives. Thus L stands for Leipzig, LB for Ludwigsburg, LU for Ludwigshafen, etc.

nun *n* Nonne *f* ▷ *She's a nun.* Sie ist Nonne.

nurse *n* Krankenpfleger *m*, Krankenschwester *f* ▷ *He's a nurse.* Er ist Krankenpfleger. ▷ *She's a nurse.* Sie ist Krankenschwester.

nursery *n* ❶ *(for children)* Kindergarten *f* (*pl* Kindergärten) ❷ *(for plants)* Baumschule *f*

nursery school *n* Kindergarten *m* (*pl* Kindergärten)

- German children go to **Kindergarten** from the age of 3 to 6.

nut *n* ❶ Nuss *f* (*pl* Nüsse) ❷ *(made of metal)* Mutter *f*

nuts *adj* **He's nuts.** *(informal)* Er spinnt.

nylon *n* Nylon *nt*

O

oak *n* Eiche *f* ▷ *an oak table* ein Eichentisch *m*
oar *n* Ruder *nt* (*pl* Ruder)
oats *npl* Hafer *m*
obedient *adj* gehorsam
obey *vb* gehorchen [**48**] (*perf* hat gehorcht) ▷ *She didn't obey her mother.* Sie hat ihrer Mutter nicht gehorcht.; **to obey the rules** die Regeln befolgen [**7**]
object *n* Gegenstand *m* (*pl* Gegenstände) ▷ *a familiar object* ein vertrauter Gegenstand
objection *n* Einspruch *m* (*pl* Einsprüche)
oboe *n* Oboe *f* ▷ *I play the oboe.* Ich spiele Oboe.
obsessed *adj* besessen ▷ *He's completely obsessed with trains.* Er ist von Zügen ganz besessen.
obsession *n* Leidenschaft *f* ▷ *Football's an obsession of mine.* Fußball ist meine Leidenschaft.
obtain *vb* erhalten [**33**] (*imperf* erhielt, *perf* hat erhalten)
obvious *adj* offensichtlich
obviously *adv* ❶ *(of course)* natürlich ▷ *Do you want to pass the exam? — Obviously!* Willst du die Prüfung bestehen? — Natürlich! ▷ *Obviously not!* Natürlich nicht! ❷ *(visibly)* offensichtlich ▷ *She was obviously exhausted.* Sie war offensichtlich erschöpft.
occasion *n* Gelegenheit *f* ▷ *a special occasion* eine besondere Gelegenheit; **on several occasions** mehrmals
occasionally *adv* ab und zu
occupation *n* Beschäftigung *f*
occupy *vb* besetzen [**7**] (*perf* hat besetzt) ▷ *That seat is occupied.* Der Platz ist besetzt.
occur *vb (happen)* passieren [**76**] (*perf* ist passiert) ▷ *The accident occurred yesterday.* Der Unfall ist gestern passiert.; **It suddenly occurred to me that ...** Plötzlich ist mir eingefallen, dass ...
OCD *abbr* (= *obsessive compulsive disorder*) Zwangsstörung *f*
ocean *n* Ozean *m* (*pl* Ozeane)
o'clock *adv* **at four o'clock** um vier Uhr; **It's five o'clock.** Es ist fünf Uhr.
October *n* Oktober *m* ▷ *in October* im Oktober
octopus *n* Tintenfisch *m* (*pl* Tintenfische)
odd *adj* ❶ eigenartig ▷ *That's odd!* Das ist eigenartig! ❷ ungerade ▷ *an odd number* eine ungerade Zahl
of *prep* von ▷ *some photos of my holiday* Fotos von meinen Ferien ▷ *three of us* drei von uns ▷ *a friend of mine* ein Freund von mir ▷ *That's very kind of you.* Das ist sehr nett von Ihnen. ▷ *Can I have half of that?* Kann ich die Hälfte davon haben?

> 'of' is not translated when specifying a quantity of something.

▷ *a kilo of oranges* ein Kilo Orangen

> 'of' is often expressed by using the genitive.

▷ *the end of the film* das Ende des Films ▷ *the top of the stairs* das obere Ende der Treppe ▷ *the front of the house* die

Vorderseite des Hauses; **a boy of ten** ein zehnjähriger Junge; **the fourteenth of September** der vierzehnte September; **It's made of wood.** Es ist aus Holz.

off *adv, prep, adj*

For other expressions with 'off', see the verbs 'get', 'take', 'turn' etc.

❶ *(heater, light, TV)* aus ▷ *All the lights are off.* Alle Lichter sind aus. ❷ *(tap, gas)* zu ▷ *Are you sure the tap is off?* Bist du sicher, dass der Hahn zu ist? ❸ *(cancelled)* abgesagt ▷ *The match is off.* Das Spiel wurde abgesagt.; **to be off sick** krank sein [**65**]; **a day off** ein freier Tag; **to take a day off work** sich einen Tag freinehmen [**52**]; **She's off school today.** Sie ist heute nicht in der Schule.; **I must be off now.** Ich muss jetzt gehen.; **I'm off.** Ich gehe jetzt.

offence *n (crime)* Vergehen *nt (pl* Vergehen)

offer *n* Angebot *nt (pl* Angebote) ▷ *a good offer* ein günstiges Angebot; **'on special offer'** 'im Sonderangebot' ▸ *vb* anbieten [**8**] *(imperf* bot an, *perf* hat angeboten) ▷ *He offered to help me.* Er bot mir seine Hilfe an. ▷ *I offered to go with them.* Ich habe ihnen angeboten mitzugehen.

office *n* Büro *nt (pl* Büros) ▷ *She works in an office.* Sie arbeitet in einem Büro.; **doctor's office** die Arztpraxis

officer *n (in army)* Offizier *m (pl* Offiziere); **a police officer** *(man)* ein Polizeibeamter

official *adj* offiziell

off-licence *n* Wein- und Spirituosenhandlung *f*

offside *adj (in football)* im Abseits

often *adv* oft ▷ *It often rains.* Es regnet oft. ▷ *How often do you go to church?* Wie oft gehst du in die Kirche? ▷ *I'd like to go skiing more often.* Ich würde gern öfter Ski fahren.

oil *n* ❶ *(for lubrication, cooking)* Öl *nt (pl* Öle); **an oil painting** ein Ölgemälde *nt* ❷ *(petroleum)* Erdöl *nt* ▷ *North Sea oil* Erdöl aus der Nordsee ▸ *vb* ölen [**38**]

oil rig *n* Bohrinsel *f* ▷ *He works on an oil rig.* Er arbeitet auf einer Bohrinsel.

ointment *n* Salbe *f*

okay *excl, adj* okay ▷ *Could you call back later?—Okay!* Kannst du später anrufen? — Okay! ▷ *I'll meet you at six o'clock, okay?* Ich treffe dich um sechs Uhr, okay? ▷ *Is that okay?* Ist das okay? ▷ *How was your holiday?—It was okay.* Wie waren die Ferien? — Okay.; **I'll do it tomorrow, if that's okay with you.** Ich mache das morgen, wenn du einverstanden bist.; **Are you okay?** Bist du in Ordnung?

old *adj* alt ▷ *an old dog* ein alter Hund ▷ *old people* alte Menschen ▷ *my old English teacher* mein alter Englischlehrer ▷ *How old are you?* Wie alt bist du? ▷ *He's ten years old.* Er ist zehn Jahre alt. ▷ *my older brother* mein älterer Bruder ▷ *my older sister* meine ältere Schwester ▷ *She's two years older than me.* Sie ist zwei Jahre älter als ich. ▷ *He's the oldest in the family.* Er ist der Älteste der Familie.

old age pensioner *n* Rentner *m (pl* Rentner), Rentnerin *f* ▷ *She's an old age pensioner.* Sie ist Rentnerin.

old-fashioned *adj* altmodisch ▷ *She wears old-fashioned clothes.* Sie trägt altmodische Kleidung. ▷ *My parents are rather old-fashioned.* Meine Eltern sind ziemlich altmodisch.

olive *n* Olive *f*

olive oil *n* Olivenöl *nt (pl* Olivenöle)

Olympic *adj* olympisch; **the Olympics** die Olympischen Spiele

omelette *n* Omelett *nt (pl* Omeletts)

on *prep, adv*

There are several ways of translating 'on'. Scan the examples to find one that is similar to what you want to say. For other expressions with 'on' see the verbs 'go', 'put', 'turn' etc.

❶ auf

Use the accusative to express movement or a change of place. Use the dative when there is no change of place.

▷ *It's on the table.* Es ist auf dem Tisch. ▷ *Please, put it on the table.* Stell es bitte auf den Tisch. ▷ *on an island* auf einer Insel ▷ *on the left* auf der linken Seite ❷ an ▷ *on Friday* am Freitag ▷ *on Christmas Day* am ersten Weihnachtsfeiertag ▷ *on the twentieth of June* am zwanzigsten Juni ▷ *on my birthday* an meinem Geburtstag; **on Fridays** freitags

Use the accusative to express movement or a change of place. Use the dative when there is no change of place.

▷ *There was not a single picture on the wall.* An der Wand hing kein einziges Bild. ▷ *She hung a picture up on the wall.* Sie hängte ein Bild an die Wand. ❸ in ▷ *on the second floor* im zweiten Stock ▷ *on TV* im Fernsehen ▷ *What's on TV?* Was kommt im Fernsehen? ▷ *I heard it on the radio.* Ich habe es im Radio gehört.; **on the bus (1)** *(by bus)* mit dem Bus ▷ *I go into town on the bus.* Ich fahre mit dem Bus in die Stadt. **(2)** *(inside)* im Bus ▷ *There were no empty seats on the bus.* Es gab keinen freien Platz im Bus.; **I go to school on my bike.** Ich fahre mit dem Fahrrad zur Schule.; **on holiday** in den Ferien ▷ *They're on holiday.* Sie sind in den Ferien.; **They are on strike.** Sie streiken.

▶ *adj* ❶ *(heater, light, TV)* an ▷ *I left the light on.* Ich habe das Licht angelassen. ▷ *Is the dishwasher on?* Ist die Spülmaschine an? ❷ *(tap, gas)* auf ▷ *Leave the tap on.* Lass den Hahn auf.; **What's on at the cinema?** Was gibt's im Kino?

once *adv* einmal ▷ *once a week* einmal pro Woche ▷ *once more* noch einmal ▷ *I've been to Germany once before.* Ich war schon einmal in Deutschland.; **Once upon a time ...** Es war einmal ...; **at once** sofort; **once in a while** ab und zu

one *num, pron*

Use **ein** for masculine and neuter nouns, **eine** for feminine nouns.

❶ ein ▷ *one man* ein Mann ▷ *one child* ein Kind ▷ *We stayed there for one day.* Wir sind einen Tag dortgeblieben. ❷ eine ▷ *one minute* eine Minute ▷ *Do you need a stamp? — No thanks, I've got one.* Brauchst du eine Briefmarke? — Nein danke, ich habe eine. ▷ *I've got one brother and one sister.* Ich habe einen Bruder und eine Schwester. ❸ eins

Use **eins** when counting.

▷ *one, two, three* eins, zwei, drei ❹ *(impersonal)* man ▷ *One never knows.* Man kann nie wissen.; **this one (1)** *(masculine)* dieser ▷ *Which foot hurts? — This one.* Welcher Fuß tut weh? — Dieser. **(2)** *(feminine)* diese ▷ *Which is your cup? — This one.* Welche ist deine Tasse? — Diese. **(3)** *(neuter)* dieses ▷ *Which is the best photo? — This one.* Welches ist das beste Foto? — Dieses.; **that one (1)** *(masculine)* der da ▷ *Which pen did you use? — That one.* Welchen Schreiber hast du benützt? — Den da. **(2)** *(feminine)* die da ▷ *Which bag is yours? — That one.* Welche ist deine Tasche? — Die da. **(3)** *(neuter)* das da ▷ *Which is your car? — That one.* Welches ist Ihr Auto? — Das da.

oneself *pron* ❶ sich ▷ *to hurt oneself* sich wehtun ❷ selbst ▷ *It's quicker to do it oneself.* Es geht schneller, wenn man es selbst macht.

one-way *adj* **a one-way street** eine Einbahnstraße

onion *n* Zwiebel *f* ▷ *onion soup* die Zwiebelsuppe

online *adj, adv* online

only *adv, adj, conj* ❶ einzig ▷ *Monday is the only day I'm free.* Montag ist mein einziger freier Tag. ▷ *German is the only subject I like.* Deutsch ist das einzige Fach, das ich mag. ❷ nur ▷ *How much was it? — Only twenty euros.* Wie viel hat es gekostet? — Nur zwanzig Euro. ▷ *We only want to stay for one night.* Wir wollen nur eine Nacht bleiben. ▷ *the same sweater, only in black* der gleiche Pullover, nur in Schwarz; **an only child** ein Einzelkind *nt*

onwards *adv* ab ▷ *from July onwards* ab Juli

open *adj* offen ▷ *The window was open.* Das Fenster war offen.; **The baker's is open on Sunday morning.** Die Bäckerei hat am Sonntagmorgen auf.; **in the open air** im Freien
▶ *vb* ❶ aufmachen [**4**] (*perf* hat aufgemacht) ▷ *Can I open the window?* Kann ich das Fenster aufmachen? ▷ *What time do the shops open?* Um wie viel Uhr machen die Geschäfte auf? ❷ aufgehen [**29**] (*imperf* ging auf, *perf* ist aufgegangen) ▷ *The door opens automatically.* Die Tür geht automatisch auf. ▷ *The door opened and in came Jim.* Die Tür ging auf und Jim kam herein.

opening hours *npl* Öffnungszeiten *fpl*

opera *n* Oper *f*

operate *vb (machine)* bedienen [**7**] (*perf* hat bedient); **to operate on someone** jemanden operieren [**76**]

operation *n* Operation *f* ▷ *a major operation* eine größere Operation; **to have an operation** operiert werden [**91**]

opinion *n* Meinung *f* ▷ *He asked me my opinion.* Er fragte mich nach meiner Meinung. ▷ *What's your opinion?* Was ist deine Meinung?; **in my opinion** meiner Meinung nach

opinion poll *n* Meinungsumfrage *f*

opponent *n* Gegner *m* (*pl* Gegner), Gegnerin *f*

opportunity *n* Gelegenheit *f*; **to have the opportunity to do something** die Gelegenheit haben [**32**], etwas zu tun

opposed *adj* **to be opposed to something** gegen etwas sein [**65**]

opposite *adj, adv, prep*
❶ entgegengesetzt ▷ *It's in the opposite direction.* Es ist in der entgegengesetzten Richtung.
❷ gegenüber ▷ *They live opposite.* Sie wohnen gegenüber. ▷ *the girl sitting opposite me* das Mädchen, das mir gegenüber saß; **the opposite sex** das andere Geschlecht

opposition *n* Opposition *f*

optician *n* Optiker *m* (*pl* Optiker), Optikerin *f* ▷ *She's an optician.* Sie ist Optikerin.

optimistic *adj* optimistisch

option *n* ❶ *(choice)* Wahl *f* ▷ *I've got no option.* Ich habe keine andere Wahl.
❷ *(optional subject)* Wahlfach *nt* (*pl* Wahlfächer) ▷ *I'm doing geology as my option.* Ich habe Geologie als Wahlfach.

or *conj* ❶ oder ▷ *Tea or coffee?* Tee oder Kaffee?

> Use **weder ... noch** in negative sentences.

▷ *I don't eat meat or fish.* Ich esse weder Fleisch noch Fisch. ❷ *(otherwise)* sonst ▷ *Hurry up or you'll miss the bus.* Beeil dich, sonst verpasst du den Bus.; **Give me the money, or else!** Gib mir das Geld, sonst gibt's was!

oral *adj* mündlich ▷ *an oral exam* eine mündliche Prüfung
▶ *n* mündliche Prüfung *f* ▷ *I've got my German oral soon.* Ich habe bald meine mündliche Prüfung in Deutsch.

orange *n* Orange *f*; **an orange juice** ein Orangensaft *m*
▶ *adj (colour)* orangerot

orchard *n* Obstgarten *m* (*pl* Obstgärten)

orchestra *n* ❶ Orchester *nt* (*pl* Orchester) ▷ *I play in the school orchestra.* Ich spiele im Schulorchester.
❷ *(stalls)* Parkett *nt* ▷ *We sat in the orchestra.* Wir saßen im Parkett.

order *n* ❶ *(sequence)* Reihenfolge *f* ▷ *in alphabetical order* in alphabetischer Reihenfolge ❷ *(at restaurant, in shop)* Bestellung *f* ▷ *The waiter took our order.* Der Ober nahm unsere Bestellung auf. ❸ *(instruction)* Befehl *m* (*pl* Befehle) ▷ *That's an order.* Das ist ein Befehl.; **in order to** um zu; **'out of order'** 'außer Betrieb'
▶ *vb* bestellen [7] (*perf* hat bestellt) ▷ *We ordered steak and chips.* Wir haben Steak mit Pommes frites bestellt. ▷ *Are you ready to order?* Möchten Sie bestellen?

order about *vb* herumkommandieren [15] (*perf* hat herumkommandiert)

ordinary *adj* ❶ gewöhnlich ▷ *an ordinary day* ein gewöhnlicher Tag ❷ *(people)* normal ▷ *an ordinary family* eine normale Familie ▷ *He's just an ordinary guy.* Er ist ein ganz normaler Mensch.

organ *n (instrument)* Orgel *f* ▷ *I play the organ.* Ich spiele Orgel.

organic *adj (fruit)* biologisch angebaut; **organic vegetables** das Biogemüse *sg*

organization *n* Organisation *f*

organize *vb* organisieren [76] (*perf* hat organisiert)

original *adj* originell ▷ *It's a very original idea.* Das ist eine sehr originelle Idee.; **Our original plan was to go camping.** Ursprünglich wollten wir zelten.

originally *adv* ursprünglich

Orkney *n* Orkneyinseln *fpl*; **in Orkney** auf den Orkneyinseln

ornament *n* Verzierung *f*

orphan *n* Waisenkind *nt* (*pl* Waisenkinder) ▷ *She's an orphan.* Sie ist ein Waisenkind.

other *adj, pron* andere ▷ *Have you got these jeans in other colours?* Haben Sie diese Jeans in anderen Farben? ▷ *on the other side of the street* auf der anderen Straßenseite; **the other day** neulich; **the other one (1)** *(masculine)* der andere ▷ *This hat? — No, the other one.* Dieser Hut? — Nein, der andere. **(2)** *(feminine)* die andere ▷ *This cup? — No, the other one.* Diese Tasse? — Nein, die andere. **(3)** *(neuter)* das andere ▷ *This photo? — No, the other one.* Dieses Foto? — Nein, das andere.; **the others** die anderen ▷ *The others are going but I'm not.* Die anderen gehen, ich nicht.

otherwise *adv, conj* sonst ▷ *Note down the number, otherwise you'll forget it.* Schreib dir die Nummer auf, sonst vergisst du sie. ▷ *Put some sunscreen on, you'll get burned otherwise.* Creme dich ein, sonst bekommst du einen Sonnenbrand. ▷ *I'm tired, but otherwise I'm fine.* Ich bin müde, aber sonst geht's mir gut.

ought *vb*

> If you want to say that you feel obliged to do something, use the conditional tense of **sollen**.

▷ *I ought to phone my parents.* Ich sollte meine Eltern anrufen. ▷ *You ought not to do that.* Du solltest das nicht tun.

> If you want to say that something is likely, use the conditional tense of **müssen**.

▷ *He ought to win.* Er müsste gewinnen.

our *adj* unser ▷ *Our boss is quite nice.* Unser Chef ist ganz nett. ▷ *Our company is going to expand.* Unsere Firma wird expandieren. ▷ *Our house is quite big.* Unser Haus ist ziemlich groß. ▷ *Our neighbours are very nice.* Unsere Nachbarn sind sehr nett.

> Do not use **unser** with parts of the body.

▷ *We had to shut our eyes.* Wir mussten die Augen zumachen.

ours *pron* ❶ unserer ▷ *Your garden is very big, ours is much smaller.* Euer Garten ist sehr groß, unserer ist viel kleiner.
unsere ▷ *Your school is very different from ours.* Eure Schule ist ganz anderes als unsere.
unseres ▷ *Your house is bigger than ours.* Euer Haus ist größer als unseres.

❷ unsere ▷ *Our teachers are strict. — Ours are too.* Unsere Lehrer sind streng. — Unsere auch.; **Is this ours?** Gehört das uns? ▷ *This car is ours.* Das Auto gehört uns. ▷ *Whose is this? — It's ours.* Wem gehört das? — Uns.

ourselves *pron* ❶ uns ▷ *We really enjoyed ourselves.* Wir haben uns wirklich amüsiert. ❷ selbst ▷ *We built our garage ourselves.* Wir haben die Garage selbst gebaut.

out *adv*

> There are several ways of translating 'out'. Scan the examples to find one that is similar to what you want to say. For other expressions with 'out', see the verbs 'go', 'put', 'turn' etc.

❶ *(outside)* draußen ▷ *It's cold out.* Es ist kalt draußen. ❷ *(light, fire)* aus ▷ *All the lights are out.* Alle Lichter sind aus.; **She's out.** Sie ist weg.; **She's out shopping.** Sie ist zum Einkaufen.; **out there** da draußen; **to go out** ausgehen [**29**]; **to go out with somebody** mit jemandem gehen [**29**]; **out of (1)** aus ▷ *to drink out of a glass* aus einem Glas trinken **(2)** von ▷ *in nine cases out of ten* in neun von zehn Fällen **(3)** außerhalb ▷ *He lives out of town.* Er wohnt außerhalb der Stadt. ▷ *three kilometres out of town* drei Kilometer außerhalb der Stadt; **out of curiosity** aus Neugier; **out of work** arbeitslos; **That is out of the question.** Das kommt nicht infrage.; **You're out!** *(in game)* Du bist draußen!; **'way out'** 'Ausgang'

outdoor *adj* im Freien ▷ *outdoor activities* Aktivitäten im Freien; **an outdoor swimming pool** ein Freibad *nt*

outdoors *adv* im Freien

outfit *n* Outfit *nt (pl* Outfits) ▷ *a cowboy outfit* ein Cowboyoutfit

outing *n* Ausflug *m (pl* Ausflüge) ▷ *to go on an outing* einen Ausflug machen

outline *n* ❶ *(summary)* Grundriss *m (gen* Grundrisses, *pl* Grundrisse) ▷ *This is an outline of the plan.* Das ist der Grundriss des Plans. ❷ *(shape)* Umriss *m (gen* Umrisses, *pl* Umrisse) ▷ *We could see the outline of the mountain.* Wir konnten den Umriss des Berges erkennen.

outside *n* Außenseite *f*
▸ *adj, adv, prep* ❶ äußere ▷ *the outside walls* die äußeren Mauern ❷ draußen ▷ *It's very cold outside.* Draußen ist es sehr kalt. ❸ außerhalb ▷ *outside the school* außerhalb der Schule ▷ *outside school hours* außerhalb der Schulzeit

outskirts *npl* Stadtrand *msg* ▷ *on the outskirts of the town* am Stadtrand

outstanding *adj* bemerkenswert

oval *adj* oval

oven *n* Backofen *m (pl* Backöfen)

over *prep, adv, adj* ❶ über

> Use the accusative to express movement or a change of place. Use the dative when there is no change of place.

▷ *The ball went over the wall.* Der Ball flog über die Mauer. ▷ *There's a mirror over the washbasin.* Über dem Becken ist ein Spiegel. ❷ *(more than)* über ▷ *It's over twenty kilos.* Es ist über zwanzig Kilo schwer. ▷ *The temperature was over thirty degrees.* Die Temperatur lag über dreißig Grad. ❸ *(finished)* vorbei ▷ *I'll be happy when the exams are over.* Ich bin froh, wenn die Prüfungen vorbei sind.; **over the holidays** die Ferien über; **over Christmas** über Weihnachten; **over here** hier; **over there** dort; **all over Scotland** in ganz Schottland

overcast *adj* bedeckt ▷ *The sky was overcast.* Der Himmel war bedeckt.

overdose *n (of drugs)* Überdosis *f (pl* Überdosen) ▷ *to take an overdose* eine Überdosis nehmen

overdraft *n* Überziehungskredit *m*

overseas *adv* ❶ im Ausland ▷ *I'd like to work overseas.* Ich würde gern im Ausland arbeiten. ❷ ins Ausland ▷ *His company has sent him overseas.* Seine Firma hat ihn ins Ausland geschickt.

overtake *vb* überholen [**18**] (*perf* hat überholt) ▷ *He overtook me.* Er hat mich überholt.
overtime *n* Überstunden *fpl* ▷ *to work overtime* Überstunden machen
overtook *vb see* **overtake**
overweight *adj* **to be overweight** Übergewicht haben [**32**]
owe *vb* schulden [**54**]; **to owe somebody something** jemandem etwas schulden [**54**]
owing to *prep* wegen ▷ *owing to bad weather* wegen des schlechten Wetters
owl *n* Eule *f*
own *adj* eigen ▷ *I've got my own bathroom.* Ich habe mein eigenes Badezimmer.; **I'd like a room of my own.** Ich hätte gern ein eigenes Zimmer.; **on one's own** allein
▸ *vb* besitzen [**68**] (*imperf* besaß, *perf* hat besessen) ▷ *My father owns a small business.* Mein Vater besitzt ein kleines Geschäft.
own up *vb* zugeben [**28**] (*pres* gibt zu, *imperf* gab zu, *perf* hat zugegeben)
owner *n* Besitzer *m* (*pl* Besitzer), Besitzerin *f*
oxygen *n* Sauerstoff *m*
oyster *n* Auster *f*
ozone layer *n* Ozonschicht *f*

p

Pacific *n* Pazifik *m*
pack *vb* packen [**38**] ▷ *I'll help you pack.* Ich helfe dir packen. ▷ *I've packed my case.* Ich habe meinen Koffer gepackt.; **Pack it in!** *(stop it)* Lass es!
▸ *n* ❶ *(packet)* Packung *f* ▷ *a pack of cigarettes* eine Packung Zigaretten ❷ *(of yoghurts, cans)* Pack *m* (*pl* Packs) ▷ *a six-pack* ein Sechserpack; **a pack of cards** ein Spiel Karten *nt*
package *n* Paket *nt* (*pl* Pakete); **a package holiday** eine Pauschalreise
packed *adj* gerammelt voll ▷ *The cinema was packed.* Das Kino war gerammelt voll.
packed lunch *n* Lunchpaket *nt* (*pl* Lunchpakete); **I take a packed lunch to school.** Ich nehme für mittags etwas zum Essen in die Schule mit.
packet *n* Packung *f* ▷ *a packet of cigarettes* eine Packung Zigaretten
pad *n* *(notepad)* Notizblock *m* (*pl* Notizblöcke)

paddle *vb* ❶ *(canoe)* paddeln [**34**] ❷ *(in water)* planschen [**48**]
▶ *n (for canoe)* Paddel *nt* (*pl* Paddel); **to go for a paddle** planschen gehen [**29**]
padlock *n* Vorhängeschloss *nt* (*gen* Vorhängeschlosses, *pl* Vorhängeschlösser)
page *n (of book)* Seite *f*
▶ *vb* **to page somebody** jemanden per Pager benachrichtigen [**7**]
pain *n* Schmerz *m* (*gen* Schmerzes, *pl* Schmerzen) ▷ *a terrible pain* ein furchtbarer Schmerz; **I've got pains in my stomach.** Ich habe Bauchschmerzen.; **to be in pain** Schmerzen haben [**32**]; **He's a real pain.** *(informal)* Er geht einem echt auf die Nerven.
painful *adj* schmerzhaft; **to suffer from painful periods** starke Periodenschmerzen haben [**32**]; **to be painful** wehtun [**81**]
painkiller *n* Schmerzmittel *nt* (*pl* Schmerzmittel)
paint *n* Farbe *f*
▶ *vb* ❶ streichen (*imperf* strich, *perf* hat gestrichen) ▷ *to paint something green* etwas grün streichen ❷ *(pictures)* malen [**38**] ▷ *She painted a picture of the house.* Sie hat von dem Haus ein Bild gemalt.
paintbrush *n* Pinsel *m* (*pl* Pinsel)
painter *n* Maler *m* (*pl* Maler), Malerin *f*; **a painter and decorator** ein Anstreicher *m*
painting *n* ❶ Malen *nt* ▷ *My hobby is painting.* Malen ist mein Hobby. ❷ *(picture)* Bild *nt* (*pl* Bilder) ▷ *a painting by Picasso* ein Bild von Picasso
pair *n* Paar *nt* (*pl* Paare) ▷ *a pair of shoes* ein Paar Schuhe; **a pair of scissors** eine Schere; **a pair of trousers** eine Hose; **a pair of jeans** eine Jeans; **in pairs** paarweise
Pakistan *n* Pakistan *nt*; **from Pakistan** aus Pakistan; **to Pakistan** nach Pakistan
Pakistani *n* Pakistani *m* (*pl* Pakistani), Pakistani *f*
▶ *adj* pakistanisch; **He's Pakistani.** Er ist Pakistani.
palace *n* Palast *m* (*pl* Paläste)
pale *adj* blass ▷ *You're very pale.* Du bist sehr blass.; **a pale blue shirt** ein hellblaues Hemd
Palestine *n* Palästina *nt*; **from Palestine** aus Palästina; **to Palestine** nach Palästina
Palestinian *adj* palästinensisch; **He's Palestinian.** Er ist Palästinenser.
▶ *n* Palästinenser *m* (*pl* Palästinenser), Palästinenserin *f*
palm *n (of hand)* Handteller *m* (*pl* Handteller); **a palm tree** eine Palme
pan *n* ❶ *(saucepan)* Topf *m* (*pl* Töpfe) ❷ *(frying pan)* Pfanne *f*
pancake *n* Pfannkuchen *m* (*pl* Pfannkuchen)
panic *n* Panik *f*
▶ *vb* in Panik geraten (*pres* gerät in Panik, *imperf* geriet in Panik, *perf* ist in Panik geraten) ▷ *She panicked.* Sie geriet in Panik.; **Don't panic!** Nur keine Panik!
panther *n* Panther *m* (*pl* Panther)
pantomime *n* Weihnachtsmärchen *nt* (*pl* Weihnachtsmärchen)
pants *npl* ❶ *(underwear)* Unterhose *f* ▷ *a pair of pants* eine Unterhose ❷ *(trousers)* Hose *f* ▷ *a pair of pants* eine Hose
pantyhose *npl (US)* Strumpfhose *f*
paper *n* ❶ Papier *nt* (*pl* Papiere) ▷ *a piece of paper* ein Stück Papier ▷ *a paper towel* ein Papierhandtuch ❷ *(newspaper)* Zeitung *f* ▷ *an advert in the paper* eine Anzeige in der Zeitung; **an exam paper** eine Klausur
paperback *n* Taschenbuch *nt* (*pl* Taschenbücher)
paper clip *n* Büroklammer *f*
paper round *n* **to do a paper round** Zeitungen austragen [**77**]
parachute *n* Fallschirm *m* (*pl* Fallschirme)

parade *n* Parade *f*
paradise *n* Paradies *nt* (*gen* Paradieses, *pl* Paradiese)
paragraph *n* Paragraf *m* (*gen* Paragrafen, *pl* Paragrafen)
parallel *adj* parallel
paralyzed *adj* gelähmt
paramedic *n* Sanitäter *m* (*pl* Sanitäter), Sanitäterin *f*
parcel *n* Paket *nt* (*pl* Pakete)
pardon *n* **Pardon?** Wie bitte?
parent *n* ❶ *(father)* Vater *m* ❷ *(mother)* Mutter *f*; **my parents** meine Eltern
Paris *n* Paris *nt*
park *n* Park *m* (*pl* Parks); **a national park** ein Nationalpark; **a theme park** ein Themenpark; **a car park** ein Parkplatz *m*
▶ *vb* parken [**38**] ▷ *Where can I park my car?* Wo kann ich mein Auto parken?; **We couldn't find anywhere to park.** Wir haben nirgends einen Parkplatz gefunden.
parking *n* Parken *nt* ▷ *'no parking'* 'Parken verboten'
parking lot *n (US)* Parkplatz *m* (*gen* Parkplatzes, *pl* Parkplätze)
parking meter *n* Parkuhr *f*
parking ticket *n* Strafzettel *m* (*pl* Strafzettel)
parliament *n* Parlament *nt* (*pl* Parlamente)
parole *n* **on parole** auf Bewährung
parrot *n* Papagei *m* (*pl* Papageien)
parsley *n* Petersilie *f*
part *n* ❶ *(section)* Teil *m* (*pl* Teile) ▷ *The first part of the film was boring.* Der erste Teil des Films war langweilig. ❷ *(component)* Teil *nt* (*pl* Teile) ▷ *spare parts* Ersatzteile ❸ *(in play, film)* Rolle *f*; **to take part in something** an etwas teilnehmen [**52**]
particular *adj* bestimmt ▷ *I am looking for a particular book.* Ich suche ein bestimmtes Buch. ▷ *Are you looking for anything particular?* Suchen Sie nach etwas Bestimmtem?; **nothing in particular** nichts Bestimmtes
particularly *adv* besonders
partly *adv* zum Teil
partner *n* Partner *m* (*pl* Partner), Partnerin *f*
part-time *adj, adv* Teilzeit ▷ *a part-time job* eine Teilzeitarbeit ▷ *She works part-time.* Sie arbeitet Teilzeit.
party *n* ❶ Party *f* (*pl* Partys) ▷ *a birthday party* eine Geburtstagsparty ▷ *a Christmas party* eine Weihnachtsparty ▷ *a New Year party* eine Silvesterparty ❷ *(political)* Partei *f* ▷ *the Conservative Party* die Konservative Partei ❸ *(group)* Gruppe *f* ▷ *a party of tourists* eine Gruppe Touristen
pass *n* Pass *m* (*gen* Passes, *pl* Pässe) ▷ *The pass was blocked with snow.* Der Pass war zugeschneit. ▷ *That was a good pass by Ferguson.* Das war ein guter Pass von Ferguson.; **to get a pass** *(in exam)* bestehen [**72**]; **a bus pass** **(1)** *(monthly)* eine Monatskarte für den Bus **(2)** *(for old-age pensioners)* eine Seniorenkarte für den Bus

Almost all German cities operate an integrated public transport system; you can buy a weekly (**Wochenkarte**), monthly (**Monatskarte**) or yearly (**Jahreskarte**) pass which is valid for that period on all buses, trams and light railway vehicles in a particular zone.

▶ *vb* ❶ *(give)* geben [**28**] (*pres* gibt, *imperf* gab, *perf* hat gegeben) ▷ *Could you pass me the salt?* Könntest du mir das Salz geben? ❷ *(go by)* vergehen [**29**] (*imperf* verging, *perf* ist vergangen) ▷ *The time has passed quickly.* Die Zeit ist schnell vergangen. ❸ *(on foot)* vorbeigehen [**29**] an (*imperf* ging vorbei, *perf* ist vorbeigegangen) ▷ *I pass his house on my way to school.* Auf dem Weg zur Schule gehe ich an seinem Haus vorbei. ❹ *(in vehicle)*

a b c d e f g h i j k l m n o p q r s t u v w x y z

vorbeifahren [**21**] an (*pres* fährt vorbei, *imperf* fuhr vorbei, *perf* ist vorbeigefahren) ▷ *We passed the post office.* Wir sind an der Post vorbeigefahren. ❺ *(exam)* bestehen [**72**] (*imperf* bestand, *perf* hat bestanden) ▷ *Did you pass?* Hast du bestanden?; **to pass an exam** eine Prüfung bestehen [**72**]

pass out *vb (faint)* ohnmächtig werden [**91**] (*pres* wird ohnmächtig, *imperf* wurde ohnmächtig, *perf* ist ohnmächtig geworden)

passage *n* ❶ *(piece of writing)* Abschnitt *m* (*pl* Abschnitte) ▷ *Read the passage carefully.* Lest den Abschnitt sorgfältig durch. ❷ *(corridor)* Gang *m* (*pl* Gänge)

passenger *n* Passagier *m* (*pl* Passagiere), Passagierin *f*

passion *n* Leidenschaft *f*

passive *adj* passiv; **passive smoking** das Passivrauchen

Passover *n* Passahfest *nt*

passport *n* Pass *m* (*gen* Passes, *pl* Pässe); **passport control** die Passkontrolle

password *n* Passwort *nt* (*pl* Passwörter)

past *adv, prep (beyond)* nach ▷ *It's on the right, just past the station.* Es ist auf der rechten Seite, gleich nach dem Bahnhof. ▷ *It's quarter past nine.* Es ist Viertel nach neun. ▷ *It's past midnight.* Es ist nach Mitternacht.; **It's half past ten.** Es ist halb elf.; **to go past (1)** *(vehicle)* vorbeifahren [**21**] ▷ *The bus went past without stopping.* Der Bus ist vorbeigefahren, ohne anzuhalten. ▷ *The bus goes past our house.* Der Bus fährt an unserem Haus vorbei. **(2)** *(on foot)* vorbeigehen [**29**] ▷ *He went past without saying hello.* Er ging vorbei, ohne Hallo zu sagen. ▷ *I went past your house yesterday.* Ich bin gestern an eurem Haus vorbeigegangen.
▸ *n* Vergangenheit *f* ▷ *She lives in the past.* Sie lebt in der Vergangenheit.; **in the past** *(previously)* früher ▷ *That was common in the past.* Das war früher üblich.

pasta *n* Teigwaren *fpl* ▷ *Pasta is easy to cook.* Teigwaren sind leicht zu kochen.

pasteurized *adj* pasteurisiert

pastry *n* Teig *m*; **pastries** *(cakes)* das Gebäck *sg*

pat *vb (dog, cat)* streicheln [**88**] (*perf* hat gestreichelt)

patch *n* ❶ Stück *nt* (*pl* Stücke) ▷ *a patch of material* ein Stück Stoff ❷ *(for flat tyre)* Flicken *m* (*pl* Flicken); **He's got a bald patch.** Er hat eine kahle Stelle.

path *n* Weg *m* (*pl* Wege)

pathetic *adj* schrecklich schlecht ▷ *Our team was pathetic.* Unsere Mannschaft war schrecklich schlecht.

patience *n* ❶ Geduld *f* ▷ *He hasn't got much patience.* Er hat nicht viel Geduld. ❷ *(card game)* Patience *f* ▷ *to play patience* Patience spielen

patient *n* Patient *m* (*gen* Patienten, *pl* Patienten), Patientin *f*
▸ *adj* geduldig

patio *n* Terrasse *f*

patrol *n* ❶ *(military)* Patrouille *f* ❷ *(of police)* Streife *f*

patrol car *n* Streifenwagen *m* (*pl* Streifenwagen)

pattern *n* Muster *nt* (*pl* Muster) ▷ *a geometric pattern* ein geometrisches Muster ▷ *a sewing pattern* ein Nähmuster

pause *n* Pause *f*

pavement *n* Bürgersteig *m* (*pl* Bürgersteige)

paw *n* Pfote *f*

pay *n* Bezahlung *f*
▸ *vb* bezahlen [**7**] (*perf* hat bezahlt) ▷ *They pay me more on Sundays.* Sie bezahlen mir sonntags mehr. ▷ *to pay by cheque* mit Scheck bezahlen ▷ *to pay by credit card* mit Kreditkarte bezahlen; **to pay for something** für etwas bezahlen [**7**]; **to pay extra for**

something für etwas extra bezahlen [7]; **to pay attention** aufpassen [31]; **Don't pay any attention to him.** Beachte ihn einfach nicht.; **to pay somebody a visit** jemanden besuchen [7]; **to pay somebody back** *(money)* es jemandem zurückzahlen [15]

payment *n* Bezahlung *f*

payphone *n* Münzfernsprecher *m* (*pl* Münzfernsprecher)

PC *n (= personal computer)* PC *m* (*pl* PCs) ▷ *She typed the report on her PC.* Sie hat den Bericht am PC erfasst.

PE *n (= physical education)* Sportunterricht *m*

pea *n* Erbse *f*

peace *n* ❶ *(after war)* Frieden *m* ❷ *(quietness)* Stille *f*

peaceful *adj* ❶ *(calm)* ruhig ▷ *a peaceful afternoon* ein ruhiger Nachmittag ❷ *(not violent)* friedlich ▷ *a peaceful protest* ein friedlicher Protest

peach *n* Pfirsich *m* (*pl* Pfirsiche)

peacock *n* Pfau *m* (*pl* Pfauen)

peak *n (of mountain)* Gipfel *m* (*pl* Gipfel); **the peak rate** der Spitzentarif; **in peak season** in der Hochsaison

peanut *n* Erdnuss *f* (*pl* Erdnüsse) ▷ *a packet of peanuts* eine Packung Erdnüsse

peanut butter *n* Erdnussbutter *f* ▷ *a peanut-butter sandwich* ein Brot mit Erdnussbutter

pear *n* Birne *f*

pearl *n* Perle *f*

pebble *n* Kieselstein *m* (*pl* Kieselsteine); **a pebble beach** ein Kieselstrand *m*

peculiar *adj* eigenartig ▷ *He's a peculiar person.* Er ist ein eigenartiger Mensch. ▷ *It tastes peculiar.* Es schmeckt eigenartig.

pedal *n* Pedal *nt* (*pl* Pedale)

pedestrian *n* Fußgänger *m* (*pl* Fußgänger), Fußgängerin *f*

pedestrian crossing *n* Fußgängerüberweg *m* (*pl* Fußgängerüberwege)

pee *n* **to have a pee** *(informal)* pinkeln [88]

peel *n (of orange)* Schale *f* ▶ *vb* ❶ schälen [38] ▷ *Shall I peel the potatoes?* Soll ich die Kartoffeln schälen? ❷ sich schälen [38] ▷ *My nose is peeling.* Meine Nase schält sich.

peg *n* ❶ *(for coats)* Haken *m* (*pl* Haken) ❷ *(clothes peg)* Wäscheklammer *f* ❸ *(tent peg)* Hering *m* (*pl* Heringe)

pelican crossing *n* Fußgängerampel *f*

pelvis *n* Becken *nt* (*pl* Becken)

pen *n* Schreiber *m* (*pl* Schreiber)

penalty *n* ❶ *(punishment)* Strafe *f* ▷ *the death penalty* die Todesstrafe ❷ *(in football)* Elfmeter *m* (*pl* Elfmeter) ❸ *(in rugby)* Strafstoß *m* (*gen* Strafstoßes, *pl* Strafstöße); **a penalty shoot-out** ein Elfmeterschießen *nt*

pence *npl* Pence *mpl*

pencil *n* Bleistift *m* (*pl* Bleistifte); **in pencil** mit Bleistift

pencil case *n* Federmäppchen *nt* (*pl* Federmäppchen)

pencil sharpener *n* Bleistiftspitzer *m* (*pl* Bleistiftspitzer)

pendant *n* Anhänger *m* (*pl* Anhänger)

pen friend *n* Brieffreund *m* (*pl* Brieffreunde), Brieffreundin *f*

penguin *n* Pinguin *m* (*pl* Pinguine)

penicillin *n* Penizillin *nt*

penis *n* Penis *m* (*gen* Penis, *pl* Penisse)

penknife *n* Taschenmesser *nt* (*pl* Taschenmesser)

penny *n* Penny *m* (*pl* Pennys *or* Pence)

pension *n* Rente *f*

pensioner *n* Rentner *m* (*pl* Rentner), Rentnerin *f*

people *npl* ❶ Leute *pl* ▷ *The people were nice.* Die Leute waren nett. ▷ *a lot of people* viele Leute ❷ *(individuals)* Menschen *mpl* ▷ *six people* sechs Menschen ▷ *several people* mehrere Menschen; **German people** die Deutschen; **People say that ...** Man sagt, dass ...

a b c d e f g h i j k l m n o p q r s t u v w x y z

pepper *n* ❶ *(spice)* Pfeffer *m* ▷ *Pass the pepper, please.* Gib mir mal bitte den Pfeffer. ❷ *(vegetable)* Paprikaschote *f* ▷ *a green pepper* eine grüne Paprikaschote
peppermill *n* Pfeffermühle *f*
peppermint *n (sweet)* Pfefferminzbonbon *nt (pl* Pfefferminzbonbons); **peppermint chewing gum** der Kaugummi mit Pfefferminzgeschmack
per *prep* pro ▷ *per day* pro Tag ▷ *per week* pro Woche; **thirty miles per hour** dreißig Meilen in der Stunde
per cent *adv* Prozent *nt* ▷ *fifty per cent* fünfzig Prozent
percentage *n* Prozentsatz *m (gen* Prozentsatzes, *pl* Prozentsätze)
percussion *n* Schlagzeug *nt (pl* Schlagzeuge) ▷ *I play percussion.* Ich spiele Schlagzeug.
perfect *adj* perfekt ▷ *He speaks perfect English.* Er spricht perfekt Englisch.
perfectly *adv* ❶ ganz ▷ *You know perfectly well what happened.* Du weißt ganz genau, was passiert ist. ❷ *(very well)* perfekt ▷ *The system worked perfectly.* Das System hat perfekt funktioniert.
perform *vb (act, play)* spielen [**38**]
performance *n* ❶ *(show)* Vorstellung *f* ▷ *The performance lasts two hours.* Die Vorstellung dauert zwei Stunden. ❷ *(acting)* Darstellung *f* ▷ *his performance as Hamlet* seine Darstellung des Hamlet ❸ *(results)* Leistung *f* ▷ *the team's poor performance* die schwache Leistung der Mannschaft
perfume *n* Parfüm *nt (pl* Parfüme)
perhaps *adv* vielleicht ▷ *a bit boring, perhaps* etwas langweilig vielleicht ▷ *Perhaps he's ill.* Vielleicht ist er krank. ▷ *perhaps not* vielleicht nicht
period *n* ❶ Zeit *f* ▷ *for a limited period* für eine begrenzte Zeit ❷ *(in history)* Epoche *f* ▷ *the Victorian period* die viktorianische Epoche ❸ *(menstruation)* Periode *f* ▷ *I'm having my period.* Ich habe meine Periode. ❹ *(lesson time)* Stunde *f* ▷ *Each period lasts forty minutes.* Jede Stunde dauert vierzig Minuten.
perm *n* Dauerwelle *f* ▷ *She's got a perm.* Sie hat eine Dauerwelle.; **to have a perm** sich eine Dauerwelle machen lassen [**42**]
permanent *adj* ❶ *(damage, solution, relationship)* dauerhaft ▷ *a permanent solution* eine dauerhafte Lösung ❷ *(difficulties, tension)* dauernd ▷ *a permanent headache* dauernde Kopfschmerzen ❸ *(job, address)* fest ▷ *a permanent job* eine feste Arbeit
permission *n* Erlaubnis *f (pl* Erlaubnisse) ▷ *to ask somebody's permission* jemanden um Erlaubnis bitten; **Could I have permission to leave early?** Darf ich früher gehen?
permit *n* Schein *m (pl* Scheine) ▷ *a fishing permit* ein Angelschein
persecute *vb* verfolgen [**84**] *(perf* hat verfolgt)
person *n* ❶ Mensch *m (gen* Menschen, *pl* Menschen) ▷ *She's a very nice person.* Sie ist ein netter Mensch. ❷ *(in grammar)* Person *f* ▷ *first person singular* erste Person Singular; **in person** persönlich
personal *adj* persönlich
personality *n* Persönlichkeit *f*
personally *adv* persönlich ▷ *I don't know him personally.* Ich kenne ihn nicht persönlich. ▷ *Personally I don't agree.* Ich persönlich bin nicht einverstanden.
personal stereo *n* Walkman® *m (pl* Walkmans)
perspiration *n* Schweiß *m*
persuade *vb* überreden [**54**] *(perf* hat überredet); **to persuade somebody to do something** jemanden überreden [**54**], etwas zu tun
Peru *n* Peru *nt*
Peruvian *adj* peruanisch
pessimistic *adj* pessimistisch

pest *n (person)* Nervensäge *f* ▷ *He's a real pest!* Er ist eine echte Nervensäge!

pester *vb* belästigen [**7**] (*perf* hat belästigt) ▷ *Stop pestering me!* Hör auf, mich zu belästigen!; **The children pestered her to take them to the zoo.** Die Kinder ließen ihr keine Ruhe, mit ihnen in den Zoo zu gehen.

pesticide *n* Pestizid *nt*

pet *n* Haustier *nt* (*pl* Haustiere) ▷ *Have you got a pet?* Hast du ein Haustier?; **She's the teacher's pet.** Sie ist das Schätzchen der Lehrerin.

petrol *n* Benzin *nt* (*pl* Benzine); **unleaded petrol** bleifreies Benzin

petrol station *n* Tankstelle *f*

pharmacy *n* Apotheke *f*

pheasant *n* Fasan *m* (*pl* Fasane)

philosophy *n* Philosophie *f*

phobia *n* Phobie *f*

phone *n* ❶ Telefon *nt* (*pl* Telefone) ▷ *Where's the phone?* Wo ist das Telefon? ▷ *Is there a phone here?* Gibt es hier ein Telefon?; **by phone** telefonisch ❷ *(mobile)* Handy *nt* (*pl* Handys) ▷ *I've got a new phone.* Ich habe ein neues Handy.; **to be on the phone** *(speaking)* telefonieren [**76**]; **Can I use the phone, please?** Kann ich mal bitte telefonieren?
▸ *vb* anrufen [**56**] (*imperf* rief an, *perf* hat angerufen) ▷ *I tried to phone you yesterday.* Ich habe gestern versucht, dich anzurufen.

phone bill *n* Telefonrechnung *f*

phone book *n* Telefonbuch *nt* (*pl* Telefonbücher)

phone box *n* Telefonzelle *f*

phone call *n* Anruf *m* (*pl* Anrufe) ▷ *There's a phone call for you.* Da ist ein Anruf für Sie.; **to make a phone call** telefonieren [**76**]

phonecard *n* Telefonkarte *f*

phone number *n* Telefonnummer *f*

photo *n* Foto *nt* (*pl* Fotos) ▷ *to take a photo* ein Foto machen ▷ *to take a photo of somebody* ein Foto von jemandem machen

photocopier *n* Fotokopierer *m* (*pl* Fotokopierer)

photocopy *n* Fotokopie *f*
▸ *vb* fotokopieren [**76**] (*perf* hat fotokopiert)

photograph *n* Foto *nt* (*pl* Fotos) ▷ *to take a photograph* ein Foto machen ▷ *to take a photograph of somebody* ein Foto von jemandem machen

> Be careful not to translate **photograph** by **Fotograf**.

▸ *vb* fotografieren [**76**] (*perf* hat fotografiert)

photographer *n* Fotograf *m* (*gen* Fotografen, *pl* Fotografen), Fotografin *f* ▷ *She's a photographer.* Sie ist Fotografin.

photography *n* Fotografie *f* ▷ *My hobby is photography.* Mein Hobby ist die Fotografie.

phrase *n* Wendung *f*

phrase book *n* Sprachführer *m* (*pl* Sprachführer)

physical *adj (of the body)* körperlich ▷ *physical exercise* körperliche Bewegung; **physical education** der Sportunterricht; **physical therapist** *(man)* der Krankengymnast
▸ *n (US)* ärztliche Untersuchung *f*

physicist *n* Physiker *m* (*pl* Physiker), Physikerin *f* ▷ *He's a physicist.* Er ist Physiker.

physics *n* Physik *f* ▷ *She teaches physics.* Sie unterrichtet Physik.

physiotherapist *n* Krankengymnast *m* (*gen* Krankengymnasten, *pl* Krankengymnasten), Krankengymnastin *f*

physiotherapy *n* Krankengymnastik *f*

pianist *n* Pianist *m* (*gen* Pianisten, *pl* Pianisten), Pianistin *f*

piano *n* Klavier *nt* (*pl* Klaviere) ▷ *I play the piano.* Ich spiele Klavier. ▷ *I have piano lessons.* Ich nehme Klavierstunden.

pick *n* **Take your pick!** Du hast die Wahl! ▸ *vb* ❶ *(choose)* auswählen [**4**] *(perf* hat ausgewählt) ▷ *I picked the biggest piece.* Ich habe das größte Stück ausgewählt. ❷ *(fruit, flowers)* pflücken [**48**]; **to pick on somebody** auf jemandem herumhacken [**15**] ▷ *She's always picking on me.* Sie hackt dauernd auf mir herum.; **to pick out** auswählen [**4**] ▷ *I like them all – it's difficult to pick one out.* Sie gefallen mir alle – es ist schwierig, eins auszuwählen.; **to pick up** **(1)** *(collect)* abholen [**4**] ▷ *We'll come to the airport to pick you up.* Wir holen dich am Flughafen ab. **(2)** *(from floor)* aufheben ▷ *Could you help me pick up the toys?* Kannst du mir helfen, die Spielsachen aufzuheben? **(3)** *(informal: learn)* aufschnappen [**4**] ▷ *I picked up some Spanish during my holiday.* Ich habe während der Ferien etwas Spanisch aufgeschnappt.

pickpocket *n* Taschendieb *m* (*pl* Taschendiebe), Taschendiebin *f*

picnic *n* Picknick *nt* (*pl* Picknicke); **to have a picnic** picknicken [**48**]

picture *n* ❶ Bild *nt* (*pl* Bilder) ▷ *The books has lots of pictures.* Das Buch ist voller Bilder.; **to draw a picture of something** etwas zeichnen [**53**] ❷ Foto *nt* (*pl* Fotos) ▷ *My picture was in the paper.* Mein Foto war in der Zeitung. ❸ *(painting)* Gemälde *nt* (*pl* Gemälde) ▷ *a famous picture* ein berühmtes Gemälde; **to paint a picture of something** etwas malen [**38**]; **the pictures** *(cinema)* das Kino ▷ *Shall we go to the pictures?* Sollen wir ins Kino gehen?

pie *n* ❶ *(savoury)* Pastete *f* ❷ *(sweet)* Obstkuchen *m* (*pl* Obstkuchen); **an apple pie** ein gedeckter Apfelkuchen

piece *n* Stück *nt* (*pl* Stücke) ▷ *A small piece, please.* Ein kleines Stück, bitte.; **a piece of furniture** ein Möbelstück *nt*; **a piece of advice** ein Ratschlag *m*

pier *n* Pier *m* (*pl* Piere)

pierced *adj* ❶ durchstochen ▷ *I've got pierced ears.* Ich habe durchstochene Ohrläppchen. ❷ gepierct ▷ *She's got a pierced nose.* Sie hat eine gepiercte Nase.

piercing *adj (cry)* durchdringend

pig *n* Schwein *nt* (*pl* Schweine)

pigeon *n* Taube *f*

piggy bank *n* Sparschwein *nt* (*pl* Sparschweine)

pigtail *n* Zopf *m* (*pl* Zöpfe)

pile *n* ❶ *(tidy)* Stapel *m* (*pl* Stapel) ❷ *(untidy)* Haufen *m* (*pl* Haufen)

pill *n* Pille *f*; **to be on the pill** die Pille nehmen [**52**]

pillow *n* Kopfkissen *nt* (*pl* Kopfkissen)

pilot *n* Pilot *m* (*gen* Piloten, *pl* Piloten), Pilotin *f* ▷ *He's a pilot.* Er ist Pilot.

pimple *n* Pickel *m* (*pl* Pickel)

PIN *n (= personal identification number)* PIN-Nummer *f*

pin *n* Stecknadel *f*; **I've got pins and needles in my foot.** Mein Fuß ist eingeschlafen.

pinball *n* Flipper *m* (*pl* Flipper); **to play pinball** flippern [**34**]; **a pinball machine** ein Flipper

pinch *vb* ❶ kneifen (*imperf* kniff, *perf* hat gekniffen) ▷ *He pinched me!* Er hat mich gekniffen! ❷ *(informal: steal)* klauen [**38**] ▷ *Who's pinched my pen?* Wer hat meinen Schreiber geklaut?

pine *n* Kiefer *f* ▷ *a pine table* ein Kieferntisch *m*

pineapple *n* Ananas *f* (*pl* Ananas)

pink *adj* rosa

rosa is invariable.

▷ *a pink shirt* ein rosa Hemd

pint *n* Pint *nt* (*pl* Pints)

In Germany measurements are in litres and centilitres. A pint is about 0.6 litres. German people don't drink pints of beer, they are more likely to order **ein großes Bier**.

to have a pint ein Bier trinken [**80**]

pipe *n* ❶ *(for water, gas)* Rohr *nt* (*pl* Rohre) ▷ *The pipes froze.* Die Rohre sind eingefroren. ❷ *(for smoking)* Pfeife *f* ▷ *He smokes a pipe.* Er raucht Pfeife.; **the pipes** *(bagpipes)* der Dudelsack *sg* ▷ *He plays the pipes.* Er spielt Dudelsack.

pirate *n* Pirat *m* (*gen* Piraten, *pl* Piraten)

pirated *adj* **a pirated video** ein Raubvideo *nt*

Pisces *nsg* Fische *mpl* ▷ *I'm Pisces.* Ich bin Fisch.

pistol *n* Pistole *f*

pitch *n* Platz *m* (*gen* Platzes, *pl* Plätze) ▷ *a football pitch* ein Fußballplatz
▶ *vb (tent)* aufschlagen **[59]** (*pres* schlägt auf, *imperf* schlug auf, *perf* hat aufgeschlagen) ▷ *We pitched our tent near the beach.* Wir haben unser Zelt in der Nähe des Strandes aufgeschlagen.

pity *n* Mitleid *nt*; **What a pity!** Wie schade!
▶ *vb* bemitleiden **[7]** (*perf* hat bemitleidet)

pizza *n* Pizza *f* (*pl* Pizzas)

place *n* ❶ *(location)* Ort *m* (*pl* Orte) ▷ *It's a quiet place.* Es ist ein ruhiger Ort. ▷ *interesting places* interessante Orte ❷ *(space)* Platz *m* (*gen* Platzes, *pl* Plätze) ▷ *a parking place* ein Parkplatz ▷ *a university place* ein Studienplatz; **to change places** die Plätze tauschen **[48]**; **to take place** stattfinden **[24]**; **at your place** bei dir; **to my place** zu mir
▶ *vb* legen **[38]** ▷ *He placed his hand on hers.* Er legte seine Hand auf ihre.; **He was placed third.** Er wurde Dritter.

plain *n* Ebene *f*
▶ *adj, adv* ❶ *(self-coloured)* einfarbig ▷ *a plain carpet* ein einfarbiger Teppich ❷ *(not fancy)* einfach ▷ *a plain white blouse* eine einfache weiße Bluse

plain chocolate *n* bittere Schokolade *f*

plait *n* Zopf *m* (*pl* Zöpfe) ▷ *She wears her hair in a plait.* Sie trägt einen Zopf.

plan *n* Plan *m* (*pl* Pläne) ▷ *What are your plans for the holidays?* Welche Ferienpläne habt ihr? ▷ *to make plans* Pläne machen ▷ *a plan of the campsite* ein Plan des Zeltplatzes; **Everything went according to plan.** Alles lief nach Plan.; **my essay plan** das Konzept für meinen Aufsatz
▶ *vb* planen **[38]** ▷ *We're planning a trip to Germany.* Wir planen eine Reise nach Deutschland. ▷ *Plan your revision carefully.* Plant eure Stoffwiederholung sorgfältig.; **to plan to do something** vorhaben **[32]**, etwas zu tun ▷ *I'm planning to get a job in the holidays.* Ich habe vor, mir einen Ferienjob zu suchen.

plane *n* Flugzeug *nt* (*pl* Flugzeuge) ▷ *by plane* mit dem Flugzeug

planet *n* Planet *m* (*gen* Planeten, *pl* Planeten)

plant *n* ❶ Pflanze *f* ▷ *to water the plants* die Pflanzen gießen ❷ *(factory)* Fabrik *f*
▶ *vb* pflanzen **[36]**

plaster *n* ❶ *(sticking plaster)* Pflaster *nt* (*pl* Pflaster) ▷ *Have you got a plaster?* Hast du ein Pflaster? ❷ *(for fracture)* Gips *m* (*gen* Gipses, *pl* Gipse) ▷ *Her leg's in plaster.* Sie hat das Bein in Gips.

plastic *n* Plastik *nt* ▷ *It's made of plastic.* Es ist aus Plastik.
▶ *adj* aus Plastik ▷ *a plastic mac* ein Regenmantel aus Plastik; **a plastic bag** eine Plastiktüte

plate *n (for food)* Teller *m* (*pl* Teller)

platform *n* ❶ *(at station)* Bahnsteig *m* (*pl* Bahnsteige) ▷ *on platform seven* auf Bahnsteig sieben ❷ *(for performers)* Podium *nt* (*pl* Podien)

play *n* Stück *nt* (*pl* Stücke) ▷ *a play by Shakespeare* ein Stück von Shakespeare ▷ *to put on a play* ein Stück aufführen
▶ *vb* ❶ spielen **[38]** ▷ *He's playing with his friends.* Er spielt mit seinen Freunden. ▷ *What sort of music do they play?* Welche Art von Musik spielen sie? ▷ *I play hockey.* Ich spiele Hockey. ▷ *I play the guitar.* Ich spiele Gitarre. ▷ *She's always playing that record.* Sie spielt dauernd diese Platte. ❷ *(against person, team)* spielen **[38]** gegen ▷ *Germany are playing Scotland.* Deutschland spielt gegen Schottland.

a b c d e f g h i j k l m n o p q r s t u v w x y z

play down *vb* herunterspielen [**15**] (*perf* hat heruntergespielt)

player *n* Spieler *m* (*pl* Spieler), Spielerin *f* ▷ *a football player* ein Fußballspieler

playground *n* ❶ (*at school*) Schulhof *m* (*pl* Schulhöfe) ❷ (*in park*) Spielplatz *m* (*gen* Spielplatzes, *pl* Spielplätze)

playgroup *n* Spielgruppe *f*

playing card *n* Spielkarte *f*

playing field *n* Sportplatz *m* (*gen* Sportplatzes, *pl* Sportplätze)

playtime *n* Pause *f*

pleasant *adj* angenehm

please *excl* bitte ▷ *Two coffees, please.* Zwei Kaffee bitte.

pleased *adj* ❶ (*happy*) erfreut ▷ *My mother's not going to be very pleased.* Meine Mutter wird nicht sehr erfreut sein. ❷ (*satisfied*) zufrieden ▷ *It's beautiful, she'll be pleased with it.* Es ist wunderschön, sie wird damit sehr zufrieden sein.; **to be pleased about something** sich über etwas freuen [**38**]; **Pleased to meet you!** Angenehm!

pleasure *n* Vergnügen *nt* (*pl* Vergnügen) ▷ *I read for pleasure.* Ich lese zum Vergnügen.

plenty *n* mehr als genug ▷ *I've got plenty.* Ich habe mehr als genug. ▷ *That's plenty, thanks.* Danke, das ist mehr als genug.; **I've got plenty to do.** Ich habe viel zu tun.; **plenty of (1)** viele ▷ *plenty of opportunities* viele Möglichkeiten **(2)** (*more than enough*) genügend ▷ *I've got plenty of money.* Ich habe genügend Geld. ▷ *We've got plenty of time.* Wir haben genügend Zeit.

pliers *npl* Zange *fsg*; **a pair of pliers** eine Zange

plot *n* ❶ (*of story, play*) Handlung *f* ❷ (*against somebody*) Verschwörung *f* ▷ *a plot against the president* eine Verschwörung gegen den Präsidenten; **a plot of land** ein Stück Land *nt*; **a vegetable plot** ein Gemüsebeet *nt*
▶ *vb* planen [**38**] ▷ *They were plotting to kill him.* Sie planten, ihn zu töten.

plough *n* Pflug *m* (*pl* Pflüge)
▶ *vb* pflügen [**38**]

plug *n* ❶ (*electrical*) Stecker *m* (*pl* Stecker) ▷ *The plug is faulty.* Der Stecker ist kaputt. ❷ (*for sink*) Stöpsel *m* (*pl* Stöpsel)

plug in *vb* einstecken [**4**] (*perf* hat eingesteckt)

plum *n* Pflaume *f* ▷ *plum jam* die Pflaumenmarmelade

plumber *n* Klempner *m* (*pl* Klempner), Klempnerin *f* ▷ *He's a plumber.* Er ist Klempner.

plump *adj* rundlich

plural *n* Plural *m* (*pl* Plurale)

plus *prep, adj* plus ▷ *four plus three equals seven.* Vier plus drei macht sieben. ▷ *I got a B plus.* Ich habe eine Zwei plus bekommen.

In Germany, grades are given from 1 to 6, with 1 being the best.

three children plus a dog drei Kinder und ein Hund

p.m. *abbr* **at eight p.m.** um acht Uhr abends

In Germany times are often given using the 24-hour clock.

pneumonia *n* Lungenentzündung *f*

poached *adj* **a poached egg** ein verlorenes Ei *nt*

pocket *n* Tasche *f*; **pocket money** das Taschengeld

podcast *n* Podcast *m* (*pl* Podcasts) ▷ *to download a podcast* einen Podcast herunterladen

poem *n* Gedicht *nt* (*pl* Gedichte)

poet *n* Dichter *m* (*pl* Dichter), Dichterin *f*

poetry *n* Gedichte *ntpl* ▷ *to write poetry* Gedichte schreiben

point *n* ❶ (*spot, score*) Punkt *m* (*pl* Punkte) ▷ *a point on the horizon* ein Punkt am Horizont ▷ *They scored five points.* Sie machten fünf Punkte. ❷ (*comment*) Bemerkung *f* ▷ *He made some interesting points.* Er machte ein

paar interessante Bemerkungen. ❸ *(tip)* Spitze *f* ▷ *a pencil with a sharp point* ein Bleistift mit einer scharfen Spitze ❹ *(in time)* Zeitpunkt *m* ▷ *At that point, we were three one up.* Zu dem Zeitpunkt lagen wir mit drei zu eins in Führung.; **a point of view** ein Gesichtspunkt *m*; **to get the point** begreifen; **That's a good point!** Da hast du recht.; **There's no point.** Das hat keinen Wert.; **What's the point?** Wozu?; **Punctuality isn't my strong point.** Pünktlichkeit ist nicht meine Stärke.; **two point five (2.5)** zwei Komma fünf (2,5)
▸ *vb* mit dem Finger zeigen [**38**] ▷ *Don't point!* Man zeigt nicht mit dem Finger!; **to point at somebody** auf jemanden zeigen [**38**]; **to point a gun at somebody** auf jemanden mit der Waffe zielen [**38**]; **to point something out (1)** *(show)* auf etwas zeigen [**38**] ▷ *The guide pointed out Big Ben.* Unser Führer zeigte auf Big Ben. **(2)** *(mention)* auf etwas hinweisen ▷ *I should point out that ...* Ich möchte darauf hinweisen, dass ...

pointless *adj* nutzlos ▷ *It's pointless to argue.* Es ist nutzlos zu streiten.

poison *n* Gift *nt* (*pl* Gifte)
▸ *vb* vergiften [**2**] (*perf* hat vergiftet)

poisonous *adj* giftig

poke *vb* **He poked me in the eye.** Er stieß mir ins Auge.

poker *n* Poker *nt* ▷ *I play poker.* Ich spiele Poker.

Poland *n* Polen *nt*; **from Poland** aus Polen; **to Poland** nach Polen

polar bear *n* Eisbär *m* (*gen* Eisbären, *pl* Eisbären)

Pole *n (Polish person)* Pole *m* (*gen* Polen, *pl* Polen), Polin *f*

pole *n* Mast *m* (*pl* Masten) ▷ *a telegraph pole* ein Telegrafenmast; **a tent pole** eine Zeltstange; **a ski pole** ein Skistock *m*; **the North Pole** der Nordpol; **the South Pole** der Südpol

police *npl* Polizei *f* ▷ *We called the police.* Wir haben die Polizei gerufen.

> Note that 'police' is used with a plural verb and **Polizei** with a singular verb.

▷ *The police haven't arrived yet.* Die Polizei ist noch nicht da.; **a police car** ein Polizeiwagen *m*; **a police station** ein Polizeirevier *nt*

policeman *n* Polizist *m* (*gen* Polizisten, *pl* Polizisten) ▷ *He's a policeman.* Er ist Polizist.

policewoman *n* Polizistin *f* ▷ *She's a policewoman.* Sie ist Polizistin.

Polish *adj* polnisch; **He's Polish.** Er ist Pole.; **She's Polish.** Sie ist Polin.
▸ *n (language)* Polnisch *nt* (*gen* Polnischen)

polish *n* ❶ *(for shoes)* Schuhcreme *f* (*pl* Schuhcremes) ❷ *(for furniture)* Politur *f*
▸ *vb* ❶ *(shoes)* eincremen [**4**] (*perf* hat eingecremt) ❷ *(glass, furniture)* polieren [**76**] (*perf* hat poliert)

polite *adj* höflich

politely *adv* höflich

political *adj* politisch

politician *n* Politiker *m* (*pl* Politiker), Politikerin *f*

politics *npl* Politik *f* ▷ *I'm not interested in politics.* Ich interessiere mich nicht für Politik.

pollute *vb* verschmutzen [**7**] (*perf* hat verschmutzt)

polluted *adj* verschmutzt

pollution *n* Umweltverschmutzung *f*; **air pollution** die Luftverschmutzung

polo-necked sweater *n* Rollkragenpullover *m* (*pl* Rollkragenpullover)

polythene bag *n* Plastiktüte *f*

pond *n* Teich *m* (*pl* Teiche) ▷ *We've got a pond in our garden.* Wir haben einen Teich im Garten.

pony *n* Pony *nt* (*pl* Ponys)

ponytail *n* Pferdeschwanz *m* (*gen* Pferdeschwanzes, *pl* Pferdeschwänze)

▷ *He's got a ponytail.* Er hat einen Pferdeschwanz.

pony trekking *n* **to go pony trekking** Pony reiten gehen [**29**]

poodle *n* Pudel *m* (*pl* Pudel)

pool *n* ❶ *(puddle)* Pfütze *f* ❷ *(pond)* Teich *m* (*pl* Teiche) ❸ *(for swimming)* Schwimmbecken *nt* (*pl* Schwimmbecken) ❹ *(game)* Poolbillard *nt* ▷ *Shall we have a game of pool?* Sollen wir eine Partie Poolbillard spielen?; **the pools** *(football)* das Toto

poor *adj* ❶ arm ▷ *a poor family* eine arme Familie ▷ *They are poorer than we are.* Sie sind ärmer als wir. ▷ *Poor David!* Der arme David!; **the poor** die Armen *mpl* ❷ *(bad)* schlecht ▷ *a poor mark* eine schlechte Note

pop *adj* **pop music** die Popmusik; **a pop star** ein Popstar *m*; **a pop group** eine Popgruppe; **a pop song** ein Popsong *m*

pop in *vb* vorbeikommen [**40**] (*imperf* kam vorbei, *perf* ist vorbeigekommen)

pop out *vb* kurz weggehen [**29**] (*imperf* ging weg, *perf* ist weggegangen)

pop round *vb* **I'm just popping round to John's.** Ich gehe nur mal kurz zu John.

popcorn *n* Popcorn *nt*

pope *n* Papst *m* (*pl* Päpste)

poppy *n* Mohn *m*

popular *adj* beliebt ▷ *She's a very popular girl.* Sie ist sehr beliebt.

population *n* Bevölkerung *f*

porch *n* Veranda *f* (*pl* Veranden)

pork *n* Schweinefleisch *nt* ▷ *I don't eat pork.* Ich esse kein Schweinefleisch.; **a pork chop** ein Schweinekotelett *nt*

porridge *n* Haferbrei *m*

port *n* ❶ *(harbour)* Hafen *m* (*pl* Häfen) ❷ *(wine)* Portwein *m* ▷ *a glass of port* ein Glas Portwein

portable *adj* tragbar ▷ *a portable TV* ein tragbarer Fernseher

porter *n* ❶ *(in hotel)* Portier *m* (*pl* Portiers) ❷ *(at station)* Gepäckträger *m* (*pl* Gepäckträger)

portion *n* Portion *f* ▷ *a large portion of chips* eine große Portion Pommes frites

portrait *n* Porträt *nt* (*pl* Porträts)

Portugal *n* Portugal *nt*; **from Portugal** aus Portugal; **to Portugal** nach Portugal

Portuguese *adj* portugiesisch; **She's Portuguese.** Sie ist Portugiesin.
▶ *n* ❶ *(person)* Portugiese *m* (*gen* Portugiesen, *pl* Portugiesen), Portugiesin *f* ❷ *(language)* Portugiesisch *nt* (*gen* Portugiesischen)

posh *adj* vornehm ▷ *a posh hotel* ein vornehmes Hotel

position *n* Stellung *f* ▷ *an uncomfortable position* eine unbequeme Stellung

positive *adj* ❶ *(good)* positiv ▷ *a positive attitude* eine positive Einstellung ❷ *(sure)* ganz sicher ▷ *I'm positive.* Ich bin ganz sicher.

possession *n* **Have you got all your possessions?** Hast du all deine Sachen?

possibility *n* Möglichkeit *f* ▷ *It's a possibility.* Das ist eine Möglichkeit.

possible *adj* möglich ▷ *as soon as possible* sobald wie möglich

possibly *adv (perhaps)* vielleicht ▷ *Are you coming to the party? — Possibly.* Kommst du zur Party? — Vielleicht.; **... if you possibly can.** ... wenn du irgend kannst.; **I can't possibly come.** Ich kann unmöglich kommen.

post *n* ❶ *(letters)* Post *f* ▷ *Is there any post for me?* Ist Post für mich da? ❷ *(pole)* Pfosten *m* (*pl* Pfosten) ▷ *The ball hit the post.* Der Ball traf den Pfosten. ❸ *(on forum, blog)* Beitrag *m* (*pl* Beiträge)
▶ *vb* ❶ aufgeben [**28**] (*pres* gibt auf, *imperf* gab auf, *perf* hat aufgegeben) ▷ *I've got some cards to post.* Ich muss ein paar Karten aufgeben. ❷ *(on website)* posten [**2**]

postbox *n* Briefkasten *m* (*pl* Briefkästen)

postcard *n* Postkarte *f*

postcode *n* Postleitzahl *f*

German postcodes consist of a 5-figure number which precedes the name of the city.

poster *n* ❶ Poster *nt* (*pl* Poster) ▷ *I've got posters on my bedroom walls.* Ich habe in meinem Zimmer Poster an den Wänden. ❷ *(advertising)* Plakat *nt* (*pl* Plakate) ▷ *There are posters all over town.* In der ganzen Stadt hängen Plakate.

postman *n* Briefträger *m* (*pl* Briefträger) ▷ *He's a postman.* Er ist Briefträger.

post office *n* Postamt *nt* (*pl* Postämter) ▷ *Where's the post office, please?* Wo ist das Postamt, bitte?; **She works for the post office.** Sie arbeitet bei der Post.

postpone *vb* verschieben (*imperf* verschob, *perf* hat verschoben) ▷ *The match has been postponed.* Das Spiel wurde verschoben.

postwoman *n* Briefträgerin *f* ▷ *She's a postwoman.* Sie ist Briefträgerin.

pot *n* ❶ Topf *m* (*pl* Töpfe) ▷ *a pot of jam* ein Marmeladentopf ❷ *(for hot drinks)* Kanne *f* ❸ *(marijuana)* Gras *nt* ▷ *to smoke pot* Gras rauchen; **pots and pans** Töpfe und Pfannen

potato *n* Kartoffel *f* ▷ *a baked potato* eine gebackene Kartoffel ▷ *potato salad* der Kartoffelsalat; **mashed potatoes** der Kartoffelbrei; **potato chips** die Kartoffelchips *mpl*

pottery *n* Keramik *f*

pound *n (weight, money)* Pfund *nt* (*pl* Pfunde *or* Pfund)

> When talking about an amount of money or specifying a quantity of something use the plural form **Pfund**.

▷ *two pounds of carrots* zwei Pfund Karotten ▷ *How many euros do you get for a pound?* Wie viel Euro bekommt man für ein Pfund? ▷ *a pound coin* eine Pfundmünze

▸ *vb* pochen [**48**] ▷ *My heart was pounding.* Mein Herz hat gepocht.

pour *vb (liquid)* gießen [**31**] (*imperf* goss, *perf* hat gegossen) ▷ *She poured some water into the pan.* Sie goss etwas Wasser in den Topf. ▷ *It's pouring.* Es gießt.; **She poured him a drink.** Sie goss ihm einen Drink ein.; **Shall I pour you a cup of tea?** Soll ich Ihnen eine Tasse Tee einschenken?; **in the pouring rain** im strömenden Regen

poverty *n* Armut *f*

powder *n* ❶ Pulver *nt* ❷ *(face powder)* Puder *m* (*pl* Puder)

power *n* ❶ *(electricity)* Strom *m* ▷ *The power's off.* Es gibt keinen Strom.; **a power cut** ein Stromausfall *m*; **a power point** eine Steckdose; **a power station** ein Kraftwerk *nt* ❷ *(energy)* Energie *f* ▷ *nuclear power* die Kernenergie ▷ *solar power* die Sonnenenergie ❸ *(authority)* Macht *f* (*pl* Mächte) ▷ *to be in power* an der Macht sein

powerful *adj* ❶ mächtig ▷ *a powerful man* ein mächtiger Mann ❷ *(physically)* kräftig ❸ *(machine)* leistungsstark

practical *adj* praktisch ▷ *a practical suggestion* ein praktischer Vorschlag ▷ *She's very practical.* Sie ist sehr praktisch.

practically *adv* praktisch ▷ *It's practically impossible.* Es ist praktisch unmöglich.

practice *n* ❶ *(for sport)* Training *nt* ▷ *football practice* das Fußballtraining ❷ Übung *f* ▷ *You need more practice.* Du brauchst mehr Übung.; **I've got to do my piano practice.** Ich muss Klavier üben.; **It's normal practice in our school.** Das ist in unserer Schule so üblich.; **in practice** in der Praxis; **a medical practice** eine Arztpraxis

practise *vb* ❶ *(music, hobby, language)* üben [**38**] ▷ *I ought to practise more.* Ich sollte mehr üben. ▷ *I practise the flute every evening.* Ich übe jeden Abend

Flöte. ▷ *I practised my German when we were on holiday.* Ich habe in den Ferien mein Deutsch geübt. ❷ *(sport)* trainieren [**76**] (*perf* hat trainiert) ▷ *The team practises on Thursdays.* Die Mannschaft trainiert donnerstags. ▷ *I don't practise enough.* Ich trainiere nicht genug.

praise *vb* loben [**38**] ▷ *The teacher praised her work.* Der Lehrer lobte ihre Arbeit.

pram *n* Kinderwagen *m* (*pl* Kinderwagen)

prawn *n* Garnele *f*

pray *vb* beten [**2**] ▷ *to pray for something* für etwas beten

prayer *n* Gebet *nt* (*pl* Gebete)

precious *adj* kostbar

precise *adj* genau ▷ *at that precise moment* genau in diesem Augenblick

precisely *adv* genau ▷ *Precisely!* Genau!; **at ten o'clock precisely** um Punkt zehn Uhr

predict *vb* vorhersagen [**15**] (*perf* hat vorhergesagt)

prefect *n*

German schools do not have prefects.

My sister's a prefect. Meine Schwester ist im letzten Schuljahr und führt die Aufsicht bei den Jüngeren.

prefer *vb* lieber mögen [**50**] (*pres* mag lieber, *imperf* mochte lieber, *perf* hat lieber gemocht) ▷ *Which would you prefer?* Was magst du lieber? ▷ *I prefer German to chemistry.* Ich mag Deutsch lieber als Chemie.; **I preferred the first version.** Die erste Version hat mir besser gefallen.

pregnant *adj* schwanger ▷ *She's six months pregnant.* Sie ist im siebten Monat schwanger.

prejudice *n* ❶ Vorurteil *nt* (*pl* Vorurteile) ▷ *That's just a prejudice.* Das ist ein Vorurteil. ❷ Vorurteile *ntpl* ▷ *There's a lot of racial prejudice.* Es gibt viele Rassenvorurteile.

prejudiced *adj* voreingenommen; **to be prejudiced against somebody** gegen jemanden voreingenommen sein [**65**]

premature *adj* verfrüht; **a premature baby** eine Frühgeburt

Premier League *n* erste Liga *f* ▷ *in the Premier League* in der ersten Liga

The 'Premier League' is similar to the German **Bundesliga**.

premises *npl* Geschäftsräume *mpl* ▷ *They're moving to new premises.* Sie ziehen in neue Geschäftsräume um.

prep *n (homework)* Hausaufgaben *fpl* ▷ *history prep* die Hausaufgaben in Geschichte

preparation *n* Vorbereitung *f*

prepare *vb* vorbereiten [**2**] (*perf* hat vorbereitet) ▷ *She prepares lessons in the evening.* Abends bereitet sie Stunden vor.; **to prepare for something** Vorbereitungen für etwas treffen [**78**]

prepared *adj* **to be prepared to do something** bereit sein [**65**], etwas zu tun

prep school *n* private Grundschule *f*

prescribe *vb (medicine)* verschreiben [**61**] (*imperf* verschrieb, *perf* hat verschrieben) ▷ *He prescribed me a course of antibiotics.* Er hat mir eine Antibiotikakur verschrieben.

prescription *n* Rezept *nt* (*pl* Rezepte) ▷ *You can't get it without a prescription.* Das bekommt man nicht ohne Rezept.

present *adj* ❶ *(in attendance)* anwesend ▷ *He wasn't present at the meeting.* Er war bei der Besprechung nicht anwesend. ❷ *(current)* gegenwärtig ▷ *the present situation* die gegenwärtige Situation; **the present tense** die Gegenwart

▶ *n* ❶ *(gift)* Geschenk *nt* (*pl* Geschenke) ▷ *I'm going to buy presents.* Ich kaufe Geschenke.; **to give somebody a present** jemandem etwas schenken [**38**] ❷ *(time)* Gegenwart *f* ▷ *She was living in the past not the present.* Sie lebte

in der Vergangenheit, nicht in der Gegenwart.; **up to the present** bis heute; **for the present** momentan; **at present** im Augenblick; **the present tense** das Präsens
▸ *vb* **to present somebody with something** *(prize, medal)* jemandem etwas verleihen

presenter *n (on TV)* Moderator *m (pl* Moderatoren), Moderatorin *f*

president *n* Präsident *m (gen* Präsidenten, *pl* Präsidenten), Präsidentin *f*

press *n* Presse *f*; **a press conference** eine Pressekonferenz
▸ *vb* ❶ drücken [**38**] ▷ *Don't press too hard!* Nicht zu fest drücken! ❷ treten [**79**] auf *(pres* tritt auf, *imperf* trat, *perf* hat getreten) ▷ *He pressed the accelerator.* Er trat aufs Gaspedal.

press-up *n* Liegestütz *m (gen* Liegestützes, *pl* Liegestütze) ▷ *I do twenty press-ups every morning.* Ich mache jeden Morgen zwanzig Liegestütze.

pressure *n* Druck *m* ▷ *He's under a lot of pressure.* Er steht unter viel Druck.; **a pressure group (1)** *(small-scale, local)* eine Bürgerinitiative **(2)** *(large-scale, more political)* eine Pressure-Group
▸ *vb* Druck ausüben [**4**] auf *(perf* hat Druck ausgeübt) ▷ *They are pressuring me.* Sie üben Druck auf mich aus.

presume *vb* annehmen [**1**] *(pres* nimmt an, *imperf* nahm an, *perf* hat angenommen) ▷ *I presume so.* Das nehme ich an.

pretend *vb* **to pretend to do something** so tun [**81**], als ob man etwas täte

Note that **als ob** is followed by the subjunctive.

pretty *adj, adv* ❶ hübsch ▷ *She's very pretty.* Sie ist sehr hübsch. ❷ *(rather)* ziemlich ▷ *That film was pretty bad.* Der Film war ziemlich schlecht.; **It's pretty much the same.** Das ist mehr oder weniger dasselbe.

prevent *vb* verhindern [**88**] *(perf* hat verhindert); **to prevent somebody from doing something** jemanden davon abhalten [**33**], etwas zu tun

previous *adj* vorherig

previously *adv* früher

price *n* Preis *m (gen* Preises, *pl* Preise)

price list *n* Preisliste *f*

prick *vb* stechen *(pres* sticht, *imperf* stach, *perf* hat gestochen) ▷ *I've pricked my finger.* Ich habe mir in den Finger gestochen.

pride *n* Stolz *m (gen* Stolzes)

priest *n* Priester *m (pl* Priester) ▷ *He's a priest.* Er ist Priester.

primarily *adv* vor allem

primary *adj* hauptsächlich

primary school *n* Grundschule *f*

Children in Germany begin **Grundschule** at the age of 6. The **Grundschule** provides primary education in school years 1 to 4.

▷ *She's still at primary school.* Sie ist noch in der Grundschule.

prime minister *n* Premierminister *m (pl* Premierminister), Premierministerin *f*

prince *n* Prinz *m (gen* Prinzen, *pl* Prinzen) ▷ *the Prince of Wales* der Prinz von Wales

princess *n* Prinzessin *f* ▷ *Princess Anne* Prinzessin Anne

principal *adj* **the principal reason** der Hauptgrund; **my principal concern** mein Hauptanliegen *nt*
▸ *n (of college)* Direktor *m (pl* Direktoren), Direktorin *f*

principle *n* Prinzip *nt (pl* Prinzipien); **on principle** aus Prinzip

print *n* ❶ *(photo)* Abzug *m (pl* Abzüge) ▷ *colour prints* Farbabzüge ❷ *(letters)* Schrift *f*; **in small print** klein gedruckt ❸ *(fingerprint)* Fingerabdruck *m (pl* Fingerabdrücke) ❹ *(picture)*

Kunstdruck *m* (*pl* Kunstdrucke) ▷ *a framed print* ein gerahmter Kunstdruck

printer *n (machine)* Drucker *m* (*pl* Drucker)

printout *n* Ausdruck *m* (*pl* Ausdrucke)

priority *n* Priorität *f*

prison *n* Gefängnis *nt* (*gen* Gefängnisses, *pl* Gefängnisse); **in prison** im Gefängnis

prisoner *n* Gefangene *m* (*gen* Gefangenen, *pl* Gefangenen), Gefangene *f* (*gen* Gefangenen) ▷ *a prisoner (man)* ein Gefangener

private *adj* privat; **a private school** eine Privatschule; **private property** das Privateigentum; **'private'** *(on envelope)* 'persönlich'; **a private bathroom** ein eigenes Badezimmer; **I have private lessons.** Ich bekomme Nachhilfestunden.

prize *n* Preis *m* (*gen* Preises, *pl* Preise) ▷ *to win a prize* einen Preis gewinnen

prize-giving *n* Preisverleihung *f*

prizewinner *n* Preisträger *m* (*pl* Preisträger), Preisträgerin *f*

pro *n* Profi *m* (*pl* Profis)

der Profi is also used for women.

▷ *This was her first year as a pro.* Dies war ihr erstes Jahr als Profi.; **the pros and cons** das Für und Wider

probability *n* Wahrscheinlichkeit *f*

probable *adj* wahrscheinlich

probably *adv* wahrscheinlich ▷ *probably not* wahrscheinlich nicht

problem *n* Problem *nt* (*pl* Probleme) ▷ *No problem!* Kein Problem!

process *n* Prozess *m* (*gen* Prozesses, *pl* Prozesse) ▷ *the peace process* der Friedensprozess; **to be in the process of doing something** gerade dabei sein [**65**], etwas zu tun

procession *n (religious)* Prozession *f*

produce *vb* ❶ *(manufacture)* herstellen [**4**] (*perf* hat hergestellt) ❷ *(play, show)* inszenieren [**76**] (*perf* hat inszeniert) ❸ *(film)* produzieren [**76**] (*perf* hat produziert)

producer *n* ❶ *(of play, show)* Regisseur *m* (*pl* Regisseure), Regisseurin *f* ❷ *(of film)* Produzent *m* (*gen* Produzenten, *pl* Produzenten), Produzentin *f*

product *n* Produkt *nt* (*pl* Produkte)

production *n* ❶ Produktion *f* ▷ *They're increasing production.* Sie erhöhen die Produktion. ❷ *(play, show)* Inszenierung *f* ▷ *a production of 'Hamlet'* eine Hamletinszenierung

profession *n* Beruf *m* (*pl* Berufe)

professional *n* Profi *m* (*pl* Profis)

der Profi is also used for women.

▷ *She now plays as a professional.* Sie spielt jetzt als Profi.

▶ *adj (player)* professionell ▷ *a very professional piece of work* eine sehr professionelle Arbeit; **a professional musician** ein Berufsmusiker *m*

professor *n* Professor *m* (*pl* Professoren), Professorin *f*; **He's the German professor.** Er hat den Lehrstuhl für Deutsch inne.

profit *n* Gewinn *m* (*pl* Gewinne)

profitable *adj* gewinnbringend

program *n* Programm *nt* (*pl* Programme) ▷ *a computer program* ein Computerprogramm

▶ *vb* programmieren [**76**] (*perf* hat programmiert) ▷ *to program a computer* einen Computer programmieren

programme *n* Programm *nt* (*pl* Programme)

programmer *n* Programmierer *m* (*pl* Programmierer), Programmiererin *f* ▷ *She's a programmer.* Sie ist Programmiererin.

progress *n* Fortschritt *m* (*pl* Fortschritte) ▷ *You're making progress!* Du machst Fortschritte!

prohibit *vb* verbieten [**8**] (*imperf* verbat, *perf* hat verboten) ▷ *Smoking is prohibited.* Das Rauchen ist verboten.

project *n* ❶ *(plan)* Projekt *nt* (*pl* Projekte) ❷ *(at school)* Referat *nt* (*pl* Referate) ▷ *I'm doing a project on Berlin.* Ich schreibe ein Referat über Berlin.

projector *n* Projektor *m* (*pl* Projektoren)

promise *n* Versprechen *nt* (*pl* Versprechen) ▷ *You didn't keep your promise.* Du hast dein Versprechen nicht gehalten.; **That's a promise!** Versprochen!
▶ *vb* versprechen **[70]** (*pres* verspricht, *imperf* versprach, *perf* hat versprochen) ▷ *She promised to write.* Sie hat versprochen zu schreiben. ▷ *I'll write, I promise!* Ich schreibe, das verspreche ich!

promote *vb* **to be promoted** befördert werden **[91]**

promotion *n* ❶ (*in job*) Beförderung *f* ❷ (*advertising*) Werbung *f*

prompt *adj, adv* schnell ▷ *a prompt reply* eine schnelle Antwort; **at eight o'clock prompt** genau um acht Uhr

pronoun *n* Pronomen *nt* (*pl* Pronomen)

pronounce *vb* aussprechen **[70]** (*pres* spricht aus, *imperf* sprach aus, *perf* hat ausgesprochen) ▷ *How do you pronounce that word?* Wie spricht man das Wort aus?

pronunciation *n* Aussprache *f*

proof *n* Beweis *m* (*gen* Beweises, *pl* Beweise)

proper *adj* ❶ (*genuine*) echt ▷ *proper German bread* echtes deutsches Brot ❷ (*decent*) ordentlich ▷ *We didn't have a proper lunch.* Wir hatten kein ordentliches Mittagessen. ▷ *It's difficult to get a proper job.* Es ist schwierig, einen ordentlichen Job zu bekommen. ▷ *We need proper training.* Wir brauchen eine ordentliche Ausbildung. ❸ (*appropriate*) richtig ▷ *You have to have the proper equipment.* Sie brauchen die richtige Ausrüstung.; **If you had come at the proper time ...** Wenn du zur rechten Zeit gekommen wärst ...

properly *adv* ❶ (*correctly*) richtig ▷ *You're not doing it properly.* Du machst das nicht richtig. ❷ (*appropriately*) anständig ▷ *Dress properly for your interview.* Zieh dich zum Vorstellungsgespräch anständig an.

property *n* Eigentum *nt*; **'private property'** 'Privateigentum'; **stolen property** das Diebesgut

propose *vb* vorschlagen **[59]** (*pres* schlägt vor, *imperf* schlug vor, *perf* hat vorgeschlagen) ▷ *I propose a new plan.* Ich schlage einen neuen Plan vor.; **to propose to do something** vorhaben **[32]**, etwas zu tun; **to propose to somebody** (*for marriage*) jemandem einen Heiratsantrag machen **[48]**

prosecute *vb* strafrechtlich verfolgen **[84]** (*perf* hat verfolgt) ▷ *They were prosecuted for murder.* Sie wurden wegen Mordes strafrechtlich verfolgt.; **'Shoplifters will be prosecuted'** 'Jeder Diebstahl wird zur Anzeige gebracht'

prostitute *n* Prostituierte *f* (*gen* Prostituierten); **a male prostitute** ein Prostituierter

protect *vb* schützen **[36]**

protection *n* Schutz *m* (*gen* Schutzes)

protein *n* Protein *nt* (*pl* Proteine)

protest *n* Protest *m* (*pl* Proteste) ▷ *He ignored their protests.* Er hat ihre Proteste ignoriert.; **a protest march** ein Protestmarsch *m*
▶ *vb* protestieren **[76]** (*perf* hat protestiert)

Protestant *n* Protestant *m* (*gen* Protestanten, *pl* Protestanten), Protestantin *f* ▷ *She's a Protestant.* Sie ist Protestantin.
▶ *adj* protestantisch ▷ *a Protestant church* eine protestantische Kirche

protester *n* Demonstrant *m* (*gen* Demonstranten, *pl* Demonstranten), Demonstrantin *f*

proud *adj* stolz ▷ *Her parents are proud of her.* Ihre Eltern sind stolz auf sie.

prove *vb* beweisen (*imperf* bewies, *perf* hat bewiesen) ▷ *The police couldn't prove it.* Die Polizei konnte es nicht beweisen.

proverb *n* Sprichwort *nt* (*pl* Sprichwörter)
provide *vb* stellen [**38**] ▷ *We'll provide the food.* Wir stellen das Essen.; **to provide somebody with something** jemandem etwas zur Verfügung stellen [**38**]
provide for *vb* versorgen [**7**] (*perf* hat versorgt)
provided *conj* vorausgesetzt, dass ▷ *He'll play provided he's fit.* Er spielt, vorausgesetzt, dass er fit ist.
prune *n* Backpflaume *f*
psychiatrist *n* Psychiater *m* (*pl* Psychiater), Psychiaterin *f* ▷ *She's a psychiatrist.* Sie ist Psychiaterin.
psychological *adj* psychologisch
psychologist *n* Psychologe *m* (*gen* Psychologen, *pl* Psychologen), Psychologin *f* ▷ *He's a psychologist.* Er ist Psychologe.
psychology *n* Psychologie *f*
PTO *abbr* (*= please turn over*) b. w. (*= bitte wenden*)
pub *n* Kneipe *f*
public *n* Öffentlichkeit *f* ▷ *open to the public* der Öffentlichkeit zugänglich; **in public** in der Öffentlichkeit
▶ *adj* öffentlich ▷ *public opinion* die öffentliche Meinung ▷ *public transport* öffentliche Verkehrsmittel *ntpl*; **a public holiday** ein gesetzlicher Feiertag; **the public address system** die Lautsprecheranlage
publicity *n* Publicity *f*
public school *n* Privatschule *f*
publish *vb* veröffentlichen [**84**] (*perf* hat veröffentlicht)
publisher *n* (*company*) Verlag *m* (*pl* Verlage)
pudding *n* Nachtisch *m* ▷ *What's for pudding?* Was gibt's zum Nachtisch?; **rice pudding** der Milchreis; **black pudding** die Blutwurst
puddle *n* Pfütze *f*
puff pastry *n* Blätterteig *m*
pull *vb* ziehen [**96**] (*imperf* zog, *perf* hat gezogen) ▷ *Pull!* Zieh!; **He pulled the trigger.** Er drückte ab.; **to pull a muscle** sich einen Muskel zerren [**38**]; **You're pulling my leg!** (*informal*) Du willst mich wohl auf den Arm nehmen!; **to pull down** abreißen; **to pull out (1)** (*tooth, weed*) herausziehen [**96**] **(2)** (*car*) ausscheren [**4**] ▷ *The car pulled out to overtake.* Das Auto scherte aus, um zu überholen. **(3)** (*withdraw*) aussteigen [**74**] ▷ *She pulled out of the tournament.* Sie ist aus dem Turnier ausgestiegen.; **to pull through** (*survive*) durchkommen [**40**]; **to pull up** (*car*) anhalten [**33**]
pullover *n* Pullover *m* (*pl* Pullover)
pulse *n* Puls *m* (*gen* Pulses, *pl* Pulse) ▷ *The nurse felt his pulse.* Die Schwester fühlte ihm den Puls.
pump *n* ❶ Pumpe *f* ▷ *a bicycle pump* eine Fahrradpumpe; **a petrol pump** eine Zapfsäule ❷ (*shoe*) Sportschuh *m* (*pl* Sportschuhe)
▶ *vb* pumpen [**38**]; **to pump up** (*tyre*) aufpumpen [**4**]
pumpkin *n* Kürbis *m* (*gen* Kürbisses, *pl* Kürbisse)
punch *n* ❶ (*blow*) Schlag *m* (*pl* Schläge) ▷ *a violent punch* ein heftiger Schlag ❷ (*drink*) Punsch *m*
▶ *vb* ❶ (*hit*) schlagen [**59**] (*pres* schlägt, *imperf* schlug, *perf* hat geschlagen) ▷ *He punched me!* Er hat mich geschlagen! ❷ (*in ticket machine*) entwerten [**18**] (*perf* hat entwertet) ▷ *Punch your ticket before you get on the train.* Entwerten Sie Ihre Fahrkarte, bevor Sie in den Zug steigen. ❸ (*by ticket inspector*) knipsen [**48**] ▷ *He forgot to punch my ticket.* Er hat vergessen, meine Fahrkarte zu knipsen.
punctual *adj* pünktlich
punctuation *n* Zeichensetzung *f*
puncture *n* Reifenpanne *f* ▷ *to have a puncture* eine Reifenpanne haben
punish *vb* bestrafen [**7**] (*perf* hat bestraft) ▷ *The teacher punished him.* Der

Lehrer bestrafte ihn.
punishment *n* Strafe *f*
punk *n (person)* Punker *m* (*pl* Punker), Punkerin *f*; **a punk rock band** eine Punkband
pupil *n* Schüler *m* (*pl* Schüler), Schülerin *f*
puppet *n* Marionette *f*
purchase *vb* erwerben **[90]** (*pres* erwirbt, *imperf* erwarb, *perf* hat erworben)
pure *adj* rein ▷ *pure orange juice* reiner Orangensaft; **He's doing pure maths.** Er macht rein theoretische Mathematik.
purple *adj* lila
purpose *n* Zweck *m* (*pl* Zwecke) ▷ *What is the purpose of these changes?* Welchen Zweck haben diese Veränderungen?; **his purpose in life** sein Lebensinhalt; **on purpose** absichtlich
purr *vb* schnurren **[48]**
purse *n* ❶ *(for money)* Geldbeutel *m* (*pl* Geldbeutel) ❷ *(US: handbag)* Handtasche *f*
pursue *vb* verfolgen **[84]** (*perf* hat verfolgt)
push *n* **to give somebody a push** jemanden stoßen
▶ *vb* ❶ *(button)* drücken **[38]** ❷ drängeln **[34]** ▷ *Don't push!* Nicht drängeln!; **to push somebody to do something** jemanden drängen **[38]**, etwas zu tun; **to push drugs** mit Drogen handeln **[34]**; **to push around** herumkommandieren **[76]**; **Push off!** *(informal)* Hau ab!; **I pushed my way through.** Ich drängelte mich durch.
pushchair *n* Sportwagen *m* (*pl* Sportwagen)
push-up *n* Liegestütz *m* (*gen* Liegestützes, *pl* Liegestütze) ▷ *I do twenty push-ups every morning.* Ich mache jeden Morgen zwanzig Liegestütze.

put *vb*

> Use **legen** when you're putting something down flat, use **stellen** when you're standing something upright.

❶ legen **[38]** ▷ *Where shall I put my things?* Wohin soll ich meine Sachen legen? ▷ *She's putting the baby to bed.* Sie legt das Baby ins Bett. ❷ stellen **[38]** ▷ *Put the vase on the table.* Stell die Vase auf den Tisch.; **Don't forget to put your name on the paper.** Vergiss nicht, deinen Namen auf das Papier zu schreiben.
put aside *vb* zurücklegen **[15]** (*perf* hat zurückgelegt)
put away *vb* wegräumen **[4]** (*perf* hat weggeräumt)
put back *vb* ❶ zurücklegen **[15]** (*perf* hat zurückgelegt) ❷ zurückstellen **[15]** (*perf* hat zurückgestellt)
put down *vb* ❶ abstellen **[4]** (*perf* hat abgestellt) ❷ *(in writing)* aufschreiben **[61]** (*imperf* schrieb auf, *perf* hat aufgeschrieben)
put forward *vb* vorstellen **[4]** (*perf* hat vorgestellt)
put in *vb (install)* einbauen **[4]** (*perf* hat eingebaut)
put off *vb* ❶ *(switch off)* ausmachen **[48]** (*perf* hat ausgemacht) ❷ *(postpone)* verschieben (*imperf* verschob, *perf* hat verschoben) ❸ *(distract)* stören **[38]** ❹ *(discourage)* entmutigen **[18]** (*perf* hat entmutigt)
put on *vb* ❶ *(clothes)* anziehen **[96]** (*imperf* zog an, *perf* hat angezogen) ❷ *(lipstick)* auftragen **[77]** (*pres* trägt auf, *imperf* trug auf, *perf* hat aufgetragen) ❸ *(record)* auflegen **[4]** (*perf* hat aufgelegt) ❹ *(light, heater, TV)* anmachen **[4]** (*perf* hat angemacht) ❺ *(play, show)* aufführen **[4]** (*perf* hat aufgeführt) ❻ aufstellen **[4]** (*perf* hat aufgestellt)
put out *vb* ❶ *(light, cigarette)* ausmachen **[48]** (*perf* hat ausgemacht)

a b c d e f g h i j k l m n o p q r s t u v w x y z

❷ *(fire)* löschen [**48**]

put through *vb* verbinden (*imperf* verband, *perf* hat verbunden)

put up *vb* ❶ *(pin up)* aufhängen [**35**] (*perf* hat aufgehängt) ❷ *(tent)* aufschlagen [**59**] (*pres* schlägt auf, *imperf* schlug auf, *perf* hat aufgeschlagen) ❸ *(price)* erhöhen [**19**] (*perf* hat erhöht) ❹ *(accommodate)* übernachten lassen [**42**](*pres* lässt übernachten, *imperf* ließ übernachten, *perf* hat übernachten lassen)

puzzle *n (jigsaw)* Puzzle *nt* (*pl* Puzzles)

puzzled *adj* verdutzt ▷ *You look puzzled!* Du siehst verdutzt aus!

pyjamas *npl* Schlafanzug *m* (*pl* Schlafanzüge) ▷ *my pyjamas* mein Schlafanzug; **a pair of pyjamas** ein Schlafanzug; **a pyjama top** ein Schlafanzugoberteil *nt*

pyramid *n* Pyramide *f*

Pyrenees *npl* **the Pyrenees** die Pyrenäen *pl*

q

quad bike *n* Quad *nt* (*pl* Quads)

qualification *n* Qualifikation *f* ▷ *vocational qualifications* die beruflichen Qualifikationen; **to leave school without any qualifications** die Schule ohne einen Abschluss verlassen [**42**]

qualified *adj* ausgebildet ▷ *a qualified driving instructor* ein ausgebildeter Fahrlehrer ▷ *a qualified nurse* eine ausgebildete Krankenschwester

qualify *vb* ❶ *(for job)* seinen Abschluss machen [**48**] ▷ *She qualified as a teacher last year.* Sie hat letztes Jahr ihren Abschluss als Lehrerin gemacht. ❷ *(in competition)* sich qualifizieren [**76**] (*perf* hat sich qualifiziert) ▷ *Our team didn't qualify.* Unsere Mannschaft konnte sich nicht qualifizieren.

quality *n* ❶ Qualität *f* ▷ *a good quality of life* eine gute Lebensqualität; **good-quality ingredients** qualitativ hochwertige Zutaten ❷ *(of person)*

Eigenschaft *f* ▷ *good qualities* gute Eigenschaften
quantity *n* Menge *f*
quarantine *n* Quarantäne *f* ▷ *in quarantine* in Quarantäne
quarrel *n* Streit *m* (*pl* Streite)
▶ *vb* sich streiten (*imperf* stritt sich, *perf* hat sich gestritten)
quarry *n* (*for stone*) Steinbruch *m* (*pl* Steinbrüche)
quarter *n* Viertel *nt* (*pl* Viertel) ▷ *three quarters* drei Viertel ▷ *a quarter of an hour* eine viertel Stunde; **three quarters of an hour** eine Dreiviertelstunde; **a quarter past ten** Viertel nach zehn; **a quarter to eleven** Viertel vor elf
quarter final *n* Viertelfinale *nt* (*pl* Viertelfinale)
quartet *n* Quartett *nt* (*pl* Quartette) ▷ *a string quartet* ein Streichquartett
quay *n* Kai *m* (*pl* Kais)
queen *n* ❶ Königin *f* ▷ *Queen Elizabeth* Königin Elisabeth ❷ (*playing card*) Dame *f* ▷ *the queen of hearts* die Herzdame
query *n* Frage *f*
▶ *vb* infrage stellen [**38**] ▷ *No one queried my decision.* Niemand hat meine Entscheidung infrage gestellt.; **They queried the bill.** Sie reklamierten die Rechnung.
question *n* Frage *f* ▷ *That's a difficult question.* Das ist eine schwierige Frage.; **Can I ask a question?** Kann ich etwas fragen?; **It's out of the question.** Das kommt nicht infrage.
▶ *vb* befragen [**7**] (*perf* hat befragt); **He was questioned by the police.** Die Polizei hat ihn vernommen.
question mark *n* Fragezeichen *nt* (*pl* Fragezeichen)
questionnaire *n* Fragebogen *m* (*pl* Fragebögen)
queue *n* Schlange *f*
▶ *vb* Schlange stehen [**72**] (*imperf* stand Schlange, *perf* hat Schlange gestanden) ▷ *We queued for an hour.* Wir haben eine Stunde lang Schlange gestanden.; **to queue for something** für etwas anstehen [**72**]
quick *adj, adv* schnell ▷ *a quick lunch* ein schnelles Mittagessen ▷ *Quick, phone the police!* Schnell, rufen Sie die Polizei! ▷ *It's quicker by train.* Mit dem Zug geht es schneller.; **Be quick!** Beeil dich!; **She's a quick learner.** Sie lernt schnell.
quickly *adv* schnell ▷ *It was all over very quickly.* Es war alles sehr schnell vorbei.
quiet *adj* ❶ (*not talkative, peaceful*) ruhig ▷ *You're very quiet today.* Du bist heute sehr ruhig. ▷ *a quiet little town* eine ruhige, kleine Stadt ❷ (*not noisy*) leise ▷ *The engine's very quiet.* Der Motor ist sehr leise.; **Be quiet!** Sei still!; **Quiet!** Ruhe!
quietly *adv* leise ▷ *He quietly opened the door.* Er öffnete leise die Tür.
quilt *n* (*duvet*) Steppdecke *f*
quit *vb* ❶ aufgeben [**28**] (*pres* gibt auf, *imperf* gab auf, *perf* hat aufgegeben) ▷ *I quit my job last week.* Ich habe meine Stelle letzte Woche aufgegeben.
❷ aufhören [**4**] ▷ *I quit smoking.* Ich habe mit dem Rauchen aufgehört.
quite *adv* ❶ (*rather*) ziemlich ▷ *It's quite warm today.* Heute ist es ziemlich warm. ▷ *I've been there quite a lot.* Ich war schon ziemlich oft da. ▷ *quite a lot of money* ziemlich viel Geld ▷ *quite a few people* ziemlich viele Leute ▷ *It costs quite a lot.* Es ist ziemlich teuer. ▷ *It's quite a long way.* Es ist ziemlich weit. ▷ *It was quite a shock.* Es war ein ziemlicher Schock.; **I quite liked the film, but ...** Der Film hat mir ganz gut gefallen, aber ... ❷ (*entirely*) ganz ▷ *I'm not quite sure.* Ich bin mir nicht ganz sicher. ▷ *It's not quite the same.* Das ist nicht ganz das Gleiche.; **quite good** ganz gut
quiz *n* Quiz *nt* (*gen* Quiz, *pl* Quiz)
quotation *n* Zitat *nt* (*pl* Zitate) ▷ *a quotation from Shakespeare* ein Shakespearezitat

quotation marks *npl* Anführungszeichen *ntpl*

quote *n* Zitat *nt* (*pl* Zitate) ▷ *a Shakespeare quote* ein Shakespearezitat; **quotes** *(quotation marks)* die Anführungszeichen
▶ *vb* zitieren [**76**] (*perf* hat zitiert)

r

rabbi *n* Rabbiner *m* (*pl* Rabbiner)

rabbit *n* Kaninchen *nt* (*pl* Kaninchen); **a rabbit hutch** ein Kaninchenstall *m*

race *n* ❶ *(sport)* Rennen *nt* (*pl* Rennen) ▷ *a cycle race* ein Radrennen ❷ *(species)* Rasse *f* ▷ *the human race* die Menschheit; **race relations** Rassenbeziehungen *fpl*
▶ *vb* ❶ rennen [**55**] (*imperf* rannte, *perf* ist gerannt) ▷ *We raced to catch the bus.* Wir sind gerannt, um den Bus zu erreichen. ❷ *(have a race)* um die Wette laufen [**43**] mit (*pres* läuft um die Wette, *imperf* lief um die Wette, *perf* ist um die Wette gelaufen) ▷ *I'll race you!* Ich laufe mit dir um die Wette!

racecourse *n* Pferderennbahn *f*

racer *n (bike)* Rennrad *nt* (*pl* Rennräder)

racetrack *n* Rennbahn *f*

racial *adj* **racial discrimination** die Rassendiskriminierung

racing car *n* Rennwagen *m* (*pl* Rennwagen)

racing driver *n* Rennfahrer *m* (*pl* Rennfahrer), Rennfahrerin *f*
racism *n* Rassismus *m* (*gen* Rassismus)
racist *adj* rassistisch; **He's racist.** Er ist ein Rassist.
▶ *n* Rassist *m* (*gen* Rassisten, *pl* Rassisten), Rassistin *f*
rack *n* (*for luggage*) Gepäckträger *m* (*pl* Gepäckträger)
racket *n* ❶ (*for sport*) Schläger *m* (*pl* Schläger) ▷ *my tennis racket* mein Tennisschläger ❷ (*noise*) Krach *m* ▷ *a terrible racket* ein furchtbarer Krach
racquet *n* Schläger *m* (*pl* Schläger)
radar *n* Radar *nt*
radiation *n* Strahlung *f*
radiator *n* Heizkörper *m* (*pl* Heizkörper)
radio *n* Radio *nt* (*pl* Radios); **on the radio** im Radio; **a radio station** ein Rundfunksender *m*
radioactive *adj* radioaktiv
radish *n* ❶ (*small red*) Radieschen *nt* (*pl* Radieschen) ❷ (*long white*) Rettich *m* (*pl* Rettiche)
RAF *n* (= *Royal Air Force*) britische Luftwaffe *f* ▷ *He's in the RAF.* Er ist bei der britischen Luftwaffe.
raffle *n* Tombola *f* (*pl* Tombolas) ▷ *a raffle ticket* ein Tombolalos *nt*
raft *n* Floß *nt* (*gen* Floßes, *pl* Flöße)
rag *n* Lumpen *m* (*pl* Lumpen) ▷ *dressed in rags* in Lumpen gekleidet; **a piece of rag** ein Lappen *m*
rage *n* Wut *f* ▷ *mad with rage* wild vor Wut; **to be in a rage** wütend sein [65]; **It's all the rage.** Es ist große Mode.
rail *n* ❶ (*on stairs, bridge, balcony*) Geländer *nt* (*pl* Geländer) ❷ (*on railway line*) Schiene *f*; **by rail** mit dem Zug
railcard *n* Bahncard® *f* (*pl* Bahncards)
railroad *n* (*US*) Eisenbahn *f*
railway *n* Eisenbahn *f*; **a railway line** eine Eisenbahnlinie; **a railway station** ein Bahnhof *m*
rain *n* Regen *m* ▷ *in the rain* im Regen
▶ *vb* regnen [53] ▷ *It rains a lot here.* Hier regnet es viel.; **It's raining.** Es regnet.
rainbow *n* Regenbogen *m* (*pl* Regenbogen)
raincoat *n* Regenmantel *m* (*pl* Regenmäntel)
rainfall *n* Niederschlag *m* (*pl* Niederschläge)
rainforest *n* Regenwald *m* (*pl* Regenwälder)
rainy *adj* regnerisch
raise *vb* ❶ (*lift*) hochheben (*imperf* hob hoch, *perf* hat hochgehoben) ▷ *He raised his hand.* Er hob die Hand hoch. ❷ (*improve*) heben (*imperf* hob, *perf* hat gehoben) ▷ *They want to raise standards in schools.* Sie wollen das Niveau in den Schulen heben.; **to raise money** Spenden sammeln [34]
raisin *n* Rosine *f*
rake *n* Rechen *m* (*pl* Rechen)
rally *n* ❶ (*of people*) Kundgebung *f* ❷ (*sport*) Rallye *f* (*pl* Rallyes) ▷ *a rally driver* ein Rallyefahrer *m* ❸ (*in tennis*) Ballwechsel *m* (*pl* Ballwechsel)
rambler *n* Wanderer *m* (*pl* Wanderer), Wanderin *f*
ramp *n* (*for wheelchairs*) Rampe *f*
ran *vb see* **run**
rang *vb see* **ring**
range *n* Auswahl *f* ▷ *a wide range of colours* eine große Auswahl an Farben; **a range of subjects** verschiedene Themen; **a mountain range** eine Bergkette
▶ *vb* **to range from ... to** gehen [29] von ... bis; **Tickets range from two to twenty pounds.** Karten kosten von zwei bis zwanzig Pfund.
rap *n* (*music*) Rap *m*
rape *n* Vergewaltigung *f*
▶ *vb* vergewaltigen [7] (*perf* hat vergewaltigt)
rapids *npl* Stromschnellen *fpl*
rare *adj* ❶ (*unusual*) selten ▷ *a rare plant* eine seltene Pflanze ❷ (*steak*) blutig
raspberry *n* Himbeere *f* ▷ *raspberry jam* die Himbeermarmelade
rat *n* Ratte *f*

rather *adv* ziemlich ▷ *I was rather disappointed.* Ich war ziemlich enttäuscht. ▷ *Twenty pounds! That's rather a lot!* Zwanzig Pfund! Das ist aber ziemlich viel!; **rather a lot of** ziemlich viel; **rather than** statt; **I'd rather ...** Ich würde lieber ...
rattlesnake *n* Klapperschlange *f*
rave *vb* schwärmen [**38**] ▷ *They raved about the film.* Sie schwärmten von dem Film.
▶ *n (party)* Raveparty *f (pl* Ravepartys); **rave music** die Ravemusik
ravenous *adj* **to be ravenous** einen Riesenhunger haben [**32**]
raw *adj (food)* roh; **raw materials** die Rohstoffe *mpl*
razor *n* Rasierapparat *m (pl* Rasierapparate); **a razor blade** eine Rasierklinge
RE *n (= religious education)* Religionsunterricht *m*
reach *n* **out of reach** außer Reichweite; **within easy reach of** leicht zu erreichen
▶ *vb* ❶ ankommen [**40**] in ▷ *We reached the hotel at ten o'clock.* Wir sind um zehn Uhr im Hotel angekommen.; **We hope to reach the final.** Wir wollen ins Endspiel kommen. ❷ *(decision)* treffen [**78**] ▷ *Eventually they reached a decision.* Sie haben schließlich eine Entscheidung getroffen.; **He reached for his gun.** Er griff nach seiner Pistole.
reaction *n* Reaktion *f*
reactor *n* Reaktor *m (pl* Reaktoren) ▷ *a nuclear reactor* ein Kernreaktor
read *vb* lesen [**45**] *(pres* liest, *imperf* las, *perf* hat gelesen) ▷ *I don't read much.* Ich lese nicht viel. ▷ *Have you read it?* Hast du es gelesen? ▷ *Read the text out loud.* Lies den Text laut.
reading *n* Lesen *nt* ▷ *Reading is one of my hobbies.* Lesen ist eines meiner Hobbies.
ready *adj* fertig ▷ *She's nearly ready.* Sie ist fast fertig.; **He's always ready to help.** Er ist immer bereit zu helfen.; **a ready meal** ein Fertiggericht *nt*; **to get ready** sich fertig machen [**48**]; **to get something ready** etwas machen [**48**]
real *adj* ❶ *(not fake)* echt ▷ *He wasn't a real policeman.* Er war kein echter Polizist. ▷ *It's real leather.* Es ist echtes Leder. ❷ wirklich ▷ *Her real name is Cordelia.* Ihr wirklicher Name ist Cordelia. ▷ *in real life* im wirklichen Leben; **It was a real nightmare.** Es war wirklich ein Albtraum.
realistic *adj* realistisch
reality *n* Wirklichkeit *f*
realize *vb* **to realize that ...** bemerken [**7**], dass ...
really *adv* wirklich ▷ *She's really nice.* Sie ist wirklich nett. ▷ *I'm learning Italian. — Really?* Ich lerne Italienisch. — Wirklich? ▷ *Do you really think so?* Meinst du wirklich?; **Do you want to go? — Not really.** Willst du gehen? — Eigentlich nicht.
realtor *n (US)* Immobilienhändler *m (pl* Immobilienhändler), Immobilienhändlerin *f*
reason *n* Grund *m (pl* Gründe) ▷ *There's no reason to think that ...* Es gibt keinen Grund zu meinen, dass ...; **for security reasons** aus Sicherheitsgründen; **That was the main reason I went.** Das war der Hauptgrund, warum ich gegangen bin.
reasonable *adj* ❶ *(sensible)* vernünftig ▷ *Be reasonable!* Sei vernünftig! ❷ *(not bad)* ganz ordentlich ▷ *He wrote a reasonable essay.* Er hat einen ganz ordentlichen Aufsatz geschrieben.
reasonably *adv* ziemlich ▷ *reasonably well* ziemlich gut; **reasonably priced accommodation** preiswerte Unterbringung
reassure *vb* beruhigen [**18**] *(perf* hat beruhigt)
reassuring *adj* beruhigend
rebel *n* Rebell *m (pl* Rebellen), Rebellin *f*
▶ *vb* rebellieren [**76**] *(perf* hat rebelliert)

rebellious *adj* aufmüpfig
receipt *n* Quittung *f*
receive *vb* erhalten [**33**] (*pres* erhält, *imperf* erhielt, *perf* hat erhalten)
receiver *n* (*of phone*) Hörer *m* (*pl* Hörer) ▷ *to pick up the receiver* den Hörer abnehmen
recent *adj* neueste ▷ *the recent developments in ...* die neuesten Entwicklungen in ...; **in recent years** in den letzten Jahren
recently *adv* in letzter Zeit ▷ *I've been doing a lot of training recently.* Ich habe in letzter Zeit viel trainiert.
reception *n* ❶ (*in hotel*) Rezeption *f* ▷ *Please leave your key at reception.* Bitte geben Sie Ihren Schlüssel an der Rezeption ab. ❷ (*party*) Empfang *m* (*pl* Empfänge) ▷ *The reception will be at a hotel.* Der Empfang findet in einem Hotel statt.
receptionist *n* Empfangschef *m* (*pl* Empfangschefs), Empfangsdame *f*
recipe *n* Rezept *nt* (*pl* Rezepte)
reckon *vb* meinen [**38**] ▷ *What do you reckon?* Was meinst du?
recognize *vb* erkennen [**39**] (*imperf* erkannte, *perf* hat erkannt) ▷ *You'll recognize me by my red hair.* Du wirst mich an meinen roten Haaren erkennen.
recommend *vb* empfehlen [**17**] (*pres* empfiehlt, *imperf* empfahl, *perf* hat empfohlen) ▷ *What do you recommend?* Was können Sie empfehlen?
reconsider *vb* **to reconsider something** sich etwas noch einmal überlegen [**82**]
record *n* ❶ (*recording*) Schallplatte *f* ▷ *my favourite record* meine Lieblingsschallplatte ❷ (*sport*) Rekord *m* (*pl* Rekorde) ▷ *the world record* der Weltrekord; **in record time** in Rekordzeit; **He's got a criminal record.** Er ist vorbestraft.; **records** (*of police, hospital*) die Akten; **There is no record of your booking.** Ihre Buchung ist nirgends belegt.
▶ *vb* (*on film, tape*) aufnehmen [**52**] (*pres* nimmt auf, *imperf* nahm auf, *perf* hat aufgenommen) ▷ *They've just recorded their new album.* Sie haben eben ihr neues Album aufgenommen.
recorded delivery *n* **to send something recorded delivery** etwas per Einschreiben senden
recorder *n* (*instrument*) Blockflöte *f* ▷ *She plays the recorder.* Sie spielt Blockflöte.; **a cassette recorder** ein Kassettenrekorder *m*; **a video recorder** ein Videorekorder *m*
recording *n* Aufnahme *f*
record player *n* Plattenspieler *m* (*pl* Plattenspieler)
recover *vb* sich erholen [**19**] (*perf* hat sich erholt) ▷ *He's recovering from a knee injury.* Er erholt sich von einer Knieverletzung.
recovery *n* Erholung *f*; **Best wishes for a speedy recovery!** Gute Besserung!
rectangle *n* Rechteck *nt* (*pl* Rechtecke)
rectangular *adj* rechteckig
recycle *vb* wiederverwerten [**7**] (*perf* hat wiederverwertet)
recycling *n* Recycling *nt*
red *adj* rot ▷ *a red rose* eine rote Rose ▷ *red meat* rotes Fleisch ▷ *Peter's got red hair.* Peter hat rote Haare.; **to go through a red light** bei Rot über die Ampel fahren [**21**]
redcurrant *n* Rote Johannisbeere *f*
redecorate *vb* renovieren [**76**] (*perf* hat renoviert)
redo *vb* noch einmal machen [**48**]
reduce *vb* ermäßigen [**7**] (*perf* hat ermäßigt) ▷ *at a reduced price* zu ermäßigtem Preis; **'reduce speed now'** 'Geschwindigkeit verringern'
reduction *n* Nachlass *m* (*gen* Nachlasses, *pl* Nachlässe) ▷ *a five per cent reduction* ein Nachlass von fünf Prozent; **'Huge reductions!'** 'Stark reduzierte Preise!'

a b c d e f g h i j k l m n o p q r s t u v w x y z

redundant *adj* **to be made redundant** entlassen werden [**91**]
refer *vb* **to refer to** anspielen [**4**] auf
referee *n* Schiedsrichter *m (pl* Schiedsrichter), Schiedsrichterin *f*
reference *n (for job application)* Arbeitszeugnis *nt (gen* Arbeitszeugnisses, *pl* Arbeitszeugnisse) ▷ *Would you please give me a reference?* Können Sie mir bitte ein Arbeitszeugnis geben?; **With reference to your letter of ...** Mit Bezug auf Ihren Brief vom ...; **a reference book** ein Nachschlagewerk *nt*
refill *vb* nachfüllen [**4**] (*perf* hat nachgefüllt) ▷ *He refilled my glass.* Er füllte mein Glas nach.
reflect *vb (light, image)* reflektieren [**76**] (*perf* hat reflektiert)
reflection *n (in mirror)* Spiegelbild *nt (pl* Spiegelbilder)
reflex *n* Reflex *m (gen* Reflexes, *pl* Reflexe)
reflexive *adj* reflexiv ▷ *a reflexive verb* ein reflexives Verb
refreshing *adj* erfrischend
refreshments *npl* Erfrischungen *fpl*
refrigerator *n* Kühlschrank *m (pl* Kühlschränke)
refuge *n* Zuflucht *f*
refugee *n* Flüchtling *m (pl* Flüchtlinge)

> **der Flüchtling** is also used for women.

refund *n* Rückvergütung *f*
▸ *vb* zurückerstatten [**2**] (*perf* hat zurückerstattet)
refuse *vb* sich weigern [**88**]
▸ *n* Müll *m*; **refuse collection** die Müllabfuhr
regain *vb* **to regain consciousness** wieder zu Bewusstsein kommen [**40**]
regard *n* **Give my regards to Alice.** Grüße an Alice.; **Martin sends his regards.** Martin lässt grüßen.; **'with kind regards'** 'mit freundlichen Grüßen'
▸ *vb* **to regard something as** etwas betrachten [**7**] als; **as regards ...** was ... betrifft
regiment *n* Regiment *nt (pl* Regimenter)
region *n* Gegend *f*
regional *adj* regional
register *n (in school)* Klassenbuch *nt (pl* Klassenbücher)
▸ *vb (at school, college)* sich einschreiben [**61**] (*imperf* schrieb sich ein, *perf* hat sich eingeschrieben)
registered *adj* **a registered letter** ein eingeschriebener Brief
registration *n (in school)* Namensaufruf *m (pl* Namensaufrufe)
regret *n* Bedauern *nt*; **I've got no regrets.** Ich bedaure nichts.
▸ *vb* bedauern [**88**] (*perf* hat bedauert) ▷ *You'll regret it!* Du wirst es bedauern!; **to regret doing something** es bedauern [**88**], etwas getan zu haben
regular *adj* ❶ regelmäßig ▷ *at regular intervals* in regelmäßigen Abständen ▷ *a regular verb* ein regelmäßiges Verb; **to take regular exercise** regelmäßig Sport machen [**48**] ❷ *(average)* normal ▷ *a regular portion of fries* eine normale Portion Pommes frites
regularly *adv* regelmäßig
regulation *n* Bestimmung *f*
rehearsal *n* Probe *f*
rehearse *vb* proben [**38**]
rein *n* Zügel *m (pl* Zügel) ▷ *the reins* die Zügel
reindeer *n* Rentier *nt (pl* Rentiere)
reject *vb (idea, suggestion)* verwerfen [**92**] (*pres* verwirft, *imperf* verwarf, *perf* hat verworfen) ▷ *We rejected the idea.* Wir haben die Idee verworfen.; **I applied but they rejected me.** Ich habe mich beworben, wurde aber abgelehnt.
related *adj (people)* verwandt ▷ *Are you related to her?* Bist du mit ihr verwandt? ▷ *We're related.* Wir sind miteinander verwandt.; **The two**

events were not related. Es bestand kein Zusammenhang zwischen den beiden Ereignissen.

relation *n* ❶ *(person)* Verwandte *m (gen* Verwandten, *pl* Verwandten), Verwandte *f (gen* Verwandten) ▷ *He's a distant relation.* Er ist ein entfernter Verwandter. ▷ *I've got relations in London.* Ich habe Verwandte in London. ▷ *my close relations* meine engsten Verwandten ❷ *(connection)* Bezug *m (pl* Bezüge) ▷ *It has no relation to reality.* Es hat keinen Bezug zur Wirklichkeit.; **in relation to** verglichen mit

relationship *n* Beziehung *f* ▷ *We have a good relationship.* Wir haben eine gute Beziehung. ▷ *I'm not in a relationship at the moment.* Ich habe im Moment keine Beziehung.

relative *n* Verwandte *m (gen* Verwandten, *pl* Verwandten), Verwandte *f (gen* Verwandten) ▷ *a relative (man)* ein Verwandter ▷ *my close relatives* meine engsten Verwandten; **all her relatives** ihre ganze Verwandtschaft

relatively *adv* relativ

relax *vb* sich entspannen **[18]** *(perf* hat sich entspannt) ▷ *I relax listening to music.* Ich entspanne mich beim Musikhören.; **Relax! Everything's fine.** Immer mit der Ruhe! Alles ist in Ordnung.

relaxation *n* Entspannung *f* ▷ *I don't have much time for relaxation.* Ich habe nicht viel Zeit für Entspannung.

relaxed *adj* entspannt

relaxing *adj* entspannend ▷ *I find cooking relaxing.* Ich finde Kochen entspannend.

relay *n* **a relay race** ein Staffellauf *m*

release *vb* ❶ *(prisoner)* freilassen **[42]** *(pres* lässt frei, *imperf* ließ frei, *perf* hat freigelassen) ❷ *(report, news)* veröffentlichen **[84]** *(perf* hat veröffentlicht) ❸ *(record, video)* herausbringen **[13]** *(imperf* brachte heraus, *perf* hat herausgebracht) ▶ *n (from prison)* Freilassung *f* ▷ *the release of Nelson Mandela* die Freilassung Nelson Mandelas; **the band's latest release** die neueste Platte der Band

relevant *adj (documents)* entsprechend; **That's not relevant.** Das ist nicht relevant.; **to be relevant to something** einen Bezug zu etwas haben **[32]**

reliable *adj* zuverlässig ▷ *a reliable car* ein zuverlässiges Auto ▷ *He's not very reliable.* Er ist nicht sehr zuverlässig.

relief *n* Erleichterung *f* ▷ *That's a relief!* Das ist eine Erleichterung!

relieved *adj* erleichtert ▷ *I was relieved to hear ...* Ich war erleichtert zu hören ...

religion *n* Religion *f* ▷ *What religion are you?* Welche Religion hast du?

religious *adj* religiös ▷ *I'm not religious.* Ich bin nicht religiös.; **my religious beliefs** mein Glaube *m*

reluctant *adj* **to be reluctant to do something** etwas nur ungern tun **[81]**

reluctantly *adv* ungern ▷ *She reluctantly accepted.* Sie hat ungern angenommen.

rely on *vb* sich verlassen **[42]** auf *(pres* verlässt sich, *imperf* verließ sich, *perf* hat sich verlassen) ▷ *I'm relying on you.* Ich verlasse mich auf dich.

remain *vb* bleiben **[10]** *(imperf* blieb, *perf* ist geblieben); **to remain silent** schweigen

remaining *adj* restlich ▷ *the remaining ingredients* die restlichen Zutaten

remark *n* Bemerkung *f*

remarkable *adj* bemerkenswert

remarkably *adv* bemerkenswert

remember *vb* sich erinnern **[88]** *(perf* hat sich erinnert) ▷ *I can't remember his name.* Ich kann mich nicht an seinen Namen erinnern. ▷ *I don't remember.* Ich erinnere mich nicht.

> In German you often say 'don't forget' rather than 'remember' when reminding somebody about something.

a b c d e f g h i j k l m n o p q r s t u v w x y z

▷ *Remember your passport!* Vergiss deinen Pass nicht! ▷ *Remember to write your name on the form.* Vergiss nicht, deinen Namen auf das Formular zu schreiben.

remind *vb* erinnern [**88**] (*perf* hat erinnert) ▷ *It reminds me of Scotland.* Es erinnert mich an Schottland. ▷ *I'll remind you tomorrow.* Ich werde dich morgen daran erinnern. ▷ *Remind me to speak to Daniel.* Erinnere mich, dass ich mit Daniel sprechen will.

remote *adj* abgelegen ▷ *a remote village* ein abgelegenes Dorf

remote control *n* Fernbedienung *f*

remotely *adv* entfernt ▷ *There was nobody remotely resembling this description.* Niemand sah dieser Beschreibung auch nur entfernt ähnlich.; **It's remotely possible that ...** Es ist gerade eben noch möglich, dass ...

remove *vb* entfernen [**18**] (*perf* hat entfernt) ▷ *Did you remove the stain?* Hast du den Fleck entfernt?

renew *vb (passport, licence)* verlängern lassen [**42**](*pres* lässt verlängern, *imperf* ließ verlängern, *perf* hat verlängern lassen) ▷ *You'll need to renew your passport.* Du musst deinen Pass verlängern lassen.; **to renew a contract** einen Vertrag verlängern [**88**]

renewable *adj (energy, resource, passport)* erneuerbar

renovate *vb* renovieren [**76**] (*perf* hat renoviert) ▷ *The building's been renovated.* Das Gebäude ist renoviert worden.

rent *n* Miete *f*

Be careful not to translate **rent** by **Rente**.

▸ *vb* mieten [**2**] ▷ *We rented a car.* Wir haben ein Auto gemietet.

reoffend *vb* erneut straffällig werden [**91**]

reorganize *vb* umorganisieren [**4**] (*perf* hat umorganisiert)

rep *n (= representative)* Vertreter *m* (*pl* Vertreter), Vertreterin *f*

repaid *vb see* **repay**

repair *vb* reparieren [**76**] (*perf* hat repariert); **to get something repaired** etwas reparieren lassen [**42**]

▸ *n* Reparatur *f*

repay *vb (money)* zurückzahlen [**15**] (*perf* hat zurückgezahlt)

repeat *vb* wiederholen [**4**] (*perf* hat wiederholt)

▸ *n* Wiederholung *f* ▷ *There are too many repeats on TV.* Es gibt zu viele Wiederholungen im Fernsehen.

repeatedly *adv* wiederholt

repetitive *adj (movement, work)* monoton

replace *vb* ersetzen [**36**] (*perf* hat ersetzt)

replay *n* **There will be a replay on Friday.** Das Spiel wird am Freitag wiederholt.

▸ *vb (match)* wiederholen [**4**] (*perf* hat wiederholt)

reply *n* Antwort *f*

▸ *vb* antworten [**2**]

report *n* ❶ *(of event)* Bericht *m* (*pl* Berichte) ▷ *a report in the paper* ein Zeitungsbericht ❷ *(at school)* Zeugnis *nt* (*gen* Zeugnisses, *pl* Zeugnisse) ▷ *I got a good report.* Ich habe ein gutes Zeugnis bekommen.; **report card** das Zeugnis

▸ *vb* ❶ melden [**54**] ▷ *I've reported the theft.* Ich habe den Diebstahl gemeldet. ❷ sich melden [**54**] ▷ *Report to reception when you arrive.* Melden Sie sich bei Ihrer Ankunft am Empfang.

reporter *n* Reporter *m* (*pl* Reporter), Reporterin *f* ▷ *She'd like to be a reporter.* Sie möchte gern Reporterin werden.

represent *vb (person)* vertreten [**79**] (*pres* vertritt, *imperf* vertrat, *perf* hat vertreten) ▷ *My lawyer represented me in court.* Mein Anwalt hat mich vor Gericht vertreten.

representative *adj* repräsentativ

reptile *n* Reptil *nt* (*pl* Reptilien)
republic *n* Republik *f*
reputation *n* Ruf *m*
request *n* Bitte *f*
▶ *vb* bitten [**9**] um (*imperf* bat, *perf* hat gebeten) ▷ *He requested information.* Er bat um Informationen.
require *vb* erfordern [**19**] (*perf* hat erfordert) ▷ *Her job requires a lot of patience.* Ihre Arbeit erfordert viel Geduld.
resat *vb see* **resit**
rescue *vb* retten [**2**]
▶ *n* Rettung *f* ▷ *a rescue operation* eine Rettungsaktion; **a mountain rescue team** ein Team der Bergwacht; **the rescue services** der Rettungsdienst *sg*; **to come to somebody's rescue** jemandem zu Hilfe kommen [**40**]
research *n* (*experimental*) Forschung *f* ▷ *He's doing research.* Er ist in der Forschung tätig.; **Research has shown that ...** Forschungen haben ergeben, dass ...; **She's doing some research in the library.** Sie sammelt in der Bibliothek Material.
resemblance *n* Ähnlichkeit *f*
resent *vb* übel nehmen [**52**] (*pres* nimmt übel, *imperf* nahm übel, *perf* hat übel genommen) ▷ *I really resent your criticism.* Ich nehme Ihnen Ihre Kritik wirklich übel.; **I resent being dependent on her.** Ich ärgere mich darüber, von ihr abhängig zu sein.
resentful *adj* verärgert ▷ *He was resentful about the way they were treated.* Er war verärgert darüber, wie sie behandelt wurden.
reservation *n* ❶ (*at restaurant*) Reservierung *f*; **I'd like to make a reservation for this evening.** Ich möchte für heute Abend einen Tisch reservieren. ❷ (*for journey, at hotel*) Buchung *f*; **I've got a reservation for two nights.** Ich habe für zwei Nächte gebucht.
reserve *n* ❶ (*place*) Schutzgebiet *nt* (*pl* Schutzgebiete) ▷ *a nature reserve* ein Naturschutzgebiet ❷ (*person*) Reservespieler *m* (*pl* Reservespieler), Reservespielerin *f* ▷ *She was reserve in the game last Saturday.* Sie war beim Spiel letzten Samstag Reservespielerin.
▶ *vb* reservieren [**76**] (*perf* hat reserviert) ▷ *I'd like to reserve a table for tomorrow evening.* Ich möchte für morgen Abend einen Tisch reservieren.
reserved *adj* reserviert ▷ *a reserved seat* ein reservierter Platz ▷ *He's quite reserved.* Er ist ziemlich reserviert.
resident *n* Bewohner *m* (*pl* Bewohner), Bewohnerin *f*
residential *adj* **a residential area** ein Wohngebiet *nt*
resign *vb* ❶ zurücktreten [**79**] (*pres* tritt zurück, *imperf* trat zurück, *perf* ist zurückgetreten) ▷ *The minister resigned.* Der Minister ist zurückgetreten. ❷ (*employee*) kündigen [**38**] ▷ *She resigned to take up a post abroad.* Sie kündigte, um einen Posten im Ausland zu übernehmen.
resit *vb* wiederholen [**4**] (*perf* hat wiederholt) ▷ *I'm resitting the exam in May.* Ich wiederhole die Prüfung im Mai.
resolution *n* (*decision*) Beschluss *m* (*gen* Beschlusses, *pl* Beschlüsse); **Have you made any New Year's resolutions?** Hast du zum neuen Jahr gute Vorsätze gefasst?
resort *n* (*at seaside*) Badeort *m* (*pl* Badeorte) ▷ *It's a resort on the Costa del Sol.* Es ist ein Badeort an der Costa del Sol.; **a ski resort** ein Skiort; **as a last resort** als letzter Ausweg
resources *npl* (*financial*) Mittel *ntpl* ▷ *We haven't the resources to build a swimming pool.* Wir haben nicht die Mittel, um ein Schwimmbad zu bauen.; **natural resources** Bodenschätze *mpl*

respect *n* Respekt *m*
▸ *vb* respektieren **[76]** (*perf* hat respektiert)

respectable *adj* ❶ anständig ▹ *respectable people* anständige Leute *pl* ❷ *(standard, marks)* ordentlich

responsibility *n* Verantwortung *f*

responsible *adj* ❶ verantwortlich ▹ *to be responsible for something* für etwas verantwortlich sein; **It's a responsible job.** Es ist ein verantwortungsvoller Posten. ❷ *(mature)* verantwortungsbewusst ▹ *You should be more responsible.* Du solltest verantwortungsbewusster sein.

rest *n* ❶ *(relaxation)* Pause *f* ▹ *five minutes' rest* eine fünfminütige Pause; **to have a rest** sich ausruhen **[4]** ❷ *(remainder)* Rest *m* (*pl* Reste) ▹ *I'll do the rest.* Ich mache den Rest. ▹ *the rest of the money* der Rest des Geldes; **the rest of them** die anderen
▸ *vb* ❶ *(relax)* sich ausruhen **[4]** (*perf* hat sich ausgeruht) ▹ *She's resting in her room.* Sie ruht sich in ihrem Zimmer aus. ❷ *(not overstrain)* schonen **[38]** ▹ *He has to rest his knee.* Er muss sein Knie schonen. ❸ *(lean)* lehnen **[38]** ▹ *I rested my bike against the window.* Ich habe mein Fahrrad ans Fenster gelehnt.

restaurant *n* Restaurant *nt* (*pl* Restaurants) ▹ *We don't often go to restaurants.* Wir gehen nicht oft ins Restaurant.; **a restaurant car** ein Speisewagen *m*

restless *adj* unruhig

restore *vb* *(building, picture)* restaurieren **[76]** (*perf* hat restauriert)

restrict *vb* beschränken **[18]** (*perf* hat beschränkt)

rest room *n* *(US)* Toilette *f*

result *n* Ergebnis *nt* (*gen* Ergebnisses, *pl* Ergebnisse) ▹ *my exam results* meine Prüfungsergebnisse; **What was the result? — One nil.** Wie ist das Spiel ausgegangen? — Eins zu null.

résumé *n* ❶ Zusammenfassung *f* ▹ *a résumé of her speech* eine Zusammenfassung ihrer Rede ❷ *(US: CV)* Lebenslauf *m* (*pl* Lebensläufe)

retire *vb* in Rente gehen **[29]** (*imperf* ging in Rente, *perf* ist in Rente gegangen) ▹ *He retired last year.* Er ist letztes Jahr in Rente gegangen.

retired *adj* im Ruhestand ▹ *She's retired.* Sie ist im Ruhestand. ▹ *a retired teacher* ein Lehrer im Ruhestand

retirement *n* Ruhestand *m*

return *n* ❶ Rückkehr *f* ▹ *after our return* nach unserer Rückkehr; **the return journey** die Rückfahrt; **a return match** ein Rückspiel *nt* ❷ *(ticket)* Rückfahrkarte *f* ▹ *A return to Freiburg, please.* Eine Rückfahrkarte nach Freiburg, bitte.; **in return** dafür; **in return for** für; **Many happy returns!** Herzlichen Glückwunsch zum Geburtstag!
▸ *vb* ❶ *(come back)* zurückkommen **[40]** (*imperf* kam zurück, *perf* ist zurückgekommen) ▹ *I've just returned from holiday.* Ich bin gerade aus den Ferien zurückgekommen.; **to return home** wieder nach Hause kommen **[40]** ❷ *(go back)* zurückkehren **[15]** (*perf* ist zurückgekehrt) ▹ *He returned to Germany the following year.* Er ist im Jahr danach nach Deutschland zurückgekehrt. ❸ *(give back)* zurückgeben **[28]** (*pres* gibt zurück, *imperf* gab zurück, *perf* hat zurückgegeben) ▹ *She borrows my things and doesn't return them.* Sie leiht sich meine Sachen aus und gibt sie dann nicht zurück.

reunion *n* Treffen *nt* (*pl* Treffen)

reveal *vb* *(truth, facts)* ans Licht bringen **[13]** (*imperf* brachte ans Licht, *perf* hat ans Licht gebracht) ▹ *The survey reveals that many people are overweight.* Die Untersuchung bringt ans Licht, dass viele Menschen Übergewicht haben.; **She refused to reveal the**

whereabouts of her daughter. Sie weigerte sich, den Aufenthaltsort ihrer Tochter preiszugeben.; **It was revealed that ...** Es wurde bekannt gegeben, dass ...

revenge *n* Rache *f* ▷ *in revenge* aus Rache; **to take revenge** sich rächen [48]

reverse *vb (car)* rückwärtsfahren [21] (*pres* fährt rückwärts, *imperf* fuhr rückwärts, *perf* ist rückwärtsgefahren) ▷ *He reversed without looking.* Er fuhr rückwärts ohne zu sehen.; **to reverse the charges** *(telephone)* ein R-Gespräch führen [38]

▶ *adj* umgekehrt ▷ *in reverse order* in umgekehrter Reihenfolge; **in reverse gear** im Rückwärtsgang

review *n* ❶ *(of policy, salary)* Überprüfung *f* ❷ *(of subject)* Prüfung *f*; **to be under review** überprüft werden [91]

revise *vb* den Stoff wiederholen [38] ▷ *I haven't started revising yet.* Ich habe noch nicht angefangen, den Stoff zu wiederholen.; **I've revised my opinion.** Ich habe meine Meinung geändert.

revision *n* Wiederholung des Stoffes *f*; **Have you done a lot of revision?** Hast du schon viel Stoff wiederholt?

revolting *adj* ekelhaft

revolution *n* Revolution *f* ▷ *the French Revolution* die Französische Revolution

reward *n* Belohnung *f*

rewarding *adj* dankbar ▷ *a rewarding job* eine dankbare Arbeit

rewind *vb* zurückspulen [15] (*perf* hat zurückgespult) ▷ *to rewind a cassette* eine Kassette zurückspulen

Rhine *n* Rhein *m*

rhinoceros *n* Nashorn *nt* (*pl* Nashörner)

rhubarb *n* Rhabarber *m* ▷ *a rhubarb tart* ein Rhabarberkuchen

rhythm *n* Rhythmus *m* (*gen* Rhythmus, *pl* Rhythmen)

rib *n* Rippe *f*

ribbon *n* Band *nt* (*pl* Bänder)

rice *n* Reis *m*; **rice pudding** der Milchreis

rich *adj* reich; **the rich** die Reichen *mpl*

rid *vb* **to get rid of** loswerden [91]

ride *n* **to go for a ride (1)** *(on horse)* reiten gehen [29] **(2)** *(on bike)* mit dem Fahrrad fahren [21]; **We went for a bike ride.** Wir haben eine Fahrt mit dem Fahrrad gemacht.; **It's a short bus ride to the town centre.** Die Stadtmitte ist nur eine kurze Busfahrt entfernt.

▶ *vb (on horse)* reiten (*imperf* ritt, *perf* ist geritten) ▷ *I'm learning to ride.* Ich lerne reiten.; **to ride a bike** Fahrrad fahren [21] ▷ *Can you ride a bike?* Kannst du Fahrrad fahren?

rider *n* ❶ *(on horse)* Reiter *m* (*pl* Reiter), Reiterin *f* ▷ *She's a good rider.* Sie ist eine gute Reiterin. ❷ *(on bike)* Fahrradfahrer *m* (*pl* Fahrradfahrer), Fahrradfahrerin *f*

ridiculous *adj* lächerlich ▷ *Don't be ridiculous!* Mach dich nicht lächerlich!

riding *n* Reiten *nt*; **to go riding** reiten gehen [29]; **a riding school** eine Reitschule

rifle *n* Gewehr *nt* (*pl* Gewehre) ▷ *a hunting rifle* ein Jagdgewehr

right *adj, adv*

> There are several ways of translating 'right'. Scan the examples to find one that is similar to what you want to say.

❶ *(correct, suitable)* richtig ▷ *the right answer* die richtige Antwort ▷ *Am I pronouncing it right?* Spreche ich das richtig aus? ▷ *It isn't the right size.* Es ist nicht die richtige Größe. ▷ *We're on the right train.* Wir sind im richtigen Zug. ▷ *It's not right to behave like that.* Es ist nicht richtig, sich so zu benehmen.; **Is this the right road for Hamburg?** Sind wir hier richtig nach Hamburg?; **I think you did the right thing.** Ich glaube, du hast das Richtige getan.; **to be right (1)** *(person)* recht haben [32] ▷ *You were*

a b c d e f g h i j k l m n o p q r s t u v w x y z

right! Du hattest recht! **(2)** *(statement, opinion)* richtig sein [**65**] ▷ *That's right!* Das ist richtig! ❷ *(accurate)* genau ▷ *Do you have the right time?* Haben Sie die genaue Zeit? ❸ *(not left)* rechte ▷ *the right foot* der rechte Fuß ▷ *my right arm* mein rechter Arm ▷ *your right hand* deine rechte Hand ▷ *her right eye* ihr rechtes Auge ❹ *(turn)* rechts ▷ *Turn right at the lights.* Biegen Sie an der Ampel rechts ab.; **Look right!** Sehen Sie nach rechts!; **Right! Let's get started.** Okay! Fangen wir an.; **right away** sofort
▸ *n* ❶ Recht *nt* (*pl* Rechte) ▷ *You've got no right to do that.* Du hast kein Recht, das zu tun. ❷ *(not left)* rechte Seite *f*; **on the right** rechts; **right of way** die Vorfahrt

right-hand *adj* **the right-hand side** die rechte Seite; **It's on the right-hand side.** Es liegt rechts.

right-handed *adj* rechtshändig

rightly *adv* richtig ▷ *If I remember rightly ...* Wenn ich mich richtig erinnere, ... ▷ *She rightly decided that he was lying.* Sie kam zu dem richtigen Schluss, dass er log.

ring *n* ❶ Ring *m* (*pl* Ringe) ▷ *a gold ring* ein goldener Ring ▷ *a diamond ring* ein Diamantring; **a wedding ring** ein Ehering ❷ *(circle)* Kreis *m* (*gen* Kreises, *pl* Kreise) ▷ *to stand in a ring* im Kreis stehen ❸ *(of bell)* Klingeln *nt*; **There was a ring at the door.** Es klingelt.; **to give somebody a ring** jemanden anrufen [**56**]
▸ *vb* ❶ anrufen [**56**] (*imperf* rief an, *perf* hat angerufen) ▷ *Your mother rang.* Deine Mutter hat heute früh angerufen.; **to ring somebody** jemanden anrufen [**56**]; **to ring somebody up** jemanden anrufen [**56**] ❷ klingeln [**34**] ▷ *The phone's ringing.* Das Telefon klingelt.; **to ring the bell** *(doorbell)* klingeln [**34**]; **to ring back** zurückrufen [**56**]

ring binder *n* Ringheft *nt* (*pl* Ringhefte)

ringtone *n* Klingelton *m* (*pl* Klingeltöne)

rinse *vb* spülen [**38**]

riot *n* Krawalle *mpl*
▸ *vb* randalieren [**76**] (*perf* hat randaliert)

rip *vb* zerreißen (*imperf* zerriss, *perf* hat zerrissen) ▷ *I've ripped my jeans.* Ich habe meine Jeans zerrissen. ▷ *My skirt's ripped.* Mein Rock ist zerrissen.

rip off *vb (informal)* ausnehmen [**52**] (*pres* nimmt aus, *imperf* nahm aus, *perf* hat ausgenommen)

rip up *vb* zerreißen (*imperf* zerriss, *perf* hat zerrissen)

ripe *adj* reif

rip-off *n* **It's a rip-off!** *(informal)* Das ist Nepp!

rise *n* ❶ *(in prices, temperature)* Anstieg *m* (*pl* Anstiege) ▷ *a sudden rise in temperature* ein plötzlicher Temperaturanstieg ❷ *(pay rise)* Gehaltserhöhung *f*
▸ *vb* ❶ *(increase)* steigen [**74**] (*imperf* stieg, *perf* ist gestiegen) ▷ *Prices are rising.* Die Preise steigen. ❷ aufgehen [**29**] (*imperf* ging auf, *perf* ist aufgegangen) ▷ *The sun rises early in June.* Die Sonne geht im Juni früh auf.

risk *n* Risiko *nt* (*pl* Risiken); **to take risks** Risiken eingehen [**29**]; **It's at your own risk.** Auf eigene Gefahr.
▸ *vb* riskieren [**76**] (*perf* hat riskiert) ▷ *You risk getting a fine.* Du riskierst einen Strafzettel. ▷ *I wouldn't risk it.* Das würde ich an deiner Stelle nicht riskieren.

rival *n* Rivale *m* (*gen* Rivalen, *pl* Rivalen), Rivalin *f*
▸ *adj* rivalisierend ▷ *a rival gang* eine rivalisierende Bande; **a rival company** ein Konkurrenzunternehmen *nt*

river *n* Fluss *m* (*gen* Flusses, *pl* Flüsse); **the river Rhine** der Rhein

road *n* Straße *f* ▷ *There's a lot of traffic on the roads.* Es herrscht viel Verkehr auf

den Straßen.; **They live across the road.** Sie wohnen gegenüber.
road map *n* Straßenkarte *f*
road rage *n* Aggressivität im Straßenverkehr *f*
road sign *n* Verkehrsschild *nt* (*pl* Verkehrsschilder)
roadworks *npl* Bauarbeiten *fpl*
roast *adj* **roast chicken** das Brathähnchen; **roast potatoes** die Bratkartoffeln; **roast pork** der Schweinebraten; **roast beef** der Rindsbraten
rob *vb* **to rob somebody** jemanden berauben [**7**]; **to rob a bank** eine Bank ausrauben [**4**]; **to rob somebody of something** jemandem etwas rauben [**38**]
robber *n* Räuber *m* (*pl* Räuber), Räuberin *f*; **a bank robber** ein Bankräuber
robbery *n* Raub *m* (*pl* Raube); **a bank robbery** ein Bankraub; **armed robbery** der bewaffnete Raubüberfall
robin *n* Rotkehlchen *nt* (*pl* Rotkehlchen)
robot *n* Roboter *m* (*pl* Roboter)
rock *n* ❶ *(substance)* Fels *m* (*gen* Fels) ▷ *They tunnelled through the rock.* Sie gruben einen Tunnel durch den Fels. ❷ *(boulder)* Felsbrocken *m* (*pl* Felsbrocken) ▷ *I sat on a rock.* Ich saß auf einem Felsbrocken. ❸ *(stone)* Stein *m* (*pl* Steine) ▷ *The crowd threw rocks.* Die Menge fing an, Steine zu werfen. ❹ *(music)* Rock *m* ▷ *a rock concert* ein Rockkonzert ▷ *He's a rock star.* Er ist ein Rockstar. ❺ *(sweet)* Zuckerstange *f* ▷ *a stick of rock* eine Zuckerstange; **rock and roll** der Rock 'n' Roll
▶ *vb* erschüttern [**19**] (*perf* hat erschüttert) ▷ *The explosion rocked the building.* Die Explosion erschütterte das Gebäude.
rocket *n* *(firework, spacecraft)* Rakete *f*
rocking horse *n* Schaukelpferd *nt* (*pl* Schaukelpferde)
rod *n* *(for fishing)* Angel *f*
rode *vb see* **ride**
role *n* Rolle *f*
role play *n* Rollenspiel *nt* (*pl* Rollenspiele) ▷ *to do a role play* ein Rollenspiel machen
roll *n* ❶ Rolle *f* ▷ *a roll of tape* eine Rolle Klebstreifen ▷ *a toilet roll* eine Rolle Toilettenpapier ❷ *(bread)* Brötchen *nt* (*pl* Brötchen)
▶ *vb* rollen [**38**]; **to roll out the pastry** den Teig ausrollen [**4**]
Rollerblade® *n* Rollerblade® *m* (*pl* Rollerblades)
roller coaster *n* Achterbahn *f*
roller skates *npl* Rollschuhe *mpl*
roller-skating *n* Rollschuhlaufen *nt*; **to go roller-skating** Rollschuh laufen [**43**]
Roman *adj, n* *(ancient)* römisch ▷ *a Roman villa* eine römische Villa ▷ *the Roman empire* das Römische Reich; **the Romans** die Römer *mpl*
Roman Catholic *n* Katholik *m* (*gen* Katholiken, *pl* Katholiken), Katholikin *f* ▷ *He's a Roman Catholic.* Er ist Katholik.
romance *n* *(novels)* Liebesroman *m* (*pl* Liebesromane) ▷ *I read a lot of romances.* Ich lese viele Liebesromane.; **a holiday romance** ein Ferienflirt *m*
Romania *n* Rumänien *nt*; **from Romania** aus Rumänien; **to Romania** nach Rumänien
Romanian *adj* rumänisch
romantic *adj* romantisch
roof *n* Dach *nt* (*pl* Dächer)
roof rack *n* Dachträger *m* (*pl* Dachträger)
room *n* ❶ Zimmer *nt* (*pl* Zimmer) ▷ *the biggest room in the house* das größte Zimmer des Hauses ▷ *She's in her room.* Sie ist in ihrem Zimmer. ▷ *the music room* das Musikzimmer; **a single room** ein Einzelzimmer; **a double room** ein Doppelzimmer ❷ *(space)* Platz *m* (*gen* Platzes) ▷ *There's no room for that box.* Es ist kein Platz für diese Schachtel.
root *n* Wurzel *f*

rope *n* Seil *nt* (*pl* Seile)
rose *vb see* **rise**
▸ *n (flower)* Rose *f*
rot *vb* verfaulen [7] (*perf* ist verfault)
rotten *adj (decayed)* faulig ▷ *a rotten apple* ein fauliger Apfel; **rotten weather** *(informal)* das Mistwetter; **That's a rotten thing to do.** Das ist gemein.; **to feel rotten** *(informal)* sich mies fühlen [38]
rough *adj* ❶ rau ▷ *My hands are rough.* Meine Hände sind rau. ▷ *It's a rough area.* Das ist eine raue Gegend. ❷ *(game)* hart ▷ *Rugby's a rough sport.* Rugby ist ein harter Sport. ❸ *(water)* stürmisch ▷ *The sea was rough.* Das Meer war stürmisch. ❹ ungefähr ▷ *I've got a rough idea.* Ich habe eine ungefähre Vorstellung.; **to feel rough** sich nicht wohlfühlen [4]
roughly *adv* ungefähr ▷ *It weighs roughly twenty kilos.* Es wiegt ungefähr zwanzig Kilo.
round *adj, adv, prep* ❶ rund ▷ *a round table* ein runder Tisch ❷ *(around)* um ▷ *We were sitting round the table.* Wir saßen um den Tisch herum. ▷ *She wore a scarf round her neck.* Sie trug einen Schal um den Hals.; **It's just round the corner.** *(very near)* Es ist gleich um die Ecke.; **to go round to somebody's house** bei jemandem vorbeigehen [29]; **to have a look round** sich umsehen [64]; **to go round a museum** sich ein Museum ansehen [64]; **round here** hier in der Gegend; **all round** ringsherum; **all year round** das ganze Jahr über; **round about** *(roughly)* etwa
▸ *n (of tournament, boxing match)* Runde *f* ▷ *a round of golf* eine Runde Golf; **a round of drinks** eine Runde
roundabout *n* ❶ *(at junction)* Kreisverkehr *m* (*pl* Kreisverkehre) ❷ *(at funfair)* Karussell *nt* (*pl* Karussells)
rounders *nsg* Schlagball *m*
round trip *n (US)* Hin- und Rückfahrt *f*; **a round-trip ticket** eine Rückfahrkarte
route *n* Route *f* ▷ *We're planning our route.* Wir planen unsere Route.
route planner *n* Routenplaner *m* (*pl* Routenplaner)
routine *n* Routine *f*
row (1) *n* Reihe *f* ▷ *a row of houses* eine Reihe Häuser ▷ *Our seats are in the front row.* Unsere Plätze sind in der ersten Reihe.; **five times in a row** fünfmal hintereinander
row (2) *n* ❶ *(noise)* Krach *m* ▷ *What's that terrible row?* Was ist das für ein furchtbarer Krach? ❷ *(quarrel)* Streit *m* (*pl* Streite); **to have a row** Streit haben [32]
row *vb* rudern [88] ▷ *We took turns to row.* Wir haben abwechselnd gerudert.
rowboat *n (US)* Ruderboot *nt* (*pl* Ruderboote)
rowing *n (sport)* Rudern *nt* ▷ *My hobby is rowing.* Rudern ist mein Hobby.; **a rowing boat** ein Ruderboot *nt*
royal *adj* königlich ▷ *the royal family* die königliche Familie
rub *vb* ❶ *(stain)* reiben (*imperf* rieb, *perf* hat gerieben) ❷ *(part of body)* sich reiben ▷ *Don't rub your eyes!* Reib dir nicht die Augen!; **I rubbed myself dry with a towel.** Ich rieb mich mit einem Handtuch trocken.; **to rub something out** etwas ausradieren [4]
rubber *n* ❶ Gummi *m* (*pl* Gummis) ▷ *rubber soles* die Gummisohlen ❷ *(eraser)* Radiergummi *m* (*pl* Radiergummis) ▷ *Can I borrow your rubber?* Kann ich deinen Radiergummi ausleihen?; **a rubber band** ein Gummiband *nt*
rubbish *n* ❶ *(refuse)* Müll *m* ▷ *When do they collect the rubbish?* Wann wird der Müll abgeholt? ❷ *(junk)* Krempel *m* ▷ *They sell a lot of rubbish at the market.* Sie verkaufen eine Menge Krempel auf dem Markt. ❸ *(nonsense)* Unsinn *m*

▷ *Don't talk rubbish!* Red keinen Unsinn!; **That's a load of rubbish!** *(informal)* Das ist doch Unsinn!; **This magazine is rubbish!** *(informal)* Die Zeitschrift ist Schrott!; **a rubbish bin** ein Mülleimer *m*; **a rubbish dump** eine Müllkippe
▶ *adj (informal)* miserabel ▷ *They're a rubbish team!* Sie sind eine miserable Mannschaft!

rucksack *n* Rucksack *m* (*pl* Rucksäcke)

rude *adj* ❶ *(impolite)* unhöflich ▷ *It's rude to interrupt.* Es ist unhöflich dazwischenzureden. ▷ *He was very rude to me.* Er war sehr unhöflich zu mir. ❷ *(offensive)* unanständig ▷ *a rude joke* ein unanständiger Witz; **a rude word** ein Schimpfwort *nt*

rug *n* ❶ Teppich *m* (*pl* Teppiche) ▷ *a Persian rug* ein Perserteppich ❷ *(blanket)* Decke *f* ▷ *a tartan rug* eine karierte Decke

rugby *n* Rugby *nt* ▷ *I play rugby.* Ich spiele Rugby.

ruin *n* Ruine *f* ▷ *the ruins of the castle* die Ruine der Burg; **My life is in ruins.** Mein Leben ist ruiniert.
▶ *vb* ruinieren **[76]** (*perf* hat ruiniert) ▷ *You'll ruin your shoes.* Du ruinierst dir deine Schuhe. ▷ *That's far too expensive. You are ruining me!* Das ist viel zu teuer. Du ruinierst mich noch!; **It ruined our holiday.** Es hat uns den Urlaub verdorben.

rule *n* ❶ Regel *f* ▷ *the rules of grammar* die Grammatikregeln; **as a rule** in der Regel ❷ *(regulation)* Vorschrift *f* ▷ *It's against the rules.* Das ist gegen die Vorschriften.
▶ *vb* regieren **[76]** (*perf* hat regiert)

rule out *vb (possibility)* ausschließen (*imperf* schloss aus, *perf* hat ausgeschlossen)

ruler *n* Lineal *nt* (*pl* Lineale) ▷ *Can I borrow your ruler?* Kann ich dein Lineal ausleihen?

rum *n* Rum *m*

rumour *n* Gerücht *nt* (*pl* Gerüchte) ▷ *It's just a rumour.* Es ist nur ein Gerücht.

run *n (in cricket)* Lauf *m* (*pl* Läufe) ▷ *to score a run* einen Lauf machen; **to go for a run** einen Dauerlauf machen **[48]**; **I did a ten-kilometre run.** Ich bin zehn Kilometer gelaufen.; **on the run** auf der Flucht; **in the long run** auf Dauer
▶ *vb* ❶ laufen **[43]** (*pres* läuft, *imperf* lief, *perf* ist gelaufen) ▷ *I ran five kilometres.* Ich bin fünf Kilometer gelaufen.; **to run a marathon** an einem Marathonlauf teilnehmen **[52]** ❷ *(manage)* leiten **[2]** ▷ *He runs a large company.* Er leitet ein großes Unternehmen. ❸ *(organize)* veranstalten **[2]** (*perf* hat veranstaltet) ▷ *They run music courses in the holidays.* Sie veranstalten Musikkurse während der Ferien. ❹ *(water)* laufen **[43]** ▷ *Don't leave the tap running.* Lass das Wasser nicht laufen.; **to run a bath** ein Bad einlaufen lassen **[42]** ❺ *(by car)* fahren **[21]** (*pres* fährt, *imperf* fuhr, *perf* hat gefahren) ▷ *I can run you to the station.* Ich kann dich zum Bahnhof fahren.; **to run away** weglaufen **[43]**; **Time is running out.** Die Zeit wird knapp.; **We ran out of money.** Uns ist das Geld ausgegangen.; **to run somebody over** jemanden überfahren **[21]**; **to get run over** überfahren werden **[91]**

rung *vb see* **ring**

runner *n* Läufer *m* (*pl* Läufer), Läuferin *f*

runner-up *n* Zweite *m* (*gen* Zweiten, *pl* Zweiten), Zweite *f* (*gen* Zweiten)

running *n* Laufen *nt* ▷ *Running is my favourite sport.* Laufen ist mein Lieblingssport.

run-up *n* **in the run-up to Christmas** in der Zeit vor Weihnachten

runway *n* Startbahn *f*

rush *n* Eile *f*; **in a rush** in Eile
▶ *vb* ❶ *(run)* rennen **[55]** (*imperf* rannte, *perf* ist gerannt) ▷ *Everyone rushed outside.* Alle rannten hinaus. ❷ *(hurry)*

sich beeilen [7] (*perf* hat sich beeilt) ▷ *There's no need to rush.* Wir brauchen uns nicht zu beeilen.

rush hour *n* Hauptverkehrszeit *f* ▷ *in the rush hour* in der Hauptverkehrszeit

Russia *n* Russland *nt*; **from Russia** aus Russland; **to Russia** nach Russland

Russian *adj* russisch; **He's Russian.** Er ist Russe.; **She's Russian.** Sie ist Russin.

▸ *n* ❶ *(person)* Russe *m* (*gen* Russen, *pl* Russen), Russin *f* ❷ *(language)* Russisch *nt* (*gen* Russischen)

rust *n* Rost *m*

rusty *adj* rostig ▷ *a rusty bike* ein rostiges Fahrrad; **My German is very rusty.** Mein Deutsch ist ziemlich eingerostet.

rye *n* Roggen *m*; **rye bread** das Roggenbrot

S

Sabbath *n* ❶ *(Christian)* Sonntag *m* (*pl* Sonntage) ❷ *(Jewish)* Sabbat *m* (*pl* Sabbate)

sack *n* Sack *m* (*pl* Säcke); **to get the sack** gefeuert werden [91]

▸ *vb* **to sack somebody** jemanden feuern [34]

sacred *adj* heilig

sacrifice *n* Opfer *nt* (*pl* Opfer)

sad *adj* traurig

saddle *n* Sattel *m* (*pl* Sättel)

saddlebag *n* Satteltasche *f*

safe *n* Safe *m* (*pl* Safes) ▷ *She put the money in the safe.* Sie tat das Geld in den Safe.

▸ *adj* ❶ sicher ▷ *It's perfectly safe.* Es ist völlig sicher. ▷ *This car isn't safe.* Das Auto ist nicht sicher. ❷ *(out of danger)* in Sicherheit ▷ *You're safe now.* Sie sind jetzt in Sicherheit.; **to feel safe** sich sicher fühlen [38]; **safe sex** Safer Sex

safety *n* Sicherheit *f*; **a safety belt** ein Sicherheitsgurt *m*; **a safety pin** eine Sicherheitsnadel

Sagittarius *n* Schütze *m* (*gen* Schützen) ▷ *I'm Sagittarius.* Ich bin Schütze.
said *vb see* **say**
sail *n* Segel *nt* (*pl* Segel) ▶ *vb* ❶ (*travel*) segeln [**34**] (*perf* ist gesegelt) ❷ (*set off*) abfahren [**21**] (*pres* fährt ab, *imperf* fuhr ab, *perf* ist abgefahren) ▷ *The boat sails at eight o'clock.* Das Schiff fährt um acht Uhr ab.
sailing *n* Segeln *nt* ▷ *His hobby is sailing.* Segeln ist sein Hobby.; **to go sailing** segeln gehen [**29**]; **a sailing boat** ein Segelboot *nt*; **a sailing ship** ein Segelschiff *nt*
sailor *n* Matrose *m* (*gen* Matrosen, *pl* Matrosen), Matrosin *f* ▷ *He's a sailor.* Er ist Matrose.
saint *n* Heilige *m* (*gen* Heiligen, *pl* Heiligen), Heilige *f* (*gen* Heiligen) ▷ *a saint (man)* ein Heiliger
sake *n* **for the sake of** um ... willen
salad *n* Salat *m* (*pl* Salate); **salad cream** die Salatmayonnaise; **salad dressing** die Salatsoße
salami *n* Salami *f* (*gen* Salami, *pl* Salamis)
salary *n* Gehalt *nt* (*pl* Gehälter)
sale *n* (*end of season reductions*) Schlussverkauf *m* (*pl* Schlussverkäufe) ▷ *There's a sale on at Harrods.* Bei Harrods ist Schlussverkauf.; **on sale** erhältlich; **'for sale'** 'zu verkaufen'
sales assistant *n* Verkäufer *m* (*pl* Verkäufer), Verkäuferin *f* ▷ *She's a sales assistant.* Sie ist Verkäuferin.
salesman *n* ❶ (*sales rep*) Vertreter *m* (*pl* Vertreter) ▷ *He's a salesman.* Er ist Vertreter.; **a double-glazing salesman** ein Vertreter für Doppelfenster ❷ (*sales assistant*) Verkäufer *m* (*pl* Verkäufer)
saleswoman *n* ❶ (*sales rep*) Vertreterin *f* ▷ *She's a saleswoman.* Sie ist Vertreterin. ❷ (*sales assistant*) Verkäuferin *f*
salmon *n* Lachs *m* (*gen* Lachses, *pl* Lachse)
salon *n* Salon *m* (*pl* Salons) ▷ *a hair salon* ein Friseursalon ▷ *a beauty salon* ein Kosmetiksalon
salt *n* Salz *nt* (*gen* Salzes, *pl* Salze)
salty *adj* salzig
Salvation Army *n* Heilsarmee *f*
same *adj* gleiche ▷ *The same coat is cheaper elsewhere.* Der gleiche Mantel ist anderswo billiger. ▷ *He asked me the same question.* Er hat mir die gleiche Frage gestellt. ▷ *I have the same car.* Ich habe das gleiche Auto. ▷ *We obviously have the same problems.* Wir haben offensichtlich die gleichen Probleme.; **at the same time** zur gleichen Zeit; **It's not the same.** Das ist nicht das Gleiche.; **They're exactly the same.** Sie sind genau gleich.
sample *n* Probe *f* ▷ *a free sample of perfume* eine kostenlose Parfümprobe
sand *n* Sand *m*
sandal *n* Sandale *f* ▷ *a pair of sandals* ein Paar Sandalen
sand castle *n* Sandburg *f*
sandwich *n* **I normally have a sandwich for lunch.** Zu Mittag esse ich meistens ein belegtes Brot.; **a cheese sandwich** ein Käsebrot
sang *vb see* **sing**
sanitary towel *n* Damenbinde *f*
sank *vb see* **sink**
Santa Claus *n* Weihnachtsmann *m* (*pl* Weihnachtsmänner)
sarcastic *adj* sarkastisch
sardine *n* Sardine *f*
sat *vb see* **sit**
satchel *n* Schulranzen *m* (*pl* Schulranzen)
satellite *n* Satellit *m* (*gen* Satelliten, *pl* Satelliten); **a satellite dish** eine Satellitenschüssel; **satellite television** das Satellitenfernsehen
satisfactory *adj* befriedigend
satisfied *adj* zufrieden
sat nav *n* GPS *nt* (*pl* GPS)
Saturday *n* Samstag *m* (*pl* Samstage) ▷ *on Saturday* am Samstag ▷ *every*

Saturday jeden Samstag ▷ *last Saturday* letzten Samstag ▷ *next Saturday* nächsten Samstag; **on Saturdays** samstags; **a Saturday job** ein Samstagsjob

sauce *n* Soße *f*

saucepan *n* Kochtopf *m* (*pl* Kochtöpfe)

saucer *n* Untertasse *f*

Saudi Arabia *n* Saudi-Arabien *nt*; **to Saudi Arabia** nach Saudi-Arabien

sausage *n* Wurst *f* (*pl* Würste); **a sausage roll** eine Wurst im Blätterteig

save *vb* ❶ *(money, time)* sparen [**38**] ▷ *I've saved fifty pounds.* Ich habe fünfzig Pfund gespart. ▷ *I saved money by waiting for the sales.* Ich habe Geld gespart, weil ich bis zum Schlussverkauf gewartet habe. ▷ *We took a taxi to save time.* Wir haben ein Taxi genommen, um Zeit zu sparen. ❷ *(rescue)* retten [**2**] ▷ *Luckily, all the passengers were saved.* Zum Glück wurden alle Passagiere gerettet. ❸ *(on computer)* speichern [**88**] ▷ *I saved the file onto the hard drive.* Ich habe die Datei auf der Festplatte gespeichert.; **to save up** sparen [**38**]

savings *npl* Ersparnisse *fpl* ▷ *She spent all her savings on a computer.* Sie gab all ihre Ersparnisse für einen Computer aus.

savoury *adj (spicy)* pikant

saw *vb see* **see**
▶ *n* Säge *f*

saxophone *n* Saxofon *nt* (*pl* Saxofone) ▷ *I play the saxophone.* Ich spiele Saxofon.

say *vb* sagen [**38**] ▷ *What did he say?* Was hat er gesagt? ▷ *Did you hear what she said?* Hast du gehört, was sie gesagt hat? ▷ *Could you say that again?* Können Sie das noch einmal sagen?; **That goes without saying.** Das ist selbstverständlich.

saying *n* Redensart *f* ▷ *It's just a saying.* Das ist so eine Redensart.

scale *n* ❶ *(of map)* Maßstab *m* (*pl* Maßstäbe) ▷ *a large-scale map* eine Karte großen Maßstabs ❷ *(size, extent)* Ausmaß *nt* (*gen* Ausmaßes, *pl* Ausmaße) ▷ *a disaster on a massive scale* eine Katastrophe von riesigem Ausmaß ❸ *(in music)* Tonleiter *f*

scales *npl (in kitchen, shop)* Waage *fsg*; **bathroom scales** die Personenwaage

scampi *npl* Scampi *pl*

scandal *n* ❶ *(outrage)* Skandal *m* (*pl* Skandale) ▷ *It caused a scandal.* Es hat einen Skandal verursacht. ❷ *(gossip)* Tratsch *m* ▷ *It's just scandal.* Das ist nur Tratsch.

Scandinavia *n* Skandinavien *nt*; **from Scandinavia** aus Skandinavien; **to Scandinavia** nach Skandinavien

Scandinavian *adj* skandinavisch; **He's Scandinavian.** Er ist Skandinavier.

scar *n* Narbe *f*

scarce *adj* ❶ knapp ▷ *scarce resources* knappe Geldmittel ❷ rar ▷ *Jobs are scarce.* Jobs sind rar.

scarcely *adv* kaum ▷ *I scarcely knew him.* Ich kannte ihn kaum.

scare *n* Schrecken *m* (*pl* Schrecken); **a bomb scare** ein Bombenalarm *m*
▶ *vb* **to scare somebody** jemandem Angst machen [**48**]

scarecrow *n* Vogelscheuche *f*

scared *adj* **to be scared** Angst haben [**32**]; **to be scared of** Angst haben [**32**] vor

scarf *n* ❶ *(long)* Schal *m* (*pl* Schals) ❷ *(square)* Halstuch *nt* (*pl* Halstücher)

scary *adj* furchterregend ▷ *It was really scary.* Es war wirklich furchterregend.

scene *n* ❶ *(place)* Ort *m* (*pl* Orte) ▷ *The police were soon on the scene.* Die Polizei war schnell vor Ort. ▷ *the scene of the crime* der Ort des Verbrechens ❷ *(event, sight)* Spektakel *nt* (*pl* Spektakel) ▷ *It was an amazing scene.* Es war ein erstaunliches Spektakel.; **to make a scene** eine Szene machen [**48**]

scenery *n (landscape)* Landschaft *f*

schedule *n* Programm *nt* (*pl* Programme) ▷ *a busy schedule* ein volles

Programm; **on schedule** planmäßig; **to be behind schedule** Verspätung haben [**32**]
scheduled flight *n* Linienflug *m* (*pl* Linienflüge)
scheme *n* ❶ (*idea*) Plan *m* (*pl* Pläne) ▷ *a crazy scheme* ein verrückter Plan ❷ (*project*) Projekt *nt* (*pl* Projekte) ▷ *a council road-widening scheme* ein Straßenverbreiterungsprojekt der Gemeinde
scholarship *n* Stipendium *nt* (*pl* Stipendien)
school *n* Schule *f*; **to go to school** in die Schule gehen [**29**]
schoolbook *n* Schulbuch *nt* (*pl* Schulbücher)
schoolboy *n* Schuljunge *m* (*gen* Schuljungen, *pl* Schuljungen)
schoolchildren *n* Schulkinder *ntpl*
schoolgirl *n* Schulmädchen *nt* (*pl* Schulmädchen)
science *n* Wissenschaft *f*
science fiction *n* Science-Fiction *f*
scientific *adj* wissenschaftlich
scientist *n* (*doing research*) Wissenschaftler *m* (*pl* Wissenschaftler), Wissenschaftlerin *f* ▷ *She's a scientist.* Sie ist Wissenschaftlerin.; **He trained as a scientist.** Er hat eine wissenschaftliche Ausbildung.
scissors *npl* Schere *f* ▷ *a pair of scissors* eine Schere
scooter *n* ❶ Motorroller *m* (*pl* Motorroller) ❷ (*child's toy*) Roller *m* (*pl* Roller)
score *n* Spielstand *m* (*pl* Spielstände); **What's the score?** Wie steht das Spiel?; **The score was three nil.** Es stand drei zu null.
▶ *vb* ❶ (*goal*) schießen (*imperf* schoss, *perf* hat geschossen) ▷ *to score a goal* ein Tor schießen ❷ (*point*) machen [**48**] ▷ *to score six out of ten* sechs von zehn Punkten machen ❸ (*keep score*) zählen [**38**] ▷ *Who's going to score?* Wer zählt?
Scorpio *n* Skorpion *m* ▷ *I'm Scorpio.* Ich bin Skorpion.
Scot *n* Schotte *m* (*gen* Schotten, *pl* Schotten), Schottin *f*
Scotch tape® *n* (*US*) Tesafilm® *m*
Scotland *n* Schottland *nt*; **from Scotland** aus Schottland; **in Scotland** in Schottland; **to Scotland** nach Schottland
Scots *adj* schottisch ▷ *a Scots accent* ein schottischer Akzent
Scotsman *n* Schotte *m* (*gen* Schotten, *pl* Schotten)
Scotswoman *n* Schottin *f*
Scottish *adj* schottisch ▷ *a Scottish accent* ein schottischer Akzent; **He's Scottish.** Er ist Schotte.; **She's Scottish.** Sie ist Schottin.
scout *n* Pfadfinder *m* (*pl* Pfadfinder) ▷ *I'm in the Scouts.* Ich bin bei den Pfadfindern.; **girl scout** die Pfadfinderin
scrambled eggs *npl* Rühreier *ntpl*
scrap *n* ❶ Stück *nt* (*pl* Stücke) ▷ *a scrap of paper* ein Stück Papier ❷ (*fight*) Schlägerei *f*; **scrap iron** das Alteisen
▶ *vb* (*plan, idea*) verwerfen [**92**] (*pres* verwirft, *imperf* verwarf, *perf* hat verworfen) ▷ *The plan was scrapped.* Der Plan wurde verworfen.
scrapbook *n* Album *nt* (*pl* Alben)
scratch *vb* kratzen [**36**] ▷ *Stop scratching!* Hör auf zu kratzen!
▶ *n* (*on skin*) Kratzer *m* (*pl* Kratzer); **to start from scratch** von vorn anfangen [**23**]
scream *n* Schrei *m* (*pl* Schreie)
▶ *vb* schreien [**62**] (*imperf* schrie, *perf* hat geschrien)
screen *n* ❶ (*cinema*) Leinwand *f* (*pl* Leinwände) ❷ (*television, computer*) Bildschirm *m* (*pl* Bildschirme) ▷ *An error message appeared on the screen.* Auf dem Bildschirm erschien eine Fehlermeldung.
screen saver *n* (*computer*) Bildschirmschoner *m* (*pl* Bildschirmschoner)

screw *n* Schraube *f*
screwdriver *n* Schraubenzieher *m* (*pl* Schraubenzieher)
scribble *vb* kritzeln [**34**]
scrub *vb* schrubben [**48**] ▷ *He scrubbed the floor.* Er schrubbte den Boden.
sculpture *n* Skulptur *f*
sea *n* Meer *nt* (*pl* Meere)
seafood *n* Meeresfrüchte *fpl* ▷ *I don't like seafood.* Ich mag Meeresfrüchte nicht.
seagull *n* Möwe *f*
seal *n* ❶ (*animal*) Seehund *m* (*pl* Seehunde) ❷ (*on container*) Siegel *nt* (*pl* Siegel)
▶ *vb* ❶ (*container*) versiegeln [**84**] (*perf* hat versiegelt) ❷ (*letter*) zukleben [**4**] (*perf* hat zugeklebt)
seaman *n* Seemann *m* (*pl* Seeleute)
search *vb* durchsuchen [**18**] (*perf* hat durchsucht) ▷ *They searched the woods for her.* Sie haben den Wald nach ihr durchsucht.; **to search for something** nach etwas suchen [**48**]
▶ *n* Suche *f*
search party *n* Suchtrupp *m* (*pl* Suchtrupps)
seashore *n* Strand *m* (*pl* Strände) ▷ *on the seashore* am Strand
seasick *adj* seekrank ▷ *to be seasick* seekrank sein
seaside *n* **at the seaside** am Meer; **We're going to the seaside.** Wir fahren ans Meer.
season *n* Jahreszeit *f* ▷ *What's your favourite season?* Welche Jahreszeit hast du am liebsten?; **out of season** außerhalb der Saison; **during the holiday season** während der Ferienzeit; **a season ticket** eine Dauerkarte
seat *n* Platz *m* (*gen* Platzes, *pl* Plätze)
seat belt *n* Sicherheitsgurt *m* (*pl* Sicherheitsgurte); **Fasten your seat belt!** Schnalle dich an!
seaweed *n* Alge *f*
second *adj* zweite ▷ *the second man from the right* der zweite Mann von rechts ▷ *her second husband* ihr zweiter Mann ▷ *on the second page* auf der zweiten Seite ▷ *my second child* mein zweites Kind; **to come second** (*in race*) Zweiter werden [**91**]; **the second of August** der zweite August
▶ *n* Sekunde *f* ▷ *It'll only take a second.* Es dauert nur eine Sekunde.
secondary school *n* ❶ Gymnasium *nt* (*pl* Gymnasien) ❷ Realschule *f*

Germans always specify the type of secondary school. **Gymnasium** takes nine years and leads to **Abitur**, **Realschule** takes six years and leads to **mittlere Reife**.

second-class *adj, adv* ❶ (*ticket, compartment*) zweiter Klasse ▷ *to travel second-class* zweiter Klasse fahren ❷ (*stamp, letter*) normal

In Germany there is no first-class or second-class post. However, letters cost more to send than postcards, so you have to remember to say what you are sending when buying stamps. There is also an express service.

▷ *to send something second-class* etwas mit normaler Post schicken
second-hand *adj* gebraucht; **a second-hand car** ein Gebrauchtwagen *m*
secondly *adv* zweitens ▷ *firstly ... secondly ...* erstens ... zweitens ...
secret *adj* geheim ▷ *a secret mission* eine geheime Mission
▶ *n* Geheimnis *nt* (*gen* Geheimnisses, *pl* Geheimnisse) ▷ *It's a secret.* Es ist ein Geheimnis. ▷ *Can you keep a secret?* Kannst du ein Geheimnis für dich behalten?; **in secret** heimlich
secretary *n* Sekretär *m* (*pl* Sekretäre), Sekretärin *f* ▷ *She's a secretary.* Sie ist Sekretärin.
secretly *adv* heimlich
section *n* ❶ Teil *m* (*pl* Teile) ▷ *I passed the written section of the exam.* Ich habe den schriftlichen Teil der Prüfung

bestanden. ❷ *(in shop)* Abteilung *f* ▷ *the food section* die Lebensmittelabteilung

security *n* Sicherheit *f* ▷ *airport security* die Sicherheit auf den Flughäfen; **to have no job security** keinen sicheren Job haben [**32**]; **a security guard** ein Sicherheitsbeamter

security guard *n* Wächter *m (pl* Wächter), Wächterin *f*; **She's a security guard.** Sie ist beim Sicherheitsdienst.

see *vb* sehen [**64**] ▷ *I can't see.* Ich kann nichts sehen. ▷ *I saw him yesterday.* Ich habe ihn gestern gesehen. ▷ *Have you seen him?* Hast du ihn gesehen?; **See you!** *(informal)* Tschüs!; **See you soon!** Bis bald!; **to see to something** sich um etwas kümmern [**38**]

seed *n* Samen *m (pl* Samen); **sunflower seeds** die Sonnenblumenkerne *mpl*

seem *vb* scheinen [**57**] *(imperf* schien, *perf* hat geschienen) ▷ *The shop seemed to be closed.* Das Geschäft schien geschlossen zu haben. ▷ *That seems like a good idea.* Das scheint eine gute Idee zu sein.; **She seems tired.** Sie wirkt müde.; **It seems that ...** Es sieht so aus, dass ...; **There seems to be a problem.** Anscheinend gibt's ein Problem.

seen *vb see* **see**

seesaw *n* Wippe *f*

seldom *adv* selten

select *vb* auswählen [**4**] *(perf* hat ausgewählt)

selection *n* Auswahl *f*

self-catering *adj* **a self-catering apartment** eine Wohnung für Selbstversorger

self-confidence *n* Selbstvertrauen *nt* ▷ *He hasn't got much self-confidence.* Er hat nicht viel Selbstvertrauen.

self-conscious *adj* gehemmt

self-defence *n* Selbstverteidigung *f* ▷ *self-defence classes* der Selbstverteidigungskurs; **She killed him in self-defence.** Sie hat ihn in Notwehr getötet.

self-employed *adj* **to be self-employed** selbstständig sein [**65**]; **the self-employed** die Selbstständigen *mpl*

selfish *adj* egoistisch ▷ *Don't be so selfish.* Sei nicht so egoistisch.

self-service *adj* **It's self-service.** *(café, shop)* Da ist Selbstbedienung.; **a self-service restaurant** ein Selbstbedienungsrestaurant *nt*

sell *vb* verkaufen [**84**] *(perf* hat verkauft) ▷ *He sold it to me.* Er hat es mir verkauft.; **to sell off** verkaufen [**84**]; **The tickets are all sold out.** Alle Karten sind ausverkauft.; **The tickets sold out in three hours.** Die Karten waren in drei Stunden ausverkauft.

sell-by date *n* Verfallsdatum *nt (pl* Verfallsdaten)

Sellotape® *n* Tesafilm® *m*

semi *n* Doppelhaushälfte *f* ▷ *We live in a semi.* Wir wohnen in einer Doppelhaushälfte.

semicircle *n* Halbkreis *m (gen* Halbkreises, *pl* Halbkreise)

semicolon *n* Strichpunkt *m (pl* Strichpunkte)

semi-detached house *n* Doppelhaushälfte *f* ▷ *We live in a semi-detached house.* Wir wohnen in einer Doppelhaushälfte.

semi-final *n* Halbfinale *nt (pl* Halbfinale)

semi-skimmed milk *n* fettarme Milch *f*

send *vb* schicken [**48**] ▷ *She sent me money.* Sie hat mir Geld geschickt.; **to send back** zurückschicken [**4**]; **to send off (1)** *(goods, letter)* abschicken [**4**] **(2)** *(in sports match)* vom Platz schicken [**48**] ▷ *He was sent off.* Er wurde vom Platz geschickt.; **to send off for something (1)** *(free)* etwas kommen lassen [**42**] ▷ *I've sent off for a brochure.* Ich habe mir eine Broschüre kommen lassen. **(2)** *(paid for)* etwas bestellen [7] ▷ *She sent off for a DVD.* Sie hat eine DVD bestellt.; **to send out** verschicken [7]

senior *adj* leitend ▷ *senior management* die leitenden Angestellten; **senior school** die weiterführende Schule; **senior pupils** die Oberstufenschüler

senior citizen *n* Senior *m* (*pl* Senioren), Seniorin *f*

sensational *adj* sensationell

sense *n* ❶ *(faculty)* Sinn *m* (*pl* Sinne) ▷ *the five senses* die fünf Sinne ▷ *the sixth sense* der sechste Sinn; **the sense of touch** der Tastsinn; **the sense of smell** der Geschmacksinn; **sense of humour** der Sinn für Humor ❷ *(wisdom)* Verstand *m*; **Use your common sense!** Benutze deinen gesunden Menschenverstand!; **It makes sense.** Das macht Sinn.; **It doesn't make sense.** Das macht keinen Sinn.

sensible *adj* vernünftig ▷ *Be sensible!* Sei vernünftig! ▷ *It would be sensible to check first.* Es wäre vernünftig, zuerst nachzusehen.

> Be careful not to translate **sensible** by **sensibel**.

sensitive *adj* sensibel ▷ *She's very sensitive.* Sie ist sehr sensibel.

sent *vb see* **send**

sentence *n* ❶ Satz *m* (*gen* Satzes, *pl* Sätze) ▷ *What does this sentence mean?* Was bedeutet dieser Satz? ❷ *(judgment)* Urteil *nt* (*pl* Urteile) ▷ *The court will pass sentence tomorrow.* Das Gericht wird morgen das Urteil verkünden. ❸ *(punishment)* Strafe *f* ▷ *the death sentence* die Todesstrafe; **He got a life sentence.** Er hat lebenslänglich bekommen.
▶ *vb* verurteilen [84] (*perf* hat verurteilt) ▷ *to sentence somebody to life imprisonment* jemanden zu einer lebenslangen Gefängnisstrafe verurteilen ▷ *to sentence somebody to death* jemanden zum Tode verurteilen

sentimental *adj* sentimental

separate *adj* getrennt ▷ *separate rooms* getrennte Zimmer; **I wrote it on a separate sheet.** Ich habe es auf ein extra Blatt geschrieben.; **on separate occasions** bei verschiedenen Gelegenheiten; **on two separate occasions** zweimal
▶ *vb* ❶ trennen [38] ❷ *(married couple)* sich trennen [38]

separately *adv* extra

separation *n* Trennung *f*

September *n* September *m* ▷ *in September* im September

sequel *n* *(book, film)* Fortsetzung *f*

sergeant *n* ❶ *(army)* Feldwebel *m* (*pl* Feldwebel), Feldwebelin *f* ❷ *(police)* Polizeimeister *m* (*pl* Polizeimeister), Polizeimeisterin *f*

serial *n* Fernsehserie *f*

series *nsg* ❶ Sendereihe *f* ▷ *a TV series* eine Sendereihe im Fernsehen ❷ *(of numbers)* Reihe *f*

serious *adj* ❶ ernst ▷ *You look very serious.* Du siehst sehr ernst aus.; **Are you serious?** Ist das dein Ernst? ❷ *(illness, mistake)* schwer

> Be careful not to translate **serious** by **seriös**.

seriously *adv* im Ernst ▷ *No, but seriously ...* Nein, aber im Ernst ...; **to take somebody seriously** jemanden ernst nehmen [52]; **seriously injured** schwer verletzt; **Seriously?** Im Ernst?

servant *n* Diener *m* (*pl* Diener), Dienerin *f*

serve *vb* ❶ servieren [76] (*perf* hat serviert) ▷ *Dinner is served.* Das Essen ist serviert. ❷ aufschlagen [59] (*pres* schlägt auf, *imperf* schlug auf, *perf* hat aufgeschlagen) ▷ *It's Murray's turn to serve.* Murray schlägt auf. ❸ *(prison sentence)* absitzen [68] (*imperf* saß ab, *perf* hat abgesessen); **to serve time** im Gefängnis sein [65]; **It serves you right.** Das geschieht dir recht.
▶ *n* *(tennis)* Aufschlag *m* (*pl* Aufschläge); **It's your serve.** Du hast Aufschlag.

service *vb (car, washing machine)* überholen [18] *(perf* hat überholt) ▸ *n* ❶ Bedienung *f* ▷ *Service is included.* Die Bedienung ist inklusive. ❷ *(of car)* Inspektion *f* ❸ *(church service)* Gottesdienst *m (pl* Gottesdienste); **the Fire Service** die Feuerwehr; **the armed services** die Streitkräfte

service charge *n* Bedienung *f* ▷ *There's no service charge.* Die Bedienung wird nicht extra berechnet.

service station *n* Tankstelle *f*

serviette *n* Serviette *f*

session *n* Sitzung *f*

set *n* Satz *m (gen* Satzes, *pl* Sätze) ▷ *a set of keys* ein Satz Schlüssel ▷ *Williams won the set. (tennis)* Williams hat den Satz gewonnen.; **a chess set** ein Schachspiel *nt*; **a train set** eine Spielzeugeisenbahn ▸ *vb* ❶ *(alarm clock)* stellen [38] ▷ *I set the alarm for seven o'clock.* Ich habe den Wecker auf sieben Uhr gestellt. ❷ *(record)* aufstellen [4] *(perf* hat aufgestellt) ▷ *The world record was set last year.* Der Weltrekord wurde letztes Jahr aufgestellt. ❸ *(sun)* untergehen [29] *(imperf* ging unter, *perf* ist untergegangen) ▷ *The sun was setting.* Die Sonne ging unter.; **The film is set in Morocco.** Der Film spielt in Marokko.; **to set off** aufbrechen [11]; **to set out** aufbrechen [11]; **to set the table** den Tisch decken [38]

settee *n* Sofa *nt (pl* Sofas)

settle *vb* ❶ *(problem)* lösen [38] ❷ *(argument)* beilegen [4] *(perf* hat beigelegt); **to settle an account** eine Rechnung begleichen; **to settle down** *(calm down)* ruhiger werden [91]; **Settle down!** Beruhige dich!; **to settle in** sich einleben [4]; **to settle on something** sich für etwas entscheiden

seven *num* sieben ▷ *She's seven.* Sie ist sieben.

seventeen *num* siebzehn ▷ *He's seventeen.* Er ist siebzehn.

seventeenth *adj* siebzehnte ▷ *the seventeenth of August* der siebzehnte August

seventh *adj* siebte ▷ *the seventh floor* der siebte Stock ▷ *the seventh of August* der siebte August

seventy *num* siebzig ▷ *She's seventy.* Sie ist siebzig.

several *adj, pron* einige ▷ *several schools* einige Schulen ▷ *several of them* einige von ihnen

sew *vb* nähen [38]; **to sew up** *(tear)* flicken [48]

sewing *n* Nähen *nt*; **I like sewing.** Ich nähe gern.; **a sewing machine** eine Nähmaschine

sewn *vb see* **sew**

sex *n* Geschlecht *nt (pl* Geschlechter); **to have sex with somebody** mit jemandem Verkehr haben [32]; **sex education** der Aufklärungsunterricht

sexism *n* Sexismus *m (gen* Sexismus)

sexist *adj* sexistisch

sexual *adj* sexuell ▷ *sexual harassment* die sexuelle Belästigung; **sexual discrimination** die Diskriminierung aufgrund des Geschlechts

sexuality *n* Sexualität *f*

sexy *adj* sexy

shabby *adj* schäbig

shade *n* ❶ Schatten *m (pl* Schatten) ▷ *in the shade* im Schatten ❷ *(colour)* Ton *m (pl* Töne) ▷ *a shade of blue* ein Blauton

shadow *n* Schatten *m (pl* Schatten)

shake *vb* ❶ ausschütteln [4] *(perf* hat ausgeschüttelt) ▷ *She shook the rug.* Sie hat den Teppich ausgeschüttelt. ❷ schütteln [34] ▷ *She shook the bottle.* Sie hat die Flasche geschüttelt. ❸ *(tremble)* zittern [88] ▷ *He was shaking with fear.* Er zitterte vor Angst.; **to shake one's head** *(in refusal)* den Kopf schütteln [34]; **to shake hands with somebody** jemandem die Hand geben [28]

a b c d e f g h i j k l m n o p q r **s** t u v w x y z

shaken *adj* mitgenommen ▷ *I was feeling a bit shaken.* Ich war etwas mitgenommen.

shall *vb* **Shall I shut the window?** Soll ich das Fenster zumachen?; **Shall we ask him to come with us?** Sollen wir ihn fragen, ob er mitkommt?

shallow *adj (water, pool)* flach

shambles *nsg* Chaos *nt (gen* Chaos) ▷ *It's a complete shambles.* Es ist ein völliges Chaos.

shame *n* Schande *f* ▷ *The shame of it!* Diese Schande!; **What a shame!** Wie schade!; **It's a shame that ...** Es ist schade, dass ...

shampoo *n* Shampoo *nt (pl* Shampoos) ▷ *a bottle of shampoo* eine Flasche Shampoo

shape *n* Form *f*

share *n* ❶ *(in company)* Aktie *f* ▷ *They've got shares in BT.* Sie haben Aktien von BT. ❷ *(portion)* Anteil *m (pl* Anteile) ▶ *vb* teilen [**38**] ▷ *to share a room with somebody* ein Zimmer mit jemandem teilen; **to share out** verteilen [**84**]

shark *n* Hai *m (pl* Haie)

sharp *adj* ❶ *(razor, knife)* scharf ▷ *I need a sharper knife.* Ich brauche ein schärferes Messer. ❷ *(spike, point)* spitz ❸ *(clever)* gescheit ▷ *She's very sharp.* Sie ist sehr gescheit.; **at two o'clock sharp** Punkt zwei Uhr

shave *vb (have a shave)* sich rasieren [**76**] *(perf* hat sich rasiert); **to shave one's legs** sich die Beine rasieren [**76**]

shaver *n* **an electric shaver** ein Elektrorasierer *m*

shaving cream *n* Rasiercreme *f (pl* Rasiercremes)

shaving foam *n* Rasierschaum *m*

she *pron* sie ▷ *She's very nice.* Sie ist sehr nett.

shed *n* Schuppen *m (pl* Schuppen)

she'd = **she had**; **she would**

sheep *n* Schaf *nt (pl* Schafe) ▷ *dozens of sheep* Dutzende von Schafen

sheepdog *n* Schäferhund *m (pl* Schäferhunde)

sheer *adj* rein ▷ *It's sheer greed.* Das ist die reine Gier.

sheet *n (on bed)* Leintuch *nt (pl* Leintücher); **a sheet of paper** ein Blatt Papier *nt*

shelf *n* Regal *nt (pl* Regale)

shell *n* ❶ *(on beach)* Muschel *f* ❷ *(of egg, nut)* Schale *f* ❸ *(explosive)* Granate *f*

she'll = **she will**

shellfish *n* Schalentier *nt (pl* Schalentiere)

shelter *n* **to take shelter** sich unterstellen [**4**]; **a bus shelter** eine überdachte Bushaltestelle

shelves *npl see* **shelf**

shepherd *n* Schäfer *m (pl* Schäfer), Schäferin *f*

sherry *n* Sherry *m (pl* Sherrys)

she's = **she is**; **she has**

Shetland Islands *npl* Shetlandinseln *fpl*

shift *n* Schicht *f* ▷ *His shift starts at eight o'clock.* Seine Schicht fängt um acht Uhr an. ▷ *the night shift* die Nachtschicht; **to do shift work** Schicht arbeiten [**2**] ▶ *vb (move)* verschieben *(imperf* verschob, *perf* hat verschoben) ▷ *I couldn't shift the wardrobe.* Ich konnte den Schrank nicht verschieben.; **Shift yourself!** *(informal)* Jetzt aber los!

shin *n* Schienbein *nt (pl* Schienbeine)

shine *vb* scheinen [**57**] *(imperf* schien, *perf* hat geschienen) ▷ *The sun was shining.* Die Sonne schien.

shiny *adj* glänzend

ship *n* Schiff *nt (pl* Schiffe)

shirt *n* ❶ *(man's)* Hemd *nt (pl* Hemden) ❷ *(woman's)* Bluse *f*

shiver *vb* zittern [**88**]

shock *n* Schock *m (pl* Schocks); **to get a shock (1)** *(surprise)* einen Schock bekommen [**40**] **(2)** *(electric)* einen Schlag bekommen [**40**]; **an electric**

shock ein elektrischer Schlag ▶ *vb (upset)* schockieren [76] (*perf* hat schockiert) ▷ *I was shocked by the tragedy.* Ich war über die Tragödie schockiert. ▷ *Nothing shocks me any more.* Mich schockiert nichts mehr.

shocked *adj* schockiert ▷ *He'll be shocked if you say that.* Wenn du das sagst, wird er schockiert sein.

shocking *adj* schockierend ▷ *It's shocking!* Es ist schockierend! ▷ *a shocking waste* eine schockierende Verschwendung

shoe *n* Schuh *m* (*pl* Schuhe)

shoelace *n* Schnürsenkel *m* (*pl* Schnürsenkel)

shoe polish *n* Schuhcreme *f* (*pl* Schuhcremes)

shoe shop *n* Schuhgeschäft *nt* (*pl* Schuhgeschäfte)

shone *vb see* **shine**

shook *vb see* **shake**

shoot *vb* ❶ *(gun, in football)* schießen (*imperf* schoss, *perf* hat geschossen) ▷ *Don't shoot!* Nicht schießen!; **to shoot at somebody** auf jemanden schießen; **He was shot in the leg.** *(wounded)* Er wurde ins Bein getroffen.; **to shoot an arrow** einen Pfeil abschießen ❷ *(kill)* erschießen (*imperf* erschoss, *perf* hat erschossen) ▷ *He was shot by a sniper.* Er wurde von einem Heckenschützen erschossen.; **to shoot oneself** *(dead)* sich erschießen ❸ *(film)* drehen [38] ▷ *The film was shot in Prague.* Der Film wurde in Prag gedreht.

shooting *n* ❶ Schüsse *mpl* ▷ *They heard shooting.* Sie hörten Schüsse.; **a shooting** eine Schießerei ❷ *(hunting)* Jagd *f* ▷ *to go shooting* auf die Jagd gehen

shop *n* Geschäft *nt* (*pl* Geschäfte) ▷ *a sports shop* ein Sportgeschäft

shop assistant *n* Verkäufer *m* (*pl* Verkäufer), Verkäuferin *f* ▷ *She's a shop assistant.* Sie ist Verkäuferin.

shopkeeper *n* Ladenbesitzer *m* (*pl* Ladenbesitzer), Ladenbesitzerin *f* ▷ *He's a shopkeeper.* Er ist Ladenbesitzer.

shoplifting *n* Ladendiebstahl *m* (*pl* Ladendiebstähle)

shopping *n (purchases)* Einkäufe *mpl* ▷ *Can you get the shopping from the car?* Kannst du die Einkäufe aus dem Auto holen?; **I love shopping.** Ich gehe gern einkaufen.; **to go shopping** einkaufen gehen [29]; **a shopping bag** eine Einkaufstasche; **a shopping centre** ein Einkaufszentrum *nt*

shop window *n* Schaufenster *nt* (*pl* Schaufenster)

shore *n* Küste *f*; **on shore** an Land

short *adj* ❶ kurz ▷ *a short skirt* ein kurzer Rock ▷ *short hair* kurze Haare ▷ *a short break* eine kurze Pause ▷ *a short walk* ein kurzer Spaziergang; **too short** zu kurz ❷ *(person)* klein ▷ *She's quite short.* Sie ist ziemlich klein.; **to be short of something** knapp an etwas sein [65]; **In short, the answer's no.** Kurz, die Antwort ist nein.; **at short notice** kurzfristig

shortage *n* Mangel *m* ▷ *a water shortage* ein Wassermangel

short cut *n* Abkürzung *f* ▷ *I took a short cut.* Ich habe eine Abkürzung genommen.

shortly *adv* ❶ bald ▷ *He'll be arriving shortly.* Er kommt bald. ❷ kurz ▷ *shortly after the accident* kurz nach dem Unfall

shorts *npl* Shorts *pl* ▷ *a pair of shorts* ein Paar Shorts

short-sighted *adj* kurzsichtig

shot *vb see* **shoot** ▶ *n* ❶ *(gunshot)* Schuss *m* (*gen* Schusses, *pl* Schüsse) ❷ *(photo)* Foto *nt* (*pl* Fotos) ▷ *a shot of the church* ein Foto der Kirche ❸ *(injection)* Spritze *f*

shotgun *n* Flinte *f*

should *vb* sollen [69] ▷ *You should take more exercise.* Du solltest mehr Sport machen.; **He should be there by now.** Er müsste jetzt da sein.; **That**

a b c d e f g h i j k l m n o p q r s t u v w x y z

shouldn't be too hard. Das dürfte nicht zu schwer sein.; **I should have told you before.** Ich hätte es dir vorher sagen sollen.

When 'should' means 'would' use **würde**.

▷ *I should go if I were you.* Ich würde gehen, wenn ich du wäre.; **I should be so lucky!** Das wäre zu schön!

shoulder *n* Schulter *f*; **a shoulder bag** eine Umhängetasche

shouldn't = **should not**

shout *vb* schreien [**62**] (*imperf* schrie, *perf* hat geschrien) ▷ *Don't shout!* Schrei doch nicht so! ▷ *'Go away!' he shouted.* 'Geh weg!' schrie er.
▶ *n* Schrei *m* (*pl* Schreie)

shovel *n* Schaufel *f*

show *n* ❶ *(performance)* Show *f* (*pl* Shows) ❷ *(programme)* Sendung *f* ❸ *(exhibition)* Ausstellung *f*
▶ *vb* ❶ zeigen [**38**]; **to show somebody something** jemandem etwas zeigen [**38**] ❷ beweisen (*imperf* bewies, *perf* hat bewiesen) ▷ *She showed great courage.* Sie hat großen Mut bewiesen.; **It shows.** Das sieht man.; **to show off** *(informal)* angeben [**28**]; **to show up** *(turn up)* aufkreuzen [**4**]

shower *n* ❶ Dusche *f*; **to have a shower** duschen [**48**] ❷ *(of rain)* Schauer *m* (*pl* Schauer)

shown *vb see* **show**

show-off *n* Angeber *m* (*pl* Angeber), Angeberin *f*

shrank *vb see* **shrink**

shriek *vb* kreischen [**38**]

shrimps *npl* Krabben *fpl*

shrink *vb (clothes, fabric)* einlaufen [**43**] (*pres* läuft ein, *imperf* lief ein, *perf* ist eingelaufen)

Shrove Tuesday *n* Fastnachtsdienstag *m*

shrug *vb* **He shrugged his shoulders.** Er zuckte mit den Schultern.

shrunk *vb see* **shrink**

shuffle *vb* **to shuffle the cards** die Karten mischen [**48**]

shut *vb* zumachen [**4**] (*perf* hat zugemacht) ▷ *What time do you shut?* Wann machen Sie zu? ▷ *What time do the shops shut?* Wann machen die Geschäfte zu?; **to shut down** schließen ▷ *The cinema shut down last year.* Das Kino hat letztes Jahr geschlossen.; **to shut up (1)** *(close)* verschließen **(2)** *(be quiet)* den Mund halten [**33**] ▷ *Shut up!* Halt den Mund!

shuttle *n* ❶ *(plane)* Pendelflugzeug *nt* (*pl* Pendelflugzeuge) ❷ *(train)* Pendelzug *m* (*pl* Pendelzüge) ❸ *(bus)* Pendelbus *m* (*gen* Pendelbusses, *pl* Pendelbusse)

shuttlecock *n (badminton)* Federball *m* (*pl* Federbälle)

shy *adj* schüchtern

Sicily *n* Sizilien *nt*; **from Sicily** aus Sizilien; **to Sicily** nach Sizilien

sick *adj* ❶ *(ill)* krank ▷ *He was sick for four days.* Er war vier Tage krank. ❷ *(joke, humour)* übel ▷ *That's really sick!* Das war wirklich übel!; **to be sick** *(vomit)* sich übergeben [**28**]; **I feel sick.** Mir ist schlecht.; **to be sick of something** etwas leid sein [**65**]

sickness *n* Krankheit *f*

side *n* ❶ Seite *f* ▷ *He was driving on the wrong side of the road.* Er fuhr auf der falschen Straßenseite. ▷ *He's on my side.* Er ist auf meiner Seite.; **side by side** nebeneinander; **the side entrance** der Seiteneingang; **to take sides** Partei ergreifen ❷ *(edge)* Rand *m* (*pl* Ränder) ▷ *by the side of the road* am Straßenrand ❸ *(of pool, river)* Ufer *nt* (*pl* Ufer) ▷ *by the side of the lake* am Ufer des Sees

sideboard *n* Anrichte *f*

side effect *n* Nebeneffekt *m* (*pl* Nebeneffekte)

sidewalk *n (US)* Bürgersteig *m* (*pl* Bürgersteige)

sideways *adv* ❶ *(look)* von der Seite ❷ *(move, be facing)* zur Seite; **sideways on** von der Seite

sieve *n* Sieb *nt* (*pl* Siebe)
sigh *n* Seufzer *m* (*pl* Seufzer)
▶ *vb* seufzen [**36**]
sight *n* Anblick *m* ▷ *an amazing sight* ein irrer Anblick; **in sight** in Sicht; **out of sight** nicht zu sehen; **to have poor sight** schlechte Augen haben [**32**]; **to know somebody by sight** jemanden vom Sehen kennen [**39**]; **the sights** *(tourist spots)* die Sehenswürdigkeiten
sightseeing *n* Sightseeing *nt*; **to go sightseeing** Sightseeing machen [**48**]
sign *n* ❶ *(notice)* Schild *nt* (*pl* Schilder) ▷ *There was a big sign saying 'private'.* Da war ein großes Schild, auf dem 'privat' stand.; **a road sign** ein Verkehrsschild ❷ *(gesture, indication)* Zeichen *nt* (*pl* Zeichen) ▷ *There's no sign of improvement.* Es gibt kein Zeichen einer Besserung.; **What sign are you?** *(star sign)* Was für ein Sternzeichen sind Sie?
▶ *vb* unterschreiben [**61**] (*imperf* unterschrieb, *perf* hat unterschrieben); **to sign on (1)** *(as unemployed)* sich arbeitslos melden [**54**] **(2)** *(for course)* sich einschreiben [**61**]
signal *n* Signal *nt* (*pl* Signale)
▶ *vb* **to signal to somebody** jemandem ein Zeichen geben [**28**]
signature *n* Unterschrift *f*
significance *n* Bedeutung *f*
significant *adj* bedeutend
sign language *n* Zeichensprache *f*
signpost *n* Wegweiser *m* (*pl* Wegweiser)
silence *n* Stille *f* ▷ *There was absolute silence.* Es herrschte absolute Stille.
silent *adj* still
silk *n* Seide *f*
▶ *adj* seiden ▷ *a silk scarf* ein seidener Schal
silky *adj* seidig
silly *adj* dumm ▷ *That's the silliest excuse I've ever heard.* Das ist die dümmste Ausrede, die ich je gehört habe.
silver *n* Silber *nt* ▷ *a silver medal* eine Silbermedaille
similar *adj* ähnlich ▷ *My sister is very similar to me.* Meine Schwester ist mir sehr ähnlich.
simple *adj* ❶ einfach ▷ *It's very simple.* Das ist sehr einfach. ❷ *(simple-minded)* einfältig ▷ *He's a bit simple.* Er ist etwas einfältig.
simply *adv* einfach ▷ *It's simply not possible.* Es ist einfach nicht möglich.
sin *n* Sünde *f*
▶ *vb* sündigen [**84**]
since *prep, adv, conj* ❶ seit ▷ *since Christmas* seit Weihnachten ▷ *I haven't seen her since she left.* Ich habe sie nicht gesehen, seit sie weggezogen ist.; **since then** seither; **ever since** seitdem ❷ *(because)* da ▷ *Since you're tired, let's stay at home.* Da du müde bist, bleiben wir doch zu Hause.
sincere *adj* aufrichtig
sincerely *adv* **Yours sincerely ...** Mit freundlichen Grüßen ...
sing *vb* singen [**66**] (*imperf* sang, *perf* hat gesungen) ▷ *He sang out of tune.* Er hat falsch gesungen. ▷ *Have you ever sung this tune before?* Hast du die Melodie schon mal gesungen?
singer *n* Sänger *m* (*pl* Sänger), Sängerin *f*
singing *n* Singen *nt*
single *adj (unmarried)* alleinstehend; **a single room** ein Einzelzimmer *nt*; **not a single thing** absolut nichts
▶ *n* ❶ *(ticket)* einfache Fahrkarte *f* ▷ *A single to Bonn, please.* Eine einfache Fahrkarte nach Bonn, bitte. ❷ *(record)* Single *f* (*pl* Singles); **a CD single** eine CD-Single
single parent *n* **She's a single parent.** Sie ist alleinerziehende Mutter.; **a single parent family** eine Einelternteilfamilie
singular *n* Singular *m* (*pl* Singulare) ▷ *in the singular* im Singular
sink *n* Spüle *f*
▶ *vb* sinken [**67**] (*imperf* sank, *perf* ist gesunken)

a b c d e f g h i j k l m n o p q r **s** t u v w x y z

sir *n*

In German no form of address is normally used apart from **Sie**.

▷ *Would you like to order, Sir?* Möchten Sie bestellen?; **Yes sir.** Ja.

siren *n* Sirene *f*

sister *n* Schwester *f* ▷ *my little sister* meine kleine Schwester ▷ *I wanted to speak to the sister on the ward.* Ich wollte die Stationsschwester sprechen.

sister-in-law *n* Schwägerin *f*

sit *vb* ❶ *(be sitting)* sitzen [**68**] (*imperf* saß, *perf* hat gesessen) ▷ *She was sitting on the floor.* Sie saß auf dem Boden. ❷ *(sit down)* sich setzen [**36**] ▷ *Sit on that chair.* Setz dich auf den Stuhl.; **to sit down** sich setzen [**36**]; **to be sitting** sitzen [**68**]; **to sit an exam** eine Prüfung machen [**48**]

site *n* ❶ Stätte *f* ▷ *an archaeological site* eine archäologische Stätte; **the site of the accident** der Unfallort ❷ *(campsite)* Campingplatz *m* (*gen* Campingplatzes, *pl* Campingplätze); **a building site** eine Baustelle

sitting room *n* Wohnzimmer *nt* (*pl* Wohnzimmer)

situation *n* Situation *f*

six *num* sechs ▷ *He's six.* Er ist sechs.

sixteen *num* sechzehn ▷ *He's sixteen.* Er ist sechzehn.

sixteenth *adj* sechzehnte ▷ *the sixteenth of August* der sechzehnte August

sixth *adj* sechste ▷ *the sixth floor* der sechste Stock ▷ *the sixth of August* der sechste August

sixty *num* sechzig ▷ *She's sixty.* Sie ist sechzig.

size *n*

Germany uses the European system for clothing and shoe sizes.

❶ *(of object, clothing)* Größe *f* ▷ *What size do you take?* Welche Größe haben Sie?; **I'm a size ten.** Ich habe Größe achtunddreißig. ❷ *(of shoes)* Schuhgröße *f* ▷ *I take size six.* Ich habe Schuhgröße neununddreißig.

skate *vb* ❶ *(ice-skate)* Schlittschuh laufen [**43**] (*pres* läuft Schlittschuh, *imperf* lief Schlittschuh, *perf* ist Schlittschuh gelaufen) ❷ *(roller-skate)* Rollschuh laufen [**43**] (*pres* läuft Rollschuh, *imperf* lief Rollschuh, *perf* ist Rollschuh gelaufen)

skateboard *n* Skateboard *nt* (*pl* Skateboards)

skateboarding *n* Skateboardfahren *nt*; **to go skateboarding** Skateboard fahren [**21**]

skates *npl* ❶ Schlittschuhe *mpl* ❷ *(roller skates)* Rollschuhe *mpl*

skating *n* ❶ Schlittschuhlaufen *nt*; **to go skating** Schlittschuh laufen [**43**]; **a skating rink** eine Eisbahn ❷ *(roller-skating)* Rollschuhlaufen *nt*; **to go skating** Rollschuh laufen [**43**]; **a skating rink** eine Rollschuhbahn

skeleton *n* Skelett *nt* (*pl* Skelette)

sketch *n (drawing)* Skizze *f* ▶ *vb* skizzieren [**76**] (*perf* hat skizziert)

ski *vb* Ski fahren [**21**] (*pres* fährt Ski, *imperf* fuhr Ski, *perf* ist Ski gefahren) ▷ *Can you ski?* Kannst du Ski fahren? ▶ *n* Ski *m* (*pl* Skier); **ski boots** die Skistiefel; **a ski lift** ein Skilift *m*; **ski pants** die Skihose *sg*; **a ski pole** ein Skistock *m*; **a ski slope** eine Skipiste; **a ski suit** ein Skianzug *m*

skid *vb* schleudern [**88**] (*perf* ist geschleudert)

skier *n* Skifahrer *m* (*pl* Skifahrer), Skifahrerin *f*

skiing *n* Skifahren *nt*; **to go skiing** Ski fahren [**21**]; **to go on a skiing holiday** in den Skiurlaub fahren [**21**]

skilful *adj* geschickt

skill *n* Können *nt* ▷ *a lot of skill* viel Können

skilled *adj* **a skilled worker** ein Facharbeiter *m*

skimmed milk *n* Magermilch *f*

skin *n* Haut *f* (*pl* Häute); **skin cancer** der Hautkrebs

skinhead *n* Skinhead *m* (*pl* Skinheads)

> **der Skinhead** is also used for women.

skinny *adj* mager

skip *n* (*container*) Container *m* (*pl* Container)

▸ *vb* ❶ (*with rope*) seilspringen [71] (*perf* ist seilgesprungen) ❷ auslassen [42] (*pres* lässt aus, *imperf* ließ aus, *perf* hat ausgelassen) ▷ *to skip a meal* eine Mahlzeit auslassen; **I skipped the maths lesson.** Ich habe die Mathestunde geschwänzt.

skirt *n* Rock *m* (*pl* Röcke)

skive *vb* (*be lazy*) faulenzen [36]; **to skive off** (*informal*) schwänzen [36]

skull *n* Schädel *m* (*pl* Schädel)

sky *n* Himmel *m* (*pl* Himmel)

skyscraper *n* Wolkenkratzer *m* (*pl* Wolkenkratzer)

slam *vb* zuknallen [4] (*perf* hat/ist zugeknallt)

> For the perfect tense use **haben** when the verb has an object and **sein** when there is no object.

▷ *The door slammed.* Die Tür ist zugeknallt. ▷ *She slammed the door.* Sie hat die Tür zugeknallt.

slang *n* Slang *m* (*pl* Slangs)

slap *n* Ohrfeige *f*

▸ *vb* **to slap somebody** jemandem einen Klaps geben [28]

slate *n* ❶ Schiefer *m* (*pl* Schiefer) ❷ (*for roof*) Schieferziegel *m* (*pl* Schieferziegel)

sledge *n* Schlitten *m* (*pl* Schlitten)

sledging *n* **to go sledging** Schlitten fahren [21]

sleep *n* Schlaf *m* ▷ *I need some sleep.* Ich brauche Schlaf.; **to go to sleep** einschlafen [58]

▸ *vb* schlafen [58] (*pres* schläft, *imperf* schlief, *perf* hat geschlafen) ▷ *I couldn't sleep.* Ich konnte nicht schlafen.; **to sleep with somebody** mit jemandem schlafen [58]; **to sleep together** miteinander schlafen [58]; **to sleep around** mit jedem schlafen [58]; **to sleep in** verschlafen [58]

sleeping bag *n* Schlafsack *m* (*pl* Schlafsäcke)

sleeping pill *n* Schlaftablette *f*

sleepover *n* Übernachtung *f*; **to have a sleepover** bei Freunden übernachten [2]

sleepy *adj* schläfrig; **to feel sleepy** schläfrig sein [65]; **a sleepy little village** ein verschlafenes kleines Dorf

sleet *n* Schneeregen *m*

▸ *vb* **It's sleeting.** Es fällt Schneeregen.

sleeve *n* ❶ Ärmel *m* (*pl* Ärmel) ▷ *long sleeves* lange Ärmel ▷ *short sleeves* kurze Ärmel ❷ (*record sleeve*) Hülle *f*

slept *vb see* **sleep**

slice *n* Scheibe *f*

▸ *vb* aufschneiden [60] (*imperf* schnitt auf, *perf* hat aufgeschnitten)

slide *n* ❶ (*in playground*) Rutschbahn *f* ❷ (*photo*) Dia *nt* (*pl* Dias) ❸ (*hair slide*) Klemme *f*

▸ *vb* rutschen [48] (*perf* ist gerutscht)

slight *adj* klein ▷ *a slight problem* ein kleines Problem ▷ *a slight improvement* eine kleine Verbesserung

slightly *adv* etwas

slim *adj* schlank

▸ *vb* (*be on a diet*) abnehmen [52] (*pres* nimmt ab, *imperf* nahm ab, *perf* hat abgenommen) ▷ *I'm slimming.* Ich nehme gerade ab.

sling *n* Schlinge *f* ▷ *She had her arm in a sling.* Sie hatte den Arm in der Schlinge.

slip *n* ❶ (*mistake*) Schnitzer *m* (*pl* Schnitzer) ❷ (*underskirt*) Unterrock *m* (*pl* Unterröcke); **a slip of paper** ein Zettel *m*; **a slip of the tongue** ein Versprecher *m*

▸ *vb* ausrutschen [4] (*perf* ist ausgerutscht) ▷ *He slipped on the ice.* Er ist auf dem Eis ausgerutscht.; **to slip up** (*make a mistake*) einen Fehler machen [48]

slipper *n* Hausschuh *m* (*pl* Hausschuhe) ▷ *a pair of slippers* ein Paar Hausschuhe
slippery *adj* glatt
slip-up *n* Schnitzer *m* (*pl* Schnitzer); **There's been a slip-up.** Da ist etwas schiefgelaufen.
slope *n* Abhang *m* (*pl* Abhänge)
slot *n* Schlitz *m* (*gen* Schlitzes, *pl* Schlitze)
slot machine *n* ❶ *(for gambling)* Geldspielautomat *m* (*gen* Geldspielautomaten, *pl* Geldspielautomaten) ❷ *(vending machine)* Automat *m* (*gen* Automaten, *pl* Automaten)
slow *adj, adv* langsam ▷ *He's a bit slow.* Er ist etwas langsam.; **to go slow** (1) *(person)* langsam gehen [29] (2) *(car)* langsam fahren [21] ▷ *Drive slower!* Fahr langsamer!; **My watch is slow.** Meine Uhr geht nach.
slow down *vb* verlangsamen [84] (*perf* hat verlangsamt)
slowly *adv* langsam
slug *n (animal)* Nacktschnecke *f*
slum *n* Slum *m* (*pl* Slums)
smack *n (slap)* Klaps *m* (*gen* Klapses, *pl* Klapse)
▶ *vb* **to smack somebody** jemandem einen Klaps geben [28]
small *adj* klein; **small change** das Kleingeld

> Be careful not to translate **small** by **schmal**.

smart *adj* ❶ *(elegant)* schick ❷ *(clever)* intelligent ▷ *a smart idea* eine intelligente Idee
smartphone *n* Smartphone *nt* (*pl* Smartphones)
smashing *adj (informal)* klasse ▷ *I think he's smashing.* Ich finde, er ist klasse.

> **klasse** is invariable.

▷ *a smashing film* ein klasse Film
smell *n* Geruch *m* (*pl* Gerüche); **the sense of smell** der Geruchsinn
▶ *vb* ❶ stinken (*imperf* stank, *perf* hat gestunken) ▷ *That old dog really smells!* Der alte Hund stinkt!; **to smell of something** nach etwas riechen ❷ *(detect)* riechen (*imperf* roch, *perf* hat gerochen) ▷ *I can't smell anything.* Ich kann nichts riechen.
smelly *adj* stinkend; **He's got smelly feet.** Seine Füße stinken.
smelt *vb see* **smell**
smile *n* Lächeln *nt*
▶ *vb* lächeln [34]
smiley *n* Smiley *nt* (*pl* Smileys)
smoke *n* Rauch *m*
▶ *vb* rauchen [48] ▷ *I don't smoke.* Ich rauche nicht. ▷ *He smokes cigars.* Er raucht Zigarren.
smoker *n* Raucher *m* (*pl* Raucher), Raucherin *f*
smoking *n* Rauchen *nt* ▷ *to give up smoking* mit dem Rauchen aufhören ▷ *Smoking is bad for you.* Rauchen schadet der Gesundheit.; **'no smoking'** 'Rauchen verboten'
smooth *adj* ❶ *(surface)* glatt ❷ *(person)* aalglatt
smoothie *n* Smoothie *m* (*pl* Smoothies)
SMS *n (= short message service)* SMS *f*
smudge *n* Dreck *m*
smuggle *vb* schmuggeln [34]
smuggler *n* Schmuggler *m* (*pl* Schmuggler), Schmugglerin *f*
smuggling *n* Schmuggeln *nt*
snack *n* Snack *m* (*pl* Snacks) ▷ *to have a snack* einen Snack zu sich nehmen
snack bar *n* Imbissstube *f*
snail *n* Schnecke *f*
snake *n* Schlange *f*
snap *vb (break)* brechen [11] (*pres* bricht, *imperf* brach, *perf* ist gebrochen) ▷ *The branch snapped.* Der Zweig brach.; **to snap one's fingers** mit dem Finger schnipsen [48]
snatch *vb* **to snatch something from somebody** jemandem etwas entreißen; **My bag was snatched.** Man hat mir meine Handtasche entrissen.

sneak *vb* **to sneak in** sich hineinschleichen; **to sneak out** sich hinausschleichen; **to sneak up on somebody** an jemanden heranschleichen
sneeze *vb* niesen [**38**]
sniff *vb* ❶ schniefen [**38**] ▷ *Stop sniffing!* Hör auf zu schniefen! ❷ schnüffeln [**88**] an ▷ *The dog sniffed my hand.* Der Hund schnüffelte an meiner Hand.; **to sniff glue** schnüffeln [**88**]
snob *n* Snob *m* (*pl* Snobs)
der Snob is also used for women.
▷ *She is such a snob.* Sie ist ein furchtbarer Snob.
snooker *n* Snooker *nt* ▷ *to play snooker* Snooker spielen
snooze *n* Nickerchen *nt* (*pl* Nickerchen) ▷ *to have a snooze* ein Nickerchen machen
snore *vb* schnarchen [**48**]
snow *n* Schnee *m*
▶ *vb* schneien [**38**] ▷ *It's snowing.* Es schneit.
snowball *n* Schneeball *m* (*pl* Schneebälle)
snowboarding *n* Snowboarding *nt*
snowflake *n* Schneeflocke *f*
snowman *n* Schneemann *m* (*pl* Schneemänner) ▷ *to build a snowman* einen Schneemann machen
so *conj, adv* ❶ also ▷ *The shop was closed, so I went home.* Das Geschäft war zu, also ging ich nach Hause. ▷ *It rained, so I got wet.* Es hat geregnet, also bin ich nass geworden. ▷ *So, have you always lived in London?* Also, hast du schon immer in London gewohnt?; **So what?** Na und? ❷ so ▷ *It was so heavy!* Es war so schwer! ▷ *It's not so heavy!* Es ist nicht so schwer! ▷ *He was talking so fast I couldn't understand.* Er hat so schnell geredet, dass ich nichts verstanden habe. ▷ *How's your father? — Not so good.* Wie geht's deinem Vater? — Nicht so gut. ▷ *He's like his sister but not so clever.* Er ist wie seine Schwester, aber nicht so klug.; **so much** (*a lot*) so sehr ▷ *I love you so much.* Ich liebe dich so sehr!; **so much ...** so viel ... ▷ *I've got so much work.* Ich habe so viel Arbeit.; **so many ...** so viele ... ▷ *I've got so many things to do today.* Ich muss heute so viele Dinge erledigen.; **so do I** ich auch ▷ *I love horses. — So do I.* Ich mag Pferde. — Ich auch.; **so have we** wir auch ▷ *I've been to Hamburg. — So have we.* Ich war schon einmal in Hamburg. — Wir auch.; **I think so.** Ich glaube schon.; **I hope so.** Hoffentlich.; **That's not so.** Das ist nicht so.; **so far** bis jetzt ▷ *It's been easy so far.* Bis jetzt war es einfach.; **so far so good** so weit, so gut; **ten or so people** so etwa zehn Leute; **at five o'clock or so** so gegen fünf Uhr
soak *vb* einweichen [**4**] (*perf* hat eingeweicht)
soaking *adj* völlig durchnässt ▷ *We were soaking.* Wir waren völlig durchnässt.; **soaking wet** patschnass
soap *n* Seife *f*
soap opera *n* Seifenoper *f*
soap powder *n* Waschpulver *nt* (*pl* Waschpulver)
sob *vb* schluchzen [**36**] ▷ *She was sobbing.* Sie schluchzte.
sober *adj* nüchtern
sober up *vb* nüchtern werden [**91**] (*pres* wird nüchtern, *imperf* wurde nüchtern, *perf* ist nüchtern geworden)
soccer *n* Fußball *m* ▷ *to play soccer* Fußball spielen; **a soccer player** ein Fußballspieler *m*
social *adj* sozial ▷ *social problems* soziale Probleme; **a social class** eine gesellschaftliche Schicht; **I have a good social life.** Ich komme viel unter Leute.
socialism *n* Sozialismus *m* (*gen* Sozialismus)
socialist *adj* sozialistisch
▶ *n* Sozialist *m* (*gen* Sozialisten, *pl* Sozialisten), Sozialistin *f* ▷ *She's a Socialist.* Sie ist Sozialistin.

social security *n* ❶ *(money)* Sozialhilfe *f*; **to be on social security** Sozialhilfe bekommen [**40**] ❷ *(organization)* Sozialversicherung *f*

social worker *n* Sozialarbeiter *m* (*pl* Sozialarbeiter), Sozialarbeiterin *f* ▷ *She's a social worker.* Sie ist Sozialarbeiterin.

society *n* ❶ Gesellschaft *f* ▷ *We live in a multicultural society.* Wir leben in einer multikulturellen Gesellschaft. ❷ Verein *m* (*pl* Vereine) ▷ *the Royal Society for the Prevention of Cruelty to Animals* der Tierschutzverein; **a drama society** eine Theatergruppe

sociology *n* Soziologie *f*

sock *n* Socke *f*

socket *n* Steckdose *f*

sofa *n* Sofa *nt* (*pl* Sofas)

soft *adj* weich; **soft cheese** der Weichkäse; **to be soft on somebody** *(be kind to)* nachsichtig mit jemandem sein [**65**]; **a soft drink** ein alkoholfreies Getränk; **soft drugs** weiche Drogen; **a soft option** eine bequeme Lösung

software *n* Software *f*

soil *n* Boden *m* (*pl* Böden)

solar *adj* **solar eclipse** die Sonnenfinsternis

solar power *n* Sonnenenergie *f*

sold *vb see* **sell**

soldier *n* Soldat *m* (*gen* Soldaten, *pl* Soldaten), Soldatin *f* ▷ *He's a soldier.* Er ist Soldat.

solicitor *n* ❶ *(for lawsuits)* Rechtsanwalt *m* (*pl* Rechtsanwälte), Rechtsanwältin *f* ▷ *He's a solicitor.* Er ist Rechtsanwalt. ❷ *(for property, wills)* Notar *m* (*pl* Notare), Notarin *f* ▷ *She's a solicitor.* Sie ist Notarin.

solid *adj* ❶ stabil ▷ *a solid wall* eine stabile Wand ❷ massiv ▷ *solid gold* massives Gold; **for three hours solid** drei geschlagene Stunden lang

solo *n* Solo *nt* (*pl* Soli) ▷ *a guitar solo* ein Gitarrensolo

solution *n* Lösung *f*

solve *vb* lösen [**38**]

some *adj, pron* ❶ ein paar

Use **ein paar** with plural nouns.

▷ *some nice pictures* ein paar nette Bilder ▷ *I only sold some of them.* Ich habe nur ein paar verkauft.; **Some people say that ...** Manche Leute sagen, dass ...; **some day** eines Tages; **some day next week** irgendwann nächste Woche ❷ *(some but not all)* einige ▷ *Are these mushrooms poisonous? — Only some.* Sind diese Pilze giftig? — Nur einige.; **I only took some of it.** Ich habe nur etwas davon genommen.; **I'm going to buy some stamps. Do you want some too?** Ich kaufe Briefmarken. Willst du auch welche?; **Would you like some coffee? — No thanks, I've got some.** Möchten Sie Kaffee? — Nein danke, ich habe schon welchen.

'some' is frequently not translated.

▷ *Would you like some bread?* Möchtest du Brot? ▷ *Have you got some mineral water?* Haben Sie Mineralwasser?

somebody *pron* jemand ▷ *Somebody stole my bag.* Jemand hat meine Tasche gestohlen.

somehow *adv* irgendwie ▷ *I'll do it somehow.* Ich mache es irgendwie. ▷ *Somehow I don't think he believed me.* Irgendwie hat er mir anscheinend nicht geglaubt.

someone *pron* jemand

something *pron* etwas ▷ *something special* etwas Besonderes ▷ *Wear something warm.* Zieh etwas Warmes an.; **That's really something!** Das ist echt toll!; **It cost a hundred pounds, or something like that.** Es kostet hundert Pfund, oder so in der Gegend.; **His name is Phil or something.** Er heißt Phil oder so ähnlich.

sometime *adv* mal ▷ *You must come and see us sometime.* Du musst uns mal besuchen.; **sometime last month** irgendwann letzten Monat

sometimes *adv* manchmal ▷ *Sometimes I think she hates me.* Manchmal denke ich, sie hasst mich.
somewhere *adv* irgendwo ▷ *I've left my keys somewhere.* Ich habe irgendwo meine Schlüssel liegen lassen. ▷ *I'd like to live somewhere sunny.* Ich würde gern irgendwo leben, wo es sonnig ist.
son *n* Sohn *m* (*pl* Söhne)
song *n* Lied *nt* (*pl* Lieder)
son-in-law *n* Schwiegersohn *m* (*pl* Schwiegersöhne)
soon *adv* bald ▷ *very soon* sehr bald; **soon afterwards** kurz danach; **as soon as possible** sobald wie möglich
sooner *adv* früher ▷ *a bit sooner* etwas früher ▷ *sooner or later* früher oder später
soprano *n* Sopran *m* (*pl* Soprane)
sore *adj* **It's sore.** Es tut weh.; **That's a sore point.** Das ist ein wunder Punkt.
▶ *n* Wunde *f*
sorry *adj* **I'm really sorry.** Es tut mir wirklich leid.; **Sorry!** Entschuldigung!; **I feel sorry for her.** Sie tut mir leid.
sort *n* Art *f* ▷ *There are different sorts of mushrooms.* Es gibt verschiedene Arten von Pilzen.; **what sort of ... (1)** was für ein ... ▷ *What sort of cake is that?* Was für ein Kuchen ist das? ▷ *What sort of bike have you got?* Was für ein Fahrrad hast du? **(2)** was für eine ... ▷ *What sort of school do you go to?* In was für eine Schule gehst du?
sort out *vb* ❶ *(objects)* sortieren **[76]** (*perf* hat sortiert) ❷ *(problems)* lösen **[38]**
soul *n* ❶ *(spirit)* Seele *f* ❷ *(music)* Soul *m*
sound *n* ❶ *(noise)* Geräusch *nt* (*pl* Geräusche); **Don't make a sound!** Still!; **I heard the sound of footsteps.** Ich hörte Schritte. ❷ Lautstärke *f* ▷ *Can I turn the sound down?* Kann ich die Lautstärke runterdrehen?
▶ *vb* klingen (*imperf* klang, *perf* hat geklungen) ▷ *That sounds interesting.* Das klingt interessant.; **It sounds as if she's doing well at school.** Allem Anschein nach ist sie gut in der Schule.; **That sounds like a good idea.** Das scheint eine gute Idee zu sein.
▶ *adj, adv* gut ▷ *That's sound advice.* Das ist ein guter Rat.; **to be sound asleep** fest schlafen **[58]**
soundtrack *n* Soundtrack *m* (*pl* Soundtracks)
soup *n* Suppe *f* ▷ *vegetable soup* die Gemüsesuppe
sour *adj* sauer
south *adj, adv* nach Süden ▷ *We were travelling south.* Wir sind nach Süden gefahren.; **the south coast** die Südküste; **a south wind** ein Südwind *m*; **south of** südlich von
▶ *n* Süden *m* ▷ *in the south* im Süden; **in the South of Germany** in Süddeutschland
South Africa *n* Südafrika *nt*; **from South Africa** aus Südafrika; **to South Africa** nach Südafrika
South America *n* Südamerika *nt*; **from South America** aus Südamerika; **to South America** nach Südamerika
South American *n* Südamerikaner *m* (*pl* Südamerikaner), Südamerikanerin *f*
▶ *adj* südamerikanisch
southeast *n* Südosten *m*; **southeast England** Südostengland *nt*
southern *adj* südlich ▷ *the southern part of the island* der südliche Teil der Insel; **Southern England** Südengland *nt*
South Pole *n* Südpol *m*
southwest *n* Südwesten *m*; **southwest Germany** Südwestdeutschland *nt*
souvenir *n* Souvenir *nt* (*pl* Souvenirs) ▷ *a souvenir shop* ein Souvenirgeschäft
soya *n* Soja *f*
soy sauce *n* Sojasoße *f*
space *n* ❶ Platz *m* (*gen* Platzes) ▷ *There's enough space.* Es ist genug Platz da.; **a parking space** ein Parkplatz ❷ *(outer space)* Raum *m*
spacecraft *n* Raumschiff *nt* (*pl* Raumschiffe)

spade *n* Spaten *m* (*pl* Spaten); **spades** *(in cards)* das Pik
Spain *n* Spanien *nt*; **from Spain** aus Spanien; **in Spain** in Spanien; **to Spain** nach Spanien
Spaniard *n* Spanier *m* (*pl* Spanier), Spanierin *f*
spaniel *n* Spaniel *m* (*pl* Spaniel)
Spanish *adj* spanisch; **He's Spanish.** Er ist Spanier.; **She's Spanish.** Sie ist Spanierin.
▸ *n (language)* Spanisch *nt* (*gen* Spanischen); **the Spanish** die Spanier *mpl*
spanner *n* Schraubenschlüssel *m* (*pl* Schraubenschlüssel)
spare *vb* **Can you spare a moment?** Hast du mal einen Moment Zeit?; **I can't spare the time.** Ich habe die Zeit nicht.; **There's no room to spare.** Es ist kein Platz übrig.; **We arrived with time to spare.** Wir waren zu früh da.
Be careful not to translate **to spare** by **sparen**.
▸ *n* Ersatzteil *nt* (*pl* Ersatzteile); **I've lost my key. — Have you got a spare?** Ich habe meinen Schlüssel verloren. — Hast du einen Ersatzschlüssel?
▸ *adj* **spare batteries** die Ersatzbatterien *fpl*; **a spare part** ein Ersatzteil *nt*; **a spare room** ein Gästezimmer *nt*; **spare time** die Freizeit ▹ *What do you do in your spare time?* Was machen Sie in Ihrer Freizeit?; **spare wheel** das Reserverad
sparkling *adj (water)* mit Kohlensäure; **sparkling wine** der Sekt
sparrow *n* Spatz *m* (*gen* Spatzen, *pl* Spatzen)
spat *vb see* **spit**
speak *vb* sprechen **[70]** (*pres* spricht, *imperf* sprach, *perf* hat gesprochen) ▹ *Do you speak English?* Sprechen Sie Englisch?; **to speak to somebody** mit jemandem reden **[54]**; **spoken German** gesprochenes Deutsch
speak up *vb* lauter sprechen **[70]** (*pres* spricht, *imperf* sprach, *perf* hat gesprochen)
speaker *n* ❶ *(loudspeaker)* Lautsprecher *m* (*pl* Lautsprecher) ❷ *(in debate)* Redner *m* (*pl* Redner), Rednerin *f*
special *adj* besondere ▹ *a special occasion* ein besonderer Anlass
specialist *n* Fachmann *m* (*pl* Fachleute), Fachfrau *f*
speciality *n* Spezialität *f*
specialize *vb* sich spezialisieren **[76]** (*perf* hat sich spezialisiert) ▹ *We specialize in skiing equipment.* Wir haben uns auf Skiausrüstung spezialisiert.
specially *adv* ❶ besonders ▹ *It can be very cold here, specially in winter.* Es kann hier sehr kalt werden, besonders im Winter. ❷ speziell ▹ *It's specially designed for teenagers.* Das ist speziell für Teenager gedacht.; **not specially** nicht besonders
species *nsg* Art *f*
specific *adj* ❶ *(particular)* speziell ▹ *certain specific issues* gewisse spezielle Fragen ❷ *(precise)* genau ▹ *Could you be more specific?* Könnten Sie sich etwas genauer ausdrücken?
specs *npl* Brille *fsg* ▹ *a pair of specs* eine Brille
spectacles *npl* Brille *fsg* ▹ *a pair of spectacles* eine Brille
spectacular *adj* spektakulär
spectator *n* Zuschauer *m* (*pl* Zuschauer), Zuschauerin *f*
speech *n* Rede *f* ▹ *to make a speech* eine Rede halten
speechless *adj* sprachlos ▹ *speechless with admiration* sprachlos vor Bewunderung ▹ *I was speechless.* Ich war sprachlos.
speed *n* ❶ Gang *m* (*pl* Gänge); **a three-speed bike** ein Dreigangrad *nt* ❷ Geschwindigkeit *f* ▹ *at top speed* mit Höchstgeschwindigkeit; **to speed up** schneller werden **[91]**
speedboat *n* Schnellboot *nt* (*pl* Schnellboote)

speed limit *n* Geschwindigkeitsbegrenzung *f* ▷ *to break the speed limit* die Geschwindigkeitsbegrenzung überschreiten

spell *vb* ❶ *(in writing)* schreiben [**61**] (*imperf* schrieb, *perf* hat geschrieben) ▷ *How do you spell that?* Wie schreibt man das? ❷ *(out loud)* buchstabieren [**76**] (*perf* hat buchstabiert) ▷ *Can you spell that please?* Können Sie das bitte buchstabieren?; **I can't spell.** Ich kann keine Rechtschreibung.
▶ *n* **to cast a spell on somebody** jemanden verhexen [**7**]; **to be under somebody's spell** von jemandem wie verzaubert sein [**65**]

spelling *n* Rechtschreibung *f* ▷ *My spelling is terrible.* Meine Rechtschreibung ist furchtbar.; **a spelling mistake** ein Rechtschreibfehler *m*

spelt *vb see* **spell**

spend *vb* ❶ *(money)* ausgeben [**28**] (*pres* gibt aus, *imperf* gab aus, *perf* hat ausgegeben) ❷ *(time)* verbringen [**13**] (*imperf* verbrachte, *perf* hat verbracht) ▷ *He spent a month in Italy.* Er verbrachte einen Monat in Italien.

> Be careful not to translate **to spend** by **spenden**.

spice *n* Gewürz *nt* (*gen* Gewürzes, *pl* Gewürze)

spicy *adj* scharf ▷ *Indian food's much spicier than German food.* Indisches Essen ist viel schärfer als deutsches.

spider *n* Spinne *f*

spill *vb (tip over)* verschütten [**7**] ▷ *He spilled his coffee.* Er hat seinen Kaffee verschüttet.; **to get spilt** verschüttet werden [**91**]

spinach *n* Spinat *m*

spine *n* Rückgrat *nt* (*pl* Rückgrate)

spire *n* Kirchturm *m* (*pl* Kirchtürme)

spirit *n* ❶ *(courage)* Mut *m* ❷ *(energy)* Energie *f*; **to be in good spirits** gut gelaunt sein [**65**]

spirits *npl* Spirituosen *pl*

spiritual *adj* geistlich ▷ *the spiritual leader of Tibet* der geistliche Führer Tibets

spit *vb* spucken [**38**]; **to spit something out** etwas ausspucken [**4**]; **It's spitting.** Es tröpfelt.

spite *n* **in spite of** trotz; **out of spite** aus Gehässigkeit
▶ *vb* ärgern [**88**] ▷ *He just did it to spite me.* Er tat es nur, um mich zu ärgern.

spiteful *adj* ❶ *(action)* gemein ❷ *(person)* gehässig

splash *vb* bespritzen [**7**] (*perf* hat bespritzt) ▷ *Don't splash me!* Bespritz mich nicht!
▶ *n* Platsch *m* ▷ *I heard a splash.* Ich hörte einen Platsch.; **a splash of colour** ein Farbfleck *m*

splendid *adj* wunderbar

splinter *n* Splitter *m* (*pl* Splitter)

split *vb* ❶ zerteilen [**95**] (*perf* hat zerteilt) ▷ *He split the wood with an axe.* Er zerteilte das Holz mit einer Axt. ❷ zerbrechen [**11**] (*pres* zerbricht, *imperf* zerbrach, *perf* ist zerbrochen) ▷ *The ship hit a rock and split in two.* Das Schiff lief auf einen Fels auf und zerbrach in zwei Teile. ❸ *(divide up)* teilen [**38**] ▷ *They split the profits.* Sie teilten den Gewinn.; **to split up (1)** *(couple)* sich trennen [**38**] **(2)** *(group)* sich auflösen [**4**]

spoil *vb* ❶ verderben (*pres* verdirbt, *imperf* verdarb, *perf* hat verdorben) ▷ *It spoiled our evening.* Es hat uns den Abend verdorben. ❷ *(child)* verwöhnen [**84**] (*perf* hat verwöhnt)

spoiled *adj* verwöhnt ▷ *a spoiled child* ein verwöhntes Kind

spoilsport *n* Spielverderber *m* (*pl* Spielverderber), Spielverderberin *f*

spoilt *adj* verwöhnt ▷ *a spoilt child* ein verwöhntes Kind
▶ *vb see* **spoil**

spoken *vb see* **speak**

spokesman *n* Sprecher *m* (*pl* Sprecher)

spokeswoman *n* Sprecherin *f*

sponge *n* Schwamm *m* (*pl* Schwämme); **a sponge bag** ein Kulturbeutel *m*; **a sponge cake** ein Rührkuchen *m*

sponsor *n* Sponsor *m* (*pl* Sponsoren), Sponsorin *f*
▸ *vb* sponsern [**88**] ▹ *The festival was sponsored by ...* Das Festival wurde gesponsert von ...

spontaneous *adj* spontan

spooky *adj* ❶ (*eerie*) gruselig ▹ *a spooky story* eine gruselige Geschichte ❷ (*strange*) komisch ▹ *a spooky coincidence* ein komischer Zufall

spoon *n* Löffel *m* (*pl* Löffel) ▹ *a spoon of sugar* ein Löffel Zucker

spoonful *n* **a spoonful of soup** ein Löffel Suppe

sport *n* Sport *m* ▹ *What's your favourite sport?* Was ist dein Lieblingssport?; **a sports bag** eine Sporttasche; **a sports car** ein Sportwagen *m*; **a sports jacket** eine Sportjacke; **Go on, be a sport!** Nun komm schon, sei kein Frosch!

sportsman *n* Sportler *m* (*pl* Sportler)

sportswear *n* Sportkleidung *f*

sportswoman *n* Sportlerin *f*

sporty *adj* sportlich ▹ *I'm not very sporty.* Ich bin nicht besonders sportlich.

spot *n* ❶ (*mark*) Fleck *m* (*pl* Flecke) ▹ *There's a spot of blood on your shirt.* Du hast einen Blutfleck auf dem Hemd. ❷ (*in pattern*) Punkt *m* (*pl* Punkte) ▹ *a red dress with white spots* ein rotes Kleid mit weißen Punkten ❸ (*pimple*) Pickel *m* (*pl* Pickel) ▹ *I've got a big spot on my chin.* Ich habe einen großen Pickel am Kinn. ❹ (*place*) Platz *m* (*gen* Platzes, *pl* Plätze) ▹ *It's a lovely spot for a picnic.* Es ist ein herrlicher Platz für ein Picknick.; **on the spot (1)** (*immediately*) sofort ▹ *They gave her the job on the spot.* Sie haben ihr den Job sofort gegeben. **(2)** (*at the same place*) an Ort und Stelle ▹ *They were able to mend the car on the spot.* Sie konnten das Auto an Ort und Stelle reparieren.
▸ *vb* entdecken [**18**] (*perf* hat entdeckt) ▹ *I spotted Jack.* Ich habe Jack entdeckt.

spotless *adj* makellos

spotlight *n* Scheinwerferlicht *nt*

spotty *adj* (*pimply*) pickelig

sprain *vb* **I've sprained my ankle.** Ich habe mir den Fuß verstaucht.
▸ *n* Verstauchung *f* ▹ *It's just a sprain.* Es ist nur eine Verstauchung.

spray *n* Spray *nt* (*pl* Sprays) ▹ *hair spray* das Haarspray
▸ *vb* sprühen [**38**] ▹ *to spray perfume on one's hand* sich Parfüm auf die Hand sprühen ▹ *Somebody had sprayed graffiti on the wall.* Irgendjemand hatte Graffiti auf die Wand gesprüht.

spread *n* **cheese spread** der Streichkäse; **chocolate spread** der Schokoladenaufstrich
▸ *vb* ❶ streichen (*imperf* strich, *perf* hat gestrichen) ▹ *to spread butter on a cracker* Butter auf einen Cracker streichen ❷ (*disease, news*) sich verbreiten [**2**] (*perf* hat sich verbreitet) ▹ *The news spread rapidly.* Die Nachricht verbreitete sich schnell.; **to spread out** (*people*) sich verteilen [**84**]

spreadsheet *n* (*computer program*) Tabellenkalkulation *f*

spring *n* ❶ (*season*) Frühling *m* (*pl* Frühlinge) ▹ *in spring* im Frühling ❷ (*metal coil*) Feder *f* ❸ (*water hole*) Quelle *f*

springtime *n* Frühjahr *nt* (*pl* Frühjahre) ▹ *in springtime* im Frühjahr

sprint *n* Sprint *m* (*pl* Sprints); **a hundred-metre sprint** ein Einhundertmeterlauf *m*
▸ *vb* rennen [**55**] (*imperf* rannte, *perf* ist gerannt) ▹ *She sprinted for the bus.* Sie rannte, um den Bus zu erreichen.

sprouts *npl* **Brussels sprouts** der Rosenkohl *sg*

spy *n* Spion *m* (*pl* Spione), Spionin *f*
▸ *vb* **to spy on somebody** jemandem nachspionieren [**4**]

spying *n* Spionage *f*

square *n* ❶ Quadrat *nt* (*pl* Quadrate) ▹ *a square and a triangle* ein Quadrat

und ein Dreieck ❷ Platz *m* (*gen* Platzes, *pl* Plätze) ▷ *the town square* der Rathausplatz
▶ *adj* **two square metres** zwei Quadratmeter; **It's two metres square.** Es misst zwei mal zwei Meter.
squash *n (sport)* Squash *nt* ▷ *I play squash.* Ich spiele Squash.; **a squash court** ein Squashcourt *m*; **a squash racket** ein Squashschläger *m*; **orange squash** der Orangensaft
▶ *vb* zerdrücken [95] (*perf* hat zerdrückt) ▷ *You're squashing me.* Du zerdrückst mich.
squeak *vb* ❶ *(mouse, child)* quieksen [48] ❷ *(creak)* quietschen [48]
squeeze *vb* ❶ *(fruit, toothpaste)* pressen [31] ❷ *(hand, arm)* drücken [38] ▷ *to squeeze somebody's arm* jemandem den Arm drücken; **to squeeze into tight jeans** sich in enge Jeans quetschen [48]
squirrel *n* Eichhörnchen *nt* (*pl* Eichhörnchen)
stab *vb* **to stab somebody (1)** *(wound)* jemanden mit dem Messer verletzen [36] **(2)** *(kill)* jemanden erstechen
stable *n* Stall *m* (*pl* Ställe)
▶ *adj* stabil ▷ *a stable relationship* eine stabile Beziehung
stack *n* Stapel *m* (*pl* Stapel) ▷ *a stack of books* ein Stapel Bücher
stadium *n* Stadion *nt* (*pl* Stadien)
staff *n* ❶ *(in company)* Belegschaft *f* ❷ *(in school)* Lehrerschaft *f*
stage *n* ❶ *(in plays)* Bühne *f* ❷ *(for speeches, lectures)* Podium *nt* (*pl* Podien); **at this stage (1)** an diesem Punkt ▷ *at this stage in the negotiations* an diesem Punkt der Verhandlungen **(2)** im Augenblick ▷ *At this stage, one can't tell.* Im Augenblick kann man das noch nicht sagen.; **to do something in stages** etwas in Etappen machen [48]
stain *n* Fleck *m* (*pl* Flecke)
▶ *vb* beflecken [7] (*perf* hat befleckt)
stainless steel *n* Edelstahl *m*
stair *n (step)* Stufe *f*
staircase *n* Treppe *f*
stairs *npl* Treppe *fsg*
stale *adj (bread)* altbacken
stalemate *n (in chess)* Patt *nt* (*pl* Patts)
stall *n* Stand *m* (*pl* Stände) ▷ *He's got a market stall.* Er hat einen Marktstand.; **the stalls** *(in cinema, theatre)* das Parkett *sg*
stammer *n* Stottern *nt*; **He's got a stammer.** Er stottert.
stamp *vb (passport)* abstempeln [4] (*perf* hat abgestempelt); **to stamp one's foot** mit dem Fuß aufstampfen [4]
▶ *n* ❶ Briefmarke *f* ▷ *I need a stamp.* Ich brauche eine Briefmarke. ▷ *a stamp album* ein Briefmarkenalbum ▷ *a stamp collection* eine Briefmarkensammlung ❷ *(rubber stamp)* Stempel *m* (*pl* Stempel)
stand *vb* ❶ *(be standing)* stehen [72] (*imperf* stand, *perf* hat gestanden) ▷ *He was standing by the door.* Er stand an der Tür. ❷ *(stand up)* aufstehen [72] (*perf* ist aufgestanden) ❸ *(tolerate, withstand)* aushalten [33] (*pres* hält aus, *imperf* hielt aus, *perf* hat ausgehalten) ▷ *I can't stand all this noise.* Ich halte diesen Lärm nicht aus.; **to stand for (1)** *(be short for)* stehen [72] für ▷ *'BT' stands for 'British Telecom'.* 'BT' steht für 'British Telecom'. **(2)** *(tolerate)* dulden [54] ▷ *I won't stand for it!* Ich dulde das nicht!; **to stand in for somebody** jemanden vertreten [79]; **to stand out** herausragen [15]; **to stand up** *(get up)* aufstehen [72]; **to stand up for** eintreten [79] für ▷ *Stand up for your rights!* Tretet für eure Rechte ein!
standard *adj* normal ▷ *the standard procedure* die normale Vorgehensweise; **standard German** das Hochdeutsch; **standard equipment** die Standardausrüstung
▶ *n* Niveau *nt* (*pl* Niveaus) ▷ *The standard is very high.* Das Niveau ist sehr

hoch.; **the standard of living** der Lebensstandard; **She's got high standards.** Sie hat hohe Ansprüche.

stands *npl (at sports ground)* Tribüne *fsg*

stank *vb see* **stink**

staple *n* Heftklammer *f*
▶ *vb* zusammenheften [**4**] (*perf* hat zusammengeheftet)

stapler *n* Heftmaschine *f*

star *n* ❶ *(in sky)* Stern *m* (*pl* Sterne) ❷ *(celebrity)* Star *m* (*pl* Stars)
der Star is also used for women.
▷ *She's a TV star.* Sie ist ein Fernsehstar.; **the stars** *(horoscope)* die Sterne
▶ *vb* die Hauptrolle spielen [**38**] ▷ *The film stars Nicole Kidman.* Nicole Kidman spielt in dem Film die Hauptrolle.; ... **starring Johnny Depp** ... mit Johnny Depp in der Hauptrolle

stare *vb* **to stare at something** etwas anstarren [**4**]

start *n* ❶ Anfang *m* (*pl* Anfänge) ▷ *It's not much, but it's a start.* Es ist nicht viel, aber es ist immerhin ein Anfang.; **Shall we make a start on the washing-up?** Sollen wir den Abwasch in Angriff nehmen? ❷ *(of race)* Start *m* (*pl* Starts)
▶ *vb* ❶ anfangen [**23**] (*pres* fängt an, *imperf* fing an, *perf* hat angefangen) ▷ *What time does it start?* Wann fängt es an?; **to start doing something** anfangen [**23**], etwas zu tun ❷ *(organization)* gründen [**54**] ▷ *He wants to start his own business.* Er möchte ein eigenes Geschäft gründen. ❸ *(campaign)* ins Leben rufen [**56**] (*imperf* rief ins Leben, *perf* hat ins Leben gerufen) ▷ *She started the campaign.* Sie hat die Kampagne ins Leben gerufen. ❹ *(car)* anlassen [**42**] (*pres* lässt an, *imperf* ließ an, *perf* hat angelassen) ▷ *He couldn't start the car.* Er konnte das Auto nicht anlassen.; **The car wouldn't start.** Das Auto ist nicht angesprungen.; **to start off** *(leave)* aufbrechen [**11**]

starter *n (first course)* Vorspeise *f*

starve *vb (die)* verhungern [**88**] (*perf* ist verhungert) ▷ *People were literally starving.* Die Menschen sind förmlich verhungert.; **I'm starving!** Ich bin am Verhungern!; **They starved us in prison.** Sie ließen uns im Gefängnis hungern.

state *n* ❶ Zustand *m* (*pl* Zustände); **He was in a real state.** *(upset)* Er ist fast durchgedreht. ❷ *(government)* Staat *m*; **the States** *(USA)* die Staaten
▶ *vb* ❶ *(say)* erklären [**19**] (*perf* hat erklärt) ▷ *He stated his intention to resign.* Er erklärte seine Absicht zurückzutreten. ❷ *(give)* angeben [**28**] (*pres* gibt an, *imperf* gab an, *perf* hat angegeben) ▷ *Please state your name and address.* Geben Sie bitte Ihren Namen und Ihre Adresse an.

statement *n* Erklärung *f*

station *n (railway)* Bahnhof *m* (*pl* Bahnhöfe); **the bus station** der Busbahnhof; **a police station** eine Polizeiwache; **a radio station** ein Rundfunksender *m*

stationer's *n* Schreibwarengeschäft *nt* (*pl* Schreibwarengeschäfte)

statue *n* Statue *f*

stay *vb* ❶ *(remain)* bleiben [**10**] (*imperf* blieb, *perf* ist geblieben) ▷ *Stay here!* Bleiben Sie hier!; **to stay in** *(not go out)* zu Hause bleiben [**10**]; **to stay up** aufbleiben [**10**] ❷ *(spend the night)* übernachten [**2**] (*perf* hat übernachtet) ▷ *to stay with friends* bei Freunden übernachten; **Where are you staying?** Wo wohnen Sie?; **to stay the night** über Nacht bleiben [**10**]; **We stayed in Belgium for a few days.** Wir waren ein paar Tage in Belgien.
▶ *n* Aufenthalt *m* (*pl* Aufenthalte) ▷ *my stay in Bonn* mein Aufenthalt in Bonn

steady *adj* ❶ stetig ▷ *steady progress* stetiger Fortschritt ❷ fest ▷ *a steady job* eine feste Arbeit ❸ *(voice, hand)* ruhig ❹ *(person)* solide; **a steady boyfriend** ein fester Freund; **a steady girlfriend**

eine feste Freundin; **Steady on!** Immer mit der Ruhe!

steak *n (beef)* Steak *nt (pl* Steaks) ▷ *steak and chips* Steak mit Pommes frites

steal *vb* stehlen [73] (*pres* stiehlt, *imperf* stahl, *perf* hat gestohlen)

steam *n* Dampf *m (pl* Dämpfe) ▷ *a steam engine* eine Dampflokomotive

steel *n* Stahl *m* ▷ *a steel door* eine Stahltür

steep *adj (slope)* steil

steeple *n* Kirchturm *m (pl* Kirchtürme)

steering wheel *n* Lenkrad *nt (pl* Lenkräder)

step *n* ❶ *(pace)* Schritt *m (pl* Schritte) ▷ *He took a step forward.* Er machte einen Schritt nach vorn. ❷ *(stair)* Stufe *f* ▷ *She tripped over the step.* Sie stolperte über die Stufe.
▶ *vb* **to step aside** zur Seite treten [79]; **to step back** zurücktreten [79]

stepbrother *n* Stiefbruder *m (pl* Stiefbrüder)

stepdaughter *n* Stieftochter *f (pl* Stieftöchter)

stepfather *n* Stiefvater *m (pl* Stiefväter)

stepladder *n* Trittleiter *f*

stepmother *n* Stiefmutter *f (pl* Stiefmütter)

stepsister *n* Stiefschwester *f*

stepson *n* Stiefsohn *m (pl* Stiefsöhne)

stereo *n* Stereoanlage *f*

sterling *adj* **five pounds sterling** fünf britische Pfund

stew *n* Eintopf *m (pl* Eintöpfe)

steward *n* Steward *m (pl* Stewards)

stewardess *n* Stewardess *f (pl* Stewardessen)

stick *n* Stock *m (pl* Stöcke)
▶ *vb (with adhesive)* kleben [38]; **I can't stick it any longer.** Ich halte das nicht mehr aus.

stick out *vb* herausstrecken [15] (*perf* hat herausgestreckt)

sticker *n* Aufkleber *m (pl* Aufkleber)

stick insect *n* Gespenstheuschrecke *f (pl* Gespenstheuschrecken)

sticky *adj* klebrig ▷ *to have sticky hands* klebrige Hände haben; **a sticky label** ein Aufkleber *m*

stiff *adj, adv (rigid)* steif; **to have a stiff neck** einen steifen Hals haben [32]; **to feel stiff (1)** steif sein [65] ▷ *I feel stiff after the long journey.* Ich bin nach der langen Reise ganz steif.
(2) Muskelkater haben [32] ▷ *I feel stiff after playing football yesterday.* Ich habe gestern Fußball gespielt und habe jetzt Muskelkater.; **to be bored stiff** sich zu Tode langweilen [38]; **to be frozen stiff** total durchgefroren sein [65]; **to be scared stiff** furchtbare Angst haben [32]

still *adv* ❶ immer noch ▷ *I still haven't finished.* Ich bin immer noch nicht fertig. ▷ *Are you still in bed?* Bist du immer noch im Bett?; **better still** noch besser ❷ *(even so)* trotzdem ▷ *She knows I don't like it, but she still does it.* Sie weiß, dass ich das nicht mag, sie macht es aber trotzdem. ❸ *(after all)* immerhin ▷ *Still, it's the thought that counts.* Es war immerhin gut gemeint.
▶ *adj* still ▷ *Keep still!* Halt still! ▷ *Sit still!* Sitz still!

sting *n* Stich *m (pl* Stiche) ▷ *a wasp sting* ein Wespenstich
▶ *vb* stechen (*pres* sticht, *imperf* stach, *perf* hat gestochen) ▷ *I've been stung.* Ich bin gestochen worden.

stink *vb* stinken (*imperf* stank, *perf* hat gestunken) ▷ *It stinks!* Es stinkt!
▶ *n* Gestank *m*

stir *vb* umrühren [4] (*perf* hat umgerührt)

stitch *vb (cloth)* nähen [38]
▶ *n* Stich *m (pl* Stiche) ▷ *I had five stitches.* Ich wurde mit fünf Stichen genäht.

stock *n* ❶ *(supply)* Vorrat *m (pl* Vorräte) ❷ *(in shop)* Lager *nt (pl* Lager) ▷ *in stock* auf Lager; **out of stock** ausverkauft ❸ Brühe *f* ▷ *chicken stock* die Hühnerbrühe

▶ *vb (have in stock)* führen [**38**] ▷ *Do you stock camping stoves?* Führen Sie Campingkocher?; **to stock up** sich eindecken [**4**]
stock cube *n* Brühwürfel *m (pl* Brühwürfel)
stocking *n* Strumpf *m (pl* Strümpfe)
stomach *n* ❶ Magen *m (pl* Mägen) ▷ *on a full stomach* mit vollem Magen ❷ Bauch *m (pl* Bäuche) ▷ *to lie on one's stomach* auf dem Bauch liegen
stomachache *n* **to have a stomachache** Bauchschmerzen haben [**32**]
stone *n (rock)* Stein *m (pl* Steine) ▷ *a stone wall* eine Steinmauer ▷ *a peach stone* ein Pfirsichstein
In Germany weight is expressed in kilos. A stone is about 6.3 kg.
▷ *I weigh eight stone.* Ich wiege fünfzig Kilo.
stood *vb see* **stand**
stool *n* Hocker *m (pl* Hocker)
stop *vb* ❶ aufhören [**4**] *(perf* hat aufgehört) ▷ *He stopped crying.* Er hörte auf zu weinen. ▷ *I think the rain's going to stop.* Ich glaube, es hört auf zu regnen. ▷ *You should stop smoking.* Du solltest aufhören zu rauchen.; **to stop somebody doing something** jemanden daran hindern [**88**], etwas zu tun; **Stop it!** Hör auf! ❷ *(bus, train, car)* halten [**33**] *(pres* hält, *imperf* hielt, *perf* hat gehalten) ▷ *The bus doesn't stop here.* Der Bus hält hier nicht. ❸ stoppen [**48**] ▷ *a campaign to stop whaling* eine Kampagne, um den Walfang zu stoppen; **Stop!** Halt!
▶ *n* Haltestelle *f* ▷ *a bus stop* eine Bushaltestelle; **This is my stop.** Ich muss jetzt aussteigen.
stopwatch *n* Stoppuhr *f*
store *n* ❶ *(shop)* Geschäft *nt (pl* Geschäfte) ▷ *a furniture store* ein Möbelgeschäft ❷ *(stock, storeroom)* Lager *nt (pl* Lager)
▶ *vb* ❶ lagern [**88**] ▷ *They store potatoes in the cellar.* Sie lagern Kartoffeln im Keller. ❷ *(information)* speichern [**88**]
storey *n* Stock *m (pl* Stock) ▷ *the first storey* der erste Stock; **a three-storey building** ein dreistöckiges Gebäude
storm *n* ❶ *(gale)* Sturm *m (pl* Stürme) ❷ *(thunderstorm)* Gewitter *nt (pl* Gewitter)
stormy *adj* stürmisch
story *n* Geschichte *f*
stove *n* ❶ *(in kitchen)* Herd *m (pl* Herde) ❷ *(camping stove)* Kocher *m (pl* Kocher)
straight *adj* ❶ gerade ▷ *a straight line* eine gerade Linie ❷ glatt ▷ *straight hair* glatte Haare ❸ *(heterosexual)* hetero; **straight away** sofort; **straight on** geradeaus
straightforward *adj* einfach
strain *n (stress)* Anstrengung *f*; **It was a strain.** Es war anstrengend.
▶ *vb* sich verrenken [**7**] *(perf* hat sich verrenkt) ▷ *I strained my back.* Ich habe mir den Rücken verrenkt.; **I strained a muscle.** Ich habe mir einen Muskel gezerrt.
strange *adj* sonderbar ▷ *That's strange!* Das ist sonderbar!
stranger *n* Fremde *m (gen* Fremden, *pl* Fremden), Fremde *f (gen* Fremden) ▷ *a stranger (man)* ein Fremder; **Don't talk to strangers.** Sprich nicht mit fremden Menschen.; **I'm a stranger here.** Ich bin hier fremd.
strangle *vb* erwürgen [**19**] *(perf* hat erwürgt)
strap *n* ❶ *(of bag, camera, shoe, suitcase)* Riemen *m (pl* Riemen) ❷ *(of bra, dress)* Träger *m (pl* Träger) ❸ *(of watch)* Armband *nt (pl* Armbänder)
straw *n* Stroh *nt*; **That's the last straw!** Jetzt reicht's aber!
strawberry *n* Erdbeere *f* ▷ *strawberry jam* die Erdbeermarmelade ▷ *a strawberry ice cream* ein Erdbeereis
stray *n* **a stray cat** eine streunende Katze
stream *n* Bach *m (pl* Bäche)

street *n* Straße *f* ▷ *in the street* auf der Straße

streetlamp *n* Straßenlampe *f*

street plan *n* Stadtplan *m* (*pl* Stadtpläne)

streetwise *adj* (*informal*) gewieft

strength *n* Kraft *f* (*pl* Kräfte)

stress *vb* betonen **[7]** (*perf* hat betont) ▷ *I would like to stress that ...* Ich möchte betonen, dass ...
▶ *n* Stress *m* (*gen* Stresses)

stretch *vb* ❶ (*person, animal*) sich strecken **[48]** ▷ *The dog woke up and stretched.* Der Hund wachte auf und streckte sich. ❷ (*get bigger*) ausleiern **[4]** (*perf* ist ausgeleiert) ▷ *My sweater stretched when I washed it.* Mein Pullover ist in der Wäsche ausgeleiert. ❸ (*stretch out*) spannen **[38]** ▷ *They stretched a rope between the trees.* Sie spannten ein Seil zwischen den Bäumen.; **to stretch out one's arms** die Arme ausbreiten **[4]**

stretcher *n* Trage *f*

stretchy *adj* elastisch

strict *adj* streng

strike *n* Streik *m* (*pl* Streiks); **to be on strike** streiken **[38]**; **to go on strike** in den Streik treten **[79]**
▶ *vb* ❶ schlagen **[59]** (*pres* schlägt, *imperf* schlug, *perf* hat geschlagen) ▷ *The clock struck three.* Die Uhr schlug drei. ▷ *She struck him across the mouth.* Sie schlug ihm auf den Mund. ❷ (*go on strike*) streiken **[38]**; **to strike a match** ein Streichholz anzünden **[54]**

striker *n* ❶ (*person on strike*) Streikende *m* (*gen* Streikenden, *pl* Streikenden), Streikende *f* (*gen* Streikenden) ▷ *a striker (man)* ein Streikender ❷ (*footballer*) Torschütze *m* (*gen* Torschützen, *pl* Torschützen)

string *n* ❶ Schnur *f* (*pl* Schnüre) ▷ *a piece of string* eine Schnur ❷ (*of violin, guitar*) Saite *f*

strip *vb* (*get undressed*) sich ausziehen **[96]** (*imperf* zog sich aus, *perf* hat sich ausgezogen)
▶ *n* Streifen *m* (*pl* Streifen); **a strip cartoon** ein Comicstrip *m*

stripe *n* Streifen *m* (*pl* Streifen)

striped *adj* gestreift ▷ *a striped skirt* ein gestreifter Rock

stroke *vb* streicheln **[88]**
▶ *n* Schlag *m* (*pl* Schläge) ▷ *to have a stroke* einen Schlag bekommen

stroll *n* **to go for a stroll** einen Spaziergang machen **[48]**

stroller *n* (*US*) (*for child*) Sportwagen *m* (*pl* Sportwagen)

strong *adj* stark ▷ *She's very strong.* Sie ist sehr stark. ▷ *Gerry is stronger than Robert.* Gerry ist stärker als Robert.

strongly *adv* dringend ▷ *We strongly recommend that ...* Wir empfehlen dringend, dass ...; **He smelt strongly of tobacco.** Er roch stark nach Tabak.; **strongly built** solide gebaut; **I don't feel strongly about it.** Das ist mir ziemlich egal.

struck *vb see* **strike**

struggle *vb* (*physically*) sich wehren **[38]** ▷ *He struggled, but he couldn't escape.* Er wehrte sich, aber er konnte sich nicht befreien.; **to struggle to do something (1)** (*fight*) kämpfen **[38]**, um etwas zu tun ▷ *He struggled to get custody of his daughter.* Er kämpfte, um das Sorgerecht für seine Tochter zu bekommen. **(2)** (*have difficulty*) Mühe haben **[32]**, etwas zu tun ▷ *She struggled to pay the bill.* Sie hatte Mühe, die Rechnung zu bezahlen.
▶ *n* (*for independence, equality*) Kampf *m* (*pl* Kämpfe) ▷ *It was a struggle.* Es war ein Kampf.

stubborn *adj* stur

stuck *vb see* **stick**
▶ *adj* **It's stuck.** Es klemmt.; **to get stuck** stecken bleiben **[10]**

stuck-up *adj* (*informal*) hochnäsig

stud *n* ❶ (*earring*) Ohrstecker *m* (*pl* Ohrstecker) ❷ (*on football boots*) Stollen *m* (*pl* Stollen)

a b c d e f g h i j k l m n o p q r s t u v w x y z

student *n* Student *m* (*gen* Studenten, *pl* Studenten), Studentin *f*

studio *n* Studio *nt* (*pl* Studios) ▷ *a TV studio* ein Fernsehstudio; **a studio flat** eine Einzimmerwohnung

study *vb* ❶ *(at university)* studieren [**76**] (*perf* hat studiert) ▷ *I plan to study biology.* Ich habe vor, Biologie zu studieren. ❷ *(do homework)* lernen [**38**] ▷ *I've got to study tonight.* Ich muss heute Abend lernen.

stuff *n* ❶ *(things)* Sachen *fpl* ▷ *There's some stuff on the table for you.* Auf dem Tisch stehen Sachen für dich. ❷ *(possessions)* Zeug *nt* ▷ *Have you got all your stuff?* Hast du all dein Zeug?

stuffy *adj (room)* stickig ▷ *It's really stuffy in here.* Hier drin ist es wirklich stickig.

stumble *vb* stolpern [**88**] (*perf* ist gestolpert)

stung *vb see* **sting**

stunk *vb see* **stink**

stunned *adj (amazed)* sprachlos ▷ *I was stunned.* Ich war sprachlos.

stunning *adj* umwerfend

stunt *n (in film)* Stunt *m* (*pl* Stunts)

stuntman *n* Stuntman *m* (*pl* Stuntmen)

stupid *adj* blöd ▷ *a stupid joke* ein blöder Witz; **Me, go jogging? Don't be stupid!** Ich und joggen? Du spinnst wohl!

stutter *vb* stottern [**88**]
▶ *n* **He's got a stutter.** Er stottert.

style *n* Stil *m* (*pl* Stile) ▷ *That's not his style.* Das ist nicht sein Stil.

subject *n* ❶ Thema *nt* (*pl* Themen) ▷ *The subject of my project was the internet.* Das Thema meines Referats war das Internet. ❷ *(at school)* Fach *nt* (*pl* Fächer) ▷ *What's your favourite subject?* Was ist dein Lieblingsfach?

subjunctive *n* Konjunktiv *m*

submarine *n* U-Boot *nt* (*pl* U-Boote)

subscription *n (to paper, magazine)* Abonnement *nt* (*pl* Abonnements); **to take out a subscription to something** etwas abonnieren [**76**]

subsidy *n* Subvention *f*

substance *n* Substanz *f*

substitute *n (player)* Ersatzspieler *m* (*pl* Ersatzspieler), Ersatzspielerin *f*
▶ *vb* ersetzen [**36**] (*perf* hat ersetzt) ▷ *to substitute wine for beer* Bier durch Wein ersetzen

subtitled *adj* mit Untertiteln

subtitles *npl* Untertitel *mpl* ▷ *an English film with German subtitles* ein englischer Film mit deutschen Untertiteln

subtle *adj* fein ▷ *a subtle difference* ein feiner Unterschied

subtract *vb* abziehen [**96**] (*imperf* zog ab, *perf* hat abgezogen) ▷ *to subtract three from five* drei von fünf abziehen

suburb *n* Vorstadt *f* (*pl* Vorstädte) ▷ *a suburb of Berlin* eine Vorstadt von Berlin ▷ *They live in the suburbs.* Sie wohnen in der Vorstadt.

subway *n* ❶ *(underpass)* Unterführung *f* ❷ *(underground)* U-Bahn *f*

succeed *vb* Erfolg haben [**32**] (*pres* hat Erfolg, *imperf* hatte Erfolg, *perf* hat Erfolg gehabt) ▷ *He succeeded in his plan.* Er hatte mit seinem Plan Erfolg.; **I succeeded in convincing him.** Es ist mir gelungen, ihn zu überzeugen.

success *n* Erfolg *m* (*pl* Erfolge) ▷ *The play was a great success.* Das Stück war ein großer Erfolg.

successful *adj* erfolgreich ▷ *a successful attempt* ein erfolgreicher Versuch ▷ *He's a successful businessman.* Er ist ein erfolgreicher Geschäftsmann.; **to be successful in doing something** etwas mit Erfolg tun [**81**]

successfully *adv* mit Erfolg

such *adj, adv* so ▷ *such nice people* so nette Leute ▷ *such a long journey* eine so lange Reise; **such a lot of (1)** *(so much)* so viel ▷ *such a lot of work* so viel Arbeit **(2)** *(so many)* so viele ▷ *such a lot of mistakes* so viele Fehler; **such as** *(like)* wie zum Beispiel; **not as such** nicht eigentlich; **There's no such thing.** So was gibt es nicht.

such-and-such *adj* der und der ▷ *such-and-such a place* der und der Ort die und die ▷ *such-and-such a time* die und die Zeit das und das ▷ *such-and-such a problem* das und das Problem

suck *vb (sweets)* lutschen [**48**] ▷ *to suck one's thumb* am Daumen lutschen

sudden *adj* plötzlich ▷ *a sudden change* eine plötzliche Änderung; **all of a sudden** plötzlich

suddenly *adv* plötzlich ▷ *Suddenly, the door opened.* Plötzlich ging die Tür auf.

suede *n* Wildleder *nt* ▷ *a suede jacket* eine Wildlederjacke

suffer *vb* leiden [**44**] (*imperf* litt, *perf* hat gelitten) ▷ *She was really suffering.* Sie hat wirklich gelitten.; **to suffer from a disease** an einer Krankheit leiden [**44**]

suffocate *vb* ersticken [**19**] (*perf* ist erstickt)

sugar *n* Zucker *m* (*pl* Zucker)

suggest *vb* vorschlagen [**59**] (*pres* schlägt vor, *imperf* schlug vor, *perf* hat vorgeschlagen) ▷ *I suggested they set off early.* Ich habe vorgeschlagen, dass sie früh aufbrechen sollen.

suggestion *n* Vorschlag *m* (*pl* Vorschläge)

suicide *n* Selbstmord *m* (*pl* Selbstmorde) ▷ *to commit suicide* Selbstmord begehen

suicide bomber *n* Selbstmordattentäter *m* (*pl* Selbstmordattentäter), Selbstmordattentäterin *f*

suicide bombing *n* Selbstmordattentat *nt* (*pl* Selbstmordattentate)

suit *n* ❶ *(man's)* Anzug *m* (*pl* Anzüge) ❷ *(woman's)* Kostüm *nt* (*pl* Kostüme) ▸ *vb* ❶ *(be convenient for)* passen [**31**] ▷ *What time would suit you?* Welche Zeit würde Ihnen passen? ▷ *That suits me fine.* Das passt mir gut.; **Suit yourself!** Wie du willst! ❷ *(look good on)* stehen [**72**] (*imperf* stand, *perf* hat gestanden) ▷ *That dress really suits you.* Das Kleid steht dir wirklich.

suitable *adj* ❶ passend ▷ *a suitable time* eine passende Zeit ❷ *(clothes)* angemessen ▷ *suitable clothing* angemessene Kleidung

suitcase *n* Koffer *m* (*pl* Koffer)

suite *n (of rooms)* Suite *f*; **a bedroom suite** eine Schlafzimmereinrichtung

sulk *vb* schmollen [**48**]

sultana *n* Sultanine *f*

sum *n* ❶ *(calculation)* Rechnen *nt*; **She's good at sums.** Sie kann gut rechnen. ❷ *(amount)* Summe *f* ▷ *a sum of money* eine Geldsumme

sum up *vb* zusammenfassen [**15**] (*perf* hat zusammengefasst)

summarize *vb* zusammenfassen [**15**] (*perf* hat zusammengefasst)

summary *n* Zusammenfassung *f*

summer *n* Sommer *m* (*pl* Sommer) ▷ *in summer* im Sommer; **summer clothes** die Sommerkleidung *sg*; **the summer holidays** die Sommerferien

summertime *n* Sommer *m* (*pl* Sommer) ▷ *in summertime* im Sommer

summit *n* Gipfel *m* (*pl* Gipfel)

sun *n* Sonne *f* ▷ *in the sun* in der Sonne

sunbathe *vb* sonnenbaden [**54**] (*perf* hat sonnengebadet)

sunblock *n* Sonnenschutzmittel *nt* (*pl* Sonnenschutzmittel)

sunburn *n* Sonnenbrand *m* (*pl* Sonnenbrände)

sunburnt *adj* **I got sunburnt.** Ich habe einen Sonnenbrand bekommen.

Sunday *n* Sonntag *m* (*pl* Sonntage) ▷ *every Sunday* jeden Sonntag ▷ *last Sunday* letzten Sonntag ▷ *next Sunday* nächsten Sonntag ▷ *on Sunday* am Sonntag; **on Sundays** sonntags

Sunday school *n* Sonntagsschule *f*

sunflower *n* Sonnenblume *f*

sung *vb see* **sing**

sunglasses *npl* Sonnenbrille *fsg* ▷ *a pair of sunglasses* eine Sonnenbrille

sunk *vb see* **sink**

sunlight *n* Sonnenlicht *nt*
sunny *adj* sonnig ▷ *a sunny morning* ein sonniger Morgen; **It's sunny.** Die Sonne scheint.
sunrise *n* Sonnenaufgang *m (pl* Sonnenaufgänge)
sunroof *n* Schiebedach *nt (pl* Schiebedächer)
sunscreen *n* Sonnenschutzcreme *f (pl* Sonnenschutzcremes)
sunset *n* Sonnenuntergang *m (pl* Sonnenuntergänge)
sunshine *n* Sonnenschein *m*
sunstroke *n* Hitzschlag *m (pl* Hitzschläge) ▷ *to get sunstroke* einen Hitzschlag bekommen
suntan *n* **to have a suntan** braun sein [65]; **suntan lotion** die Sonnenmilch; **suntan oil** das Sonnenöl
super *adj* klasse
klasse is invariable.
▷ *a super film* ein klasse Film
supermarket *n* Supermarkt *m (pl* Supermärkte)
supernatural *adj* übernatürlich
superstitious *adj* abergläubisch
supervise *vb* beaufsichtigen [84] *(perf* hat beaufsichtigt)
supervisor *n* ❶ *(in factory)* Vorarbeiter *m (pl* Vorarbeiter), Vorarbeiterin *f* ❷ *(in department store)* Abteilungsleiter *m (pl* Abteilungsleiter), Abteilungsleiterin *f*
supper *n* Abendessen *nt (pl* Abendessen)
supplement *n* ❶ *(of newspaper, magazine)* Beilage *f* ❷ *(money)* Zuschlag *m (pl* Zuschläge)
supplies *npl (food)* Vorräte *mpl*
supply *vb* ❶ *(goods, material)* liefern [88] ▷ *The farm supplied us with food.* Der Bauernhof lieferte uns die Lebensmittel. ❷ *(put at somebody's disposal)* stellen [38] ▷ *The centre supplied all the necessary equipment.* Das Zentrum hat die ganze notwendige Ausrüstung gestellt.
▶ *n* Vorrat *m (pl* Vorräte) ▷ *a supply of paper* ein Papiervorrat; **the water supply** *(to town)* die Wasserversorgung
supply teacher *n* Aushilfslehrer *m (pl* Aushilfslehrer), Aushilfslehrerin *f*
support *vb* ❶ unterstützen [36] ▷ *My mum has always supported me.* Meine Mutti hat mich immer unterstützt.; **What team do you support?** Für welche Mannschaft bist du?
❷ *(financially)* sorgen [38] für ▷ *She had to support five children on her own.* Sie musste allein für ihre fünf Kinder sorgen.
▶ *n (backing)* Unterstützung *f*
supporter *n* ❶ Fan *m (pl* Fans)
der Fan is also used for women.
▷ *a Liverpool supporter* ein Liverpool-Fan
❷ Anhänger *m (pl* Anhänger), Anhängerin *f* ▷ *She's a supporter of the Labour Party.* Sie ist Anhängerin der Labour-Party.
suppose *vb* annehmen [1] *(pres* nimmt an, *imperf* nahm an, *perf* hat angenommen) ▷ *I suppose he's late.* Ich nehme an, er kommt zu spät. ▷ *Suppose you won the lottery.* Nimm mal an, du gewinnst im Lotto. ▷ *I suppose so.* Das nehme ich an.; **to be supposed to do something** etwas tun sollen [69]; **You're supposed to show your passport.** Sie müssen Ihren Pass zeigen.
supposing *conj* angenommen
▷ *Supposing you won the lottery ...* Angenommen, du gewinnst im Lotto ...
sure *adj* sicher ▷ *Are you sure?* Bist du sicher?; **Sure!** Klar!; **to make sure that ...** sich vergewissern [88], dass ...
surely *adv* sicherlich ▷ *Surely you've been to London?* Du warst doch sicherlich schon in London? ▷ *The church is open on Sundays, surely?* Die Kirche ist sonntags doch sicherlich geöffnet?
surf *n* Brandung *f*
▶ *vb* surfen [38] *(perf* hat gesurft); **to surf the Net** im Internet surfen [38]

surface *n* Oberfläche *f*
surfboard *n* Surfbrett *nt* (*pl* Surfbretter)
surfing *n* Surfen *nt*; **to go surfing** surfen gehen [**29**]
surgeon *n* Chirurg *m* (*gen* Chirurgen, *pl* Chirurgen), Chirurgin *f* ▷ *She's a surgeon.* Sie ist Chirurgin.
surgery *n (doctor's surgery)* Arztpraxis *f* (*pl* Arztpraxen); **surgery hours** die Sprechstunden
surname *n* Nachname *m* (*gen* Nachnamens, *pl* Nachnamen)
surprise *n* Überraschung *f*
surprised *adj* überrascht ▷ *I was surprised to see him.* Ich war überrascht, ihn zu sehen.
surprising *adj* überraschend
surrender *vb* sich ergeben [**28**] (*pres* ergibt sich, *imperf* ergab sich, *perf* hat sich ergeben)
surrogate mother *n* Leihmutter *f* (*pl* Leihmütter)
surround *vb* umstellen [**4**] (*perf* hat umstellt) ▷ *The police surrounded the house.* Die Polizei hat das Haus umstellt. ▷ *You're surrounded!* Sie sind umstellt!; **surrounded by** umgeben von
surroundings *npl* Umgebung *fsg* ▷ *a hotel in beautiful surroundings* ein Hotel in wunderschöner Umgebung
survey *n (research)* Umfrage *f*
survive *vb* überleben [**18**] (*perf* hat überlebt)
survivor *n* Überlebende *m* (*gen* Überlebenden, *pl* Überlebenden), Überlebende *f* (*gen* Überlebenden) ▷ *There were no survivors.* Es gab keine Überlebenden.
suspect *vb* verdächtigen [**84**] (*perf* hat verdächtigt)
▶ *n* Verdächtige *m* (*gen* Verdächtigen, *pl* Verdächtigen), Verdächtige *f* (*gen* Verdächtigen) ▷ *a suspect (man)* ein Verdächtiger
suspend *vb* ❶ *(from school)* verweisen (*imperf* verwies, *perf* hat verwiesen) ▷ *He was suspended.* Er wurde von der Schule verwiesen. ❷ *(from team)* sperren [**38**] ❸ *(from job)* suspendieren [**76**] (*perf* hat suspendiert)
suspense *n* ❶ *(waiting)* Ungewissheit *f* ▷ *The suspense was terrible.* Die Ungewissheit war furchtbar. ❷ *(in story)* Spannung *f*; **a film with lots of suspense** ein sehr spannender Film
suspicious *adj* ❶ argwöhnisch ▷ *He was suspicious at first.* Zuerst war er argwöhnisch. ❷ *(suspicious-looking)* verdächtig ▷ *a suspicious person* eine verdächtige Person
swallow *vb* schlucken [**48**]
swam *vb see* **swim**
swan *n* Schwan *m* (*pl* Schwäne)
swap *vb* tauschen [**48**] ▷ *Do you want to swap?* Willst du tauschen?; **to swap an apple for a sweet** einen Apfel für ein Bonbon eintauschen [**4**]
swear *vb* ❶ *(make an oath)* schwören (*imperf* schwor, *perf* hat geschworen) ❷ *(curse)* fluchen [**38**]
swearword *n* Kraftausdruck *m* (*pl* Kraftausdrücke)
sweat *n* Schweiß *m* (*gen* Schweißes)
▶ *vb* schwitzen [**36**]
sweater *n* Pullover *m* (*pl* Pullover)
sweaty *adj* ❶ *(person, face)* verschwitzt ▷ *I'm all sweaty.* Ich bin ganz verschwitzt. ❷ *(hands)* feucht
Swede *n (person)* Schwede *m* (*gen* Schweden, *pl* Schweden), Schwedin *f*
Sweden *n* Schweden *nt*; **from Sweden** aus Schweden; **to Sweden** nach Schweden
Swedish *adj* schwedisch; **He's Swedish.** Er ist Schwede.; **She's Swedish.** Sie ist Schwedin.
▶ *n (language)* Schwedisch *nt* (*gen* Schwedischen)
sweep *vb* fegen [**38**] ▷ *to sweep the floor* den Boden fegen
sweet *n* ❶ *(candy)* Bonbon *nt* (*pl* Bonbons) ▷ *a bag of sweets* eine Tüte Bonbons ❷ *(pudding)* Nachtisch *m*

a b c d e f g h i j k l m n o p q r s t u v w x y z

▷ *What sweet did you have?* Was für einen Nachtisch hattest du?
▶ *adj* ❶ süß ▷ *Isn't she sweet?* Ist sie nicht süß? ❷ *(kind)* nett ▷ *That was really sweet of you.* Das war wirklich nett von dir.; **sweet and sour pork** Schweinefleisch süß-sauer

sweetcorn *n* Mais *m*

swept *vb see* **sweep**

swerve *vb* ausscheren [**4**] (*perf* ist ausgeschert) ▷ *He swerved to avoid the cyclist.* Er scherte aus, um dem Fahrradfahrer auszuweichen.

swim *n* **to go for a swim** schwimmen gehen [**29**]
▶ *vb* schwimmen [**63**] (*imperf* schwamm, *perf* ist geschwommen) ▷ *Can you swim?* Kannst du schwimmen? ▷ *She swam across the river.* Sie schwamm über den Fluss.

swimmer *n* Schwimmer *m* (*pl* Schwimmer), Schwimmerin *f* ▷ *She's a good swimmer.* Sie ist eine gute Schwimmerin.

swimming *n* Schwimmen *nt*; **to go swimming** schwimmen gehen [**29**]; **Do you like swimming?** Schwimmst du gern?; **a swimming cap** eine Bademütze; **a swimming costume** ein Badeanzug *m*; **a swimming pool** ein Schwimmbad *nt*; **swimming trunks** die Badehose *sg*

swimsuit *n* Badeanzug *m* (*pl* Badeanzüge)

swing *n (in playground, garden)* Schaukel *f*
▶ *vb* schaukeln [**34**]

Swiss *adj* Schweizer ▷ *I like Swiss cheese.* Ich mag Schweizer Käse.; **Andreas is Swiss.** Andreas ist Schweizer.; **Claudie is Swiss.** Claudie ist Schweizerin.
▶ *n (person)* Schweizer *m* (*pl* Schweizer), Schweizerin *f*; **the Swiss** die Schweizer

switch *n (for light, radio etc)* Schalter *m* (*pl* Schalter)
▶ *vb* tauschen [**48**] ▷ *to switch A for B* A gegen B tauschen

switch off *vb* ausschalten [**2**] (*perf* hat ausgeschaltet)

switch on *vb* anschalten [**2**] (*perf* hat angeschaltet)

Switzerland *n* Schweiz *f* (*gen* Schweiz)

> Note that the definite article is used in German for countries which are feminine.

from Switzerland aus der Schweiz; **in Switzerland** in der Schweiz; **to Switzerland** in die Schweiz

swollen *adj (arm, leg)* geschwollen

swop *vb* tauschen [**48**] ▷ *Do you want to swop?* Willst du tauschen?; **to swop an apple for a sweet** einen Apfel für ein Bonbon eintauschen [**4**]

sword *n* Schwert *nt* (*pl* Schwerter)

swore *vb see* **swear**

sworn *vb see* **swear**

swot *vb (informal)* pauken [**38**] ▷ *I'll have to swot for the maths exam.* Ich muss für die Matheprüfung pauken.
▶ *n (informal)* Streber *m* (*pl* Streber), Streberin *f*

swum *vb see* **swim**

swung *vb see* **swing**

syllabus *n* Lehrplan *m* (*pl* Lehrpläne) ▷ *on the syllabus* auf dem Lehrplan

symbol *n* Symbol *nt* (*pl* Symbole)

sympathetic *adj* verständnisvoll

> Be careful not to translate **sympathetic** by **sympathisch**.

sympathize *vb* **to sympathize with somebody** *(pity)* Mitgefühl mit jemandem haben [**32**]

sympathy *n* Mitleid *nt*

symptom *n* Symptom *nt*

syringe *n* Spritze *f*

system *n* System *nt* (*pl* Systeme)

t

table *n* Tisch *m* (*pl* Tische) ▷ *to lay the table* den Tisch decken
tablecloth *n* Tischdecke *f*
tablespoon *n* Esslöffel *m* (*pl* Esslöffel) ▷ *a tablespoon of sugar* ein Esslöffel Zucker
tablespoonful *n* **a tablespoonful of sugar** ein Esslöffel Zucker
tablet *n* ❶ *(medicine)* Tablette *f* ❷ *(computer)* Tablet *nt* (*pl* Tablets)
table tennis *n* Tischtennis *nt* (*gen* Tischtennis) ▷ *to play table tennis* Tischtennis spielen
tact *n* Takt *m*
tactful *adj* taktvoll
tactics *npl* Taktik *fsg*
tadpole *n* Kaulquappe *f*
tag *n (label)* Etikett *nt* (*pl* Etiketts)
tail *n* Schwanz *m* (*gen* Schwanzes, *pl* Schwänze); **Heads or tails?** Kopf oder Zahl?
tailor *n* Schneider *m* (*pl* Schneider), Schneiderin *f* ▷ *He's a tailor.* Er ist Schneider.
take *vb* ❶ nehmen **[52]** (*pres* nimmt, *imperf* nahm, *perf* hat genommen) ▷ *He took a plate from the cupboard.* Er nahm einen Teller aus dem Schrank. ▷ *We took a taxi.* Wir haben ein Taxi genommen. ❷ *(take along)* mitnehmen **[52]** (*pres* nimmt mit, *imperf* nahm mit, *perf* hat mitgenommen) ▷ *Are you taking your camera?* Nimmst du deine Kamera mit? ▷ *Don't take anything valuable with you.* Nehmen Sie nichts Wertvolles mit. ▷ *He goes to London every week, but he never takes me.* Er fährt jede Woche nach London, aber er nimmt mich nie mit. ▷ *Do you take your exercise books home?* Nehmt ihr eure Hefte mit nach Hause? ❸ *(to a certain place)* bringen **[13]** (*imperf* brachte, *perf* hat gebracht) ▷ *She always takes him to school.* Sie bringt ihn immer zur Schule. ▷ *I'm taking my coat to the cleaner's.* Ich bringe meinen Mantel in die Reinigung. ❹ *(require)* brauchen **[48]** ▷ *She always takes hours to get ready.* Sie braucht immer Stunden, bis sie fertig ist. ▷ *It takes five people to do this job.* Für diese Arbeit braucht man fünf Leute. ▷ *That takes a lot of courage.* Dazu braucht man viel Mut.; **It takes a lot of money to do that.** Das kostet viel Geld. ❺ *(last)* dauern **[88]** ▷ *The journey took three hours.* Die Fahrt dauerte drei Stunden. ▷ *It won't take long.* Das dauert nicht lange. ❻ *(tolerate)* ertragen **[77]** (*pres* erträgt, *imperf* ertrug, *perf* hat ertragen) ▷ *He can't take being criticized.* Er kann es nicht ertragen, kritisiert zu werden. ❼ *(exam, test, subject)* machen **[48]** ▷ *Have you taken your driving test yet?* Hast du deine Fahrprüfung schon gemacht? ▷ *I'm taking German instead of French.* Ich mache Deutsch statt Französisch.
take after *vb* nachschlagen **[59]** (*pres* schlägt nach, *imperf* schlug nach, *perf* hat nachgeschlagen)
take apart *vb* **to take something apart** etwas auseinandernehmen **[52]**

take away *vb* ❶ *(object)* wegnehmen [**52**] (*pres* nimmt weg, *imperf* nahm weg, *perf* hat weggenommen) ❷ *(person)* wegbringen [**13**] (*imperf* brachte weg, *perf* hat weggebracht)

take back *vb* zurückbringen [**13**] (*imperf* brachte zurück, *perf* hat zurückgebracht)

take down *vb* herunternehmen [**52**] (*pres* nimmt herunter, *imperf* nahm herunter, *perf* hat heruntergenommen)

take in *vb (understand)* verstehen [**72**] (*imperf* verstand, *perf* hat verstanden)

take off *vb* ❶ *(plane)* abfliegen [**25**] (*imperf* flog ab, *perf* ist abgeflogen) ❷ *(clothes)* ausziehen [**96**] (*imperf* zog aus, *perf* hat ausgezogen)

take out *vb (from container, pocket)* herausnehmen [**52**] (*pres* nimmt heraus, *imperf* nahm heraus, *perf* hat herausgenommen)

take over *vb* übernehmen [**52**] (*pres* übernimmt, *imperf* übernahm, *perf* hat übernommen)

takeaway *n* ❶ *(meal)* Essen zum Mitnehmen *nt* (*pl* Essen zum Mitnehmen) ❷ *(shop)* Imbissstube *f* ▷ *a Chinese takeaway* eine chinesische Imbissstube

takeoff *n (of plane)* Abflug *m* (*pl* Abflüge)

tale *n (story)* Geschichte *f*

talent *n* Talent *nt* (*pl* Talente) ▷ *She's got lots of talent.* Sie hat sehr viel Talent.; **to have a talent for something** eine Begabung für etwas haben [**32**]; **He's got a real talent for languages.** Er ist wirklich sprachbegabt.

talented *adj* begabt

talk *n* ❶ *(speech)* Vortrag *m* (*pl* Vorträge) ▷ *She gave a talk on rock climbing.* Sie hielt einen Vortrag über das Klettern. ❷ *(conversation)* Gespräch *nt* (*pl* Gespräche) ▷ *We had a talk about her problems.* Wir hatten ein Gespräch über ihre Probleme.; **I had a talk with my Mum about it.** Ich habe mit meiner Mutti darüber gesprochen. ❸ *(gossip)* Gerede *nt* ▷ *It's just talk.* Das ist nur Gerede.
▶ *vb* reden [**54**] ▷ *We talked about the weather.* Wir haben über das Wetter geredet.; **to talk something over with somebody** etwas mit jemandem besprechen [**70**]

talkative *adj* redselig

tall *adj* ❶ *(person, tree)* groß ▷ *They've cut down the tallest tree in the park.* Sie haben den größten Baum im Park gefällt. ▷ *He's two metres tall.* Er ist zwei Meter groß. ❷ *(building)* hoch

Before a noun or after an article, use **hohe**.

▷ *a tall building* ein hohes Gebäude

tame *adj (animal)* zahm

tampon *n* Tampon *m* (*pl* Tampons)

tan *n* **She's got a lovely tan.** Sie ist schön braun.

tangerine *n* Mandarine *f*

tank *n* ❶ *(for water, petrol)* Tank *m* (*pl* Tanks) ❷ *(military)* Panzer *m* (*pl* Panzer); **a fish tank** ein Aquarium *nt*

tanker *n* ❶ *(ship)* Tanker *m* (*pl* Tanker) ▷ *an oil tanker* ein Öltanker ❷ *(truck)* Tankwagen *m* (*pl* Tankwagen) ▷ *a petrol tanker* ein Benzintankwagen

tap *n* ❶ *(water tap)* Wasserhahn *m* (*pl* Wasserhähne) ❷ *(gentle blow)* Klaps *m* (*pl* Klapse)

tap-dancing *n* Stepptanzen *nt*; **I do tap-dancing.** Ich mache Stepptanz.

tape *vb (record)* aufnehmen [**52**] (*pres* nimmt auf, *imperf* nahm auf, *perf* hat aufgenommen) ▷ *Did you tape that film last night?* Hast du den Film gestern Abend aufgenommen?
▶ *n* ❶ Kassette *f* ▷ *a tape of Tom Jones* eine Kassette von Tom Jones ❷ *(sticky tape)* Klebstreifen *m* (*pl* Klebstreifen)

tape measure *n* Maßband *nt* (*pl* Maßbänder)

tape recorder *n* Kassettenrekorder *m* (*pl* Kassettenrekorder)

target *n* Ziel *nt* (*pl* Ziele)

tart *n* Kuchen *m* (*pl* Kuchen) ▷ *an apple tart* ein Apfelkuchen
tartan *adj* im Schottenkaro ▷ *a tartan scarf* ein Schal im Schottenkaro
task *n* Aufgabe *f*
taste *n* Geschmack *m* (*pl* Geschmäcke) ▷ *It's got a really strange taste.* Es hat einen sehr eigenartigen Geschmack. ▷ *She has good taste.* Sie hat einen guten Geschmack.; **a joke in bad taste** ein geschmackloser Witz; **Would you like a taste?** Möchtest du mal probieren?
▶ *vb* ❶ probieren [**76**] (*perf* hat probiert) ▷ *Would you like to taste it?* Möchtest du mal probieren? ❷ schmecken [**48**] ▷ *You can taste the garlic in it.* Man kann den Knoblauch schmecken.; **to taste of something** nach etwas schmecken [**48**]
tasty *adj* schmackhaft
tattoo *n* Tätowierung *f*
taught *vb see* **teach**
Taurus *n* Stier *m* ▷ *I'm Taurus.* Ich bin Stier.
tax *n* (*on goods, income*) Steuer *f*
taxi *n* Taxi *nt* (*pl* Taxis) ▷ *a taxi driver* ein Taxifahrer
taxi rank *n* Taxistand *m* (*pl* Taxistände)
TB *n* (= *tuberculosis*) TB *f* (= *Tuberkulose*)
tea *n* ❶ Tee *m* (*pl* Tees) ▷ *a cup of tea* eine Tasse Tee

Usually, tea is not drunk with milk and sugar in Germany, but is served with lemon, and is referred to as **Schwarztee**. Fruit teas and herbal teas are also very widespread.

a tea bag ein Teebeutel *m* ❷ (*evening meal*) Abendessen *nt* (*pl* Abendessen) ▷ *We were having tea.* Wir saßen beim Abendessen.
teach *vb* ❶ beibringen [**13**] (*imperf* brachte bei, *perf* hat beigebracht) ▷ *My sister taught me to swim.* Meine Schwester hat mir das Schwimmen beigebracht.; **That'll teach you!** Das wird dir eine Lehre sein! ❷ (*in school*) unterrichten [**2**] (*perf* hat unterrichtet) ▷ *She teaches physics.* Sie unterrichtet Physik.
teacher *n* Lehrer *m* (*pl* Lehrer), Lehrerin *f* ▷ *a maths teacher* ein Mathelehrer ▷ *She's a teacher.* Sie ist Lehrerin. ▷ *He's a primary school teacher.* Er ist Grundschullehrer.
team *n* Mannschaft *f* ▷ *a football team* eine Fußballmannschaft ▷ *She was in my team.* Sie war in meiner Mannschaft.
teapot *n* Teekanne *f*
tear *n* Träne *f* ▷ *She was in tears.* Sie war in Tränen aufgelöst.
▶ *vb* zerreißen (*imperf* zerriss, *perf* hat/ist zerrissen) ▷ *Mind you don't tear the page.* Pass auf, dass du die Seite nicht zerreißt.

For the perfect tense use **haben** when the verb has an object and **sein** when there is no object.

▷ *You've torn your shirt.* Du hast dein Hemd zerrissen. ▷ *Your shirt is torn.* Dein Hemd ist zerrissen. ▷ *It won't tear, it's very strong.* Es zerreißt nicht, es ist sehr stark.; **to tear up** zerreißen
tease *vb* ❶ (*unkindly*) quälen [**38**] ▷ *Stop teasing that poor animal!* Hör auf, das arme Tier zu quälen! ❷ (*jokingly*) necken [**48**] ▷ *He's teasing you.* Er neckt dich nur.; **I was only teasing.** Ich habe nur einen Scherz gemacht.
teaspoon *n* Teelöffel *m* (*pl* Teelöffel) ▷ *a teaspoon of sugar* ein Teelöffel Zucker
teaspoonful *n* **a teaspoonful of sugar** ein Teelöffel Zucker
teatime *n* (*in evening*) Abendessenszeit *f* ▷ *It was nearly teatime.* Es war fast Abendessenszeit.; **Teatime!** Abendessen!
tea towel *n* Geschirrtuch *nt* (*pl* Geschirrtücher)
technical *adj* technisch; **a technical college** eine Fachhochschule
technician *n* Techniker *m* (*pl* Techniker), Technikerin *f*
technological *adj* technologisch

a b c d e f g h i j k l m n o p q r s t u v w x y z

technology *n* Technologie *f*
teddy bear *n* Teddybär *m* (*gen* Teddybären, *pl* Teddybären)
teenage *adj* ❶ für Teenager ▷ *a teenage magazine* eine Zeitschrift für Teenager ❷ *(boys, girls)* heranwachsend ▷ *She has two teenage daughters.* Sie hat zwei heranwachsende Töchter.
teenager *n* Teenager *m* (*pl* Teenager)
der Teenager is also used for girls.
teens *npl* **She's in her teens.** Sie ist ein Teenager.
tee-shirt *n* T-Shirt *nt* (*pl* T-Shirts)
teeth *npl see* **tooth**
teleconferencing *n* Telekonferenzen *fpl*
telephone *n* Telefon *nt* (*pl* Telefone) ▷ *on the telephone* am Telefon; **a telephone box** eine Telefonzelle; **a telephone call** ein Anruf *m*; **the telephone directory** das Telefonbuch; **a telephone number** eine Telefonnummer
telescope *n* Teleskop *nt* (*pl* Teleskope)
television *n* Fernsehen *nt*; **on television** im Fernsehen; **a television programme** eine Fernsehsendung
tell *vb* sagen [**38**]; **to tell somebody something** jemandem etwas sagen [**38**]; **to tell somebody to do something** jemandem sagen [**38**], er solle etwas tun; **to tell lies** lügen [**47**]; **to tell a story** eine Geschichte erzählen [**19**]; **I can't tell the difference between them.** Ich kann sie nicht unterscheiden.
tell off *vb* schimpfen [**38**]
telly *n* Fernseher *m* (*pl* Fernseher); **to watch telly** fernsehen [**64**]; **on telly** im Fernsehen
temper *n* **to be in a temper** wütend sein [**65**]; **to lose one's temper** wütend werden [**91**]; **He's got a terrible temper.** Er ist furchtbar jähzornig.
temperature *n (of oven, water, person)* Temperatur *f*; **The temperature was thirty degrees.** Es waren dreißig Grad.; **to have a temperature** Fieber haben [**32**]
temple *n* Tempel *m* (*pl* Tempel)
temporary *adj* vorläufig
temptation *n* Versuchung *f*
tempting *adj* verlockend
ten *num* zehn ▷ *She's ten.* Sie ist zehn.
tend to *vb* **to tend to do something** dazu neigen [**38**], etwas zu tun
tennis *n* Tennis *nt* (*gen* Tennis) ▷ *Do you play tennis?* Spielst du Tennis?; **a tennis ball** ein Tennisball *m*; **a tennis court** ein Tennisplatz *m*
tennis player *n* Tennisspieler *m* (*pl* Tennisspieler), Tennisspielerin *f* ▷ *He's a tennis player.* Er ist Tennisspieler.
tenor *n* Tenor *m* (*pl* Tenöre)
tenpin bowling *n* Bowling *nt*; **to go tenpin bowling** Bowling spielen [**38**]
tense *adj* angespannt ▷ *a tense situation* eine angespannte Situation
▶ *n* **the present tense** das Präsens; **the future tense** das Futur
tension *n* Spannung *f*
tent *n* Zelt *nt* (*pl* Zelte)
tenth *adj* zehnte ▷ *the tenth floor* der zehnte Stock ▷ *the tenth of August* der zehnte August
term *n (at school)* Trimester *nt* (*pl* Trimester)
In Germany the school and university year is divided into two semesters rather than three terms.
to come to terms with something sich mit etwas abfinden [**24**]
terminal *adj (illness, patient)* unheilbar
▶ *n (of computer)* Terminal *nt* (*pl* Terminals); **an oil terminal** ein Ölterminal *m*; **an air terminal** ein Terminal *m*
terminally *adv* **to be terminally ill** unheilbar krank sein [**65**]
terrace *n* ❶ *(patio)* Terrasse *f* ❷ *(row of houses)* Häuserreihe *f*; **the terraces** *(at stadium)* die Ränge
terraced *adj* **a terraced house** ein Reihenhaus *nt*

terrible *adj* furchtbar ▷ *My German is terrible.* Mein Deutsch ist furchtbar.
terribly *adv* furchtbar ▷ *He suffered terribly.* Er litt furchtbar. ▷ *I'm terribly sorry.* Es tut mir furchtbar leid.
terrific *adj (wonderful)* super
super is invariable.
▷ *That's terrific!* Das ist super! ▷ *You look terrific!* Du siehst super aus!
terrified *adj* **I was terrified!** Ich hatte furchtbare Angst!
terrorism *n* Terrorismus *m (gen* Terrorismus)
terrorist *n* Terrorist *m (gen* Terroristen, *pl* Terroristen), Terroristin *f*; **a terrorist attack** ein Terrorangriff *m*
test *n* ❶ *(at school)* Arbeit *f* ▷ *I've got a test tomorrow.* Ich schreibe morgen eine Arbeit. ❷ *(trial, check)* Test *m (pl* Tests) ▷ *nuclear tests* Atomtests ❸ *(medical)* Untersuchung *f* ▷ *a blood test* eine Blutuntersuchung ▷ *They're going to do some more tests tomorrow.* Sie machen morgen noch weitere Untersuchungen.; **driving test** die Fahrprüfung
▶ *vb* ❶ probieren **[76]** *(perf* hat probiert); **to test something out** etwas ausprobieren **[4]** ❷ *(class)* abfragen **[4]** *(perf* hat abgefragt) ▷ *He tested us on the new vocabulary.* Er hat uns die neuen Wörter abgefragt.; **She was tested for drugs.** Man hat bei ihr ein Drogentest gemacht.
test tube *n* Reagenzglas *nt (gen* Reagenzglases, *pl* Reagenzgläser)
text *n (text message)* SMS *f (pl* SMS)
▶ *vb* eine SMS schicken **[48]** ▷ *I'll text you.* Ich schicke dir eine SMS.
textbook *n* Lehrbuch *nt (pl* Lehrbücher); **a German textbook** ein Deutschbuch
textiles *npl* Textilien *fpl*; **a textiles factory** eine Textilfabrik
text message *n* SMS *f (pl* SMS)
text messaging *n* Versenden von SMS *nt*
Thames *n* Themse *f*
than *conj* als ▷ *She's taller than me.* Sie ist größer als ich. ▷ *I've got more books than him.* Ich habe mehr Bücher als er. ▷ *more than ten years* mehr als zehn Jahre ▷ *more than once* mehr als einmal
thank *vb* sich bedanken **[7]** bei *(perf* hat sich bedankt) ▷ *Don't forget to write and thank them.* Vergiss nicht, ihnen zu schreiben und dich bei ihnen zu bedanken.; **thank you** danke; **thank you very much** vielen Dank
thanks *excl* danke; **thanks to** dank
that *adj, pron, conj* ❶ dieser ▷ *that man* dieser Mann; diese ▷ *that woman* diese Frau; dieses ▷ *that book* dieses Buch; **that one (1)** *(masculine)* der da ▷ *This man? — No, that one.* Dieser Mann? — Nein, der da. **(2)** *(feminine)* die da ▷ *This woman? — No, that one.* Diese Frau? — Nein, die da. **(3)** *(neuter)* das da ▷ *Do you like this photo? — No, I prefer that one.* Gefällt dir dieses Foto? — Nein, das da gefällt mir besser. ❷ das ▷ *Did you see that?* Hast du das gesehen? ▷ *What's that?* Was ist das? ▷ *Who's that?* Wer ist das? ▷ *Is that you?* Bist du das?; **That's ...** Das ist ... ▷ *That's my German teacher.* Das ist meine Deutschlehrerin.; **That's what he said.** Das hat er gesagt.
In relative clauses use **der**, **die** or **das**, depending on the gender of the noun 'that' refers to.
❸ der ▷ *the man that saw us* der Mann, der uns sah; die ▷ *the woman that saw us* die Frau, die uns sah; das ▷ *the child that saw us* das Kind, das uns sah; die ▷ *the people that helped us* die Leute, die uns geholfen haben ❹ dass ▷ *He thought that Henry was ill.* Er dachte, dass Henry krank war. ▷ *I know that she likes chocolate.* Ich weiß, dass sie Schokolade mag. ❺ so ▷ *It was that big.* Es war so groß. ▷ *It's about that high.* Es ist etwa so hoch. ▷ *It's not that difficult.* Es ist nicht so schwierig.

the *art*

> Use **der** with a masculine noun, **die** with a feminine noun, and **das** with a neuter noun. For plural nouns always use **die**.

❶ der ▷ *the boy* der Junge; die ▷ *the orange* die Orange; das ▷ *the girl* das Mädchen ❷ die ▷ *the children* die Kinder

theatre *n* Theater *nt* (*pl* Theater)

theft *n* Diebstahl *m* (*pl* Diebstähle)

their *adj* ihr ▷ *their father* ihr Vater ▷ *their mother* ihre Mutter ▷ *their child* ihr Kind ▷ *their parents* ihre Eltern

> Do not use **ihr** with parts of the body.

▷ *They can't bend their arms.* Sie können die Arme nicht bewegen.

theirs *pron* ❶ ihrer ▷ *This is our computer, not theirs.* Das ist unser Computer, nicht ihrer.
ihre ▷ *It's not our garage, it's theirs.* Das ist nicht unsere Garage, sondern ihre.
ihres ▷ *It's not our car, it's theirs.* Das ist nicht unser Auto, sondern ihres. ❷ ihre ▷ *These are not our ideas, they're theirs.* Das sind nicht unsere Ideen, sondern ihre.; **Is this theirs?** Gehört das ihnen?

them *pron* ❶ sie ▷ *I didn't see them.* Ich habe sie nicht gesehen.

> Use **sie** after prepositions which take the accusative.

▷ *It's for them.* Es ist für sie. ❷ ihnen

> Use **ihnen** when 'them' means 'to them'.

▷ *I gave them some brochures.* Ich habe ihnen ein paar Broschüren gegeben. ▷ *I told them the truth.* Ich habe ihnen die Wahrheit gesagt.

> Use **ihnen** after prepositions which take the dative.

▷ *Ann and Sophie came. Graham was with them.* Ann und Sophie sind gekommen. Graham war bei ihnen.

themselves *pron* ❶ sich ▷ *Did they hurt themselves?* Haben sie sich verletzt? ❷ selbst ▷ *They did it themselves.* Sie haben es selbst gemacht.

then *adv, conj* ❶ dann ▷ *I get dressed. Then I have breakfast.* Ich ziehe mich an. Dann frühstücke ich. ▷ *My pen's run out. — Use a pencil then!* Mein Kugelschreiber ist leer. — Dann nimm einen Bleistift! ❷ *(at that time)* damals ▷ *There was no electricity then.* Damals gab es keinen Strom.; **now and then** ab und zu ▷ *Do you play chess? — Now and then.* Spielst du Schach? — Ab und zu.; **By then it was too late.** Da war es schon zu spät.

there *adv*

> Use **dort** when something is in a fixed position, **dorthin** when there is movement involved.

❶ dort ▷ *Can you see that house there?* Siehst du das Haus dort? ▷ *Berlin? I've never been there.* Berlin? Ich war noch nie dort.; **over there** dort drüben; **in there** dort drin; **on there** darauf; **up there** dort oben; **down there** dort unten ❷ dorthin ▷ *Put it there.* Stell es dorthin. ▷ *He went there on Friday.* Er ging am Freitag dorthin.; **There he is!** Da ist er ja!; **There is ... (1)** Es ist ... ▷ *There's a factory near my house.* In der Nähe von meinem Haus ist eine Fabrik. **(2)** Es gibt ... ▷ *There is a lot of poverty in the world.* Es gibt viel Armut auf der Welt.; **There are ... (1)** Es sind ... ▷ *There are five people in my family.* In meiner Familie sind fünf Leute. **(2)** Es gibt ... ▷ *There are many schools in this city.* In dieser Stadt gibt es viele Schulen.; **There has been an accident.** Es hat einen Unfall gegeben.

therefore *adv* deshalb

there's = **there is**; **there has**

thermometer *n* Thermometer *nt* (*pl* Thermometer)

Thermos® *n* Thermosflasche® *f*

these *adj, pron* ❶ die ▷ *these shoes* die Schuhe; **THESE shoes** diese Schuhe hier ❷ die hier ▷ *I want these!* Ich möchte die hier! ▷ *I'm looking for some sandals. Can I try these?* Ich suche Sandalen. Kann ich die hier anprobieren?

they *pron* sie ▷ *Are there any tickets left? — No, they're all sold.* Gibt es noch Karten? — Nein, sie sind schon alle verkauft. ▷ *Do you like those shoes? — No, they're horrible.* Gefallen dir die Schuhe? — Nein, sie sind furchtbar.; **They say that ...** Man sagt, dass ...

they'd = **they had**; **they would**

they'll = **they will**

they're = **they are**

they've = **they have**

thick *adj* ❶ *(not thin)* dick ▷ *one metre thick* einen Meter dick ❷ *(stupid)* dumm

thief *n* Dieb *m* (*pl* Diebe), Diebin *f*

thigh *n* Schenkel *m*

thin *adj* dünn

thing *n* Ding *nt* (*pl* Dinge) ▷ *beautiful things* schöne Dinge ▷ *What's that thing called?* Wie heißt das Ding da?; **my things** *(belongings)* meine Sachen; **You poor thing! (1)** *(man)* Du Armer! **(2)** *(woman)* Du Arme!

think *vb* ❶ denken **[14]** (*imperf* dachte, *perf* hat gedacht) ▷ *I think you're wrong.* Ich denke, du hast unrecht. ▷ *What are you thinking about?* Woran denkst du?; **What do you think about the suggestion?** Was halten Sie von dem Vorschlag? ❷ glauben **[38]** ▷ *I don't think I can come.* Ich glaube nicht, dass ich kommen kann.; **I think so.** Ich glaube schon.; **I don't think so.** Ich glaube nicht. ❸ *(spend time thinking)* nachdenken **[14]** (*perf* hat nachgedacht) ▷ *Think carefully before you reply.* Denk gut nach, bevor du antwortest. ▷ *I'll think about it.* Ich denke darüber nach. ❹ *(imagine)* sich vorstellen **[4]** (*perf* hat sich vorgestellt) ▷ *Think what life would be like without cars.* Stell dir vor, wie es wäre, wenn es keine Autos gäbe.; **I'll think it over.** Ich werde es mir überlegen.

third *adj* dritte ▷ *the third day* der dritte Tag ▷ *the third time* das dritte Mal ▷ *the third of August* der dritte August; **He came third.** Er wurde Dritter.
▶ *n* Drittel *nt* (*pl* Drittel) ▷ *a third of the population* ein Drittel der Bevölkerung

thirdly *adv* drittens

Third World *n* Dritte Welt *f*

thirst *n* Durst *m*

thirsty *adj* **to be thirsty** Durst haben **[32]**

thirteen *num* dreizehn ▷ *I'm thirteen.* Ich bin dreizehn.

thirteenth *adj* dreizehnte ▷ *the thirteenth of August* der dreizehnte August

thirty *num* dreißig ▷ *She's thirty.* Sie ist dreißig.

this *adj, pron* ❶ dieser ▷ *this man* dieser Mann; diese ▷ *this woman* diese Frau; dieses ▷ *this child* dieses Kind; **this one (1)** *(masculine)* der hier ▷ *That man over there? — No, this one.* Der Mann dort? — Nein, der hier. **(2)** *(feminine)* die hier ▷ *That woman over there? — No, this one.* Die Frau dort? — Nein, die hier. **(3)** *(neuter)* das hier ▷ *I don't like that picture over there, I prefer this one.* Das Bild dort gefällt mir nicht, das hier gefällt mir besser. ❷ das ▷ *You see this?* Siehst du das? ▷ *What's this?* Was ist das? ▷ *This is my mother. (introduction)* Das ist meine Mutter.; **This is Gavin speaking.** *(on the phone)* Hier spricht Gavin.

thistle *n* Distel *f*

thorough *adj* gründlich ▷ *She's very thorough.* Sie ist sehr gründlich.

those *adj, pron* ❶ diese ▷ *those shoes* diese Schuhe; **THOSE shoes** diese Schuhe dort ❷ die da ▷ *I want those!* Ich möchte die da! ▷ *I'm looking for some sandals. Can I try those?* Ich suche Sandalen. Kann ich die da anprobieren?

though *conj, adv* obwohl ▷ *It's warm, though it's raining.* Es ist warm, obwohl es regnet.; **He's nice, though not very clever.** Er ist nett, aber nicht besonders klug.

thought *vb see* **think**
▶ *n (idea)* Gedanke *m* (*gen* Gedankens, *pl* Gedanken) ▷ *I've just had a thought.* Mir

ist eben ein Gedanke gekommen.; **It was a nice thought, thank you.** Das war nett, vielen Dank.; **It's the thought that counts.** Es war gut gemeint.

thoughtful *adj* ❶ *(deep in thought)* nachdenklich ▷ *You look thoughtful.* Du siehst nachdenklich aus. ❷ *(considerate)* aufmerksam ▷ *She's very thoughtful.* Sie ist sehr aufmerksam.

thoughtless *adj* gedankenlos

thousand *num* **a thousand** eintausend; **two thousand pounds** zweitausend Pfund; **thousands of people** Tausende von Menschen

thousandth *adj* tausendste

thread *n* Faden *m* (*pl* Fäden)

threat *n* Drohung *f*

threaten *vb* drohen [**38**] ▷ *He threatened me.* Er hat mir gedroht. ▷ *to threaten to do something* drohen, etwas zu tun

three *num* drei ▷ *She's three.* Sie ist drei.

three-piece suite *n* dreiteilige Polstergarnitur *f*

threw *vb see* **throw**

thrilled *adj* **I was thrilled.** *(pleased)* Ich habe mich unheimlich gefreut.

thriller *n* Thriller *m* (*pl* Thriller)

thrilling *adj* spannend

throat *n* Hals *m* (*gen* Halses, *pl* Hälse); **to have a sore throat** Halsweh haben [**32**]

through *prep, adj, adv* durch ▷ *through the window* durch das Fenster ▷ *to go through Leeds* durch Leeds fahren ▷ *to go through a tunnel* durch einen Tunnel fahren; **I know her through my sister.** Ich kenne sie über meine Schwester.; **The window was dirty and I couldn't see through.** Das Fenster war schmutzig, und ich konnte nicht durchsehen.; **a through train** ein durchgehender Zug; **'no through road'** 'keine Durchfahrt'

throughout *prep* **throughout Britain** in ganz Großbritannien; **throughout the year** das ganze Jahr über

throw *vb* werfen [**92**] (*pres* wirft, *imperf* warf, *perf* hat geworfen) ▷ *He threw the ball to me.* Er warf mir den Ball zu.; **to throw a party** eine Party machen [**48**]; **That really threw him.** Das hat ihn aus der Fassung gebracht.; **to throw away (1)** *(rubbish)* wegwerfen [**92**] **(2)** *(chance)* vergeben [**28**]; **to throw out (1)** *(throw away)* wegwerfen [**92**] **(2)** *(person)* rauswerfen [**92**] ▷ *I threw him out.* Ich habe ihn rausgeworfen.; **to throw up** sich übergeben [**28**]

thumb *n* Daumen *m* (*pl* Daumen)

thumb tack *n (US)* Reißzwecke *f*

thump *vb* **to thump somebody** *(informal)* jemandem eine verpassen [**7**]

thunder *n* Donner *m* (*pl* Donner)

thunderstorm *n* Gewitter *nt* (*pl* Gewitter)

Thursday *n* Donnerstag *m* (*pl* Donnerstage) ▷ *on Thursday* am Donnerstag ▷ *every Thursday* jeden Donnerstag ▷ *last Thursday* letzten Donnerstag ▷ *next Thursday* nächsten Donnerstag; **on Thursdays** donnerstags

tick *n* ❶ *(mark)* Häkchen *nt* (*pl* Häkchen) ❷ *(of clock)* Ticken *nt*; **in a tick** in einer Sekunde
▶ *vb* ❶ ankreuzen [**36**] (*perf* hat angekreuzt) ▷ *Tick the appropriate box.* Kreuzen Sie das entsprechende Kästchen an. ❷ *(clock)* ticken [**48**]; **to tick off (1)** *(on list)* abhaken [**4**] **(2)** *(scold)* ausschimpfen [**4**]

ticket *n* ❶ *(for bus, tube, train)* Fahrkarte *f* ▷ *an underground ticket* eine Fahrkarte für die U-Bahn ❷ *(for plane)* Ticket *nt* (*pl* Tickets) ❸ *(for theatre, concert, cinema, museum)* Eintrittskarte *f*; **a parking ticket** ein Strafzettel *m*

ticket inspector *n* Fahrscheinkontrolleur *m* (*pl* Fahrscheinkontrolleure), Fahrscheinkontrolleurin *f*

ticket office *n* ❶ *(for travel)* Fahrkartenschalter *m* (*pl*

Fahrkartenschalter) ❷ *(for theatre, cinema)* Kasse *f*

tickle *vb* kitzeln [**34**]

tide *n* **high tide** die Flut; **low tide** die Ebbe

tidy *adj* ordentlich ▷ *Your room is very tidy.* Dein Zimmer ist sehr ordentlich. ▷ *She's very tidy.* Sie ist sehr ordentlich.
▶ *vb* aufräumen [**4**] (*perf* hat aufgeräumt) ▷ *Go and tidy your room.* Geh und räum dein Zimmer auf.; **to tidy up** aufräumen [**4**]

tie *n (necktie)* Krawatte *f*; **It was a tie.** *(in sport)* Es gab ein Unentschieden.
▶ *vb* ❶ *(ribbon, shoelaces)* zubinden (*imperf* band zu, *perf* hat zugebunden); **I tied a knot in the rope.** Ich machte einen Knoten in das Seil. ❷ *(in sport)* unentschieden spielen [**38**]; **They tied three all.** Sie haben drei zu drei gespielt.; **to tie up (1)** *(parcel)* zuschnüren [**4**] **(2)** *(dog, boat)* anbinden **(3)** *(prisoner)* fesseln [**34**]

tiger *n* Tiger *m* (*pl* Tiger)

tight *adj* ❶ *(tight-fitting)* eng ▷ *tight jeans* enge Jeans ❷ *(too tight)* zu eng ▷ *This dress is a bit tight.* Das Kleid ist etwas zu eng.

tighten *vb* ❶ *(rope)* spannen [**38**] ❷ *(screw)* anziehen [**96**] (*imperf* zog an, *perf* hat angezogen)

tightly *adv (hold)* fest

tights *npl* Strumpfhose *fsg* ▷ *a pair of tights* eine Strumpfhose

tile *n* ❶ *(on roof)* Dachziegel *m* (*pl* Dachziegel) ❷ *(on wall, floor)* Fliese *f*

till *n* Kasse *f*
▶ *prep, conj* ❶ bis ▷ *I waited till ten o'clock.* Ich habe bis zehn Uhr gewartet.; **till now** bis jetzt; **till then** bis dann ❷ vor

> Use **vor** if the sentence you want to translate contains a negative such as 'not' or 'never'.

▷ *It won't be ready till next week.* Vor nächster Woche wird es nicht fertig. ▷ *Till last year I'd never been to Germany.* Vor letztem Jahr war ich nie in Deutschland.

time *n* ❶ Zeit *f* ▷ *It's time to get up.* Es ist Zeit zum Aufstehen. ▷ *It was two o'clock, German time.* Es war zwei Uhr, deutsche Zeit. ▷ *I'm sorry, I haven't got time.* Ich habe leider keine Zeit.; **What time is it?** Wie viel Uhr ist es?; **What time do you get up?** Um wie viel Uhr stehst du auf?; **on time** pünktlich; **from time to time** von Zeit zu Zeit; **in time** rechtzeitig; **just in time** gerade noch rechtzeitig; **in no time** im Nu ❷ *(moment)* Moment *m* (*pl* Momente) ▷ *This isn't a good time to ask him.* Das ist kein guter Moment, um ihn zu fragen.; **for the time being** momentan ❸ *(occasion)* Mal *nt* (*pl* Male) ▷ *next time* nächstes Mal; **this time** diesmal; **two at a time** jeweils zwei; **How many times?** Wie oft?; **at times** manchmal; **a long time** lange; **in a week's time** in einer Woche; **Come and see us any time.** Besuchen sie uns, wann Sie wollen.; **to have a good time** sich amüsieren [**76**]; **two times two** zwei mal zwei

time off *n* Freizeit *f*

timetable *n* ❶ *(for train, bus)* Fahrplan *m* (*pl* Fahrpläne) ❷ *(at school)* Stundenplan *m* (*pl* Stundenpläne)

tin *n* ❶ Dose *f* ▷ *a tin of beans* eine Dose Bohnen ▷ *a biscuit tin* eine Keksdose ❷ *(type of metal)* Zinn *nt*

tin opener *n* Dosenöffner *m* (*pl* Dosenöffner)

tiny *adj* winzig

tip *n* ❶ *(money)* Trinkgeld *nt* (*pl* Trinkgelder) ▷ *Shall I give him a tip?* Soll ich ihm ein Trinkgeld geben? ❷ *(advice)* Tipp *m* (*pl* Tipps) ▷ *a useful tip* ein guter Tipp ❸ *(end)* Spitze *f*; **It's on the tip of my tongue.** Es liegt mir auf der Zunge.; **a rubbish tip** eine Müllkippe; **This place is a complete tip!** *(informal)* Was für ein Saustall!
▶ *vb* **to tip somebody** jemandem ein Trinkgeld geben [**28**]

tipsy *adj* beschwipst ▷ *I'm feeling a bit tipsy.* Ich bin etwas beschwipst.
tiptoe *n* **on tiptoe** auf Zehenspitzen
tired *adj* müde ▷ *I'm tired.* Ich bin müde.; **to be tired of something** etwas leid sein [**65**]
tiring *adj* ermüdend
tissue *n* Papiertaschentuch *nt* (*pl* Papiertaschentücher) ▷ *Have you got a tissue?* Hast du ein Papiertaschentuch?
title *n* Titel *m* (*pl* Titel)
to *prep* ❶ nach ▷ *to go to Munich* nach München fahren ▷ *We went to Italy.* Wir sind nach Italien gefahren. ▷ *the train to London* der Zug nach London ▷ *the road to Edinburgh* die Straße nach Edinburgh ▷ *to the left* nach links; **I've never been to Munich.** Ich war noch nie in München. ❷ in ▷ *to go to school* in die Schule gehen ▷ *to go to the theatre* ins Theater gehen ❸ zu

> Use **zu** when you talk about going to a particular place or person.

▷ *We drove to the station.* Wir fuhren zum Bahnhof. ▷ *to go to the doctor's* zum Arzt gehen ▷ *to go to the baker's* zum Bäcker gehen ▷ *Let's go to Anne's house.* Lass uns zu Anne nach Hause gehen.; **a letter to his mother** ein Brief an seine Mutter; **It's hard to say.** Es ist schwer zu sagen.; **It's easy to criticize.** Es ist leicht zu kritisieren.; **something to drink** etwas zu trinken ❹ (*as far as, until*) bis ▷ *to count to ten* bis zehn zählen ▷ *It's ninety kilometres to the border.* Es sind neunzig Kilometer bis zur Grenze.; **from ... to** von ... bis; **ten to nine** zehn vor neun

> Use the dative when you say or give something to somebody.

▷ *Give it to me!* Gib es mir! ▷ *That's what he said to me.* Das ist, was er zu mir gesagt hat.; **to talk to somebody** mit jemandem reden [**54**]

> When 'to' is used with the infinitive, it is often not translated.

▷ *I'd like to go.* Ich würde gern gehen. ❺ (*in order to*) um ... zu

> **um ... zu** is used with the infinitive.

▷ *I did it to help you.* Ich tat es, um dir zu helfen. ▷ *She's too young to go to school.* Sie ist noch zu jung, um in die Schule zu gehen.; **the key to the front door** der Schlüssel für die Haustür; **the answer to the question** die Antwort auf die Frage
toad *n* Kröte *f*
toast *n* ❶ Toast *m* (*pl* Toasts) ▷ *a piece of toast* eine Scheibe Toast ❷ (*speech*) Trinkspruch *m* (*pl* Trinksprüche) ▷ *to drink a toast to somebody* einen Trinkspruch auf jemanden ausbringen
toaster *n* Toaster *m* (*pl* Toaster)
toastie *n* Toast *m* (*pl* Toasts) ▷ *a cheese toastie* ein Käsetoast
tobacco *n* Tabak *m*
tobacconist's *n* Tabakladen *m* (*pl* Tabakläden)
today *adv* heute ▷ *What did you do today?* Was hast du heute gemacht?
toddler *n* Kleinkind *nt* (*pl* Kleinkinder)
toe *n* Zeh *m* (*pl* Zehen) ▷ *my big toe* mein großer Zeh
toffee *n* Karamell *m*
together *adv* ❶ zusammen ▷ *Are they still together?* Sind sie noch zusammen? ❷ (*at the same time*) gleichzeitig ▷ *Don't all speak together!* Redet nicht alle gleichzeitig!; **together with** (*with person*) zusammen mit
toilet *n* Toilette *f*
toilet paper *n* Toilettenpapier *nt*
toiletries *npl* Toilettenartikel *mpl*
toilet roll *n* Rolle Toilettenpapier *f*
told *vb see* **tell**
toll *n* (*on bridge, motorway*) Benutzungsgebühr *f*
tomato *n* Tomate *f* ▷ *tomato soup* die Tomatensuppe
tomorrow *adv* morgen ▷ *tomorrow morning* morgen früh ▷ *tomorrow night* morgen Abend; **the day after tomorrow** übermorgen

ton *n* Tonne *f* ▷ *That old bike weighs a ton.* Das alte Fahrrad wiegt ja eine Tonne.
tongue *n* Zunge *f*; **to say something tongue in cheek** etwas nicht so ernst meinen [**38**]
tonic *n (tonic water)* Tonic *nt (pl* Tonics); **a gin and tonic** ein Gin Tonic *m*
tonight *adv* ❶ *(this evening)* heute Abend ▷ *Are you going out tonight?* Gehst du heute Abend aus? ❷ *(during the night)* heute Nacht ▷ *I'll sleep well tonight.* Ich werde heute Nacht gut schlafen.
tonsillitis *n* Mandelentzündung *f* ▷ *She's got tonsillitis.* Sie hat eine Mandelentzündung.
tonsils *npl* Mandeln *fpl*
too *adv, adj* ❶ *(as well)* auch ▷ *My sister came too.* Meine Schwester ist auch mitgekommen. ❷ *(excessively)* zu ▷ *The water's too hot.* Das Wasser ist zu heiß. ▷ *We arrived too late.* Wir sind zu spät gekommen.; **too much** zu viel; **too many** zu viele; **Too bad!** Da kann man nichts machen!
took *vb see* **take**
tool *n* Werkzeug *nt (pl* Werkzeuge); **a tool box** ein Werkzeugkasten *m*
tooth *n* Zahn *m (pl* Zähne)
toothache *n* Zahnschmerzen *mpl* ▷ *to have toothache* Zahnschmerzen haben
toothbrush *n* Zahnbürste *f*
toothpaste *n* Zahnpasta *f (pl* Zahnpasten)
top *n* ❶ *(of tree)* Spitze *f* ❷ *(of mountain)* Gipfel *m (pl* Gipfel) ❸ *(of garment)* Oberteil *nt (pl* Oberteile) ▷ *a bikini top* ein Bikinioberteil ❹ *(of table)* Kopfende *nt (pl* Kopfenden) ❺ *(of box, jar)* Deckel *m (pl* Deckel) ❻ *(of bottle)* Verschluss *m (gen* Verschlusses, *pl* Verschlüsse); **at the top of the page** oben auf der Seite; **to reach the top of the ladder** oben auf der Leiter ankommen [**40**]; **on top of** *(on)* oben auf; **There's a surcharge on top of that.** Es kommt noch ein Zuschlag dazu.; **from top to bottom** von oben bis unten
▶ *adj (first-class)* erstklassig ▷ *a top hotel* ein erstklassiges Hotel; **a top surgeon** ein Spitzenchirurg *m*; **a top model** *(fashion)* ein Topmodel *nt*; **He always gets top marks.** Er bekommt immer Spitzennoten.; **the top floor** der oberste Stock
topic *n* Thema *nt (pl* Themen) ▷ *The essay can be on any topic.* Der Aufsatz kann über ein beliebiges Thema sein.
torch *n* Taschenlampe *f*
tortoise *n* Schildkröte *f*
torture *n* Folter *f*; **It was pure torture.** *(informal)* Es war die Hölle.
▶ *vb* quälen [**38**] ▷ *Stop torturing that poor animal!* Hör auf, das arme Tier zu quälen!
total *adj* gesamt ▷ *the total amount* der gesamte Betrag
▶ *n* ❶ *(amount)* Gesamtmenge *f* ❷ *(money, figures)* Endsumme *f*; **the grand total** die Gesamtsumme
totally *adv* völlig ▷ *He's totally useless.* Er ist völlig unfähig.
touch *n* **to get in touch with somebody** sich mit jemandem in Verbindung setzen [**36**]; **to keep in touch with somebody** mit jemandem in Verbindung bleiben [**10**]; **Keep in touch!** Lass von dir hören!; **to lose touch** sich aus den Augen verlieren [**85**]; **to lose touch with somebody** jemanden aus den Augen verlieren [**85**]
▶ *vb* berühren [**18**] *(perf* hat berührt); **'Do not touch'** 'Nicht berühren'; **Don't touch that!** Fass das nicht an!
tough *adj* ❶ hart ▷ *It was tough, but I managed OK.* Es war hart, aber ich habe es geschafft. ▷ *It's a tough job.* Das ist eine harte Arbeit. ▷ *He thinks he's a tough guy.* Er meint, er sei ein harter Bursche. ❷ *(meat)* zäh ▷ *The meat's tough.* Das Fleisch ist zäh. ❸ *(strong)* fest ▷ *tough leather gloves* feste Lederhandschuhe; **Tough luck!** Das ist Pech!

tour *n* ❶ *(of town, museum)* Besichtigung *f*; **We went on a tour of the city.** Wir haben die Stadt besichtigt.; **a guided tour** eine Führung; **a package tour** eine Pauschalreise ❷ *(by singer, group)* Tournee *f* ▷ *on tour* auf Tournee ▷ *to go on tour* auf Tournee gehen
▸ *vb* **Sting's touring Europe.** *(singer, artiste)* Sting ist auf Europatournee.
tourism *n* Tourismus *m* (*gen* Tourismus)
tourist *n* Tourist *m* (*gen* Touristen, *pl* Touristen), Touristin *f*; **tourist information office** das Verkehrsbüro
towards *prep* ❶ *(in the direction of)* auf ... zu ▷ *He came towards me.* Er kam auf mich zu. ❷ *(of attitude)* gegenüber ▷ *my feelings towards him* meine Empfindungen ihm gegenüber
towel *n* Handtuch *nt* (*pl* Handtücher)
tower *n* Turm *m* (*pl* Türme); **a tower block** ein Hochhaus *nt*
town *n* Stadt *f* (*pl* Städte); **a town plan** ein Stadtplan *m*; **the town centre** die Stadtmitte; **the town hall** das Rathaus
tow truck *n (US)* Abschleppwagen *m* (*pl* Abschleppwagen)
toy *n* Spielzeug *nt* (*pl* Spielzeuge); **a toy shop** ein Spielwarengeschäft *nt*; **a toy car** ein Spielzeugauto *nt*
trace *n* Spur *f* ▷ *There was no trace of him.* Von ihm fehlte jede Spur.
▸ *vb (draw)* nachziehen [**96**] (*imperf* zog nach, *perf* hat nachgezogen)
tracing paper *n* Pauspapier *nt*
track *n* ❶ *(dirt road)* Pfad *m* (*pl* Pfade) ❷ *(railway line)* Gleis *nt* (*gen* Gleises, *pl* Gleise) ❸ *(in sport)* Rennbahn *f* ▷ *two laps of the track* zwei Runden der Rennbahn ❹ *(song)* Stück *nt* (*pl* Stücke) ▷ *This is my favourite track.* Das ist mein Lieblingsstück. ❺ *(trail)* Spur *f* ▷ *They followed the tracks for miles.* Sie folgten der Spur meilenweit.
track down *vb* **to track somebody down** jemanden finden [**24**] ▷ *The police never tracked down the killer.* Die Polizei hat den Mörder nie gefunden.
tracksuit *n* Jogginganzug *m* (*pl* Jogginganzüge)
tractor *n* Traktor *m* (*pl* Traktoren)
trade *n (skill, job)* Handwerk *nt* ▷ *to learn a trade* ein Handwerk erlernen
trade union *n* Gewerkschaft *f*
Unions in Germany are organized within the **Deutscher Gewerkschaftsbund (DGB)**.
tradition *n* Tradition *f*
traditional *adj* traditionell
traffic *n* Verkehr *m* ▷ *The traffic was terrible.* Es war furchtbar viel Verkehr.
traffic circle *n (US)* Kreisverkehr *m* (*pl* Kreisverkehre)
traffic jam *n* Stau *m* (*pl* Staus)
traffic lights *npl* Ampel *fsg*
traffic warden *n* ❶ *(man)* Hilfspolizist *m* (*gen* Hilfspolizisten, *pl* Hilfspolizisten) ❷ *(woman)* Politesse *f*
tragedy *n* Tragödie *f*
tragic *adj* tragisch
trailer *n* ❶ *(vehicle)* Anhänger *m* (*pl* Anhänger) ❷ *(caravan)* Wohnwagen *m* (*pl* Wohnwagen) ❸ *(advert for film)* Vorschau *f*
train *n* Zug *m* (*pl* Züge)
▸ *vb (sport)* trainieren [**76**] (*perf* hat trainiert) ▷ *to train for a race* für ein Rennen trainieren; **to train as a teacher** eine Lehrerausbildung machen [**48**]; **to train an animal to do something** ein Tier dressieren [**76**], etwas zu tun
trained *adj* gelernt ▷ *She's a trained nurse.* Sie ist gelernte Krankenschwester.
trainee *n* ❶ *(in profession)* Praktikant *m* (*gen* Praktikanten, *pl* Praktikanten), Praktikantin *f* ▷ *She's a trainee.* Sie ist Praktikantin. ❷ *(apprentice)* Lehrling *m* (*pl* Lehrlinge)
der Lehrling is also used for women.
▷ *She's a trainee plumber.* Sie ist Klempnerlehrling.
trainer *n* ❶ *(sports coach)* Trainer *m* (*pl* Trainer), Trainerin *f* ❷ *(of animals)* Dresseur *m* (*pl* Dresseure), Dresseuse *f*

trainers *npl* Turnschuhe *mpl* ▷ *a pair of trainers* ein Paar Turnschuhe
training *n* ❶ Ausbildung *f* ▷ *a training course* ein Ausbildungskurs *m* ❷ *(sport)* Training *nt* (*pl* Trainings)
tram *n* Straßenbahn *f*
tramp *n* Landstreicher *m* (*pl* Landstreicher), Landstreicherin *f*
trampoline *n* Trampolin *nt* (*pl* Trampoline)
transfer *n (sticker)* Abziehbild *nt* (*pl* Abziehbilder)
transit lounge *n* Transithalle *f*
translate *vb* übersetzen [**36**] (*perf* hat übersetzt) ▷ *to translate something into English* etwas ins Englische übersetzen
translation *n* Übersetzung *f*
translator *n* Übersetzer *m* (*pl* Übersetzer), Übersetzerin *f* ▷ *Anita's a translator.* Anita ist Übersetzerin.
transparent *adj* durchsichtig
transplant *n* Transplantation *f* ▷ *a heart transplant* eine Herztransplantation
transport *n* Transport *m* (*pl* Transporte) ▷ *the transport of goods* der Warentransport
▶ *vb* transportieren [**76**] (*perf* hat transportiert)
trap *n* Falle *f*
trash *n (US)* Müll *m*
trash can *n (US)* Mülleimer *m* (*pl* Mülleimer)
travel *n* Reisen *nt*
▶ *vb* reisen [**36**] (*perf* ist gereist) ▷ *I prefer to travel by train.* Ich reise lieber mit dem Zug.; **I'd like to travel round the world.** Ich würde gern eine Weltreise machen.; **We travelled over eight hundred kilometres.** Wir haben über achthundert Kilometer zurückgelegt.; **News travels fast!** Neuigkeiten sprechen sich schnell herum!
travel agency *n* Reisebüro *nt* (*pl* Reisebüros)
travel agent *n* Reisebürokaufmann *m* (*pl* Reisebürokaufleute), Reisebürokauffrau *f* ▷ *She's a travel agent.* Sie ist Reisebürokauffrau.; **at the travel agent's** im Reisebüro
traveller *n* ❶ *(on bus, train)* Fahrgast *m* (*pl* Fahrgäste)

> **der Fahrgast** is also used for women.

❷ *(on plane)* Passagier *m* (*pl* Passagiere), Passagierin *f*
traveller's cheque *n* Reisescheck *m* (*pl* Reiseschecks)
travelling *n* **I love travelling.** Ich reise sehr gern.
travel sickness *n* Reisekrankheit *f*
tray *n* Tablett *nt* (*pl* Tabletts)
tread *vb* treten [**79**] (*pres* tritt, *imperf* trat, *perf* ist getreten) ▷ *to tread on something* auf etwas treten ▷ *He trod on her foot.* Er ist ihr auf den Fuß getreten.
treasure *n* Schatz *m* (*gen* Schatzes, *pl* Schätze)
treat *n* ❶ *(present)* Geschenk *nt* (*pl* Geschenke) ❷ *(food)* Leckerbissen *m* (*pl* Leckerbissen); **to give somebody a treat** jemandem eine besondere Freude machen [**48**]
▶ *vb (well, badly)* behandeln [**34**] (*perf* hat behandelt); **to treat somebody to something** jemandem etwas spendieren [**76**]
treatment *n* Behandlung *f*
treble *vb* sich verdreifachen [**7**] (*perf* hat sich verdreifacht) ▷ *The price has trebled.* Der Preis hat sich verdreifacht.
tree *n* Baum *m* (*pl* Bäume)
tremble *vb* zittern [**88**]
tremendous *adj* ❶ fantastisch ▷ *Gordon is a tremendous person.* Gordon ist fantastisch. ❷ gewaltig ▷ *a tremendous success* ein gewaltiger Erfolg
trend *n* ❶ *(tendency)* Tendenz *f* ❷ *(fashion)* Trend *m* (*pl* Trends)
trendy *adj* modisch
trial *n (in court)* Prozess *m* (*gen* Prozesses, *pl* Prozesse)
triangle *n* Dreieck *nt* (*pl* Dreiecke)
tribe *n* Stamm *m* (*pl* Stämme)

a b c d e f g h i j k l m n o p q r s t u v w x y z

trick *n* ❶ Streich *m* (*pl* Streiche) ▷ *to play a trick on somebody* jemandem einen Streich spielen ❷ *(knack)* Trick *m* (*pl* Tricks) ▷ *It's not easy: there's a trick to it.* Das ist nicht leicht: Da ist ein Trick dabei.
▶ *vb* **to trick somebody** jemanden reinlegen [**4**]

tricky *adj* knifflig

tricycle *n* Dreirad *nt* (*pl* Dreiräder)

trip *n* Reise *f* ▷ *to go on a trip* eine Reise machen ▷ *Have a good trip!* Gute Reise!; **a day trip** ein Tagesausflug *m*
▶ *vb* *(stumble)* stolpern [**88**]

triple *adj* dreifach

triplets *npl* Drillinge *mpl*

trivial *adj* trivial

troll *n (internet)* Troll *m* (*pl* Trolle)

trolley *n* ❶ *(for shopping)* Einkaufswagen *m* (*pl* Einkaufswagen) ❷ *(for luggage)* Kofferkuli *m* (*pl* Kofferkulis)

trolling *n (internet)* Trolling *nt*

trombone *n* Posaune *f* ▷ *I play the trombone.* Ich spiele Posaune.

troops *npl* Truppen *fpl* ▷ *British troops* die britischen Truppen

trophy *n* Trophäe *f* ▷ *to win a trophy* eine Trophäe gewinnen

tropical *adj* tropisch ▷ *tropical plants* tropische Pflanzen; **The weather was tropical.** Es war tropisch heiß.

trouble *n* Problem *nt* (*pl* Probleme) ▷ *The trouble is ...* Das Problem ist ...; **What's the trouble?** Was ist das Problem?; **to be in trouble** in Schwierigkeiten sein [**65**]; **stomach trouble** die Magenbeschwerden *fpl*; **to take a lot of trouble over something** sich mit etwas viel Mühe geben [**28**]; **Don't worry, it's no trouble.** Keine Sorge, das macht keine Mühe.

troublemaker *n* Unruhestifter *m* (*pl* Unruhestifter), Unruhestifterin *f*

trousers *npl* Hose *fsg* ▷ *a pair of trousers* eine Hose

trout *n* Forelle *f*

truant *n* **to play truant** die Schule schwänzen [**36**]

truck *n* Lastwagen *m* (*pl* Lastwagen); **He's a truck driver.** Er ist Lastwagenfahrer.

true *adj* wahr ▷ *true love* wahre Liebe ▷ *That's true.* Das ist wahr.; **to come true** wahr werden [**91**]

trumpet *n* Trompete *f* ▷ *She plays the trumpet.* Sie spielt Trompete.

trunk *n* ❶ *(of tree)* Stamm *m* (*pl* Stämme) ❷ *(of elephant)* Rüssel *m* (*pl* Rüssel) ❸ *(luggage)* Schrankkoffer *m* (*pl* Schrankkoffer) ❹ *(boot of car)* Kofferraum *m* (*pl* Kofferräume)

trunks *npl* **swimming trunks** die Badehose *sg*

trust *n* Vertrauen *nt* ▷ *to have trust in somebody* Vertrauen zu jemandem haben
▶ *vb* **to trust somebody** jemandem vertrauen [**84**]; **Trust me!** Glaub mir!

truth *n* Wahrheit *f*

try *n* Versuch *m* (*pl* Versuche) ▷ *his third try* sein dritter Versuch; **to have a try** es versuchen [**84**]; **It's worth a try.** Der Versuch lohnt sich.; **to give something a try** etwas versuchen [**84**]
▶ *vb* ❶ *(attempt)* versuchen [**84**] (*perf* hat versucht) ▷ *to try to do something* versuchen, etwas zu tun; **to try again** es noch einmal versuchen [**84**] ❷ *(taste)* probieren [**76**] (*perf* hat probiert) ▷ *Would you like to try some?* Möchtest du etwas probieren?; **to try on** *(clothes)* anprobieren [**76**]; **to try something out** etwas ausprobieren [**4**]

T-shirt *n* T-Shirt *nt* (*pl* T-Shirts)

tube *n* Tube *f*; **the Tube** *(underground)* die U-Bahn

tuberculosis *n* Tuberkulose *f*

Tuesday *n* Dienstag *m* (*pl* Dienstage) ▷ *on Tuesday* am Dienstag ▷ *every Tuesday* jeden Dienstag ▷ *last Tuesday* letzten Dienstag ▷ *next Tuesday* nächsten Dienstag; **on Tuesdays** dienstags

tug of war *n* Tauziehen *nt*

tuition *n* ❶ Unterricht *m*; **extra tuition** die Nachhilfestunden *fpl* ❷ *(tuition fees)* Studiengebühren *fpl*
tulip *n* Tulpe *f*
tumble dryer *n* Wäschetrockner *m* (*pl* Wäschetrockner)
tummy *n* Bauch *m* (*pl* Bäuche) ▷ *I've got a sore tummy.* Ich habe Bauchschmerzen.
tuna *n* Thunfisch *m* (*pl* Thunfische)
tune *n (melody)* Melodie *f*; **to play in tune** richtig spielen [**38**]; **to sing out of tune** falsch singen [**66**]
Tunisia *n* Tunesien *nt*; **in Tunisia** in Tunesien
tunnel *n* Tunnel *m* (*pl* Tunnel); **the Tunnel** *(Chunnel)* der Kanaltunnel
Turk *n* Türke *m* (*gen* Türken, *pl* Türken), Türkin *f*
Turkey *n* Türkei *f*

> Note that the definite article is used in German for countries which are feminine.

from Turkey aus der Türkei; **in Turkey** in der Türkei; **to Turkey** in die Türkei
turkey *n* Truthahn *m* (*pl* Truthähne)
Turkish *adj* türkisch
▶ *n (language)* Türkische *nt* (*gen* Türkischen)
turn *n (in road)* Abbiegung *f*; **'no left turn'** 'links abbiegen verboten'; **Whose turn is it?** Wer ist an der Reihe?; **It's my turn!** Ich bin an der Reihe!
▶ *vb* ❶ abbiegen (*imperf* bog ab, *perf* ist abgebogen) ▷ *Turn right at the lights.* Biegen Sie an der Ampel rechts ab. ❷ *(become)* werden [**91**] (*pres* wird, *imperf* wurde, *perf* ist geworden) ▷ *to turn red* rot werden; **to turn into something** sich in etwas verwandeln [**34**]
turn back *vb* umkehren [**4**] (*perf* ist umgekehrt)
turn down *vb* ❶ *(offer)* ablehnen [**4**] (*perf* hat abgelehnt) ❷ *(radio, TV)* leiser stellen [**38**] ❸ *(heating)* herunterdrehen [**15**] (*perf* hat heruntergedreht)
turn off *vb* ❶ *(light, radio)* ausmachen [**48**] (*perf* hat ausgemacht) ❷ *(tap)* zudrehen [**15**] (*perf* hat zugedreht) ❸ *(engine)* ausschalten [**2**] (*perf* hat ausgeschaltet)
turn on *vb* ❶ *(light, radio)* anmachen [**4**] (*perf* hat angemacht) ❷ *(tap)* aufdrehen [**15**] (*perf* hat aufgedreht) ❸ *(engine)* anlassen [**42**] (*pres* lässt an, *imperf* ließ an, *perf* hat angelassen)
turn out *vb* **It turned out to be a mistake.** Es stellte sich heraus, dass das ein Fehler war.
turn round *vb* ❶ *(car)* umkehren [**4**] (*perf* ist umgekehrt) ❷ *(person)* sich umdrehen [**4**] (*perf* hat sich umgedreht)
turn up *vb* ❶ *(arrive)* aufkreuzen [**4**] (*perf* ist aufgekreuzt) ❷ *(heater)* höherstellen [**15**] ❸ *(radio, TV)* lauter machen [**48**]
turning *n* **It's the third turning on the left.** Es ist die dritte Straße links.; **We took the wrong turning.** Wir sind falsch abgebogen.
turnip *n* Steckrübe *f*
turquoise *adj (colour)* türkis
turtle *n* Meeresschildkröte *f*
tutor *n (private teacher)* Lehrer *m* (*pl* Lehrer), Lehrerin *f*
TV *n* Fernsehen *nt*
tweet *vb (internet)* twittern [**88**]
tweezers *npl* Pinzette *fsg* ▷ *a pair of tweezers* eine Pinzette
twelfth *adj* zwölfte ▷ *the twelfth floor* der zwölfte Stock ▷ *the twelfth of August* der zwölfte August
twelve *num* zwölf ▷ *She's twelve.* Sie ist zwölf. ▷ *at twelve o'clock* um zwölf Uhr
twentieth *adj* zwanzigste ▷ *the twentieth of August* der zwanzigste August
twenty *num* zwanzig ▷ *He's twenty.* Er ist zwanzig.
twice *adv* zweimal; **twice as much** doppelt so viel
twin *n* Zwilling *m* (*pl* Zwillinge)

> **der Zwilling** is also used for women.

my twin brother mein Zwillingsbruder *m*; **her twin sister** ihre Zwillingsschwester; **identical twins** eineiige Zwillinge; **a twin room** ein Doppelzimmer mit zwei Betten

twinned *adj* **Oxford is twinned with Bonn.** Oxford und Bonn sind Partnerstädte.

twist *vb* ❶ *(bend)* biegen *(imperf* bog, *perf* hat gebogen); **I've twisted my ankle.** Ich habe mir den Fuß vertreten. ❷ *(distort)* verdrehen [**84**] *(perf* hat verdreht) ▷ *You're twisting my words.* Sie verdrehen meine Worte.

Twitter® *n* Twitter® *nt*

two *num* zwei ▷ *She's two.* Sie ist zwei.

type *n* Art *f* ▷ *What type of camera have you got?* Welche Art von Fotoapparat hast du?
▶ *vb* Schreibmaschine schreiben [**61**] ▷ *Can you type?* Kannst du Schreibmaschine schreiben?; **to type a letter** einen Brief tippen [**38**]

typewriter *n* Schreibmaschine *f*

typical *adj* typisch ▷ *That's just typical!* Das ist typisch!

tyre *n* Reifen *m (pl* Reifen) ▷ *the tyre pressure* der Reifendruck

U

UFO *n (= unidentified flying object)* UFO *nt (pl* UFOs) *(= unbekanntes Flugobjekt)*

ugly *adj* hässlich

UK *n (= United Kingdom)* **the UK** das Vereinigte Königreich; **from the UK** aus dem Vereinigten Königreich; **in the UK** im Vereinigten Königreich; **to the UK** in das Vereinigte Königreich

ulcer *n* Geschwür *nt (pl* Geschwüre)

Ulster *n* Ulster *nt*; **from Ulster** aus Ulster; **in Ulster** in Ulster; **to Ulster** nach Ulster

umbrella *n* ❶ Regenschirm *m (pl* Regenschirme) ❷ *(for sun)* Sonnenschirm *m (pl* Sonnenschirme)

umlaut *n* Umlaut *m* ▷ *The plural of 'Haus' is written with an umlaut.* Der Plural von 'Haus' wird mit Umlaut gebildet.; **a umlaut** ä; **o umlaut** ö; **u umlaut** ü

umpire *n* Schiedsrichter *m (pl* Schiedsrichter), Schiedsrichterin *f*

UN *n (= United Nations)* UN *pl*

unable *adj* **to be unable to do something** etwas nicht tun können [**41**]
unanimous *adj* einstimmig ▷ *a unanimous decision* ein einstimmiger Beschluss
unavoidable *adj* unvermeidlich
unbearable *adj* unerträglich
unbelievable *adj* unglaublich
unbreakable *adj* unzerbrechlich
uncertain *adj* ungewiss ▷ *The future is uncertain.* Die Zukunft ist ungewiss.; **to be uncertain about something** sich über etwas nicht im Klaren sein [**65**]
uncle *n* Onkel *m* (*pl* Onkel) ▷ *my uncle* mein Onkel
uncomfortable *adj* unbequem ▷ *The seats are rather uncomfortable.* Die Sitze sind ziemlich unbequem.
unconscious *adj* bewusstlos
uncontrollable *adj* unkontrollierbar
under *prep* unter

Use the accusative to express movement or a change of place. Use the dative when there is no change of place.

▷ *The ball rolled under the table.* Der Ball rollte unter den Tisch. ▷ *The cat's under the table.* Die Katze ist unter dem Tisch. ▷ *children under ten* Kinder unter zehn; **under there** da drunter; **under twenty people** weniger als zwanzig Leute
underage *adj* minderjährig
underdog *n* Underdog *m* (*pl* Underdogs) ▷ *We were the underdogs on this occasion.* Wir waren diesmal die Underdogs.
underground *adj, adv* ❶ unterirdisch ▷ *underground water pipes* unterirdische Wasserrohre; **an underground car park** eine Tiefgarage ❷ unter der Erde ▷ *Moles live underground.* Maulwürfe leben unter der Erde.
▶ *n* U-Bahn *f* ▷ *Is there an underground in Bonn?* Gibt es in Bonn eine U-Bahn?
underline *vb* unterstreichen (*imperf* unterstrich, *perf* hat unterstrichen)
underneath *prep, adv* ❶ unter

Use the accusative to express movement or a change of place. Use the dative when there is no change of place.

▷ *I put it underneath that pile.* Ich habe es unter diesen Stapel gelegt. ▷ *It was hidden underneath the carpet.* Es war unter dem Teppich versteckt.
❷ darunter ▷ *I got out of the car and looked underneath.* Ich stieg aus dem Auto aus und sah darunter.
underpants *npl* Unterhose *fsg* ▷ *a pair of underpants* eine Unterhose
underpass *n* Unterführung *f*
undershirt *n (US)* Unterhemd *nt* (*pl* Unterhemden)
understand *vb* verstehen [**72**] (*imperf* verstand, *perf* hat verstanden) ▷ *Do you understand?* Verstehst du? ▷ *I don't understand this word.* Ich verstehe dieses Wort nicht. ▷ *Is that understood?* Ist das verstanden?
understanding *adj* verständnisvoll ▷ *She's very understanding.* Sie ist sehr verständnisvoll.
understood *vb see* **understand**
undertaker *n* Beerdigungsunternehmer *m* (*pl* Beerdigungsunternehmer), Beerdigungsunternehmerin *f*
underwater *adj, adv* unter Wasser ▷ *It was filmed underwater.* Es wurde unter Wasser gefilmt.; **an underwater camera** eine Unterwasserkamera
underwear *n* Unterwäsche *f*
undo *vb* aufmachen [**4**] (*perf* hat aufgemacht)
undress *vb (get undressed)* sich ausziehen [**96**] (*imperf* zog sich aus, *perf* hat sich ausgezogen) ▷ *The doctor told me to get undressed.* Der Arzt bat mich, mich auszuziehen.
unemployed *adj* arbeitslos ▷ *He's unemployed.* Er ist arbeitslos. ▷ *He's been unemployed for a year.* Er ist seit einem

a b c d e f g h i j k l m n o p q r s t u v w x y z

Jahr arbeitslos.; **the unemployed** die Arbeitslosen *mpl*

unemployment *n* Arbeitslosigkeit *f*

unexpected *adj* unerwartet ▷ *an unexpected visitor* ein unerwarteter Gast

unexpectedly *adv* überraschend ▷ *They arrived unexpectedly.* Sie sind überraschend gekommen.

unfair *adj* unfair ▷ *It's unfair to girls.* Es ist Mädchen gegenüber unfair.

unfamiliar *adj* unbekannt ▷ *I heard an unfamiliar voice.* Ich hörte eine unbekannte Stimme.

unfashionable *adj* unmodern

unfit *adj* nicht fit ▷ *I'm rather unfit at the moment.* Ich bin im Moment nicht sehr fit.

unfold *vb* auseinanderfalten [**15**] (*perf* hat auseinandergefaltet) ▷ *She unfolded the map.* Sie faltete die Karte auseinander.

unforgettable *adj* unvergesslich

unfortunately *adv* leider ▷ *Unfortunately, I arrived late.* Ich bin leider zu spät gekommen.

unfriendly *adj* unfreundlich ▷ *They're a bit unfriendly.* Sie sind etwas unfreundlich.

ungrateful *adj* undankbar

unhappy *adj* unglücklich ▷ *He was very unhappy as a child.* Er war als Kind sehr unglücklich. ▷ *to look unhappy* unglücklich aussehen

unhealthy *adj* ungesund

uni *n* Uni *f* (*pl* Unis) ▷ *to go to uni* zur Uni gehen

uniform *n* Uniform *f* ▷ *the school uniform* die Schuluniform

School uniforms are virtually nonexistent in Germany.

uninhabited *adj* unbewohnt

union *n (trade union)* Gewerkschaft *f*

Union Jack *n* britische Flagge *f*

unique *adj* einzigartig

unit *n* Einheit *f* ▷ *a unit of measurement* eine Maßeinheit; **a kitchen unit** ein Kücheneinbauschrank *m*

United Kingdom *n* **the United Kingdom** das Vereinigte Königreich; **from the United Kingdom** aus dem Vereinigten Königreich; **in the United Kingdom** im Vereinigten Königreich; **to the United Kingdom** in das Vereinigte Königreich

United Nations *npl* **The United Nations are extremely important.** Die Vereinten Nationen sind äußerst wichtig.

United States *n* **The United States play a big role.** Die Vereinigten Staaten spielen eine große Rolle.; **from the United States** aus den Vereinigten Staaten; **in the United States** in den Vereinigten Staaten; **to the United States** in die Vereinigten Staaten

universe *n* Universum *nt*

university *n* Universität *f* ▷ *Do you want to go to university?* Möchtest du auf die Universität gehen? ▷ *Lancaster University* die Universität von Lancaster; **She's at university.** Sie studiert.

unless *conj* es sei denn ▷ *unless he leaves* es sei denn, er geht ▷ *I won't come unless you phone me.* Ich komme nicht, es sei denn, du rufst an.

unlikely *adj* unwahrscheinlich ▷ *It's possible, but unlikely.* Es ist möglich, aber unwahrscheinlich.

unload *vb* ausladen (*pres* lädt aus, *imperf* lud aus, *perf* hat ausgeladen) ▷ *We unloaded the car.* Wir haben das Auto ausgeladen.; **The lorries go there to unload.** Die Lastwagen fahren dorthin um abzuladen.

unlock *vb* aufschließen (*imperf* schloss auf, *perf* hat aufgeschlossen) ▷ *He unlocked the door.* Er schloss die Tür auf.

unlucky *adj* **to be unlucky (1)** *(number, object)* Unglück bringen [**13**] ▷ *They say thirteen is an unlucky number.* Es heißt, dass die Zahl dreizehn Unglück bringt. **(2)** *(person)* kein Glück haben [**32**] ▷ *Did* *you win? — No, I was unlucky.* Hast du gewonnen? — Nein, ich habe kein Glück gehabt.

unmarried *adj (person)* unverheiratet ▷ *an unmarried couple* ein unverheiratetes Paar; **an unmarried mother** eine ledige Mutter

unnatural *adj* unnatürlich

unnecessary *adj* unnötig

unpack *vb (clothes, case)* auspacken [**4**] (*perf* hat ausgepackt) ▷ *I went to my room to unpack.* Ich ging auf mein Zimmer, um auszupacken.

unpleasant *adj* unangenehm

unplug *vb* ausstecken [**4**] (*perf* hat ausgesteckt) ▷ *She unplugged the TV.* Sie hat den Fernseher ausgesteckt.

unpopular *adj* unbeliebt

unrealistic *adj* unrealistisch

unreasonable *adj* unmöglich ▷ *Her attitude was completely unreasonable.* Ihre Haltung war völlig unmöglich.

unreliable *adj* unzuverlässig ▷ *He's completely unreliable.* Er ist total unzuverlässig.

unroll *vb* aufrollen [**4**] (*perf* hat aufgerollt)

unscrew *vb* aufschrauben [**4**] (*perf* hat aufgeschraubt) ▷ *She unscrewed the top of the bottle.* Sie schraubte den Flaschenverschluss auf.

unskilled *adj* ungelernt ▷ *an unskilled worker* ein ungelernter Arbeiter

unsuccessful *adj (attempt)* erfolglos ▷ *an unsuccessful artist* ein erfolgloser Künstler; **to be unsuccessful in doing something** keinen Erfolg bei etwas haben [**32**]

unsuitable *adj (clothes, equipment)* ungeeignet

untidy *adj* unordentlich

untie *vb* ❶ *(knot, parcel)* aufmachen [**4**] (*perf* hat aufgemacht) ❷ *(animal)* losbinden (*imperf* band los, *perf* hat losgebunden)

until *prep, conj* ❶ bis ▷ *I waited until ten o'clock.* Ich habe bis zehn Uhr gewartet.; **until now** bis jetzt; **until then** bis dahin ❷ vor

> Use **vor** if the sentence you want to translate contains a negative, such as 'not' or 'never'.

▷ *It won't be ready until next week.* Es wird nicht vor nächster Woche fertig sein. ▷ *Until last year I'd never been to Germany.* Vor letztem Jahr war ich noch nie in Deutschland.

unusual *adj* ungewöhnlich ▷ *an unusual shape* eine ungewöhnliche Form ▷ *It's unusual to get snow at this time of year.* Es ist ungewöhnlich, dass es um diese Jahreszeit schneit.

unwilling *adj* **to be unwilling to do something** nicht gewillt sein [**65**], etwas zu tun

unwrap *vb* auspacken [**4**] (*perf* hat ausgepackt) ▷ *Let's unwrap the presents.* Packen wir die Geschenke aus.

up *prep, adv* auf

> Use the accusative to express movement or a change of place. Use the dative when there is no change of place.

▷ *He drove me up the hill.* Er hat mich den Berg hinaufgefahren. ▷ *the chapel up on the hill* die Kapelle auf dem Berg; **up here** hier oben; **up there** dort oben; **up north** oben im Norden; **to be up** *(out of bed)* auf sein [**65**]; **What's up?** Was gibt's?; **What's up with her?** Was ist los mit ihr?; **to get up** *(in the morning)* aufstehen [**72**]; **to go up** **(1)** hinauffahren [**4**] ▷ *The bus went up the hill.* Der Bus ist den Berg hinaufgefahren. **(2)** *(on foot)* hinaufgehen [**29**] ▷ *We went up the hill.* Wir sind den Berg hinaufgegangen.; **to go up to somebody** auf jemanden zugehen [**29**]; **She came up to me.** Sie kam auf mich zu.; **up to** *(as far as)* bis; **It's up to you.** Das ist dir überlassen.

> For other expressions with 'up', see the verbs 'go', 'come', 'put', 'turn' etc.

uphill *adv* bergauf
upper sixth *n* **the upper sixth** die dreizehnte Klasse
upright *adj* **to stand upright** aufrecht stehen [**72**]
upset *n* **a stomach upset** eine Magenverstimmung
▶ *adj* ❶ *(hurt)* gekränkt ▷ *She was upset when he said that.* Sie fühlte sich gekränkt, als er das sagte. ❷ *(sad)* betrübt ▷ *I was very upset when my father died.* Ich war sehr betrübt, als mein Vater starb.; **an upset stomach** eine Magenverstimmung
▶ *vb* aufregen [**4**] (*perf* hat aufgeregt) ▷ *Don't say anything to upset her!* Sag nichts, was sie aufregen könnte.
upside down *adv* verkehrt herum ▷ *It's upside down.* Es ist verkehrt herum.
upstairs *adv* oben ▷ *Where's your coat? — It's upstairs.* Wo ist dein Mantel? — Er ist oben.; **the people upstairs** die Leute von oben; **to go upstairs** hinaufgehen [**29**]
up-to-date *adj* ❶ *(car, stereo)* modern ❷ *(information)* aktuell ▷ *an up-to-date timetable* ein aktueller Fahrplan; **to bring something up to date** etwas auf den neuesten Stand bringen [**13**]; **to keep somebody up to date** jemanden auf dem Laufenden halten [**33**]
upwards *adv* hinauf ▷ *to look upwards* hinaufsehen
urgent *adj* dringend ▷ *Is it urgent?* Ist es dringend?
US *nsg* USA *pl*; **from the US** aus den USA; **in the US** in den USA; **to the US** in die USA
us *pron* uns ▷ *They saw us.* Sie haben uns gesehen. ▷ *They gave us a map.* Sie gaben uns eine Karte.; **Who is it? — It's us!** Wer ist da? — Wir sind's!
USA *n* USA *pl*; **from the USA** aus den USA; **in the USA** in den USA; **to the USA** in die USA
use *n* **It's no use.** Es hat keinen Zweck.; **to make use of something** etwas benützen [**7**]
▶ *vb* benützen [**7**] (*perf* hat benützt) ▷ *Can we use a dictionary in the exam?* Können wir in der Prüfung ein Wörterbuch benützen?; **Can I use your phone?** Kann ich mal telefonieren?; **to use the toilet** auf die Toilette gehen [**29**]; **to use up** aufbrauchen [**4**]; **I used to live in London.** Ich habe früher mal in London gelebt.; **I used not to like maths, but now ...** Früher habe ich Mathe nicht gemocht, aber jetzt ...; **to be used to something** an etwas gewöhnt sein [**65**]; **a used car** ein Gebrauchtwagen *m*
useful *adj* nützlich
useless *adj* nutzlos ▷ *This map is just useless.* Diese Karte ist echt nutzlos.; **You're useless!** Du bist zu nichts zu gebrauchen!; **It's useless asking her!** Es ist zwecklos, sie zu fragen!
user *n* Benutzer *m* (*pl* Benutzer), Benutzerin *f*
user-friendly *adj* benutzerfreundlich
usual *adj* üblich ▷ *as usual* wie üblich
usually *adv* normalerweise ▷ *I usually get to school at half past eight.* Ich bin normalerweise um halb neun in der Schule.

V

vacancy *n (job)* freie Stelle *f*; **'Vacancies'** 'Zimmer frei'; **'No vacancies'** 'Belegt'

vacant *adj* ❶ *(seat, job)* frei ❷ *(building)* leer stehend ❸ *(look)* leer ▷ *a vacant look* ein leerer Blick

vacation *n (US)* ❶ *(from school)* Ferien *pl* ▷ *They went on vacation to Mexico.* Sie haben in Mexiko Ferien gemacht. ❷ *(from work)* Urlaub *m* (*pl* Urlaube) ▷ *I have thirty days' vacation a year.* Ich habe dreißig Tage Urlaub im Jahr.

vaccinate *vb* impfen [**38**]

vacuum *vb* staubsaugen [**38**] (*imperf* staubsaugte, *perf* hat gestaubsaugt) ▷ *to vacuum the hall* den Flur staubsaugen

vacuum cleaner *n* Staubsauger *m* (*pl* Staubsauger)

vagina *n* Vagina *f* (*pl* Vaginen)

vague *adj* vage

vain *adj* eitel ▷ *He's so vain!* Er ist so eitel!; **in vain** umsonst

Valentine card *n* Valentinskarte *f*

- Germans celebrate Valentine's Day by giving flowers rather than sending cards.

Valentine's Day *n* Valentinstag *m* (*pl* Valentinstage)

valid *adj* gültig ▷ *This ticket is valid for three months.* Dieser Fahrschein ist drei Monate lang gültig.

valley *n* Tal *nt* (*pl* Täler)

valuable *adj* wertvoll ▷ *a valuable picture* ein wertvolles Bild ▷ *valuable help* wertvolle Hilfe

value *n* Wert *m* (*pl* Werte)

van *n* Lieferwagen *m* (*pl* Lieferwagen)

vandal *n* Vandale *m* (*gen* Vandalen, *pl* Vandalen), Vandalin *f*

vandalism *n* Vandalismus *m* (*gen* Vandalismus)

vandalize *vb* mutwillig zerstören [**95**] (*perf* hat mutwillig zerstört)

vanilla *n* Vanille *f*; **vanilla ice cream** das Vanilleeis

vape *vb* dampfen [**48**]

vaping *n* Dampfen *nt*

vanish *vb* verschwinden [**86**] (*imperf* verschwand, *perf* ist verschwunden)

variety *n* ❶ Abwechslung *f* ▷ *She likes variety in her life.* Sie hat gern Abwechslung im Leben. ❷ *(kind)* Sorte *f* ▷ *a new variety of rose* eine neue Rosensorte; **a variety of CDs** eine Vielzahl von CDs

various *adj* verschieden ▷ *We visited various villages.* Wir haben verschiedene Dörfer besucht.

vary *vb* schwanken [**38**] ▷ *It varies between two and four per cent.* Es schwankt zwischen zwei und vier Prozent.; **It varies.** Das ist unterschiedlich.

vase *n* Vase *f*

VAT *n* (= *value added tax*) Mehrwertsteuer *f*

VCR *n* (= *video cassette recorder*) Videorekorder *m* (*pl* Videorekorder)

VDU *n* (= *visual display unit*) Bildschirm *m* (*pl* Bildschirme)

veal *n* Kalbfleisch *nt*

vegan *n* Veganer *m* (*pl* Veganer), Veganerin *f* ▷ *I'm a vegan.* Ich bin Veganerin.
vegetable *n* Gemüsesorte *f*; **vegetables** das Gemüse *sg*; **vegetable soup** die Gemüsesuppe
vegetarian *adj* vegetarisch ▷ *vegetarian lasagne* die vegetarische Lasagne; **He's vegetarian.** Er ist Vegetarier.
▶ *n* Vegetarier *m* (*pl* Vegetarier), Vegetarierin *f* ▷ *She's a vegetarian.* Sie ist Vegetarierin.
vehicle *n* Fahrzeug *nt* (*pl* Fahrzeuge)
vein *n* Vene *f*
velvet *n* Samt *m*
vending machine *n* Automat *m* (*gen* Automaten, *pl* Automaten)
verb *n* Verb *nt* (*pl* Verben)
verdict *n* Urteil *nt* (*pl* Urteile)
vertical *adj* senkrecht
vertigo *n* Schwindelgefühl *nt*; **He had an attack of vertigo.** Ihm wurde schwindlig.
very *adv* sehr ▷ *very tall* sehr groß ▷ *not very interesting* nicht sehr interessant; **very much (1)** sehr viel ▷ *He didn't eat very much.* Er hat nicht sehr viel gegessen. **(2)** *(like, love, respect)* sehr ▷ *I love her very much.* Ich liebe sie sehr.; **Thank you very much.** Vielen Dank.
vest *n* ❶ Unterhemd *nt* (*pl* Unterhemden) ❷ *(waistcoat)* Weste *f*
vet *n* Tierarzt *m* (*gen* Tierarztes, *pl* Tierärzte), Tierärztin *f* ▷ *She's a vet.* Sie ist Tierärztin.
via *prep* über ▷ *We went to Munich via Ulm.* Wir sind über Ulm nach München gefahren.
vicar *n* Pastor *m* (*pl* Pastoren), Pastorin *f* ▷ *He's a vicar.* Er ist Pastor.
vicious *adj* ❶ brutal ▷ *a vicious attack* ein brutaler Überfall ❷ *(dog)* bissig ❸ *(person)* bösartig; **a vicious circle** ein Teufelskreis *m*
victim *n* Opfer *nt* (*pl* Opfer) ▷ *He was the victim of a mugging.* Er wurde das Opfer eines Straßenüberfalls.
victory *n* Sieg *m* (*pl* Siege)
video *vb* auf Video aufnehmen **[52]** (*pres* nimmt auf Video auf, *imperf* nahm auf Video auf, *perf* hat auf Video aufgenommen)
▶ *n* ❶ *(film)* Video *nt* (*pl* Videos) ▷ *to watch a video* ein Video ansehen ▷ *a video of my family on holiday* ein Video von meiner Familie in den Ferien ❷ *(video recorder)* Videorekorder *m* (*pl* Videorekorder) ▷ *Have you got a video?* Habt ihr einen Videorekorder?; **a video camera** eine Videokamera; **a video cassette** eine Videokassette; **a video game** ein Videospiel *nt*; **a video recorder** ein Videorekorder; **a video shop** eine Videothek
Vienna *n* Wien *nt*; **to Vienna** nach Wien
Vietnamese *n* Vietnamese *m* (*pl* Vietnamesen), Vietnamesin *f*
▶ *adj* vietnamesisch
view *n* ❶ Aussicht *f* ▷ *There's an amazing view.* Man hat dort eine tolle Aussicht. ❷ *(opinion)* Meinung *f* ▷ *in my view* meiner Meinung nach
viewer *n* Fernsehzuschauer *m* (*pl* Fernsehzuschauer), Fernsehzuschauerin *f*
viewpoint *n* Standpunkt *m* (*pl* Standpunkte)
vile *adj (smell, food)* ekelhaft
villa *n* Villa *f* (*pl* Villen)
village *n* Dorf *nt* (*pl* Dörfer)
vine *n* Weinrebe *f*
vinegar *n* Essig *m*
vineyard *n* Weinberg *m* (*pl* Weinberge)
viola *n* Bratsche *f* ▷ *I play the viola.* Ich spiele Bratsche.
violence *n* Gewalt *f*
violent *adj* ❶ *(person, film)* gewalttätig; **a violent crime** ein Gewaltverbrechen *nt* ❷ *(explosion)* gewaltig
violin *n* Geige *f* ▷ *I play the violin.* Ich spiele Geige.
violinist *n* Geigenspieler *m* (*pl* Geigenspieler), Geigenspielerin *f*

virgin *n* Jungfrau *f* ▷ *to be a virgin* Jungfrau sein
Virgo *n* Jungfrau *f* ▷ *I'm Virgo.* Ich bin Jungfrau.
virtual reality *n* virtuelle Realität *f*
virus *n* Virus *nt* (*gen* Virus, *pl* Viren)
visa *n* Visum *nt* (*pl* Visa)
visible *adj* sichtbar
visit *n* ❶ Besuch *m* (*pl* Besuche) ▷ *my last visit to her* mein letzter Besuch bei ihr ❷ *(to country)* Aufenthalt *m* (*pl* Aufenthalte) ▷ *Did you enjoy your visit to Germany?* Hat euer Deutschlandaufenthalt Spaß gemacht?
▶ *vb* ❶ *(person)* besuchen [**7**] (*perf* hat besucht) ❷ *(place)* besichtigen [**18**] (*perf* hat besichtigt) ▷ *We'd like to visit the castle.* Wir würden gern die Burg besichtigen.
visitor *n* Besucher *m* (*pl* Besucher), Besucherin *f*; **to have a visitor** Besuch haben [**32**]
visual *adj* visuell
vital *adj* äußerst wichtig ▷ *It's vital for you to take these tablets.* Es ist äußerst wichtig, dass du diese Tabletten nimmst.; **of vital importance** äußerst wichtig
vitamin *n* Vitamin *nt* (*pl* Vitamine)
vivid *adj* lebhaft ▷ *to have a vivid imagination* eine lebhafte Fantasie haben
vocabulary *n* Wortschatz *m* (*gen* Wortschatzes, *pl* Wortschätze)
vocational *adj* beruflich ▷ *vocational training* die berufliche Ausbildung; **a vocational college** eine Berufsschule
vodka *n* Wodka *m* (*pl* Wodkas)
voice *n* Stimme *f*
voice mail *n* Voicemail *f*
volcano *n* Vulkan *m* (*pl* Vulkane)
volleyball *n* Volleyball *m* ▷ *to play volleyball* Volleyball spielen
voluntary *adj (contribution, statement)* freiwillig; **to do voluntary work** ehrenamtlich tätig sein [**65**]
volunteer *n* Freiwillige *m* (*gen* Freiwilligen, *pl* Freiwilligen), Freiwillige *f* (*gen* Freiwilligen) ▷ *a volunteer (man)* ein Freiwilliger
▶ *vb* **to volunteer to do something** sich freiwillig melden [**54**], etwas zu tun
vomit *vb* sich übergeben [**28**] (*pres* übergibt sich, *imperf* übergab sich, *perf* hat sich übergeben)
vote *n* Stimme *f*
▶ *vb* wählen [**38**] ▷ *to vote Labour* Labour wählen; **to vote for somebody** für jemanden stimmen [**38**]
voucher *n* Gutschein *m* (*pl* Gutscheine) ▷ *a gift voucher* ein Geschenkgutschein
vowel *n* Vokal *m* (*pl* Vokale)
vulgar *adj* vulgär

W

wage *n* Lohn *m* (*pl* Löhne) ▷ *He collected his wages.* Er hat seinen Lohn abgeholt.
waist *n* Taille *f*
waistcoat *n* Weste *f*
wait *vb* warten [**2**]; **to wait for something** auf etwas warten [**2**]; **to wait for somebody** auf jemanden warten [**2**]; **Wait a minute!** Einen Augenblick!; **to keep somebody waiting** jemanden warten lassen [**42**]; **I can't wait for the holidays.** Ich kann die Ferien kaum erwarten.; **I can't wait to see him again.** Ich kann's kaum erwarten, bis ich ihn wiedersehe.
wait up *vb* aufbleiben [**10**] (*imperf* blieb auf, *perf* ist aufgeblieben)
waiter *n* Kellner *m* (*pl* Kellner)
waiting list *n* Warteliste *f*
waiting room *n* Wartezimmer *nt* (*pl* Wartezimmer)
waitress *n* Kellnerin *f*
wake up *vb* aufwachen [**4**] (*perf* ist aufgewacht) ▷ *I woke up at six o'clock.* Ich bin um sechs Uhr aufgewacht.; **to wake somebody up** jemanden wecken [**38**]
Wales *n* Wales *nt* ▷ *the Prince of Wales* der Prinz von Wales; **from Wales** aus Wales; **in Wales** in Wales; **to Wales** nach Wales
walk *vb* ❶ gehen [**29**] (*imperf* ging, *perf* ist gegangen) ▷ *He walks fast.* Er geht schnell. ❷ *(go on foot)* zu Fuß gehen ▷ *Are you walking or going by bus?* Geht ihr zu Fuß oder nehmt ihr den Bus? ▷ *We walked ten kilometres.* Wir sind zehn Kilometer zu Fuß gegangen.; **to walk the dog** mit dem Hund spazieren gehen [**29**]
▶ *n* Spaziergang *m* (*pl* Spaziergänge) ▷ *to go for a walk* einen Spaziergang machen; **It's ten minutes' walk from here.** Von hier ist es zehn Minuten zu Fuß.
walking *n* Wandern *nt*; **I did some walking in the Alps last summer.** Ich bin letzten Sommer in den Alpen gewandert.
walking stick *n* Spazierstock *m* (*pl* Spazierstöcke)
wall *n* ❶ Mauer *f* ▷ *There's a wall round the garden.* Um den Garten ist eine Mauer. ❷ Wand *f* (*pl* Wände) ▷ *They have lots of pictures on the wall.* Sie haben viele Bilder an der Wand.
wallet *n* Brieftasche *f*
wallpaper *n* Tapete *f*
walnut *n* Walnuss *f* (*pl* Walnüsse)
wander *vb* **to wander around** herumlaufen
want *vb* möchten (*pres* mag, *imperf* mochte, *perf* hat gemocht) ▷ *Do you want some cake?* Möchtest du Kuchen?; **to want to do something** etwas tun wollen [**94**] ▷ *What do you want to do?* Was willst du machen?
war *n* Krieg *m* (*pl* Kriege)
ward *n (room in hospital)* Krankensaal *m* (*pl* Krankensäle)

wardrobe *n (piece of furniture)* Kleiderschrank *m* (*pl* Kleiderschränke)

warehouse *n* Lagerhaus *nt* (*gen* Lagerhauses, *pl* Lagerhäuser)

warm *adj* ❶ warm ▷ *warm water* warmes Wasser ▷ *It's warm in here.* Hier drin ist es warm. ▷ *It's warmer in the kitchen.* In der Küche ist es wärmer.

When you talk about a person being 'warm', you use the impersonal construction.

▷ *I'm warm.* Mir ist warm. ▷ *I'm too warm.* Mir ist zu warm. ❷ herzlich ▷ *a warm welcome* ein herzlicher Empfang; **to warm up (1)** *(for sport)* sich aufwärmen **(2)** *(food)* aufwärmen ▷ *I'll warm up some lasagne for you.* Ich wärme dir etwas Lasagne auf.; **to warm over** aufwärmen

warn *vb* warnen [38] ▷ *Well, I warned you!* Ich habe dich ja gewarnt.; **to warn somebody not to do something** jemanden davor warnen, etwas zu tun [81]

warning *n* Warnung *f*

wart *n* Warze *f*

was *vb see* **be**

wash *n* **to have a wash** sich waschen [89]; **to give something a wash** etwas waschen [89]

▶ *vb* ❶ waschen [89] (*pres* wäscht, *imperf* wusch, *perf* hat gewaschen) ▷ *to wash something* etwas waschen ❷ *(have a wash)* sich waschen [89] ▷ *Every morning I get up, wash and get dressed.* Jeden Morgen stehe ich auf, wasche mich und ziehe mich an.; **to wash one's hands** sich die Hände waschen [89]; **to wash one's hair** sich die Haare waschen [89]; **to wash up** abwaschen [89]

washbasin *n* Waschbecken *nt* (*pl* Waschbecken)

washcloth *n (US)* Waschlappen *m* (*pl* Waschlappen)

washing *n (clothes)* Wäsche *f*; **Have you got any washing?** Hast du etwas zu waschen?; **to do the washing** Wäsche waschen [89]

washing machine *n* Waschmaschine *f*

washing powder *n* Waschpulver *nt* (*pl* Waschpulver)

washing-up *n* Abwasch *m* ▷ *to do the washing-up* den Abwasch machen

washing-up liquid *n* Spülmittel *nt* (*pl* Spülmittel)

wasn't = **was not**

wasp *n* Wespe *f*

waste *n* ❶ Verschwendung *f* ▷ *It's such a waste!* Es ist so eine Verschwendung! ▷ *It's a waste of time.* Es ist Zeitverschwendung! ❷ *(rubbish)* Müll *m* ▷ *nuclear waste* der Atommüll

▶ *vb* verschwenden [7] (*perf* hat verschwendet) ▷ *I don't like wasting money.* Ich verschwende nicht gerne Geld. ▷ *There's no time to waste.* Wir haben keine Zeit zu verschwenden.

wastepaper basket *n* Papierkorb *m* (*pl* Papierkörbe)

watch *n* Uhr *f*

▶ *vb* ❶ *(film, video)* ansehen [64] (*pres* sieht an, *imperf* sah an, *perf* hat angesehen) ▷ *Did you watch that film last night?* Hast du dir gestern Abend den Film angesehen?; **to watch television** fernsehen [64] ❷ zusehen [64] (*pres* sieht zu, *imperf* sah zu, *perf* hat zugesehen) ▷ *Watch me!* Sieh mir zu! ❸ *(keep a watch on)* beobachten [2] (*perf* hat beobachtet) ▷ *The police were watching the house.* Die Polizei beobachtete das Haus.; **to watch out** aufpassen [31]; **Watch out!** Pass auf!

water *n* Wasser *nt* (*pl* Wasser)

▶ *vb* ❶ *(plant)* gießen (*imperf* goss, *perf* hat gegossen) ▷ *He was watering his tulips.* Er goss seine Tulpen. ❷ *(garden)* sprengen ▷ *We should water the lawn.* Wir sollten den Rasen sprengen.

waterfall *n* Wasserfall *m* (*pl* Wasserfälle)

watering can *n* Gießkanne *f*

watermelon *n* Wassermelone *f*

waterproof *adj* wasserdicht ▷ *Is this jacket waterproof?* Ist die Jacke wasserdicht?
water-skiing *n* Wasserskifahren *nt*; **to go water-skiing** Wasserski fahren [**21**]
wave *n (in water)* Welle *f*; **We gave him a wave.** Wir haben ihm zugewinkt. ▶ *vb* winken [**38**]; **to wave at somebody** jemandem zuwinken; **to wave goodbye** zum Abschied winken [**38**]
wax *n* Wachs *nt (gen* Wachses)
way *n* ❶ *(manner)* Art und Weise *f* ▷ *That's no way to talk to your mother!* Das ist keine Art und Weise, mit deiner Mutter zu reden!; **She looked at me in a strange way.** Sie sah mich sonderbar an.; **This book tells you the right way to do it.** Dieses Buch erklärt, wie man es machen muss.; **You're doing it the wrong way.** Du machst das falsch.; **In a way you're right.** In gewisser Weise hast du recht.; **a way of life** eine Art zu leben ❷ *(route)* Weg *m* ▷ *I don't know the way.* Ich kenne den Weg nicht.; **on the way** unterwegs; **It's a long way.** Es ist weit.; **Which way is it?** In welcher Richtung ist es?; **The supermarket is this way.** Zum Supermarkt geht es in diese Richtung.; **Do you know the way to the hotel?** Wissen Sie, wie man zum Hotel kommt?; **'way in'** 'Eingang'; **'way out'** 'Ausgang'; **by the way ...** übrigens ...
we *pron* wir ▷ *We're staying here for a week.* Wir sind eine Woche lang hier.
weak *adj* schwach ▷ *Maths is my weakest subject.* In Mathe bin ich am schwächsten.
wealthy *adj* reich
weapon *n* Waffe *f*
wear *vb (clothes)* tragen [**77**] *(pres* trägt, *imperf* trug, *perf* hat getragen) ▷ *She was wearing a hat.* Sie trug einen Hut. ▷ *She was wearing black.* Sie trug Schwarz.
weather *n* Wetter *nt* ▷ *What was the weather like?* Wie war das Wetter? ▷ *The weather was lovely.* Das Wetter war herrlich.
weather forecast *n* Wettervorhersage *f*
Web *n* **the Web** das Web
web address *n* Internetadresse *f*
webcam *n* Webcam *f (pl* Webcams)
web page *n* Webseite *f*
website *n* Website *f (pl* Websites)
we'd = **we had**; **we would**
wedding *n* Hochzeit *f*; **wedding anniversary** der Hochzeitstag; **wedding dress** das Brautkleid; **wedding ring** der Ehering
Wednesday *n* Mittwoch *m (pl* Mittwoche) ▷ *on Wednesday* am Mittwoch ▷ *every Wednesday* jeden Mittwoch ▷ *last Wednesday* letzten Mittwoch ▷ *next Wednesday* nächsten Mittwoch; **on Wednesdays** mittwochs
weed *n* Unkraut *nt* ▷ *The garden's full of weeds.* Der Garten ist voller Unkraut.
week *n* Woche *f* ▷ *last week* letzte Woche ▷ *every week* jede Woche ▷ *next week* nächste Woche ▷ *in a week's time* in einer Woche; **a week on Friday** Freitag in einer Woche
weekday *n* **on weekdays** werktags
weekend *n* Wochenende *nt (pl* Wochenenden) ▷ *at the weekend* am Wochenende ▷ *at weekends* am Wochenende ▷ *last weekend* letztes Wochenende ▷ *next weekend* nächstes Wochenende
weigh *vb* wiegen *(imperf* wog, *perf* hat gewogen) ▷ *How much do you weigh?* Wie viel wiegst du? ▷ *First, weigh the flour.* Wiegen Sie zuerst das Mehl.; **to weigh oneself** sich wiegen
weight *n* Gewicht *nt (pl* Gewichte); **to lose weight** abnehmen [**52**]; **to put on weight** zunehmen [**52**]
weightlifting *n* Gewichtheben *nt*
weird *adj* sonderbar
welcome *n* **They gave her a warm welcome.** Sie haben sie herzlich

empfangen.; **Welcome!** Herzlich willkommen! ▷ *Welcome to Germany!* Herzlich willkommen in Deutschland!
▶ *vb* **to welcome somebody** jemanden begrüßen [**31**]; **Thank you! — You're welcome!** Danke! — Bitte!

well *adj, adv* ❶ gut ▷ *You did that really well.* Das hast du wirklich gut gemacht.; **to do well** gut sein [**65**]; **to be well** *(in good health)* gesund sein [**65**]; **Get well soon!** Gute Besserung!; **Well done!** Gut gemacht! ❷ na ja ▷ *It's enormous! Well, quite big anyway.* Es ist riesig! Na ja, jedenfalls ziemlich groß.; **as well** auch
▶ *n* Brunnen *m (pl* Brunnen)

we'll = **we will**

well-behaved *adj* artig

wellingtons *npl* Gummistiefel *mpl*

well-known *adj* bekannt ▷ *a well-known film star* ein bekannter Filmstar

well-off *adj* gut situiert

Welsh *adj* walisisch; **He's Welsh.** Er ist Waliser.; **She's Welsh.** Sie ist Waliserin.; **Welsh people** die Waliser *mpl*
▶ *n (language)* Walisisch *nt (gen* Walisischen)

Welshman *n* Waliser *m (pl* Waliser)

Welshwoman *n* Waliserin *f*

went *vb see* **go**

were *vb see* **be**

we're = **we are**

weren't = **were not**

west *n* Westen *m* ▷ *in the west* im Westen
▶ *adj, adv* nach Westen ▷ *We were travelling west.* Wir fuhren nach Westen.; **the west coast** die Westküste; **a west wind** ein Westwind *m*; **west of** westlich von; **the West Country** der Südwesten Englands

western *n (film)* Western *m (gen* Western, *pl* Western)
▶ *adj* westlich; **the western part of the island** der westliche Teil der Insel; **Western Europe** Westeuropa *nt*

West Indian *adj* westindisch; **He's West Indian.** Er ist aus Westindien.
▶ *n (person)* Westinder *m (pl* Westinder), Westinderin *f*

wet *adj* nass ▷ *wet clothes* nasse Kleider ▷ *to get wet* nass werden; **wet weather** regnerisches Wetter; **dripping wet** klatschnass; **It was wet all week.** Es hat die ganze Woche geregnet.

wet suit *n* Neoprenanzug *m (pl* Neoprenanzüge)

we've = **we have**

whale *n* Wal *m (pl* Wale)

what *adj, pron* ❶ was ▷ *What are you doing?* Was tust du? ▷ *What did you say?* Was hast du gesagt? ▷ *What is it?* Was ist das? ▷ *What's the matter?* Was ist los? ▷ *What happened?* Was ist passiert? ▷ *I saw what happened.* Ich habe gesehen, was passiert ist. ▷ *I heard what he said.* Ich habe gehört, was er gesagt hat.; **What?** Was? ❷ welcher ▷ *What name?* Welcher Name? welche ▷ *What colour is it?* Welche Farbe hat es? welches ▷ *What book do you want?* Welches Buch möchten Sie? welche ▷ *What subjects are you studying?* Welche Fächer studierst du?; **What's the capital of Finland?** Wie heißt die Hauptstadt von Finnland?; **What a mess!** So ein Chaos!

wheat *n* Weizen *m*

wheel *n* Rad *nt (pl* Räder); **the steering wheel** das Lenkrad

wheelchair *n* Rollstuhl *m (pl* Rollstühle)

when *adv, conj* ❶ wann ▷ *When did he go?* Wann ist er gegangen? ❷ als ▷ *She was reading when I came in.* Sie las, als ich hereinkam.

where *adv, conj* wo ▷ *Where's Emma today?* Wo ist Emma heute? ▷ *Where do you live?* Wo wohnst du? ▷ *a shop where you can buy gardening tools* ein Geschäft, wo man Gartengeräte kaufen kann; **Where are you from?** Woher sind Sie?; **Where are you going?** Wohin gehst du?

a b c d e f g h i j k l m n o p q r s t u v w x y z

Be careful not to translate **where** by **wer**.

whether *conj* ob ▷ *I don't know whether to go or not.* Ich weiß nicht, ob ich gehen soll oder nicht.

which *adj, pron* ❶ welcher ▷ *Which coat is yours?* Welcher Mantel ist deiner?
welche ▷ *Which CD did you buy?* Welche CD hast du gekauft?
welches ▷ *Which book do you want?* Welches Buch willst du?
welche ▷ *Which shoes should I wear?* Welche Schuhe soll ich anziehen?

When asking 'which one' use **welcher** or **welche** or **welches**, depending on whether the noun is masculine, feminine or neuter.

I know his brother. — Which one? Ich kenne seinen Bruder. — Welchen?; **I know his sister. — Which one?** Ich kenne seine Schwester. — Welche?; **I took one of your books. — Which one?** Ich habe eines deiner Bücher genommen. — Welches?; **Which would you like?** Welches möchtest du?; **Which of these are yours?** Welche davon gehören dir?

In relative clauses use **der**, **die** or **das**, depending on the gender of the noun 'which' refers to.

❷ der ▷ *the film which is on now* der Film, der gerade läuft
die ▷ *the CD which is playing now* die CD, die gerade läuft
das ▷ *the book which I am reading* das Buch, das ich lese
die ▷ *the sweets which I ate* die Süßigkeiten, die ich gegessen habe

while *conj* während ▷ *You hold the torch while I look inside.* Halt du die Taschenlampe, während ich hineinsehe. ▷ *She's dynamic, while he's more laid-back.* Sie ist dynamisch, während er eher lässig ist.
▶ *n* Weile *f* ▷ *after a while* nach einer Weile; **a while ago** vor einer Weile; **for a while** eine Zeit lang; **quite a while** ziemlich lange

whip *n* Peitsche *f*
▶ *vb* ❶ peitschen ▷ *She whipped her horse.* Sie peitschte ihr Pferd.
❷ *(eggs)* schlagen **[59]** (*pres* schlägt, *imperf* schlug, *perf* hat geschlagen)

whipped cream *n* Schlagsahne *f*

whiskers *npl* Schnurrhaare *ntpl*

whisky *n* Whisky *m* (*pl* Whiskys)

whisper *vb* flüstern **[88]**

whistle *n* Pfeife *f*; **The referee blew his whistle.** Der Schiedsrichter hat gepfiffen.
▶ *vb* pfeifen (*imperf* pfiff, *perf* hat gepfiffen)

white *adj* weiß ▷ *He's got white hair.* Er hat weiße Haare.; **white wine** der Weißwein; **white bread** das Weißbrot; **white coffee** der Kaffee mit Milch; **a white man** ein Weißer; **a white woman** eine Weiße; **white people** die Weißen *mpl*

whiteboard *n* Weißwandtafel *f* ▷ *an interactive whiteboard* eine interaktive Weißwandtafel

Whitsun *n* Pfingsten *nt* (*gen* Pfingsten, *pl* Pfingsten)

who *pron* ❶ wer ▷ *Who said that?* Wer hat das gesagt? ▷ *Who's he?* Wer ist er?

In relative clauses use **der**, **die** or **das**, depending on the gender of the noun 'who' refers to.

❷ der ▷ *the man who saw us* der Mann, der uns gesehen hat ▷ *the man who we saw* der Mann, den wir gesehen haben
die ▷ *the woman who saw us* die Frau, die uns gesehen hat ▷ *the woman who we saw* die Frau, die wir gesehen haben
das ▷ *the child who saw us* das Kind, das uns gesehen hat ▷ *the child who we saw* das Kind, das wir gesehen haben
die ▷ *the people who saw us* die Leute, die uns gesehen haben

Be careful not to translate **who** by **wo**.

whole *adj* ganz ▷ *the whole class* die ganze Klasse ▷ *the whole day* den ganzen Tag ▷ *the whole world* die ganze Welt
▶ *n* **The whole of Wales was affected.** Ganz Wales war davon betroffen.; **on the whole** im Großen und Ganzen

wholemeal *adj* **wholemeal bread** das Vollkornbrot; **wholemeal flour** das Vollkornmehl

wholewheat *adj (US)* **wholewheat bread** das Vollkornbrot

whom *pron* wen ▷ *Whom did you see?* Wen hast du gesehen?; **the man to whom I spoke** der Mann, mit dem ich gesprochen habe; **the woman to whom I spoke** die Frau, mit der ich gesprochen habe

whose *pron, adj* wessen ▷ *Whose book is this?* Wessen Buch ist das?; **Whose is this?** Wem gehört das?; **I know whose it is.** Ich weiß, wem das gehört.; **the man whose picture was in the paper** der Mann, dessen Bild in der Zeitung war; **the woman whose picture was in the paper** die Frau, deren Bild in der Zeitung war; **the girl whose picture was in the paper** das Mädchen, dessen Bild in der Zeitung war

why *adv* warum ▷ *Why did you do that?* Warum hast du das getan? ▷ *Tell me why.* Sag mir warum. ▷ *Why not?* Warum nicht? ▷ *All right, why not?* Also gut, warum auch nicht?; **That's why he did it.** Deshalb hat er es getan.

wicked *adj* ❶ *(evil)* böse ❷ *(informal: really great)* geil

wide *adj, adv* breit ▷ *a wide road* eine breite Straße; **wide open** weit offen; **wide awake** hellwach

widow *n* Witwe *f* ▷ *She's a widow.* Sie ist Witwe.

widower *n* Witwer *m* (*pl* Witwer) ▷ *He's a widower.* Er ist Witwer.

width *n* Breite *f*

wife *n* Frau *f* ▷ *his wife* seine Frau

Wi-Fi *n* Wi-Fi *nt*

wig *n* Perücke *f*

wild *adj* ❶ wild ▷ *a wild animal* ein wildes Tier ❷ *(crazy)* verrückt ▷ *She's a bit wild.* Sie ist ein bisschen verrückt.

wild card *n* Wildcard *f* (*pl* Wildcards)

wildlife *n* Tierwelt *f* ▷ *I'm interested in wildlife.* Ich interessiere mich für die Tierwelt.

will *n* Testament *nt* (*pl* Testamente) ▷ *He left me some money in his will.* Er hat mir in seinem Testament Geld vermacht.; **He came of his own free will.** Er ist freiwillig gekommen.
▶ *vb*

> In German the present tense is often used to express somebody's intention to do something.

▷ *I'll show you your room.* Ich zeige Ihnen Ihr Zimmer. ▷ *I'll give you a hand.* Ich helfe dir.; **Will you help me?** Hilfst du mir?; **Will you wash up? — No, I won't.** Wäschst du ab? — Nein.

> Use the German future tense when referring to the more distant future.

▷ *I will come back one day.* Ich werde eines Tages zurückkommen. ▷ *It won't take long.* Es wird nicht lange dauern.; **That'll be Dave.** Das wird Dave sein.; **Will you be quiet!** Werdet ihr wohl still sein!

willing *adj* **to be willing to do something** bereit sein, etwas zu tun **[81]**

win *vb* gewinnen **[30]** (*imperf* gewann, *perf* hat gewonnen) ▷ *Did you win?* Hast du gewonnen?; **to win a prize** einen Preis bekommen **[40]**
▶ *n* Sieg *m* (*pl* Siege)

wind *vb* ❶ *(rope, wool, wire)* wickeln ▷ *He wound the rope round the tree.* Er wickelte das Seil um den Baum. ❷ *(river, path)* sich schlängeln ▷ *The road winds through the valley.* Die Straße schlängelt sich durch das Tal.
▶ *n* Wind *m* (*pl* Winde) ▷ *a strong wind* ein starker Wind; **a wind farm** eine

Windfarm; **a wind instrument** ein Blasinstrument *nt*; **wind power** die Windkraft

window *n* Fenster *nt* (*pl* Fenster) ▷ *to break a window* ein Fenster kaputt machen ▷ *a broken window* ein kaputtes Fenster; **a shop window** ein Schaufenster

windscreen *n* Windschutzscheibe *f*

windscreen wiper *n* Scheibenwischer *m* (*pl* Scheibenwischer)

windshield *n (US)* Windschutzscheibe *f*

windy *adj (place)* windig ▷ *It's windy.* Es ist windig.

wine *n* Wein *m* (*pl* Weine) ▷ *a bottle of wine* eine Flasche Wein ▷ *a glass of wine* ein Glas Wein; **white wine** der Weißwein; **red wine** der Rotwein; **a wine bar** eine Weinstube; **a wine glass** ein Weinglas *nt*; **the wine list** die Getränkekarte

wing *n* Flügel *m* (*pl* Flügel)

wink *vb* **to wink at somebody** jemandem zublinzeln

winner *n* Sieger *m* (*pl* Sieger), Siegerin *f*

winning *adj* **the winning team** die Siegermannschaft; **the winning goal** das entscheidende Tor

winter *n* Winter *m* (*pl* Winter) ▷ *in winter* im Winter

wipe *vb* abwischen [**4**] (*perf* hat abgewischt); **to wipe one's feet** sich die Füße abstreifen; **to wipe up** aufwischen

wire *n* Draht *m* (*pl* Drähte)

wisdom tooth *n* Weisheitszahn *m* (*pl* Weisheitszähne)

wise *adj* weise

wish *vb* **to wish for something** sich etwas wünschen [**48**]; **to wish to do something** etwas tun möchten; **I wish you were here!** Ich wünschte, du wärst da!; **I wish you'd told me!** Wenn du mir das doch nur gesagt hättest! ▶ *n* Wunsch *m* (*pl* Wünsche); **to make a wish** sich etwas wünschen [**48**]; **'best wishes'** *(on greetings card)* 'Alles Gute'; **'with best wishes, Jo'** 'alles Liebe, Jo'

with *prep* ❶ mit ▷ *Come with me.* Komm mit mir. ▷ *a woman with blue eyes* eine Frau mit blauen Augen; **Fill the jug with water.** Tu Wasser in den Krug.; **He walks with a stick.** Er geht am Stock. ❷ *(at the home of)* bei ▷ *We stayed with friends.* Wir haben bei Freunden übernachtet. ❸ vor ▷ *green with envy* grün vor Neid ▷ *to shake with fear* vor Angst zittern

without *prep* ohne ▷ *without a coat* ohne einen Mantel ▷ *without speaking* ohne etwas zu sagen

witness *n* Zeuge *m* (*gen* Zeugen, *pl* Zeugen), Zeugin *f* ▷ *There were no witnesses.* Es gab keine Zeugen.; **witness box** der Zeugenstand; **witness stand** der Zeugenstand

witty *adj* geistreich

wives *npl see* **wife**

woken up *vb see* **wake up**

woke up *vb see* **wake up**

wolf *n* Wolf *m* (*pl* Wölfe)

woman *n* Frau *f*; **a woman doctor** eine Ärztin

won *vb see* **win**

wonder *vb* sich fragen [**38**] ▷ *I wonder why she said that.* Ich frage mich, warum sie das gesagt hat. ▷ *I wonder what that means.* Ich frage mich, was das bedeutet.; **I wonder where Caroline is.** Wo Caroline wohl ist?

wonderful *adj* wunderbar

won't = **will not**

wood *n* ❶ *(timber)* Holz *nt* (*pl* Hölzer) ▷ *It's made of wood.* Es ist aus Holz. ❷ *(forest)* Wald *m* (*pl* Wälder) ▷ *We went for a walk in the wood.* Wir sind im Wald spazieren gegangen.

wooden *adj* hölzern; **a wooden chair** ein Holzstuhl *m*

woodwork *n* Schreinern *nt* ▷ *Dieter's hobby is woodwork.* Schreinern ist Dieters Hobby.

wool *n* Wolle *f* ▷ *It's made of wool.* Es ist aus Wolle.

word *n* Wort *nt* (*pl* Wörter) ▷ *a difficult word* ein schwieriges Wort; **What's the word for 'shop' in German?** Wie heißt 'shop' auf Deutsch?; **in other words** in anderen Worten; **to have a word with somebody** mit jemandem reden [**54**]; **the words** *(lyrics)* der Text *sg*

word processing *n* Textverarbeitung *f*

word processor *n* Textverarbeitungssystem *nt* (*pl* Textverarbeitungssysteme)

wore *vb see* **wear**

work *n* Arbeit *f* ▷ *She's looking for work.* Sie sucht Arbeit. ▷ *He's at work at the moment.* Er ist zurzeit bei der Arbeit. ▷ *It's hard work.* Das ist harte Arbeit.; **to be off work** *(sick)* krank sein [**65**]; **He's out of work.** Er ist arbeitslos.
▶ *vb* ❶ *(person)* arbeiten [**2**] ▷ *She works in a shop.* Sie arbeitet in einem Laden. ▷ *to work hard* hart arbeiten ❷ *(machine, plan)* funktionieren [**76**] (*perf* hat funktioniert) ▷ *The heating isn't working.* Die Heizung funktioniert nicht. ▷ *My plan worked perfectly.* Mein Plan hat prima funktioniert.; **to work out** **(1)** *(exercise)* trainieren [**76**] ▷ *I work out twice a week.* Ich trainiere zweimal pro Woche. **(2)** *(turn out)* klappen [**48**] ▷ *In the end it worked out really well.* Am Ende hat es richtig gut geklappt.; **to work something out** *(figure out)* auf etwas kommen [**40**] ▷ *I just couldn't work it out.* Ich bin einfach nicht darauf gekommen.; **It works out at ten pounds each.** Das macht für jeden zehn Pfund.

worker *n* Arbeiter *m* (*pl* Arbeiter), Arbeiterin *f* ▷ *He's a factory worker.* Er ist Fabrikarbeiter.; **She's a good worker.** Sie macht gute Arbeit.

work experience *n* Praktikum *nt* (*pl* Praktika) ▷ *work experience in a factory* ein Praktikum in einer Fabrik

working-class *adj* Arbeiterklasse *m* ▷ *a working-class family* eine Familie der Arbeiterklasse

workman *n* Arbeiter *m* (*pl* Arbeiter)

worksheet *n* Arbeitsblatt *nt* (*pl* Arbeitsblätter)

workshop *n* Werkstatt *f* (*pl* Werkstätten); **a drama workshop** ein Theaterworkshop *m*

workspace *n* Arbeitsplatz *m* (*gen* Arbeitsplatzes, *pl* Arbeitsplätze)

workstation *n* Arbeitsplatzcomputer *m* (*pl* Arbeitsplatzcomputer)

world *n* Welt *f*; **He's the world champion.** Er ist der Weltmeister.

World Wide Web *n* **the World Wide Web** das World Wide Web

worm *n* Wurm *m* (*pl* Würmer)

worn *vb see* **wear**
▶ *adj* abgenutzt ▷ *The carpet is a bit worn.* Der Teppich ist etwas abgenutzt.; **worn out** *(tired)* erschöpft

worried *adj* besorgt ▷ *She's very worried.* Sie ist sehr besorgt.; **to be worried about something** sich wegen etwas Sorgen machen [**48**]; **to look worried** besorgt aussehen [**64**]

worry *vb* sich Sorgen machen ▷ *You worry too much.* Du machst dir zu viele Sorgen.; **Don't worry!** Keine Sorge!

worse *adj, adv* schlechter ▷ *My results were bad, but his were even worse.* Meine Noten waren schlecht, aber seine waren noch schlechter. ▷ *I'm feeling worse.* Mir geht es schlechter.; **It was even worse than that.** Es war sogar noch schlimmer.

worst *adj* **the worst (1)** der schlechteste ▷ *the worst student in the class* der schlechteste Schüler der Klasse **(2)** die schlechteste ▷ *He got the worst mark in the whole class.* Er hat von der ganzen Klasse die schlechteste Note bekommen. **(3)** das schlechteste ▷ *the worst report I've ever had* das schlechteste Zeugnis, das ich je hatte; **my worst enemy** mein schlimmster Feind; **Maths is my worst subject.** In Mathe bin ich am schlechtesten.
▶ *n* Schlimmste *nt* (*gen* Schlimmsten)

▷ *The worst of it is that ...* Das Schlimmste daran ist, dass ...; **at worst** schlimmstenfalls; **if the worst comes to the worst** schlimmstenfalls

worth *adj* **to be worth** wert sein [**65**]; **It's worth it.** Das lohnt sich.

would *vb* **Would you like ...?** Möchtest du ...? ▷ *Would you like a biscuit?* Möchtest du einen Keks? ▷ *Would you like to go and see a film?* Möchtest du ins Kino gehen?; **Would you close the door please?** Würden Sie bitte die Tür zumachen?; **I'd like ...** Ich würde gern ... ▷ *I'd like to go to America.* Ich würde gern nach Amerika fahren.; **Shall we go and see a film? — Yes, I'd like that.** Sollen wir ins Kino gehen? — Au ja!; **I said I'd do it.** Ich sagte, ich würde es tun.; **If you asked him he'd do it.** Wenn du ihn fragen würdest, würde er es tun.; **If you had asked him he would have done it.** Wenn du ihn gefragt hättest, hätte er es getan.

wouldn't = **would not**

wound *vb see* **wind**

▶ *vb* verwunden [**7**] (*perf* hat verwundet) ▷ *He was wounded.* Er wurde verwundet.

▶ *n* Wunde *f*

wrap *vb* einpacken [**4**] (*perf* hat eingepackt) ▷ *She's wrapping the present.* Sie packt das Geschenk ein.; **Can you wrap it for me please?** (*in shop*) Können Sie es mir bitte in Geschenkpapier einpacken?; **to wrap up** einpacken [**4**]

wrapping paper *n* Geschenkpapier *nt*

wreck *n* Wrack *nt* (*pl* Wracks) ▷ *That car is a wreck!* Das Auto ist ein Wrack. ▷ *After the exam I was a complete wreck.* Nach der Prüfung war ich ein totales Wrack.

▶ *vb* ❶ (*building*) zerstören [**95**] (*perf* hat zerstört) ▷ *The explosion wrecked the whole house.* Die Explosion hat das ganze Haus zerstört. ❷ (*car*) kaputt fahren (*pres* fährt kaputt, *imperf* fuhr kaputt, *perf* hat kaputt gefahren) ▷ *He's wrecked his car.* Er hat sein Auto kaputt gefahren. ❸ (*plan, holiday*) verderben (*pres* verdirbt, *imperf* verdarb, *perf* hat verdorben) ▷ *Our trip was wrecked by bad weather.* Das schlechte Wetter hat uns den Ausflug verdorben.

wrestler *n* Ringer *m* (*pl* Ringer), Ringerin *f*

wrestling *n* Ringen *nt* ▷ *His hobby is wrestling.* Ringen ist sein Hobby.

wrinkled *adj* faltig

wrist *n* Handgelenk *nt* (*pl* Handgelenke)

write *vb* schreiben [**61**] (*imperf* schrieb, *perf* hat geschrieben) ▷ *to write a letter* einen Brief schreiben; **to write to somebody** jemandem schreiben [**61**]; **to write down** aufschreiben [**61**]

writer *n* Schriftsteller *m* (*pl* Schriftsteller), Schriftstellerin *f* ▷ *She's a writer.* Sie ist Schriftstellerin.

writing *n* Schrift *f* ▷ *I can't read your writing.* Ich kann deine Schrift nicht lesen.; **in writing** schriftlich

written *vb see* **write**

wrong *adj, adv* ❶ (*incorrect*) falsch ▷ *The information was wrong.* Die Information war falsch. ▷ *the wrong answer* die falsche Antwort; **You've got the wrong number.** Sie haben sich verwählt. ❷ (*morally bad*) unrecht ▷ *I think fox hunting is wrong.* Ich meine, dass Fuchsjagden unrecht sind.; **to be wrong** (*mistaken*) unrecht haben [**32**]; **to do something wrong** etwas falsch machen [**48**]; **to go wrong** (*plan*) schiefgehen [**29**]; **What's wrong?** Was ist los?; **What's wrong with her?** Was ist mit ihr los?

wrote *vb see* **write**

WWW *abbr* (= *World Wide Web*); **the WWW** das WWW

X

Y

Xmas *n* (= *Christmas*) Weihnachten *nt*
X-ray *vb* röntgen [**54**] ▷ *They X-rayed my arm.* Sie haben meinen Arm geröntgt.
▶ *n* Röntgenaufnahme *f*; **to have an X-ray** geröntgt werden [**91**]

yacht *n* ❶ *(sailing boat)* Segelboot *nt* (*pl* Segelboote) ❷ *(luxury motorboat)* Jacht *f*
yawn *vb* gähnen [**38**]
year *n* Jahr *nt* (*pl* Jahre) ▷ *last year* letztes Jahr ▷ *next year* nächstes Jahr ▷ *to be fifteen years old* fünfzehn Jahre alt sein; **an eight-year-old child** ein achtjähriges Kind

In Germany secondary schools, years are counted from the **fünfte Klasse** (youngest) to the **dreizehnte Klasse** (oldest).

He's a first-year. Er ist in der fünften Klasse.
yell *vb* schreien [**62**] (*imperf* schrie, *perf* hat geschrien)
yellow *adj* gelb
yes *adv* ❶ ja ▷ *Do you like it? — Yes.* Gefällt es dir? — Ja. ▷ *Yes please.* Ja bitte.
❷ doch

Use **doch** to contradict a negative statement or question.

▷ *Don't you like it? — Yes!* Gefällt es dir nicht? — Doch! ▷ *You're not Swiss, are you?* — *Yes I am!* Sie sind nicht Schweizer, oder? — Doch, ich bin Schweizer. ▷ *That's not true.* — *Yes it is!* Das ist nicht wahr. — Doch!

yesterday *adv* gestern ▷ *yesterday morning* gestern früh ▷ *yesterday afternoon* gestern Nachmittag ▷ *yesterday evening* gestern Abend ▷ *all day yesterday* gestern den ganzen Tag; **the day before yesterday** vorgestern

yet *adv* ❶ noch ▷ *It has yet to be proved that ...* Es muss noch bewiesen werden, dass ... ❷ *(in questions)* schon ▷ *Has the murderer been caught yet?* Ist der Mörder schon gefasst worden?; **not yet** noch nicht; **not as yet** noch nicht; **Have you finished yet?** Bist du fertig?

yoga *n* Yoga *nt*

yoghurt *n* Joghurt *m (pl* Joghurts)

yolk *n* Eigelb *nt (pl* Eigelbe)

you *pron*

> Only use **du** when speaking to one person, and when the person is your own age or younger. Use **ihr** for several people of your own age or younger. If in doubt use the polite form **Sie**.

❶ *(polite form, singular and plural)* Sie ▷ *Do you like football?* Mögen Sie Fußball? ▷ *Can I help you?* Kann ich Ihnen behilflich sein? ▷ *I saw you yesterday.* Ich habe Sie gestern gesehen. ▷ *It's for you.* Das ist für Sie. ❷ *(familiar singular)* du ▷ *Do you like football?* Magst du Fußball? ▷ *She's younger than you.* Sie ist jünger als du. ▷ *I know you.* Ich kenne dich. ▷ *I gave it to you.* Ich habe es dir gegeben. ▷ *It's for you.* Es ist für dich. ▷ *I'll come with you.* Ich komme mit dir mit. ❸ *(familiar plural)* ihr ▷ *Do you two like football?* Mögt ihr beiden Fußball? ▷ *I told you to be quiet.* Ich habe euch gesagt, ihr sollt still sein. ▷ *This is for you two.* Es ist für euch beide. ▷ *Can I come with you?* Kann ich mit euch mitkommen?

young *adj* jung ▷ *young people* junge Leute

younger *adj* jünger ▷ *He's younger than me.* Er ist jünger als ich. ▷ *my younger brother* mein jüngerer Bruder ▷ *my younger sister* meine jüngere Schwester

youngest *adj* jüngste ▷ *his youngest brother* sein jüngster Bruder ▷ *She's the youngest.* Sie ist die Jüngste.

your *adj*

> Only use **dein** when speaking to one person, and when the person is your own age or younger. For several people of your own age or younger use **euer**. If in doubt use the polite form **Ihr**.

❶ *(polite form, singular and plural)* Ihr ▷ *your father* Ihr Vater ▷ *your mother* Ihre Mutter ▷ *your house* Ihr Haus ▷ *your seats* Ihre Plätze ❷ *(familiar singular)* dein ▷ *your brother* dein Bruder ▷ *your sister* deine Schwester ▷ *your book* dein Buch ▷ *your parents* deine Eltern ❸ *(familiar plural)* euer ▷ *your father* euer Vater ▷ *your mother* eure Mutter ▷ *your car* euer Auto ▷ *your teachers* eure Lehrer

> Do not use **Ihr**, **dein** or **euer** with parts of the body.

▷ *Would you like to wash your hands?* Möchten Sie sich die Hände waschen? ▷ *Do you want to wash your hair?* Möchtest du dir die Haare waschen? ▷ *You two, go upstairs and brush your teeth.* Ihr beide geht nach oben und putzt euch die Zähne.

yours *pron*

> Only use **deiner/deine/deines** when talking to one person of your own age or younger. Use **euer/eure/eures** when talking to several people of your own age or younger. If in doubt use the polite form **Ihrer/Ihre/Ihres**.

❶ *(polite form, singular and plural)* Ihrer ▷ *That's a nice coat. Is it yours?* Das ist ein hübscher Mantel. Ist es Ihrer?; Ihre ▷ *What a pretty jacket. Is it yours?* Was für eine hübsche Jacke. Ist das Ihre?; Ihres ▷ *I like that car. Is it yours?* Das Auto gefällt mir. Ist es Ihres?; Ihre ▷ *my parents and yours* meine Eltern und Ihre; **Is this yours?** Gehört das Ihnen?; **Yours sincerely, ...** Mit freundlichen Grüßen ... ❷ *(familiar singular)* deiner ▷ *I've lost my pen. Can I use yours?* Ich habe meinen Schreiber verlegt. Kann ich deinen benützen?; deine ▷ *Nice jacket. Is it yours?* Hübsche Jacke. Ist das deine?; deines ▷ *I like that car. Is it yours?* Das Auto gefällt mir. Ist das deines?; deine ▷ *my parents and yours* meine Eltern und deine ▷ *My hands are dirty, yours are clean.* Meine Hände sind schmutzig, deine sind sauber.; **Is this yours?** Gehört das dir? ❸ *(familiar plural)* euer ▷ *My computer is broken. Can I use yours?* Mein Computer ist kaputt. Kann ich euren benutzen?; eure ▷ *I haven't got a torch. Can I use yours?* Ich habe keine Taschenlampe. Kann ich eure benutzen?; eures ▷ *Our house is bigger than yours.* Unser Haus ist größer als eures.; eure ▷ *our parents and yours* unsere Eltern und eure; **Is this yours?** Gehört das euch?

yourself *pron*

> Only use **dich/dir** when talking to one person of your own age or younger. If in doubt use the polite form **sich**.

❶ *(polite form)* sich ▷ *Have you hurt yourself?* Haben Sie sich verletzt? ▷ *Tell me about yourself!* Erzählen Sie etwas von sich! ❷ *(familiar form)* dich ▷ *Have you hurt yourself?* Hast du dich verletzt? ❸ *(familiar form)* dir ▷ *Tell me about yourself!* Erzähl mir etwas von dir! ▷ *If you are not happy with yourself ...* Wenn du mit dir selbst nicht zufrieden bist ... ❹ selbst; **Do it yourself! (1)** Machen Sie es selbst! **(2)** Mach's selbst!

yourselves *pron*

> Only use **euch** when talking to people of your own age or younger. If in doubt use the polite form **sich**.

❶ *(polite form)* sich ▷ *Did you enjoy yourselves?* Haben Sie sich amüsiert? ❷ *(familiar form)* euch ▷ *Did you enjoy yourselves?* Habt ihr euch amüsiert? ❸ selbst; **Did you make it yourselves? (1)** Haben Sie es selbst gemacht? **(2)** Habt ihr es selbst gemacht?

youth club *n* Jugendzentrum *nt (pl* Jugendzentren)

youth hostel *n* Jugendherberge *f*

Yugoslavia *n* Jugoslawien *nt*; **in the former Yugoslavia** im ehemaligen Jugoslawien

Z

zany *adj* irre komisch ▷ *a zany film* ein irre komischer Film
zebra *n* Zebra *nt* (*pl* Zebras)
zebra crossing *n* Zebrastreifen *m* (*pl* Zebrastreifen)
zero *n* Null *f*
Zimmer frame® *n* Gehapparat *m* (*pl* Gehapparate)
zip *n* Reißverschluss *m* (*gen* Reißverschlusses, *pl* Reißverschlüsse)
zip code *n* (*US*) Postleitzahl *f*
zip drive *n* Zip-Laufwerk *nt* (*pl* Zip-Laufwerke)
zipper *n* (*US*) Reißverschluss *m* (*gen* Reißverschlusses, *pl* Reißverschlüsse)
zodiac *n* Tierkreis *m* (*gen* Tierkreises); **the signs of the zodiac** die Sternzeichen
zone *n* Zone *f*
zoo *n* Zoo *m* (*pl* Zoos)
zoom lens *n* Zoomobjektiv *nt* (*pl* Zoomobjektive)
zucchini *npl* (*US*) Zucchini *pl*

VERB TABLES

Introduction

The verb tables in the following section contain 97 tables of German verbs (some regular and some irregular) in alphabetical order.
Each table shows you the following forms:

Present	*eg* ich arbeite = **I work** *or* **I'm working**
Present Subjunctive	*eg* ich arbeite = **I work**
Perfect	*eg* ich habe gearbeitet = **I worked** *or* **I have worked**
Imperfect	*eg* ich arbeitete = **I was working** *or* **I worked**
Future	*eg* ich werde arbeiten = **I will work**
Conditional	*eg* ich würde arbeiten = **I would work**
Imperative	*eg* arbeite = **work**
Present Participle	*eg* arbeitend = **working**
Past Participle	*eg* gearbeitet = **worked**

On both sides of the dictionary, most of the German verbs are followed by a number (e.g. **holen** [38] *vb* to fetch). This number corresponds to a verb table number in this verbs section, where the pattern followed by the model verb is shown. When you come across **kämpfen** [38] *vb* to fight, for example, you will see that it follows the same pattern as that of model verb **holen**, shown in verb table **38**. For other verbs, a summary of the main forms is given after the word (*eg* **heben** (*imperf* **hob**, *perf* **hat gehoben**) *vb* to lift).

In the verb tables, you will find examples of **weak**, **strong** and **mixed** verb forms. **Weak** verbs follow regular patterns, **strong** verbs follow irregular patterns and **mixed** verbs follow a mixture of regular and irregular patterns.

In order to help you use the verbs shown in the verb tables correctly, there are also a number of example phrases at the bottom of each page to show the sense as it is used in context.

Remember:	**ich**	=	I
	du	=	you (*to one person you know well*)
	er	=	he/it
	sie	=	she/it
	es	=	it/he/she
	wir	=	we
	ihr	=	you (*to more than one person you know well*)
	Sie	=	you (*polite form, to one or more people*)
	sie	=	they

Table 1

annehmen *to accept*

strong, separable, *formed with* **haben**

PRESENT

ich	nehme an
du	nimmst an
er/sie/es	nimmt an
wir	nehmen an
ihr	nehmt an
sie/Sie	nehmen an

PRESENT SUBJUNCTIVE

ich	nehme an
du	nehmest an
er/sie/es	nehme an
wir	nehmen an
ihr	nehmet an
sie/Sie	nehmen an

PERFECT

ich	habe angenommen
du	hast angenommen
er/sie/es	hat angenommen
wir	haben angenommen
ihr	habt angenommen
sie/Sie	haben angenommen

IMPERFECT

ich	nahm an
du	nahmst an
er/sie/es	nahm an
wir	nahmen an
ihr	nahmt an
sie/Sie	nahmen an

FUTURE

ich	werde annehmen
du	wirst annehmen
er/sie/es	wird annehmen
wir	werden annehmen
ihr	werdet annehmen
sie/Sie	werden annehmen

CONDITIONAL

ich	würde annehmen
du	würdest annehmen
er/sie/es	würde annehmen
wir	würden annehmen
ihr	würdet annehmen
sie/Sie	würden annehmen

IMPERATIVE

nimm an! / nehmen wir an! / nehmt an! / nehmen Sie an!

PRESENT PARTICIPLE

annehmend

PAST PARTICIPLE

angenommen

EXAMPLE PHRASES

Ich **nehme an**, dass er heute nicht mehr kommt.	*I assume that he isn't coming today.*
Ich **habe** die neue Stelle **angenommen**.	*I have accepted the new job.*

weak,
formed with **haben**

to work **arbeiten**

PRESENT	
ich	arbeite
du	arbeitest
er/sie/es	arbeitet
wir	arbeiten
ihr	arbeitet
sie/Sie	arbeiten

PRESENT SUBJUNCTIVE	
ich	arbeite
du	arbeitest
er/sie/es	arbeite
wir	arbeiten
ihr	arbeitet
sie/Sie	arbeiten

PERFECT	
ich	habe gearbeitet
du	hast gearbeitet
er/sie/es	hat gearbeitet
wir	haben gearbeitet
ihr	habt gearbeitet
sie/Sie	haben gearbeitet

IMPERFECT	
ich	arbeitete
du	arbeitetest
er/sie/es	arbeitete
wir	arbeiteten
ihr	arbeitetet
sie/Sie	arbeiteten

FUTURE	
ich	werde arbeiten
du	wirst arbeiten
er/sie/es	wird arbeiten
wir	werden arbeiten
ihr	werdet arbeiten
sie/Sie	werden arbeiten

CONDITIONAL	
ich	würde arbeiten
du	würdest arbeiten
er/sie/es	würde arbeiten
wir	würden arbeiten
ihr	würdet arbeiten
sie/Sie	würden arbeiten

IMPERATIVE

arbeite! / arbeiten wir! / arbeitet! / arbeiten Sie!

PRESENT PARTICIPLE

arbeitend

PAST PARTICIPLE

gearbeitet

EXAMPLE PHRASES

Er **hat** früher als Elektriker **gearbeitet**.	*He used to work as an electrician.*
Sie **arbeitete** wochenlang an dem Projekt.	*She worked for weeks on the project.*
Ich **würde** nicht gern sonntags **arbeiten**.	*I wouldn't like to work on Sundays.*

atmen *to breathe*

weak, *formed with* **haben**

PRESENT

ich	atme
du	atmest
er/sie/es	atmet
wir	atmen
ihr	atmet
sie/Sie	atmen

PRESENT SUBJUNCTIVE

ich	atme
du	atmest
er/sie/es	atme
wir	atmen
ihr	atmet
sie/Sie	atmen

PERFECT

ich	habe geatmet
du	hast geatmet
er/sie/es	hat geatmet
wir	haben geatmet
ihr	habt geatmet
sie/Sie	haben geatmet

IMPERFECT

ich	atmete
du	atmetest
er/sie/es	atmete
wir	atmeten
ihr	atmetet
sie/Sie	atmeten

FUTURE

ich	werde atmen
du	wirst atmen
er/sie/es	wird atmen
wir	werden atmen
ihr	werdet atmen
sie/Sie	werden atmen

CONDITIONAL

ich	würde atmen
du	würdest atmen
er/sie/es	würde atmen
wir	würden atmen
ihr	würdet atmen
sie/Sie	würden atmen

IMPERATIVE

atme! / atmen wir! / atmet! / atmen Sie!

PRESENT PARTICIPLE

atmend

PAST PARTICIPLE

geatmet

EXAMPLE PHRASES

Sie **atmet** jetzt wieder etwas freier. — *She is now breathing a bit more freely again.*

Wir **atmeten** tief ein und aus. — *We took deep breaths.*

Dort **werden** wir frischere Luft **atmen**. — *We'll breathe fresher air there.*

weak, separable,
formed with **haben**

to be enough **ausreichen**

PRESENT

ich	reiche aus
du	reichst aus
er/sie/es	reicht aus
wir	reichen aus
ihr	reicht aus
sie/Sie	reichen aus

PRESENT SUBJUNCTIVE

ich	reiche aus
du	reichest aus
er/sie/es	reiche aus
wir	reichen aus
ihr	reichet aus
sie/Sie	reichen aus

PERFECT

ich	habe ausgereicht
du	hast ausgereicht
er/sie/es	hat ausgereicht
wir	haben ausgereicht
ihr	habt ausgereicht
sie/Sie	haben ausgereicht

IMPERFECT

ich	reichte aus
du	reichtest aus
er/sie/es	reichte aus
wir	reichten aus
ihr	reichtet aus
sie/Sie	reichten aus

FUTURE

ich	werde ausreichen
du	wirst ausreichen
er/sie/es	wird ausreichen
wir	werden ausreichen
ihr	werdet ausreichen
sie/Sie	werden ausreichen

CONDITIONAL

ich	würde ausreichen
du	würdest ausreichen
er/sie/es	würde ausreichen
wir	würden ausreichen
ihr	würdet ausreichen
sie/Sie	würden ausreichen

IMPERATIVE

reiche(e) aus! / reichen wir aus! / reicht aus! / reichen Sie aus!

PRESENT PARTICIPLE

ausreichend

PAST PARTICIPLE

ausgereicht

EXAMPLE PHRASES

Er meint, das Geld **reiche** nicht **aus**.	*He thinks the money isn't enough.*
Die Zeit **reichte** nie **aus**.	*There was never enough time.*
Das **wird** uns nicht **ausreichen**.	*That won't be enough for us.*

beginnen *to begin*

strong, inseparable, *formed with* **haben**

PRESENT

ich	beginne
du	beginnst
er/sie/es	beginnt
wir	beginnen
ihr	beginnt
sie/Sie	beginnen

PRESENT SUBJUNCTIVE

ich	beginne
du	beginnest
er/sie/es	beginne
wir	beginnen
ihr	beginnet
sie/Sie	beginnen

PERFECT

ich	habe begonnen
du	hast begonnen
er/sie/es	hat begonnen
wir	haben begonnen
ihr	habt begonnen
sie/Sie	haben begonnen

IMPERFECT

ich	begann
du	begannst
er/sie/es	begann
wir	begannen
ihr	begannt
sie/Sie	begannen

FUTURE

ich	werde beginnen
du	wirst beginnen
er/sie/es	wird beginnen
wir	werden beginnen
ihr	werdet beginnen
sie/Sie	werden beginnen

CONDITIONAL

ich	würde beginnen
du	würdest beginnen
er/sie/es	würde beginnen
wir	würden beginnen
ihr	würdet beginnen
sie/Sie	würden beginnen

IMPERATIVE

beginn(e)! / beginnen wir! / beginnt! / beginnen Sie!

PRESENT PARTICIPLE

beginnend

PAST PARTICIPLE

begonnen

EXAMPLE PHRASES

Die Vorstellung **beginnt** gleich. — *The performance is about to begin.*

Er **hat** als Lehrling **begonnen**. — *He started off as an apprentice.*

Wir **würden** nicht ohne dich **beginnen**. — *We wouldn't start without you.*

PRESENT

ich	beiße
du	beißt
er/sie/es	beißt
wir	beißen
ihr	beißt
sie/Sie	beißen

PRESENT SUBJUNCTIVE

ich	beiße
du	beißest
er/sie/es	beiße
wir	beißen
ihr	beißet
sie/Sie	beißen

PERFECT

ich	habe gebissen
du	hast gebissen
er/sie/es	hat gebissen
wir	haben gebissen
ihr	habt gebissen
sie/Sie	haben gebissen

IMPERFECT

ich	biss
du	bissest
er/sie/es	biss
wir	bissen
ihr	bisst
sie/Sie	bissen

FUTURE

ich	werde beißen
du	wirst beißen
er/sie/es	wird beißen
wir	werden beißen
ihr	werdet beißen
sie/Sie	werden beißen

CONDITIONAL

ich	würde beißen
du	würdest beißen
er/sie/es	würde beißen
wir	würden beißen
ihr	würdet beißen
sie/Sie	würden beißen

IMPERATIVE

beiß(e)! / beißen wir! / beißt! / beißen Sie!

PRESENT PARTICIPLE

beißend

PAST PARTICIPLE

gebissen

EXAMPLE PHRASES

Er versichert uns, sein Hund **beiße** nicht.	*He assures us his dog doesn't bite.*
Sie **biss** in den Apfel.	*She bit into the apple.*
Er **wird** dich schon nicht **beißen**!	*He won't bite you!*

bestellen *to order*

weak, inseparable, *formed with* **haben**

PRESENT

ich	bestelle
du	bestellst
er/sie/es	bestellt
wir	bestellen
ihr	bestellt
sie/Sie	bestellen

PRESENT SUBJUNCTIVE

ich	bestelle
du	bestellest
er/sie/es	bestelle
wir	bestellen
ihr	bestellet
sie/Sie	bestellen

PERFECT

ich	habe bestellt
du	hast bestellt
er/sie/es	hat bestellt
wir	haben bestellt
ihr	habt bestellt
sie/Sie	haben bestellt

IMPERFECT

ich	bestellte
du	bestelltest
er/sie/es	bestellte
wir	bestellten
ihr	bestelltet
sie/Sie	bestellten

FUTURE

ich	werde bestellen
du	wirst bestellen
er/sie/es	wird bestellen
wir	werden bestellen
ihr	werdet bestellen
sie/Sie	werden bestellen

CONDITIONAL

ich	würde bestellen
du	würdest bestellen
er/sie/es	würde bestellen
wir	würden bestellen
ihr	würdet bestellen
sie/Sie	würden bestellen

IMPERATIVE

bestelle(e)! / bestellen wir! / bestellt! / bestellen Sie!

PRESENT PARTICIPLE

bestellend

PAST PARTICIPLE

bestellt

EXAMPLE PHRASES

Ich **bestelle** uns schon mal ein Bier.	*I'll go and order a beer for us.*
Haben Sie schon **bestellt**?	*Have you ordered yet?*
Wir **bestellten** einen Tisch für zwei.	*We reserved a table for two.*

PRESENT

ich	biete
du	bietest
er/sie/es	bietet
wir	bieten
ihr	bietet
sie/Sie	bieten

PRESENT SUBJUNCTIVE

ich	biete
du	bietest
er/sie/es	biete
wir	bieten
ihr	bietet
sie/Sie	bieten

PERFECT

ich	habe geboten
du	hast geboten
er/sie/es	hat geboten
wir	haben geboten
ihr	habt geboten
sie/Sie	haben geboten

IMPERFECT

ich	bot
du	bot(e)st
er/sie/es	bot
wir	boten
ihr	botet
sie/Sie	boten

FUTURE

ich	werde bieten
du	wirst bieten
er/sie/es	wird bieten
wir	werden bieten
ihr	werdet bieten
sie/Sie	werden bieten

CONDITIONAL

ich	würde bieten
du	würdest bieten
er/sie/es	würde bieten
wir	würden bieten
ihr	würdet bieten
sie/Sie	würden bieten

IMPERATIVE

biet(e)! / bieten wir! / bietet! / bieten Sie!

PRESENT PARTICIPLE

bietend

PAST PARTICIPLE

geboten

EXAMPLE PHRASES

Er **bot** ihm die Hand.	*He held out his hand to him.*
Was **werden** sie uns **bieten**?	*What will they offer us?*
Wir **würden** ihm gern mehr **bieten**.	*We would like to offer him more.*

bitten *to ask (for)* strong, *formed with* **haben**

PRESENT

ich	bitte
du	bittest
er/sie/es	bittet
wir	bitten
ihr	bittet
sie/Sie	bitten

PRESENT SUBJUNCTIVE

ich	bitte
du	bittest
er/sie/es	bitte
wir	bitten
ihr	bittet
sie/Sie	bitten

PERFECT

ich	habe gebeten
du	hast gebeten
er/sie/es	hat gebeten
wir	haben gebeten
ihr	habt gebeten
sie/Sie	haben gebeten

IMPERFECT

ich	bat
du	bat(e)st
er/sie/es	bat
wir	baten
ihr	batet
sie/Sie	baten

FUTURE

ich	werde bitten
du	wirst bitten
er/sie/es	wird bitten
wir	werden bitten
ihr	werdet bitten
sie/Sie	werden bitten

CONDITIONAL

ich	würde bitten
du	würdest bitten
er/sie/es	würde bitten
wir	würden bitten
ihr	würdet bitten
sie/Sie	würden bitten

IMPERATIVE

bitt(e)! / bitten wir! / bittet! / bitten Sie!

PRESENT PARTICIPLE

bittend

PAST PARTICIPLE

gebeten

EXAMPLE PHRASES

Ich **bitte** Sie, uns in Ruhe zu lassen. — *I'm asking you to leave us alone.*

Sie **bat** ihn um Hilfe. — *She asked him for help.*

PRESENT

ich	bleibe
du	bleibst
er/sie/es	bleibt
wir	bleiben
ihr	bleibt
sie/Sie	bleiben

PRESENT SUBJUNCTIVE

ich	bleibe
du	bleibest
er/sie/es	bleibe
wir	bleiben
ihr	bleibet
sie/Sie	bleiben

PERFECT

ich	bin geblieben
du	bist geblieben
er/sie/es	ist geblieben
wir	sind geblieben
ihr	seid geblieben
sie/Sie	sind geblieben

IMPERFECT

ich	blieb
du	bliebst
er/sie/es	blieb
wir	blieben
ihr	bliebt
sie/Sie	blieben

FUTURE

ich	werde bleiben
du	wirst bleiben
er/sie/es	wird bleiben
wir	werden bleiben
ihr	werdet bleiben
sie/Sie	werden bleiben

CONDITIONAL

ich	würde bleiben
du	würdest bleiben
er/sie/es	würde bleiben
wir	würden bleiben
ihr	würdet bleiben
sie/Sie	würden bleiben

IMPERATIVE

bleib(e)! / bleiben wir! / bleibt! / bleiben Sie!

PRESENT PARTICIPLE

bleibend

PAST PARTICIPLE

geblieben

EXAMPLE PHRASES

Hoffentlich **bleibt** das Wetter schön.	*I hope the weather stays fine.*
Dieses Erlebnis **blieb** in meiner Erinnerung.	*This experience stayed with me.*

brechen *to break*

strong, *formed with* **haben/sein***

PRESENT

ich	breche
du	brichst
er/sie/es	bricht
wir	brechen
ihr	brecht
sie/Sie	brechen

PRESENT SUBJUNCTIVE

ich	breche
du	brechest
er/sie/es	breche
wir	brechen
ihr	brechet
sie/Sie	brechen

PERFECT

ich	habe gebrochen
du	hast gebrochen
er/sie/es	hat gebrochen
wir	haben gebrochen
ihr	habt gebrochen
sie/Sie	haben gebrochen

IMPERFECT

ich	brach
du	brachst
er/sie/es	brach
wir	brachen
ihr	bracht
sie/Sie	brachen

FUTURE

ich	werde brechen
du	wirst brechen
er/sie/es	wird brechen
wir	werden brechen
ihr	werdet brechen
sie/Sie	werden brechen

CONDITIONAL

ich	würde brechen
du	würdest brechen
er/sie/es	würde brechen
wir	würden brechen
ihr	würdet brechen
sie/Sie	würden brechen

IMPERATIVE

brich! / brechen wir! / brecht! / brechen Sie!

PRESENT PARTICIPLE

brechend

PAST PARTICIPLE

gebrochen

*When **brechen** is used with no direct object, it is formed with **sein**.

EXAMPLE PHRASES

Sie **hat** ihr Versprechen **gebrochen**.	*She broke her promise.*
Der Sturz **brach** ihm fast den Arm.	*The fall almost broke his arm.*
Ich **würde** ihm nie die Treue **brechen**.	*I would never break his trust.*

PRESENT

ich	brenne
du	brennst
er/sie/es	brennt
wir	brennen
ihr	brennt
sie/Sie	brennen

PRESENT SUBJUNCTIVE

ich	brenne
du	brennest
er/sie/es	brenne
wir	brennen
ihr	brennet
sie/Sie	brennen

PERFECT

ich	habe gebrannt
du	hast gebrannt
er/sie/es	hat gebrannt
wir	haben gebrannt
ihr	habt gebrannt
sie/Sie	haben gebrannt

IMPERFECT

ich	brannte
du	branntest
er/sie/es	brannte
wir	brannten
ihr	branntet
sie/Sie	brannten

FUTURE

ich	werde brennen
du	wirst brennen
er/sie/es	wird brennen
wir	werden brennen
ihr	werdet brennen
sie/Sie	werden brennen

CONDITIONAL

ich	würde brennen
du	würdest brennen
er/sie/es	würde brennen
wir	würden brennen
ihr	würdet brennen
sie/Sie	würden brennen

IMPERATIVE

brenn(e)! / brennen wir! / brennet! / brennen Sie!

PRESENT PARTICIPLE

brennend

PAST PARTICIPLE

gebrannt

EXAMPLE PHRASES

Das Streichholz **brennt** nicht.	*The match won't light.*
Das ganze Haus **brannte**.	*The entire house was on fire.*
Wir **werden** diese CD zuerst **brennen**.	*We'll burn this CD first.*

bringen *to bring* mixed, *formed with* **haben**

PRESENT		PRESENT SUBJUNCTIVE	
ich	bringe	ich	bringe
du	bringst	du	bringest
er/sie/es	bringt	er/sie/es	bringe
wir	bringen	wir	bringen
ihr	bringt	ihr	bringet
sie/Sie	bringen	sie/Sie	bringen

PERFECT		IMPERFECT	
ich	habe gebracht	ich	brachte
du	hast gebracht	du	brachtest
er/sie/es	hat gebracht	er/sie/es	brachte
wir	haben gebracht	wir	brachten
ihr	habt gebracht	ihr	brachtet
sie/Sie	haben gebracht	sie/Sie	brachten

FUTURE		CONDITIONAL	
ich	werde bringen	ich	würde bringen
du	wirst bringen	du	würdest bringen
er/sie/es	wird bringen	er/sie/es	würde bringen
wir	werden bringen	wir	würden bringen
ihr	werdet bringen	ihr	würdet bringen
sie/Sie	werden bringen	sie/Sie	würden bringen

IMPERATIVE
bring(e)! / bringen wir! / bringt! / bringen Sie!

PRESENT PARTICIPLE
bringend

PAST PARTICIPLE
gebracht

EXAMPLE PHRASES

Bringst du mich zum Flughafen? — *Can you take me to the airport?*
Max **hat** mir Blumen **gebracht**. — *Max brought me flowers.*
Das **brachte** mich auf eine Idee. — *It gave me an idea.*

PRESENT

ich	denke
du	denkst
er/sie/es	denkt
wir	denken
ihr	denkt
sie/Sie	denken

PRESENT SUBJUNCTIVE

ich	denke
du	denkest
er/sie/es	denke
wir	denken
ihr	denket
sie/Sie	denken

PERFECT

ich	habe gedacht
du	hast gedacht
er/sie/es	hat gedacht
wir	haben gedacht
ihr	habt gedacht
sie/Sie	haben gedacht

IMPERFECT

ich	dachte
du	dachtest
er/sie/es	dachte
wir	dachten
ihr	dachtet
sie/Sie	dachten

FUTURE

ich	werde denken
du	wirst denken
er/sie/es	wird denken
wir	werden denken
ihr	werdet denken
sie/Sie	werden denken

CONDITIONAL

ich	würde denken
du	würdest denken
er/sie/es	würde denken
wir	würden denken
ihr	würdet denken
sie/Sie	würden denken

IMPERATIVE

denk(e)! / denken wir! / denkt! / denken Sie!

PRESENT PARTICIPLE

denkend

PAST PARTICIPLE

gedacht

EXAMPLE PHRASES

Wie **denken** Sie darüber? — *What do you think about it?*

Er **hat** an sie **gedacht**. — *He thought of her.*

Es war das Erste, woran ich **dachte**. — *It was the first thing I thought of.*

Table 15

durchsetzen *to enforce*

weak, separable, *formed with* **haben**

PRESENT

ich	setze durch
du	setzt durch
er/sie/es	setzt durch
wir	setzen durch
ihr	setzt durch
sie/Sie	setzen durch

PRESENT SUBJUNCTIVE

ich	setze durch
du	setzest durch
er/sie/es	setze durch
wir	setzen durch
ihr	setzet durch
sie/Sie	setzen durch

PERFECT

ich	habe durchgesetzt
du	hast durchgesetzt
er/sie/es	hat durchgesetzt
wir	haben durchgesetzt
ihr	habt durchgesetzt
sie/Sie	haben durchgesetzt

IMPERFECT

ich	setzte durch
du	setztest durch
er/sie/es	setzte durch
wir	setzten durch
ihr	setztet durch
sie/Sie	setzten durch

FUTURE

ich	werde durchsetzen
du	wirst durchsetzen
er/sie/es	wird durchsetzen
wir	werden durchsetzen
ihr	werdet durchsetzen
sie/Sie	werden durchsetzen

CONDITIONAL

ich	würde durchsetzen
du	würdest durchsetzen
er/sie/es	würde durchsetzen
wir	würden durchsetzen
ihr	würdet durchsetzen
sie/Sie	würden durchsetzen

IMPERATIVE

setz(e) durch! / setzen wir durch! / setzt durch! / setzen Sie durch!

PRESENT PARTICIPLE

durchsetzend

PAST PARTICIPLE

durchgesetzt

EXAMPLE PHRASES

Er **setzte** sich mit seinem Plan **durch**. — *He was successful with his plan.*

Ich **würde** dieses Ziel gern bald **durchsetzen**. — *I would like to achieve this aim soon.*

PRESENT		PRESENT SUBJUNCTIVE	
ich	darf	ich	dürfe
du	darfst	du	dürfest
er/sie/es	darf	er/sie/es	dürfe
wir	dürfen	wir	dürfen
ihr	dürft	ihr	dürfet
sie/Sie	dürfen	sie/Sie	dürfen

PERFECT		IMPERFECT	
ich	habe gedurft /dürfen	ich	durfte
du	hast gedurft/dürfen	du	durftest
er/sie/es	hat gedurft/dürfen	er/sie/es	durfte
wir	haben gedurft/dürfen	wir	durften
ihr	habt gedurft/dürfen	ihr	durftet
sie/Sie	haben gedurft/dürfen	sie/Sie	durften

FUTURE		CONDITIONAL	
ich	werde dürfen	ich	würde dürfen
du	wirst dürfen	du	würdest dürfen
er/sie/es	wird dürfen	er/sie/es	würde dürfen
wir	werden dürfen	wir	würden dürfen
ihr	werdet dürfen	ihr	würdet dürfen
sie/Sie	werden dürfen	sie/Sie	würden dürfen

PRESENT PARTICIPLE
dürfend

PAST PARTICIPLE
gedurft / dürfen*

*This form is used when combined with another infinitive.

EXAMPLE PHRASES

Er meint, er **dürfe** das nicht.	*He thinks he isn't allowed to.*
Wir **durften** nicht ausgehen.	*We weren't allowed to go out.*
Das **würde** ich zu Hause nicht **dürfen**.	*I wouldn't be allowed to do that at home.*

empfehlen *to recommend*

strong, inseparable, *formed with* **haben**

PRESENT

ich	empfehle
du	empfiehlst
er/sie/es	empfiehlt
wir	empfehlen
ihr	empfehlt
sie/Sie	empfehlen

PRESENT SUBJUNCTIVE

ich	empfehle
du	empfehlest
er/sie/es	empfehle
wir	empfehlen
ihr	empfehlet
sie/Sie	empfehlen

PERFECT

ich	habe empfohlen
du	hast empfohlen
er/sie/es	hat empfohlen
wir	haben empfohlen
ihr	habt empfohlen
sie/Sie	haben empfohlen

IMPERFECT

ich	empfahl
du	empfahlst
er/sie/es	empfahl
wir	empfahlen
ihr	empfahlt
sie/Sie	empfahlen

FUTURE

ich	werde empfehlen
du	wirst empfehlen
er/sie/es	wird empfehlen
wir	werden empfehlen
ihr	werdet empfehlen
sie/Sie	werden empfehlen

CONDITIONAL

ich	würde empfehlen
du	würdest empfehlen
er/sie/es	würde empfehlen
wir	würden empfehlen
ihr	würdet empfehlen
sie/Sie	würden empfehlen

IMPERATIVE

empfiehl! / empfehlen wir! / empfehlt! / empfehlen Sie!

PRESENT PARTICIPLE

empfehlend

PAST PARTICIPLE

empfohlen

EXAMPLE PHRASES

Was **empfiehlst** du mir zu tun? *What would you recommend I do?*

PRESENT

ich	entdecke
du	entdeckst
er/sie/es	entdeckt
wir	entdecken
ihr	entdeckt
sie/Sie	entdecken

PRESENT SUBJUNCTIVE

ich	entdecke
du	entdeckest
er/sie/es	entdecke
wir	entdecken
ihr	entdecket
sie/Sie	entdecken

PERFECT

ich	habe entdeckt
du	hast entdeckt
er/sie/es	hat entdeckt
wir	haben entdeckt
ihr	habt entdeckt
sie/Sie	haben entdeckt

IMPERFECT

ich	entdeckte
du	entdecktest
er/sie/es	entdeckte
wir	entdeckten
ihr	entdecktet
sie/Sie	entdeckten

FUTURE

ich	werde entdecken
du	wirst entdecken
er/sie/es	wird entdecken
wir	werden entdecken
ihr	werdet entdecken
sie/Sie	werden entdecken

CONDITIONAL

ich	würde entdecken
du	würdest entdecken
er/sie/es	würde entdecken
wir	würden entdecken
ihr	würdet entdecken
sie/Sie	würden entdecken

IMPERATIVE

entdeck(e)! / entdecken wir! / entdeckt! / entdecken Sie!

PRESENT PARTICIPLE

entdeckend

PAST PARTICIPLE

entdeckt

EXAMPLE PHRASES

Kolumbus **hat** Amerika **entdeckt**. *Columbus discovered America.*

Table 19

erzählen *to tell*

weak, inseparable,
formed with **haben**

PRESENT

ich	erzähle
du	erzählst
er/sie/es	erzählt
wir	erzählen
ihr	erzählt
sie/Sie	erzählen

PRESENT SUBJUNCTIVE

ich	erzähle
du	erzählest
er/sie/es	erzähle
wir	erzählen
ihr	erzählet
sie/Sie	erzählen

PERFECT

ich	habe erzählt
du	hast erzählt
er/sie/es	hat erzählt
wir	haben erzählt
ihr	habt erzählt
sie/Sie	haben erzählt

IMPERFECT

ich	erzählte
du	erzähltest
er/sie/es	erzählte
wir	erzählten
ihr	erzähltet
sie/Sie	erzählten

FUTURE

ich	werde erzählen
du	wirst erzählen
er/sie/es	wird erzählen
wir	werden erzählen
ihr	werdet erzählen
sie/Sie	werden erzählen

CONDITIONAL

ich	würde erzählen
du	würdest erzählen
er/sie/es	würde erzählen
wir	würden erzählen
ihr	würdet erzählen
sie/Sie	würden erzählen

IMPERATIVE

erzähl(e)! / erzählen wir! / erzählt! / erzählen Sie!

PRESENT PARTICIPLE

erzählend

PAST PARTICIPLE

erzählt

EXAMPLE PHRASES

Er denkt, sie **erzähle** nur Lügen. — *He thinks all she tells is lies.*
Sie **erzählte** uns ihren Traum. — *She told us about her dream.*

PRESENT

ich	esse
du	isst
er/sie/es	isst
wir	essen
ihr	esst
sie/Sie	essen

PRESENT SUBJUNCTIVE

ich	esse
du	essest
er/sie/es	esse
wir	essen
ihr	esset
sie/Sie	essen

PERFECT

ich	habe gegessen
du	hast gegessen
er/sie/es	hat gegessen
wir	haben gegessen
ihr	habt gegessen
sie/Sie	haben gegessen

IMPERFECT

ich	aß
du	aßest
er/sie/es	aß
wir	aßen
ihr	aßt
sie/Sie	aßen

FUTURE

ich	werde essen
du	wirst essen
er/sie/es	wird essen
wir	werden essen
ihr	werdet essen
sie/Sie	werden essen

CONDITIONAL

ich	würde essen
du	würdest essen
er/sie/es	würde essen
wir	würden essen
ihr	würdet essen
sie/Sie	würden essen

IMPERATIVE

iss! / essen wir! / esst! / essen Sie!

PRESENT PARTICIPLE

essend

PAST PARTICIPLE

gegessen

EXAMPLE PHRASES

Ich **esse** kein Fleisch. — *I don't eat meat.*

Ich **aß** den ganzen Kuchen. — *I ate the whole cake.*

fahren *to drive; to go*

strong, *formed with* **haben/sein***

PRESENT

ich	fahre
du	fährst
er/sie/es	fährt
wir	fahren
ihr	fahrt
sie/Sie	fahren

PRESENT SUBJUNCTIVE

ich	fahre
du	fahrest
er/sie/es	fahre
wir	fahren
ihr	fahret
sie/Sie	fahren

PERFECT

ich	bin gefahren
du	bist gefahren
er/sie/es	ist gefahren
wir	sind gefahren
ihr	seid gefahren
sie/Sie	sind gefahren

IMPERFECT

ich	fuhr
du	fuhrst
er/sie/es	fuhr
wir	fuhren
ihr	fuhrt
sie/Sie	fuhren

FUTURE

ich	werde fahren
du	wirst fahren
er/sie/es	wird fahren
wir	werden fahren
ihr	werdet fahren
sie/Sie	werden fahren

CONDITIONAL

ich	würde fahren
du	würdest fahren
er/sie/es	würde fahren
wir	würden fahren
ihr	würdet fahren
sie/Sie	würden fahren

IMPERATIVE

fahr(e)! / fahren wir! / fahrt! / fahren Sie!

PRESENT PARTICIPLE

fahrend

PAST PARTICIPLE

gefahren

*When **fahren** is used with a direct object, it is formed with **haben**.

EXAMPLE PHRASES

In Deutschland **fährt** man rechts.	*In Germany they drive on the right.*
Ich **bin** mit der Familie nach Spanien **gefahren**.	*I went to Spain with my family.*

PRESENT

ich	falle
du	fällst
er/sie/es	fällt
wir	fallen
ihr	fallt
sie/Sie	fallen

PRESENT SUBJUNCTIVE

ich	falle
du	fallest
er/sie/es	falle
wir	fallen
ihr	fallet
sie/Sie	fallen

PERFECT

ich	bin gefallen
du	bist gefallen
er/sie/es	ist gefallen
wir	sind gefallen
ihr	seid gefallen
sie/Sie	sind gefallen

IMPERFECT

ich	fiel
du	fielst
er/sie/es	fiel
wir	fielen
ihr	fielt
sie/Sie	fielen

FUTURE

ich	werde fallen
du	wirst fallen
er/sie/es	wird fallen
wir	werden fallen
ihr	werdet fallen
sie/Sie	werden fallen

CONDITIONAL

ich	würde fallen
du	würdest fallen
er/sie/es	würde fallen
wir	würden fallen
ihr	würdet fallen
sie/Sie	würden fallen

IMPERATIVE

fall(e)! / fallen wir! / fallt! / fallen Sie!

PRESENT PARTICIPLE

fallend

PAST PARTICIPLE

gefallen

EXAMPLE PHRASES

Er meint, der Euro **falle** im Wert.	*He thinks the euro is going down in value.*
Er **fiel** vom Fahrrad.	*He fell off his bike.*
Ihr **werdet** noch **fallen** und euch wehtun.	*You'll end up falling and hurting yourselves.*

fangen *to catch*

strong, *formed with* **haben**

PRESENT

ich	fange
du	fängst
er/sie/es	fängt
wir	fangen
ihr	fangt
sie/Sie	fangen

PRESENT SUBJUNCTIVE

ich	fange
du	fangest
er/sie/es	fange
wir	fangen
ihr	fanget
sie/Sie	fangen

PERFECT

ich	habe gefangen
du	hast gefangen
er/sie/es	hat gefangen
wir	haben gefangen
ihr	habt gefangen
sie/Sie	haben gefangen

IMPERFECT

ich	fing
du	fingst
er/sie/es	fing
wir	fingen
ihr	fingt
sie/Sie	fingen

FUTURE

ich	werde fangen
du	wirst fangen
er/sie/es	wird fangen
wir	werden fangen
ihr	werdet fangen
sie/Sie	werden fangen

CONDITIONAL

ich	würde fangen
du	würdest fangen
er/sie/es	würde fangen
wir	würden fangen
ihr	würdet fangen
sie/Sie	würden fangen

IMPERATIVE

fang(e)! / fangen wir! / fangt! / fangen Sie!

PRESENT PARTICIPLE

fangend

PAST PARTICIPLE

gefangen

EXAMPLE PHRASES

Ich **fing** den Ball. *I caught the ball.*

PRESENT

ich	finde
du	findest
er/sie/es	findet
wir	finden
ihr	findet
sie/Sie	finden

PRESENT SUBJUNCTIVE

ich	finde
du	findest
er/sie/es	finde
wir	finden
ihr	findet
sie/Sie	finden

PERFECT

ich	habe gefunden
du	hast gefunden
er/sie/es	hat gefunden
wir	haben gefunden
ihr	habt gefunden
sie/Sie	haben gefunden

IMPERFECT

ich	fand
du	fand(e)st
er/sie/es	fand
wir	fanden
ihr	fandet
sie/Sie	fanden

FUTURE

ich	werde finden
du	wirst finden
er/sie/es	wird finden
wir	werden finden
ihr	werdet finden
sie/Sie	werden finden

CONDITIONAL

ich	würde finden
du	würdest finden
er/sie/es	würde finden
wir	würden finden
ihr	würdet finden
sie/Sie	würden finden

IMPERATIVE

find(e)! / finden wir! / findet! / finden Sie!

PRESENT PARTICIPLE

findend

PAST PARTICIPLE

gefunden

EXAMPLE PHRASES

Sie sagt, sie **finde** ihn attraktiv.	*She says she finds him attractive.*
Hast du deine Brieftasche **gefunden**?	*Have you found your wallet?*
Wir **werden** dieses Dorf nie **finden**.	*We'll never find that village.*

fliegen *to fly*

strong, *formed with* **haben/sein***

PRESENT

ich	fliege
du	fliegst
er/sie/es	fliegen
wir	fliegen
ihr	fliegt
sie/Sie	fliegen

PRESENT SUBJUNCTIVE

ich	fliege
du	fliegest
er/sie/es	fliege
wir	fliegen
ihr	flieget
sie/Sie	fliegen

PERFECT

ich	habe geflogen
du	hast geflogen
er/sie/es	hat geflogen
wir	haben geflogen
ihr	habt geflogen
sie/Sie	haben geflogen

IMPERFECT

ich	flog
du	flogst
er/sie/es	flog
wir	flogen
ihr	flogt
sie/Sie	flogen

FUTURE

ich	werde fliegen
du	wirst fliegen
er/sie/es	wird fliegen
wir	werden fliegen
ihr	werdet fliegen
sie/Sie	werden fliegen

CONDITIONAL

ich	würde fliegen
du	würdest fliegen
er/sie/es	würde fliegen
wir	würden fliegen
ihr	würdet fliegen
sie/Sie	würden fliegen

IMPERATIVE

flieg(e)! / fliegen wir! / fliegt! / fliegen Sie!

PRESENT PARTICIPLE

fliegend

PAST PARTICIPLE

geflogen

*When **fliegen** is used with no direct object, it is formed with **sein**.

EXAMPLE PHRASES

Wir **flogen** zusammen nach Spanien. — *We flew to Spain together.*

Es war, als **würde** ich **fliegen**. — *It was as if I was flying.*

strong,
formed with **haben/sein***

to flee **fliehen**

PRESENT

ich	fliehe
du	fliehst
er/sie/es	flieht
wir	fliehen
ihr	flieht
sie/Sie	fliehen

PRESENT SUBJUNCTIVE

ich	fliehe
du	fliehest
er/sie/es	fliehe
wir	fliehen
ihr	fliehet
sie/Sie	fliehen

PERFECT

ich	bin geflohen
du	bist geflohen
er/sie/es	ist geflohen
wir	sind geflohen
ihr	seid geflohen
sie/Sie	sind geflohen

IMPERFECT

ich	floh
du	flohst
er/sie/es	floh
wir	flohen
ihr	floht
sie/Sie	flohen

FUTURE

ich	werde fliehen
du	wirst fliehen
er/sie/es	wird fliehen
wir	werden fliehen
ihr	werdet fliehen
sie/Sie	werden fliehen

CONDITIONAL

ich	würde fliehen
du	würdest fliehen
er/sie/es	würde fliehen
wir	würden fliehen
ihr	würdet fliehen
sie/Sie	würden fliehen

IMPERATIVE

flieh(e)! / fliehen wir! / flieht! / fliehen Sie!

PRESENT PARTICIPLE

fliehend

PAST PARTICIPLE

geflohen

*When **fliehen** is used with a direct object, it is formed with **haben**.

EXAMPLE PHRASES

Sie **floh** vor der Polizei.	*She fled from the police.*

fließen *to flow*

strong, *formed with* **sein**

PRESENT

ich	fließe
du	fließt
er/sie/es	fließt
wir	fließen
ihr	fließt
sie/Sie	fließen

PRESENT SUBJUNCTIVE

ich	fließe
du	fließest
er/sie/es	fließe
wir	fließen
ihr	fließet
sie/Sie	fließen

PERFECT

ich	bin geflossen
du	bist geflossen
er/sie/es	ist geflossen
wir	sind geflossen
ihr	seid geflossen
sie/Sie	sind geflossen

IMPERFECT

ich	floss
du	flossest
er/sie/es	floss
wir	flossen
ihr	flosst
sie/Sie	flossen

FUTURE

ich	werde fließen
du	wirst fließen
er/sie/es	wird fließen
wir	werden fließen
ihr	werdet fließen
sie/Sie	werden fließen

CONDITIONAL

ich	würde fließen
du	würdest fließen
er/sie/es	würde fließen
wir	würden fließen
ihr	würdet fließen
sie/Sie	würden fließen

IMPERATIVE

fließ(e)! / fließen wir! / fließt! / fließen Sie!

PRESENT PARTICIPLE

fließend

PAST PARTICIPLE

geflossen

EXAMPLE PHRASES

Welcher Fluss **fließt** durch Hamburg? — *Which river flows through Hamburg?*

strong, *formed with* **haben** *to give* **geben**

PRESENT

ich	gebe
du	gibst
er/sie/es	gibt
wir	geben
ihr	gebt
sie/Sie	geben

PRESENT SUBJUNCTIVE

ich	gebe
du	gebest
er/sie/es	gebe
wir	geben
ihr	gebet
sie/Sie	geben

PERFECT

ich	habe gegeben
du	hast gegeben
er/sie/es	hat gegeben
wir	haben gegeben
ihr	habt gegeben
sie/Sie	haben gegeben

IMPERFECT

ich	gab
du	gabst
er/sie/es	gab
wir	gaben
ihr	gabt
sie/Sie	gaben

FUTURE

ich	werde geben
du	wirst geben
er/sie/es	wird geben
wir	werden geben
ihr	werdet geben
sie/Sie	werden geben

CONDITIONAL

ich	würde geben
du	würdest geben
er/sie/es	würde geben
wir	würden geben
ihr	würdet geben
sie/Sie	würden geben

IMPERATIVE

gib! / geben wir! / gebt! / geben Sie!

PRESENT PARTICIPLE

gebend

PAST PARTICIPLE

gegeben

EXAMPLE PHRASES

Er **gab** mir das Geld für die Bücher. — *He gave me the money for the books.*

Wir **würden** alles dafür **geben**, ins Finale zu kommen. — *We would give anything to reach the finals.*

gehen *to go*

strong, *formed with* **haben**

PRESENT

ich	gehe
du	gehst
er/sie/es	geht
wir	gehen
ihr	geht
sie/Sie	gehen

PRESENT SUBJUNCTIVE

ich	gehe
du	gehest
er/sie/es	gehe
wir	gehen
ihr	gehet
sie/Sie	gehen

PERFECT

ich	bin gegangen
du	bist gegangen
er/sie/es	ist gegangen
wir	sind gegangen
ihr	seid gegangen
sie/Sie	sind gegangen

IMPERFECT

ich	ging
du	gingst
er/sie/es	ging
wir	gingen
ihr	gingt
sie/Sie	gingen

FUTURE

ich	werde gehen
du	wirst gehen
er/sie/es	wird gehen
wir	werden gehen
ihr	werdet gehen
sie/Sie	werden gehen

CONDITIONAL

ich	würde gehen
du	würdest gehen
er/sie/es	würde gehen
wir	würden gehen
ihr	würdet gehen
sie/Sie	würden gehen

IMPERATIVE

geh(e)! / gehen wir! / geht! / gehen Sie!

PRESENT PARTICIPLE

gehend

PAST PARTICIPLE

gegangen

EXAMPLE PHRASES

Wir **sind** gestern schwimmen **gegangen**. — *We went swimming yesterday.*

Die Kinder **gingen** ins Haus. — *The children went into the house.*

In diesen Kleidern **würde** ich nicht ins Theater **gehen**. — *I wouldn't go to the theatre in these clothes.*

PRESENT

ich	gewinne
du	gewinnst
er/sie/es	gewinnt
wir	gewinnen
ihr	gewinnt
sie/Sie	gewinnen

PRESENT SUBJUNCTIVE

ich	gewinne
du	gewinnest
er/sie/es	gewinne
wir	gewinnen
ihr	gewinnet
sie/Sie	gewinnen

PERFECT

ich	habe gewonnen
du	hast gewonnen
er/sie/es	hat gewonnen
wir	haben gewonnen
ihr	habt gewonnen
sie/Sie	haben gewonnen

IMPERFECT

ich	gewann
du	gewannst
er/sie/es	gewann
wir	gewannen
ihr	gewannt
sie/Sie	gewannen

FUTURE

ich	werde gewinnen
du	wirst gewinnen
er/sie/es	wird gewinnen
wir	werden gewinnen
ihr	werdet gewinnen
sie/Sie	werden gewinnen

CONDITIONAL

ich	würde gewinnen
du	würdest gewinnen
er/sie/es	würde gewinnen
wir	würden gewinnen
ihr	würdet gewinnen
sie/Sie	würden gewinnen

IMPERATIVE

gewinn(e)! / gewinnen wir! / gewinnt! / gewinnen Sie!

PRESENT PARTICIPLE

gewinnend

PAST PARTICIPLE

gewonnen

EXAMPLE PHRASES

Er **gewinnt** immer beim Kartenspielen. — *He always wins at cards.*

Er **hat** den ersten Preis **gewonnen**. — *He won first prize.*

grüßen *to greet*

weak, *formed with* **haben**

PRESENT

ich	grüße
du	grüßt
er/sie/es	grüßt
wir	grüßen
ihr	grüßt
sie/Sie	grüßen

PRESENT SUBJUNCTIVE

ich	grüße
du	grüßest
er/sie/es	grüße
wir	grüßen
ihr	grüßet
sie/Sie	grüßen

PERFECT

ich	habe gegrüßt
du	hast gegrüßt
er/sie/es	hat gegrüßt
wir	haben gegrüßt
ihr	habt gegrüßt
sie/Sie	haben gegrüßt

IMPERFECT

ich	grüßte
du	grüßtest
er/sie/es	grüßte
wir	grüßten
ihr	grüßtet
sie/Sie	grüßten

FUTURE

ich	werde grüßen
du	wirst grüßen
er/sie/es	wird grüßen
wir	werden grüßen
ihr	werdet grüßen
sie/Sie	werden grüßen

CONDITIONAL

ich	würde grüßen
du	würdest grüßen
er/sie/es	würde grüßen
wir	würden grüßen
ihr	würdet grüßen
sie/Sie	würden grüßen

IMPERATIVE

grüß(e)! / grüßen wir! / grüßt! / grüßen Sie!

PRESENT PARTICIPLE

grüßend

PAST PARTICIPLE

gegrüßt

EXAMPLE PHRASES

Sie **grüßte** mich mit einem Lächeln. — *She greeted me with a smile.*

PRESENT

ich	habe
du	hast
er/sie/es	hat
wir	haben
ihr	habt
sie/Sie	haben

PRESENT SUBJUNCTIVE

ich	habe
du	habest
er/sie/es	habe
wir	haben
ihr	habet
sie/Sie	haben

PERFECT

ich	habe gehabt
du	hast gehabt
er/sie/es	hat gehabt
wir	haben gehabt
ihr	habt gehabt
sie/Sie	haben gehabt

IMPERFECT

ich	hatte
du	hattest
er/sie/es	hatte
wir	hatten
ihr	hattet
sie/Sie	hatten

FUTURE

ich	werde haben
du	wirst haben
er/sie/es	wird haben
wir	werden haben
ihr	werdet haben
sie/Sie	werden haben

CONDITIONAL

ich	würde haben
du	würdest haben
er/sie/es	würde haben
wir	würden haben
ihr	würdet haben
sie/Sie	würden haben

IMPERATIVE

hab(e)! / haben wir! / habt! / haben Sie!

PRESENT PARTICIPLE

habend

PAST PARTICIPLE

gehabt

EXAMPLE PHRASES

Hast du eine Schwester? — *Have you got a sister?*
Er sagt, er **habe** keine Zeit. — *He says he has no time.*
Er **hatte** Hunger. — *He was hungry.*

halten *to hold*

strong, *formed with* **haben**

PRESENT

ich	halte
du	hältst
er/sie/es	hält
wir	halten
ihr	haltet
sie/Sie	halten

PRESENT SUBJUNCTIVE

ich	halte
du	haltest
er/sie/es	halte
wir	halten
ihr	haltet
sie/Sie	halten

PERFECT

ich	habe gehalten
du	hast gehalten
er/sie/es	hat gehalten
wir	haben gehalten
ihr	habt gehalten
sie/Sie	haben gehalten

IMPERFECT

ich	hielt
du	hielt(e)st
er/sie/es	hielt
wir	hielten
ihr	hieltet
sie/Sie	hielten

FUTURE

ich	werde halten
du	wirst halten
er/sie/es	wird halten
wir	werden halten
ihr	werdet halten
sie/Sie	werden halten

CONDITIONAL

ich	würde halten
du	würdest halten
er/sie/es	würde halten
wir	würden halten
ihr	würdet halten
sie/Sie	würden halten

IMPERATIVE

halt(e)! / halten wir! / haltet! / halten Sie!

PRESENT PARTICIPLE

haltend

PAST PARTICIPLE

gehalten

EXAMPLE PHRASES

Hältst du das mal für mich? *Can you hold that for me?*

weak,
formed with **haben**

to trade; to act **handeln**

PRESENT

ich	handle
du	handelst
er/sie/es	handelt
wir	handeln
ihr	handelt
sie/Sie	handeln

PRESENT SUBJUNCTIVE

ich	handle
du	handlest
er/sie/es	handle
wir	handlen
ihr	handlet
sie/Sie	handlen

PERFECT

ich	habe gehandelt
du	hast gehandelt
er/sie/es	hat gehandelt
wir	haben gehandelt
ihr	habt gehandelt
sie/Sie	haben gehandelt

IMPERFECT

ich	handelte
du	handeltest
er/sie/es	handelte
wir	handelten
ihr	handeltet
sie/Sie	handelten

FUTURE

ich	werde handeln
du	wirst handeln
er/sie/es	wird handeln
wir	werden handeln
ihr	werdet handeln
sie/Sie	werden handeln

CONDITIONAL

ich	würde handeln
du	würdest handeln
er/sie/es	würde handeln
wir	würden handeln
ihr	würdet handeln
sie/Sie	würden handeln

IMPERATIVE

handle! / handeln wir! / handelt! / handeln Sie!

PRESENT PARTICIPLE

handelnd

PAST PARTICIPLE

gehandelt

EXAMPLE PHRASES

Die Polizei **handelte** schnell.	*The police acted quickly.*
Er **würde** nie mit Drogen **handeln.**	*He would never deal in drugs.*

Table 35

hängen *to hang*

strong*, *formed with* **haben**

PRESENT

ich	hänge
du	hängst
er/sie/es	hängt
wir	hängen
ihr	hängt
sie/Sie	hängen

PRESENT SUBJUNCTIVE

ich	hänge
du	hängest
er/sie/es	hänge
wir	hängen
ihr	hänget
sie/Sie	hängen

PERFECT

ich	habe gehangen
du	hast gehangen
er/sie/es	hat gehangen
wir	haben gehangen
ihr	habt gehangen
sie/Sie	haben gehangen

IMPERFECT

ich	hing
du	hingst
er/sie/es	hing
wir	hingen
ihr	hingt
sie/Sie	hingen

FUTURE

ich	werde hängen
du	wirst hängen
er/sie/es	wird hängen
wir	werden hängen
ihr	werdet hängen
sie/Sie	werden hängen

CONDITIONAL

ich	würde hängen
du	würdest hängen
er/sie/es	würde hängen
wir	würden hängen
ihr	würdet hängen
sie/Sie	würden hängen

IMPERATIVE

häng(e)! / hängen wir! / hängt! / hängen Sie!

PRESENT PARTICIPLE

hängend

PAST PARTICIPLE

gehangen

*Conjugated as a weak verb when it has a direct object.

EXAMPLE PHRASES

Das Bild **hing** an der Wand. — *The picture was hanging on the wall.*

Wir **werden** die Wäsche auf die Leine **hängen**. — *We'll hang the washing on the line.*

PRESENT		PRESENT SUBJUNCTIVE	
ich	heize	ich	heize
du	heizt	du	heizest
er/sie/es	heizt	er/sie/es	heize
wir	heizen	wir	heizen
ihr	heizt	ihr	heizet
sie/Sie	heizen	sie/Sie	heizen

PERFECT		IMPERFECT	
ich	habe geheizt	ich	heizte
du	hast geheizt	du	heiztest
er/sie/es	hat geheizt	er/sie/es	heizte
wir	haben geheizt	wir	heizten
ihr	habt geheizt	ihr	heiztet
sie/Sie	haben geheizt	sie/Sie	heizten

FUTURE		CONDITIONAL	
ich	werde heizen	ich	würde heizen
du	wirst heizen	du	würdest heizen
er/sie/es	wird heizen	er/sie/es	würde heizen
wir	werden heizen	wir	würden heizen
ihr	werdet heizen	ihr	würdet heizen
sie/Sie	werden heizen	sie/Sie	würden heizen

IMPERATIVE

heiz(e)! / heizen wir! / heizt! / heizen Sie!

PRESENT PARTICIPLE

heizend

PAST PARTICIPLE

geheizt

EXAMPLE PHRASES

Der Ofen **heizt** gut. — *The stove gives off a good heat.*

An Ihrer Stelle **würde** ich das Haus besser **heizen**. — *If I were you, I would heat the house better.*

helfen *to help*

strong, dative,
formed with **haben**

PRESENT		PRESENT SUBJUNCTIVE	
ich	helfe	ich	helfe
du	hilfst	du	helfest
er/sie/es	hilft	er/sie/es	helfe
wir	helfen	wir	helfen
ihr	helft	ihr	helfet
sie/Sie	helfen	sie/Sie	helfen

PERFECT		IMPERFECT	
ich	habe geholfen	ich	half
du	hast geholfen	du	halfst
er/sie/es	hat geholfen	er/sie/es	half
wir	haben geholfen	wir	halfen
ihr	habt geholfen	ihr	halft
sie/Sie	haben geholfen	sie/Sie	halfen

FUTURE		CONDITIONAL	
ich	werde helfen	ich	würde helfen
du	wirst helfen	du	würdest helfen
er/sie/es	wird helfen	er/sie/es	würde helfen
wir	werden helfen	wir	würden helfen
ihr	werdet helfen	ihr	würdet helfen
sie/Sie	werden helfen	sie/Sie	würden helfen

IMPERATIVE

hilf! / helfen wir! / helft! / helfen Sie!

PRESENT PARTICIPLE

helfend

PAST PARTICIPLE

geholfen

EXAMPLE PHRASES

Sie sagt, sie **helfe** gern anderen. — *She says she likes to help others.*

Er **hat** mir dabei **geholfen**. — *He helped me with it.*

Er **wird** mir **helfen**, den Aufsatz zu schreiben. — *He will help me write the essay.*

PRESENT

ich	hole
du	holst
er/sie/es	holt
wir	holen
ihr	holt
sie/Sie	holen

PRESENT SUBJUNCTIVE

ich	hole
du	holest
er/sie/es	hole
wir	holen
ihr	holet
sie/Sie	holen

PERFECT

ich	habe geholt
du	hast geholt
er/sie/es	hat geholt
wir	haben geholt
ihr	habt geholt
sie/Sie	haben geholt

IMPERFECT

ich	holte
du	holtest
er/sie/es	holte
wir	holten
ihr	holtet
sie/Sie	holten

FUTURE

ich	werde holen
du	wirst holen
er/sie/es	wird holen
wir	werden holen
ihr	werdet holen
sie/Sie	werden holen

CONDITIONAL

ich	würde holen
du	würdest holen
er/sie/es	würde holen
wir	würden holen
ihr	würdet holen
sie/Sie	würden holen

IMPERATIVE

hol(e)! / holen wir! / holt! / holen Sie!

PRESENT PARTICIPLE

holend

PAST PARTICIPLE

geholt

EXAMPLE PHRASES

Er **holt** jeden Tag frische Milch vom Supermarkt. — *He gets fresh milk from the supermarket every day.*

Ich **habe** mir eine Erkältung **geholt**. — *I caught a cold.*

kennen *to know (be acquainted with)*

mixed, *formed with* **haben**

PRESENT

ich	kenne
du	kennst
er/sie/es	kennt
wir	kennen
ihr	kennt
sie/Sie	kennen

PRESENT SUBJUNCTIVE

ich	kenne
du	kennest
er/sie/es	kenne
wir	kennen
ihr	kennet
sie/Sie	kennen

PERFECT

ich	habe gekannt
du	hast gekannt
er/sie/es	hat gekannt
wir	haben gekannt
ihr	habt gekannt
sie/Sie	haben gekannt

IMPERFECT

ich	kannte
du	kanntest
er/sie/es	kannte
wir	kannten
ihr	kanntet
sie/Sie	kannten

FUTURE

ich	werde kennen
du	wirst kennen
er/sie/es	wird kennen
wir	werden kennen
ihr	werdet kennen
sie/Sie	werden kennen

CONDITIONAL

ich	würde kennen
du	würdest kennen
er/sie/es	würde kennen
wir	würden kennen
ihr	würdet kennen
sie/Sie	würden kennen

IMPERATIVE

kenn(e)! / kennen wir! / kennt! / kennen Sie!

PRESENT PARTICIPLE

kennend

PAST PARTICIPLE

gekannt

EXAMPLE PHRASES

Ich **kenne** ihn nicht. — *I don't know him.*

Er sprach von ihr, als **würde** er sie kennen. — *He spoke of her as if he knew her.*

PRESENT

ich	komme
du	kommst
er/sie/es	kommt
wir	kommen
ihr	kommt
sie/Sie	kommen

PRESENT SUBJUNCTIVE

ich	komme
du	kommest
er/sie/es	komme
wir	kommen
ihr	kommet
sie/Sie	kommen

PERFECT

ich	bin gekommen
du	bist gekommen
er/sie/es	ist gekommen
wir	sind gekommen
ihr	seid gekommen
sie/Sie	sind gekommen

IMPERFECT

ich	kam
du	kamst
er/sie/es	kam
wir	kamen
ihr	kamt
sie/Sie	kamen

FUTURE

ich	werde kommen
du	wirst kommen
er/sie/es	wird kommen
wir	werden kommen
ihr	werdet kommen
sie/Sie	werden kommen

CONDITIONAL

ich	würde kommen
du	würdest kommen
er/sie/es	würde kommen
wir	würden kommen
ihr	würdet kommen
sie/Sie	würden kommen

IMPERATIVE

komm(e)! / kommen wir! / kommt! / kommen Sie!

PRESENT PARTICIPLE

kommend

PAST PARTICIPLE

gekommen

EXAMPLE PHRASES

Ich **komme** zu deiner Party. — *I'm coming to your party.*

Er **kam** die Straße entlang. — *He was coming along the street.*

können *to be able to*

modal, *formed with* **haben**

PRESENT

ich	kann
du	kannst
er/sie/es	kann
wir	können
ihr	könnt
sie/Sie	können

PRESENT SUBJUNCTIVE

ich	könne
du	könnest
er/sie/es	könne
wir	können
ihr	könnet
sie/Sie	können

PERFECT

ich	habe gekonnt/können
du	hast gekonnt/können
er/sie/es	hat gekonnt/können
wir	haben gekonnt/können
ihr	habt gekonnt/können
sie/Sie	haben gekonnt/können

IMPERFECT

ich	konnte
du	konntest
er/sie/es	konnte
wir	konnten
ihr	konntet
sie/Sie	konnten

FUTURE

ich	werde können
du	wirst können
er/sie/es	wird können
wir	werden können
ihr	werdet können
sie/Sie	werden können

CONDITIONAL

ich	würde können
du	würdest können
er/sie/es	würde können
wir	würden können
ihr	würdet können
sie/Sie	würden können

PRESENT PARTICIPLE

könnend

PAST PARTICIPLE

gekonnt / können*

*This form is used when combined with another infinitive.

EXAMPLE PHRASES

Er **kann** gut schwimmen.	*He can swim well.*
Sie sagt, ich **könne** jetzt noch nicht gehen.	*She says I can't leave yet.*
Morgen **werde** ich nicht kommen können.	*I won't be able to come tomorrow.*

PRESENT

ich	lasse
du	lässt
er/sie/es	lässt
wir	lassen
ihr	lasst
sie/Sie	lassen

PRESENT SUBJUNCTIVE

ich	lasse
du	lassest
er/sie/es	lasse
wir	lassen
ihr	lasset
sie/Sie	lassen

PERFECT

ich	habe gelassen/lassen
du	hast gelassen/lassen
er/sie/es	hat gelassen/lassen
wir	haben gelassen/lassen
ihr	habt gelassen/lassen
sie/Sie	haben gelassen/lassen

IMPERFECT

ich	ließ
du	ließest
er/sie/es	ließ
wir	ließen
ihr	ließt
sie/Sie	ließen

FUTURE

ich	werde lassen
du	wirst lassen
er/sie/es	wird lassen
wir	werden lassen
ihr	werdet lassen
sie/Sie	werden lassen

CONDITIONAL

ich	würde lassen
du	würdest lassen
er/sie/es	würde lassen
wir	würden lassen
ihr	würdet lassen
sie/Sie	würden lassen

IMPERATIVE

lass! / lassen wir! / lasst! / lassen Sie!

PRESENT PARTICIPLE

lassend

PAST PARTICIPLE

gelassen / lassen*

*This form is used when combined with another infinitive.

EXAMPLE PHRASES

Ich **lasse** den Hund nicht auf das Sofa. — *I won't let the dog on the sofa.*

Ich **würde** das Baby nie allein lassen. — *I would never leave the baby alone.*

laufen *to run*

strong, *formed with* **sein**

PRESENT

ich	laufe
du	läufst
er/sie/es	läuft
wir	laufen
ihr	lauft
sie/Sie	laufen

PRESENT SUBJUNCTIVE

ich	laufe
du	laufest
er/sie/es	laufe
wir	laufen
ihr	laufet
sie/Sie	laufen

PERFECT

ich	bin gelaufen
du	bist gelaufen
er/sie/es	ist gelaufen
wir	sind gelaufen
ihr	seid gelaufen
sie/Sie	sind gelaufen

IMPERFECT

ich	lief
du	liefst
er/sie/es	lief
wir	liefen
ihr	lieft
sie/Sie	liefen

FUTURE

ich	werde laufen
du	wirst laufen
er/sie/es	wird laufen
wir	werden laufen
ihr	werdet laufen
sie/Sie	werden laufen

CONDITIONAL

ich	würde laufen
du	würdest laufen
er/sie/es	würde laufen
wir	würden laufen
ihr	würdet laufen
sie/Sie	würden laufen

IMPERATIVE

lauf(e)! / laufen wir! / lauft! / laufen Sie!

PRESENT PARTICIPLE

laufend

PAST PARTICIPLE

gelaufen

EXAMPLE PHRASES

Er sagt, ihm **laufe** die Nase. — *He says he's got a runny nose.*
Er **lief** so schnell er konnte. — *He ran as fast as he could.*

PRESENT

ich	leide
du	leidest
er/sie/es	leidet
wir	leiden
ihr	leidet
sie/Sie	leiden

PRESENT SUBJUNCTIVE

ich	leide
du	leidest
er/sie/es	leide
wir	leiden
ihr	leidet
sie/Sie	leiden

PERFECT

ich	habe gelitten
du	hast gelitten
er/sie/es	hat gelitten
wir	haben gelitten
ihr	habt gelitten
sie/Sie	haben gelitten

IMPERFECT

ich	litt
du	litt(e)st
er/sie/es	litt
wir	litten
ihr	littet
sie/Sie	litten

FUTURE

ich	werde leiden
du	wirst leiden
er/sie/es	wird leiden
wir	werden leiden
ihr	werdet leiden
sie/Sie	werden leiden

CONDITIONAL

ich	würde leiden
du	würdest leiden
er/sie/es	würde leiden
wir	würden leiden
ihr	würdet leiden
sie/Sie	würden leiden

IMPERATIVE

leid(e)! / leiden wir! / leidet! / leiden Sie!

PRESENT PARTICIPLE

leidend

PAST PARTICIPLE

gelitten

EXAMPLE PHRASES

Wir **leiden** sehr unter der Hitze. — *We're suffering badly from the heat.*

Sie **litt** an Asthma. — *She suffered from asthma.*

lesen *to read*

strong, *formed with* **haben**

PRESENT

ich	lese
du	liest
er/sie/es	liest
wir	lesen
ihr	lest
sie/Sie	lesen

PRESENT SUBJUNCTIVE

ich	lese
du	lesest
er/sie/es	lese
wir	lesen
ihr	leset
sie/Sie	lesen

PERFECT

ich	habe gelesen
du	hast gelesen
er/sie/es	hat gelesen
wir	haben gelesen
ihr	habt gelesen
sie/Sie	haben gelesen

IMPERFECT

ich	las
du	lasest
er/sie/es	las
wir	lasen
ihr	last
sie/Sie	lasen

FUTURE

ich	werde lesen
du	wirst lesen
er/sie/es	wird lesen
wir	werden lesen
ihr	werdet lesen
sie/Sie	werden lesen

CONDITIONAL

ich	würde lesen
du	würdest lesen
er/sie/es	würde lesen
wir	würden lesen
ihr	würdet lesen
sie/Sie	würden lesen

IMPERATIVE

lies! / lesen wir! / lest! / lesen Sie!

PRESENT PARTICIPLE

lesend

PAST PARTICIPLE

gelesen

EXAMPLE PHRASES

Er sagt, er **lese** jeden Tag zwei Zeitungen.	*He says he reads two newspapers every day.*
Das **habe** ich in der Zeitung **gelesen**.	*I read it in the newspaper.*
Morgen **werde** ich Harry Potter **lesen**.	*I'll read Harry Potter tomorrow.*

strong, *formed with* **haben** *to lie* **liegen**

PRESENT

ich	liege
du	liegst
er/sie/es	liegt
wir	liegen
ihr	liegt
sie/Sie	liegen

PRESENT SUBJUNCTIVE

ich	liege
du	liegest
er/sie/es	liege
wir	liegen
ihr	lieget
sie/Sie	liegen

PERFECT

ich	habe gelegen
du	hast gelegen
er/sie/es	hat gelegen
wir	haben gelegen
ihr	habt gelegen
sie/Sie	haben gelegen

IMPERFECT

ich	lag
du	lagst
er/sie/es	lag
wir	lagen
ihr	lagt
sie/Sie	lagen

FUTURE

ich	werde liegen
du	wirst liegen
er/sie/es	wird liegen
wir	werden liegen
ihr	werdet liegen
sie/Sie	werden liegen

CONDITIONAL

ich	würde liegen
du	würdest liegen
er/sie/es	würde liegen
wir	würden liegen
ihr	würdet liegen
sie/Sie	würden liegen

IMPERATIVE

lieg(e)! / liegen wir! / liegt! / liegen Sie!

PRESENT PARTICIPLE

liegend

PAST PARTICIPLE

gelegen

EXAMPLE PHRASES

Wir **lagen** den ganzen Tag am Strand. *We lay on the beach all day.*

lügen *to (tell a) lie*

strong, *formed with* **haben**

PRESENT

ich	lüge
du	lügst
er/sie/es	lügt
wir	lügen
ihr	lügt
sie/Sie	lügen

PRESENT SUBJUNCTIVE

ich	lüge
du	lügest
er/sie/es	lüge
wir	lügen
ihr	lüget
sie/Sie	lügen

PERFECT

ich	habe gelogen
du	hast gelogen
er/sie/es	hat gelogen
wir	haben gelogen
ihr	habt gelogen
sie/Sie	haben gelogen

IMPERFECT

ich	log
du	logst
er/sie/es	log
wir	logen
ihr	logt
sie/Sie	logen

FUTURE

ich	werde lügen
du	wirst lügen
er/sie/es	wird lügen
wir	werden lügen
ihr	werdet lügen
sie/Sie	werden lügen

CONDITIONAL

ich	würde lügen
du	würdest lügen
er/sie/es	würde lügen
wir	würden lügen
ihr	würdet lügen
sie/Sie	würden lügen

IMPERATIVE

lüg(e)! / lügen wir! / lügt! / lügen Sie!

PRESENT PARTICIPLE

lügend

PAST PARTICIPLE

gelogen

EXAMPLE PHRASES

Er **hat gelogen**! — *He told a lie!*

Ich **würde lügen**, wenn ich das sagen würde. — *I would be lying if I said that.*

PRESENT

ich	mache
du	machst
er/sie/es	macht
wir	machen
ihr	macht
sie/Sie	machen

PRESENT SUBJUNCTIVE

ich	mache
du	machest
er/sie/es	mache
wir	machen
ihr	machet
sie/Sie	machen

PERFECT

ich	habe gemacht
du	hast gemacht
er/sie/es	hat gemacht
wir	haben gemacht
ihr	habt gemacht
sie/Sie	haben gemacht

IMPERFECT

ich	machte
du	machtest
er/sie/es	machte
wir	machten
ihr	machtet
sie/Sie	machten

FUTURE

ich	werde machen
du	wirst machen
er/sie/es	wird machen
wir	werden machen
ihr	werdet machen
sie/Sie	werden machen

CONDITIONAL

ich	würde machen
du	würdest machen
er/sie/es	würde machen
wir	würden machen
ihr	würdet machen
sie/Sie	würden machen

IMPERATIVE

mach! / machen wir! / macht! / machen Sie!

PRESENT PARTICIPLE

machend

PAST PARTICIPLE

gemacht

EXAMPLE PHRASES

Was **machst** du?	*What are you doing?*
Ich **habe** die Betten **gemacht**.	*I made the beds.*
Ich **werde** es morgen **machen**.	*I'll do it tomorrow.*

misstrauen *to mistrust*

weak, inseparable, *formed with* **haben**

PRESENT

ich	misstraue
du	misstraust
er/sie/es	misstraut
wir	misstrauen
ihr	misstraut
sie/Sie	misstrauen

PRESENT SUBJUNCTIVE

ich	misstraue
du	misstrauest
er/sie/es	misstraue
wir	misstrauen
ihr	misstrauet
sie/Sie	misstrauen

PERFECT

ich	habe misstraut
du	hast misstraut
er/sie/es	hat misstraut
wir	haben misstraut
ihr	habt misstraut
sie/Sie	haben misstraut

IMPERFECT

ich	misstraute
du	misstrautest
er/sie/es	misstraute
wir	misstrauten
ihr	misstrautet
sie/Sie	misstrauten

FUTURE

ich	werde misstrauen
du	wirst misstrauen
er/sie/es	wird misstrauen
wir	werden misstrauen
ihr	werdet misstrauen
sie/Sie	werden misstrauen

CONDITIONAL

ich	würde misstrauen
du	würdest misstrauen
er/sie/es	würde misstrauen
wir	würden misstrauen
ihr	würdet misstrauen
sie/Sie	würden misstrauen

IMPERATIVE

misstrau(e)! / misstrauen wir! / misstraut! / misstrauen Sie!

PRESENT PARTICIPLE

misstrauend

PAST PARTICIPLE

misstraut

EXAMPLE PHRASES

Er sagt, er **misstraue** allen Politikern.	*He says he mistrusts all politicians.*
Ich **habe** ihr von Anfang an **misstraut**.	*I didn't trust her from the start.*

PRESENT		PRESENT SUBJUNCTIVE	
ich	mag	ich	möge
du	magst	du	mögest
er/sie/es	mag	er/sie/es	möge
wir	mögen	wir	mögen
ihr	mögt	ihr	möget
sie/Sie	mögen	sie/Sie	mögen

PERFECT		IMPERFECT	
ich	habe gemocht/mögen	ich	mochte
du	hast gemocht/mögen	du	mochtest
er/sie/es	hat gemocht/mögen	er/sie/es	mochte
wir	haben gemocht/mögen	wir	mochten
ihr	habt gemocht/mögen	ihr	mochtet
sie/Sie	haben gemocht/mögen	sie/Sie	mochten

FUTURE		CONDITIONAL	
ich	werde mögen	ich	würde mögen
du	wirst mögen	du	würdest mögen
er/sie/es	wird mögen	er/sie/es	würde mögen
wir	werden mögen	wir	würden mögen
ihr	werdet mögen	ihr	würdet mögen
sie/Sie	werden mögen	sie/Sie	würden mögen

PRESENT PARTICIPLE
mögend

PAST PARTICIPLE
gemocht / mögen*

*This form is used when combined with another infinitive.

EXAMPLE PHRASES

Ich **mag** gern Vanilleeis.	*I like vanilla ice cream.*
Er **mochte** sie nicht danach fragen.	*He didn't want to ask her about it.*

müssen *to have to* modal, *formed with* **haben**

PRESENT		PRESENT SUBJUNCTIVE	
ich	muss	ich	müsse
du	musst	du	müssest
er/sie/es	muss	er/sie/es	müsse
wir	müssen	wir	müssen
ihr	müsst	ihr	müsset
sie/Sie	müssen	sie/Sie	müssen

PERFECT		IMPERFECT	
ich	habe gemusst/müssen	ich	musste
du	hast gemusst/müssen	du	musstest
er/sie/es	hat gemusst/müssen	er/sie/es	musste
wir	haben gemusst/müssen	wir	mussten
ihr	habt gemusst/müssen	ihr	musstet
sie/Sie	haben gemusst/müssen	sie/Sie	mussten

FUTURE		CONDITIONAL	
ich	werde müssen	ich	würde müssen
du	wirst müssen	du	würdest müssen
er/sie/es	wird müssen	er/sie/es	würde müssen
wir	werden müssen	wir	würden müssen
ihr	werdet müssen	ihr	würdet müssen
sie/Sie	werden müssen	sie/Sie	würden müssen

PRESENT PARTICIPLE
müssend

PAST PARTICIPLE
gemusst / müssen*

*This form is used when combined with another infinitive.

EXAMPLE PHRASES

Er meint, er **müsse** jetzt gehen.	*He thinks he'll have to leave now.*
Sie **hat** abwaschen **müssen**.	*She had to wash up.*

PRESENT

ich	nehme
du	nimmst
er/sie/es	nimmt
wir	nehmen
ihr	nehmt
sie/Sie	nehmen

PRESENT SUBJUNCTIVE

ich	nehme
du	nehmest
er/sie/es	nehme
wir	nehmen
ihr	nehmet
sie/Sie	nehmen

PERFECT

ich	habe genommen
du	hast genommen
er/sie/es	hat genommen
wir	haben genommen
ihr	habt genommen
sie/Sie	haben genommen

IMPERFECT

ich	nahm
du	nahmst
er/sie/es	nahm
wir	nahmen
ihr	nahmt
sie/Sie	nahmen

FUTURE

ich	werde nehmen
du	wirst nehmen
er/sie/es	wird nehmen
wir	werden nehmen
ihr	werdet nehmen
sie/Sie	werden nehmen

CONDITIONAL

ich	würde nehmen
du	würdest nehmen
er/sie/es	würde nehmen
wir	würden nehmen
ihr	würdet nehmen
sie/Sie	würden nehmen

IMPERATIVE

nimm / nehmen wir! / nehmt! / nehmen Sie!

PRESENT PARTICIPLE

nehmend

PAST PARTICIPLE

genommen

EXAMPLE PHRASES

Hast du den Bus in die Stadt **genommen**? *Did you take the bus into town?*

Wir **werden** den Bus in die Stadt **nehmen**. *We'll take the bus into town.*

rechnen *to work out*

weak, *formed with* **haben**

PRESENT

ich	rechne
du	rechnest
er/sie/es	rechnet
wir	rechnen
ihr	rechnet
sie/Sie	rechnen

PRESENT SUBJUNCTIVE

ich	rechne
du	rechnest
er/sie/es	rechne
wir	rechnen
ihr	rechnet
sie/Sie	rechnen

PERFECT

ich	habe gerechnet
du	hast gerechnet
er/sie/es	hat gerechnet
wir	haben gerechnet
ihr	habt gerechnet
sie/Sie	haben gerechnet

IMPERFECT

ich	rechnete
du	rechnetest
er/sie/es	rechnete
wir	rechneten
ihr	rechnetet
sie/Sie	rechneten

FUTURE

ich	werde rechnen
du	wirst rechnen
er/sie/es	wird rechnen
wir	werden rechnen
ihr	werdet rechnen
sie/Sie	werden rechnen

CONDITIONAL

ich	würde rechnen
du	würdest rechnen
er/sie/es	würde rechnen
wir	würden rechnen
ihr	würdet rechnen
sie/Sie	würden rechnen

IMPERATIVE

rechne! / rechnen wir! / rechnet! / rechnen Sie!

PRESENT PARTICIPLE

rechnend

PAST PARTICIPLE

gerechnet

EXAMPLE PHRASES

Ich **werde** mal schnell **rechnen**, wie viel das wird. — *I'll work out quickly how much that's going to be.*

PRESENT

ich	rede
du	redest
er/sie/es	redet
wir	reden
ihr	redet
sie/Sie	reden

PRESENT SUBJUNCTIVE

ich	rede
du	redest
er/sie/es	rede
wir	reden
ihr	redet
sie/Sie	reden

PERFECT

ich	habe geredet
du	hast geredet
er/sie/es	hat geredet
wir	haben geredet
ihr	habt geredet
sie/Sie	haben geredet

IMPERFECT

ich	redete
du	redetest
er/sie/es	redete
wir	redeten
ihr	redetet
sie/Sie	redeten

FUTURE

ich	werde reden
du	wirst reden
er/sie/es	wird reden
wir	werden reden
ihr	werdet reden
sie/Sie	werden reden

CONDITIONAL

ich	würde reden
du	würdest reden
er/sie/es	würde reden
wir	würden reden
ihr	würdet reden
sie/Sie	würden reden

IMPERATIVE

red(e)! / reden wir! / redet! / reden Sie!

PRESENT PARTICIPLE

redend

PAST PARTICIPLE

geredet

EXAMPLE PHRASES

Er meint, ich **rede** Unsinn. — *He thinks I'm talking nonsense.*

Ich **werde** mit deinem Vater **reden**. — *I'll speak to your father.*

rennen *to run*

mixed, *formed with* **sein**

PRESENT

ich	renne
du	rennst
er/sie/es	rennt
wir	rennen
ihr	rennt
sie/Sie	rennen

PRESENT SUBJUNCTIVE

ich	renne
du	rennest
er/sie/es	renne
wir	rennen
ihr	rennet
sie/Sie	rennen

PERFECT

ich	bin gerannt
du	bist gerannt
er/sie/es	ist gerannt
wir	sind gerannt
ihr	seid gerannt
sie/Sie	sind gerannt

IMPERFECT

ich	rannte
du	ranntest
er/sie/es	rannte
wir	rannten
ihr	ranntet
sie/Sie	rannten

FUTURE

ich	werde rennen
du	wirst rennen
er/sie/es	wird rennen
wir	werden rennen
ihr	werdet rennen
sie/Sie	werden rennen

CONDITIONAL

ich	würde rennen
du	würdest rennen
er/sie/es	würde rennen
wir	würden rennen
ihr	würdet rennen
sie/Sie	würden rennen

IMPERATIVE

renn(e)! / rennen wir! / rennt! / rennen Sie!

PRESENT PARTICIPLE

rennend

PAST PARTICIPLE

gerannt

EXAMPLE PHRASES

Sie **rannte** schnell weg.	*She ran away fast.*
Ich **werde** die 100 Meter nicht **rennen**.	*I won't run the 100 metres.*

PRESENT

ich	rufe
du	rufst
er/sie/es	ruft
wir	rufen
ihr	ruft
sie/Sie	rufen

PRESENT SUBJUNCTIVE

ich	rufe
du	rufest
er/sie/es	rufe
wir	rufen
ihr	rufet
sie/Sie	rufen

PERFECT

ich	habe gerufen
du	hast gerufen
er/sie/es	hat gerufen
wir	haben gerufen
ihr	habt gerufen
sie/Sie	haben gerufen

IMPERFECT

ich	rief
du	riefst
er/sie/es	rief
wir	riefen
ihr	rieft
sie/Sie	riefen

FUTURE

ich	werde rufen
du	wirst rufen
er/sie/es	wird rufen
wir	werden rufen
ihr	werdet rufen
sie/Sie	werden rufen

CONDITIONAL

ich	würde rufen
du	würdest rufen
er/sie/es	würde rufen
wir	würden rufen
ihr	würdet rufen
sie/Sie	würden rufen

IMPERATIVE

ruf(e)! / rufen wir! / ruft! / rufen Sie!

PRESENT PARTICIPLE

rufend

PAST PARTICIPLE

gerufen

EXAMPLE PHRASES

Sie **ruft** um Hilfe. — *She is shouting for help.*
Ich **habe** dir ein Taxi **gerufen**. — *I called you a taxi.*

scheinen *to shine; to seem*

strong, *formed with* **haben**

PRESENT

ich	scheine
du	scheinst
er/sie/es	scheint
wir	scheinen
ihr	scheint
sie/Sie	scheinen

PRESENT SUBJUNCTIVE

ich	scheine
du	scheinest
er/sie/es	scheine
wir	scheinen
ihr	scheinet
sie/Sie	scheinen

PERFECT

ich	habe geschienen
du	hast geschienen
er/sie/es	hat geschienen
wir	haben geschienen
ihr	habt geschienen
sie/Sie	haben geschienen

IMPERFECT

ich	schien
du	schienst
er/sie/es	schien
wir	schienen
ihr	schient
sie/Sie	schienen

FUTURE

ich	werde scheinen
du	wirst scheinen
er/sie/es	wird scheinen
wir	werden scheinen
ihr	werdet scheinen
sie/Sie	werden scheinen

CONDITIONAL

ich	würde scheinen
du	würdest scheinen
er/sie/es	würde scheinen
wir	würden scheinen
ihr	würdet scheinen
sie/Sie	würden scheinen

IMPERATIVE

schein(e)! / scheinen wir! / scheint! / scheinen Sie!

PRESENT PARTICIPLE

scheinend

PAST PARTICIPLE

geschienen

EXAMPLE PHRASES

Gestern **hat** die Sonne nicht **geschienen**. — *The sun wasn't shining yesterday.*

Sie **schienen** glücklich zu sein. — *They seemed to be happy.*

PRESENT

ich	schlafe
du	schläfst
er/sie/es	schläft
wir	schlafen
ihr	schlaft
sie/Sie	schlafen

PRESENT SUBJUNCTIVE

ich	schlafe
du	schlafest
er/sie/es	schlafe
wir	schlafen
ihr	schlafet
sie/Sie	schlafen

PERFECT

ich	habe geschlafen
du	hast geschlafen
er/sie/es	hat geschlafen
wir	haben geschlafen
ihr	habt geschlafen
sie/Sie	haben geschlafen

IMPERFECT

ich	schlief
du	schliefst
er/sie/es	schlief
wir	schliefen
ihr	schlieft
sie/Sie	schliefen

FUTURE

ich	werde schlafen
du	wirst schlafen
er/sie/es	wird schlafen
wir	werden schlafen
ihr	werdet schlafen
sie/Sie	werden schlafen

CONDITIONAL

ich	würde schlafen
du	würdest schlafen
er/sie/es	würde schlafen
wir	würden schlafen
ihr	würdet schlafen
sie/Sie	würden schlafen

IMPERATIVE

schlaf(e)! / schlafen wir! / schlaft! / schlafen Sie!

PRESENT PARTICIPLE

schlafend

PAST PARTICIPLE

geschlafen

EXAMPLE PHRASES

Sie **schläft** immer noch. — *She's still asleep.*

Hast du gut **geschlafen**? — *Did you sleep well?*

schlagen *to beat* — strong, *formed with* **haben**

PRESENT

ich	schlage
du	schlägst
er/sie/es	schlägt
wir	schlagen
ihr	schlagt
sie/Sie	schlagen

PRESENT SUBJUNCTIVE

ich	schlage
du	schlagest
er/sie/es	schlage
wir	schlagen
ihr	schlaget
sie/Sie	schlagen

PERFECT

ich	habe geschlagen
du	hast geschlagen
er/sie/es	hat geschlagen
wir	haben geschlagen
ihr	habt geschlagen
sie/Sie	haben geschlagen

IMPERFECT

ich	schlug
du	schlugst
er/sie/es	schlug
wir	schlugen
ihr	schlugt
sie/Sie	schlugen

FUTURE

ich	werde schlagen
du	wirst schlagen
er/sie/es	wird schlagen
wir	werden schlagen
ihr	werdet schlagen
sie/Sie	werden schlagen

CONDITIONAL

ich	würde schlagen
du	würdest schlagen
er/sie/es	würde schlagen
wir	würden schlagen
ihr	würdet schlagen
sie/Sie	würden schlagen

IMPERATIVE

schlag(e)! / schlagen wir! / schlagt! / schlagen Sie!

PRESENT PARTICIPLE

schlagend

PAST PARTICIPLE

geschlagen

EXAMPLE PHRASES

Mein Herz **schlägt** schneller.	*My heart is beating faster.*
England **hat** Deutschland **geschlagen**.	*England beat Germany.*

PRESENT

ich	schneide
du	schneidest
er/sie/es	schneidet
wir	schneiden
ihr	schneidet
sie/Sie	schneiden

PRESENT SUBJUNCTIVE

ich	schneide
du	schneidest
er/sie/es	schneide
wir	schneiden
ihr	schneidet
sie/Sie	schneiden

PERFECT

ich	habe geschnitten
du	hast geschnitten
er/sie/es	hat geschnitten
wir	haben geschnitten
ihr	habt geschnitten
sie/Sie	haben geschnitten

IMPERFECT

ich	schnitt
du	schnittst
er/sie/es	schnitt
wir	schnitten
ihr	schnittet
sie/Sie	schnitten

FUTURE

ich	werde schneiden
du	wirst schneiden
er/sie/es	wird schneiden
wir	werden schneiden
ihr	werdet schneiden
sie/Sie	werden schneiden

CONDITIONAL

ich	würde schneiden
du	würdest schneiden
er/sie/es	würde schneiden
wir	würden schneiden
ihr	würdet schneiden
sie/Sie	würden schneiden

IMPERATIVE

schneid(e)! / schneiden wir! / schneidet! / schneiden Sie!

PRESENT PARTICIPLE

schneidend

PAST PARTICIPLE

geschnitten

EXAMPLE PHRASES

Ich **habe** mir in den Finger **geschnitten**. — *I've cut my finger.*

Ich **werde** das Brot in Scheiben **schneiden**. — *I'll slice the bread.*

Table 61

schreiben *to write*

strong, *formed with* **haben**

PRESENT

ich	schreibe
du	schreibst
er/sie/es	schreibt
wir	schreiben
ihr	schreibt
sie/Sie	schreiben

PRESENT SUBJUNCTIVE

ich	schreibe
du	schreibest
er/sie/es	schreibe
wir	schreiben
ihr	schreibet
sie/Sie	schreiben

PERFECT

ich	habe geschrieben
du	hast geschrieben
er/sie/es	hat geschrieben
wir	haben geschrieben
ihr	habt geschrieben
sie/Sie	haben geschrieben

IMPERFECT

ich	schrieb
du	schriebst
er/sie/es	schrieb
wir	schrieben
ihr	schriebt
sie/Sie	schrieben

FUTURE

ich	werde schreiben
du	wirst schreiben
er/sie/es	wird schreiben
wir	werden schreiben
ihr	werdet schreiben
sie/Sie	werden schreiben

CONDITIONAL

ich	würde schreiben
du	würdest schreiben
er/sie/es	würde schreiben
wir	würden schreiben
ihr	würdet schreiben
sie/Sie	würden schreiben

IMPERATIVE

schreib(e)! / schreiben wir! / schreibt! / schreiben Sie!

PRESENT PARTICIPLE

schreibend

PAST PARTICIPLE

geschrieben

EXAMPLE PHRASES

Sie **hat** mir einen Brief **geschrieben**.	*She wrote me a letter.*
Er **schrieb** das Wort an die Tafel.	*He wrote the word on the blackboard.*

PRESENT

ich	schreie
du	schreist
er/sie/es	schreit
wir	schreien
ihr	schreit
sie/Sie	schreien

PRESENT SUBJUNCTIVE

ich	schreie
du	schreiest
er/sie/es	schreie
wir	schreien
ihr	schreiet
sie/Sie	schreien

PERFECT

ich	habe geschrien
du	hast geschrien
er/sie/es	hat geschrien
wir	haben geschrien
ihr	habt geschrien
sie/Sie	haben geschrien

IMPERFECT

ich	schrie
du	schriest
er/sie/es	schrie
wir	schrieen
ihr	schriet
sie/Sie	schrieen

FUTURE

ich	werde schreien
du	wirst schreien
er/sie/es	wird schreien
wir	werden schreien
ihr	werdet schreien
sie/Sie	werden schreien

CONDITIONAL

ich	würde schreien
du	würdest schreien
er/sie/es	würde schreien
wir	würden schreien
ihr	würdet schreien
sie/Sie	würden schreien

IMPERATIVE

schrei(e)! / schreien wir! / schreit! / schreien Sie!

PRESENT PARTICIPLE

schreiend

PAST PARTICIPLE

geschrien

EXAMPLE PHRASES

Sie sagt, er **schreie** zu laut. — *She says he's shouting too loud.*

Wir **haben geschrien**, er hat uns aber nicht gehört. — *We shouted but he didn't hear us.*

Table 63

schwimmen *to swim*

strong, *formed with* **sein**

PRESENT

ich	schwimme
du	schwimmst
er/sie/es	schwimmt
wir	schwimmen
ihr	schwimmt
sie/Sie	schwimmen

PRESENT SUBJUNCTIVE

ich	schwimme
du	schwimmest
er/sie/es	schwimme
wir	schwimmen
ihr	schwimmet
sie/Sie	schwimmen

PERFECT

ich	bin geschwommen
du	bist geschwommen
er/sie/es	ist geschwommen
wir	sind geschwommen
ihr	seid geschwommen
sie/Sie	sind geschwommen

IMPERFECT

ich	schwamm
du	schwammst
er/sie/es	schwamm
wir	schwammen
ihr	schwammt
sie/Sie	schwammen

FUTURE

ich	werde schwimmen
du	wirst schwimmen
er/sie/es	wird schwimmen
wir	werden schwimmen
ihr	werdet schwimmen
sie/Sie	werden schwimmen

CONDITIONAL

ich	würde schwimmen
du	würdest schwimmen
er/sie/es	würde schwimmen
wir	würden schwimmen
ihr	würdet schwimmen
sie/Sie	würden schwimmen

IMPERATIVE

schwimm(e)! / schwimmen wir! / schwimmt! / schwimmen Sie!

PRESENT PARTICIPLE

schwimmend

PAST PARTICIPLE

geschwommen

EXAMPLE PHRASES

Er **ist** über den Fluss **geschwommen**.	*He swam across the river.*
Ich **würde** gern öfter **schwimmen**.	*I'd like to swim more often.*

PRESENT		PRESENT SUBJUNCTIVE	
ich	sehe	ich	sehe
du	siehst	du	sehest
er/sie/es	sieht	er/sie/es	sehe
wir	sehen	wir	sehen
ihr	seht	ihr	sehet
sie/Sie	sehen	sie/Sie	sehen

PERFECT		IMPERFECT	
ich	habe gesehen	ich	sah
du	hast gesehen	du	sahst
er/sie/es	hat gesehen	er/sie/es	sah
wir	haben gesehen	wir	sahen
ihr	habt gesehen	ihr	saht
sie/Sie	haben gesehen	sie/Sie	sahen

FUTURE		CONDITIONAL	
ich	werde sehen	ich	würde sehen
du	wirst sehen	du	würdest sehen
er/sie/es	wird sehen	er/sie/es	würde sehen
wir	werden sehen	wir	würden sehen
ihr	werdet sehen	ihr	würdet sehen
sie/Sie	werden sehen	sie/Sie	würden sehen

IMPERATIVE

sieh(e)! / sehen wir! / seht! / sehen Sie!

PRESENT PARTICIPLE

sehend

PAST PARTICIPLE

gesehen

EXAMPLE PHRASES

Ich **habe** diesen Film noch nicht **gesehen**. — *I haven't seen this film yet.*

Wir **werden sehen**, wie sich die Dinge entwickeln. — *We'll see how things develop.*

sein *to be*

strong, *formed with* **sein**

PRESENT

ich	bin
du	bist
er/sie/es	ist
wir	sind
ihr	seid
sie/Sie	sind

PRESENT SUBJUNCTIVE

ich	sei
du	sei(e)st
er/sie/es	sei
wir	seien
ihr	seiet
sie/Sie	seien

PERFECT

ich	bin gewesen
du	bist gewesen
er/sie/es	ist gewesen
wir	sind gewesen
ihr	seid gewesen
sie/Sie	sind gewesen

IMPERFECT

ich	war
du	warst
er/sie/es	war
wir	waren
ihr	wart
sie/Sie	waren

FUTURE

ich	werde sein
du	wirst sein
er/sie/es	wird sein
wir	werden sein
ihr	werdet sein
sie/Sie	werden sein

CONDITIONAL

ich	würde sein
du	würdest sein
er/sie/es	würde sein
wir	würden sein
ihr	würdet sein
sie/Sie	würden sein

IMPERATIVE

sei! / seien wir! / seid! / seien Sie!

PRESENT PARTICIPLE

seiend

PAST PARTICIPLE

gewesen

EXAMPLE PHRASES

Er **ist** zehn Jahre.	*He's ten years old.*
Wir **waren** gestern im Theater.	*We were at the theatre yesterday.*
Morgen **werde** ich in Berlin **sein**.	*I'll be in Berlin tomorrow.*

PRESENT

ich	singe
du	singst
er/sie/es	singt
wir	singen
ihr	singt
sie/Sie	singen

PRESENT SUBJUNCTIVE

ich	singe
du	singest
er/sie/es	singe
wir	singen
ihr	singet
sie/Sie	singen

PERFECT

ich	habe gesungen
du	hast gesungen
er/sie/es	hat gesungen
wir	haben gesungen
ihr	habt gesungen
sie/Sie	haben gesungen

IMPERFECT

ich	sang
du	sangst
er/sie/es	sang
wir	sangen
ihr	sangt
sie/Sie	sangen

FUTURE

ich	werde singen
du	wirst singen
er/sie/es	wird singen
wir	werden singen
ihr	werdet singen
sie/Sie	werden singen

CONDITIONAL

ich	würde singen
du	würdest singen
er/sie/es	würde singen
wir	würden singen
ihr	würdet singen
sie/Sie	würden singen

IMPERATIVE

sing(e)! / singen wir! / singt! / singen Sie!

PRESENT PARTICIPLE

singend

PAST PARTICIPLE

gesungen

EXAMPLE PHRASES

Er **singt** nicht gut.	*He's a bad singer.*
Wir **werden** jetzt die Nationalhymne **singen**.	*We will sing the national anthem now.*

sinken *to sink*

strong, *formed with* **sein**

PRESENT

ich	sinke
du	sinkst
er/sie/es	sinkt
wir	sinken
ihr	sinkt
sie/Sie	sinken

PRESENT SUBJUNCTIVE

ich	sinke
du	sinkest
er/sie/es	sinke
wir	sinken
ihr	sinket
sie/Sie	sinken

PERFECT

ich	bin gesunken
du	bist gesunken
er/sie/es	ist gesunken
wir	sind gesunken
ihr	seid gesunken
sie/Sie	sind gesunken

IMPERFECT

ich	sank
du	sankst
er/sie/es	sank
wir	sanken
ihr	sankt
sie/Sie	sanken

FUTURE

ich	werde sinken
du	wirst sinken
er/sie/es	wird sinken
wir	werden sinken
ihr	werdet sinken
sie/Sie	werden sinken

CONDITIONAL

ich	würde sinken
du	würdest sinken
er/sie/es	würde sinken
wir	würden sinken
ihr	würdet sinken
sie/Sie	würden sinken

IMPERATIVE

sink(e)! / sinken wir! / sinkt! / sinken Sie!

PRESENT PARTICIPLE

sinkend

PAST PARTICIPLE

gesunken

EXAMPLE PHRASES

Die Preise für Handys **sinken**. — *Prices of mobile phones are falling.*

Wann **ist** die Titanic **gesunken**? — *When did the Titanic sink?*

PRESENT

ich	sitze
du	sitzt
er/sie/es	sitzt
wir	sitzen
ihr	sitzt
sie/Sie	sitzen

PRESENT SUBJUNCTIVE

ich	sitze
du	sitzest
er/sie/es	sitze
wir	sitzen
ihr	sitzet
sie/Sie	sitzen

PERFECT

ich	habe gesessen
du	hast gesessen
er/sie/es	hat gesessen
wir	haben gesessen
ihr	habt gesessen
sie/Sie	haben gesessen

IMPERFECT

ich	saß
du	saßest
er/sie/es	saß
wir	saßen
ihr	saßt
sie/Sie	saßen

FUTURE

ich	werde sitzen
du	wirst sitzen
er/sie/es	wird sitzen
wir	werden sitzen
ihr	werdet sitzen
sie/Sie	werden sitzen

CONDITIONAL

ich	würde sitzen
du	würdest sitzen
er/sie/es	würde sitzen
wir	würden sitzen
ihr	würdet sitzen
sie/Sie	würden sitzen

IMPERATIVE

sitz(e)! / sitzen wir! / sitzt! / sitzen Sie!

PRESENT PARTICIPLE

sitzend

PAST PARTICIPLE

gesessen

EXAMPLE PHRASES

Er **saß** auf meinem Stuhl.	*He was sitting on my chair.*
Wo **wird** der Präsident **sitzen**?	*Where will the president be sitting?*
Wir **würden** gern in der ersten Reihe **sitzen**.	*We'd like to sit in the front row.*

sollen *to be supposed to*

modal, *formed with* **haben**

PRESENT

ich	soll
du	sollst
er/sie/es	soll
wir	sollen
ihr	sollt
sie/Sie	sollen

PRESENT SUBJUNCTIVE

ich	solle
du	sollest
er/sie/es	solle
wir	sollen
ihr	sollet
sie/Sie	sollen

PERFECT

ich	habe gesollt/sollen
du	hast gesollt/sollen
er/sie/es	hat gesollt/sollen
wir	haben gesollt/sollen
ihr	habt gesollt/sollen
sie/Sie	haben gesollt/sollen

IMPERFECT

ich	sollte
du	solltest
er/sie/es	sollte
wir	sollten
ihr	solltet
sie/Sie	sollten

FUTURE

ich	werde sollen
du	wirst sollen
er/sie/es	wird sollen
wir	werden sollen
ihr	werdet sollen
sie/Sie	werden sollen

CONDITIONAL

ich	würde sollen
du	würdest sollen
er/sie/es	würde sollen
wir	würden sollen
ihr	würdet sollen
sie/Sie	würden sollen

PRESENT PARTICIPLE

sollend

PAST PARTICIPLE

gesollt / sollen*

*This form is used when combined with another infinitive.

EXAMPLE PHRASES

Ich **soll** um 5 Uhr dort sein. — *I'm supposed to be there at 5 o'clock.*

Ich **sollte** draußen bleiben. — *I was supposed to stay outside.*

PRESENT

ich	spreche
du	sprichst
er/sie/es	spricht
wir	sprechen
ihr	sprecht
sie/Sie	sprechen

PRESENT SUBJUNCTIVE

ich	spreche
du	sprechest
er/sie/es	spreche
wir	sprechen
ihr	sprechet
sie/Sie	sprechen

PERFECT

ich	habe gesprochen
du	hast gesprochen
er/sie/es	hat gesprochen
wir	haben gesprochen
ihr	habt gesprochen
sie/Sie	haben gesprochen

IMPERFECT

ich	sprach
du	sprachst
er/sie/es	sprach
wir	sprachen
ihr	spracht
sie/Sie	sprachen

FUTURE

ich	werde sprechen
du	wirst sprechen
er/sie/es	wird sprechen
wir	werden sprechen
ihr	werdet sprechen
sie/Sie	werden sprechen

CONDITIONAL

ich	würde sprechen
du	würdest sprechen
er/sie/es	würde sprechen
wir	würden sprechen
ihr	würdet sprechen
sie/Sie	würden sprechen

IMPERATIVE

sprich! / sprechen wir! / sprecht! / sprechen Sie!

PRESENT PARTICIPLE

sprechend

PAST PARTICIPLE

gesprochen

EXAMPLE PHRASES

Er **spricht** kein Italienisch.	*He doesn't speak Italian.*
Sie sagt, sie **spreche** aus Erfahrung.	*She says she's speaking from experience.*
Ich **werde** mit ihm darüber **sprechen**.	*I'll speak to him about it.*

springen *to jump*

strong, *formed with* **sein**

PRESENT

ich	springe
du	springst
er/sie/es	springt
wir	springen
ihr	springt
sie/Sie	springen

PRESENT SUBJUNCTIVE

ich	springe
du	springest
er/sie/es	springe
wir	springen
ihr	springet
sie/Sie	springen

PERFECT

ich	bin gesprungen
du	bist gesprungen
er/sie/es	ist gesprungen
wir	sind gesprungen
ihr	seid gesprungen
sie/Sie	sind gesprungen

IMPERFECT

ich	sprang
du	sprangst
er/sie/es	sprang
wir	sprangen
ihr	sprangt
sie/Sie	sprangen

FUTURE

ich	werde springen
du	wirst springen
er/sie/es	wird springen
wir	werden springen
ihr	werdet springen
sie/Sie	werden springen

CONDITIONAL

ich	würde springen
du	würdest springen
er/sie/es	würde springen
wir	würden springen
ihr	würdet springen
sie/Sie	würden springen

IMPERATIVE

spring(e)! / springen wir! / springt! / springen Sie!

PRESENT PARTICIPLE

springend

PAST PARTICIPLE

gesprungen

EXAMPLE PHRASES

Er **sprang** über den Zaun. He jumped over the fence.

PRESENT

ich	stehe
du	stehst
er/sie/es	steht
wir	stehen
ihr	steht
sie/Sie	stehen

PRESENT SUBJUNCTIVE

ich	stehe
du	stehest
er/sie/es	stehe
wir	stehen
ihr	stehet
sie/Sie	stehen

PERFECT

ich	habe gestanden
du	hast gestanden
er/sie/es	hat gestanden
wir	haben gestanden
ihr	habt gestanden
sie/Sie	haben gestanden

IMPERFECT

ich	stand
du	stand(e)st
er/sie/es	stand
wir	standen
ihr	standet
sie/Sie	standen

FUTURE

ich	werde stehen
du	wirst stehen
er/sie/es	wird stehen
wir	werden stehen
ihr	werdet stehen
sie/Sie	werden stehen

CONDITIONAL

ich	würde stehen
du	würdest stehen
er/sie/es	würde stehen
wir	würden stehen
ihr	würdet stehen
sie/Sie	würden stehen

IMPERATIVE

steh(e)! / stehen wir! / steht! / stehen Sie!

PRESENT PARTICIPLE

stehend

PAST PARTICIPLE

gestanden

EXAMPLE PHRASES

Die Vase **steht** auf dem Tisch.	*The vase is on the table.*
Wir **standen** an der Bushaltestelle.	*We stood at the bus stop.*
Dieses Kleid **würde** dir gut **stehen**.	*This dress would suit you.*

Table 73

stehlen *to steal*

strong, *formed with* **haben**

PRESENT

ich	stehle
du	stiehlst
er/sie/es	stiehlt
wir	stehlen
ihr	stehlt
sie/Sie	stehlen

PRESENT SUBJUNCTIVE

ich	stehle
du	stehlest
er/sie/es	stehle
wir	stehlen
ihr	stehlet
sie/Sie	stehlen

PERFECT

ich	habe gestohlen
du	hast gestohlen
er/sie/es	hat gestohlen
wir	haben gestohlen
ihr	habt gestohlen
sie/Sie	haben gestohlen

IMPERFECT

ich	stahl
du	stahlst
er/sie/es	stahl
wir	stahlen
ihr	stahlt
sie/Sie	stahlen

FUTURE

ich	werde stehlen
du	wirst stehlen
er/sie/es	wird stehlen
wir	werden stehlen
ihr	werdet stehlen
sie/Sie	werden stehlen

CONDITIONAL

ich	würde stehlen
du	würdest stehlen
er/sie/es	würde stehlen
wir	würden stehlen
ihr	würdet stehlen
sie/Sie	würden stehlen

IMPERATIVE

stiehl! / stehlen wir! / stehlt! / stehlen Sie!

PRESENT PARTICIPLE

stehlend

PAST PARTICIPLE

gestohlen

EXAMPLE PHRASES

Er **hat** das ganze Geld **gestohlen**. *He stole all the money.*
Ich **würde** euch nichts **stehlen**. *I wouldn't steal anything from you.*

strong, *formed with* **sein** *to climb* **steigen**

PRESENT

ich	steige
du	steigst
er/sie/es	steigt
wir	steigen
ihr	steigt
sie/Sie	steigen

PRESENT SUBJUNCTIVE

ich	steige
du	steigest
er/sie/es	steige
wir	steigen
ihr	steiget
sie/Sie	steigen

PERFECT

ich	bin gestiegen
du	bist gestiegen
er/sie/es	ist gestiegen
wir	sind gestiegen
ihr	seid gestiegen
sie/Sie	sind gestiegen

IMPERFECT

ich	stieg
du	stiegst
er/sie/es	stieg
wir	stiegen
ihr	stiegt
sie/Sie	stiegen

FUTURE

ich	werde steigen
du	wirst steigen
er/sie/es	wird steigen
wir	werden steigen
ihr	werdet steigen
sie/Sie	werden steigen

CONDITIONAL

ich	würde steigen
du	würdest steigen
er/sie/es	würde steigen
wir	würden steigen
ihr	würdet steigen
sie/Sie	würden steigen

IMPERATIVE

steig(e)! / steigen wir! / steigt! / steigen Sie!

PRESENT PARTICIPLE

steigend

PAST PARTICIPLE

gestiegen

EXAMPLE PHRASES

Sie **ist** auf die Leiter **gestiegen**. *She climbed up the ladder.*
Die Temperatur **stieg** auf 28 Grad. *The temperature rose to 28 degrees.*

sterben *to die*

strong, *formed with* **sein**

PRESENT

ich	sterbe
du	stirbst
er/sie/es	stirbt
wir	sterben
ihr	sterbt
sie/Sie	sterben

PRESENT SUBJUNCTIVE

ich	sterbe
du	sterbest
er/sie/es	sterbe
wir	sterben
ihr	sterbet
sie/Sie	sterben

PERFECT

ich	bin gestorben
du	bist gestorben
er/sie/es	ist gestorben
wir	sind gestorben
ihr	seid gestorben
sie/Sie	sind gestorben

IMPERFECT

ich	starb
du	starbst
er/sie/es	starb
wir	starben
ihr	starbt
sie/Sie	starben

FUTURE

ich	werde sterben
du	wirst sterben
er/sie/es	wird sterben
wir	werden sterben
ihr	werdet sterben
sie/Sie	werden sterben

CONDITIONAL

ich	würde sterben
du	würdest sterben
er/sie/es	würde sterben
wir	würden sterben
ihr	würdet sterben
sie/Sie	würden sterben

IMPERATIVE

stirb! / sterben wir! / sterbt! / sterben Sie!

PRESENT PARTICIPLE

sterbend

PAST PARTICIPLE

gestorben

EXAMPLE PHRASES

Ich **sterbe** hier vor Langeweile. — *I'm dying of boredom here.*
Er **starb** eines natürlichen Todes. — *He died a natural death.*
Daran **wirst** du nicht **sterben**! — *It won't kill you!*

PRESENT

ich	studiere
du	studierst
er/sie/es	studiert
wir	studieren
ihr	studiert
sie/Sie	studieren

PRESENT SUBJUNCTIVE

ich	studiere
du	studierest
er/sie/es	studiere
wir	studieren
ihr	studieret
sie/Sie	studieren

PERFECT

ich	habe studiert
du	hast studiert
er/sie/es	hat studiert
wir	haben studiert
ihr	habt studiert
sie/Sie	haben studiert

IMPERFECT

ich	studierte
du	studiertest
er/sie/es	studierte
wir	studierten
ihr	studiertet
sie/Sie	studierten

FUTURE

ich	werde studieren
du	wirst studieren
er/sie/es	wird studieren
wir	werden studieren
ihr	werdet studieren
sie/Sie	werden studieren

CONDITIONAL

ich	würde studieren
du	würdest studieren
er/sie/es	würde studieren
wir	würden studieren
ihr	würdet studieren
sie/Sie	würden studieren

IMPERATIVE

studiere! / studieren wir! / studiert! / studieren Sie!

PRESENT PARTICIPLE

studierend

PAST PARTICIPLE

studiert

EXAMPLE PHRASES

Mein Bruder **studiert** Deutsch. — *My brother is studying German.*

Sie **hat** in Köln **studiert**. — *She was a student at Cologne University.*

tragen *to wear; to carry*

strong, *formed with* **haben**

PRESENT

ich	trage
du	trägst
er/sie/es	trägt
wir	tragen
ihr	tragt
sie/Sie	tragen

PRESENT SUBJUNCTIVE

ich	trage
du	tragest
er/sie/es	trage
wir	tragen
ihr	traget
sie/Sie	tragen

PERFECT

ich	habe getragen
du	hast getragen
er/sie/es	hat getragen
wir	haben getragen
ihr	habt getragen
sie/Sie	haben getragen

IMPERFECT

ich	trug
du	trugst
er/sie/es	trug
wir	trugen
ihr	trugt
sie/Sie	trugen

FUTURE

ich	werde tragen
du	wirst tragen
er/sie/es	wird tragen
wir	werden tragen
ihr	werdet tragen
sie/Sie	werden tragen

CONDITIONAL

ich	würde tragen
du	würdest tragen
er/sie/es	würde tragen
wir	würden tragen
ihr	würdet tragen
sie/Sie	würden tragen

IMPERATIVE

trag(e)! / tragen wir! / tragt! / tragen Sie!

PRESENT PARTICIPLE

tragend

PAST PARTICIPLE

getragen

EXAMPLE PHRASES

Er sagt, er **trage** nie neue Kleider.	*He says he never wears new clothes.*
Ich **trug** ihren Koffer zum Bahnhof.	*I carried her case to the station.*
Ich **würde** meine Haare gern länger **tragen**.	*I'd like to wear my hair longer.*

PRESENT

ich	treffe
du	triffst
er/sie/es	trifft
wir	treffen
ihr	trefft
sie/Sie	treffen

PRESENT SUBJUNCTIVE

ich	treffe
du	treffest
er/sie/es	treffe
wir	treffen
ihr	treffet
sie/Sie	treffen

PERFECT

ich	habe getroffen
du	hast getroffen
er/sie/es	hat getroffen
wir	haben getroffen
ihr	habt getroffen
sie/Sie	haben getroffen

IMPERFECT

ich	traf
du	trafst
er/sie/es	traf
wir	trafen
ihr	traft
sie/Sie	trafen

FUTURE

ich	werde treffen
du	wirst treffen
er/sie/es	wird treffen
wir	werden treffen
ihr	werdet treffen
sie/Sie	werden treffen

CONDITIONAL

ich	würde treffen
du	würdest treffen
er/sie/es	würde treffen
wir	würden treffen
ihr	würdet treffen
sie/Sie	würden treffen

IMPERATIVE

triff! / treffen wir! / trefft! / treffen Sie!

PRESENT PARTICIPLE

treffend

PAST PARTICIPLE

getroffen

EXAMPLE PHRASES

Sie **trifft** sich zweimal pro Woche mit ihm. — *She meets with him twice a week.*

Wir **werden** uns am Bahnhof **treffen**. — *We'll meet at the station.*

treten *to kick; to step*

strong, *formed with* **haben/sein***

PRESENT

ich	trete
du	trittst
er/sie/es	tritt
wir	treten
ihr	tretet
sie/Sie	treten

PRESENT SUBJUNCTIVE

ich	trete
du	tretest
er/sie/es	trete
wir	treten
ihr	tretet
sie/Sie	treten

PERFECT

ich	habe getreten
du	hast getreten
er/sie/es	hat getreten
wir	haben getreten
ihr	habt getreten
sie/Sie	haben getreten

IMPERFECT

ich	trat
du	trat(e)st
er/sie/es	trat
wir	traten
ihr	tratet
sie/Sie	traten

FUTURE

ich	werde treten
du	wirst treten
er/sie/es	wird treten
wir	werden treten
ihr	werdet treten
sie/Sie	werden treten

CONDITIONAL

ich	würde treten
du	würdest treten
er/sie/es	würde treten
wir	würden treten
ihr	würdet treten
sie/Sie	würden treten

IMPERATIVE

tritt! / treten wir! / tretet! / treten Sie!

PRESENT PARTICIPLE

tretend

PAST PARTICIPLE

getreten

*When **treten** is used with no direct object, it is formed with **sein**.

EXAMPLE PHRASES

Pass auf, wohin du **trittst**! — *Watch your step!*

Er **hat** mich **getreten**. — *He kicked me.*

PRESENT

ich	trinke
du	trinkst
er/sie/es	trinkt
wir	trinken
ihr	trinkt
sie/Sie	trinken

PRESENT SUBJUNCTIVE

ich	trinke
du	trinkest
er/sie/es	trinke
wir	trinken
ihr	trinket
sie/Sie	trinken

PERFECT

ich	habe getrunken
du	hast getrunken
er/sie/es	hat getrunken
wir	haben getrunken
ihr	habt getrunken
sie/Sie	haben getrunken

IMPERFECT

ich	trank
du	trankst
er/sie/es	trank
wir	tranken
ihr	trankt
sie/Sie	tranken

FUTURE

ich	werde trinken
du	wirst trinken
er/sie/es	wird trinken
wir	werden trinken
ihr	werdet trinken
sie/Sie	werden trinken

CONDITIONAL

ich	würde trinken
du	würdest trinken
er/sie/es	würde trinken
wir	würden trinken
ihr	würdet trinken
sie/Sie	würden trinken

IMPERATIVE

trink(e)! / trinken wir! / trinkt! / trinken Sie!

PRESENT PARTICIPLE

trinkend

PAST PARTICIPLE

getrunken

EXAMPLE PHRASES

Er **trank** die ganze Flasche leer. — *He drank the whole bottle.*

Ich **würde** gern ein Bier mit Ihnen trinken. — *I'd like to have a beer with you.*

tun *to do*

strong, *formed with* **haben**

PRESENT

ich	tue
du	tust
er/sie/es	tut
wir	tun
ihr	tut
sie/Sie	tun

PRESENT SUBJUNCTIVE

ich	tue
du	tuest
er/sie/es	tue
wir	tuen
ihr	tuet
sie/Sie	tuen

PERFECT

ich	habe getan
du	hast getan
er/sie/es	hat getan
wir	haben getan
ihr	habt getan
sie/Sie	haben getan

IMPERFECT

ich	tat
du	tat(e)st
er/sie/es	tat
wir	taten
ihr	tatet
sie/Sie	taten

FUTURE

ich	werde tun
du	wirst tun
er/sie/es	wird tun
wir	werden tun
ihr	werdet tun
sie/Sie	werden tun

CONDITIONAL

ich	würde tun
du	würdest tun
er/sie/es	würde tun
wir	würden tun
ihr	würdet tun
sie/Sie	würden tun

IMPERATIVE

tu(e)! / tun wir! / tut! / tun Sie!

PRESENT PARTICIPLE

tuend

PAST PARTICIPLE

getan

EXAMPLE PHRASES

Er **hat** den ganzen Tag nichts **getan**. — *He hasn't done anything all day.*

Ich **werde** das auf keinen Fall **tun**. — *There is no way I'll do that.*

weak, inseparable, reflexive, *formed with* **haben** *to think about* **sich überlegen**

PRESENT

ich	überlege mir
du	überlegst dir
er/sie/es	überlegt sich
wir	überlegen uns
ihr	überlegt euch
sie/Sie	überlegen sich

PRESENT SUBJUNCTIVE

ich	überlege mir
du	überlegest dir
er/sie/es	überlege sich
wir	überlegen uns
ihr	überleget euch
sie/Sie	überlegen sich

PERFECT

ich	habe mir überlegt
du	hast dir überlegt
er/sie/es	hat sich überlegt
wir	haben uns überlegt
ihr	habt euch überlegt
sie/Sie	haben sich überlegt

IMPERFECT

ich	überlegte mir
du	überlegtest dir
er/sie/es	überlegte sich
wir	überlegten uns
ihr	überlegtet euch
sie/Sie	überlegten sich

FUTURE

ich	werde mir überlegen
du	wirst dir überlegen
er/sie/es	wird sich überlegen
wir	werden uns überlegen
ihr	werdet euch überlegen
sie/Sie	werden sich überlegen

CONDITIONAL

ich	würde mir überlegen
du	würdest dir überlegen
er/sie/es	würde sich überlegen
wir	würden uns überlegen
ihr	würdet euch überlegen
sie/Sie	würden sich überlegen

IMPERATIVE

überleg(e) dir! / überlegen wir uns! / überlegt euch! / überlegen Sie sich!

PRESENT PARTICIPLE

überlegend

PAST PARTICIPLE

überlegt

EXAMPLE PHRASES

Er **überlegte sich** einen schlauen Plan.	*He thought of a clever plan.*
Das **werde** ich **mir überlegen**.	*I'll have a think about it.*

vergessen *to forget*

strong, inseparable, *formed with* **haben**

PRESENT

ich	vergesse
du	vergisst
er/sie/es	vergisst
wir	vergessen
ihr	vergesst
sie/Sie	vergessen

PRESENT SUBJUNCTIVE

ich	vergesse
du	vergessest
er/sie/es	vergesse
wir	vergessen
ihr	vergesset
sie/Sie	vergessen

PERFECT

ich	habe vergessen
du	hast vergessen
er/sie/es	hat vergessen
wir	haben vergessen
ihr	habt vergessen
sie/Sie	haben vergessen

IMPERFECT

ich	vergaß
du	vergaßest
er/sie/es	vergaß
wir	vergaßen
ihr	vergaßt
sie/Sie	vergaßen

FUTURE

ich	werde vergessen
du	wirst vergessen
er/sie/es	wird vergessen
wir	werden vergessen
ihr	werdet vergessen
sie/Sie	werden vergessen

CONDITIONAL

ich	würde vergessen
du	würdest vergessen
er/sie/es	würde vergessen
wir	würden vergessen
ihr	würdet vergessen
sie/Sie	würden vergessen

IMPERATIVE

vergiss! / vergessen wir! / vergesst! / vergessen Sie!

PRESENT PARTICIPLE

vergessend

PAST PARTICIPLE

vergessen

EXAMPLE PHRASES

Er sagt, er **vergesse** nie ein Gesicht.	*He says he never forgets a face.*
Ich **habe** seinen Namen vergessen.	*I've forgotten his name.*

PRESENT

ich	verlange
du	verlangst
er/sie/es	verlangt
wir	verlangen
ihr	verlangt
sie/Sie	verlangen

PRESENT SUBJUNCTIVE

ich	verlange
du	verlangest
er/sie/es	verlange
wir	verlangen
ihr	verlanget
sie/Sie	verlangen

PERFECT

ich	habe verlangt
du	hast verlangt
er/sie/es	hat verlangt
wir	haben verlangt
ihr	habt verlangt
sie/Sie	haben verlangt

IMPERFECT

ich	verlangte
du	verlangtest
er/sie/es	verlangte
wir	verlangten
ihr	verlangtet
sie/Sie	verlangten

FUTURE

ich	werde verlangen
du	wirst verlangen
er/sie/es	wird verlangen
wir	werden verlangen
ihr	werdet verlangen
sie/Sie	werden verlangen

CONDITIONAL

ich	würde verlangen
du	würdest verlangen
er/sie/es	würde verlangen
wir	würden verlangen
ihr	würdet verlangen
sie/Sie	würden verlangen

IMPERATIVE

verlang(e)! / verlangen wir! / verlangt! / verlangen Sie!

PRESENT PARTICIPLE

verlangend

PAST PARTICIPLE

verlangt

EXAMPLE PHRASES

Wie viel **hat** er dafür **verlangt**? — *How much did he want for it?*

Sie **verlangten**, dass man sie anhört. — *They demanded to be heard.*

Table 85

verlieren *to lose*

strong, inseparable, *formed with* **haben**

PRESENT

ich	verliere
du	verlierst
er/sie/es	verliert
wir	verlieren
ihr	verliert
sie/Sie	verlieren

PRESENT SUBJUNCTIVE

ich	verliere
du	verlierest
er/sie/es	verliere
wir	verlieren
ihr	verlieret
sie/Sie	verlieren

PERFECT

ich	habe verloren
du	hast verloren
er/sie/es	hat verloren
wir	haben verloren
ihr	habt verloren
sie/Sie	haben verloren

IMPERFECT

ich	verlor
du	verlorst
er/sie/es	verlor
wir	verloren
ihr	verlort
sie/Sie	verloren

FUTURE

ich	werde verlieren
du	wirst verlieren
er/sie/es	wird verlieren
wir	werden verlieren
ihr	werdet verlieren
sie/Sie	werden verlieren

CONDITIONAL

ich	würde verlieren
du	würdest verlieren
er/sie/es	würde verlieren
wir	würden verlieren
ihr	würdet verlieren
sie/Sie	würden verlieren

IMPERATIVE

verlier(e)! / verlieren wir! / verliert! / verlieren Sie!

PRESENT PARTICIPLE

verlierend

PAST PARTICIPLE

verloren

EXAMPLE PHRASES

Wenn du **verlierst**, musst du mir 10 Euro zahlen. — *If you lose, you'll have to pay me 10 euros.*

Wir **haben** drei Spiele hintereinander **verloren**. — *We lost three matches in a row.*

strong, inseparable,
formed with **sein**

to disappear verschwinden

PRESENT

ich	verschwinde
du	verschwindest
er/sie/es	verschwindet
wir	verschwinden
ihr	verschwindet
sie/Sie	verschwinden

PRESENT SUBJUNCTIVE

ich	verschwinde
du	verschwindest
er/sie/es	verschwinde
wir	verschwinden
ihr	verschwindet
sie/Sie	verschwinden

PERFECT

ich	bin verschwunden
du	bist verschwunden
er/sie/es	ist verschwunden
wir	sind verschwunden
ihr	seid verschwunden
sie/Sie	sind verschwunden

IMPERFECT

ich	verschwand
du	verschwand(e)st
er/sie/es	verschwand
wir	verschwanden
ihr	verschwandet
sie/Sie	verschwanden

FUTURE

ich	werde verschwinden
du	wirst verschwinden
er/sie/es	wird verschwinden
wir	werden verschwinden
ihr	werdet verschwinden
sie/Sie	werden verschwinden

CONDITIONAL

ich	würde verschwinden
du	würdest verschwinden
er/sie/es	würde verschwinden
wir	würden verschwinden
ihr	würdet verschwinden
sie/Sie	würden verschwinden

IMPERATIVE

verschwind(e)! / verschwinden wir! / verschwindet! / verschwinden Sie!

PRESENT PARTICIPLE

verschwindend

PAST PARTICIPLE

verschwunden

EXAMPLE PHRASES

Er **ist** seit Sonntag **verschwunden**.	*He has been missing since Sunday.*
Unsere Sorgen **werden** bald **verschwinden**.	*Our worries will soon disappear.*

wachsen *to grow*

strong, *formed with* **sein**

PRESENT

ich	wachse
du	wächst
er/sie/es	wächst
wir	wachsen
ihr	wachst
sie/Sie	wachsen

PRESENT SUBJUNCTIVE

ich	wachse
du	wachsest
er/sie/es	wachse
wir	wachsen
ihr	wachset
sie/Sie	wachsen

PERFECT

ich	bin gewachsen
du	bist gewachsen
er/sie/es	ist gewachsen
wir	sind gewachsen
ihr	seid gewachsen
sie/Sie	sind gewachsen

IMPERFECT

ich	wuchs
du	wuchsest
er/sie/es	wuchs
wir	wuchsen
ihr	wuchst
sie/Sie	wuchsen

FUTURE

ich	werde wachsen
du	wirst wachsen
er/sie/es	wird wachsen
wir	werden wachsen
ihr	werdet wachsen
sie/Sie	werden wachsen

CONDITIONAL

ich	würde wachsen
du	würdest wachsen
er/sie/es	würde wachsen
wir	würden wachsen
ihr	würdet wachsen
sie/Sie	würden wachsen

IMPERATIVE

wachs(e)! / wachsen wir! / wachst! / wachsen Sie!

PRESENT PARTICIPLE

wachsend

PAST PARTICIPLE

gewachsen

EXAMPLE PHRASES

Der Baum **wächst** nicht mehr.	*The tree has stopped growing.*
Ich **bin** im letzten Jahr 10 Zentimeter **gewachsen**.	*I've grown 10 centimetres in the past year.*
Meine Probleme **werden** weiter **wachsen**.	*My problems will keep on growing.*

PRESENT

ich	wand(e)re
du	wanderst
er/sie/es	wandert
wir	wandern
ihr	wandert
sie/Sie	wandern

PRESENT SUBJUNCTIVE

ich	wand(e)re
du	wandrest
er/sie/es	wand(e)re
wir	wandern
ihr	wandert
sie/Sie	wandern

PERFECT

ich	bin gewandert
du	bist gewandert
er/sie/es	ist gewandert
wir	sind gewandert
ihr	seid gewandert
sie/Sie	sind gewandert

IMPERFECT

ich	wanderte
du	wandertest
er/sie/es	wanderte
wir	wanderten
ihr	wandertet
sie/Sie	wanderten

FUTURE

ich	werde wandern
du	wirst wandern
er/sie/es	wird wandern
wir	werden wandern
ihr	werdet wandern
sie/Sie	werden wandern

CONDITIONAL

ich	würde wandern
du	würdest wandern
er/sie/es	würde wandern
wir	würden wandern
ihr	würdet wandern
sie/Sie	würden wandern

IMPERATIVE

wandre! / wandern wir! / wandert! / wandern Sie!

PRESENT PARTICIPLE

wandernd

PAST PARTICIPLE

gewandert

EXAMPLE PHRASES

Im Urlaub **werden** wir jeden Tag **wandern**. — *On our holiday we'll go hiking every day.*

waschen *to wash*

strong, *formed with* **haben**

PRESENT

ich	wasche
du	wäschst
er/sie/es	wäscht
wir	waschen
ihr	wascht
sie/Sie	waschen

PRESENT SUBJUNCTIVE

ich	wasche
du	waschest
er/sie/es	wasche
wir	waschen
ihr	waschet
sie/Sie	waschen

PERFECT

ich	habe gewaschen
du	hast gewaschen
er/sie/es	hat gewaschen
wir	haben gewaschen
ihr	habt gewaschen
sie/Sie	haben gewaschen

IMPERFECT

ich	wusch
du	wuschest
er/sie/es	wusch
wir	wuschen
ihr	wuscht
sie/Sie	wuschen

FUTURE

ich	werde waschen
du	wirst waschen
er/sie/es	wird waschen
wir	werden waschen
ihr	werdet waschen
sie/Sie	werden waschen

CONDITIONAL

ich	würde waschen
du	würdest waschen
er/sie/es	würde waschen
wir	würden waschen
ihr	würdet waschen
sie/Sie	würden waschen

IMPERATIVE

wasche(e)! / waschen wir! / wascht! / waschen Sie!

PRESENT PARTICIPLE

waschend

PAST PARTICIPLE

gewaschen

EXAMPLE PHRASES

Ich **habe** mir die Hände **gewaschen**.	*I washed my hands.*
Die Katze **wusch** sich in der Sonne.	*The cat was washing itself in the sunshine.*
Ich **werde** mir jetzt die Haare **waschen**.	*I'll go and wash my hair now.*

PRESENT

ich	werbe
du	wirbst
er/sie/es	wirbt
wir	werben
ihr	werbt
sie/Sie	werben

PRESENT SUBJUNCTIVE

ich	werbe
du	werbest
er/sie/es	werbe
wir	werben
ihr	werbet
sie/Sie	werben

PERFECT

ich	habe geworben
du	hast geworben
er/sie/es	hat geworben
wir	haben geworben
ihr	habt geworben
sie/Sie	haben geworben

IMPERFECT

ich	warb
du	warbst
er/sie/es	warb
wir	warben
ihr	warbt
sie/Sie	warben

FUTURE

ich	werde werben
du	wirst werben
er/sie/es	wird werben
wir	werden werben
ihr	werdet werben
sie/Sie	werden werben

CONDITIONAL

ich	würde werben
du	würdest werben
er/sie/es	würde werben
wir	würden werben
ihr	würdet werben
sie/Sie	würden werben

IMPERATIVE

wirb! / werben wir! / werbt! / werben Sie!

PRESENT PARTICIPLE

werbend

PAST PARTICIPLE

geworben

EXAMPLE PHRASES

Die Partei **wirbt** zur Zeit Mitglieder. — *The party is currently recruiting members.*

Wir **werden** für unser neues Produkt **werben**. — *We will advertise our new product.*

werden *to become*

strong, *formed with* **sein**

PRESENT

ich	werde
du	wirst
er/sie/es	wird
wir	werden
ihr	werdet
sie/Sie	werden

PRESENT SUBJUNCTIVE

ich	werde
du	werdest
er/sie/es	werde
wir	werden
ihr	werdet
sie/Sie	werden

PERFECT

ich	bin geworden
du	bist geworden
er/sie/es	ist geworden
wir	sind geworden
ihr	seid geworden
sie/Sie	sind geworden

IMPERFECT

ich	wurde
du	wurdest
er/sie/es	wurde
wir	wurden
ihr	wurdet
sie/Sie	wurden

FUTURE

ich	werde werden
du	wirst werden
er/sie/es	wird werden
wir	werden werden
ihr	werdet werden
sie/Sie	werden werden

CONDITIONAL

ich	würde werden
du	würdest werden
er/sie/es	würde werden
wir	würden werden
ihr	würdet werden
sie/Sie	würden werden

IMPERATIVE

werde! / werden wir! / werdet! / werden Sie!

PRESENT PARTICIPLE

werdend

PAST PARTICIPLE

geworden

EXAMPLE PHRASES

Mir **wird** schlecht. — *I feel ill.*

Ich **werde** Lehrerin **werden**. — *I'll become a teacher.*

PRESENT

ich	werfe
du	wirfst
er/sie/es	wirft
wir	werfen
ihr	werft
sie/Sie	werfen

PRESENT SUBJUNCTIVE

ich	werfe
du	werfest
er/sie/es	werfe
wir	werfen
ihr	werfet
sie/Sie	werfen

PERFECT

ich	habe geworfen
du	hast geworfen
er/sie/es	hat geworfen
wir	haben geworfen
ihr	habt geworfen
sie/Sie	haben geworfen

IMPERFECT

ich	warf
du	warfst
er/sie/es	warf
wir	warfen
ihr	warft
sie/Sie	warfen

FUTURE

ich	werde werfen
du	wirst werfen
er/sie/es	wird werfen
wir	werden werfen
ihr	werdet werfen
sie/Sie	werden werfen

CONDITIONAL

ich	würde werfen
du	würdest werfen
er/sie/es	würde werfen
wir	würden werfen
ihr	würdet werfen
sie/Sie	würden werfen

IMPERATIVE

wirf! / werfen wir! / werft! / werfen Sie!

PRESENT PARTICIPLE

werfend

PAST PARTICIPLE

geworfen

EXAMPLE PHRASES

Er drohte ihm, er **werfe** ihn aus dem Haus. — *He threatened to throw him out of the house.*

Am liebsten **würde** ich das Handtuch **werfen**. — *I feel like throwing in the towel.*

wissen *to know*

mixed, *formed with* **haben**

PRESENT

ich	weiß
du	weißt
er/sie/es	weiß
wir	wissen
ihr	wisst
sie/Sie	wissen

PRESENT SUBJUNCTIVE

ich	wisse
du	wissest
er/sie/es	wisse
wir	wissen
ihr	wisset
sie/Sie	wissen

PERFECT

ich	habe gewusst
du	hast gewusst
er/sie/es	hat gewusst
wir	haben gewusst
ihr	habt gewusst
sie/Sie	haben gewusst

IMPERFECT

ich	wusste
du	wusstest
er/sie/es	wusste
wir	wussten
ihr	wusstet
sie/Sie	wussten

FUTURE

ich	werde wissen
du	wirst wissen
er/sie/es	wird wissen
wir	werden wissen
ihr	werdet wissen
sie/Sie	werden wissen

CONDITIONAL

ich	würde wissen
du	würdest wissen
er/sie/es	würde wissen
wir	würden wissen
ihr	würdet wissen
sie/Sie	würden wissen

IMPERATIVE

wisse! / wissen wir! / wisset! / wissen Sie!

PRESENT PARTICIPLE

wissend

PAST PARTICIPLE

gewusst

EXAMPLE PHRASES

Ich **weiß** nicht.	*I don't know.*
Er **hat** nichts davon **gewusst**.	*He didn't know anything about it.*
Morgen **werden** wir **wissen**, wer gewonnen hat.	*Tomorrow we'll know who has won.*

PRESENT

ich	will
du	willst
er/sie/es	will
wir	wollen
ihr	wollt
sie/Sie	wollen

PRESENT SUBJUNCTIVE

ich	wolle
du	wollest
er/sie/es	wolle
wir	wollen
ihr	wollet
sie/Sie	wollen

PERFECT

ich	habe gewollt/wollen
du	hast gewollt/wollen
er/sie/es	hat gewollt/wollen
wir	haben gewollt/wollen
ihr	habt gewollt/wollen
sie/Sie	haben gewollt/wollen

IMPERFECT

ich	wollte
du	wolltest
er/sie/es	wollte
wir	wolten
ihr	wolltet
sie/Sie	wollten

FUTURE

ich	werde wollen
du	wirst wollen
er/sie/es	wird wollen
wir	werden wollen
ihr	werdet wollen
sie/Sie	werden wollen

CONDITIONAL

ich	würde wollen
du	würdest wollen
er/sie/es	würde wollen
wir	würden wollen
ihr	würdet wollen
sie/Sie	würden wollen

IMPERATIVE

wolle! / wollen wir! / wollt! / wollen Sie!

PRESENT PARTICIPLE

wollend

PAST PARTICIPLE

gewollt / wollen*

*This form is used when combined with another infinitive.

EXAMPLE PHRASES

Er **will** nach London gehen. — *He wants to go to London.*
Sie **wollten** nur mehr Geld. — *All they wanted was more money.*

zerstören *to destroy*

weak, inseparable, *formed with* **haben**

PRESENT

ich	zerstöre
du	zerstörst
er/sie/es	zerstört
wir	zerstören
ihr	zerstört
sie/Sie	zerstören

PRESENT SUBJUNCTIVE

ich	zerstöre
du	zerstörest
er/sie/es	zerstöre
wir	zerstören
ihr	zerstöret
sie/Sie	zerstören

PERFECT

ich	habe zerstört
du	hast zerstört
er/sie/es	hat zerstört
wir	haben zerstört
ihr	habt zerstört
sie/Sie	haben zerstört

IMPERFECT

ich	zerstörte
du	zerstörtest
er/sie/es	zerstörte
wir	zerstörten
ihr	zerstörtet
sie/Sie	zerstörten

FUTURE

ich	werde zerstören
du	wirst zerstören
er/sie/es	wird zerstören
wir	werden zerstören
ihr	werdet zerstören
sie/Sie	werden zerstören

CONDITIONAL

ich	würde zerstören
du	würdest zerstören
er/sie/es	würde zerstören
wir	würden zerstören
ihr	würdet zerstören
sie/Sie	würden zerstören

IMPERATIVE

zerstör(e)! / zerstören wir! / zerstört! / zerstören Sie!

PRESENT PARTICIPLE

zerstörend

PAST PARTICIPLE

zerstört

EXAMPLE PHRASES

Er **hat** ihr Selbstvertrauen zerstört.	*He has destroyed her self-confidence.*
Das **würde** unsere Freundschaft zerstören.	*It would destroy our friendship.*

strong,
formed with **sein/haben***

to go; to pull **ziehen**

PRESENT

ich	ziehe
du	ziehst
er/sie/es	zieht
wir	ziehen
ihr	zieht
sie/Sie	ziehen

PRESENT SUBJUNCTIVE

ich	ziehe
du	ziehest
er/sie/es	ziehe
wir	ziehen
ihr	ziehet
sie/Sie	ziehen

PERFECT

ich	bin/habe gezogen
du	bist/hast gezogen
er/sie/es	ist/hat gezogen
wir	sind/haben gezogen
ihr	seid/habt gezogen
sie/Sie	sind/haben gezogen

IMPERFECT

ich	zog
du	zogst
er/sie/es	zog
wir	zogen
ihr	zogt
sie/Sie	zogen

FUTURE

ich	werde ziehen
du	wirst ziehen
er/sie/es	wird ziehen
wir	werden ziehen
ihr	werdet ziehen
sie/Sie	werden ziehen

CONDITIONAL

ich	würde ziehen
du	würdest ziehen
er/sie/es	würde ziehen
wir	würden ziehen
ihr	würdet ziehen
sie/Sie	würden ziehen

IMPERATIVE

zieh(e)! / ziehen wir! / zieht! / ziehen Sie!

PRESENT PARTICIPLE

ziehend

PAST PARTICIPLE

gezogen

*When **ziehen** is used with a direct object, it is formed with **haben**.

EXAMPLE PHRASES

Sie **zog** mich am Ärmel.	*She pulled at my sleeve.*
Ich **würde** nie nach Bayern ziehen.	*I would never move to Bavaria.*

zwingen *to force*

strong, *formed with* **haben**

PRESENT

ich	zwinge
du	zwingst
er/sie/es	zwingt
wir	zwingen
ihr	zwingt
sie/Sie	zwingen

PRESENT SUBJUNCTIVE

ich	zwinge
du	zwingest
er/sie/es	zwinge
wir	zwingen
ihr	zwinget
sie/Sie	zwingen

PERFECT

ich	habe gezwungen
du	hast gezwungen
er/sie/es	hat gezwungen
wir	haben gezwungen
ihr	habt gezwungen
sie/Sie	haben gezwungen

IMPERFECT

ich	zwang
du	zwangst
er/sie/es	zwang
wir	zwangen
ihr	zwangt
sie/Sie	zwangen

FUTURE

ich	werde zwingen
du	wirst zwingen
er/sie/es	wird zwingen
wir	werden zwingen
ihr	werdet zwingen
sie/Sie	werden zwingen

CONDITIONAL

ich	würde zwingen
du	würdest zwingen
er/sie/es	würde zwingen
wir	würden zwingen
ihr	würdet zwingen
sie/Sie	würden zwingen

IMPERATIVE

zwing(e)! / zwingen wir! / zwingt! / zwingen Sie!

PRESENT PARTICIPLE

zwingend

PAST PARTICIPLE

gezwungen

EXAMPLE PHRASES

Ich **zwinge** mich dazu. — *I force myself to do it.*

Er **hat** ihn **gezwungen**, das zu tun. — *He forced him to do it.*